The Language of Composition

The Language of Composition
Reading • Writing • Rhetoric

Renée H. Shea
Bowie State University, Maryland

Lawrence Scanlon
Brewster High School, New York

Robin Dissin Aufses
John F. Kennedy High School, New York

Bedford/St. Martin's   Boston • New York

For Bedford/St. Martin's

Developmental Editor: Nathan Odell
Senior Production Editor: Irwin Zucker
Production Supervisor: Andrew Ensor
Marketing Manager: Daniel McDonough
Art Director: Lucy Krikorian
Text Design: Linda M. Robertson
Copy Editor: Patricia Phelan
Indexer: Kirsten Kite
Photo Research: Helane Prottas
Cover Design: Donna Lee Dennison
Cover Art: The Gay Science, R. B. Kitaj. © R. B. Kitaj, courtesy, Marlborough Gallery, New York.
 © Bolton Museum and Art Gallery, Lancashire, UK
Composition: Stratford/TexTech
Printing and Binding: R. R. Donnelley & Sons Company

President: Joan E. Feinberg
Editorial Director: Denise B. Wydra
Editor in Chief: Karen S. Henry
Director of Development: Erica T. Appel
Director of Marketing: Karen Melton Soeltz
Director of Editing, Design, and Production: Marcia Cohen
Managing Editor: Shuli Traub

Library of Congress Control Number: 2007924372

Manufactured in the United States of America.

1 2 3 4 5 6   11 10 09 08 07

For information, write: Bedford/St. Martin's, 75 Arlington Street, Boston, MA 02116 (617-399-4000)

ISBN-10: 0-312-45094-X
ISBN-13: 978-0-312-45094-6

To Michael Shea, William and Mary Scanlon,
and Arthur Aufses

Preface

We have designed *The Language of Composition: Reading • Writing • Rhetoric* to be the first college-level textbook designed for upper-level high school English courses, in particular the Advanced Placement* English Language and Composition course. Its goal is to help high school students read, analyze, and write with the same level of skill and sophistication of thought as they would in a first-year composition course in college. *The Language of Composition* offers a diverse collection of over 100 college-level readings — including nonfiction, fiction, and poetry — that are both interesting and suitable for a high school audience; practical advice on rhetoric, reading, and writing; and special attention to synthesis and visual analysis skills in keeping with the changes to the AP English Language and Composition course and exam for 2007.

The Language of Composition is the product of years of experience and collaboration. The three of us met through workshops where we were learning how to incorporate the theory and practice of rhetoric into high school curricula and sharing strategies that worked in both high school and college courses. What began in summer workshops extended to years of discussions about what worked with eleventh- or twelfth-graders and how better to prepare students to succeed in, or place out of first-year composition. The more we taught our students and worked with teachers, the more we came to appreciate the interrelationship among the three main components of this book: rhetoric, reading, and writing.

Rhetoric

Introductory chapters teach the skills essential for success in the AP English Language and Composition course.

In the three opening chapters of *The Language of Composition*, we introduce students to the principles and language of rhetorical analysis that they will use throughout the following ten chapters of readings.

---

*AP and Advanced Placement Program are registered trademarks of the College Entrance Examination Board, which was not involved in the publication of and does not endorse this product.

- Chapter 1, "An Introduction to Rhetoric: Using the 'Available Means,'" provides explanations and examples of rhetorical concepts including the rhetorical triangle; ethos, pathos, and logos; visual rhetoric; and more.
- Chapter 2, "Close Reading: The Art and Craft of Analysis," guides students through the analysis of diction and syntax with an emphasis on their rhetorical effects.
- Chapter 3, "Synthesizing Sources: Entering the Conversation," introduces students to the use of sources. We ask them first to analyze texts that demonstrate skillful writers using sources; then we walk them through the process of using sources to develop and articulate their own viewpoints.

When developing these introductory chapters, we asked ourselves what students need to know to analyze rhetoric in the writing of others and to use it in their own writing. We wanted to provide sufficient terminology to make the language of rhetorical analysis accessible, but we also wanted the instructional method to remain practical and example-based. Once students have an understanding of how professional writers use rhetorical strategies (in both nonfiction and fiction), we provide opportunities for them to take rhetorical stances and try out strategies to support their own arguments.

Throughout these introductory chapters, we incorporate instruction in the rhetorical and stylistic analysis of visual texts. Just as a writer uses verbal humor to make a point, a political cartoonist might use visual humor. Just as a writer uses evocative language to engage her audience, so might a photographer use evocative images. Especially in this information-rich age, facts and figures, statistics and numerical data of all kinds are just as likely to be presented in visual form — in charts, tables, graphs — as in prose.

Reading

The thematic organization encourages students to explore the complexities of a single issue and synthesize the different viewpoints represented.

We chose the ten chapter themes — Education, Work, Community, Gender, Sports and Fitness, Language, Science and Technology, Popular Culture, Nature, and Politics — because they are ones that students will find interesting and relevant, and that teachers can easily supplement with literary works or with materials from current events. The **essential question** at the beginning of each chapter — for example, "How does the language we use reveal who we are?" or "What is the relationship of the individual to the community?" — invites students to enter the chapter's conversation and begin thinking critically about the chapter's theme.

The thematic arrangement means that in each chapter, students read about and discuss one broad issue. By analyzing the readings, understanding the complexity of the issue, synthesizing multiple perspectives, and developing their own viewpoint, students get experience with synthesis and the critical use of sources that is expected in college courses.

Diverse and engaging readings in each thematic chapter focus on topics of interest to students and serve as excellent rhetorical models.

We selected readings for *The Language of Composition* that exemplify excellent writing. Whether a text is narrative, expository, argumentative, or fictional, we believe that students benefit from reading and analyzing exceptional rhetoric from contemporary and classic authors. We also selected readings that are important, and relevant to students, because we believe that interesting, provocative topics promote active, critical reading.

Each thematic chapter is anchored by a central essay and a classic essay, and includes a range of additional nonfiction readings, poetry and fiction, and visual texts:

- The **central essays** are rich rhetorical and stylistic models, ideally suited to the AP English Language course, such as Martin Luther King Jr.'s "Letter from Birmingham Jail," Stephen Jay Gould's "Women's Brains," Richard Rodriguez's "Aria," and Jamaica Kincaid's "On Seeing England for the First Time."

- The **classic essays** are canonical works written between the eighteenth century and the early twentieth century, giving students experience analyzing writing styles from different periods. Among the classic essays are Ralph Waldo Emerson's "Education," Virginia Woolf's "Professions for Women," Mark Twain's "Corn-Pone Opinions," and Jonathan Swift's "A Modest Proposal."

- Additional **nonfiction readings** by well-known and emerging writers in each chapter include essays, autobiographies and memoirs, biographies, newspaper columns, speeches, journals, letters, government documents, academic journal articles, and editorials. This range of rhetorical contexts and types of readings will inspire students to become agile readers and versatile writers.

- **Poetry** and **fiction** relating to the chapter's theme add richness and new perspectives to the issue under discussion. We love imaginative literature and want to imbue a similar appreciation in our students. And we believe that the principles and practice of rhetoric are useful when reading both nonfiction and imaginative literature. That is why, after a series of provocative and probing nonfiction readings in each chapter, we include short stories, selections from novels, classic and contemporary poetry — even a "not quite poem" by Nikki Giovanni.

Visual texts in each chapter give students an opportunity to hone the visual analysis skills learned in the opening chapters.

Knowing how important visuals have become as rhetorical texts in college study, and in our society as a whole, we feature visual texts in every chapter. Among these we include political cartoons, photographs, public monuments, tables or graphs, or even paintings. We approach these texts rhetorically, as we do the written ones, encouraging students to read them closely and to ask questions about the ways artists and designers achieve their purposes.

Writing

Carefully crafted apparatus accompanying the readings reinforces the content of the book's introductory chapters and provides opportunities for discussion and interpretation, for rhetorical and stylistic analysis, and for writing.

In *The Language of Composition*, we have tried to build bridges that enable students to read with a writer's eye — that is, to see how they can use the techniques of professional and published writers in their own writing. Thus, we intend the apparatus in *The Language of Composition* to link reading with writing. Always promoting active reading, the questions guide students from understanding what a text is about to how the content is presented as it is and why — the rhetorical strategies. The next step, then, is to encourage students to use those strategies in their own writing. **Exploring the Text,** the apparatus that accompanies the additional nonfiction readings, the poetry and fiction, and the visual texts include both critical thinking and rhetorical analysis questions.

The apparatus for the central and classic essays is more elaborate:

- **Questions for Discussion** probe content and connections and support students' careful reading to comprehend ideas, understand cultural and historical context, and make connections to compelling contemporary issues or influences.
- **Questions on Rhetoric and Style** address the *how* and *why* issues by examining the choices the writer makes and the effect those choices have. These take into account the micro level of diction and syntax as well as the macro

level of a piece's patterns of organization. While Questions for Discussion are generally open-ended, Questions on Rhetoric and Style are close reading inquiries, requiring precise answers similar to analytical essay or multiple-choice responses.

- **Suggestions for Writing** guide students toward written responses that extend the conversation from the reading and suggest ways that students might practice some of the strategies that the writer uses.

Writer on Writing sections give students a glimpse of how the authors in the book deal with the challenges of writing.

A Writer on Writing section in each chapter includes an interview — that we conducted ourselves — with a prominent author from the chapter who shares his or her unique perspective on the writing process. We think that hearing how professional writers talk about their writing process helps bridge the gap between the polished (and what for students might seem impossibly polished) work of a writer and the student's own work. When journalist Samuel Freedman talks about how deadlines affect his writing and how he approaches them, students are hearing advice from a mentor as well as a fellow writer. He outlines just like the rest of us! We hope that as students hear writers reflecting on how they write, students will begin to think more deeply about their own writing process.

Conversation sections give students practice writing the kind of synthesis essay now required on the AP English Language and Composition exam.

Designed to help students succeed on the new synthesis essay question on the AP English Language and Composition exam, the Conversation section in each chapter provides source material and guiding questions to help students use the words and ideas of others to support their own arguments. For example, the chapter on sports and fitness includes a cluster of readings and a visual text focused on body image, exploring the consequences of cultural expectations on both men and women. After synthesizing the written and visual texts provided, students are ready to develop their own voice and viewpoint. The Conversation section gives students an opportunity to develop confidence and facility in working with multiple texts.

Student Writing sections serve as guided peer-review sessions encouraging students to think critically about revision strategies.

Student Writing sections use papers by high school and first-year college students to model the types of writing essential to success in the AP English Language course and in college, from writing a rhetorical analysis to incorporating sources in support of an argument. These writings demonstrate the students' skill and creativity, yet they are all in-process. We provide questions that encourage revision and expansion, not mere editing or proofreading. We have found that such student work is more accessible and often provokes suggestions and comments that students would be reluctant to venture about a professional author's work.

Grammar as Rhetoric and Style sections bring grammar to life, going beyond *dos* and *don'ts* to explore why grammar is important and how writers can use it to persuade.

Grammar as Rhetoric and Style sections use examples from the chapter's readings to reinforce students' understanding of grammar and show how to use grammar to achieve a rhetorical purpose or stylistic effect. In each chapter, we focus on one issue — such as coordination, parallel structure, or pronouns — and explore how what might seem a mechanical point can, in fact, be approached rhetorically. In these sections, we draw on examples from the readings in the chapter so that students can see, for instance, how Martin Luther King Jr. uses parallel structure and to what effect, or how Gay Talese uses precise, active verbs.

Ancillaries

The Language of Composition TEACHER'S MANUAL includes solid support and exciting classroom ideas from the veteran author team of *The Language of Composition*.

The Language of Composition TEACHER'S MANUAL (ISBN-10: 0-312-45942-4; ISBN-13: 978-0-312-45942-0)   The teacher's manual to *The Language of Composition* is a wealth of teaching resources, including suggested approaches to teaching the chapters and the central and classic essays; connections to longer works of nonfiction and fiction, as well as film; sample synthesis exercises; one sure-fire lesson plan for each chapter; answers to Questions on Rhetoric and Style and Grammar as Rhetoric and Style exercises; and much more.

Affordable New Media resources give students innovative ways to improve their skills in writing, rhetoric, and use of sources.

The Language of Composition book companion site <bedfordstmartins.com/languageofcomp>   This free resource includes the *Language of Composition* Media Library with links to audio, video, and texts referred to in *The Language of Composition*; templates for the dialectical journal and graphic organizer in Chapter 2; a customized lesson plan for *Exercise Central*, the world's largest collection of online interactive grammar exercises; and a portal to *Re:Writing*, a free collection of Bedford/St. Martin's most popular online materials for writing, grammar, and research.

i•claim visualizing argument   The i•claim CD-ROM offers a new way to see argument. With tutorials, interactive assignments, and over 70 multimedia arguments (including Lou Gehrig's farewell speech), i•claim brings argument to life.

i•cite visualizing sources   The i•cite CD-ROM presents a new way to see sources. With its animated introduction to using sources, concrete tutorials, and practice exercises, i•cite helps students understand the hows and whys of working with sources.

To bundle i•claim and i•cite with *The Language of Composition* for only $2, use: ISBN-10: 0-312-47357-5; ISBN-13: 978-0-312-47357-0.

Acknowledgments

We want to extend our heartfelt appreciation to the team at Bedford/St. Martin's. We've enjoyed the support, guidance, and encouragement of many talented professionals, starting with the leadership of president Joan Feinberg, editorial director Denise Wydra, editor-in-chief Karen Henry, and director of development Erica Appel, who have been committed to this project from the start. We say a special thanks to Nancy Perry, former editor-in-chief and current editorial director of custom publishing, for encouraging us to explore this idea that became *The Language of Composition*. It is no exaggeration to call her role in this project visionary; *The Language of Composition* would truly not exist without her initial ideas and continuing belief in it. To our gifted editor Nathan Odell, we would like to present an academy award for his exceptional judgment, appreciation for language, energy, and enthusiasm — and patience. Assigned to this project as our editor, he became our dear friend. We thank Dan McDonough, high school marketing manager, for his creativity and faith. He brought us together at Bedford/St. Martin's and from the very start understood what we had in mind for this project. We hope the finished product lives up to his ideal. A sincere thank you to Fran Weinberg for her meticulous attention to detail and sound editorial advice. We also want to thank our many dedicated and innovative colleagues in the Advanced Placement Program at the College Board, Educational Testing Service, and classrooms across the country for sharing their knowledge of their subject matter and their passion for preparing students for success in college. We want to single out Janet Heller, formerly director of the AP Program in the Middle States Office of the College Board, for giving us incredible opportunities to teach and learn. A remarkable teacher in her own right, Janet encouraged us by example and common classroom sense to seek better ways to motivate and move all students to do their best work, work that would make them as well as us proud. We would like to thank our reviewers, whose expertise guided us at every turn, Tim Averill, Nelina Backman, Ronnie Campagna, Margaret D. Devaney, Timothy Donahue, Dr. Thomas Humble, Carol Jago, Renée Lepley, Patricia A. Rand, Dee Schulten, Becky Talk, Karla Walters, and Jason Webb. We also want to thank our colleagues who model the high school–college partnerships that are fundamental to *The Language of Composition*: Mary-Grace Gannon, Kathleen L. Bell, Elizabeth Higgins, Mary McManus, David Jolliffe, Hephzibah Roskelly, Robert DiYanni, Marilyn Elkins, Ed Schmieder, and George Gadda. Their suggestions, advice, and insights have made *The Language of Composition* a better book. We thank our families for their unflagging support and encouragement through every stage of this project. A longer list of co-authors should include our children Meredith Barnes, Christopher Shea, Kate Aufses, Michael Aufses, Alison Scanlon, Lindsay Prezzano, Maura Scanlon, and Kaitlin Scanlon. Finally, we are grateful to our students — the ones in our classrooms and the colleagues in our workshops — for teaching us well.

RENÉE H. SHEA
LAWRENCE SCANLON
ROBIN DISSIN AUFSES

Contents

3 SYNTHESIZING SOURCES: Entering the Conversation   61

4 EDUCATION   87

To what extent do our schools serve the goals of a true education?

CENTRAL ESSAY

> *I find myself, each September, increasingly appalled by the dismal lists of texts that my sons are doomed to waste a school year reading. What I get as compensation is a measure of insight into why our society has come to admire Montel Williams and Ricki Lake so much more than Dante and Homer.*

CLASSIC ESSAY

> *I believe that our own experience instructs us that the secret of Education lies in respecting the pupil. It is not for you to choose what he shall know, what he shall do. It is chosen and foreordained, and he only holds the key to his own secret.*

> *I learned to read with a Superman comic book. Simple enough, I suppose. I cannot recall which particular Superman comic book I read, nor can I remember which villain he fought in that isssue. I cannot remember the plot, nor the means by which I obtained the comic book. What I can remember is this: I was 3 years old, a Spokane Indian boy living with his family on the Spokane Indian Resrvation in eastern Washington state.*

6 **COMMUNITY** 259

What is the relationship of the individual to the community?

CENTRAL ESSAY

MARTIN LUTHER KING JR., *Letter from Birmingham Jail* 260

(with the public statement by eight Alabama clergymen)
> Abused and scorned though we may be, our destiny is tied up with the destiny of America. Before the pilgrims landed at Plymouth, we were here. Before the pen of Jefferson etched across the pages of history the majestic words of the Declaration of Independence, we were here.

CLASSIC ESSAY

HENRY DAVID THOREAU, *Where I Lived, and What I Lived for* 276
> I went to the woods because I wished to live deliberately, to front only the essential facts of life, and see if I could not learn what it had to teach, and not, when I came to die, discover that I had not lived.

8   SPORTS AND FITNESS   429

How do the values of sports affect the way we see ourselves?

10   SCIENCE AND TECHNOLOGY   599

How are advances in science and technology affecting the way we define our humanity?

11 POPULAR CULTURE 707

To what extent does pop culture reflect our society's values?

Rhetorical Contents

Narration

Description

Exemplification

Comparison and Contrast

Classification and Division

Definition

Process Analysis

Cause and Effect

Argument

The Language of Composition

1

An Introduction to Rhetoric: Using the "Available Means"

To many people, the word *rhetoric* automatically signals that trickery or deception is afoot. They assume that an advertiser is trying to manipulate a consumer, a politician wants to obscure a point, or a spin doctor is spinning. "Empty rhetoric!" is a common criticism — and at times an indictment. Yet Greek philosopher Aristotle (384–322 B.C.E.) defined **rhetoric** as "the faculty of observing in any given case the available means of persuasion." At its best, rhetoric is a thoughtful, reflective activity leading to effective communication, including rational exchange of opposing viewpoints. In Aristotle's day and in ours, those who understand and can use the available means to appeal to an **audience** of one or many find themselves in a position of strength. They have the tools to resolve conflicts without confrontation, to persuade readers or listeners to support their position, or to move others to take action.

Key Elements of Rhetoric

Let's start out by looking at a speech that nearly everyone has read or heard: the speech baseball player Lou Gehrig gave at an Appreciation Day held in his honor on July 4, 1939. Gehrig had recently learned that he was suffering from amyotrophic lateral sclerosis (ALS), a neurological disorder that has no cure (today it is known as "Lou Gehrig's disease"). Although Gehrig was a reluctant speaker, the fans' chant of "We want Lou!" brought him to the podium to deliver one of the all-time most powerful, heartfelt — and brief (under three hundred words) — speeches.

> Watch it on the Web: bedfordstmartins.com/languageofcomp

Fans, for the past two weeks you have been reading about a bad break I got. Yet today I consider myself the luckiest man on the face of the earth. I have been in ballparks for seventeen years and have never received anything but

1

kindness and encouragement from you fans. Look at these grand men. Which of you wouldn't consider it the highlight of his career just to associate with them for even one day?

Sure, I'm lucky. Who wouldn't consider it an honor to have known Jacob Ruppert; also the builder of baseball's greatest empire, Ed Barrow; to have spent six years with that wonderful little fellow, Miller Huggins; then to have spent the next nine years with that outstanding leader, that smart student of psychology — the best manager in baseball today, Joe McCarthy? Who wouldn't feel honored to have roomed with such a grand guy as Bill Dickey?

Sure, I'm lucky. When the New York Giants, a team you would give your right arm to beat, and vice versa, sends you a gift — that's something! When everybody down to the groundskeepers and those boys in white coats remember you with trophies — that's something!

When you have a wonderful mother-in-law who takes sides with you in squabbles against her own daughter — that's something! When you have a father and mother who work all their lives so that you can have an education and build your body — it's a blessing! When you have a wife who has been a tower of strength and shown more courage than you dreamed existed — that's the finest I know!

So I close in saying that I might have been given a bad break, but I have an awful lot to live for! Thank you.

Why is this an effective speech? First of all, Lou Gehrig understood that rhetoric is always situational: it has a **context** — the occasion or the time and place it was written or spoken — and a **purpose** or goal that the speaker or writer wants to achieve. Gehrig delivered the speech between games of a doubleheader. The more important context, though, is the poignant contrast between the celebration of his athletic career and the life-threatening diagnosis he had received. Within this context, his purpose is to remain positive by looking on the bright side — his past luck and present optimism — and downplaying the bleak outlook. He makes a single reference to the diagnosis and does so in the straightforward language of strength: he got a "bad break" — there is no blame, no self-pity, no plea for sympathy. Throughout, he maintains his focus: to celebrate the occasion and get back to work — that is, playing baseball. While in our time the word *rhetoric* may suggest deception, this speech reminds us that rhetoric can serve sincerity as well.

Context and purpose are easy to spot in Gehrig's speech; identifying them in more complex situations is harder, but it is essential to analyzing effective rhetoric. When we read any text, we ask about the context in which it was written. Then we consider the purpose: is the speaker trying to win agreement, persuade us to take action, evoke sympathy, make someone laugh, inform, provoke, celebrate, repudiate, put forth a proposal, secure support, or bring about a favorable decision? Keep in mind too that sometimes the context arises from current events or cultural **bias**. For example, someone writing about freedom of speech in a community that has experienced hate graffiti must take that context into account and adjust the purpose of the piece so as not to offend the audience.

Another reason this speech is effective is that Gehrig has a crystal clear main idea: he's the "luckiest man on the face of the earth." Whether you call this idea a **thesis**, a **claim**, or an **assertion**, it is a clear and focused statement. Further, Gehrig knows his **subject** — baseball in general, the New York Yankees in particular. Though he is a champion baseball player, he is not a polished orator or a highly sophisticated writer; therefore, as a **speaker** he presents himself as a common man, modest and glad for the life he's lived. His audience is his fans and fellow athletes, those in the stadium as well as those who will hear the speech from afar, people rooting for him on and off the field. Gehrig's understanding of how these factors — subject (and main idea), speaker, and audience — interact determines his speech: a plainspoken, positive appreciation for what he has had, and a champion's courageous acceptance of the challenges that lie before him. No wonder one commentator wrote, "Lou Gehrig's speech almost rocked Yankee Stadium off its feet."

The Rhetorical Triangle

One way to consider the elements in Gehrig's speech is through the **rhetorical triangle** below. Some refer to it as the **Aristotelian triangle**, so-called because Aristotle described the interaction among subject, speaker, and audience (or subject, writer, and reader), as well as how this interaction determines the

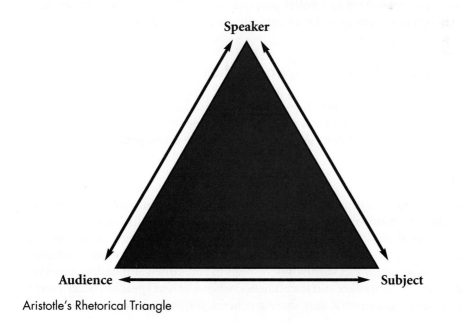

Aristotle's Rhetorical Triangle

structure and language of the argument — that is, a text or image that establishes a position.

Thus far, we've been analyzing a speech from the viewpoint of the audience, or readers, but skilled writers consider this interaction as they are developing an essay, speech, letter, or other text. Writers or speakers must first choose a **subject** and then evaluate what they already know about it, what others have said about it, and what kind of evidence or proof will sufficiently develop their position.

You might think the identity of the speaker in your own writing is obvious, but that's not necessarily so. Writers often assume what Aristotle called a **persona** — the character the speaker creates when he or she writes or speaks — depending on the context, purpose, subject, and audience. Are you speaking as a poet, comedian, or scholar? Are you speaking as an expert on ice skating, popular music, or a specific software program? Are you speaking as a literary critic in your English class or as a concerned citizen in your local community?

Before you proceed with these explorations and begin to craft an essay, however, it's important to think about the audience. What does the audience know about the subject? What is the audience's attitude toward it? Is there common ground between the writer's and reader's views on the subject? Each audience requires you to use different information to shape your argument effectively.

Imagine you are writing an essay for a college application. Who will read it? What will they be expecting? What is likely to impress them enough to admit you to their school? Or perhaps you're addressing peers you're working with on a collaborative project. Maybe you are writing a letter to a prospective employer who has never met you. If you are writing to a newspaper to express an environmental concern or opposition to a policy proposed by an elected official, your audience might be a larger group — for example, the whole community.

Appeals to Ethos, Logos, and Pathos

After analyzing the relationship of speaker to subject, audience to speaker, and audience to subject, a writer is ready to make some strategic choices. One is how to persuade the audience by appealing to **ethos**, **logos**, and **pathos**.

Ethos

Speakers and writers appeal to ethos, or character, to demonstrate that they are credible and trustworthy. Think, for example, of a speech discouraging children from using alcohol. Speakers might appeal to ethos by stressing that they are concerned parents, psychologists specializing in alcoholism or adolescent behavior, or recovering alcoholics themselves. Appeals to ethos often emphasize shared values between the speaker and the audience: when a parent speaks to other parents in the same community, they share a concern for their children's education or well-being. Lou Gehrig establishes ethos quite simply because he is a good sport, a regular guy who shares the audience's love of baseball and family, and like them, he has known good luck and bad breaks.

In some instances, a speaker's reputation immediately establishes ethos. For example, the speaker may be a scholar in Russian history and economics as well as the secretary of state. Or the speaker may be "the dog whisperer," a well-known animal behaviorist. In other cases, the speaker establishes ethos through the discourse itself, whether written or spoken, by making a good impression. That impression may result from a **tone** of reason and goodwill or from the type and thoroughness of information presented. The speaker's ethos — expertise and knowledge, experience, training, sincerity, or a combination of these — gives the audience a reason for listening.

Logos

Writers and speakers appeal to logos, or reason, by offering clear, rational ideas. Appealing to logos (Greek, "embodied thought") means having a clear main idea, or thesis, with specific details, examples, facts, statistical data, or expert testimony as support. Of course, the idea must be logical. Although on first reading or hearing, Gehrig's speech may seem largely emotional, it is actually based on irrefutable logic. He starts with the thesis that he is "the luckiest man on the face of the earth" and supports it with two points: (1) his seventeen years of playing baseball and (2) his belief that he has "never received anything but kindness and encouragement from [his] fans." Specifically, he has worked with good people on the field, he's been part of a sterling team, and he has the "blessing" of a supportive family. That he has gotten a "bad break" neither negates nor even lessens any of these experiences. What **assumption**, or underlying belief, links these seemingly contrasting ideas? It's that Gehrig is lucky even though he's had a bad break. He assumes, no doubt as his audience does, that bad breaks are a natural and inevitable part of life.

Another way to appeal to logos is to acknowledge a **counterargument** — that is, to anticipate objections or opposing views. While you might worry that raising an opposing view will weaken your argument, you'll be vulnerable if you ignore ideas that run counter to your own. In acknowledging a counterargument, you agree (**concede**) that an opposing argument may be true, but then you deny (**refute**) the validity of all or part of the argument. This concession and refutation actually strengthens your argument; it appeals to logos by demonstrating that you considered your subject carefully before making your argument.

In longer, more complex texts, the writer may address the counterargument in greater depth. Lou Gehrig, however, simply concedes what some of his listeners may think — that his bad break is cause for discouragement or even giving up; he disagrees because he has "an awful lot to live for!" Granted, he implies his concession rather than stating it outright, but in addressing it at all, he acknowledges a contrasting way of viewing his situation, that is a counterargument.

Pathos

Without question, Gehrig's speech gains power with its appeal to pathos, or emotion. Although writing that relies exclusively on emotional appeals is rarely effective in the long term, choosing language (such as figurative language or personal anecdotes) that engages the emotions of the audience can add an important dimension. Obviously, Gehrig uses the first person (*I*) because he is speaking about himself, but he also chooses a sequence of words with strong positive **connotations**: *greatest, wonderful, honored, grand, blessing.* He uses one image — *tower of strength* — that may not seem very original but strikes the right note. It is a well-known description that his audience understands — in fact, they probably have used it themselves.

Although an argument that appeals only to the emotions is by definition weak — it's generally **propagandistic** in purpose and more **polemical** than persuasive — an effective speaker or writer understands the power of evoking an audience's emotions. Emotional appeals usually include vivid, concrete description and figurative language. In addition, visual elements often carry a strong emotional appeal. A striking photograph, for example, may strengthen an argument. Advertisers certainly make the most of photos and other visual images to entice or persuade audiences.

Ethos, Logos, and Pathos in Practice

Let's go through an argument that appeared in a newspaper and analyze the elements we've just discussed. In the following article, which appeared in the *Washington Post* on Mother's Day in 2006, Jody Heyman takes an interesting approach: she organizes her main argument around the counterargument.

We Can Afford to Give Parents a Break

In an era when the mythology of motherhood is slowly yielding to the realities, it seems only appropriate to disabuse ourselves of some of the myths surrounding our government's treatment of mothers.

Perhaps the most obvious yardstick of governmental respect for mothers is maternity leave policy. Of 168 countries on which I collected data — for Harvard University's Project on Global Working Families and at McGill University — 164 have found a way to guarantee paid maternity leave. The only ones that haven't are Papua New Guinea, Swaziland, Lesotho and the United States. In most high-income countries, moms can receive help from dads who have paid parental leave. Indeed, in 27 countries fathers have a right to at least three months of paid leave at the birth of a child. Not in America.

Breast-feeding is crucial because it lowers infant morbidity and mortality three- to five-fold. But in America, there is no guarantee that mothers will be able to safeguard their infants in this way. While 76 countries ensure that mothers can take time from work to breast-feed their infants, America does not.

When children get sick, parents in 37 countries are guaranteed at least a minimum amount of paid leave to care for them. This is affordable because children get out of the hospital faster and recover from both chronic and acute illnesses more rapidly when parents are involved in their care. But the United States does not provide leave to any Americans for their own health problems — despite the fact that personal sick leave is a basic right of citizens in more than 150 countries around the world.

While a low-income mother in the United States is twice as likely as a   5
middle-class one to have a child with asthma or another chronic condition and twice as likely to be providing 30 hours or more of care a month for elderly or sick parents, she is less likely to have the work flexibility she needs to provide that care. Half of middle-class Americans can rely on getting a job with sick leave; three quarters of low-income Americans cannot.

While American women and men agree that women still do more of the housework and provide more of the care both for children and aging parents, they have fewer benefits — less sick leave, annual leave, flexibility at work. The United States has engaged in a unique private-sector experiment — as opposed to any partnership between the public and private. The experiment has tested what companies can and will offer voluntarily. This means that companies that want to do the right thing by mothers are stymied. If they offer paid maternity leave, they have to compete with a company across the street that doesn't — an uneven playing field that does not exist in most nations.

The conventional wisdom that the United States cannot afford to adopt more progressive and humane policies toward its own mothers and remain competitive in the global economy is upheld by certain myths.

Myth 1: The United States can't compete while offering policies that would markedly improve the lives of most American parents and children. The World Economic Forum rated the four most competitive nations as Finland, the United States, Sweden and Denmark. All but the United States provide at least a month of paid annual leave, six months of paid parental leave and paid sick leave.

Myth 2: Decent working conditions will lead to high unemployment. Iceland enjoys among the world's lowest unemployment rates, at 3.4 percent, yet ensures that all its working citizens enjoy a month of paid annual leave and extensive paid sick leave.

Myth 3: Decent working conditions will inhibit economic growth. Ire-   10
land got the nickname "Celtic Tiger" because its growth rate is among the world's highest — 6.4 percent per year throughout the 1990s and in the early years of this decade. It achieved this growth rate while ensuring six months of paid parental leave, four weeks of paid annual leave, short- and long-term paid sick leave and unpaid leave to meet children's health needs.

If politicians of either mainstream persuasion in the United States really valued mothers and families on Mother's Day or any other day, they would commit to finally ensuring rights for American mothers and fathers that most parents around the world already enjoy. They would ensure that American mothers receive paid maternity leave, as mothers in 164 other nations do. They would ensure that moms have breast-feeding breaks and sick leave. They would support early childhood education and after-school programs. Then the United States could be truly competitive in the most meaningful sense, and "Happy Mother's Day" would be more than just another myth.

The writer is director of the McGill University Institute for Health and Social Policy, founder of the Project on Global Working Families at Harvard, and author of Forgotten Families: Ending the Growing Crisis Confronting Children and Working Parents in a Global Economy.

Jody Heyman establishes ethos from the outset by referring to "our government," indicating that even though she is being critical, she is doing so on behalf of the audience. Then immediately in the next paragraph, she provides information that establishes her as an expert: she has "collected data — for Harvard University's Project on Global Working Families and at McGill University." Working with projects associated with two prestigious universities gives her strong credibility to speak on the subject. Further, at the end of the article, a biographical note states that Heyman was the director or founder of each project and indicates she has written a book on the topic at hand. Without question, her voice is an informed one.

Note that *where* something is published affects its credibility. In Heyman's case, her opinion piece appeared in a newspaper based in the nation's capital (where the legislation that Heyman calls for would be enacted). Moreover, it is a well-respected publication. In addition, this newspaper is associated more with liberal than conservative views, so Heyman can assume that her audience will be more receptive than hostile to her position. Although her readers may not agree with everything, they are likely to be willing to consider her views regarding family leave. Articles such as Heyman's are often reprinted in other publications, so it's always good to note where they originally appeared in order to understand who the writer was targeting.

Perhaps Heyman's strongest appeal to logos is her decision to frame her viewpoint not as a women's rights issue but as an economic one. She develops her argument for several paragraphs with facts and figures, presumably from the data she has collected. In fact, she begins the second paragraph by citing policies in other countries. She then goes on to write, for example, "When children get sick, parents in 37 countries are guaranteed at least a minimum amount of paid leave to care for them," and "personal sick leave is a basic right of citizens in more than 150 countries around the world."

She also appeals to reason by carefully analyzing cause and effect. When she compares the situations of low- and middle-income mothers, for instance, she emphasizes the effect on each group of not having paid sick leave or "work flexibility." Then she points out the disparity between men's and women's working conditions in order to emphasize the burdens carried by women, who are less likely to have the means to shoulder them.

After Heyman appeals to logos through facts, figures, and analysis, she focuses on what she expects to be the central objection to her call for an expanded maternity leave policy: "that the United States cannot afford to adopt more progressive and humane policies toward its own mothers and remain competitive in the global economy." She presents this concern in the form of three counterarguments — which she calls "myths" — and addresses them one by one. She refutes each with more facts, figures, and analysis. For instance, one of the myths is that "Decent working conditions will lead to high unemployment." Her refutation is to cite the case of Iceland, which "enjoys among the world's lowest unemployment rates, at 3.4 percent, yet ensures that all its working citizens enjoy a month of paid annual leave and extensive paid sick leave."

Does Heyman ignore pathos? She does not, for instance, identify herself as a mother or call on her personal experience with motherhood in any way, which might tug at the reader's heartstrings. Yet, she uses the occasion of Mother's Day and the warm feelings surrounding it to appeal to the audience's emotions. "If politicians . . . in the United States really valued mothers and families on Mother's Day," she suggests, they would enact the policies she advocates. And by writing in her final sentence, "'Happy Mother's Day' would be more than just another myth," Heyman uses the emotional power of Mother's Day to compel readers to consider her argument.

• ASSIGNMENT •

Widely considered the greatest scientist of the twentieth century, Albert Einstein (1879–1955) is responsible for the theory of relativity. He won the Nobel Prize in Physics in 1921. In 1936, he wrote the following letter to a sixth-grade student, Phyllis Wright, in response to her question as to whether scientists pray, and if so, what they pray for. How rhetorically effective do you find Einstein's response? Explain your answer in terms of subject, speaker, audience; context and purpose; and appeals to logos, ethos, and pathos.

January 24, 1936

Dear Phyllis,

   I have tried to respond to your question as simply as I could. Here is my answer.

   Scientific research is based on the idea that everything that takes place is determined by laws of nature, and therefore this holds for the actions of people. For this reason, a research scientist will hardly be inclined to believe that events could be influenced by a prayer, i.e., by a wish addressed to a supernatural being.

However, it must be admitted that our actual knowledge of these laws is only imperfect and fragmentary, so that, actually, the belief in the existence of basic all-embracing laws in Nature also rests on a sort of faith. All the same this faith has been largely justified so far by the success of scientific research.

But, on the other hand, every one who is seriously involved in the pursuit of science becomes convinced that a spirit is manifest in the laws of the Universe — a spirit vastly superior to that of man, and one in the face of which we with our modest powers must feel humble. In this way the pursuit of science leads to a religious feeling of a special sort, which is indeed quite different from the religiosity of someone more naive.

I hope this answers your question.

Best wishes

Yours,

Albert Einstein

Visual Rhetoric

So far we've been discussing texts that consist of words, either written or spoken, but the same elements of rhetoric are at work with visual texts, like political cartoons. Although political cartoons are often **satiric**, they may also comment without any hint of sarcasm or criticism. Consider the accompanying cartoon, which cartoonist Tom Toles drew after the death of civil-rights icon Rosa Parks in 2006. Parks was the woman who refused in 1955 to give up her seat on the bus in Montgomery, Alabama; that act came to symbolize the struggle for racial equality in the United States.

We can discuss the cartoon in the terms we've been using to examine texts that are exclusively verbal: The subject is the death of Rosa Parks, a well-known person loved by many. The speaker is Tom Toles, a respected and award-winning political cartoonist. The audience is made up of readers of the *Washington Post* and other newspapers; that is, it's a very broad audience. The speaker can assume his audience shares his admiration and respect for Parks and that they view her passing as the loss of a public figure as well as a private woman. And finally, the context is a memorial for a well-loved civil rights activist, and Toles's purpose is to remember Parks as an ordinary citizen whose courage and determination brought extraordinary results.

As you can see in this example, it's not uncommon for one passage or image to use more than one appeal. Readers' familiarity with Toles — along with his obvious respect for his subject — establishes his ethos. The image in the cartoon appeals primarily to pathos. Toles shows Rosa Parks, who was a devout Christian, as she is about to enter heaven through the pearly gates; they are attended by an angel, probably Saint Peter, who is reading a ledger. Toles depicts Parks wearing a simple coat and carrying her pocketbook, as she did while sitting on the bus so many years ago. The commentary at the bottom right reads, "We've been holding it [the front row in heaven] open since 1955," a reminder that more than fifty years have elapsed since Parks resolutely sat where she pleased. The caption can be seen as an appeal to both pathos and logos. Its emotional appeal is its acknowledgment that, of course, heaven would have been waiting for this good woman, but the mention of "the front row" appeals to logic because Parks made her mark in history for refusing to sit in the back of the bus. Some might even read the caption as a criticism of how slow the country was both to integrate and to pay tribute to Parks.

• **ASSIGNMENT** •

Analyze a political cartoon in terms of the rhetorical triangle and its appeals to logos, pathos, and ethos. As part of your analysis of audience, note if possible where the cartoon first appeared, and describe that source's political leanings. Finally, examine the interaction of written text and visual images.

An Example of Rhetoric from Literature

Rhetoric is by no means limited to nonfiction. Poetry, fiction, and drama also seek to persuade. For example, in Book 24 of Homer's epic *The Iliad*, the story of the Trojan War, the Greek warrior Achilles has defeated the Trojan prince Hector. Achilles has not only refused to return his rival's body to Troy for burial, but he has also dishonored it by lashing it to a chariot and pulling it through the dirt. This is the context. The purpose is that Priam, king of Troy and Hector's aged father, wants to reclaim his son's body from the brutal Achilles. In this scene, old meets young; the defeated meets the conqueror. Priam knows that his success depends on the strength of his rhetoric. He begins:

> Remember your own father,
> Achilles, in your godlike youth: his years
> like mine are many, and he stands upon
> the fearful doorstep of old age. He, too,
> is hard pressed it may be, by those around him,   5
> there being no one able to defend
> him from bane of war and ruin. Ah, but he
> may nonetheless hear news of you alive,
> and so with glad heart hope through all his days
> for sight of his dear son, come back from Troy,   10
> while I have deathly fortune. . . .
> And he who stood alone among them all,
> their champion, and Troy's, ten days ago
> you killed him, fighting for his land, my prince, Hector.
> It is for him that I have come   15
> among these ships, to beg him back from you,
> and I bring ransom without stint.
> Achilles, be reverent toward the great gods! And take
> pity on me, remember your own father.
> Think me more pitiful by far, since I   20
> have brought myself to do what no man else
> has done before — to lift to my lips the hand
> of one who killed my son.

In this powerfully moving passage, Priam, the speaker, knows that his audience, Achilles, will resist the subject, Priam's request for his son's body. He knows that his ethos cannot be his kingship, since he is king of a nearly vanquished country. Thus he assumes the persona of an aging and grieving father and appeals to Achilles by beginning, "Remember your own father." Knowing that a logical appeal is unlikely to move the rash Achilles, Priam appeals to pathos, reminding the "godlike" warrior that his father's "years / like mine are many, and he stands upon / the fearful doorstep of old age." Priam repeats this appeal as he asks for pity, reminding his audience that Achilles' father can still hope to see his son alive, while Priam cannot. Priam appeals to logos, to Achilles' reason, when he offers "ransom" and reminds him to "be reverent toward the great gods." Note that he wisely saves these points for last, after he has engaged Achilles' emotion. Priam is successful, Homer tells us later, in stirring in Achilles "new longing, and an ache of grief." Achilles grants Priam's request.

Arrangement

Another element of rhetoric is the organization of a piece, what classical rhetoricians called arrangement. Whether you're analyzing a text or writing your own, consider how the essay and its individual paragraphs or sections are arranged. Is the text organized in the best possible way in order to achieve its purpose? An essay always has a beginning, middle, and end: an introduction, developmental paragraphs, and conclusion. But how a writer structures the argument within that framework depends upon his or her intended purpose and effect. In the following sections, we'll look at a formal classical model of arrangement; then we'll examine rhetorical patterns of development.

The Classical Model

Classical rhetoricians outlined a five-part structure for an oratory, or speech, that writers still use today, although perhaps not always consciously:

- The introduction (*exordium*) introduces the reader to the subject under discussion. In Latin, *exordium* means "beginning a web," which is an apt description for an introduction. Whether it is a single paragraph or several, the introduction draws the readers into the text by piquing their interest, challenging them, or otherwise getting their attention. Often the introduction is where the writer establishes ethos.

- The narration (*narratio*) provides factual information and background material on the subject at hand, thus beginning the developmental paragraphs, or establishes why the subject is a problem that needs addressing. The level of detail a writer uses in this section depends largely on the audience's knowledge of the subject. Although classical rhetoric describes narration as appealing to logos, in actuality it often appeals to pathos because the writer attempts to evoke an emotional response about the importance of the issue being discussed.

• The confirmation (*confirmatio*), usually the major part of the text, includes the development or the proof needed to make the writer's case — the nuts and bolts of the essay, containing the most specific and concrete detail in the text. The confirmation generally makes the strongest appeal to logos.

• The refutation (*refutatio*), which addresses the counterargument, is in many ways a bridge between the writer's proof and conclusion. Although classical rhetoricians recommended placing this section at the end of the text as a way to anticipate objections to the proof given in the confirmation section, this is not a hard-and-fast rule. Earlier we analyzed an essay about working mothers in which the author, Jody Heyman, used counterarguments as an overall organization. If opposing views are well known or valued by the audience, a writer will address them before presenting his or her own argument. The counterargument's appeal is largely to logos.

• The conclusion (*peroratio*) — whether it is one paragraph or several — brings the essay to a satisfying close. Here the writer usually appeals to pathos and reminds the reader of the ethos established earlier. Rather than simply repeating what has gone before, the conclusion brings all the writer's ideas together and answers the question, so what? Writers should remember the classical rhetoricians' advice that the last words and ideas of a text are those the audience is most likely to remember.

An example of the classical model at work is the piece below written in 2006 by Sandra Day O'Connor, a former Supreme Court justice, and Roy Romer, superintendent of the Los Angeles Unified School District.

Not by Math Alone

Fierce global competition prompted President Bush to use the State of the Union address to call for better math and science education, where there's evidence that many schools are falling short.

    We should be equally troubled by another shortcoming in American schools: Most young people today simply do not have an adequate understanding of how our government and political system work, and they are thus not well prepared to participate as citizens.

Introduction

    This country has long exemplified democratic practice to the rest of the world. With the attention we are paying to advancing democracy abroad, we ought not neglect it at home.

Narration

Two-thirds of 12th-graders scored below "proficient" on the last national civics assessment in 1998, and only 9 percent could list two ways a democracy benefits from citizen participation. Yes, young people remain highly patriotic, and many volunteer in their communities. But most are largely disconnected from current events and issues.

A healthy democracy depends on the participation of citizens, and that participation is learned behavior; it doesn't just happen. As the 2003 report "The Civic Mission of Schools" noted: "Individuals do not automatically become free and responsible citizens, but must be educated for citizenship." That means civic learning — educating students for democracy — needs to be on par with other academic subjects.

5

This is not a new idea. Our first public schools saw education for citizenship as a core part of their mission. Eighty years ago, John Dewey said, "Democracy needs to be reborn in every generation and education is its midwife."

But in recent years, civic learning has been pushed aside. Until the 1960s, three courses in civics and government were common in American high schools, and two of them ("civics" and "problems of democracy") explored the role of citizens and encouraged students to discuss current issues. Today those courses are very rare.

What remains is a course on "American government" that usually spends little time on how people can — and why they should — participate. The effect of reduced civic learning on civic life is not theoretical. Research shows that the better people understand our history and system of government, the more likely they are to vote and participate in the civic life.

We need more and better classes to impart the knowledge of government, history, law and current events that students need to understand and participate in a democratic republic. And we also know that much effective civic learning takes place beyond the classroom — in extracurricular activity, service work that is connected to class work, and other ways students experience civic life.

Confirmation

Preserving our democracy should be reason enough to promote civic learning. But there are other benefits. Understanding society and how we relate to each other fosters the attitudes essential for success in college, work and communities; it enhances student learning in other subjects.

10

Economic and technological competitiveness is essential, and America's economy and technology have flourished because of the rule of law and the "assets" of a free and open society. Democracy has been good for business and for economic well-being. By the same token, failing to hone the civic tools of democracy will have economic consequences.

Bill Gates — a top business and technology leader — argues strongly that schools have to prepare students not only for college and career but for citizenship as well.

None of this is to diminish the importance of improving math and science education. This latest push, as well as the earlier emphasis on literacy, deserves support. It should also be the occasion for a broader commitment, and that means restoring education for democracy to its central place in school.

Refutation

We need more students proficient in math, science and engineering. We also need them to be prepared for their role as citizens. Only then can self-government work. Only then will we not only be more competitive but also remain the beacon of liberty in a tumultuous world.

Conclusion

Sandra Day O'Connor retired as an associate justice of the Supreme Court. Roy Romer, a former governor of Colorado, is superintendent of the Los Angeles Unified School District. They are co-chairs of the national advisory council of the Campaign for the Civic Mission of Schools.

Sandra Day O'Connor and Roy Romer follow the classical model very closely. The opening two paragraphs are an introduction to the main idea the authors develop. In fact, the last sentence is their two-part claim, or thesis: "Most young people today simply do not have an adequate understanding of how our government and political system work, and they are thus not well prepared to participate as citizens." O'Connor's position as a former Supreme Court justice establishes her ethos as a reasonable person, an advocate for justice, and a concerned citizen. Romer's biographical note at the end of the article suggests similar qualities. The authors use the pronoun "we" to refer not only to themselves but to all of "us" who are concerned about American society. The opening phrase "Fierce global competition" connotes a sense of urgency, and the warning that we are not adequately preparing our young people to participate as citizens is sure to evoke an emotional response of concern, even alarm.

In paragraphs 3 to 6 — the narration — the authors provide background information, including facts that add urgency to their point. They cite statistics, quote from research reports, even call on the well-known educator John Dewey. They also include a definition of "civic learning," a key term in their argument. Their facts-and-figures appeal is largely to logos, though the language of "a healthy democracy" certainly engages the emotions.

Paragraphs 7 to 12 present the bulk of the argument — the confirmation — by offering reasons and examples to support the case that young people lack the knowledge necessary for them to be informed citizens. The authors link civic learning to other subjects as well as to economic development. They quote Bill Gates, chairman of Microsoft, who has spoken about the economic importance of a well-informed citizenry.

In paragraph 13, O'Connor and Romer briefly address a major objection — the refutation — that we need to worry more about math and science education than about civic learning. While they concede the importance of math, science, and literacy, they point out that it is possible to increase civic education without undermining the gains made in those other fields.

The final paragraph — the conclusion — emphasizes the importance of a democracy to a well-versed citizenry, a point that stresses the shared values of the authors with their audience. The appeal to pathos is primarily through the vivid language, particularly the final sentence with its emotionally charged description "beacon of liberty," a view of their nation that most Americans hold dear.

Patterns of Development

Another way to consider arrangement is according to purpose. Is the writer's purpose to compare and contrast, to narrate an event, to define a term? Each of these purposes suggests a method of organization, or arrangement. These patterns of development include a range of logical ways to organize an entire text or, more likely, individual paragraphs or sections. In the following pages, we'll discuss the major patterns of development by examining excerpts from the essays in this book.

Narration

Narration refers to telling a story or recounting a series of events. It can be based on personal experience or on knowledge gained from reading or observation. Chronology usually governs narration, which includes concrete detail, a point of view, and sometimes such elements as dialogue. Narration is not simply crafting an appealing story; it is crafting a story that supports your thesis.

Writers often use narration as a way to enter into their topics. In the following example, Rebecca Walker tells a story about her son to lead into her explanation of why she put together the anthology *Putting Down the Gun* (p. 412).

> The idea for this book was born one night after a grueling conversation with my then eleven-year-old son. He had come home from his progressive middle school unnaturally quiet and withdrawn, shrugging off my questions of concern with uncharacteristic irritability. Where was the sunny, chatty boy I dropped off that morning? What had befallen him in the perilous halls of middle school? I backed off but kept a close eye on him, watching for clues.

After a big bowl of his favorite pasta, he sat on a sofa in my study and read his science textbook as I wrote at my desk. We both enjoyed this simple yet profound togetherness, the two of us focused on our own projects yet palpably connected. As we worked under the soft glow of paper lanterns, with the heat on high and our little dog snoring at his feet, my son began to relax. I could feel a shift as he began to remember, deep in his body, that he was home, that he was safe, that he did not have to brace to protect himself from the expectations of the outside world.

Walker brings her audience into her experience with her son by narrating step-by-step what happened and what she noticed when he returned from school. It's not only a personal story but also one that she will show has wider significance in the culture. Narration has the advantage of drawing readers in because everyone loves a good story.

Description

Description is closely allied with narration because both include many specific details. However, unlike narration, description emphasizes the senses by painting a picture of how something looks, sounds, smells, tastes, or feels. Description is often used to establish a mood or atmosphere. Rarely is an entire essay descriptive, but clear and vivid description can make writing more persuasive. By asking readers to see what you see and feel what you feel, you make it easy for them to empathize with you, your subject, or your argument. In the following example from "Serving in Florida" (p. 179), Barbara Ehrenreich describes her coworkers:

> I make friends, over time, with the other "girls" who work my shift: Nita, the tattooed twenty-something who taunts us by going around saying brightly, "Have we started making money yet?" Ellen, whose teenage son cooks on the graveyard shift and who once managed a restaurant in Massachusetts but won't try out for management here because she prefers being a "common worker" and not "ordering people around." Easy-going fiftyish Lucy, with the raucous laugh, who limps toward the end of the shift because of something that has gone wrong with her leg, the exact nature of which cannot be determined without health insurance. We talk about the usual girl things — men, children, and the sinister allure of Jerry's chocolate peanut-butter cream pie.

Ehrenreich's primary purpose here is to humanize her coworkers and make her readers understand their struggle to survive on the minimum wage. To achieve this, she makes them specific living-and-breathing human beings who are "tattooed" or have a "raucous laugh."

Narration and description often work hand in hand, as in the following paragraph from "Shooting an Elephant" (p. 979) by George Orwell. The author narrates the death throes of the elephant in such dense and vivid detail that we mourn the loss and realize that something extraordinary has died, and the narrator (Orwell), like all of us, is diminished by that passing — which is the point Orwell wants us to understand:

> When I pulled the trigger I did not hear the bang or feel the kick — one never does when a shot goes home — but I heard the devilish roar of glee that went up from the crowd. In that instant, in too short a time, one would have thought, even for the bullet to get there, a mysterious, terrible change had come over the elephant. He neither stirred nor fell, but every line of his body had altered. He looked suddenly stricken, shrunken, immensely old, as though the frightful impact of the bullet had paralysed him without knocking him down. At last, after what seemed a long time — it might have been five seconds, I dare say — he sagged flabbily to his knees. His mouth slobbered. An enormous senility seemed to have settled upon him. One could have imagined him thousands of years old. I fired again into the same spot. At the second shot he did not collapse but climbed with desperate slowness to his feet and stood weakly upright, with legs sagging and head drooping. I fired a third time. That was the shot that did for him. You could see the agony of it jolt his whole body and knock the last remnant of strength from his legs. But in falling he seemed for a moment to rise, for as his hind legs collapsed beneath him he seemed to tower upward like a huge rock toppling, his trunk reaching skyward like a tree. He trumpeted, for the first and only time. And then down he came, his belly towards me, with a crash that seemed to shake the ground even where I lay.

Note the emotionally charged language, such as "devilish roar of glee," and the strong verbs such as "slobbered," "did not collapse but climbed." Note the descriptive details: "jolt," "sagging," "drooping," "desperate slowness." The language is so vivid that we feel as though a drawing or painting is emerging with each detail the author adds.

Process Analysis

Process analysis explains how something works, how to do something, or how something was done. We use process analysis when we explain how to bake bread or set up an Excel spreadsheet, how to improve a difficult situation or assemble a treadmill. Many self-help books are essentially process analysis. The key to successful process analysis is clarity: it's important to explain a subject clearly and logically, with transitions that mark the sequence of major steps, stages, or phases of the process.

In the essay "Transsexual Frogs" (p. 655), Elizabeth Royte uses process analysis to explain the research of Tyrone Hayes, a biologist at the University of California at Berkeley investigating the impact of the pesticide atrazine.

> The next summer Hayes headed into the field. He loaded a refrigerated 18-wheel truck with 500 half-gallon buckets and drove east, followed by his students. He parked near an Indiana farm, a Wyoming river, and a Utah pond, filled his buckets with 18,000 pounds of water, and then turned his rig back toward Berkeley. He thawed the frozen water, poured it into hundreds of individual tanks, and dropped in thousands of leopard-frog eggs collected en route. To find out if frogs in the wild showed hermaphroditism, Hayes dissected juveniles from numerous sites. To see if frogs were vulnerable as adults, and if the effects were reversible, he exposed them to atrazine at different stages of their development.

In this example, Royte explains how something was done, that is, the actual physical journey that Hayes took when he "headed into the field": he traveled from California to Indiana, Wyoming, Utah, and back to California. The verbs themselves emphasize the process of his work: he "loaded," "parked," "filled," "turned . . . back," "thawed," "poured," and "dropped."

Exemplification

Providing a series of examples — facts, specific cases, or instances — turns a general idea into a concrete one; this makes your argument both clearer and more persuasive to a reader. A writer might use one extended example or a series of related ones to illustrate a point. You're probably familiar with this type of development. How many times have you tried to explain something by saying, "Let me give you an example"?

Aristotle taught that examples are a type of logical proof called **induction**. That is, a series of specific examples leads to a general conclusion. If you believe, for example, that hip-hop culture has gone mainstream, you might cite a series of examples that leads to that conclusion. For example, you could discuss hip-hop music in chain-store advertising, the language of hip-hop gaining widespread acceptance, and entertainers from many different backgrounds integrating elements of hip-hop into their music.

In the following paragraph from "I Know Why the Caged Bird Cannot Read" (p. 89), Francine Prose establishes the wide and, she believes, indiscriminate range of readings assigned in high school classes by giving many examples of those her own sons have read:

> My own two sons, now twenty-one and seventeen, have read (in public and private schools) Shakespeare, Hawthorne, and Melville. But they've also slogged repeatedly through the manipulative melodramas of Alice Walker and Maya Angelou, through sentimental middlebrow favorites (*To Kill a Mockingbird* and *A Separate Peace*), the weaker novels of John Steinbeck, the fantasies of Ray Bradbury. My older son spent the first several weeks of sophomore English discussing the class's summer assignment, *Ordinary People*, a

weeper and former bestseller by Judith Guest about a "dysfunctional" family recovering from a teenage son's suicide.

Prose develops her point by giving examples of authors, novels, and types of novels. But only in the case of *Ordinary People* does she discuss the example. The others are there to support her point about the rather random nature of books assigned in high school classrooms.

In the following paragraph, instead of giving several examples, Prose uses one extended example to make the point that even so-called great literature is often poorly taught. Note how she mines the example of *Huckleberry Finn* to discuss the various objections and concerns she has about teaching:

> It's cheering that so many lists include *The Adventures of Huckleberry Finn* — but not when we discover that this moving, funny novel is being taught not as a work of art but as a piece of damning evidence against that bigot, Mark Twain. A friend's daughter's English teacher informed a group of parents that the only reason to study *Huckleberry Finn* was to decide whether it was a racist text. Instructors consulting *Teaching Values Through Teaching Literature* will have resolved this debate long before they walk into the classroom to supervise "a close reading of *Huckleberry Finn* that will reveal the various ways in which Twain undercuts Jim's humanity: in the minstrel routines with Huck as the 'straight man'; in generalities about Blacks as unreliable, primitive and slow-witted. . . ."

By examining one case in depth — *Huckleberry Finn* — Prose considers the novel itself, ways it is taught, and the suggestions in one book of how to teach it. Note that she might have brought in other examples, treating each briefly, but focusing on one book allows her to examine the issue more closely.

Comparison and Contrast

A common pattern of development is comparison and contrast: juxtaposing two things to highlight their similarities and differences. Writers use comparison and contrast to analyze information carefully, which often reveals insights into the nature of the information being analyzed. Comparison and contrast is often required on examinations where you have to discuss the subtle differences or similarities in the method, style, or purpose of two texts.

In the following excerpt from "Walking the Path between Worlds" (p. 300), Lori Arviso Alvord compares and contrasts the landscape and culture of her home in the Southwest with that of New England and Dartmouth College:

> My memories of my arrival in Hanover, New Hampshire, are mostly of the color green. Green cloaked the hillsides, crawled up the ivied walls, and was reflected in the river where the Dartmouth crew students sculled. For

a girl who had never been far from Crownpoint, New Mexico, the green felt incredibly juicy, lush, beautiful, and threatening. Crownpoint had had vast acreage of sky and sand, but aside from the pastel scrub brush, mesquite, and chamiso, practically the only growing things there were the tiny stunted pines called pinion trees. Yet it is beautiful; you can see the edges and contours of red earth stretching all the way to the boxshaped faraway cliffs and the horizon. No horizon was in sight in Hanover, only trees. I felt claustrophobic.

If the physical contrasts were striking, the cultural ones were even more so. Although I felt lucky to be there, I was in complete culture shock. I thought people talked too much, laughed too loud, asked too many personal questions, and had no respect for privacy. They seemed overly competitive and put a higher value on material wealth than I was used to. Navajos placed much more emphasis on a person's relations to family, clan, tribe, and the other inhabitants of the earth, both human and nonhuman, than on possessions. Everyone at home followed unwritten codes for behavior. We were taught to be humble and not to draw attention to ourselves, to favor cooperation over competition (so as not to make ourselves "look better" at another's expense or hurt someone's feelings), to value silence over words, to respect our elders, and to reserve our opinions until they were asked for.

In the first paragraph, Arviso emphasizes the physical details of the landscape, so her comparison and contrast relies on description. In the second paragraph, she is more analytical as she examines the behavior. Although she does not make a judgment directly, in both paragraphs she leads her readers to understand her conclusion that her New Mexico home — the landscape and its inhabitants — is what she prefers.

Comparisons and contrasts, whether as a full essay or a paragraph, can be organized in two ways: subject-by-subject or point by point. In a subject by subject analysis, the writer discusses all elements of one subject, then turns to another. For instance, a comparison and contrast of two presidential candidates by subject would present a full discussion of the first candidate, then the second candidate. A point-by-point analysis is organized around the specific points of a discussion. So, a point-by-point analysis of two presidential candidates might discuss their education, then their experience, then the vision each has for the country. Arviso uses point-by-point analysis as she first compares and contrasts the landscapes and then the cultures of both places.

Classification and Division

It is important for readers as well as writers to be able to sort material or ideas into major categories. By answering the question, What goes together and why?

writers and readers can make connections between things that might otherwise seem unrelated. In some cases, the categories are ready-made, such as *single, married, divorced*, or *widowed*. In other cases, you might be asked either to analyze an essay that offers categories or to apply them. For instance, you might classify the books you're reading in class according to the categories Francis Bacon defined: "Some books are meant to be tasted, others to be swallowed, and some few to be chewed and digested."

Most of the time, a writer's task is to develop his or her own categories, to find a distinctive way of breaking down a larger idea or concept into parts. For example, in "Politics and the English Language" (p. 529), George Orwell sets up categories of imprecise and stale writing: "dying metaphors," "operators of verbal false limbs," "pretentious diction," and "meaningless words." He explains each in a paragraph with several examples and analysis. Classification and division is not the organization for his entire essay, however, because he is making a larger cause-and-effect argument that sloppy language leads to sloppy thinking; nevertheless, his classification scheme allows him to explore in a systematic way what he sees as problems.

In Amy Tan's essay "Mother Tongue" (p. 542) she classifies the "Englishes" she speaks into categories of public and private spheres:

> Recently, I was made keenly aware of the different Englishes I do use. I was giving a talk to a large group of people, the same talk I had already given to half a dozen other groups. The nature of the talk was about my writing, my life, and my book, *The Joy Luck Club*. The talk was going along well enough, until I remembered one major difference that made the whole talk sound wrong. My mother was in the room. And it was perhaps the first time she had heard me give a lengthy speech, using the kind of English I have never used with her. I was saying things like "The intersection of memory upon imagination" and "There is an aspect of my fiction that related to thus-and-thus" — speech filled with carefully wrought grammatical phrases, burdened, it suddenly seemed to me, with nominalized forms, past perfect tenses, conditional phrases, all the forms of standard English that I had learned in school and through books, the forms of English I did not use at home with my mother.
>
> Just last week, I was walking down the street with my mother, and I again found myself conscious of the English I was using, the English I do use with her. We were talking about the price of new and used furniture and I heard myself saying this: "Not waste money that way." My husband was with us as well, and he didn't notice any switch in my Englishes. And then I realized why. It's because over the twenty years we've been together I've often used that same kind of English with him, and sometimes he even uses it with me. It has become our language of intimacy, a different sort of English that related to family talk, the language I grew up with.

Tan does not start out by identifying two categories, but as she describes them she classifies her "Englishes" as the English she learned in school and in books and the language of intimacy she learned at home.

Definition

So many discussions depend upon definition. In examining the benefits of attending an Ivy League school, for instance, we need to define *Ivy League* before we can have a meaningful conversation. If we are evaluating a program's *success*, we must define what qualifies as success. Before we can determine whether certain behavior is or is not *patriotic*, we must define the term. Ratings systems for movies must carefully define *violence*. To ensure that writers and their audiences are speaking the same language, definition may lay the foundation to establish common ground or identifying areas of conflict.

Defining a term is often the first step in a debate or disagreement. In some cases, definition is only a paragraph or two that clarify terms, but in other cases, the purpose of an entire essay is to establish a definition. In Jane Howard's essay "In Search of the Good Family" (p. 283), she explores the meaning of *family*, a common enough term, yet one she redefines. She opens by identifying similar terms: "Call it a clan, call it a network, call it a tribe, call it a family." She contrasts the traditional "blood family" with "new families . . . [that] consist of friends of the road, ascribed by chance, or friends of the heart, achieved by choice." She develops her essay by first establishing the need we all have for a network of "kin" who may or may not be blood relatives. Then she analyzes ten characteristics that define a family. Here is one:

> Good families prize their rituals. Nothing welds a family more than these. Rituals are vital especially for clans without histories because they evoke a past, imply a future, and hint at continuity. No line in the seder service at Passover reassures more than the last: "Next year in Jerusalem!" A clan becomes more of a clan each time it gathers to observe a fixed ritual (Christmas, birthdays, Thanksgiving, and so on), grieves at a funeral (anyone may come to most funerals; those who do declare their tribalness), and devises a new rite of its own. Equinox breakfasts can be at least as welding as Memorial Day parades. Several of my colleagues and I used to meet for lunch every Pearl Harbor Day, preferably to eat some politically neutral fare like smorgasbord, to "forgive" our only ancestrally Japanese friend, Irene Kubota Neves. For that and other things we became, and remain, a sort of family.

Howard explains the purpose of rituals in her opening paragraph and then provides specific examples to explain what she means by *rituals*. She offers such a variety of them that her readers cannot fail to understand the flexibility and openness she associates with her definition of *family*.

Cause and Effect

Analyzing the causes that lead to a certain effect or, conversely, the effects that result from a cause is a powerful foundation for argument. Rachel Carson's case for the unintended and unexpected effects of the pesticide DDT in *Silent Spring* is legendary (p. 798). Although she uses a number of different methods to organize and develop her analysis, this simple — or not so simple — causal link is the basis of everything that follows. On a similar topic, Terry Tempest Williams in "The Clan of One-Breasted Women" (p. 816) proceeds from the effect she sees — the breast cancer that has affected the women in her family — to argue that the cause is environmental.

Since causal analysis depends upon crystal clear logic, it is important to carefully trace a chain of cause and effect and to recognize possible contributing causes. You don't want to jump to the conclusion that there is only one cause or one result, nor do you want to mistake an effect for an underlying cause. In "Letter from Birmingham Jail" (p. 260), for instance, Martin Luther King Jr. points out that his critics had mistaken a cause for an effect: the protests of the civil rights movement were not the cause of violence but the effect of segregation.

Cause and effect is often signaled by a *why* in the title or the opening paragraph. In "I Know Why the Caged Bird Cannot Read" (p. 89), Francine Prose sets out what she believes are the causes for high school students' lack of enthusiasm for reading: "Given the dreariness with which literature is taught in many American classrooms, it seems miraculous that any sentient teenager would view reading as a source of pleasure." In the following paragraph, she explains the positive effects of reading classical literature:

> Great novels can help us master the all-too-rare skill of tolerating — of being able to hold in mind — ambiguity and contradiction. Jay Gatsby has a shady past, but he's also sympathetic. Huck Finn is a liar, but we come to love him. A friend's student once wrote that Alice Munro's characters weren't people he'd choose to hang out with but that reading her work always made him feel "a little less petty and judgmental." Such benefits are denied to the young reader exposed only to books with banal, simple-minded moral equations as well as to the students encouraged to come up with reductive, wrong-headed readings of multilayered texts.

In her analysis, Prose argues for the positive effects of reading canonical literature, and she provides several examples. She concludes by pointing out that teaching less challenging works, or teaching more challenging works without acknowledging their complexity, has the effect of encouraging unclear or superficial thinking.

• ASSIGNMENT •

Reread Jody Heyman's essay "We Can Afford to Give Parents a Break" (p. 6), and discuss the patterns of development she uses. Which of these patterns prevails in the overall essay? Which does she use in specific sections or paragraphs?

When Rhetoric Misses the Mark

Not every attempt at effective rhetoric hits its mark. Actually, whether a speech or letter or essay is rhetorically effective is often a matter of opinion. When former president Bill Clinton addressed the nation on August 17, 1998, he described his relationship with Monica Lewinsky as "not appropriate." Some found the speech effective, while others thought he had not been sufficiently apologetic or even contrite. (Audio and full text of the speech is at <bedfordstmartins.com/languageofcomp>.)

In 2006, at the funeral of Coretta Scott King, widow of Martin Luther King Jr., a number of those who eulogized her also spoke about racism, the futility of the war in Iraq, and military spending that exceeded funding for the poor. Some listeners criticized such discussions, arguing that a funeral held in a church should acknowledge only the life and accomplishments of the deceased; others asserted that any occasion honoring the commitment of Mrs. King and her husband to racial and economic justice was an appropriate venue for social criticism.

A famous example of humorously ineffective rhetoric is the proposal of Mr. Collins to the high-spirited heroine Elizabeth Bennet in the nineteenth-century novel *Pride and Prejudice* by Jane Austen. Mr. Collins, a foolish and sycophantic minister, stands to inherit the Bennet estate; thus he assumes that any of the Bennet sisters, including Elizabeth, will be grateful for his offer of marriage. So he crafts his offer as a business proposal that is a series of reasons. Following is a slightly abridged version of Mr. Collins's proposal:

> My reasons for marrying are, first, that I think it a right thing for every clergyman in easy circumstances (like myself) to set the example of matrimony in his parish. Secondly, that I am convinced it will add very greatly to my happiness; and thirdly — which perhaps I ought to have mentioned earlier, that it is the particular advice and recommendation of the very noble lady whom I have the honour of calling patroness. . . . But the fact is, that being, as I am, to inherit this estate after the death of your honoured father (who, however, may live many years longer), I could not satisfy myself without resolving to chuse a wife from among his daughters, that the loss to them might be as little as possible, when the melancholy event takes place — which, however, as I have already said, may not be for several years. This has been my motive,

my fair cousin, and I flatter myself it will not sink me in your esteem. And now nothing remains for me but to assure you in the most animated language of the violence of my affection. To fortune I am perfectly indifferent, and shall make no demand of that nature on your father, since I am well aware that it could not be complied with; and that one thousand pounds in the 4 per cents, which will not be yours till after your mother's decease, is all that you may ever be entitled to. On that head, therefore, I shall be uniformly silent; and you may assure yourself that no ungenerous reproach shall ever pass my lips when we are married.

Mr. Collins appeals to logos with a sequence of reasons that support his intent to marry: ministers should be married, marriage will add to his happiness, and his patroness wants him to marry. Of course, these are all advantages to himself. Ultimately, he claims that he can assure Elizabeth "in the most animated language of the violence of [his] affection," yet he offers no language at all about his emotional attachment. Finally, as if to refute the counterargument that she would not reap many benefits from the proposed alliance, he reminds her that her financial future is grim unless she accepts his offer and promises to be "uniformly silent" rather than to remind her of that fact once they are married.

Where did he go wrong? Without devaluing the wry humor of Austen in her portrayal of Mr. Collins, we can conclude that at the very least he failed to understand his audience. He offers reasons for marriage that would have little appeal to Elizabeth, who does not share his businesslike and self-serving assumptions. No wonder she can hardly wait to extricate herself from the exchange or that he responds with shocked indignation.

Understanding your audience is just as important in visual texts, especially ones meant to be humorous. Consider the accompanying cartoon by Roz Chast that was published in the *New Yorker*. Its humor depends upon the artist's confidence that her audience is familiar with popular culture, Greek mythology, and the Bible. Chast's point is that the ancient legends and stories many of us hold sacred might be considered as sensational as the highly dramatic, often amazing headlines of the *National Enquirer*; however, this would be lost on someone unfamiliar with her three sources. She even pokes gentle fun at the publication by dating it May 17, 8423, B.C. (even though it costs a rather contemporary fifty cents).

The headline "Woman Turns into Pillar of Salt!" alludes to the story in Genesis of Lot's wife defying warnings not to look back on the destruction of the kingdom of Sodom and Gomorrah. The reference to the man living in the whale's stomach is to the biblical story of Jonah. The bottom left story alludes to the ancient Greek myth that Athena sprang fully grown (and in full armor) from the head of her father Zeus. And the headline on the bottom right refers to Cerberus, the three-headed dog who guards the entrance to Hades.

The cartoon would lack its amusing punch if the audience did not understand the references to the popular newspaper that specializes in sensational stories, as well as characters and stories from the Bible and Greek mythology.

R. CL

• ASSIGNMENT •

Following are four texts related to the death of Diana, Princess of Wales, in 1997. Divorced from England's Prince Charles, she was the mother of Princes William and Harry. During her life the princess was known for both her philanthropy and her scandal-plagued marriage. The first text here is a news report from the British Broadcasting Company on the morning of Diana's death. The second is the televised speech Queen Elizabeth gave several days later. The third is the eulogy Lord Spencer, Diana's brother, delivered at her funeral service. The fourth is an entry in <www.wikipedia.com>. Discuss the purpose of each text and how the interaction of speaker, audience, and subject affects the text. Consider how effective each text is in achieving its purpose.

Princess Diana Dies in Paris Crash

BBC, August 31, 1997

Diana, Princess of Wales, has died after a car crash in Paris.

She was taken to hospital in the early hours of Sunday morning where surgeons tried for two hours to save her life but she died at 0300 BST.

In a statement Buckingham Palace said the Queen and the Prince of Wales were "deeply shocked and distressed." Prince Charles broke the news of their mother's death to Princes William and Harry at Balmoral Castle in Scotland where the royal family had been spending the summer.

The accident happened after the princess left the Ritz Hotel in the French capital with her companion, Dodi Al Fayed — son of Harrods owner, Mohammed Al Fayed. Dodi Al Fayed and the vehicle's driver were also killed in the collision in a tunnel under the Place de l'Alma in the centre of the city.

The princess' Mercedes car was apparently being pursued at high speed by photographers on motorbikes when it hit a pillar and smashed into a wall. Mr. Al Fayed and the chauffeur died at the scene but the princess and her bodyguard were cut from the wreckage and rushed to hospital. The French authorities have begun a criminal investigation and are questioning seven photographers.

Tributes to the princess have been pouring in from around the world. Speaking from his home in South Africa, the princess' brother, Lord Charles Spencer, said his sister had been "unique." While it was not the time for recriminations there was no doubt the press had played a part in her death, the earl added.

Hundreds of mourners have gathered at the princess' London home, Kensington Palace, and many have laid flowers at the gates.

Queen Elizabeth's Televised Speech

September 5, 1997

Watch it on the Web: bedfordstmartins.com/languageofcomp

Since last Sunday's dreadful news we have seen, throughout Britain and around the world, an overwhelming expression of sadness at Diana's death.

We have all been trying in our different ways to cope. It is not easy to express a sense of loss, since the initial shock is often succeeded by a mixture of other feelings: disbelief, incomprehension, anger — and concern for those who remain.

We have all felt those emotions in these last few days. So what I say to you now, as your queen and as a grandmother, I say from my heart.

First, I want to pay tribute to Diana myself. She was an exceptional and gifted human being. In good times and bad, she never lost her capacity to smile and laugh, nor to inspire others with her warmth and kindness.

I admired and respected her — for her energy and commitment to others, and especially for her devotion to her two boys. This week at Balmoral, we have all been trying to help William and Harry come to terms with the devastating loss that they and the rest of us have suffered.

No one who knew Diana will ever forget her. Millions of others who never met her, but felt they knew her, will remember her. I for one believe that there are lessons to be drawn from her life and from the extraordinary and moving reaction to her death.

I share in your determination to cherish her memory.

This is also an opportunity for me, on behalf of my family, and especially Prince Charles and William and Harry, to thank all of you who have brought flowers, sent messages, and paid your respects in so many ways to a remarkable person. These acts of kindness have been a huge source of help and comfort.

Our thoughts are also with Diana's family and the families of those who died with her. I know that they too have drawn strength from what has happened since last weekend, as they seek to heal their sorrow and then to face the future without a loved one.

I hope that tomorrow we can all, wherever we are, join in expressing our grief at Diana's loss, and gratitude for her all-too-short life. It is a chance to show to the whole world the British nation united in grief and respect.

Earl Spencer's Eulogy for Diana
September 6, 1997

> Watch it on the Web: bedfordstmartins.com/languageofcomp

I stand before you today, the representative of a family in grief, in a country in mourning, before a world in shock.

We are all united, not only in our desire to pay our respects to Diana but rather in our need to do so. For such was her extraordinary appeal that the tens of millions of people taking part in this service all over the world, via television and radio, who never actually met her, feel that they, too, lost someone close to them in the early hours of Sunday morning. It is a more remarkable tribute to Diana than I can ever hope to offer her today.

Diana was the very essence of compassion, of duty, of style, of beauty. All over the world, she was a symbol of selfless humanity. All over the world, a standard bearer for the rights of the truly downtrodden, a very British girl who transcended nationality. Someone with a natural nobility who was classless and who proved in the last year that she needed no royal title to continue to generate her particular brand of magic.

Today is our chance to say thank you for the way you brightened our lives, even though God granted you but half a life. We will all feel cheated, always, that you were taken from us so young, and yet we must learn to be grateful that you came along at all. Only now that you are gone do we truly appreciate what we are now without and we want you to know that life without you is very, very difficult.

We have all despaired at our loss over the past week and only the strength of the message you gave us through your years of giving has afforded us the strength to move forward. There is a temptation to rush to canonize your memory; there is no need to do so. You stand tall enough as a human being of unique qualities not to need to be seen as a saint. Indeed, to sanctify your memory would be to miss out on the very core of your being, your wonderfully mischievous sense of humor, with a laugh that bent you double. Your joy for life, transmitted wherever you took your smile and the sparkle in those unforgettable eyes. Your boundless energy which you could barely contain. But your greatest gift was your intuition and it was a gift you used wisely. This is what underpinned all your other wonderful attributes, and if we look to analyze what it was about you that had such a wide appeal, we find it in your instinctive feel for what was really important in all our lives.

Without your God-given sensitivity, we would be immersed in greater ignorance at the anguish of AIDS and HIV sufferers, the plight of the homeless, the isolation of lepers, the random destruction of land mines. Diana explained to me once that it was her innermost feelings of suffering that made it possible for her to connect with her constituency of the rejected.

And here we come to another truth about her. For all the status, the glamour, the applause, Diana remained throughout a very insecure person at heart, almost childlike in her desire to do good for others so she could release herself from deep feelings of unworthiness, of which her eating disorders were merely a symptom. The world sensed this part of her character and cherished her for her vulnerability, while admiring her for her honesty.

The last time I saw Diana was on July 1, her birthday, in London, when, typically, she was not taking time to celebrate her special day with friends but was guest of honor at a special charity fundraising evening. She sparkled, of course, but I would rather cherish the days I spent with her in March when she came to visit me and my children in our home in South Africa. I am proud of the fact, apart from when she was on display meeting President [Nelson] Mandela, we managed to contrive to stop the ever-present paparazzi from getting a single picture of her — that meant a lot to her.

These were days I will always treasure. It was as if we had been transported back to our childhood, when we spent such an enormous amount of time together — the two youngest in the family. Fundamentally, she had not changed at all from the big sister who mothered me as a baby, fought with me at school and endured those long train journeys between our parents' homes with me at weekends.

It is a tribute to her level-headedness and strength that despite the most bizarre life imaginable after her childhood, she remained intact, true to herself.

There is no doubt that she was looking for a new direction in her life at this time. She talked endlessly of getting away from England, mainly because of the treatment that she received at the hands of the newspapers.

I don't think she ever understood why her genuinely good intentions were sneered at by the media, why there appeared to be a permanent quest on their behalf to bring her down. It is baffling.

My own and only explanation is that genuine goodness is threatening to those at the opposite end of the moral spectrum. It is a point to remember that of all the ironies about Diana, perhaps the greatest was this — a girl given the name of the ancient goddess of hunting was, in the end, the most hunted person of the modern age.

She would want us today to pledge ourselves to protecting her beloved boys, William and Harry, from a similar fate, and I do this here, Diana, on your behalf. We will not allow them to suffer the anguish that was used regularly to drive you to tearful despair.

And, beyond that, on behalf of your mother and sisters, I pledge that we, your blood family, will do all we can to continue the imaginative way in which you were steering these two exceptional young men, so that their souls are not simply immersed by duty and tradition but can sing openly, as you planned. We fully respect the heritage into which they have both been born and will always respect and encourage them in their royal role, but we, like you, recognize the need for them to experience as many different aspects of life as possible to arm them spiritually and emotionally for the years ahead. I know you would have expected nothing less from us.

William and Harry, we all care desperately for you today. We are all chewed up with the sadness at the loss of a woman who was not even our mother. How great your suffering is, we cannot even imagine.

I would like to end by thanking God for the small mercies he has shown us at this dreadful time. For taking Diana at her most beautiful and radiant and when she had joy in her private life.

Above all, we give thanks for the life of a woman I am so proud to be able to call my sister — the unique, the complex, the extraordinary and irreplaceable Diana, whose beauty, both internal and external, will never be extinguished from our minds.

Wikipedia entry for Princess Diana (accessed September 15, 2006)

On 31 August 1997 Diana was involved in a car accident in the Pont de l'Alma road tunnel in Paris, along with her new lover Dodi Al-Fayed, and their driver Henri Paul. Their Mercedes crashed on the thirteenth pillar of the tunnel. Fayed's bodyguard Trevor Rees-Jones was closest to the point of impact and yet the only survivor of the crash, since he was the only occupant of the car who was wearing a seatbelt. Henri Paul and Dodi Fayed were killed instantly. Diana, unbelted in the back seat, slid forward during the impact and "submarined" under the seat in front, causing massive internal bleeding. She was transported to the Pitié-Salpêtrière Hospital where, despite lengthy resuscitation attempts, she died. Her funeral on 6 September 1997 was broadcast and watched by over 1 billion people worldwide. . . .

Controversy

The death of Diana has been the subject of widespread theories, supported by Mohamed Al-Fayed, whose son died in the accident. These were rejected by French investigators and British officials, who stated that the driver, Henri Paul, was drunk and on drugs. Among Mr. Fayed's suggestions were that Diana was pregnant by Dodi at the time of her death and that Dodi had just bought her an engagement ring, although witnesses to autopsies reported that the princess had not been pregnant and the jeweller cited by Mr. Fayed denied knowledge of the engagement ring. Nonetheless, in 2004 the authorities ordered an independent inquiry by Lord Stevens, a former chief of the Metropolitan Police, and he suggested that the case was "far more complex than any of us thought" and reported "new forensic evidence" and witnesses [*Telegraph*, May 2006]. The inquiry is expected to report its findings in 2007. The French authorities have also decided to reopen the case.

Several press photos were taken of the crash scene within moments of the crash. On 13 July 2006 Italian magazine *Chi* published photographs showing Diana in her "last moments" despite an unofficial blackout on such photographs being published. The photographs were taken minutes after the accident and show the Princess slumped in the back seat while a paramedic attempts to fit an oxygen mask over her face. The photographs were also published in other Italian and Spanish magazines and newspapers.

The editor of *Chi* defended his decision by saying he published the photographs for the "simple reason that they haven't been seen before" and that he felt the images do not disrespect the memory of the Princess. The British media publicly refused to publish the images, with the notable exception of *The Sun*, which printed the picture but with the face blacked out. . . .

Final Resting Place

Princess Diana's final resting place is said to be in the grounds of Althorp Park, her family home. The original plan was for her to be buried in the Spencer family vault at the local church in nearby Great Brington, but Diana's brother, Charles, the 9th Earl Spencer, said that he was concerned about public safety and security and the onslaught of visitors that might overwhelm Great Brington. He decided that he wanted his sister to be buried where her grave could be easily cared for and visited in privacy by her sons and other relatives.

Lord Spencer selected a burial site on an island in an ornamental lake known as The Oval within Althorp Park's Pleasure Garden. A path with 36 oak trees, marking each year of her life, leads to the Oval. Four black swans swim in the lake, symbolizing sentinels guarding the island. In the water there are several water lilies. White roses and lilies were Diana's favorite flowers. On the southern verge of the Round Oval sits the Summerhouse, previously in the gardens of Admiralty House, London, and now serving as a memorial to Princess Diana. An ancient arboretum stands nearby, which contains trees planted by Prince William and Prince Harry, other members of her family and the princess herself. . . .

Close Reading:
The Art and Craft of Analysis

Do you ever wonder how your teachers can teach the same books year after year and not be bored by them? One reason is that the works we study in school have many layers of meaning, revealing something new each time we read them. That quality is what distinguishes them from literary potato chips, writings that are satisfying — even delicious — but offer little nutritional value. A mystery or a romance may absorb us completely, but usually we do not read it a second time.

How do you find the "nutritional value" in the books, stories, essays, and poems you study in school? Your teacher may lead you through a work, putting it in context, focusing your attention on themes and techniques, asking for a response. Or, you might do these things yourself through a process called **close reading,** or analysis of a text. When you read closely, you develop an understanding of a text that is based first on the words themselves and then on the larger ideas those words suggest. That is, you start with the small details, and as you think about them, you discover how they affect the text's larger meaning. When you *write* about close reading, you start with the larger meaning you've discovered and use the small details — the language itself — to support your interpretation.

As with any skill, close reading becomes easier with practice, but it's important to remember that we use it unconsciously — and instantaneously — every day as we respond to people and situations. We are aware of the interaction of subject, speaker, and audience (remember the rhetorical triangle in Chapter 1?), and we instinctively respond to the context and purpose of our interactions. We also consider style: body language, gestures, facial expressions, tone of voice, volume, sentence structure, **colloquialisms,** vocabulary, and more. And when we recount a conversation or describe a situation, we often analyze it in the same way we would write about a text we have read closely.

Take a look at the concluding paragraphs of "Where Nothing Says Everything," an essay by Suzanne Berne about visiting Ground Zero, the site of the terrorist attacks on the World Trade Center, several months after September 11,

35

2001. In the essay, which appeared in the *New York Times* travel section in April 2002, Berne writes that she had trouble getting a ticket to the official viewing platform, so she went into a deli that advertised a view of Ground Zero from its second floor. She brought her sandwich upstairs to a table next to a large window.

> And there, at last, I got my ticket to the disaster.
>
> I could see not just into the pit now, but also its access ramp, which trucks had been traveling up and down since I had arrived that morning. Gathered along the ramp were firefighters in their black helmets and black coats. Slowly they lined up, and it became clear that this was an honor guard, and that someone's remains were being carried up the ramp toward the open door of an ambulance.
>
> Everyone in the dining room stopped eating. Several people stood up, whether out of respect or to see better, I don't know. For a moment, everything paused.
>
> Then the day flowed back into itself. Soon I was outside once more, joining the tide of people washing around the site. Later, as I huddled with a little crowd on the viewing platform, watching people scrawl their names or write "God Bless America" on the plywood walls, it occurred to me that a form of repopulation was taking effect, with so many visitors to this place, thousands of visitors, all of us coming to see the wide emptiness where so many were lost. And by the act of our visiting — whether we are motivated by curiosity or horror or reverence or grief, or by something confusing that combines them all — that space fills up again.

Using what you learned in Chapter 1, you can probably identify the passage's context and purpose: the writer, not a New Yorker, visits Ground Zero and is awed by the emptiness that was once the World Trade Center; her purpose is to describe the experience to readers who seven months later still feel the immediacy of that September morning.

You can analyze the passage through the rhetorical triangle, considering the interaction of subject, speaker, and audience. Berne's audience, readers of the travel section of a national newspaper, may be planning their own visit and thus may be interested in her personal experience. You can also consider the ways Berne appeals to ethos, pathos, and logos. She establishes ethos by actually going to Ground Zero, not simply musing about it; her emotion-laden subject appeals to pathos; and in an original way, she uses logos, or logic, to show that visitors to the site are repopulating the area that was decimated on September 11.

And there's more. Using close-reading techniques, we can also examine Berne's **style.** Doing so provides information about the choices she makes at the word and sentence levels, some of which we may use to further analyze this piece.

Analyzing Style

Just as we pay attention to more than the spoken words during a conversation, when we read closely, we look beyond the words on the page. And just as we notice body language, gestures, facial expressions, and volume in our conversations, we can understand a text better by examining its **tone,** sentence structure, and vocabulary. These elements make up the **style** of the written piece and help us to discover layers of meaning. Style contributes to the meaning, purpose, and effect of a text, whether it is visual or written.

Look back at the excerpt from Berne's essay. Here are some questions about style that might come to mind based on your first impressions of the passage:

- Why is the first paragraph one sentence?
- In that paragraph, why does Berne call the empty space "the disaster"?
- Why does the third sentence begin with "Gathered" rather than "Firefighters"?
- What examples of figurative language appear in the fourth paragraph?
- Does the word *huddled* in the fourth paragraph remind you of anything else you've read?
- What is the effect of the dashes in the final sentence?

You may notice that these questions fall into two categories: the choice of words and how the words are arranged. We call the choice of words **diction** and the arrangement of words **syntax.** Sometimes we talk about style as a matter of *tropes* and *schemes.* A **trope** is essentially artful diction. A trope could be a **metaphor,** a **simile, personification,** and **hyperbole.** A **scheme** is artful syntax. **Parallelisms, juxtapositions,** and **antitheses** are common schemes.

Here are some questions to ask when you analyze diction:

1. Which of the important words in the passage (verbs, nouns, adjectives, and adverbs) are general and abstract? Which are specific and concrete?
2. Are the important words formal, informal, colloquial, or slang?
3. Are some words nonliteral or figurative, creating **figures of speech** such as metaphors?

When you analyze syntax, you might ask:

1. What is the order of the parts of the sentence? Is it the usual (subject-verb-object), or is it inverted?
2. Which part of speech is more prominent — nouns or verbs?
3. What are the sentences like? Are they **periodic** (moving toward something important at the end) or **cumulative** (adding details that support an important idea in the beginning of the sentence)?
4. How does the sentence connect its words, phrases, and clauses?

These first-impression questions can be categorized as shown in the accompanying table.

FIRST-IMPRESSION QUESTIONS	DICTION	SYNTAX
Why is the first paragraph one sentence?		✓
In that paragraph, why does Berne call the empty space "the disaster"?	✓	
Why does the third sentence begin with "Gathered" rather than "Firefighters"?		✓
What examples of figurative language appear in the fourth paragraph?	✓	
Does the word *huddled* in the fourth paragraph remind you of anything else you've read?	✓	
What is the effect of the dashes in the final sentence?		✓

If you can answer these questions, you will be well on your way toward an analysis of an author's style and how that style is part of the text's message.

Talking with the Text

By now, you may be wondering how to generate your own questions to do a close reading. Just start by paying close attention to the choices a writer makes in the way he or she connects subject, speaker, and audience, as well as the choices the writer makes about style. Remember that style is a subset of rhetoric — it is a means of persuasion.

Let's look at three different approaches to close reading a passage by Joan Didion about California's Santa Ana winds from her essay "Los Angeles Notebook." As you interact with the text, keep in mind that you're not only identifying techniques and strategies, but you are also analyzing their effect. In other words, how do Didion's choices in diction and syntax help her achieve a particular purpose? To answer this, you must determine what the purpose is, what the choices are, and what effect those choices create.

> There is something uneasy in the Los Angeles air this afternoon, some unnatural stillness, some tension. What it means is that tonight a Santa Ana will begin to blow, a hot wind from the northeast whining down through the

Cajon and San Gorgonio Passes, blowing up sand storms out along Route 66, drying the hills and the nerves to flash point. For a few days now we will see smoke back in the canyons, and hear sirens in the night. I have neither heard nor read that a Santa Ana is due, but I know it, and almost everyone I have seen today knows it too. We know it because we feel it. The baby frets. The maid sulks. I rekindle a waning argument with the telephone company, then cut my losses and lie down, given over to whatever it is in the air. To live with the Santa Ana is to accept, consciously or unconsciously, a deeply mechanistic view of human behavior.

I recall being told, when I first moved to Los Angeles and was living on an isolated beach, that the Indians would throw themselves into the sea when the bad wind blew. I could see why. The Pacific turned ominously glossy during a Santa Ana period, and one woke in the night troubled not only by the peacocks screaming in the olive trees but by the eerie absence of surf. The heat was surreal. The sky had a yellow cast, the kind of light sometimes called "earthquake weather." My only neighbor would not come out of her house for days, and there were no lights at night, and her husband roamed the place with a machete. One day he would tell me that he had heard a trespasser, the next a rattlesnake.

"On nights like that," Raymond Chandler once wrote about the Santa Ana, "every booze party ends in a fight. Meek little wives feel the edge of the carving knife and study their husbands' necks. Anything can happen." That was the kind of wind it was. I did not know then that there was any basis for the effect it had on all of us, but it turns out to be another of those cases in which science bears out folk wisdom. The Santa Ana, which is named for one of the canyons it rushes through, is a *foehn* wind, like the *foehn* of Austria and Switzerland and the *hamsin* of Israel. There are a number of persistent malevolent winds, perhaps the best known of which are the *mistral* of France and the Mediterranean *sirocco*, but a *foehn* wind has distinct characteristics: it occurs on the leeward slope of a mountain range and, although the air begins as a cold mass, it is warmed as it comes down the mountain and appears finally as a hot dry wind. Whenever and wherever *foehn* blows, doctors hear about headaches and nausea and allergies, about "nervousness," about "depression." In Los Angeles some teachers do not attempt to conduct formal classes during a Santa Ana, because the children become unmanageable. In Switzerland the suicide rate goes up during the *foehn*, and in the courts of some Swiss cantons the wind is considered a mitigating circumstance for crime. Surgeons are said to watch the wind, because blood does not clot normally during a *foehn*. A few years ago an Israeli physicist discovered that not only during such winds, but for the ten or twelve hours which precede them, the air carries an unusually high ratio of positive to negative ions. No one seems to know exactly why that should be; some talk about friction and others suggest solar disturbances. In any case the positive ions are there, and what an excess of positive ions does, in the simplest terms, is make people unhappy. One cannot get much more mechanistic than that.

Annotation

One technique you can use is **annotation.** Annotating a text requires reading with a pen or pencil in hand. If you are not allowed to write in your book, write on Post-it notes. As you read, circle words you don't know, or write them on the Post-it notes. Identify main ideas — **thesis statements, topic sentences** — and also words, phrases, or sentences that appeal to you or that you don't understand. Look for figures of speech, or tropes, such as metaphors, similes, and personification — as well as **imagery** and detail. If you don't know the technical term for something, just describe it. For example, if you come across an adjective-and-noun combination that seems contradictory, such as "meager abundance," and you don't know that the term for it is **oxymoron,** you might still note the juxtaposition of two words that have opposite meanings. Use the margins or Post-it notes to ask questions or to comment on what you have read. In short, as you read, listen to the voice in your head, and write down what that voice is saying.

Following is an annotated version of the Didion passage:

There is something (uneasy) in the Los Angeles air this afternoon, some (unnatural) stillness, some tension. What it means is that tonight a Santa Ana will begin to blow, a hot wind from the northeast (whining) down through the Cajon and San Gorgonio Passes, blowing up sand storms out along Route 66, drying the hills and the nerves to (flash point.) For a few days now we will (see) smoke back in the canyons, and (hear) sirens in the night. I have neither heard nor read that a Santa Ana is due, but I know it, and almost everyone I have seen today knows it too. We know it because we (feel) it. (The baby frets. The maid sulks.) I rekindle a waning argument with the telephone company, then cut my losses and lie down, given over to whatever it is in the air. To live with the Santa Ana is to accept, consciously or unconsciously, a deeply (mechanistic) view of human behavior.

I recall being told, when I first moved to Los Angeles and was living on an isolated beach, that the Indians would throw themselves into the sea when the bad wind blew. I could see why. The Pacific turned (ominously) glossy during a Santa Ana

Margin annotations:

Long sentence

Related words. Anxiety, foreboding

Appeal to senses

Short sentences

Look up word

Folktale?

Echo of foreboding in opening

period, and one woke in the night troubled not only by the *Vivid images*
peacocks screaming in the olive trees but by the eerie absence
of surf. The heat was surreal. The sky had a yellow cast, the
kind of light sometimes called "earthquake weather." My
only neighbor would not come out of her house for days, and
there were no lights at night, and her husband roamed the *Personal anecdote*
More anxiety words place with a machete. One day he would tell me that he had
heard a trespasser, the next a rattlesnake. *— Look up name*

"On nights like that," Raymond Chandler once wrote
about the Santa Ana, "every booze party ends in a fight. Meek
little wives feel the edge of the carving knife and study their
husbands' necks. Anything can happen." That was the kind of
wind it was. I did not know then that there was any basis for
the effect it had on all of us, but it turns out to be another of
those cases in which science bears out folk wisdom. The *— Seemingly contradictory sources of information*
Santa Ana, which is named for one of the canyons it rushes
through, is a *foehn* wind, like the *foehn* of Austria and
Switzerland and the *hamsin* of Israel. There are a number of
Good description persistent malevolent winds, perhaps the best known of
which are the *mistral* of France and the Mediterranean
sirocco, but a *foehn* wind has distinct characteristics: ① it
occurs on the leeward slope of a mountain range and,
although the air begins as a cold mass, it is warmed as it
comes down the mountain and appears finally as a hot dry
wind. Whenever and wherever *foehn* blows, ② doctors hear
about headaches and nausea and allergies, about "nervous-
At least 7 scientific facts ness," about "depression." ③ In Los Angeles some teachers do *Why in quotes?*
not attempt to conduct formal classes during a Santa Ana, ④
because the children become unmanageable. In Switzerland
the suicide rate goes up during the *foehn*, and in the courts of
some Swiss cantons the wind is considered a ⑤ mitigating circumstance for crime. Surgeons are said to watch the wind,
because ⑥ blood does not clot normally during a *foehn*. A few
years ago an Israeli physicist discovered that not only during
such winds, but for the ten or twelve hours which precede
them, the air carries an unusually ⑦ high ratio of positive to
negative ions. No one seems to know exactly why that should

be; some talk about friction and others suggest solar disturbances. In any case the positive ions are there, and <u>what an</u>

Strange — <u>excess of positive ions does, in the simplest terms, is make</u>
should be positive <u>people unhappy.</u> One cannot get much more mechanistic
than that.

Dialectical Journal

Another way to interact with a text is to keep a **dialectical journal,** or double-
entry notebook. Dialectical journals use columns to represent visually the conversation between the text and the reader. Let's look at a dialectical journal set up
with note taking on the left (in this case, sections of the text you think are important) and with note making on the right (your comments).

NOTE TAKING	PARA.	NOTE MAKING
What it means is that tonight a Santa Ana will begin to blow, a hot wind from the northeast whining down through the Cajon and San Gorgonio Passes, blowing up sand storms out along Route 66, drying the hills and the nerves to flash point.	1	"drying the hills and the nerves" — example of zeugma, makes connection between nature and human behavior. Long sentence *winding* to the end — a "flash point" — like the winds "whining" down the passes and causing humans to act crazy.
"On nights like that," Raymond Chandler once wrote about the Santa Ana, "every booze party ends in a fight. Meek little wives feel the edge of the carving knife and study their husbands' necks. Anything can happen."	3	Chandler, who wrote crime fiction, was known for his hard-boiled style and cynicism. His quotation offers another image that supports Didion's view of the Santa Ana winds' effects on human behavior.
Whenever and wherever *foehn* blows, doctors hear about headaches and nausea and allergies, about "nervous-ness," about "depression." In Los Angeles some teachers do not attempt to conduct formal classes during a Santa Ana, because the children become unmanageable. In Switzerland the	3	These are impressive reports, from all over the world, and they make Didion's argument about the effects of winds on behavior convincing. They're basically a list — they could almost be bullet points.

NOTE TAKING	PARA.	NOTE MAKING
suicide rate goes up during the *foehn*, and in the courts of some Swiss cantons the wind is considered a mitigating circumstance for crime. Surgeons are said to watch the wind, because blood does not clot normally during a *foehn*.		
A few years ago an Israeli physicist discovered that not only during such winds, but for the ten or twelve hours which precede them, the air carries an unusually high ratio of positive to negative ions.	3	Sounds pretty scientific; an Israeli physicist sounds like an expert. Another scientific fact for Didion's argument.

Breaking the text into small sections helps you notice the details in Didion's writing: specific word and sentence choices. For example, she connects two seemingly different things in the same grammatical construction ("drying the hills and the nerves"; the technical name for this figure of speech is **zeugma**). She also alludes to crime writer Raymond Chandler, to facts, even to some scientific data. Collecting these bits of information from the text and considering their impression on you prepares you to answer the following questions about Didion's style: What effect is she striving for? How does the effect serve the purpose of her writing?

Graphic Organizer

A third way to organize your thoughts about a specific text is to use a **graphic organizer.** Your teacher may divide the text for you, or you may divide it yourself as you begin your analysis. Use the paragraph divisions in the text as natural breaking points, or perhaps consider smaller sections that reveal interesting stylistic choices. Although a graphic organizer takes time to complete, it lets you gather a great deal of information to analyze as you prepare to write an essay.

The accompanying graphic organizer below asks you to copy something the writer has said, then restate it in your own words; next you analyze how the writer makes the point and what the effect on the reader is. Note that you become increasingly analytical as you move across the columns to the right.

QUOTATION	PARAPHRASE OR SUMMARIZE
There is something uneasy in the Los Angeles air this afternoon, some unnatural stillness, some tension. What it means is that tonight a Santa Ana will begin to blow, a hot wind from the northeast whining down through the Cajon and San Gorgonio Passes, blowing up sand storms out along Route 66, drying the hills and the nerves to flash point. For a few days now we will see smoke back in the canyons, and hear sirens in the night. I have neither heard nor read that a Santa Ana is due, but I know it, and almost everyone I have seen today knows it too. We know it because we feel it. The baby frets. The maid sulks. I rekindle a waning argument with the telephone company, then cut my losses and lie down, given over to whatever it is in the air. To live with the Santa Ana is to accept, consciously or unconsciously, a deeply mechanistic view of human behavior.	The winds are creepy. They bring sand storms and cause fires. People know they're coming without being told because babies and maids act strange. The speaker picks a fight and then gives up. The Santa Ana winds make us aware that human behavior can be explained in terms of physical causes and processes.
I recall being told, when I first moved to Los Angeles and was living on an isolated beach, that the Indians would throw themselves into the sea when the bad wind blew. I could see why. The Pacific turned ominously glossy during a Santa Ana period, and one woke in the night troubled not only by the peacocks screaming in the olive trees but by the eerie absence of surf. The heat was surreal. The sky had a yellow cast, the kind of light sometimes called "earthquake weather." My only neighbor would not come out of her house for days, and there were no lights at night, and her husband roamed the place with a machete. One day he would tell me that he had heard a trespasser, the next a rattlesnake.	Didion talks about her early experiences with the winds, plus the folklore about them. She mentions things that seem weird — peacocks screeching and a very quiet ocean. She says her neighbors are strange too; one stays indoors, and the other walks around with a big knife.

RHETORICAL STRATEGY OR STYLE ELEMENT	EFFECT OR FUNCTION
Personification: the wind whines	Giving the wind a human quality makes it even more threatening.
Cumulative sentence	Makes her point by accumulating details about what it means that the Santa Ana is beginning to blow.
Two short sentences: "The baby frets. The maid sulks."	Those simple sentences reduce human behavior to irrefutable evidence. We can't argue with what we see so clearly.
"rekindle"	Though she's talking about restarting an argument with the phone company, the word makes us think of starting a fire, like the wind does up in the hills.
Subordinate clause in the middle of that first sentence: "when I first moved to Los Angeles and was living on an isolated beach."	The clause accentuates Didion's isolation and because it's so long almost makes her experience more important than the Indians who threw themselves into the ocean.
"peacocks screaming in the olive trees"	Kind of an upside-down image. Peacocks are usually regal and elegant; these are screaming. Also olive trees are associated with peace (the olive branch). Supports the idea that the Santa Ana turns everything upside down. "And" as the coordinating conjunction makes the wife hiding and the husband with the machete equally important.
Compound sentence: My only neighbor would not come out of her house for days, and there were no lights at night, and her husband roamed the place with a machete.	
"machete"	"Machete" is associated with revolutions in banana republics, vigilantes. Suggests danger.

(continued on next page)

QUOTATION	PARAPHRASE OR SUMMARIZE
"On nights like that," Raymond Chandler once wrote about the Santa Ana, "every booze party ends in a fight. Meek little wives feel the edge of the carving knife and study their husbands' necks. Anything can happen." That was the kind of wind it was. I did not know then that there was any basis for the effect it had on all of us, but it turns out to be another of those cases in which science bears out folk wisdom.	Didion quotes a writer who describes the effects of the wind as causing women to want to kill their husbands. She says that folklore sometimes has a basis in science.
The Santa Ana, which is named for one of the canyons it rushes through, is a *foehn* wind, like the *foehn* of Austria and Switzerland and the *hamsin* of Israel . . . A few years ago an Israeli physicist discovered that not only during such winds, but for the ten or twelve hours which precede them, the air carries an unusually high ratio of positive to negative ions.	This section gives scientific facts about the Santa Ana wind, including its generic name, *foehn*. Didion names other winds like it in other parts of the world, but says the *foehn* has its own characteristics. She names some of the effects the *foehn* has on people in various places.

The following essay analyzes how Joan Didion creates a sense of foreboding that, in turn, helps her to develop her argument about the winds' effects on human behavior.

Joan Didion's Santa Ana Winds: A Mechanistic View of Nature

by Jane Knobler

The ominous description of Los Angeles preceding the arrival of the Santa Ana wind, juxtaposed with a scientific-sounding explanation develops Joan Didion's view that human behavior is basically a result of mechanics. She recreates the tense, stifling atmosphere that precedes the wind and argues that its effect on the people of Los Angeles can be explained by science. The eerie atmosphere, like a 1930s detective film based on a Raymond Chandler novel, highlights the strangeness of a wind affecting behavior even before the wind has begun to blow.

The effect of Didion's diction in the first part of the essay is to create foreboding; terror is just over the horizon. The wind cranks the nerves to a "flash point," causing arguments to be "rekindle[d]"; one needs a "machete" for protection. The reader is reminded of the ease with which disaster visits the West Coast. Forest fires, mudslides, snakebite, murder can happen in a moment.

RHETORICAL STRATEGY OR STYLE ELEMENT	EFFECT OR FUNCTION
Allusion to Raymond Chandler	Chandler, who wrote crime fiction, was known for his hard-boiled style and cynical views. The allusion to Chandler helps create the ominous tone.
Complex sentence: "There are a number of persistent malevolent winds, perhaps the best known of which are the *mistral* of France and the Mediterranean *sirocco*, but a *foehn* wind has distinct characteristics: it occurs on the leeward slope of a mountain range and, although the air begins as a cold mass, it is warmed as it comes down the mountain and appears finally as a hot dry wind."	The details accumulate, ending in "hot dry wind" to create a picture of the "persistent malevolent wind."

The word choice in the second part of the essay is more scientific; Didion provides names for these dangerous winds as well as statistics and facts about the "suicide rate," "unmanageable" children, and a "mitigating circumstance for crime." She supports her view that living in Los Angeles requires an understanding that human behavior is often out of our control. The dark atmosphere the Santa Ana wind creates has concrete, dire consequences that can be reported in terms of misbehavior and death. The vivid description of the impending terror that precedes the Santa Ana wind is highlighted when it is followed by the facts about the evil wind.

Didion's choice and accumulation of detail also heighten the sense of foreboding. The coming of the wind has negative effects on the baby who "frets" and the maid who "sulks"; it causes the "eerie absence of surf." The world is in an unnatural state. One cannot trust one's expectations or perceptions. The long cumulative sentence that describes the "persistent malevolent winds" begins by naming other winds, moves to the wind's beginning as a "cold mass," and ends with the increasingly frightening "hot dry wind." Those last three words reinforce what is "malevolent" in the beginning of the sentence. The wind's "positive ions" seem at first a scientific explanation, but a second look shows them to be another perversion of nature. Wind should be cool; this wind blows hot. Something positive should bring happiness. These positive ions make us unhappy. Nature is a force to be reckoned with; all of our good intentions cannot stand up to the Santa Ana wind.

The evil Santa Ana winds have a negative effect on human behavior. When they are coming, the only course is to take to one's bed. Otherwise, one may risk behaving badly or becoming the victim of someone else's bad behavior. It won't be our fault. It will be the fault of the Santa Ana winds.

• ASSIGNMENT •

The following observation of the wind comes from the 1545 book *Toxophilus* by English scholar Roger Ascham, who served as tutor to Princess Elizabeth, later Elizabeth I. Although Ascham, like Didion, contemplates the effect of unusual winds, the writing is vastly different in some measure because of the more than 400 years between the pieces. Use one of the close reading techniques we've discussed — annotation, dialectical journal, or graphic organizer — to analyze the Ascham text. Explain how the technique you selected helped to make Ascham more accessible to a twenty-first-century reader.

To see the wind, with a man his eyes, it is unpossible, the nature of it is so fine, and subtile; yet this experience of the wind had I once myself, and that was in the great snow that fell four years ago: I rode in the highway betwixt Topcliff-upon-Swale, and Borowe Bridge, the way being somewhat trodden afore, by wayfaring men. The fields on both sides were plain and lay almost yard deep with snow, the night afore had been a little frost, so that the snow was hard and crusted above. That morning the sun shone bright and clear, the wind was whistling aloft, and sharp according to the time of the year. The snow in the highway lay loose and trodden with horse feet: so as the wind blew, it took the loose snow with it, and made it so slide upon the snow in the field which was hard and crusted by reason of the frost overnight, that thereby I might see very well the whole nature of the wind as it blew that day. And I had a great delight and pleasure to mark it, which maketh me now far better to remember it. Sometime the wind would be not past two yards broad, and so it would carry the snow as far as I could see. Another time the snow would blow over half the field at once. Sometime the snow would tumble softly, by and by it would fly wonderful fast. And this I perceived also, that the wind goeth by streams and not whole together. For I should see one stream within a score on me, then the space of two score no snow would stir, but after so much quantity of ground, another stream of snow at the same very time should be carried likewise, but not equally. For the one would stand still when the other flew apace, and so continue sometime swiftlier, sometime slowlier, sometime broader, sometime narrower, as far as I could see. Nor it flew not straight, but sometime it crooked this way, sometime that way, and sometime it ran round about in a compass. And sometime the snow would be lift clean from the ground and up into the air, and by and by it would be all clapped to the ground as though there had been no wind at all, straightaway it would rise and fly again.

And that which was the most marvel of all, at one time two drifts of snow flew, the one out of the West into the East, the other out of the North into the

East: and I saw two winds by reason of the snow the one cross over the other, as it had been two highways. And again I should hear the wind blow in the air, when nothing was stirred at the ground. And when all was still where I rode, not very far from me the snow should be lifted wonderfully. This experience made me more marvel at the nature of the wind, than it made me cunning in the knowledge of the wind: but yet thereby I learned perfectly that it is no marvel at all though men in a wind lose their length in shooting, seeing so many ways the wind is so variable in blowing.

Analyzing a Visual Text

Many of the same tools of rhetorical analysis and close reading that we have practiced on written texts are also useful for detecting the underlying messages in visual texts, such as advertisements. Let's look at the accompanying ad for the Dodge Durango.

The rhetorical triangle still applies: what are the relationships among the text's subject (a powerful sport utility vehicle), its audience (the potential SUV buyer), and the speaker (in this case, the artwork and words)? The advertisement appeals to ethos in the text at the top left: it banks on associations to Dodge cars and trucks — power, dependability, toughness. Its appeal to pathos plays on our notion of the cheeseburger as a guilty pleasure; we're meant to associate tofu with wimpy, energy-efficient cars. As for logos, the Durango is affordable; it makes sense to own one. Why not enjoy life, drive an affordable SUV, and eat big juicy cheeseburgers?

When we analyze a visual text, we still look at the words, both individually and in the way they are placed on the page. And we study the images the same way.

Look at the text on the top left part of the ad.

Dodge Durango. This is the most affordable SUV with a V-8. Dodge Durango. With nearly four tons of towing, this baby carries around chunks of those wimpy wanna-bes in its tail pipe.

Note the aggressive tone. How is that sense of aggressiveness created? It may be the repetition of "Dodge Durango" with its hard consonant sounds; it may be the prepositional phrase announcing that the vehicle can tow four tons. It's a "baby" that carries "chunks" of its competitors in its tailpipe. The use of the colloquialism "baby" contrasts nicely with the image of the car as a predator eating the competition. The owner of a Dodge Durango will be the kind of person whose car is his or her "baby" and who is the leader of the pack, not one "of those wimpy wanna-bes."

The Dodge logo — a ram's head — and the slogan "grab life by the horns" appears at the top right of the ad. Both the image and the words play with the

DODGE DURANGO. This is the most affordable SUV with a V-8. Dodge Durango. With nearly four tons of towing,* this baby carries around chunks of those wimpy wanna-bes in its tail pipe. For more info, call 800-4 A DODGE or visit dodge.com

GRAB LIFE BY THE HORNS

DODGE

IT'S A BIG FAT JUICY CHEESEBURGER IN A LAND OF TOFU.

*Depending on model and when properly equipped.

connotations of horns: strength, masculinity, and noise. The imperative sentence is a call to action that can be paraphrased as "Don't be a wimp! Enjoy life now!"

The photo, however, is less aggressive. Perhaps it is a pitch to the rising number of female car buyers. In fact, the photo shows a man and a woman in the car, pulling a vintage Airstream motor home, thus suggesting not only a family atmosphere but also good taste, as Airstreams are collectibles. Though the front of the Dodge Durango is outsized, a reminder of the power under the hood, the ocean and sky in the background temper the aggressiveness of the looming SUV; it looks like a beautiful day for a cool couple with great taste to be out for a ride.

Finally, the text at the bottom of the ad has yet another message. The large white letters on the dark road are boldly designed but the message is gentle and even funny. "[B]ig fat juicy cheeseburger" acknowledges our natural desire for pleasures that are not always healthy. But who can resist when the alternative is tofu? The antecedent of *it* in *it's* is, of course, the SUV, but the pronoun suggests an understanding, an insider's wink.

So what is the advertisement's message? Or are there a few different messages? If you were to write an essay analyzing the "language" of the visual text, you might consider a thesis that argues for the ad's multiple messages. Here's one example:

> The Dodge Durango ad balances aggressiveness with humor; it appeals to men and women with its reminder that life is too short not to enjoy its guilty pleasures.

• ASSIGNMENT •

Find an ad that either appeals to you or provokes you, and analyze it as we have done with the Durango ad.

From Analysis to Essay: Writing about Close Reading

The more we examine the elements of diction and syntax and consider their effects, the deeper our understanding of an essay, a speech, or a visual text becomes. We also have to reach that deeper understanding when we write about rhetoric and style, or we will end up merely summarizing rather than analyzing the strategies a writer uses to achieve a particular purpose.

Let's take one text — President John F. Kennedy's inaugural address — through the various stages: from reading it, to analyzing it, to writing about it. Given on a cold January afternoon in 1961, the address was hailed as a return to the tradition of political eloquence. It offers great pleasures to students of rhetoric, rewarding the close reader's efforts with details large and small that lend themselves to analysis, that inspire imitation, and that have withstood the test of time. As you read the speech for the first time, consider the notion maintained by the ancient Romans and Greeks that eloquence is indispensable to politics. When you read it a second time, have a conversation with the text by annotating it, creating a dialectical journal, or using a graphic organizer.

Watch it on the Web: bedfordstmartins.com/languageofcomp

Vice President Johnson, Mr. Speaker, Mr. Chief Justice, President Eisenhower, Vice President Nixon, President Truman, Reverend Clergy, fellow citizens:

We observe today not a victory of party but a celebration of freedom — symbolizing an end as well as a beginning — signifying renewal as well as change. For I have sworn before you and Almighty God the same solemn oath our forebears prescribed nearly a century and three-quarters ago.

The world is very different now. For man holds in his mortal hands the power to abolish all forms of human poverty and all forms of human life. And yet the same revolutionary beliefs for which our forebears fought are still at issue around the globe — the belief that the rights of man come not from the generosity of the state but from the hand of God.

We dare not forget today that we are the heirs of that first revolution. Let the word go forth from this time and place, to friend and foe alike, that the torch has been passed to a new generation of Americans — born in this century, tempered by war, disciplined by a hard and bitter peace, proud of our ancient heritage — and unwilling to witness or permit the slow undoing of those human rights to which this nation has always been committed, and to which we are committed today at home and around the world.

Let every nation know, whether it wishes us well or ill, that we shall pay any price, bear any burden, meet any hardship, support any friend, oppose any foe to assure the survival and the success of liberty.   5

This much we pledge — and more.

To those old allies whose cultural and spiritual origins we share, we pledge the loyalty of faithful friends. United there is little we cannot do in a host of cooperative ventures. Divided there is little we can do — for we dare not meet a powerful challenge at odds and split asunder.

To those new states whom we welcome to the ranks of the free, we pledge our word that one form of colonial control shall not have passed away merely to be replaced by a far more iron tyranny. We shall not always expect to find them supporting our view. But we shall always hope to find them strongly supporting their own freedom — and to remember that, in the past, those who foolishly sought power by riding the back of the tiger ended up inside.

To those people in the huts and villages of half the globe struggling to break the bonds of mass misery, we pledge our best efforts to help them help themselves, for whatever period is required — not because the communists may be doing it, not because we seek their votes, but because it is right. If a free society cannot help the many who are poor, it cannot save the few who are rich.

To our sister republics south of our border, we offer a special pledge —   10
to convert our good words into good deeds — in a new alliance for

progress — to assist free men and free governments in casting off the chains of poverty. But this peaceful revolution of hope cannot become the prey of hostile powers. Let all our neighbors know that we shall join with them to oppose aggression or subversion anywhere in the Americas. And let every other power know that this Hemisphere intends to remain the master of its own house.

To that world assembly of sovereign states, the United Nations, our last best hope in an age where the instruments of war have far outpaced the instruments of peace, we renew our pledge of support — to prevent it from becoming merely a forum for invective — to strengthen its shield of the new and the weak — and to enlarge the area in which its writ may run.

Finally, to those nations who would make themselves our adversary, we offer not a pledge but a request: that both sides begin anew the quest for peace, before the dark powers of destruction unleashed by science engulf all humanity in planned or accidental self-destruction.

We dare not tempt them with weakness. For only when our arms are sufficient beyond doubt can we be certain beyond doubt that they will never be employed.

But neither can two great and powerful groups of nations take comfort from our present course — both sides overburdened by the cost of modern weapons, both rightly alarmed by the steady spread of the deadly atom, yet both racing to alter that uncertain balance of terror that stays the hand of mankind's final war.

So let us begin anew — remembering on both sides that civility is not a   15
sign of weakness, and sincerity is always subject to proof. Let us never negotiate out of fear. But let us never fear to negotiate.

Let both sides explore what problems unite us instead of belaboring those problems which divide us.

Let both sides, for the first time, formulate serious and precise proposals for the inspection and control of arms — and bring the absolute power to destroy other nations under the absolute control of all nations.

Let both sides seek to invoke the wonders of science instead of its terrors. Together let us explore the stars, conquer the deserts, eradicate disease, tap the ocean depths and encourage the arts and commerce.

Let both sides unite to heed in all corners of the earth the command of Isaiah — to "undo the heavy burdens . . . (and) let the oppressed go free."

And if a beachhead of cooperation may push back the jungle of suspi-   20
cion, let both sides join in creating a new endeavor, not a new balance of power, but a new world of law, where the strong are just and the weak secure and the peace preserved.

All this will not be finished in the first one hundred days. Nor will it be finished in the first one thousand days, nor in the life of this Administration, nor even perhaps in our lifetime on this planet. But let us begin.

In your hands, my fellow citizens, more than mine, will rest the final success or failure of our course. Since this country was founded, each generation of Americans has been summoned to give testimony to its national loyalty. The graves of young Americans who answered the call to service surround the globe.

Now the trumpet summons us again — not as a call to bear arms, though arms we need — not as a call to battle, though embattled we are — but a call to bear the burden of a long twilight struggle, year in and year out, "rejoicing in hope, patient in tribulation" — a struggle against the common enemies of man: tyranny, poverty, disease and war itself.

Can we forge against these enemies a grand and global alliance, North and South, East and West, that can assure a more fruitful life for all mankind? Will you join in that historic effort?

In the long history of the world, only a few generations have been   25
granted the role of defending freedom in its hour of maximum danger. I do not shrink from this responsibility — I welcome it. I do not believe that any of us would exchange places with any other people or any other generation. The energy, the faith, the devotion which we bring to this endeavor will light our country and all who serve it — and the glow from that fire can truly light the world.

And so, my fellow Americans: ask not what your country can do for you — ask what you can do for your country.

My fellow citizens of the world: ask not what America will do for you, but what together we can do for the freedom of man.

Finally, whether you are citizens of America or citizens of the world, ask of us here the same high standards of strength and sacrifice which we ask of you. With a good conscience our only sure reward, with history the final judge of our deeds, let us go forth to lead the land we love, asking His blessing and His help, but knowing that here on earth God's work must truly be our own.

Let's look at the big ideas in Kennedy's inaugural address by going back to the Aristotelian triangle. The speaker, the youngest U.S. president, the country's first Roman Catholic president, having won by a small margin, makes his subject common heritage and purpose, human rights and obligations, rather than policy. Thus, his appeal is less to logos, or logic, than it is to pathos (connecting with his audience emotionally) and to ethos (establishing his own ethical credentials). The audience — those there on that icy morning and the millions watching on television — is vast and diverse. The speech is short, only 1,343 words; its length is, perhaps, the new president's nod to the live audience standing in the cold on the Capitol grounds. Kennedy appeals to pathos, in part, by reaching his audience psychologically, asking them to consider what they can do for their country. He establishes ethos by offering America as a partner with the "citizens of the world" to champion the "freedom of man." Now it's your turn to analyze the specific language and arrangement of the speech and to consider the tone that results.

• ASSIGNMENT •

Annotate the inaugural address by John F. Kennedy, or use a graphic organizer or a dialectical journal. Once you've identified the diction and syntax, answer the following close-reading questions. Consider how Kennedy's diction and syntax create the tone of the speech. Also consider how you can use Kennedy's tone as a basis for an essay on the speech.

Diction

1. Why are so many of the words abstract? How do words like *freedom, poverty, devotion, loyalty,* and *sacrifice* set the tone of the speech?

2. Find examples of formal rhetorical tropes such as metaphor and personification.

3. Does Kennedy use any figures of speech that might be considered clichés? Which metaphors are fresher? Is there a pattern to their use?

4. Do any words in the speech seem **archaic**, or old-fashioned? If so, what are they? What is their effect?

Syntax

1. The speech is a succession of twenty-eight short paragraphs. Twelve paragraphs have only one sentence, eight have two, and six have three sentences. Why do you think Kennedy used these short paragraphs?

2. The speech contains two extremes of sentence length, ranging from eighty words (para. 4) to six words (para. 6). A high proportion of the sentences are on the short side. Why?

3. More than twenty sentences are **complex sentences** — that is, sentences that contain a subordinate clause. How do complex sentences suggest hidden energy?

4. The speech has many examples of antithesis in parallel grammatical structures: "To those old allies"; "to those new states"; "If a free society cannot help the many who are poor, it cannot save the few who are rich"; and of course, "[A]sk not what your country can do for you — ask what you can do for your country." What does this use of opposites suggest about the purpose of Kennedy's speech?

5. Why is the dominance of **declarative sentences,** which make statements, appropriate in an inaugural address?

6. Paragraph 24 consists of two rhetorical questions. How do they act as a transition to Kennedy's call for action?

7. Find examples of rhetorical schemes such as **anaphora** (the repetition of a word or phrase at the beginning of successive phrases, clauses, or lines) and zeugma (use of two different words in a grammatically similar way but producing different, often incongruous, meanings).

8. Consider the speech's many examples of parallelism: "born in this country, tempered by war, disciplined by a hard and bitter peace, proud of our ancient heritage"; "pay any price, bear any burden, meet any hardship, support any friend, oppose any foe". How do they lend themselves to Kennedy's purpose?

9. Kennedy uses **hortative** sentences (language that urges or calls to action) in paragraphs 2–21: "let us," "Let both sides." Later, in paragraphs 26–27, he uses the **imperative:** "ask" and "ask not." What is the difference between the two forms, and why did he start with one and end with the other?

Look at your answers to the preceding questions. Even if you weren't able to answer them all, you may be able to see one or more patterns.

Kennedy's address is formal; the archaic diction (*asunder, foe, writ, forebears*) underscores the formality. The figures of speech make traditional yet powerful connections — *tyranny* and *iron, power* and *tiger, poverty* and *chains* — and they are a strong source of emotional persuasion. Such figures of speech as personification ("our sister republics") elevate the speech to a grand style. The "beachhead of cooperation" pushing back the "jungle of suspicion" is especially rich and vivid.

The speech's syntax reveals other meanings and adds to the development of the speech's tone. Formality is sustained by a scheme such as anaphora: "Not as a call to bear arms, though arms we need; not as a call to battle, though embattled we are." The many examples of parallelism and especially the antitheses — "If a free society cannot help the many who are poor, it cannot save the few who are rich," juxtaposing the many and the few, the poor with the rich — are intended to unite disparate groups and also to reassure the country that despite Kennedy's narrow margin of victory, he will be everyone's president.

This short address covers a lot of ground. Each of its short paragraphs reveals another one of Kennedy's principles or promises — an early version of what we now call bullet points. There are a variety of sentence types: many are very short, declarative sentences; a few are compound; and more than twenty are complex. Beginning a sentence with a subordinate clause allows steam to build and energizes the sentence's main idea. The speech is a call to action, but Kennedy uses hortatory forms ("let us") more than imperatives ("ask" and "ask not"); his intention is to persuade rather than coerce. And the rhetorical questions in paragraph 24 are also reminders that the young president was building consensus rather than dictating. Finally, many sentences begin with coordinating conjunctions, such as *so*, *for*, and *but*. These transitional words move us smoothly from one sentence into the next and represent continuity — the passing of the torch — in the same way an inauguration helps the country make the transition to a new era.

So how do you come up with an idea for an essay about Kennedy's rhetoric and style? One approach is to identify the passage's tone, which is the feeling behind the words. Tone is closely connected to attitude, the speaker's feelings about the subject matter and the audience. And both tone and attitude are created by diction and syntax. His attitude is one of respect for the grand occasion, its history, and the legacy it is carrying forward. The tone of his speech is a combination of respectful eloquence and youthful idealism.

Following is a possible thesis for an essay that synthesizes the preceding observations on Kennedy's inaugural address:

> While the speech's respectful eloquence is appropriate for the occasion of an inauguration, its youthful energy and look to the future make it distinctly John F. Kennedy's.

Your close reading has probably revealed all or most of the significant rhetorical and stylistic features in Kennedy's speech. Recognizing the tropes and schemes in a text as rich as this one is good; identifying their purpose and effect is very good. It's fine, for example, if you know that when Kennedy enjoins his listeners to "ask not what your country can do for you — ask what you can do for your country," he is employing **antimetabole.** It would be better though to explain what the statement *does* in the speech and how it is likely to affect the audience. Writing an excellent essay takes you a step further, from stating *that* to explaining *how*.

Consider what an analysis does. A mere dissection or a disassembly separates something into its component parts, but an analysis explains how it works. This applies as much to a written text as it does to a biological specimen or a machine. In other words, in your essay you should not only describe what the speaker (or writer) is saying, but you should also explain how the diction and syntax serve the speaker's (or writer's) purpose, enrich the text, and affect the audience. You should also consider the rhetorical triangle as it applies to your own compositions: the relationship that you, the speaker, have with your subject and with your audience. Craft your writing so that it deserves to be read and so that it will engage your reader. If you think it's not quite as eloquent as President Kennedy's, don't worry; you're on your way.

• ASSIGNMENT •

Using the preceding thesis or creating your own, write an essay analyzing the rhetorical strategies John F. Kennedy uses in his inaugural address to achieve his purpose.

Glossary of Selected Tropes and Schemes

John F. Kennedy's inaugural address is almost a textbook of stylistic devices. The following brief glossary of terms gives examples from Kennedy's speech.

alliteration   Repetition of the same sound beginning several words in sequence

> [L]et us go forth to lead the land we love.

allusion   Brief reference to a person, event, or place, real or fictitious, or to a work of art

> Let both sides unite to heed in all corners of the earth the command of Isaiah.

anaphora   Repetition of a word or phrase at the beginning of successive phrases, clauses, or lines

> not as a call to bear arms, though arms we need — not as a call to battle, though embattled we are.

antimetabole   Repetition of words in reverse order

> [A]sk not what your country can do for you — ask what you can do for your country.

antithesis   Opposition, or contrast, of ideas or words in a balanced or parallel construction

> [W]e shall support any friend, oppose any foe.

archaic diction   Old-fashioned or outdated choice of words

> beliefs for which our forebears fought

asyndeton   Omission of conjunctions between coordinate phrases, clauses, or words

> [W]e shall pay any price, bear any burden, meet any hardship, support any friend, oppose any foe to assure the survival and the success of liberty.

cumulative sentence   Sentence that completes the main idea at the beginning of the sentence, and then builds and adds on

> But neither can two great and powerful groups of nations take comfort from our present course — both sides overburdened by the cost of modern weapons, both rightly alarmed by the steady spread of the deadly atom, yet both racing to alter that uncertain balance of terror that stays the hand of mankind's final war.

hortative sentence   Sentence that exhorts, advises, calls to action

> Let both sides explore what problems unite us instead of belaboring those problems which divide us.

imperative sentence   Sentence used to command, enjoin, implore, or entreat

> My fellow citizens of the world: ask not what America will do for you, but what together we can do for the freedom of man.

inversion   Inverted order of words in a sentence (variation of the subject-verb-object order)

> United there is little we cannot do in a host of cooperative ventures. Divided there is little we can do.

juxtaposition   Placement of two things closely together to emphasize comparisons or contrasts

> *[W]e are the* heirs of that first revolution. *Let the word go forth . . . that the torch has been passed to* a new generation of Americans — *born in this century.* [emphasis added]

metaphor   Figure of speech that says one thing is another in order to explain by comparison

> *And if a beachhead of cooperation may push back the jungle of suspicion.*

metonymy   Using a single feature to represent the whole

> *In your hands, my fellow citizens, more than mine, will rest the final success or failure of our course.*

oxymoron   Paradoxical juxtaposition of words that seem to contradict one another

> *But this peaceful revolution.*

parallelism   Similarity of structure in a pair or series of related words, phrases, or clauses

> *Let both sides explore . . . Let both sides, for the first time, formulate serious and precise proposals . . . Let both sides seek to invoke . . . Let both sides unite to heed.*

periodic sentence   Sentence whose main clause is withheld until the end

> *To that world assembly of sovereign states, the United Nations, our last best hope in an age where the instruments of war have far outpaced the instruments of peace, we renew our pledge of support.*

personification   Attribution of a lifelike quality to an inanimate object or idea

> *with history the final judge of our deeds*

rhetorical question   Figure of speech in the form of a question posed for rhetorical effect rather than for the purpose of getting an answer

> *Will you join in that historic effort?*

zeugma   Use of two different words in a grammatically similar way but producing different, often incongruous, meanings

> *Now the trumpet summons us again — not as a call to bear arms, though arms we need — not as a call to battle, though embattled we are — but a call to bear the burden.*

3

Synthesizing Sources: Entering the Conversation

All writers draw on the work of others as they develop their own positions, regardless of their topic. Whether you are explaining your opinion about an issue specific to your community such as whether the prom should be abolished, or you are developing a position on a larger, more controversial issue such as the AIDS epidemic in Africa, you should know as much as possible about the topic. Rather than make a quick response that reflects an opinion based only on what you already know, you must research and read sources — what others have written. Then you can develop your own informed opinion, a measured response that considers multiple perspectives and possibilities.

Essentially, research into sources lets you enter the conversation that society is having about your topic. What have other schools decided about the prom? Why? Have some developed alternative events? What has been the response? What responsibility does the United States have to help control AIDS epidemics in other countries? What preventive measures are working to slow the spread of AIDS?

To answer questions posed by your topic and to develop new questions, locate and read such sources as articles, editorials, and reports. Don't look for a pro-and-con debate that represents only polarized views; instead, explore a range of viewpoints.

You already use sources quite naturally. For example, when you decide to purchase a computer, you gather information by exploring different sources. Before choosing between a Mac and a PC, you might consult *Consumer Reports* in print or online. You would compare prices. You'd ask your friends for their opinions, and you might go to a computer store and talk with the experts. You might read reviews online, or use forums as a quick source for many opinions. You go through this process when making a big decision, such as choosing a college, or a relatively minor one, such as deciding which movie to see. The final result of your inquiry might not be an essay, but you are joining a conversation that is already ongoing.

You'll do something similar as you approach the readings in this textbook. For example, when you read "Mother Tongue," Amy Tan's essay about bias against

61

nonnative English speakers, you may have a similar story to add or an experience that contrasts with hers. When you consider Ralph Waldo Emerson's definition of what constitutes a true education, you might enter the conversation by pointing out the shortcomings in the classes you've taken; or you might suggest that Emerson's perspective is dated and doesn't apply to today's schools. You enter the conversation by carefully reading and understanding the writer's perspective and ideas, by examining your own ideas in light of the writer's, and by synthesizing these views into a more informed position than the one you began with.

Types of Support

When writing essays, particularly persuasive ones, you should use many types of information to support your argument. You will make your position more specific — and more convincing — by adding details and examples. You might cite, or refer to, an *anecdote* — that is, a brief story that illustrates a point you are making. An anecdote can be about a personal experience or about something that happened to someone else. For instance, if you are writing about the pros and cons of single-sex schools, you might cite your own experience in an all-boys or all-girls classroom.

You might also develop your ideas with *facts* — information that is verifiable through general sources, such as an encyclopedia, a history book, or a biographical dictionary. The dates of Jimmy Carter's presidency, the number of American soldiers killed on D-Day, the years that Nelson Mandela was in prison, for example, are the kinds of facts that work as examples but do not require you to state where you located them.

A third kind of information is *quantitative data*, especially statistical information. Often quantitative data is more than just numbers. You might report on trends, such as high-school graduation rates over the last ten years, by including such variables as males versus females, urban versus suburban schools, or American versus Japanese schools. In most cases, you should **document** — that is, give credit to — the sources where you find this information.

Another valuable kind of information is *expert testimony*. In an essay on the impact of video games on preschool children, for example, you might cite a neurologist, pediatrician, or psychologist who has written on the topic. You could quote the expert directly or put his or her points in your own words by summarizing or paraphrasing them. Citing anecdotes, facts, statistics, and experts is one way to appeal to logos. In addition, documenting such information establishes your ethos. You may not be a neurologist, but when you cite one and then document who the neurologist is or where you found his or her observation, you demonstrate a serious approach to the topic at hand; you show you understand the conversation in process.

Writers at Work

In this section, we'll examine the way four authors develop their ideas or positions by using anecdotes, facts, quantitative data, expert testimony, or a combination of these. In *The Cheating Culture*, author David Callahan argues, "In one area of American life after another — sports, business, law, education, science, medicine — more people seem to be cutting corners." He cites an anecdote about LeBron James, which was much talked about in 2003.

> A leading high school basketball player named LeBron James, the next Michael Jordan some say, shows up one day at his school in Akron driving a new $50,000 Hummer H2 sports utility vehicle crammed with three TVs. The Ohio High School Athletic Association immediately launches an investigation, suspecting that the Hummer is a gift from a sports agent or university recruiter. James denies everything. My mom gave it to me, he says. Few believe that James's middle-class mother can afford a top-of-the-line Hummer, but no one can prove a violation of state rules. It's a typical episode in the money-saturated world of collegiate and professional sports, where recruiting violations, drug use, and other kinds of cheating — like Sammy Sosa's corked bat — are pervasive.

The anecdote supports Callahan's argument that cheating is pervasive, with appeals to logos, pathos, and ethos. The facts (James got a Hummer) and quantitative data (the cost of the Hummer) appeal to logos because of the improbability of a middle-class person being able to afford a Hummer. The anecdote also appeals to pathos because the possibility that LeBron James, a popular athlete, cheated is likely to evoke an emotional response from readers. Callahan's marshaling of supporting evidence establishes ethos; the reader is ready to accept his bigger argument that cheating is pervasive.

In her book, *Nickel and Dimed*, Barbara Ehrenreich discusses the difficulty that rich people have understanding what it takes to live on the minimum wage. To explain why they might have such difficulty, she cites two articles published in the *New York Times*, including one by an expert on the topic.

> In a 2000 article on the "disappearing poor," journalist James Fallows reports that, from the vantage point of the Internet's nouveaux riches, it is "hard to understand people for whom a million dollars would be a fortune . . . not to mention those for whom $246 is a full week's earning." Among the reasons he and others have cited for the blindness of the affluent is the fact that they are less and less likely to share spaces and services with the poor. As public schools and other public services deteriorate, those who can afford to do so send their children to private schools and spend their off-hours in private

spaces — health clubs, for example, instead of the local park. They don't ride on public buses and subways. They withdraw from mixed neighborhoods into distant suburbs, gated communities, or guarded apartment towers; they shop in stores that, in line with the prevailing "market segmentation," are designed to appeal to the affluent alone. Even the affluent young are increasingly unlikely to spend their summers learning how the "other half" lives, as lifeguards, waitresses, or housekeepers at resort hotels. The *New York Times* reports that they now prefer career-relevant activities like summer school or interning in an appropriate professional setting to the "sweaty, low-paid and mind-numbing slots that have long been their lot."

In her book, Ehrenreich documents at the bottom of the page exactly where and when the *Times* article appeared. How do these sources support Ehrenreich's position on "the blindness of the affluent"? First, both add credibility to her argument. The *New York Times* and the journalist James Fallows are both known for in-depth research and reporting. Second, by using direct quotations, Ehrenreich shows that she's not just giving us her personal viewpoint but one that is supported by the findings of others who have investigated this topic.

In the book's conclusion, Ehrenreich writes, "According to a recent poll conducted by Jobs for the Future, a Boston-based employment research firm, 94 percent of Americans agree that 'people who work full-time should be able to earn enough to keep their families out of poverty.'" She could have simply said, "Most people think that those with full-time jobs should be able to earn enough to keep themselves and their families out of the category of poverty." Instead, she documents the source of her information and provides a statistic — 94 percent. This adds the authority of a research study to her argument and strengthens her appeals to ethos and logos.

In some instances, such as the following excerpt from "The Clan of One-Breasted Women," documented sources can act as counterweight to an emotional example or anecdote. Author Terry Tempest Williams is writing about a volatile issue — the effect of nuclear testing on the health of citizens — and her viewpoint is highly personal because several women in her family have suffered from breast cancer. By providing full information about her sources in her notes, Williams guards against being accused of making up or exaggerating information, or expressing an opinion that has no basis in fact.

> Much has been written about this "American nuclear tragedy." Public health was secondary to national security. The Atomic Energy Commissioner, Thomas Murray, said, "Gentlemen, we must not let anything interfere with this series of tests, nothing."[2]
>
> Again and again, the American public was told by its government, in spite of burns, blisters, and nausea. "It has been found that the tests may be conducted with adequate assurance of safety under conditions prevailing at the bombing reservations."[3] Assuaging public fears was simply a matter of

public relations. "Your best action," an Atomic Energy Commission booklet read, "is not to be worried about fallout." A news release typical of the times stated, "We find no basis for concluding that harm to any individual has resulted from radioactive fallout."[4]

On August 30, 1979, during Jimmy Carter's presidency, a suit was filed entitled "Irene Allen vs. the United States of America." Mrs. Allen was the first to be alphabetically listed with twenty-four test cases, representative of nearly 1200 plaintiffs seeking compensation from the United States government for cancers caused from nuclear testing in Nevada.

Irene Allen lived in Hurricane, Utah. She was the mother of five children and had been widowed twice. Her first husband with their two oldest boys had watched the tests from the roof of the local high school. He died of leukemia in 1956. Her second husband died of pancreatic cancer in 1978.

In a town meeting conducted by Utah Senator Orrin Hatch, shortly before the suit was filed, Mrs. Allen said, "I am not blaming the government, I want you to know that, Senator Hatch. But I thought if my testimony could help in any way so this wouldn't happen again to any of the generations coming up after us . . . I am really happy to be here this day to bear testimony of this."[5]

---

2. Szasz, Ferenc M., "Downwind from the Bomb," *Nevada Historical Society Quarterly*, Fall 1987, Vol. XXX, No. 3, p. 185.

3. Fradkin, Philip L., *Fallout* (Tucson: University of Arizona Press, 1989), 98.

4. Ibid., 109.

5. Town meeting held by Senator Orrin Hatch in St. George, Utah, April 17, 1979, transcript 26–28.

In the essay, Williams includes the above references for the sources she cites in the text.

Sources should enhance, not replace, your argument. As you include different sources, you may start to feel that the ideas of others are so persuasive that you have nothing new to say. Or you may think that the more sources you cite, the more impressed your reader, especially your teacher, will be. But make no mistake: while sources inform your own ideas, support or illustrate them, or demonstrate your understanding of opposing views, what *you* have to say is the main event; *your* position is central.

In the following example, Laura Hillenbrand, author of *Seabiscuit*, a Pulitzer Prize–winning book about a champion racehorse who beat the odds, maintains her own voice throughout. She validates her statements by identifying her sources in a section at the end of the book, but whether she is quoting directly or paraphrasing, she never gets lost in the sources or allows them to overwhelm her ideas.

To pilot a racehorse is to ride a half-ton catapult. It is without question one of the most formidable feats in sport. The extraordinary athleticism of the jockey is unparalleled: A study of the elements of athleticism conducted by Los Angeles exercise physiologists and physicians found that of all major sports competitors, jockeys may be, pound for pound, the best overall athletes. They have to be. To begin with, there are the demands on balance, coordination, and reflex. A horse's body is a constantly shifting topography, with a bobbing head and neck and roiling muscle over the shoulders, back, and rump. On a running horse, a jockey does not sit in the saddle, he crouches over it, leaning all of his weight on his toes, which rest on the thin metal bases of stirrups dangling about a foot from the horse's topline. When a horse is in full stride, the only parts of the jockey that are in continuous contact with the animal are the insides of the feet and ankles — everything else is balanced in midair. In other words, jockeys squat on the pitching backs of their mounts, a task much like perching on the grille of a car while it speeds down a twisting, potholed freeway in traffic. The stance is, in the words of University of North Carolina researchers, "a situation of dynamic imbalance and ballistic opportunity." The center of balance is so narrow that if jockeys shift only slightly rearward, they will flip right off the back. If they tip more than a few inches forward, a fall is almost inevitable. A thoroughbred's neck, while broad from top to bottom, is surprisingly narrow in width, like the body of a fish. Pitching up and down as the horse runs, it offers little for the jockey to grab to avoid plunging to the ground and under the horse's hooves.

Jockey (video), Tel-Air Productions, 1980.

A. E. Waller et al., "Jockey Injuries in the United States," *Journal of the American Medical Association*, 2000; vol. 283, no. 10.

At the end of *Seabiscuit*, Hillenbrand includes the above information about the sources she cites. The first item is a videotape about the study by Los Angeles exercise physiologists and physicians; the second is an article in a medical journal.

• ASSIGNMENT •

The following selection comes from the best-selling 2000 book, *Bowling Alone: The Collapse and Revival of American Community* by Harvard professor Robert D. Putnam. In this passage Putnam discusses the nature of television in American life, but not in the usual way. Putnam is not attacking its influence on our attention span; he is not claiming anything about how it's dumbing us down. Rather, he is interested in how TV affects our relationship with our community.

Read the passage carefully, noting Putnam's citation of sources and his footnotes regarding those sources. Then answer the questions that follow.

Most studies estimate that the average American now watches roughly four hours per day, very nearly the highest viewership anywhere in the world. Time

researchers John Robinson and Geoffrey Godbey, using the more conservative time diary technique for determining how people allocate their time, offer
an estimate closer to three hours per day but conclude that as a primary activity, television absorbed almost 40 percent of the average American's free time
in 1995, an increase of roughly one-third since 1965. Between 1965 and
1995 we gained an average of six hours a week in added leisure time, and
we spent almost all of those additional hours watching TV. In short, as Robinson and Godbey conclude, "Television is the 800-pound gorilla of leisure
time."[13]

Moreover, multiple sets per household have proliferated: by the late
1990's three-quarters of all U.S. homes had more than one set, allowing ever
more private viewing. The fraction of sixth-graders with a TV set in their bedroom grew from 6 percent in 1970 to 77 percent in 1999. (Two kids in three
aged 8–18 say that TV is usually on during meals in their home.) At the same
time, during the 1980s the rapid diffusion of videocassette players and video
games into American households added yet other forms of "screen time."
Finally, during the 1990s personal computers and Internet access dramatically
broadened the types of information and entertainment brought into the American home.[14]

The single most important consequence of the television revolution has
been to bring us home. As early as 1982, a survey by Scripps-Howard
reported that eight out of the ten most popular leisure activities were typically
based at home. Amid all the declining graphs for social and community
involvement traced in the DDB Needham Life Style surveys from 1975 to
1999, one line stands out: The number of Americans who reported a preference for "spending a quiet evening at home" rose steadily. Not surprisingly,
those who said so were heavily dependent on televised entertainment.[15]
While early enthusiasts for this new medium spoke eagerly of television as an
"electronic hearth" that would foster family togetherness, the experience of the
last half century is cautionary.

Social critic James Howard Kunstler's polemic is not far off target:

> The American house has been TV-centered for three generations. It is the
> focus of family life, and the life of the house correspondingly turns inward,
> away from whatever occurs beyond its four walls. (TV rooms are called
> "family rooms" in builders' lingo. A friend who is an architect explained to
> me: "People don't want to admit that what the family does together is
> watch TV.") At the same time, the television is the family's chief connection
> with the outside world. The physical envelope of the house itself no longer
> connects their lives to the outside in any active way; rather, it seals them
> off from it. The outside world has become an abstraction filtered through
> television, just as the weather is an abstraction filtered through air condi-
> tioning.[16]

Notes

13. Data in this paragraph exclude time when television is merely on in the background. Comstock, *Evolution of American Television*, 17, reports that "on any fall day in the late 1980s, the set in the average television owning household was on for about eight hours." According to Eurodata TV (*One Television Year in the World: Audience Report*, April 1999), the United States ranks third out of forty-seven nations in viewing hours per day, behind only Japan and Mexico. Thanks to Pippa Norris for advice about the media and participation. Robinson and Godbey, *Time for Life*, 136–153, 340–341.

14. *Statistical Abstract of the United States* (various years); *Kids & Media @ The New Millennium* (Menlo Park, Calif.: Henry J. Kaiser Family Foundation, 1999), 13.

15. *Where Does the Time Go? The United Media Enterprises Report on Leisure in America* (New York: Newspaper Enterprise Association, 1983), 10; author's analysis of DDB Needham Life Style archive. Preference for a quiet evening at home rose from 68 percent in 1975 to 77 percent in 1999. Those who agreed were also more likely to agree that "TV is my primary form of entertainment."

16. Kunstler, *Geography of Nowhere*, 167.

Questions

1. How does Robert Putnam establish credibility?

2. Among the names in the Notes — Comstock, Robinson, Godbey, Needham, and Kunstler — which ones are cited in the selection? Match the names with their texts.

3. In footnote 13, Putnam identifies three separate sources. What effect does the additional information have?

4. What is the purpose of footnote 14? Why does it include information that may seem obvious to the reader?

5. How does Putnam use the source given in footnote 15 to support his claim about the relationship between TV watching and staying at home?

6. James Howard Kunstler's view is more extreme than Putnam's. How does citing Kunstler affect Putnam's argument?

7. What do Putnam's notes and sources suggest about his research?

The Relationship of Sources to Audience

If you were writing an in-class essay, would you take the time to put together a bibliography? Of course not. But you would prepare a bibliography for a formal research paper because that writing has a different purpose and the audience has different expectations. A writer must analyze the rhetorical situation in order to determine what is appropriate, even when it comes to sources and documentation. (See The Rhetorical Triangle, p. 3.)

Now let's consider a topic and examine how sources were used and identified for three different audiences. The following excerpts are from three pieces about the contemporary author Edwidge Danticat, whose short story "New York Day Women" is included in Chapter 6.

The first example is a newspaper article written for a general audience, casual readers interested primarily in personal information about Danticat. Note that the quotations are from interviews conducted with her and with people who have known her rather than statistics or other more formal evidence. The author's in-text citations include enough information about the sources to show that they have the credibility to speak about Danticat's past.

Paul Moses, "Haitian Dream, Brooklyn Memory"
New York Newsday, 21 May 1995

Guidance counselor Mariann Finn recalled Danticat, who graduated in 1986 [from Clara Barton High School] as a very quiet and family-oriented young lady. "She pretty much stood in the background, very shy, extremely reticent about speaking up," she said. Then she saw Danticat on the MacNeil-Lehrer NewsHour, speaking out on immigration issues: "I said this is not the Edwidge I knew, by no means."

Danticat got her bachelor's degree from Barnard College and then a master of Fine Arts degree from Brown University — the novel was her thesis — before returning home to live with her parents and brothers. . . .

Danticat's work has been "extremely well received in the Caribbean community, especially in the Haitian community," said Regine Latortue, chairwoman of the Africana Studies Department and professor of comparative black literature at Brooklyn College.

The next example is the introduction from a piece in a literary magazine for writers. The audience expects a more formal approach. Consequently, the type of evidence that author Renée Shea uses is more formal and wide-ranging; she cites information from a number of other publications, including newspapers, magazines, and literary journals. Shea's documentation style is more formal as well. She uses in-text documentation that includes titles and, in some cases, dates for her sources.

Renée Shea, "Traveling Worlds with Edwidge Danticat"

Poets & Writers Magazine, January/February 1997

Within the past two years, Haitian-born Edwidge Danticat has published her first novel *Breath, Eyes, Memory* (Soho Press, 1994) and *Krik? Krak!*, a short story collection (Soho Press, 1995), both to reviews running from favorable to raves. Vintage Books published a "Reading Group Guide" for the popular *Breath, Eyes, Memory*, and *Krik? Krak!* hasn't stopped winning prizes: a finalist for the National Book Award in 1995 and *People Magazine*'s choice as one of the "Best of Pages" for that same year. Danticat is proving *The New York Times* right on target in its inclusion of her in a November 1994 article entitled "30 artists, 30 and under . . . likely to (gulp!) change the culture for the next 30 years." Last summer in *Newsweek* an article on the new American identity began: "Thomas Wolfe, shake hands with Edwidge Danticat, your spiritual heir." And *Granta* magazine named Danticat among the 20 "Best of Young American Novelists." She has been featured in *Elle, Essence, Ms.* and *Mirabella* magazines and was the focus of major articles in *The Boston Globe, San Francisco Guardian, Washington Post, San Antonio Express,* and *The Miami Herald*, where she made front-page news under the banner headline "The Healing Art of Writing." In 1995, she inaugurated a literary series on emerging women writers sponsored by the National Museum of Women in the Arts. . . . In 1996, Danticat spent a semester teaching at New York University. She has done book tours in the U.S. and abroad, and students are writing about her. She speaks at professional meetings as well as high school graduations. Danticat has not just arrived: she presides.

The third example is from the academic journal *Meridians: feminism, race, transnationalism*. For this audience of scholars and researchers, the author chooses other scholarly works as her sources and documents them thoroughly, providing parenthetical documentation for many sources and including a lengthy endnote offering further commentary on a key point the author, Valérie Loichot, is making.

Valérie Loichot, "Edwidge Danticat's Kitchen History"

Meridians: feminism, race, transnationalism 5.1 (2004): 92–116

Another split no longer in value in the context of Caribbean American women is between the private and the political. The communal memory that is passed on from mothers to daughters is not only that of good cookin' but also that of political activism: "In this ma world you got to take yuh mouth and make a gun!" (Marshall 1983, 7). This discourse of empowerment, as Marshall describes, takes place in the kitchen. Danticat's heroines, like Marshall's, participate in this politicizing of the private kitchen.[16] Writing, perceived as a humiliating "spit in [the] face" or as a degrading "dark rouge" by the mothers, becomes a war mask that daughters put on the palimpsest of their mothers' indelible text: their cooking history.

Unifying the themes of gender and physical and cultural healing, Danticat's writing is described alternatively as cooking or as a female activity. It is writing which, like Marshall's, originated in the mother's kitchen: "Your mother, she introduced you to the first echoes of the tongue you now speak when at the end of the day she would braid your hair while you sat between her legs, scrubbing the kitchen pots" (Danticat 1996, 224). It brings the memory of the past just like cooking does, it braids women together just like food reunites them in an action of solidarity:

> When you write, it's like braiding your hair . . . some of the braids are long, others are short. Some are thick, others are thin. Some are heavy, others are light, like the diverse women in your family. Those fables and metaphors, those similes and those soliloquies, whose diction and je ne sais quoi daily slip into your survival soup, by way of their finger (Danticat 1996, 220).

The action of cooking, in this dense paragraph, is presented as the writing of a collectivity, the difficult braiding of histories of women. Writing is a "survival soup" made by these women's hands. Chancy shows that Caribbean women escape what she calls "culture-lacune" "through the written text, through the actualization of identity in language, the world of words shaping a new reality within the inviolable space of the imagination" (1997, 115). The action of cooking projected within Danticat's novel doubles and reinforces this liberating function of writing.

16. For Jeffrey Pilcher (*¡Qué Vivan los Tamales!* 1998), women cooks participate directly in the construction or "imagination," to use Benedict Anderson's term, of the Mexican nation. Since culinary products are central to nation building, "by proclaiming their culinary patriotism, women have established their claim to citizenship, and thereby gained a basis for political participation." . . . Danticat's novel certainly leads in that direction since remaining Haitian in exile relies heavily on speaking Creole and cooking Haitian. For a more explicit equivalence between food and nation building, see Ntozake Shange's *If I Can Cook/You Know God Can* (1998) where the author proves by food the existence of an African American nation. . . .

As you can see, the type of evidence and the way it is documented depends on audience and situation.

• ASSIGNMENT •

Columnists for print and online publications comment on culture and current events. They establish a viewpoint and style. One of their rhetorical strategies is their use of sources, which is dictated in part by their audience. Using a minimum of four columns by one writer, analyze the columnist's audience by examining the type of sources he or she uses. You might consider syndicated columnists such as Richard Rodriguez, George Will, Ellen Goodman, William Safire, Maureen Dowd, or David Brooks, or a sportswriter, a movie or music reviewer, or a columnist in a local publication.

The Synthesis Essay

What do sources have to do with the writing you are doing? The texts we have examined in this chapter were written by journalists, professors, and scholars; the sources they use and the ways they document them are appropriate for their audiences. In school, you have probably written a "synthesis essay," which requires you to use outside sources, sources that have been assigned to you, or sources that are part of your classroom readings. Keep in mind that your goal is the same as that of the more experienced writers: to use sources to support and illustrate your own ideas and to establish your credibility as a member of the academic community that values the "conversation" created by different voices. Whether your teacher wants you to make informal in-text citations or to use formal in-text parenthetical documentation and an end-of-paper Works Cited list, as prescribed by the Modern Language Association (MLA), you must document sources to give credit where credit is due.

In the following brief essay, college freshman Domenek Hawkins responds to a controversial topic in 2006: the Spanish version of the U.S. national anthem. For an in-class writing assignment, she was given three articles on the topic and asked to develop her own position on whether "Nuestro Himno" should be accepted as an alternative to "The Star-Spangled Banner" at ceremonial events. Because she is using three specific sources that her teacher already knows, she does not provide formal in-text documentation, but she does list the sources at the end of the essay. Note that Domenek's own ideas and opinions dominate the essay; the sources support and inform, but they do not overwhelm.

Nuestro Himno

Domenek Hawkins

As a person of mixed race, I proudly support both of my countries. My coffee skin tones lead most people to assume I am African American, but only those who know me realize that I am, in fact, an Afro-Latina who represents La Republica Dominicana as well as the United States of America. I am a bilingual Spanish-English person who loves to listen to *la bachata* and *merengue y salsa* as much as rap, R & B, and soul. Sometimes living in the U.S. makes it seem difficult to preserve who I am and where I come from because America — a home for many immigrants — does not seem to welcome cultural diversity. Embracing the Spanish version of "The Star-Spangled Banner" would be a step in the right direction toward full acceptance of differences.

The editorial in the *Herald News* speaks for many people who believe that everyone should speak English, and that those who do not are being disrespectful. This article asserts that immigrants and others who call America their new home must observe "boundaries — and the national anthem is one." Those who oppose the so-called Spanish national anthem see "The Star-Spangled Banner" as a sacred icon of the English language. They apparently see learning the English words as a test of loyalty.

I agree with one point made in this editorial, that "Learning the national anthem in English is a tribute to the history of this nation." However, couldn't singing it in Spanish be the first step toward learning it in English? One of the problems I've seen in my own family is mastering English. My brother Jesus recently came to the U.S., and as he would say, "My English es no very good looking." It helps him to be around people who speak both English and Spanish, as I do, because he can switch as he learns more English words and expressions. It would be easier for people like my brother and my *abuelita* (my grandmother) to learn "The Star-Spangled Banner" in Spanish first and then in English. Then they would understand the meaning even before they understood the English words.

According to David Goldstein, a reporter for *The Seattle Times*, this is not the first time our national anthem has been translated. In 1919 there was a Spanish version, and he points out that the Library of Congress Web site has "vintage translations in Polish, French, Italian, Portuguese, and Armenian, among others. A little Googling will turn up versions in Samoan and Yiddish, too." It seems that this opposition to "El Nuestro Himno" might be related to the current controversy over immigration laws rather than a real concern over the purity of the words to a patriotic song.

I feel that hearing a Spanish version of the national anthem on ceremonial occasions will benefit all citizens of the U.S. by letting freedom ring in diverse voices. I want to ask those who are opposed to "El Nuestro Himno," who it is hurting. It is "a respectful, recognizable, stirring version of a familiar song" (*Washington Post* editorial) — a song that I believe shows the gratitude of immigrants to the United States of America for opening its doors and giving them opportunities that they were not offered in other countries. America should welcome the gesture!

Works Cited

Editorial, *Herald News* (New Jersey). 4 May 2006: E06.

Editorial, *Washington Post*. 4 May 2006: A24.

Goldstein, David. "National Anthem in Other Languages? Heard This Before." *Seattle Times*. 6 May 2006: A1.

Domenek has used all three sources to add authority to her viewpoint, yet she emphasizes her personal experience and involvement as a bicultural, bilingual person. She opens with an anecdote about her own heritage, which leads to her thesis, or claim. In the second paragraph, she presents objections to this position, and she opens the third paragraph by conceding one of the points of a counter-argument. She uses that point to develop her own argument: that a Spanish version allows those not proficient in English to understand the spirit of the national anthem, that there have already been many translations, and that accepting "El Nuestro Himno" symbolizes acceptance of diversity. Domenek returns to her personal experience in both her development and conclusion. Throughout the essay, she cites other writers, yet she never forfeits or dilutes her own ideas. She has entered the conversation as an informed and reasonable voice.

Conversation
Focus on Community Service

In this section, we will walk you through the process of writing a synthesis essay: understanding the assignment, analyzing a series of readings, and writing an argument using them.

Following is the type of prompt you may encounter. It asks you to write a synthesis essay.

> Using the following documents on community service requirements in high schools, write an essay explaining whether you believe that high schools in general — or your specific school or district — should make community service mandatory. Incorporate references to or quotations from a minimum of three of these sources in your essay.

Before reading the texts, think about how the sources will help you fulfill the assignment. As we've discussed, sources can illustrate or support your own ideas. If you think that community service requirements are worthwhile, then you can look to your sources to help you make that point. But it's important that you do not reject texts that do not support your position or are not directly relevant to it. In fact, you might use a text that presents an opinion in opposition to yours as a counterargument, and then concede and refute it. Most important, keep an open mind while you read the sources so your thesis shows that you understand the complexity of the subject of community service.

1. From *Millennials Rising*

NEIL HOWE AND WILLIAM STRAUSS

The definition of "community service" has morphed from one generation to the next, dating back to World War II. For the Silent [generation that came of age in the 1940s], community deed-doing was channeled by the Selective Service law, which pushed young males toward socially acceptable deferments such as teaching, science, or even marriage. For leading-edge Boomers, the term "community service" often meant cleaning hospital bedpans to avoid Vietnam — or for the more radically minded, spurring oppressed neighborhoods to vent their grievances against the "establishment." When the draft ended, in 1973, first-wave Boomers had eliminated mandatory civic duty for their later cohorts and the generation to follow. Growing up in the era of the Volunteer Army, Gen Xers developed their own ethic of volunteerism, de-emphasizing great crusades in favor of simple acts of charity to help needy people. For teenagers, "community service" came to mean punishment for drunk drivers and Breakfast Club miscreants.

By the Millennial era [people born between 1982 and 2002], the notion of volunteering gave way to a more compulsory "service learning," which is now often required for graduation from middle or high school. Bolstered by Acts of Congress in 1990 and 1993, which created the Learn and Serve America program, the integration of community service with academic study has spread to schools everywhere. From 1984 to 1999, the share of high schools offering any kind of community service program grew from 17 to 83 percent, and the share with "service learning" grew from 9 to 46 percent. Two-thirds of all public schools at all grade levels now have students engaged in community work, often . . . as part of the curriculum.

A new Millennial service ethic is emerging, built around notions of collegial (rather than individual) action, support for (rather than resistance against) civic institutions, and the tangible doing of good deeds. Surveys show that five of every six Millennials believe their generation has the greatest duty to improve the environment — and that, far more than older people, Millennials would impose extra civic duties on themselves, including taxes to achieve results.

2. *Community Service Mission Statement*

THE DALTON SCHOOL (A SMALL PRIVATE HIGH SCHOOL)

Community Service is something that needs to be done. Community Service situates our moral center; it teaches us through experience — about the relationship between empathy and responsibility, about what it takes to be part of a community, in essence, about being human. Inherent in the notion of community service are the feelings of optimism and empowerment: we are optimistic that the world can change for the better and when empowered to effect that change, we as individuals can make a difference. There are no more important lessons that we can learn and teach.

For Survival

We are members of many communities: family, school, neighborhood, city, country, religion, and ethnic group. It is from these communities that we gain our sustenance. We must each play a role in contributing to our communities so that these communities can continue to survive and prosper. Benevolent action is essential to the survival and prosperity of any community. We must engage in community service because it needs to be done and because we need our communities to survive.

For a Moral Center

Community Service is vital to the healthy community. A community that takes without giving back, that is indifferent to the needs of its fellow members, that is only concerned with individual measures of success, is a weak, unsound community. The strength of a community can be found in its moral center; the ability to articulate and act upon a defined moral center will fortify a community. The moral center of a community, that place where we can find the values of empathy, compassion, and caring, is the basis for civic responsibility and the success of that community.

For Personal Enrichment

Doing Community Service is empowering. When an individual goes out in the world and interacts with other people in the spirit of bettering, that individual makes a contribution and will feel a sense of accomplishment.

We are reminded all too often of the cynicism, indifference, and isolation that exists in our society. Community Service, the taking of physical action, reminds us of our connection and ability to connect. It is important to study the great actions of others, but participating in community service enables the individual to learn for himself and to teach herself.

For the Institutional Community

Our school is a place of learning; we need to integrate the ideals of Community Service into our academic curriculum. Because Community Service embodies experiential learning, locating a moral center, community health, because it is about empowerment and making the world a better place, because these issues are at the core of being, we need to do it. The desire to act comes from a pride, caring, and respect for a community. Community Service must be harnessed to foster a sense of community in a school, a neighborhood, and beyond.

3. *Volunteer Work Opens Teen's Eyes to Nursing*

THE DETROIT NEWS, APRIL 16, 2005

If you asked 13-year-olds to make a list of their favorite after-school activities, visiting with the elderly probably wouldn't be a top choice. But it would be for John Prueter, son of Keith and Barbara Prueter of Essexville, who says he'd spend time with older generations every day if he could.

"All the older people are nice people," he said. "They like to see young people come visit in these homes." Prueter, a seventh-grader at Cramer Junior High School, spends much of his after-school time at the Alterra Sterling House, an assisted-living home in Hampton Township.

Prueter got into volunteering with the elderly almost two years ago when his great-grandmother, Mable Post, suffered a stroke. Always close to her, Prueter visited her regularly when she was in the hospital. After 100 days, she was transferred to Alterra, where she still lives. Now, instead of coming just to visit a relative, he comes to volunteer and visit with everyone. He is the youngest of Alterra's regular volunteers and one of the most frequent visitors.

Prueter spends his time there helping with activities such as cooking and gardening, playing games with residents and just chatting with them. He speaks to the residents on a level that makes them feel good, said Pam O'Laughlin, executive director for Alterra's Bay City campus. "He has a unique ability to communicate with these folks," she said. "He's not timid. They look forward to him coming." Prueter sometimes takes the residents small gifts, such as cake on a birthday, and often calls them when he cannot come in.

He's willing to help Alterra's staff with any activities, O'Laughlin said. For example, he helped residents make cheesecakes for Easter. He helps with garden- 5 ing and crafts, and calls the bingo games each Sunday. He also helps with mail delivery, assists nurses and helps residents get ready for special trips or concerts.

Virginia Ball, an 85-year-old resident, says Prueter visits with her regularly when he stops in. He runs and answers her phone when he hears it ringing down the hall and helps out with other tasks. "He'll offer to fold laundry," she said. But if there is nothing to do to help, Prueter will just sit in her room and chat. "He seems to enjoy talking to older people," Ball said.

His service at Alterra earned him an outstanding youth volunteer award from Veterans of Foreign Wars Post 6950. Prueter wants to be in the marching band when he moves up to Garber High School. But he says he doesn't plan on letting practice get in the way of his visits to Alterra. Even after high school, Prueter hopes to continue working with the elderly by studying nursing. He says he became interested in the field because of his volunteer work.

His dream job, he says, is working where he volunteers now.

4. *In the Good Name of Community Service* (summary)

TARA BAHRAMPOUR, *WASHINGTON POST*, MARCH 7, 2005

Willie Grothman and Tim Phang of Washington-Lee High School in Arlington, Virginia have formed a student service organization called the Willie Grothman Club, which involves community service without minimum hours or mandatory attendance or even formal enrollment. Anyone can join, even if only to participate in a single activity. They have held ten events, many of which have involved walking — for AIDS, for the homeless and for breast cancer in an event in which they took turns walking relays all night around a track in the rain. The group plans to go bowling soon to benefit cystic fibrosis research. For such events they collect pledges of money from friends and family members for each mile walked or each bowling pin knocked over.

Club members remind potential recruits that besides offering a chance to be helpful and make friends, participation in the Willie Grothman Club looks good on college applications. "All the college people I've been talking to have been fairly impressed," Grothman said. To add luster to that aura, they are generous in bestowing titles and offices. "I won't lie — I mean, we created a lot of positions," Grothman said. "But when you're putting it on a college application, you want to at least have an officer position." He admits that the club began "as a ridiculous joke," but is proud that "we made something of it, which is more than a lot of school clubs do."

5. *Mandatory Volunteerism*

ARTHUR STUKAS, MARK SNYDER, AND E. GIL CLARY

PSYCHOLOGICAL SCIENCE, JANUARY 1999

Two studies suggest that community service requirements can have negative effects on students' intentions to volunteer freely in the future but only when students feel that they aren't ready to volunteer or that the requirement is too controlling. Students who are ready to volunteer should be less influenced by requirements to serve.

Students who were not "ready" to volunteer were less affected by the free choice condition — that is, researchers were able to persuade them to volunteer while making sure that they still felt that it was their free choice and they were more likely to want to volunteer in the future than "not ready" students who had been required. Students were just as likely to want to continue volunteering after being required as after having a free choice to volunteer. To avoid the negative effects of mandatory volunteer programs on students' motivation, institutions should design these programs to contain an element of free choice and to offer programs that allow students to choose the type of volunteer activity they will engage in or allow them to combine personal interests and skills with their service requirements. Researchers found that students who initially did not want to volunteer found that they actually enjoyed helping others if requirements were applied gently and with their input and involvement in the process.

6. *Volunteer* (cartoon)

THE *BREEZE,* JAMES MADISON UNIVERSITY NEWSPAPER

7. From *Youth Attitudes toward Civic Education and Community Service Requirements* (graphs)

MARK HUGO LOPEZ, THE CENTER FOR INFORMATION AND RESEARCH ON CIVIC LEARNING AND ENGAGEMENT, 2002

Graph 1 Attitudes toward Requiring Community Service for a High School Diploma, by Age

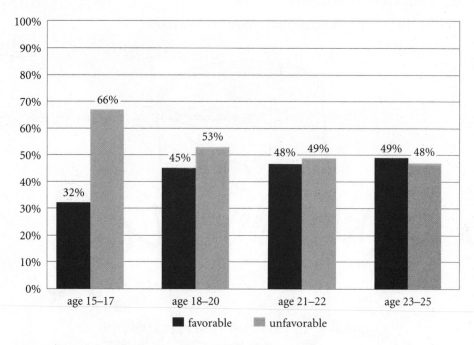

SOURCE: CIRCLE/Council for Excellence in Government Youth Survey, 2002.

Graph 2 Attitudes toward Requiring Community Service for a High School Diploma, by Level of Educational Success

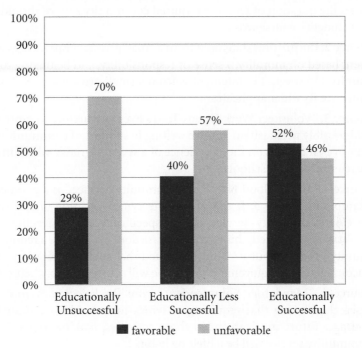

SOURCE: CIRCLE/Council for Excellence in Government Youth Survey, 2002.

Identifying the Issues: Recognizing Complexity

To engage your audience, present your position as reasonable, and perhaps valuable, in a voice that is reasoned, sincere, and informed, using the classic appeals to ethos, logos, and pathos. Written argument, after all, is not likely to change the view of the reader, at least not radically or immediately. Rather, a compelling argument leaves the reader thinking, questioning, considering, and reconsidering.

Keep in mind that the reasonable voice is usually a qualified one, one that is both challenged and informed by others. To write a qualified argument, you must anticipate objections to your position and recognize and respect the complexities of your topic. A reasonable voice recognizes that there are more than two sides to an issue, more than pro–con — which is the written equivalent of a shouting match — but multiple perspectives.

Careful reading has already revealed some of the complexities of required community service. Let's explore a few.

- Source 1, the excerpt from *Millennials Rising*, points out that legislation supports "the integration of community service with academic study." This raises the question of whether required community service should be part of a student's course work.

- Source 2, the mission statement from a small private school, offers an argument based on morality, a sense of responsibility, and belonging to a community. However, the statement is from a small private school. Might this influence its wider application?

- Source 3, "Volunteer Work Opens Teen's Eyes to Nursing," is quite positive and possibly persuasive if you are writing in support of community service. However, it focuses on the experience of a seventh-grader, which might not be relevant to high schools.

- Source 4, "In the Good Name of Community Service," is a good counterexample to Source 3. It reports on the cynical attitude of students who develop community service efforts specifically to bolster their college applications. Granted, this particular case does not involve a required community program, but it could be argued that such exploitation might be encouraged by a requirement that some will satisfy only for their own gain.

- Source 5, "Mandatory Volunteerism" from *Psychological Science*, reports research showing that requiring activities that should be voluntary discourages future involvement in those activities, making it less likely that community service will be a lifelong habit.

- Source 6, "Volunteer" the flyer, emphasizes an upbeat, try-it-you'll-like-it advertising claim. It could be interpreted as questioning the motivation for performing community service or even whether "mandatory volunteering" is an oxymoron.

- Source 7, the graphs from a study by Mark Hugo Lopez, a researcher from the University of Maryland, raises further questions about required community service. Graph 1 shows that support for requiring such service is weakest among those currently in school and is evenly split among those over the age of twenty-one. Does this finding suggest that community service is "good medicine" for high school students, who will eventually appreciate the experience? Graph 2 shows that young people with greater levels of education (completion of a BA or some college work, as opposed to only a high school education) are more likely to support a community service requirement in high schools.

Formulating Your Position

Before you formulate your position, it may be helpful to take stock of the issues. In analyzing the texts on community service, the following issues emerge:

- Does requiring community service devalue it?
- Does requiring it discourage future participation?
- Does the positive experience that most volunteers have offset their initial reluctance to participate?
- How does the structure of the community service program — is it part of academic study? are there choices? — affect its perceived value?
- Can such a requirement be safeguarded from exploitation for an individual's personal gain? If so, how?
- What values about community and education underlie a service requirement?
- What influence does socioeconomic situation play in such a requirement? For example, if students need to earn money, can required community service programs be designed to accommodate them?
- How does a school system determine how many hours of service to require?

These questions — and others you might have — illustrate the complexity of the issue and ensure that you do not develop an argument that is one-sided or even polarized between yes and no. Instead, you are now prepared to write a documented essay that reflects the complexities surrounding the topic.

With these questions and issues in mind, you can begin to formulate a thesis, or claim, that captures your position on the topic. Consider the following working thesis statements:

- Community service can be extremely valuable in the development of both character and academics, but the negative effects of forcing students to participate by making such programs a graduation requirement offset the benefits.
- Though students may not recognize the value of community service until later in life, ——— High School should require community service to instill a sense of civic responsibility and encourage a lifelong habit of helping others.
- High schools should encourage students to participate in community service and reward those who do so without making participation mandatory for graduation.
- Required community service programs are beneficial to both the individuals who participate and the communities being served, as long as students have some choice in the type of service they engage in.

Although you might want to tailor these working thesis statements to use in your essay, each one suggests a clear focus while acknowledging the complexities of the issue.

Incorporating Sources:
Inform Rather than Overwhelm

Once you have formulated your thesis, you will develop your ideas by incorporating sources into your essay. Don't simply summarize or paraphrase a series of texts, but rather cite sources — by paraphrasing or quoting directly — in the service of your own argument. As emphasized throughout, you do not want to represent ideas or words as your own if they are not: give credit where it is due. But you're in charge of the sources, not the other way around.

In the following pages, we consider two uses of sources for an essay on community service. Here is a sample paragraph that takes a positive view of the long-term benefits of community service.

Participation in community service contributes to a person's belief that he or she can make a positive change in the world. According to the excerpt from "Millennials Rising," five out of six Millennials, the youngest generation, "believe their generation has the greatest duty to improve the environment" and would accept additional "civic duties" to bring about needed change. Furthermore, those who have achieved educational success tend to support a community service requirement in high school, according to a study of attitudes toward community service conducted by University of Maryland researcher Mark Hugo Lopez. That finding suggests that people who pursue their education through college perceive community service as a positive influence in their experience, perhaps even one that has promoted their educational goals.

The preceding paragraph uses direct quotations and paraphrases from *Millennials Rising,* and an analysis of one of the graphs from Lopez's study. Notice that the sources are identified within the text.

In the following paragraph, a source is used as the counterargument. Note the concession and refutation.

The ideal of community service often falls short of the reality. A school may institute required community service with the optimistic belief that students will develop a sense of responsibility toward others and feel a connection to others whose immediate situation is dissimilar to theirs. The Dalton School, a small private high school, developed a mission statement that includes utopian goals, such as community service, as a means toward "empowerment" and a belief that "the world can change for the better." It asserts that community service will "foster a sense of community in a school, a neighborhood, and beyond." While those lofty goals may be achieved at least to some extent in certain situations, the practical reality is far different in most cases. Students may simply "put in their time" because the service is a graduation requirement, or they may actually exploit the requirement for their own gain. An article in the *Washington Post* reported on students in a Virginia high school, for instance, who formed their own clubs, with many officer positions, in order to impress college admissions committees. They "empowered" themselves, though hardly in the idealistic way described in the mission statement.

Note that the mission statement was cited to develop the counterargument — that required community service builds a citizenry of people committed to reciprocal responsibilities and confident of their ability to make a difference. After the concession — "those lofty goals may be achieved at least to some extent in certain situations" — the paragraph continues as a refutation, which also includes a reference to another text.

As you go through the readings and other texts in the following chapters, you will join conversations on a range of topics, reflecting on and integrating the ideas of others from different times and places into your own thinking and writing. Each chapter includes a section called Conversation in which you will practice this skill with a series of texts (including visuals) related to the theme of the chapter. Keep in mind the rhetorical triangle; the traditional appeals to logos, pathos, and ethos; and your skill at close reading.

Now, enter the conversations.

4

Education

To what extent do our schools serve the goals
of a true education?

Education remains a concept as difficult to define and as open to debate as it is essential to our identity. What makes a person educated? Is a skilled artisan with no formal schooling educated? Is a wise grandmother with eighty years of life experience but only a third-grade education educated? Is Bill Gates, who dropped out of Harvard as a junior to found Microsoft, more or less educated than his classmates who stayed in school? When we are seeking education, are we looking for knowledge, wisdom, skills, or all three?

Perhaps these questions can all be answered once we define the purpose of education. But formulating that definition generates more questions. Is the purpose of education to prepare citizens to participate in a democracy so they can vote wisely? Is it to teach practical skills that prepare students for the workforce? Or is it to make us more knowledgeable about ourselves and our culture — to know, in the words of the British poet Matthew Arnold (1822–1888), "the best that is known and thought in the world"?

Even Arnold's focus begs several questions: What is "best"? Who decides? How do we balance a skills-based education — what the American educator John Dewey (1859–1952) called "mechanical efficiency" — with a deep understanding of "democratic ideals"? Should schools impart values as well as knowledge? Do mainstream ideas take precedence over concerns of individual groups? Can both be represented?

Such philosophical questions are often lost in the practical realities of school and schooling. Our national rhetoric has gone "back to basics," promised that "no child [will be] left behind," and declared that a "digital divide" threatens to further separate the haves from the have-nots. At the same time advocates of standardized testing are praising the positive impact of accountability, critics are sounding alarms about the negative effects of competition and ranking. We are far from agreement about the best way to teach and learn. And in the twenty-first century, the herculean task of educating the populace is made even more challenging by globalization and the demands of the international marketplace. What information and skills do students need to compete in a global economy, to make decisions that have a global impact?

The selections in this chapter explore many of these issues. For example, they ask how choices of required reading affect students and whether the humdrum routine of drill contributes to an education. The writers give us an insider's view of what it means to feel excluded from mainstream education by attitude, textbooks, economics, or choice. They discuss how U.S. schools compare with those in other countries. And they ask whether the American high school is obsolete. Together, they lead us to reflect on what education means and whether — and how — our schools embody that vision.

I Know Why the Caged Bird Cannot Read

How American High School Students
Learn to Loathe Literature

FRANCINE PROSE

 Francine Prose, who was born in the late 1940s, is a reporter, essayist, critic, and editor. She has also written more than twenty books, including poetry, fiction, and children's literature. Her novel *Blue Angel* (2000) was a finalist for the National Book Award, and her nonfiction work *The Lives of the Muses: Nine Women and the Artists They Inspired* (2002) was a national best seller and a *New York Times* Notable Book. She has received numerous grants and awards, including Guggenheim and Fulbright fellowships. She is also the author of *Reading Like a Writer: A Guide for People Who Love Books and Those Who Want to Write Them* (2006). Prose is currently a book reviewer for a number of magazines and periodicals, including the *New York Times Book Review* and *O*. The following essay, published in *Harper's* in September, 1999, is a critique of the quality of required reading in American high schools.

Books discussed in this essay include:

I Know Why the Caged Bird Sings by Maya Angelou. Bantam Books, 1983.

To Kill a Mockingbird by Harper Lee. Warner Books, 1988.

Teaching Values through Teaching Literature by Margaret Dodson. Eric/Edinfo Press, 1993.

Teaching the Novel by Becky Alano. Eric/Edinfo Press, 1989.

Teaching Literature by Women Authors by Carolyn Smith McGowen. Eric/Edinfo Press, 1993.

Like most parents who have, against all odds, preserved a lively and still evolving passion for good books, I find myself, each September, increasingly appalled by the dismal lists of texts that my sons are doomed to waste a school year reading. What I get as compensation is a measure of insight into why our society has come to admire Montel Williams and Ricki Lake so much more than Dante and Homer. Given the dreariness with which literature is taught in many American classrooms, it seems miraculous that any sentient teenager would view reading as a source of pleasure. Traditionally, the love of reading has been born and nurtured in high school English class — the last time many students will find themselves in a roomful of people who have all read the same text and are, in theory, prepared to discuss it. High school — even more than college — is where literary tastes and allegiances are formed; what we read in adolescence is imprinted on our brains as the dreamy notions of childhood crystallize into hard data.

The intense loyalty adults harbor for books first encountered in youth is one probable reason for the otherwise baffling longevity of vintage mediocre novels, books that teachers may themselves have read in adolescence; it is also the most plausible explanation for the peculiar [1998] Modern Library list of the "100 Best Novels of the 20th Century," a roster dominated by robust survivors from the tenth-grade syllabus. *Darkness at Noon, Lord of the Flies, Brave New World,* and *The Studs Lonigan Trilogy* all speak, in various ways, to the vestigial teenage psyches of men of a certain age. The parallel list drawn up by students (younger, more of them female) in the Radcliffe Publishing Course reflects the equally romantic and tacky tastes (*Gone with the Wind, The Fountainhead*) of a later generation of adolescent girls.

Given the fact that these early encounters with literature leave such indelible impressions, it would seem doubly important to make sure that high school students are actually reading literature. Yet every opportunity to instill adolescents with a lifelong affinity for narrative, for the ways in which the vision of an artist can percolate through an idiosyncratic use of language, and for the supple gymnastics of a mind that exercises the mind of the reader is being squandered on regimens of trash and semi-trash, taught for reasons that have nothing to do with how well a book is written. In fact, less and less attention is being paid to what has been written, let alone how; it's become a rarity for a teacher to suggest that a book might be a work of art composed of words and sentences, or that the choice of these words and sentences can inform and delight us. We hear that more books are being bought and sold than ever before, yet no one, as far as I know, is arguing that we are producing and becoming a nation of avid readers of serious literature.

Much has been made of the lemminglike fervor with which our universities have rushed to sacrifice complexity for diversity; for decades now, critics have decried our plummeting scholastic standards and mourned the death of cultural literacy without having done one appreciable thing to raise the educational bar or revive our moribund culture. Meanwhile, scant notice has been paid, except by exasperated parents, to the missed opportunities and misinformation that form the true curriculum of so many high school English classes.

My own two sons, now twenty-one and seventeen, have read (in public and private schools) Shakespeare, Hawthorne, and Melville. But they've also slogged repeatedly through the manipulative melodramas of Alice Walker and Maya Angelou, through sentimental, middlebrow favorites (*To Kill a Mockingbird* and *A Separate Peace*), the weaker novels of John Steinbeck, the fantasies of Ray Bradbury. My older son spent the first several weeks of sophomore English discussing the class's summer assignment, *Ordinary People,* a weeper and former bestseller by Judith Guest about a "dysfunctional" family recovering from a teenage son's suicide attempt.

Neither has heard a teacher suggest that he read Kafka, though one might suppose that teenagers might enjoy the transformative science-fiction aspects of *The Metamorphosis*, a story about a young man so alienated from *his* "dysfunctional" family that he turns — embarrassingly for them — into a giant beetle. No instructor has ever asked my sons to read Alice Munro, who writes so lucidly and beautifully about the hypersensitivity that makes adolescence a hell.

In the hope of finding out that my children and my friends' children were exceptionally unfortunate, I recently collected eighty or so reading lists from high schools throughout the country. Because of how overworked teachers are, how hard to reach during the school day, as well as the odd, paranoid defensiveness that pervades so many schools, obtaining these documents seemed to require more time and dogged perseverance than obtaining one's FBI surveillance files — and what I came away with may not be a scientifically accurate survey. Such surveys have been done by the National Council of Teachers of English (published in the 1993 NCTE research report, *Literature in the Secondary Schools*), with results that both underline and fail to reflect what I found.

What emerges from these photocopied pages distributed in public, private, and Catholic schools as well as in military academies, in Manhattan and Denver, in rural Oregon and urban Missouri, is a numbing sameness, unaffected by geography, region, or community size. Nearly every list contains at least one of Shakespeare's plays. Indeed, in the NCTE report, Shakespeare (followed closely by John Steinbeck) tops the rosters of "Ten Most Frequently Required Authors of Book-Length Works, Grades 9–12."

Yet in other genres — fiction and memoir — the news is far more upsetting. On the lists sampled, Harper Lee's *To Kill a Mockingbird* and Maya Angelou's *I Know Why the Caged Bird Sings* are among the titles that appear most often, a grisly fact that in itself should inspire us to examine the works that dominate our children's literary education.

First published in 1970, *I Know Why the Caged Bird Sings* is what we have since learned to recognize as a "survivor" memoir, a first-person narrative of victimization and recovery. Angelou transports us to her childhood in segregated Arkansas, where she was raised by her grandmother and was mostly content, despite the unpleasantness of her white neighbors, until, after a move to St. Louis, eight-year-old Maya was raped by her mother's boyfriend.

One can see why this memoir might appeal to the lazy or uninspired teacher, who can conduct the class as if the students were the studio audience for Angelou's guest appearance on *Oprah*. The author's frequently vented distrust of white society might rouse even the most sluggish or understandably disaffected ninth-graders to join a discussion of racism; her victory over poverty and abuse can be used to address what one fan, in a customer book review on Amazon.com, celebrated as "transcending that pain, drawing from it deeper levels of meaning about being truly human and truly alive." Many chapters end with sententious

10

epigrams virtually begging to serve as texts for sophomoric rumination on such questions as: What does Angelou mean when she writes, "If growing up is painful for the Southern Black girl, being aware of her displacement is rust on the razor that threatens the throat"?

But much more terrifying than the prospect of Angelou's pieties being dissected for their deeper meaning is the notion of her language being used as a model of "poetic" prose style. Many of the terrible mysteries that confront teachers of college freshman composition can be solved simply by looking at Angelou's writing. Who told students to combine a dozen mixed metaphors in one paragraph? Consider a typical passage from Angelou's opaque prose: "Weekdays revolved on a sameness wheel. They turned into themselves so steadily and inevitably that each seemed to be the original of yesterday's rough draft. Saturdays, however, always broke the mold and dared to be different." Where do students learn to write stale, inaccurate similes? "The man's dead words fell like bricks around the auditorium and too many settled in my belly." Who seriously believes that murky, turgid, convoluted language of this sort constitutes good writing? "Youth and social approval allied themselves with me and we trammeled memories of slights and insults. The wind of our swift passage remodeled my features. Lost tears were pounded to mud and then to dust. Years of withdrawal were brushed aside and left behind, as hanging ropes of parasitic moss."

To hold up this book as a paradigm of memoir, of thought — of literature — is akin to inviting doctors convicted of malpractice to instruct our medical students. If we want to use Angelou's work to educate our kids, let's invite them to parse her language, sentence by sentence; ask them precisely what it means and ask why one would bother obscuring ideas that could be expressed so much more simply and felicitously.

Narrated affably enough by a nine-year-old girl named Scout, *To Kill a Mockingbird* is the perennially beloved and treacly account of growing up in a small Southern town during the Depression. Its hero is Scout's father, the saintly Atticus Finch, a lawyer who represents everything we cherish about justice and democracy and the American Way, and who defends a black man falsely accused of rape by a poor white woman. The novel has a shadow hero, too, the descriptively named Boo Radley, a gooney recluse who becomes the occasion for yet another lesson in tolerance and compassion.

Such summary reduces the book, but not by all that much. To read the novel   15 is, for most, an exercise in wish-fulfillment and self-congratulation, a chance to consider thorny issues of race and prejudice from a safe distance and with the comfortable certainty that the reader would *never* harbor the racist attitudes espoused by the lowlifes in the novel. We (the readers) are Scout, her childhood is our childhood, and Atticus Finch is our brave, infinitely patient American Daddy. And that creepy big guy living alone in the scary house turns out to have been watching over us with protective benevolent attention.

Maya Angelou and Harper Lee are not the only authors on the lists. The other most popular books are *The Great Gatsby*, *The Scarlet Letter*, *The Adventures of*

Huckleberry Finn, and *The Catcher in the Rye*. John Steinbeck (*The Pearl, Of Mice and Men, The Red Pony, The Grapes of Wrath*) and Toni Morrison (*Song of Solomon, Sula, The Bluest Eye, Beloved*) are the writers — after Shakespeare — represented by the largest number of titles. Also widely studied are novels of more dubious literary merit: John Knowles's *A Separate Peace*, William Golding's *Lord of the Flies*, Elie Wiesel's *Night*, and Ray Bradbury's *Fahrenheit 451, Dandelion Wine, The October Country*, and *Something Wicked This Way Comes*. Trailing behind these favorites, Orwell (*Nineteen Eighty-Four* and *Animal Farm*) is still being read, as are the Brontës (*Wuthering Heights* and *Jane Eyre*).

How astonishing then that students exposed to such a wide array of masterpieces and competent middlebrow entertainments are not mobbing their libraries and bookstores, demanding heady diets of serious or semi-serious fiction! And how puzzling that I should so often find myself teaching bright, eager college undergraduate and graduate students, would-be writers handicapped not merely by how little literature they have read but by their utter inability to read it; many are nearly incapable of doing the close line-by-line reading necessary to disclose the most basic information in a story by Henry James or a seemingly more straightforward one by Katherine Mansfield or Paul Bowles.

The explanation, it turns out, lies in how these books, even the best of them, are being presented in the classroom. My dogged search for reading lists flushed out, in addition to the lists themselves, course descriptions, teaching guides, and anecdotes that reveal how English literature is being taught to high school students. Only rarely do teachers propose that writing might be worth reading closely. Instead, students are informed that literature is principally a vehicle for the soporific moral blather they suffer daily from their parents. The present vogue for teaching "values" through literature uses the novel as a springboard for the sort of discussion formerly conducted in civics or ethics classes — areas of study that, in theory, have been phased out of the curriculum but that, in fact, have been retained and cleverly substituted for what we used to call English. English — and everything about it that is inventive, imaginative, or pleasurable — is beside the point in classrooms, as is everything that constitutes style and that distinguishes writers, one from another, as precisely as fingerprints or DNA mapping.

The question is no longer what the writer has written but rather who the writer is — specifically, what ethnic group or gender identity an author represents. A motion passed by the San Francisco Board of Education in March 1998 mandates that "works of literature read in class in grades nine to eleven by each high school student must include works by writers of color which reflect the diversity of culture, race, and class of the students of the San Francisco Unified School District. . . . The writers who are known to be lesbian, gay, bisexual or transgender, shall be appropriately identified in the curriculum." Meanwhile, aesthetic beauty — felicitous or accurate language, images, rhythm, wit, the satisfaction of recognizing something in fiction that seems fresh and true — is simply too frivolous, suspect, and elitist even to mention.

Thus the fragile *To Kill a Mockingbird* is freighted with tons of sociopolitical   20
ballast. A "Collaborative Program Planning Record of Learning Experience,"
which I obtained from the Internet, outlines the "overall goal" of teaching the
book ("To understand problems relating to discrimination and prejudice that
exist in our present-day society. To understand and apply these principles to our
own lives") and suggests topics for student discussion: "What type of people make
up your community? Is there any group of people . . . a person (NO NAMES
PLEASE) or type of person in your community that you feel uncomfortable
around?"

A description of "The Family in Literature," an elective offered by the Princeton Day School — a course including works by Sophocles and Eugene O'Neill —
begins: "Bruce Springsteen once tried to make us believe that, 'No one can break
the ties that bind/You can't for say-yay-yay-yay-yay-yay-yake the ties that bind.'
He has since divorced his wife and married his back-up singer. So what are these
ties and just how strong are they, after all?" With its chilling echoes of New Age
psychobabble, Margaret Dodson's *Teaching Values through Teaching Literature*, a
sourcebook for high school English teachers, informs us that the point of Steinbeck's *Of Mice and Men* is "to show how progress has been made in the treatment
of the mentally disadvantaged, and that more and better roles in society are being
devised for them [and to] establish that mentally retarded people are human
beings with the same needs and feelings that everyone else experiences."

An eighth-grader studying Elie Wiesel's overwrought *Night* in a class taught
by a passionate gay-rights advocate came home with the following notes: "Many
Jews killed during the Holocaust, but many *many* homosexuals murdered by
Nazis. Pink triangle — Silence equals death."

It's cheering that so many lists include *The Adventures of Huckleberry Finn* —
but not when we discover that this moving, funny novel is being taught not as a
work of art but as a piece of damning evidence against that bigot, Mark Twain. A
friend's daughter's English teacher informed a group of parents that the only reason to study *Huckleberry Finn* was to decide whether it was a racist text. Instructors consulting *Teaching Values through Teaching Literature* will have resolved this
debate long before they walk into the classroom to supervise "a close reading of
Huckleberry Finn that will reveal the various ways in which Twain undercuts Jim's
humanity: in the minstrel routines with Huck as the 'straight man'; in generalities
about Blacks as unreliable, primitive and slow-witted. . . ."

Luckily for the teacher and students required to confront this fictional equivalent of a minstrel show, Mark Twain can be rehabilitated — that is to say,
revised. In classes that sound like test screenings used to position unreleased
Hollywood films, focus groups in which viewers are invited to choose among
variant endings, students are polled for possible alternatives to Huck's and Tom
Sawyer's actions — should Tom have carried out his plan to "free" Jim? — and
asked to speculate on what the fictional characters might have or should have
done to become better people and atone for the sins of their creators.

In the most unintentionally hilarious of these lesson plans, a chapter entitled   25
"*Ethan Frome:* An Avoidable Tragedy," Dodson warns teachers to expect resistance to their efforts to reform Wharton's characters and thus improve her novel's outcome: "Students intensely dislike the mere suggestion that Ethan should have honored his commitment to Zeena and encouraged Mattie to date Dennie Eady, yet this would surely have demonstrated greater love than the suicide attempt."

Thus another puzzle confronting college and even graduate school instructors — Why do students so despise dead writers? — is partly explained by the adversarial stance that these sourcebooks adopt toward authors of classic texts. Teachers are counseled "to help students rise above Emerson's style of stating an idea bluntly, announcing reservations, and sometimes even negating the original idea" and to present "a method of contrasting the drab, utilitarian prose of *Nineteen Eighty-four* with a lyric poem 'To a Darkling Thrush,' by Thomas Hardy." Why not mention that such works have been read for years — for a reason! — and urge students to figure out what that reason is? Doesn't it seem less *valuable* to read Emily Dickinson's work as the brain-damaged mumblings of a demented agoraphobic than to approach the subject of Dickinson, as Richard Sewell suggests in his biography of her, on our knees? No one's suggesting that canonical writers should be immune to criticism. Dickens's anti-Semitism, Tolstoy's overly romantic ideas about the peasantry, Kipling's racism, are all problematic, and merit discussion. But to treat the geniuses of the past as naughty children, amenable to reeducation by the children of the present, evokes the educational theory of the Chinese Cultural Revolution.

No wonder students are rarely asked to consider what was actually written by these hopeless racists and sociopaths. Instead, they're told to write around the books, or, better yet, write their own books. Becky Alano's depressing *Teaching the Novel* advises readers of Sylvia Plath's *The Bell Jar* to construct a therapeutic evaluation of its suicidal heroine ("Do you think she is ready to go home? What is your prognosis for her future?") and lists documents to be written as supplements to *Macbeth* (a script of the TV evening news announcing the murders; a psychiatrist's report on Lady Macbeth, or her suicide note to her husband; Macbeth's entry in *Who's Who*, or his obituary).

How should prospective readers of Anne Frank's *The Diary of a Young Girl* prepare? Carolyn Smith McGowen's *Teaching Literature by Women Authors* suggests: "Give each student a paper grocery bag. Explain that to avoid being sent to a concentration camp, many people went into hiding. Often they could take with them only what they could carry. . . . Ask your students to choose the items they would take into hiding. These items must fit into the grocery bag." A class attempting to interpret an Emily Dickinson poem can be divided into three groups, each group interpreting the poem based on one of Freud's levels of consciousness; thus the little ids, egos, and superegos can respond to the Dickinson poem according to the category of awareness to which their group has been assigned.

Those who might have supposed that one purpose of fiction was to deploy the powers of language to connect us, directly and intimately, with the hearts and souls of others, will be disappointed to learn that the whole point is to make us examine ourselves. According to Alano, *The Catcher in the Rye* will doubtless suggest an incident "in which you felt yourself to be an 'outsider' like Holden. Why did you feel outside? What finally changed your situation?" Stephen Crane's *The Red Badge of Courage* should make us compare our anxieties ("Describe an event that you anticipated with fear. . . . Was the actual event worth the dread?") with those of its Civil War hero. And what does *The Great Gatsby* lead us to consider? "Did you ever pursue a goal with single-minded devotion? . . . Would you have gained your end in any other way?" Are we to believe that the average eleventh-grader has had an experience comparable to that of Jay Gatsby — or F. Scott Fitzgerald? And is it any wonder that teenagers should complete these exercises with little but contempt for the writer who so pointlessly complicated and obfuscated a personal true story that sixteen-year-olds could have told so much more interestingly themselves?

I remember when it dawned on me that I might, someday, grow old. I was in the   30
eleventh grade. Our marvelous and unusual English teacher had assigned us to read *King Lear* — that is, to read every line of *King Lear*. (As I recall, we were asked to circle every word or metaphor having to do with eyes and vision, a tedious process we grumbled about but that succeeded in focusing our attention.) Although I knew I would never ever resemble the decrepit adults around me, Shakespeare's genius, his poetry, his profound, encyclopedic understanding of personality, managed to persuade me that I could *be* that mythical king — an imaginative identification very different from whatever result I might have obtained by persuading myself that my own experience was the *same* as Lear's. I recall the hallucinatory sense of having left my warm bedroom, of finding myself — old, enraged, alone, despised — on that heath, in that dangerous storm. And I remember realizing, after the storm subsided, that language, that mere words on the page, had raised that howling tempest.

Lear is still the Shakespeare play I like best. I reread it periodically, increasingly moved now that age is no longer a theoretical possibility, and now that its portrayal of Lear's behavior so often seems like reportage. A friend whose elderly boss is ruining his company with irrational tests of fealty and refusals to cede power needs only six words to describe the situation at work: *King Lear*, Act One, Scene One.

Another high school favorite was the King James Version of the Book of Revelation. I don't think I'd ever heard of Armageddon, nor did I believe that when the seals of a book were opened horses would fly out. What delighted me was the language, the cadences and the rhythms, and the power of the images: the four horsemen, the beast, the woman clothed with the sun.

But rather than exposing students to works of literature that expand their capacities and vocabularies, sharpen their comprehension, and deepen the level at which they think and feel, we either offer them "easy" (Steinbeck, Knowles, Angelou, Lee) books that "anyone" can understand, or we serve up the tougher works predigested. We no longer believe that books were written one word at a time, and deserve to be read that way. We've forgotten the difference between a student who has never read a nineteenth-century novel and an idiot incapable of reading one. When my son was assigned *Wuthering Heights* in tenth-grade English, the complex sentences, archaisms, multiple narrators, and interwoven stories seemed, at first, like a foreign language. But soon enough, he caught on and reported being moved almost to tears by the cruelty of Heathcliff's treatment of Isabella.

In fact, it's not difficult to find fiction that combines clear, beautiful, accessible, idiosyncratic language with a narrative that conveys a complex worldview. But to use such literature might require teachers and school boards to make fresh choices, selections uncontaminated by trends, clichés, and received ideas. If educators continue to assume that teenagers are interested exclusively in books about teenagers, there *is* engaging, truthful fiction about childhood and adolescence, written in ways that remind us why someone might like to read. There is, for example, Charles Baxter's precise and evocative "Gryphon." And there are the carefully chosen details, the complex sentences, and the down-to-earth diction in Stuart Dybek's great Chicago story, "Hot Ice."

If English class is the only forum in which students can talk about racism and 35 ethnic identity, why not teach Hilton Als's *The Women*, Flannery O'Connor's "Everything That Rises Must Converge," or any of the stories in James Alan McPherson's *Hue and Cry*, all of which eloquently and directly address the subtle, powerful ways in which race affects every tiny decision and gesture? Why not introduce our kids to the clarity and power of James Baldwin's great story "Sonny's Blues"?

My suspicion is that the reason such texts are not used as often as *I Know Why the Caged Bird Sings* is precisely the reason why they *should* be taught — that is, because they're complicated. Baldwin, Als, and McPherson reject obvious "lessons" and familiar arcs of abuse, self-realization, and recovery; they actively refute simplistic prescriptions about how to live.

Great novels can help us master the all-too-rare skill of tolerating — of being able to hold in mind — ambiguity and contradiction. Jay Gatsby has a shady past, but he's also sympathetic. Huck Finn is a liar, but we come to love him. A friend's student once wrote that Alice Munro's characters weren't people he'd choose to hang out with but that reading her work always made him feel "a little less petty and judgmental." Such benefits are denied to the young reader exposed only to books with banal, simple-minded moral equations as well as to the student encouraged to come up with reductive, wrong-headed readings of multilayered texts.

The narrator of *Caged Bird* is good, her rapist is bad; Scout and Atticus Finch are good, their bigoted neighbors are bad. But the characters in James Alan McPherson's "Gold Coast" are a good deal more lifelike. The cantankerous, bigoted, elderly white janitor and the young African American student, his temporary assistant, who puts up with the janitor's bullshit and is simultaneously cheered and saddened by the knowledge that he's headed for greater success than the janitor will ever achieve, both embody mixtures of admirable and more dubious qualities. In other words, they're more like humans. It's hard to imagine the lesson plans telling students exactly how to feel about these two complex plausible characters.

No one's suggesting that every existing syllabus be shredded; many books on the current lists are great works of art. But why not *tell* the students that, instead of suggesting that Mark Twain be posthumously reprimanded? Why not point out how convincingly he captured the workings of Huck's mind, the inner voice of a kid trying desperately to sew a crazy quilt of self together from the ragged scraps around him? Why not celebrate the accuracy and vigor with which he translated the rhythms of American speech into written language?

In simplifying what a book is allowed to tell us — Twain's novel is wholly about racism and not at all about what it's like to *be* Huck Finn — teachers pretend to spark discussion but actually prevent it. They claim to relate the world of the book to the world of experience, but by concentrating on the student's own history they narrow the world of experience down to the personal and deny students *other* sorts of experience — the experience of what's in the book, for starters. One reason we read writers from other times or cultures is to confront alternatives — of feeling and sensibility, of history and psyche, of information and ideas. To experience the heartbreaking matter-of-factness with which Anne Frank described her situation seems more useful than packing a paper bag with Game Boys, cigarettes, and CDs so that we can go into hiding and avoid being sent to the camps.

The pleasure of surrender to the world of a book is only one of the pleasures that this new way of reading — and teaching — denies. In blurring the line between reality and fiction (What happened to you that was exactly like what happened to Hester Prynne?), it reduces our respect for imagination, beauty, art, thought, and for the way that the human spirit expresses itself in words.

Writers have no choice but to believe that literature will survive, that it's worth some effort to preserve the most beautiful, meaningful lyrics or narratives, the record of who we were, and are. And if we want our children to begin an extended love affair with reading and with what great writing can do, we *want* them to get an early start — or any start, at all. Teaching students to value literary masterpieces is our best hope of awakening them to the infinite capacities and complexities of human experience, of helping them acknowledge and accept complexity and ambiguity, and of making them love and respect the language that allows us to smuggle out, and send one another, our urgent, eloquent dispatches from the prison of the self.

That may be what writers — and readers — desire. But if it's not occurring, perhaps that's because our culture wants it less urgently than we do. Education, after all, is a process intended to produce a product. So we have to ask ourselves:

40

What sort of product is being produced by the current system? How does it change when certain factors are added to, or removed from, our literature curriculum? And is it really in the best interests of our consumer economy to create a well-educated, smart, highly literate society of fervent readers? Doesn't our epidemic dumbing-down have undeniable advantages for those institutions (the media, the advertising industry, the government) whose interests are better served by a population not trained to read too closely or ask too many questions?

On the most obvious level, it's worth noting that books are among the few remaining forms of entertainment not sustained by, and meant to further, the interests of advertising. Television, newspapers, and magazines are busily instilling us with new desires and previously unsuspected needs, while books sell only themselves. Moreover, the time we spend reading is time spent away from media that have a greater chance of alchemically transmuting attention into money.

But of course what's happening is more complex and subtle than that, more closely connected to how we conceive of the relation between intellect and spirit. The new-model English-class graduate — the one who has been force-fed the gross oversimplifications proffered by these lesson plans and teaching manuals — values empathy and imagination less than the ability to make quick and irreversible judgments, to entertain and maintain simplistic immovable opinions about guilt and innocence, about the possibilities and limitations of human nature. Less comfortable with the gray areas than with sharply delineated black and white, he or she can work in groups and operate by consensus, and has a resultant, residual distrust for the eccentric, the idiosyncratic, the annoyingly . . . individual. 45

What I've described is a salable product, tailored to the needs of the economic and political moment. What results from these educational methods is a mode of thinking (or, more accurately, of *not* thinking) that equips our kids for the future: Future McDonald's employees. Future corporate board members. Future special prosecutors. Future makers of 100-best-books lists who fondly recall what they first read in high school — and who may not have read anything since. And so the roster of literary masterpieces we pass along to future generations will continue its downward shift, and those lightweight, mediocre high school favorites will continue to rise, unburdened by gravity, to the top of the list.

Questions for Discussion

1. Francine Prose states, "Traditionally, the love of reading has been born and nurtured in high school English class" (para. 1). Do you think this is generally the case? Describe your experience on this subject.
2. What does Prose mean when she writes, "[B]y concentrating on the student's own history they [teachers] narrow the world of experience down to the personal and deny students *other* sorts of experience — the experience of what's in the book, for starters" (para. 40)? Do you agree with Prose's statement? Why or why not?

3. What is Prose implying in the following statement about what she calls the "new-model English-class graduate": "But of course what's happening is more complex and subtle than that [seeing books as unconnected to advertising], more closely connected to how we conceive of the relation between intellect and spirit" (para. 45)?
4. Whom does Prose blame for this state of affairs? Does assigning blame affect the cogency of her argument?
5. This essay was written in 1999. Do you think Prose would or could make the same argument today? Why or why not?

Questions on Rhetoric and Style

1. Discuss three appeals to ethos in this essay. What different roles, or personae, does Prose use to establish her ethos?
2. Prose's opening paragraph includes such words as *appalled*, *dismal*, and *dreariness* — all with negative connotations. Why does she start out with such strong language? Does she risk putting off readers who do not share her views? Why or why not? What other examples of strongly emotional language do you find in the essay?
3. Prose makes several key assumptions about the role and impact of reading literary works in high school. What are they?
4. What appeals does she make to logos?
5. Prose cites many different novels and plays. Does she assume her audience is familiar with some of them? All of them? Explain why it matters whether the audience knows the works.
6. According to Prose, "To hold up [*I Know Why the Caged Bird Sings*] as a paradigm of memoir, of thought — of literature — is akin to inviting doctors convicted of malpractice to instruct our medical students" (para. 13). Do you agree with this analogy? Explain your answer. What other examples of figurative language can you find in this essay?
7. Toward the end of the essay (paras. 35, 39, and 43), Prose uses a series of rhetorical questions. What is her purpose in piling one rhetorical question on top of the other?
8. Would Prose have strengthened her argument by including interviews with a few high school students or teachers? Why or why not?
9. According to Prose, why are American high school students learning to loathe literature? Try to find at least four or five reasons.
10. Does she propose a solution or recommendations to change this situation? If she does not offer a solution, is her argument weakened? Explain your answer.

Suggestions for Writing

1. Prose is highly critical of the quality of both *I Know Why the Caged Bird Sings* and *To Kill a Mockingbird*. If you have read either, write an evaluation of her criticism

of the book. Pay particular attention to the quotations she selects; is she setting up a straw man — that is, an argument easily refuted?

2. Prose is skeptical of the practice of using literary works to teach values. Write an essay in which you support or challenge her position. Be specific in your references to novels, plays, or poems.

3. Prose writes, "Great novels can help us master the all-too-rare skill of tolerating — of being able to hold in mind — ambiguity and contradiction" (para. 37). Select a novel you know well, and explain the "ambiguity and contradiction" at its heart.

4. Collect the required reading lists from several schools (or classes) in different geographical regions, and compare and contrast them. Are there differences in quality as well as quantity? Are any of the books Prose discusses included on them? Do the books appeal to boys as well as girls? Is there opportunity for choice? Write an essay analyzing these lists from Prose's point of view.

From *Education*

RALPH WALDO EMERSON

Ralph Waldo Emerson (1803–1882), perhaps best known for his essay "Self-Reliance" (1841), was one of America's most influential thinkers and writers. After graduating from Harvard Divinity School, he followed nine generations of his family into the ministry but practiced for only a few years. In 1836, he and other like-minded intellectuals, including Henry David Thoreau, founded the Transcendental Club, and that same year he published his influential essay "Nature" (1836). Known as a great orator, Emerson made his living as a popular lecturer on a wide range of topics. From 1821 to 1826, he taught in city and country schools and later served on a number of school boards, including the Concord School Committee and the Board of Overseers of Harvard College. Emerson's essay "Education," from which the following excerpt is taken, was put together posthumously from his writings published in *The American Scholar* and from his commencement addresses.

I believe that our own experience instructs us that the secret of Education lies in respecting the pupil. It is not for you to choose what he shall know, what he shall do. It is chosen and foreordained, and he only holds the key to his own secret. By your tampering and thwarting and too much governing he may be hindered from his end and kept out of his own. Respect the child. Wait and see the new product of Nature. Nature loves analogies, but not repetitions. Respect the child. Be not too much his parent. Trespass not on his solitude.

But I hear the outcry which replies to this suggestion — Would you verily throw up the reins of public and private discipline; would you leave the young child to the mad career of his own passions and whimsies, and call this anarchy a respect for the child's nature? I answer — Respect the child, respect him to the end, but also respect yourself. Be the companion of his thought, the friend of his friendship, the lover of his virtue — but no kinsman of his sin. Let him find you so true to yourself that you are the irreconcilable hater of his vice and the imperturbable slighter of his trifling.

The two points in a boy's training are, to keep his *naturel* and train off all but that — to keep his *naturel*, but stop off his uproar, fooling, and horseplay — keep his nature and arm it with knowledge in the very direction to which it points. Here are the two capital facts, Genius and Drill. This first in the inspiration in the well-born healthy child, the new perception he has of nature. Somewhat he sees in forms or hears in music or apprehends in mathematics, or believes practicable in mechanics or possible in political society, which no one else sees or hears or believes. This is the perpetual romance of new life, the invasion of God into the old dead world, when he sends into quiet houses a young soul with a thought which is not met, looking for something which is not there, but which ought to be there: the thought is dim but it is sure, and he casts about restless for means and masters to verify it; he makes wild attempts to explain himself and invoke the aid and consent of the by-standers. Baffled for want of language and methods to convey his meaning, not yet clear to himself, he conceives that thought not in this house or town, yet in some other house or town is the wise master who can put him in possession of the rules and instruments to execute his will. Happy this child with a bias, with a thought which entrances him, leads him, now into deserts now into cities, the fool of an idea. Let him follow it in good and in evil report, in good or bad company; it will justify itself; it will lead him at last into the illustrious society of the lovers of truth.

In London, in a private company, I became acquainted with a gentleman, Sir Charles Fellowes, who, being at Xanthos, in the Aegean Sea, had seen a Turk point with his staff to some carved work on the corner of a stone almost buried in the soil. Fellowes scraped away the dirt, was struck with the beauty of the sculptured ornaments, and, looking about him, observed more blocks and fragments like this. He returned to the spot, procured laborers and uncovered many blocks. He went back to England, bought a Greek grammar and learned the language; he read history and studied ancient art to explain his stones; he interested Gibson the sculptor; he invoked the assistance of the English Government; he called in the succor of Sir Humphry Davy to analyze the pigments; of experts in coins, of scholars and connoisseurs; and at last in his third visit brought home to England such statues and marble reliefs and such careful plans that he was able to reconstruct, in the British Museum where it now stands, the perfect model of the Ionic trophy-monument, fifty years older than the Parthenon of Athens, and which had been destroyed by earthquakes, then by iconoclast Christians, then by savage Turks. But mark that in the task he had achieved an excellent education, and become associated with distinguished scholars whom he had interested in his pursuit; in short, had formed a college for himself; the enthusiast had found the master, the masters, whom he sought. Always genius seeks genius, desires nothing so much as to be a pupil and to find those who can lend it aid to perfect itself.

Nor are the two elements, enthusiasm and drill, incompatible. Accuracy is 5 essential to beauty. The very definition of the intellect is Aristotle's: "that by which we know terms or boundaries." Give a boy accurate perceptions. Teach him the difference between the similar and the same. Make him call things by their right names. Pardon in him no blunder. Then he will give you solid satisfaction as long as he lives. It is better to teach the child arithmetic and Latin grammar than rhetoric or moral philosophy, because they require exactitude of performance; it is made certain that the lesson is mastered, and that power of performance is worth more than the knowledge. He can learn anything which is important to him now that the power to learn is secured: as mechanics say, when one has learned the use of tools, it is easy to work at a new craft.

Letter by letter, syllable by syllable, the child learns to read, and in good time can convey to all the domestic circle the sense of Shakespeare. By many steps each just as short, the stammering boy and the hesitating collegian, in the school debates, in college clubs, in mock court, comes at last to full, secure, triumphant unfolding of his thought in the popular assembly, with a fullness of power that makes all the steps forgotten.

But this function of opening and feeding the human mind is not to be fulfilled by any mechanical or military method; is not to be trusted to any skill less large than Nature itself. You must not neglect the form, but you must secure the essentials. It is curious how perverse and intermeddling we are, and what vast pains and cost we incur to do wrong. Whilst we all know in our own experience and apply natural methods in our own business — in education our common sense fails us, and we are continually trying costly machinery against nature, in patent schools and academies and in great colleges and universities.

The natural method forever confutes our experiments, and we must still come back to it. The whole theory of the school is on the nurse's or mother's knee. The child is as hot to learn as the mother is to impart. There is mutual delight. The joy of our childhood in hearing beautiful stories from some skillful aunt who loves to tell them, must be repeated in youth. The boy wishes to learn to skate; to coast, to catch a fish in the brook, to hit a mark with a snowball or a stone; and a boy a little older is just as well pleased to teach him these sciences. Not less delightful is the mutual pleasure of teaching and learning the secret of algebra, or of chemistry, or of good reading and good recitation of poetry or of prose, or of chosen facts in history or in biography.

Nature provided for the communication of thought by planting with it in the receiving mind a fury to impart it. 'Tis so in every art, in every science. One burns to tell the new fact, the other burns to hear it. See how far a young doctor will ride or walk to witness a new surgical operation. I have seen a carriage-maker's shop emptied of all its workmen into the street, to scrutinize a new pattern from New York. So in literature, the young man who has taste for poetry, for fine images, for noble thoughts, is insatiable for this nourishment, and forgets all the world for the more learned friend — who finds equal joy in dealing out his treasures.

Happy the natural college thus self-instituted around every natural teacher;   10
the young men of Athens around Socrates; of Alexander around Plotinus; of Paris around Abelard; of Germany around Fichte, or Niebuhr, or Goethe: in short the natural sphere of every leading mind. But the moment this is organized, difficulties begin. The college was to be the nurse and home of genius; but, though every young man is born with some determination in his nature, and is a potential genius; is at last to be one; it is, in the most, obstructed and delayed, and, whatever they may hereafter be, their senses are now opened in advance of their minds. They are more sensual than intellectual. Appetite and indolence they have, but no

enthusiasm. These come in numbers to the college: few geniuses: and the teaching comes to be arranged for these many, and not for those few. Hence the instruction seems to require skillful tutors, of accurate and systematic mind, rather than ardent and inventive masters. Besides, the youth of genius are eccentric, won't drill, are irritable, uncertain, explosive, solitary, not men of the world, not good for every-day association. You have to work for large classes instead of individuals; you must lower your flag and reef your sails to wait for the dull sailors; you grow departmental, routinary, military almost with your discipline and college police. But what doth such a school to form a great and heroic character? What abiding Hope can it inspire? What Reformer will it nurse? What poet will it breed to sing to the human race? What discoverer of Nature's laws will it prompt to enrich us by disclosing in the mind the statute which all matter must obey? What fiery soul will it send out to warm a nation with his charity? What tranquil mind will it have fortified to walk with meekness in private and obscure duties, to wait and to suffer? Is it not manifest that our academic institutions should have a wider scope; that they should not be timid and keep the ruts of the last generation, but that wise men thinking for themselves and heartily seeking the good of mankind, and counting the cost of innovation, should dare to arouse the young to a just and heroic life; that the moral nature should be addressed in the schoolroom, and children should be treated as the high-born candidates of truth and virtue?

So to regard the young child, the young man, requires, no doubt, rare patience: a patience that nothing but faith in the medial forces of the soul can give. You see his sensualism; you see his want of those tastes and perceptions which make the power and safety of your character. Very likely. But he has something else. If he has his own vice, he has its correlative virtue. Every mind should be allowed to make its own statement in action, and its balance will appear. In these judgments one needs that foresight which was attributed to an eminent reformer, of whom it was said "his patience could see in the bud of the aloe the blossom at the end of a hundred years." Alas for the cripple Practice when it seeks to come up with the bird Theory, which flies before it. Try your design on the best school. The scholars are of all ages and temperaments and capacities. It is difficult to class them, some are too young, some are slow, some perverse. Each requires so much consideration, that the morning hope of the teacher, of a day of love and progress, is often closed at evening by despair. Each single case, the more it is considered, shows more to be done; and the strict conditions of the hours, on one side, and the number of tasks, on the other. Whatever becomes of our method, the conditions stand fast — six hours, and thirty, fifty, or a hundred and fifty pupils. Something must be done, and done speedily, and in this distress the wisest are tempted to adopt violent means, to proclaim martial law, corporal punishment, mechanical arrangement, bribes, spies, wrath, main strength and ignorance, in lieu of that wise genial providential influence they had hoped, and yet hope at some future day to adopt. Of course the devotion to details reacts injuriously on the teacher. He cannot indulge his genius, he cannot delight in personal relations with young friends, when his eye is always on the clock, and twenty classes are to be dealt with before the day is done. Besides, how can he please himself with genius, and foster modest virtue? A sure proportion of rogue and dunce finds its way into every school and requires a cruel share of time, and the gentle teacher, who wished to be a Providence to youth, is grown a martinet, sore with suspicions; knows as much vice as the judge of a police court, and his love of learning is lost in the routine of grammars and books of elements.

A rule is so easy that it does not need a man to apply it; an automaton, a machine, can be made to keep a school so. It facilitates labor and thought so much that there is always the temptation in large schools to omit the endless task of meeting the wants of each single mind, and to govern by steam. But it is at frightful cost. Our modes of Education aim to expedite, to save labor; to do for masses what cannot be done for masses, what must be done reverently, one by one: say rather, the whole world is needed for the tuition of each pupil. The advantages of this system of emulation and display are so prompt and obvious, it is such a time-saver, it is so energetic on slow and on bad natures, and is of so easy application, needing no sage or poet, but any tutor or schoolmaster in his first term can apply it — that it is not strange that this calomel[1] of culture should be a popular medicine. On the other hand, total abstinence from this drug, and the adoption of simple discipline and the following of nature involves at once immense claims on the time, the thoughts, on the Life of the teacher. It requires time, use, insight, event, all the great lessons and assistances of God; and only to think of using it implies character and profoundness; to enter on this course of discipline is to be good and great. It is precisely analogous to the difference between the use of corporal punishment and the methods of love. It is so easy to bestow on a bad boy a blow, overpower him, and get obedience without words, that in this world of hurry and distraction, who can wait for the returns of reason and the conquest of self; in the uncertainty too whether that will ever come? And yet the familiar observation of the universal compensations might suggest the fear that so summary a stop of a bad humor was more jeopardous than its continuance.

Now the correction of this quack practice is to import into Education the wisdom of life. Leave this military hurry and adopt the pace of Nature. Her secret is patience. Do you know how the naturalist learns all the secrets of the forest, of plants, of birds, of beasts, of reptiles, of fishes, of the rivers and the sea? When he goes into the woods the birds fly before him and he finds none; when he goes to the river bank, the fish and the reptile swim away and leave him alone. His secret is patience; he sits down, and sits still; he is a statue; he is a log. These creatures have no value for their time, and he must put as low a rate on his. By dint of obstinate sitting still, reptile, fish, bird and beast, which all wish to return to their haunts, begin to return. He sits still; if they approach, he remains passive as the

---

[1] A mercury compound once used as a laxative, purgative, or disinfectant. — Eds.

stone he sits upon. They lose their fear. They have curiosity too about him. By and by the curiosity masters the fear, and they come swimming, creeping and flying towards him; and as he is still immovable, they not only resume their haunts and their ordinary labors and manners, show themselves to him in their work-day trim, but also volunteer some degree of advances towards fellowship and good understanding with a biped who behaves so civilly and well. Can you not baffle the impatience and passion of the child by your tranquility? Can you not wait for him, as Nature and Providence do? Can you not keep for his mind and ways, for his secret, the same curiosity you give to the squirrel, snake, rabbit, and the sheldrake and the deer? He has a secret; wonderful methods in him; he is — every child — a new style of man; give him time and opportunity. Talk of Columbus and Newton! I tell you the child just born in yonder hovel is the beginning of a revolution as great as theirs. But you must have the believing and prophetic eye. Have the self-command you wish to inspire. Your teaching and discipline must have the reserve and taciturnity of Nature. Teach them to hold their tongues by holding your own. Say little; do not snarl; do not chide; but govern by the eye. See what they need, and that the right thing is done.

I confess myself utterly at a loss in suggesting particular reforms in our ways of teaching. No discretion that can be lodged with a school-committee, with the overseers or visitors of an academy, of a college, can at all avail to reach these difficulties and perplexities, but they solve themselves when we leave institutions and address individuals. The will, the male power, organizes, imposes its own thought and wish on others, and makes that military eye which controls boys as it controls men; admirable in its results, a fortune to him who has it, and only dangerous when it leads the workman to overvalue and overuse it and precludes him from finer means. Sympathy, the female force — which they must use who have not the first — deficient in instant control and the breaking down of resistance, is more subtle and lasting and creative. I advise teachers to cherish mother-wit. I assume that you will keep the grammar, reading, writing and arithmetic in order; 'tis easy and of course you will. But smuggle in a little contraband wit, fancy, imagination, thought. If you have a taste which you have suppressed because it is not shared by those about you, tell them that. Set this law up, whatever becomes of the rules of the school: they must not whisper, much less talk; but if one of the young people says a wise thing, greet it, and let all the children clap their hands. They shall have no book but school-books in the room; but if one has brought in a Plutarch or Shakespeare or Don Quixote or Goldsmith or any other good book, and understands what he reads, put him at once at the head of the class. Nobody shall be disorderly, or leave his desk without permission, but if a boy runs from his bench, or a girl, because the fire falls, or to check some injury that a little dastard is indicting behind his desk on some helpless sufferer, take away the medal from the head of the class and give it on the instant to the brave rescuer. If a child happens to show that he knows any fact about astronomy, or plants, or birds, or rocks, or history, that interests him and you, hush all the classes and encourage him to tell it so that all may hear. Then you have made your school-room like the world. Of course you will insist on modesty in the children, and respect to their teachers, but if the boy stops you in your speech, cries out that you are wrong and sets you right, hug him!

To whatsoever upright mind, to whatsoever beating heart I speak, to you it is   15
committed to educate men. By simple living, by an illimitable soul, you inspire, you correct, you instruct, you raise, you embellish all. By your own act you teach the beholder how to do the practicable. According to the depth from which you draw your life, such is the depth not only of your strenuous effort, but of your manners and presence. The beautiful nature of the world has here blended your happiness with your power. Work straight on in absolute duty, and you lend an arm and an encouragement to all the youth of the universe. Consent yourself to be an organ of your highest thought, and lo! suddenly you put all men in your debt, and are the fountain of an energy that goes pulsing on with waves of benefit to the borders of society, to the circumference of things.

Questions for Discussion

1. In this essay, Ralph Waldo Emerson describes his view of an ideal education. What are its defining characteristics?
2. In what ways is Emerson's advice appropriate to a child's first teacher — his or her parents?
3. Why does Emerson believe "[i]t is better to teach the child arithmetic and Latin grammar than rhetoric or moral philosophy" (para. 5)?
4. In what ways does this essay point out the education system's effect on teachers as well as students?
5. Why does Emerson criticize schools as bureaucratic institutions (para. 10)?
6. Emerson refers to educating "a boy" and "a man" and uses masculine pronouns when referring to students. As a reader, does this gender bias affect how receptive you are to Emerson's ideas?
7. Describe the adult that Emerson imagines would emerge from an education based on the principles he supports.

Questions on Rhetoric and Style

1. What does Emerson mean when he says, "Nature loves analogies, but not repetitions" (para. 1)?
2. Why is the relationship between "Genius and Drill," as Emerson explains it, paradoxical (para. 3)?
3. Paragraph 4 is taken up almost entirely by an extended example. What is Emerson's purpose in developing this long explanation?
4. Identify at least five examples of figurative language that Emerson uses to advance his argument, and explain their effect. In responding, consider the fol-

lowing line from paragraph 11: "Alas for the cripple Practice when it seeks to come up with the bird Theory, which flies before it."

5. What exactly is the "natural method" to which Emerson refers (para. 8)?

6. Identify examples of the following rhetorical strategies in paragraph 13, and explain their effect: rhetorical questions, sentence variety and pacing, analogy, allusion, and imperative sentences.

7. Point out appeals to pathos through highly emotional and evocative diction.

8. Explain why you do or do not interpret the opening line of paragraph 14 as ironic: "I confess myself utterly at a loss in suggesting particular reforms in our ways of teaching."

9. Why does Emerson believe that the "will, the male power" (para. 14) will be of less benefit to the child than "[s]ympathy, the female force"?

10. Rephrase the following sentence in contemporary language: "And yet the familiar observation of the universal compensations might suggest the fear that so summary a stop of a bad humor was more jeopardous than its continuance" (para. 12).

11. What is Emerson's purpose in shifting among the pronouns *I*, *we*, and *you*?

12. How would you describe Emerson's tone in this essay?

Suggestions for Writing

1. In paragraph 12, Emerson makes the following assertion about education in his time: "Our modes of Education aim to expedite, to save labor; to do for masses what cannot be done for masses, what must be done reverently, one by one: say rather, the whole world is needed for the tuition of each pupil." What does he mean? (You might have to look up the meaning of *tuition* in this context.) Do you think that public education today still resembles Emerson's description? Explain.

2. If you were responsible for the education of a child — your own or one for whom you serve as guardian — which of Emerson's assertions about education would you choose as your guiding principle? Write an essay explaining why you would choose that principle over another of Emerson's principles.

3. Explain why you agree or disagree with Emerson's assertion that "every young man [and woman] is born with some determination in his [or her] nature, and is a potential genius" (para. 10).

4. Write a response to Emerson in the voice of Francine Prose, explaining why you agree or disagree with the issues he raises and the positions he takes.

5. Evaluate your own schooling according to the criteria presented in paragraph 10.

Superman and Me

SHERMAN ALEXIE

> Sherman J. Alexie Jr. (b. 1966), a member of the Spokane and the Coeur d'Alene
> tribes, grew up on the Spokane Reservation in Washington state. A graduate of
> Washington State University, he has published eighteen books, including *The Lone
> Ranger and Tonto Fistfight in Heaven* (1983), a short-story collection that received
> a PEN/Hemingway Award for Best First Book of Fiction. One of the stories in this
> collection was the basis for the movie *Smoke Signals* (1999), for which Alexie
> wrote the screenplay. An activist for Native American rights and culture, Alexie
> wrote the following essay describing the impact of reading on his life. It was origi-
> nally published in the *Los Angeles Times* in 1998.

I learned to read with a Superman comic book. Simple enough, I suppose.
I cannot recall which particular Superman comic book I read, nor can I
remember which villain he fought in that issue. I cannot remember the plot, nor
the means by which I obtained the comic book. What I can remember is this:
I was 3 years old, a Spokane Indian boy living with his family on the Spokane
Indian Reservation in eastern Washington state. We were poor by most standards,
but one of my parents usually managed to find some minimum-wage job or
another, which made us middle-class by reservation standards. I had a brother
and three sisters. We lived on a combination of irregular paychecks, hope, fear
and government surplus food.

My father, who is one of the few Indians who went to Catholic school on purpose, was an avid reader of westerns, spy thrillers, murder mysteries, gangster
epics, basketball player biographies and anything else he could find. He bought
his books by the pound at Dutch's Pawn Shop, Goodwill, Salvation Army and
Value Village. When he had extra money, he bought new novels at supermarkets,
convenience stores and hospital gift shops. Our house was filled with books. They
were stacked in crazy piles in the bathroom, bedrooms and living room. In a fit of
unemployment-inspired creative energy, my father built a set of bookshelves and
soon filled them with a random assortment of books about the Kennedy assassination, Watergate, the Vietnam War and the entire 23-book series of the Apache
westerns. My father loved books, and since I loved my father with an aching devotion, I decided to love books as well.

I can remember picking up my father's books before I could read. The words
themselves were mostly foreign, but I still remember the exact moment when I
first understood, with a sudden clarity, the purpose of a paragraph. I didn't have
the vocabulary to say "paragraph," but I realized that a paragraph was a fence that
held words. The words inside a paragraph worked together for a common pur-

pose. They had some specific reason for being inside the same fence. This knowledge delighted me. I began to think of everything in terms of paragraphs. Our reservation was a small paragraph within the United States. My family's house was a paragraph, distinct from the other paragraphs of the LeBrets to the north, the Fords to our south and the Tribal School to the west. Inside our house, each family member existed as a separate paragraph but still had genetics and common experiences to link us. Now, using this logic, I can see my changed family as an essay of seven paragraphs: mother, father, older brother, the deceased sister, my younger twin sisters and our adopted little brother.

At the same time I was seeing the world in paragraphs, I also picked up that Superman comic book. Each panel, complete with picture, dialogue and narrative was a three-dimensional paragraph. In one panel, Superman breaks through a door. His suit is red, blue and yellow. The brown door shatters into many pieces. I look at the narrative above the picture. I cannot read the words, but I assume it tells me that "Superman is breaking down the door." Aloud, I pretend to read the words and say, "Superman is breaking down the door." Words, dialogue, also float out of Superman's mouth. Because he is breaking down the door, I assume he says, "I am breaking down the door." Once again, I pretend to read the words and say aloud, "I am breaking down the door." In this way, I learned to read.

This might be an interesting story all by itself. A little Indian boy teaches 5 himself to read at an early age and advances quickly. He reads *Grapes of Wrath* in kindergarten when other children are struggling through *Dick and Jane*. If he'd been anything but an Indian boy living on the reservation, he might have been called a prodigy. But he is an Indian boy living on the reservation and is simply an oddity. He grows into a man who often speaks of his childhood in the third-person, as if it will somehow dull the pain and make him sound more modest about his talents.

A smart Indian is a dangerous person, widely feared and ridiculed by Indians and non-Indians alike. I fought with my classmates on a daily basis. They wanted me to stay quiet when the non-Indian teacher asked for answers, for volunteers, for help. We were Indian children who were expected to be stupid. Most lived up to those expectations inside the classroom but subverted them on the outside. They struggled with basic reading in school but could remember how to sing a few dozen powwow songs. They were monosyllabic in front of their non-Indian teachers but could tell complicated stories and jokes at the dinner table. They submissively ducked their heads when confronted by a non-Indian adult but would slug it out with the Indian bully who was 10 years older. As Indian children, we were expected to fail in the non-Indian world. Those who failed were ceremonially accepted by other Indians and appropriately pitied by non-Indians.

I refused to fail. I was smart. I was arrogant. I was lucky. I read books late into the night, until I could barely keep my eyes open. I read books at recess, then during lunch and in the few minutes left after I had finished my classroom assignments. I read books in the car when my family traveled to powwows or basketball games. In shopping malls, I ran to the bookstores and read bits and pieces of as many books as I could. I read the books my father brought home from the pawnshops and secondhand. I read the books I borrowed from the library. I read the backs of cereal boxes. I read the newspaper. I read the bulletins posted on the walls of the school, the clinic, the tribal offices, the post office. I read junk mail. I read auto-repair manuals. I read magazines. I read anything that had words and paragraphs. I read with equal parts joy and desperation. I loved those books, but I also knew that love had only one purpose. I was trying to save my life.

Despite all the books I read, I am still surprised I became a writer. I was going to be a pediatrician. These days, I write novels, short stories, and poems. I visit schools and teach creative writing to Indian kids. In all my years in the reservation school system, I was never taught how to write poetry, short stories or novels. I was certainly never taught that Indians wrote poetry, short stories and novels. Writing was something beyond Indians. I cannot recall a single time that a guest teacher visited the reservation. There must have been visiting teachers. Who were they? Where are they now? Do they exist? I visit the schools as often as possible. The Indian kids crowd the classroom. Many are writing their own poems, short stories and novels. They have read my books. They have read many other books. They look at me with bright eyes and arrogant wonder. They are trying to save their lives. Then there are the sullen and already defeated Indian kids who sit in the back rows and ignore me with theatrical precision. The pages of their notebooks are empty. They carry neither pencil nor pen. They stare out the window. They refuse and resist. "Books," I say to them. "Books," I say. I throw my weight against their locked doors. The door holds. I am smart. I am arrogant. I am lucky. I am trying to save our lives.

Exploring the Text

1. What figure of speech is the following: "We lived on a combination of irregular paychecks, hope, fear and government surplus food"? What is its effect?
2. In what ways does the description of Sherman Alexie's father play against the stereotype?
3. What is the effect of Alexie's analogy of a paragraph to a fence (para. 3)?
4. What does Alexie mean when he describes "an Indian boy" who "grows into a man who often speaks of his childhood in the third-person" (para. 5)?
5. In paragraph 7, Alexie deliberately uses a number of short, simple sentences. What effect is he trying to achieve?
6. This eight-paragraph essay is divided into two distinct sections. Why? How would you describe the arrangement of material? How does it suit Alexie's overall purpose?

7. Discuss Alexie's use of parallel structure and repetition in the last two paragraphs. Pay particular attention to the final sentence in each.
8. Who is the audience for this essay? Cite specific passages to support your response.

Best in Class

MARGARET TALBOT

A senior fellow at the New America Foundation, a nonpartisan think tank, Margaret Talbot (b. 1961) writes about the cultural politics of the United States in the twenty-first century. She has been an editor at *Lingua Franca* and the *New Republic*, and she has received a Whiting Writers' Award. Currently she is a contributing writer for the *New Yorker*. In the following selection, which appeared in 2005 in the *New Yorker*, Talbot examines the impact of naming a single valedictorian, multiple valedictorians, or none at all.

Daniel Kennedy remembers when he still thought that valedictorians were a good thing. Kennedy, a wiry fifty-nine-year-old who has a stern buzz cut, was in 1997 the principal of Sarasota High School, in Sarasota, Florida. Toward the end of the school year, it became apparent that several seniors were deadlocked in the race to become valedictorian. At first, Kennedy saw no particular reason to worry. "My innocent thought was[,] What possible problem could those great kids cause?" he recalled last month, during a drive around Sarasota. "And I went blindly on with my day."

The school had a system in place to break ties. "If the G.P.A.s were the same, the award was supposed to go to the kid with the most credits," Kennedy explained. It turned out that one of the top students, Denny Davies, had learned of this rule, and had quietly arranged to take extra courses during his senior year, including an independent study in algebra. "The independent study was probably a breeze, and he ended up with the most credits," Kennedy said.

Davies was named valedictorian. His chief rivals for the honor were furious — in particular, a girl named Kylie Barker, who told me recently that she had wanted to be valedictorian "pretty much forever."

Kennedy recalled, "Soon, the kids were doing everything they could to battle it out." As we drove past sugary-white beaches, high-rise hotels, and prosperous strip malls, he told me that the ensuing controversy "effectively divided the school and the community." Kennedy took the position that Davies had followed the school's own policy, which he had been resourceful enough to figure out, and whether he should have been allowed to load on an easy extra class was beside the point. He'd done it, and he hadn't broken any rules. Davies's guidance counsellor, Paul Storm, agreed. In an interview with the Sarasota *Herald-Tribune* at the time,

he said of Davies, "He's very clever. He said, 'I want to be valedictorian. I've figured out I need to do this and that. Can you help me?' Denny had a good strategy,
and this strategy was available to anyone who was a competitor."

Barker's supporters argued that what Davies had done was a sneaky way of   5
gaming the system. "It never crossed my mind to approach it as a *strategy*," Barker,
who is . . . pursuing a Ph.D. in chemistry at Northwestern University, said. "I just
thought it was something you worked really hard for." Kimberly Belcher, who was
ranked third that year, and who is now studying for a doctorate in theology at
Notre Dame University, told me, "Among our friends, who were sort of the Academic Olympics and National Honor Society types, it was a big deal. Most of the
people I knew thought that it was unfair of Denny to use what we thought of as a
loophole to take a class that was too easy for him, and to do it secretly. We felt
betrayed. I'm not angry anymore, but, boy, I was angry then." Davies, who is now
a captain in the Air Force, and is stationed in Germany, said that he didn't care to
comment about the dispute, except to say that he was a "firm believer in the idea
that people benefit from healthy competition."

During the final weeks of the school year, Kennedy was meeting with both
sets of riled parents, and students were buttonholing him in the hallway. "I'm
telling you, it was hostile!" he said. Some teachers considered boycotting graduation; students talked about booing Davies when he walked out onstage. Kylie
Barker's mom, Cheryl, said that she recalls getting a call in the middle of the day
from Kylie's chemistry teacher, Jim Harshman, who asked her to pick up Kylie
from school, saying, "She's in a pressure cooker here, and she's about to burst."

Kennedy tried to broker a compromise. Davies had suggested that he and
Barker be named co-valedictorians, and Kennedy embraced the idea. But the
Barkers weren't excited about it. "The principal was trying to make everybody
happy, and when you do that there's always somebody who isn't," Cheryl Barker
said. "I guess it was me."

Kennedy remembers finally "convincing everybody to agree reluctantly —
and I do mean *extremely* reluctantly — to have co-valedictorians." He went on, "I
have been in education basically my whole life, and I've been to a lot of graduations in my time. But I dreaded this one. Sarasota High is a big school — three
thousand kids — and there were probably seven thousand people in the audience. At that time, it felt like half of the students in the room hated one of those
two valedictorians and half hated the other. The tension was so thick that I was
sitting up there in my cap and gown sweating buckets the whole time." In the
end, both students got through their speeches — Kylie's was about integrity —
without incident. But Kennedy, a likeable traditionalist who has been married to
his childhood sweetheart for thirty-seven years, concluded that it was time to get
rid of valedictorians at Sarasota High.

Kennedy convened a committee to consider various alternatives, and it was
decided that from then on all students in the top ten per cent of the class —
which at Sarasota means about seventy-five people — would march in first dur-

ing graduation and have an asterisk printed next to their names on the program. "Students and parents got to see more kids recognized," Kennedy said. "It made everybody feel better."

Sarasota is a competitive school district — while visiting the area, I saw a car with a bumper sticker that read, "My Child Was Student of the Month at Tuttle Elementary" — but most of the local high schools have followed Kennedy's lead. Riverview High School has also eliminated valedictorians and salutatorians; Booker High School ended the tradition last year. Four years ago, North Port High opened near Sarasota. George Kennedy, its principal, recalled thinking that it "would be easier to just start out without valedictorians, so we wouldn't be taking something away later on." He added, "There's an awful lot of clawing and scratching to get to the top. You have families at some schools coming in freshman year saying, 'How can my kid get to No. 1?' And the pressure that puts on teachers is inexcusable. 'Valedictorian' is an antiquated title, and I think it has more negative connotations and effects than positive ones."

When Kennedy left Sarasota High to form a charter school, the Sarasota Military Academy, in 2001, he did not even consider having a valedictorian. Kennedy has an amiable way about him, but he's not kidding when he says, "My advice to other principals is, Whatever you do, do *not* name a valedictorian. Any principal who does is facing peril."

At one time, it was obvious who the best students in a school were. But now the contenders for the valedictorian title, especially at large, top-performing suburban high schools, are numerous and determined. Many schools offer Advanced Placement courses — and sometimes honors and International Baccalaureate classes — extra weight when a student's G.P.A. is calculated, so that an A earns 5.0 points, versus 4.0 in a regular class. Students who fill their schedules with A.P. classes, as the ambitious ones tend to do, can end up with G.P.A.s well above 4.0.

Jim Conrey is the director of public information at Adlai Stevenson High School, in Lincolnshire, Illinois — a public school with forty-five hundred students that is well funded enough to have such a thing as a director of public information. Students at the top of their class, Conrey said, are often separated by one thousandth of a decimal point. A few years ago, a school committee issued a report saying that "parents routinely phone the principal's office to express their concern over the competitive nature of our numerical ranking practice. Minuscule differences between the ranks of two students can often be perceived as major differences. Is a student ranked No. 1 in a given class really the 'best' student in that class?" As of this year, Stevenson High will no longer have a valedictorian and a salutatorian. Instead, students can apply to speak at graduation, and a faculty panel will select two winners. "If you go to a really good school, you could be ranked a hundred and thirty-fourth in your class and still be a really good student," Conrey said.

Between 1990 and 2000, the over-all mean G.P.A. of high-school students increased from 2.68 to 2.94, which is attributable in part to grade inflation and in part to the fact that students are working harder. Last year, more than a million students took at least one A.P. course. During the nineteen-nineties, the percentage of students taking A.P. or International Baccalaureate classes in math more than doubled, from 4.4 per cent of graduating seniors to 9.5 per cent. My own high school, North Hollywood High, in Los Angeles, had three or four A.P. classes when I graduated, in 1979 (a time when we were told that our most illustrious alumnus was Bert Convy, the game-show host; Susan Sontag had gone there, too, but nobody mentioned her). Now it has twenty-two.

Some schools, responding to the critique that competition has got too bruis-   15
ing, have decided that naming a single valedictorian is part of the reason that today's students have become so anxious. (Many small private schools came to this conclusion long ago, and never adopted the valedictorian tradition.) An organization called Stressed Out Students, which is headed by Denise Clark Pope, a Stanford education professor, has a list of about twenty-five schools, mostly in the Bay Area and Silicon Valley, that have pledged to try to make students and their parents less driven. Pope told me that "it would be healthier to eliminate valedictorians or change the rules, so that, for example, anyone who wants to can put their hat in the ring, and then there can be a vote for the best gradua- tion speaker. Then you get a person who really wants to give a speech. It's not an academic contest."

A number of schools now call everyone who gets a 4.0 or higher a valedicto- rian. At Cleveland High School, in the San Fernando Valley, there will be thirty- two valedictorians this year. At Mission San Jose, in Northern California, there will be twenty-three. "We have such an outstanding student body that it was just hard to get that definitive," Stuart Kew, the principal of Mission San Jose, said. "Occasionally, we get the criticism that it's so watered down it doesn't mean any- thing. But the students don't feel that way." On graduation day, each of the school's many valedictorians will speak at a ceremony, where, one hopes, the chairs will be comfortable.

The single-valedictorian tradition is also being endangered by lawsuits. In 2003, Brian Delekta, who narrowly missed having the highest G.P.A. in his class, sued his school district, near Port Huron, Michigan, asking that he be credited with an A-plus, instead of an A, for a work-study class that he took at his mother's law firm. (In addition, Delekta asked for a restraining order on the publication of class rankings.) In another case that year, Blair Hornstine, a senior at Moores- town High School, in New Jersey, and the daughter of a New Jersey superior- court judge, sued the local board of education to be named the school's sole valedictorian; she also asked for two hundred thousand dollars in compensatory damages and more than two million dollars in punitive damages. Hornstine had an unspecified illness that caused "substantial fatigue," and, with the consent of the school district, she had taken many of her classes at home, with private tutors.

Her transcript showed twenty-three A-pluses, nine A's, and a single A-minus; two-thirds of her classes were A.P. courses. Her weighted G.P.A. was 4.6894, which reportedly put her .055 points ahead of her closest competitor, Kenneth Mirkin.

The school board, however, decided that Hornstine's home instruction had given her an unfair advantage and that she should share the valedictorian title with Mirkin. Judge Freda Wolfson sided with Hornstine. The defendants, she wrote, "should revel in the success," of their accommodation to a student's disability "and the academic star it has produced," instead of seeking "to diminish the honor that she has rightly earned." In her ruling, Judge Wolfson nevertheless made a larger point about the insidious effects of naming a top student. "The fierceness of the competition in Moorestown High School is evidenced by the widespread involvement of parents in this dispute, which may have been fueled by the school's emphasis on grade-based distinctions," she wrote. "While the school's Handbook states that it seeks to minimize competition by no longer reporting class rank . . . elsewhere it heightens the levels of competition by naming a valedictorian." The case inspired a mocking Web site, the Blair Hornstine Project, and a flood of vitriolic Internet commentary; Hornstine was so excoriated by critics in her home town that she did not even attend graduation. The Moorestown Board of Education acknowledged no wrongdoing but eventually agreed to an out-of-court settlement, under which Hornstine was reportedly paid sixty thousand dollars. (Harvard, which had admitted her to the Class of 2007, rescinded the offer not long after a local paper for which Hornstine had written a column revealed that she had plagiarized material.)

I recently spoke to some students who had been involved in legal actions over the naming of a valedictorian, and they seemed to share a common attitude toward the experience. On the one hand, they shrugged off the importance of the honor — they had gone on to colleges where valedictorians were so plentiful that to have claimed bragging rights would have been seriously uncool. On the other hand, they could easily recall their high-school state of mind, and feel indignant all over again, utterly convinced that they had done the right thing. In 2003, Sarah Bird, a senior at Plano West Senior High School, in Plano, Texas, requested a hearing before the local school board. Another student, Jennifer Wu, had been named sole valedictorian, although her G.P.A. was virtually identical to Bird's. Bird had played on the school's basketball team. The sport was treated like a physical-education course by the school, and for several semesters she had been given unweighted A's. This had put her at a disadvantage, Bird felt. The hearing, at which Bird's lawyer asked that the two students be named co-valedictorians, involved some very close parsing. Brent William Bailey, Bird's lawyer, told me, "Going in, the other girl had a G.P.A. of 4.46885 and Sarah had 4.46731 — so that was a difference of .00154. Then the calculations were redone and Sarah came out with a G.P.A. of 4.47647." The school board granted Bird's request. "I was prepared to go ahead with a lawsuit if it hadn't gone our way," Bailey recalled. Wu, who expressed unhappiness over the decision to the *Dallas Morning News*, then requested a hearing of her own, to question the way the process was handled. Wu is now a sophomore at Harvard, where she is a premed student. We spoke just before finals, and she clearly had other things on her mind. "Nobody in college cares about your having been valedictorian," she said. "My roommate had no idea I was valedictorian. It doesn't come up, and I don't think about it." Still, when I asked Wu why she had complained to the school board, she said, "I wanted to make sure the school knew how traumatic something like this can be — thinking you're competing under one set of rules, and having an expectation because of that, and then finding out you're competing under another."

Stephanie Klotz's academic ambitions made her stand out at Valley View High, in   20
Germantown, Ohio, from which she graduated in 2001. "We weren't from here originally," Klotz told me. "My dad had been in the military, and we'd lived in Pennsylvania, Idaho, Texas, and upstate New York. I knew there was a big world out there, and I was going to go out and conquer it. I wasn't going to get married right out of high school and be a housewife with twenty kids." Klotz paused, but not for long. "I mean, Germantown is a place with only three stoplights. I come from a very educated family, and expectations are set at a higher level than they are in a small farming town." Then, too, Klotz said, she was always kind of a "nerd — a science nerd, a nature nerd." She continued, "My dad went deer hunting when I was three years old, and they were cutting up the deer next door, because my mom wouldn't let it in the house, and I was, like, 'Daddy, can I play with the head?'" As a young girl, she loved accompanying her father, an anesthetist, to the hospital, where she was allowed to observe surgeries. At Valley View, where football is very popular — T-shirts bear the slogan "Valley View Football Is Life. Nothing Else Matters" — Klotz was often unhappy. She doesn't like football, and was captain of the dance team, which, she said, "got me made fun of — that and being smart. I'd say, 'I want to see *you* do a kick line for an hour!'" She also worked with the town's rescue squad ("I was so service-oriented; I did hundreds and hundreds of hours of service work"), loved science, and hated English and history. She was often "bored to tears" in classes that she found insufficiently challenging, but she got straight A's anyway, as well as tens of thousands of dollars in college-scholarship money.

Several weeks before the school year ended, the principal of Valley View told Klotz that she and four other students would share the valedictorian title. Klotz thought the decision was odd — as she recalled, one of the girls had got a B — but she let it go. "Notices were sent out, relatives notified," her father, Randy Klotz, said. Three of the students had G.P.A.s above 4.0 because they'd taken at least one A.P. course, whereas Stephanie, whose G.P.A. was 4.0, had not. (Instead of taking A.P. history in her junior year, Stephanie, who hoped to become a doctor, had decided to take another chemistry course.) Three weeks before graduation, Stephanie was told that the school was reversing its decision: she and Megan

Keener, another girl with a 4.0 G.P.A. wouldn't be valedictorians after all. (Keener, too, lacked A.P. credits, though she had been taking classes at local colleges.) Two students with G.P.A.s above 4.0 would be named co-valedictorians, and a third would be salutatorian. "I would be nothing," Klotz recalled.

When Klotz told her parents, they complained first to the principal, then several times to the school board. Finally, the family hired a lawyer and sued the school district, the superintendent, and the principal of Valley View. A judge in the Common Plea Court of Montgomery County, Ohio, sided with the Klotzes, and, days before graduation, issued an order reinstating Klotz and Keener as valedictorians.

"At first, I was, like, I'm seventeen, I can't be dealing with this before I graduate from high school," Klotz told me. "I'm not strong enough. And then I thought, I need to fight for the people who are coming after me, who really aren't strong enough to fight." Graduation day, she recalled, "was kind of a comedy event, really. I was sitting there, bored, twirling my tassels." Klotz said that she wasn't allowed to speak, because the decision to reinstate her title was made just before graduation day. One of the valedictorians who did speak, she recalled, "read that Dr. Seuss book 'Oh, the Places You'll Go!' to the audience. I mean, she read practically the entire book." Klotz remembers being given "so many academic awards and plaques, it was ridiculous. Every time I sat down, I had to get up again to get an award. I had so many plaques I literally couldn't carry them off the stage, and I'm, like, 'Oh, yeah, right, I'm not valedictorian?'"

Klotz graduated magna cum laude from the University of Dayton in May, and will start medical school at the University of Cincinnati in August. At college, Klotz realized that she was "a little fish in a big sea with a lot of valedictorians." But she's glad that she sued: she learned that she could be a fighter when she needed to be, and she showed Germantown that she couldn't be "walked all over." Klotz, who is engaged to be married to a social worker, is working as a waitress until school starts. To her fiancé's chagrin, she's been watching a lot of "trauma-and-E.R. shows" at home. (He lacks her strong stomach.) "There's so much focus on all the terrible things youths in our society do — murdering each other, using drugs — that I think it's good to focus on the positive things, as opposed to people who are dropping out and are failures," she said. "There are all these special programs to keep kids in school, give them a special experience, make them feel special. So much of classroom experience is focussed on these kids who are *lacking*. There's nothing to reward the kids who are self-motivated and are working hard."

The first public high school in the United States, Boston's English Classical School, was founded in 1821. Within a few decades, the practice of designating a valedictorian had become an established tradition in American high schools. There was little public financing of secondary schools and a good deal of hostility to them, at least until the eighteen-eighties. High schools were so widely criticized 25 as palaces of privilege, teaching Latin to the children of the rich, that Horace Mann, the education reformer, tried for a while to come up with a new name for "high school," reasoning that perhaps the phrase implied "superior and exclusive," William J. Reese notes in his 1995 history "The Origins of the American High School." (In fact, many high-school students in the nineteenth century were middle-class girls training to support themselves as teachers.) By 1900, roughly ten per cent of American adolescents were enrolled in high school, and public funding remained relatively small.

The graduation ceremony, and in particular the valedictory, served an important purpose for proponents of publicly funded secondary education. A clever graduate declaiming loftily was something to show off to the local taxpayers, and, besides, graduation ceremonies were popular entertainments in an age that lacked television and radio and honored elocution and oratory. "By the late eighteen-fifties, approximately four thousand spectators attended the graduation exercises at Philadelphia's Central High School — and twice that number was turned away," Reese writes. "Eight to ten thousand citizens arrived for the event in Cleveland in the eighteen-seventies." In smaller towns, five hundred or more people might show up to see five or six graduates.

The valedictorian prize also celebrated people who weren't often publicly recognized: studious girls. In the nineteenth century, young women largely outperformed young men in American high schools. They generally won more prizes, graduated at higher rates, and displayed lovelier penmanship. At graduation, girls would read while sitting or standing on a low step, since it wasn't considered proper for them to speak from a platform. Still, the opportunity to appear before an audience of hundreds or thousands, to be singled out for one's academic achievements, must have been heady at a time when modesty and self-effacement were the constant counsel for young women.

In 1981, two professors, Terry Denny and Karen Arnold, began following the lives of eighty-one high-school valedictorians — forty-six women and thirty-five men from Illinois. (Their sample is, admittedly, narrow.) According to Arnold's 1995 book "Lives of Promise: What Becomes of High School Valedictorians," these students continued to distinguish themselves academically in college; a little less than sixty per cent pursued graduate studies. By their early thirties, most were "working in high-level, prestigious, secure professions" — they were lawyers, accountants, professors, doctors, engineers. Arnold totted up fifteen Ph.D.s, six law degrees, three medical degrees, and twenty-two master's degrees in her group. The valedictorians got divorced at a lower rate than did the population at large, were less likely to use alcohol and drugs, and tended to be active in their communities. At the same time, Arnold, who stays in touch with her cohort, has found that few of the valedictorians seem destined for intellectual eminence or for creative work outside of familiar career paths. Dedicated to the well-rounded ideal — to be a valedictorian, after all, you must excel in classes that don't interest you or are poorly taught — the valedictorians had "used their strong work ethic to pursue multiple academic and extracurricular interests. None was obsessed with a single talent area to which he or she subordinated school and social involvement." This marks a difference, Arnold said, from what we know about many eminent achievers, who tend to evince an early passion for a particular field. For these people, Arnold writes, a "powerful early interest evolves into life-long, intensive, even obsessive involvement in the talent area." She goes on, "Exceptional adult achievers often recall formal schooling as a disliked distraction." Valedictorians, by contrast, conformed to the expectations of school and carefully chose careers that were likely to be socially and financially secure: "As a rule, valedictorians relegated their early interests to hobbies, second majors, or regretted dead ends. The serious athletes among the valedictorians never pursued sports occupations. Most of the high school musicians hung up their instruments during college."

Becoming a valedictorian at a top high school is a gruelling trajectory — involving perhaps a dozen A.P. classes and hours of study each night. Sometimes students cave in to the pressure. In 2002, Audrey Lin, one of Mission San Jose's many valedictorians, admitted that she had cheated to get to the top in high school, and gave back her valedictorian plaque. Lin, who is now a student at Berkeley, made her confession in conjunction with the release of a study by the Josephson Institute of Ethics, in which three-quarters of the high-school students surveyed acknowledged having cheated on a test the previous year; ten years earlier, the number had been sixty-one per cent.

In some ways, it seems that the valedictorian is a status designed for a simpler 30 time, when few people aspired to college. It isn't entirely suited to a brutally competitive age in which the dividing line between those who go to college and those who don't may be the most significant fissure in American society, and in which the children (and parents) of the upper middle classes have been convinced that going to an exceedingly selective college is the only way to insure wealth and happiness.

Still, perhaps something is lost if schools eliminate valedictorians. Like spelling bees, the contest for valedictorian offers a pleasing image of a purer meritocracy, in which learning and performing by the rules leave one hard-working person standing. It seems sad to abolish the tradition — and faintly ridiculous to honor too large a group. (If we're trying to be more sensitive, doesn't it make ordinary students feel *worse* when they can't be one of several dozen valedictorians?) Maybe the answer is to stick to one valedictorian but to make the rules of the contest clear, and to be sure everyone knows them. Maybe the honor should go to the student who is not necessarily the smartest but the most adept at running a peculiarly American kind of academic marathon, one that requires prodigious energy, tactical savvy, and a Tracy Flick–like determination. (Remember the Reese Witherspoon character from "Election"?)

"Over the past ten years, a lot of school districts have been abolishing the valedictorian, and I'm against that," Karen Arnold told me. "On the day we allow anybody who's always wanted to be a quarterback to play on the high-school football team, *then* we can get rid of valedictorians. If we rank anything, we ought to rank what we say is most central to school, which is to say, academic learning."

A few weeks ago, I met Cheryl Barker, the mother of Kylie, the girl at Sarasota High School who, as it turned out, was one of the last two valedictorians at the school. Her daughter went to Furman University, in South Carolina, then to Northwestern. Cheryl Barker was a waitress when Kylie was in high school, and she is now the manager of a family-style restaurant in Sarasota. Her husband owns a print shop, and they have two younger children, a daughter who is graduating from Florida State this year and plans to go to law school, and a son who just graduated in the top ten per cent from Sarasota High.

Cheryl Barker still marvels at how hard Kylie worked, how determined she was, how she never missed a day of school, how she'd go to the library all the time to use the computer because they didn't have one at home. Barker thinks that it was a mistake for the high school to stop naming a valedictorian and a salutatorian. "Those kids all know who the No. 1 and 2 are, anyway," she told me over coffee. "Everyone's so afraid of getting sued or losing their jobs these days that they try too hard to candy-coat things." But, she added, "there are some kids who what they're good at is studying. That's what they do. They deserve something special to strive for. They do."

Exploring the Text

1. Margaret Talbot spends a good deal of time at the outset of the essay describing the situation at Sarasota High School, yet her primary subject is neither that school nor its students. What is her rhetorical strategy in examining this one school in such depth?
2. In paragraph 14, Talbot refers to her own experience in high school. What is the effect of this personal element?
3. In this essay, Talbot surveys a range of perspectives on the issue of valedictorians. Identify at least four of them.
4. Why does Talbot rely so heavily on interviews with students? Why would this approach appeal to her audience?
5. Beginning with paragraph 25, Talbot presents some historical background on the American high school. How would the effect of this information have changed if she had opened the article with it?
6. Is the analogy Karen Arnold draws in paragraph 32 valid? She says, "On the day we allow anybody who's always wanted to be a quarterback to play on the high-school football team, *then* we can get rid of valedictorians."
7. Does this essay rely more heavily on logos or pathos?
8. Where do Talbot's sympathies lie? Does she believe that naming a single valedictorian is right or wrong? How would you describe her tone?

A Talk to Teachers

JAMES BALDWIN

James Baldwin (1924–1987) was one of the most influential figures in American literature during the latter half of the twentieth century. His novels include *Go Tell It on the Mountain* (1953), *Giovanni's Room* (1956), *If Beale Street Could Talk* (1974), and *Just Above My Head* (1979). A sharp social critic of race relations and sexual identity, Baldwin wrote numerous essays that were collected in *Notes of a Native Son* (1955), *The Fire Next Time* (1963), and *The Devil Finds Work* (1976). He also wrote poetry and plays. By the late 1940s, Baldwin had moved to Europe, where he lived in France and Turkey for most of the rest of his life. He returned at times to the United States to lecture and participate in the civil rights movement. Some maintain that Baldwin considered himself a "commuter" rather than an expatriate. He delivered the following speech to a group of New York City schoolteachers in 1963, the height of the movement for equality for African Americans.

Let's begin by saying that we are living through a very dangerous time. Everyone in this room is in one way or another aware of that. We are in a revolutionary situation, no matter how unpopular that word has become in this country. The society in which we live is desperately menaced, not by [Nikita] Khrushchev,[1] but from within. So any citizen of this country who figures himself as responsible — and particularly those of you who deal with the minds and hearts of young people — must be prepared to "go for broke." Or to put it another way, you must understand that in the attempt to correct so many generations of bad faith and cruelty, when it is operating not only in the classroom but in society, you will meet the most fantastic, the most brutal, and the most determined resistance. There is no point in pretending that this won't happen.

Since I am talking to schoolteachers and I am not a teacher myself, and in some ways am fairly easily intimidated, I beg you to let me leave that and go back to what I think to be the entire purpose of education in the first place. It would seem to me that when a child is born, if I'm the child's parent, it is my obligation and my high duty to civilize that child. Man is a social animal. He cannot exist without a society. A society, in turn, depends on certain things which everyone within that society takes for granted. Now, the crucial paradox which confronts us here is that the whole process of education occurs within a social framework and is designed to perpetuate the aims of society. Thus, for example, the boys and girls who were born during the era of the Third Reich, when educated to the purposes of the Third Reich, became barbarians. The paradox of education is precisely this — that as one begins to become conscious one begins to examine the society in which he is being educated. The purpose of education, finally, is to

---

[1]Premier of the Soviet Union, 1958–64. — Eds.

create in a person the ability to look at the world for himself, to make his own decisions, to say to himself this is black or this is white, to decide for himself whether there is a God in heaven or not. To ask questions of the universe, and then learn to live with those questions, is the way he achieves his own identity. But no society is really anxious to have that kind of person around. What societies really, ideally, want is a citizenry which will simply obey the rules of society. If a society succeeds in this, that society is about to perish. The obligation of anyone who thinks of himself as responsible is to examine society and try to change it and to fight it — at no matter what risk. This is the only hope society has. This is the only way societies change.

Now, if what I have tried to sketch has any validity, it becomes thoroughly clear, at least to me, that any Negro who is born in this country and undergoes the American educational system runs the risk of becoming schizophrenic. On the one hand he is born in the shadow of the stars and stripes and he is assured it represents a nation which has never lost a war. He pledges allegiance to that flag which guarantees "liberty and justice for all." He is part of a country in which anyone can become president, and so forth. But on the other hand he is also assured by his country and his countrymen that he has never contributed anything to civilization — that his past is nothing more than a record of humiliations gladly endured. He is assumed by the republic that he, his father, his mother, and his ancestors were happy, shiftless, watermelon-eating darkies who loved Mr. Charlie and Miss Ann,[2] that the value he has as a black man is proven by one thing only — his devotion to white people. If you think I am exaggerating, examine the myths which proliferate in this country about Negroes.

All this enters the child's consciousness much sooner than we as adults would like to think it does. As adults, we are easily fooled because we are so anxious to be fooled. But children are very different. Children, not yet aware that it is dangerous to look too deeply at anything, look at everything, look at each other, and draw their own conclusions. They don't have the vocabulary to express what they see, and we, their elders, know how to intimidate them very easily and very soon. But a black child, looking at the world around him, though he cannot know quite what to make of it, is aware that there is a reason why his mother works so hard, why his father is always on edge. He is aware that there is some reason why, if he sits down in the front of the bus, his father or mother slaps him and drags him to the back of the bus. He is aware that there is some terrible weight on his parents' shoulders which menaces him. And it isn't long — in fact it begins when he is in school — before he discovers the shape of his oppression.

Let us say that the child is seven years old and I am his father, and I decide to take him to the zoo, or to Madison Square Garden, or to the U.N. Building, or to

5

---

[2]Figurative characters invented by African slaves to represent male and female slave masters, respectively. — Eds.

any of the tremendous monuments we find all over New York. We get into a bus and we go from where I live on 131st Street and Seventh Avenue downtown through the park and we get into New York City, which is not Harlem. Now, where the boy lives — even if it is a housing project — is in an undesirable neighborhood. If he lives in one of those housing projects of which everyone in New York is so proud, he has at the front door, if not closer, the pimps, the whores, the junkies — in a word, the danger of life in the ghetto. And the child knows this, though he doesn't know why.

I still remember my first sight of New York. It was really another city when I was born — where I was born. We looked down over the Park Avenue streetcar tracks. It was Park Avenue, but I didn't know what Park Avenue meant *downtown*. The Park Avenue I grew up on, which is still standing, is dark and dirty. No one would dream of opening a Tiffany's on that Park Avenue, and when you go downtown you discover that you are literally in the white world. It is rich — or at least it looks rich. It is clean — because they collect garbage downtown. There are doormen. People walk about as though they owned where they are — and indeed they do. And it's a great shock. It's very hard to relate yourself to this. You don't know what it means. You know — you know instinctively — that none of this is for you. You know this before you are told. And who is it for and who is paying for it? And why isn't it for you?

Later on when you become a grocery boy or messenger and you try to enter one of those buildings a man says, "Go to the back door." Still later, if you happen by some odd chance to have a friend in one of those buildings, the man says, "Where's your package?" Now this by no means is the core of the matter. What I'm trying to get at is that by this time the Negro child has had, effectively, almost all the doors of opportunity slammed in his face, and there are very few things he can do about it. He can more or less accept it with an absolutely inarticulate and dangerous rage inside — all the more dangerous because it is never expressed. It is precisely those silent people whom white people see every day of their lives — I mean your porter and your maid, who never say anything more than "Yes, Sir" and "No, Ma'am." They will tell you it's raining if that is what you want to hear, and they will tell you the sun is shining if *that* is what you want to hear. They really hate you — really hate you because in their eyes (and they're right) you stand between them and life. I want to come back to that in a moment. It is the most sinister of the facts, I think, which we now face.

There is something else the Negro child can do, too. Every street boy — and I was a street boy, so I know — looking at the society which has produced him, looking at the standards of that society which are not honored by anybody, looking at your churches and the government and the politicians, understands that this structure is operated for someone else's benefit — not for his. And there's no reason in it for him. If he is really cunning, really ruthless, really strong — and many of us are — he becomes a kind of criminal. He becomes a kind of criminal because that's the only way he can live. Harlem and every ghetto in this city — every ghetto in this country — is full of people who live outside the law. They wouldn't dream of calling a policeman. They wouldn't, for a moment, listen to any of those professions of which we are so proud on the Fourth of July. They have turned away from this country forever and totally. They live by their wits and really long to see the day when the entire structure comes down.

The point of all this is that black men were brought here as a source of cheap labor. They were indispensable to the economy. In order to justify the fact that men were treated as though they were animals, the white republic had to brainwash itself into believing that they were, indeed, animals and *deserved* to be treated like animals. Therefore it is almost impossible for any Negro child to discover anything about his actual history. The reason is that this "animal," once he suspects his own worth, once he starts believing that he is a man, has begun to attack the entire power structure. This is why America has spent such a long time keeping the Negro in his place. What I am trying to suggest to you is that it was not an accident, it was not an act of God, it was not done by well-meaning people muddling into something which they didn't understand. It was a deliberate policy hammered into place in order to make money from black flesh. And now, in 1963, because we have never faced this fact, we are in intolerable trouble.

The Reconstruction, as I read the evidence, was a bargain between the North and South to this effect: "We've liberated them from the land — and delivered them to the bosses." When we left Mississippi to come North we did not come to freedom. We came to the bottom of the labor market, and we are still there. Even the Depression of the 1930s failed to make a dent in Negroes' relationship to white workers in the labor unions. Even today, so brainwashed is this republic that people seriously ask in what they suppose to be good faith, "What does the Negro want?" I've heard a great many asinine questions in my life, but that is perhaps the most asinine and perhaps the most insulting. But the point here is that people who ask that question, thinking that they ask it in good faith, are really the victims of this conspiracy to make Negroes believe they are less than human.

In order for me to live, I decided very early that some mistake had been made somewhere. I was not a "nigger" even though you called me one. But if I was a "nigger" in your eyes, there was something about *you* — there was something *you* needed. I had to realize when I was very young that I was none of those things I was told I was. I was not, for example, happy. I never touched a watermelon for all kinds of reasons that had been invented by white people, and I knew enough about life by this time to understand that whatever you invent, whatever you project, is you! So where we are now is that a whole country of people believe I'm a "nigger," and I *don't*, and the battle's on! Because if I am not what I've been told I am, then it means that *you're* not what you thought *you* were *either*! And that is the crisis.

It is not really a "Negro revolution" that is upsetting the country. What is upsetting the country is a sense of its own identity. If, for example, one managed to change the curriculum in all the schools so that Negroes learned more about themselves and their real contributions to this culture, you would be liberating not only Negroes, you'd be liberating white people who know nothing about their own history. And the reason is that if you are compelled to lie about one aspect of anybody's history, you must lie about it all. If you have to lie about my real role here, if you have to pretend that I hoed all that cotton just because I loved you, then you have done something to yourself. You are mad.

Now let's go back a minute. I talked earlier about those silent people — the porter and the maid — who, as I said, don't look up at the sky if you ask them if it is raining, but look into your face. My ancestors and I were very well trained. We understood very early that this was not a Christian nation. It didn't matter what you said or how often you went to church. My father and my mother and my grandfather and my grandmother knew that Christians didn't act this way. It was as simple as that. And if that was so there was no point in dealing with white people in terms of their own moral professions, for they were not going to honor them. What one did was to turn away, smiling all the time, and tell white people what they wanted to hear. But people always accuse you of reckless talk when you say this.

All this means that there are in this country tremendous reservoirs of bitterness which have never been able to find an outlet, but may find an outlet soon. It means that well-meaning white liberals place themselves in great danger when they try to deal with Negroes as though they were missionaries. It means, in brief, that a great price is demanded to liberate all those silent people so that they can breathe for the first time and *tell* you what they think of you. And a price is demanded to liberate all those white children — some of them near forty — who have never grown up, and who never will grow up, because they have no sense of their identity.

What passes for identity in America is a series of myths about one's heroic an- 15
cestors. It's astounding to me, for example, that so many people really appear to believe that the country was founded by a band of heroes who wanted to be free. That happens not to be true. What happened was that some people left Europe because they couldn't stay there any longer and had to go someplace else to make it. That's all. They were hungry, they were poor, they were convicts. Those who were making it in England, for example, did not get on the *Mayflower*. That's how the country was settled. Not by Gary Cooper. Yet we have a whole race of people, a whole republic, who believe the myths to the point where even today they select political representatives, as far as I can tell, by how closely they resemble Gary Cooper. Now this is dangerously infantile, and it shows in every level of national life. When I was living in Europe, for example, one of the worst revelations to me was the way Americans walked around Europe buying this and buying that and insulting everybody — not even out of malice, just because they didn't know any better. Well, that is the way they have always treated me. They

weren't cruel, they just didn't know you were alive. They didn't know you had any feelings.

What I am trying to suggest here is that in the doing of all this for 100 years or more, it is the American white man who has long since lost his grip on reality. In some peculiar way, having created this myth about Negroes, and the myth about his own history, he created myths about the world so that, for example, he was astounded that some people could prefer [Fidel] Castro, astounded that there are people in the world who don't go into hiding when they hear the word "Communism," astounded that Communism is one of the realities of the twentieth century which we will not overcome by pretending that it does not exist. The political level in this country now, on the part of people who should know better, is abysmal.

The Bible says somewhere that where there is no vision the people perish. I don't think anyone can doubt that in this country today we are menaced — intolerably menaced — by a lack of vision.

It is inconceivable that a sovereign people should continue, as we do so abjectly, to say, "I can't do anything about it. It's the government." The government is the creation of the people. It is responsible to the people. And the people are responsible for it. No American has the right to allow the present government to say, when Negro children are being bombed and hosed and shot and beaten all over the Deep South, that there is nothing we can do about it. There must have been a day in this country's life when the bombing of the children in Sunday School would have created a public uproar and endangered the life of a Governor [George] Wallace. It happened here and there was no public uproar.

I began by saying that one of the paradoxes of education was that precisely at the point when you begin to develop a conscience, you must find yourself at war with your society. It is your responsibility to change society if you think of yourself as an educated person. And on the basis of the evidence — the moral and political evidence — one is compelled to say that this is a backward society. Now if I were a teacher in this school, or any Negro school, and I was dealing with Negro children, who were in my care only a few hours of every day and would then return to their homes and to the streets, children who have an apprehension of their future which with every hour grows grimmer and darker, I would try to teach them — I would try to make them know — that those streets, those houses, those dangers, those agonies by which they are surrounded, are criminal. I would try to make each child know that these things are the result of a criminal conspiracy to destroy him. I would teach him that if he intends to get to be a man, he must at once decide that he is stronger than this conspiracy and that he must never make his peace with it. And that one of his weapons for refusing to make his peace with it and for destroying it depends on what he decides he is worth. I would teach him that there are currently very few standards in this country which are worth a man's respect. That it is up to him to begin to change these standards for the sake of the life and the health of the country. I would suggest to him that the popular culture — as represented, for example, on television and in comic books and in movies — is based on fantasies created by very ill people, and he must be aware that these are fantasies that have nothing to do with reality. I would teach him that the press he reads is not as free as it says it is — and that he can do something about that, too. I would try to make him know that just as American history is longer, larger, more various, more beautiful, and more terrible than anything anyone has ever said about it, so is the world larger, more daring, more beautiful and more terrible, but principally larger — and that it belongs to him. I would teach him that he doesn't have to be bound by the expediencies of any given administration, any given policy, any given morality; that he has the right and the necessity to examine everything. I would try to show him that one has not learned anything about Castro when one says, "He is a Communist." This is a way of his learning something about Castro, something about Cuba, something, in time, about the world. I would suggest to him that he is living, at the moment, in an enormous province. America is not the world and if America is going to become a nation, she must find a way — and this child must help her to find a way to use the tremendous potential and tremendous energy which this child represents. If this country does not find a way to use that energy, it will be destroyed by that energy.

Exploring the Text

1. What relationship does James Baldwin establish with his audience in the opening two paragraphs? How does he establish his ethos?
2. What is the "crucial paradox which confronts us here" (para. 2)?
3. Identify four appeals to pathos in paragraphs 3–5.
4. What is the effect of Baldwin's emphasizing his personal experience when he begins paragraph 6 with "I still remember my first sight of New York"?
5. Analyze Baldwin's use of pronouns in paragraphs 8 and 9. What is his purpose in alternating between first, second, and third person?
6. How would you describe Baldwin's perspective on history? What is the effect of using historical events to support his argument?
7. Why, in paragraph 11, does Baldwin use the term *nigger*? What effect would have been lost — or gained — had he used a less provocative term?
8. What does Baldwin mean by "What passes for identity in America is a series of myths about one's heroic ancestors" (para. 15)?
9. What is the effect of the short two-sentence paragraph 17?
10. Identify examples of parallelism and repetition in the final, long paragraph. Discuss how Baldwin uses these strategies to achieve his purpose.
11. Where in this speech does Baldwin appeal to logos?
12. How would you describe Baldwin's overall tone? Cite specific passages to support your position.

School

KYOKO MORI

Kyoko Mori, who was born in Kobe, Japan, in 1957, earned both an MA and a PhD from the University of Wisconsin. She was a Briggs-Copeland lecturer at Harvard University for several years; she joined the creative writing faculty at George Mason University in Virginia in 2005. She is the author of two nonfiction books, several novels, and numerous essays, many of which have appeared in the annual *Best American Essays*. In her memoir, *Polite Lies: On Being a Woman Caught between Cultures* (1999), she reflects on the differences between Japanese and American approaches to education. The following selection is a chapter from that book.

During our senior year at college, some of my classmates said they could hardly wait to graduate, to join "the real world." They couldn't concentrate on classes, knowing that they would soon be out of school forever. I didn't feel the same way at all. School seemed as "real" to me as "the outside world" — only more interesting.

I still don't trust the distinction often made between school and "the real world," which implies that there is something insubstantial or artificial about school. The business meetings I attended in Milwaukee as an interpreter confirmed my suspicion that arcane and "academic" discussions don't happen only at colleges. The directors of two small companies, one Japanese and the other American, once had a twenty-minute debate about whether the plastic cover of a particular camera lens should be "pumpkin yellow" or "the yellow of raincoats." What each man meant by these terms was unclear to the other and had to be redefined many times over. This is the conversation I recall now when I attend academic conferences and cannot understand what is being said about a book I have read more than once.

School and "the real world" both have their absurd moments, but school is where people go when they are not satisfied with their "real world" lives and want a change. Many Americans in their thirties and forties go back to college to get trained for a different line of work or to pursue a lifelong interest they couldn't afford to study earlier. Until they are in need of such second chances, most Americans take colleges for granted because they are always there — almost any adult can get into some college at any age.

Being able to go back to school is a particularly American opportunity. My Japanese friends will never be able to do the same. In Japan, school does not give anyone a second chance. Many of my Japanese friends are married women with money who already have college degrees. But none of them can go back to college to earn a second degree in art, education, or social work, as their American counterparts may do.

Recently, a few Japanese colleges have started accepting applications from ⁵ adults who have been out of school for years, but these colleges are exceptions. The only way most people can get into a college in Japan is to take and pass the entrance examination for that particular college immediately after graduating from high school. The number of exams a student can sit for in a given year is limited since many schools give their exams on the same day.

A student who does not get into any college will have to wait a year, attending a cram school. There is a word for a student in this situation — *ronin* (floating person). In feudal times, the word referred to samurai whose clan had been dissolved. Feudal *ronin* had to roam around until they could find a new master to serve. To be a modern *ronin* is scarcely better: while their friends move on to colleges or jobs, *ronin* must float around for a year without any allegiance. In Japan, anyone who doesn't belong to the right group at the right time feels like a failure. If a *ronin* can't get into a college after a year at a cram school, he or she usually gives up and settles for a low-paying job rather than spending another year floating around.

In the States, young people who don't feel ready for college can work for a few years and then apply when they feel more motivated or mature. Young Japanese people don't have the same chance. For older adults to go back to school to have a second chance — at a job or an artistic career or personal fulfillment — is practically impossible.

The very accessibility of schools in America adds to the perception that they are not real or substantial enough. Many Americans who criticize their own school system for being "too easy" idealize the Japanese school system because they are drawn to its rough image. The details Americans cite as the merits of the Japanese system actually reflect their ideal of the mythical "real world" where people must work hard — long hours, the emphasis on discipline and basic skills, the tough competition among peers. These people admire the Japanese school system because they see it as a samurai version of their own fantasies about the American work ethic.

My education at a traditional Japanese grade school was nothing so glorious. Day-to-day life at a Japanese public school was harsh but also boring. Until I transferred to a private school in seventh grade, I didn't learn anything that I couldn't have learned at home by reading and memorizing the same books with my mother's help.

Recently when I was in Japan, I was asked why I did not write my novels in ¹⁰ Japanese, why I did not at least translate my own work. The question surprised me at first. The people who asked knew that for twelve years I have lived in a small Wisconsin town where I have few opportunities to speak Japanese. No one can write novels in a language she has not spoken every day for more than a decade. But there is another reason I could not possibly have written my novels or poems in Japanese: I was never taught to write in what was my native language.

My public education in Japan prepared me to make the correct letters to spell out the correct sounds, but that is not the same as teaching me how to write.

When I started the first grade at six, I had not been taught to read at home — at least not in a formal way. Because my mother read to me all the time, I had memorized my favorite books and could read along with her. Sometimes, when my mother and I were standing on the street corner waiting for a taxi, I noticed that I could read the license plates of the cars passing by. I would read the plates and she would nod and smile because I was right, but no big fuss was made about my being able to read. Most of the other kids starting school with me were the same way: we sort of knew how to read because of our mothers, but we hadn't been formally trained.

In first grade, we were taught the fifty phonetic signs that make up the Japanese alphabet, a dozen simple pictorial characters, and the basic numbers. By the end of the year, everyone in our class could read our textbooks and write simple messages to our family and friends in our sprawling, uneven handwriting. People who admire the Japanese education system are partially right. Japanese schools *are* very good at teaching skills like basic writing — which can only be learned through memorization and repeated practice.

Once we learned the alphabet and some pictorial characters, my classmates and I wrote compositions about our families, our vacations, our friends. Occasionally, our teachers had us write stories and poems as well. In summer, we were given notebooks in which we had to keep "picture diaries": on the upper, blank, half we drew pictures, and on the lower, lined, half we wrote sentences about what we did every day. These assignments gave us a lot of practice at writing.

When we got to the upper grades, though, our assignments changed. We no longer wrote stories or poems; our compositions weren't about our personal experiences or feelings. Almost every writing assignment was a book report or a summary of our reading. We had to follow a very strict formula, organizing our thoughts under predetermined headings like "plot," "characters," "setting," "themes," "what we learned from the book." If we didn't follow the format, we got poor grades.

The grades didn't always make sense. Luckily, I did well most of the time, but I wasn't sure what I did right aside from adhering to the format. The only suggestions I got were circled corrections where I had used the wrong pictorial characters or general remarks about my bad penmanship.

A few of my friends didn't do so well, but they were never given suggestions for improvement. They would simply get low grades and comments like "Your writing needs improvement," "You didn't really follow the directions for the assignment," or "I can see you tried some but you still have a long way to go." Often, our teachers openly scolded pupils. In front of the whole class, my friends were told to "pay better attention" and to "try harder." It didn't matter that most of them were serious and well-behaved students, not lazy and inattentive troublemakers; they were already trying hard, trying to pay attention.

15

No matter what the subject, our teachers never gave us very clear advice about how to do better. When I couldn't understand long division or fractions and decimals in math, I felt bad at first. On the timed tests we had every day, I could finish only half the problems before the teacher's stopwatch beeped, telling us to put down our pencils. The results were put up on the wall, and my name was always near the bottom. I was told to "try harder," but none of my teachers spent extra time with me to go over what I was doing wrong. Since I wasn't given a real chance to improve, I decided after a while that I didn't really care how I did.

Over and over again, our Japanese education offered this sort of harsh judgment combined with vague exhortation. In every subject, kids who didn't do well were made to feel ashamed and yet given no chance to improve. The humiliation was especially obvious in physical education classes. At our grade school we were expected to learn to swim in the same way we were expected to learn to write: by sheer repetition and "trying harder." We were left to swim around on our own, but the pool hours weren't just for fun. Each of us had to wear a cloth swim-cap with the symbol that indicated our skill level. Students who couldn't swim at all were singled out by the big red circle sewn on top of their caps. "Red mark, red mark, you'll sink like a big hammer," some of the other kids taunted, and the teachers did nothing to stop them. I was glad that I already knew how to swim by the time I started school.

For those of us who could swim, there were monthly tests to determine how far we could go without stopping. For every five or ten meters we could swim, our mothers sewed red or black lines on the side of our caps. Those who could swim fifty meters in the crawl, sidestroke, or breaststroke got the best marks on their caps: five all-black lines. In fifth grade, when I passed the test for fifty meters, my teachers praised me for having "tried so hard," even though I was able to do so well only because my mother had taught me to swim in the river near her parents' home. Unlike my teachers, my mother enjoyed giving specific instructions. She drew diagrams on paper to show me what my arms and legs should be doing for crawl and sidestroke. Then she made me lie down on the sand on the river bank to practice the arm and leg movements. Once I was in the water, she stood on the bank shouting out instructions like "Stretch your arms all the way," "Turn your head sideways." When my form was wrong, she showed me by imitating me — exaggerating my awkward movements and making me laugh. "I don't look like *that*," I protested, but I knew exactly what I needed to improve.

I did not learn how to write in Japanese because even at the private school I attended after seventh grade, Japanese language classes were taught by older men who had studied classical Japanese literature or Chinese poetry at the national universities before the war. They were the most conservative and traditional of all our teachers. In their classes, we read the works of famous authors and wrote essays to answer questions like: "What is the theme?" "When does the main character realize the importance of morality?" "What important Buddhist philosophy is expressed in this passage?" All the writing we did for our extracurricular   20 activities — for skits or school newspapers and magazines — was supervised by younger teachers who did not teach Japanese.

During those same years, we learned how to write in English. Our English teachers were young Japanese women who had studied in the States or England, and American women from small Midwestern towns who had just graduated from college. In their classes, we wrote essays about our families, friends, hobbies, future dreams — personal subjects we had not written about at school since third grade. We were given plenty of instruction about the specifics of writing: word choice, description, style. Our essays came back with comments both about our writing and about the thoughts we had expressed. I looked forward to writing essays and reading my teachers' comments. By the time I was a high school senior, I wanted to be a writer, and English was the only language I could write in.

To study writing, I had to go to an American college. Creative writing was not — and still is not — offered at Japanese colleges, in English or in Japanese. I don't know how Japanese writers learn to write, since most of them, as children, must have had the same kind of education I had. There are no schools or writers' conferences where a person can study creative writing as an adult. I have never heard of people getting together to form a writing group or workshop.

Writing is not something that comes naturally to the chosen few. Most American writers of my generation didn't just learn to write on their own. Without the classes we took in creative writing and modern literature, we wouldn't have known what to read, how to read it, how to pay attention to form and content. We needed to be shown how to write good dialogue, smooth transitions, pared-down but vivid character descriptions. These things didn't come naturally. It would have taken us thirty years to learn, on our own, the same skills we learned in eight years of college and graduate school. My friends at graduate school came from average Midwestern homes; they were not children of famous writers. School gave us a chance we would never have had otherwise. In America, we are proof that the romantic notion of the natural writer is a myth. In Japan, where no formal training is offered in writing, the myth may be a sad reality that prevents many people from becoming writers.

My stepmother used the traditional method of harsh judgment even though she was not a teacher. When Michiko came to live with my family, I was twelve and already knew how to cook and bake simple foods like omelettes and chocolate chip cookies and how to clean up the kitchen. But my attempts to help Michiko always ended in disaster. She complained endlessly about how I had not been taught to do things the "proper way." Everything I did, from drying the dishes to sweeping the floor, was wrong. "I can't believe that you don't know how to do this," she would scold in her shrill voice, and yet she never showed me exactly what the "proper way" was. When I asked, "What do you mean? What am I doing wrong?" she would scream, "If I have to tell you, then it's no good. I can't show you something you should already know." I was supposed to watch her silently and learn on my own through observation, but she made me too nervous to concentrate. I had no idea what I was supposed to be looking for. If I gave up and asked, "Do you mean the way I am holding the broom or are you saying that I should start over there instead of here?" she would stomp out of the kitchen without a word.

I know that Michiko's silent and judgmental manner was a manifestation of her meanspiritedness, but she didn't invent the method. The tradition of not giving specific instruction comes from Zen. In traditional Zen philosophy, satori or enlightenment is considered to be beyond human description. Since no one can describe satori or ways to attain it, the teacher-monk asks his disciples a series of koans — questions meant to puzzle and disturb rather than to provide answers. The whole purpose of the koan is to break down the disciples' reliance on their own intellect by humiliating them. At its worst, the teaching technique amounts to intellectual or spiritual hazing. The disciples are supposed to hit bottom and suffer terrible despair before they can open their eyes to satori and experience beauty and peace that is beyond logic or description.

To my American friends who took up Zen in college, this style of teaching seemed liberating because of its apparent emphasis on a larger and unexplainable truth instead of minute and trivial details. After years of American education, my friends were tired of specific instruction. All the rules they had to learn about writing good paragraphs or improving their tennis swings struck them as fussy and superficial. Zen taught them that everything they had learned in their Western education was an illusion that needed to be shattered. The very destructiveness and uncertainty of enlightenment sounded uplifting.

But in the Zen-style teaching actually practiced in Japan, students are not liberated from minute details. The details are everything. A beginning calligraphy student writes the same letters over and over, trying to make her brush strokes look exactly like her master's. If she puts one dot five millimeters too far to the right, her work is considered flawed. The master does not point out her mistake. "No, not right yet," he grunts. "Do it over." Until the student can see for herself that her dot is in the wrong place, she will have to keep copying the same letters — she has not reached "enlightenment."

In America, students are often drilled on the details of grammar or form and yet are forgiven for the minor mistakes they make in their writing. Their teacher might say, "You have a couple of awkward sentences and punctuation mistakes here, but your paper is excellent overall. Your ideas are good and you write with a wonderful voice." Hearing comments like these, my friends concluded that their teachers were being inconsistent. If the minor details weren't important in the end, why did the teachers spend so much time on them?

The paradox about the two styles of teaching is that neither emphasizes what it considers to be truly important. In calligraphy and other traditional arts derived from Zen, following the correct form is everything — there is no possibility that you can make a few minor mistakes and still "get" the spirit or the essence of the "truth" — and yet instruction consists of vague exhortation about "following the right balance" and "working hard." In America, where teachers actually value the overall spirit of the work, they spend most of their time talking about details.

This paradox reflects a common ground all teachers share. No matter what and how we teach, we believe that what we value the most is beyond our meager ability to describe. We are struck dumb with admiration at the things we value, so we try to teach the secondary things that we think are easier to talk about. Like most American writing teachers, I value the overall spirit or genuine voice in my students' work and yet nag them about the smaller details of technique like trimming their lines or writing better dialogue. Mine is a Western approach — the same method of instruction is apparent even in the Bible, which gives God a name that cannot be spoken, while offering book after book detailing the laws about how to build a temple or what foods should not be eaten together.

My Japanese teachers, who thought that detail was everything, must have felt that precision was so important that it could not be described: only the truly enlightened can be in perfect harmony with the correct form. In the meantime, they must have reasoned, they could at least talk about the value of hard work, something everyone can easily understand. The contradiction we share points to the difficulty of teaching anything: trying to pass on knowledge that seems so clear to ourselves to people who don't have that knowledge. When my stepmother complained, "How can I teach you something you should already know?" she was expressing in its meanest form the universal frustration of teachers.

In spite of our shared frustration, though, I have a hard time forgiving some of my former teachers in Japan because they never seemed humbled by the near impossibility of their task. Many of my teachers felt entitled to be both strict and arbitrary — strict about their own authority and the rules of the system and yet so arbitrary and lax about helping us.

In Japan, whether you are in school or at your private karate, judo, or *ikebana*[1] lesson, you can never question the authority of the teacher, whom you address simply as "sensei," literally, "one whose life comes first." Unless there are multiple teachers who need to be distinguished from one another, you do not even use their family names, much less first names (which you most likely do not know). The teacher is like the biblical God, whom you cannot name.

Students are not expected to question the competence of their teachers or the usefulness of their assignments, any more than Zen disciples can rebel against their master and his koans. Japanese students who study at American universities are amazed that at the end of the semester most universities ask their students to evaluate their teachers. Even though students in Japan complain to each other

---

[1]Japanese art of flower arrangement. — Eds.

about their teachers, they would never think of writing an evaluation or filing official grievances.

In the teaching of many traditional Japanese art forms, the teacher's author- 35 ity is backed up by a complete hierarchy called *ie* that controls instruction. Even the choice of this word, since it means both "house" and "family origin," reflects high expectations of allegiance. What is described in English as a "school" (such as a school of writing or painting) is actually a "family" in Japanese. Each *ie* is structured like a family hierarchy: at the top is the head teacher, called *iemoto* (source of the house), and under him are various assistant teachers who, in turn, take their own assistants. All these teachers are licensed by the *ie*. A beginner in *ikebana* or Japanese dance will study with a minor assistant teacher for a few years and then move on to a more advanced teacher. There are various levels of competence awarded along the way, but every advancement must be approved by the *ie*.

The system makes it impossible for a student to challenge any teacher's decision, since the teacher can invoke the authority of the whole clanlike hierarchy. Teachers can make any arbitrary decision so long as it can be backed up by the *ie*. When my cousin Kazumi studied *ikebana*, she was disillusioned by the unfair judgments her teachers made every year about who should be allowed to advance to the next level of competence. There were no tests or lists of tasks and qualities that determined the advancements. Who advanced and who didn't seemed entirely up to the teachers' whims. People who were related to any of the teachers rose through the ranks much faster than those who weren't.

Whether or not they won an advancement to the next level, all the students were required to attend the annual certificate ceremony in their best kimonos. The year of the Kobe earthquake Kazumi received a letter from her *ie* advising students to rent a good kimono to attend the annual ceremony if theirs had been destroyed in the earthquake.

"I had been disillusioned with *ikebana* for some time anyway," Kazumi told me, "but the letter was the last straw. I couldn't believe that the teachers thought this was a time for people to be worrying about their kimonos. Even though the letter said that we didn't necessarily have to have a nice kimono if our family had suffered such a great damage that we had no money, the tone was very condescending — and it was obvious that they were really saying that we should rent one no matter what the cost. They didn't write and say, 'We are so sorry about the earthquake. We would be so happy if you could still come to the annual ceremony in spite of the damage many of you must have suffered, and of course, you can wear whatever you would like.'"

She switched to Dutch-style flower arrangement even though it, too, has a nationwide association that oversees its teaching and licensing. Like *ikebana*, Dutch flower arrangement has different levels of teachers and different levels of competence, but Kazumi sees a big difference between the two. To advance from one to the next in the Dutch style, people take tests in which each person is given a bucket of flowers to make into a table arrangement, a small bouquet, and a corsage; a group of judges scores the results. Everybody has the same amount of time, the same number of arrangements to complete, similar flowers in the bucket, and the same group of judges. Evaluation isn't arbitrary the way it was for *ikebana*. In the lessons she took — mostly from Dutch teachers — plenty of specific instruction was given about colors, textures, shapes, and the flowers themselves. Her teachers looked at her work and gave her suggestions — something none of her *ikebana* teachers ever did.

Until I talked to Kazumi, I was hoping that even though my Japanese friends   40
could not go back to school in their thirties and forties, they might be able to take private lessons or receive training through volunteer work in order to pursue some of their interests. Even in small towns like Green Bay, many people my age can learn new skills, pursue their hobbies, or work for causes they believe in without enrolling in school.

My Japanese friends do not have similar chances to learn something new or feel useful. There are very few volunteer organizations in Japan for nature conservation, crisis intervention, helping children, or working with families who are poor or homeless. The few soup kitchens one might find in big Japanese cities are operated by international organizations like the Salvation Army. People who work at them are mostly foreigners. A nice Japanese housewife is not expected to do volunteer work for strangers. "If she has time to help people she doesn't even know," her relatives would grumble, "why doesn't she do more to help her own kids study? Why doesn't she run for an office in the P.T.A. at their school?" Most middle-class Japanese people seem to think that poor people deserve to be poor — it's their own fault or the fault of their families and relatives. Nobody should expect help from total strangers. As for conserving nature, that is the job of biologists. My friends have a hard time justifying their passion for gardening to their husbands and in-laws. If they were to spend their afternoons taking care of injured wildlife or clearing marshes of trash instead of cleaning their houses and preparing special meals for their children, their families would probably disown them.

Nice housewives like my friends can take private lessons only if they can be justified as genteel means of cultivating fine, feminine tastes — like *ikebana*, tea, koto and samisen music — but these are the traditional Japanese arts with the strict *ie* structure. Joining the *ie* would involve my friends in another burdensome system of duties and obligations, something they already experience in every facet of their lives.

In so many ways, Japan is a place of no second chances. Many of my friends are in very unhappy marriages. They write to me about the shouting and shoving matches they have with their husbands, about the night they tried to run away, only to have the husband chase them down the street, catch them, and drag them home. Unable to run away, my friends lock themselves up in the guest room or sleep in their daughters' rooms to avoid sleeping with their husbands. For most American women, leaving a bad marriage like theirs would be nothing but happiness. My friends stay because divorce still carries a big stigma in Japan. If they leave their husbands, they may never be able to see their children again. Certainly, they will not be able to marry again and try another chance at marriage. Nobody marries a divorced middle-aged woman in Japan.

Life in Japan is like an unending stint at a school where you have to keep taking tests — giving your answers under pressure without help or guidance, knowing that you will get no second chance if you make a mistake. Japanese people have to make many of the big decisions of their lives — whom to marry, what company to join — without detailed information, since it is rude to ask direct questions even at *omiai* meetings and job interviews. They have no choice but to trust authority and do their best, just as they were supposed to do in school. If their job or marriage turns out to be a disappointment, they will be given the same vague exhortations they heard from their teachers: keep trying, work hard, pay attention.

There is nothing intrinsically wrong with trying harder. Sometimes when I 45 see my former students in Green Bay seeming to flounder — waiting on tables or working clerical jobs they hate, the whole time talking about their big plans to "go back to school" soon — I think maybe a little Japanese perseverance might not hurt them. I know that for them or for anyone else, going back to school does not guarantee a job or happiness. Within school, too, when my students complain that everything we read in a modern American literature class is depressing or that I simply do not "like" their work (when every poem they wrote in the class is a love poem in couplets), I long for a little Japanese respect for authority. Some of my students would be better off if they trusted me a little rather than questioning my decisions at every turn. Still, I would rather have students who question too much than those who assume that I know best and don't owe them any explanations. No one should have power that is unjustified and unjustifiable, regardless of how convenient or efficient it may seem for the smooth running of the classroom, the educational system, or the country.

The problem with the Japanese system, ultimately, is that individual freedom — to question the teacher, to disagree — is sacrificed for the supposed convenience and protection of the whole group. The system works well for people who feel no desire to rebel. The Japanese *ie* system my cousin complained about does ensure that anyone who perseveres in a given art form will have some recognition; periodically, every student is asked to take part in public exhibitions or concerts. Most Japanese students have public-performance opportunities many of my American friends — artists and musicians — don't.

But for me — as well as for my cousin — the price is too high. The security comes with too many obligations. The *ie* system asks that you trust your teachers who have not earned or deserved your trust. What you are required to have is blind faith in the *ie*: like the church or the mosque, the *ie* is an institution that is designed to inspire total obedience to its rules. In Japan, if you reject your chance to enjoy the security that comes from joining the right group such as an *ie*, an elite school, a good company, or a respectable family, you will have to leave the country or live in it as an outcast. Life in Japan resembles the harshest interpretation of a religious faith: the Koran or the sword, either you are with Christ or against him, either you join the sheltering umbrella of Japanese security or you have nothing. In school and elsewhere, people are rewarded for obeying the rules diligently, never for taking a chance and being different, or for asking good questions.

But words like *security* and *uncertainty* are misleading. Because Dutch-style flower arrangement is not as popular as *ikebana* and the association does not provide the same kind of protection that a traditional *ie* gives its teachers, my cousin is struggling to get enough students for the classes she offers. She has quit her clerical job, which she did not like, and committed herself to the life of a flower-arrangement teacher. She isn't going to get a second chance at being a clerk or going back to *ikebana*. My cousin's life is uncertain and insecure. But daily, as she arranges her own flowers and watches her students cutting and arranging theirs, she is certain of other things. She knows when she is making a good arrangement and when she is not. In Dutch-style arrangements, my cousin has learned what colors and shapes look pleasing; she has a firm sense of what she considers beautiful. She also knows that she will tell her students exactly what she thinks about their work rather than keeping her criticism to herself or being vague. Kazumi feels a certainty about truth, beauty, honesty. That is the only certainty worth choosing.

Exploring the Text

1. According to Kyoko Mori, what are the major differences between the Japanese and American educational systems? Summarize them.
2. What is the effect of Mori's introducing Japanese terms, especially *ronin* (para. 6), at the beginning of the essay?
3. Why does she place the phrase "the real world" in quotation marks (para. 1)?
4. Does Mori's reliance on personal experience limit or enhance her analysis? Explain.
5. What is the "paradox" that Mori refers to in paragraph 30?
6. What is Mori's purpose in including her cousin Kazumi's experience (paras. 36–39)?
7. Describe the arrangement of this essay. At the most general level, it is organized as a comparison/contrast, but it is made up of eight sections that are separated by space within the text. Would you say that this structure is governed more by logos or pathos?
8. Apart from the fact that her book is written in English, how do you know that Mori's audience are Western readers?

9. How would you describe Mori's attitude toward Japan in this essay? Is she judgmental? Harsh? Objective? Cite specific passages to support your response.

10. How does your own experience in school compare with Mori's as she describes it in paragraphs 15–19?

KYOKO MORI ON WRITING

In the following interview, Kyoko Mori responds to questions about statements in her essay "School" (p. 130).

Renee Shea (RS): When you point out that the Japanese don't really teach creative writing, you write, "In America, we are proof that the romantic notion of the natural writer is a myth." But don't you believe that talent in writing is in many ways inborn, a gift some of us have, others of us just don't, regardless of how well we're taught?

Kyoko Mori (KM): I do believe that talent may play a large part in who becomes a successful lifelong writer and who becomes a successful published writer (I'm not sure if these two things are exactly the same). But while talent is necessary, it's not enough to make someone a writer. Some people learn to be writers without going to school because school is not the only place that provides instruction and community — for instance, someone might come from a family of writers, study biology, and become a novelist without studying writing in a formal way because she or he was exposed to writing and literature all the time and had a community of like-minded people. Most of us are not that lucky. We go to school to belong to a community of writers and to get suggestions about what to read, as well as how to improve our own writing.

RS: You point out that in the United States "students are often drilled on the details of grammar or form and yet are forgiven for the minor mistakes they make in writing." Do you believe that our schools have failed by not holding students accountable for precision in grammar, mechanics, and sentence structure? Do you think that we should "return to basics" in the teaching of grammar?

KM: I don't think we should "return to the basics" because that presupposes that we have completely abandoned the basics. I've known a lot of elementary school teachers, for example, who emphasized the whole-language philosophy of teaching reading and writing — and they don't think of that as abandoning the basics in any way. Starting with a story that kids can really enjoy, rather than with phonics drills, is not to abandon the basics but to inspire the desire to learn them. I do think that attention to detail is important, and that includes knowing the fundamentals of spelling and grammar and sentence-, paragraph-, and essay-construction. But I don't think correctness in these areas is what makes for good writing. Being correct is not an end in itself. I'd rather read an essay or a short story that has a few minor mistakes but tells a lively story and has some insights than an essay or a short story that contains no mistakes and yet offers no new insights.

RS: You say, "I value the overall spirit or genuine voice in my students' work." What do you mean by *spirit* and *voice*? What can an aspiring writer do to develop those seemingly elusive qualities?

KM: I know that *voice* is almost impossible to define. It's more than style, it's more than thought, and it's much more than any measurements we can apply to it, such as sentence lengths or recurring expressions and imagery. But we do know a voice or a spirit when we see or hear it in other people's writing, just as we recognize each person as having his or her own personality. Maybe the way to think about it is this: when people don't feel comfortable with the act of writing, they feel that words actually prevent them from saying what they really mean. They string together words that they would never say in their real lives, to make awkward sentences that sound nothing like their real thoughts. There are things that prevent students from expressing not only their thoughts but their personalities in writing, and I do think that the fear of failure or making mistakes has something to do with this disconnect between the self and the words. I don't think people should write in the same way, or in the same voice, they would use for everyday speech. If someone recorded our everyday speech, we would all sound like bad writing — full of repetitions and interjections and inarticulate phrases. But I do think that we should try to write with the ease we feel in speaking to people we feel comfortable with — or out of faith that what we say will be understood.

Follow-up

After you have discussed Kyoko Mori's responses to the interviewer, choose another selection from this chapter. Then develop several questions, based on quotations from the piece, that you would like to ask the author in order to learn more about his or her views on education.

The History Teacher (poetry)

BILLY COLLINS

Billy Collins (b. 1941) served two terms as poet laureate of the United States, beginning in 2001. He has written more than ten books of poetry, including *Nine Horses* (2003), *Picnic, Lightning* (1998), and *The Art of Drowning* (1995). A distinguished professor of English at Lehman College in New York City, Collins has received fellowships from the National Endowment for the Arts and the Guggenheim Foundation. He was chosen in 1992 as a Literary Lion of the New York Public Library. Collins, who actively promotes poetry in the schools, edited *Poetry 180: A Turning Back to Poetry* (2003), an anthology of contemporary poems that aims to increase high school students' appreciation and enjoyment of poetry.

Trying to protect his students' innocence
he told them the Ice Age was really just
the Chilly Age, a period of a million years
when everyone had to wear sweaters.

And the Stone Age became the Gravel Age,   5
named after the long driveways of time.

The Spanish Inquisition was nothing more
than an outbreak of questions such as
"How far is it from here to Madrid?"
"What do you call the matador's hat?"   10

The War of the Roses took place in a garden,
and the Enola Gay dropped one tiny atom
on Japan.

The children would leave his classroom
for the playground to torment the weak   15
and the smart,
mussing up their hair and breaking their glasses,

while he gathered up his notes and walked home
past flower beds and white picket fences,
wondering if they would believe that soldiers   20
in the Boer War told long, rambling stories
designed to make the enemy nod off.

Exploring the Text

1. How would you describe the approach the history teacher takes toward his teaching?
2. What is the effect of juxtaposing the teacher's version of historical events with the description of the children when they "would leave his classroom / for the playground" (ll. 14–15)?
3. What is the speaker's attitude toward the history teacher? Is he critical? Admiring? Amused? Cite specific lines to support your response.
4. Does this poem make an argument *or* ask a question? What is the argument or the question? Consider the title as you explore these questions.
5. What is your attitude toward the history teacher? When does protection become lying? Is it a matter of degree? Intent? How do you think this teacher would present the events of September 11, 2001?

Eleven (fiction)

SANDRA CISNEROS

One of the first Latina writers to achieve commercial success, Sandra Cisneros (b. 1954) is a novelist, short-story writer, and poet, best known for *The House on Mango Street* (1983), a collection of connected stories and sketches. Recipient of many awards including a MacArthur Fellowship (the so-called "genius grant"), Cisneros has published the short-story collection *Woman Hollering Creek* (1991), the poetry collections *My Wicked Wicked Ways* (1987) and *Loose Woman* (1994), and the novel *Caramelo* (2002). The *New York Times Book Review* says Cisneros "embraces . . . the endless variety of Mexican and American culture — songs and stories, jokes and legends, furniture and food." The story "Eleven" explores the nature of power in the classroom.

What they don't understand about birthdays and what they never tell you is that when you're eleven, you're also ten, and nine, and eight, and seven, and six, and five, and four, and three, and two, and one. And when you wake up on your eleventh birthday you expect to feel eleven, but you don't. You open your eyes and everything's just like yesterday, only it's today. And you don't feel eleven at all. You feel like you're still ten. And you are — underneath the year that makes you eleven.

Like some days you might say something stupid, and that's the part of you that's still ten. Or maybe some days you might need to sit on your mama's lap because you're scared, and that's the part of you that's five. And maybe one day when you're all grown up maybe you will need to cry like if you're three, and that's okay. That's what I tell Mama when she's sad and needs to cry. Maybe she's feeling three.

Because the way you grow old is kind of like an onion or like the rings inside a tree trunk or like my little wooden dolls that fit one inside the other, each year inside the next one. That's how being eleven years old is.

You don't feel eleven. Not right away. It takes a few days, weeks even, sometimes even months before you say Eleven when they ask you. And you don't feel smart eleven, not until you're almost twelve. That's the way it is.

Only today I wish I didn't have only eleven years rattling inside me like pennies in a tin Band-Aid box. Today I wish I was one hundred and two instead of eleven because if I was one hundred and two I'd have known what to say when Mrs. Price put the red sweater on my desk. I would've known how to tell her it wasn't mine instead of just sitting there with that look on my face and nothing coming out of my mouth.

"Whose is this?" Mrs. Price says, and she holds the red sweater up in the air for all the class to see. "Whose? It's been sitting in the coatroom for a month."

"Not mine," says everybody. "Not me."

"It has to belong to somebody," Ms. Price keeps saying, but nobody can remember. It's an ugly sweater with red plastic buttons and a collar and sleeves all stretched out like you could use it for a jump rope. It's maybe a thousand years old and even if it belonged to me I wouldn't say so.

Maybe because I'm skinny, maybe because she doesn't like me, that stupid Sylvia Saldívar says, "I think it belongs to Rachel." An ugly sweater like that, all raggedy and old, but Mrs. Price believes her. Mrs. Price takes the sweater and puts it right on my desk, but when I open my mouth nothing comes out.

"That's not, I don't, you're not . . . Not mine," I finally say in a little voice that was maybe me when I was four.

"Of course it's yours," Mrs. Price says. "I remember you wearing it once." Because she's older and the teacher, she's right and I'm not.

Not mine, not mine, not mine, but Mrs. Price is already turning to page thirty-two, and math problem number four. I don't know why but all of a sudden I'm feeling sick inside, like the part of me that's three wants to come out of my eyes, only I squeeze them shut tight and bite down on my teeth real hard and try to remember today I am eleven, eleven. Mama is making a cake for me tonight, and when Papa comes home everybody will sing Happy birthday, happy birthday to you.

But when the sick feeling goes away and I open my eyes, the red sweater's still sitting there like a big red mountain. I move the red sweater to the corner of my desk with my ruler. I move my pencil and books and eraser as far from it as possible. I even move my chair a little to the right. Not mine, not mine, not mine.

In my head I'm thinking how long till lunchtime, how long till I can take the red sweater and throw it over the schoolyard fence, or leave it hanging on a parking meter, or bunch it up into a little ball and toss it in the alley. Except when math period ends Mrs. Price says loud and in front of everybody, "Now, Rachel, that's enough," because she sees I've shoved the red sweater to the tippy-tip corner of my desk and it's hanging all over the edge like a waterfall, but I don't care.

"Rachel," Mrs. Price says. She says it like she's getting mad. "You put that   15
sweater on right now and no more nonsense."

"But it's not —"

"Now!" Mrs. Price says.

This is when I wish I wasn't eleven, because all the years inside of me — ten, nine, eight, seven, six, five, four three, two, and one — are pushing at the back of my eyes when I put one arm through one sleeve of the sweater that smells like cottage cheese, and then the other arm through the other and stand there with my arms apart like if the sweater hurts me and it does, all itchy and full of germs that aren't even mine.

That's when everything I've been holding in since this morning, since when Mrs. Price put the sweater on my desk, finally lets go, and all of a sudden I'm crying in front of everybody. I wish I was invisible but I'm not. I'm eleven and it's my birthday today and I'm crying like I'm three in front of everybody. I put my head down on the desk and bury my face in my stupid clown-sweater arms. My face all hot and spit coming out of my mouth because I can't stop the little animal noises from coming out of me, until there aren't any more tears left in my eyes, and it's just my body shaking like when you have the hiccups, and my whole head hurts like when you drink milk too fast.

But the worst part is right before the bell rings for lunch. That stupid Phyllis   20
Lopez, who is even dumber than Sylvia Saldívar, says she remembers the red sweater is hers! I take it off right away and give it to her, only Mrs. Price pretends like everything's okay.

Today I'm eleven. There's a cake Mama's making for tonight, and when Papa comes home from work we'll eat it. There'll be candles and presents and everybody will sing Happy birthday, happy birthday to you, Rachel, only it's too late.

I'm eleven today. I'm eleven, ten, nine, eight, seven six, five, four, three, two, and one, but I wish I was one hundred and two. I wish I was anything but eleven, because I want today to be far away already, far away like a runaway balloon, like a tiny *o* in the sky, so tiny-tiny you have to close your eyes to see it.

Exploring the Text

1. Why do you think Sandra Cisneros chose to tell "Eleven" from the viewpoint of the young girl rather than of an omniscient narrator? What effect does this have?
2. What is the source of Mrs. Price's authority? Is it solely "because she's older and the teacher" (para. 11)?
3. In what ways does Cisneros's juxtaposition of home life and school life make for an effective rhetorical strategy?

4. Discuss the figurative language in this story, especially the similes. What purposes do they serve?
5. In which ways is this a story about having a voice in society, about who gets to talk and who gets heard?

From *Reading at Risk* (tables)

NATIONAL ENDOWMENT FOR THE ARTS

The following tables summarize the findings from *Reading at Risk*, a report of the National Endowment for the Arts on trends in literary reading. *Literary reading* is defined as "reading of novels, short stories, poetry, or drama in any print format, including the Internet. Any type was admitted, from romance novels to classical poetry." Overall, the tables show that the percentage of adult Americans reading literature declined 10 percent, from nearly 57 percent of the population in 1982 to 47 percent in 2002.

Trends in Book and Literary Reading

	Percentage of U.S. Adult Population		Change, 1992 to 2002 Percentage Point (pp)	
	1992	2002	Difference	Rate of Decline
Read Any Book	60.9	56.6	-4.3 pp	-7%
Read Literature	54.0	46.7	-7.3 pp	-14%

Literary Reading by Gender

	Percentage by Group			Percentage Point (pp) Change	
	1982	1992	2002	1992-2002	1982-2002
Men	49.1	47.4	37.6	-9.8 pp	-11.5 pp
Women	63.0	60.3	55.1	-5.2 pp	-7.9 pp

Literary Reading by Age

	Percentage by Group			Percentage Point (pp) Change	
	1982	1992	2002	1992-2002	1982-2002
18-24	59.8	53.3	42.8	-10.5 pp	-17.0 pp
25-34	62.1	54.6	47.7	-6.9 pp	-14.4 pp
35-44	59.7	58.9	46.6	-12.3 pp	-13.1 pp
45-54	54.9	56.9	51.6	-5.3 pp	-3.3 pp
55-64	52.8	52.9	48.9	-4.0 pp	-3.9 pp
65-74	47.2	50.8	45.3	-5.5 pp	-1.9 pp
75 & Older	40.9	40.4	36.7	-3.7 pp	-4.2 pp

Participation in Cultural and Social Activities

	Percentage of U.S. Adult Population	
	Literary Readers	Non-Literary Readers
Perform Volunteer and Charity Work	43.0	17.0
Visit Art Museums	44.0	12.0
Attend Performing Arts Events	49.0	17.0
Attend Sporting Events	45.0	27.0

Exploring the Texts

1. Study each of the National Endowment for the Arts tables. What does each table conclude about the variable being examined, such as gender or age?
2. Given the correlation between gender and literary reading, what would you recommend schools do about their choice of required readings?
3. What implications does the correlation between age and literary reading have for America's elementary and secondary classrooms?

4. Generate a series of hypotheses about the reason(s) for the correlation between reading and participation in cultural and social activities, including sports events.

5. Choose one of the tables and pose a series of questions that would lead to further research.

Conversation

Each of the following texts presents a viewpoint on the American high school.

Sources
1. **Horace Mann,** From *Report of the Massachusetts Board of Education*
2. **Leon Botstein,** *Let Teenagers Try Adulthood*
3. **Todd Gitlin,** *The Liberal Arts in an Age of Info-Glut*
4. **David S. Broder,** *A Model for High Schools*
5. **Floyd Norris,** *U.S. Students Fare Badly in International Survey of Math Skills*
6. **Norman Rockwell,** *The Spirit of Education* (painting)

After you have read, studied, and synthesized these pieces, enter the conversation with one of the suggested topics on pp. 163–164.

1. From *Report of the Massachusetts Board of Education*

HORACE MANN

The following selection is taken from an official policy document by Horace Mann (1796–1859), who is known as the father of American public education.

Intellectual Education as a Means of Removing Poverty, and Securing Abundance

. . . According to the European theory, men are divided into classes, — some to toil and earn, others to seize and enjoy. According to the Massachusetts theory, all are to have an equal chance for earning, and equal security in the enjoyment of what they earn. The latter tends to equality of condition; the former, to the grossest inequalities. . . .

But is it not true that Massachusetts, in some respects, instead of adhering more and more closely to her own theory, is becoming emulous of the baneful examples of Europe? The distance between the two extremes of society is lengthening, instead of being abridged. With every generation, fortunes increase on the one hand, and some new privation is added to poverty on the other. We are verging towards those extremes of opulence and of penury, each of which unhumanizes the human mind. A perpetual struggle for the bare necessaries of life, without the ability to obtain them, makes men wolfish. Avarice, on the other hand, sees, in all the victims of misery around it, not objects for pity and succor, but only crude materials to be worked up into more money.

I suppose it to be the universal sentiment of all those who mingle any ingredient of benevolence with their notions on political economy, that vast and overshadowing private fortunes are among the greatest dangers to which the happiness of the people in a republic can be subjected. Such fortunes would create a feudalism of a new kind, but one more oppressive and unrelenting than that of the middle ages. The feudal lords in England and on the Continent never held their retainers in a more abject condition of servitude than the great majority of foreign manufacturers and capitalists hold their operatives and laborers at the present day. The means employed are different; but the similarity in results is striking. What force did then, money does now. The villein[1] of the middle ages had no spot of earth on which he could live, unless one were granted to him by his lord. The operative or laborer of the present day has no employment, and therefore no bread, unless the capitalist will accept his services. The vassal had no shelter but such as his master provided for him. Not one in five thousand of English operatives or farm-laborers is able to build or own even a hovel; and therefore they must accept such shelter as capital offers them. The baron prescribed his own terms to his retainers: those terms were peremptory, and the serf must submit or perish. The British manufacturer or farmer prescribes the rate of wages he will give to his work-people; he reduces these wages under whatever pretext he pleases; and they, too, have no alternative but submission or starvation. In some respects, indeed, the condition of the modern dependent is more forlorn than that of the corresponding serf class in former times. Some attributes of the patriarchal relation did spring up between the lord and his lieges to soften the harsh relations subsisting between them. Hence came some oversight of the condition of children, some relief in sickness, some protection and support in the decrepitude of age. But only in instances comparatively few have kindly offices smoothed the rugged relation between British capital and British labor. The children of the work-people are abandoned to their fate; and notwithstanding the privations they suffer, and the dangers they threaten, no power in the realm has yet been able to secure them an education; and when the adult laborer is prostrated by sickness, or eventually worn out by toil and age, the poorhouse, which has all along been his destination, becomes his destiny. . . .

Now, surely nothing but universal education can counterwork this tendency to the domination of capital and servility of labor. If one class possesses all the wealth and the education, while the residue of society is ignorant and poor, it matters not by what name the relation between them may be called: the latter, in fact and in truth, will be the servile dependants and subjects of the former. But, if

---

[1]In a feudal society, a serf who has the right to own property.

education be equally diffused, it will draw property after it by the strongest of all attractions, for such a thing never did happen, and never can happen, as that an intelligent and practical body of men should be permanently poor. Property and labor in different classes are essentially antagonistic; but property and labor in the same class are essentially fraternal. The people of Massachusetts have, in some degree, appreciated the truth, that the unexampled prosperity of the State — its comfort, its competence, its general intelligence and virtue — is attributable to the education, more or less perfect, which all its people have received: but are they sensible of a fact equally important; namely, that it is to this same education that two-thirds of the people are indebted for not being today the vassals of as severe a tyranny, in the form of capital, as the lower classes of Europe are bound to in the form of brute force?

Education, then, beyond all other devices of human origin, is the great equal-   5
izer of the conditions of men, — the balance-wheel of the social machinery. I do not here mean that it so elevates the moral nature as to make men disdain and abhor the oppression of their fellow-men. This idea pertains to another of its attributes. But I mean that it gives each man the independence and the means by which he can resist the selfishness of other men. It does better than to disarm the poor of their hostility towards the rich: it prevents being poor. Agrarianism is the revenge of poverty against wealth. The wanton destruction of the property of others — the burning of hay-ricks and corn-ricks, the demolition of machinery because it supersedes hand-labor, the sprinkling of vitriol on rich dresses — is only agrarianism run mad. Education prevents both the revenge and the mad-ness. On the other hand, a fellow-feeling for one's class or caste is the common instinct of hearts not wholly sunk in selfish regards for person or for family. The spread of education, by enlarging the cultivated class or caste, will open a wider area over which the social feelings will expand; and, if this education should be universal and complete, it would do more than all things else to obliterate facti-tious distinctions in society. . . .

For the creation of wealth, then, — for the existence of a wealthy people and a wealthy nation, — intelligence is the grand condition. The number of im-provers will increase as the intellectual constituency, if I may call it, increases. In former times, and in most parts of the world even at the present day, not one man in a million has ever had such a development of mind as made it possible for him to become a contributor to art or science. Let this development precede, and contributions, numberless, and of inestimable value, will be sure to follow. That political economy, therefore, which busies itself about capital and labor, supply and demand, interest and rents, favorable and unfavorable balances of trade, but leaves out of account the element of a widespread mental development, is nought but stupendous folly. The greatest of all the arts in political economy is to change a consumer into a producer; and the next greatest is to increase the producer's producing power, — an end to be directly attained by increasing his intelligence. For mere delving, an ignorant man is but little better than a swine, whom he so much resembles in his appetites, and surpasses in his powers of mischief.

Questions

1. Why does Horace Mann begin with a description of the "feudal lords in England and on the Continent" (para. 3)?
2. What does Mann mean by "Property and labor in different classes are essentially antagonistic; but property and labor in the same class are essentially fraternal" (para. 4)?
3. What metaphor does Mann use to describe education in a democracy? Is it effective?
4. When Mann uses the term *intelligence*, does he mean innate ability or developed skill?
5. Describe Mann's style in this excerpt. In what ways is it appropriate for his audience?

2. *Let Teenagers Try Adulthood*

LEON BOTSTEIN

The following opinion piece was written by Leon Botstein, president of Bard College and author of *Jefferson's Children: Education and the Promise of American Culture* (1997).

The national outpouring after the Littleton [Columbine High School in Colorado,] shootings has forced us to confront something we have suspected for a long time: the American high school is obsolete and should be abolished. In the . . . month [after the shootings] high school students present and past [came] forward with stories about cliques and the artificial intensity of a world defined by insiders and outsiders, in which the insiders hold sway because of superficial definitions of good looks and attractiveness, popularity and sports prowess.

The team sports of high school dominate more than student culture. A community's loyalty to the high school system is often based on the extent to which varsity teams succeed. High school administrators and faculty members are often former coaches, and the coaches themselves are placed in a separate, untouchable category. The result is that the culture of the inside elite is not contested by the adults in the school. Individuality and dissent are discouraged.

But the rules of high school turn out not to be the rules of life. Often the high school outsider becomes the more successful and admired adult. The definitions of masculinity and femininity go through sufficient transformation to make the game of popularity in high school an embarrassment. No other group of adults young or old is confined to an age-segregated environment, much like a gang in which individuals of the same age group define each other's world. In no workplace, not even in colleges or universities, is there such a narrow segmentation by chronology.

Given the poor quality of recruitment and training for high school teachers, it is no wonder that the curriculum and the enterprise of learning hold so little sway over young people. When puberty meets education and learning in modern

America, the victory of puberty masquerading as popular culture and the tyranny of peer groups based on ludicrous values meet little resistance.

By the time those who graduate from high school go on to college and realize what really is at stake in becoming an adult, too many opportunities have been lost and too much time has been wasted. Most thoughtful young people suffer the high school environment in silence and in their junior and senior years mark time waiting for college to begin. The Littleton killers, above and beyond the psychological demons that drove them to violence, felt trapped in the artificiality of the high school world and believed it to be real. They engineered their moment of undivided attention and importance in the absence of any confidence that life after high school could have a different meaning.

Adults should face the fact that they don't like adolescents and that they have used high school to isolate the pubescent and hormonally active adolescent away from both the picture-book idealized innocence of childhood and the more accountable world of adulthood. But the primary reason high school doesn't work anymore, if it ever did, is that young people mature substantially earlier in the late 20th century than they did when the high school was invented. For example, the age of first menstruation has dropped at least two years since the beginning of this century, and not surprisingly, the onset of sexual activity has dropped in proportion. An institution intended for children in transition now holds young adults back well beyond the developmental point for which high school was originally designed.

Furthermore, whatever constraints to the presumption of adulthood among young people may have existed decades ago have now fallen away. Information and images, as well as the real and virtual freedom of movement we associate with adulthood, are now accessible to every 15- and 16-year-old.

Secondary education must be rethought. Elementary school should begin at age 4 or 5 and end with the sixth grade. We should entirely abandon the concept of the middle school and junior high school. Beginning with the seventh grade, there should be four years of secondary education that we may call high school. Young people should graduate at 16 rather than 18.

They could then enter the real world, the world of work or national service, in which they would take a place of responsibility alongside older adults in mixed company. They could stay at home and attend junior college, or they could go away to college. For all the faults of college, at least the adults who dominate the world of colleges, the faculty, were selected precisely because they were exceptional and different, not because they were popular. Despite the often cavalier attitude toward teaching in college, at least physicists know their physics, mathematicians know and love their mathematics, and music is taught by musicians, not by graduates of education schools, where the disciplines are subordinated to the study of classroom management.

For those 16-year-olds who do not want to do any of the above, we might construct new kinds of institutions, each dedicated to one activity, from science to dance, to which adolescents could devote their energies while working together with professionals in those fields.

At 16, young Americans are prepared to be taken seriously and to develop the motivations and interests that will serve them well in adult life. They need to enter a world where they are not in a lunchroom with only their peers, estranged from other age groups and cut off from the game of life as it is really played. There is nothing utopian about this idea; it is immensely practical and efficient, and its implementation is long overdue. We need to face biological and cultural facts and not prolong the life of a flawed institution that is out of date.

Questions

1. In the first paragraph, Leon Botstein states, "[T]he American high school is obsolete and should be abolished." Why? What specific reasons does he provide?
2. What does Botstein mean by "the rules of high school turn out not to be the rules of life" (para. 3)?
3. What is Botstein's proposed solution?
4. Where does Botstein address a counterargument? Does he refute (or concede) in sufficient detail to be persuasive?
5. Which parts of Botstein's reasoning do you find the strongest? the weakest? Explain.

3. *The Liberal Arts in an Age of Info-Glut*

TODD GITLIN

In the following selection, author and university professor Todd Gitlin argues that studying the liberal arts is even more important now in this age of mass media.

The glut of images is, in many respects, unprecedented, and so is the challenge it poses for education and the arts. On average, Americans watch television, or are in its presence, for more than four hours a day — half the waking hours that are not taken up with work (and sometimes even then). For the sake of argument, let us suppose that, during those hours of watching television, the representative American tunes in to six fictional programs. Those might include half-hour comedies, hour-long dramas, and two-hour movies. (Actually, thanks to remote-control devices, many viewers see more than one program at a time. More than two-thirds of cable subscribers surf channels, and the younger they are, the more they surf.)

For simplicity's sake, assume 16 minutes of commercials per hour on commercial channels — say, 40 distinct commercials per hour. That gives us roughly

160 more short units of mass-mediated message per day. For viewers who watch news shows, throw in, as a conservative estimate, 30 separate news items every day. Add trailers for upcoming shows and trivia quizzes. Add sporting events. Add videocassettes. Add billboards along the highway, on street corners, on buses. Add newspaper and magazine stories and advertisements, video and computer games, books — especially lightweight fiction. Add the photo-studded displays of wiggling, potentially meaningful units of information and disinformation that flood into millions of households and offices through the Internet. Read me! Notice me! Click on me! All told, we are exposed to thousands of mass-produced stories a month, not counting thousands more freestanding images and labels that flash into the corners of our consciousness.

Note, too, that this imagescape has a sound track — the vast quantities of performed music and other auditory stimuli, including songs, sound effects, tapes, compact disks, voice-mail filler — all the currents and ejaculations of organized sound that have become the background of our lives.

Now, it is true that no one but impressionable psychotics could be held in thrall for long by most of the minuscule dramas and depictions we find in popular culture. We experience most of the messages minimally, as sensations of the moment. But some part of the imagescape is nearly always clamoring for attention. Caught in the cross hairs of what the comedy writer Larry Gelbart has called "weapons of mass distraction," how shall we know, deeply, who we are? How shall we find still points in a turning world? How shall we learn to govern ourselves?

What does it mean, this information for which we are to be grateful and 5 upgrade our facilities? When a neo-Nazi creates a World-Wide Web site that maintains that Auschwitz was not a death camp, he is, technically, adding as much "information" to the gross informational product as when someone posts an analysis of global warming. Garbage in, garbage sloshing around. When people "chat" about the weather in Phoenix or Paris, they are circulating information, but this does not mean they are either deepening their sensibilities or improving their democratic capacity to govern themselves. Long before Hollywood or computers, the French observer Alexis de Tocqueville wrote of America: "What is generally sought in the productions of mind is easy pleasure and information without labor." Toward that very end, the genius of our consumer-oriented marketplace has been to produce the Walkman, the remote-control device, and the computer mouse.

When information piles up higgledy-piggledy — when information becomes the noise of our culture — the need to teach the lessons of the liberal arts is urgent. Students need "chaff detectors." They need some orientation to philosophy, history, language, literature, music, and arts that have lasted more than 15 minutes. In a high-velocity culture, the liberal arts have to say, "Take your time." They have to tell students, "Trends are fine, but you need to learn about what endures."

Faculty members in the liberal arts need to say: "We don't want to add to your information glut, we want to offer some ground from which to perceive the rest of what you will see. Amid the weightless fluff of a culture of obsolescence, here is Jane Austen on psychological complication, Balzac on the pecuniary squeeze. Here is Dostoyevsky wrestling with God, Melville with nothingness, Douglass with slavery. Here is Rembrandt's religious inwardness, Mozart's exuberance, Beethoven's longing. In a culture of chaff, here is wheat."

The point is not simply to help us find our deepest individual beings. It is also to help new generations discover that they are not that different from the common run of humanity. Common concerns about life and death, right and wrong, beauty and ugliness persist throughout the vicissitudes of individual life, throughout our American restlessness, global instabilities, the multiple livelihoods that we must shape in an age of retraining, downsizing, and resizing. We badly need continuities to counteract vertigo as we shift identities, careen through careers and cultural changes.

Finally, we need to cultivate the liberal arts in a democratic spirit — not necessarily for the sake of piety before the past (though that spirit is hardly ruled out), but to pry us out of parochialism. In preparation for citizenship, the liberal arts tell us that human beings have faced troubles before; they tell us how people have managed, well and badly. Access to a common, full-blooded humanities curriculum will help our students cross social boundaries in their imaginations. Studying a common core of learning will help orient them to common tasks as citizens; it will challenge or bolster — make them think through — their views and, in any case, help them understand why not everyone in the world (or in their classroom) agrees with them.

Regardless of one's views of the curricular conflicts of our time, surely no one   10
who is intellectually serious can help but notice how students of all stripes arrive at college with shallow and scattered educations, ill-prepared to learn. They are greeted by budget pressures and shortsighted overseers. A strong liberal-arts curriculum could teach them about their history, their social condition, themselves. Today's common curriculum would not be that of 1950 — anymore than 1950's was that of 1900. What overlap it would have with the past would generate cultural ballast. Surely the academic left and right (and center) might find some common ground in the quest to offer a higher education that is democratically useful, citizenly, and smart.

Questions

1. Why does Todd Gitlin explain in detail the television-watching habits of most Americans? How does this information lay the foundation for his argument?
2. How does the style of paragraph 2, which begins "For simplicity's sake," reflect its content? Pay special attention to the sentence structure.

3. What effect does Gitlin's use of such emotional terms and references as "impressionable psychotics" and "neo-Nazi" have on his audience?
4. Why does he quote nineteenth-century critic Alexis de Tocqueville (para. 5)?
5. Gitlin offers several reasons for the importance of the liberal arts. What are they? Why does he present them in the order that he does?
6. This selection is from a longer article about the need for a common core curriculum in colleges. Do you think that its argument is relevant to high schools as well?

4. *A Model for High Schools*

DAVID S. BRODER

In the following article, Pulitzer Prize–winning journalist David S. Broder, a political correspondent for the *Washington Post*, discusses alternative high schools.

The assigned readings for Aurora del Val's students . . . were sections of the writings of Greek philosopher Plato and black nationalist Malcolm X. For 90 minutes her 14 young scholars wrestled verbally with twin paradoxes: Plato's insistence that prisoners in a cave might find the shadows on the wall more real than the outside world, and Malcolm's declaration that his intellectual freedom began when he entered prison.

Prodded by their teacher's questions, the students grappled with the issues of appearance. The oddity is that these teenagers were all high school dropouts, kids who had walked out or been tossed out of their previous schools, kids with attitude problems, behavioral problems, drug or alcohol problems, kids whose teachers and families had often marked them off as hopeless losers.

And here they were in a voluntary program, run by the Portland Community College [in Oregon], where a single breach of discipline — an unexcused absence, an unfinished assignment, a blown test — would mean automatic expulsion, but where the curriculum was stiff enough to challenge an undergraduate at any of Portland's elite private colleges.

The Gateway to College program . . . is one of eight "early-college high school" programs supported in part by the Bill and Melinda Gates Foundation and four other charities. They represent diverse approaches to a problem drawing increasing attention from the Bush administration and governors of both parties: how to make high school education more rigorous and ease the transition from high school to college or the workplace.

[In 2005] in Washington there [was] an "education summit" sponsored by 5 the National Governors Association and Achieve Inc., a business-backed school reform group trying to stiffen high-school graduation requirements and improve the quality of the workforce.

Their concern [was] prompted by the fact that too many students are dropping out of high school, bored or dissatisfied with what it offers, and too many of those who graduate lack the skills needed for well-paying jobs or, if they go on to college, need remedial classes in English and math.

The Gateway experiment suggests that even for the hardest cases — teenagers with few credits, low grade-point averages and a host of personal problems — the challenge of a tough curriculum, backed by skillful teaching in small classes and plenty of personal counseling, can be a path to success.

Each new cohort of 20 or fewer students spends a semester together, with intensive focus on basic skills, including study techniques and classroom communication. Bonding during this term builds mutual support and helps motivate students to keep up their work. "They've become like family," del Val said of her students. "They are real supportive of each other."

After one term, the students move into the regular community-college adult classes, with the goal not only of completing their 12th-grade requirements but picking up enough college credits to qualify for an associate (two-year) degree.

The program has been judged a success. Among the first 600 students enrolled, attendance in the first term averaged 92 percent, and 71 percent successfully completed it. Almost nine out of 10 continued in regular community-college classes, working toward their diplomas and two-year degrees.

The Gates Foundation was impressed enough to double the original $5 million grant [in 2004], enabling Gateway to expand its national network from eight campuses to 17, including one in Maryland's Montgomery County.

But the most important testimonials come from the students whose lives have been changed. Kathy Kraus, dressed all in black and wearing a bowler hat, said, "The teachers here have encouraged me to write poems and essays. I never had that."

Scott Weidlich said he was being home-schooled but his parents "never really cared and I wasn't motivated." Jessica Smidt said, "My old classes were so full of kids and most of the teachers didn't want to be there. Here, you don't get lost in the crowd."

Chris Marks said, "My high school was swamped with drugs — and so was I. Here, I feel a real sense of responsibility. You're not being watched. It's your ass, and your life, and you either make the most of this opportunity or you don't. It's up to you."

Del Val, who almost abandoned teaching after seeing how "overwhelmed and overworked" her friends were, shuffling students through five large classes a day in typical high schools in California, said it is enormously satisfying to see the way students respond in this environment.

It is clear that even high school dropouts are capable of much more than most of them are being asked to do. The question is whether the country can afford to waste their talents.

Questions

1. How do the first two paragraphs serve David Broder's purpose of writing about alternative high schools?
2. What does Broder do to emphasize the academic rigor of the Gateway to College program?
3. How does he dispel or at least challenge the image of these students as "hopeless losers" (para. 2)?
4. According to Broder, why is it important to the community, even on a national level, to keep students from dropping out of high school?
5. In paragraph 10, Broder claims that the program he is describing "has been judged a success." How does he support this claim?

5. *U.S. Students Fare Badly in International Survey of Math Skills*

Floyd Norris

In the following article, Floyd Norris reports on a study comparing the math skills of American students with those from different countries.

High school students in Hong Kong, Finland and South Korea do best in mathematics among those in 40 surveyed countries while students in the United States finished in the bottom half, according to a new international comparison of mathematical skills shown by 15-year-olds.

The United States was also cited as having the poorest outcomes per dollar spent on education. It ranked 28th of 40 countries in math and 18th in reading.

The study, released [December 7, 2004] by the Organization for Economic Cooperation and Development, a group based in Paris representing 30 nations, used tests given to students in 2003 and was intended to assess relative performance and to try to determine reasons for it.

"The gap between the best and worst performing countries has widened," said Andreas Schleicher, the official who directed the study and wrote the report.

The study compared student performance in 29 of the 30 countries in the organization, which includes all major industrialized nations, and in 11 other countries that chose to participate. Because of insufficient participation in the study, figures for Britain were not reported. 5

The study devoted less attention to reading than did a previous one in 2000, but it provided rankings that showed relatively little change.

Over all in reading, the top countries were Finland, South Korea, Canada and Australia. The United States finished 18th, higher than nations like Denmark, Germany and Hungary, all of which had students who performed better in math than American students did.

Fuzzy on Math

Results of international testing on the mathematic skills of 15-year-olds show the skills of teenagers in the United States trailing those of their foreign counterparts.

Percentage of students whose scores fell into the top two scoring groups or the bottom two:

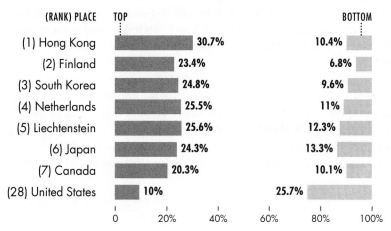

(RANK) PLACE	TOP	BOTTOM
(1) Hong Kong	30.7%	10.4%
(2) Finland	23.4%	6.8%
(3) South Korea	24.8%	9.6%
(4) Netherlands	25.5%	11%
(5) Liechtenstein	25.6%	12.3%
(6) Japan	24.3%	13.3%
(7) Canada	20.3%	10.1%
(28) United States	10%	25.7%

0   20%   40%   60%   80%   100%

Source: Organization for Economic Cooperation and Development. Reprinted by permission of the *New York Times.*

The study looked not only at the average performance of students, but also at how many from each country were top performers. It separated students into seven groups, ranging from Level 6, the best, to Level 1, which the authors viewed as a minimal level of competence. The remaining students were below the first level, a category that included more than half the students in Brazil, Indonesia and Tunisia.

In the United States, 10 percent of the students were in one of the top two groups, less than half as many as in Canada and a third the total of the leader, Hong Kong, which had 30.7 percent of its students in the top two categories.

Finland had the smallest percentage of underperforming students, with 6.8 percent.

The evaluation asked questions that were intended to test the ability of students to recognize what mathematical calculations were needed, and then to perform them, and to deal with questions that they would confront as citizens. Mr. Schleicher said that students in countries that emphasized theorems and rote learning tended not to do as well as those that emphasized the more practical aspects of mathematics.

The survey also questioned students about their own views of themselves and their work, and found that while good students were more likely to think

10

they were good, countries that did well often had a large number of students who did not feel they were doing well. In the United States, 36 percent of the students agreed with the statement, "I am just not good at mathematics," while in Hong Kong, 57 percent agreed. In South Korea the figure was 62 percent.

Of the United States students, 72 percent said they got good grades in mathematics, more than in any other country. In Hong Kong, only 25 percent of the students said they got good marks, the lowest of any country.

The study said that while girls typically did only a little worse than boys on the test, "they consistently report much lower interest in and enjoyment of mathematics" and "much higher levels of helplessness and stress in mathematics classes."

Regarding spending, the study concluded that "while spending on educa-   15
tional institutions is a necessary prerequisite for the provision of high-quality education, spending alone is not sufficient to achieve high levels of outcomes."

It noted that while the Czech Republic spent only one third as much per student as the United States did, it was one of the top 10 performing nations in the study, while the United States performed below the average of the nations surveyed.

Questions

1. Summarize the major findings of the study reported in Floyd Norris's article. Identify who was assessed, how, and by whom.
2. What were the major findings in this study regarding both the performance and attitude of U.S. students?
3. According to this study, how did money spent per student correlate with student performance?

6. *The Spirit of Education* (painting)

NORMAN ROCKWELL

Following is a Norman Rockwell painting, *The Spirit of Education*, that was featured on the cover of *The Saturday Evening Post* in 1934. A popular and prolific artist in his own time, Rockwell was known for his depiction of positive American values.

Questions

1. Examine the props carefully. What are the "tools" of education, according to Norman Rockwell's image?
2. On the basis of the visual depiction alone, who is excluded from Rockwell's vision of education?

3. What assumptions about education does Rockwell make in this illustration?
4. In 1934, the United States was in the midst of the Great Depression. How does this painting encourage an optimistic outlook on the future?

Entering the Conversation

As you respond to the following prompts, support your argument with references to at least three of the sources in Conversation: Focus on the American High School. For help using sources, see Chapter 3.

1. Write an essay explaining whether you agree with Leon Botstein's critique of the American high school (p. 153).

2. Using the texts in Conversation: Focus on the American High School, as well as your own insights into high school, identify two serious problems,

and propose recommendations for addressing them. Cite at least two sources from the Conversation in your response.

3. John Dewey, the father of experiential education, described the interaction of education and democracy as follows:

> Democratic society is peculiarly dependent for its maintenance upon the use in forming a course of study of criteria which are broadly human. Democracy cannot flourish where the chief influences in selecting subject matter of instruction are utilitarian ends narrowly conceived for the masses, and, for the higher education of the few, the traditions of a specialized cultivated class. The notion that the "essentials" of elementary education are the three R's mechanically treated, is based upon ignorance of the essentials needed for realization of democratic ideals. . . . A curriculum which acknowledges the social responsibilities of education must present situations where problems are relevant to the problems of living together, and where observation and information are calculated to develop social insight and interest.
>
> — *Democracy and Education*, 1916

Write an essay explaining the extent to which you believe that high schools today are preparing citizens to achieve Dewey's vision. Draw on your experience and observation, and cite at least three of the sources from the Conversation to develop your argument.

4. Suppose you could choose to attend either a high school that emphasizes vocational education, including training in specific job skills and required internships, or a high school that emphasizes the liberal arts. Which would better prepare you to participate in a global economy? Explain why.

Student Writing

Argument: Using Personal Experiences as Evidence

The following essay is one AP student's response to the following prompt.

> James Baldwin delivered "A Talk to Teachers" to a group of educators in New York City in 1963 — over forty years ago. Do the problems and prejudices he discussed still exist, or are they history?

As you read, consider how the student explains and supports his viewpoint.

A Talk to High School Teachers

Tyler Wilchek

In James Baldwin's "A Talk to Teachers," he writes a social criticism of public schools and describes how the problems are reflected in the larger society. Forty-two years later, some of the problems Baldwin mentions still exist in public schools. If I were to give a talk to teachers today, I would be sure to talk about segregation in different parts of a typical school such as class level, athletics, and social situations. Regular, honors, and Advanced Placement classes definitely have trends linking race to the difficulty of the class. Also, sports are often dominated by particular races, so teams end up with predominantly one race. Last, social situations during lunch prove race is still a factor.

In my school a link can be made between the race of students and the level of classes enrolled in. Often in AP and honors classes, the students are predominantly white. In regular classes, the students are predominantly African American and Hispanic. This trend reflects the experiences Baldwin discusses in his essay. Baldwin is in awe when he encounters the "whiter" parts of Park Avenue. Used to the more unclean and unkempt part of the city that he grew up in, he knows that this other part of town is not really meant for him. Baldwin writes, "You know — you know instinctively — that none of this is for you. You know this before you are told." He points out that he feels unwelcome and shunned from this part of Park Avenue. I feel as if this is how African American students feel today towards advanced-level classes. The low enrollment of African American students in upper-level classes can perhaps be explained by the premise that Baldwin brings up. Minority students believe that they cannot be accepted in the society of advanced-level classes. Although expectations can sometime define how much a person can push himself, if students believe that they are not meant for honors classes, they will not attempt to try them. African American students often do not have people raising their expectations. Therefore, when they look at honors courses, their perception is already denying any chance for success. They instinctively believe that these classes are not for them.

Another problem in high schools today is segregation in athletics. As an active member of two varsity sports at my high school for three years, I have noticed the "white sports" and the "black sports." Participating in two almost exclusively white sports (swimming and lacrosse) has shown me that sports teams are just as segregated as classes. In the sports that I play, involvement and encouragement from parents is essential for success. Swimming requires parents to volunteer at meets and pay for membership to pools, while lacrosse is just not as popular a sport as basketball or football. It is much harder for black people to succeed in swimming and lacrosse because of the lack of opportunities. Baldwin agrees that black children are not given a fair opportunity to succeed in life. Baldwin states that "the Negro child has had, effectively, almost all the doors of opportunity slammed in his face, and there are very few things he can do about it." African American children do not have these doors of opportunity in sports such as swimming and lacrosse. Many black students do not have the thousand dollars a year to swim or hundreds of dollars to purchase lacrosse equipment. These doors of opportunity are just not available for minority students in high school. At my school, basketball and football are dominated by African Americans students because the equipment is more readily available and there are more opportunities to play.

Last, public high schools are segregated in social situations, such as where students choose to eat lunch in the cafeteria. Each and every student has his own group of friends, his own place to sit, his home sweet home, during every lunch period. There are very distinct areas for each group of students. But usually these students are linked by more than common interests; they are also linked by race. The most distinct areas in my school are probably the Asian math-and-science magnet section, the Gothic (white) students near the trophy cases, the African American students near the lunch line, and the Hispanic students in the hallway. Students today feel a sense of security when they are with people of their own race, and so they choose to isolate themselves with people of their own race.

Segregation is the core problem that exists in public high schools today. Although Baldwin wrote his essay many years ago, the issue of race still plays a large part in public education. The lack of African American enrollment in advanced classes, segregation in sports teams, and racial isolation in the cafeteria illustrate that this is still very much a problem today. Although there have been improvements over the past forty years, segregation is still a concern for public schools.

Questions

1. How has Tyler drawn connections to James Baldwin's essay? Examine places where he refers specifically to Baldwin's essay. Should Tyler have added more explicit references, perhaps even quotations? Explain.
2. Assuming that the third sentence ("If I were to give a talk to teachers today . . .") is Tyler's thesis, would you recommend eliminating the following three sentences? If so, why? If not, what do you think they add to the introductory paragraph?
3. Are the specific details in this essay one of its strengths or weaknesses? Explain.
4. Try rewriting a paragraph of this essay in the third person. Do you think Tyler's decision to write in the first person is more effective, or would the distance achieved by the third person have given his position greater weight?
5. Tyler opens his final paragraph with the statement, "Segregation is the core problem that exists in public high schools today." How well do you think he has prepared for and supported this conclusion?

Grammar as Rhetoric and Style
The Appositive

An appositive is a noun or noun phrase that tells you something about a nearby noun or pronoun. In each sentence below, the appositive is bracketed. The arrow shows the noun or pronoun that the appositive details.

It turned out that one of the top students, *Denny Davies*, had learned of this rule.

— Margaret Talbot

Kennedy, *a wiry fifty-nine-year-old who has a stern buzz cut*, was in 1997 the principal of Sarasota High School.

— Margaret Talbot

In 1981, two professors . . . began following the lives of eighty-one high-school valedictorians — *forty-six women and thirty-five men from Illinois*.

— Margaret Talbot

Japanese people have to make many of the big decisions of their lives — *whom to marry, what company to join* — without detailed information.

— Kyoko Mori

We were given plenty of instruction about the specifics of writing: *word choice, description, style*.

— Kyoko Mori

When my cousin *Kazumi* studied *ikebana*, she was disillusioned by the unfair judgments her teachers made every year.

— Kyoko Mori

Punctuation and Appositives

The last example given does not use punctuation to set off the appositive from the rest of the sentence, but the others do. Here's why: If the sentence can be understood without the appositive, the writer uses punctuation to set off the appositive. If the sentence cannot be understood without the appositive, the writer does *not* set off the appositive with punctuation marks. In the first example given, the name of the top student is a minor detail, so Margaret Talbot sets off the appositive with commas. In the final sentence, Kyoko Mori has several cousins; it is essential that she tell the reader *which* cousin she is describing, so she does not punctuate the appositive.

Choosing Punctuation

If your appositive needs punctuation, you can set off the appositive in one of three ways. First, you can use one or two commas.

> The principal of Sarasota High School in 1997 was Daniel Kennedy, *a wiry fifty-nine-year-old who has a stern buzz cut.*
>
> — MARGARET TALBOT

> Kennedy, *a wiry fifty-nine-year-old who has a stern buzz cut,* was in 1997 the principal of Sarasota High School.
>
> — MARGARET TALBOT

Second, you can use one or two dashes.

> In 1981, two professors . . . began following the lives of eighty-one high-school valedictorians — *forty-six women and thirty-five men from Illinois.*
>
> — MARGARET TALBOT

> Japanese people have to make many of the big decisions of their lives — *whom to marry, what company to join* — without detailed information.
>
> — KYOKO MORI

Third, you can use a colon.

> We were given plenty of instruction about the specifics of writing: *word choice, description, style.*
>
> — KYOKO MORI

Dashes emphasize the appositive more than commas do. Furthermore, if an appositive contains its own internal commas, then one dash, two dashes, or a colon makes it easier to read the complete sentence.

Position of Appositive: Before or after the Noun?

All the examples so far in this lesson have shown an appositive coming *after* the noun or pronoun it details. Although that is the most common way that an appositive is used, it can come before the noun or pronoun as well.

> *A wiry fifty-nine-year-old who has a stern buzz cut,* Daniel Kennedy was in 1997 the principal of Sarasota High School.

Whether you put the appositive before or after the noun it details is a stylistic choice. If in doubt, read the sentence aloud with several surrounding sentences to determine which placement sounds better.

Rhetorical and Stylistic Strategy

An appositive serves two rhetorical and stylistic functions:

- First, an appositive can *clarify* a term by providing a proper noun or a synonym for the term, by defining or explaining the term, or by getting more specific.

PROPER NOUN   Its hero is Scout's father, *the saintly Atticus Finch.*

         — FRANCINE PROSE

SYNONYM   . . . an automaton, *a machine,* can be made to keep a school so.

         — RALPH WALDO EMERSON

LONGER DEFINITION   First published in 1970, *I Know Why the Caged Bird Sings* is what we have since learned to recognize as a "survivor" memoir — *a first-person narrative of victimization and recovery.*

         — FRANCINE PROSE

EXPLANATION   [O]ne might suppose that teenagers might enjoy the transformative science-fiction aspects of *The Metamorphosis, a story about a young man so alienated from his "dysfunctional" family that he turns . . . into a giant beetle.*

         — FRANCINE PROSE

SPECIFICITY   Yet in other genres — *fiction and memoir* — the news is far more upsetting.

         — FRANCINE PROSE

- Second, an appositive can *smooth* choppy writing. Note how stilted each of the following items is compared with the preceding versions.

   Its hero is Scout's father. His name is Atticus Finch. He is saintly.

   An automaton is a machine. An automaton can be made to keep a school so.

   I Know Why the Caged Bird Sings was first published in 1970. It is what we have since learned to recognize as a "survivor" memoir. A "survivor" memoir is a first-person narrative. The narrative deals with victimization and recovery.

[O]ne might suppose that teenagers might enjoy the transformative science-fiction aspects of *The Metamorphosis. The Metamorphosis* is a story about a young man.

Yet in other genres the news is far more upsetting. Other genres are fiction and memoir.

• EXERCISE 1

Identify the appositive in the following sentences and the word or phrase it details.

1. My father, a truly exceptional man, worked at an ordinary job and was unknown outside the small town where he lived.

2. His rage passes description — the sort of rage that is only seen when rich folk that have more than they can enjoy suddenly lose something that they have long had but have never before used or wanted.
   — J. R. R. Tolkein, *The Hobbit*

3. [W. E. B.] DuBois saw the grandeur and degradation in a single unifying thought — slavery was the West's tragic flaw; yet it was tragic precisely because of the greatness of the civilization that encompassed it.
   — Dinesh D'Souza, "Equality and the Classics"

4. The eruptions in the early part of our century — the time of world wars and emergent modernity — were premonitions of a sort.
   — Sven Birkerts, *The Gutenberg Elegies*

5. Evidently I need this starting point — the world as it appeared before people bent it to their myriad plans — from which to begin dreaming up my own myriad, imaginary hominid agendas.
   — Barbara Kingsolver, "Knowing Our Place"

6. The war America waged in Vietnam, the first to be witnessed day after day by television cameras, introduced the home front to new tele-intimacy with death and destruction.
   — Susan Sontag, *Regarding the Pain of Others*

7. The restaurant's signature dish, a tantalizing fish taco, is also one of the least expensive entrees on the menu.

• EXERCISE 2

Provide the correct punctuation for each of the following sentences by using a dash, comma, or colon to separate the appositives from the rest of the sentence. Or, if a sentence does not need punctuation around the appositive,

for that sentence, write "NP" for "no punctuation." Be ready to explain why your choice of punctuation is the most effective in each case.

1. Several West African countries Nigeria, Ghana, Benin, Cameroon, and Togo were at some time in their history under colonial rule.

2. The mayoral candidate's rally opened to throngs of people an unusually large turnout for a cold, rainy day.

3. The British parliamentary system has two branches the House of Lords and the House of Commons.

4. The fifth canon of rhetoric style includes a writer's choices of diction and syntax.

5. One of our most popular poets Billy Collins is also one of our most gifted.

6. The surgeons reconstructed his hand the most damaged part of his body.

7. The rewards of hard work both physical and mental are often intangible.

8. Homer the Greek poet was blind.

9. Don't you think that businesses should close on July 4 the birthday of our country?

• EXERCISE 3

Combine each of the following pairs of sentences into one more fluent and coherent sentence by using an appositive. Be sure to punctuate correctly.

1. The *Times* is a world-renowned newspaper. It is delivered to my house every day.

2. Dolores Cunningham is the first mayor in our town's history to increase jobs during her four-year term. She is an advocate of the supply-side theory of economics.

3. A major health problem for teenagers is bulimia. Bulimia is an eating disorder.

4. My car is in the parking lot. It's an old blue station wagon with a dent in the fender.

5. That call was from Bridget. She's the top student in my calculus class.

6. The Edwardsville Tigers are the only baseball team ever to lose a series that it had led three games to none. They will be forever remembered for this colossal choke.

7. Warren G. Harding defeated James Cox in the 1920 presidential election by 26 percentage points. This was the biggest landslide victory in the history of U.S. presidential elections.

8. The service opened to the choir's rendition of Handel's "Hallelujah Chorus." That performance was a smashing success.

• EXERCISE 4

Identify the appositives in the following sentences from "I Know Why the Caged Bird Can't Read," and explain their effect. Note that all are direct quotations.

1. Traditionally, the love of reading has been born and nurtured in high school English class — the last time many students will find themselves in a roomful of people who have all read the same text and are, in theory, prepared to discuss it.

2. The intense loyalty adults harbor for books first encountered in youth is one probable reason for the otherwise baffling longevity of vintage mediocre novels, books that teachers may themselves have read in adolescence. . . .

3. Yet in other genres — fiction and memoir — the news is far more upsetting.

4. First published in 1970, *I Know Why the Caged Bird Sings* is what we have since learned to recognize as a "survivor" memoir, a first-person narrative of victimization and recovery.

5. My older son spent the first several weeks of sophomore English discussing the class's summer assignment, *Ordinary People,* a weeper and former bestseller by Judith Guest about a "dysfunctional" family recovering from a teenage son's suicide attempt.

6. Its hero is Scout's father, the saintly Atticus Finch, a lawyer who represents everything we cherish about justice and democracy and the American Way.

7. The novel has a shadow hero, too, the descriptively named Boo Radley, a gooney recluse who becomes the occasion for yet another lesson in tolerance and compassion.

8. To read the novel is, for most, an exercise in wish-fulfillment and self-congratulation, a chance to consider thorny issues of race and prejudice from a safe distance and with the comfortable certainty that the reader would *never* harbor the racist attitudes espoused by the lowlifes in the novel.

9. The question is no longer what the writer has written but rather who the writer is — specifically, what ethnic group or gender identity an author represents.

10. Meanwhile, aesthetic beauty — felicitous or accurate language, images, rhythm, wit, the satisfaction of recognizing something in fiction that seems fresh and true — is simply too frivolous, suspect, and elitist even to mention.

• EXERCISE 5

Each of the following sentences includes one or more appositives. Identify the appositives, explain their effect, and then write a sentence of your own using that sentence as a model.

1. And on the basis of this evidence — the moral and political evidence — one is compelled to say that this is a backward society.
   — James Baldwin, "A Talk to Teachers"

2. So to regard the young child, the young man, requires, no doubt, rare patience: a patience that nothing but faith in the remedial forces of the soul can give.   — Ralph Waldo Emerson, "Education"

3. Mr. Somervell — a most delightful man, to whom my debt is great — was charged with the duty of teaching the stupidest boys the most regarded thing — namely, to write mere English.
   — Winston Churchill, *A Roving Commission: My Early Life*

4. In their classes, we wrote essays about our families, friends, hobbies, future dreams — personal subjects we had not written about at school since third grade.   — Kyoko Mori, "School"

5. I am also other selves: a late starter, a casualty of the culture wars of the 1960s, an alienated adolescent sopping up pop culture and dreaming of escape, an American kid growing up in the 1950s, playing touch football and watching *I Love Lucy*.
   — Sven Birkerts, *The Gutenberg Elegies*

Suggestions for Writing

Education

Now that you have examined a number of readings and other texts that focus on education, explore this topic yourself by synthesizing your own ideas and the readings. You might want to do more research or use readings from other classes as you write.

1. Many see standardized testing as the answer to improving public education in the United States. Thus, students face district- and state-mandated

tests as well as national ones. What do you think? Write a personal essay discussing whether standardized testing is an effective way to bring about improved instruction and performance. Then, research the topic, and revise your essay by broadening its scope beyond your own experience.

2. Homeschooling has become an effective alternative to public or private school for an increasingly large number of students in the United States. Research this trend by consulting print and electronic resources and, if possible, by interviewing someone involved with homeschooling. Would Ralph Waldo Emerson, whose essay "Education" appears on page 102, support or oppose this method of education? Write an essay exploring both the benefits and liabilities of homeschooling.

3. Many people believe that children should be required to attend at least one year of school prior to kindergarten. Write an essay explaining why tax dollars should or should not be used to pay for mandatory, government-funded preschool. You might want to do some research to develop and support your position.

4. Write your own "Talk to Teachers," addressing either the teachers in your school or teachers in general. To start this assignment, replace the name *Khrushchev* with *Al Qaeda* in the opening paragraph of James Baldwin's "A Talk to Teachers" (page 123). How does this substitution set the stage for your more contemporary view?

5. Write a roundtable discussion among three or four of the authors in this chapter as they discuss *one* of the following quotations:

   • The only real education comes from what goes counter to you.

   — ANDRÉ GIDE

   • I have never let my schooling interfere with my education.

   — MARK TWAIN

   • Education is not filling a bucket but lighting a fire.

   — WILLIAM BUTLER YEATS

   • Rewards and punishments are the lowest form of education.

   — CHUANG-TZU

6. According to Francine Prose, "Education, after all, is a process intended to produce a product." Examine your school or another part of an educational system (for example, your school district, a Montessori class, a private religion-affiliated school). Describe specific parts of the educational process, and the "product" they strive to produce. Think of this as a cause-effect essay, with the process as the cause and the product as the effect.

7. According to numerous reports, including *Reading at Risk* (p. 147), reading is simply not the pastime of choice for many — especially not young people. One way to stimulate interest in books is through Community

Reads programs, where a group — for example, an entire city or town — agree to read and discuss a particular book, usually a novel, in such contexts as libraries, churches, PTA meetings, and classrooms. In some cases, the author visits the community for a discussion. If you have participated in one of these Community Reads projects, write an essay evaluating your experience, paying particular attention to whether the experience encouraged you to become a more enthusiastic reader. If you have not participated in one of these projects, write an essay explaining why you believe it would or would not be a worthwhile experience for your community.

8. Write a comparison/contrast of the high school classroom as you've experienced it in the United States with the high school experience in another country. If you've attended school in another country, you can use your own experience; if you know someone who has, you might interview that person; or you can research the topic in print and electronic sources. Consider how the classroom, including the relationship of teacher and student, reflects the values of the larger society. Kyoko Mori's essay "School" (p. 130) might guide you as you write.

9. High school class of 2035! What will high school be like for the next generation? Write an essay explaining what changes you anticipate for high schools in the not-too-distant future. Will the high school be pretty much the same as yours? Will students interact with teachers solely online? Or will future students face a backlash to a more traditional model? What books will students be reading? Will they be reading at all? Can you imagine yourself as one of the teachers?

5

Work

How does our work shape or influence our lives?

A pleasure for some, a necessity for most, a virtue for many, a curse for a few. Work means different things to different people. Whether a paycheck is the prime motivation, or the job is both vocation and avocation, work is at the center of most people's lives. What we do, how much we do, and where we do it greatly affects our identities and values.

Some cultures pride themselves on having a strong work ethic. What is a *work ethic*? How did the concept evolve? Does our twenty-first-century life lack a work ethic, as many have argued? Or, as others have claimed, have we become a society of workaholics? Does a strong work ethic make us better people, or is it rooted in materialism? Our national mythology — the American Dream — is based on the belief that hard work will not go unrewarded. That belief is reinforced by rags-to-riches stories, such as those written by nineteenth-century author Horatio Alger. The tales of Benjamin Franklin's hard work and perseverance have been passed down in aphorisms such as "A stitch in time saves nine." The great industrial dynasties — the Carnegies, the Rockefellers — and business giants such as Donald Trump and Bill Gates are presented as evidence that the American Dream is still a reality. What is the social responsibility, if any, of people like Trump and Gates, whose work has made them more than merely successful?

The authors and artists in this chapter offer different perspectives on the meaning and motivation of work. Thomas Carlyle (p. 209) argues that work itself is ennobling and dignifies the worker. Richard Selzer (p. 197) asks whether secular work can become a religious calling. Annie Dillard (p. 212) looks at the work of an artist, not a poet or painter, but a gifted pilot. Other authors in this chapter, however, consider work a necessity, perhaps even a necessary evil, rather than its own reward. They describe the hardship of forced labor and of blue-collar occupations that offer low pay and little autonomy for the employee whose work choices are severely limited by a lack of education or training. Finally, we enter a conversation about the plight of working parents as they try to balance the benefits of the unpaid work of caring for family with the intangible profits such work brings.

As you plan for your life after high school, what sort of work is most important to you? Do you expect your work to define you, to provide financial security, to support you while you explore other goals, or to be some combination of these three? Do you want a job or a career? What is the difference? Or might you take the approach of the speaker in Robert Frost's poem "Two Tramps in Mud Time"? He says, "My object in living is to unite / My avocation and my vocation / As my two eyes make one in sight."

From *Serving in Florida*

BARBARA EHRENREICH

Best-selling author Barbara Ehrenreich (b. 1941) started out as a scientist. But after receiving her PhD in biology from Rockefeller University, she pursued a career in the academic world only briefly before starting to write for magazines such as *Time* and the *Progressive*. A social critic with a decidedly liberal bent, her sardonic sensibility often animates her writing. Her books include *The American Health Empire: Power, Profits, and Politics* (1971), *Women in the Global Factory* (1983), *Fear of Falling: The Inner Life of the Middle Class* (1989), and *The Snarling Citizen: Essays* (1995). To research her two most recent books, Ehrenreich went undercover. For *Nickel and Dimed* (2001), a study of the working poor in the United States, she relocated to several cities; worked as a server, maid, and salesclerk; and tried to live on the wages she received. In *Bait and Switch: The (Futile) Pursuit of the American Dream* (2005), she documents the difficulty of a woman over fifty trying to find a white-collar job. The following excerpt from "Serving in Florida," a chapter in *Nickel and Dimed*, describes her experience working in a restaurant named Jerry's.

Picture a fat person's hell, and I don't mean a place with no food. Instead there is everything you might eat if eating had no bodily consequences — the cheese fries, the chicken-fried steaks, the fudge-laden desserts — only here every bite must be paid for, one way or another, in human discomfort. The kitchen is a cavern, a stomach leading to the lower intestine that is the garbage and dishwashing area, from which issue bizarre smells combining the edible and the offal: creamy carrion, pizza barf, and that unique and enigmatic Jerry's scent, citrus fart. The floor is slick with spills, forcing us to walk through the kitchen with tiny steps, like Susan McDougal[1] in leg irons. Sinks everywhere are clogged with scraps of lettuce, decomposing lemon wedges, water-logged toast crusts. Put your hand down on any counter and you risk being stuck to it by the film of ancient syrup spills, and this is unfortunate because hands are utensils here, used for scooping up lettuce onto the salad plates, lifting out pie slices, and even moving hash browns from one plate to another. The regulation poster in the single unisex rest room admonishes us to wash our hands thoroughly, and even offers instructions for doing so, but there is always some vital substance missing —

---

[1]Susan McDougal was imprisoned for contempt of court, fraud, and conspiracy in connection with the failed Whitewater land deal involving President Bill Clinton and First Lady Hillary Rodham Clinton. The Clintons were never charged with any wrongdoing. — Eds.

soap, paper towels, toilet paper — and I never found all three at once. You learn to stuff your pockets with napkins before going in there, and too bad about the customers, who must eat, although they don't realize it, almost literally out of our hands.

The break room summarizes the whole situation: there is none, because there are no breaks at Jerry's. For six to eight hours in a row, you never sit except to pee. Actually, there are three folding chairs at a table immediately adjacent to the bathroom, but hardly anyone ever sits in this, the very rectum of the gastroarchitectural system. Rather, the function of the peri-toilet area is to house the ashtrays in which servers and dishwashers leave their cigarettes burning at all times, like votive candles, so they don't have to waste time lighting up again when they dash back here for a puff. Almost everyone smokes as if their pulmonary well-being depended on it — the multinational mélange of cooks; the dishwashers, who are all Czechs here; the servers, who are American natives — creating an atmosphere in which oxygen is only an occasional pollutant. My first morning at Jerry's, when the hypoglycemic shakes set in, I complain to one of my fellow servers that I don't understand how she can go so long without food. "Well, I don't understand how *you* can go so long without a cigarette," she responds in a tone of reproach. Because work is what you do for others; smoking is what you do for yourself. I don't know why the antismoking crusaders have never grasped the element of defiant self-nurturance that makes the habit so endearing to its victims — as if, in the American workplace, the only thing people have to call their own is the tumors they are nourishing and the spare moments they devote to feeding them.

Now, the Industrial Revolution is not an easy transition, especially, in my experience, when you have to zip through it in just a couple of days. I have gone from craft work straight into the factory, from the air-conditioned morgue of the Hearthside directly into the flames. Customers arrive in human waves, sometimes disgorged fifty at a time from their tour buses, peckish and whiny. Instead of two "girls" on the floor at once, there can be as many as six of us running around in our brilliant pink-and-orange Hawaiian shirts. Conversations, either with customers or with fellow employees, seldom last more than twenty seconds at a time. On my first day, in fact, I am hurt by my sister servers' coldness. My mentor for the day is a supremely competent, emotionally uninflected twenty-three-year-old, and the others, who gossip a little among themselves about the real reason someone is out sick today and the size of the bail bond someone else has had to pay, ignore me completely. On my second day, I find out why. "Well, it's good to see *you* again," one of them says in greeting. "Hardly anyone comes back after the first day." I feel powerfully vindicated — a survivor — but it would take a long time, probably months, before I could hope to be accepted into this sorority.

I start out with the beautiful, heroic idea of handling the two jobs at once, and for two days I almost do it: working the breakfast/lunch shift at Jerry's from 8:00 till 2:00, arriving at the Hearthside a few minutes late, at 2:10, and attempting to hold out until 10:00. In the few minutes I have between jobs, I pick up a spicy chicken sandwich at the Wendy's drive-through window, gobble it down in the car, and change from khaki slacks to black, from Hawaiian to rust-colored polo. There is a problem, though. When, during the 3:00–4:00 o'clock dead time, I finally sit down to wrap silver, my flesh seems to bond to the seat: I try to refuel with a purloined cup of clam chowder, as I've seen Gail and Joan do dozens of times, but Stu catches me and hisses "No *eating*!" although there's not a customer around to be offended by the sight of food making contact with a server's lips. So I tell Gail I'm going to quit, and she hugs me and says she might just follow me to Jerry's herself.

But the chances of this are minuscule. She has left the flophouse and her 5 annoying roommate and is back to living in her truck. But, guess what, she reports to me excitedly later that evening, Phillip has given her permission to park overnight in the hotel parking lot, as long as she keeps out of sight, and the parking lot should be totally safe since it's patrolled by a hotel security guard! With the Hearthside offering benefits like that, how could anyone think of leaving? This must be Phillip's theory, anyway. He accepts my resignation with a shrug, his main concern being that I return my two polo shirts and aprons.

Gail would have triumphed at Jerry's, I'm sure, but for me it's a crash course in exhaustion management. Years ago, the kindly fry cook who trained me to waitress at a Los Angeles truck stop used to say: Never make an unnecessary trip; if you don't have to walk fast, walk slow; if you don't have to walk, stand. But at Jerry's the effort of distinguishing necessary from unnecessary and urgent from whenever would itself be too much of an energy drain. The only thing to do is to treat each shift as a one-time-only emergency: you've got fifty starving people out there, lying scattered on the battlefield, so get out there and feed them! Forget that you will have to do this again tomorrow, forget that you will have to be alert enough to dodge the drunks on the drive home tonight — just burn, burn, burn! Ideally, at some point you enter what servers call a "rhythm" and psychologists term a "flow state," where signals pass from the sense organs directly to the muscles, bypassing the cerebral cortex, and a Zen-like emptiness sets in. I'm on a 2:00–10:00 P.M. shift now, and a male server from the morning shift tells me about the time he "pulled a triple" — three shifts in a row, all the way around the clock — and then got off and had a drink and met this girl, and maybe he shouldn't tell me this, but they had sex right then and there and it was like *beautiful.*

But there's another capacity of the neuromuscular system, which is pain. I start tossing back drugstore-brand ibuprofens as if they were vitamin C, four before each shift, because an old mouse-related repetitive-stress injury in my upper back has come back to full-spasm strength, thanks to the tray carrying. In my ordinary life, this level of disability might justify a day of ice packs and stretching. Here I comfort myself with the Aleve commercial where the cute blue-collar guy asks: If you quit after working four hours, what would your boss say? And the not-so-cute blue-collar guy, who's lugging a metal beam on his back, answers: He'd fire me, that's what. But fortunately, the commercial tells us, we workers can exert the same kind of authority over our painkillers that our bosses exert over us. If Tylenol doesn't want to work for more than four hours, you just fire its ass and switch to Aleve.

True, I take occasional breaks from this life, going home now and then to catch up on e-mail and for conjugal visits (though I am careful to "pay" for everything I eat here, at $5 for a dinner, which I put in a jar), seeing *The Truman Show* with friends and letting them buy my ticket. And I still have those what-am-I-doing-here moments at work, when I get so homesick for the printed word that I obsessively reread the six-page menu. But as the days go by, my old life is beginning to look exceedingly strange. The e-mails and phone messages addressed to my former self come from a distant race of people with exotic concerns and far too much time on their hands. The neighborly market I used to cruise for produce now looks forbiddingly like a Manhattan yuppie emporium. And when I sit down one morning in my real home to pay bills from my past life, I am dazzled by the two- and three-figure sums owed to outfits like Club Body Tech and Amazon.com.

Management at Jerry's is generally calmer and more "professional" than at the Hearthside, with two exceptions. One is Joy, a plump, blowsy woman in her early thirties who once kindly devoted several minutes of her time to instructing me in the correct one-handed method of tray carrying but whose moods change disconcertingly from shift to shift and even within one. The other is B.J., aka B.J. the Bitch, whose contribution is to stand by the kitchen counter and yell, "Nita, your order's up, move it!" or "Barbara, didn't you see you've got another table out there? Come *on*, girl!" Among other things, she is hated for having replaced the whipped cream squirt cans with big plastic whipped-cream-filled baggies that have to be squeezed with both hands — because, reportedly, she saw or thought she saw employees trying to inhale the propellant gas from the squirt cans, in the hope that it might be nitrous oxide. On my third night, she pulls me aside abruptly and brings her face so close that it looks like she's planning to butt me with her forehead. But instead of saying, "You're fired," she says, "You're doing fine." The only trouble is I'm spending time chatting with customers: "That's how they're getting you." Furthermore I am letting them "run me," which means harassment by sequential demands: you bring the catsup and they decide they want extra Thousand Island; you bring that and they announce they now need a side of fries, and so on into distraction. Finally she tells me not to take her wrong. She tries to say things in a nice way, but "you get into a mode, you know, because everything has to move so fast."[2]

---

[2]In *Workers in a Lean World: Unions in the International Economy* (Verso, 1997), Kim Moody cites studies finding an increase in stress-related workplace injuries and illness between the mid-1980s and the early 1990s. He argues that rising stress levels reflect a new system of "management by stress" in which workers in a variety of industries are being squeezed to extract maximum productivity, to the detriment of their health.

I mumble thanks for the advice, feeling like I've just been stripped naked by   10
the crazed enforcer of some ancient sumptuary law: No chatting for *you*, girl. No
fancy service ethic allowed for the serfs. Chatting with customers is for the good-
looking young college-educated servers in the downtown carpaccio and ceviche
joints, the kids who can make $70–$100 a night. What had I been thinking? My
job is to move orders from tables to kitchen and then trays from kitchen to tables.
Customers are in fact the major obstacle to the smooth transformation of information into food and food into money — they are, in short, the enemy. And the
painful thing is that I'm beginning to see it this way myself. There are the traditional asshole types — frat boys who down multiple Buds and then make a fuss
because the steaks are so emaciated and the fries so sparse — as well as the variously impaired — due to age, diabetes, or literacy issues — who require patient
nutritional counseling. The worst, for some reason, are the Visible Christians —
like the ten-person table, all jolly and sanctified after Sunday night service, who
run me mercilessly and then leave me $1 on a $92 bill. Or the guy with the crucifixion T-shirt (SOMEONE TO LOOK UP TO) who complains that his baked potato is
too hard and his iced tea too icy (I cheerfully fix both) and leaves no tip at all. As a
general rule, people wearing crosses or WWJD? ("What Would Jesus Do?") buttons
look at us disapprovingly no matter what we do, as if they were confusing waitressing with Mary Magdalene's original profession.

I make friends, over time, with the other "girls" who work my shift: Nita, the
tattooed twenty-something who taunts us by going around saying brightly, "Have
we started making money yet?" Ellen, whose teenage son cooks on the graveyard
shift and who once managed a restaurant in Massachusetts but won't try out for
management here because she prefers being a "common worker" and not "ordering people around." Easygoing fiftyish Lucy, with the raucous laugh, who limps
toward the end of the shift because of something that has gone wrong with her
leg, the exact nature of which cannot be determined without health insurance.
We talk about the usual girl things — men, children, and the sinister allure of
Jerry's chocolate peanut-butter cream pie — though no one, I notice, ever brings
up anything potentially expensive, like shopping or movies. As at the Hearthside,
the only recreation ever referred to is partying, which requires little more than
some beer, a joint, and a few close friends. Still, no one is homeless, or cops to it
anyway, thanks usually to a working husband or boyfriend. All in all, we form
a reliable mutual-support group: if one of us is feeling sick or overwhelmed, another one will "bev" a table or even carry trays for her. If one of us is off sneaking
a cigarette or a pee, the others will do their best to conceal her absence from the
enforcers of corporate rationality.[3]

---

[3]Until April 1998, there was no federally mandated right to bathroom breaks. According to
Marc Linder and Ingrid Nygaard, authors of *Void Where Prohibited: Rest Breaks and the Right to
Urinate on Company Time* (Cornell University Press, 1997), "The right to rest and void at

But my saving human connection — my oxytocin [hormone] receptor, as it were — is George, the nineteen-year-old Czech dishwasher who has been in this country exactly one week. We get talking when he asks me, tortuously, how much cigarettes cost at Jerry's. I do my best to explain that they cost over a dollar more here than at a regular store and suggest that he just take one from the half-filled packs that are always lying around on the break table. But that would be unthinkable. Except for the one tiny earring signaling his allegiance to some vaguely alternative point of view, George is a perfect straight arrow — crew-cut, hardworking, and hungry for eye contact. "Czech Republic," I ask, "or Slovakia?" and he seems delighted that I know the difference. "Vaclav Havel," I try, "Velvet Revolution, Frank Zappa?" "Yes, yes, 1989," he says, and I realize that for him this is already history.

My project is to teach George English. "How are you today, George?" I say at the start of each shift. "I am good, and how are you today, Barbara?" I learn that he is not paid by Jerry's but by the "agent" who shipped him over — $5 an hour, with the agent getting the dollar or so difference between that and what Jerry's pays dishwashers. I learn also that he shares an apartment with a crowd of other Czech "dishers," as he calls them, and that he cannot sleep until one of them goes off for his shift, leaving a vacant bed. We are having one of our ESL sessions late one afternoon when B.J. catches us at it and orders "Joseph" to take up the rubber mats on the floor near the dishwashing sinks and mop underneath. "I thought your name was George," I say loud enough for B.J. to hear as she strides off back to the counter. Is she embarrassed? Maybe a little, because she greets me back at the counter with "George, Joseph — there are so many of them!" I say nothing, neither nodding nor smiling, and for this I am punished later, when I think I am ready to go and she announces that I need to roll fifty more sets of silverware, and isn't it time I mixed up a fresh four-gallon batch of blue-cheese dressing? May you grow old in this place, B.J., is the curse I beam out at her when I am finally permitted to leave. May the syrup spills glue your feet to the floor.

I make the decision to move closer to Key West. First, because of the drive. Second and third, also because of the drive: gas is eating up $4–$5 a day, and although Jerry's is as high-volume as you can get, the tips average only 10 percent, and not just for a newbie like me. Between the base pay of $2.15 an hour and the

---

work is not high on the list of social or political causes supported by professional or executive employees, who enjoy personal workplace liberties that millions of factory workers can only dream about. . . . While we were dismayed to discover that workers lacked an acknowledged right to void at work, [the workers] were amazed by outsiders' naïve belief that their employers would permit them to perform this basic bodily function when necessary. . . . A factory worker, not allowed a break for six-hour stretches, voided into pads worn inside her uniform; and a kindergarten teacher in a school without aides had to take all twenty children with her to the bathroom and line them up outside the stall door while she voided."

obligation to share tips with the busboys and dishwashers, we're averaging only about $7.50 an hour. Then there is the $30 I had to spend on the regulation tan slacks worn by Jerry's servers — a setback it could take weeks to absorb. (I had combed the town's two downscale department stores hoping for something cheaper but decided in the end that these marked-down Dockers, originally $49, were more likely to survive a daily washing.) Of my fellow servers, everyone who lacks a working husband or boyfriend seems to have a second job: Nita does something at a computer eight hours a day; another welds. Without the forty-five-minute commute, I can picture myself working two jobs and still having the time to shower between them.

So I take the $500 deposit I have coming from my landlord, the $400 I have earned toward the next month's rent, plus the $200 reserved for emergencies, and use the $1,100 to pay the rent and deposit on trailer number 46 in the Overseas Trailer Park, a mile from the cluster of budget hotels that constitute Key West's version of an industrial park. Number 46 is about eight feet in width and shaped like a barbell inside, with a narrow region — because of the sink and the stove — separating the bedroom from what might optimistically be called the "living" area, with its two-person table and half-sized couch. The bathroom is so small my knees rub against the shower stall when I sit on the toilet, and you can't just leap out of the bed, you have to climb down to the foot of it in order to find a patch of floor space to stand on. Outside, I am within a few yards of a liquor store, a bar that advertises "free beer tomorrow," a convenience store, and a Burger King — but no supermarket or, alas, Laundromat. By reputation, the Overseas park is a nest of crime and crack, and I am hoping at least for some vibrant multicultural street life. But desolation rules night and day, except for a thin stream of pedestrians heading for their jobs at the Sheraton or the 7-Eleven. There are not exactly people here but what amounts to canned labor, being preserved between shifts from the heat.

In line with my reduced living conditions, a new form of ugliness arises at Jerry's. First we are confronted — via an announcement on the computers through which we input orders — with the new rule that the hotel bar, the Driftwood, is henceforth off-limits to restaurant employees. The culprit, I learn through the grapevine, is the ultraefficient twenty-three-year-old who trained me — another trailer home dweller and a mother of three. Something had set her off one morning, so she slipped out for a nip and returned to the floor impaired. The restriction mostly hurts Ellen, whose habit it is to free her hair from its rubber band and drop by the Driftwood for a couple of Zins before heading home at the end of her shift, but all of us feel the chill. Then the next day, when I go for straws, I find the dry-storage room locked. It's never been locked before; we go in and out of it all day — for napkins, jelly containers, Styrofoam cups for takeout. Vic, the portly assistant manager who opens it for me, explains that he caught one of the dishwashers attempting to steal something and, unfortunately, the miscreant will be with us until a replacement can be found — hence the locked door. I neglect to ask what he had been trying to steal but Vic tells me who he is — the kid with the buzz cut and the earring, you know, he's back there right now.

I wish I could say I rushed back and confronted George to get his side of the story. I wish I could say I stood up to Vic and insisted that George be given a translator and allowed to defend himself or announced that I'd find a lawyer who'd handle the case pro bono. At the very least I should have testified as to the kid's honesty. The mystery to me is that there's not much worth stealing in the dry-storage room, at least not in any fenceable quantity: "Is Gyorgi here, and am having 200 — maybe 250 — catsup packets. What do you say?" My guess is that he had taken — if he had taken anything at all — some Saltines or a can of cherry pie mix and that the motive for taking it was hunger.

So why didn't I intervene? Certainly not because I was held back by the kind of moral paralysis that can mask as journalistic objectivity. On the contrary, something new — something loathsome and servile — had infected me, along with the kitchen odors that I could still sniff on my bra when I finally undressed at night. In real life I am moderately brave, but plenty of brave people shed their courage in POW camps, and maybe something similar goes on in the infinitely more congenial milieu of the low-wage American workplace. Maybe, in a month or two more at Jerry's, I might have regained my crusading spirit. Then again, in a month or two I might have turned into a different person altogether — say, the kind of person who would have turned George in.

Questions for Discussion

1. Does Barbara Ehrenreich seem to be exaggerating the workplace as she describes it in this selection? If you have worked in a restaurant, does her description of the environment match your experience?
2. What is Ehrenreich's attitude toward her coworkers? Does she appreciate them? Is she condescending? How do you react to her observations?
3. Early in the selection, as Ehrenreich pays bills left over from her "real life," she reflects, "[My] old life is beginning to look exceedingly strange" (para. 8). At the end, she asks, "So why didn't I intervene [with George]?" (para. 18). Does the experience of "serving in Florida" change Ehrenreich? Cite specific passages to support your response.
4. According to Ehrenreich, who is to blame for the situation of those who work at low-paying jobs in restaurants? Are there heroes and villains, or does the workplace itself change the people who are part of it?
5. Overall, what is your attitude toward Ehrenreich and her method of research? Does choosing to live as one of the working poor for a short time — as a kind of visitor or tourist — give her an accurate picture of their lives? Explain whether you find her presentation of them respectful, convincing, sympathetic, patronizing, superficial, or some combination of these. Cite specific passages.

Questions on Rhetoric and Style

1. Ehrenreich opens the selection with "Picture a fat person's hell . . ." (para. 1). What is the intended effect? Does she want to shock or disgust the reader? Is she being humorous?
2. Ehrenreich describes the kitchen in terms of bodily organs and functions. What response is she trying to evoke? Is she successful? (See paras. 1 and 2.)
3. Ehrenreich provides fairly extensive commentary in footnotes. What is the effect of this strategy? In the footnotes, is her tone different from the one used in the body of the piece?
4. Ehrenreich uses lively, emotionally charged language throughout. Identify one passage and analyze the diction, especially the connotations of the words. Suggestions: the paragraph beginning "Now, the Industrial Revolution is not an easy transition . . ." (para. 3) or "I make friends, over time, with the other 'girls' who work my shift . . ." (para. 11).
5. Ehrenreich occasionally uses crude expressions. Are they appropriate? What is her intended effect in shifting to diction that is not only informal but, some would say, crass?
6. Ehrenreich is both outsider and insider in this selection; that is, she is the writer observing the environment in which she is playing a role. How does she make this narrative stance work? Does she shift abruptly between describing what is going on and commenting about it, or does she move smoothly between the two? Discuss by citing specific passages.
7. Discuss specific instances of humor in this selection. Is it primarily ironic humor? Aggressively sarcastic? Affectionately amusing? Cite specific passages in your response.
8. What elements of fiction does Ehrenreich employ? Consider such elements as figurative language, dialogue, narrative commentary, and description of people and settings.
9. In this selection, Ehrenreich does not state a thesis or indicate directly what her purpose is; instead, she works by inference and implication. What is her purpose? State it directly in a sentence that begins, "In this selection, Ehrenreich . . ."
10. At times, Ehrenreich seems to raise tangential issues. When she describes her coworker smoking, for instance, she writes: "Because work is what you do for others; smoking is what you do for yourself. I don't know why the antismoking crusaders have never grasped the element of defiant self-nurturance that makes the habit so endearing to its victims — as if, in the American workplace, the only thing people have to call their own is the tumors they are nourishing and the spare moments they devote to feeding them" (para. 2). What is the effect of this commentary? What is its relevance to Ehrenreich's overall purpose?
11. How does Ehrenreich establish her ethos in this selection? What part does her relationship with George play in her appeal to ethos?
12. Who is Ehrenreich's audience? Base your answer on the tone you detect in specific passages.

Suggestions for Writing

1. How much is the minimum wage? Develop a budget for living for one month as a single person earning the minimum wage (plus tips if applicable) in your geographical area. What kind of living accommodations could you afford? How much money would you have available for food? What would your transportation costs be?

2. Using Ehrenreich as a model, describe a negative work experience (for example, you may have found a boss arrogant or you may have encountered prejudice or bias). You can narrate — and comment — but also use dialogue, as Ehrenreich does, to make the situation come alive for your readers.

3. In "Evaluation," the final chapter of *Nickel and Dimed*, Ehrenreich observes:

   > Some odd optical property of our highly polarized and unequal society makes the poor almost invisible to their economic superiors. The poor can see the affluent easily enough — on television, for example, or on the covers of magazines. But the affluent rarely see the poor or, if they do catch sight of them in some public space, rarely know what they're seeing, since — thanks to consignment stores and, yes, Wal-Mart — the poor are usually able to disguise themselves as members of the more comfortable classes.

   Write an essay supporting or challenging Ehrenreich's analysis.

4. *Nickel and Dimed* takes place from 1998 to 2000. Write an essay explaining whether the author's experience would be the same or different in today's economy.

5. Write an editorial for a newspaper on a topic related to the issues Ehrenreich raises — for example, a minimum wage, health care, working conditions.

BARBARA EHRENREICH ON WRITING

For this interview, Renée Shea asked Barbara Ehrenreich, author of "Serving in Florida," questions submitted by a class of high school juniors.

Renée Shea (RS): Why do you think it's more effective to view an issue through firsthand experience rather than basing it more on hard data like statistics?

Barbara Ehrenreich (BE): I don't think that at all. Most of my work as a journalist has involved conventional research — interviewing people, gathering facts, etc. I actually did a lot of that for *Nickel and Dimed* too, but I put the facts and statistics in the footnotes and conclusion so that they wouldn't interrupt the narrative.

Nickel and Dimed was my first venture into what is called immersion journalism, where you put yourself bodily into the situation you're investigating. The big disadvantage of this kind of journalism, I discovered, is that you can't suddenly break out of your role and say, "Hey, I'm a journalist, and I'd like to ask you some questions." You have to be pretty quiet and unobtrusive.

But the advantage of this kind of journalism is that I learned things I could not have learned by interviewing people — like just how hard the work is. If I had interviewed people about this, they probably would have said that, yes, the work is pretty hard and they're tired at the end of the day. It was another thing to actually do the work myself and discover how exhausted — mentally and physically — I was at the end of a shift. And I'm a physically very strong person!

RS: Did you find it difficult to call up specific events to use in your writing? For example, did you find yourself able to reconstruct conversations easily from memory, or did you have to reinvent parts of them?

BE: I would rush "home" to my motel or whatever every day to write up in my journal everything that had happened that day while it was still fresh in my mind. Sometimes I could also find time to jot down some notes while I was at work. So, no, I didn't invent anything.

RS: Did you find it hard to write about people you worked with once you had become their friend? (How did you come up with the names of your female characters?)

BE: I had two rules for writing about my coworkers: (1) change their names (the names chosen are pretty arbitrary) and omit any identifying characteristics, and (2) don't include anything that they might find embarrassing, even without their real names being used. Some people confided rather personal things to me — for example, problems with domestic violence — which I did not put in the book. Also, I did not relate occasions where I had socialized with coworkers. I figured that was not related to the theme of the book and was nobody's business.

RS: Were there facts or events in your experience that you left out because they didn't support the rest of your story?

BE: No. What kind of a journalist would I be if I did that? The great adventure in a project like this is that you get to learn new things, you get to be surprised. And how could I have known what the "rest of the story" would be until I'd experienced it?

RS: Did your perspective change as you became involved in this project, or did it always stay aligned with what you saw initially as your prime goal?

BE: It depends what you mean by my "perspective." I started out thinking that wages are too low and that too many Americans live in poverty — and everything I experienced reinforced that view. What I didn't know at the start was just how bad things are. For example, I had initially calculated I could live on $7 an hour, and that didn't turn out to be true. I was stunned by how expensive housing was everywhere I went.

So I started out thinking something was wrong, and I ended up being furious about just how wrong it is.

Follow-up

Were you surprised by Ehrenreich's responses? How so? What do her responses add to your understanding of the excerpt from "Serving in Florida"?

The Atlanta Exposition Address

Booker T. Washington

Born a slave in West Virginia, Booker T. Washington (1856–1915) was an influential educator and the founder of Tuskegee Normal and Industrial Institute in Alabama. After emancipation, he worked in salt mines and coal mines and then literally walked two hundred miles to attend the Hampton Institute in Virginia, which was then an industrial school for African Americans and Native Americans. There, he paid his tuition and board by working as a janitor. Graduating with honors in 1875, Washington taught at the Hampton Institute until 1881. Stressing the importance of learning a trade and developing self-confidence, Washington appealed to African Americans living in the post-Reconstruction South. He was criticized by the NAACP and other organizations for being a pragmatist who promoted accommodation rather than resistance to Southern white supremacy. He worked behind the scenes, however, to sponsor civil rights suits and advocate on behalf of Historically Black Colleges and Universities. Washington delivered the following speech in 1895 before the Cotton States and International Exposition in Atlanta to promote the economic ascendancy of the South.

Hear it on the Web: bedfordstmartins.com/languageofcomp

Mr. President and Gentlemen of the Board of Directors and Citizens.

One-third of the population of the South is of the Negro race. No enterprise seeking the material, civil, or moral welfare of this section can disregard this element of our population and reach the highest success. I but convey to you, Mr. President and Directors, the sentiment of the masses of my race when I say that in no way have the value and manhood of the American Negro been more fittingly and generously recognized than by the managers of this magnificent Exposition at every stage of its progress. It is a recognition that will do more to cement the friendship of the two races than any occurrence since the dawn of our freedom.

Not only this, but the opportunity here afforded will awaken among us a new era of industrial progress. Ignorant and inexperienced, it is not strange that in the first years of our new life we began at the top instead of at the bottom; that a seat in Congress or the state legislature was more sought than real estate or industrial skill; that the political convention of stump speaking had more attractions than starting a dairy farm or truck garden.

A ship lost at sea for many days suddenly sighted a friendly vessel. From the mast of the unfortunate vessel was seen a signal, "Water, water; we die of thirst!" The answer from the friendly vessel at once came back, "Cast down your bucket where you are." A second time the signal, "Water, water; send us water!" ran up from the distressed vessel, and was answered, "Cast down your bucket where you are." And a third and fourth signal for water was answered, "Cast down your bucket where you are." The captain of the distressed vessel, at last heeding the injunction, cast down his bucket, and it came up full of fresh, sparkling water from the mouth of the Amazon River. To those of my race who depend on bettering their condition in a foreign land or who underestimate the importance of cultivating friendly relations with the Southern white man, who is their next-door neighbour, I would say: "Cast down your bucket where you are" — cast it down in making friends in every manly way of the people of all races by whom we are surrounded.

Cast it down in agriculture, mechanics, in commerce, in domestic service, and in the professions. And in this connection it is well to bear in mind that whatever other sins the South may be called to bear, when it comes to business pure and simple, it is in the South that the Negro is given a man's chance in the commercial world, and in nothing is this Exposition more eloquent than in emphasizing this chance. Our greatest danger is that in the great leap from slavery to freedom we may overlook the fact that the masses of us are to live by the productions of our hands, and fail to keep in mind that we shall prosper in proportion as we learn to dignify and glorify common labour and put brains and skill into the common occupations of life; shall prosper in proportion as we learn to draw the line between the superficial and the substantial, the ornamental gewgaws of life and the useful. No race can prosper till it learns that there is as much dignity in tilling a field as in writing a poem. It is at the bottom of life we must begin, and not at the top. Nor should we permit our grievances to overshadow our opportunities.

To those of the white race who look to the incoming of those of foreign birth and strange tongue and habits for the prosperity of the South, were I permitted I would repeat what I say to my own race, "Cast down your bucket where you are." Cast it down among the eight millions of Negroes whose habits you know, whose fidelity and love you have tested in days when to have proved treacherous meant the ruin of your firesides. Cast down your bucket among these people who have, without strikes and labour wars, tilled your fields, cleared your forests, builded your railroads and cities, and brought forth treasures from the bowels of the earth, and helped make possible this magnificent representation of the progress of the South. Casting down your bucket among my people, helping and encouraging them as you are doing on these grounds, and to education of head, hand, and heart, you will find that they will buy your surplus land; make blossom the waste places in your fields, and run your factories. While doing, this, you can be sure in the future, as in the past, that you and your families will be surrounded by the most patient, faithful, law-abiding, and unresentful people that the world has seen. As we have proved our loyalty to you in the past, in nursing your children, watching by the sickbed of your mothers and fathers, and often following them with tear-dimmed eyes to their graves, so in the future, in our humble way, we

5

shall stand by you with a devotion that no foreigner can approach, ready to lay down our lives, if need be, in defence of yours, interlacing our industrial, commercial, civil, and religious life with yours in a way that shall make the interests of both races one. In all things that are purely social we can be as separate as the fingers, yet one as the hand in all things essential to mutual progress.

There is no defence or security for any of us except in the highest intelligence and development of all. If anywhere there are efforts tending to curtail the fullest growth of the Negro, let these efforts be turned into stimulating, encouraging, and making him the most useful and intelligent citizen. Effort or means so invested will pay a thousand per cent interest. These efforts will be twice blessed — "blessing him that gives and him that takes."

There is no escape through law of man or God from the inevitable: —

The laws of changeless justice bind
  Oppressor with oppressed;
And close as sin and suffering joined
  We march to fate abreast.

Nearly sixteen millions of hands will aid you in pulling the load upward, or they will pull against you the load downward. We shall constitute one-third and more of the ignorance and crime of the South, or one-third its intelligence and progress; we shall contribute one-third to the business and industrial prosperity of the South, or we shall prove a veritable body of death, stagnating, depressing, retarding every effort to advance the body politic.

Gentlemen of the Exposition, as we present to you our humble effort at an exhibition of our progress, you must not expect overmuch. Starting thirty years ago with ownership here and there in a few quilts and pumpkins and chickens (gathered from miscellaneous sources), remember the path that has led from these to the inventions and production of agricultural implements, buggies, steam-engines, newspapers, books, statuary, carving, paintings, the management of drug-stores and banks, has not been trodden without contact with thorns and thistles. While we take pride in what we exhibit as a result of our independent efforts, we do not for a moment forget that our part in this exhibition would fall far short of your expectations but for the constant help that has come to our educational life, not only from the Southern states, but especially from Northern philanthropists, who have made their gifts a constant stream of blessing and encouragement.

The wisest among my race understand that the agitation of questions of social equality is the extremest folly, and that progress in the enjoyment of all the privileges that will come to us must be the result of severe and constant struggle rather than of artificial forcing. No race that has anything to contribute to the markets of the world is long in any degree ostracized. It is important and right that all privileges of the law be ours, but it is vastly more important that we be prepared for the exercises of these privileges. The opportunity to earn a dollar in a factory just now is worth infinitely more than the opportunity to spend a dollar in an opera-house.

In conclusion, may I repeat that nothing in thirty years has given us more hope and encouragement, and drawn us so near to you of the white race, as this opportunity offered by the Exposition; and here bending, as it were, over the altar that represents the results of the struggles of your race and mine, both starting practically empty-handed three decades ago. I pledged that in your effort to work out the great and intricate problem which God has laid at the doors of the South, you shall have at all times the patient, sympathetic help of my race; only let this be constantly in mind, that, while from representations in these buildings of the product of field, of forest, of mine, of factory, letters, and art, much good will come, yet far above and beyond material benefits will be that higher good, that, let us pray God, will come, in a blotting out of sectional differences and racial animosities and suspicions, in a determination to administer absolute justice, in a willing obedience among all classes to the mandates of law. This, then, coupled with our material prosperity, will bring into our beloved South a new heaven and new earth.

Questions for Discussion

1. What are Booker T. Washington's goals, as articulated in this speech? What does he believe is the best way to achieve them?
2. This speech has come to be known by the sentence "Cast down your bucket where you are" (para. 3). What does Washington mean by this exhortation?
3. In what types of work does Washington want African Americans to engage?
4. How do you interpret Washington's concluding statement in paragraph 5: "In all things that are purely social we can be as separate as the fingers, yet one as the hand in all things essential to mutual progress"?
5. Discuss two possible — and contrasting — interpretations of Washington's assertion, "The opportunity to earn a dollar in a factory just now is worth infinitely more than the opportunity to spend a dollar in an opera-house" (para. 10).
6. Where in this speech does Washington implicitly argue against racial stereotypes and advocate American values of rugged individualism and a strong work ethic?
7. In the introduction to Washington's autobiography, *Up from Slavery*, Henry Louis Gates Jr. and Nellie McKay make the following observation: "To some, Washington's autobiography seems to paper over centuries of accumulated white responsibility for the evils of slavery, and instead of demanding the reform of white American institutions, it calls for African American conformity to the dominant myth of individualism in the United States. To other readers, however, Washington's message in *Up from Slavery* puts its priorities exactly where they had to be — on the necessity of self-help within the African American community" (*Norton Anthology of African American Literature*). Which view is yours? Cite specific passages to support your position.

Questions on Rhetoric and Style

1. Washington opens his speech with a simple factual statement. Why is this an effective beginning?

2. What appeals to ethos does Washington make in the opening paragraphs? What additional appeals to ethos does he make as the speech proceeds?

3. What is the point of the story Washington tells in paragraph 3 about a "ship lost at sea"? What is the rhetorical effect?

4. In paragraph 5, identify examples of parallel structure, synecdoche, periodic sentence, and analogy. Discuss the effect of these stylistic techniques.

5. Why is the biblical quotation in paragraph 6 ("'blessing him that gives and him that takes'") appropriate to the point Washington is making?

6. What is the main idea in paragraph 7?

7. What is the tone of paragraph 8? How does it set the paragraph apart from the rest of the speech?

8. What is the prevailing imagery of the final paragraph? Why do you think Washington chose to end this way?

9. Identify appeals to both logos and pathos in this speech. Which one is more prevalent? Why do you think Washington emphasized that appeal?

10. Discuss the importance of the occasion and audience of this speech. How do these factors influence its form and content?

11. In the chapter of Washington's autobiography, *Up from Slavery*, that includes this speech, Washington writes of the enthusiastic response he received, including a letter from President Grover Cleveland, who he felt "is not conscious of possessing any color prejudice." Washington continues:

    > [A]s a rule, it is only the little, narrow people who live for themselves, who never read good books, who do not travel, who never open up their souls in a way to permit them to come into contact with other souls — with the great outside world. No man whose vision is bounded by color can come into contact with what is highest and best in the world. In meeting men, in many places, I have found that the happiest people are those who do the most for others; the most miserable are those who do the least. I have also found that few things, if any, are capable of making one so blind and narrow as race prejudice. I often say to our students, in the course of my talks to them on Sunday evenings in the chapel, that the longer I live and the more experience I have of the world, the more I am convinced that, after all, the one thing that is most worth living for — and dying for, if need be — is the opportunity of making some one else more happy and more useful.

    Does the language of the speech support or undermine this reflection? Cite specific passages to illustrate your response.

12. Listen to an excerpt from this speech, the only surviving record of Washington's voice, at <http://bedfordstmartins.com/languageofcomp>. Which rhetorical techniques does hearing the speech call attention to?

Suggestions for Writing

1. In his autobiography, *Up from Slavery*, Washington writes that as he began this speech, "[T]he thing that was uppermost in my mind was the desire to say something that would cement the friendship of the races and bring about hearty cooperation between them." Write an essay in which you analyze the rhetorical strategies he uses to achieve this goal, and discuss how effective you believe he is.

2. In *The Souls of Black Folk* (1903), African American intellectual W. E. B. DuBois took Washington to task. Acknowledging that Washington "stands as the one recognized spokesman of his ten million fellows and one of the most notable figures in a nation of seventy million," DuBois criticizes him for promoting "a gospel of Work and Money to such an extent as apparently almost completely to overshadow the higher aims of life." Read this chapter at <bedfordstmartins.com/languageofcomp>, and then explain whether you agree with Washington or DuBois.

3. The poem "Booker T. and W.E.B." (1969) by Dudley Randall captures and comments on the debate between Washington and W. E. B. DuBois. Write an essay (1) analyzing the way in which Randall frames the debate and (2) discussing with whom the speaker is more sympathetic. The poem can be found at <bedfordstmartins.com/languageofcomp>.

4. Do you think Washington was visionary or misguided in his emphasis on what has come to be known as vocational education or job training? As you write your response, consider the increasing interest in many high schools in training programs and internships that emphasize preparation for specific jobs in business and industry (such as construction, electronics, and the hospitality industry) rather than preparation for college only.

5. Write a letter (or e-mail) to Washington in the persona of a prominent contemporary African American, pointing out how Washington's values and strategies were right for his day and how they were wrong. Consider using a persona such as Condoleeza Rice, Barack Obama, Bill Cosby, or Oprah Winfrey.

The Surgeon as Priest

Richard Selzer

Born in 1928, Richard Selzer is both an accomplished surgeon and a writer. He earned his MD at Albany Medical College, completed an internship and residency at Yale University, and continued as a faculty member there until 1985 while also practicing medicine. His writing career began with *Rituals of Surgery* (1974), a collection of short stories. He went on to publish numerous essays and stories in magazines and collected his essays in *Mortal Lessons: Notes on the Art of Surgery* (1977) and *Confessions of a Knife* (1979). In 1990, he published *Imagine a Woman*, a collection of novellas, and *A Mile and a Half of Ink*, a journal. Selzer documented his recovery from Legionnaires' disease in *Raising the Dead: A Doctor's Encounter with His Own Mortality* (1994). He is the recipient of numerous honors, including an American Medical Writers Association award and a Guggenheim Fellowship. In the following essay from *Mortal Lessons*, Selzer reflects on the spiritual link between physicians and "healers."

In the foyer of a great medical school there hangs a painting of Vesalius. Lean, ascetic, possessed, the anatomist stands before a dissecting table upon which lies the naked body of a man. The flesh of the two is silvery. A concentration of moonlight, like a strange rain of virus, washes them. The cadaver has dignity and reserve; it is distanced by its death. Vesalius reaches for his dissecting knife. As he does so, he glances over his shoulder at a crucifix on the wall. His face wears an expression of guilt and melancholy and fear. He knows that there is something wrong, forbidden in what he is about to do, but he cannot help himself, for he is a fanatic. He is driven by a dark desire. To see, to feel, to discover is all. His is a passion, not a romance.

I understand you, Vesalius. Even now, after so many voyages within, so much exploration, I feel the same sense that one must not gaze into the body, the same irrational fear that it is an evil deed for which punishment awaits. Consider. The sight of our internal organs is denied us. To how many men is it given to look upon their own spleens, their hearts, and live? The hidden geography of the body is a Medusa's head, one glimpse of which would render blind the presumptuous eye. Still, rigid rules are broken by the smallest inadvertencies: I pause in the midst of an operation being performed under spinal anesthesia to observe the face of my patient, to speak a word or two of reassurance. I peer above the screen separating his head from his abdomen, in which I am most deeply employed. He is not asleep, but rather stares straight upward, his attention riveted, a look of terrible discovery, of wonder upon his face. Watch him. This man is violating a taboo. I follow his gaze upward, and see in the great operating lamp suspended above his belly the reflection of his viscera. There is the liver, dark and turgid above, there the loops of his bowel winding slow, there his blood runs extravagantly. It is that which he sees and studies with so much horror and fascination. Something primordial in him has been aroused — a fright, a longing. I feel it, too, and quickly bend above his open body to shield it from his view. How dare he look within the Ark! Cover his eyes! But it is too late; he has already *seen*; that which no man should; he has trespassed. And I am no longer a surgeon, but a hierophant who must do magic to ward off the punishment of the angry gods.

I feel some hesitation to invite you to come with me into the body. It seems a reckless, defiant act. Yet there is more than dread reflected from these rosy coasts, these restless estuaries of pearl. And it is time to share it, the way the catbird shares the song which must be a joy to him and is a living truth to those who hear it. So shall I make of my fingers, words; of my scalpel, a sentence; of the body of my patient, a story.

One enters the body in surgery, as in love, as though one were an exile returning at last to his hearth, daring uncharted darkness in order to reach home. Turn sideways, if you will, and slip with me into the cleft I have made. Do not fear the yellow meadows of fat, the red that sweats and trickles where you step. Here, give me your hand. Lower between the beefy cliffs. Now rest a bit upon the peritoneum. All at once, gleaming, the membrane parts . . . and you are *in*.

It is the stillest place that ever was. As though suddenly you are struck deaf.   5
Why, when the blood sluices fierce as Niagara, when the brain teems with electricity, and the numberless cells exchange their goods in ceaseless commerce — why is it so quiet? Has some priest in charge of these rites uttered the command "Silence"? This is no silence of the vacant stratosphere, but the awful quiet of ruins, of rainbows, full of expectation and holy dread. Soon you shall know surgery as a Mass served with Body and Blood, wherein disease is assailed as though it were sin.

Touch the great artery. Feel it bound like a deer in the might of its lightness, and know the thunderless boil of the blood. Lean for a bit against this bone. It is the only memento you will leave to the earth. Its tacitness is everlasting. In the hush of the tissue wait with me for the shaft of pronouncement. Press your ear against his body, the way you did as a child holding a seashell and heard faintly the half-remembered, longed-for sea. Now strain to listen *past* the silence. In the canals, cilia paddle quiet as an Iroquois canoe. Somewhere nearby a white whip-slide of tendon bows across a joint. Fire burns here but does not crackle. Again, listen. Now there *is* sound — small splashings, tunneled currents of air, slow gaseous bubbles ascend through dark, unlit lakes. Across the diaphragm and into the chest . . . here at last it is all noise; the whisper of the lungs, the *lubdup, lubdup* of the garrulous heart.

But it is good you do not hear the machinery of your marrow lest it madden like the buzzing of a thousand coppery bees. It is frightening to lie with your ear in the pillow, and hear the beating of your heart. Not that it beats . . . but that it might stop, even as you listen. For anything that moves must come to rest, no rhythm is endless but must one day lurch . . . then halt. Not that it is a disservice to a man to be made mindful of his death, but . . . at three o'clock in the morning it is less than philosophy. It is Fantasy, replete with dreadful images forming in the smoke of alabaster crematoria. It is then that one thinks of the bristlecone pines, and envies them for having lasted. It is their slowness, I think. Slow down, heart, and drub on.

What is to one man a coincidence is to another a miracle. It was one or the other of these that I saw last spring. While the rest of nature was in flux, Joe Riker remained obstinate through the change of seasons. "No operation," said Joe. "I don't want no operation."

Joe Riker is a short-order cook in a diner where I sometimes drink coffee. Each week for six months he had paid a visit to my office, carrying his affliction like a pet mouse under his hat. Every Thursday at four o'clock he would sit on my examining table, lift the fedora from his head, and bend forward to show me the hole. Joe Riker's hole was as big as his mouth. You could have dropped a plum in it. Gouged from the tonsured top of his head was a mucky puddle whose meaty heaped edge rose above the normal scalp about it. There was no mistaking the announcement from this rampart.

The cancer had chewed through Joe's scalp, munched his skull, then opened   10
the membranes underneath — the dura mater, the pia mater, the arachnoid — until it had laid bare this short-order cook's brain, pink and gray, and pulsating so that with each beat a little pool of cerebral fluid quivered. Now and then a drop would manage the rim to run across his balding head, and Joe would reach one burry hand up to wipe it away, with the heel of his thumb, the way such a man would wipe away a tear.

I would gaze then upon Joe Riker and marvel. How dignified he was, as though that tumor, gnawing him, denuding his very brain, had given him a grace that a lifetime of good health had not bestowed.

"Joe," I say, "let's get rid of it. Cut out the bad part, put in a metal plate, and you're cured." And I wait.

"No operation," says Joe. I try again.

"What do you mean, 'no operation'? You're going to get meningitis. Any day now. And die. That thing is going to get to your brain."

I think of it devouring the man's dreams and memories. I wonder what they   15
are. The surgeon knows all the parts of the brain, but he does not know his patient's dreams and memories. And for a moment I am tempted . . . to take the man's head in my hands, hold it to my ear, and listen. But his dreams are none of my business. It is his flesh that matters.

"No operation," says Joe.

"You give me a headache," I say. And we smile, not because the joke is funny anymore, but because we've got something between us, like a secret.

"Same time next week?" Joe asks. I wash out the wound with peroxide, and apply a dressing. He lowers the fedora over it.

"Yes," I say, "same time." And the next week he comes again.

There came the week when Joe Riker did not show up; nor did he the week [20] after that, nor for a whole month. I drive over to his diner. He is behind the counter, shuffling back and forth between the grill and the sink. He is wearing the fedora. He sets a cup of coffee in front of me.

"I want to see your hole," I say.

"Which one?" he asks, and winks.

"Never mind that," I say. "I want to see it." I am all business.

"Not here," says Joe. He looks around, checking the counter, as though I have made an indecent suggestion.

"My office at four o'clock," I say. [25]

"Yeah," says Joe, and turns away.

He is late. Everyone else has gone for the day. Joe is beginning to make me angry. At last he arrives.

"Take off your hat," I say, and he knows by my voice that I am not happy. He does, though, raise it straight up with both hands the way he always does, and I see . . . that the wound has healed. Where once there had been a bitten-out excavation, moist and shaggy, there is now a fragile bridge of shiny new skin.

"What happened?" I manage.

"You mean that?" He points to the top of his head. "Oh well," he says, "the [30] wife's sister, she went to France, and brought me a bottle of water from Lourdes. I've been washing it out with that for a month."

"Holy water?" I say.

"Yeah," says Joe. "Holy water."

I see Joe now and then at the diner. He looks like anything but a fleshly garden of miracles. Rather, he has taken on a terrible ordinariness — Eden after the Fall, and minus its most beautiful creatures. There is a certain slovenliness, a dishevelment of the tissues. Did the disease ennoble him, and now that it is gone, is he somehow diminished? Perhaps I am wrong. Perhaps the only change is just the sly wink with which he greets me, as though to signal that we have shared something furtive. Could such a man, I think as I sip my coffee, could such a man have felt the brush of wings? How often it seems that the glory leaves as soon as the wound is healed. But then it is only saints who bloom in martyrdom, becoming less and less the flesh that pains, more and more ghost-colored weightlessness.

It was many years between my first sight of the living human brain and Joe Riker's windowing. I had thought then, long ago: Could this one-pound loaf of sourdough be the pelting brain? *This*, along whose busy circuitry run Reason and Madness in perpetual race — a race that most often ends in a tie? But the look deceives. What seems a fattish snail drowsing in its shell, in fact lives in quickness, where all is dart and stir and rapids of electricity.

Once again to the operating room . . . [35]

How to cut a paste that is less solid than a cheese — Brie, perhaps? And not waste any of it? For that would be a decade of remembrances and wishes lost there, wiped from the knife. Mostly it is done with cautery, burning the margins of the piece to be removed, coagulating with the fine electric current these blood vessels that course everywhere. First a spot is burned, then another alongside the first, and the cut is made between. One does not stitch — one cannot sew custard. Blood is blotted with little squares of absorbent gauze. These are called patties. Through each of these a long black thread has been sewn, lest a blood-soaked patty slip into some remote fissure, or flatten against a gyrus like a starfish against a coral reef, and go unnoticed come time to close the incision. A patty abandoned brainside does not benefit the health, or improve the climate of the intelligence. Like the bodies of slain warriors, they must be retrieved from the field, and carried home, so they do not bloat and mortify, poisoning forever the plain upon which the battle was fought. One pulls them out by their black thread and counts them.

Listen to the neurosurgeon: "Patty, buzz, suck, cut," he says. Then "Suck, cut, patty, buzz." It is as simple as a nursery rhyme.

The surgeon knows the landscape of the brain, yet does not know how a thought is made. Man has grown envious of this mystery. He would master and subdue it electronically. He would construct a computer to rival or surpass the brain. He would harness Europa's bull to a plow. There are men who implant electrodes into the brain, that part where anger is kept — the rage center, they call it. They press a button, and a furious bull halts in mid-charge, and lopes amiably to nuzzle his matador. Anger has turned to sweet compliance. Others sever whole tracts of brain cells with their knives, to mollify the insane. Here is surgery grown violent as rape. These men cannot know the brain. They have not the heart for it.

I last saw the brain in the emergency room. I wiped it from the shoulder of a young girl to make her smashed body more presentable to her father. Now I stand with him by the stretcher. We are arm in arm, like brothers. All at once there is that terrible silence of discovery. I glance at him, follow his gaze and see that there is more brain upon her shoulder, newly slipped from the cracked skull. He bends forward a bit. He must make certain. It *is* her brain! I watch the knowledge expand upon his face, so like hers. I, too, stare at the fragment flung wetly, now drying beneath the bright lights of the emergency room, its cargo of thoughts evaporating from it, mingling for this little time with his, with mine, before dispersing in the air.

On the east coast of the Argolid, in the northern part of the Peloponnesus, lies Epidaurus. O bury my heart there, in that place I have never seen, but that I love as a farmer loves his home soil. In a valley nearby, in the fourth century B.C., there was built the temple of Asclepius, the god of medicine. To a great open colonnaded room, the abaton, came the sick from all over Greece. Here they lay down on pallets. As night fell, the priests, bearing fire for the lamps, walked among them, commanding them to sleep. They were told to dream of the god, and that he would come to them in their sleep in the form of a serpent, and that he would heal them. In the morning they arose cured. . . .

Walk the length of the abaton; the sick are in their places, each upon his pallet. Here is one that cannot sleep. See how his breath rises and falls against some burden that presses upon it. At last, he dozes, only to awaken minutes later, unrefreshed. It is toward dawn. The night lamps flicker low, casting snaky patterns across the colonnade. Already the chattering swallows swoop in and our among the pillars. All at once the fitful eyes of the man cease their roving, for he sees between the candle-lamp and the wall the shadow of an upraised serpent, a great yellow snake with topaz eyes. It slides closer. It is arched and godlike. It bends above him, swaying, the tongue and the lamplight flickering as one. Exultant, he raises himself upon one arm, and with the other, reaches out for the touch that heals.

On the bulletin board in the front hall of the hospital where I work, there appeared an announcement. "Yeshi Dhonden," it read, "will make rounds at six o'clock on the morning of June 10." The particulars were then given, followed by a notation: "Yeshi Dhonden is Personal Physician to the Dalai Lama." I am not so leathery a skeptic that I would knowingly ignore an emissary from the gods. Not only might such sangfroid be inimical to one's earthly well-being, it could take care of eternity as well. Thus, on the morning of June 10, I join the clutch of whitecoats waiting in the small conference room adjacent to the ward selected for the rounds. The air in the room is heavy with ill-concealed dubiety and suspicion of bamboozlement. At precisely six o'clock, he materializes, a short, golden, barrelly man dressed in a sleeveless robe of saffron and maroon. His scalp is shaven, and the only visible hair is a scanty black line above each hooded eye.

He bows in greeting while his young interpreter makes the introduction. Yeshi Dhonden, we are told, will examine a patient selected by a member of the staff. The diagnosis is as unknown to Yeshi Dhonden as it is to us. The examination of the patient will take place in our presence, after which we will reconvene in the conference room where Yeshi Dhonden will discuss the case. We are further informed that for the past two hours Yeshi Dhonden has purified himself by bathing, fasting, and prayer. I, having breakfasted well, performed only the most desultory of ablutions, and given no thought at all to my soul, glance furtively at my fellows. Suddenly, we seem a soiled, uncouth lot.

The patient had been awakened early and told that she was to be examined by a foreign doctor, and had been asked to produce a fresh specimen of urine, so when we enter her room, the woman shows no surprise. She has long ago taken on that mixture of compliance and resignation that is the facies of chronic illness. This was to be but another in an endless series of tests and examinations. Yeshi Dhonden steps to the bedside while the rest stand apart, watching. For a long time he gazes at the woman, favoring no part of her body with his eyes, but seeming to fix his glance at a place just above her supine form. I, too, study her. No physical sign nor obvious symptom gives a clue to the nature of her disease.

At last he takes her hand, raising it in both of his own. Now he bends over the bed in a kind of crouching stance, his head drawn down into the collar of his 45 robe. His eyes are closed as he feels for her pulse. In a moment he has found the spot, and for the next half hour he remains thus, suspended above the patient like some exotic golden bird with folded wings, holding the pulse of the woman beneath his fingers, cradling her hand in his. All the power of the man seems to have been drawn down into this one purpose. It is palpation of the pulse raised to the state of ritual. From the foot of the bed, where I stand, it is as though he and the patient have entered a special place of isolation, of apartness, about which a vacancy hovers, and across which no violation is possible. After a moment the woman rests back upon her pillow. From time to time, she raises her head to look at the strange figure above her, then sinks back once more. I cannot see their hands joined in a correspondence that is exclusive, intimate, his fingertips receiving the voice of her sick body through the rhythm and throb she offers at her wrist. All at once I am envious — not of him, not of Yeshi Dhonden for his gift of beauty and holiness, but of her. I want to be held like that, touched so, *received*. And I know that I, who have palpated a hundred thousand pulses, have not felt a single one.

At last Yeshi Dhonden straightens, gently places the woman's hand upon the bed, and steps back. The interpreter produces a small wooden bowl and two sticks. Yeshi Dhonden pours a small portion of the urine specimen into the bowl, and proceeds to whip the liquid with the two sticks. This he does for several minutes until a foam is raised. Then, bowing above the bowl, he inhales the odor three times. He sets down the bowl and turns to leave. All this while, he has not uttered a single word. As he nears the door, the woman raises her head and calls out to him in a voice at once urgent and serene. "Thank you, doctor," she says, and touches with her other hand the place he had held on her wrist, as though to recapture something that had visited there. Yeshi Dhonden turns back for a moment to gaze at her, then steps into the corridor. Rounds are at an end.

We are seated once more in the conference room. Yeshi Dhonden speaks now for the first time, in soft Tibetan sounds that I have never heard before. He has barely begun when the young interpreter begins to translate, the two voices continuing in tandem — a bilingual fugue, the one chasing the other. It is like the chanting of monks. He speaks of winds coursing through the body of the woman, currents that break against barriers, eddying. These vortices are in her blood, he says. The last spendings of an imperfect heart. Between the chambers of her heart, long, long before she was born, a wind had come and blown open a deep gate that must never be opened. Through it charge the full waters of her river, as the mountain stream cascades in the springtime, battering, knocking loose the land, and flooding her breath. Thus he speaks, and is silent.

"May we now have the diagnosis?" a professor asks.

The host of these rounds, the man who knows, answers.

"Congenital heart disease," he says. "Interventricular septal defect, with resultant heart failure." 50

A gateway in the heart, I think. That must not be opened. Through it charge the full waters that flood her breath. So! Here then is the doctor listening to the sounds of the body to which the rest of us are deaf. He is more than doctor. He is priest.

I know . . . I know . . . the doctor to the gods is pure knowledge, pure healing. The doctor to man stumbles, must often wound; his patient must die, as must he.

Now and then it happens, as I make my own rounds, that I hear the sounds of his voice, like an ancient Buddhist prayer, its meaning long since forgotten, only the music remaining. Then a jubilation possesses me, and I feel myself touched by something divine.

Exploring the Text

1. Do you agree with Richard Selzer's metaphor that the job of being a surgeon is tantamount to a religious calling? Why or why not?

2. Why does Selzer open the essay by invoking Vesalius, a sixteenth-century Belgian physician whose seven-volume work, *On the Structure of the Human Body*, is credited with laying the foundation for modern anatomical science? If you did not have that biographical information, would the allusion still work rhetorically?

3. What does Selzer mean when he states, "And I am no longer a surgeon, but a hierophant who must do magic to ward off the punishment of the angry gods" (para. 2)? Is this as a literal statement or hyperbole?

4. What is your response to the metaphor in paragraph 5: "Soon you shall know surgery as a Mass served with Body and Blood, wherein disease is assailed as though it were sin"? What suggestions does Selzer make by creating that metaphor?

5. What is Selzer's purpose in telling the story of Joe Riker (paras. 8–34)? Why does he present this example through elements of fiction, including dialogue and description?

6. What is Selzer's original attitude toward Yeshi Dhonden (para. 42)? Does it change? If so, how? Cite specific passages.

7. Selzer is known for fusing subjective poetic images with precise technical details. Identify two or three passages that illustrate this fusion, and discuss the impact of bringing together two different types of descriptions.

8. This essay is divided into five sections. How do they work together so that the whole is greater than the sum of its five parts? Pay particular attention to the short (two-paragraph) fourth section; what effect would eliminating it have? How would you describe the overall organization of this essay?

9. Critics have called this essay risky for two reasons. First, some readers object to visualizing the medical details that Selzer describes. Second, some see his framing surgery as religious ritual to be exaggeration. How valid do you find these two criticisms in view of what you see as Selzer's purpose in this essay?

The Traveling Bra Salesman's Lesson

Claudia O'Keefe

Claudia O'Keefe (b. 1958) lives in Frankford, West Virginia, and is the author of several novels and short stories, primarily science fiction. She has edited several collections, including *Mother: Famous Writers Celebrate Motherhood with a Treasury of Short Stories, Essays, and Poems* (1996), *Forever Sisters: Famous Writers Celebrate the Power of Sisterhood with Short Stories, Essays, and Memoirs* (1999), and *Father: Famous Writers Celebrate the Bond between Father and Child* (2000). The following essay won first prize from among nearly twenty-five hundred entries in a competition sponsored by the *Economist* and the Shell Oil Company on the topic "Import workers or export jobs?"

It's a little after 10 A.M. at a 20-vehicle flea market in rural West Virginia. I'm getting worried. I haven't sold enough merchandise to pay for my $7 space fee and I didn't have any money to bring with me, not even to make change. I reach into a carton of vintage clothing to mark down my prices. My fingers grasp something silky and slippery, a lacy slip Elizabeth Taylor could have worn in *Cat on a Hot Tin Roof*. Instead of the thin, cheesy polyester and shoddy workmanship I'm used to seeing in contemporary lingerie from the same manufacturer, the older slip features quality fabric and lace that is not only sewn on straight, but will survive a hundred washings and remain looking near new.

This isn't what I notice first, however. It's the original price tag from 1966. I'm amazed because 38 years later I can still decipher the sales codes printed on it, codes which were on the thousands of tags exactly like it and part of my first paying job, given to me when I was eight years old.

The Good Life

My stepfather was a salesman during the 1960s, traveling California and the American southwest in his big, hulking Buick, selling bras, slips, and girdles to small department stores and five-and-dimes. Whenever he returned from one of his two-week trips, he brought several lunch sacks full of torn price tags with him, evidence of product sold. My job was to sort and count the tags, at a nickel for every hundred I recorded.

We lived in a three-bedroom home in an upscale Los Angeles suburb, owned two cars, and took annual vacations. My brother, sister, and I never lacked any of the benefits of a middle-class upbringing, a new school wardrobe each year, copious Christmas presents, private lessons, even horses when we were older. In a medical emergency we worried more about how to get to a doctor quickly than we did about paying the bill. All of this was affordable on my dad's one sales job without incurring vast amounts of debt.

These days the same lingerie lines my dad marketed are now sold primarily in Wal-Mart. Instead of being crafted in the U.S.A. by American workers they are manufactured almost exclusively in China. Gone are the traveling salesmen who ferried clothing to small-town variety stores across the nation, and their buyers who used to decide which lines to stock. Most of the old independent retailers no longer exist. A handful of chains have replaced them, with buying decisions made at the corporate level. Jobs which comfortably supported a family have been eliminated in favor of new ones paying so little employees are encouraged to apply for food stamps.

I have more in common today with the minimum-wage employees at my local supercenter, than my dad in his Buick cruising Route 66 with a trunk full of bras. Why? I'm currently stuck living in job-poor West Virginia. With the exception of the occasional social worker position advertised at $19K a year, the positions listed in my local paper pay $6 or less per hour. When I held one of the area's top professional jobs, as a 70-hour-per-week PR director for an arts organization, I earned just $1103 each month after taxes, no health insurance, no benefits. I understand too well the desire of unemployed and low-wage workers throughout the world who will make any sacrifice necessary, even to the point of moving some place where they are resented and vilified, in order to find work. I sympathize with the talented and skilled employees in India and Russia who are currently gobbling up my country's offshored tech jobs. Given these nations' past and current struggles with poverty or economic turmoil, I would do exactly as they are doing.

Unfortunately, few companies want to outsource quality jobs to West Virginia. Though I've spent the last two years trying to put together the $3,000 necessary to move myself and my mother, *Grapes of Wrath*–style, to another state with decent employment, I can't even manage to keep our utilities and rent current.

Feeling isolated here, I've looked outward for answers and become a financial news junkie. I comb each new statistic, wait just as eagerly for the U.S. monthly payroll report as I would if I owned stock. I take it all in, the arguments for and against free trade, the fears of those who feel the exportation of jobs will lead to a "race to the bottom," where America loses superpower status and becomes a third-world nation. I watch corporate spokespeople madly spinning their version of outsourcing's benefits, cheaper prices and increased jobs at home. I note Alan Greenspan's testimony suggesting that displaced workers must retrain themselves for the new jobs which will appear on the horizon to replace ones lost and unlikely to return. None who support this belief, however, can offer a list of the positions for which the jobless should school themselves. I sit in front of the TV where verbal combatants are engaged in a heated exchange over immigration reform. Should we be more compassionate, open our borders wider to financially depressed people willing to fill all those jobs Americans don't want? Or do we need a 50-foot razor-wire fence to protect native-born and naturalized citizens from the downward pressure on wages caused by tides of illegal aliens crossing into the U.S.?

I suck in as much information as I can take before crying uncle, the attack dog political ads about job creation, the surveys and polls and yelling and screaming from experts and average Americans alike.

Two realities stand out from all the rest. 10

Moving On

Geography can no longer prevent jobs in developed regions such as North America and Europe from migrating to cheaper, emerging markets. The outsourcing jet has already left the terminal, cleared international airspace, and has enough fuel onboard to reach the far ends of the earth nonstop.

Meanwhile, those workers whose jobs have fled are crowding into that empty terminal, clamoring for protections against what they perceive as theft. They see a worker in China being paid pennies for a job that use to guarantee a nice middle-class life for their families and they're so frustrated they don't know which they want to do more, cry or shoot something, preferably a politician. They may cry, but thankfully they don't shoot. Instead they pour every ounce of their attention into complaining to those same politicians, charging them with an impossible task, returning things to the way they were.

I know firsthand the dangers of refusing to let go of the past. A decade ago I was a published writer with a promising career in fiction. Fiction publishing at that time was in the midst of a corporate sea change devastating to authors of the type of books I wrote. Not only wasn't pay increasing, fewer and fewer books were being bought. Not wanting to give up a career that was my whole life, I sought to adjust to my shrinking income by progressively relocating to areas of the country with cheaper and cheaper costs of living. I moved from pricey California to a slightly less expensive northern New Mexico to Florida, rural Virginia, and finally, with my money gone, any momentum I'd once had long expended, and all contacts evaporated, I came to a disgruntled rest four years ago in West Virginia.

Similar to my experience with publishing, Americans who have lost their jobs since January 2001 are having to adjust to the idea that the next one they find is likely to involve a pay cut. According to the U.S. Labor Department, 57 percent of those workers who found re-employment earned less than they did at their old jobs. One third took a cut of 20 percent or more in order to be employed.

What happens if, as several studies suggest, outsourcing continues to ramp 15 up and those same workers are thrown on the street once more? Will their next job pay even less? Could scores of computer programmers, financial analysts, and paralegals end up like my West Virginia neighbors, huddled around a card table in a supercenter break room, using a Styrofoam cup for an ashtray while they grouse about their lives?

Back in the 1970s, my stepfather saw his career as a traveling bra salesman coming to an end. Though he adored the freedom of the open road, he didn't balk. He mourned and moved on. He studied for a real estate license and found a new life as a highly successful broker.

A New Dream

The question is not whether it is good or bad to import workers or export jobs. The problem is that society has hit an emotional road block. My country is one tremendously divided, with pro-business and pro-worker stubbornly pitted against each other. We're anxious. We're angry. Neither side wants to give and nothing can be solved until we acknowledge one crucial fact.

The past is dust. Those mythic decades, during which The American Dream was considered to be our natural right, are over. We need to wake from our state of denial, accept this golden era's passing, and get on with life. Once we agree that the past cannot be recaptured, we will at last open ourselves to solutions we haven't yet considered, to business and immigration models which are still waiting to be invented. Working as willing participants of change, we will devise ways to keep businesses from discarding employees like so much surplus machinery, while making certain there is profit for all. Ingenuity will be given free reign and the synergies we so badly need to solve this international crisis can finally come together.

Standing in that West Virginia flea market, I look at the vintage, never-worn slip in my hands. Back in my home state of California, at the Rose Bowl Flea Market, it would fetch $35 or more. Here, I'll have to price it at $1. In fact while I'm doing this, a woman approaches me.

"How much?" she asks.

I tell her, while pointing out that the slip is in mint condition and of a superior quality to comparable ones made today.

"Will you take a quarter?" she asks.

Hurry, I urge my country. Before it's too late. Only when we admit that the future awaits us can we embrace a more inclusive and thrilling successor to outmoded twentieth-century ideals, a goal without boundaries or limits, not The American Dream, but The Global Dream.

20

Exploring the Text

1. Claudia O'Keefe frames the essay with a scene in a flea market in West Virginia. Why does she employ this rhetorical strategy? How does she prevent this autobiographical scene from making her essay seem subjective or overly personal?

2. Where in the essay does O'Keefe begin appealing to logos? What elements of hard data or other quantitative information does she include? Cite specific instances.

3. How does O'Keefe establish her ethos within the first several paragraphs? How would you describe that ethos?

4. O'Keefe is careful not to sound xenophobic or to be overly critical of workers in other countries. How does she do this? Cite specific passages where she describes or refer to these workers. What is her attitude toward them?

5. Find examples of the following in this essay, and discuss the effect of each: metaphor, rhetorical question, cumulative sentence, short simple sentence, informal diction.

6. Where does O'Keefe address counterargument(s)? Does she concede or refute them?

7. What does O'Keefe mean when she says, "The past is dust" (para. 18)? Explain why you agree or disagree with her.

8. In a sentence or two, state in your own words what O'Keefe's answer is to the topic, "Import workers or export jobs?"

9. Identify a section or passage of this essay where O'Keefe combines appeals to both emotion and reason. Explain how she does so, and discuss the effect.

10. How would you describe O'Keefe's tone in this essay? Cite specific passages to support your description.

From *Labour*

Thomas Carlyle

Thomas Carlyle (1795–1881) was one of the preeminent figures of the Victorian era. Born in Scotland, he attended the University of Edinburgh. Carlyle is known as a rigorous thinker and vivid stylist. His *Sartor Resartus* (1833–1834) was especially influential on American transcendentalists Ralph Waldo Emerson and Henry David Thoreau. In fact, Carlyle exerted an influence on a number of notable Victorian thinkers, including John Stuart Mill, John Ruskin, and Charles Dickens, who dedicated his novel *Hard Times* to Carlyle. Among Carlyle's best-known works are *Chartism* (1840) and *Past and Present* (1843). Both works explain Carlyle's opposition to the industrial society beginning to emerge in Britain. In *Past and Present*, he extols the virtues of the past and warns against the loss of spiritual connection and community in an increasingly urban, capitalistic society. In addition to this loss, Carlyle claims, a changed attitude toward work was manifesting itself, as he discusses in this excerpt from the chapter Labour.

For there is a perennial nobleness, and even sacredness, in Work. Were he never so benighted, forgetful of his high calling, there is always hope in a man that actually and earnestly works: in Idleness alone is there perpetual despair. Work, never so Mammonish, mean, is in communication with Nature;

the real desire to get Work done will itself lead one more and more to truth, to Nature's appointments and regulations, which are truth.

The latest Gospel in this world is, Know thy work and do it. "Know thyself": long enough has that poor "self" of thine tormented thee; thou wilt never get to "know" it, I believe! Think it not thy business, this of knowing thyself; thou art an unknowable individual: know what thou canst work at; and work at it, like a Hercules! That will be thy better plan.

It has been written, "an endless significance lies in Work"; a man perfects himself by working. Foul jungles are cleared away, fair seedfields rise instead, and stately cities; and withal the man himself first ceases to be a jungle and foul unwholesome desert thereby. Consider how, even in the meanest sorts of Labour, the whole soul of a man is composed into a kind of real harmony, the instant he sets himself to work! Doubt, Desire, Sorrow, Remorse, Indignation, Despair itself, all these like helldogs lie beleaguering the soul of the poor dayworker, as of every man: but he bends himself with free valour against his task, and all these are stilled, all these shrink murmuring far off into their caves. The man is now a man. The blessed glow of Labour in him, is it not as purifying fire, wherein all poison is burnt up, and of sour smoke itself there is made bright blessed flame!

Destiny, on the whole, has no other way of cultivating us. A formless Chaos, once set it revolving, grows round and ever rounder; ranges itself, by mere force of gravity, into strata, spherical courses; is no longer a Chaos, but a round compacted World. What would become of the Earth, did she cease to revolve? In the poor old Earth, so long as she revolves, all inequalities, irregularities disperse themselves; all irregularities are incessantly becoming regular. Hast thou looked on the Potter's wheel, — one of the venerablest objects; old as the Prophet Ezechiel and far older? Rude lumps of clay, how they spin themselves up, by mere quick whirling, into beautiful circular dishes. And fancy the most assiduous Potter, but without his wheel; reduced to make dishes, or rather amorphous botches, by mere kneading and baking! Even such a Potter were Destiny, with a human soul that would rest and lie at ease, that would not work and spin! Of an idle unrevolving man the kindest Destiny, like the most assiduous Potter without wheel, can bake and knead nothing other than a botch; let her spend on him what expensive colouring, what gilding and enamelling she will, he is but a botch. Not a dish; no, a bulging, kneaded, crooked, shambling, squint-cornered, amorphous botch, — a mere enamelled vessel of dishonour! Let the idle think of this.

Blessed is he who has found his work; let him ask no other blessedness. He ⁵ has a work, a life-purpose; he has found it, and will follow it! How, as a freeflowing channel, dug and torn by noble force through the sour mud-swamp of one's existence, like an ever-deepening river there, it runs and flows; — draining off the sour festering water, gradually from the root of the remotest grass-blade; making, instead of pestilential swamp, a green fruitful meadow with its clearflowing stream. How blessed for the meadow itself, let the stream and its value be great or small! Labour is Life: from the inmost heart of the Worker rises his god-given Force, the sacred celestial Life-essence breathed into him by Almighty God; from his inmost heart awakens him to all nobleness, — to all knowledge, "self-knowledge" and much else, so soon as Work fitly begins. Knowledge? The knowledge that will hold good in working, cleave thou to that; for Nature herself accredits that, says Yea to that. Properly thou hast no other knowledge but what thou hast got by working: the rest is yet all a hypothesis of knowledge; a thing to be argued of in schools, a thing floating in the clouds, in endless logic-vortices, till we try it and fix it. "Doubt, of whatever kind, can be ended by Action alone."

Exploring the Text

1. What is Thomas Carlyle's definition of *work*? Does Carlyle define *work* more narrowly or more broadly than we usually do today?
2. Discuss why you agree or disagree with Carlyle's opening assertion that "there is a perennial nobleness, and even sacredness, in Work." Do you believe that this statement applies more logically to certain professions, such as artistic or service ones? Does it matter to Carlyle what type of work a person does?
3. In the opening paragraph, Carlyle establishes that true work is a means to an end. Explain the logic that leads to his conclusion that work is both noble and sacred. Pay attention to Carlyle's assumptions.
4. What is Carlyle's point in paragraph 2? How is he adding to his definition of work?
5. Discuss the appeals to pathos in paragraph 3. Pay particular attention to connotation, imagery, and figurative language.
6. In paragraph 4, Carlyle develops an extended metaphor about the "Potter's wheel" and destiny. Explain the figure and its effect.
7. Carlyle ends paragraph 4 with the admonition, "Let the idle think of this." What is his point? Why is that short, imperative sentence an effective way to make the point?
8. Identify the following rhetorical strategies in paragraph 5, and explain their effect: emotional language, sentence variety and pacing, analogy, rhetorical question, and personification.
9. Why, according to Carlyle, is "every noble work . . . at first 'impossible'"?
10. How would you describe Carlyle's tone in this excerpt? Cite specific passages to support your position.
11. In what ways is Carlyle's thinking utopian?

From *The Writing Life*

ANNIE DILLARD

In 1975, when she was twenty-nine, Annie Dillard won the Pulitzer Prize for *Pilgrim at Tinker Creek* (1974). Written in the tradition of Henry David Thoreau's *Walden* (the subject of Dillard's MA thesis), *Pilgrim* established her as a contemporary nature writer and philosopher. She is known for her metaphysical leaps, beginning with meticulous description of natural phenomena and expanding into spiritual musings. Dillard, formerly a professor of English and writer-in-residence at Wesleyan University in Connecticut, is also the author of many books, including *An American Childhood* (1987), an autobiography; *The Writing Life* (1989); and *For the Time Being* (1999). This chapter from *The Writing Life*, often called "The Stunt Pilot," explores what it means when work becomes art.

Dave Rahm lived in Bellingham, Washington, north of Seattle. Bellingham, a harbor town, lies between the San Juan Islands in Haro Strait and the alpine North Cascade Mountains. I lived there between stints on the island. Dave Rahm was a stunt pilot, the air's own genius.

In 1975, with a newcomer's willingness to try anything once, I attended the Bellingham Air Show. The Bellingham airport was a wide clearing in a forest of tall Douglas firs; its runways suited small planes. It was June. People wearing blue or tan zipped jackets stood loosely on the concrete walkways and runways outside the coffee shop. At that latitude in June, you stayed outside because you could, even most of the night, if you could think up something to do. The sky did not darken until ten o'clock or so, and it never got very dark. Your life parted and opened in the sunlight. You tossed your dark winter routines, thought up mad projects, and improvised everything from hour to hour. Being a stunt pilot seemed the most reasonable thing in the world; you could wave your arms in the air all day and all night, and sleep next winter.

I saw from the ground a dozen stunt pilots; the air show scheduled them one after the other, for an hour of aerobatics. Each pilot took up his or her plane and performed a batch of tricks. They were precise and impressive. They flew upside down, and straightened out; they did barrel rolls, and straightened out; they drilled through dives and spins, and landed gently on a far runway.

For the end of the day, separated from all other performances of every sort, the air show director had scheduled a program titled "Dave Rahm." The leaflet said that Rahm was a geologist who taught at Western Washington University. He had flown for King Hussein in Jordan. A tall man in the crowd told me Hussein had seen Rahm fly on a visit the king made to the United States; he had invited him to Jordan to perform at ceremonies. Hussein was a pilot, too. "Hussein thought he was the greatest thing in the world."

Idly, paying scant attention, I saw a medium-sized, rugged man dressed in   5
brown leather, all begoggled, climb in a black biplane's open cockpit. The plane
was a Bücker Jungman, built in the thirties. I saw a tall, dark-haired woman seize
a propeller tip at the plane's nose and yank it down till the engine caught. He was
off; he climbed high over the airport in his biplane, very high until he was barely
visible as a mote, and then seemed to fall down the air, diving headlong, and
streaming beauty in spirals behind him.

The black plane dropped spinning, and flattened out spinning the other way;
it began to carve the air into forms that built wildly and musically on each other
and never ended. Reluctantly, I started paying attention. Rahm drew high above
the world an inexhaustibly glorious line; it piled over our heads in loops and
arabesques. It was like a Saul Steinberg fantasy; the plane was the pen. Like Steinberg's contracting and billowing pen line, the line Rahm spun moved to form
new, punning shapes from the edges of the old. Like a Klee line, it smattered the
sky with landscapes and systems.

The air show announcer hushed. He had been squawking all day, and now he
quit. The crowd stilled. Even the children watched dumbstruck as the slow, black
biplane buzzed its way around the air. Rahm made beauty with his whole body; it
was pure pattern, and you could watch it happen. The plane moved every way a
line can move, and it controlled three dimensions, so the line carved massive and
subtle slits in the air like sculptures. The plane looped the loop, seeming to arch
its back like a gymnast; it stalled, dropped, and spun out of it climbing; it spiraled
and knifed west on one side's wings and back east on another; it turned cartwheels, which must be physically impossible; it played with its own line like a cat
with yarn. How did the pilot know where in the air he was? If he got lost, the
ground would swat him.

Rahm did everything his plane could do: tailspins, four-point rolls, flat spins,
figure 8's, snap rolls, and hammerheads. He did pirouettes on the plane's tail. The
other pilots could do these stunts, too, skillfully, one at a time. But Rahm used the
plane inexhaustibly, like a brush marking thin air.

His was pure energy and naked spirit. I have thought about it for years.
Rahm's line unrolled in time. Like music, it split the bulging rim of the future
along its seam. It pried out the present. We watchers waited for the split-second
curve of beauty in the present to reveal itself. The human pilot, Dave Rahm,
worked in the cockpit right at the plane's nose; his very body tore into the future
for us and reeled it down upon us like a curling peel.

Like any fine artist, he controlled the tension of the audience's longing. You   10
desired, unwittingly, a certain kind of roll or climb, or a return to a certain portion of the air, and he fulfilled your hope slantingly, like a poet, or evaded it until
you thought you would burst, and then fulfilled it surprisingly, so you gasped and
cried out.

The oddest, most exhilarating and exhausting thing was this: he never quit.
The music had no periods; no rests or endings; the poetry's beautiful sentence
never ended; the line had no finish; the sculptured forms piled overhead, one into

another without surcease. Who could breathe, in a world where rhythm itself had no periods?

It had taken me several minutes to understand what an extraordinary thing I was seeing. Rahm kept all that embellished space in mind at once. For another twenty minutes I watched the beauty unroll and grow more fantastic and unlikely before my eyes. Now Rahm brought the plane down slidingly, and just in time, for I thought I would snap from the effort to compass and remember the line's long intelligence; I could not add another curve. He brought the plane down on a far runway. After a pause, I saw him step out, an ordinary man, and make his way back to the terminal.

The show was over. It was late. Just as I turned from the runway, something caught my eye and made me laugh. It was a swallow, a blue-green swallow, having its own air show, apparently inspired by Rahm. The swallow climbed high over the runway, held its wings oddly, tipped them, and rolled down the air in loops. The inspired swallow. I always want to paint, too, after I see the Rembrandts. The blue-green swallow tumbled precisely, and caught itself and flew up again as if excited, and looped down again, the way swallows do, but tensely, holding its body carefully still. It was a stunt swallow.

I went home and thought about Rahm's performance that night, and the next day, and the next.

I had thought I knew my way around beauty a little bit. I knew I had devoted a good part of my life to it, memorizing poetry and focusing my attention on complexity of rhythm in particular, on force, movement, repetition, and surprise, in both poetry and prose. Now I had stood among dandelions between two asphalt runways in Bellingham, Washington, and begun learning about beauty. Even the Boston Museum of Fine Arts was never more inspiriting than this small northwestern airport on this time-killing Sunday afternoon in June. Nothing on earth is more gladdening than knowing we must roll up our sleeves and move back the boundaries of the humanly possible once more. 15

Later I flew with Dave Rahm; he took me up. A generous geographer, Dick Smith, at Western Washington University, arranged it, and came along. Rahm and Dick Smith were colleagues at the university. In geology, Rahm had published two books and many articles. Rahm was handsome in a dull sort of way, blunt-featured, wide-jawed, wind-burned, keen-eyed, and taciturn. As anyone would expect. He was forty. He wanted to show me the Cascade Mountains; these enormous peaks, only fifty miles from the coast, rise over nine thousand feet; they are heavily glaciated. Whatcom County has more glaciers than the lower forty-eight states combined; the Cascades make the Rocky Mountains look like hills. Mount Baker is volcanic, like most Cascade peaks. That year, Mount Baker was acting up. Even from my house at the shore I could see, early in the morning on clear days, volcanic vapor rise near its peak. Often the vapor made a cloud which swelled all morning and hid the snows. Every day the newspapers reported on Baker's activity: would it blow? (A few years later, Mount St. Helens did blow.)

Rahm was not flying his trick biplane that day, but a faster, enclosed plane, a single-engine Cessna. We flew from a bumpy grass airstrip near my house, out over the coast and inland. There was coastal plain down there, but we could not see it for clouds. We were over the clouds at five hundred feet and inside them too, heading for an abrupt line of peaks we could not see. I gave up on everything, the way you do in airplanes; it was out of my hands. Every once in a while Rahm saw a peephole in the clouds and buzzed over for a look. "That's Larsen's pea farm," he said, or "That's Nooksack Road," and he changed our course with a heave.

When we got to the mountains, he slid us along Mount Baker's flanks sideways.

Our plane swiped at the mountain with a roar. I glimpsed a windshield view of dirty snow traveling fast. Our shaking, swooping belly seemed to graze the snow. The wings shuddered; we peeled away and the mountain fell back and the engines whined. We felt flung, because we were in fact flung; parts of our faces and internal organs trailed pressingly behind on the curves. We came back for another pass at the mountain, and another. We dove at the snow headlong like suicides; we jerked up, down, or away at the last second, so late we left our hearts, stomachs, and lungs behind. If I forced myself to hold my heavy head up against the g's, and to raise my eyelids, heavy as barbells, and to notice what I saw, I could see the wrinkled green crevasses cracking the glaciers' snow.

Pitching snow filled all the windows, and shapes of dark rock. I had no notion which way was up. Everything was black or gray or white except the fatal crevasses; everything made noise and shook. I felt my face smashed sideways and saw rushing abstractions of snow in the windshield. Patches of cloud obscured the snow fleetingly. We straightened out, turned, and dashed at the mountainside for another pass, which we made, apparently, on our ear, an inch or two away from the slope. Icefalls and cornices jumbled and fell away. If a commercial plane's black box, such as the FAA painstakingly recovers from crash sites, could store videotapes as well as pilots' last words, some videotapes would look like this: a mountainside coming up at the windows from all directions, ice and snow and rock filling the screen up close and screaming by.

Rahm was just being polite. His geographer colleague wanted to see the fissure on Mount Baker from which steam escaped. Everybody in Bellingham wanted to see that sooty fissure, as did every geologist in the country; no one on earth could fly so close to it as Rahm. He knew the mountain by familiar love and feel, like a face; he knew what the plane could do and what he dared to do.

When Mount Baker inexplicably let us go, he jammed us into cloud again and soon tilted. "The Sisters!" someone shouted, and I saw the windshield fill with red rock. This mountain looked infernal, a drear and sheer plane of lifeless rock. It was red and sharp; its gritty blades cut through the clouds at random. The

20

mountain was quiet. It was in shade. Careening, we made sideways passes at these brittle peaks too steep for snow. Their rock was full of iron, somebody shouted at me then or later; the iron had rusted, so they were red. Later, when I was back on the ground, I recalled that, from a distance, the two jagged peaks called the Twin Sisters looked translucent against the sky; they were sharp, tapered, and fragile as arrowheads.

I talked to Rahm. He was flying us out to the islands now. The islands were fifty or sixty miles away. Like many other people, I had picked Bellingham, Washington, by looking at an atlas. It was clear from the atlas that you could row in the salt water and see snow-covered mountains; you could scale a glaciated mountainside with an ice ax in August, skirting green crevasses two hundred feet deep, and look out on the islands in the sea. Now, in the air, the clouds had risen over us; dark forms lay on the glinting water. There was almost no color to the day, just blackened green and some yellow. I knew the islands were forested in dark Douglas firs the size of skyscrapers. Bald eagles scavenged on the beaches; robins the size of herring gulls sang in the clearings. We made our way out to the islands through the layer of air between the curving planet and its held, thick clouds.

"When I started trying to figure out what I was going to do with my life, I decided to become an expert on mountains. It wasn't much to be, it wasn't everything, but it was something. I was going to know everything about mountains from every point of view." So I started out in geography." Geography proved too pedestrian for Rahm, too concerned with "how many bushels of wheat an acre." So he ended up in geology. Smith had told me that geology departments throughout the country used Rahm's photographic slides — close-ups of geologic features from the air.

"I used to climb mountains. But you know, you can get a better feel for a   25
mountain's power flying around it, flying all around it, than you can from climbing it tied to its side like a flea."

He talked about his flying performances. He thought of the air as a line, he said. "This end of the line, that end of the line — like a rope." He improvised. "I get a rhythm going and stick with it." While he was performing in a show, he paid attention, he said, to the lighting. He didn't play against the sun. That was all he said about what he did.

In aerobatic maneuvers, pilots pull about seven positive g's on some stunts and six negative g's on others. Some gyrations push; others pull. Pilots alternate the pressures carefully, so they do not gray out or black out.

Later I learned that some stunt pilots tune up by wearing gravity boots. These are boots made to hook over a doorway; wearing them, you hang in the doorway upside-down. It must startle a pilot's children, to run into their father or mother in the course of their home wandering — the parent hanging wide-eyed upside-down in the doorway like a bat.

We were landing; here was the airstrip on Stuart Island — that island to which Ferrar Burn was dragged by the tide. We put down, climbed out of the plane, and walked. We wandered a dirt track through fields to a lee shore where yellow sandstone ledges slid into the sea. The salt chuck, people there called salt water. The sun came out. I caught a snake in the salt chuck; the snake, eighteen inches long, was swimming in the green shallows.

I had a survivor's elation. Rahm had found Mount Baker in the clouds before 30 Mount Baker found the plane. He had wiped it with the fast plane like a cloth and we had lived. When we took off from Stuart Island and gained altitude, I asked if we could turn over — could we do a barrel roll? The plane was making a lot of noise, and Dick Smith did not hear any of this, I learned later. "Why not?" Rahm said, and added surprisingly, "It won't hurt the plane." Without ado he leaned on the wheel and the ring went down and we went somersaulting over it. We upended with a roar. We stuck to the plane's sides like flung paint. All the blood in my body bulged on my face; it piled up between my skull and skin. Vaguely I could see the chrome sea twirling over Rahm's head like a baton, and the dark islands sliding down the skies like rain.

The g's slammed me into my seat like thugs and pinned me while my heart pounded and the plane turned over slowly and compacted each organ in turn. My eyeballs were newly spherical and full of heartbeats. I seemed to hear a crescendo; the wing rolled shuddering down the last ninety degrees and settled on the flat. There were the islands, admirably below us, and the clouds, admirably above. When I could breathe, I asked if we could do it again, and we did. He rolled the other way. The brilliant line of the sea slid up the side window bearing its heavy islands. Through the shriek of my blood and the plane's shakes I glimpsed the line of the sea over the windshield, thin as a spear. How in performance did Rahm keep track while his brain blurred and blood roared in his ears without ceasing? Every performance was a tour de force and a show of will, a *machtspruch*.[1] I had seen the other stunt pilots straighten out after a trick or two; their blood could drop back and the planet simmer down. An Olympic gymnast, at peak form, strings out a line of spins ten stunts long across a mat, and is hard put to keep his footing at the end. Rahm endured much greater pressure on his faster spins, using the plane's power, and he could spin in three dimensions and keep twirling till he ran out of sky room or luck.

When we straightened out, and had flown straightforwardly for ten minutes toward home, Dick Smith, clearing his throat, brought himself to speak. "What was that we did out there?"

"The barrel rolls?" Rahm said. "They were barrel rolls." He said nothing else. I looked at the back of his head; I could see the serious line of his cheek and jaw. He was in shirtsleeves, tanned, strong-wristed. I could not imagine loving him under any circumstance; he was alien to me, unfazed. He looked like G.I. Joe. He flew with that matter-of-fact, bored gesture pilots use. They click overhead switches

---

[1]German, an authoritative pronouncement. — Eds.

and turn dials as if only their magnificent strength makes such dullness endurable. The half circle of wheel in their big hands looks like a toy they plan to crush in a minute; the wiggly stick the wheel mounts seems barely attached.

A crop-duster pilot in Wyoming told me the life expectancy of a crop-duster pilot is five years. They fly too low. They hit buildings and power lines. They have no space to fly out of trouble, and no space to recover from a stall. We were in Cody, Wyoming, out on the North Fork of the Shoshone River. The crop duster had wakened me that morning flying over the ranch house and clearing my bedroom roof by half an inch. I saw the bolts on the wheel assembly a few feet from my face. He was spraying with pesticide the plain old grass. Over breakfast I asked him how long he had been dusting crops. "Four years," he said, and the figure stalled in the air between us for a moment. "You know you're going to die at it someday," he added. "We all know it. We accept that; it's part of it." I think now that, since the crop duster was in his twenties, he accepted only that he had to say such stuff; privately he counted on skewing the curve.

I suppose Rahm knew the fact, too. I do not know how he felt about it. "It's worth it," said the early French aviator [Jean] Mermoz. He was Antoine de Saint-Exupéry's friend. "It's worth the final smashup." 35

Rahm smashed up in front of King Hussein, in Jordan, during a performance. The plane spun down and never came out of it; it nosedived into the ground and exploded. He bought the farm. I was living then with my husband out on that remote island in the San Juans, cut off from everything. Battery radios picked up the Canadian Broadcasting Company out of Toronto, half a continent away; island people would, in theory, learn if the United States blew up, but not much else. There were no newspapers. One friend got the Sunday *New York Times* by mailboat on the following Friday. He saved it until Sunday and had a party, every week; we all read the Sunday *Times* and no one mentioned that it was last week's.

One day, Paul Glenn's brother flew out from Bellingham to visit; he had a seaplane. He landed in the water in front of the cabin and tied up to our mooring. He came in for coffee, and he gave out news of this and that, and — Say, did we know that stunt pilot Dave Rahm had cracked up? In Jordan, during a performance: he never came out of a dive. He just dove right down into the ground, and his wife was there watching. "I saw it on CBS News last night." And then — with a sudden sharp look at my filling eyes — "What, did you know him?" But no, I did not know him. He took me up once. Several years ago. I admired his flying. I had thought that danger was the safest thing in the world, if you went about it right.

Later I found a newspaper. Rahm was living in Jordan that year; King Hussein invited him to train the aerobatics team, the Royal Jordanian Falcons. He was also visiting professor of geology at the University of Jordan. In Amman that day he had been flying a Pitt Special, a plane he knew well. Katy Rahm, his wife of six months, was sitting beside Hussein in the viewing stands, with her daughter.

Rahm died performing a Lomcevak combined with a tail slide and hammerhead. In a Lomcevak, the pilot brings the plane up on a slant and pirouettes. I had seen Rahm do this: the falling plane twirled slowly like a leaf. Like a ballerina, the plane seemed to hold its head back stiff in concentration at the music's slow, painful beauty. It was one of Rahm's favorite routines. Next the pilot flies straight up, stalls the plane, and slides down the air on his tail. He brings the nose down — the hammerhead — kicks the engine, and finishes with a low loop.

It is a dangerous maneuver at any altitude, and Rahm was doing it low. He hit the ground on the loop; the tail slide had left him no height. When Rahm went down, King Hussein dashed to the burning plane to pull him out, but he was already dead.

A few months after the air show, and a month after I had flown with Rahm, I was 40 working at my desk near Bellingham, where I lived, when I heard a sound so odd it finally penetrated my concentration. It was the buzz of an airplane, but it rose and fell musically, and it never quit; the plane never flew out of earshot. I walked out on the porch and looked up: it was Rahm in the black and gold biplane, looping all over the air. I had been wondering about his performance flight: could it really have been so beautiful? It was, for here it was again. The little plane twisted all over the air like a vine. It trailed a line like a very long mathematical proof you could follow only so far, and then it lost you in its complexity. I saw Rahm flying high over the Douglas firs, and out over the water, and back over farms. The air was a fluid, and Rahm was an eel.

It was as if Mozart could move his body through his notes, and you could walk out on the porch, look up, and see him in periwig and breeches, flying around in the sky. You could hear the music as he dove through it; it streamed after him like a contrail.

I lost myself; standing on the firm porch, I lost my direction and reeled. My neck and spine rose and turned, so I followed the plane's line kinesthetically. In his open-cockpit, black plane, Rahm demonstrated curved space. He slid down ramps of air, he vaulted and wheeled. He piled loops in heaps and praised height. He unrolled the scroll of the air, extended it, and bent it into Möbius strips; he furled line in a thousand new ways, as if he were inventing a script and writing it in one infinitely recurring utterance until I thought the bounds of beauty must break.

From inside, the looping plane had sounded tinny, like a kazoo. Outside, the buzz rose and fell to the Doppler effect as the plane looped near or away. Rahm cleaved the sky like a prow and tossed out time left and right in his wake. He performed for forty minutes; then he headed the plane, as small as a wasp, back to the airport inland. Later I learned Rahm often practiced acrobatic flights over this shore. His idea was that if he lost control and was going to go down, he could ditch in the salt chuck, where no one else would get hurt.

If I had not turned two barrel rolls in an airplane, I might have fancied Rahm felt good up there, and playful. Maybe Jackson Pollock felt a sort of playfulness, in addition to the artist's usual deliberate and intelligent care. In my limited experience, painting, unlike writing, pleases the senses while you do it, and more while you do it than after it is done. Drawing lines with an airplane, unfortunately, tortures the senses. Jet bomber pilots black out. I knew Rahm felt as if his brain were bursting his eardrums, felt that if he let his jaws close as tight as centrifugal force pressed them, he would bite through his lungs.

"All virtue is a form of acting," Yeats said. Rahm deliberately turned himself into a figure. Sitting invisible at the controls of a distant airplane, he became the agent and the instrument of art and invention. He did not tell me how he felt, when we spoke of his performance flying; he told me instead that he paid attention to how his plane and its line looked to the audience against the lighted sky. If he had noticed how he felt, he could not have done the work. Robed in his airplane, he was as featureless as a priest. He was lost in his figural aspect like an actor or a king. Of his flying, he had said only, "I get a rhythm and stick with it." In its reticence, this statement reminded me of Veronese's "Given a large canvas, I enhanced it as I saw fit." But Veronese was ironic, and Rahm was not; he was literal as an astronaut; the machine gave him tongue.

When Rahm flew, he sat down in the middle of art, and strapped himself in. He spun it all around him. He could not see it himself. If he never saw it on film, he never saw it at all — as if Beethoven could not hear his final symphonies not because he was deaf, but because he was inside the paper on which he wrote. Rahm must have felt it happen, that fusion of vision and metal, motion and idea. I think of this man as a figure, a college professor with a Ph.D. upside down in the loud band of beauty. What are we here for? *Propter chorum*, the monks say: for the sake of the choir.

"Purity does not lie in separation from but in deeper penetration into the universe," Teilhard de Chardin[2] wrote. It is hard to imagine a deeper penetration into the universe than Rahm's last dive in his plane, or than his inexpressible wordless selfless line's inscribing the air and dissolving. Any other art may be permanent. I cannot recall one Rahm sequence. He improvised. If Christo wraps a building or dyes a harbor, we join his poignant and fierce awareness that the work will be gone in days. Rahm's plane shed a ribbon in space, a ribbon whose end unraveled in memory while its beginning unfurled as surprise. He may have acknowledged that what he did could be called art, but it would have been, I think, only in the common misusage, which holds art to be the last extreme of skill. Rahm rode the point of the line to the possible; he discovered it and wound it down to show. He made his dazzling probe on the run. "The world is filled, and filled with the Absolute," Teilhard de Chardin wrote. "To see this is to be made free."

....

---

[2]Pierre Teilhard de Chardin (1881–1955), was a French paleontologist, geologist, and philosopher. — Eds.

Exploring the Text

1. Annie Dillard opens her essay with a factual and objective style. Why does she use this approach?

2. Dillard uses many similes, especially in paragraphs 30–31 and 40–43. How does this serve her rhetorical purpose? What points is she making about Dave Rahm's work?

3. Dillard frequently uses syntactical inversions. Find several examples of them, and discuss their effect.

4. In this essay Dillard uses numerous and varied allusions (for example, to Paul Klee, Mozart, William Butler Yeats, Rembrandt, Jackson Pollock). Why does Dillard make these allusions? What effect does she achieve? In your response, consider the quotation that closes the essay.

5. What is the purpose of paragraph 13, where Dillard describes a swallow? Could this description have been placed elsewhere in the essay? Why or why not?

6. In paragraph 36, Dillard writes, "He bought the farm." What is the effect of using this cliché? Try rewriting the sentence using a more formal expression; how does the effect change?

7. What does Dillard mean when she says, "When Rahm flew, he sat down in the middle of art, and strapped himself in" (para. 46)?

8. According to Dillard, what sets Rahm apart from mere skilled pilots and makes him an artist? At what point does skill become art?

9. How would you describe Dillard's attitude toward the stunt pilot? Cite specific passages to support your position.

10. Which characteristics does Dave Rahm, as described by Annie Dillard, share with the surgeon, as described by Richard Selzer (p. 197)?

In Praise of a Snail's Pace

ELLEN GOODMAN

Pulitzer Prize–winning journalist Ellen Goodman (b. 1941) has been a syndicated columnist since 1976. She received her BA from Radcliffe College and later was a fellow at the Nieman Foundation for Journalism at Harvard. She began her career as a researcher for *Newsweek* and was later a reporter for the *Detroit Free Press* and the *Boston Globe*. She published her first book, *Turning Points*, in 1979 and then collections of her columns, including *Making Sense* (1989), *Value Judgments* (1993), and *Paper Trail: Common Sense in Uncommon Times* (2004). She is co-author of *I Know Just What You Mean: The Power of Friendship in Women's Lives* (2000). In 1994, Goodman was the first Lorry I. Lokey Visiting Professor of Professional Journalism at Stanford University. The following essay originally appeared in the *Washington Post* in 2005.

I arrive at the [Casco Bay, Maine] island post office carrying an artifact from another age. It's a square envelope, handwritten, with return address that can be found on a map. Inside is a condolence note, a few words of memory and sympathy to a wife who has become a widow. I could have sent these words far more efficiently through e-mail than through this "snail mail." But I am among those who still believe that sympathy is diluted by two-thirds when it arrives over the Internet transom.

I would no more send an e-condolence than an e-thank you or an e-wedding invitation. There are rituals you cannot speed up without destroying them. It would be like serving Thanksgiving dinner at a fast-food restaurant.

My note goes into the old blue mailbox and I walk home wondering if slowness isn't the only way we pay attention now in a world of hyperactive technology.

Weeks ago, a friend lamented the trouble she had communicating with her grown son. It wasn't that her son was out of touch. Hardly. They were connected across miles through e-mail and cell phone, instant-messaging and text-messaging. But she had something serious to say and feared that an e-mail would elicit a reply that said: I M GR8. Was there no way to get undivided attention in the full in-box of his life? She finally chose a letter, a pen on paper, a stamp on envelope.

How do you describe the times we live in, so connected and yet fractured? 5
Linda Stone, a former Microsoft techie, characterizes ours as an era of "continuous partial attention." At the extreme end are teenagers instant-messaging while they are talking on the cell phone, downloading music and doing homework. But adults too live with all systems go, interrupted and distracted, scanning everything, multi-technological-tasking everywhere.

We suffer from the illusion, Stone says, that we can expand our personal bandwidth, connecting to more and more. Instead, we end up overstimulated, overwhelmed and, she adds, unfulfilled. Continuous partial attention inevitably feels like a lack of full attention.

But there are signs of people searching for ways to slow down and listen up. We are told that experienced e-mail users are taking longer to answer, freeing themselves from the tyranny of the reply button. Caller ID is used to find out who we don't have to talk to. And the next "killer ap," they say, will be e-mail software that can triage the important from the trivial.

Meanwhile, at companies where technology interrupts creativity and online contact prevents face-to-face contact, there are now e-mail-free Fridays. At others, there are bosses who require that you check your BlackBerry at the meeting door.

If a ringing cell phone once signaled your importance to a client, now that client is impressed when you turn off the cell phone. People who stayed connected 10 ways, 24-7, now pride themselves on "going dark."

"People hunger for more attention," says Stone, whose message has been wel- 10
comed even at a conference of bloggers. "Full attention will be the aphrodisiac of the future."

Indeed, at the height of our romance with e-mail, *You've Got Mail* was the cinematic love story. Now e-mail brings less thrill — "who will be there?" And more dread — "how many are out there?" Today's romantics are couples who leave their laptops behind on the honeymoon.

As for text-message flirtation, a young woman ended hers with a man who wrote, "C U L8R." He didn't have enough time to spell out Y-O-U?

Slowness guru Carl Horlore began *In Praise of Slowness* after he found himself seduced by a book of condensed classic fairy tales to read to his son. One-minute bedtime stories? We are relearning that paying attention briefly is as impossible as painting a landscape from a speeding car.

It is not just my trip to the mailbox that has brought this to mind. I come here each summer to stop hurrying. My island is no Brigadoon: WiFi is on the way, and some people roam the island with their cell phones, looking for a hot spot. But I exchange the Internet for the country road.

Georgia O'Keeffe once said that it takes a long time to see a flower. No technology can rush the growth of the leeks in the garden. All the speed in the Internet cannot hurry the healing of a friend's loss. Paying attention is the coin of this realm. 15

Sometimes, a letter becomes the icon of an old-fashioned new fashion. And sometimes, in this technological whirlwind, it takes a piece of snail mail to carry the stamp of authenticity.

Exploring the Text

1. What is the effect of the framing device Ellen Goodman employs — that is, beginning and ending her article with the same incident?
2. What does Goodman mean by "a world of hyperactive technology" (para. 3)?
3. Who are the experts Goodman quotes? How do they illustrate or strengthen her viewpoint?
4. What effect does Goodman achieve by lacing her writing with allusions, including ones to *You've Got Mail*, *Brigadoon*, and Georgia O'Keeffe?
5. What does Goodman mean by "Continuous partial attention inevitably feels like a lack of full attention" (para. 6)? Do you agree, or do you think that primarily members of an older generation have this perspective?
6. Why does Goodman assert that our times are "so connected and yet fractured" (para. 5)?
7. Although Goodman is not writing about work per se, what point is she making in paragraph 5 about the world of work infiltrating our lives 24/7 — what she describes as "multi-technological-tasking everywhere"?
8. What is Goodman's tone in this selection? Why is it appropriate for the point she is making?

I Stand Here Ironing (fiction)

TILLIE OLSEN

> The daughter of political refugees who fled from czarist Russia, Tillie Olsen
> (1912–2007) was born in Omaha, Nebraska. Although she began writing in
> the 1930s, she did not receive widespread attention until the 1960s, when the
> women's movement celebrated her depiction of working-class women. Politically
> active in unionist movements, she stopped writing in 1936 and began again only
> in 1953, after she followed her oldest daughter's suggestion to take a writing
> class. Soon she began work on the collection of short stories that was published as
> *Tell Me a Riddle* (1961); the partially autobiographical "I Stand Here Ironing" is
> one of those stories. In 1974, Olsen published *Yonnondio*, the novel she had
> begun in the 1930s and that is often compared with John Steinbeck's *Grapes of
> Wrath*. In 1978, Olsen recounted her experiences raising and supporting small
> children in her essay collection, *Silences*. Although she never graduated from high
> school, Olsen nevertheless went on to an academic career at Stanford University,
> Amherst College, Massachusetts Institute of Technology, and Kenyon College.

I stand here ironing, and what you asked me moves tormented back and
forth with the iron.

"I wish you would manage the time to come in and talk with me about your
daughter. I'm sure you can help me understand her. She's a youngster who needs
help and whom I'm deeply interested in helping."

"Who needs help." . . . Even if I came, what good would it do? You think
because I am her mother I have a key, or that in some way you could use me as a
key? She has lived for nineteen years. There is all that life that has happened outside of me, beyond me.

And when is there time to remember, to sift, to weigh, to estimate, to total? I
will start and there will be an interruption and I will have to gather it all together
again. Or I will become engulfed with all I did or did not do, with what should
have been and what cannot be helped.

She was a beautiful baby. The first and only one of our five that was beautiful 5
at birth. You do not guess how new and uneasy her tenancy in her now-loveliness.
You did not know her all those years she was thought homely, or see her poring
over her baby pictures, making me tell her over and over how beautiful she had
been — and would be, I would tell her — and was now, to the seeing eye. But the
seeing eyes were few or nonexistent. Including mine.

I nursed her. They feel that's important nowadays, I nursed all the children,
but with her, with all the fierce rigidity of first motherhood, I did like the books
then said. Though her cries battered me to trembling and my breasts ached with
swollenness, I waited till the clock decreed.

Why do I put that first? I do not even know if it matters, or if it explains anything.

She was a beautiful baby. She blew shining bubbles of sound. She loved motion, loved light, loved color and music and textures. She would lie on the floor in her blue overalls patting the surface so hard in ecstasy her hands and feet would blur. She was a miracle to me, but when she was eight months old I had to leave her daytimes with the woman downstairs to whom she was no miracle at all, for I worked or looked for work and for Emily's father, who "could no longer endure" (he wrote in his good-bye note) "sharing want with us."

I was nineteen. It was the pre-relief, pre-WPA world of the depression. I would start running as soon as I got off the streetcar, running up the stairs, the place smelling sour, and awake or asleep to startle awake, when she saw me she would break into a clogged weeping that could not be comforted, a weeping I can hear yet.

After a while I found a job hashing at night so I could be with her days, and it   10
was better. But it came to where I had to bring her to his family and leave her.

It took a long time to raise the money for her fare back. Then she got chicken pox and I had to wait longer. When she finally came, I hardly knew her, walking quick and nervous like her father, looking like her father, thin, and dressed in a shoddy red that yellowed her skin and glared at the pockmarks. All the baby love-liness gone.

She was two. Old enough for nursery school they said, and I did not know then what I know now — the fatigue of the long day, and the lacerations of group life in the kinds of nurseries that are only parking places for children.

Except that it would have made no difference if I had known. It was the only place there was. It was the only way we could be together, the only way I could hold a job.

And even without knowing, I knew. I knew the teacher that was evil because all these years it has curdled into my memory, the little boy hunched in the cor-ner, her rasp, "why aren't you outside, because Alvin hits you? that's no reason, go out, scaredy." I knew Emily hated it even if she did not clutch and implore "don't go Mommy" like the other children, mornings.

She always had a reason why we should stay home. Momma, you look sick.   15
Momma, I feel sick. Momma, the teachers aren't there today, they're sick. Momma, we can't go, there was a fire there last night. Momma, it's a holiday today, no school, they told me.

But never a direct protest, never rebellion. I think of our others in their three-, four-year-oldness — the explosions, the tempers, the denunciations, the demands — and I feel suddenly ill. I put the iron down. What in me demanded that goodness in her? And what was the cost, the cost to her of such goodness?

The old man living in the back once said in his gentle way: "You should smile at Emily more when you look at her." What *was* in my face when I looked at her? I loved her. There were all the acts of love.

It was only with the others I remembered what he said, and it was the face of joy, and not of care or tightness or worry I turned to them — too late for Emily. She does not smile easily, let alone almost always as her brothers and sisters do. Her face is closed and sombre, but when she wants, how fluid. You must have seen it in her pantomimes, you spoke of her rare gift for comedy on the stage that rouses laughter out of the audience so dear they applaud and applaud and do not want to let her go.

Where does it come from, that comedy? There was none of it in her when she came back to me that second time, after I had to send her away again. She had a new daddy now to learn to love, and I think perhaps it was a better time.

Except when we left her alone nights, telling ourselves she was old enough.   20

"Can't you go some other time, Mommy, like tomorrow?" she would ask. "Will it be just a little while you'll be gone? Do you promise?"

The time we came back, the front door open, the clock on the floor in the hall. She rigid awake. "It wasn't just a little while. I didn't cry. Three times I called you, just three times, and then I ran downstairs to open the door so you could come faster. The clock talked loud. I threw it away, it scared me what it talked."

She said the clock talked loud again that night I went to the hospital to have Susan. She was delirious with the fever that comes before red measles, but she was fully conscious all the week I was gone and the week after we were home when she could not come near the new baby or me.

She did not get well. She stayed skeleton thin, not wanting to eat, and night after night she had nightmares. She would call for me, and I would rouse from exhaustion to sleepily call back: "You're all right, darling, go to sleep, it's just a dream," and if she still called, in a sterner voice, "now go to sleep, Emily, there's nothing to hurt you." Twice, only twice, when I had to get up for Susan anyhow, I went in to sit with her.

Now when it is too late (as if she would let me hold her and comfort her like I   25 do the others) I get up and go to her at once at her moan or restless stirring. "Are you awake, Emily? Can I get you something?" And the answer is always the same: "No, I'm all right, go back to sleep, Mother."

They persuaded me at the clinic to send her away to a convalescent home in the country where "she can have the kind of food and care you can't manage for her, and you'll be free to concentrate on the new baby." They still send children to that place. I see pictures on the society page of sleek young women planning affairs to raise money for it, or dancing at the affairs, or decorating Easter eggs or filling Christmas stockings for the children.

They never have a picture of the children so I do not know if the girls still wear those gigantic red bows and the ravaged looks on the every other Sunday when parents can come to visit "unless otherwise notified" — as we were notified the first six weeks.

Oh it is a handsome place, green lawns and tall trees and fluted flower beds. High up on the balconies of each cottage the children stand, the girls in their red bows and white dresses, the boys in white suits and giant red ties. The parents stand below shrieking up to be heard and the children shriek down to be heard, and between them the invisible wall "Not To Be Contaminated by Parental Germs or Physical Affection."

There was a tiny girl who always stood hand in hand with Emily. Her parents never came. One visit she was gone. "They moved her to Rose Cottage," Emily shouted in explanation. "They don't like you to love anybody here."

She wrote once a week, the labored writing of a seven-year-old. "I am fine. How is the baby. If I write my leter nicly I will have a star. Love." There never was a star. We wrote every other day, letters she could never hold or keep but only hear read — once. "We simply do not have room for children to keep any personal possessions," they patiently explained when we pieced one Sunday's shrieking together to plead how much it would mean to Emily, who loved so to keep things, to be allowed to keep her letters and cards.

Each visit she looked frailer. "She isn't eating," they told us.

(They had runny eggs for breakfast or mush with lumps, Emily said later, I'd hold it in my mouth and not swallow. Nothing ever tasted good, just when they had chicken.)

It took us eight months to get her released home, and only the fact that she gained back so little of her seven lost pounds convinced the social worker.

I used to try to hold and love her after she came back, but her body would stay stiff, and after a while she'd push away. She ate little. Food sickened her, and I think much of life too. Oh she had physical lightness and brightness, twinkling by on skates, bouncing like a ball up and down up and down over the jump rope, skimming over the hill; but these were momentary.

She fretted about her appearance, thin and dark and foreign-looking at a time when every little girl was supposed to look or thought she should look a chubby blonde replica of Shirley Temple. The doorbell sometimes rang for her, but no one seemed to come and play in the house or to be a best friend. Maybe because we moved so much.

There was a boy she loved painfully through two school semesters. Months later she told me how she had taken pennies from my purse to buy him candy. "Licorice was his favorite and I brought him some every day, but he still liked Jennifer better'n me. Why, Mommy?" The kind of question for which there is no answer.

School was a worry for her. She was not glib or quick in a world where glibness and quickness were easily confused with ability to learn. To her overworked and exasperated teachers she was an overconscientious "slow learner" who kept trying to catch up and was absent entirely too often.

I let her be absent, though sometimes the illness was imaginary. How different from my now-strictness about attendance with the others. I wasn't working. We had a new baby. I was home anyhow. Sometimes, after Susan grew old enough, I would keep her home from school, too, to have them all together.

Mostly Emily had asthma, and her breathing, harsh and labored, would fill the house with a curiously tranquil sound. I would bring the two old dresser mirrors and her boxes of collections to her bed. She would select beads and single earrings, bottle tops and shells, dried flowers and pebbles, old postcards and scraps, all sorts of oddments; then she and Susan would play Kingdom, setting up landscapes and furniture, peopling them with action.

Those were the only times of peaceful companionship between her and   40
Susan. I have edged away from it, that poisonous feeling between them, that terrible balancing of hurts and needs I had to do between the two, and did so badly, those earlier years.

Oh there were conflicts between the others too, each one human, needing, demanding, hurting, taking — but only between Emily and Susan, no, Emily toward Susan that corroding resentment. It seems so obvious on the surface, yet it is not obvious; Susan, the second child, Susan, golden- and curly-haired and chubby, quick and articulate and assured, everything in appearance and manner Emily was not; Susan, not able to resist Emily's precious things, losing or sometimes clumsily breaking them; Susan telling jokes and riddles to company for applause while Emily sat silent (to say to me later: that was *my* riddle, Mother, I told it to Susan); Susan, who for all the five years' difference in age was just a year behind Emily in developing physically.

I am glad for that slow physical development that widened the difference between her and her contemporaries, though she suffered over it. She was too vulnerable for that terrible world of youthful competition, of preening and parading, of constant measuring of yourself against every other, of envy, "If I had that copper hair," "If I had that skin. . . ." She tormented herself enough about not looking like the others, there was enough of unsureness, the having to be conscious of words before you speak, the constant caring — what are they thinking of me? without having it all magnified by the merciless physical drives.

Ronnie is calling. He is wet and I change him. It is rare there is such a cry now. That time of motherhood is almost behind me when the ear is not one's own but must always be racked and listening for the child cry, the child call. We sit for a while and I hold him, looking out over the city spread in charcoal with its soft aisles of light. "*Shoogily,*" he breathes and curls closer. I carry him back to bed, asleep. *Shoogily.* A funny word, a family word, inherited from Emily, invented by her to say: *comfort.*

In this and other ways she leaves her seal, I say aloud. And startle at my saying it. What do I mean? What did I start to gather together, to try and make coherent? I was at the terrible, growing years. War years. I do not remember them well. I was working, there were four smaller ones now, there was not time for her. She had to help be a mother, and housekeeper, and shopper. She had to get her seal. Mornings of crisis and near hysteria trying to get lunches packed, hair combed, coats and shoes found, everyone to school or Child Care on time, the baby ready for transportation. And always the paper scribbled on by a smaller one, the book looked at by Susan then mislaid, the homework not done. Running out to that huge school where she was one, she was lost, she was a drop; suffering over the unpreparedness, stammering and unsure in her classes.

There was so little time left at night after the kids were bedded down. She would struggle over books, always eating (it was in those years she developed her enormous appetite that is legendary in our family) and I would be ironing, or preparing food for the next day, or writing V-mail to Bill, or tending the baby. Sometimes, to make me laugh, or out of her despair, she would imitate happenings or types at school.

I think I said once: "Why don't you do something like this in the school amateur show?" One morning she phoned me at work, hardly understandable through the weeping. "Mother, I did it. I won, I won; they gave me first prize; they clapped and clapped and wouldn't let me go."

Now suddenly she was Somebody, and as imprisoned in her difference as she had been in anonymity.

She began to be asked to perform at other high schools, even in colleges, then at city and statewide affairs. The first one we went to, I only recognized her that first moment when thin, shy, she almost drowned herself into the curtains. Then: Was this Emily? The control, the command, the convulsing and deadly clowning, the spell, then the roaring, stamping audience, unwilling to let this rare and precious laughter out of their lives.

Afterwards: You ought to do something about her with a gift like that — but without money or knowing how, what does one do? We have left it all to her, and the gift has so often eddied inside, clogged and clotted, as been used and growing.

She is coming. She runs up the stairs two at a time with her light graceful step, and I know she is happy tonight. Whatever it was that occasioned your call did not happen today.

"Aren't you ever going to finish the ironing, Mother? Whistler painted his mother in a rocker. I'd have to paint mine standing over an ironing board." This is one of her communicative nights and she tells me everything and nothing as she fixes herself a plate of food out of the icebox.

She is so lovely. Why did you want me to come in at all? Why were you concerned? She will find her way.

She starts up the stairs to bed. "Don't get me up with the rest in the morning." "But I thought you were having midterms." "Oh, those," she comes back in, kisses me, and says quite lightly, "in a couple of years when we'll all be atom-dead they won't matter a bit."

She has said it before. She *believes* it. But because I have been dredging the past, and all that compounds a human being is so heavy and meaningful in me, I cannot endure it tonight.

I will never total it all. I will never come in to say: She was a child seldom smiled at. Her father left me before she was a year old. I had to work her first six years when there was work, or I sent her home and to his relatives. There were

45

50

55

years she had care she hated. She was dark and thin and foreign-looking in a world where the prestige went to blondeness and curly hair and dimples, she was slow where glibness was prized. She was a child of anxious, not proud, love. We were poor and could not afford for her the soil of easy growth. I was a young mother, I was a distracted mother. There were other children pushing up, demanding. Her younger sister seemed all that she was not. There were years she did not want me to touch her. She kept too much in herself, her life was such she had to keep too much in herself. My wisdom came too late. She has much to her and probably little will come of it. She is a child of her age, of depression, of war, of fear.

Let her be. So all that is in her will not bloom — but in how many does it? There is still enough left to live by. Only help her to know — help make it so there is cause for her to know — that she is more than this dress on the ironing board, helpless before the iron.

Exploring the Text

1. Who is the speaker of this stream-of-consciousness monologue? Describe her in terms of age, circumstances, and frame of mind. Why is her socioeconomic situation important?
2. Who is the speaker in paragraph 2 ("'I wish you would manage the time to come in . . .'")? In what ways is this speaker the audience for the narrator's response?
3. What does the narrator mean when she asks, "And when is there time to remember, to sift, to weigh, to estimate, to total" (para. 4)?
4. How does the narrator view herself as a mother? Cite specific passages to support your interpretation.
5. In paragraph 55, the narrator describes her daughter Emily as "a child of her age, of depression, of war, of fear." In what ways does this description also apply to the narrator?
6. How do you interpret the final paragraph? Is it a hopeful ending?
7. Why is ironing a fitting metaphor for this story?

Harvest Song (poetry)

Jean Toomer

A writer and philosopher of the Harlem Renaissance and the Lost Generation, Jean Toomer (1894–1967) is best known for his experimental work *Cane* (1923). That book is a series of poems and short stories about the African American experience in the rural South and the northern cities where many migrated during the first part of the twentieth century. Toomer was born Nathan Pinchback Toomer, the son of Nathan Toomer, a planter, and Nina Pinchback, the daughter of Pinckney Benton Stewart Pinchback, governor of Louisiana during Reconstruction and the first U.S. governor of African American descent. Toomer graduated from high school in Washington, D.C., and attended several colleges, including the University of Chicago and New York University. "Harvest Song" is one of the poems from *Cane*.

I am a reaper whose muscles set at sundown. All my oats are cradled.
But I am too chilled, and too fatigued to bind them. And I hunger.

I crack a grain between my teeth. I do not taste it.
I have been in the fields all day. My throat is dry. I hunger.

My eyes are caked with dust of oatfields at harvest-time. 5
I am a blind man who stares across the hills, seeking stack'd fields of other
    harvesters.

It would be good to see them . . . crook'd, split, and iron-ring'd handles of the
    scythes. It would be good to see them, dust-caked and blind. I hunger.

(Dusk is a strange fear'd sheath their blades are dull'd in.)
My throat is dry. And should I call, a cracked grain like the oats . . . eoho —

I fear to call. What should they hear me, and offer me their grain, oats, or wheat, 10
    or corn? I have been in the fields all day. I fear I could not taste it.
    I fear knowledge of my hunger.

My ears are caked with dust of oatfields at harvest-time.
I am a deaf man who strains to hear the calls of other harvesters whose throats
    are also dry.

It would be good to hear their songs . . . reapers of the sweet-stalk'd cane, cutters
    of the corn . . . even though their throats cracked and the strangeness of their
    voices deafened me.

I hunger. My throat is dry. Now that the sun has set and I am chilled, I fear
    to call. (Eoho, my brothers!)

I am a reaper. (Eoho!) All my oats are cradled. But I am too fatigued to bind 15
    them. And I hunger. I crack a grain. It has no taste to it. My throat is dry . . .

O my brothers, I beat my palms, still soft, against the stubble of my harvesting.
    (You beat your soft palms, too.) My pain is sweet. Sweeter than the oats or
    wheat or corn. It will not bring me knowledge of my hunger.

Exploring the Text

1. Who is the speaker in Jean Toomer's poem?
2. What is the setting of the poem, and why is it important?
3. What patterns of repetition does the poem contain? What is their effect?
4. At various points, the speaker indicates that he is blind, he is deaf, he cannot taste. Are these claims literally true? Why does the speaker make these statements?
5. Why does he say, "My pain is sweet" (l. 16)?
6. Trace the development of the concept of hunger throughout the poem. As a reader, when do you begin realizing that this hunger is not entirely literal?
7. Why is this poem called a song?
8. What is the relationship between the work and the worker in the poem?

We Can Do It! (poster)

J. HOWARD MILLER

> J. Howard Miller, a graphic designer at Westinghouse, created this poster in 1942. During World War II, women in the United States entered the workplace in unprecedented numbers because increased production was necessary to meet the war effort and so many men were serving in the military. From 1940 to 1945, the number of women in the workforce rose from twelve to eighteen million. In 1940, women made up 8 percent of workers employed in the production of durable goods; by 1945, they made up 45 percent. The woman in this poster became known as "Rosie the Riveter," the symbol of women workers in the World War II defense industry. Miller's poster was one of those used during the war to recruit women into the workforce.

Exploring the Text

1. How does the written text reinforce the visual in the poster?
2. What characteristics do you associate with the woman depicted in the poster?
3. Which stereotypes of women are being addressed (and perhaps refuted) by the woman in the poster?
4. Discuss this poster as an argument for women working outside the home. How does it appeal to logos as well as pathos?
5. Compare and contrast this image with one done by Norman Rockwell for a 1943 cover of *The Saturday Evening Post*; you can see the Rockwell painting at <bedfordstmartins.com/languageofcomp>.

The Great GAPsby Society (cartoon)

JEFF PARKER

Jeff Parker (b. 1959) is an editorial cartoonist for *Florida Today*. A member of the National Cartoonists Society and the Association of American Editorial Cartoonists, he was nominated in 1997 and 1998 for the NCS Reuben Award for editorial cartooning. His cartoons have been included in many editions of Pelican Books' *Best Editorial Cartoons of the Year*.

Exploring the Text

1. The title of this cartoon alludes to the novel *The Great Gatsby* by F. Scott Fitzgerald. Why is the allusion appropriate? If you haven't read the novel to which the title alludes, does the cartoon still make sense?

2. Try summarizing the point, or message, of the cartoon. How does the verbal summary change the impact of the visual?

3. What does the audience have to know in order to get the full impact of the cartoon? Will readers who have jobs in the "quickee mart" or places such as McDonald's feel insulted or mocked? Explain.

4. What is the purpose of the expression "old sport"? How does it contribute to the characterization of the man in the suit?

5. How do you think Barbara Ehrenreich, whose "From *Serving in Florida*" appears on page 179, would respond to this cartoon? Would the cartoon effectively illustrate her work? Which other readings from this chapter would the cartoon enhance?

Conversation

Focus on Working Parents

Each of the following texts presents a viewpoint on working parents:

Sources

1. **Marilyn Gardner,** *More Working Parents Play "Beat the Clock"*
2. **Amelia Warren Tyagi,** *Why Women Have to Work*
3. **Claudia Wallis,** *The Case for Staying Home*
4. **Christopher Mele,** *Sick Parents Go to Work, Stay Home When Kids Are Ill*
5. **Kimberly Palmer,** *My Mother, Myself, Her Career, My Questions*
6. **Buzz McClain,** *Don't Call Me Mr. Mom*

After you have read, studied, and synthesized these pieces, enter the conversation by responding to one of the prompts on page 248.

1. *More Working Parents Play "Beat the Clock"*

MARILYN GARDNER

In the following selection, Marilyn Gardner discusses the challenges faced by families with two working parents.

Scott Fulgham, a night-shift police officer in Chattanooga, Tenn., knows a lot about strange schedules. He eats breakfast when he wakes up at 2 P.M. He joins his family for dinner at 6:30 P.M., then grabs "lunch" on the job at 2 A.M. When the sun comes up, he pulls down the shades and goes to bed.

"My sleep cycle gets a little crazy," says Mr. Fulgham, a patrol sergeant who spends 10 nights on duty, then four nights off. "Your body's having to adjust all the time."

That isn't the only adjustment taking place in the Fulgham household. Like many families living with America's 24 million shift workers, his wife, Kathie, and two daughters must adapt their schedules to accommodate his. "It puts challenges on the whole family," Mrs. Fulgham says.

By one count, 40 percent of employed Americans work late hours or weekends or both. As more families like the Fulghams inhabit a topsy-turvy world that turns nights into days and weekends into just another time to punch the clock, some are paying a price.

These unconventional schedules can "undermine the stability of marriages, 5 increase the amount of housework to be done, reduce family cohesiveness, and require elaborate child-care arrangements," warns Harriet Presser, a sociologist at the University of Maryland.

Parents working nights are more likely to separate or divorce than those on other work schedules, she finds.

As the ranks of extended-hours employees grow, so does the recognition among sociologists, labor specialists, and employers that off-hour workers and families need more attention than they are getting, says Dr. Presser, author of the book "Working in a 24/7 Economy: Challenges for American Families."

For decades, nontraditional schedules were largely the province of blue-collar workers, many of whom had a family history of shift work. Today, half of those on nonstandard hours are white-collar, technical, or service-industry workers.

"It's a huge change," says David Mitchell, director of publications for Circadian Technologies in Lexington, Mass. "A lot of these people just don't think of themselves as shift workers." Because these new white-collar employees have no personal or family history of shifts, he adds, "it just slams them. The [realities] are so different from what all their years of education led them to expect."

The Fulghams both have college degrees, as do their parents. Referring to her   10
husband's schedule, Mrs. Fulgham, public-relations director of the Tennessee Aquarium, says, "We weren't prepared for it."

Neither was Kacey Powers of Bakersfield, Calif. A week after she and her husband, Chris, were married 10 years ago, he started a job at a shingle manufacturing plant.

He works 12-hour shifts, rotating between days and nights. This involves four nights on the "graveyard" shift from 7 P.M. to 7 A.M. Then he has 1½ days off, after which he works 7 A.M. to 7 P.M. for three days. After two days off, he puts in three graveyard shifts. Then he has 1½ days off and four days on, capped by a meeting day that starts at 7 A.M. A calendar by the phone keeps the family on track.

"The kids are used to it," Mrs. Powers says of their two sons, ages 6 and 7. "They know when he sleeps graveyard. They're quiet. They tend to play outside."

But that kind of easy acceptance can be harder for adults. Powers observes a high divorce rate at her husband's plant, as well as other problems. "I've seen men lose their jobs because they're losing their family," Powers says. "They neglect their work, call in sick, and have high absenteeism."

To resolve problems, she says, "You have to talk, you have to relay things to   15
each other. A lot of wives don't get up with their husbands at 5 A.M. I try to go the extra mile, and he does the same for me."

They also carve out family time. Two weeks ago they visited Universal Studios. On Mr. Powers's weekends off, they set aside a day with their sons, perhaps going to a lake or renting videos.

Who Watches the Children?

For two-career couples and single parents, nonstandard schedules make child care complex. Nearly a third of extended-hours employees have children under

18. And more than a quarter of employed women regularly work nights, evenings, and weekends, when quality care is least available.

"People are really struggling with the question, What do you do with your kids?" says Netsy Firestein, executive director of the Labor Project for Working Families in Berkeley, Calif. "They're making all kinds of informal arrangements, whether it's early in the morning or in the evening. There are no great solutions to this."

Teri Ransom, director of Happy Kids 'Round the Clock Child Care in Denver, says that because parents have such difficulty finding after-hours child care, she even accepted children on Mother's Day this year. "Restaurants are open then, and waitresses have to work," she explains.

Yet even extended-hours care does not solve all problems. Most parents do not want their children to spend all night at a center.   20

To avoid such dilemmas, a third of married mothers with preschool children say they and their spouses deliberately work different shifts so their husbands or parents can care for the children. Yet most married mothers who work evenings, nights, or weekends do so because the job demands it, Presser says. Many parents simply cannot choose their schedules.

When parents work different shifts, Presser wonders whether the father or mother who worked all night is coming home and sleeping, leaving the children essentially unsupervised.

She does find some benefits when parents work different shifts. Child care costs less. Fathers often spend more time with children, and many men do more housework. Mr. Fulgham, for one, cooks dinner more than half the time, shares the grocery shopping, and does some laundry. He picks up 5-year-old Jilly after school, and in the evening gives her a bath and reads to her.

Still, "tag-team parenting" can create its own challenges. Jo Browning, who works at the B. F. Goodrich plant in Opelika, Ala., watches husbands and wives who work on different shifts meeting in the parking lot or at the time clock. "There's no family time together when you both rotate," she says.

Divorced and the mother of a 13-year-old daughter, Ms. Browning also knows how nonstandard hours affect parents with older children.   25

"If you're a single mom and you have a 14-year-old, what do you do?" she asks. "You don't want to hire a baby sitter, but you don't want to leave them alone, either. You depend on family and friends and neighbors to help you."

Health concerns also rank high for some shift workers. Because sleep deprivation is common, a handful of companies are starting to teach these employees how to sleep in the daytime. The average man who works nights sleeps 5.5 hours during the day, Mitchell says, while the average woman on the night shift sleeps only 4.8 hours because of domestic responsibilities.

Some employers are also educating night workers about nutrition. "They're eating the wrong food — fried chicken, spicy burritos, and coffee," Mitchell explains.

But even practical help like this doesn't address other issues affecting many employees on nonstandard hours.

"When he works 10 days straight, it's a strain," Mrs. Fulgham says. "It's not just a lack of intimacy. It's a lack of communication. You just seem to be speaking in this code of getting through life."   30

Challenges can be even more acute for single parents. Forty percent of single mothers work shifts, and more than a third work weekends. They are also more likely to hold lower-paying jobs with fewer benefits and less flexibility.

Family Mealtime Sacrificed

Researchers still have much to learn about the ramifications of these schedules, Presser says. This includes their long-term effects on children.

Noting that many shiftwork families lose their dinner hour, she says, "Dinnertime is the most important family ritual in togetherness time. Working evenings clearly leads to the absence of a parent during dinnertime."

Presser expects jobs with off-hours schedules to increase. "We like stores to be open around the clock, medical services to be available continuously, and people to answer the phone when we make travel reservations late at night," she says.

For now, some parents take a philosophical, you-do-what-you-gotta-do   35 approach. As Mr. Fulgham puts it, "You've got to look at the positives. You've got to manipulate the negatives and make them more positive."

To which his wife adds, "In a family like ours, everybody learns that they're all part of the solution. Our family has adapted."

Questions

1. In this essay, Marilyn Gardner uses several types of evidence: expert testimony, statistical data, facts, and personal anecdotes. Identify an example of each. Does she rely on one type of evidence more than on others?
2. What does Gardner mean by "nontraditional schedules" (para. 8)?
3. What is "tag-team parenting" (para. 24)? Does it have a negative connotation?
4. According to Gardner, what are some of the effects of parents working unusual hours and shifts?
5. What appeals to pathos does Gardner make?

2. *Why Women Have to Work*

AMELIA WARREN TYAGI

In the following reading, which originally appeared in *Time* in 2004, Amelia Warren Tyagi looks at the economic realities that require both parents to work.

Why are today's mothers working so hard, putting in long hours at home and at the office? For the money.

Oh, sure, those ladies who took their grandmothers' advice and married a doctor, a lawyer or an Enron executive may show up for work to "fulfill themselves" or to "expand their horizons." But for most women who, like me, came of age in the '90s, it comes down to dollars and cents, and the calculation is brutal.

In one column sits that big-eyed slobbery youngster, and a mother's heart beating to be there so she can give him everything. And in the other column sits the mother's heart . . . beating to give him everything.

Because in most of the U.S. it is no longer possible to support a middle-class family on Dad's income alone. This isn't a question of having enough cash to buy Game Boys and exotic trips. It is a question of having enough to buy the basics.

Like a home. Anyone who hasn't been hiding under a rock in Montana knows   5
that it costs more to purchase a house than it used to. But what many do not realize is that this increase has become a *family* problem, with mothers caught in the cross hairs. Over the past generation, home prices have risen twice as fast for couples with young children as for those without kids. Why? Confidence in the public schools has dwindled, leaving millions of families to conclude that the only way to ensure Junior a slot in a safe, quality school is to snatch up a home in a good school district. In most cities that means paying more for the family home. Since the mid-'70s, the amount of the average family budget earmarked for the mortgage has increased a whopping 69% (adjusted for inflation). At the same time, the average father's income increased less than 1%. How to make up the difference? With Mom's paycheck, of course.

These moms aren't marching to the office so they can get into brand-new McMansions. In fact, the average family today lives in a house that is older than the one Mom and Dad grew up in, and scarcely half a room bigger. The average couple with young children now shells out more than $127,000 for a home, up from $72,000 (adjusted for inflation) less than 20 years ago.

Then there is preschool. No longer an optional "Mother's Day Out" enterprise, preschool is widely viewed as a prerequisite for elementary school. But that prerequisite isn't offered at most public schools, which means that any mother who wants her kids to have access to this "essential start to early education," as the experts call it, has to come up with cold, hard cash. A full-time preschool program can cost over $5,000 a year — more than a year's tuition at most state universities! Add the cost of health insurance (for those lucky enough to have it) and the eventual price of sending a kid to college (double — when adjusted for inflation — what it was a generation ago), and most middle-class moms find they have no choice but to get a job if they want to make ends meet.

To be sure, there are plenty of mothers who scrimp and save and find a way to stay home (at least for a few years). But there are plenty more who decide that the cost is just too high, and the choice of whether to stay home is no choice at all.

Questions

1. What viewpoint does Amelia Warren Tyagi present? Are her sympathies with women, particularly working mothers, or with families as a whole? Cite specific passages to support your response.

2. What does Tyagi mean when she points out that the increase in housing prices "has become a *family* problem, with mothers caught in the cross hairs" (para. 5)?
3. Tyagi presents the issue in a personal way, but how does she also appeal to logos? Cite specific examples.
4. What is the tone of the first three paragraphs? Does the tone change as the essay continues? What is the overall tone?

3. *The Case for Staying at Home*

Claudia Wallis

In the following excerpt from a 2006 article in *Time*, Claudia Wallis explains why women with young children are choosing to stay at home rather than go out to work.

Ten, 15 years ago, it all seemed so doable. Bring home the bacon, fry it up in a pan, split the second shift with some sensitive New Age man. But slowly the snappy, upbeat work-life rhythm has changed for women in high-powered posts. . . . The U.S. workweek still averages around 34 hours, thanks in part to a sluggish manu-facturing sector. but for those in financial services, it's 55 hours; for top executives in big corporations, it's 60 to 70, says Catalyst, a research and consulting group that focuses on women in business. For dual-career couples with kids under 18, the combined work hours have grown from 81 a week in 1977 to 91 in 2002, according to the Families and Work Institute. E-mail, pagers and cell phones promised to allow execs to work from home. Who knew that would mean that home was no longer a sanctuary? Today BlackBerrys sprout on the sidelines of Little League games. Cell phones vibrate at the school play. And it's back to the e-mail after *Goodnight Moon.* "We are now the workaholism capital of the world, surpassing the Japanese," laments sociologist Arlie Hochschild, author of *The Time Bind: When Work Becomes Home and Home Becomes Work.*

Meanwhile, the pace has quickened on the home front, where a mother's job has expanded to include managing a packed schedule of child-enhancement activities. In their new book *The Mommy Myth*, Susan Douglas, a professor of communication studies at the University of Michigan, and Meredith Michaels, who teaches philosophy at Smith College, label the phenomenon the New Momism. Nowadays, they write, our culture insists that "to be a remotely decent mother, a woman has to devote her entire physical, psychological, emotional, and intellectual being, 24/7, to her children." It's a standard of success that's "impos-sible to meet," they argue. But that sure doesn't stop women from trying.

For most mothers — and fathers, for that matter — there is little choice but to persevere on both fronts to pay the bills. Indeed, 72% of mothers with children under 18 are in the work force — a figure that is up sharply from 47% in 1975 but has held steady since 1997. And thanks in part to a dodgy economy, there's growth in another category, working women whose husbands are unemployed, which has risen to 6.4% of all married couples.

But in the professional and managerial classes, where higher incomes permit more choices, a reluctant revolt is under way. Today's women execs are less willing to play the juggler's game, especially in its current high-speed mode, and more willing to sacrifice paychecks and prestige for time with their family. . . . [M]ost of these women are choosing not so much to drop out as to stop out, often with every intention of returning. Their mantra: You can have it all, just not all at the same time. Their behavior, contrary to some popular reports, is not a June Cleaver–ish embrace of old-fashioned motherhood but a new, nonlinear approach to building a career and an insistence on restoring some kind of sanity. "What this group is staying home from is the 80-hour-a-week job," says Hochschild. "They are committed to work, but many watched their mothers and fathers be ground up by very long hours, and they would like to give their own children more than they got. They want a work-family balance."

Because these women represent a small and privileged sector, the dimensions 5 of the exodus are hard to measure. What some experts are zeroing in on is the first-ever drop-off in workplace participation by married mothers with a child less than 1 year old. That figure fell from 59% in 1997 to 53% in 2000. The drop may sound modest, but, says Howard Hayghe, an economist at the Bureau of Labor Statistics, "that's huge," and the figure was roughly the same in 2002. Significantly, the drop was mostly among women who were white, over 30 and well educated.

Census data reveal an uptick in stay-at-home moms who hold graduate or professional degrees — the very women who seemed destined to blast through the glass ceiling. Now 22% of them are home with their kids. A study by Catalyst found that 1 in 3 women with M.B.A.s are not working full-time (it's 1 in 20 for their male peers). Economist and author Sylvia Ann Hewlett, who teaches at Columbia University, says she sees a brain drain throughout the top 10% of the female labor force (those earning more than $55,000). "What we have discovered in looking at this group over the last five years," she says, "is that many women who have any kind of choice are opting out."

Other experts say the drop-out rate isn't climbing but is merely more visible now that so many women are in high positions. In 1971 just 9% of medical degrees, 7% of law degrees and 4% of M.B.A.s were awarded to women; 30 years later, the respective figures were 43%, 47% and 41%.

Questions

1. Which socioeconomic group is the focus of this reading? Why is that focus significant?
2. In paragraph 4, what does Claudia Wallis mean by "a reluctant revolt"? by "the juggler's game, especially in its current high-speed mode"? by "a new, nonlinear approach to building a career"?

3. Who are the people Wallis cites?

4. What point(s) does Wallis make with the statistical evidence she cites?

4. *Sick Parents Go to Work, Stay Home When Kids Are Ill*

CHRISTOPHER MELE

In the following 2002 article from *USA Today*, Christopher Mele talks about how working parents use their sick leave.

Got the sniffles? Low-grade temperature? Hacking cough? If you're a working mom or dad, chances are you're dragging yourself to work rather than taking a day off.

The payoff for parents who go to the office feeling lousy? They save a day that they may need to take off in the future if their son or daughter gets sick and needs to stay home.

It's all part of the juggling act of working parents who are trying to raise a family and maintain their careers, especially in an uncertain economic environment that demands productivity.

"Everybody's competing because they're afraid if they don't show up, their desk won't be there tomorrow," said Jeannette Lofas, president and founder of the Stepfamily Foundation Inc.

Lee DeNigris of Tallman, N.Y., has already had to take three weeks off from   5
her job as a field technician for Verizon to care for her 5-month-old daughter, Amanda. Day care has been a breeding ground of germs for Amanda, who has had three ear infections, an upper respiratory infection and a long-lasting cold since February.

DeNigris, who also has two sons, ages 13 and 11, had been a stay-at-home mom. Now, economics dictate that both she and her husband work. That means going to work on days that she otherwise would have stayed home sick.

"I have to have the days available," she said. "When I got the stomach flu that she had and the boys had, I had to go into work with that. That was nasty."

Productivity ultimately suffers — to say nothing of the chances of infecting co-workers on the job — when sick parents head to work, Lofas said. "The bottom-line result is that corporations get less of their employees," she said.

Studies show that working parents give up personal care time, sleep and recovery time from illnesses to be with their kids, said Stephanie Coontz, national co-chairwoman of the Council on Contemporary Families.

"They will often go into work with colds or illnesses that, before they had   10
kids, they would have grabbed at the opportunity to stay home," she said. "The evidence is pretty overwhelming that working parents neglect themselves first."

"Family issues" ranked as the second most cited reason for workers to take an unscheduled absence, according to a survey last year by CCH Inc., a provider of employment law and human resources information. Personal illness topped the list of reasons at 32%, followed by family issues at 21%.

Yolanda Rios of Garnerville, N.Y., can vouch for that. The single mother of 16- and 12-year-old sons works as an accountant for Daikin, a chemical manufacturer. "I would have to feel really, really sick to stay home," she said.

Rios credits the company with being family-oriented and flexible so that she can make up time and leave early or late if she needs to. "I know not all companies are like that, so I count myself lucky," she said.

The drive to give up personal and sick days has a broader historical backdrop. In 21st century America, parents are responsible for their children longer than in decades past. In the 1920s and 1930s, kids were sent into the work force at ages ranging from 10 to 15 to support the household.

"Now, kids are an economic drain rather than an economic resource," Coontz said.   15

Flexible work arrangements or sick-day policies help ease the work-life balancing act. Sonja Brown, director of patient services for the American Cancer Society in White Plains, N.Y., has two daughters, 10-year-old Tayleur and 3-year-old SoMauri.

Brown said her employer recently adopted a new policy where workers get a block of time off to use as needed. No longer are days off called "sick" or "personal" days. The simple act of changing how the days are classified has made a world of difference. Brown said she now feels less guilty about calling in sick when one of her daughters is ill and she's more likely to take the day off if she needs it for herself.

"Before, it was like, 'Oh my God. I need to save the time for my child,'" she said. "Thank God my job has made it easier for us."

Questions

1. What is the central issue in Christopher Mele's article?
2. Does his emphasis on specific cases undermine or strengthen Mele's larger point?
3. According to Mele, who or what needs to change?

5. *My Mother, Myself, Her Career, My Questions*

KIMBERLY PALMER

In the following selection, Kimberly Palmer gives a personal account of her experience as the daughter of a working mother.

A few months ago, after my husband and I started discussing the career vs. family balancing act that we see in our future, I quizzed my mother about the decisions she had made when she was starting out as a working woman and a mother. She shocked me when she said she had decided to sacrifice some of her professional ambitions for my two younger sisters and me. I had always thought of her as a total career woman and also a total mom — and that she had managed to do, er, everything. I have come to realize that she'd been able to hide the struggle from me because she had support not only from inside the family, but also because other educated women at the time were also trying to do both things.

It's a small but telling example of a much broader issue. My friends and I, now in our late twenties, have begun performing the same balancing act as our mothers and even grandmothers — but without the staunchly careerist back-drop of a few years back. Not only have there been pendulum swings in feminist theory about where a woman's rightful place is (in the office? or should she have the "choice" to stay home?); but I hear about younger women rejecting their mother's decisions and favoring hearth and home over the office. Reacting to this apparent trend, Linda Hirshman recently documented in *American Prospect* mag-azine that highly educated women in their thirties and forties do, in fact, decide to stay at home with their children. They've even earned a name — the opt-out gen-eration. Now I find a new magazine called *Total 180! The Magazine for the Profes-sional Woman Turned Stay-at-Home Mom*.

I don't want to criticize the three stay-at-home moms who founded the new magazine, but its very title, *Total 180!*, alarms me. Are we just dismantling the very real gains our mothers' generation made to work both inside and outside the house?

When I talked with my mom, who has spent most of her career working part time on health policy at a nonprofit in Washington, she was surprised that I didn't realize she had made sacrifices for her kids. Didn't I remember all those times when I was sick and she stayed home with me? Yes, I did; and her attention had always seemed focused on bringing me ginger ale and saltines. Only now did I realize that her thoughts might have been wandering to the repercussions of missing work.

But I soon discovered that few of my girlfriends knew why their parents 5 decided to have children when they did or how they balanced conflicting am-bitions.

One told me that she was afraid to bring up the question with her mom, who had mostly stayed at home, because she thought the subject might be too painful. What if she learned that her mom wished she had been more focused on a career all those years?

Another, whose mother was a doctor, told me that the question made her uncomfortable: "From as early as I can remember, my mom made clear to me that having children was the biggest nuisance one could bring to one's life as a woman. She tells me that when she would come home from her job, tired and exhausted from being with patients she would force herself to play with us."

Yet another worried about being a disappointment: "In talking with my mom about the future, I could always sense that she would get nervous about me not wanting a family. I think her worry is that I get too focused on career issues and forget about all the positives that come from having a family," this married, 26-year-old economic consultant told me.

Mary Pipher, author of "Reviving Ophelia: Saving the Selves of Adolescent Girls," thinks these kinds of discussions between mothers and daughters are vital in shaping a young woman's approach to the vexing issues she will face as an adult woman in our society. When mothers talk about their own choices, she says, they "teach [their] children not what to think but how to think." She says that "Mothers are often the best teachers for their daughters on matters of sex, love, relationships, work, childbearing, time management, wellness and spirituality."

The value of mother-daughter communication when daughters are young seems widely recognized: A survey released last year by the Century Council, a nonprofit organization dedicated to fighting drunk driving and illegal drinking, showed a lack of communication between mothers and daughters on underage drinking. As a result, the council launched a Web site and is planning a blog to help spark conversations. Universities, including Northwestern and the University of Texas, offer mother-daughter programs for teenaged girls and their moms. But this emphasis on mother-daughter bonding seems to dwindle as we progress from our teens to our twenties.

Our moms, after all, have survived what the founders of *Total 180!* have fallen for: the all-or-nothing mentality that has been regaining strength in recent years. My mom tells stories about how she dealt with it. For example, when one boss left "See me" notes for her if she was five minutes late after delayed preschool openings, she sped up her search for a new job. She also says she and my dad think the fact that they both worked helped their marriage, because it let them both develop careers that gave them something to talk about — along with the children — at the end of the day.

My mother was backed by a philosophy that encouraged a woman to pursue a career *and* have a family if she wished to. I don't think that a "total 180" will ever be for me — going, as the magazine puts it, "from briefcase to diaper bag." So I'm hoping for a switch back to the feminism of my mom's generation, which says that you can keep both your job and your family — as long as you know which one takes priority when fever strikes.

Questions

1. Summarize the personal experience that Kimberly Palmer draws on for this essay. Does it seem typical for a woman in her twenties?
2. What is Palmer's attitude toward the magazine *Total 180!* (para. 2)?
3. According to Palmer, what changes in societal attitudes have made it more difficult for younger women to balance career and family?
4. What is Palmer's attitude toward her own mother?
5. What is Palmer's central thesis? State it in one sentence.

6. *Don't Call Me Mr. Mom*

BUZZ MCCLAIN

In the following selection, which was originally posted on <www.slowlane .com>, Buzz McClain discusses attitudes toward stay-at-home dads.

Men who choose to stay at home to raise the children while the mothers commute to work experience things most fathers do not. Not the least of these are the insensitive comments by people who can't comprehend the concept.

It's the price at-home dads pay for being daring and non-traditional. After all, it's not everyday you encounter an at-home dad — then again, maybe you do and just don't realize it because they look like ordinary fathers, except they have slightly more spit-up on their shoulders — so you can't be blamed for saying the wrong thing. Well, we're here to help.

Here are a few things that make at-home fathers cringe, according to the members of the National At-Home Dads Association, who have heard it all.

1. *"What are you going to do when you go back to work in the real world?"* Oh, how at-home dads hate this. It implies raising children isn't real and it isn't work. It is lots of both.

2. *"Wouldn't it be better for the kids if the mother stayed at home?"* No offense, but no. Studies show that working mothers are more involved in their children's lives when the father stays at home than when given over to professional day care; and because of the circumstances, the fathers are far more involved with the children than the dads who see their children only briefly after work and on weekends. The kids get two parents with strong influences.

3. *"What do you do with all your spare time?"* No matter the ages and numbers of the kids, the statement is baloney: There is no spare time. Besides seeing to the children's feeding, clothing, bedding, amusement and education, at-home dads typically assume command of household chores, from laundry to kitchen duty to lawn care. And you can't punch a clock after eight hours and go home. You ARE home.

4. *"Who wears the pants in the family?"* This implies staying at home with the children makes you less masculine; true, at-home dads are likely to wash more dishes, fold more laundry and go to the tot lot more than the father who commutes, but when mom is home dads play and watch just as much sports, ogle just as many women and perform just as many testosterone-driven activities [as] other fathers. And they do it with more gusto because getting out of the house means more to them.

5. *"Oh, so you're Mr. Mom."* Don't call us Mr. Mom. The kids already have a mother. At-home fathers do not replace mothers; they simply assume

duties traditionally performed by them. If you must call at-home dads something, try Mr. Dad.

6. *"That's a nice Mommy Wagon you drive."* Ahem. It is NOT a Mommy Wagon. It's a marvelously functional all-purpose utility vehicle that just happens to have enough room to seat more than half of the Stingers Little League soccer team.

7. *"What does your wife think about you not working?"* Ordinarily a fair question, but often asked to see how the woman is handling the pressure of being the primary breadwinner. Get real: The empowerment is a heady sensation, one most women don't get to experience, and she loves it. As a bonus, she goes to the office each day knowing her baby is in good hands. Real men deal with the role change just fine, thank you.

8. *"How can you stand to change diapers all the time?"* This is likely to be asked by the "traditional man," the kind who will overhaul a greasy auto engine but can't bring himself to wipe a baby's butt. We know of one such man who, when confronted with a messy diaper, put the baby in the bathtub until the mother came home. Diapers are easy, pal. (Plum–and–sweet potato spit-up is another thing altogether.)

9. *"Do you miss the security of having a job?"* Maybe at first, but who isn't disillusioned by the general lack of loyalty companies express these days? Mergers, takeovers, layoffs, forced relocations and a slavish devotion by corporations to the bottom line are enough to rattle anyone's sense of security. An at-home dad has the job of a lifetime — you can't be fired or transferred to a lesser position.

10. *"What do you mean you didn't get a chance to finish the laundry?"* Most often asked by frazzled wives coming home from work. Well, honey, things got really fun at the tot lot with the playgroup and we stayed a few hours longer than we expected . . .

Questions

1. Of what importance is it that Buzz McClain's article appeared on <www.slowlane .com>, "the online resource for stay-at-home dads"? Who is its audience?
2. Although McClain uses humor, he makes serious points. What are they?
3. What is the tone of this piece? Why do you think the author chose that tone?

Entering the Conversation

As you respond to the following prompts, support your argument with references to at least three of the sources in Conversation: Focus on Working Parents. For help using sources, see Chapter 3.

1. Write an essay identifying the major issues facing working parents. Do not include your own opinion; just synthesize the information in the readings.

2. Suppose that you are a parent of two preschool children and are in your early thirties, just getting established in your career. Write an essay explaining why you would or would not choose to stay at home with your children.

3. Using the readings in "Conversation: Focus on Working Parents," and your own knowledge, write an essay describing the difficulties facing working parents with young children. Propose at least three measures that employers might enact to become more family-friendly.

4. Using your own experience growing up, as well as at least three of the sources in "Conversation: Focus on Working Parents," explain what you consider the two most important issues a person faces trying to balance family and work.

5. What stereotypes or prejudices exist toward stay-at-home moms or stay-at-home dads? Write an essay in which you discuss the attitudes of society in general — and employers in particular — toward men or women who choose to stay at home with young children rather than work. Then make recommendations that will help stay-at-home parents overcome such bias.

Student Writing

Analyzing Styles in Paired Passages

Following is a prompt that requires close reading of two passages: Ellen Goodman's article on page 221 and the following excerpt from a novel by George Eliot, the pseudonym of Mary Anne Evans.

> Novelist George Eliot in "Old Leisure," which follows, and newspaper columnist Ellen Goodman in "In Praise of a Snail's Pace" (p. 221) consider changes in the pace and occupations of their societies — in 1859 and 2005, respectively. After reading both selections carefully, write an essay in which you compare and contrast how each writer conveys her purpose.

After you have read and discussed both passages, read the student essay, which was written outside class by high school junior Teresa Ingraham without specific time constraints. Pay special attention to the way the student supports her analysis with examples from the two texts.

Old Leisure

Leisure is gone — gone where the spinning-wheels are gone, and the pack-horses, and the slow wagons, and the pedlars, who brought bargains to the door on sunny afternoons. Ingenious philosophers tell you, perhaps that the great work of the steam-engine is to create leisure for mankind. Do not believe them: it only creates a vacuum for eager thought to rush in. Even idleness is eager now — eager for amusement: prone to excursion — trains, art-museums, periodical literature, and exciting novels: prone even to scientific theorizing, and cursory peeps through microscopes. Old Leisure was quite a different personage: he only read one newspaper, innocent of leaders, and was free from that periodicity of sensations which we call post-time. He was a contemplative, rather stout gentleman, of excellent digestion, — of quiet perceptions, undiseased by hypothesis: happy in his inability to know the causes of things, preferring the things themselves. He lived chiefly in the country, among pleasant seats and homesteads, and was fond of sauntering by the fruit-tree wall, and scenting the apricots when they were warmed by the morning sunshine, or of sheltering himself under the orchard boughs at noon, when the summer pears were falling. He knew nothing of weekday services, and thought none the worse of the Sunday sermon if it allowed him to sleep from the text to the blessing — liking the afternoon service best, because the prayers were the shortest, and not ashamed to say so; for he had an easy, jolly conscience, broadbacked like himself, and able to carry a great deal of beer or port-wine, — not being made squeamish by doubts and qualms and lofty aspirations. Life was not a task to him, but a sinecure: he fingered the guineas in his pocket, and ate his dinners, and slept the sleep of the irresponsible; for had he not kept up his charter by going to church on the Sunday afternoons?

Fine old Leisure! Do not be severe upon him, and judge him by our standard: he never went to Exeter Hall, or heard a popular preacher, or read *Tracts for the Times* or *Sartor Resartus*.[1]

---

[1]Works published between 1833 and 1841; *Sartor Resartus* was written by Thomas Carlyle (see p. 209). — Eds.

Student Response

No Leisure Then or Now

Teresa Ingraham

While both passages employ elements of satire to convey an understanding of the necessity of progress against a sense of nostalgia for the past, Ellen Goodman's column "In Praise of a Snail's Pace" is a more humorous and personal approach than the sermonizing tone and personification in George Eliot's "Old Leisure."

Eliot begins her piece with an illustration of "old Leisure" and a series of outdated images that are almost humorous to the modern reader. This old version of leisure time is said to be "gone," vanished along with the "slow wagons" and "pack-horses" that served to bring "pedlars" to one's door and remind one of the enjoyable slow-paced life that advancement in technology seems to deplete. Eliot creates a character to demonstrate her conflicting feelings on these advancements: she personifies leisure time as "old Leisure." She describes old Leisure as a "contemplative," "stout gentleman," who enjoys nothing more than sleeping during church, drinking a "great deal of beer or port-wine," and never worrying about investigating questions about the more complicated aspects of life. Eliot's nostalgia for this past, simplified way of life is evident as she defends old Leisure, warning others not to "be severe upon him," and identifies many amiable qualities of his "personage" such as his "easy, jolly conscience." She also goes on to criticize this new form of leisure that "creates a vacuum for eager thought to rush in," and she pokes fun as she sarcastically describes philosophers who promote great works of technology such as "the steam-engine" as "ingenious." The phrase "idleness is eager" serves as a paradoxical personification that furthers Eliot's opinion that true complacent leisure is no longer existent; it has been replaced by an addiction and urgency for "scientific theorizing" and "cursory peeps through microscopes" in an attempt to find the answers to questions "doubts and qualms and lofty aspirations" bring. The speed of this progress as it has overcome mankind is portrayed in its "eagerness" and "rush" and is contrasted with the "slow" and "sauntering" pace of old leisure. While all these points initially seem to support the argument that Eliot prefers this past version of life, she also demonstrates that she feels the necessity of progress and introspection. Her conflicting feelings are present as she characterizes old Leisure as "irresponsible" and includes herself in the "standard" by which old Leisure might be judged harshly. Additionally, she ends her description of old Leisure's views with a rhetorical question that ironically works both to make fun of Leisure's thoughts and to defend him from modern critics. As Eliot preaches to her audience that one should always appreciate the small, simpler things in life and occasionally look on life as a sort of "sinecure," she also points out the flaws in never asking "to know the causes of things" or immersing oneself in such works as *Sartor Resartus*.

Ellen Goodman writes her opinion on progress with a more direct, personal, and humorous approach. Her reference to the "square envelope" that carries her condolences as "an artifact from another age" succeeds to amusingly identify the current generation's view of "snail mail" as anachronistic. Because her preference is clearly inclined toward past forms of communication, Goodman's incorporation of these descriptions creates a satirical effect. Her use of humor pokes fun at a reader opposed to her view, but does so lightly enough that her message rings clear of resentment. She states that "there are rituals you cannot speed up without destroying them," but avoids sounding as though she is giving a lecture by comparing this idea to the image of "Thanksgiving dinner at a fast-food restaurant." Goodman illustrates how "hyperactive technology" has taken over the current generation's lives by metaphorically describing a friend's son's busy schedule as "the full in-box of his life." When "e-mail users" step away from the computer, Goodman depicts them as "freeing themselves from the tyranny of the reply button." Many times she points out the conflicting ideas that accompany the "times we live in" by describing it as an era of "continuous partial attention." While technology of today has made communication and worldwide connection a problem of the past, Goodman feels that individuals have never been more separated. Paying full attention to someone is so rare that the pleasure of it is likened to an "aphrodisiac." Irony is again evident in the way she contrasts past admiration of "a ringing cell phone" to the present reverence of people who turn their cell phones off. Goodman's "exchange" of the "Internet for the country road" is comparable to Eliot's use of a rural countryside to represent the old form of leisure, but she narrates her views in first person to help the reader identify her opinion more directly. Still, along with Goodman's affection for "snail mail" and her belief that it alone carries "the stamp of authenticity," is her optimism for the reform of the "technological whirlwind" of today. Even among all of this progress are "signs of people searching for ways to slow down and listen up." Goodman understands that humankind will always continue to advance, to question, and to use the best technology available, but she also wishes to impose upon her audience the importance of revering the old-fashioned, timeless practices that define what everyone longs for in this life.

Both of these pieces of writing aim to open readers' eyes to a nostalgia and veneration for past ways of life that should accompany a desire for innovation and improvement for the future. Though written in different time periods and in different styles, these selections make their audiences question their hasty judgment of a simpler, slower way of life as unfulfilled and frivolous.

Questions

1. The prompt calls for a comparison and contrast of how each writer conveys her purpose. What does Teresa identify as the purpose of these essays?
2. What are the resources of language that Teresa focuses on in her analysis? Identify specific ones that she names.

3. Teresa begins her essay with a clear opening statement that addresses the prompt. How might this paragraph be developed into a fuller introduction?

4. Does Teresa develop her analysis more through (a) paraphrase and reference to the two readings, (b) long quotations taken from the two, or (c) briefer quotations interwoven into her own writing? Why do you think her method of development is or is not effective?

5. Does Teresa find more comparison or contrast between these two pieces? Explain why you agree or disagree with her analysis.

Grammar as Rhetoric and Style
Short Simple Sentences and Fragments

Short Simple Sentences

A simple sentence, strictly defined, has a subject and verb: it consists of one independent clause. A simple sentence may have a compound subject, a compound verb, a modifier, and an object or a complement, but it still is one independent clause.

The following examples of simple sentences appear in Barbara Ehrenreich's "Serving in Florida."

> There is a problem, though.
> But the chances of this are minuscule.
> This must be Phillip's theory, anyway.
> Finally she tells me not to worry.
> What had I been thinking?

Sometimes simple sentences can be rather long:

> The e-mails and phone messages addressed to my former self come from a distant race of people with exotic concerns and far too much time on their hands.

This example from Ehrenreich is twenty-eight words. This lesson focuses on *short* simple sentences, ones that run no more than seven words.

Sentence Fragments

A sentence fragment is an incomplete sentence that readers understand to be complete. Some fragments are missing a subject, verb, or both; other fragments have a subject and verb, but are dependent clauses. Consider the underlined fragment in the following example.

"Wouldn't it be better for the kids if the mother stayed at home?" <u>No offense, but no.</u>

— BUZZ MCCLAIN

This fragment has neither a subject nor a verb. If we added a subject and verb to make it a complete sentence, it might read like this:

> "Wouldn't it be better for the kids if the mother stayed at home?" No offense, but no it would not be better.

Following is an example of a fragment created by a freestanding dependent clause:

> *Hurry,* I urge my country. <u>Before it's too late.</u>

— CLAUDIA O'KEEFE

If we were to rewrite this as a complete sentence, we might connect the dependent clause to the simple sentence (that is, the independent clause) that precedes it:

> *Hurry,* I urge my country, before it's too late.

Rhetorical and Stylistic Strategy

A series of simple sentences can become monotonous, but one or two short simple sentences can be rhetorically effective in a number of situations:

- after several long sentences
- as a summary of what the writer has just said
- as a transition between sentences or paragraphs

Essentially, one or two short simple sentences create emphasis by contrast. As a writer, when you juxtapose one or two short simple sentences with several longer ones, you call attention to the short simple ones. Consider this paragraph from Claudia O'Keefe's essay "The Traveling Bra Salesman's Lesson."

> The question is not whether it is good or bad to import workers or export jobs. The problem is that society has hit an emotional roadblock. My country is one tremendously divided, with pro-business and pro-worker stubbornly pitted against each other. <u>We're anxious. We're angry.</u> Neither side wants to give and nothing can be solved until we acknowledge one crucial fact.

Notice that the short simple sentences (both structured simply as subject + linking verb) stand out among the longer sentences in the paragraph. Their similar structure adds even more emphasis.

In some instances, writers choose to use sentence fragments, especially short ones. Although most of the time you will avoid fragments, occasionally you might use one for effect. What's important is that you use the fragment as you use a short simple sentence, *deliberately*, for a special reason:

- to make a transition
- to signal a conclusion
- to emphasize an important point.

Both the short simple sentence and an effective fragment focus your reader. Consider this example, the conclusion from Claudia O'Keefe's essay:

> *Hurry*, I urge my country. <u>Before it's too late.</u> Only when we admit that the future awaits us can we embrace a more inclusive and thrilling successor to outmoded 20th century ideals, a goal without boundaries or limits, not The American Dream, but The Global Dream.

The underlined fragment could easily have been part of the sentence that precedes it. However, by presenting it as a fragment, O'Keefe slows her reader down and emphasizes the importance of time.

A word of caution! Use both short simple sentences and fragments sparingly. Used intentionally and infrequently, both can be effective. Overused, they lose their punch or become more of a gimmick than a valuable technique. Also, consider whether your audience will interpret a fragment as a grammatical error. If you are confident that your audience will recognize your deliberate use of a fragment, then use it. But if you think your teacher or reader will assume you made a mistake, then it's better to write a complete sentence. Again, if you use fragments infrequently, then your audience is more likely to know you're deliberately choosing what is technically an incomplete sentence.

· EXERCISE 1

Identify the simple sentences in the following paragraph from Annie Dillard's essay "The Writing Life." What is their effect?

The air show announcer hushed. He had been squawking all day, and now he quit. The crowd stilled. Even the children watched dumbstruck as the slow, black biplane buzzed its way around the air. Rahm made beauty with his whole body; it was pure pattern, and you could watch it happen. The plane moved every way a line can move, and it controlled three dimensions, so the line carved massive and subtle slits in the air like sculptures. The plane looped the loop, seeming to arch its back like a gymnast; it stalled, dropped, and spun out of it climbing; it spiraled and knifed west on one side's wings and back east on another; it turned cartwheels, which must be physically impossible; it played with its own line like a cat with yarn. How did the pilot know where in the air he was? If he got lost, the ground would swat him.

• EXERCISE 2

Revise the paragraph in Exercise 1 either by turning it into a series of short simple sentences or by eliminating the simple sentences entirely. How do your revisions change the effect? Read the original paragraph; then read your revised paragraph aloud, and listen to the difference.

• EXERCISE 3

Identify the short simple sentences and the fragment in the following paragraphs reproduced here from Tillie Olsen's short story "I Stand Here Ironing." Discuss their effect. In your analysis, keep in mind that fiction writers use these syntactical strategies for the same reasons as nonfiction writers, yet they also employ short sentences and fragments to evoke disconnected thoughts of the narrator.

Why do I put that first? I do not even know if it matters, or if it explains anything.

She was a beautiful baby. She blew shining bubbles of sound. She loved motion, loved light, loved color and music and textures. She would lie on the floor in her blue overalls patting the surface so hard in ecstasy her hands and feet would blur. She was a miracle to me, but when she was eight months old I had to leave her daytimes with the woman downstairs to whom she was no miracle at all, for I worked or looked for work and for Emily's father, who "could no longer endure" (he wrote in his good-bye note) "sharing want with us."

I was nineteen. It was the pre-relief, pre-WPA world of the depression. I would start running as soon as I got off the streetcar, running up the stairs, the place smelling sour, and awake or asleep to startle awake, when she saw me she would break into a clogged weeping that could not be comforted, a weeping I can hear yet.

After a while I found a job hashing at night so I could be with her days, and it was better. But it came to where I had to bring her to his family and leave her.

It took a long time to raise the money for her fare back. Then she got chicken pox and I had to wait longer. When she finally came, I hardly knew her, walking quick and nervous like her father, looking like her father, thin, and dressed in a shoddy red that yellowed her skin and glared at the pockmarks. All the baby loveliness gone.

• **EXERCISE 4**

Find examples of short simple sentences or fragments that are used effectively in this textbook or that you find in magazines, newspapers, or novels.

Suggestions for Writing
Work

Now that you have examined a number of readings and other texts focusing on work, explore one dimension of this topic by synthesizing your own ideas and the readings. You might want to do more research or use readings from other classes as you prepare for the following assignments.

1. What is the difference between a job and a career? Write an essay explaining the distinction. Use support drawn from the readings in this chapter and from your own experience or observation.

2. How do the popular media — either today or in the past — depict the workplace? Select one genre, such as the movies or cartoons.

3. These days many complain that young people no longer have a *work ethic*. What does that term mean to you? Do you believe that you and your peers are motivated by a work ethic? Why or why not? Explain your response in terms of your own experience and your reading.

4. Write a response to Thomas Carlyle (p. 209) by a financially successful or powerful contemporary person, such as Donald Trump or Bill Gates. Indicate areas of common ground as well as disagreement.

5. Thomas Carlyle, whose view of work you read on page 209, believed that a society's worth could be measured by the attitude of its citizens toward work. Write an essay explaining the conclusions you would draw about the society you're living in right now. Focus on either your local community or a larger, national community.

6. How is telecommuting changing our concept of the workplace? In the past, many people felt like part of a "workplace family" of people they saw nearly every day and got to know well. Is the idea of a workplace family outdated, redefined, or simply impossible in a world where physical proximity is not necessary for successful working relationships? Write an essay explaining your view.

7. Write an argument defending exorbitant salaries or fees paid to athletes and movie stars. Develop a logical argument with clearly drawn reasons — or write your response as a satire.

8. Abraham Maslow (1908–1970) was one of the founders of a field known as humanistic psychology. Research Maslow's "hierarchy of needs," and discuss the ways in which work fulfills some or all human needs. Explain whether you believe there is a correlation between the number of needs work fulfills and the status of the work.

9. Which of the following quotations most accurately captures your attitude toward work or the professional life you hope to have? Write an essay about why the quotation speaks to you.

- "Work consists of whatever a body is obliged to do, and Play consists of whatever a body is not obliged to do."   — MARK TWAIN

- "There is dignity in work only when it is work freely accepted."
                                                                    — ALBERT CAMUS

- "Never work just for money or for power. They won't save your soul or help you sleep at night."   — MARIAN WRIGHT EDELMAN

- "Work for something because it is good, not just because it stands a chance to succeed."   — VACLAV HAVEL

- "In order that people may be happy in their work, these three things are needed: They must be fit for it: They must not do too much of it: And they must have a sense of success in it."   — JOHN RUSKIN

6

Community

*What is the relationship of the individual
to the community?*

How can an individual maintain integrity and pursue personal dreams while contributing to the overall society? This is the central question facing every community. In the United States, we pride ourselves on rugged individualism and the pioneering spirit; at the same time, we believe in collective values. In other parts of the world, people perceive the balance of the individual and the community differently, but the history and literature of most societies depict the struggle of the individual to live life in good faith or conscience while being part of a community.

In the twenty-first century, the speed of our lives and an increasingly global perspective are redefining what a community is. The word *community* itself is changing, coming to mean a group of like-minded people sharing common interests, when in the past it referred to a group of people of various skills and interests cooperating with one another in order to survive. Geography and uniformity, once the main criteria of a community, now bow to technology and diversity, which today underlie the definition of ethnic communities, the intelligence community, or online communities, for example. Consider the notion of the "gated community." Is the phrase an expression of a different kind of community, one defined not by inclusion but rather exclusion?

We find — and forge — communities based on geography, ethnicity, race, religion, marital status, occupation, class, economic status, gender, political affiliation, shared interest, or even language. Are those features more important than values, principles, and ideals? Or do we belong to various communities based on distinct criteria? How can we belong to several communities simultaneously?

The readings in this chapter explore the balance of individual concerns and community values, and examine how different types of communities arise, some intentionally, some coincidentally. As you discuss these ideas, consider how people form communities, how individuals gain membership, how the community contributes to an individual's identity, and how outsiders perceive the community. Such discussions will help you formulate questions about the meaning of community in your own life.

Letter from Birmingham Jail

MARTIN LUTHER KING JR.

 Martin Luther King Jr. (1929–1968) was one of the most influential leaders of the civil rights movement of the 1950s and 1960s. Dr. King was born in Atlanta, Georgia, and grew up in the Ebenezer Baptist Church, where his father and grandfather were ministers. He earned a BA at Morehouse College, a divinity degree at Crozer Theological Seminary, and a PhD in theology at Boston University, all by the age of 26. In 1957, he founded the Southern Christian Leadership Conference and later led numerous protests against segregation by practicing the Gandhian doctrine of nonviolent resistance. In 1963, while King was in Birmingham, Alabama, eight clergymen published a letter in the *Post-Herald* criticizing his presence and his strategies. From the cell where he was jailed for demonstrating, King responded by writing what has come to be known as "Letter from Birmingham Jail."

The following is the public statement directed to Martin Luther King Jr. by eight Alabama clergymen that occasioned King's letter.

We the undersigned clergymen are among those who, in January, issued "an appeal for law and order and common sense," in dealing with racial problems in Alabama. We expressed understanding that honest convictions in racial matters could properly be pursued in the courts, but urged that decisions of those courts should in the meantime be peacefully obeyed.

Since that time there has been some evidence of increased forbearance and a willingness to face facts. Responsible citizens have undertaken to work on various problems which cause racial friction and unrest. In Birmingham, recent public events have given indication that we all have opportunity for a new constructive and realistic approach to racial problems.

However, we are now confronted by a series of demonstrations by some of our Negro citizens, directed and led in part by outsiders. We recognize the natural impatience of people who feel that their hopes are slow in being realized. But we are convinced that these demonstrations are unwise and untimely.

We agree rather with certain local Negro leadership which has called for honest and open negotiation of racial issues in our area. And we believe this kind of facing of issues can best be accomplished by citizens of our own metropolitan area, white and Negro, meeting with their knowledge and experience of the local situation. All of us need to face that responsibility and find proper channels for its accomplishment.

Just as we formerly pointed out that "hatred and violence have no sanction in our religious and political traditions," we also point out that such actions as incite to hatred and violence, however technically peaceful those actions may be, have not contributed to the resolution of our local problems. We do not believe that these days of new hope are days when extreme measures are justified in Birmingham.

We commend the community as a whole, and the local news media and law enforcement officials in particular, on the calm manner in which these demonstrations have been handled. We urge the public to continue to show restraint should the demonstrations continue, and the law enforcement officials to remain calm and continue to protect our city from violence.

We further strongly urge our own Negro community to withdraw support from these demonstrations, and to unite locally in working peacefully for a better Birmingham. When rights are consistently denied, a cause should be pressed in the courts and in negotiations among local leaders, and not in the streets. We appeal to both our white and Negro citizenry to observe the principles of law and order and common sense.

BISHOP C. C. J. CARPENTER, D.D., LL.D., Episcopalian Bishop of Alabama

BISHOP JOSEPH A. DURICK, D.D., Auxiliary Bishop, Roman Catholic Diocese of Mobile, Birmingham

RABBI MILTON L. GRAFMAN, Temple Emanu-El, Birmingham, Alabama

BISHOP PAUL HARDIN, Methodist Bishop of the Alabama–West Florida Conference

BISHOP NOLAN B. HARMON, Bishop of the North Alabama Conference of the Methodist Church

REV. GEORGE M. MURRAY, D.D., LL.D., Bishop Coadjutor, Episcopal Diocese of Alabama

REV. EDWARD V. RAMAGE, Moderator, Synod of the Alabama Presbyterian Church in the United States

REV. EARL STALLINGS, Pastor, First Baptist Church, Birmingham, Alabama

April 12, 1963

My Dear Fellow Clergymen:

While confined here in the Birmingham city jail, I came across your recent statement calling my present activities "unwise and untimely." Seldom do I pause to answer criticism of my work and ideas. If I sought to answer all the criticisms that cross my desk, my secretaries would have little time for anything other than such correspondence in the course of the day, and I would have no time for constructive work. But since I feel that you are men of genuine good will and that your criticisms are sincerely set forth, I want to try to answer your statement in what I hope will be patient and reasonable terms.

I think I should indicate why I am here in Birmingham, since you have been influenced by the view which argues against "outsiders coming in." I have the honor of serving as president of the Southern Christian Leadership Conference, an organization operating in every southern state, with headquarters in Atlanta, Georgia. We have some eighty-five affiliated organizations across the South, and one of them is the Alabama Christian Movement for Human Rights. Frequently we share staff, educational, and financial resources with our affiliates. Several months ago the affiliate here in Birmingham asked us to be on call to engage in a nonviolent direct-action program if such were deemed necessary. We readily consented, and when the hour came we lived up to our promise. So I, along with several members of my staff, am here because I was invited here. I am here because I have organizational ties here.

But more basically, I am in Birmingham because injustice is here. Just as the prophets of the eighth century B.C. left their villages and carried their "thus saith the Lord" far beyond the boundaries of their home towns, and just as the Apostle Paul left his village of Tarsus and carried the gospel of Jesus Christ to the far corners of the Greco-Roman world, so am I compelled to carry the gospel of freedom beyond my own home town. Like Paul, I must constantly respond to the Macedonian call for aid.

Moreover, I am cognizant of the interrelatedness of all communities and states. I cannot sit idly by in Atlanta and not be concerned about what happens in Birmingham. Injustice anywhere is a threat to justice everywhere. We are caught in an inescapable network of mutuality, tied in a single garment of destiny. Whatever affects one directly, affects all indirectly. Never again can we afford to live with the narrow, provincial "outside agitator" idea. Anyone who lives inside the United States can never be considered an outsider anywhere within its bounds.

You deplore the demonstrations taking place in Birmingham. But your statement, I am sorry to say, fails to express a similar concern for the conditions that brought about the demonstrations. I am sure that none of you would want to rest content with the superficial kind of social analysis that deals merely with effects and does not grapple with underlying causes. It is unfortunate that demonstrations are taking place in Birmingham, but it is even more unfortunate that the city's white power structure left the Negro community with no alternative.

In any nonviolent campaign there are four basic steps: collection of the facts to determine whether injustices exist; negotiation; self-purification; and direct action. We have gone through all these steps in Birmingham. There can be no gainsaying the fact that racial injustice engulfs this community. Birmingham is probably the most thoroughly segregated city in the United States. Its ugly record of brutality is widely known. Negroes have experienced grossly unjust treatment in the courts. There have been more unsolved bombings of Negro homes and churches in Birmingham than in any other city in the nation. These are the hard,

5

brutal facts of the case. On the basis of these conditions, Negro leaders sought to negotiate with the city fathers. But the latter consistently refused to engage in good-faith negotiation.

Then, last September, came the opportunity to talk with leaders of Birmingham's economic community. In the course of the negotiations, certain promises were made by the merchants — for example, to remove the stores' humiliating racial signs. On the basis of these promises, the Reverend Fred Shuttlesworth and the leaders of the Alabama Christian Movement for Human Rights agreed to a moratorium on all demonstrations. As the weeks and months went by, we realized that we were the victims of a broken promise. A few signs, briefly removed, returned; the others remained.

As in so many past experiences, our hopes had been blasted, and the shadow of deep disappointment settled upon us. We had no alternative except to prepare for direct action, whereby we would present our very bodies as a means of laying our case before the conscience of the local and the national community. Mindful of the difficulties involved, we decided to undertake a process of self-purification. We began a series of workshops on nonviolence, and we repeatedly asked ourselves: "Are you able to accept blows without retaliating?" "Are you able to endure the ordeal of jail?" We decided to schedule our direct-action program for the Easter season, realizing that except for Christmas, this is the main shopping period of the year. Knowing that a strong economic withdrawal program would be the by-product of direct action, we felt that this would be the best time to bring pressure to bear on the merchants for the needed change.

Then it occurred to us that Birmingham's mayoral election was coming up in March, and we speedily decided to postpone action until after election day. When we discovered that the Commissioner of Public Safety, Eugene "Bull" Connor, had piled up enough votes to be in the runoff, we decided again to postpone action until the day after the runoff so that the demonstrations could not be used to cloud the issues. Like many others, we wanted to see Mr. Connor defeated, and to this end we endured postponement after postponement. Having aided in this community need, we felt that our direct-action program could be delayed no longer.

You may well ask, "Why direct action? Why sit-ins, marches, and so forth? Isn't negotiation a better path?" You are quite right in calling for negotiation. Indeed, this is the very purpose of direct action. Nonviolent direct action seeks to create such a crisis and foster such a tension that a community which has constantly refused to negotiate is forced to confront the issue. It seeks so to dramatize the issue that it can no longer be ignored. My citing the creation of tension as part of the work of the nonviolent-resister may sound rather shocking. But I must confess that I am not afraid of the word "tension." I have earnestly opposed violent tension, but there is a type of constructive, nonviolent tension which is necessary for growth. Just as Socrates felt that it was necessary to create a tension in the mind so that individuals could rise from the bondage of myths and half-

10

truths to the unfettered realm of creative analysis and objective appraisal, so must we see the need for nonviolent gadflies to create the kind of tension in society that will help men rise from the dark depths of prejudice and racism to the majestic heights of understanding and brotherhood.

The purpose of our direct-action program is to create a situation so crisis-packed that it will inevitably open the door to negotiation. I therefore concur with you in your call for negotiation. Too long has our beloved Southland been bogged down in a tragic effort to live in monologue rather than dialogue.

One of the basic points in your statement is that the action that I and my associates have taken in Birmingham is untimely. Some have asked: "Why didn't you give the new city administration time to act?" The only answer that I can give to this query is that the new Birmingham administration must be prodded about as much as the outgoing one, before it will act. We are sadly mistaken if we feel that the election of Albert Boutwell as mayor will bring the millennium to Birmingham. While Mr. Boutwell is a much more gentle person than Mr. Connor, they are both segregationists, dedicated to maintenance of the status quo. I have hoped that Mr. Boutwell will be reasonable enough to see the futility of massive resistance to desegregation. But he will not see this without pressure from devotees of civil rights. My friends, I must say to you that we have not made a single gain in civil rights without determined legal and nonviolent pressure. Lamentably, it is an historical fact that privileged groups seldom give up their privileges voluntarily. Individuals may see the moral light and voluntarily give up their unjust posture, but, as Reinhold Niebuhr[1] has reminded us, groups tend to be more immoral than individuals.

We know through painful experience that freedom is never voluntarily given by the oppressor; it must be demanded by the oppressed. Frankly, I have yet to engage in a direct-action campaign that was "well timed" in the view of those who have not suffered unduly from the disease of segregation. For years now I have heard the word "Wait!" It rings in the ear of every Negro with piercing familiarity. This "Wait" has almost always meant "Never." We must come to see, with one of our distinguished jurists, that "justice too long delayed is justice denied."

We have waited for more than 340 years for our constitutional and God-given rights. The nations of Asia and Africa are moving with jet-like speed toward gaining political independence, but we still creep at horse-and-buggy pace toward gaining a cup of coffee at a lunch counter. Perhaps it is easy for those who have never felt the stinging darts of segregation to say, "Wait." But when you have seen vicious mobs lynch your mothers and fathers at will and drown your sisters and brothers at whim; when you have seen hate-filled policemen curse, kick, and even kill your black brothers and sisters; when you see the vast majority of your twenty million Negro brothers smothering in an airtight cage of poverty in the

---

[1]Neibuhr (1892–1971) was a U.S. clergyman and a Protestant theologian. — Eds.

midst of an affluent society; when you suddenly find your tongue twisted and your speech stammering as you seek to explain to your six-year-old daughter why she can't go to the public amusement park that has just been advertised on television, and see tears welling up in her eyes when she is told that Funtown is closed to colored children, and see ominous clouds of inferiority beginning to form in her little mental sky, and see her beginning to distort her personality by developing an unconscious bitterness toward white people; when you have to concoct an answer for a five-year-old son who is asking, "Daddy, why do white people treat colored people so mean?"; when you take a cross-country drive and find it necessary to sleep night after night in the uncomfortable corners of your automobile because no motel will accept you; when you are humiliated day in and day out by nagging signs reading "white" and "colored"; when your first name becomes "nigger," your middle name becomes "boy" (however old you are) and your last name becomes "John," and your wife and mother are never given the respected title "Mrs."; when you are harried by day and haunted by night by the fact that you are a Negro, living constantly at tiptoe stance, never quite knowing what to expect next, and are plagued with inner fears and outer resentments; when you are forever fighting a degenerating sense of "nobodiness" — then you will understand why we find it difficult to wait. There comes a time when the cup of endurance runs over, and men are no longer willing to be plunged into the abyss of despair. I hope, sirs, you can understand our legitimate and unavoidable impatience.

You express a great deal of anxiety over our willingness to break laws. This is 15 certainly a legitimate concern. Since we so diligently urge people to obey the Supreme Court's decision of 1954 outlawing segregation in the public schools, at first glance it may seem rather paradoxical for us consciously to break laws. One may well ask: "How can you advocate breaking some laws and obeying others?" The answer lies in the fact that there are two types of laws: just and unjust. I would be the first to advocate obeying just laws. One has not only a legal but a moral responsibility to obey just laws. Conversely, one has a moral responsibility to disobey unjust laws. I would agree with St. Augustine that "an unjust law is no law at all."

Now, what is the difference between the two? How does one determine whether a law is just or unjust? A just law is a man-made code that squares with the moral law or the law of God. An unjust law is a code that is out of harmony with the moral law. To put it in the terms of St. Thomas Aquinas: An unjust law is a human law that is not rooted in eternal law and natural law. Any law that uplifts human personality is just. Any law that degrades human personality is unjust. All segregation statutes are unjust because segregation distorts the soul and damages the personality. It gives the segregator a false sense of superiority and the segregated a false sense of inferiority. Segregation, to use the terminology of the Jewish philosopher Martin Buber, substitutes an "I-it" relationship for an "I-thou" relationship and ends up relegating persons to the status of things. Hence segregation is not only politically, economically, and sociologically unsound, it is morally wrong and sinful. Paul Tillich[2] has said that sin is separation. Is not segregation an existential expression of man's tragic separation, his awful estrangement, his terrible sinfulness? Thus it is that I can urge men to obey the 1954 decision of the Supreme Court, for it is morally right; and I can urge them to disobey segregation ordinances, for they are morally wrong.

Let us consider a more concrete example of just and unjust laws. An unjust law is a code that a numerical or power majority group compels a minority group to obey but does not make binding on itself. This is *difference* made legal. By the same token, a just law is a code that a majority compels a minority to follow and that it is willing to follow itself. This is *sameness* made legal.

Let me give another explanation. A law is unjust if it is inflicted on a minority that, as a result of being denied the right to vote, had no part in enacting or devising the law. Who can say that the legislature of Alabama which set up that state's segregation laws was democratically elected? Throughout Alabama all sorts of devious methods are used to prevent Negroes from becoming registered voters, and there are some counties in which, even though Negroes constitute a majority of the population, not a single Negro is registered. Can any law enacted under such circumstances be considered democratically structured?

Sometimes a law is just on its face and unjust in its application. For instance, I have been arrested on a charge of parading without a permit. Now, there is nothing wrong in having an ordinance which requires a permit for a parade. But such an ordinance becomes unjust when it is used to maintain segregation and to deny citizens the First-Amendment privilege of peaceful assembly and protest.

I hope you are able to see the distinction I am trying to point out. In no sense do I advocate evading or defying the law, as would the rabid segregationist. That would lead to anarchy. One who breaks an unjust law must do so openly, lovingly, and with a willingness to accept the penalty. I submit that an individual who breaks a law that conscience tells him is unjust, and who willingly accepts the penalty of imprisonment in order to arouse the conscience of the community over its injustice, is in reality expressing the highest respect for law. 20

Of course, there is nothing new about this kind of civil disobedience. It was evidenced sublimely in the refusal of Shadrach, Meshach, and Abednego to obey the laws of Nebuchadnezzar, on the ground that a higher moral law was at stake. It was practiced superbly by the early Christians, who were willing to face hungry lions and the excruciating pain of chopping blocks rather than submit to certain unjust laws of the Roman Empire. To a degree, academic freedom is a reality today because Socrates practiced civil disobedience. In our own nation, the Boston Tea Party represented a massive act of civil disobedience.

We should never forget that everything Adolf Hitler did in Germany was "legal" and everything the Hungarian freedom fighters did in Hungary was "ille-

---

[2]Tillich (1886–1965) was a German American philosopher and a Christian theologian. —Eds.

gal." It was "illegal" to aid and comfort a Jew in Hitler's Germany. Even so, I am sure that, had I lived in Germany at the time, I would have aided and comforted my Jewish brothers. If today I lived in a Communist country where certain principles dear to the Christian faith are suppressed, I would openly advocate disobeying that country's antireligious laws.

I must make two honest confessions to you, my Christian and Jewish brothers. First, I must confess that over the past few years I have been gravely disappointed with the white moderate. I have almost reached the regrettable conclusion that the Negro's great stumbling block in his stride toward freedom is not the White Citizen's Counciler or the Ku Klux Klanner, but the white moderate, who is more devoted to "order" than to justice; who prefers a negative peace which is the absence of tension to a positive peace which is the presence of justice; who constantly says, "I agree with you in the goal you seek, but I cannot agree with your methods of direct action"; who paternalistically believes he can set the timetable for another man's freedom; who lives by a mythical concept of time and who constantly advises the Negro to wait for a "more convenient season." Shallow understanding from people of good will is more frustrating than absolute misunderstanding from people of ill will. Lukewarm acceptance is much more bewildering than outright rejection.

I had hoped that the white moderate would understand that law and order exist for the purpose of establishing justice and that when they fail in this purpose they become the dangerously structured dams that block the flow of social progress. I had hoped that the white moderate would understand that the present tension in the South is a necessary phase of the transition from an obnoxious negative peace, in which the Negro passively accepted his unjust plight, to a substantive and positive peace, in which all men will respect the dignity and worth of human personality. Actually, we who engage in nonviolent direct action are not the creators of tension. We merely bring to the surface the hidden tension that is already alive. We bring it out in the open, where it can be seen and dealt with. Like a boil that can never be cured so long as it is covered up but must be opened with all its ugliness to the natural medicines of air and light, injustice must be exposed, with all the tension its exposure creates, to the light of human conscience and the air of national opinion, before it can be cured.

In your statement you assert that our actions, even though peaceful, must be condemned because they precipitate violence. But is this a logical assertion? Isn't this like condemning a robbed man because his possession of money precipitated the evil act of robbery? Isn't this like condemning Socrates because his unswerving commitment to truth and his philosophical inquiries precipitated the act by the misguided populace in which they made him drink hemlock? Isn't this like condemning Jesus because his unique God-consciousness and never-ceasing devotion to God's will precipitated the evil act of crucifixion? We must come to see that, as the federal courts have consistently affirmed, it is wrong to urge an individual to cease his efforts to gain his basic constitutional rights because the quest may precipitate violence. Society must protect the robbed and punish the robber.

I had also hoped that the white moderate would reject the myth concerning time in relation to the struggle for freedom. I have just received a letter from a white brother in Texas. He writes: "All Christians know that the colored people will receive equal rights eventually, but it is possible that you are in too great a religious hurry. It has taken Christianity almost two thousand years to accomplish what it has. The teachings of Christ take time to come to earth." Such an attitude stems from a tragic misconception of time, from the strangely irrational notion that there is something in the very flow of time that will inevitably cure all ills. Actually, time itself is neutral; it can be used either destructively or constructively. More and more I feel that the people of ill will have used time much more effectively than have the people of good will. We will have to repent in this generation not merely for the hateful words and actions of the bad people, but for the appalling silence of the good people. Human progress never rolls in on wheels of inevitability; it comes through the tireless efforts of men willing to be co-workers with God, and without this hard work, time itself becomes an ally of the forces of social stagnation. We must use time creatively, in the knowledge that the time is always ripe to do right. Now is the time to make real the promise of democracy and transform our pending national elegy into a creative psalm of brotherhood. Now is the time to lift our national policy from the quicksand of racial injustice to the solid rock of human dignity.

You speak of our activity in Birmingham as extreme. At first I was rather disappointed that fellow clergymen would see my nonviolent efforts as those of an extremist. I began thinking about the fact that I stand in the middle of two opposing forces in the Negro community. One is a force of complacency, made up in part of Negroes who, as a result of long years of oppression, are so drained of self-respect and a sense of "somebodiness" that they have adjusted to segregation; and in part of a few middle-class Negroes who, because of a degree of academic and economic security and because in some ways they profit by segregation, have become insensitive to the problems of the masses. The other force is one of bitterness and hatred, and it comes perilously close to advocating violence. It is expressed in the various black nationalist groups that are springing up across the nation, the largest and best-known being Elijah Muhammad's Muslim movement. Nourished by the Negro's frustration over the continued existence of racial discrimination, this movement is made up of people who have lost faith in America, who have absolutely repudiated Christianity, and who have concluded that the white man is an incorrigible "devil."

I have tried to stand between these two forces, saying that we need emulate neither the "do-nothingism" of the complacent nor the hatred and despair of the black nationalist. For there is the more excellent way of love and nonviolent protest. I am grateful to God that, through the influence of the Negro church, the way of nonviolence became an integral part of our struggle.

If this philosophy had not emerged, by now many streets of the South would, I am convinced, be flowing with blood. And I am further convinced that if our white brothers dismiss as "rabble-rousers" and "outside agitators" those of us who employ nonviolent direct action, and if they refuse to support our nonviolent efforts, millions of Negroes will, out of frustration and despair, seek solace and security in black-nationalist ideologies — a development that would inevitably lead to a frightening racial nightmare.

Oppressed people cannot remain oppressed forever. The yearning for free-   30
dom eventually manifests itself, and that is what has happened to the American Negro. Something within has reminded him of his birthright of freedom, and something without has reminded him that it can be gained. Consciously or unconsciously, he has been caught up by the *Zeitgeist*,[3] and with his black broth-ers of Africa and his brown and yellow brothers of Asia, South America, and the Caribbean, the United States Negro is moving with a sense of great urgency toward the promised land of racial justice. If one recognizes this vital urge that has engulfed the Negro community, one should readily understand why public demonstrations are taking place. The Negro has many pent-up resentments and latent frustrations, and he must release them. So let him march; let him make prayer pilgrimages to the city hall; let him go on freedom rides — and try to understand why he must do so. If his repressed emotions are not released in non-violent ways, they will seek expression through violence; this is not a threat but a fact of history. So I have not said to my people, "Get rid of your discontent." Rather, I have tried to say that this normal and healthy discontent can be chan-neled into the creative outlet of nonviolent direct action. And now this approach is being termed extremist.

But though I was initially disappointed at being categorized as an extremist, as I continued to think about the matter I gradually gained a measure of satisfac-tion from the label. Was not Jesus an extremist for love: "Love your enemies, bless them that curse you, do good to them that hate you, and pray for them which despitefully use you, and persecute you." Was not Amos an extremist for justice: "Let justice roll down like waters and righteousness like an ever-flowing stream." Was not Paul an extremist for the Christian gospel: "I bear in my body the marks of the Lord Jesus." Was not Martin Luther an extremist: "Here I stand; I cannot do otherwise, so help me God." And John Bunyan: "I will stay in jail to the end of my days before I make a butchery of my conscience." And Abraham Lincoln: "This nation cannot survive half slave and half free." And Thomas Jefferson: "We hold these truths to be self-evident, that all men are created equal. . . ." So the question is not whether we will be extremists, but what kind of extremists we will be. Will we be extremists for hate or for love? Will we be extremists for the preservation of injustice or for the extension of justice? In that dramatic scene on Calvary's hill

---

[3]German, "spirit of the time." — Eds.

three men were crucified. We must never forget that all three were crucified for the same crime — the crime of extremism. Two were extremists for immorality, and thus fell below their environment. The other, Jesus Christ, was an extremist for love, truth, and goodness, and thereby rose above his environment. Perhaps the South, the nation, and the world are in dire need of creative extremists.

I had hoped that the white moderate would see this need. Perhaps I was too optimistic; perhaps I expected too much. I suppose I should have realized that few members of the oppressor race can understand the deep groans and passionate yearnings of the oppressed race, and still fewer have the vision to see that injustice must be rooted out by strong, persistent, and determined action. I am thankful, however, that some of our white brothers in the South have grasped the meaning of this social revolution and committed themselves to it. They are still all too few in quantity, but they are big in quality. Some — such as Ralph McGill, Lillian Smith, Harry Golden, James McBridge Dabbs, Ann Braden, and Sarah Patton Boyle — have written about our struggle in eloquent and prophetic terms. Others have marched with us down nameless streets of the South. They have languished in filthy, roach-infested jails, suffering the abuse and brutality of policemen who view them as "dirty nigger-lovers." Unlike so many of their moderate brothers and sisters, they have recognized the urgency of the moment and sensed the need for powerful "action" antidotes to combat the disease of segregation.

Let me take note of my other major disappointment. I have been so greatly disappointed with the white church and its leadership. Of course, there are some notable exceptions. I am not unmindful of the fact that each of you has taken some significant stands on this issue. I commend you, Reverend [Earl] Stallings, for your Christian stand on this past Sunday, in welcoming Negroes to your worship service on a nonsegregated basis. I commend the Catholic leaders of this state for integrating Spring Hill College several years ago.

But despite these notable exceptions, I must honestly reiterate that I have been disappointed with the church. I do not say this as one of those negative critics who can always find something wrong with the church. I say this as a minister of the gospel, who loves the church; who was nurtured in its bosom; who has been sustained by its spiritual blessings and who will remain true to it as long as the cord of life shall lengthen.

When I was suddenly catapulted into the leadership of the bus protest in   35
Montgomery, Alabama, a few years ago, I felt we would be supported by the white church. I felt that the white ministers, priests, and rabbis of the South would be among our strongest allies. Instead, some have been outright opponents, refusing to understand the freedom movement and misrepresenting its leaders; all too many others have been more cautious than courageous and have remained silent behind the anesthetizing security of stained-glass windows.

In spite of my shattered dreams, I came to Birmingham with the hope that the white religious leadership of this community would see the justice of our cause and, with deep moral concern, would serve as the channel through which our just grievances could reach the power structure. I had hoped that each of you would understand. But again I have been disappointed.

I have heard numerous southern religious leaders admonish their worshipers to comply with a desegregation decision because it is the law, but I have longed to hear white ministers declare: "Follow this decree because integration is morally right and because the Negro is your brother." In the midst of blatant injustices inflicted upon the Negro, I have watched white church men stand on the sideline and mouth pious irrelevancies and sanctimonious trivialities. In the midst of a mighty struggle to rid our nation of racial and economic injustice, I have heard many ministers say: "Those are social issues, with which the gospel has no real concern." And I have watched many churches commit themselves to a completely otherworldly religion which makes a strange, un-Biblical distinction between body and soul, between the sacred and the secular.

I have traveled the length and breadth of Alabama, Mississippi, and all the other southern states. On sweltering summer days and crisp autumn mornings I have looked at the South's beautiful churches with their lofty spires pointing heavenward. I have beheld the impressive outlines of her massive religious-education buildings. Over and over I have found myself asking: "What kind of people worship here? Who is their God? Where were their voices when the lips of Governor [Ross] Barnett dripped with words of interposition and nullification? Where were they when Governor [George] Wallace gave a clarion call for defiance and hatred? Where were their voices of support when bruised and weary Negro men and women decided to rise from the dark dungeons of complacency to the bright hills of creative protest?"

Yes, these questions are still in my mind. In deep disappointment I have wept over the laxity of the church. But be assured that my tears have been tears of love. There can be no deep disappointment where there is not deep love. Yes, I love the church. How could I do otherwise? I am in the rather unique position of being the son, the grandson, and the great-grandson of preachers. Yes, I see the church as the body of Christ. But, oh! How we have blemished and scarred that body through social neglect and through fear of being nonconformists.

There was a time when the church was very powerful — in the time when 40 the early Christians rejoiced at being deemed worthy to suffer for what they believed. In those days the church was not merely a thermometer that recorded the ideas and principles of popular opinion; it was a thermostat that transformed the mores of society. Whenever the early Christians entered a town, the people in power became disturbed and immediately sought to convict the Christians for being "disturbers of the peace" and "outside agitators." But the Christians pressed on, in the conviction that they were "a colony of heaven," called to obey God rather than man. Small in number, they were big in commitment. They were too God-intoxicated to be "astronomically intimidated." By their effort and example they brought an end to such ancient evils as infanticide and gladiatorial contests.

Things are different now. So often the contemporary church is a weak, ineffectual voice with an uncertain sound. So often it is an archdefender of the status quo. Far from being disturbed by the presence of the church, the power structure of the average community is consoled by the church's silent — and often even vocal — sanction of things as they are.

But the judgment of God is upon the church as never before. If today's church does not recapture the sacrificial spirit of the early church, it will lose its authenticity, forfeit the loyalty of millions, and be dismissed as an irrelevant social club with no meaning for the twentieth century. Every day I meet young people whose disappointment with the church has turned into outright disgust.

Perhaps I have once again been too optimistic. Is organized religion too inextricably bound to the status quo to save our nation and the world? Perhaps I must turn my faith to the inner spiritual church, the church within the church, as the true *ekklesia* and the hope of the world. But again I am thankful to God that some noble souls from the ranks of organized religion have broken loose from the paralyzing chains of conformity and joined us as active partners in the struggle for freedom. They have left their secure congregations and walked the streets of Albany, Georgia, with us. They have gone down the highways of the South on tortuous rides for freedom. Yes, they have gone to jail with us. Some have been dismissed from their churches, have lost the support of their bishops and fellow ministers. But they have acted in the faith that right defeated is stronger than evil triumphant. Their witness has been the spiritual salt that has preserved the true meaning of the gospel in these troubled times. They have carved a tunnel of hope through the dark mountain of disappointment.

I hope the church as a whole will meet the challenge of this decisive hour. But even if the church does not come to the aid of justice, I have no despair about the future. I have no fear about the outcome of our struggle in Birmingham, even if our motives are at present misunderstood. We will reach the goal of freedom in Birmingham and all over the nation, because the goal of America is freedom. Abused and scorned though we may be, our destiny is tied up with America's destiny. Before the pilgrims landed at Plymouth, we were here. Before the pen of Jefferson etched the majestic words of the Declaration of Independence across the pages of history, we were here. For more than two centuries our forebears labored in this country without wages: they made cotton king; they built the homes of their masters while suffering gross injustice and shameful humiliation — and yet out of a bottomless vitality they continued to thrive and develop. If the inexpressible cruelties of slavery could not stop us, the opposition we now face will surely fail. We will win our freedom because the sacred heritage of our nation and the eternal will of God are embodied in our echoing demands.

Before closing I feel impelled to mention one other point in your statement that has troubled me profoundly. You warmly commended the Birmingham police force for keeping "order" and "preventing violence." I doubt that you would have so warmly commended the police force if you had seen its dogs sinking their teeth into unarmed, nonviolent Negroes. I doubt that you would so quickly com-

45

mend the policemen if you were to observe their ugly and inhumane treatment of Negroes here in the city jail; if you were to watch them push and curse old Negro women and young Negro girls; if you were to see them slap and kick old Negro men and young boys; if you were to observe them, as they did on two occasions, refuse to give us food because we wanted to sing our grace together. I cannot join you in your praise of the Birmingham police department.

It is true that the police have exercised a degree of discipline in handling the demonstrators. In this sense they have conducted themselves rather "nonviolently" in public. But for what purpose? To preserve the evil system of segregation. Over the past few years I have consistently preached that nonviolence demands that the means we use must be as pure as the ends we seek. I have tried to make clear that it is wrong to use immoral means to attain moral ends. But now I must affirm that it is just as wrong, or perhaps even more so, to use moral means to preserve immoral ends. Perhaps Mr. Connor and his policemen have been rather nonviolent in public, as was Chief Pritchett in Albany, Georgia, but they have used the moral means of nonviolence to maintain the immoral end of racial injustice. As T. S. Eliot has said, "The last temptation is the greatest treason: To do the right deed for the wrong reason."

I wish you had commended the Negro sit-inners and demonstrators of Birmingham for their sublime courage, their willingness to suffer, and their amazing discipline in the midst of great provocation. One day the South will recognize its real heroes. They will be the James Merediths, with the noble sense of purpose that enables them to face jeering and hostile mobs, and with the agonizing loneliness that characterizes the life of the pioneer. They will be old, oppressed, battered Negro women, symbolized in a seventy-two-year-old woman in Montgomery, Alabama, who rose up with a sense of dignity and with her people decided not to ride segregated buses, and who responded with ungrammatical profundity to one who inquired about her weariness: "My feets is tired, but my soul is at rest." They will be the young high school and college students, the young ministers of the gospel and a host of their elders, courageously and nonviolently sitting in at lunch counters and willingly going to jail for conscience' sake. One day the South will know that when these disinherited children of God sat down at lunch counters, they were in reality standing up for what is best in the American dream and for the most sacred values in our Judaeo-Christian heritage, thereby bringing our nation back to those great wells of democracy which were dug deep by the founding fathers in their formulation of the Constitution and the Declaration of Independence.

Never before have I written so long a letter. I'm afraid it is much too long to take your precious time. I can assure you that it would have been much shorter if I had been writing from a comfortable desk, but what else can one do when he is alone in a narrow jail cell, other than write long letters, think long thoughts, and pray long prayers?

If I have said anything in this letter that overstates the truth and indicates an unreasonable impatience, I beg you to forgive me. If I have said anything that understates the truth and indicates my having a patience that allows me to settle for anything less than brotherhood, I beg God to forgive me.

I hope this letter finds you strong in the faith. I also hope that circumstances 50 will soon make it possible for me to meet each of you, not as an integrationist or a civil-rights leader but as a fellow clergyman and a Christian brother. Let us all hope that the dark clouds of racial prejudice will soon pass away and the deep fog of misunderstanding will be lifted from our fear-drenched communities, and in some not too distant tomorrow the radiant stars of love and brotherhood will shine over our great nation with all their scintillating beauty.

Yours for the cause of Peace and Brotherhood,
Martin Luther King Jr.

Questions for Discussion

1. Martin Luther King writes as a member of several communities, some overlapping, some in conflict. What are they? Focusing on two or three, explain how he defines himself within each.
2. What is the meaning of *ekklesia* (para. 43)? What does King mean when he invokes "the true *ekklesia*"?
3. How does King balance the twin appeals to religion and patriotism throughout "Letter from Birmingham Jail"? Do you think he puts more emphasis on religion or patriotism? Why do you think he makes that choice?
4. In the later 1960s, Alice Walker wrote an essay titled "The Civil Rights Movement: What Good Was It?" How would you answer her question today? What good do you believe has resulted from the civil rights movement?

Questions on Rhetoric and Style

1. What is King's tone in the opening paragraph? How might you make an argument for its being ironic?
2. Why does King arrange paragraphs 2–4 in the order that he does? How would reversing the order change the impact?
3. How do King's allusions to biblical figures and events appeal to both ethos and pathos?
4. Why does King go into such detail to explain the basic principles and process of the nonviolent protest movement?
5. In sentence 2 of paragraph 14, what is the effect of juxtaposing the rate of change in Asian and African cultures with the rate of change in American culture?
6. In the long sentence in paragraph 14 (beginning with "But when you have seen"), why does King arrange the "when" clauses in the order that he does? Try repositioning them, and then discuss the difference in effect.
7. What rhetorical strategies are used in paragraph 25? Identify at least four.

8. What are the chief rhetorical strategies used in paragraph 31? Identify at least five.
9. Why does King wait until paragraph 45 to address the alleged commendable behavior of the Birmingham police in "preventing violence"?
10. Trace one of the following patterns of figurative language throughout King's letter: darkness and light, high and low, sickness and health.
11. King uses repetition of single words or phrases, of sentence structures, and of sounds. Focusing on a passage of one or more paragraphs, discuss the effect of this use of repetition.
12. Considering the final three paragraphs as King's conclusion, discuss whether you believe it is rhetorically effective.

Suggestions for Writing

1. Compare and contrast the rhetorical strategies King employs in "Letter from Birmingham Jail" with those he uses in another piece, such as the "I Have a Dream" speech or the introduction to *Why We Can't Wait* (which appeared on the 1989 AP Language exam). Why are certain strategies more appropriate for a speech than for an essay or a letter?
2. Select a quotation from King's letter, and explain (1) why you find it compelling or (2) on what grounds you would challenge it. Cite evidence from your own experience or reading to support your position. Possible quotations to focus on include:
   a. "Injustice anywhere is a threat to justice everywhere." (para. 4)
   b. ". . . freedom is never voluntarily given by the oppressor; it must be demanded by the oppressed." (para. 13)
   c. "Shallow understanding from people of good will is more frustrating than absolute misunderstanding from people of ill will." (para. 23)
3. Describe a time when your participation in, or loyalty to, two different communities conflicted. Explain the nature of the conflict and how you resolved it.

Where I Lived, and What I Lived For

Henry David Thoreau

 Henry David Thoreau (1817–1862) was a philosopher, poet, essayist, and naturalist as well as an outspoken social critic. He was born in Concord, Massachusetts, and was educated at Harvard. He worked at a variety of professions, from land surveyor to teacher to pencil maker. Strongly influenced by his neighbor and friend Ralph Waldo Emerson, Thoreau considered himself a fierce patriot who honored his country and its ideals, if not always its government. He spoke out against the war against Mexico, and slavery — specifically the Fugitive Slave Act — and defended the abolitionist John Brown. He is best known for *Walden, or Life in the Woods*, published in 1854, which is his account of living in a cabin on Walden Pond for two years. This selection is from the second chapter of *Walden*.

I went to the woods because I wished to live deliberately, to front only the essential facts of life, and see if I could not learn what it had to teach, and not, when I came to die, discover that I had not lived. I did not wish to live what was not life, living is so dear; nor did I wish to practice resignation, unless it was quite necessary. I wanted to live deep and suck out all the marrow of life, to live so sturdily and Spartan-like as to put to rout all that was not life, to cut a broad swath and shave close, to drive life into a corner, and reduce it to its lowest terms, and, if it proved to be mean, why then to get the whole and genuine meanness of it, and publish its meanness to the world; or if it were sublime, to know it by experience, and be able to give a true account of it in my next excursion. For most men, it appears to me, are in a strange uncertainty about it, whether it is of the devil or of God, and have *somewhat hastily* concluded that it is the chief end of man here to "glorify God and enjoy him forever."[1]

Still we live meanly, like ants; though the fable tells us that we were long ago changed into men; like pygmies we fight with cranes;[2] it is error upon error, and clout upon clout, and our best virtue has for its occasion a superfluous and evitable wretchedness. Our life is frittered away by detail. An honest man has

---

[1] The first question and answer in the Westminster Catechism, a statement of religious doctrine that came out of the Protestant Reformation, is "Q: What is the chief end of man? A: To glorify God and enjoy him forever." — Eds.

[2] Allusions to the Greek fable of the Myrmidons (ant-people), and to Book III of the *Iliad*, respectively. The *Iliad* draws a parallel between the Trojan War and the mythological war between the cranes and the Pygmies. — Eds.

hardly need to count more than his ten fingers, or in extreme cases he may add his ten toes, and lump the rest. Simplicity, simplicity, simplicity! I say, let your affairs be as two or three, and not a hundred or a thousand; instead of a million count half a dozen, and keep your accounts on your thumb-nail. In the midst of this chopping sea of civilized life, such are the clouds and storms and quicksands and thousand-and-one items to be allowed for, that a man has to live, if he would not founder and go to the bottom and not make his port at all, by dead reckoning, and he must be a great calculator indeed who succeeds. Simplify, simplify. Instead of three meals a day, if it be necessary eat but one; instead of a hundred dishes, five; and reduce other things in proportion. Our life is like a German Confederacy, made of up petty states, with its boundary forever fluctuating, so that even a German cannot tell you how it is bounded at any moment. The nation itself, with all its so-called internal improvements, which, by the way are all external and superficial, is just such an unwieldy and overgrown establishment, cluttered with furniture and tripped up by its own traps, ruined by luxury and heedless expense, by want of calculation and a worthy aim, as the million households in the land; and the only cure for it, as for them, is in a rigid economy, a stern and more than Spartan simplicity of life and elevation of purpose. It lives too fast. Men think that it is essential that the *Nation* have commerce, and export ice, and talk through a telegraph, and ride thirty miles an hour, without a doubt, whether *they* do or not; but whether we should live like baboons or like men, is a little uncertain. If we do not get out sleepers,[3] and forge rails, and devote days and nights to the work, but go to tinkering upon our *lives* to improve *them*, who will build railroads? And if railroads are not built, how shall we get to heaven in season? But if we stay at home and mind our business, who will want railroads? We do not ride on the railroad; it rides upon us. Did you ever think what those sleepers are that underlie the railroad? Each one is a man, an Irishman, or a Yankee man. The rails are laid on them, and they are covered with sand, and the cars run smoothly over them. They are sound sleepers, I assure you. And every few years a new lot is laid down and run over, so that, if some have the pleasure of riding on a rail, others have the misfortune to be ridden upon. And when they run over a man that is walking in his sleep, a supernumerary sleeper in the wrong position, and wake him up, they suddenly stop the cars, and make a hue and cry about it, as if this were an exception. I am glad to know that it takes a gang of men for every five miles to keep the sleepers down and level in their beds as it is, for this is a sign that they may sometimes get up again.

Why should we live with such hurry and waste of life? We are determined to be starved before we are hungry. Men say that a stitch in time saves nine, and so they take a thousand stitches today to save nine tomorrow. As for *work*, we haven't any of any consequence. We have the Saint Vitus' dance, and cannot possibly keep

---

[3]Here, *sleepers* means "railroad ties." — Eds.

our heads still. If I should only give a few pulls at the parish bell-rope, as for a fire, that is, without setting the bell, there is hardly a man on his farm in the outskirts of Concord, notwithstanding that press of engagements which was his excuse so many times this morning, nor a boy, nor a woman, I might almost say, but would foresake all and follow that sound, not mainly to save property from the flames, but, if we will confess the truth, much more to see it burn, since burn it must, and we, be it known, did not set it on fire — or to see it put out, and have a hand in it, if that is done as handsomely; yes, even if it were the parish church itself. Hardly a man takes a half-hour's nap after dinner, but when he wakes he holds up his head and asks, "What's the news?" as if the rest of mankind had stood his sentinels. Some give directions to be waked every half-hour, doubtless for no other purpose; and then, to pay for it, they tell what they have dreamed. After a night's sleep the news is as indispensable as the breakfast. "Pray tell me anything new that has happened to a man anywhere on this globe" — and he reads it over his coffee and rolls, that a man has had his eyes gouged out this morning on the Wachito River; never dreaming the while that he lives in the dark unfathomed mammoth cave of this world, and has but the rudiment of an eye himself.

For my part, I could easily do without the post-office. I think that there are very few important communications made through it. To speak critically, I never received more than one or two letters in my life — I wrote this some years ago — that were worth the postage. The penny-post is, commonly, an institution through which you seriously offer a man that penny for his thoughts which is so often safely offered in jest. And I am sure that I never read any memorable news in a newspaper. If we read of one man robbed, or murdered, or killed by accident, or one house burned, or one vessel wrecked or one steamboat blown up, or one cow run over on the Western Railroad, or one mad dog killed, or one lot of grasshoppers in the winter — we never need read of another. One is enough. If you are acquainted with the principle, what do you care for a myriad instances and applications? To a philosopher all *news*, as it is called, is gossip, and they who edit and read it are old women over their tea. Yet not a few are greedy after this gossip. There was such a rush, as I hear, the other day at one of the offices to learn the foreign news by the last arrival, that several large squares of plate glass belonging to the establishment were broken by the pressure — news which I seriously think a ready wit might write a twelvemonth, or twelve years, beforehand with sufficient accuracy. As for Spain, for instance, if you know how to throw in Don Carlos and the Infanta, and Don Pedro and Seville and Granada, from time to time in the right proportions — they may have changed the names a little since I saw the papers — and serve up a bullfight when other entertainments fail, it will be true to the letter, and give us as good an idea of the exact state or ruin of things in Spain as the most succinct and lucid reports under this head in the newspapers; and as for England, almost the last significant scrap of news from that quarter was the revolution of 1649; and if you have learned the history of her crops for an average year, you never need attend to that thing again, unless your speculations are of a merely pecuniary character. If one may judge who rarely looks into the newspapers, nothing new does ever happen in foreign parts, a French revolution not excepted.

What news! how much more important to know what that is which was   5 never old! "Kieou-pe-yu (great dignitary of the state of Wei) sent a man to Khoung-tseu to know his news. Khoung-tseu caused the messenger to be seated near him, and questioned him in these terms: What is your master doing? The messenger answered with respect: My master desires to diminish the number of his faults, but he cannot come to the end of them. The messenger being gone, the philosopher remarked: What a worthy messenger! What a worthy messenger!" The preacher, instead of vexing the ears of drowsy farmers on their day of rest at the end of the week — for Sunday is the fit conclusion of an ill-spent week, and not the fresh and brave beginning of a new one — with this one other draggle-tail of a sermon, should shout with thundering voice, "Pause! Avast! Why so seeming fast, but deadly slow?"

Shams and delusions are esteemed for soundless truths, while reality is fabulous. If men would steadily observe realities only, and not allow themselves to be deluded, life, to compare it with such things as we know, would be like a fairy tale and the Arabian Nights' Entertainments. If we respected only what is inevitable and has a right to be, music and poetry would resound along the streets. When we are unhurried and wise, we perceive that only great and worthy things have any permanent and absolute existence, that petty fears and petty pleasures are but the shadow of the reality. This is always exhilarating and sublime. By closing the eyes and slumbering, and consenting to be deceived by shows, men establish and confirm their daily life of routine and habit everywhere, which still is built on purely illusory foundations. Children, who play life, discern its true law and relations more clearly than men, who fail to live it worthily, but who think that they are wiser by experience, that is, by failure. I have read in a Hindoo book, that "there was a king's son, who, being expelled in infancy from his native city, was brought up by a forester, and, growing up to maturity in that state, imagined himself to belong to the barbarous race with which he lived. One of his father's ministers having discovered him, revealed to him what he was, and the misconception of his character was removed, and he knew himself to be a prince. So soul," continues the Hindoo philosopher, "from the circumstances in which it is placed, mistakes its own character, until the truth is revealed to it by some holy teacher and then it knows itself to be *Brahme*."[4] I perceive that we inhabitants of New England live this mean life that we do because our vision does not penetrate the surface of things. We think that that *is* which *appears* to be. If a man should walk through this town and see only the reality, where, think you, would the "Milldam"[5] go to? If he should give us an account of the realities he beheld there, we should not recognize the place in his description. Look at the meetinghouse, or a courthouse, or

---

[4]One of the three main Hindu gods, now spelled *Brahma*. — Eds.
[5]Concord's business center. — Eds.

a jail, or a shop, or a dwelling-house, and say what that thing really is before a true gaze, and they would all go to pieces in your account of them. Men esteem truth remote, in the outskirts of the system behind the farthest star, before Adam and after the last man. In eternity there is indeed something true and sublime. But all these times and places and occasions are now and here. God himself culminates in the present moment, and will never be more divine in the lapse of all the ages. And we are enabled to apprehend at all what is sublime and noble only by the perpetual instilling and drenching of the reality that surrounds us. The universe constantly and obediently answers to our conceptions; whether we travel fast or slow, the track is laid for us. Let us spend our lives in conceiving then. The poet or the artist never yet had so fair and noble a design but some of his posterity at least could accomplish it.

Let us spend one day as deliberately as Nature, and not be thrown off the track by every nutshell and mosquito's wing that falls on the rails. Let us rise early and fast, or breakfast, gently and without perturbation; let company come and let company go, let the bells ring and the children cry — determined to make a day of it. Why should we knock under and go with the stream? Let us not be upset and overwhelmed in that terrible rapid and whirlpool called a dinner, situated in the meridian shallows. Weather this danger and you are safe, for the rest of the way is downhill. With unrelaxed nerves, with morning vigor, sail by it, looking another way, tied to the mast like Ulysses. If the engine whistles, let it whistle till it is hoarse for its pains. If the bell rings, why should we run? We will consider what kind of music they are like. Let us settle ourselves and work and wedge our feet downward through the mud and slush of opinion, and prejudice, and tradition, and delusion, and appearance, that alluvion which covers the globe, through Paris and London, through New York and Boston and Concord, through Church and State, through poetry and philosophy and religion, till we come to a hard bottom and rocks in place, which we can call *reality*, and say, This is, and no mistake; and then begin, having a *point d'appui*,[6] below freshet and frost and fire, a place where you might found a wall or a state, or set a lamppost safely, or perhaps a gauge, not a Nilometer, but a Realometer, that future ages might know how deep a freshet of shams and appearances had gathered from time to time. If you stand right fronting and face to face to a fact, you will see the sun glimmer on both its surfaces, as if it were a cimeter, and feel its sweet edge dividing you through the heart and marrow, and so you will happily conclude your mortal career. Be it life or death, we crave only reality. If we are really dying, let us hear the rattle in our throats and feel cold in the extremities; if we are alive, let us go about our business.

Time is but the stream I go afishing in. I drink at it; but while I drink I see the sandy bottom and detect how shallow it is. Its thin current slides away but eter-

---

[6]French, "foundation." — Eds.

nity remains. I would drink deeper; fish in the sky, whose bottom is pebbly with stars. I cannot count one. I know not the first letter of the alphabet. I have always been regretting that I was not as wise as the day I was born. The intellect is a cleaver; it discerns and rifts its way into the secret of things. I do not wish to be any more busy with my hands than is necessary. My head is hands and feet. I feel all my best faculties concentrated in it. My instinct tells me that my head is an organ for burrowing, as some creatures use their snout and fore paws, and with it I would mine and burrow my way through these hills. I think that the richest vein is somewhere hereabouts, so by the divining-rod and thin rising vapors, I judge; and here I will begin to mine.

Questions for Discussion

1. What is Henry David Thoreau calling for early in paragraph 2 when he writes, "Simplicity, simplicity, simplicity!"?
2. Thoreau writes, "We do not ride on the railroad; it rides upon us" (para. 2). Consider an electronic device (such as a notebook computer, a cell phone, a PDA, or an mp3 player). What would Thoreau say about it? Has this device helped to simplify our lives, or has it had a negative impact on them?
3. What does Thoreau mean when he says, "As for *work*, we haven't any of any consequence" (para. 3)? What is his definition of *work*?
4. How do you interpret this assertion: "Shams and delusions are esteemed for soundless truths, while reality is fabulous" (para. 6)? Use that as a topic sentence, and develop it with examples from your own experience.
5. Do you think Thoreau's advice and sentiments in this essay are meant as recommendations for living one's entire life or as suggestions for periodically reflecting on life's true meaning? Is he suggesting isolation as a lifestyle?
6. In today's terms, how would you characterize Thoreau's politics? Is he very conservative or very progressive? Is he somewhere in between?

Questions on Rhetoric and Style

1. In the first paragraph, what does Thoreau declare as his higher purpose?
2. Cite and explain the antitheses in the first paragraph.
3. What are the meanings of *dear* and *mean* as used in paragraph 1?
4. What is the rhetorical effect of the similes in paragraph 2?
5. Describe the extended metaphor in paragraph 2. What effect does it have?
6. What effect does Thoreau create with his repetitions? Cite several examples.
7. What paradox does Thoreau develop concerning the railroad in paragraph 2?
8. Paragraph 3 begins with a rhetorical question. How effectively does the rest of the paragraph answer it?

9. Discuss the meaning of the phrase "starved before we are hungry" in sentence 2 of paragraph 3.

10. Compare the probable rhetorical effect of paragraph 4 at the time it was written with its effect today.

11. Sometimes even the slightest stylistic feature can work effectively as a rhetorical strategy. What is the effect of the alliterative phrase "freshet and frost and fire" in paragraph 7?

12. In the concluding paragraph, Thoreau develops two metaphors regarding time and the intellect. What are they? What is their effect?

Suggestions for Writing

1. In paragraph 5, Thoreau writes, "What news! how much more important to know what that is which was never old!" Write an essay in which you evaluate Thoreau's own writing according to this thought. Consider how this essay appeals to two audiences: Thoreau's contemporaries and today's readers.

2. In this essay, Thoreau extols the virtues of individualism and self-sufficiency. Discuss how living according to these virtues can jeopardize the community; consider specific circumstances when such jeopardy might occur.

3. Write a response to Thoreau, telling him how modern technology has influenced how we communicate. Acknowledge how he did or did not anticipate our modern condition.

4. Using the reflective style of Thoreau, write your own philosophical essay entitled "Where I Live, and What I Live For" (note present tense).

In Search of the Good Family

JANE HOWARD

Jane Howard (1935–1996) was a journalist who wrote about the changing American scene. A frequent contributor to *Life*, the *New York Times*, and *Smithsonian*, she is the author of *Please Touch: A Guided Tour of the Human Potential Movement* (1970), *A Different Woman* (1973), *Families* (1978), and *Margaret Mead: A Life* (1984). The following selection, adapted for *Atlantic Monthly* from *Families*, explores the characteristics that make conventional families and new kinds of families meaningful communities.

Call it a clan, call it a network, call it a tribe, call it a family. Whatever you call it, whoever you are, you need one. You need one because you are human. You didn't come from nowhere. Before you, around you, and presumably after you, too, there are others. Some of these others must matter a lot — to you, and if you are very lucky, to one another. Their welfare must be nearly as important to you as your own. Even if you live alone, even if your solitude is elected and ebullient, you still cannot do without a clan or tribe.

The trouble with the clans and tribes many of us were born into is not that they consist of meddlesome ogres but that they are too far away. In emergencies we rush across continents and if need be oceans to their sides, as they do to ours. Maybe we even make a habit of seeing them, once or twice a year, for the sheer pleasure of it. But blood ties seldom dictate our addresses. Our blood kin are often too remote to ease us from our Tuesdays to our Wednesdays. For this we must rely on our families of friends. If our relatives are not, do not wish to be, or for whatever reasons cannot be our friends, then by some complex alchemy we must try to transform our friends into our relatives. If blood and roots don't do the job, then we must look to water and branches, and sort ourselves into new constellations, new families.

These new families, to borrow the terminology of an African tribe (the Bangwa of the Cameroons), may consist either of friends of the road, ascribed by chance, or friends of the heart, achieved by choice. Ascribed friends are those we happen to go to school with, work with, or live near. They know where we went last weekend and whether we still have a cold. Just being around gives them a provisional importance in our lives, and us in theirs. Maybe they will still matter to us when we or they move away; quite likely they won't. Six months or two years will probably erase us from each other's thoughts, unless by some chance they and we have become friends of the heart.

Wishing to be friends, as Aristotle wrote, is quick work, but friendship is a slowly ripening fruit. An ancient proverb he quotes in his *Ethics* had it that you cannot know a man until you and he together have eaten a peck of salt. Now a peck, a quarter of a bushel, is quite a lot of salt — more, perhaps, than most pairs of people ever have occasion to share. We must try though. We must sit together at as many tables as we can. We must steer each other through enough seasons and weathers so that sooner or later it crosses our minds that one of us, God knows which or with what sorrow, must one day mourn the other.

We must devise new ways, or revive old ones, to equip ourselves with kinfolk. 5 Maybe such an impulse prompted whoever ordered the cake I saw in my neighborhood bakery to have it frosted to say "Happy Birthday Surrogate." I like to think that this cake was decorated not for a judge but for someone's surrogate mother or surrogate brother: loathsome jargon, but admirable sentiment. If you didn't conceive me or if we didn't grow up in the same house, we can still be related, if we decide we ought to be. It is never too late, I like to hope, to augment our families in ways nature neglected to do. It is never too late to choose new clans.

The best-chosen clans, like the best friendships and the best blood families, endure by accumulating a history solid enough to suggest a future. But clans that don't last have merit too. We can lament them but we shouldn't deride them. Better an ephemeral clan or tribe than none at all. A few of my life's most tribally joyous times, in fact, have been spent with people whom I have yet to see again. This saddens me, as it may them too, but dwelling overlong on such sadness does no good. A more fertile exercise is to think back on those times and try to figure out what made them, for all their brevity, so stirring. What can such times teach us about forming new and more lasting tribes in the future?

New tribes and clans can no more be willed into existence, of course, than any other good thing can. We keep trying, though. To try, with gritted teeth and girded loins, is after all American. That is what the two Helens and I were talking about the day we had lunch in a room way up in a high-rise motel near the Kansas City airport. We had lunch there at the end of a two-day conference on families. The two Helens were social scientists, but I liked them even so, among other reasons because they both objected to that motel's coffee shop even more than I did. One of the Helens, from Virginia, disliked it so much that she had brought along homemade whole wheat bread, sesame butter, and honey from her parents' farm in South Dakota, where she had visited before the conference. Her picnic was the best thing that happened, to me at least, those whole two days.

"If you're voluntarily childless and alone," said the other Helen, who was from Pennsylvania by way of Puerto Rico, "it gets harder and harder with the passage of time. It's stressful. That's why you need support systems." I had been hearing quite a bit of talk about "support systems." The term is not among my favorites, but I can understand its currency. Whatever "support systems" may be, the need for them is clearly urgent, and not just in this country. Are there not thriving "mega-families" of as many as three hundred people in Scandinavia? Have not the Japanese for years had an honored, enduring — if perhaps by our standards rather rigid — custom of adopting nonrelatives to fill gaps in their families? Should we not applaud and maybe imitate such ingenuity?

And consider our own Unitarians. From Santa Barbara to Boston they have been earnestly dividing their congregations into arbitrary "extended families" whose members are bound to act like each other's relatives. Kurt Vonnegut, Jr. plays with a similar train of thought in his fictional *Slapstick*. In that book every newborn baby is assigned a randomly chosen middle name, like Uranium or Daffodil or Raspberry. These middle names are connected with hyphens to numbers between one and twenty, and any two people who have the same middle name are automatically related. This is all to the good, the author thinks, because "human beings need all the relatives they can get — as possible donors or receivers not of love but of common decency." He envisions these extended families as "one of the four greatest inventions by Americans," the others being *Robert's Rules of Order*, the Bill of Rights, and the principles of Alcoholics Anonymous.

This charming notion might even work, if it weren't so arbitrary. Already   10
each of us is born into one family not of our choosing. If we're going to devise new ones, we might as well have the luxury of picking the members ourselves. Clever picking might result in new families whose benefits would surpass or at least equal those of the old. As a member in reasonable standing of six or seven tribes in addition to the one I was born to, I have been trying to figure which characteristics are common to both kinds of families.

1. Good families have a chief, or a heroine, or a founder — someone around whom others cluster, whose achievements, as the Yiddish word has it, let them *kvell*,[1] and whose example spurs them on to like feats. Some blood dynasties produce such figures regularly; others languish for as many as five generations between demigods, wondering with each new pregnancy whether this, at last, might be the messianic baby who will redeem them. Look, is there not something gubernatorial about her footstep, or musical about the way he bangs with his spoon on his cup? All clans, of all kinds, need such a figure now and then. Sometimes clans based on water rather than blood harbor several such personages at one time.

2. Good families have a switchboard operator — someone who cannot help but keep track of what all the others are up to, who plays Houston Mission Control to everyone else's Apollo. This role is assumed rather than assigned. The person who volunteers for it often has the instincts of an archivist, and feels driven to keep scrapbooks and photograph albums up to date, so that the clan can see proof of its own continuity.

3. Good families are much to all their members, but everything to none. Good families are fortresses with many windows and doors to the outer world. The blood clans I feel most drawn to were founded by parents who are nearly as devoted to what they do outside as they are to each other and their children. Their curiosity and passion are contagious. Everybody, where they live, is busy. Paint is

---

[1]Yiddish, "exclaim proudly, especially in boasting about a member of a family." — Eds.

spattered on eyeglasses. Mud lurks under fingernails. Person-to-person calls come in the middle of the night from Tokyo and Brussels. Catcher's mitts, ballet slippers, overdue library books, and other signs of extrafamilial concerns are everywhere.

4. Good families are hospitable. Knowing that hosts need guests as much as guests need hosts, they are generous with honorary memberships for friends, whom they urge to come early and often and to stay late. Such clans exude a vivid sense of surrounding rings of relatives, neighbors, teachers, students, and godparents, any of whom at any time might break or slide into the inner circle. Inside that circle a wholesome, tacit emotional feudalism develops: you give me protection, I'll give you fealty. Such pacts begin with, but soon go far beyond, the jolly exchange of pie at Thanksgiving or cake on a birthday. They mean that you can ask me to supervise your children for the fortnight you will be in the hospital, and that however inconvenient this might be for me, I shall manage to do so. It means I can phone you on what for me is a dreary, wretched Sunday afternoon and for you is the eve of a deadline, knowing you will tell me to come right over, if only to watch you type. It means we need not dissemble. ("To yield to seeming," as Martin Buber[2] wrote, "is man's essential cowardice, to resist it is his essential courage . . . one must at times pay dearly for life lived from the being, but it is never too dear.")

5. Good families deal squarely with direness. Pity the tribe that doesn't have, and cherish, at least one flamboyant eccentric. Pity too the one that supposes it can avoid for long the woes to which all flesh is heir. Lunacy, bankruptcy, suicide, and other unthinkable fates sooner or later afflict the noblest of clans with an undertow of gloom. Family life is a set of givens, someone once told me, and it takes courage to see certain givens as blessings rather than as curses. It surely does. Contradictions and inconsistencies are givens, too. So is the battle against what the Oregon patriarch Kenneth Babbs calls malarkey. "There's always malarkey lurking, bubbles in the cesspool, fetid bubbles that pop and smell. But I don't put up with malarkey, between my stepkids and my natural ones or anywhere else in the family."

6. Good families prize their rituals. Nothing welds a family more than these. Rituals are vital especially for clans without histories, because they evoke a past, imply a future, and hint at continuity. No line in the seder service at Passover reassures more than the last: "Next year in Jerusalem!" A clan becomes more of a clan each time it gathers to observe a fixed ritual (Christmas, birthdays, Thanksgiving, and so on), grieves at a funeral (anyone may come to most funerals; those who do declare their tribalness), and devises a new rite of its own. Equinox breakfasts can be at least as welding as Memorial Day parades. Several of my colleagues and I used to meet for lunch every Pearl Harbor Day, preferably to eat some polit-

15

---

[2]Buber (1878–1965) was an Austrian-Israeli philosopher and Jewish theologian. — Eds.

ically neutral fare like smorgasbord, to "forgive" our only ancestrally Japanese friend, Irene Kubota Neves. For that and other things we became, and remain, a sort of family. . . .

7. Good families are affectionate. This of course is a matter of style. I know clans whose members greet each other with gingerly handshakes or, in what pass for kisses, with hurried brushes of jawbones, as if the object were to touch not the lips but the ears. I don't see how such people manage. "The tribe that does not hug," as someone who has been part of many *ad hoc* families recently wrote to me, "is no tribe at all. More and more I realize that everybody, regardless of age, needs to be hugged and comforted in a brotherly or sisterly way now and then. Preferably now."

8. Good families have a sense of place, which these days is not achieved easily. As Susanne Langer wrote in 1957, "Most people have no home that is a symbol of their childhood, not even a definite memory of one place to serve that purpose . . . all the old symbols are gone." Once I asked a roomful of supper guests if anyone felt a strong pull to any certain spot on the face of the earth. Everyone was silent, except for a visitor from Bavaria. The rest of us seemed to know all too well what Walker Percy means in *The Moviegoer* when he tells of the "genie-soul of a place, which every place has or else is not a place [and which] wherever you go, you must meet and master or else be met and mastered." All that meeting and mastering saps plenty of strength. It also underscores our need for tribal bases of the sort which soaring real estate taxes and splintering families have made all but obsolete.

So what are we to do, those of us whose habit and pleasure and doom is our tendency, as a Georgia lady put it, to "fly off at every other whipstitch"? Think in terms of movable feasts, that's what. Live here, wherever here may be, as if we were going to belong here for the rest of our lives. Learn to hallow whatever ground we happen to stand on or land on. Like medieval knights who took their tapestries along on Crusades, like modern Afghanis with their yurts, we must pack such totems and icons as we can to make short-term quarters feel like home. Pillows, small rugs, watercolors can dispel much of the chilling anonymity of a motel room or sublet apartment. When we can, we should live in rooms with stoves or fireplaces or at least candlelight. The ancient saying is still true: Extinguished hearth, extinguished family.

Round tables help too, and as a friend of mine once put it, so do "too many comfortable chairs, with surfaces to put feet on, arranged so as to encourage a maximum of eye contact." Such rooms inspire good talk, of which good clans can never have enough.

9. Good families, not just the blood kind, find some way to connect with posterity. "To forge a link in the humble chain of being, encircling heirs to ancestors," as Michael Novak has written, "is to walk within a circle of magic as primitive as humans knew in caves." He is talking of course about babies, feeling them leap in wombs, giving them suck. Parenthood, however, is a state which some

miss by chance and others by design, and a vocation to which not all are called. Some of us, like the novelist Richard P. Brickner, look on as others "name their children and their children in turn name their own lives, devising their own flags from their parents' cloth." What are we who lack children to do? Build houses? Plant trees? Write books or symphonies or laws? Perhaps, but even if we do these things, there should be children on the sidelines if not at the center of our lives.

It is a sadly impoverished tribe that does not allow access to, and make much of, some children. Not too much, of course; it has truly been said that never in history have so many educated people devoted so much attention to so few children. Attention, in excess, can turn to fawning, which isn't much better than neglect. Still, if we don't regularly see and talk to and laugh with people who can expect to outlive us by twenty years or so, we had better get busy and find some.

10. Good families also honor their elders. The wider the age range, the stronger the tribe. Jean-Paul Sartre and Margaret Mead, to name two spectacularly confident former children, have both remarked on the central importance of grandparents in their own early lives. Grandparents are now in much more abundant supply than they were a generation or two ago, when old age was more rare. If actual grandparents are not at hand, no family should have too hard a time finding substitute ones to whom to pay unfeigned homage. The Soviet Union's enchantment with day-care centers, I have heard, stems at least in part from the state's eagerness to keep children away from their presumably subversive grandparents. Let that be a lesson to clans based on interest as well as to those based on genes.

Exploring the Text

1. Identify the sentence in which Jane Howard first states the thesis of her essay. Then note the places where she restates her thesis, and discuss whether you find the repetition effective.
2. How do you react to the traditional terms Howard uses that refer to *family* (*clan, tribe, kin, dynasty, blood, roots, patriarch*)? How do you react to her more contemporary terms (*network, surrogate mother, support system, extended family*)? What do your reactions tell you about your own idea of family?
3. What is the impact of the sources Howard cites and quotes? Consider her allusion to Aristotle (para. 4), her conversation with "the two Helens" (paras. 7–8), her illustration from novelist Kurt Vonnegut Jr. (para. 9), and the quotations from the authors Susanne Langer (para. 18), Walker Percy (para. 18), and Michael Novak (para. 21).
4. Examine the various figures of speech Howard uses, such as a family member "who plays Houston Mission Control to everyone else's Apollo" (para. 12) and "a wholesome, tacit emotional feudalism" (para. 14). What is their cumulative effect?
5. What rhetorical modes does Howard draw on in the overall organization of her essay? Does one dominate? Explain.

6. How would you describe the order in which Howard discusses the characteristics of "good families"?
7. In the years since Howard published *Families*, how have developments regarding family and communications undercut or reinforced her thesis?
8. Of the characteristics that Howard lists, which two do you think are most important to a family?

The New Community

AMITAI ETZIONI

Sociologist Amitai Etzioni (b. 1929) escaped Nazi Germany and as a teenager fought in the Israeli War for Independence. After getting a PhD from the University of California at Berkeley in 1958, he taught at Columbia University for twenty years. Later, he became director of the Institute for Communitarian Policy Studies at George Washington University. He has written over twenty-four books, including *The Limits of Privacy* (1999), *The Moral Dimension: Toward a New Economics* (1988), and *From Empire to Community: A New Approach to International Relations* (2004). In 1990, he founded the Communitarian Network, described on his Web site as "a not-for-profit, non-partisan organization dedicated to shoring up the moral, social, and political foundations of society." In the following excerpt from *The Spirit of Community: Rights, Responsibilities, and the Communitarian Agenda* (1993), he examines changes in the concept of community as American society has shifted from primarily rural to urban and argues for "new communities in which people have choices . . . but still maintain common bonds."

It's hard to believe now, but for a long time the loss of community was considered to be liberating. Societies were believed to progress from closely knit, "primitive," or rural villages to unrestrictive, "modern," or urban societies. The former were depicted as based on kinship and loyalty in an age in which both were suspect; the latter, however, were seen as based on reason (or "rationality") in an era in which reason's power to illuminate was admired with little attention paid to the deep shadows it casts. The two types of social relations have often been labeled with the terms supplied by a German sociologist, Ferdinand Tönnies. One is gemeinschaft, the German term for community, and the other is gesellschaft, the German word for society, which he used to refer to people who have rather few bonds, like people in a crowd or a mass society (*Community and Society*).

Far from decrying the loss of community, this sanguine approach to the rise of modernity depicted small towns and villages as backward places that confined behavior. American writers such as Sinclair Lewis and John O'Hara satirized small towns as insular, claustrophobic places, inhabited by petty, mean-spirited people. They were depicted as the opposite of "big cities," whose atmosphere was said to set people free. Anonymity would allow each person to pursue what he or she wished rather than what the community dictated. It was further argued that relations in the *gesellschaft* would be based not on preexisting, "ascribed" social bonds, such as between cousins, but on contractual relations, freely negotiated among autonomous individuals.

Other major forms of progress were believed to accompany the movement from a world of villages to one of cities. Magic, superstition, alchemy, and religion — "backward beliefs" — would be replaced by bright, shining science and technology. There would be no more villagers willing to sell their wares only to their own kind and not to outsiders — a phenomenon anthropologists have often noted. Old-fashioned values and a sense of obligation were expected to yield to logic and calculation. Social bonds dominating all relations (you did not charge interest on a loan to members of your community because such a charge was considered indecent usury) were pushed aside to make room for a free market, with prices and interest rates set according to market logic. By the same token, the network of reciprocal obligations and care that is at the heart of communities would give way to individual rights protected by the state. The impersonal right to social services and welfare payments, for instance, would replace any reliance on members of one's family, tribe, or ethnic benevolent association.

The sun, moon, and stars of the new universe would be individuals, not the community. In a typical case, the U.S. Supreme Court ruled that the Sierra Club had no legal standing to argue for the preservation of parkland as a community resource (Glendon 112). Rather, if the Sierra Club wished to show standing, it would have to demonstrate that particular individuals were harmed.

Throughout twentieth-century America, as the transition to *gesellschaft*   5 evolved, even its champions realized that it was not the unmitigated blessing they had expected. Although it was true that those who moved from villages and small towns into urban centers often shed tight social relations and strong community bonds, the result for many was isolation, lack of caring for one another, and exposure to rowdiness and crime.

Criminologists report that young farmhands in rural America in the early nineteenth-century did not always work on their parents' land. However, when they were sent to work outside their home they usually lived with other farmers and were integrated into their family life. In this way they were placed in a community context that sustained the moral voice, reinforced the values of their upbringing, and promoted socially constructive behavior. It was only when these farmhands went to work in factories in cities — and were housed on their own in barracks without established social networks, elders, and values — that rowdy and criminal behavior, alcoholism, and prostitution became common. Even in those early days attempts to correct these proclivities were made not by returning these young people to their families and villages, but by trying to generate Communitarian elements in the cities. Among the best analysts of these developments is James Q. Wilson, a leading political scientist. He notes that associations such as the Young Men's Christian Association (YMCA), temperance societies, and the Children's Aid society sought to provide a socially appropriate, morality-sustaining context for young people ("Rediscovery" 13).

Other experiences paralleled those of the factory hands. The migration to the American West, for example, is usually thought of as a time when individuals were free to venture forth and carve out a life of their own in the Great Plains. Actually, many people traveled in caravans and settled as communities, although each family claimed its own plot of land. Mutual assistance in such rough terrain was an absolute requirement. Mining towns and trading posts, however, in which rampant individualism often did prevail, were places of much chicanery. People who had mined gold often lost their stakes to unscrupulous traders; those who owned land were driven off it with little compensation by railroad companies, among others. Fly-by-night banks frequently welshed on notes that they themselves had issued. An unfettered market, one without a community context, turned out to lack the essential moral underpinnings that trade requires, and not just by sound social relations.

In many ways these frontier settlements — with their washed-out social bonds, loose morals, and unbridled greed — were the forerunners of Wall Street in the 1980s. The Street became a "den of thieves," thick with knaves who held that anything went as long as you made millions more than the next guy. Moreover, the mood of self-centered "making it" of the me generation spilled over into large segments of society. It was celebrated by the White House and many in Congress, who saw in an unfettered pursuit of self-interest the social force that revitalizes economies and societies. By the end of the eighties even some of the proponents of me-ism felt that the pursuit of greed had run amok.

By the early nineties the waning of community, which had long concerned sociologists, became more pronounced and drew more attention. As writer Jonathan Rowe put it: "It was common to think about the community as we used to think about air and water. It is there. It takes care of itself, and it can and will absorb whatever we unleash into it" ("Left and Right"). Now it became evident that the social environment needed fostering just as nature did. Responding to the new cues, George Bush evoked the image of a "kinder, gentler" society as a central theme for his first presidential campaign in 1988. The time was right to return to community and the moral order it harbored. Bill Clinton made the spirit of community a theme of his 1992 campaign.

The prolonged recession of 1991–1992 and the generally low and slowing   10
growth of the American economy worked against this new concern with we-ness. Interracial and interethnic tensions rose considerably, not only between blacks and whites, but also between blacks and Hispanics and among various segments of the community and Asian-Americans. This is one more reason why the United States will have to work its way to a stronger, growing, more competitive economy: interracial and ethnic peace are much easier to maintain in a rising than in a stagnant economy. However, it does not mean that community rebuilding has to

be deferred until the economy is shored up. It does indicate that enhancing we-ness will require greater commitment and effort from both the government and the people, if community rebuilding is to take place in a sluggish economy.

Does this mean that we all have to move back to live in small towns and villages in order to ensure the social foundations of morality, to rebuild and shore up we-ness? Can one not bring up decent young people in the city? Isn't it possible to have a modern society, which requires a high concentration of labor and a great deal of geographic mobility — and still sustain a web of social bonds, a Communitarian nexus? There is more than one sociological answer to these queries.

First, many cities have sustained (or reclaimed) some elements of community. Herbert Gans, a Columbia University sociologist, observed that within cities there were what he called "urban villages." He found communities where, generally speaking, "neighbors were friendly and quick to say hello to each other," where the various ethnic groups, transients, and bohemians "could live together side by side without much difficulty." Gans further noted that "for most West Enders (in Boston) . . . life in the area resembled that found in the village or small town, and even in the suburb" (*The Urban Villagers*, 14–15). Even in large metropolises, such as New York City, there are neighborhoods in which many people know their neighbors, their shopkeepers, and their local leaders. They are likely to meet one another in neighborhood bars, bowling alleys, and places of worship. They watch out for each other's safety and children. They act in concert to protect their parks and bus stops. They form political clubs and are a force in local politics. (Jim Sleeper's *Closest of Strangers* provides a fine description of these New York City communities.)

In some instances members of one ethnic group live comfortably next to one another, as in New York City's Chinatown and Miami's Little Havana. In other cities ethnic groups are more geographically dispersed but sustain ethnic-community bonds around such institutions as churches and synagogues, social clubs, and private schools. In recent decades a measure of return to community has benefited from the revival of loyalty to ethnic groups. While the sons and daughters of immigrants, the so-called second generation, often sought to assimilate, to become Americanized to the point that their distinct backgrounds were lost in a new identity, *their* children, the third generation and onward, often seek to reestablish their ethnic identity and bonds.

How does one reconcile the two sociological pictures — the James Q. Wilson concept of the city as *gesellschaft*, with little community or moral base, and the Herbert Gans image of *gemeinschaft*, of urban villages? The answer, first of all, is that both exist side by side. Between the urban villages, in row houses and high rises, you find large pockets of people who do not know their next-door neighbors, with whom they may have shared a floor, corridors, and elevators for a generation. Elderly people especially, who have no social bonds at work and are largely abandoned by their families, often lead rather isolated lives. In 1950 14.4 percent of those sixty-five years of age and older lived alone (Monk 534); by 1990 the percentage stood at nearly 31 percent (U.S. Bureau of the Census, table L, 12).

Also, to some extent a welcome return to small-town life of sorts has been occurring in modern America. Although not all suburbs, which attracted millions of city dwellers, make for viable communities, as a rule the movement to the suburbs has enhanced the Communitarian nexus. 15

In addition, postmodern technology helps. More people are again able to work at home or nearby, and a high concentration of labor is less and less necessary, in contrast with the industrial age. People can use their computers and modems at home to do a good part of their office work, from processing insurance claims to trading worldwide commodities, stocks, and bonds. Architects can design buildings and engineers monitor faraway power networks from their places of residence.

It used to be widely observed that Americans, unlike Europeans, move around so much that they are hard-pressed to put down real community roots. On average, it is said, the whole country moves about once every five years. These figures, however, may be a bit obsolete. For various reasons, in recent years Americans seem to move somewhat less often (Barringer A16). One explanation is a growing desire to maintain the bonds of friendship and local social roots of their children, spouses, and themselves. In effect there is little reason to believe that the economy will suffer if this trend continues, and it may actually benefit from less shuttling around of people. Surely the Communitarian nexus will benefit.

Finally, there are new, nongeographic, communities made up of people who do not live near one another. Their foundations may not be as stable and deep-rooted as residential communities, but they fulfill many of the social and moral functions of traditional communities. Work-based and professional communities are among the most common of these. That is, people who work together in a steel mill or a high-tech firm such as Lotus or Microsoft often develop work-related friendships and community webs; groups of co-workers hang around together, help one another, play and party together, and go on joint outings. As they learn to know and care for one another, they also form and reinforce moral expectations.

Other communities are found in some law firms, on many campuses (although one community may not encompass everyone on campus), among physicians at the same hospital or with the same specialty in a town, and among some labor union members.

Some critics have attacked these communities as being artificially constructed, because they lack geographical definition or because they are merely social networks, without a residential concentration. Ray Oldenburg, author of *The Great Good Place*, decries the new definitions of community that encompass co-workers and even radio call-in show audiences. "Can we really create a satisfactory community apart from geography?" he asks (Baldwin 17). "My answer is 20 'no.'" But people who work every day in the same place spend more hours together and in closer proximity than people who live on the same village street. Most important, these nongeographic communities often provide at least some elements of the Communitarian nexus, and hence they tend to have the moral infrastructure we consider essential for a civil and humane society.

In short, our society is neither without community nor sufficiently Communitarian; it is neither *gemeinschaft* nor *gesellschaft*, but a mixture of the two sociological conditions. America does not need a simple return to gemeinschaft, to the traditional community. Modern economic prerequisites preclude such a shift, but even if it were possible, such backpedaling would be undesirable because traditional communities have been too constraining and authoritarian. Such traditional communities were usually homogeneous. What we need now are communities that balance both diversity and unity. As John W. Gardner has noted: "To prevent the wholeness from smothering diversity, there must be a philosophy of pluralism, an open climate for dissent, and an opportunity for subcommunities to retain their identity and share in the setting of larger group goals" (*Building Community* 11). Thus, we need to strengthen the communitarian elements in the urban and suburban centers, to provide the social bonds that sustain the moral voice, but at the same time avoid tight networks that suppress pluralism and dissent. James Pinkerton, who served in the Bush White House, speaks eloquently about a new paradigm focused around what he calls a "new *gemeinschaft*." It would be, he says, neither oppressive nor hierarchical. In short, we need new communities in which people have choices and readily accommodate divergent *sub*communities but still maintain common bonds.

Notes

Deborah Baldwin, "Creating Community," *Common Cause Magazine*, July/August 1990, 17.

Felicity Barringer, "18 Percent of Households in U.S. Moved in '89," *New York Times*, December 20, 1991, A16.

Herbert Gans, *The Urban Villagers: Group and Class in the Life of Italian-Americans* (New York: The Free Press, 1962, 1982), 14–15.

John W. Gardner, *Building Community* (Washington, D.C.: Independent Sector, 1991), 11.

Mary Ann Glendon, *Rights Talk* (New York: The Free Press, 1991), 112.

Abraham Monk, "Aging, Loneliness, and Communications," *American Behavioral Scientist* 31 (5): 534.

Jonathan Rowe, "Left and Right: The Emergence of a New Politics in the 1990s?" sponsored by the Heritage Foundation and the Progressive Foundation, October 30, 1991, Washington, D.C.

Jim Sleeper, *Closest of Strangers: Liberalism and the Politics of Race in New York* (New York: W. W. Norton & Company, 1990).

Ferdinand Tönnies, *Community and Society*, translated and edited by Charles P. Loomis (East Lansing: Michigan State University Press, 1957).

U.S. Bureau of the Census, Current Population Reports, series P-20, no. 450, *Marital Status and Living Arrangements: March 1990* (Washington, D.C.: U.S. Government Printing Office, 1991), table L, 12.

James Q. Wilson, "The Rediscovery of Character: Private Virtue and Public Policy," *The Public Interest* 81 (Fall 1985): 13.

Exploring the Text

1. Who is Amitai Etzioni's audience for this excerpt (or for *The Spirit of Community*, the book in which it appeared)? Cite specific elements of the text to support your answer.

2. What do the German terms *gemeinschaft* and *gesellschaft* mean? Why does Etzioni use them? How does their use reinforce your analysis of his audience?

3. The first ten paragraphs describe the history of American communities. Based on the information in these paragraphs and the presentation of it, what assumptions do you think Etzioni makes about his audience's knowledge?

4. What is the rhetorical effect of the questions that make up the bulk of paragraph 11?

5. Where in this excerpt does Etzioni address the counterargument, or at least a perspective different from his own?

6. What does Etzioni mean by "the moral infrastructure we consider essential for a civil and humane society" (para. 20)?

7. While Etzioni presents historical background, he does not do so chronologically. How would you describe his organizational structure? How does it contribute to achieving his purpose?

8. What kinds of evidence does Etzioni use to develop his argument? Cite specific examples of at least three types.

9. Etzioni uses both formal and informal language. Cite several examples of each, and explain the likely effect of this mixture on his intended audience.

10. What observations do you have about the sources listed at the end of the excerpt — both the number and the type? What kind of relationship is Etzioni trying to establish with his audience?

11. Ethos and logos prevail in this excerpt, but what appeals, perhaps more subtle, does Etzioni make to pathos?

Commencement Speech at Mount Holyoke College

Anna Quindlen

Beginning as a general assignment reporter, Anna Quindlen (b. 1953) went on to win the Pulitzer Prize for Commentary in 1992 for her opinion column "Public and Private" in the *New York Times*. She is the author of many novels, including *Object Lessons* (1991), *One True Thing* (1995), *Black and Blue* (1998), *Blessings* (2003), and *Rise and Shine* (2006). Her nonfiction includes *How Reading Changed My Life* and *A Short Guide to a Happy Life*. She currently writes a biweekly column for *Newsweek*. In 1994, Quindlen gave up her job at the *New York Times* to write fiction full-time and spend more time with her three children, a decision for which many soundly criticized her. In the following speech, she considers the impact of making individual decisions that do not conform to prevailing community values.

I look at all of you today and I cannot help but see myself twenty-five years ago, at my own Barnard commencement. I sometimes seem, in my mind, to have as much in common with that girl as I do with any stranger I might pass in the doorway of a Starbucks or in the aisle of an airplane. I cannot remember what she wore or how she felt that day. But I can tell you this about her without question: she was perfect.

Let me be very clear what I mean by that. I mean that I got up every day and tried to be perfect in every possible way. If there was a test to be had, I had studied for it; if there was a paper to be written, it was done. I smiled at everyone in the dorm hallways, because it was important to be friendly, and I made fun of them behind their backs because it was important to be witty. And I worked as a residence counselor and sat on housing council. If anyone had ever stopped and asked me why I did those things — well, I'm not sure what I would have said. But I can tell you, today, that I did them to be perfect, in every possible way.

Being perfect was hard work, and the hell of it was, the rules of it changed. So that while I arrived at college in 1970 with a trunk full of perfect pleated kilts and perfect monogrammed sweaters, by Christmas vacation I had another perfect uniform: overalls, turtlenecks, Doc Martens, and the perfect New York City Barnard College affect — part hyperintellectual, part ennui. This was very hard work indeed. I had read neither Sartre nor Sappho, and the closest I ever came to being bored and above it all was falling asleep. Finally, it was harder to become perfect because I realized, at Barnard, that I was not the smartest girl in the world. Eventually being perfect day after day, year after year, became like always carrying a backpack filled with bricks on my back. And oh, how I secretly longed to lay my burden down.

So what I want to say to you today is this: if this sounds, in any way, familiar to you, if you have been trying to be perfect in one way or another, too, then make today, when for a moment there are no more grades to be gotten, classmates to be met, terrain to be scouted, positioning to be arranged — make today the day to put down the backpack. Trying to be perfect may be sort of inevitable for people like us, who are smart and ambitious and interested in the world and in its good opinion. But at one level it's too hard, and at another, it's too cheap and easy. Because it really requires you mainly to read the zeitgeist[1] of wherever and whenever you happen to be, and to assume the masks necessary to be the best of whatever the zeitgeist dictates or requires. Those requirements shape-shift, sure, but when you're clever you can read them and do the imitation required.

But nothing important, or meaningful, or beautiful, or interesting, or great   5 ever came out of imitations. The thing that is really hard, and really amazing, is giving up on being perfect and beginning the work of becoming yourself.

This is more difficult, because there is no zeitgeist to read, no template to follow, no mask to wear. Set aside what your friends expect, what your parents demand, what your acquaintances require. Set aside the messages this culture sends, through its advertising, its entertainment, its disdain and its disapproval, about how you should behave.

Set aside the old traditional notion of female as nurturer and male as leader; set aside, too, the new traditional notions of female as superwoman and male as oppressor. Begin with that most terrifying of all things, a clean slate. Then look, every day, at the choices you are making, and when you ask yourself why you are making them, find this answer: for me, for me. Because they are who and what I am, and mean to be.

This is the hard work of your life in the world, to make it all up as you go along, to acknowledge the introvert, the clown, the artist, the reserved, the distraught, the goofball, the thinker. You will have to bend all your will not to march to the music that all of those great "theys" out there pipe on their flutes. They want you to go to professional school, to wear khakis, to pierce your navel, to bare your soul. These are the fashionable ways. The music is tinny, if you listen close enough. Look inside. That way lies dancing to the melodies spun out by your own heart. This is a symphony. All the rest are jingles.

This will always be your struggle whether you are twenty-one or fifty-one. I know this from experience. When I quit the *New York Times* to be a full-time mother, the voices of the world said that I was nuts. When I quit it again to be a full-time novelist, they said I was nuts again. But I am not nuts. I am happy. I am successful on my own terms. Because if your success is not on your own terms, if it looks good to the world but does not feel good in your heart, it is not success at all. Remember the words of Lily Tomlin: If you win the rat race, you're still a rat.

Look at your fingers. Hold them in front of your face. Each one is crowned   10 by an abstract design that is completely different than those of anyone in this

---

[1]German, "spirit of the time."

crowd, in this country, in this world. They are a metaphor for you. Each of you is as different as your fingerprints. Why in the world should you march to any lockstep?

The lockstep is easier, but here is why you cannot march to it. Because nothing great or even good ever came of it. When young writers write to me about following in the footsteps of those of us who string together nouns and verbs for a living, I tell them this: every story has already been told. Once you've read *Anna Karenina*, *Bleak House*, *The Sound and the Fury*, *To Kill a Mockingbird* and *A Wrinkle in Time*, you understand that there is really no reason to ever write another novel. Except that each writer brings to the table, if she will let herself, something that no one else in the history of time has ever had. And that is herself, her own personality, her own voice. If she is doing Faulkner imitations, she can stay home. If she is giving readers what she thinks they want instead of what she is, she should stop typing.

But if her books reflect her character, who she really is, then she is giving them a new and wonderful gift. Giving it to herself, too.

And that is true of music and art and teaching and medicine. Someone sent me a T-shirt not long ago that read "Well-Behaved Women Don't Make History." They don't make good lawyers, either, or doctors or businesswomen. Imitations are redundant. Yourself is what is wanted.

You already know this. I just need to remind you. Think back. Think back to first or second grade, when you could still hear the sound of your own voice in your head, when you were too young, too unformed, too fantastic to understand that you were supposed to take on the protective coloration of the expectations of those around you. Think of what the writer Catherine Drinker Bowen once wrote, more than half a century ago: "Many a man who has known himself at ten forgets himself utterly between ten and thirty." Many a woman, too.

You are not alone in this. We parents have forgotten our way sometimes, too. I say this as the deeply committed, often flawed mother of three. When you were first born, each of you, our great glory was in thinking you absolutely distinct from every baby who had ever been born before. You were a miracle of singularity, and we knew it in every fiber of our being.   15

But we are only human, and being a parent is a very difficult job, more difficult than any other, because it requires the shaping of other people, which is an act of extraordinary hubris. Over the years we learned to want for you things that you did not want for yourself. We learned to want the lead in the play, the acceptance to our own college, the straight and narrow path that often leads absolutely nowhere. Sometimes we wanted those things because we were convinced it would make life better, or at least easier for you. Sometimes we had a hard time distinguishing between where you ended and we began.

So that another reason that you must give up on being perfect and take hold of being yourself is because sometime, in the distant future, you may want to be parents, too. If you can bring to your children the self that you truly are, as opposed to some amalgam of manners and mannerisms, expectations and fears that you have acquired as a carapace along the way, you will give them, too, a great gift. You will teach them by example not to be terrorized by the narrow and parsimonious expectations of the world, a world that often likes to color within the lines when a spray of paint, a scrawl of crayon, is what is truly wanted.

Remember yourself, from the days when you were younger and rougher and wilder, more scrawl than straight line. Remember all of yourself, the flaws and faults as well as the many strengths. Carl Jung once said, "If people can be educated to see the lowly side of their own natures, it may be hoped that they will also learn to understand and to love their fellow men better. A little less hypocrisy and a little more tolerance toward oneself can only have good results in respect for our neighbors, for we are all too prone to transfer to our fellows the injustice and violence we inflict upon our own natures."

Most commencement speeches suggest you take up something or other: the challenge of the future, a vision of the twenty-first century. Instead I'd like you to give up. Give up the backpack. Give up the nonsensical and punishing quest for perfection that dogs too many of us through too much of our lives. It is a quest that causes us to doubt and denigrate ourselves, our true selves, our quirks and foibles and great leaps into the unknown, and that is bad enough.

But this is worse: that someday, sometime, you will be somewhere, maybe   20
on a day like today — a berm overlooking a pond in Vermont, the lip of the Grand Canyon at sunset. Maybe something bad will have happened: you will have lost someone you loved, or failed at something you wanted to succeed at very much.

And sitting there, you will fall into the center of yourself. You will look for that core to sustain you. If you have been perfect all your life, and have managed to meet all the expectations of your family, your friends, your community, your society, chances are excellent that there will be a black hole where your core ought to be.

Don't take that chance. Begin to say no to the Greek chorus that thinks it knows the parameters of a happy life when all it knows is the homogenization of human experience. Listen to that small voice from inside you, that tells you to go another way. George Eliot wrote, "It is never too late to be what you might have been." It is never too early, either. And it will make all the difference in the world. Take it from someone who has left the backpack full of bricks far behind. Every day feels light as a feather.

Exploring the Text

1. What rhetorical strategies does Anna Quindlen use to tailor her speech to a specific occasion and audience?
2. How does she use her own experience without sounding judgmental or didactic?
3. What does she mean when says, "I'd like you to give up. Give up the backpack" (para. 19)?

4. Beyond the backpack, Quindlen introduces the metaphor of fingerprints (para. 10). Which metaphor works better for you? Why?

5. Is Quindlen suggesting that the graduates should lower their expectations and goals? Explain your answer.

6. Quindlen quotes Lily Tomlin (actress, comedian, writer), Catherine Drinker Bowen (writer of semifictional biographies), Carl Jung (psychiatrist), and George Eliot (novelist) (paras. 9, 14, 18, 22). What is the effect of citing such a variety of sources?

7. In her speech, does Quindlen sympathize more with the values of the community or the individual? Explain.

Walking the Path between Worlds

LORI ARVISO ALVORD

> The first Navajo woman surgeon, Lori Arviso Alvord (b. 1958) is currently the associate dean of student and minority affairs and assistant professor of surgery at Dartmouth Medical School. She received her BA from Dartmouth College and her MD from Stanford University. At the start of her career, she served as a general surgeon in the Indian Health Service in her native New Mexico. She has been honored with numerous awards, including the Governor's Award for Outstanding Women from the State of New Mexico (1992) and the Outstanding Women in Medicine Award from the University of Missouri–Kansas City School of Medicine (2001). Her autobiography, *The Scalpel and the Silver Bear*, describes her efforts to combine Navajo healing practices with Western medicine. The following passage from that book focuses on her journey from the reservation to Dartmouth.

Today Navajo children are still standing on the playgrounds where I stood, facing the critical decision I would face after I graduated from high school: to leave the rez, or to stay and cleave to traditional ways. To let the desert live inside them, or to try to wash it away. They too hear the voice of the wind and the desert, smell the strong smells of our people, and feel the ways we came from. "*Decide,*" the world whispers to them, "*you must choose.*"

I chose to leave and get an education, following the path of the books I loved so much. But leaving Dinetah was a frightening prospect. Navajo people believe we are safe within the four sacred mountains that bound the Navajo reservation — Mount Taylor, San Francisco Peak, Blanca Peak, and the La Plata Range. In our creation stories it is the place of our origins, of our emergence to the surface of the earth from other worlds below, the place where Changing Woman and First Man, Coyote, the Twins, and the monsters in our legends roamed. These mountains are central to everything in our lives. To leave this place is to invite imbalance, to break our precious link with the tribe, to leave the Walk of Beauty, and to court danger. It was a dangerous step, that into the unknown, unguarded world.

In our song called the Mountain Chant, each of the sacred mountains is honored. The words describe each mountain and its special qualities.

> The mountain to the east is Sisna'jin
> It is standing out.
> The strong White Bead is standing out
> A living mountain is standing out . . .
> The mountain to the south is Tsoodził
> It is standing out.
> The strong turquoise is standing out
> A living mountain is standing out . . .
> The mountain to the west is Dook'o'oosłííd.
> It is standing out.
> The strong white shell is standing out.
> A living mountain is standing out . . .
> The mountain to the north is Dibé Ntsaa.
> It is standing out.
> The strong jet is standing out.
> A living mountain is standing out . . .[1]

If I left, I would leave the enclosed and sacred world within the strong mountains, standing out.

I made good grades in high school, but I had received a very marginal education. I had a few good teachers, but teachers were difficult to recruit to our schools and they often didn't stay long. Funding was often inadequate. I spent many hours in classrooms where, I now see, very little was being taught. Nevertheless my parents always assumed, quite optimistically, that all their children would go to college. I don't remember any lectures from my father on the importance of higher education — just the quiet assurance that he and my mother and Grandmother all believed in us.

My college plans were modest; I assumed I would attend a nearby state school.   5
But then I happened to meet another Navajo student who was attending Princeton. I had heard of Princeton but had no idea where it was. I asked him how many Indians were there. He replied, "Five." I couldn't even imagine a place with only five Indians, since our town was 98 percent Indian. Then he mentioned Dartmouth, which had about fifty Indians on campus, and I felt a little better. *Ivy League* was a term I had heard, but I had no concept of its meaning. No one from my high school had ever attended an Ivy League college.

---

[1]Aileen O'Bryan, *Navajo Indian Myths* (New York: Dover, 1994).

At my request, my high school counselor gave me the applications for all the Ivy League schools, but I only completed Dartmouth's because I knew there were fifty Indians there.

I waited anxiously, and one day the letter came. I was accepted, early decision. I was only sixteen years old. As I was only half Navajo in blood, I wondered if this meant it would be only half as dangerous to me to leave Dinetah, the place between the sacred mountains. Half of me belonged in Dinetah, but the other half of me belonged in that other world too, I figured. Still, in my heart I was all Navajo, and I instinctively felt afraid of the move. I had seen those who went away and came back: the Vietnam veterans, broken and lost, who aimlessly wandered the streets of Gallup, the others who came back but had forgotten Navajo ways.

My memories of my arrival in Hanover, New Hampshire, are mostly of the color green. Green cloaked the hillsides, crawled up the ivied walls, and was reflected in the river where the Dartmouth crew students sculled. For a girl who had never been far from Crownpoint, New Mexico, the green felt incredibly juicy, lush, beautiful, and threatening. Crownpoint had had vast acreage of sky and sand, but aside from the pastel scrub brush, mesquite, and chamiso, practically the only growing things there were the tiny stunted pines called piñon trees. Yet it is beautiful; you can see the edges and contours of red earth stretching all the way to the box-shaped faraway cliffs and the horizon. No horizon was in sight in Hanover, only trees. I felt claustrophobic.

If the physical contrasts were striking, the cultural ones were even more so. Although I felt lucky to be there, I was in complete culture shock. I thought people talked too much, laughed too loud, asked too many personal questions, and had no respect for privacy. They seemed overly competitive and put a higher value on material wealth than I was used to. Navajos placed much more emphasis on a person's relations to family, clan, tribe, and the other inhabitants of the earth, both human and nonhuman, than on possessions. Everyone at home followed unwritten codes for behavior. We were taught to be humble and not to draw attention to ourselves, to favor cooperation over competition (so as not to make ourselves "look better" at another's expense or hurt someone's feelings), to value silence over words, to respect our elders, and to reserve our opinions until they were asked for.

Understanding the culture of Dartmouth was like taking a course in itself. I didn't know the meaning of fraternities or the class system (divided into the haves and the have-nots) which were so important there at first. Had the parents of my fellow students taught them survival skills through camping, tracking, and hunting? Did I have any interest in making four-story-high sculptures out of ice for Winter Carnival? Did they respect their elders, their parents? Did I know which fork to use at a formal dinner? What sort of ceremonies did their "tribes" practice? While they pondered such burning questions as the opening day of ski season, I was struggling just to stay warm during the frozen New Hampshire winter and not slip on the ice!   10

Indian reservations and pueblos could almost be seen as tiny Third World countries, lacking as they did electricity, indoor plumbing, and paved roads. When the Native American students arrived at Dartmouth, one of the first things we were told was that we could attend high tea at Sanborn Hall at four o'clock daily. I walked around the campus in awe, like a peasant visiting the castle of a great king.

The very stately, beautiful, and affluent campus could be intimidating and alienating. The college's unofficial mascot was the "Dartmouth Indian," a tomahawk-wielding red man whose presence was everywhere on the campus, in spite of the Native community's protests. He was like those TV Indians we had watched when we were little and thought so alien. Imagine young Native students seeing white students wearing loincloths and paint on their faces, jumping around with toy tomahawks. Like the rest of the Native community, I was shocked by this caricature.

I remember, distinctly, feeling alienated while walking around Dartmouth's campus that first year. By my sophomore year I understood what it meant to be invisible. People looked right through me — I moved around the campus as unseen as the air. Outside of my freshman roommate, Anne, I never made a close non-Indian friend. I wonder if other students of color felt the same way.

I was very homesick, wishing I didn't have to miss so many familiar events: the Navajo tribal fairs, the Zuni Shalako, the Laguna feast days, the Santa Fe Indian market, the Gallup ceremonial. Everyone at home was having a great time eating wonderful food — roasted corn from the Shiprock market, posole, red chile stew, venison jerky — and I was stuck in a library far away. I missed watching the Apache Devil Dancers and the Pueblo Buffalo Dancers. I missed the sight of Navajo traditional clothing, emblazoned with silver and turquoise, and the pink-and-purple-splashed sunsets of New Mexico. I missed that smell — that smell we had tried to wash away at our laundromat so long ago — the smell of wildness, the desert, and the Navajo world.

Sometimes I wondered: If I'd had a *kinaałdá* ceremony, could I have been 15 stronger, more independent, better able to face this loneliness and alienation, less unassured. The *kinaałdá* is part of the Blessing Way set of ceremonies performed for girls when they reach puberty. Blessing Way tells the story of Changing Woman (a central Navajo deity), and the *kinaałdá* celebrates her coming into womanhood. The family and community gather around her, she is sung to, and her female relatives massage her from head to toe, giving her the power and strength of womanhood. A large corn cake is baked underground in a corn husk–lined pit, and the girl sprinkles cornmeal over the top. Each day for four days, she runs for a mile toward the new sun, toward her new life. It gives a young woman strength and power, confidence and security, as she goes through menses for the first time. She takes that strength and those "good thoughts" with her into the world. I could have used that assurance. Because my family was less traditional, my sisters and I did not have *kinaałdá* ceremonies, although we attended those of our cousins. Nevertheless, since the Navajo culture is matriarchal, I think I was better prepared as a woman in a "man's world" than many white women I met.

A few things at Dartmouth, however, were comforting and did make me feel at home. For one thing, dogs roamed the campus freely. They didn't belong to anybody in particular but to everybody and were fed and cared for by the entire campus. Muttlike, wily, always after something to eat, they reminded me naturally of rez dogs. And everywhere I looked[,] playful squirrels ran around, reminding me of the prairie dogs who run around their prairie dog cities on the mesas and sit up on their hind legs to watch the cars drive by.

Academically, due to my strong reading background, I held my own in classes like literature and social sciences, but I was totally unprepared for the physical and life sciences. After receiving the only D of my entire life in calculus, I retreated from the sciences altogether. The high school at Crownpoint had not prepared me adequately to compete with the Ivy Leaguers. Furthermore, I had an additional problem. As I mentioned earlier, Navajos are taught from the youngest age never to draw attention to ourselves. So Navajo children do not raise their hands in class. At a school like Dartmouth, the lack of participation was seen as a sign not of humility but lack of interest and a disengaged attitude. My Navajo humility was combined with a deep feeling of academic inferiority; it was hard to compete with students who had taken calculus and read Chaucer in high school. I sat in the back and tried not to reveal my ignorance.

This sense of being torn between worlds was reflected even in my studies: I chose a double major, psychology and sociology, modified with Native American studies. I received honors in my freshman seminar as well as in two Native American studies courses that stressed writing. As a result, I found myself thinking of teaching Native American studies as a career, and perhaps also becoming a writer.

In fact, I loved Dartmouth's Native American program. It had the tough job of recruiting students like us, who were very high risk. We frequently had had only marginal high school preparation; many were reluctant to come to school so far from home; and like skittish wild horses, some would turn tail and run home at the least provocation. We found great comfort in one another, for although we came from many different tribes, our experiences at Dartmouth were similar: We all felt disconnected from the mainstream student body. For the women, it was even worse. At the time I arrived on the scene, Dartmouth had only recently changed from an all-male to a coed student body, and many of the men resented the presence of women on campus. Referred to as cohogs instead of coeds, women were shunned for dates; instead girls were bused in from nearby women's colleges on weekends. Social life was dominated by the fraternities, and, if we went to their parties at all, we were often ignored.

For all these reasons, the few Native American students at Dartmouth coalesced into a solid community who did almost everything together. Our group was made up of Paiutes, Sioux, Cherokees, Chippewas, Navajos, Pueblos, and many other tribes. We were friends, lovers, rivals, enemies. I have been a part of

20

many other groups since then, but nothing compared in intensity to the experience of being a member of that Native American student group.

Though we often felt as though we didn't belong at Dartmouth, the ironic truth is that we did belong, or rather, we were entitled to be there. Eleazar Wheelock, the Connecticut minister who founded Dartmouth College in 1769, did so with funds that came from King George II, who wished to establish a place to "educate the savages." The college flourished, but for literally hundreds of years its original founding purpose was not honored. "Educating savages" was not on the real agenda; it had simply been a way to get land and money. Before the 1960s fewer than twenty Native students graduated from Dartmouth. Then in the 1970s the Native American studies program was developed by college president John Kemeny and writer Michael Dorris, and Dartmouth began to take its mission in earnest.

We Indian students all knew why we were there. Without the vision of Kemeny and Dorris, we would never have had an opportunity to set foot on the grounds of such an institution, let alone actually enroll. We were there because of the generous scholarships the college had given us, and the money from our tribes.

Some years later, reflecting back on my college experiences, I realized something else. The outside, non-Indian world is tribeless, full of wandering singular souls, seeking connection through societies, clubs, and other groups. White people know what it is to be a family, but to be a tribe is something of an altogether different sort. It provides a feeling of inclusion in something larger, of having a set place in the universe where one always belongs. It provides connectedness and a blueprint for how to live.

At Dartmouth the fraternities and sororities seemed to be attempts to claim or create tribes. Their wild and crazy parties that often involved drugs and sex seemed to me to be unconscious re-creations of rituals and initiation ceremonies. But the fraternities emphasized exclusion as much as inclusion, and their rituals involved alcohol and hazing initiations. Although they developed from a natural urge for community, they lacked much that a real tribe has.

I began to honor and cherish my tribal membership, and in the years that followed I came to understand that such membership is central to mental health, to spiritual health, to physical health. A tribe is a community of people connected by blood or heart, by geography and tradition, who help one another and share a belief system. Community and tribe not only reduce the alienation people feel but in doing so stave off illness. In a sense they are a form of preventive medicine. Most Americans have lost their tribal identities, although at one time, most likely, everyone belonged to a tribe. One way to remedy this is to find and establish groups of people who can nurture and support one another. The Native American students at Dartmouth had become such a group.

Our new "tribe" had its ceremonies. Each year, in a primitive outdoor amphitheater called the Bema where concerts and plays were sometimes put on, we held a campus powwow. Feathered fancy dancers and women in "jingle

25

dresses" or in beaded and brightly colored fabric would spin and step to the drums of Plains Indians or to songs from an invited singer from a pueblo. The women would whirl, their shawls swirling and twisting into corkscrew shapes around them. They'd dance to two big hide-stretched drums, encircled by the men, who struck the drums rhythmically and sang. Their voices wove and resonated, rose and fell above the steady heartbeat of the drums. This ceremony was a chance for the Native and non-Native communities to come together as one. I felt then, briefly, that I belonged.

In the evening after the powwow the singing and drumming would continue at a party called a "49" — but here the ancient rhythms were mixed with modern English lyrics. The songs we sang could be romantic, funny, or political; they could be about reservation life and pickup trucks or the Bureau of Indian Affairs. They always sounded the same though, with a blend of voices rising around a drumbeat, and a melody that pulled out our memories of childhood songs.

Dartmouth was good for me. Singing with the other students melted some of my historical grief and anger into a larger powerful force, a force I would take with me into the world. I gained a new kind of family and tribe, with new songs that held us together. Once again, songs had the power to heal.

Exploring the Text

1. What different views of community did Lori Arviso Alvord experience as she moved from her home in New Mexico to college at Dartmouth?

2. What is Alvord's primary method of organization in this essay?

3. What is the effect of including the Mountain Chant?

4. What impact does the physical landscape in Hanover have on Alvord? Why does she describe the landscape in such detail?

5. Which details of life on the reservation does Alvord recall in paragraph 15? Cite specific ones, and explain their importance. Why is the *kinaałdá* ceremony especially significant?

6. Describe Alvord's tone in the two paragraphs on the history of Dartmouth and its Native American studies program (paras. 21–22)? Cite specific language and examples to support your response.

7. Ultimately, what is Alvord's attitude toward Dartmouth? Cite specific paragraphs to support your response.

8. What does Alvord mean in the concluding paragraph by "my historical grief and anger"?

New York Day Women (fiction)

EDWIDGE DANTICAT

> Born in Haiti in 1969, Edwidge Danticat immigrated to the United States when she was twelve. She received her BA from Barnard College and her MFA from Brown University, where her thesis project became her first novel, *Breath, Eyes, Memory* (1994); it was an Oprah Winfrey Book Club selection in 1998. Her other fiction includes *Krik? Krak!* (1995), *The Farming of Bones* (1998), and *The Dew Breaker* (2004). In her work, Danticat often explores themes of cultural dislocation from the perspective of immigrants of different generations. In this story, she focuses on a mother and daughter whose life in America pulls them toward separate communities.

Today, walking down the street, I see my mother. She is strolling with a happy gait, her body thrust toward the DON'T WALK sign and the yellow taxicabs that make forty-five-degree turns on the corner of Madison and Fifty-seventh Street.

I have never seen her in this kind of neighborhood, peering into Chanel and Tiffany's and gawking at the jewels glowing in the Bulgari windows. My mother never shops outside of Brooklyn. She has never seen the advertising office where I work. She is afraid to take the subway, where you may meet those young black militant street preachers who curse black women for straightening their hair.

Yet, here she is, my mother, who I left at home that morning in her bathrobe, with pieces of newspapers twisted like rollers in her hair. My mother, who accuses me of random offenses as I dash out of the house.

Would you get up and give an old lady like me your subway seat? In this state of mind, I bet you don't even give up your seat to a pregnant lady.

My mother, who is often right about that. Sometimes I get up and give my seat. Other times, I don't. It all depends on how pregnant the woman is and whether or not she is with her boyfriend or husband and whether or not *he* is sitting down.

As my mother stands in front of Carnegie Hall, one taxi driver yells to another, "What do you think this is, a dance floor?"

My mother waits patiently for this dispute to be settled before crossing the street.

In Haiti when you get hit by a car, the owner of the car gets out and kicks you for getting blood on his bumper.

※※

My mother who laughs when she says this and shows a large gap in her mouth where she lost three more molars to the dentist last week. My mother, who at fifty-nine, says dentures are okay.

※※

You can take them out when they bother you. I'll like them. I'll like them fine.   10

※※

Will it feel empty when Papa kisses you?

※※

Oh no, he doesn't kiss me that way anymore.

※※

My mother, who watches the lottery drawing every night on channel 11 without ever having played the numbers.

※※

A third of that money is all I would need. We would pay the mortgage, and your father could stop driving that taxicab all over Brooklyn.

※※

I follow my mother, mesmerized by the many possibilities of her journey. Even in   15
a flowered dress, she is lost in a sea of pinstripes and gray suits, high heels and elegant short skirts, Reebok sneakers, dashing from building to building.
    My mother, who won't go out to dinner with anyone.

※※

If they want to eat with me, let them come to my house, even if I boil water and give it to them.

※※

My mother, who talks to herself when she peels the skin off poultry.

※※

Fat, you know, and cholesterol. Fat and cholesterol killed your aunt Hermine.

※※

My mother, who makes jam with dried grapefruit peel and then puts in cinna-   20
mon bark that I always think is cockroaches in the jam. My mother, whom I have
always bought household appliances for, on her birthday. A nice rice cooker, a
blender.

I trail the red orchids in her dress and the heavy faux leather bag on her
shoulders. Realizing the ferocious pace of my pursuit, I stop against a wall to rest.
My mother keeps on walking as though she owns the sidewalk under her feet.

As she heads toward the Plaza Hotel, a bicycle messenger swings so close to
her that I want to dash forward and rescue her, but she stands dead in her tracks
and lets him ride around her and then goes on.

My mother stops at a corner hot-dog stand and asks for something. The
vendor hands her a can of soda that she slips into her bag. She stops by another
vendor selling sundresses for seven dollars each. I can tell that she is looking at
an African print dress, contemplating my size. I think to myself, Please Ma, don't
buy it. It would be just another thing that I would bury in the garage or give to
Goodwill.

**Why should we give to Goodwill when there are so many people back home who
need clothes? We save our clothes for the relatives in Haiti.**

Twenty years we have been saving all kinds of things for the relatives in Haiti. I   25
need the place in the garage for an exercise bike.

You are pretty enough to be a stewardess. Only dogs like bones.

This mother of mine, she stops at another hot-dog vendor's and buys a frank-
furter that she eats on the street. I never knew that she ate frankfurters. With her
blood pressure, she shouldn't eat anything with sodium. She has to be careful
with her heart, this day woman.

I cannot just swallow salt. Salt is heavier than a hundred bags of shame.

She is slowing her pace, and now I am too close. If she turns around, she night see
me. I let her walk into the park before I start to follow again.

My mother walks toward the sandbox in the middle of the park. There a   30
woman is waiting with a child. The woman is wearing a leotard with biker's shorts

and has small weights in her hands. The woman kisses the child good-bye and surrenders him to my mother; then she bolts off, running on the cemented stretches in the park.

The child given to my mother has frizzy blond hair. His hand slips into hers easily, like he's known her for a long time. When he raises his face to look at my mother, it is as though he is looking at the sky.

My mother gives this child the soda that she bought from the vendor on the street corner. The child's face lights up as she puts in a straw in the can for him. This seems to be a conspiracy just between the two of them.

My mother and the child sit and watch the other children play in the sandbox. The child pulls out a comic book from a knapsack with Big Bird on the back. My mother peers into his comic book. My mother, who taught herself to read as a little girl in Haiti from the books that her brothers brought home from school.

My mother, who has now lost six of her seven sisters in Ville Rose and has never had the strength to return for their funerals.

Many graves to kiss when I go back. Many graves to kiss.   35

She throws away the empty soda can when the child is done with it. I wait and watch from a corner until the woman in the leotard and biker's shorts returns, sweaty and breathless, an hour later. My mother gives the woman back her child and strolls farther into the park.

I turn around and start to walk out of the park before my mother can see me. My lunch hour is long since gone. I have to hurry back to work. I walk through a cluster of joggers, then race to a *Sweden Tours* bus. I stand behind the bus and take a peek at my mother in the park. She is standing in a circle, chatting with a group of women who are taking other people's children on an afternoon outing. They look like a Third World Parent-Teacher Association meeting.

I quickly jump into a cab heading back to the office. Would Ma have said hello had she been the one to see me first?

As the cab races away from the park, it occurs to me that perhaps one day I would chase an old woman down a street by mistake and that old woman would be somebody else's mother, who I would have mistaken for mine.

Day women come out when nobody expects them.   40

Tonight on the subway, I will get up and give my seat to a pregnant woman or a lady about Ma's age.

My mother, who stuffs thimbles in her mouth and then blows up her cheeks like Dizzy Gillespie while sewing yet another Raggedy Ann doll that she names Suzette after me.

I will have all these little Suzettes in case you never have any babies, which looks more and more like it is going to happen.

My mother who had me when she was thirty-three — *l'âge du Christ* — at the age that Christ died on the cross.

That's a blessing, believe you me, even if American doctors say by that time you 45 **can make retarded babies.**

My mother, who sews lace collars on my company softball T-shirts when she does my laundry.

Why, you can't you look like a lady playing softball?

My mother, who never went to any of my Parent-Teacher Association meetings when I was in school.

You're so good anyway. What are they going to tell me? I don't want to make you ashamed of this day woman. Shame is heavier than a hundred bags of salt.

Exploring the Text

1. What different communities do the narrator and her mother belong to?
2. How does Edwidge Danticat attach a geography or physical setting to community? In what ways does the mother transcend geography in her firm commitment to her Haitian community?
3. How do the two type styles (bold and regular font) and the white space and icons between sections create a structure for this story?
4. Who are the "New York day women"?

5. How does the narrator react when she sees her mother with the little boy?
6. How would you describe the narrator's attitude toward her mother?
7. How does Danticat develop tension between the narrator's home community and the communities that education and economic opportunity have brought her into?
8. Why do you think the author gave the narrator the following words: "perhaps one day I would chase an old woman down a street by mistake and that old woman would be somebody else's mother, who I would have mistaken for mine" (para. 39)?

EDWIDGE DANTICAT ON WRITING

English is not the first language of Edwidge Danticat, whose "New York Day Women" immediately precedes this section. Danticat's formal education in Haiti was in French, though she spoke Haitian Creole at home. In the following interview, she comments on learning English and on writing in the language of her adopted homeland, the United States.

I had an uncle in Haiti who was always trying to learn English, so he would play those Berlitz-type records in the morning when he was shaving. That was the only time I really heard English. But I started learning right away when I came [to the United States]. I immediately went to school: I came on a Friday and went to school [Clara Barton High School in New York] on Monday. My parents were serious about education. I was in a bilingual class, but there were other classes where I just kind of went in and tried to figure out what was happening . . . at home, we always spoke Creole. With my brother, we speak something of a mix, but we never really spoke French at home.

I once read an ad in *Poets & Writers* [magazine] for an anthology called *The Stepmother Tongue*, and I remember thinking, "That's what it is to me. English is my stepmother tongue." I don't mean it derogatively, though; I never thought of those images of the wicked stepmother. I thought of a stepmother tongue in the sense that you have a mother tongue and then an adopted language that you take on because your family circumstances have changed, sometimes not by your own choice. But I don't think of it as something ugly.

I've always thought my relationship to language is precarious because in the first part of my life, I was balancing languages. As I was growing up, we spoke Creole at home, but when you go out, you speak French in the office, at the bank. If you didn't speak French at my school, the teacher would act like she didn't hear what you were saying. French is the socially valid and accepted language [in Haiti], but then the people who speak

Creole are not validated and in some way are being told their voice isn't heard. So I've always felt the dichotomy in language anyway.

I've been reading Richard Rodriguez's book *Hunger of Memory* . . . I'm still struggling with some of the same issues. People sometimes say to me, "Why do you write in English?" It's the circumstances of my life that led to this. If you grew up in the United States and ended up in Mexico and wrote in Spanish, is your doing that saying you are rejecting something else? It's not to say that if you write in English, you don't think Creole or French should be written in. This is where I am at this point, and a lot of the people I feel I'm writing for are like me.

Follow-up

How does the language you use — spoken or written — reflect your participation in more than one community? Even if you speak only one language, consider the variations that you use — at home, with your friends, in school, on the Internet. Why do you use so many variations?

Child of the Americas (poetry)

AURORA LEVINS MORALES

Daughter of a Puerto Rican mother and a Jewish father, Aurora Levins Morales (b. 1954) lived in Puerto Rico until she was thirteen, when her family moved to Chicago. She received her undergraduate degree from Franconia University in New Hampshire and her MA and PhD from the Union Institute in Ohio. She coauthored with her mother *Getting Home Alive* (1986), a collection of short stories, essays, and poetry. In 1998, she published *Remedios: Stories of Earth and Iron from the History of Puertorriqueñas* and *Medicine Stories: History, Culture, and the Politics of Integrity.* An activist and writer, Morales currently divides her time between the San Francisco Bay Area and Minneapolis. In the poem that follows, she celebrates her mixed heritage.

I am a child of the Americas,
a light-skinned mestiza of the Caribbean,
a child of many diaspora, born into this continent at a crossroads.

I am a U.S. Puerto Rican Jew,
a product of the ghettos of New York I have never known.   5

An immigrant and the daughter and granddaughter of immigrants.
I speak English with passion: it's the tongue of my consciousness,
a flashing knife blade of crystal, my tool, my craft.

I am Caribeña, island grown. Spanish is in my flesh,
ripples from my tongue, lodges in my hips: 10
the language of garlic and mangoes,
the singing in my poetry, the flying gestures of my hands.
I am of Latinoamerica, rooted in the history of my continent:
I speak from that body.

I am not africa. Africa is in me, but I cannot return.   15
I am not taína. Taíno is in me, but there is no way back.
I am not european. Europe lives in me, but I have no home there.

I am new. History made me. My first language was spanglish.
I was born at the crossroads
and I am whole.   20

Exploring the Text

1. How does the speaker describe herself? What characteristics does she emphasize?
2. Why does Aurora Levins Morales introduce those characteristics in the order that she does? That is, why does she choose not to open with her Jewish or African heritage, for instance?
3. What examples of parallel structure do you find? What is their effect?
4. How do you interpret the line "Europe lives in me, but I have no home there" (l. 17)?
5. What is the tone of the poem? Is the speaker defiant, hopeful, angry, confused, ambivalent, proud? Cite specific words and phrases to support your response.
6. Which of the following descriptions of the United States do you think the speaker would prefer: melting pot, salad bowl, mosaic? Why? To which community or communities would the speaker say she belongs?

Reflections (painting)

LEE TETER

Born in the Appalachian Mountains in 1959, Lee Teter is a self-taught painter. He is known for his "frontier art" — portrayals of Native Americans and frontiersmen — and his work has appeared on magazine covers. Teter, who acted as a visual arts consultant to the 1991 film *The Last of the Mohicans*, currently lives with his family in Wyoming, where he continues to produce his realistic art in oils, pencil, and platinum prints. Although he had just begun to enjoy commercial success at the time he painted *Reflections*, he gave the rights for prints to a veterans' group. The painting depicts a visitor to the Vietnam Veterans Memorial in Washington, D.C.

Three Servicemen (sculpture)

FREDERICK HART

Frederick Hart (1943–1999), an award-winning figurative sculptor who worked primarily in bronze and acrylic, was born in Atlanta and grew up in South Carolina. He received a degree in philosophy from the University of South Carolina, and in 1993, the university awarded him an honorary doctorate of fine arts. Hart studied art at the Corcoran College of Art and Design and at American University, both in Washington, D.C. In 1987, the National Sculpture Society honored him for his stonework at the Washington National Cathedral, and in 1988 he received a Presidential Design Excellence Award for *Three Servicemen*, a realistic bronze sculpture that is located near the Vietnam Veterans Memorial.

Exploring the Texts

1. What images converge in *Reflections*?
2. Describe the sense of community evoked in the painting *Reflections*.
3. The sculpture *Three Servicemen*, which depicts soldiers from three different ethnic backgrounds, has also been called *Three Fighting Men* and *Three Infantrymen*. Why do you think that *Three Servicemen* is the preferred title?
4. The choice of Maya Lin's abstract design for the Vietnam Veterans Memorial, which is featured in *Reflections*, occasioned considerable controversy; one result was the commissioning of Frederick Hart to do a more realistic piece. Do some research into this controversy. Be sure to read Lin's description of her vision for the memorial, included in her book *Boundaries* and excerpted at <bedfordstmartins .com/languageofcomp>. Then write a paragraph in which you support, challenge, or qualify the negative opinions held by the original critics of Lin's work.
5. Consider another public monument (for example, one in your own community, one you have visited in another city, or one you have learned about through your research). How does that visual text bring together — or perhaps define — a community?

Conversation

Each of the following texts presents a view of the individual's responsibility to the larger human community.

Sources
1. Bertrand Russell, *The Happy Life*
2. Peter Singer, *The Singer Solution to World Poverty*
3. Garrett Hardin, *Lifeboat Ethics: The Case against Helping the Poor*
4. John Betjeman, *In Westminster Abbey*

After using the questions to discuss individual selections, synthesize the pieces through one of the suggested assignments on pages 334–35.

1. *The Happy Life*

BERTRAND RUSSELL

In the following selection, British philosopher Bertrand Russell reflects on the meaning of happiness.

The happy life is to an extraordinary extent the same as the good life. Professional moralists have made too much of self-denial, and in so doing have put the emphasis in the wrong place. Conscious self-denial leaves a man self-absorbed and vividly aware of what he has sacrificed; in consequence it fails often of its immediate object and almost always of its ultimate purpose. What is needed is not self-denial, but that kind of direction of interest outward which will lead spontaneously and naturally to the same acts that a person absorbed in the pursuit of his own virtue could only perform by means of conscious self-denial. I have written in this book [*The Conquest of Happiness*] as a hedonist, that is to say, as one who regards happiness as the good, but the acts to be recommended from the point of view of the hedonist are on the whole the same as those to be recommended by the sane moralist. The moralist, however, is too apt, though this is not, of course, universally true, to stress the act rather than the state of mind. The effects of an act upon the agent will be widely different according to his state of mind at the moment. If you see a child drowning and save it as the result of a direct impulse to bring help, you will emerge none the worse morally. If, on the other hand, you say to yourself, "It is the part of virtue to succor the helpless, and

317

I wish to be a virtuous man, therefore I must save this child," you will be an even worse man afterwards than you were before. What applies in this extreme case, applies in many other instances that are less obvious.

There is another difference, somewhat more subtle, between the attitude towards life that I have been recommending and that which is recommended by the traditional moralists. The traditional moralist, for example, will say that love should be unselfish. In a certain sense he is right, that is to say, it should not be selfish beyond a point, but it should undoubtedly be of such a nature that one's own happiness is bound up in its success. If a man were to invite a lady to marry him on the ground that he ardently desired her happiness and at the same time considered that she would afford ideal opportunities of self-abnegation, I think it may be doubted whether she would be altogether pleased. Undoubtedly we should desire the happiness of those whom we love, but not as an alternative to our own. In fact, the whole antithesis between self and the rest of the world, which is implied in the doctrine of self-denial, disappears as soon as we have any genuine interest in persons or things outside ourselves. Through such interests a man comes to feel himself part of the stream of life, not a hard separate entity like a billiard ball, which can have no relation with other such entities except that of collision. All unhappiness depends upon some kind of disintegration or lack of integration; there is disintegration within the self through lack of coordination between the conscious and the unconscious mind; there is lack of integration between the self and society, where the two are not knit together by the force of objective interests and affections. The happy man is the man who does not suffer from either of these failures of unity, whose personality is neither divided against itself nor pitted against the world. Such a man feels himself a citizen of the universe; enjoying freely the spectacle that it offers and the joys that it affords, untroubled by the thought of death because he feels himself not really separate from those who will come after him. It is in such profound instinctive union with the stream of life that the greatest joy is to be found.

Questions

1. In the opening paragraph, Bertrand Russell says, "The happy life is to an extraordinary extent the same as the good life." What does he mean? Is this statement paradoxical?
2. According to Russell, what would the traditional moralist say about the belief that "love should be unselfish" (para. 2)?
3. What does Russell mean by his claim that "the whole antithesis between self and the rest of the world . . . disappears as soon as we have any genuine interest in persons or things outside ourselves" (para. 2)?
4. In the second paragraph, how does Russell construct his argument?
5. Do you find Russell's simile of the billiard ball effective or ineffective? Explain why.
6. What does Russell mean by "a citizen of the universe" (para. 2)?

2. *The Singer Solution to World Poverty*

PETER SINGER

In the following selection, bioethicist Peter Singer argues for the individual's responsibility to the world community.

In the Brazilian film *Central Station*, Dora is a retired schoolteacher who makes ends meet by sitting at the station writing letters for illiterate people. Suddenly she has an opportunity to pocket $1,000. All she has to do is persuade a homeless 9-year-old boy to follow her to an address she has been given. (She is told he will be adopted by wealthy foreigners.) She delivers the boy, gets the money, spends some of it on a television set and settles down to enjoy her new acquisition. Her neighbor spoils the fun, however, by telling her that the boy was too old to be adopted — he will be killed and his organs sold for transplantation. Perhaps Dora knew this all along, but after her neighbor's plain speaking, she spends a troubled night. In the morning Dora resolves to take the boy back.

Suppose Dora had told her neighbor that it is a tough world, other people have nice new TV's too, and if selling the kid is the only way she can get one, well, he was only a street kid. She would then have become, in the eyes of the audience, a monster. She redeems herself only by being prepared to bear considerable risks to save the boy.

At the end of the movie, in cinemas in the affluent nations of the world, people who would have been quick to condemn Dora if she had not rescued the boy go home to places far more comfortable than her apartment. In fact, the average family in the United States spends almost one-third of its income on things that are no more necessary to them than Dora's new TV was to her. Gong out to nice restaurants, buying new clothes because the old ones are no longer stylish, vacationing at beach resorts — so much of our income is spent on things not essential to the preservation of our lives and health. Donated to one of a number of charitable agencies, that money could mean the difference between life and death for children in need.

All of which raises a question: In the end, what is the ethical distinction between a Brazilian who sells a homeless child to organ peddlers and an American who already has a TV and upgrades to a better one — knowing that the money could be donated to an organization that would use it to save the lives of kids in need?

Of course, there are several differences between the two situations that could 5 support different moral judgments about them. For one thing, to be able to consign a child to death when he is standing right in front of you takes a chilling kind of heartlessness; it is much easier to ignore an appeal for money to help children you will never meet. Yet for a utilitarian philosopher like myself — that is, one who judges whether acts are right or wrong by their consequences — if the upshot of the American's failure to donate the money is that one more kid dies on the streets of a Brazilian city, then it is, in some sense, just as bad as selling the kid to the organ peddlers. But one doesn't need to embrace my utilitarian ethic to see that, at the very least, there is a troubling incongruity in being so quick to condemn Dora for taking the child to the organ peddlers while, at the same time, not regarding the American consumer's behavior as raising a serious moral issue.

In his 1996 book, *Living High and Letting Die*, the New York University philosopher Peter Unger presented an ingenious series of imaginary examples designed to probe our intuitions about whether it is wrong to live well without giving substantial amounts of money to help people who are hungry, malnourished or dying from easily treatable illnesses like diarrhea. Here's my paraphrase of one of these examples:

Bob is close to retirement. He has invested most of his savings in a very rare and valuable old car, a Bugatti, which he has not been able to insure. The Bugatti is his pride and joy. In addition to the pleasure he gets from driving and caring for his car, Bob knows that its rising market value means that he will always be able to sell it and live comfortably after retirement. One day when Bob is out for a drive, he parks the Bugatti near the end of a railway siding and goes for a walk up the track. As he does so, he sees that a runaway train, with no one aboard, is running down the railway track. Looking farther down the track, he sees the small figure of a child very likely to be killed by the runaway train. He can't stop the train and the child is too far away to warn of the danger, but he can throw a switch that will divert the train down the siding where his Bugatti is parked. Then nobody will be killed — but the train will destroy his Bugatti. Thinking of his joy in owning the car and the financial security it represents, Bob decides not to throw the switch. The child is killed. For many years to come, Bob enjoys owning his Bugatti and the financial security it represents.

Bob's conduct, most of us will immediately respond, was gravely wrong. Unger agrees. But then he reminds us that we, too, have opportunities to save the lives of children. We can give to organizations like Unicef or Oxfam America. How much would we have to give one of these organizations to have a high probability of saving the life of a child threatened by easily preventable diseases? (I do not believe that children are more worth saving than adults, but since no one can argue that children have brought their poverty on themselves, focusing on them simplifies the issues.) Unger called up some experts and used the information they provided to offer some plausible estimates that include the cost of raising money, administrative expenses and the cost of delivering aid where it is most needed. By his calculation, $200 in donations would help a sickly 2-year-old transform into a healthy 6-year-old — offering safe passage through childhood's most dangerous years. To show how practical philosophical argument can be, Unger even tells his readers that they can easily donate funds by using their credit card and calling one of these toll-free numbers: (800) 367-5437 for Unicef; (800) 693-2687 for Oxfam America.

Now you, too, have the information you need to save a child's life. How should you judge yourself if you don't do it? Think again about Bob and his Bugatti. Unlike Dora, Bob did not have to look into the eyes of the child he was sacrificing for his own material comfort. The child was a complete stranger to him and too far away to relate to in an intimate, personal way. Unlike Dora, too, he did not mislead the child or initiate the chain of events imperiling him. In all these respects, Bob's situation resembles that of people able but unwilling to donate to overseas aid and differs from Dora's situation.

If you still think that it was very wrong of Bob not to throw the switch that 10 would have diverted the train and saved the child's life, then it is hard to see how you could deny that it is also very wrong not to send money to one of the organizations listed above. Unless, that is, there is some morally important difference between the two situations that I have overlooked.

Is it the practical uncertainties about whether aid will really reach the people who need it? Nobody who knows the world of overseas aid can doubt that such uncertainties exist. But Unger's figure of $200 to save a child's life was reached after he had made conservative assumptions about the proportion of the money donated that will actually reach its target.

One genuine difference between Bob and those who can afford to donate to overseas aid organizations but don't is that only Bob can save the child on the tracks, whereas there are hundreds of millions of people who can give $200 to overseas aid organizations. The problem is that most of them aren't doing it. Does this mean that it is all right for you not to do it?

Suppose that there were more owners of priceless vintage cars — Carol, Dave, Emma, Fred and so on, down to Ziggy — all in exactly the same situation as Bob, with their own siding and their own switch, all sacrificing the child in order to preserve their own cherished car. Would that make it all right for Bob to do the same? To answer this question affirmatively is to endorse follow-the-crowd ethics — the kind of ethics that led many Germans to look away when the Nazi atrocities were being committed. We do not excuse them because others were behaving no better.

We seem to lack a sound basis for drawing a clear moral line between Bob's situation and that of any reader of this article with $200 to spare who does not donate it to an overseas aid agency. These readers seem to be acting at least as badly as Bob was acting when he chose to let the runaway train hurtle toward the unsuspecting child. In the light of this conclusion, I trust that many readers will reach for the phone and donate that $200. Perhaps you should do it before reading further.

Now that you have distinguished yourself morally from people who put their vin- 15 tage cars ahead of a child's life, how about treating yourself and your partner to dinner at your favorite restaurant? But wait. The money you will spend at the restaurant could also help save the lives of children overseas! True, you weren't planning to blow $200 tonight, but if you were to give up dining out just for one month, you would easily save that amount. And what is one month's dining out, compared to a child's life? There's the rub. Since there are a lot of desperately needy children in the world, there will always be another child whose life you could save for another $200. Are you therefore obliged to keep giving until you have nothing left? At what point can you stop?

Hypothetical examples can easily become farcical. Consider Bob. How far past losing the Bugatti should he go? Imagine that Bob had got his foot stuck in the track of the siding, and if he diverted the train, then before it rammed the car it would also amputate his big toe. Should he still throw the switch? What if it would amputate his foot? His entire leg?

As absurd as the Bugatti scenario gets when pushed to extremes, the point it raises is a serious one: only when the sacrifices become very significant indeed would most people be prepared to say that Bob does nothing wrong when he decides not to throw the switch. Of course, most people could be wrong; we can't decide moral issues by taking opinion polls. But consider for yourself the level of sacrifice that you would demand of Bob, and then think about how much money you would have to give away in order to make a sacrifice that is roughly equal to that. It's almost certainly much, much more than $200. For most middle-class Americans, it could easily be more like $200,000.

Isn't it counterproductive to ask people to do so much? Don't we run the risk that many will shrug their shoulders and say that morality, so conceived, is fine for saints but not for them? I accept that we are unlikely to see, in the near or even medium-term future, a world in which it is normal for wealthy Americans to give the bulk of their wealth to strangers. When it comes to praising or blaming people for what they do, we tend to use a standard that is relative to some conception of normal behavior. Comfortably off Americans who give, say, 10 percent of their income to overseas aid organizations are so far ahead of most of their equally comfortable fellow citizens that I wouldn't go out of my way to chastise them for not doing more. Nevertheless, they should be doing much more, and they are in no position to criticize Bob for failing to make the much greater sacrifice of his Bugatti.

At this point various objections may crop up. Someone may say: "If every citizen living in the affluent nations contributed his or her share I wouldn't have to make such a drastic sacrifice, because long before such levels were reached, the resources would have been there to save the lives of all those children dying from lack of food or medical care. So why should I give more than my fair share?" Another, related, objection is that the Government ought to increase its overseas aid allocations, since that would spread the burden more equitably across all taxpayers.

Yet the question of how much we ought to give is a matter to be decided in 20 the real world — and that, sadly, is a world in which we know that most people do not, and in the immediate future will not, give substantial amounts to overseas aid agencies. We know, too, that at least in the next year, the United States Government is not going to meet even the very modest United Nations–recommended target of 0.7 percent of gross national product; at the moment it lags far below that, at 0.09 percent, not even half of Japan's 0.22 percent or a tenth of Denmark's 0.97 percent. Thus, we know that the money we can give beyond that theoretical "fair share" is still going to save lives that would otherwise be lost. While the idea that no one need do more than his or her fair share is a powerful one, should it prevail if we know that others are not doing their fair share and that children will die preventable deaths unless we do more than our fair share? That would be taking fairness too far.

Thus, this ground for limiting how much we ought to give also fails. In the world as it is now, I can see no escape from the conclusion that each one of us with wealth surplus to his or her essential needs should be giving most of it to help people suffering from poverty so dire as to be life-threatening. That's right: I'm saying that you shouldn't buy that new car, take that cruise, redecorate the house or get that pricey new suit. After all, a $1,000 suit could save five children's lives.

So how does my philosophy break down in dollars and cents? An American household with an income of $50,000 spends around $30,000 annually on necessities, according to the Conference Board, a nonprofit economic research organization. Therefore, for a household bringing in $50,000 a year, donations to help the world's poor should be as close as possible to $20,000. The $30,000 required for necessities holds for higher incomes as well. So a household making $100,000 could cut a yearly check for $70,000. Again, the formula is simple: whatever money you're spending on luxuries, not necessities, should be given away.

Now, evolutionary psychologists tell us that human nature just isn't sufficiently altruistic to make it plausible that many people will sacrifice so much for strangers. On the facts of human nature, they might be right, but they would be wrong to draw a moral conclusion from those facts. If it is the case that we ought to do things that, predictably, most of us won't do, then let's face that fact head-on. Then, if we value the life of a child more than going to fancy restaurants, the next time we dine out we will know that we could have done something better with our money. If that makes living a morally decent life extremely arduous, well, then that is the way things are. If we don't do it, then we should at least know that we are failing to live a morally decent life — not because it is good to wallow in guilt but because knowing where we should be going is the first step toward heading in that direction.

When Bob first grasped the dilemma that faced him as he stood by that railway switch, he must have thought how extraordinarily unlucky he was to be placed in a situation in which he must choose between the life of an innocent child and the sacrifice of most of his savings. But he was not unlucky at all. We are all in that situation.

Questions

1. Peter Singer opens his essay by describing a situation from a movie, yet it could be argued that seeing movies is, in fact, a luxury that one advocating his position should forgo. To what extent does this interpretation undermine Singer's argument?

2. The example of Bob and his Bugatti is hypothetical. Is this a rhetorical strategy that strengthens or weakens Singer's argument? Explain why you believe that.

3. Note the places where Singer addresses the counterargument. Where does he concede, and where does he refute?

4. When does Singer use the pronoun *we*? When does he use *you*? How does this shift reflect and contribute to appeals to ethos and pathos?

5. This selection appeared in the *New York Times Magazine* (1999). What does that fact tell you about the audience to whom Singer is appealing? To what extent do you think he is effective in reaching them?

3. *Lifeboat Ethics: The Case against Helping the Poor*

GARRETT HARDIN

In the following selection, human ecologist Garrett Hardin presents a classic argument on the implications of population growth.

Environmentalists use the metaphor of the earth as a "spaceship" in trying to persuade countries, industries, and people to stop wasting and polluting our natural resources. Since we all share life on this planet, they argue, no single person or institution has the right to destroy, waste, or use more than a fair share of its resources.

But does everyone on earth have an equal right to an equal share of its resources? The spaceship metaphor can be dangerous when used by misguided idealists to justify suicidal policies for sharing our resources through uncontrolled immigration and foreign aid. In their enthusiastic but unrealistic generosity, they confuse the ethics of a spaceship with those of a lifeboat.

A true spaceship would have to be under the control of a captain, since no ship could possibly survive if its course were determined by committee. Spaceship Earth certainly has no captain; the United Nations is merely a toothless tiger, with little power to enforce any policy upon its bickering members.

If we divide the world crudely into rich nations and poor nations, two thirds of them are desperately poor, and only one third comparatively rich, with the United States the wealthiest of all. Metaphorically each rich nation can be seen as a lifeboat full of comparatively rich people. In the ocean outside each lifeboat swim the poor of the world, who would like to get in, or at least to share some of the wealth. What should the lifeboat passengers do?

First, we must recognize the limited capacity of any lifeboat. For example, a nation's land has a limited capacity to support a population and as the current [1974] energy crisis has shown us, in some ways we have already exceeded the carrying capacity of our land.

5

Adrift in a Moral Sea

So here we sit, say 50 people in our lifeboat. To be generous, let us assume it has room for 10 more, making a total capacity of 60. Suppose the 50 of us in the lifeboat see 100 others swimming in the water outside, begging for admission to our boat or for handouts. We have several options: we may be tempted to try to live by the Christian ideal of being "our brother's keeper," or by the Marxist ideal of "to each according to his needs." Since the needs of all in the water are the same, and since they can all be seen as "our brothers," we could take them all into our boat, making a total of 150 in a boat designed for 60. The boat swamps, everyone drowns. Complete justice, complete catastrophe.

Since the boat has an unused excess capacity of 10 more passengers, we could admit just 10 more to it. But which 10 do we let in? How do we choose? Do we pick the best 10, "first come, first served"? And what do we say to the 90 we exclude? If we do let an extra 10 into our lifeboat, we will have lost our "safety factor," an engineering principle of critical importance. For example, if we don't leave room for excess capacity as a safety factor in our country's agriculture, a new plant disease or a bad change in the weather could have disastrous consequences.

Suppose we decide to preserve our small safety factor and admit no more to the lifeboat. Our survival is then possible although we shall have to be constantly on guard against boarding parties.

While this last solution clearly offers the only means of our survival, it is morally abhorrent to many people. Some say they feel guilty about their good luck. My reply is simple: "Get out and yield your place to others." This may solve the problem of the guilt-ridden person's conscience, but it does not change the ethics of the lifeboat. The needy person to whom the guilt-ridden person yields his place will not himself feel guilty about his good luck. If he did, he would not climb aboard. The net result of conscience-stricken people giving up their unjustly held seats is the elimination of that sort of conscience from the lifeboat.

This is the basic metaphor within which we must work out our solutions. Let us now enrich the image, step by step, with substantive additions from the real world, a world that must solve real and pressing problems of overpopulation and hunger.   10

The harsh ethics of the lifeboat become even harsher when we consider the reproductive differences between the rich nations and the poor nations. The people inside the lifeboats are doubling in numbers every 87 years; those swimming around outside are doubling, on the average, every 35 years, more than twice as fast as the rich. And since the world's resources are dwindling, the difference in prosperity between the rich and the poor can only increase.

As of 1973, the U.S. had a population of 210 million people, who were increasing by 0.8 percent per year. Outside our lifeboat, let us imagine another 210 million people (say the combined populations of Colombia, Ecuador, Venezuela, Morocco, Pakistan, Thailand and the Philippines) who are increasing at a rate of 3.3 percent per year. Put differently, the doubling time for this aggregate population is 21 years, compared to 87 years for the U.S.

The harsh ethics of the lifeboat become harsher when we consider the reproductive differences between rich and poor.

Multiplying the Rich and the Poor

Now suppose the U.S. agreed to pool its resources with those seven countries, with everyone receiving an equal share. Initially the ratio of Americans to non-Americans in this model would be one-to-one. But consider what the ratio would be after 87 years, by which time the Americans would have doubled to a population of 420 million. By then, doubling every 21 years, the other group would have swollen to 354 billion. Each American would have to share the available resources with more than eight people.

But, one could argue, this discussion assumes that current population trends   15
will continue, and they may not. Quite so. Most likely the rate of population increase will decline much faster in the U.S. than it will in the other countries, and there does not seem to be much we can do about it. In sharing with "each according to his needs," we must recognize that needs are determined by population size, which is determined by the rate of reproduction, which at present is regarded as a sovereign right of every nation, poor or not. This being so, the philanthropic load created by the sharing ethic of the spaceship can only increase.

The Tragedy of the Commons

The fundamental error of spaceship ethics, and the sharing it requires, is that it leads to what I call "the tragedy of the commons." Under a system of private property, the men who own property recognize their responsibility to care for it, for if they don't they will eventually suffer. A farmer, for instance, will allow no more cattle in a pasture than its carrying capacity justifies. If he overloads it, erosion sets in, weeds take over, and he loses the use of the pasture.

If a pasture becomes a commons open to all, the right of each to use it may not be matched by a corresponding responsibility to protect it. Asking everyone to use it with discretion will hardly do, for the considerate herdsman who refrains from overloading the commons suffers more than a selfish one who says his needs are greater. If everyone would restrain himself, all would be well; but it takes only one less than everyone to ruin a system of voluntary restraint. In a crowded world of less than perfect human beings, mutual ruin is inevitable if there are no controls. This is the tragedy of the commons.

One of the major tasks of education today should be the creation of such an acute awareness of the dangers of the commons that people will recognize its many varieties. For example, the air and water have become polluted because they are treated as commons. Further growth in the population or per-capita conversion of natural resources into pollutants will only make the problem worse. The same holds true for the fish of the oceans. Fishing fleets have nearly disappeared in many parts of the world, technological improvements in the art of fishing are hastening the day of complete ruin. Only the replacement of the system of the commons with a responsible system of control will save the land, air, water and oceanic fisheries.

The World Food Bank

In recent years there has been a push to create a new commons called a World Food Bank, an international depository of food reserves to which nations would contribute according to their abilities and from which they would draw according to their needs. This humanitarian proposal has received support from many liberal international groups, and from such prominent citizens as Margaret Mead, U.N. Secretary General Kurt Waldheim, and Senators Edward Kennedy and George McGovern.

A world food bank appeals powerfully to our humanitarian impulses. But [20] before we rush ahead with such a plan, let us recognize where the greatest political push comes from, lest we be disillusioned later. Our experience with the "Food for Peace program," or Public Law 480, gives us the answer. This program moved billions of dollars worth of U.S. surplus grain to food-short, population-long countries during the past two decades. But when P.L. 480 first became law, a headline in the business magazine *Forbes* revealed the real power behind it: "Feeding the World's Hungry Millions: How It Will Mean Billions for U.S. Business."

And indeed it did. In the years 1960 to 1970, U.S. taxpayers spent a total of $7.9 billion on the Food for Peace program. Between 1948 and 1970, they also paid an additional $50 billion for other economic-aid programs, some of which went for food and food-producing machinery and technology. Though all U.S. taxpayers were forced to contribute to the cost of P.L. 480, certain special interest groups gained handsomely under the program. Farmers did not have to contribute the grain; the Government, or rather the taxpayers, bought it from them at full market prices. The increased demand raised prices of farm products generally. The manufacturers of farm machinery, fertilizers and pesticides benefited by the farmers' extra efforts to grow more food. Grain elevators profited from storing the surplus until it could be shipped. Railroads made money hauling it to ports, and shipping lines profited from carrying it overseas. The implementation of P.L. 480 required the creation of a vast Government bureaucracy, which then acquired its own vested interest in continuing the program regardless of its merits.

Extracting Dollars

Those who proposed and defended the Food for Peace program in public rarely mentioned its importance to any of these special interests. The public emphasis was always on its humanitarian effects. The combination of silent selfish interests and highly vocal humanitarian apologists made a powerful and successful lobby for extracting money from taxpayers. We can expect the same lobby to push now for the creation of a World Food Bank.

However great the potential benefit to selfish interests, it should be not be a decisive argument against a truly humanitarian program. We must ask if such a program would actually do more good than harm, not only momentarily but also in the long run. Those who propose the food bank usually refer to a current "emergency" or "crisis" in terms of world food supply. But what is an emergency? Although they may be infrequent and sudden, everyone knows that emergencies will occur from time to time. A well-run family, company, organization or country prepares for the likelihood of accidents and emergencies. It expects them, it budgets for them, it saves for them.

Learning the Hard Way

What happens if some organizations or countries budget for accidents and others do not? If each country is solely responsible for its own well-being, poorly managed ones will suffer. But they can learn from experience. They may mend their ways, and learn to budget for infrequent but certain emergencies. For example, the weather varies from year to year, and periodic crop failures are certain. A wise and competent government saves out of the production of the good years in anticipation of bad years to come. Joseph taught this policy to Pharaoh in Egypt more than 2,000 years ago. Yet the great majority of the governments in the world today do not follow such a policy. They lack either the wisdom or the competence, or both. Should those nations that do manage to put something aside be forced to come to the rescue each time an emergency occurs among the poor nations?

"But it isn't their fault!" Some kind-hearted liberals argue. "How can we blame the poor people who are caught in an emergency? Why must they suffer for the sins of their governments?" The concept of blame is simply not relevant here. The real question is, what are the operational consequences of establishing a world food bank? If it is open to every country every time a need develops, slovenly rulers will not be motivated to take Joseph's advice. Someone will always come to their aid. Some countries will deposit food in the world food bank, and others will withdraw it. There will be almost no overlap. As a result of such solutions to food shortage emergencies, the poor countries will not learn to mend their ways, and will suffer progressively greater emergencies as their populations grow.

Population Control the Crude Way

On the average poor countries undergo a 2.5 percent increase in population each year; rich countries about 0.8 percent. Only rich countries have anything in the way of food reserves set aside, and even they do not have as much as they should. Poor countries have none. If poor countries received no food from the outside, the rate of their population growth would be periodically checked by crop failures and famines. But if they can always draw on a world food bank in time of need, their population can continue to grow unchecked, and so will their "need" for aid. In the short run, a world food bank may diminish that need, but in the long run it actually increases the need without limit.

Without some system of worldwide food sharing, the proportion of people in the rich and poor nations might eventually stabilize. The overpopulated poor countries would decrease in numbers, while the rich countries that had room for more people would increase. But with a well-meaning system of sharing, such as a world food bank, the growth differential between the rich and the poor countries will not only persist, it will increase. Because of the higher rate of population growth in the poor countries of the world, 88 percent of today's children are born poor, and only 12 percent rich. Year by year the ratio becomes worse, as the fast-reproducing poor outnumber the slow-reproducing rich.

A world food bank is thus a commons in disguise. People will have more motivation to draw from it than to add to any common store. The less provident and less able will multiply at the expense of the abler and more provident, bringing eventual ruin upon all who share in the commons. Besides, any system of "sharing" that amounts to foreign aid from the rich nations to the poor nations will carry the taint of charity, which will contribute little to the world peace so devoutly desired by those who support the idea of a world food bank.

As past U.S. foreign-aid programs have amply and depressingly demonstrated, international charity frequently inspires mistrust and antagonism rather than gratitude on the part of the recipient nation.

Chinese Fish and Miracle Rice

The modern approach to foreign aid stresses the export of technology and advice, rather than money and food. As an ancient Chinese proverb goes: "Give a man a fish and he will eat for a day; teach him how to fish and he will eat for the rest of his days." Acting on this advice, the Rockefeller and Ford Foundations have financed a number of programs for improving agriculture in the hungry nations. Known as the "Green Revolution," these programs have led to the development of "miracle rice" and "miracle wheat," new strains that offer bigger harvests and greater resistance to crop damage. Norman Borlaug, the Nobel Prize winning agronomist who, supported by the Rockefeller Foundation, developed "miracle wheat," is one of the most prominent advocates of a world food bank.

Whether or not the Green Revolution can increase food production as much as its champions claim is a debatable but possibly irrelevant point. Those who support this well-intended humanitarian effort should first consider some of the fundamentals of human ecology. Ironically, one man who did was the late Alan Gregg, a vice president of the Rockefeller Foundation. Two decades ago he expressed strong doubts about the wisdom of such attempts to increase food production. He likened the growth and spread of humanity over the surface of the earth to the spread of cancer in the human body, remarking that "cancerous growths demand food; but, as far as I know, they have never been cured by getting it."

Overloading the Environment

Every human born constitutes a draft on all aspects of the environment: food, air, water, forests, beaches, wildlife, scenery and solitude. Food can, perhaps, be significantly increased to meet a growing demand. But what about clean beaches, unspoiled forests, and solitude? If we satisfy a growing population's need for food, we necessarily decrease its per capita supply of the other resources needed by men.

India, for example, now has a population of 600 million, which increases by 15 million each year. This population already puts a huge load on a relatively impoverished environment. The country's forests are now only a small fraction of what they were three centuries ago and floods and erosion continually destroy the insufficient farmland that remains. Every one of the 15 million new lives added to India's population puts an additional burden on the environment, and increases the economic and social costs of crowding. However humanitarian our intent, every Indian life saved through medical or nutritional assistance from abroad diminishes the quality of life for those who remain, and for subsequent generations. If rich countries make it possible, through foreign aid, for 600 million Indians to swell to 1.2 billion in a mere 28 years, as their current growth rate threatens, will future generations of Indians thank us for hastening the destruction of their environment? Will our good intentions be sufficient excuse for the consequences of our actions?

My final example of a commons in action is one for which the public has the least desire for rational discussion — immigration. Anyone who publicly questions the wisdom of current U.S. immigration policy is promptly charged with bigotry, prejudice, ethnocentrism, chauvinism, isolationism or selfishness. Rather than encounter such accusations, one would rather talk about other matters leaving immigration policy to wallow in the crosscurrents of special interests that take no account of the good of the whole, or the interests of posterity.

Perhaps we still feel guilty about things we said in the past. Two generations ago the popular press frequently referred to Dagos, Wops, Polacks, Chinks, and Krauts in articles about how America was being "overrun" by foreigners of supposedly inferior genetic stock. But because the implied inferiority of foreigners was used then as justification for keeping them out, people now assume that restrictive policies could only be based on such misguided notions. There are other grounds.

A Nation of Immigrants

Just consider the numbers involved. Our Government acknowledges a net inflow of 400,000 immigrants a year. While we have no hard data on the extent of illegal entries, educated guesses put the figure at about 600,000 a year. Since the natural increase (excess of births over deaths) of the resident population now runs about 1.7 million per year, the yearly gain from immigration amounts to at least 19 percent of the total annual increase, and may be as much as 37 percent if we include the estimate for illegal immigrants. Considering the growing use of birth-control devices, the potential effect of education campaigns by such organizations as Planned Parenthood Federation of America and Zero Population Growth, and the influence of inflation and the housing shortage, the fertility rate of American women may decline so much that immigration could account for all the yearly increase in population. Should we not at least ask if that is what we want?

For the sake of those who worry about whether the "quality" of the average immigrant compares favorably with the quality of the average resident, let us assume that immigrants and native-born citizens are of exactly equal quality, however one defines that term. We will focus here only on quantity; and since our conclusions will depend on nothing else, all charges of bigotry and chauvinism become irrelevant.

Immigration vs. Food Supply

World food banks move food to the people, hastening the exhaustion of the environment of the poor countries. Unrestricted immigration, on the other hand, moves people to the food, thus speeding up the destruction of the environment of the rich countries. We can easily understand why poor people should want to make this latter transfer, but why should rich hosts encourage it?

As in the case of foreign-aid programs, immigration receives support from selfish interests and humanitarian impulses. The primary selfish interest in unimpeded immigration is the desire of employers for cheap labor, particularly in industries and trades that offer degrading work. In the past, one wave of foreigners after another was brought into the U.S. to work at wretched jobs for wretched wages. In recent years the Cubans, Puerto Ricans and Mexicans have had this dubious honor. The interests of the employers of cheap labor mesh well with the guilty silence of the country's liberal intelligentsia. White Anglo-Saxon Protestants are particularly reluctant to call for a closing of the doors to immigration for fear of being called bigots.

But not all countries have such reluctant leadership. Most educated Hawaiians, for example, are keenly aware of the limits of their environment, particularly in terms of population growth. There is only so much room on the islands, and the islanders know it. To Hawaiians, immigrants from the other 49 states present as great a threat as those from other nations. At a recent meeting of Hawaiian government officials in Honolulu, I had the ironic delight of hearing a speaker who like most of his audience was of Japanese ancestry, ask how the country might practically and constitutionally close its doors to further immigration. One member of the audience countered: "How can we shut the doors now? We have many friends and relatives in Japan that we'd like to bring here some day so that they can enjoy Hawaii too." The Japanese-American speaker smiled sympathetically and answered: "Yes, but we have children now, and someday we'll have grandchildren too. We can bring more people here from Japan only by giving away some of the land that we hope to pass on to our grandchildren some day. What right do we have to do that?"

At this point, I can hear U.S. liberals asking: "How can you justify slamming the door once you're inside? You say that immigrants should be kept out. But aren't we all immigrants or the descendants of immigrants? If we insist on staying, must we not admit all others?" Our craving for intellectual order leads us to seek and prefer symmetrical rules and morals: a single rule for me and everybody else; the same rule yesterday, today and tomorrow. Justice, we feel, should not change with time and place.

We Americans of non-Indian ancestry can look upon ourselves as the descendants of thieves who are guilty morally, if not legally, of stealing this land from its Indian owners. Should we then give back the land to the now living American descendants of those Indians? However morally or logically sound this proposal may be, I, for one, am unwilling to live by it and I know no one else who is. Besides, the logical consequence would be absurd. Suppose that, intoxicated with a sense of pure justice, we should decide to turn our land over to the Indians. Since all our other wealth has also been derived from the land, wouldn't we be morally obliged to give that back to the Indians too?

Pure Justice vs. Reality

Clearly, the concept of pure justice produces an infinite regression to absurdity. Centuries ago, wise men invented statutes of limitations to justify the rejection of such pure justice, in the interest of preventing continual disorder. The law zealously defends property rights, but only relatively recent property rights. Drawing a line after an arbitrary time has elapsed may be unjust, but the alternatives are worse.

We are all the descendants of thieves, and the world's resources are inequitably distributed. But we must begin the journey to tomorrow from the point where we are today. We cannot remake the past. We cannot safely divide the wealth equitably among all peoples so long as people reproduce at different rates. To do so would guarantee that our grandchildren and everyone else's grandchildren would have only a ruined world to inhabit.

To be generous with one's own possessions is quite different from being generous with those of posterity. We should call this point to the attention of those who from a commendable love of justice and equality, would institute a system of the commons, either in the form of a world food bank, or of unrestricted immigration. We must convince them if we wish to save at least some parts of the world from environmental ruin. 45

Without a true world government to control reproduction and the use of available resources, the sharing ethic of the spaceship is impossible. For the foreseeable future, our survival demands that we govern our actions by the ethics of a lifeboat, harsh though they may be. Posterity will be satisfied with nothing less.

Questions

1. What are the implications of the two central metaphors — the spaceship and the lifeboat — that Garrett Hardin uses for his argument? Is contrasting these two an effective rhetorical strategy? Discuss your answer.
2. Hardin uses population growth statistics to make projections to support his argument. Have these projections proven true? (You will need to do some research.)
3. What does Hardin mean by "the tragedy of the commons" (para. 16)?
4. Hardin relies mainly on the logic of his arguments, but he also uses strong connotative language. How do expressions such as "toothless tiger" (para. 3), "conscience-stricken people" (para. 9), and "spread of cancer" (para. 31) affect the reader?
5. What does Hardin mean by "pure justice" (para. 43)? Do you agree with his use of the phrase? Why or why not?
6. Hardin's essay was published in *Psychology Today* in 1974. To what extent do you think Hardin's basic argument can apply to today's world?

4. *In Westminster Abbey*

JOHN BETJEMAN

In this satiric poem, former British poet laureate John Betjeman addresses the individual's response to the threat of war. It appeared in the collection *Old Lights for New Chancels* (1940).

Let me take this other glove off
　　As the vox humana swells,
And the beauteous fields of Eden
　　Bask beneath the Abbey bells.
Here, where England's statesmen lie,　　　5
Listen to a lady's cry.

Gracious Lord, oh bomb the Germans.
　　Spare their women for Thy Sake,
And if that is not too easy
　　We will pardon Thy Mistake.　　　10
But, gracious Lord, whate'er shall be,
Don't let anyone bomb me.

Keep our Empire undismembered
　　Guide our Forces by Thy Hand,
Gallant blacks from far Jamaica,　　　15
　　Honduras and Togoland;

Protect them Lord in all their fights,
And, even more, protect the whites.

Think of what our Nation stands for,
  Books from Boots and country lanes,   *20*
Free speech, free passes, class distinction,
  Democracy and proper drains.
Lord, put beneath Thy special care
One-eighty-nine Cadogan Square.

Although dear Lord I am a sinner,   *25*
  I have done no major crime;
Now I'll come to Evening Service
  Whensoever I have the time.
So, Lord, reserve for me a crown.
And do not let my shares go down.   *30*

I will labour for Thy Kingdom,
  Help our lads to win the war,
Send white flowers to the cowards
  Join the Women's Army Corps,
Then wash the Steps around Thy Throne   *35*
In the Eternal Safety Zone.

Now I feel a little better,
  What a treat to hear Thy word,
Where the bones of leading statesmen,
  Have so often been interr'd.   *40*
And now, dear Lord, I cannot wait
Because I have a luncheon date.

Questions

1. John Betjeman is known for his humorous, often satirical, poetry. Which elements of this poem suggest that we should not read the poem literally?
2. Why is it important that this poem be read within the context of post–World War II England?
3. Comment on the poet's use of a woman speaker as a rhetorical device.

Entering the Conversation

As you respond to the following prompts, support your argument with references to at least two of the four sources in Conversation: Focus on the Individual's Responsibility to the Community. For help using sources, see Chapter 3.

1. How can "the good life" be lived well? Explain your position, first by defining the term and then by presenting your own view within the context of the sources.

2. Write an essay explaining which of the four perspectives represented in these readings you find most compelling. Make sure you explain why you have come to this conclusion.

3. Suppose that a proposal is made to vary college tuition according to the student's (or parent's) annual income. Essentially, tuition payment would be determined according to criteria similar to that used to levy income tax, so that those who earn the most will pay the most. Write an essay explaining why you would support or oppose this proposal.

4. Pose a question on a controversial issue, such as "Should the United States intervene in a conflict in another region?" or "Should individual citizens of affluent countries contribute a portion of their income to fight AIDS in Africa?" Then write a roundtable discussion that includes four participants: Bertrand Russell, Peter Singer, Garrett Hardin, and John Betjeman. You might do this assignment as a group, with different members role-playing the authors.

Student Writing

Synthesis: Incorporating Sources into a Revision

Following are two versions of an essay. The first is a draft that student Martin Copeland wrote in response to this prompt:

> Explain why you believe that fraternities, sororities, or both do or do not build community or provide a positive community environment for their members.

The second essay is Martin's revision after he researched the topic of fraternities and sororities further. Using the questions following each version of the essay, discuss specific ways in which the second is an improvement over the first, and suggest ways for further improvement. (Note: Both the draft and the revision were written outside class without time constraints.)

Draft

From the outside, it is very difficult to tell exactly what fraternities and sororities do or don't do for their members. What an outsider can do, however, is give an honest opinion of his or her perception of fraternities and sororities, which I feel, is very valuable to the organizations. It can allow members to understand how their organizations are perceived, what are the misconceptions, and why they may or may not be attracting new members.

Having established my outside perspective, I believe that the general idea and philosophy of fraternities and sororities is to provide a positive community environment for their members, and that in their purest form, fraternities and sororities can do just that. Unfortunately, most fraternities and sororities are not in their "purest form," and have been corrupted by wayward members so that now, they do not provide a positive community environment for their members.

It is important to understand the language of "positive community environment." Were the question only concerned with providing a community environment for their members, my answer would have been an enthusiastic "yes." Fraternities and sororities are perhaps the closest groups on college campuses. On many campuses, they live, study, and party together. The "rush" process alone is enough to bring several wannabe members together as one cohesive unit. Often, within fraternities and sororities, students make lifetime friends and professional contacts; they build a support system away from home that for many students is the ship that keeps them afloat in the vast ocean that is college.

The problem, however, lies in the fact that the question included the word "positive." For all of the great things fraternities and sororities do for their members, much of it, though pleasurable, does not seem positive. We have all heard stories of fraternities and sororities placing their pledges in compromising and even dangerous situations all for the sake of brotherhood or sisterhood. Well, such stories are more frequent than these organizations would have the general public believe. The process that pledges have to endure to make it to the positive community environment can often humiliate them, bringing them down to the point that they feel that walking away from such a group would make the person less than the others. Admittedly, that brings into question the self-esteem of the pledge, but it also makes me question why an overwhelming number of students with self-esteem issues are drawn to fraternities and sororities. Instead of being uplifting societies focused on the growth and maturity of its members, the community environment can often become a crutch, which is anything but positive.

In essence, my argument is not that fraternities and sororities are bad, because without more specific definition of the terms analyzed, of course bad examples will run rampant. My argument, however, is that as a whole, it seems that fraternities and sororities have departed from their true purposes; they have lost touch with the principles and values upon which they were founded. Finding those principles again and rebuilding their lost legacies would be an amazing step toward becoming truly positive community environments, and it would take work from all such groups in order to fix the way outsiders perceive the groups as a whole.

Questions

1. The student has written in the first person, using both *I* and *we*. Is that decision appropriate or inappropriate for this assignment and topic? Why?

2. The thesis statement is "closed," with specification of the essay's major points clearly identified. As a reader, do you find this type of thesis helpful or limiting?
3. What effect does the figurative language ("the ship that keeps them afloat," para. 3) have on you as a reader?
4. What attempts does the student make to develop a balanced tone and perspective?

Revision

After writing the draft, Martin did some reading and research on the topic. The following revision shows his more expanded view. The sources he used are available online for you to skim.

- The following two essays were presented as a debate in the alumni magazine of the University of Washington (September 2001): "Why I'm Proud I'm a Greek" by Douglas A. Luetjen and "Why I'm Proud I'm Not a Greek" by Charles R. Cross.
- "It's All Greek to Me" by Anne Remington appeared in *Parent Times Online* from the University of Iowa (Winter 2004–2005).
- The statistical data were taken from a report of the Higher Education Center for Alcohol and Other Drug Prevention.

Fraternities and Sororities
Martin Copeland

From the outside, it is very difficult to tell exactly what fraternities and sororities do or don't do for their members. What an outsider can do, however, is give an honest opinion of his or her perception to members to help them understand how their organizations are perceived, what the misconceptions are, and why they may have difficulty attracting new members. The general idea and philosophy of fraternities and sororities is to provide a positive community environment for their members, and in their purest form, they can do just that. Unfortunately, most fraternities and sororities are not in their "purest form" and have been corrupted by what might be a minority of highly visible members.

It is important to understand the language of "positive community environment." Were the question concerned only with sororities and fraternities providing a community environment for their members, my answer would have been an enthusiastic yes. Fraternities and sororities are perhaps the closest groups on college campuses. On many campuses, they live, study, and party together. The "rush" process alone is enough to bring several wannabe members together as one cohesive unit. Often, within fraternities and sororities, students make lifetime friends and professional contacts. In his explanation of why he is proud to be part of a fraternity, Douglas Luetjen points out that "all but eight U.S. presidents since 1856 have been regular or honorary members of a college fraternity. And . . . 85% of the Fortune 500 executives are fraternity members."

Furthermore, in a sorority or a fraternity, students can build a support system away from home that for many is the ship that keeps them afloat in the vast ocean that is college. Anne Remington begins her article for *Parent Times*, an online magazine from the University of Iowa, with a story about a freshman who felt that no one remembered her birthday until her Alpha Chi Omega sisters began singing to her: "And in that instance, she knew she had found a new 'home.'" Remington continues to describe Greek-letter organizations that appeal to specific minorities and that provide a "sense of belonging" for many students who are away from home for the first time.

The problem, however, lies in the fact that the question included the word "positive." For all of the great things fraternities and sororities do for their members, much of it, though pleasurable, does not always seem positive. We have all heard stories of fraternities and sororities placing their pledges in compromising and even dangerous situations all for the sake of brotherhood or sisterhood. Such stories are more frequent than these organizations would have the general public believe. The process that pledges have to endure to make it to the positive community environment can often humiliate them, bringing them down to the point that they feel that walking away from such a group would make them less than the others.

A major problem with fraternities and sororities is drinking and the negative behaviors that accompany it. According to a study at the University of Washington that was reported on the Web site <www.campusblues.com/drugs5.asp>, 85% of those living in Greek houses drank at least one to two times per week, 37% three to four times. That same study reported that sorority members are nearly twice as likely to become binge drinkers than their nonsorority counterparts, and 75% of fraternity members were self-described binge drinkers. This study also reported higher incidences of missed classes and unprotected sex among fraternity and sorority members.

In essence, my argument is not that fraternities and sororities are necessarily a negative community environment, but they do promote negative and potentially dangerous behaviors. As a whole, it seems that too many fraternities and sororities have become "organized saloons" (Cross) and departed from the principles and values upon which they were founded: "scholarship, relationships, leadership, and service" (Remington). Finding those principles again and rebuilding their lost legacies will be a step toward becoming truly positive community environments, though it will take the work of many individuals to change the way outsiders perceive fraternities and sororities.

Questions

1. Cite three changes Martin has made, and discuss their effect.
2. The revised essay is written primarily in the third person. Is this point of view more effective? Why or why not?

3. Do the sources Martin has chosen help to balance his argument, or do they favor one viewpoint?

4. Do the sources give Martin's voice more authority? If so, explain how. If you do not think so, explain why not.

5. Is the revision more effective as an argument? Explain your answer, with specific references to the initial draft and the revision.

6. Find and read one or more of the sources. Are the quotations and references effective? Would you have made other choices? Why or why not?

Grammar as Rhetoric and Style
Parallel Structures

Sentences or parts of a sentence are parallel when structures within them take the same form. Parallelism is important at the level of the word, the phrase, and the clause.

Words

> Why should we live with such hurry and waste of life?
>
> — HENRY DAVID THOREAU

In this sentence, the words *hurry* and *waste*, both nouns, follow the preposition *with*; *hurry* and *waste* are parallel.

> In eternity there is indeed something true and sublime.
>
> — HENRY DAVID THOREAU

In this sentence, the words *true* and *sublime*, both adjectives, modify the pronoun *something*; *true* and *sublime* are parallel.

Phrases

> Men esteem truth remote, in the outskirts of the system, behind the farthest star, before Adam and after the last man.
>
> — HENRY DAVID THOREAU

To modify the adjective *remote* in this first sentence, Thoreau uses parallel prepositional phrases: *in the outskirts, before the farthest star, before Adam*, and *after the last man*.

[I]t has truly been said that never in history have so many educated people de-voted so much attention to so few children.

— Jane Howard

In the next example, Jane Howard uses three parallel noun phrases, each begin-ning with *so: so many educated people, so much attention, so few children.*

This is more difficult, because there is no zeitgeist to read, no template to follow, no mask to wear.

— Anna Quindlen

And in the preceding sentence, Anna Quindlen uses three parallel nouns each preceded by *no* and each followed by an infinitive: *no zeitgeist to read, no template to follow,* and *no mask to wear.*

Clauses

"Where I Lived, and What I Lived For"

— Title of an essay by Henry David Thoreau

The title of Thoreau's essay consists of two parallel dependent, or subordinate, clauses; one begins with *where,* and the other begins with *what.*

[W]e perceive that only great and worthy things have any permanent and absolute existence, that petty fears and petty pleasures are but the shadow of the reality.

— Henry David Thoreau

The preceding example contains two parallel dependent clauses, each beginning with *that* and functioning as an object of the verb *perceive.*

If we are really dying, let us hear the rattle in our throats and feel cold in the extremities; if we are alive, let us go about our business.

— Henry David Thoreau

This example begins with a dependent clause (*If . . . dying*) followed by an inde-pendent, or main, clause (*let . . . extremities*); then after the semicolon, Thoreau presents another dependent-independent construction, parallel to the first.

Lack of Parallelism

To fully appreciate the power of the parallelism created by Thoreau, Howard, and Quindlen in the preceding examples, consider what happens when supposedly equal elements of a sentence do not follow the same grammatical or syntactical form — that is, when they are not parallel with each other.

Why should we live with such hurry and to waste life?

This version of Thoreau's sentence tries to modify the verb *should live* by coordinating a prepositional phrase, *with such hurry*, with an infinitive phrase, *to waste life*. The two phrases are not parallel with each other, and as a result, the sentence lacks balance and force.

Here's another sentence that lacks parallelism:

> It has truly been said that never in history have a lot of people who are well educated devoted their attention to such a small number of children.

The preceding sentence, like the actual sentence by Howard, still has a dependent clause with a subject (*a lot of people who are well educated*), a verb (*have devoted*), and an object (*their attention*) followed by a prepositional phrase (*to such a small number*). But the subject, verb, object, and prepositional phrase no longer share one arrangement of words; they are no longer parallel. As a result, the sentence is harder to read and easier to forget.

Rhetorical and Stylistic Strategy

Looking first at the parallel sentences at the beginning of this lesson and then at the rewrites that lack parallelism, you can see that writers use parallelism on the level of the word, phrase, or clause as a rhetorical and stylistic device to emphasize ideas, to contrast ideas, or to connect ideas.

Following are the names, definitions, and examples of specific types of parallelism:

anaphora: The deliberate repetition of a word or phrase at the beginning of successive clauses.

> *But when you have seen vicious mobs lynch your mothers and fathers at will and drown your sisters and brothers at whim; when you have seen hate-filled policemen curse, kick and even kill your black brothers and sisters; . . . when you are forever fighting a degenerating sense of "nobodiness" — then you will understand why we find it difficult to wait.*
>
> — Martin Luther King Jr.

In this example, form follows function. Just as King is saying that African Americans have had to endure unjust treatment as they waited for full civil rights, this series of parallel clauses makes the reader wait — and wait — for the main point in the independent clause.

antithesis: The contrast of thoughts in two phrases, clauses, or sentences.

> *[F]reedom is never voluntarily given by the oppressor; it must be demanded by the oppressed.*
>
> — Martin Luther King Jr.
>
> *One has not only a legal but a moral responsibility to obey just laws. Conversely, one has a moral responsibility to disobey unjust laws.*
>
> — Martin Luther King Jr.

That's one small step for man, one giant leap for mankind.

—NEIL ARMSTRONG

In all three of these examples, the parallel structure creates a clear comparison between two things in order to emphasize the difference between them. *Given by the oppressor* is contrasted in meaning and in placement with *demanded by the oppressed*. Notice also how the parallel prepositional phrases *by the oppressor* and *by the oppressed* call attention to the tension between oppressor and oppressed.

antimetabole: The identical or near repetition of words in one phrase or clause in reverse order in the next phrase or clause.

We do not ride on the railroad; it rides upon us.

—HENRY DAVID THOREAU

Ask not what your country can do for you; ask what you can do for your country.

—JOHN F. KENNEDY

The example above from President Kennedy is, perhaps, his most famous quote. Part of what makes this quote so "quotable" is that the repetition inherent in antimetabole makes it dramatic and easy to remember. Because the pattern of the two clauses is so similar, the listener only needs to remember one pattern. Because that sentence pattern is repeated, it gives the listener two chances to understand the entire sentence and places extra emphasis on the second part. It is almost as if Kennedy is repeating a point for emphasis. Keep an eye out for antimetabole in modern political soundbites.

zeugma: A figure of speech made when one part of speech (usually a verb, but sometimes a noun or an adjective) is related to another part of speech in a way that is consistent in terms of grammar but incongruous in terms of meaning. Such use is often humorous and usually ironic.

Someone sent me a T-shirt not long ago that read "Well-Behaved Women Don't Make History." They don't make good lawyers, either, or doctors or businesswomen.

—ANNA QUINDLEN

In this example, the zeugma is created when the verb *make* takes many different nouns as its direct object: *history*, but also, *lawyers, doctors,* and *businesswomen*. While all of these words are nouns, they do not have the same meanings — *history* is not an occupation, while all the other nouns are. There is a consistency in the pattern, but an inconsistency in the meaning of the words. Quindlen exploits the ironic inconsistency of the zeugma to draw a connection between two things that her audience might not otherwise think of as connected: activists who fought for women's rights, and women today who are trying to build their careers.

• EXERCISE 1

Identify the parallel structure in words, phrases, or clauses in each of the following sentences.

1. "A penny saved is a penny earned." (Benjamin Franklin)
2. Was this act the work of a genius or a lunatic?
3. This situation is a problem not only for the students but also for the teachers.
4. Heather learned to work fast, ask few questions, and generally keep a low profile.
5. After you finish your homework and before you check your email, please do your chores.

• EXERCISE 2

Correct the faulty parallelism in the following sentences.

1. My new exercise program and going on a strict diet will help me lose the weight I gained over the holidays.
2. As part of his accounting business, Rick has private clients, does some pro bono work, and corporations.
3. Try not to focus on the mistakes that you've made; what you've learned from them should be your focus instead.
4. A new job is likely to cause a person anxiety and working extra hours to make a good impression.
5. A competent physician will assess a patient's physical symptoms, and mental attitude will also be considered.

• EXERCISE 3

Identify the examples of parallel structure in the following sentences from Martin Luther King Jr.'s "Letter from Birmingham Jail," and explain their effect. Note that all are direct quotations.

1. So I, along with several members of my staff, am here because I was invited here. I am here because I have organizational ties here.
2. We are caught in an inescapable network of mutuality, tied in a single garment of destiny.
3. Whatever affects one directly, affects all indirectly.

4. In any nonviolent campaign there are four basic steps: collection of the facts to determine whether injustices exist; negotiation; self-purification; and direct action.

5. An unjust law is a code that a numerical or power majority group compels a minority group to obey but does not make binding on itself. This is a difference made legal. By the same token, a just law is a code that a majority compels a minority to follow and that it is willing to follow itself. This is sameness made legal.

6. Was not Jesus an extremist for love: "Love your enemies, bless them that curse you, do good to them that hate you, and pray for them which despitefully use you, and persecute you." Was not Amos an extremist for justice: "Let justice roll down like waters and righteousness like an ever-flowing stream." Was not Paul an extremist for the Christian gospel: "I bear in my body the marks of the Lord Jesus." Was not Martin Luther an extremist: "Here I stand; I cannot do otherwise, so help me God." And John Bunyan: "I will stay in jail to the end of my days before I make a butchery of my conscience." And Abraham Lincoln: "This nation cannot survive half slave and half free." And Thomas Jefferson: "We hold these truths to be self-evident, that all men are created equal. . . ."

7. If I have said anything in this letter that overstates the truth and indicates an unreasonable impatience, I beg you to forgive me. If I have said anything that understates the truth and indicates my having a patience that allows me to settle for anything less than brotherhood, I beg God to forgive me.

• EXERCISE 4

The following paragraph is from Toni Morrison's Nobel Lecture, delivered in 1993 when she won the Nobel Prize for Literature. Find examples of parallel structure; identify whether the construction is a word, clause, or phrase; and explain its effect.

🎧 Hear it on the Web: bedfordstmartins.com/languageofcomp

The systematic looting of language can be recognized by the tendency of its users to forgo its nuanced, complex, mid-wifery properties for menace and subjugation. Oppressive language does more than represent violence; it is violence; does more than represent the limits of knowledge; it limits knowledge. Whether it is obscuring state language or the faux-language of mindless media; whether it is the proud but calcified language of the academy or the commodity driven language of science; whether it is the malign language of law-without-ethics, or language designed for the estrangement of minorities, hiding its racist plunder in its literary cheek — it must be rejected, altered and exposed. It is the language that drinks blood, laps vulnerabilities, tucks its fascist boots under crinolines of respectability and patriotism as it moves relentlessly toward the bottom line and the bottomed-out mind. Sexist language, racist language, theistic language — all are typical of the policing languages of mastery, and cannot, do not permit new knowledge or encourage the mutual exchange of ideas.

• EXERCISE 5

Each of the following sentences is an example of parallelism. Identify the type of parallelism, explain its effect, and then model a sentence of your own on the example.

1. "To spend too much time in studies is sloth; to use them too much for ornament is affectation; to make judgment wholly by their rules is the humour of a scholar." — FRANCIS BACON

2. "Alas, art is long, and life is short." — BENJAMIN FRANKLIN

3. "Flowers are as common here . . . as people are in London." — OSCAR WILDE

4. "Where justice is denied, where poverty is enforced, where ignorance prevails, and where any one class is made to feel that society is in an organized conspiracy to oppress, rob, and degrade them, neither persons nor property will be safe." — FREDERICK DOUGLASS

5. "He carried a strobe light and the responsibility for the lives of his men." — TIM O'BRIEN

Suggestions for Writing

Community

Now that you have examined a number of texts that focus on community, explore this topic yourself by synthesizing your own ideas and the readings. You might want to do more research or use readings from other classes as you write.

1. Cell phones, email, chat rooms, social networking sites, blogs, and other electronic communication have made our world smaller and increased the pace at which we live life. Have these inventions also given us a new sense of community or opened up communities that would otherwise be closed to us? Or have they lowered our standards of what *community* means?

2. According to the Web site <www.ic.org>, an "intentional community" is

"a group of people who have chosen to live together with a common purpose, working cooperatively to create a lifestyle that reflects their shared core values." Assume you have the opportunity to develop an intentional community. How will you design it? What values will unite the group? How will the group live and work cooperatively? Write a proposal for the development of such a community.

3. Creating a community of like-minded people is the principle behind the development of many charter schools. Select a charter school in your area, and examine it as an intentional community, as defined in no. 2.

4. Write about the discussion that might ensue among several of the writers you have studied in this chapter if they were to focus on the following question: What are the characteristics of a productive and successful community at the start of the twenty-first century?

5. Was the Ku Klux Klan in the nineteenth and twentieth centuries a community? Many would argue yes, that it fit most definitions of *community*. It was, however, one of many so-called communities that might be seen as counterproductive. Choose another controversial community (such as the hip-hop community, a country club, or a secret society), examine its structure and purpose, and argue for or against its value to its members and to the larger community.

6. Many colleges and universities are developing what they call living-learning communities, in which students choose to live together as a group centered around a theme, which could be anything from Chinese culture to women in science. Some critics believe such groupings are limiting because the students are not exposed to different viewpoints and interests. Others object because they believe segregation based on race, ethnicity, or religion does not contribute to the mission of higher education. What do you think of living-learning communities? Will you choose to live in one when you go to college? Why or why not?

7. Examine a community that is organized around shared values but not geographic proximity. What holds that community together? What do members gain from it? Why does it continue?

8. Following is a description of a coffeehouse from the novel *Queen of Dreams* by Chitra Banerjee Divakaruni.

> Java demands nothing from them [customers] except their money. It allows them to remain unknown. . . . And yet they have community, too, as much of it as they want: the comfortable company of a roomful of nameless-faceless folks just like themselves, happy to be alone, to gaze into middle distance, to notice no one.

Discuss this concept of community, explain how it can function for some, and describe examples of it that you have seen.

Gender

*What is the impact of the gender roles
that society creates and enforces?*

"Why can't a woman be more like a man?" asks the exasperated Henry Higgins in *My Fair Lady*, the musical version of George Bernard Shaw's play *Pygmalion*, when he fails to understand his indomitable pupil, Eliza Doolittle. Why, indeed! The question of gender differences and roles has baffled and angered us, delighted and confused us, in life as well as in literature.

What is the distinction between sex and gender? The former refers to biological identity; the latter has come to mean behavior that is learned. Some "socially constructed" gender roles result from beliefs and pressures about the proper way to behave. When do gender roles become stereotypical views of what it means to be a woman or a man? Such views are not universal but vary according to culture and time. A look at men in the eighteenth century wearing wigs of curls tells us that what is considered appropriate for a gender in one context is wholly inappropriate in another.

What other forces define gender roles? How does ethnicity contribute to the expectations of what is masculine or feminine behavior? How does setting — a small town, an athletic field, a formal dinner — reflect a group's expectations and values?

Such issues take on even greater importance in the context of bias that results from assumptions about gender roles. When do socially constructed roles hinder individual expression or choice? Why are certain professions dominated by men and others by women? How do beliefs about sex or gender differences affect public policy, including education?

These are the questions taken up in this chapter, starting with an exploration into what "scientific evidence" has been marshaled to "prove" the intellectual superiority of men over women. Other selections focus on the repercussions of social pressures to behave "like a man," and on the profound communication barriers that result from differences in how men and women talk and listen. The serious economic and even medical consequences of beliefs about gender — and of the failure to take gender differences into account — are also considered.

The fictional Professor Higgins was, in fact, asking a rhetorical question, but the authors presented in this chapter answer his question in specific and provocative ways that are bound to challenge — and deepen — our thinking about gender roles.

Women's Brains

STEPHEN JAY GOULD

Paleontologist and evolutionary biologist Stephen Jay Gould (1941–2002) was a professor of geology and zoology at Harvard University from 1967 until his death. His major scientific work was the theory of punctuated equilibrium, a theory of evolutionary biology that builds on the work of Charles Darwin by suggesting that evolution occurs sporadically, rather than gradually over a long period of time. Gould is the author of numerous scientific texts, including *The Mismeasure of Man* (1981); *Wonderful Life: The Burgess Shale and the Nature of History* (1989); his magnum opus, *The Structure of Evolutionary Theory* (2002); and *The Hedgehog, the Fox, and the Magister's Pox: Mending the Gap between Science and the Humanities* (2003). Gould also wrote for a more general audience in his column in *Natural History*, where the following essay originally appeared.

In the Prelude to *Middlemarch*, George Eliot lamented the unfulfilled lives of talented women:

Some have felt that these blundering lives are due to the inconvenient indefiniteness with which the Supreme Power has fashioned the natures of women: if there were one level of feminine incompetence as strict as the ability to count three and no more, the social lot of women might be treated with scientific certitude.

Eliot goes on to discount the idea of innate limitation, but while she wrote in 1872, the leaders of European anthropometry were trying to measure "with scientific certitude" the inferiority of women. Anthropometry, or measurement of the human body, is not so fashionable a field these days, but it dominated the human sciences for much of the nineteenth century and remained popular until intelligence testing replaced skull measurement as a favored device for making invidious comparisons among races, classes, and sexes. Craniometry, or measurement of the skull, commanded the most attention and respect. Its unquestioned leader, Paul Broca (1824–80), professor of clinical surgery at the Faculty of Medicine in Paris, gathered a school of disciples and imitators around himself. Their work, so meticulous and apparently irrefutable, exerted great influence and won high esteem as a jewel of nineteenth-century science.

Broca's work seemed particularly invulnerable to refutation. Had he not measured with the most scrupulous care and accuracy? (Indeed, he had. I have the greatest respect for Broca's meticulous procedure. His numbers are sound. But science is an inferential exercise, not a catalog of facts. Numbers, by themselves, specify nothing. All depends upon what you do with them.) Broca depicted himself as an apostle of objectivity, a man who bowed before facts and cast aside superstition and sentimentality. He declared that "there is no faith, however respectable, no interest, however legitimate, which must not accommodate itself to the progress of human knowledge and bend before truth." Women, like it or not, had smaller brains than men and, therefore, could not equal them in intelligence. This fact, Broca argued, may reinforce a common prejudice in male society, but it is also a scientific truth. L. Manouvrier, a black sheep in Broca's fold, rejected the inferiority of women and wrote with feeling about the burden imposed upon them by Broca's numbers:

> Women displayed their talents and their diplomas. They also invoked philosophical authorities. But they were opposed by *numbers* unknown to Condorcet or to John Stuart Mill. These numbers fell upon poor women like a sledge hammer, and they were accompanied by commentaries and sarcasms more ferocious than the most misogynist imprecations of certain church fathers. The theologians had asked if women had a soul. Several centuries later, some scientists were ready to refuse them a human intelligence.

Broca's argument rested upon two sets of data: the larger brains of men in modern societies, and a supposed increase in male superiority through time. His most extensive data came from autopsies performed personally in four Parisian hospitals. For 292 male brains, he calculated an average weight of 1,325 grams; 140 female brains averaged 1,144 grams for a difference of 181 grams, or 14 percent of the male weight. Broca understood, of course, that part of this difference could be attributed to the greater height of males. Yet he made no attempt to measure the effect of size alone and actually stated that it cannot account for the entire difference because we know, a priori, that women are not as intelligent as men (a premise that the data were supposed to test, not rest upon):

> We might ask if the small size of the female brain depends exclusively upon the small size of her body. Tiedemann has proposed this explanation. But we must not forget that women are, on the average, a little less intelligent than men, a difference which we should not exaggerate but which is, nonetheless, real. We are therefore permitted to suppose that the relatively small size of the female brain depends in part upon her physical inferiority and in part upon her intellectual inferiority.

In 1873, the year after Eliot published *Middlemarch*, Broca measured the cranial capacities of prehistoric skulls from L'Homme Mort cave. Here he found a difference of only 99.5 cubic centimeters between males and females, while modern populations range from 129.5 to 220.7. Topinard, Broca's chief disciple, explained the increasing discrepancy through time as a result of differing evolutionary pressures upon dominant men and passive women:

> The man who fights for two or more in the struggle for existence, who has all the responsibility and the cares of tomorrow, who is constantly active in combating

5

the environment and human rivals, needs more brain than the woman whom he must protect and nourish, the sedentary woman, lacking any interior occupations, whose role is to raise children, love, and be passive.

In 1879, Gustave Le Bon, chief misogynist of Broca's school, used these data to publish what must be the most vicious attack upon women in modern scientific literature (no one can top Aristotle). I do not claim his views were representative of Broca's school, but they were published in France's most respected anthropological journal. Le Bon concluded:

> In the most intelligent races, as among the Parisians, there are a large number of women whose brains are closer in size to those of gorillas than to the most developed male brains. This inferiority is so obvious that no one can contest it for a moment; only its degree is worth discussion. All psychologists who have studied the intelligence of women, as well as poets and novelists, recognize today that they represent the most inferior forms of human evolution and that they are closer to children and savages than to an adult, civilized man. They excel in fickleness, inconstancy, absence of thought and logic, and incapacity to reason. Without doubt there exist some distinguished women, very superior to the average man, but they are as exceptional as the birth of any monstrosity, as, for example, of a gorilla with two heads; consequently, we may neglect them entirely.

Nor did Le Bon shrink from the social implications of his views. He was horrified by the proposal of some American reformers to grant women higher education on the same basis as men:

> A desire to give them the same education, and, as a consequence, to propose the same goals for them, is a dangerous chimera. . . . The day when, misunderstanding the inferior occupations which nature has given her, women leave the home and take part in our battles; on this day a social revolution will begin, and everything that maintains the sacred ties of the family will disappear.

Sound familiar?[1]

I have reexamined Broca's data, the basis for all this derivative pronouncement, and I find his numbers sound but his interpretation ill-founded, to say the least. The data supporting his claim for increased difference through time can be easily dismissed. Broca based his contention on the samples from L'Homme Mort alone — only seven male and six female skulls in all. Never have so little data yielded such far-ranging conclusions.

---

[1]When I wrote this essay, I assumed that Le Bon was a marginal, if colorful, figure. I have since learned that he was a leading scientist, one of the founders of social psychology, and best known for a seminal study on crowd behavior, still cited today (*La psychologie des foules*, 1895), and for his work on unconscious motivation.

In 1888, Topinard published Broca's more extensive data on the Parisian hospitals. Since Broca recorded height and age as well as brain size, we may use modern statistics to remove their effect. Brain weight decreases with age, and Broca's women were, on average, considerably older than his men. Brain weight increases with height, and his average man was almost half a foot taller than his average woman. I used multiple regression, a technique that allowed me to assess simultaneously the influence of height and age upon brain size. In an analysis of the data for women, I found that, at average male height and age, a woman's brain would weigh 1,212 grams. Correction for height and age reduces Broca's measured difference of 181 grams by more than a third, to 113 grams.

I don't know what to make of this remaining difference because I cannot assess other factors known to influence brain size in a major way. Cause of death has an important effect: degenerative disease often entails a substantial diminution of brain size. (This effect is separate from the decrease attributed to age alone.) Eugene Schreider, also working with Broca's data, found that men killed in accidents had brains weighing, on average, 60 grams more than men dying of infectious diseases. The best modern data I can find (from American hospitals) records a full 100-gram difference between death by degenerative arteriosclerosis and by violence or accident. Since so many of Broca's subjects were very elderly women, we may assume that lengthy degenerative disease was more common among them than among the men.

More importantly, modern students of brain size still have not agreed on a proper measure for eliminating the powerful effect of body size. Height is partly adequate, but men and women of the same height do not share the same body build. Weight is even worse than height, because most of its variation reflects nutrition rather than intrinsic size — fat versus skinny exerts little influence upon the brain. Manouvrier took up this subject in the 1880s and argued that muscular mass and force should be used. He tried to measure this elusive property in various ways and found a marked difference in favor of men, even in men and women of the same height. When he corrected for what he called "sexual mass," women actually came out slightly ahead in brain size.

Thus, the corrected 113-gram difference is surely too large; the true figure is probably close to zero and may as well favor women as men. And 113 grams, by the way, is exactly the average difference between a 5 foot 4 inch and a 6 foot 4 inch male in Broca's data. We would not (especially us short folks) want to ascribe greater intelligence to tall men. In short, who knows what to do with Broca's data? They certainly don't permit any confident claim that men have bigger brains than women.

To appreciate the social role of Broca and his school, we must recognize that his statements about the brains of women do not reflect an isolated prejudice toward a single disadvantaged group. They must be weighed in the context of a general theory that supported contemporary social distinctions as biologically ordained. Women, blacks, and poor people suffered the same disparagement, but women bore the brunt of Broca's argument because he had easier access to data on

10

women's brains. Women were singularly denigrated but they also stood as surrogates for other disenfranchised groups. As one of Broca's disciples wrote in 1881: "Men of the black races have a brain scarcely heavier than that of white women." This juxtaposition extended into many other realms of anthropological argument, particularly to claims that, anatomically and emotionally, both women and blacks were like white children — and that white children, by the theory of recapitulation, represented an ancestral (primitive) adult stage of human evolution. I do not regard as empty rhetoric the claim that women's battles are for all of us.

Maria Montessori did not confine her activities to educational reform for young children. She lectured on anthropology for several years at the University of Rome, and wrote an influential book entitled *Pedagogical Anthropology* (English edition, 1913). Montessori was no egalitarian. She supported most of Broca's work and the theory of innate criminality proposed by her compatriot Cesare Lombroso. She measured the circumference of children's heads in her schools and inferred that the best prospects had bigger brains. But she had no use for Broca's conclusions about women. She discussed Manouvrier's work at length and made much of his tentative claim that women, after proper correction of the data, had slightly larger brains than men. Women, she concluded, were intellectually superior, but men had prevailed heretofore by dint of physical force. Since technology has abolished force as an instrument of power, the era of women may soon be upon us: "In such an epoch there will really be superior human beings, there will really be men strong in morality and in sentiment. Perhaps in this way the reign of women is approaching, when the enigma of her anthropological superiority will be deciphered. Woman was always the custodian of human sentiment, morality and honor."

This represents one possible antidote to "scientific" claims for the constitutional inferiority of certain groups. One may affirm the validity of biological distinctions but argue that the data have been misinterpreted by prejudiced men with a stake in the outcome, and that disadvantaged groups are truly superior. In recent years, Elaine Morgan has followed this strategy in her *Descent of Woman*, a speculative reconstruction of human prehistory from the woman's point of view — and as farcical as more famous tall tales by and for men. 15

I prefer another strategy. Montessori and Morgan followed Broca's philosophy to reach a more congenial conclusion. I would rather label the whole enterprise of setting a biological value upon groups for what it is: irrelevant and highly injurious. George Eliot well appreciated the special tragedy that biological labeling imposed upon members of disadvantaged groups. She expressed it for people like herself — women of extraordinary talent. I would apply it more widely — not only to those whose dreams are flouted but also to those who never realize that they may dream — but I cannot match her prose. In conclusion, then, the rest of Eliot's prelude to *Middlemarch*:

> The limits of variation are really much wider than anyone would imagine from the sameness of women's coiffure and the favorite love stories in prose and verse.

Here and there a cygnet is reared uneasily among the ducklings in the brown pond, and never finds the living stream in fellowship with its own oary-footed kind. Here and there is born a Saint Theresa, foundress of nothing, whose loving heartbeats and sobs after an unattained goodness tremble off and are dispersed among hindrances instead of centering in some long-recognizable deed.

Questions for Discussion

1. Stephen Jay Gould's argument focuses on research about women's brain size, but — more importantly — what does he say about the nature of scientific inquiry — that is, about how scientists think?
2. What does Gould mean when he says, "Women were singularly denigrated but they also stood as surrogates for other disenfranchised groups" (para. 13)?
3. Why does Gould say, "I do not regard as empty rhetoric the claim that women's battles are for all of us" (para. 13)? Is he being patronizing? Does such a personal comment undermine his scientific credibility? Explain.
4. Gould's essay was published in 1980, and it centers on research conducted a century before that. What case can you make that Gould's true subject was not women, but assumptions about the abilities of certain groups?
5. Would individuals accustomed to science texts have an easier time reading this essay? Why or why not? How do your experience and prior knowledge of a topic affect your reading process?

Questions on Rhetoric and Style

1. What purposes do the quotations in this essay from George Eliot's novel *Middlemarch* serve? Why does Gould, when introducing the quotation from Broca in paragraph 5, refer to Eliot? Why are quotations from Eliot, whose real name was Mary Anne Evans, especially appropriate for Gould's essay?
2. In paragraph 3, Gould states, "I have the greatest respect for Broca's meticulous procedure. His numbers are sound." Despite this praise, Gould goes on to refute Broca's findings. What vulnerability does Gould find in Broca's conclusions? Does Gould's praise of Broca strengthen or weaken his own argument? Explain.
3. Gould builds two parallel arguments, one on scientific method, another on speculative conclusions. In which passages does he question the scientific method(s) rather than the findings themselves? How does Gould weave these sources together in order to make his own point?
4. How does each of the individuals Gould cites — Paul Broca, Gustave Le Bon, L. Manouvrier, and Maria Montessori — contribute to the development of his argument? Does each make a separate point, or do they reinforce one another? Could Gould have eliminated any of them without damaging his argument? Explain your reasoning.

5. At the end of paragraph 7, Gould adds a footnote reassessing an earlier point. Does this admission add or detract from his credibility?

6. Paragraphs 9 through 12 work as a unit to develop a single point that is integral to the overall essay. What is this point? How do paragraphs 9–12 develop the point?

7. In paragraph 13, Gould shows how Broca and his colleagues extended their conclusions to other groups. What is Gould's purpose in developing this point as elaborately as he does?

8. Why is questioning Maria Montessori's research and conclusions an effective strategy? What criticism might Gould be guarding against in doing so?

9. In the final two paragraphs, how does Gould bring together both of his arguments — that is, his argument against the actual scientific research and his argument about the conclusions drawn from that research?

10. This essay has a strong appeal to logos, as would be expected of a scientific argument. How does Gould also appeal to pathos? How does that appeal add to the persuasiveness of his argument?

11. Most of the time Gould writes in the third person, but he uses first person occasionally. Explain why you think this shift strengthens or weakens the essay.

12. How would you characterize the audience for whom Gould is writing? Do you think fellow scientists are among them? Explain why or why not.

Suggestions for Writing

1. In paragraph 3, Gould asserts that "science is an inferential exercise, not a catalog of facts. Numbers, by themselves, specify nothing. All depends upon what you do with them." Support, challenge, or qualify Gould's assertion by referring to statistics used in science, politics, economics, sports, or another applicable field.

2. Find an essay written for a specialized audience (for example, an essay about technology in a scientific journal or a computer magazine). Rewrite it for a more general audience.

3. Gould refers to "a general theory that supported contemporary social distinctions as biologically ordained" in the late nineteenth century. In the twenty-first century, many continue to argue for nature over nurture — that is, for biology rather than socialization — as the causal agent for skills and talents of specific groups of people. Write an essay explaining whether you believe heredity or environment is the principal determinant of human characteristics. You may use yourself as an example and may cite Gould's essay, but you should also do research in other sources to explore how the nature-nurture debate has fared in particular historical contexts.

4. Write an essay using scientific data to develop an argument that has ethical or social implications. For example, use statistical data to make (a) a case about the impact of global warming or (b) a proposal to address what is being called the obesity epidemic in the United States. Frame the essay with a quotation (as Gould does), a description, or an anecdote.

Professions for Women

VIRGINIA WOOLF

 A prolific novelist, critic, and essayist, Virginia Woolf was born in London in 1882. Her novels, particularly *Mrs. Dalloway* (1925) and *To the Lighthouse* (1927), are renowned for their penetrating psychological insight. Her novels are known for their use of interior monologue, or stream of consciousness. Woolf is also noted for her nonfiction, especially for such works as *The Common Reader* (1925), *A Room of One's Own* (1929), and *Three Guineas* (1938). Having struggled with mental illness for much of her life, she drowned herself in 1941. "Professions for Women," delivered as a talk in 1931 to the Women's Service League, was included in *Death of a Moth and Other Essays* (1942).

When your secretary invited me to come here, she told me that your Society is concerned with the employment of women and she suggested that I might tell you something about my own professional experiences. It is true I am a woman; it is true I am employed; but what professional experiences have I had? It is difficult to say. My profession is literature; and in that profession there are fewer experiences for women than in any other, with the exception of the stage — fewer, I mean, that are peculiar to women. For the road was cut many years ago — by Fanny Burney, by Aphra Behn, by Harriet Martineau, by Jane Austen, by George Eliot — many famous women, and many more unknown and forgotten, have been before me, making the path smooth, and regulating my steps. Thus, when I came to write, there were very few material obstacles in my way. Writing was a reputable and harmless occupation. The family peace was not broken by the scratching of a pen. No demand was made upon the family purse. For ten and sixpence one can buy paper enough to write all the plays of Shakespeare — if one has a mind that way. Pianos and models, Paris, Vienna and Berlin, masters and mistresses, are not needed by a writer. The cheapness of writing paper is, of course, the reason why women have succeeded as writers before they have succeeded in the other professions.

But to tell you my story — it is a simple one. You have only got to figure to yourselves a girl in a bedroom with a pen in her hand. She had only to move that pen from left to right — from ten o'clock to one. Then it occurred to her to do what is simple and cheap enough after all — to slip a few of those pages into an envelope, fix a penny stamp in the corner, and drop the envelope into the red box at the corner. It was thus that I became a journalist; and my effort was rewarded on the first day of the following month — a very glorious day it was for me — by a letter from an editor containing a cheque for one pound ten shillings and sixpence. But to show you how little I deserve to be called a professional woman, how little I know of the struggles and difficulties of such lives, I have to admit that instead of spending that sum upon bread and butter, rent, shoes and stockings, or butcher's bills, I went out and bought a cat — a beautiful cat, a Persian cat, which very soon involved me in bitter disputes with my neighbours.

What could be easier than to write articles and to buy Persian cats with the profits? But wait a moment. Articles have to be about something. Mine, I seem to remember, was about a novel by a famous man. And while I was writing this review, I discovered that if I were going to review books I should need to do battle with a certain phantom. And the phantom was a woman, and when I came to know her better I called her after the heroine of a famous poem, The Angel in the House.[1] It was she who used to come between me and my paper when I was writing reviews. It was she who bothered me and wasted my time and so tormented me that at last I killed her. You who come of a younger and happier generation may not have heard of her — you may not know what I mean by the Angel in the House. I will describe her as shortly as I can. She was intensely sympathetic. She was immensely charming. She was utterly unselfish. She excelled in the difficult arts of family life. She sacrificed herself daily. If there was chicken, she took the leg; if there was a draught she sat in it — in short she was so constituted that she never had a mind or a wish of her own, but preferred to sympathize always with the minds and wishes of others. Above all — I need not say it — she was pure. Her purity was supposed to be her chief beauty — her blushes, her great grace. In those days — the last of Queen Victoria — every house had its Angel. And when I came to write I encountered her with the very first words. The shadow of her wings fell on my page; I heard the rustling of her skirts in the room. Directly, that is to say, I took my pen in my hand to review that novel by a famous man, she slipped behind me and whispered: "My dear, you are a young woman. You are writing about a book that has been written by a man. Be sympathetic; be tender; flatter; deceive; use all the arts and wiles of our sex. Never let anybody guess that you have a mind of your own. Above all, be pure." And she made as if to guide my pen. I now record the one act for which I take some credit to myself, though the credit rightly belongs to some excellent ancestors of mine who left me a certain sum of money — shall we say five hundred pounds a year? — so that it was not necessary for me to depend solely on charm for my living. I turned upon her and caught her by the throat. I did my best to kill her. My excuse, if I were to be had up in a court of law, would be that I acted in self-defence. Had I not killed her she would have killed me. She would have plucked the heart out of my writing. For, as I found, directly I put pen to paper, you cannot review even a novel without having a mind of your own, without expressing what you think to be the truth

---

[1]"The Angel in the House" is a nineteenth-century poem about a self-sacrificing heroine; for many, she represented the ideal Victorian woman. — Eds.

about human relations, morality, sex. And all these questions, according to the Angel of the House, cannot be dealt with freely and openly by women; they must charm, they must conciliate, they must — to put it bluntly — tell lies if they are to succeed. Thus, whenever I felt the shadow of her wing or the radiance of her halo upon my page, I took up the inkpot and flung it at her. She died hard. Her fictitious nature was of great assistance to her. It is far harder to kill a phantom than a reality. She was always creeping back when I thought I had despatched her. Though I flatter myself that I killed her in the end, the struggle was severe; it took much time that had better have been spent upon learning Greek grammar; or in roaming the world in search of adventures. But it was a real experience; it was an experience that was found to befall all women writers at that time. Killing the Angel in the House was part of the occupation of a woman writer.

But to continue my story. The Angel was dead; what then remained? You may say that what remained was a simple and common object — a young woman in a bedroom with an inkpot. In other words, now that she had rid herself of false-hood, that young woman had only to be herself. Ah, but what is "herself"? I mean, what is a woman? I assure you, I do not know. I do not believe that you know. I do not believe that anybody can know until she has expressed herself in all the arts and professions open to human skill. That indeed is one of the reasons why I have come here — out of respect for you, who are in process of showing us by your experiments what a woman is, who are in process of providing us, by your failures and successes, with that extremely important piece of information.

But to continue the story of my professional experiences. I made one pound ten and six by my first review; and I bought a Persian cat with the proceeds. Then I grew ambitious. A Persian cat is all very well, I said; but a Persian cat is not enough. I must have a motor car. And it was thus that I became a novelist — for it is a very strange thing that people will give you a motor car if you will tell them a story. It is a still stranger thing that there is nothing so delightful in the world as telling stories. It is far pleasanter than writing reviews of famous novels. And yet, if I am to obey your secretary and tell you my professional experiences as a novel-ist, I must tell you about a very strange experience that befell me as a novelist. And to understand it you must try first to imagine a novelist's state of mind. I hope I am not giving away professional secrets if I say that a novelist's chief desire is to be as unconscious as possible. He has to induce in himself a state of perpetual lethargy. He wants life to proceed with the utmost quiet and regularity. He wants to see the same faces, to read the same books, to do the same things day after day, month after month, while he is writing, so that nothing may break the illusion in which he is living — so that nothing may disturb or disquiet the mysterious nos-ings about, feelings round, darts, dashes and sudden discoveries of that very shy and illusive spirit, the imagination. I suspect that this state is the same both for men and women. Be that as it may, I want you to imagine me writing a novel in a state of trance. I want you to figure to yourselves a girl sitting with a pen in her hand, which for minutes, and indeed for hours, she never dips into the inkpot.

5

The image that comes to my mind when I think of this girl is the image of a fisherman lying sunk in dreams on the verge of a deep lake with a rod held out over the water. She was letting her imagination sweep unchecked round every rock and cranny of the world that lies submerged in the depths of our unconscious being. Now came the experience, the experience that I believe to be far commoner with women writers than with men. The line raced through the girl's fingers. Her imagination had rushed away. It had sought the pools, the depths, the dark places where the largest fish slumber. And then there was a smash. There was an explosion. There was foam and confusion. The imagination had dashed itself against something hard. The girl was roused from her dream. She was indeed in a state of the most acute and difficult distress. To speak without figure she had thought of something, something about the body, about the passions which it was unfitting for her as a woman to say. Men, her reason told her, would be shocked. The consciousness of what men will say of a woman who speaks the truth about her passions had roused her from her artist's state of unconsciousness. She could write no more. The trance was over. Her imagination could work no longer. This I believe to be a very common experience with women writers — they are impeded by the extreme conventionality of the other sex. For though men sensibly allow themselves great freedom in these respects, I doubt that they realize or can control the extreme severity with which they condemn such freedom in women.

These then were two very genuine experiences of my own. These were two of the adventures of my professional life. The first — killing the Angel in the House — I think I solved. She died. But the second, telling the truth about my own experiences as a body, I do not think I solved. I doubt that any woman has solved it yet. The obstacles against her are still immensely powerful — and yet they are very difficult to define. Outwardly, what is simpler than to write books? Outwardly, what obstacles are there for a woman rather than for a man? Inwardly, I think, the case is very different; she has still many ghosts to fight, many prejudices to overcome. Indeed it will be a long time still, I think, before a woman can sit down to write a book without finding a phantom to be slain, a rock to be dashed against. And if this is so in literature, the freest of all professions for women, how is it in the new professions which you are now for the first time entering?

Those are the questions that I should like, had I time, to ask you. And indeed, if I have laid stress upon these professional experiences of mine, it is because I believe that they are, though in different forms, yours also. Even when the path is nominally open — when there is nothing to prevent a woman from being a doctor, a lawyer, a civil servant — there are many phantoms and obstacles, as I believe, looming in her way. To discuss and define them is I think of great value and importance; for thus only can the labour be shared, the difficulties be solved. But besides this, it is necessary also to discuss the ends and the aims for which we are fighting, for which we are doing battle with these formidable obstacles. Those aims cannot be taken for granted; they must be perpetually questioned and examined. The whole position, as I see it — here in this hall surrounded by women practising for the first time in history I know not how many different professions — is one of extraordinary interest and importance. You have won rooms of your own in the house hitherto exclusively owned by men. You are able, though not without great labour and effort, to pay the rent. You are earning your five hundred pounds a year. But this freedom is only a beginning; the room is your own, but it is still bare. It has to be furnished; it has to be decorated; it has to be shared. How are you going to furnish it, how are you going to decorate it? With whom are you going to share it, and upon what terms? These, I think are questions of the utmost importance and interest. For the first time in history you are able to ask them; for the first time you are able to decide for yourselves what the answers should be. Willingly would I stay and discuss those questions and answers — but not tonight. My time is up; and I must cease.

Questions for Discussion

1. According to Virginia Woolf, what are the two main obstacles to women's professional identity? Are these still the two main obstacles, or does the contemporary woman face different hurdles? Explain.

2. What is the origin of the "Angel in the House" (para. 3)? Consult the *Language of Composition* Web site for background information: <bedfordstmartins.com/languageofcomp>. Why is this an appropriate or effective frame of reference for Woolf?

3. What do you think Woolf means in paragraph 5 when she asserts that "a novelist's chief desire is to be as unconscious as possible"? Do you agree that someone who writes fiction should be "unconscious"? Why do you think a novelist would want to be "unconscious" or would benefit from being "unconscious"?

4. In paragraphs 5 and 6, Woolf explores the consequences of being unable to tell "the truth" about her own "experiences as a body." What does she mean? Why does she believe that surmounting this obstacle is more difficult — perhaps impossible at the time she was writing — than "killing the Angel in the House"?

5. In her final paragraph, Woolf apologizes to a certain extent for dwelling on her own experience, and then points out that her "professional experiences" "are, though in different forms" also the experiences of her audience. What exactly is she asking of her audience here?

6. In an online essay at <bedfordstmartins.com/languageofcomp>, Barbara Wahl Ledingham makes the following assertion about the relevance of Woolf's essay to women in the twenty-first century:

   We must claim and have knowledge of our feminists, our artists, our mothers, our leaders, and our organizers, women like Susan B. Anthony . . . or Margaret Sanger. . . . All of these women acted despite persecution. Their sacrifice is responsible for many of the rights we take for granted today, but the biggest challenge is confronting our own Angel in the House, our own inner phantom, the one that keeps us from . . . defining and owning our own lives.

With a kind of uncanny prescience, Woolf's words follow us seventy years later, haunting us with their veracity and timelessness. They are a gauge by which to measure not only our exterior accomplishments but also our inner state, and they serve as a warning not to lose consciousness or become apathetic about either realm.

After summarizing what Ledingham is saying, explain why you agree or disagree with her analysis.

Questions on Rhetoric and Style

1. How does Woolf present herself in the opening paragraph? What relationship is she establishing with her audience?
2. Identify an example in the opening paragraph of each of the following, and explain its effect: understatement, parallel structure, rhetorical question, irony, and metonymy.
3. What is the effect of the personal anecdote in paragraph 2? Does the anecdote appeal mainly to logos or pathos? Why is it especially effective for Woolf's audience?
4. What does Woolf mean in the following description of the Angel in the House: "The shadow of her wings fell on my page; I heard the rustling of her skirts in the room" (para. 3)?
5. Discuss the effect of the short simple sentences that Woolf uses in paragraph 3. How do they contribute to her tone as she describes the Angel in the House?
6. In paragraph 3, Woolf tells how she did her "best to kill [the Angel in the House]." Examine the words and images she uses to describe this act. Do you believe the violence of her descriptions to be appropriate? Explain why or why not.
7. How does the shift in person in paragraph 4 serve Woolf's purpose? In what ways is this a transitional paragraph?
8. What is the effect in paragraph 5 of Woolf's referring to a novelist as *he*? Should Woolf have used *she* as though she were referring to herself? Why or why not?
9. Summarize the extended analogy Woolf develops in paragraph 5 to describe "a girl sitting with a pen in her hand." Explain its effect.
10. Would you characterize the language at the end of paragraph 5, where Woolf writes about "the body," to be delicate and genteel or euphemistic? Explain, keeping in mind the historical context of the work.
11. By the time of this speech, Woolf's extended essay *A Room of One's Own* was well known as a feminist manifesto: Woolf claimed that every woman requires a separate income and a room of her own if she is to become an independent, productive woman. How does Woolf embellish this metaphor of a room of one's own in paragraph 7? What is the effect?

12. What is Woolf's overall tone in this speech? Because the tone evolves and shifts throughout the text, determining the overall tone is complex. Identify passages where Woolf displays various tones, sometimes in order to assume a specific persona, and then develop a description of the overall tone. You will probably need to use two words (possibly joined with *but* or *yet*) or a phrase rather than a single word. Does Woolf display anger, bitterness, resignation, aggression, apology, combativeness? Or does she show a combination of these emotions or others?

Suggestions for Writing

1. Write an essay analyzing the rhetorical strategies Woolf uses in this speech to reach her specific audience. Pay attention to the way she uses the tools of the novelist, such as characterization, scene setting, highly textured and specific descriptive detail, and figurative language.
2. You have been invited to deliver a speech entitled "Professions for Women" to an audience of your peers, male and female. Cite Woolf to support your speech's thesis, or propose a counterargument to Woolf's position. Also, be sure to describe the audience and occasion of your speech.
3. If you have read any of Virginia Woolf's fiction (either her short stories or the novels *Mrs. Dalloway* or *To the Lighthouse*, for example), discuss how this essay informs them.
4. In *A Room of One's Own*, Woolf asks, what if Shakespeare had had a sister? She calls her Judith and considers whether circumstances would have encouraged or allowed Judith to write great plays. Read the essay at <bedfordstmartins.com/languageofcomp>, and write an essay comparing and contrasting the ideas and style of that essay with those in "Professions for Women."
5. In the final paragraph of her speech, Woolf says, "Even when the path is nominally open — when there is nothing to prevent a woman from being a doctor, a lawyer, a civil servant — there are many phantoms and obstacles, as I believe, looming in her way." Write an essay in which you defend, challenge, or modify that statement with regard to women today in the United States *or* to women in another country where gender equality might be more problematic. Pay particular attention to what you see as the "phantoms and obstacles."

Letters

JOHN AND ABIGAIL ADAMS

John Adams (1735–1826), one of America's founding fathers, was the second president of the United States. His wife, Abigail Smith Adams (1744–1818), was also dedicated to the cause of independence and wrote frequently to him on the conditions of wartime Boston, which was held by the British for most of the war. The city was liberated by George Washington's army just before these letters were written. In the following two letters, Abigail writes to her husband in Philadelphia, where he is serving in the Continental Congress, and John responds as both husband and politician. Abigail presses her husband to "remember the ladies" as he and his colleagues are discussing freedom from tyranny. Given the time period, her exhortation did not refer to woman's suffrage but rather to laws regarding such matters as inheritance and spousal abuse. You can view these letters at <bedfordstmartins.com/languageofcomp>.

From Abigail to John

Braintree, March 31, 1776

I wish you would ever write me a Letter half as long as I write you; and tell me if you may where your Fleet are gone? What sort of Defence Virginia can make against our common Enemy? Whether it is so situated as to make an able Defence? Are not the Gentery Lords and the common people vassals, are they not like the uncivilized Natives Brittain represents us to be? I hope their Riffel Men who have shewen themselves very savage and even Blood thirsty; are not a specimen of the Generality of the people.

I . . . am willing to allow the Colony great merrit for having produced a Washington but they have been shamefully duped by a Dunmore.[1]

I have sometimes been ready to think that the passion for Liberty cannot be Eaqually Strong in the Breasts of those who have been accustomed to deprive their fellow Creatures of theirs. Of this I am certain that it is not founded upon that generous and christian principal of doing to others as we would that others should do unto us.

Do not you want to see Boston; I am fearfull of the small pox, or I should have been in before this time. I got Mr. Crane to go to our House and see what state it was in. I find it has been occupied by one of the Doctors of a Regiment,

---

[1]The Fourth Earl of Dunmore (John Murray) was the British colonial governor of Virginia from 1771 to 1776. He opposed independence for the colonies and was forced to return to England. — Eds.

very dirty, but no other damage has been done to it. The few things which were left in it are all gone. Cranch has the key which he never deliverd up. I have wrote to him for it and am determined to get it cleand as soon as possible and shut it up. I look upon it a new acquisition of property, a property which one month ago I did not value at a single Shilling, and could with pleasure have seen it in flames.

The Town in General is left in a better state than we expected, more oweing to a percipitate flight than any Regard to the inhabitants, tho some individuals discoverd a sense of honour and justice and have left the rent of the Houses in which they were, for the owners and the furniture unhurt, or if damaged sufficent to make it good.

Others have committed abominable Ravages. The Mansion House of your President is safe and the furniture unhurt whilst both the House and Furniture of the Solisiter General have fallen a prey to their own merciless party. Surely the very Fiends feel a Reverential awe for Virtue and patriotism, whilst they Detest the paricide and traitor.

I feel very differently at the approach of spring to what I did a month ago. We knew not then whether we could plant or sow with safety, whether when we had toild we could reap the fruits of our own industery, whether we could rest in our own Cottages, or whether we should not be driven from the sea coasts to seek shelter in the wilderness, but now we feel as if we might sit under our own vine and eat the good of the land.

I feel a gaieti de Coar[2] to which before I was a stranger. I think the Sun looks brighter, the Birds sing more melodiously, and Nature puts on a more chearfull countanance. We feel a temporary peace, and the poor fugitives are returning to their deserted habitations.

Tho we felicitate ourselves, we sympathize with those who are trembling least the Lot of Boston should be theirs. But they cannot be in similar circumstances unless pusilanimity and cowardise should take possession of them. They have time and warning given them to see the Evil and shun it. — I long to hear that you have declared an independency — and by the way in the new Code of Laws which I suppose it will be necessary for you to make I desire you would Remember the Ladies, and be more generous and favourable to them than your ancestors. Do not put such unlimited power into the hand of the Husbands. Remember all Men would be tyrants if they could. If perticuliar care and attention is not paid to the Laidies we are determined to foment a Rebelion, and will not hold ourselves bound by any Laws in which we have no voice, or Representation.

That your Sex are Naturally Tyrannical is a Truth so thoroughly established as to admit of no dispute, but such of you as wish to be happy willingly give up the harsh title of Master for the more tender and endearing one of Friend. Why then, not put it out of the power of the vicious and the Lawless to use us with cru-

---

[2]French (correctly spelled gaieté de coeur), happiness of heart. — Eds.

elty and indignity with impunity. Men of Sense in all Ages abhor those customs which treat us only as the vassals of your Sex. Regard us then as Beings placed by providence under your protection and in immitation of the Supreem Being make use of that power only for our happiness.

From John to Abigail

April 14, 1776

You justly complain of my short Letters, but the critical State of Things and the Multiplicity of Avocations must plead my Excuse. You ask where the Fleet is. The inclosed Papers will inform you. You ask what Sort of Defence Virginia can make. I believe they will make an able Defence. Their Militia and minute Men have been some time employed in training them selves and they have Nine Battallions of regulars as they call them, maintained among them, under good Officers, at the Continental Expence. They have set up a Number of Manufactories of Fire Arms, which are busily employed. They are tolerably supplied with Powder, and are successfull and assiduous, in making Salt Petre. Their neighbouring Sister or rather Daughter Colony of North Carolina, which is a warlike Colony, and has several Battallions at the Continental Expence, as well as a pretty good Militia, are ready to assist them, and they are in very good Spirits, and seem determined to make a brave Resistance. — The Gentry are very rich, and the common People very poor.

This Inequality of Property, gives an Aristocratical Turn to all their Proceedings, and occasions a strong Aversion in their Patricians, to Common Sense. But the Spirit of these Barons, is coming down, and it must submit.

It is very true, as you observe they have been duped by Dunmore. But this is a Common Case. All the Colonies are duped, more or less, at one Time and another. A more egregious Bubble was never blown up, than the Story of Commissioners coming to treat with the Congress. Yet it has gained Credit like a Charm, not only without but against the clearest Evidence. I never shall forget the Delusion, which seized our best and most sagacious Friends the dear Inhabitants of Boston, the Winter before last. Credulity and the Want of Foresight, are Imperfections in the human Character, that no Politician can sufficiently guard against.

You have given me some Pleasure, by your Account of a certain House in Queen Street. I had burned it, long ago, in Imagination. It rises now to my View like a Phoenix. — What shall I say of the Solicitor General? I pity his pretty Children, I pity his Father, and his sisters. I wish I could be clear that it is no moral Evil to pity him and his Lady. Upon Repentance they will certainly have a large Share in the Compassions of many. But . . . let Us take Warning and give it to our Children. Whenever Vanity, and Gaiety, a Love of Pomp and Dress, Furniture, Equipage, Buildings, great Company, expensive Diversions, and elegant Entertainments get the better of the Principles and Judgments of Men or Women there is no knowing where they will stop, nor into what Evils, natural, moral, or political, they will lead us.

Your Description of your own Gaiety de Coeur, charms me. Thanks be to   15
God you have just Cause to rejoice — and may the bright Prospect be obscured
by no Cloud.

As to Declarations of Independency, be patient. Read our Privateering Laws,
and our Commercial Laws. What signifies a Word.

As to your extraordinary Code of Laws, I cannot but laugh. We have been
told that our Struggle has loosened the bands of Government every where. That
Children and Apprentices were disobedient — that schools and Colledges were
grown turbulent — that Indians slighted their Guardians and Negroes grew inso-
lent to their Masters.

But your Letter was the first Intimation that another Tribe more numerous
and powerfull than all the rest were grown discontented. — This is rather too
coarse a Compliment but you are so saucy, I wont blot it out.

Depend upon it, We know better than to repeal our Masculine systems. Altho
they are in full Force, you know they are little more than Theory. We dare not
exert our Power in its full Latitude. We are obliged to go fair, and softly, and in
Practice you know We are the subjects. We have only the Name of Masters, and
rather than give up this, which would compleatly subject Us to the Despotism of
the Peticoat, I hope General Washington, and all our brave Heroes would fight. I
am sure every good Politician would plot, as long as he would against Despotism,
Empire, Monarchy, Aristocracy, Oligarchy, or Ochlocracy. — A fine Story indeed.
I begin to think the Ministry as deep as they are wicked. After stirring up Tories,
Landjobbers, Trimmers, Bigots, Canadians, Indians, Negroes, Hanoverians, Hes-
sians, Russians, Irish Roman Catholicks, Scotch Renegadoes, at last they have
stimulated the[e] to demand new Priviledges and threaten to rebell.

Exploring the Text

1. What ethos does Abigail Adams establish in the opening paragraph? How do the
   questions contribute to the persona she presents?
2. Abigail describes Boston in considerable detail. What is the general impression she
   tries to convey? Why do you think she chose the details she did?
3. When Abigail exhorts John Adams to "[r]emember the Ladies," she also points out
   that "all Men would be tyrants if they could" (para. 9) and that "your Sex are Naturally Tyrannical" (para. 10). How does she make such statements without sounding accusatory or alienating her husband? Explain.
4. Based on the details John provides in his letter to Abigail, what can you conclude
   about his attitude toward her?
5. When John tells Abigail that he "cannot but laugh" (para. 17) at her suggestions for
   laws, is he dismissing her? Is he disrespectful to her? Explain.
6. Is the last paragraph of John's letter written tongue-in-cheek, or is he serious? What
   does he mean by "the Despotism of the Peticoat"? How do you interpret this ending?

7. Describe the overall tone of each of these letters. Based on the tone and the information in the letters, describe the relationship between John and Abigail Adams. What evidence of intimacy do you find in each letter?
8. Imagine that Abigail and John Adams had access to e-mail, and rewrite these two letters as e-mail correspondence.

About Men

GRETEL EHRLICH

> In nearly everything that native Californian Gretel Ehrlich (b. 1946) writes, she reflects on the interaction of humans and their natural environment. After studying at Bennington College and New York University, she went to Wyoming as a documentary filmmaker and stayed for seventeen years. Her first book *The Solace of Open Spaces* (1984), written while she was working on a 250,000-acre ranch, describes her love for the land and people in that Western landscape. After being hit by lightning on the ranch, Ehrlich experienced an uncertain and slow recovery, which she chronicles in *A Match to the Heart* (1994). In addition, she is the author of *Questions from Heaven* (1994), a book begun as a spiritual journey to Buddhist shrines in China that evolved into a study of the effects of the Cultural Revolution; *This Cold Heaven: Seven Seasons in Greenland;* and *John Muir: Nature's Visionary* (2000). The following essay from *The Solace of Open Spaces* compares the popular view of the cowboy with Ehrlich's own experiences.

When I'm in New York but feeling lonely for Wyoming I look for the Marlboro ads in the subway. What I'm aching to see is horseflesh, the glint of a spur, a line of distant mountains, brimming creeks, and a reminder of the ranchers and cowboys I've ridden with for the last eight years. But the men I see in those posters with their stern, humorless looks remind me of no one I know here. In our hellbent earnestness to romanticize the cowboy we've ironically disesteemed his true character. If he's "strong and silent" it's because there's probably no one to talk to. If he "rides away into the sunset" it's because he's been on horseback since four in the morning moving cattle and he's trying, fifteen hours later, to get home to his family. If he's "a rugged individualist" he's also part of a team: ranch work is teamwork and even the glorified open-range cowboys of the 1880s rode up and down the Chisholm Trail in the company of twenty or thirty other riders. Instead of the macho, trigger-happy man our culture has perversely wanted him to be, the cowboy is more apt to be convivial, quirky, and softhearted. To be "tough" on a ranch has nothing to do with conquests and displays of power. More often than not, circumstances — like the colt he's riding or an unexpected blizzard — are overpowering him. It's not toughness but "toughing it out" that counts. In other words, this macho, cultural artifact the cowboy has become is simply a man who possesses resilience, patience, and an instinct for survival. "Cowboys are just like a pile of rocks — everything happens to them. They get climbed on, kicked, rained and snowed on, scuffed up by wind. Their job is 'just to take it,'" one old-timer told me.

A cowboy is someone who loves his work. Since the hours are long — ten to fifteen hours a day — and the pay is $30 he has to. What's required of him is an odd mixture of physical vigor and maternalism. His part of the beef-raising industry is to birth and nurture calves and take care of their mothers. For the most part his work is done on horseback and in a lifetime he sees and comes to know more animals than people. The iconic myth surrounding him is built on American notions of heroism: the index of a man's value as measured in physical courage. Such ideas have perverted manliness into a self-absorbed race for cheap thrills. In a rancher's world, courage has less to do with facing danger than with acting spontaneously — usually on behalf of an animal or another rider. If a cow is stuck in a boghole he throws a loop around her neck, takes his dally (a half hitch around the saddle horn), and pulls her out with horsepower. If a calf is born sick, he may take her home, warm her in front of the kitchen fire, and massage her legs until dawn. One friend, whose favorite horse was trying to swim a lake with hobbles on, dove under water and cut her legs loose with a knife, then swam her to shore, his arm around her neck lifeguard-style, and saved her from drowning. Because these incidents are usually linked to someone or something outside himself, the westerner's courage is selfless, a form of compassion.

The physical punishment that goes with cowboying is greatly underplayed. Once fear is dispensed with, the threshold of pain rises to meet the demands of the job. When Jane Fonda asked Robert Redford (in the film *Electric Horseman*) if he was sick as he struggled to his feet one morning, he replied, "No, just bent." For once the movies had it right. The cowboys I was sitting with laughed in agreement. Cowboys are rarely complainers; they show their stoicism by laughing at themselves.

If a rancher or cowboy has been thought of as a "man's man" — laconic, hard-drinking, inscrutable — there's almost no place in which the balancing act between male and female, manliness and femininity, can be more natural. If he's gruff, handsome, and physically fit on the outside, he's androgynous at the core. Ranchers are midwives, hunters, nurturers, providers, and conservationists all at once. What we've interpreted as toughness — weathered skin, calloused hands, a squint in the eye and a growl in the voice — only masks the tenderness inside. "Now don't go telling me these lambs are cute," one rancher warned me the first day I walked into the football-field-sized lambing sheds. The next thing I knew he was holding a black lamb. "Ain't this little rat good-lookin'?"

So many of the men who came to the West were southerners — men looking 5 for work and a new life after the Civil War — that chivalrousness and strict codes of honor were soon thought of as western traits. There were very few women in Wyoming during territorial days, so when they did arrive (some as mail-order brides from places like Philadelphia) there was a stand-offishness between the sexes and a formality that persists now. Ranchers still tip their hats and say, "Howdy, ma'am" instead of shaking hands with me.

Even young cowboys are often evasive with women. It's not that they're Jekyll and Hyde creatures — gentle with animals and rough on women — but rather, that they don't know how to bring their tenderness into the house and lack the vocabulary to express the complexity of what they feel. Dancing wildly all night becomes a metaphor for the explosive emotions pent up inside, and when these are, on occasion, released, they're so battery-charged and potent that one caress of the face or one "I love you" will peal for a long while.

The geographical vastness and the social isolation here make emotional evolution seem impossible. Those contradictions of the heart between respectability, logic, and convention on the one hand, and impulse, passion, and intuition on the other, played out wordlessly against the paradisical beauty of the West, give cowboys a wide-eyed but drawn look. Their lips pucker up, not with kisses but with immutability. They may want to break out, staying up all night with a lover just to talk, but they don't know how and can't imagine what the consequences will be. Those rare occasions when they do bare themselves result in confusion. "I feel as if I'd sprained my heart," one friend told me a month after such a meeting.

My friend Ted Hoagland wrote, "No one is as fragile as a woman but no one is as fragile as a man." For all the women here who use "fragileness" to avoid work or as a sexual ploy, there are men who try to hide theirs, all the while clinging to an adolescent dependency on women to cook their meals, wash their clothes, and keep the ranch house warm in winter. But there is true vulnerability in evidence here. Because these men work with animals, not machines or numbers, because they live outside in landscapes of torrential beauty, because they are confined to a place and a routine embellished with awesome variables, because calves die in the arms that pulled others into life, because they go to the mountains as if on a pilgrimage to find out what makes a herd of elk tick, their strength is also a softness, their toughness, a rare delicacy.

Exploring the Text

1. Gretel Ehrlich opens with a reference to the Marlboro man, a lone and rugged-looking cowboy who represented Marlboro in its cigarette advertising for many years. With this reference and her description of the Wyoming landscape, what effect does she achieve in the first three sentences of her essay?
2. In the opening paragraph, Ehrlich puts several descriptions in quotation marks. Why? How does she treat each as a sort of counterargument?
3. In the first paragraph, Ehrlich claims that by romanticizing the cowboy, we have "disesteemed his true character" (para. 1). How does she define that "true character"?
4. What does Ehrlich mean when she calls the cowboy "an odd mixture of physical vigor and maternalism" (para. 2)?

5. In paragraphs 5 and 6, Ehrlich analyzes the cowboy's relationship with women. How has the cowboy's history defined the way he interacts with women?

6. How does the paradoxical statement by Ted Hoagland that "[n]o one is as fragile as a woman but no one is as fragile as a man" distill the points Ehrlich makes throughout the essay?

7. How does the syntax of the final sentence represent Ehrlich's purpose in this essay — that is, how does the form of this sentence emphasize the content?

8. Ehrlich describes a number of stereotypes of the cowboy. How do some of the classic cowboy movies (for example, John Wayne or Clint Eastwood films) embody these stereotypes? Do any of them challenge these stereotypes? Consider more contemporary depictions of cowboys in television and film. Which elements of the stereotypes remain? Which are challenged?

The Myth of the Latin Woman: I Just Met a Girl Named María

Judith Ortiz Cofer

Poet, novelist, and essayist Judith Ortiz Cofer was born in Puerto Rico in 1952 and grew up in New Jersey. She is currently the Regents' and Franklin Professor of English and Creative Writing at the University of Georgia. Among her many publications are the poetry collection *A Love Story Beginning in Spanish* (2005), the novel *The Meaning of Consuelo* (2004), her memoirs *Silent Dancing: A Partial Remembrance of a Puerto Rican Childhood* (1990), and *Woman in Front of the Sun: Becoming a Writer* (2000), and her collection of prose and poetry, *The Latin Deli* (1993). She has won many awards, including the Anisfield-Wolf Award for Race Relations and the Americas Award for Children's and Young Adult Literature; she was nominated for the Pulitzer Prize in 1989. In the following selection, originally published in *Glamour* in 1992, Cofer examines the impact of stereotyping.

On a bus trip to London from Oxford University where I was earning some graduate credits one summer, a young man, obviously fresh from a pub, spotted me and as if struck by inspiration went down on his knees in the aisle. With both hands over his heart he broke into an Irish tenor's rendition of "María" from *West Side Story*.[1] My politely amused fellow passengers gave his

---

[1] *West Side Story* was a Broadway musical (1957) and then a feature film (1961). Based on *Romeo and Juliet*, the story deals with the conflicts between two New York City gangs — a Puerto Rican gang and a white ethnic gang. The Puerto Rican actress Rita Moreno, mentioned later in this paragraph, had a major role in the movie. — Eds.

lovely voice the round of gentle applause it deserved. Though I was not quite as amused, I managed my version of an English smile: no show of teeth, no extreme contortions of the facial muscles — I was at this time of my life practicing reserve and cool. Oh, that British control, how I coveted it. But María had followed me to London, reminding me of a prime fact of my life; you can leave the Island, master the English language, and travel as far as you can, but if you are a Latina, especially one like me who so obviously belongs to Rita Moreno's gene pool, the Island travels with you.

This is sometimes a very good thing — it may win you that extra minute of someone's attention. But with some people, the same things can make *you* an island — not so much a tropical paradise as an Alcatraz, a place nobody wants to visit. As a Puerto Rican girl growing up in the United States and wanting like most children to "belong," I resented the stereotype that my Hispanic appearance called forth from many people I met.

Our family lived in a large urban center in New Jersey during the sixties, where life was designed as a microcosm of my parents' casas on the island. We spoke in Spanish, we ate Puerto Rican food bought at the bodega, and we practiced strict Catholicism complete with Saturday confession and Sunday mass at a church where our parents were accommodated into a one-hour Spanish mass slot, performed by a Chinese priest trained as a missionary for Latin America.

As a girl I was kept under strict surveillance, since virtue and modesty were, by cultural equation, the same as family honor. As a teenager I was instructed on how to behave as a proper señorita. But it was a conflicting message girls got, since the Puerto Rican mothers also encouraged their daughters to look and act like women and to dress in clothes our Anglo friends and their mothers found too "mature" for our age. It was, and is, cultural, yet I often felt humiliated when I appeared at an American friend's party wearing a dress more suitable to a semi-formal than to a playroom birthday celebration. At Puerto Rican festivities, neither the music nor the colors we wore could be too loud. I still experience a vague sense of letdown when I'm invited to a "party" and it turns out to be a marathon conversation in hushed tones rather than a fiesta with salsa, laughter, and dancing — the kind of celebration I remember from my childhood.

I remember Career Day in our high school, when teachers told us to come 5
dressed as if for a job interview. It quickly became obvious that to the barrio girls, "dressing up" sometimes meant wearing ornate jewelry and clothing that would be more appropriate (by mainstream standards) for the company Christmas party than as daily office attire. That morning I had agonized in front of my closet, trying to figure out what a "career girl" would wear because, essentially, except for Marlo Thomas on TV, I had no models on which to base my decision. I knew how to dress for school: at the Catholic school I attended we all wore uniforms; I knew how to dress for Sunday mass, and I knew what dresses to wear for parties at my relatives' homes. Though I do not recall the precise details of my Career Day outfit, it must have been a composite of the above choices. But I

remember a comment my friend (an Italian-American) made in later years that coalesced my impressions of that day. She said that at the business school she was attending the Puerto Rican girls always stood out for wearing "everything at once." She meant, of course, too much jewelry, too many accessories. On that day at school, we were simply made the negative models by the nuns who were them-selves not credible fashion experts to any of us. But it was painfully obvious to me that to the others, in their tailored skirts and silk blouses, we must have seemed "hopeless" and "vulgar." Though I now know that most adolescents feel out of step much of the time, I also know that for the Puerto Rican girls of my genera-tion that sense was intensified. The way our teachers and classmates looked at us that day in school was just a taste of the culture clash that awaited us in the real world, where prospective employers and men on the street would often misinter-pret our tight skirts and jingling bracelets as a come-on.

Mixed cultural signals have perpetuated certain stereotypes — for example, that of the Hispanic woman as the "Hot Tamale" or sexual firebrand. It is a one-dimensional view that the media have found easy to promote. In their special vocabulary, advertisers have designated "sizzling" and "smoldering" as the adjec-tives of choice for describing not only the foods but also the women of Latin America. From conversations in my house I recall hearing about the harassment that Puerto Rican women endured in factories where the "boss men" talked to them as if sexual innuendo was all they understood and, worse, often gave them the choice of submitting to advances or being fired.

It is custom, however, not chromosomes, that leads us to choose scarlet over pale pink. As young girls, we were influenced in our decisions about clothes and colors by the women — older sisters and mothers who had grown up on a tropi-cal island where the natural environment was a riot of primary colors, where showing your skin was one way to keep cool as well as to look sexy. Most impor-tant of all, on the island, women perhaps felt freer to dress and move more provocatively, since, in most cases, they were protected by the traditions, mores, and laws of a Spanish/Catholic system of morality and machismo whose main rule was: *You may look at my sister, but if you touch her I will kill you.* The extended family and church structure could provide a young woman with a circle of safety in her small pueblo on the island; if a man "wronged" a girl, everyone would close in to save her family honor.

This is what I have gleaned from my discussions as an adult with older Puerto Rican women. They have told me about dressing in their best party clothes on Saturday nights and going to the town's plaza to promenade with their girlfriends in front of the boys they liked. The males were thus given an opportunity to admire the women and to express their admiration in the form of *piropos*: eroti-cally charged street poems they composed on the spot. I have been subjected to a few piropos while visiting the Island, and they can be outrageous, although cus-tom dictates that they must never cross into obscenity. This ritual, as I understand it, also entails a show of studied indifference on the woman's part; if she is "decent," she must not acknowledge the man's impassioned words. So I do understand how things can be lost in translation. When a Puerto Rican girl dressed in her idea of what is attractive meets a man from the mainstream culture who has been trained to react to certain types of clothing as a sexual signal, a clash is likely to take place. The line I first heard based on this aspect of the myth happened when the boy who took me to my first formal dance leaned over to plant a sloppy overeager kiss painfully on my mouth, and when I didn't respond with sufficient passion said in a resentful tone: "I thought you Latin girls were supposed to mature early" — my first instance of being thought of as a fruit or vegetable — I was supposed to *ripen*, not just grow into womanhood like other girls.

It is surprising to some of my professional friends that some people, including those who should know better, still put others "in their place." Though rarer, these incidents are still commonplace in my life. It happened to me most recently during a stay at a very classy metropolitan hotel favored by young professional couples for their weddings. Late one evening after the theater, as I walked toward my room with my new colleague (a woman with whom I was coordinating an arts program), a middle-aged man in a tuxedo, a young girl in satin and lace on his arm, stepped directly into our path. With his champagne glass extended toward me, he exclaimed, "Evita!"

Our way blocked, my companion and I listened as the man half-recited, half-bellowed "Don't Cry for Me, Argentina." When he finished, the young girl said: "How about a round of applause for my daddy?" We complied, hoping this would bring the silly spectacle to a close. I was becoming aware that our little group was attracting the attention of the other guests. "Daddy" must have perceived this too, and he once more barred the way as we tried to walk past him. He began to shout-sing a ditty to the tune of "La Bamba" — except the lyrics were about a girl named María whose exploits all rhymed with her name and gonorrhea. The girl kept saying "Oh, Daddy" and looking at me with pleading eyes. She wanted me to laugh along with the others. My companion and I stood silently waiting for the man to end his offensive song. When he finished, I looked not at him but at his daughter. I advised her calmly never to ask her father what he had done in the army. Then I walked between them and to my room. My friend complimented me on my cool handling of the situation. I confessed to her that I really had wanted to push the jerk into the swimming pool. I knew that this same man — probably a corporate executive, well educated, even worldly by most standards — would not have been likely to regale a white woman with a dirty song in public. He would perhaps have checked his impulse by assuming that she could be somebody's wife or mother, or at least *somebody* who might take offense. But to him, I was just an Evita or a María: merely a character in his cartoon-populated universe.

Because of my education and my proficiency with the English language, I have acquired many mechanisms for dealing with the anger I experience. This was not true for my parents, nor is it true for the many Latin women working at menial jobs who must put up with stereotypes about our ethnic group such as:

10

"They make good domestics." This is another facet of the myth of the Latin woman in the United States. Its origin is simple to deduce. Work as domestics, waitressing, and factory jobs are all that's available to women with little English and few skills. The myth of the Hispanic menial has been sustained by the same media phenomenon that made "Mammy" from *Gone with the Wind* America's idea of the black woman for generations: María, the housemaid or counter girl, is now indelibly etched into the national psyche. The big and the little screens have presented us with the picture of the funny Hispanic maid, mispronouncing words and cooking up a spicy storm in a shiny California kitchen.

This media-engendered image of the Latina in the United States has been documented by feminist Hispanic scholars, who claim that such portrayals are partially responsible for the denial of opportunities for upward mobility among Latinas in the professions. I have a Chicana friend working on a Ph.D. in philosophy at a major university. She says her doctor still shakes his head in puzzled amazement at all the "big words" she uses. Since I do not wear my diplomas around my neck for all to see, I too have on occasion been sent to that "kitchen," where some think I obviously belong.

One such incident that has stayed with me, though I recognize it as a minor offense, happened on the day of my first public poetry reading. It took place in Miami in a boat-restaurant where we were having lunch before the event. I was nervous and excited as I walked in with my notebook in my hand. An older woman motioned me to her table. Thinking (foolish me) that she wanted me to autograph a copy of my brand-new slender volume of verse, I went over. She ordered a cup of coffee from me, assuming that I was the waitress. Easy enough to mistake my poems for menus, I suppose. I know that it wasn't an intentional act of cruelty, yet of all the good things that happened that day, I remember that scene most clearly, because it reminded me of what I had to overcome before anyone would take me seriously. In retrospect I understand that my anger gave my reading fire, that I have almost always taken doubts in my abilities as a challenge — and that the result is, most times, a feeling of satisfaction at having won a convert when I see the cold, appraising eyes warm to my words, the body language change, the smile that indicates that I have opened some avenue for communication. That day I read to that woman and her lowered eyes told me that she was embarrassed at her little faux pas, and when I willed her to look up at me, it was my victory, and she graciously allowed me to punish her with my full attention. We shook hands at the end of the reading, and I never saw her again. She has probably forgotten the whole thing but maybe not.

Yet I am one of the lucky ones. My parents made it possible for me to acquire a stronger footing in the mainstream culture by giving me the chance at an education. And books and art have saved me from the harsher forms of ethnic and racial prejudice that many of my Hispanic *compañeras* have had to endure. I travel a lot around the United States, reading from my books of poetry and my novel, and the reception I most often receive is one of positive interest by people who want to know more about my culture. There are, however, thousands of Latinas without the privilege of an education or the entrée into society that I have. For them life is a struggle against the misconceptions perpetuated by the myth of the Latina as whore, domestic or criminal. We cannot change this by legislating the way people look at us. The transformation, as I see it, has to occur at a much more individual level. My personal goal in my public life is to try to replace the old pervasive stereotypes and myths about Latinas with a much more interesting set of realities. Every time I give a reading, I hope the stories I tell, the dreams and fears I examine in my work, can achieve some universal truth which will get my audience past the particulars of my skin color, my accent, or my clothes.

I once wrote a poem in which I called us Latinas "God's brown daughters." 15 This poem is really a prayer of sorts, offered upward, but also, through the human-to-human channel of art, outward. It is a prayer for communication, and for respect. In it, Latin women pray "in Spanish to an Anglo God / With a Jewish heritage," and they are "fervently hoping / that if not omnipotent / at least He be bilingual."

Exploring the Text

1. What is the effect of Judith Ortiz Cofer's opening paragraph? Does her anger draw you in or distance you?
2. Note the times when Cofer explains rather than denies the basis for stereotyping. For instance, rather than deny that Latinas prefer vivid colors, she explains that this preference reflects the bright landscape of their homelands. Does this strategy work, or do you think Cofer is playing to the stereotype?
3. Note the sections of the essay that refer to personal experience. Does Cofer's use of personal experience weaken her argument or make it more effective? Explain. Would the essay be more effective with less — or more — personal experience? Explain your view.
4. What do Cofer's experiences on the bus, in the hotel, and at the poetry reading have in common? Could she have omitted any of them from her essay? Do you find her behavior toward the man in the "very classy metropolitan hotel" unnecessarily cruel? Explain.
5. How does Cofer broaden the argument from her personal experience to larger concerns, including other stereotypes (or stereotypes of other communities)?
6. Cofer ends by quoting one of her own poems. Is this effective? Why or why not?
7. Who do you think is Cofer's audience for this essay? Does it include the woman at the poetry reading who asks Cofer for a cup of coffee?
8. According to Cofer, "Mixed cultural signals have perpetuated certain stereotypes — for example, that of the Hispanic woman as the 'Hot Tamale' or sexual firebrand. It is a one-dimensional view that the media have found easy to promote. In their special vocabulary, advertisers have designated 'sizzling' and 'smoldering'

as the adjectives of choice for describing not only the foods but also the women of Latin America" (para. 6). Does this assertion — that the media promotes stereo-types — apply today? In answering, consider Cofer's example of Latin American women, or choose another group, such as African Americans, older people, or people from the Middle East.

JUDITH ORTIZ COFER ON WRITING

In this interview, writer Judith Ortiz Cofer, whose essay "The Myth of the Latin Woman" appears on page 370, talks about her writing patterns and how she writes and revises.

Renée Shea (RS): In your essay "5:00 A.M." (in *The Latin Deli*), you said that you carved out writing time for yourself by reserving 5 to 7 A.M. every day, starting when your daughter was a baby. Do you still do that?

Judith Ortiz Cofer (JOC): I do — mainly because I've trained myself. As a child of working-class immigrants, I was determined to get a college education, but I also knew I wanted a family of my own. Then I realized I also needed art in my life. I needed writing. It's hard to explain without sounding mystical. It wasn't some feathered creature that came to tell me I was a writer, but I felt a physical, intellectual, and emotional need to write. I have talked to dancers and athletes who say they have this same feeling.

People who run or do one thing obsessively or compulsively at a certain hour find that it becomes a need. I find that my best work comes when I have not spoken to anyone yet — when I've just been asleep the whole night before, I can easily move into this realm right from dreams. It doesn't always end at 7 now because I have more leisure [since my daughter is an adult], but I find that about three hours at a time is all I can do.

RS: How do you get started on days or at times when you just don't feel the muse, just do not feel like writing a word?

JOC: Let me quote three writers:

All my major works have been written in prison . . . I would recommend prison not only to aspiring writers but to politicians too.

—Jawaharlal Nehru

Touch the page at your peril: it is you who are blank and innocent. Nevertheless you want to know, nothing will stop you. You touch the page, it's as if you've drawn a knife across it, the page has been hurt now, a sinuous wound opens, a thin incision. Darkness wells through.

— MARGARET ATWOOD

The page, the page, that eternal blankness, the blankness of eternity which you cover slowly, affirming time's scrawl as a right and your daring as necessity.

— ANNIE DILLARD

These quotations contain two words that come to my mind on the days I cannot work: *prison* and *darkness*.

I work in the dark, literally. I get up at 5 A.M., drink a lot of coffee, then go to my table. I turn on one small light over my work. The world disappears around the blank page. The darkness shields me from distractions. Most days, the blank page beckons to me. I have a plan, an idea; it will not be blank for long. Other times, the blank page is a dreaded sight, an accusation, a reminder of my limits, a demand I cannot meet. I stare at it; it stares back. I blink first.

On the days when I cannot make myself create, I still stay at my post, within a small circle of light, surrounded by the dark. I prepare myself for these blank days by having within my reach work that I *can* do when I cannot summon an original thought into my head: I can revise the previous day's work, I can take notes on what I wish to work on, I can read from works that I wish I had written, take notes on how to do what I wish I were doing; I can focus on what I need to do as soon as I can. I stay at my post for the duration of the time I had allotted my work. Two to three hours if I can manage it. I do not admit defeat until my time is up. I keep trying to work. Most important of all for me is keeping the promise I made to myself many years ago — that in each of my workdays there would be a place and a time dedicated solely to my writing, and that with the exception of emergency, illness, fire, or other major disasters, I would be there, writing, trying to write, thinking about writing, never giving it up to any other activity. Eventually I face the blank page with excitement again. I never know if I will be able to do good work. I only know that I have to be ready at my workstation, or it will certainly never happen.

RS: How do you know when what you've written is finished?

JOC: The key to perfecting a piece of work is to rewrite it and rewrite it until you hardly recognize the end product. I go through many many drafts. In fact, I just mailed out a poem that's gone through seventeen drafts! Revision meant changing one word, ending a line differently, adding a comma. There's no room for sloppiness, so if you have an excess word or anything wrong in a poem, it's as evident as a false note in a musical piece. With prose, it's finished when I read it aloud and it sounds to me as I want it to sound to others. Then I let a couple of other people read it, people I trust. After I get their opinion, I either make the revisions or not and then send it out. It's finished when I have reached my level of *incompetence*: I look at it and look at it and cannot think of anything else to do to it.

Follow-up

After you have read the interview, describe your own patterns as a writer. Do you write best at a specific time of day? Do you need utter quiet, or do you prefer writing with music or conversations in the background? Do you read your work aloud to yourself or share it with another person? When do you know you're finished? Find a quotation about writing that applies to (or inspires) you.

Being a Man

PAUL THEROUX

Paul Theroux (b. 1941) grew up in Massachusetts and graduated from the University of Massachusetts, but he has lived in and written about Malawi and Uganda in Africa and about Singapore, among other places. Theroux has written numerous novels, including *The Mosquito Coast* (1981) and *Dr. Slaughter* (1984), which were made into films. *The Great Railway Bazaar* (1975), a travel novel, became a best seller. Theroux divides his time between Cape Cod and Hawaii, where he has taken up a second profession as a beekeeper. In the following essay, part of the collection *Sunrise with Seamonsters* (1985), Theroux examines society's views of masculinity.

There is a pathetic sentence in the chapter "Fetishism" in Dr. Norman Cameron's book *Personality Development and Psychopathology*. It goes, "Fetishists are nearly always men; and their commonest fetish is a woman's shoe." I cannot read that sentence without thinking that it is just one more awful thing about being a man — and perhaps it is an important thing to know about us.

I have always disliked being a man. The whole idea of manhood in America is pitiful, in my opinion. This version of masculinity is a little like having to wear an ill-fitting coat for one's entire life (by contrast, I imagine femininity to be an oppressive sense of nakedness). Even the expression "Be a man!" strikes me as insulting and abusive. It means: Be stupid, be unfeeling, obedient, soldierly and stop thinking. Man means "manly" — how can one think about men without considering the terrible ambition of manliness? And yet it is part of every man's life. It is a hideous and crippling lie; it not only insists on difference and connives at superiority, it is also by its very nature destructive — emotionally damaging and socially harmful.

The youth who is subverted, as most are, into believing in the masculine ideal is effectively separated from women and he spends the rest of his life finding women a riddle and a nuisance. Of course, there is a female version of this male affliction. It begins with mothers encouraging little girls to say (to other adults) "Do you like my new dress?" In a sense, little girls are traditionally urged to please adults with a kind of coquettishness, while boys are enjoined to behave like monkeys towards each other. The nine-year-old coquette proceeds to become womanish in a subtle power game in which she learns to be sexually indispensable, socially decorative and always alert to a man's sense of inadequacy.

Femininity — being lady-like — implies needing a man as witness and seducer; but masculinity celebrates the exclusive company of men. That is why it is so grotesque; and that is also why there is no manliness without inadequacy — because it denies men the natural friendship of women.

It is very hard to imagine any concept of manliness that does not belittle 5 women, and it begins very early. At an age when I wanted to meet girls — let's say the treacherous years of thirteen to sixteen — I was told to take up a sport, get more fresh air, join the Boy Scouts, and I was urged not to read so much. It was the 1950s and if you asked too many questions about sex you were sent to camp — boy's camp, of course: the nightmare. Nothing is more unnatural or prison-like than a boy's camp, but if it were not for them we would have no Elks' Lodges, no pool rooms, no boxing matches, no Marines.

And perhaps no sports as we know them. Everyone is aware of how few in number are the athletes who behave like gentlemen. Just as high school basketball teaches you how to be a poor loser, the manly attitude towards sports seems to be little more than a recipe for creating bad marriages, social misfits, moral degenerates, sadists, latent rapists and just plain louts. I regard high school sports as a drug far worse than marijuana, and it is the reason that the average tennis champion, say, is a pathetic oaf.

Any objective study would find the quest for manliness essentially rightwing, puritanical, cowardly, neurotic and fueled largely by a fear of women. It is also certainly philistine. There is no book-hater like a Little League coach. But indeed all the creative arts are obnoxious to the manly ideal, because at their best the arts are pursued by uncompetitive and essentially solitary people. It makes it very hard for a creative youngster, for any boy who expresses the desire to be alone seems to be saying that there is something wrong with him.

It ought to be clear by now that I have something of an objection to the way we turn boys into men. It does not surprise me that when the President of the United States has his customary weekend off he dresses like a cowboy — it is both a measure of his insecurity and his willingness to please. In many ways, American culture does little more for a man than prepare him for modeling clothes in the L. L. Bean catalogue. I take this as a personal insult because for many years I found it impossible to admit to myself that I wanted to be a writer. It was my guilty secret, because being a writer was incompatible with being a man.

There are people who might deny this, but that is because the American writer, typically, has been so at pains to prove his manliness that we have come to see literariness and manliness as mingled qualities. But first there was a fear that writing was not a manly profession — indeed, not a profession at all. (The paradox in American letters is that it has always been easier for a woman to write and for a man to be published.) Growing up, I had thought of sports as wasteful and humiliating, and the idea of manliness was a bore. My wanting to become a writer was not a flight from that oppressive role-playing, but I quickly saw that it was at odds with it. Everything in stereotyped manliness goes against the life of the mind. The Hemingway personality is too tedious to go into here, and in any case his exertions are well-known, but certainly it was not until this aberrant behavior was examined by feminists in the 1960s that any male writer dared question the pugnacity in Hemingway's fiction. All the bullfighting and arm wrestling and elephant shooting diminished Hemingway as a writer, but it is consistent with a prevailing attitude in American writing: one cannot be a male writer without first proving that one is a man.

It is normal in America for a man to be dismissive or even somewhat apologetic about being a writer. Various factors make it easier. There is a heartiness about journalism that makes it acceptable — journalism is the manliest form of American writing and, therefore, the profession the most independent-minded women seek (yes, it is an illusion, but that is my point). Fiction-writing is equated with a kind of dispirited failure and is only manly when it produces wealth — money is masculinity. So is drinking. Being a drunkard is another assertion, if misplaced, of manliness. The American male writer is traditionally proud of his heavy drinking. But we are also a very literal-minded people. A man proves his manhood in America in old-fashioned ways. He kills lions, like Hemingway; or he hunts ducks, like Nathanael West; or he makes pronouncements like, "A man should carry enough knife to defend himself with," as James Jones once said to a *Life* interviewer. Or he says he can drink you under the table. But even tiny drunken William Faulkner loved to mount a horse and go fox hunting, and Jack Kerouac roistered up and down Manhattan in a lumberjack shirt (and spent

10

every night of *The Subterraneans*[1] with his mother in Queens). And we are familiar with the lengths to which Norman Mailer[2] is prepared, in his endearing way, to prove that he is just as much a monster as the next man.

When the novelist John Irving was revealed as a wrestler, people took him to be a very serious writer; and even a bubble reputation like Erich (*Love Story*) Segal's was enhanced by the news that he ran the marathon in a respectable time. How surprised we would be if Joyce Carol Oates were revealed as a sumo wrestler or Joan Didion active in pumping iron. "Lives in New York City with her three children" is the typical woman writer's biographical note, for just as the male writer must prove he has achieved a sort of muscular manhood, the woman writer — or rather her publicists — must prove her motherhood.

There would be no point in saying any of this if it were not generally accepted that to be a man is somehow — even now in feminist-influenced America — a privilege. It is on the contrary an unmerciful and punishing burden. Being a man is bad enough; being manly is appalling (in this sense, women's lib has done much more for men than for women). It is the sinister silliness of men's fashions, and a clubby attitude in the arts. It is the subversion of good students. It is the so-called "Dress Code" of the Ritz-Carlton Hotel in Boston, and it is the institutionalized cheating in college sports. It is the most primitive insecurity.

And this is also why men often object to feminism but are afraid to explain why: of course women have a justified grievance, but most men believe — and with reason — that their lives are just as bad.

Exploring the Text

1. What is the effect of the opening paragraph? Does it encourage you to read on? Does it provoke you? Does it intrigue you?

2. So much of this essay consists of negative descriptions of what it means to Paul Theroux to be masculine or a man. Why does he offer such strong images and assertions?

3. Note the parenthetical comments. What do they contribute to the essay? Are they rhetorically effective, or could they have been omitted?

4. How does Theroux prepare his readers for the turn the essay takes in paragraph 12 when he says, "There would be no point in saying any of this if it were not generally accepted that to be a man is somehow — even now in feminist-influenced America — a privilege." What does this reveal about Theroux's overall purpose in this piece?

---

[1] *The Subterraneans* is a 1960 film based on Jack Kerouac's novel about the lifestyle of 1950s Beats. — Eds.

[2] Norman Mailer is an American journalist and novelist. — Eds.

5. How would you describe the tone of Theroux's essay? Answer using a phrase instead of one word. Cite specific passages to support your description.
6. Do you agree or disagree with Theroux when he writes, "It is very hard to imagine any concept of manliness that does not belittle women, and it begins very early" (para. 5)? Explain.
7. In paragraph 6, Theroux describes the negative consequences of participating in competitive sports. Do you agree with him? How does the increase in women's participation in such sports affect his argument?
8. Theroux's essay was written in 1983. Which of his points are outdated? Which remain true today?

AIDS Has a Woman's Face

STEPHEN LEWIS

> Stephen Lewis (b. 1937), former Canadian ambassador to the United Nations, served as deputy director of UNICEF from 1995 to 1999. Since 2001, he has been the UN Special Envoy for HIV/AIDS in Africa, drawing attention to the HIV/AIDS crisis and calling for public responsibility. Lewis has set up his own charitable foundation, the Stephen Lewis Foundation. In the following keynote address, which Lewis delivered at the Microbicides 2004 Conference, he stresses the sexism he believes is at the heart of the pandemic.

There is, I will admit, a touch of amiable irrationality in racing across the ocean for a half hour speech. I want to assure you that I don't do it as a matter of course. But in this instance, it seemed to me that your kind invitation to address the Conference could not possibly be forfeited. I'm here because I think the work in which you're collectively engaged . . . the discovery and availability of microbicides . . . is one of the great causes of this era, and I want to be a part of it. It is in this room that morality and science will join together.

I've been in the Envoy job for nearly three years. If there is one constant throughout that time, a large part of which has been spent traversing the African continent, it is the thus-far irreversible vulnerability of women. It goes without saying that the virus has targeted women with a raging and twisted Darwinian ferocity. It goes equally without saying that gender inequality is what sustains and nurtures the virus, ultimately causing women to be infected in ever greater disproportionate numbers.

And the numbers tell a story. It was the report issued by UNAIDS on the eve of the International AIDS Conference in Barcelona in 2002 that identified the startling percentages of infected women. And it was during a panel, at the same conference, when Carol Bellamy of UNICEF used a phrase — for the first time in my hearing — that was to become a repetitive mantra: "AIDS has a woman's face."

But the problem is that the phenomenon of women's acute vulnerability did not happen overnight. It grew relentlessly over the twenty years of the pandemic. What should shock us all, what should stop us in our tracks, is how long it took to focus the world on what was happening. Why wasn't the trend identified so much earlier? Why, when it emerged in cold statistical print did not the emergency alarm bells ring out in the narrative text which accompanied the numbers? Why has it taken to 2004 — more than twenty years down the epidemiological road — to put in place a Global Coalition on Women and AIDS? Why was it only in 2003 that a UN Task Force on the plight of women in Southern Africa was appointed to do substantive work? Why have we allowed a continuing pattern of sexual carnage among young women so grave as to lose an entire generation of women and girls?

Ponder this set of figures if you will: in 2003, Botswana did a new sentinel site   5
study to establish HIV prevalence, male and female, amongst all age groups. In urban areas, for young women and girls, ages 15 to 19, the prevalence rate was 15.4%. For young men and boys of the same age, it was 1.2%. For young women between 20 and 24, the rate was 29.7%. For young men of that age it was 8.4%. For young women between the ages of 25 and 29, the rate was 54.1% (it boggles the mind); for young men of the same age, it was 29.7%.

Have I not addressed the fundamental question? The reason we have observed — and still observe without taking decisive action — this wanton attack on women is because it's women. You know it and I know it. The African countries themselves, the major external powers, the influential bilateral donors, even my beloved United Nations. No one shouted from the rhetorical rooftops, no one called an international conference and said what in God's name is going on, even though it felt in the 1990s that all we ever had time for were international conferences? It amounts to the ultimate vindication of the feminist analysis. When the rights of women are involved, the world goes into reverse.

For more than twenty years, the numbers of infected women grew exponentially, so that now virtually half the infections in the world are amongst women, and in Africa it stands at 58%, rising to 67% between the ages of 15 and 24. This is a cataclysm, plain and simple. We are depopulating parts of the continent of its women.

And while finally, after the doomsday clock has passed midnight, we're starting to be engaged and agitated, very little is changing. Please believe me: on the ground, where women live and die, very little is changing. Everything takes so excruciatingly long when we're responding to the needs and rights of women.

Between three and four years ago, I visited the well-known pre-natal health clinic in Kigali, Rwanda. I met with three women who had decided to take a course of nevirapine; they were excited and hopeful, but they asked a poignant question which haunts me to this day: they said "We'll do anything to save our babies, but what about us?" Back then, more than four years after antiretrovirals were in widespread use in the west, we simply watched the mothers die.

Well, thanks to the Columbia School of Public Health, funded by several Foundations and USAID, and working with the Elizabeth Glazer Foundation, UNICEF and governments, the strategy of PMTCT PLUS (Prevention of Mother to Child Transmission Plus) has been carefully put into place in several countries, where the "Plus" represents treatment of the mothers and partners; indeed, of the entire family. But it's a slow process, and though Columbia will roll it out as quickly as possible, it is necessarily incremental. In principle, the majority of such women will one day fall under the rubric of public antiretroviral treatment, through Ministries of Health, when it's finally introduced in most countries. But there's no clear guarantee of when that day will dawn, or that women will get the treatment to which they're entitled. It's entirely possible that the men will be at the front of the bus.

Everything proceeds at glacial speed for women, if it proceeds at all, in the face of this global health emergency.

And that's what I want to drive home. We deplore the patterns of sexual violence against women, violence which transmits the virus, but all you have to do is read the remarkable monographs by Human Rights Watch to know that for all the earnest blather, the same malevolent patterns continue. We lament the use of rape as an instrument of war, passing the virus, one hideous assault upon another, but in Eastern Congo and Western Sudan, possibly the worst episodes of sexual cruelty and mutilation are taking place on a daily basis as anywhere in the world, and the world is raising barely a finger. We have the women victims of Rwanda, now suffering full-blown AIDS, to show the ending of that story. We talk ad nauseam of amending property rights and introducing laws on inheritance rights, but I've yet to see marked progress. We speak of empowering women, and paying women for unacknowledged and uncompensated work, and ushering in a cornucopia of income generating activities . . . and in tiny pockets it's happening, especially where an indigenous local women's leadership is strong enough to take hold . . . but for the most part, in Churchill's phrase, it's all "Jaw, Jaw, Jaw."

For much of my adult life, I have felt that the struggle for gender equality is the toughest struggle of all, and never have I felt it more keenly than in the battle against HIV/AIDS. The women of Africa and beyond: they run the household, they grow the food, they assume virtually the entire burden of care, they look after the orphans, they do it all with an almost unimaginable stoicism, and as recompense for a life of almost supernatural hardship and devotion, they die agonizing deaths.

Undoubtedly — and I must acknowledge this — with the sudden growing awareness internationally of what the virus hath wrought, we will all make increasing efforts to rally to the side of women. It's entirely possible that we will make more progress over the next five years than we have made in the past twenty. But I cannot emphasize strongly enough that the inertia and sexism which plague our response are incredibly, almost indelibly engrained, and in this desperate race against time we will continue to lose vast numbers of women. That is not to suggest for a moment that we shouldn't make every conceivable effort to turn the tide; it is only to acknowledge the terrible reality of what we're up against.

People say to me, Stephen what about the men? We have to work with the men. Of course we do. But please recognize that it's going to take generations to change predatory male sexual behaviour, and the women of Africa don't have generations. They're dying today, now, day in and day out. Something dramatic has to happen which turns the talk of generations into mere moments in the passage of time.

And that, ladies and gentlemen, is where all of you come in. I'm not pretending that microbicides are a magic bullet. Microbicides aren't a vaccine. Nor do I dispute the powerful point made . . . at the opening of the conference, that we can neither forget nor diminish the structural cultural changes so urgently required. But when so many interventions have failed, when the landscape for women is so bleak, the prospect of a microbicide in five to ten years is positively intoxicating.

The idea that women will have a way of re-asserting control over their own sexuality, the idea that they will be able to defend their bodily health, the idea that women will have a course of prevention to follow which results in saving their lives, the idea that women may have a microbicide which prevents infection but allows for conception, the idea that women can use microbicides without bowing to male dictates — indeed the idea that men will not even know the microbicide is in use — these are ideas whose time has come.

For me, while microbicides are not a salvation, they come as close to salvation as anything else I've heard about. I pray that everyone at this conference understands that the women of Africa and many other parts of the world are counting on you. It is impossible to overstate how vital is the discovery of a microbicide. If we were making progress on several other fronts, microbicides would pale. But we're not making progress, or we are making progress in such painfully minute installments, that it feels as though we're moving from paralysis to immobility. The resources of the international community should flow, torrentially, into the hands of the scientists and researchers and advocates and activists assembled here who fight the good fight, because in those hands lies life.

I admit: I have a proclivity for hyperbole. It's a molecular disability, with one exception. This subject is the exception. I don't know how to convey to you what's happening out there. I move from country to country, from rural hinterland to rural hinterland, from project to project, and everywhere I go the lives of women are compromised. And it's not changing. How do you get governments and international financial institutions and bilateral development donors to understand? It's not changing. Three merciless years, and women face today exactly what they faced in yesteryear and yesteryear before that.

I travel and absorb incidents and moments that sear themselves into the mind. Some of the following anecdotes I've used before, but I cannot shake them. I meet a grandmother of 73 in Alexandria Township in Johannesburg. She lost all five of her children between 2001 and 2003. She's looking after four orphans, all of them HIV positive. Her life is in ruins. She stands for the legion of grandmothers on the continent who bury their children in a perverse reversal of the rhythm of life, and then, heroically, look after the grandchildren. How has it come to this?

I travel with Graça Machel to ground zero of the pandemic in Uganda, to visit a child headed household . . . a young girl of 14, looking after two sisters of 12 and 10, and two brothers of 11 and 8. Graça and I sit on the floor of the hut; I have the two boys on my left and Graça has the three girls on her right. She shoos everyone out of the hut except for one translator. And then she turns to the two older girls and in a gentle voice asks: "Have you started to menstruate yet?" And shyly, oh so shyly, in whispered fragments, the little girls say yes. And then Graça asks a series of questions: Do you know what it means? Do you talk to your teacher about it? Do you talk to the other kids at school? Do you talk to the villagers? Does anyone ever give you any pads? And as I sat there listening, I realized that these girls were receiving the first act of mothering around an experience that must surely be one of the most important moments of a young girl's life. And I thought to myself: this is what's happening across the continent: the mothers and fathers are gone. The mothers especially are gone. The transfer of knowledge, love and care from one generation to the next is going. How has it come to this?

I stand outside a clinic in Lusaka, Zambia, where mothers have come for testing, and the possible use of nevirapine during birth. The mothers approach me: "Mr. Lewis, you have drugs in your country to keep your people alive, why can't we have the drugs to keep ourselves alive?" I cannot tell you how often women have asked me that question. Their sense of collective dismay and vulnerability, their panic-stricken tremors at the prospect of leaving their children as orphans is palpable. I don't know how to answer the question. How do you explain that we're dealing with one of the ugliest chasms between the developing and developed world on the face of the planet? How did it come to this? How is it that we can't seem to get the world to understand that if you want to reduce the deluge of orphans, with which deluge no country can cope, you keep the mothers alive. Treatment is one way. Microbicides are the preferred way.

Just ten days ago, with my colleague Anurita Bains, who is here at the conference, I traveled to Swaziland. On a Thursday afternoon, we trekked into the hinterland to visit a small community of women living with AIDS, looking after hordes of orphan children. They led us along a narrow footpath, for what seemed an eternity, into the surrounding brush, until we'd reached the home of a woman who lay dying. I've spent a lot of time in huts where women lie dying; I don't know why this particular encounter had such a profound effect on me, but I haven't been able to get the image out of my head. I guess I've never seen anyone quite so ill before, the face a mask of death; a young woman in her twenties —

they're always in their twenties — valiantly raising her head a few inches to acknowledge the visitors. You touch her hand; utter soothing words; she's unaware. Sometimes I think I make such gestures more for my own benefit than for the person who's so desperately ill. And around her were children, watching her die. That's what children in Africa do: they don't become orphans after their parents die; they become orphans while their parents are dying; and then they watch the death itself; and then they attend the funeral.

How has it come to this?

For myself, I'm filled with rage. I can barely contain it. I know it reduces my   25
effectiveness, but there's nothing I can do about it. The madness of what is happening, the fact that it is so completely unnecessary, the fact that we could subdue this pandemic if the world put its mind to it — all of that renders me almost incoherent with the roiling blood of anger. We must find a way to bring this nightmare to an end. Africans and the world will obviously work with every instrument at our collective command to reduce the heart-breaking decimation of individuals, families and communities. But the women, certainly the women of Africa need huge quotients of additional help, and that help lies, in significant extent, in the discovery of a microbicide.

I don't have to tell anyone here — God knows, I'm way out of my depth — about the science and the trials and the timetable and the resources. I've read the materials, and as much as a layperson can grasp such things, I have grasped them. I ask only that you see microbicides, not merely as one of the great scientific pursuits of the age, but as a significant emancipation for women whose cultural and social and economic inheritance have put them so gravely at risk.

Never in human history have so many died for so little reason. You have a chance to alter the course of that history. Can there be any task more noble?

Exploring the Text

1. At the outset of his speech, Stephen Lewis says the availability of microbicides is "where morality and science join." Discuss how the rest of the speech demonstrates the joining of moral and scientific concerns.
2. Lewis delivers an impassioned speech, yet it contains statistical and other factual information. Does he balance appeals to emotion and reason, or does one outweigh the other? Cite specific passages to discuss how he appeals to both. Would the speech have been more effective had Lewis been more objective?
3. In paragraph 6, Lewis confronts the international community's refusal to acknowledge and act upon what he calls "this wanton attack on women." Why does he claim that this "amounts to the ultimate vindication of the feminist analysis"?
4. Lewis states the counterargument quite starkly; that is, "We have to work with the men" (para. 15). How does he concede and refute this counterargument? Cite specific passages.
5. Discuss at least four rhetorical strategies found in paragraph 12.

6. Discuss the various ways in which Lewis establishes his ethos: as a diplomat and public servant, as a nonscientist, as a man, as a citizen of the world. Cite specific passages that support these personae.

7. Lewis writes, "For myself, I'm filled with rage" (para. 25). He goes on to describe the level and manifestations of that rage. Do you believe this admission undermines or strengthens his argument? Explain.

8. Lewis's tone is complex. He moves between straightforward analysis and raw emotion, yet he is rarely ambivalent about his topic or his position. How would you describe his tone? Refer to specific words and passages to support your response, characterizing the tone as a phrase rather than a single word.

9. Would this speech have been more or less effective if its author were a woman — even one who holds the same professional position as Lewis does? Discuss.

10. Does AIDS still "have a woman's face"? Follow up on Lewis's research to see if the situation has changed.

There Is No Unmarked Woman

Deborah Tannen

A linguist by training, Deborah Tannen (b. 1945) is the best-selling author of more than fifteen books including *You Just Don't Understand: Women and Men in Conversation* (1990), in which she argues that "communication between men and women can be like cross-cultural communication, prey to a clash of conversational styles." She also wrote *Talking from 9 to 5: How Women's and Men's Conversational Styles Affect Who Gets Heard, Who Gets Credit, and What Gets Done at Work* (1995), *Women and Men in the Workplace: Language, Sex, and Power* (1994); *The Argument Culture: Moving from Debate to Dialogue* (1998); *I Only Say This Because I Love You: How the Way We Talk Can Make or Break Family Relationships throughout Our Lives* (2001); and *You're Wearing That? Understanding Mothers and Daughters in Conversation* (2005). Winner of numerous fellowships and awards, Dr. Tannen is a professor of linguistics at Georgetown University. The following essay is part of a longer piece Tannen wrote for the *New York Times*, "Wears Jump Suit. Sensible Shoes. Uses Husband's Last Name." She contrasts the impact that appearance, especially clothing, has in perceptions of men and women.

Some years ago I was at a small working conference of four women and eight men. Instead of concentrating on the discussion I found myself looking at the three other women at the table, thinking how each had a different style and how each style was coherent.

One woman had dark brown hair in a classic style, a cross between Cleopatra and Plain Jane. The severity of her straight hair was softened by wavy bangs and ends that turned under. Because she was beautiful, the effect was more Cleopatra than plain.

The second woman was older, full of dignity and composure. Her hair was cut in a fashionable style that left her with only one eye, thanks to a side part that let a curtain of hair fall across half her face. As she looked down to read her pre-pared paper, the hair robbed her of bifocal vision and created a barrier between her and the listeners.

The third woman's hair was wild, a frosted blond avalanche falling over and beyond her shoulders. When she spoke she frequently tossed her head, calling attention to her hair and away from her lecture.

Then there was makeup. The first woman wore facial cover that made her skin smooth and pale, a black line under each eye and mascara that darkened already dark lashes. The second wore only a light gloss on her lips and a hint of shadow on her eyes. The third had blue bands under her eyes, dark blue shadow, mascara, bright red lipstick, and rouge; her fingernails flashed red.

I considered the clothes each woman had worn during the three days of the conference: In the first case, man-tailored suits in primary colors with solid-color blouses. In the second, casual but stylish black T-shirts, a floppy collarless jacket and baggy slacks or a skirt in neutral colors. The third wore a sexy jumpsuit; tight sleeveless jersey and tight yellow slacks; a dress with gaping armholes and an indulged tendency to fall off one shoulder.

Shoes? No. 1 wore string sandals with medium heels; No. 2, sensible, com-fortable walking shoes; No. 3, pumps with spike heels. You can fill in the jewelry, scarves, shawls, sweaters — or lack of them.

As I amused myself finding coherence in these styles, I suddenly wondered why I was scrutinizing only the women. I scanned the eight men at the table. And then I knew why I wasn't studying them. The men's styles were unmarked.

The term "marked" is a staple of linguistic theory. It refers to the way language alters the base meaning of a word by adding a linguistic particle that has no meaning on its own. The unmarked form of a word carries the meaning that goes without saying — what you think of when you're not thinking anything special.

The unmarked tense of verbs in English is the present — for example, *visit.* To indicate past, you mark the verb by adding *ed* to yield *visited.* For future, you add a word: *will visit.* Nouns are presumed to be singular until marked for plural, typically by adding *s* or *es,* so *visit* becomes *visits* and *dish* becomes *dishes.*

The unmarked forms of most English words also convey "male." Being male is the unmarked case. Endings like *ess* and *ette* mark words as "female." Unfortu-nately, they also tend to mark them for frivolousness. Would you feel safe entrust-ing your life to a doctorette? Alfre Woodard, who was an Oscar nominee for best supporting actress, says she identifies herself as an actor because "actresses worry about eyelashes and cellulite, and women who are actors worry about the charac-ters we are playing." Gender markers pick up extra meanings that reflect common associations with the female gender: not quite serious, often sexual.

Each of the women at the conference had to make decisions about hair, clothing, makeup, and accessories, and each decision carried meaning. Every style available to us was marked. The men in our group had made decisions, too, but the range from which they chose was incomparably narrower. Men can choose styles that are marked, but they don't have to, and in this group none did. Unlike the women, they had the option of being unmarked.

Take the men's hair styles. There was no marine crew cut or oily longish hair falling into eyes, no asymmetrical, two-tiered construction to swirl over a bald top. One man was unabashedly bald; the others had hair of standard length, parted on one side, in natural shades of brown or gray or graying. Their hair obstructed no views, left little to toss or push back or run fingers through and, consequently, needed and attracted no attention. A few men had beards. In a business setting, beards might be marked. In this academic gathering, they weren't.

There could have been a cowboy shirt with string tie or a three-piece suit or a necklaced hippie in jeans. But there wasn't. All eight men wore brown or blue slacks and nondescript shirts of light colors. No man wore sandals or boots; their shoes were dark, closed, comfortable, and flat. In short, unmarked.

Although no man wore makeup, you couldn't say the men didn't wear   15
makeup in the sense that you could say a woman didn't wear makeup. For men, no makeup is unmarked.

I asked myself what style we women could have adopted that would have been unmarked, like the men's. The answer was none. There is no unmarked woman.

There is no woman's hairstyle that can be called standard, that says nothing about her. The range of women's hairstyles is staggering, but a woman whose hair has no particular style is perceived as not caring about how she looks, which can disqualify her from many positions, and will subtly diminish her as a person in the eyes of some.

Women must choose between attractive shoes and comfortable shoes. When our group made an unexpected trek, the woman who wore flat, laced shoes arrived first. Last to arrive was the woman in spike heels, shoes in hand and a handful of men around her.

If a woman's clothing is tight or revealing (in other words, sexy), it sends a message — an intended one of wanting to be attractive, but also a possibly unintended one of availability. If her clothes are not sexy, that too sends a message, lent meaning by the knowledge that they could have been. There are thousands of cosmetic products from which women can choose and myriad ways of applying them. Yet no makeup at all is anything but unmarked. Some men see it as a hostile refusal to please them.

Women can't even fill out a form without telling stories about themselves.   20
Most forms give four titles to choose from. "Mr." carries no meaning other than that the respondent is male. But a woman who checks "Mrs." or "Miss" communi-

cates not only whether she has been married but also whether she has conservative tastes in forms of address — and probably other conservative values as well. Checking "Ms." declines to let on about marriage (checking "Mr." declines nothing since nothing was asked), but it also marks her as either liberated or rebellious, depending on the observer's attitudes and assumptions.

I sometimes try to duck these variously marked choices by giving my title as "Dr." — and in so doing risk marking myself as either uppity (hence sarcastic responses like "Excuse *me*!") or an overachiever (hence reactions of congratulatory surprise like "Good for you!").

All married women's surnames are marked. If a woman takes her husband's name, she announces to the world that she is married and has traditional values. To some it will indicate that she is less herself, more identified by her husband's identity. If she does not take her husband's name, this too is marked, seen as worthy of comment: She has *done* something; she has "kept her own name." A man is never said to have "kept his own name" because it never occurs to anyone that he might have given it up. For him using his own name is unmarked.

A married woman who wants to have her cake and eat it too may use her surname plus his, with or without a hyphen. But this too announces her marital status and often results in a tongue-tying string. In a list (Harvey O'Donovan, Jonathan Feldman, Stephanie Woodbury McGillicutty), the woman's multiple name stands out. It is marked.

I have never been inclined toward biological explanations of gender differences in language, but I was intrigued to see Ralph Fasold bring biological phenomena to bear on the question of linguistic marking in his book *The Sociolinguistics of Language*. Fasold stresses that language and culture are particularly unfair in treating women as the marked case because biologically it is the male that is marked. While two X chromosomes make a female, two Y chromosomes make nothing. Like the linguistic markers *s*, *es*, or *ess*, the Y chromosome doesn't "mean" anything unless it is attached to a root form — an X chromosome.

Developing this idea elsewhere Fasold points out that girls are born with fully 25 female bodies, while boys are born with modified female bodies. He invites men who doubt this to lift up their shirts and contemplate why they have nipples.

In his book, Fasold notes "a wide range of facts which demonstrates that female is the unmarked sex." For example, he observes that there are a few species that produce only females, like the whiptail lizard. Thanks to parthenogenesis, they have no trouble having as many daughters as they like. There are no species, however, that produce only males. This is no surprise, since any such species would become extinct in its first generation.

Fasold is also intrigued by species that produce individuals not involved in reproduction, like honeybees and leaf-cutter ants. Reproduction is handled by the queen and a relatively few males; the workers are sterile females. "Since they do not reproduce," Fasold said, "there is no reason for them to be one sex or the other, so they default, so to speak, to female."

Fasold ends his discussion of these matters by pointing out that if language reflected biology, grammar books would direct us to use "she" to include males and females and "he" only for specifically male referents. But they don't. They tell us that "he" means "he or she," and that "she" is used only if the referent is specifically female. This use of "he" as the sex-indefinite pronoun is an innovation introduced into English by grammarians in the eighteenth and nineteenth centuries, according to Peter Mühlhäusler and Rom Harré in *Pronouns and People*. From at least about 1500, the correct sex-indefinite pronoun was "they," as it still is in casual spoken English. In other words, the female was declared by grammarians to be the marked case.

Writing this article may mark me not as a writer, not as a linguist, not as an analyst of human behavior, but as a feminist — which will have positive or negative, but in any case powerful, connotations for readers. Yet I doubt that anyone reading Ralph Fasold's book would put that label on him.

I discovered the markedness inherent in the very topic of gender after writing   30
a book on differences in conversational style based on geographical region, ethnicity, class, age, and gender. When I was interviewed, the vast majority of journalists wanted to talk about the differences between women and men. While I thought I was simply describing what I observed — something I had learned to do as a researcher — merely mentioning women and men marked me as a feminist for some.

When I wrote a book devoted to gender differences in ways of speaking, I sent the manuscript to five male colleagues, asking them to alert me to any interpretation, phrasing, or wording that might seem unfairly negative toward men. Even so, when the book came out, I encountered responses like that of the television talk show host who, after interviewing me, turned to the audience and asked if they thought I was male-bashing.

Leaping upon a poor fellow who affably nodded in agreement, she made him stand and asked, "Did what she say accurately describe you?" "Oh, yes," he answered. "That's me exactly." "And what she said about women — does that sound like your wife?" "Oh yes," he responded. "That's her exactly." "Then why do you think she's male-bashing?" He answered, with disarming honesty, "Because she's a woman and she's saying things about men."

To say anything about women and men without marking oneself as either feminist or anti-feminist, male-basher or apologist for men seems as impossible for a woman as trying to get dressed in the morning without inviting interpretations of her character.

Sitting at the conference table musing on these matters, I felt sad to think that we women didn't have the freedom to be unmarked that the men sitting next to us had. Some days you just want to get dressed and go about your business. But if you're a woman, you can't, because there is no unmarked woman.

Exploring the Text

1. What is the effect of opening the essay with elaborate descriptions of the women's dress?
2. Do Deborah Tannen's references to her personal experiences strengthen or weaken the argument about marked versus unmarked people? Explain.
3. What is the effect of Tannen's turning to "biological explanations of gender differences in language" (para. 24)? Does this discussion support or challenge her thesis about marked women?
4. In paragraph 32, what is the impact of Tannen's presenting the television anecdote as a conversation rather than a straight narrative?
5. Identify examples of subjective description, technical explanation, personal opinion, and argumentative conclusions in the essay. How effective is Tannen in embedding a technical analysis into a social commentary? Discuss.
6. Tannen uses the framing, or envelope, technique — opening and closing an essay with the same reference, quotation, or anecdote. What effect does this have?
7. Tannen wrote this essay in 1993. Is it outdated, or is it even more relevant today? Consider her thesis in light of other cultures or ethnicities or time periods. In a country where women's choices in dress are restricted by social mores, for example, is Tannen's claim applicable?
8. In the last paragraph, Tannen argues that women should have the "freedom to be unmarked." What does she mean by this? Do you think an unmarked woman is possible in our culture today?

Sweat (fiction)

ZORA NEALE HURSTON

Zora Neale Hurston (1891–1960) came to prominence in the 1920s during the Harlem Renaissance, a flowering of African American culture. A novelist, folklorist, and anthropologist, she first gained attention with her short stories, including "Sweat" and "Spunk." She is best known for her novel *Their Eyes Were Watching God* (1937), set in Eatonville, Florida, where Hurston grew up; the town was the first incorporated African American community in the United States. Her writing is known for its celebration of African American folk culture, as well as its use of authentic vernacular speech. Hurston's other works include the novel *Jonah's Gourd Vine* (1934); her autobiography, *Dust Tracks on a Road* (1942); and an anthropological study of Jamaican and Haitian folk religion, *Tell My Horse* (1938). Hurston, who died in poverty, was all but forgotten until Alice Walker took an interest in her. Walker's essay "Looking for Zora," described her personal journey to find Hurston's unmarked grave. The publication of this essay prompted a resurgence of interest in Hurston, including republication of many of her books.

I

It was eleven o'clock of a Spring night in Florida. It was Sunday. Any other night, Delia Jones would have been in bed for two hours by this time. But she was a washwoman, and Monday morning meant a great deal to her. So she collected the soiled clothes on Saturday when she returned the clean things. Sunday night after church, she sorted and put the white things to soak. It saved her almost a half-day's start. A great hamper in the bedroom held the clothes that she brought home. It was so much neater than a number of bundles lying around.

She squatted on the kitchen floor beside the great pile of clothes, sorting them into small heaps according to color, and humming a song in a mournful key, but wondering through it all where Sykes, her husband, had gone with her horse and buckboard.

Just then something long, round, limp, and black fell upon her shoulders and slithered to the floor beside her. A great terror took hold of her. It softened her knees and dried her mouth so that it was a full minute before she could cry out or move. Then she saw that it was the big bull whip her husband liked to carry when he drove.

She lifted her eyes to the door and saw him standing there bent over with laughter at her fright. She screamed at him.

"Sykes, what you throw dat whip on me like dat? You know it would skeer me — looks just like a snake, an' you knows how skeered Ah is of snakes." 5

"Course Ah knowed it! That's how come Ah done it." He slapped his leg with his hand and almost rolled on the ground in his mirth. "If you such a big fool dat you got to have a fit over a earth worm or a string, Ah don't keer how bad Ah skeer you."

"You ain't got no business doing it. Gawd knows it's a sin. Some day Ah'm gointuh drop dead from some of yo' foolishness. 'Nother thing, where you been wid mah rig? Ah feeds dat pony. He ain't fuh you to be drivin' wid no bull whip."

"You sho' is one aggravatin' nigger woman!" he declared and stepped into the room. She resumed her work and did not answer him at once. "Ah done tole you time and again to keep them white folks' clothes outa dis house."

He picked up the whip and glared at her. Delia went on with her work. She went out into the yard and returned with a galvanized tub and set it on the wash-bench. She saw that Sykes had kicked all of the clothes together again, and now stood in her way truculently, his whole manner hoping, *praying*, for an argument. But she walked calmly around him and commenced to re-sort the things.

"Next time, Ah'm gointer kick 'em outdoors," he threatened as he struck a 10 match along the leg of his corduroy breeches.

Delia never looked up from her work, and her thin, stooped shoulders sagged further.

"Ah ain't for no fuss t'night, Sykes. Ah just come from taking sacrament at the church house."

He snorted scornfully. "Yeah, you just come from de church house on a Sunday night, but heah you is gone to work on them clothes. You ain't nothing but a hypocrite. One of them amen-corner Christians — sing, whoop, and shout, then come home and wash white folks' clothes on the Sabbath."

He stepped roughly upon the whitest pile of things, kicking them helter-skelter as he crossed the room. His wife gave a little scream of dismay, and quickly gathered them together again.

"Sykes, you quit grindin' dirt into these clothes! How can Ah git through by 15 Sat'day if Ah don't start on Sunday?"

"Ah don't keer if you never git through. Anyhow, Ah done promised Gawd and a couple of other men, Ah ain't gointer have it in mah house. Don't gimme no lip neither, else Ah'll throw 'em out and put mah fist up side yo' head to boot."

Delia's habitual meekness seemed to slip from her shoulders like a blown scarf. She was on her feet; her poor little body, her bare knuckly hands bravely defying the strapping hulk before her.

"Looka heah, Sykes, you done gone too fur. Ah been married to you fur fifteen years, and Ah been takin' in washin' fur fifteen years. Sweat, sweat, sweat! Work and sweat, cry and sweat, pray and sweat!"

"What's that got to do with me?" he asked brutally.

"What's it got to do with you, Sykes? Mah tub of suds is filled yo' belly with 20 vittles more times than yo' hands is filled it. Mah sweat is done paid for this house and Ah reckon Ah kin keep on sweatin' in it."

She seized the iron skillet from the stove and struck a defensive pose, which act surprised him greatly, coming from her. It cowed him and he did not strike her as he usually did.

"Naw you won't," she panted, "that ole snaggle-toothed black woman you runnin' with ain't comin' heah to pile up on *mah* sweat and blood. You ain't paid for nothin' on this place, and Ah'm gointer stay right heah till Ah'm toted out foot foremost."

"Well, you better quit gittin' me riled up, else they'll be totin' you out sooner than you expect. Ah'm so tired of you Ah don't know whut to do. Gawd! How Ah hates skinny wimmen!"

A little awed by this new Delia, he sidled out of the door and slammed the back gate after him. He did not say where he had gone, but she knew too well. She knew very well that he would not return until nearly daybreak also. Her work over, she went on to bed but not to sleep at once. Things had come to a pretty pass!

She lay awake, gazing upon the debris that cluttered their matrimonial trail. 25 Not an image left standing along the way. Anything like flowers had long ago been drowned in the salty stream that had been pressed from her heart. Her tears, her sweat, her blood. She had brought love to the union and he had brought a longing after the flesh. Two months after the wedding, he had given her the first brutal beating. She had the memory of his numerous trips to Orlando with all of his wages when he had returned to her penniless, even before the first year had passed. She was young and soft then, but now she thought of her knotty, muscled limbs, her harsh knuckly hands, and drew herself up into an unhappy little ball in the middle of the big feather bed. Too late now to hope for love, even if it were not Bertha it would be someone else. This case differed from the others only in that she was bolder than the others. Too late for everything except her little home. She had built it for her old days, and planted one by one the trees and flowers there. It was lovely to her, lovely.

Somehow, before sleep came, she found herself saying aloud: "Oh well, whatever goes over the Devil's back, is got to come under his belly. Sometime or ruther, Sykes, like everybody else, is gointer reap his sowing." After that she was able to build a spiritual earthworks against her husband. His shells could no longer reach her. AMEN. She went to sleep and slept until he announced his presence in bed by kicking her feet and rudely snatching the covers away.

"Gimme some kivah heah, an' git yo' damn foots over on yo' own side! Ah oughter mash you in yo' mouf fuh drawing dat skillet on me."

Delia went clear to the rail without answering him. A triumphant indifference to all that he was or did.

II

The week was full of work for Delia as all other weeks, and Saturday found her behind her little pony, collecting and delivering clothes.

It was a hot, hot day near the end of July. The village men on Joe Clarke's porch even chewed cane listlessly. They did not hurl the cane-knots as usual. They let them dribble over the edge of the porch. Even conversation had collapsed under the heat.

"Heah come Delia Jones," Jim Merchant said, as the shaggy pony came 'round the bend of the road toward them. The rusty buckboard was heaped with baskets of crisp, clean laundry.

"Yep," Joe Lindsay agreed. "Hot or col', rain or shine, jes 'ez reg'lar ez de weeks roll roun' Delia carries 'em an' fetches 'em on Sat'day."

"She better if she wanter eat," said Moss. "Syke Jones ain't wuth de shot an' powder hit would tek tuh kill 'em. Not to *huh* he ain't."

"He sho' aint," Walter Thomas chimed in. "It's too bad, too, cause she wuz a right pretty li'l trick when he got huh. Ah'd uh mah'ied huh mahself if he hadnter beat me to it."

Delia nodded briefly at the men as she drove past.

"Too much knockin' will ruin *any* 'oman. He done beat huh 'nough tuh kill three women, let 'lone change they looks," said Elijah Moseley. "How Syke kin stommuck dat big black greasy Mogul he's layin' roun' wid, gits me. Ah swear dat eight-rock couldn't kiss a sardine can Ah done thowed out de back do' 'way las' yeah."

"Aw, she's fat, thass how come. He's allus been crazy 'bout fat women," put in Merchant. "He'd a' been tied up wid one long time ago if he could a' found one

30

35

tuh have him. Did Ah tell yuh 'bout him come sidlin' roun' *mah* wife — bringin' her a basket uh peecans outa his yard fuh a present? Yessir, mah wife! She tol' him tuh take 'em right straight back home, 'cause Delia works so hard ovah dat washtub she reckon everything on de place taste lak sweat an' soapsuds. Ah jus' wisht Ah'd a' caught 'im 'roun' dere! Ah'd a' made his hips ketch on fiah down dat shell road."

"Ah know he done it, too. Ah sees 'im grinnin' at every 'oman dat passes," Walter Thomas said. "But even so, he useter eat some mighty big hunks uh humble pie tuh git dat li'l 'oman he got. She wuz ez pritty ez a speckled pup! Dat wuz fifteen years ago. He useter be so skeered uh losin' huh, she could make him do some parts of a husband's duty. Dey never wuz de same in de mind."

"There oughter be a law about him," said Lindsay. "He ain't fit tuh carry guts tuh a bear."

Clarke spoke for the first time. "Tain't no law on earth dat kin make a man be decent if it ain't in 'im. There's plenty men dat takes a wife lak dey do a joint uh sugar-cane. It's round, juicy, an' sweet when dey gits it. But dey squeeze an' grind, squeeze an' grind an' wring tell dey wring every drop uh pleasure dat's in 'em out. When dey's satisfied dat dey is wrung dry, dey treats 'em jes' lak dey do a cane-chew. Dey throws 'em away. Dey knows whut dey is doin' while dey is at it, an' hates theirselves fuh it but they keeps on hangin' after huh tell she's empty. Den dey hates huh fuh bein' a cane-chew an' in de way." 40

"We oughter take Syke an' dat stray 'oman uh his'n down in Lake Howell swamp an' lay on de rawhide till they cain't say Lawd a' mussy. He allus wuz uh ovahbearin niggah, but since dat white 'oman from up north done teached 'im how to run a automobile, he done got too beggety to live — an' we oughter kill 'im," Old Man Anderson advised.

A grunt of approval went around the porch. But the heat was melting their civic virtue and Elijah Moseley began to bait Joe Clarke.

"Come on, Joe, git a melon outa dere an' slice it up for yo' customers. We'se all sufferin' wid de heat. De bear's done got *me*!"

"Thass right, Joe, a watermelon is jes' whut Ah needs tuh cure de eppizu-dicks," Walter Thomas joined forces with Moseley. "Come on dere, Joe. We all is steady customers an' you ain't set us up in a long time. Ah chooses dat long, bow-legged Floridy favorite."

"A god, an' be dough. You all gimme twenty cents and slice away," Clarke retorted. "Ah needs a col' slice m'self. Heah, everybody chip in. Ah'll lend y'all mah meat knife." 45

The money was all quickly subscribed and the huge melon brought forth. At that moment, Sykes and Bertha arrived. A determined silence fell on the porch and the melon was put away again.

Merchant snapped down the blade of his jacknife and moved toward the store door.

"Come on in, Joe, an' gimme a slab uh sow belly an' uh pound uh coffee — almost fuhgot 'twas Sat'day. Got to git on home." Most of the men left also.

Just then Delia drove past on her way home, as Sykes was ordering magnificently for Bertha. It pleased him for Delia to see.

"Git whutsoever yo' heart desires, Honey. Wait a minute, Joe. Give huh two 50 bottles uh strawberry soda-water, uh quart parched ground-peas, an' a block uh chewin' gum."

With all this they left the store, with Sykes reminding Bertha that this was his town and she could have it if she wanted it.

The men returned soon after they left, and held their watermelon feast.

"Where did Syke Jones git da 'oman from nohow?" Lindsay asked.

"Ovah Apopka. Guess dey musta been cleanin' out de town when she lef'. She don't look lak a thing but a hunk uh liver wid hair on it."

"Well, she sho' kin squall," Dave Carter contributed. "When she gits ready tuh 55 laff, she jes' opens huh mouf an' latches it back tuh de las' notch. No ole granpa alligator down in Lake Bell ain't got nothin' on huh."

III

Bertha had been in town three months now. Sykes was still paying her room-rent at Della Lewis' — the only house in town that would have taken her in. Sykes took her frequently to Winter Park to "stomps." He still assured her that he was the swellest man in the state.

"Sho' you kin have dat li'l ole house soon's Ah git dat 'oman outa dere. Everything b'longs tuh me an' you sho' kin have it. Ah sho' 'bominates uh skinny 'oman. Lawdy, you sho' is got one portly shape on you! You kin git *anything* you wants. Dis is *mah* town an' you sho' kin have it."

Delia's work-worn knees crawled over the earth in Gethsemane and up the rocks of Calvary many, many times during these months. She avoided the villagers and meeting places in her efforts to be blind and deaf. But Bertha nullified this to a degree, by coming to Delia's house to call Sykes out to her at the gate.

Delia and Sykes fought all the time now with no peaceful interludes. They slept and ate in silence. Two or three times Delia had attempted a tepid friendliness, but she was repulsed each time. It was plain that the breaches must remain agape.

The sun had burned July to August. The heat streamed down like a million 60 hot arrows, smiting all things living upon the earth. Grass withered, leaves browned, snakes went blind in shedding, and men and dogs went mad. Dog days!

Delia came home one day and found Sykes there before her. She wondered, but started to go on into the house without speaking, even though he was standing in the kitchen door and she must either stoop under his arm or ask him to move. He made no room for her. She noticed a soap box beside the steps, but paid no particular attention to it, knowing that he must have brought it there. As she was stooping to pass under his outstretched arm, he suddenly pushed her backward, laughingly.

"Look in de box dere Delia, Ah done brung yuh somethin'!"

She nearly fell upon the box in her stumbling, and when she saw what it held, she all but fainted outright.

"Syke! Syke, mah Gawd! You take dat rattlesnake 'way from heah! You *gottuh.* Oh, Jesus, have mussy!"

"Ah ain't got tuh do nuthin' uh de kin' — fact is Ah ain't got tuh do nothin' but die. Tain't no use uh you puttin' on airs makin' out lak you skeered uh dat snake — he's gointer stay right heah tell he die. He wouldn't bite me cause Ah knows how tuh handle 'im. Nohow he wouldn't risk breakin' out his fangs 'gin *yo* skinny laigs."

"Naw, now Syke, don't keep dat thing 'round tryin' tuh skeer me tuh death. You knows Ah'm even feared uh earth worms. Thass de biggest snake Ah evah did se. Kill 'im Syke, please."

"Doan ast me tuh do nothin' fuh yuh. Goin' 'round tryin' tuh be so damn asterperious. Naw, Ah ain't gonna kill it. Ah think uh damn sight mo' uh him dan you! Dat's a nice snake an' anybody doan lak 'im kin jes' hit de grit."

The village soon heard that Sykes had the snake, and came to see and ask questions.

"How de hen-fire did you ketch dat six-foot rattler, Syke?" Thomas asked.

"He's full uh frogs so he cain't hardly move, thass how Ah eased up on 'm. But Ah'm a snake charmer an' knows how tuh handle 'em. Shux, dat ain't nothin'. Ah could ketch one eve'y day if Ah so wanted tuh."

"Whut he needs is a heavy hick'ry club leaned real heavy on his head. Dat's de bes' way tuh charm a rattlesnake."

"Naw, Walt, y'all jes' don't understand dese diamon' backs lak Ah do," said Sykes in a superior tone of voice.

The village agreed with Walter, but the snake stayed on. His box remained by the kitchen door with its screen wire covering. Two or three days later it had digested its meal of frogs and literally came to life. It rattled at every movement in the kitchen or the yard. One day as Delia came down the kitchen steps she saw his chalky-white fangs curved like scimitars hung in the wire meshes. This time she did not run away with averted eyes as usual. She stood for a long time in the doorway in a red fury that grew bloodier for every second that she regarded the creature that was her torment.

That night she broached the subject as soon as Sykes sat down to the table.

"Syke, Ah wants you tuh take dat snake 'way fum heah. You done starved me an' Ah put up widcher, you done beat me an Ah took dat, but you don kilt all mah insides bringin' dat varmint heah."

Sykes poured out a saucer full of coffee and drank it deliberately before he answered her.

"A whole lot Ah keer 'bout how you feels inside uh out. Dat snake ain't goin' no damn wheah till Ah gits ready fuh 'im tuh go. So fur as beatin' is concerned, yuh ain't took near all dat you gointer take ef yuh stay 'round *me.*"

Delia pushed back her plate and got up from the table. "Ah hates you, Sykes," she said calmly. "Ah hates you tuh de same degree dat Ah useter love yuh. Ah done took an' took till mah belly is full up tuh mah neck. Dat's de reason Ah got mah letter fum de church an' moved mah membership tuh Woodbridge — so Ah don't haftuh take no sacrament wid yuh. Ah don't wantuh see yuh 'round me atall. Lay 'round wid dat 'oman all yuh wants tuh, but gwan 'way from me an' mah house. Ah hates yuh lak uh suck-egg dog."

Sykes almost let the huge wad of corn bread and collard greens he was chewing fall out of his mouth in amazement. He had a hard time whipping himself up to the proper fury to try to answer Delia.

"Well, Ah'm glad you does hate me. Ah'm sho' tiahed uh you hangin' ontuh me. Ah don't want yuh. Look at yuh stringey ole neck! Yo' rawbony laigs an' arms is enough tuh cut uh man tuh death. You looks jes' lak de devvul's doll-baby tuh *me*. You cain't hate me no worse dan Ah hates you. Ah been hatin' *you* fuh years." 80

"Yo' ole black hide don't look lak nothin' tuh me, but uh passle uh wrinkled up rubber, wid yo' big ole yeahs flappin' on each side lak uh paih uh buzzard wings. Don't think Ah'm gointuh be run 'way fum mah house neither. Ah'm goin' tuh de white folks 'bout *you*, mah young man, de very nex' time you lay yo' han's on me. Mah cup is done run ovah." Delia said this with no signs of fear and Sykes departed from the house, threatening her, but made not the slightest move to carry out any of them.

That night he did not return at all, and the next day being Sunday, Delia was glad she did not have to quarrel before she hitched up her pony and drove the four miles to Woodbridge.

She stayed to the night service — "love feast" — which was very warm and full of spirit. In the emotional winds her domestic trials were borne far and wide so that she sang as she drove homeward,

> Jurden water, black an' col
> Chills de body, not de soul
> An' Ah wantah cross Jurden in uh calm time.

She came from the barn to the kitchen door and stopped.

"Whut's de mattah, ol' Satan, you ain't kicken' up yo' racket?" She addressed the snake's box. Complete silence. She went on into the house with a new hope in its birth struggles. Perhaps her threat to go to the white folks had frightened Sykes! Perhaps he was sorry! Fifteen years of misery and suppression had brought Delia to the place where she would hope *anything* that looked towards a way over or through her wall of inhibitions.

She felt in the match-safe behind the stove at once for a match. There was only one there. 85

"Dat niggah wouldn't fetch nothin' heah tuh save his rotten neck, but he kin run thew whut Ah brings quick enough. Now he done toted off nigh on tuh haff uh box uh matches. He done had dat 'oman heah in mah house, too."

Nobody but a woman could tell how she knew this even before she struck the match. But she did and it put her into a new fury.

Presently she brought in the tubs to put the white things to soak. This time she decided she need not bring the hamper out of the bedroom; she would go in there and do the sorting. She picked up the pot-bellied lamp and went in. The room was small and the hamper stood hard by the foot of the white iron bed. She could sit and reach through the bedposts — resting as she worked.

"Ah wantah cross Jurden in uh calm time." She was singing again. The mood of the "love feast," had returned. She threw back the lid of the basket almost gaily. Then, moved by both horror and terror, she sprang back toward the door. *There lay the snake in the basket!* He moved sluggishly at first, but even as she turned round and round, jumped up and down in an insanity of fear, he began to stir vigorously. She saw him pouring his awful beauty from the basket upon the bed, then she seized the lamp and ran as fast as she could to the kitchen. The wind from the open door blew out the light and the darkness added to her terror. She sped to the darkness of the yard, slamming the door after her before she thought to set down the lamp. She did not feel safe even on the ground, so she climbed up in the hay barn.

There for an hour or more she lay sprawled upon the hay a gibbering wreck. 90

Finally she grew quiet, and after that came coherent thought. With this stalked through her a cold, bloody rage. Hours of this. A period of introspection, a space of retrospection, then a mixture of both. Out of this an awful calm.

"Well, Ah done de bes' Ah could. If things ain't right, Gawd knows tain't mah fault."

She went to sleep — a twitch sleep — and woke up to a faint gray sky. There was a loud hollow sound below. She peered out. Sykes was at the woodpile, demolishing a wire-covered box.

He hurried to the kitchen door, but hung outside there some minutes before he entered, and stood some minutes more inside before he closed it after him.

The gray in the sky was spreading. Delia descended without fear now, and 95 crouched beneath the low bedroom window. The drawn shade shut out the dawn, shut in the night. But the thin walls held back no sound.

"Dat ol' scratch is woke up now!" She mused at the tremendous whirr inside, which every woodsman knows, is one of the sound illusions. The rattler is a ventriloquist. His whirr sounds to the right, to the left, straight ahead, behind, close under foot — everywhere but where it is. Woe to him who guesses wrong unless he is prepared to hold up his end of the argument! Sometimes he strikes without rattling at all.

Inside, Sykes heard nothing until he knocked a pot lid off the stove while trying to reach the match-safe in the dark. He had emptied his pockets at Bertha's.

The snake seemed to wake up under the stove and Sykes made a quick leap into the bedroom. In spite of the gin he had had, his head was clearing now.

"Mah Gawd!" he chattered, "ef Ah could on'y strack uh light!"

The rattling ceased for a moment as he stood paralyzed. He waited. It seemed   100
that the snake waited also.

"Oh, fuh de light! Ah thought he'd be too sick" — Sykes was muttering to
himself when the whirr began again, closer, right underfoot this time. Long
before this, Sykes' ability to think had been flattened down to primitive instinct
and he leaped — onto the bed.

Outside Delia heard a cry that might have come from a maddened chim-
panzee, a stricken gorilla. All the terror, all the horror, all the rage that man possibly could express, without a recognizable human sound.

A tremendous stir inside there, another series of animal screams, the intermittent whirr of the reptile. The shade torn violently down from the window, letting in the red dawn, a huge brown hand seizing the window stick, great dull
blows upon the wooden floor punctuating the gibberish of sound long after the
rattle of the snake had abruptly subsided. All this Delia could see and hear from
her place beneath the window, and it made her ill. She crept over to the four
o'clocks and stretched herself on the cool earth to recover.

She lay there. "Delia, Delia!" She could hear Sykes calling in a most despairing
tone as one who expected no answer. The sun crept on up, and he called. Delia
could not move — her legs had gone flabby. She never moved, he called, and the
sun kept rising.

"Mah Gawd!" She heard him moan, "Mah Gawd fum Heben!" She heard him   105
stumbling about and got up from her flower-bed. The sun was growing warm. As
she approached the door she heard him call out hopefully, "Delia, is dat you Ah
heah?"

She saw him on his hands and knees as soon as she reached the door. He crept
an inch or two toward her — all that he was able, and she saw his horribly swollen
neck and his one open eye shining with hope. A surge of pity too strong to support bore her away from that eye that must, could not, fail to see the tubs. He
would see the lamp. Orlando with its doctors was too far. She could scarcely reach
the chinaberry tree, where she waited in the growing heat while inside she knew
the cold river was creeping up and up to extinguish that eye which must know by
now that she knew.

Exploring the Text

1. What qualities in Delia does Hurston emphasize from the beginning of the story?
2. Why is Sykes bothered by the income that Delia brings to their marriage? What
   gender stereotypes play into his resentment and anger?
3. In paragraph 25, beginning "She lay awake," Delia recalls her expectations for marriage. In what ways do her expectations reflect stereotypes?
4. What does Hurston mean when she describes Delia as "able to build a spiritual
   earthworks against her husband" (para. 26)?

5. How do the two scenes where Delia reaches into the hamper serve as contrasting parallels to emphasize changes in her character?
6. Hurston develops Delia as a good Christian woman so that readers can accept her final action. How does she accomplish this?
7. How does the dialect affect your reading and understanding of the story? Does it add authenticity? increase reading difficulty? both? How does reading the story aloud make a difference?
8. In what ways is this story a retelling of the fall of Adam and Eve? What biblical symbols do you find? Are these simply allusions, or is Hurston suggesting thematic parallels? What is Hurston's purpose?

Barbie Doll (poetry)

MARGE PIERCY

American poet, novelist, and activist Marge Piercy (b. 1936) grew up in Michigan in a working-class family during the Depression. She graduated from Northwestern University with an MA and went on to write seventeen volumes of poetry and fifteen novels, including *Sex Wars: A Novel of the Turbulent Post–Civil War Period* (2005); *City of Darkness, City of Light* (1996); and *The Longings of Women* (1994). She is known for her highly personal free verse and her themes of feminism and social protest. "Barbie Doll" both comments and reflects on the popular icon — and children's toy — of the same name.

This girlchild was born as usual
and presented dolls that did pee-pee
and miniature GE stoves and irons
and wee lipsticks the color of cherry candy.
Then in the magic of puberty, a classmate said: 5
You have a great big nose and fat legs.

She was healthy, tested intelligent,
possessed strong arms and back,
abundant sexual drive and manual dexterity.
She went to and fro apologizing.   10
Everyone saw a fat nose on thick legs.

She was advised to play coy,
exhorted to come on hearty,
exercise, diet, smile and wheedle.
Her good nature wore out   15
like a fan belt.

So she cut off her nose and her legs
and offered them up.

In the casket displayed on satin she lay
with the undertaker's cosmetics painted on,   *20*
a turned-up putty nose,
dressed in a pink and white nightie.
Doesn't she look pretty? everyone said.
Consummation at last.
To every woman a happy ending.   *25*

Exploring the Text

1. Identify several stereotypes that Marge Piercy draws on in this poem. Why is *girl-child* — one word — an appropriate term?
2. What images and colors does Piercy use to depict the girlchild?
3. Who is the speaker in the poem?
4. How does the way the girl is encouraged to behave run counter to her natural inclinations?
5. How does the speaker entwine other commentaries into the poem? Why? Are these voices in the mind of the girlchild real or imagined?
6. What is the speaker's tone in this poem? What specific lines and images lead you to your understanding of tone?

Cathy (cartoon)

CATHY GUISEWITE

After graduating from the University of Michigan, Cathy Guisewite (b. 1950) began work as an advertising copywriter. Eventually, she made a career out of drawing and became one of the first women to have a syndicated comic strip. In 1976, she created the character of Cathy, a young, single career woman obsessed with her weight, clothes, mother, and dating. In 1987, Guisewite received an Emmy for Outstanding Animated Program for the television special *Cathy*, and in 1993 she received the Reuben Award for Outstanding Cartoonist of the Year. The following cartoon, which appeared in 1997, was published in over fifteen hundred newspapers worldwide.

Exploring the Text

1. What story is being told in this comic strip?
2. How do the two opening frames set a tone for that story? Consider the relationship between word and image.

3. What point is Cathy Guisewite making? State it in one sentence.
4. How does Guisewite support her point with visual images, wordplay, stereotypes, and allusions?
5. This cartoon is clearly meant to be funny, but is the humorous tone ironic, acerbic, sarcastic, witty, or amusing?
6. How is the audience's identification with the character of Cathy and her various predicaments likely to affect their response to this specific cartoon?

New and Newer Versions of Scripture (table)

BILL BROADWAY

This selection by Bill Broadway, staff writer for the *Washington Post*, ran in February 2005.

Criticism of Today's New International Version of the Bible began [in 2002] with the publication of the TNIV New Testament. Opponents accused the translation committee, an independent group of evangelical scholars, of bowing to political correctness and feminist theology in using "gender neutral" or "inclusive" language.

The committee made adjustments to the 2002 text before [the February 2005] publication of the complete Bible. But committee members said they did not abandon their goal of providing an accurate translation. Critics call the effort a failure, many preferring TNIV's precursor, the best-selling New International Version [NIV] published in 1978. Here are some passages they cite:

Isaiah 19:16

NIV: "In that day Egyptians will be like women. They will shudder with fear at the uplifted hand that the Lord Almighty raises against them."

TNIV: "In that day the Egyptians will become weaklings. They will shudder with fear at the uplifted hand that the Lord Almighty raises against them."

Hebrews 12:7

NIV: "Endure hardship as discipline: God is treating you as sons. For what son is not disciplined by his father?"

TNIV: "Endure hardship as discipline; God is treating you as his children. For what children are not disciplined by their father?"

James 1:12

NIV: "Blessed is the man who perseveres under trial, because when he has stood the test, he will receive the crown of life that God has promised to those who love him."

TNIV: "Blessed are those who persevere under trial, because when they have stood the test, they will receive the crown of life that God has promised to those who love him."

Acts 20:30 (Paul is saying farewell to Ephesian elders.)

NIV: "Even from your own number men will arise and distort the truth in order to draw away the disciples after them."

TNIV: "Even from your own number some will arise and distort the truth in order to draw away the disciples after them."

Psalm 119:9

NIV: "How can a young man keep his way pure? By living according to your word."

TNIV: "How can those who are young keep their way pure? By living according to your word."

Mark 1:17 (An example of a verse revised after release of the New Testament)

NIV: "'Come, follow me,' Jesus said, 'and I will make you fishers of men.'"

TNIV (2002): "'Come, follow me,' Jesus said, 'and I will send you out to catch people.'"

TNIV (2005): "'Come, follow me,' Jesus said, 'and I will send you out to fish for people.'"

Exploring the Text

1. Identify the major changes in the new versions of scripture. How would you characterize them? Does the meaning change in any of them?
2. Select one or two examples and read them aloud — first, the original, then the revision. What is the aural impact?
3. Rewrite a passage from a historic document, such as the Gettysburg Address, with gender-neutral, or more inclusive, language. What is lost? What is gained?
4. After this selection appeared in the *Washington Post*, letters to the editor both supported and challenged the changes. One writer who opposed the changes said: "The idea of rewriting the Bible, or any text, with gender-neutral language is deplorable. We should be proud of the progress of our civilization, but falsifying history is a foolish and futile effort to make the past compliant with modern standards." A supporter wrote: "Making our translation of the Bible more inclusive strengthens its message. Perhaps centuries from now, society will have endorsed these gender-neutral Bibles and the world will be a better place . . . we may see that the male-dominant society from which Scripture was written is no longer and that we are indeed all equal in God's eyes." Discuss these two views, and then explain your own view on whether the Bible — or any sacred or political text (such as the Gettysburg Address or the Constitution) — should be revised with language that avoids specifying gender.

Conversation

Focus on Defining Masculinity

The following four texts comment directly or indirectly on definitions and images of masculinity in today's society:

Sources
1. **Mark Bauerlein and Sandra Stotsky,** *Why Johnny Won't Read*
2. **David Brooks,** *Mind over Muscle*
3. **Rebecca Walker,** *Putting Down the Gun*
4. **Ann Hulbert,** *Boy Problems*

After you have read, studied, and synthesized these pieces, enter the conversation by responding to one of the prompts on page 417.

1. *Why Johnny Won't Read*

MARK BAUERLEIN AND SANDRA STOTSKY

In the following essay, Mark Bauerlein and Sandra Stotsky, researchers involved in the National Endowment for the Arts and the National Assessment of Educational Progress, examine the reading habits and preferences of boys.

When the National Endowment for the Arts last summer [2004] released "Reading at Risk: A Survey of Literary Reading in America," journalists and commentators were quick to seize on the findings as a troubling index of the state of literary culture. The survey showed a serious decline in both literary reading and book reading in general by adults of all ages, races, incomes, education levels and regions.

But in all the discussion, one of the more worrisome trends went largely unnoticed. From 1992 to 2002, the gender gap in reading by young adults widened considerably. In overall book reading, young women slipped from 63 percent to 59 percent, while young men plummeted from 55 percent to 43 percent.

Placed in historical perspective, these findings fit with a gap that has existed in the United States since the spread of mass publishing in the mid-19th century. But for the gap to have grown so much in so short a time suggests that what was formerly a moderate difference is fast becoming a decided marker of gender identity: Girls read; boys don't.

The significance of the gender gap is echoed in two other recent studies. In September the Bureau of Labor Statistics issued the "American Time Use Survey,"

408

a report on how Americans spend their hours, including work, school, sleep and leisure. The survey found that in their leisure time young men and women both read only eight minutes per day. But the equality is misleading, because young men enjoy a full 56 minutes more leisure than young women — approximately six hours for men and five for women.

The other report, "Trends in Educational Equity of Girls and Women: 2004," 5 is from the Education Department. Between 1992 and 2002, among high school seniors, girls lost two points in reading scores and boys six points, leaving a 16-point differential in their averages on tests given by the National Assessment of Educational Progress. In the fall semester of kindergarten in 1998, on a different test, girls outperformed boys by 0.9 points. By the spring semester, the difference had nearly doubled, to 1.6 points.

Although one might expect the schools to be trying hard to make reading appealing to boys, the K-12 literature curriculum may in fact be contributing to the problem. It has long been known that there are strong differences between boys and girls in their literary preferences. According to reading interest surveys, both boys and girls are unlikely to choose books based on an "issues" approach, and children are not interested in reading about ways to reform society — or themselves. But boys prefer adventure tales, war, sports and historical nonfiction, while girls prefer stories about personal relationships and fantasy. Moreover, when given choices, boys do not choose stories that feature girls, while girls frequently select stories that appeal to boys.

Unfortunately, the textbooks and literature assigned in the elementary grades do not reflect the dispositions of male students. Few strong and active male role models can be found as lead characters. Gone are the inspiring biographies of the most important American presidents, inventors, scientists and entrepreneurs. No military valor, no high adventure. On the other hand, stories about adventurous and brave women abound. Publishers seem to be more interested in avoiding "masculine" perspectives or "stereotypes" than in getting boys to like what they are assigned to read.

At the middle school level, the kind of quality literature that might appeal to boys has been replaced by Young Adult Literature, that is, easy-to-read, short novels about teenagers and problems such as drug addiction, teenage pregnancy, alcoholism, domestic violence, divorced parents and bullying. Older literary fare has also been replaced by something called "culturally relevant" literature — texts that appeal to students' ethnic group identification on the assumption that sharing the leading character's ethnicity will motivate them to read.

There is no evidence whatsoever that either of these types of reading fare has turned boys into lifelong readers or learners. On the contrary, the evidence is accumulating that by the time they go on to high school, boys have lost their interest in reading about the fictional lives, thoughts and feelings of mature individuals in works written in high-quality prose, and they are no longer motivated by an exciting plot to persist in the struggle they will have with the vocabulary that goes with it.

Last year the National Assessment Governing Board approved a special study   10
of gender differences in reading as part of its research agenda over the next five
years. The study will examine how differences in theme, the leading character's
gender, and genre, among other factors, bear upon the relative reading performance of boys and girls. With its focus on the content of reading rather than
process, this study will, one hopes, give us some ideas on what needs to be done to
get boys reading again.

Questions

1. What types of evidence dominate in this essay? Is the purpose of the essay to
   inform or to persuade?
2. Do you agree with the authors' analysis of the literary preferences of girls and
   boys? Explain.
3. Taking the opening two paragraphs as the authors' introduction, how do they capture their readers' interest?

2. *Mind over Muscle*

DAVID BROOKS

The following is an editorial from the *New York Times* by columnist David
Brooks.

Once upon a time, it was a man's world. Men possessed most of the tools one
needed for power and success: muscles, connections, control of the crucial social
institutions.

But then along came the information age to change all that. In the information age, education is the gateway to success. And that means this is turning into a
woman's world, because women are better students than men.

From the first days of school, girls outperform boys. The gap is sometimes small, but over time slight advantages accumulate into big ones. In surveys,
kindergarten teachers report that girls are more attentive than boys and more
persistent at tasks. Through elementary school, girls are less likely to be asked
to repeat a grade. They are much less likely to be diagnosed with a learning
disability.

In high school, girls get higher grades in every subject, usually by about a
quarter of a point, and have a higher median class rank. They are more likely to
take advanced placement courses and the hardest math courses, and are more
likely to be straight-A students. They have much higher reading and writing
scores on national assessment tests. Boys still enjoy an advantage on math and
science tests, but that gap is smaller and closing.

Girls are much more likely to be involved in the school paper or yearbook, to   5
be elected to student government and to be members of academic clubs. They set
higher goals for their post–high-school career. (This data is all from the Department of Education.)

The differences become monumental in college. Women are more likely
to enroll in college and they are more likely to have better applications, so now
there are hundreds of schools where the female-male ratio is 60 to 40. About
80 percent of the majors in public administration, psychology and education
are female. And here's the most important piece of data: Until 1985 or so, male
college graduates outnumbered female college graduates. But in the mid-80's,
women drew even, and ever since they have been pulling away at a phenome-
nal rate.

This year [2005], 133 women will graduate from college for every 100 men.
By decade's end, according to Department of Education projections, there will be
142 female graduates for every 100 male graduates. Among African-Americans,
there are 200 female grads for every 100 male grads.

The social consequences are bound to be profound. The upside is that by
sheer force of numbers, women will be holding more and more leadership jobs.
On the negative side, they will have a harder and harder time finding marriageable men with comparable education levels. One thing is for sure: in 30 years the
notion that we live in an oppressive patriarchy that discriminates against women
will be regarded as a quaint anachronism.

There are debates about why women have thrived and men have faltered.
Some say men are imprisoned by their anti-intellectual machismo. Others say the
educational system has been overly feminized. Boys are asked to sit quietly for
hours at a stretch under conditions where they find it harder to thrive.

But Thomas G. Mortensen of the Pell Institute observes that these same   10
trends — thriving women, faltering men — are observable across the world. In
most countries, and in nearly all developed countries, women are graduating
from high school and college at much higher rates than men. Mortensen writes,
"We conclude that the issue is far less driven by a nation's culture than it is by
basic differences between males and females in the modern world."

In other words, if we want to help boys keep up with girls, we have to have an
honest discussion about innate differences between the sexes. We have to figure
out why poor girls who move to middle-class schools do better, but poor boys
who make the same move often do worse. We have to absorb the obvious lesson
of every airport bookstore, which is that men and women like to read totally different sorts of books, and see if we can apply this fact when designing curricu-
lums. If boys like to read about war and combat, why can't there be books about
combat on the curriculum?

Would elementary school boys do better if they spent more time outside the
classroom and less time chained to a desk? Or would they thrive more in a rigorous, competitive environment?

For 30 years, attention has focused on feminine equality. During that time honest discussion of innate differences has been stifled (ask Larry Summers[1]). It's time to look at the other half.

Questions

1. What is David Brooks's main point in this essay? Why doesn't he state it directly at the outset?
2. What is the effect of using the standard fairy-tale opening, "Once upon a time . . ."?
3. Do you agree with Brooks's cause-effect analysis that in the information age, "this is turning into a woman's world" (para. 2)? Why or why not?
4. Do you agree with Brooks that in the near future "women will be holding more and more leadership jobs" and "will have a harder and harder time finding marriageable men with comparable education levels" (para. 8)? Why or why not?
5. What type of evidence does Brooks cite in order to give his position weight?

3. *Putting Down the Gun*

REBECCA WALKER

In the following excerpt from her introduction to the essay collection *What Makes a Man: 22 Writers Imagine the Future* (2004), Rebecca Walker, journalist, activist, and author of the memoir *Black White Jewish*, looks at the pressures boys experience to conform to certain societal expectations.

The idea for this book was born one night after a grueling conversation with my then eleven-year-old son. He had come home from his progressive middle school unnaturally quiet and withdrawn, shrugging off my questions of concern with uncharacteristic irritability. Where was the sunny, chatty boy I dropped off that morning? What had befallen him in the perilous halls of middle school? I backed off but kept a close eye on him, watching for clues.

After a big bowl of his favorite pasta, he sat on a sofa in my study and read his science textbook as I wrote at my desk. We both enjoyed this simple yet profound togetherness, the two of us focused on our own projects yet palpably connected. As we worked under the soft glow of paper lanterns, with the heat on high and our little dog snoring at his feet, my son began to relax. I could feel a shift as he began to remember, deep in his body, that he was home, that he was safe, that he didn't have to brace to protect himself from the expectations of the outside world.

---

[1]Lawrence Summers was president of Harvard University when he claimed that differences in ability were one reason why women were underrepresented in scientific fields. Summers eventually resigned his post. — Eds.

An hour or so passed like this before he announced that he had a question. He had morphed back into the child I knew, and was lying down with a colorful blanket over his legs, using one hand to scratch behind the dog's ears. "I've been thinking that maybe I should play sports at school."

"Sports?" I replied with surprise, swiveling around and leaning back in my chair. "Any sport in mind, or just sports in general?"

A nonchalant shrug. "Maybe softball, I like softball."   5

I cocked my head to one side. "What brought this on?"

"I don't know," he said. "Maybe girls will like me if I play sports."

Excuse me?

My boy is intuitive, smart, and creative beyond belief. At the time he loved animals, Japanese anime, the rap group Dead Prez, and everything having to do with snowboarding. He liked to help both of his grandmothers in the garden. He liked to read science fiction. He liked to climb into bed with me and lay his head on my chest. He liked to build vast and intricate cities with his Legos, and was beginning what I thought would be a lifelong love affair with chess.

Maybe girls would like him if he played sports?   10

Call me extreme, but I felt like my brilliant eleven-year-old daughter had come home and said, "Maybe boys will like me if I stop talking in class." Or my gregarious African-American son had told me, "Maybe the kids will like me if I act white."

I tried to stay calm as he illuminated the harsh realities of his sixth grade social scene. In a nutshell, the girls liked the jocks the best, and sometimes deigned to give the time of day to the other team, the computer nerds. Since he wasn't allowed to play violent computer games — we forbade them in our house — he was having trouble securing his place with the latter, hence his desire to assume the identity of the former. When I asked about making friends based on common interests rather than superficial categories, he got flustered. "You don't understand," he said huffily. "Boys talk about sports, like their matches and who scored what and stuff, or they talk about new versions of computer games or tricks they learned to get to higher levels." Tears welled up in his eyes. "I don't have anything to talk about."

He was right; until that moment I had had no idea, but suddenly the truth of being a sixth-grade boy in America crystallized before me. My beautiful boy and every other mother's beautiful boy had what essentially boiled down to two options: fight actually in sport, or fight virtually on the computer. Athlete, gladiator, secret agent, Tomb Raider. The truth of his existence, his many likes and dislikes, none of them having to do with winning or killing of any kind, had no social currency. My son could compete and score, perform and win, or be an outcast or worse, invisible, his unique gifts unnoticed and unharvested, the world around him that much more impoverished.

That night I went to sleep with several things on my mind; the conversation I planned to have with the head of my son's school about the need for a comprehensive, curricular interrogation of the contours of masculinity; the way girls find themselves drawn to more "traditional" displays of masculinity because they are more unsure than ever about how to experience their own femininity; and the many hours and endless creativity I would have to devote to ensuring that my son's true self would not be entirely snuffed out by the cultural imperative.

And then there was the final and most chilling thought of all: 15

A bat, a "joy stick." What's next, a gun?

It occurred to me that my son was being primed for war, was being prepared to pick up a gun. The first steps were clear: Tell him that who he is authentically is not enough; tell him that he will not be loved unless he abandons his own desires and picks up a tool of competition; tell him that to really be of value he must stand ready to compete, dominate, and, if necessary, kill, if not actually then virtually, financially, athletically.

If one's life purpose is obscured by the pressure to conform to a generic type and other traces of self are ostracized into shadow, then just how difficult is it to pick up a gun, metaphoric or literal, as a means of self-definition, as a way of securing what feels like personal power?

Questions

1. Rebecca Walker focuses on her own son as she develops her thesis. Is doing so an effective strategy to reach her audience? Explain whether the addition of quantitative evidence would have strengthened or weakened the introduction. As you develop your response take into account what you believe Walker's purpose is.
2. Do you think the pressure Walker's son was expressing was simply standard peer pressure, or do you agree with her that the pressure was tied to gender roles? Explain.
3. Do you agree with this statement: "My beautiful boy and every other mother's beautiful boy had what essentially boiled down to two options: fight actually in sport, or fight virtually on the computer" (para. 13)?
4. What does Walker mean by "the cultural imperative" (para. 14)?
5. Trace the causal links that Walker makes in order to move from the pressure her son feels to participate in competitive sports to her worry that he "was being primed for war" (para. 17). Do you find any faulty linkages in her logic?

4. *Boy Problems*

ANN HULBERT

The following essay from the *New York Times Magazine* by Ann Hulbert, one of its contributing writers, is accompanied by a table taken from the National Center for Education Statistics.

"It's her future. Do the math," instructs a poster that is part of the Girl Scouts of the U.S.A.'s two-year-old "Girls Go Tech" campaign. Accompanying the message — which belongs to a series of public service announcements also spon-

---

How Long Do You Expect to Stay in School?

High-School Sophomores' Educational Expectations, by Sex

	Male	Female
Graduate/professional degree	29.4%	42.3%
College graduate	37.2	34.4
Some college	11.8	8.9
High school or less	11.1	5.4

Source: "A Profile of the American High-School Sophomore in 2002: Initial Results from the Base Year of the Education Longitudinal Study of 2002" (NCES 2005–330). U.S. Department of Education: National Center for Education Statistics.

---

sored by the Ad Council — is a photograph of an adorable little girl reading a book called "Charlotte's Web Site." The cover of the E. B. White takeoff shows Fern and Wilbur looking intently at Charlotte on a computer screen. The text below warns that "by sixth grade, an alarming number of girls lose interest in math, science and technology. Which means they won't qualify for most future jobs."

But they don't lose interest in reading, this particular ad presumes — nor do girls lose interest in school, certainly not at the rate boys do. The recent [2005] controversy over comments made by Lawrence Summers, the president of Harvard, about the gender gap in science and engineering has eclipsed a different educational disparity: boys perform consistently below girls on most tests of reading and verbal skills and lag in college enrollment and degree attainment. After dominating postsecondary education through the late 1970's, young American men now earn 25 percent fewer bachelor's degrees than young women do.

Who knows what Summers would say about this phenomenon, which is the flip side of the underrepresentation of female scientists at the top that he was addressing. Male achievement, as he explained, tends toward the extremes when it comes to testing, while females' scores are more concentrated in the middle of the range. What Summers didn't spell out is that boys owe their edge in math to the unusually high performance of a relatively small number of boys in a pool that also has more than its share of low-scoring students. In assessments of verbal literacy, the clumping of boys toward the bottom is more pronounced.

The gender disparity widens among low-income and minority students. And it is especially dramatic among African-Americans, a recent Urban Institute study shows. Black women now earn twice as many college degrees as black men do. They also receive double the number of master's degrees. But the female lead isn't just a black phenomenon; among whites, women earn 30 percent more bachelor's degrees than men and some 50 percent more master's degrees.

It's his future. Do the math — but, as the Boy Scouts warn, be prepared. This 5 trend doesn't lend itself to clear-cut treatment. Ignore the male lag, some advocates of girls are inclined to argue, on the grounds that men on average still end up outearning women. Bring back old-fashioned competition and more hard-boiled reading matter, urge advocates for boys like Christina Hoff Sommers, who in "The War Against Boys: How Misguided Feminism Is Harming Our Young Men" (2000) denounces a touchy-feeling, cooperative, progressive ethos that she says undermines boys' performance and school engagement. Males come from Mars and thrive instead on no-nonsense authority, accountability, clarity and peer rivalry.

What both of these views — feminist and antifeminist alike — fail to appreciate is how much patient attentiveness (in the Venus vein) it takes to boost stragglers rather than strivers. In the "do the math" mission under way with girls, the overarching goal has been surprisingly competitive: to maintain the momentum of female math students (who do just as well as boys early on in school) and to keep the top achievers in the academic pipeline for those "future jobs" in our technological world. The payoff for efforts that have been directed toward school performance has been gratifying. Girls are taking more math and science courses in high school and majoring with greater frequency in those fields in college. (Look at the 40 Intel finalists: [in 2005] 38 percent of them were girls.)

The educational predicament of boys is fuzzier by comparison and likely to elude tidy empirical diagnosis and well-focused remedies. At the National Bureau of Economic Research (under whose auspices Summers delivered his remarks about women), analysts have been puzzling over the whys behind "Where the Boys Aren't," the title of one working paper. There are some obvious explanations: men in the Army and in prison and more job options for males (in construction and manufacturing) that don't require a college education but pay relatively well.

Yet there are also murkier social and behavioral — and biological — issues at stake that don't augur well for a quick-fix approach. On the front end, boys appear to be later verbal bloomers than girls, which sets them up for early encounters with academic failure — and which makes early-intervention gambits like the Bush administration's push to emphasize more literacy skills in preschool look misdirected. Down the road, there is evidence that poorer "noncognitive skills" (not academic capacity but work habits and conduct) may be what hobble males most, and that growing up in single-parent families takes more of an educational toll on boys than girls.

Those are challenges that beg for more than school-based strategies. To give her credit, Laura Bush hasn't shied away from them as she starts a boy-focused youth initiative, which runs the gamut from dealing with gangs to financing fatherhood programs to improving remedial English programs. Rewards for such efforts aren't likely to be prompt and aren't aimed at the top — two reasons they deserve the spotlight. Females have yet more strides to make in the sciences, but they're building on success. A boost-the-boys educational endeavor faces the challenge of dealing with downward drift. Clearly the nation needs an impetus to tackle the larger problem of growing social inequality. Worries that it is boys who are being left behind could be the goad we need.

Questions

1. Ann Hulbert writes within the context of Harvard president Lawrence Summers's remarks suggesting that the paucity of women in math and science may be the result of innate differences in ability. How does this context affect the way she presents her views? Does she argue against him? Agree with him?
2. What is Hulbert's thesis? Restate it in a sentence or two.
3. Hulbert discusses several hypotheses for the "gender disparity." What are they?
4. What are the "murkier social and behavioral" issues (para. 8) that Hulbert believes are important to understanding the disparity in academic achievement between boys and girls?
5. Does Hulbert believe that the gains girls and young women have made are at the expense of boys and young men?
6. How does the table on educational expectations by sex affirm and expand Hulbert's analysis? Does Hulbert specifically refer to information in the table?

Entering the Conversation

As you respond to each of the following prompts, support your argument with references to at least three of the sources in Conversation: Focus on Defining Masculinity. For help using sources, see Chapter 3.

1. Write an essay explaining whether you agree or disagree that the public school system, as currently organized, holds boys back from achieving academic success and contributes to what Ann Hulbert ("Boy Problems") calls "the gender disparity."

2. Using these documents and your own knowledge and research, write an argument defining what you see as the central issue facing boys and young men in our society. Recommend at least one way to address the issue.

3. Rebecca Walker edited the anthology *What Makes a Man*. Write an essay answering that question. Cite authors in Conversation: Focus on Defining

Masculinity who support your point of view, or explain why you disagree with authors in these Conversations.

4. Choose one or two assertions that authors in this Conversation section make that you believe are questionable, perhaps even stereotypes. Write an essay illustrating how popular culture and the media promote or reinforce such beliefs. For example, David Brooks writes, "[W]omen are better students than men"; Rebecca Walker speculates that boys' choices "boiled down to two options: fight actually in sport, or fight virtually on the computer."

Student Writing

Argument: Supporting an Assertion

In the following prompt, the writer is asked to take a side in the debate over single-sex education.

> In "Fee-Paying Parents Lose Faith in Single Sex Education," an article filed on telegraph.co.uk, the online version of an English newspaper, John Clare covers the debate about single-sex schools, citing examples of formerly single-sex private schools that have become, or are planning to become, coeducational. Read the excerpt from the article below, and then choose one side of the argument to defend in an essay.

The head teachers of co-educational schools say that girls' parents are increasingly rejecting the arguments of those such as Brenda Despontin, this year's president of the Girls' Student Association (GSA), who maintains that "girls' brains are wired differently; it follows that adolescents need to be taught differently."

Girls, insists Dr. Despontin, the head of Haberdashers', Monmouth, are "short-changed" in co-ed classrooms. "Boys dominate teacher time, organising themselves quickly to the task, often with a degree of ruthlessness, while girls sharing a classroom with boys hold back, through shyness or a desire to cooperate," she says.

"Oh, no they don't," chorus co-educational school heads. "They learn how to succeed in a co-ed world." Boys' parents, they add, recognise and welcome the "civilising" influence of the opposite sex.

Read the entire article at <bedfordstmartins.com/languageofcomp>

Brian Tannenbaum, an eleventh-grade student, argues for coeducation in his response. Read his essay, and consider its strengths and weaknesses. Then answer the questions about how Brian develops his argument.

Co-educational Schools

Brian Tannenbaum

"In a world that taught them how to think, she showed them how to live." This is the tagline from *Mona Lisa Smile*, a movie set in 1953 when freethinking art-history teacher Katherine Watson came to teach at Wellesley College, arguably at that time the best women's college in the nation, and one of the top colleges in the world. From the beginning of the movie, it is evident that the Wellesley women are both intelligent and competitive. As Ms. Watson discovers in her very first class, every single student had read the art history textbook before being given any assignments. Would these women have read the textbook if they were at Yale, Harvard, or Princeton? Is it imaginable that these brilliant thinkers would take a secondary position to their male counterparts at coeducational universities? Why should women be separated from men in learning environments? Single-sex schools are both discriminatory and do not prepare their students for the real adult world where both males and females live mutually.

Segregation existed throughout the south until the 1950s, when *Brown v. Board of Education* argued that segregation of black children in the public schools was unconstitutional because it violated the Fourteenth Amendment. Is being denied admission to a school because of race any different from being denied because of sex? It seems unconstitutional that a college, such as Wellesley, has a right to deny a potential student because the applicant is a male. A person is born with both a sex and a race, and since denying someone of the black race is unconstitutional, denying someone of the male sex must be also. How would the world react if a university only admitted white students?

Advocates of single-sex education argue that males distract females and vice versa in coeducational schools. If only one sex is taught in a school, they believe, there will be no distractions and the students can focus on their studies. Although this position may seem logical, there is one major flaw. The workforce is composed of both males and females. If men and women are not able to interact as adolescents, how can they possibly interact as adults? Boys and girls must be exposed to each other so they can learn how to coexist and cooperate. Our world is based on the fundamental relationship between a man and a female. This relationship must be formed from the beginning so our world can continue to function. If the sexes are considered a distraction to each other in elementary and secondary schools, imagine the disturbance if they are first introduced to each other in the working world.

Dr. Brenda Despontin believes that "girls' brains are wired differently" and "boys dominate teacher time" in coeducational schools. Dr. Despontin sets the male brain as the standard norm and, therefore, declares the female brain to be a deviation. Ironically, this female scholar is reverting to ancient times when women were considered inferior to men. I happen to know, firsthand, that female students are outspoken in the classroom and realize they must assert their beliefs in front of males to ensure that they will not be considered the inferior sex. Young girls must be around young boys to develop the social and emotional skills that will prepare them for the coeducational world. And on the other end of the spectrum, young boys must be around young girls to guarantee healthy relationships between males and females.

The second part of the *Mona Lisa Smile* tagline says that Ms. Watson taught the Wellesley women another way of living, helping them become more than what my mother declares herself to be — a domestic engineer. Males and females must interact at a young age to ensure proper relationships between the sexes. Perhaps what is most wrong with single-sex schools is the loss of diversity. Should anyone go to school with people who are just the same as they are?

Questions

1. What is most appealing or effective about this essay? As you respond, reflect on how your own view (that is, whether you agree or disagree with Brian) affects what you find most appealing or effective.
2. Are Brian's outside sources — a film, two Supreme Court cases — helpful in making his argument? Explain why or why not.
3. Brian draws an analogy between segregation by race and sex. Explain whether you think this strategy strengthens or weakens his argument.
4. If you were making suggestions for revision, would you recommend adding additional external sources? If so, what kind would you suggest?
5. Does referring to his mother as a domestic engineer strengthen or weaken Brian's argument?
6. What is the effect of the rhetorical questions in the essay's first and last paragraphs?

Grammar as Rhetoric and Style

Pronouns

As you well know, a pronoun takes the place of a noun (called the *antecedent*). Unlike a noun, however, a pronoun defines the viewpoint in your writing. Are you talking about yourself (first person), are you talking directly to the audience (second person), or are you referring to a person who is neither the speaker nor the audience (third person)? This section considers two points of pronoun usage that affect viewpoint: (1) consistency of pronouns in a sentence or passage, and

(2) sexist pronouns, an issue touched on in Bill Broadway's piece about updating biblical texts.

Consistency: Viewpoint and Number

Pronouns must agree with one another and with their antecedents in number and in viewpoint (person). The following table summarizes which personal pronouns are singular and which are plural, as well as which are first person, second person, and third person:

VIEWPOINT	NUMBER	
	SINGULAR	PLURAL
First person	*I, me, my, mine*	*we, us, our, ours*
Second person	*you, your, yours*	*you, your, yours*
Third person	*he, him, his*	*they, them, their, theirs*
	she, her, hers	
	it, its	
	one, one's	

If you use pronouns to refer to an antecedent more than once in a sentence or paragraph, it's important that they be consistent in person and number. Consider the sentence below:

> The way *our* teachers and classmates looked at *us* that day in school was just a taste of the culture clash that awaited *you* in the real world.

This sentence shifts viewpoint from first-person plural to second-person singular, and as a result it is confusing to the reader.

When corrected, the sentence maintains a consistent first-person plural viewpoint:

> The way *our* teachers and classmates looked at *us* that day in school was just a taste of the culture clash that awaited *us* in the real world.
>
> —Judith Ortiz Cofer

Consistency is also important when using *indefinite pronouns.* (An indefinite pronoun is one that does not have a specific antecedent.) Consider the singular indefinite pronoun *one* as it is used here:

> *One* cannot think well, love well, sleep well, if *one* has not dined well.
>
> —Virginia Woolf

This sentence begins with the singular indefinite pronoun *one* and sticks with *one*. The sentence would be much less effective if it said:

> *One* cannot think well, love well, sleep well, if *you* have not dined well.

Note, though, that Virginia Woolf could have opted to use the second person:

> *You* cannot think well, love well, sleep well, if *you* have not dined well.

Woolf's use of the third person adds a formality to the tone — through the more distanced *one* — while the second-person *you* sounds more conversational.

Sexist Pronoun Usage

When a third-person singular pronoun (*he, she, it*) could refer to either a male or a female, writers have several options: they can combine the male and female pronouns, using *or*; they can use the plural form of the pronoun, being careful to adjust the rest of the sentence accordingly; or they can alternate the gender of the pronouns.

Consider the following sentences from Virginia Woolf's "Professions for Women."

> I hope I am not giving away professional secrets if I say that a *novelist*'s chief desire is to be as unconscious as possible. *He* has to induce in *himself* a state of perpetual lethargy.

The pronouns *he* and *himself* in the second sentence refer to the antecedent *novelist* in the first sentence. In using *he* and *himself*, Woolf was not only following standard grammatical practice of the 1930s but was also underscoring the reality that during her lifetime most published novelists were indeed male. But the world and the English language have changed, and using the generic *he, his, him, himself* to refer to any individual is not as acceptable today as it was when Woolf wrote (see "New and Newer Versions of Scripture" p. 405). How would writers today handle a discussion of an unidentified novelist? One possibility would be to use the term *his/her* or *his or her*:

> I hope I am not giving away professional secrets if I say that a *novelist*'s chief desire is to be as unconscious as possible. *He or she* has to induce in *himself or herself* a state of perpetual lethargy.

If writers need to make only one or two references to an unspecified antecedent, perhaps they can get away with *he or she* and *himself or herself*, though even the two references in this sentence are awkward. But if there are many references to the antecedent, as in the Woolf passage that follows, the *or* construction becomes monotonous or downright annoying:

> I hope I am not giving away professional secrets if I say that a *novelist*'s chief desire is to be as unconscious as possible. *He or she* has to induce in *himself or*

herself a state of perpetual lethargy. *He or she* wants life to proceed with the utmost quiet and regularity. *He or she* wants to see the same faces, to read the same books, to do the same things day after day, month after month, while *he or she* is writing, so that nothing may break the illusion in which *he or she* is living.

The most straightforward revision would be to change the unspecified singular noun to an unspecified plural noun:

I hope I am not giving away professional secrets if I say that the chief desire of *novelists* is to be as unconscious as possible. *They* have to induce in *themselves* a state of perpetual lethargy. *They* want life to proceed with the utmost quiet and regularity. *They* want to see the same faces, to read the same books, to do the same things day after day, month after month, while *they* are writing, so that nothing may break the illusion in which *they* are living.

Another possibility for large sections of an essay is to shift between male and female pronouns, using *he* or *him* or *his* for a while, then shifting to *she* or *her* or *hers*, and shifting yet again. Generally, writers seem to like this approach more than readers, who can lose track of what they are reading about, especially if the shift in gender happens too frequently.

Rhetorical and Stylistic Strategy

Although maintaining a consistent viewpoint is a matter of grammatical accuracy, selecting which viewpoint to use is a rhetorical decision. If the writing is formal, then the third person is generally the most appropriate choice. For example, most teachers expect a research paper to be written in the third person. If the essay is more informal and draws on the writer's personal experience, then the first person (singular or plural) works well. The second person — *you* — is generally reserved for informal writing, such as a newspaper column, where the writer is addressing readers as though they are in conversation, or for speeches, where the writer is directly addressing an audience.

In the second part of this section, we focused on sexist pronouns. Why do we recommend that you eliminate pronouns that some people think of as sexist? After all, there is nothing grammatically wrong with Virginia Woolf's use of a male pronoun to refer to an indefinite singular noun such as *novelist*. But language choice sometimes involves more than grammatical correctness. Throughout this book, you are reading about how to appeal to audiences and how to make audiences find you credible. One way to impress readers is to be sensitive to their likes and dislikes — in this case, to their own attitudes toward sexist language. Many of your readers will appreciate any steps you take in your writing to establish common ground with them. In pronoun usage, meet your readers' expectations that an indefinite singular noun might just as easily refer to a woman as to a man.

Remember, grammatical correctness and a writer's purpose go hand in hand.

• EXERCISE 1

Correct all errors in the following sentences that result from sexist pronouns or inconsistencies in pronoun person or number.

1. Popular culture once provided us with a common vocabulary, but now you have a hard time keeping up with the jargon.
2. For a runner to keep up his pace, he must pay attention to his nutrition.
3. If one measures her country's commitment to education by dollars allocated, you can see that it's not our top priority.
4. Baseball fans pay so much attention to percentages that you almost always have a sense of the improbability or likelihood of an event actually occurring.
5. Most of the time a teacher tries to tailor writing assignments to interest his students.
6. Everyone is wondering who the next Democratic presidential candidate will be and if he will be a charismatic leader.
7. A doctor should treat his patients respectfully by listening to them no matter how busy he or she is.
8. We hoped to get a free pass to the movie, but the mall was so crowded that you didn't have a chance.
9. You should try to stop arguments before they start; otherwise, one might become involved in a conflict that gets more complicated than we thought possible.
10. When one is as strong a student as Chong is, you're not surprised that he passed the bar on his first try.

• EXERCISE 2

The following paragraph is taken from the essay "I Want a Wife" by Judy Brady. (The full text is available online at <bedfordstmartins.com/languageofcomp>.) Discuss the effect of the pronouns *I* and *my*. How many times does Brady use them? How does this repetition help to achieve her purpose?

I would like to go back to school so that I can become economically independent, support myself, and, if need be, support those dependent upon me. I want a wife who will work and send me to school. And while I am going to school, I want a wife to take care of my children. I want a wife to keep track of the children's doctor and dentist appointments. And to keep track of mine, too. I want a wife to make sure my children eat properly and are kept clean. I want a wife who will wash the children's clothes and keep them mended. I want a wife who is a good nurturant attendant to my children, who arranges for their schooling, makes sure that they have an adequate social life with their peers, takes them to the park, the zoo, etc. I want a wife who takes care of the children when they are sick, a wife who arranges to be around when the children need special care, because, of course, I cannot miss classes at school. My wife must arrange to lose time at work and not lose the job. It may mean a small cut in my wife's income from time to time, but I guess I can tolerate that. Needless to say, my wife will arrange and pay for the care of the children while my wife is working.

● EXERCISE 3

The following excerpt is from "Professions for Women" by Virginia Woolf, the Classic Essay in this chapter. It includes both the first and third person. Rewrite it entirely in the first person — for example, with *I* and *we women*. Then discuss the effect of your changes. Consider the excerpt in the context of the entire essay.

These then were two very genuine experiences of my own. These were two of the adventures of my professional life. The first — killing the Angel in the House — I think I solved. She died. But the second, telling the truth about my own experiences as a body, I do not think I solved. I doubt that any woman has solved it yet. The obstacles against her are still immensely powerful — and yet they are very difficult to define. Outwardly, what is simpler than to write books? Outwardly, what obstacles are there for a woman rather than for a man? Inwardly, I think, the case is very different; she has still many ghosts to fight, many prejudices to overcome. Indeed it will be a long time still, I think, before a woman can sit down to write a book without finding a phantom to be slain, a rock to be dashed against. And if this is so in literature, the freest of all professions for women, how is it in the new professions which you are now for the first time entering?

● EXERCISE 4

Occasionally, a writer will deliberately shift from one person to another or between singular and plural to make a point. The writer might, for instance, shift from *I* when referring to a personal view to *we* when referring to membership in a particular group. Discuss the shifts in pronoun reference as a rhetorical strategy in the final three paragraphs of Steven Lewis's speech. Keep in mind the context in which he delivered the speech.

For myself, I'm filled with rage. I can barely contain it. I know it reduces my effectiveness, but there's nothing I can do about it. The madness of what is happening, the fact that it is so completely unnecessary, the fact that we could subdue this pandemic if the world put its mind to it — all of that renders me almost incoherent with the roiling blood of anger. We must find a way to bring this nightmare to an end. Africans and the world will obviously work with every instrument at our collective command to reduce the heart-breaking decimation of individuals, families and communities. But the women, certainly the women of Africa need huge quotients of additional help, and that help lies, in significant extent, in the discovery of a microbicide.

I don't have to tell anyone here — God knows, I'm way out of my depth — about the science and the trials and the timetable and the resources. I've read the materials, and as much as a layperson can grasp such things, I have grasped them. I ask only that you see microbicides, not merely as one of the great scientific pursuits of the age, but as a significant emancipation for women whose cultural and social and economic inheritance have put them so gravely at risk.

Never in human history have so many died for so little reason. You have a chance to alter the course of that history. Can there be any task more noble?

Suggestions for Writing

Gender

Now that you have examined a number of readings and other texts that focus on gender, including gender stereotypes and their consequences, explore one dimension of this topic by synthesizing your own ideas and the readings. You might want to do more research or use readings from other classes as you prepare for the following projects.

1. From popular magazines and newspapers, collect ads that reflect stereotypes about the roles of men and women, as well as ads that show men and women in a more progressive light. You might work in groups to collect and analyze the ads. Make lists of both kinds of ads. Determine which kinds of products show men and women in stereotyped roles and which show men and women breaking gender stereotypes. Which stereotypes are more common in these ads — stereotypes about women or about men? Then, working individually, write a report that discusses what the ads show about American values, beliefs, and attitudes toward gender roles.

2. Write a personal narrative in which you describe a role that your family or friends expected of you but that you either refused to play or struggled against. Explain the origin and nature of the expectation, as well as your

reasons for not wanting to fulfill it. Include a discussion of the reactions you have gotten as you challenged the role or expectation.

3. To explore the idea that gender roles are socially constructed rather than biologically determined, do some research into other cultures and times. Report on a role that our society believes is gender-specific (for example, the nurturing mother, the protective male) but that another culture or people from another period view quite differently.

4. The Internet is arguably gender-neutral. When you do not know another user's background, physical traits, style of dress, and so on, you have to judge them only by their words. Some observers believe that the anonymity of the Internet allows people to move outside of expected gender roles. Does the Internet affect you that way? Are you more willing to be confrontational online, for example? Are you funnier? Does your online voice resemble who you are in person? Write an essay exploring how gender does or does not influence your online communication style.

5. Write a roundtable conversation that you might have with three authors in this chapter about *one* of the following quotations:
   a. "The curse of too many women has been that they have this privilege of refuge in the home." — Pearl Buck
   b. "There are two kinds of spiritual law, two kinds of conscience, one in man and another, altogether different, in women. They do not understand each other." — Henrik Ibsen
   c. "The discovery is, of course, that 'man' and 'woman' are fictions, caricatures, cultural constructs. As models they are reductive, totalitarian, inappropriate to human becoming. As roles they are static, demeaning to the female, dead-ended for males and females both."
      — Andrea Dworkin
   d. "You see a lot of smart guys with dumb women but you hardly ever see a smart woman with a dumb guy." — Erica Jong

6. Examine a popular movie in terms of gender roles, and write about it. In what ways do the characters reflect conventional roles, and in what ways do they step out of those roles?

7. Write a "myth-buster" essay. Take a stereotype based on gender (such as "women are bad drivers" or "men are more prone to violent behavior than women"), and debunk it by conducting research. Use quantitative information as well as anecdotal or personal experience as evidence. Consider how this myth originated and who benefits from perpetuating it.

8. In his book *Men Are from Mars, Women Are from Venus*, John Gray writes, "A man's sense of self is defined through his ability to achieve results. . . . A woman's sense of self is defined through her feelings and the quality of her relationships." Write an essay supporting, challenging, or modifying

these statements. Use examples from your own experience and selections from this chapter.

9. Several of the authors in Conversation: Focus on Defining Masculinity raise questions about the reading required in school. Working in groups, develop a list of books the girls like, and one the boys like; then try to reach a consensus on at least two or three selections that both groups find interesting. Write an essay analyzing the process and explaining the results. As part of your inquiry, you might visit <www.guysread.com>.

8

Sports and Fitness

How do the values of sports affect the way we see ourselves?

It would be difficult to live in the modern world without somehow being involved with sports. Athletes are cultural icons; sports dominate television, radio, even film; there is mounting evidence that physical fitness is the key to health and longevity. Once the purview of men and boys, the subject of sports — opinions on its ethics, its future, its place in society — is now open to everyone. And in some ways, the line separating the professional from the spectator has blurred. Weekend athletes train like professionals; even couch potatoes participate in fantasy leagues. Scandals surrounding steroid use among high school and college athletes mirror the scandals involving Olympic and major league athletes.

From our first days in school we are asked to play to win, play by the rules, play fair, be team players, be good sports. We're taught to be good losers; we're reminded that the best defense is a good offense — and the other way around. We're told that life is a game of chance, but we can sometimes level the playing field. These exhortations are as at home in a grade school kickball game as they are in politics and business. Why are we so comfortable with this shorthand? What are the bigger issues connected to our fascination with sports?

A tiny number of people play professional sports, but huge numbers follow the professionals as spectators at both live and televised events. Professional athletes are front and center in the news and earn salaries that top those of movie stars. At their best, they are hailed as role models; at their worst, as scourges on society. Is our attraction to professional athletes healthy? Do we learn from their grit, from their strength and commitment to training, or do they encourage unhealthy narcissism and dangerous habits?

The selections in this chapter explore many of the questions raised by our interest in sports and the effect of that interest on everyday life. The readings look at the star power of our professional athletes and the thrill of tapping into our own potential for athletic achievement. They ask, at what point does an interest in athletes and sports become an unhealthy obsession and in what circumstances can athletic competition be therapeutic? As you read and discuss these pieces, consider the relationship between the dream of some athletes to play sports professionally

429

and the reality of a healthy personal lifestyle for the rest of us. Is the marketing of sports paraphernalia and the widespread participation in fantasy sports leagues a way for us to spend money and avoid, at least temporarily, the demands of real life? Or does the language of the playing field and the model of the professional athlete enliven communication and help us become better people?

The Silent Season of a Hero

GAY TALESE

 Gay Talese (b. 1932) began life on the small island of Ocean City, New Jersey. As the son of a southern Italian immigrant growing up Catholic in a Protestant town, Talese identified himself as an outsider. He is known for writing the "unnoticed story," reporting the angle ignored by others or the news that others thought was not newsworthy. Recognized for his elegant style, Talese is considered one of the founders of *New Journalism*, a term coined in the 1960s to describe the work of writers like Talese, Tom Wolfe, and Hunter S. Thompson. New Journalism is characterized by the use of elements of fiction to get at the story behind the story. New Journalists set scenes, include dialogue, and accept their own presence as part of the drama of the story. The following selection appeared in *Esquire* in 1966.

"I would like to take the great DiMaggio fishing," the old man said. "They say his father was a fisherman. Maybe he was as poor as we are and would understand."
— ERNEST HEMINGWAY, *The Old Man and the Sea*

It was not quite spring, the silent season before the search for salmon, and the old fishermen of San Francisco were either painting their boats or repairing their nets along the pier or sitting in the sun talking quietly among themselves, watching the tourists come and go, and smiling, now, as a pretty girl paused to take their picture. She was about 25, healthy and blue-eyed and wearing a turtleneck sweater, and she had long, flowing blonde hair that she brushed back a few times before clicking her camera. The fishermen, looking at her, made admiring comments, but she did not understand because they spoke a Sicilian dialect; nor did she understand the tall gray-haired man in a dark suit who stood watching her from behind a big bay window on the second floor of DiMaggio's Restaurant that overlooks the pier.

He watched until she left, lost in the crowd of newly arrived tourists that had just come down the hill by cable car. Then he sat down again at the table in the restaurant, finishing his tea and lighting another cigarette, his fifth in the last half hour. It was 11:30 in the morning. None of the other tables was occupied, and the only sounds came from the bar, where a liquor salesman was laughing at something the headwaiter had said. But then the salesman, his briefcase under his arm, headed for the door, stopping briefly to peek into the dining room and call out, "See you later, Joe." Joe DiMaggio turned and waved at the salesman. Then the room was quiet again.

At 51, DiMaggio was a most distinguished-looking man, aging as gracefully as he had played on the ball field, impeccable in his tailoring, his nails manicured, his 6-foot-2 body seeming as lean and capable as when he posed for the portrait that hangs in the restaurant and shows him in Yankee Stadium, swinging from the heels at a pitch thrown 20 years ago. His gray hair was thinning at the crown, but just barely, and his face was lined in the right places, and his expression, once as sad and haunted as a matador's, was more in repose these days, though, as now, tension had returned and he chain-smoked and occasionally paced the floor and looked out the window at the people below. In the crowd was a man he did not wish to see.

The man had met DiMaggio in New York. This week he had come to San Francisco and had telephoned several times, but none of the calls had been returned because DiMaggio suspected that the man, who had said he was doing research on some vague sociological project, really wanted to delve into DiMaggio's private life and that of DiMaggio's former wife, Marilyn Monroe. DiMaggio would never tolerate this. The memory of her death is still very painful to him, and yet, because he keeps it to himself, some people are not sensitive to it. One night in a supper club, a woman who had been drinking approached his table, and when he did not ask her to join him, she snapped:

"All right, I guess I'm *not* Marilyn Monroe." 5

He ignored her remark, but when she repeated it, he replied, barely controlling his anger, "No — I wish you were, but you're not."

The tone of his voice softened her, and she asked, "Am I saying something wrong?"

"You already have," he said. "Now will you please leave me alone?"

His friends on the wharf, understanding him as they do, are very careful when discussing him with strangers, knowing that should they inadvertently betray a confidence, he will not denounce them but rather will never speak to them again; this comes from a sense of propriety not inconsistent in the man who also, after Marilyn Monroe's death, directed that fresh flowers be placed on her grave "forever."

Some of the older fishermen who have known DiMaggio all his life remem- 10 ber him as a small boy who helped clean his father's boat, and as a young man who sneaked away and used a broken oar as a bat on the sandlots nearby. His father, a small mustachioed man known as Zio Pepe, would become infuriated and call him *lagnuso*, lazy, *meschino*, good-for-nothing, but in 1936 Zio Pepe was among those who cheered when Joe DiMaggio returned to San Francisco after his first season with the New York Yankees and was carried along the wharf on the shoulders of the fishermen.

The fishermen also remember how, after his retirement in 1951, DiMaggio brought his second wife, Marilyn, to live near the wharf, and sometimes they would be seen early in the morning fishing off DiMaggio's boat, the *Yankee Clipper*, now docked quietly in the marina, and in the evening they would be sitting and talking on the pier. They had arguments, too, the fishermen knew, and one night Marilyn was seen running hysterically, crying, as she ran, along the road away from the pier, with Joe following. But the fishermen pretended they did not see this; it was none of their affair. They knew that Joe wanted her to stay in San Francisco and avoid the sharks in Hollywood, but she was confused and torn then — "She was a child," they said — and even today DiMaggio loathes Los Angeles and many of the people in it. He no longer speaks to his onetime friend, Frank Sinatra, who had befriended Marilyn in her final years, and he also is cool to Dean Martin and Peter Lawford and Lawford's former wife, Pat, who once gave a party at which she introduced Marilyn Monroe to Robert Kennedy, and the two of them danced often that night, Joe heard, and he did not take it well. He was possessive of her that year, his close friends say, because Marilyn and he had planned to remarry; but before they could she was dead, and DiMaggio banned the Lawfords and Sinatra and many Hollywood people from her funeral. When Marilyn Monroe's attorney complained that DiMaggio was keeping her friends away, DiMaggio answered coldly, "If it weren't for those friends persuading her to stay in Hollywood, she would still be alive."

Joe DiMaggio now spends most of the year in San Francisco, and each day tourists, noticing the name on the restaurant, ask the men on the wharf if they ever see him. Oh, yes, the men say, they see him nearly every day; they have not seen him yet this morning, they add, but he should be arriving shortly. So the tourists continue to walk along the piers past the crab vendors, under the circling sea gulls, past the fish-'n'-chip stands, sometimes stopping to watch a large vessel steaming toward the Golden Gate Bridge, which, to their dismay, is painted red. Then they visit the Wax Museum, where there is a life-size figure of DiMaggio in uniform, and walk across the street and spend a quarter to peer through the silver telescopes focused on the island of Alcatraz, which is no longer a federal prison. Then they return to ask the men if DiMaggio has been seen. Not yet, the men say, although they notice his blue Impala parked in the lot next to the restaurant. Sometimes tourists will walk into the restaurant and have lunch and will see him sitting calmly in a corner signing autographs and being extremely gracious with everyone. At other times, as on this particular morning when the man from New York chose to visit, DiMaggio was tense and suspicious.

When the man entered the restaurant from the side steps leading to the dining room, he saw DiMaggio standing near the window, talking with an elderly maître d' named Charles Friscia. Not wanting to walk in and risk intrusion, the man asked one of DiMaggio's nephews to inform Joe of his presence. When DiMaggio got the message, he quickly turned and left Friscia and disappeared through an exit leading down to the kitchen.

Astonished and confused, the visitor stood in the hall. A moment later Friscia appeared and the man asked, "Did Joe leave?"

"Joe who?" Friscia replied.

"Joe DiMaggio!" 15

"Haven't seen him," Friscia said.

"You haven't *seen* him! He was standing right next to you a second ago!"

"It wasn't me," Friscia said.

"You were standing next to him. I saw you. In the dining room." 20

"You must be mistaken," Friscia said, softly, seriously. "It wasn't me."

"You *must* be kidding," the man said angrily, turning and leaving the restaurant. Before he could get to his car, however, DiMaggio's nephew came running after him and said, "Joe wants to see you."

He returned, expecting to see DiMaggio waiting for him. Instead he was handed a telephone. The voice was powerful and deep and so tense that the quick sentences ran together.

"*You are invading my rights. I did not ask you to come. I assume you have a lawyer. You must have a lawyer, get your lawyer!*"

"I came as a friend," the man interrupted. 25

"That's beside the point," DiMaggio said. "I have my privacy. I do not want it violated. You'd better get a lawyer. . . ." Then, pausing, DiMaggio asked, "Is my nephew there?"

He was not.

"Then wait where you are."

A moment later DiMaggio appeared, tall and red-faced, erect and beautifully dressed in his dark suit and white shirt with the gray silk tie and the gleaming silver cuff links. He moved with his big steps toward the man and handed him an airmail envelope unopened that the man had written from New York.

"Here," DiMaggio said. "This is yours." 30

Then DiMaggio sat down at a small table. He said nothing, just lit a cigarette and waited, legs crossed, his head held high and back so as to reveal the intricate construction of his nose, a fine sharp tip above the big nostrils and tiny bones built out from the bridge, a great nose.

"Look," DiMaggio said, more calmly, "I do not interfere with other people's lives. And I do not expect them to interfere with mine. There are things about my life, personal things, that I refuse to talk about. And even if you asked my brothers, they would be unable to tell you about them because they do not know. There are things about me, so many things, that they simply do not know. . . ."

"I don't want to cause trouble," the man said. "I think you're a great man, and . . ."

"I'm not great," DiMaggio cut in. "I'm not great," he repeated softly. "I'm just a man trying to get along."

Then DiMaggio, as if realizing that he was intruding upon his own privacy, 35
abruptly stood up. He looked at his watch.

"I'm late," he said, very formal again. "I'm 10 minutes late. You're making me late."

The man left the restaurant. He crossed the street and wandered over to the pier, briefly watching the fishermen hauling their nets and talking in the sun, seemingly very calm and contented. Then, after he turned and was headed back toward the parking lot, a blue Impala stopped in front of him and Joe DiMaggio leaned out the window and asked, "Do you have a car?" His voice was very gentle.

"Yes," the man said.

"Oh," DiMaggio said. "I would have given you a ride."

Joe DiMaggio was not born in San Francisco but in Martinez, a small fishing   40
village 25 miles northeast of the Golden Gate. Zio Pepe had settled there after leaving Isola delle Femmine, an islet off Palermo where the DiMaggios had been fishermen for generations. But in 1915, hearing of the luckier waters off San Francisco's wharf, Zio Pepe left Martinez, packing his boat with furniture and family, including Joe, who was one year old.

San Francisco was placid and picturesque when the DiMaggios arrived, but there was a competitive undercurrent and struggle for power along the pier. At dawn the boats would sail out to where the bay meets the ocean and the sea is rough, and later the men would race back with their hauls, hoping to beat their fellow fishermen to shore and sell it while they could. Twenty or 30 boats would sometimes be trying to gain the channel shoreward at the same time, and a fisherman had to know every rock in the water, and later know every bargaining trick along the shore, because the dealers and restaurateurs would play one fisherman off against the other, keeping the prices down. Later the fishermen became wiser and organized, predetermining the maximum amount each fisherman would catch, but there were always some men who, like the fish, never learned, and so heads would sometimes be broken, nets slashed, gasoline poured onto their fish, flowers of warning placed outside their doors.

But these days were ending when Zio Pepe arrived, and he expected his five sons to succeed him as fishermen, and the first two, Tom and Michael, did; but a third, Vincent, wanted to sing. He sang with such magnificent power as a young man that he came to the attention of the great banker, A. P. Giannini, and there were plans to send him to Italy for tutoring and the opera. But there was hesitation around the DiMaggio household and Vince never went; instead, he played ball with the San Francisco Seals and sports writers misspelled his name.

It was DeMaggio until Joe, at Vince's recommendation, joined the team and became a sensation, being followed later by the youngest brother, Dominic, who was also outstanding. All three later played in the big leagues, and some writers like to say that Joe was the best hitter, Dom the best fielder, Vince the best singer, and Casey Stengel once said: "Vince is the only player I ever saw who could strike out three times in one game and not be embarrassed. He'd walk into the clubhouse whistling. Everybody would be feeling sorry for him, but Vince always thought he was doing good."

After he retired from baseball Vince became a bartender, then a milkman, now a carpenter. He lives 40 miles north of San Francisco in a house he partly built, has been happily married for 34 years, has four grandchildren, has in the closet one of Joe's tailor-made suits that he has never had altered to fit, and when people ask him if he envies Joe he always says, "No, maybe Joe would like to have what I have." The brother Vincent most admired was Michael, "a big earthy man, a dreamer, a fisherman who wanted things but didn't want to take from Joe, or to work in the restaurant. He wanted a bigger boat, but wanted to earn it on his own. He never got it." In 1953, at the age of 44, Michael fell from his boat and drowned.

Since Zio Pepe's death at 77 in 1949, Tom at 62, the oldest brother — two of   45
his four sisters are older — has become nominal head of the family and manages the restaurant that was opened in 1937 as Joe DiMaggio's Grotto. Later Joe sold out his share, and now Tom is the co-owner with Dominic. Of all the brothers, Dominic, who was known as the "Little Professor" when he played with the Boston Red Sox, is the most successful in business. He lives in a fashionable Boston suburb with his wife and three children and is president of a firm that manufactures fiber cushion materials and grossed more than $3,500,000 last year.

Joe DiMaggio lives with his widowed sister, Marie, in a tan stone house on a quiet residential street not far from Fisherman's Wharf. He bought the house almost 30 years ago for his parents, and after their deaths he lived there with Marilyn Monroe. Now it is cared for by Marie, a slim and handsome dark-eyed woman who has an apartment on the second floor, Joe on the third. There are some baseball trophies and plaques in the small room off DiMaggio's bedroom, and on his dresser are photographs of Marilyn Monroe, and in the living room downstairs is a small painting of her that DiMaggio likes very much; it reveals only her face and shoulders and she is wearing a wide-brimmed sun hat, and there is a soft, sweet smile on her lips, an innocent curiosity about her that is the way he saw her and the way he wanted her to be seen by others — a simple girl, "a warm, big-hearted girl," he once described her, "that everybody took advantage of."

The publicity photographs emphasizing her sex appeal often offend him, and a memorable moment for Billy Wilder, who directed her in *The Seven-Year Itch*, occurred when he spotted DiMaggio in a large crowd of people gathered on Lexington Avenue in New York to watch a scene in which Marilyn, standing over a subway grating to cool herself, had her skirts blown high by a sudden wind blow. "What the hell is going on here?" DiMaggio was overheard to have said in the crowd, and Wilder recalled, "I shall never forget the look of death on Joe's face."

He was then 39, she was 27. They had been married in January of that year, 1954, despite disharmony in temperament and time; he was tired of publicity, she was thriving on it; he was intolerant of tardiness, she was always late. During their honeymoon in Tokyo an American general had introduced himself and asked if, as a patriotic gesture, she would visit the troops in Korea. She looked at Joe. "It's your honeymoon," he said, shrugging, "go ahead if you want to."

She appeared on 10 occasions before 100,000 servicemen, and when she returned, she said, "It was so wonderful, Joe. You never heard such cheering."

"Yes, I have," he said.   50

Across from her portrait in the living room, on a coffee table in front of a sofa, is a sterling-silver humidor that was presented to him by his Yankee teammates at a time when he was the most talked-about man in America, and when Les Brown's band had recorded a hit that was heard day and night on the radio.

> From Coast to Coast, that's all you hear
> Of Joe the One-Man Show.
> He's glorified the horsehide sphere,
> Jolting Joe DiMaggio . . .
> Joe . . . Joe . . . DiMaggio . . .
> we want you on our side . . .

The year was 1941, and it began for DiMaggio in the middle of May after the Yankees had lost four games in a row, seven of their last nine, and were in fourth place, five and a half games behind the leading Cleveland Indians. On May 15, DiMaggio hit only a first-inning single in a game that New York lost to Chicago 13–1; he was barely hitting .300, and had greatly disappointed the crowds that had seen him finish with a .352 average the year before and .381 in 1939.

He got a hit in the next game, and the next, and the next. On May 24, with the Yankees losing 6–5 to Boston, DiMaggio came up with runners on second and third and singled them home, winning the game, extending his streak to 10 games. But it went largely unnoticed. Even DiMaggio was not conscious of it until it had reached 29 games in mid-June. Then the newspapers began to dramatize it, the public became aroused, they sent him good-luck charms of every description, and DiMaggio kept hitting, and radio announcers would interrupt programs to announce the news, and then the song again: "Joe . . . Joe . . . DiMaggio . . . we want you on our side . . ."

Sometimes DiMaggio would be hitless his first three times up, the tension would build, it would appear that the game would end without his getting another chance — but he always would, and then he would hit the ball against the left-field wall, or through the pitcher's legs, or between two leaping infielders. In the forty-first game, the first of a doubleheader in Washington, DiMaggio tied an American League record that George Sisler had set in 1922. But before the second game began, a spectator sneaked onto the field and into the Yankees' dugout and stole DiMaggio's favorite bat. In the second game, using another of his bats, DiMaggio lined out twice and flied out. But in the seventh inning, borrowing one of his old bats that a teammate was using, he singled and broke Sisler's record, and he was only three games away from surpassing the major-league record of 44 set in 1897 by Willie Keeler while playing for Baltimore when it was a National League franchise.

An appeal for the missing bat was made through the newspapers. A man   55 from Newark admitted the crime and returned it with regrets. And on July 2 at Yankee Stadium, DiMaggio hit a home run into the left-field stands. The record was broken.

He also got hits on the next 11 games, but on July 17 in Cleveland, at a night game attended by 67,468, he failed against two pitchers, Al Smith and Jim Bagby, Jr., although Cleveland's hero was really its third baseman, Ken Keltner, who in the first inning lunged to his right to make a spectacular backhanded stop of a drive and, from the foul line behind third base, threw DiMaggio out. DiMaggio received a walk in the fourth inning. But in the seventh he again hit a hard shot at Keltner, who again stopped it and threw him out. DiMaggio hit sharply toward the shortstop in the eighth inning, the ball taking a bad hop, but Lou Boudreau speared it off his shoulder and threw to the second baseman to start a double play and DiMaggio's streak was stopped at 56 games. But the New York Yankees were on their way to winning the pennant by 17 games, and the World Series too, and so in August, in a hotel suite in Washington, the players threw a surprise party for DiMaggio and toasted him with champagne and presented him with his Tiffany silver humidor that is now in San Francisco in his living room. . . .

Marie was in the kitchen making toast and tea when DiMaggio came down for breakfast; his gray hair was uncombed but, since he wears it short, it was not untidy. He said good morning to Marie, sat down, and yawned. He lit a cigarette. He wore a blue wool bathrobe over his pajamas. It was 8:00 A.M. He had many things to do today and he seemed cheerful. He had a conference with the president of Continental Television, Inc., a large retail chain in California of which he is a partner and vice-president; later he had a golf date, and then a big banquet to attend, and, if that did not go on too long and if he were not too tired afterward, he might have a date.

Picking up the morning paper, not rushing to the sports page, DiMaggio read the front-page news, the people problems of 1966; Kwame Nkrumah was overthrown in Ghana, students were burning their draft cards (DiMaggio shook his head), the flu epidemic was spreading through the whole state of California. Then he flipped inside through the gossip columns, thankful they did not have him in there today — they had printed an item about his dating "an electrifying airline hostess" not long ago, and they also spotted him at dinner with Dori Lane, "the frantic frugger" in Whisky à Go Go's glass cage — and then he turned to the sports page and read a story about how the injured Mickey Mantle may never regain his form.

It happened all so quickly, the passing of Mantle, or so it seemed; he had succeeded DiMaggio, who had succeeded Ruth, but now there was no great young power hitter coming up, and the Yankee management, almost desperate, had talked Mantle out of retirement, and on September 18, 1965, they gave him a "day" in New York during which he received several thousand dollars' worth of gifts — an automobile, two quarter horses, free vacation trips to Rome, Nassau, Puerto Rico — and DiMaggio had flown to New York to make the introduction before 50,000: it had been a dramatic day, an almost holy day for the believers who had jammed the grandstands early to witness the canonization of a new stadium saint. Cardinal [Francis] Spellman was on the committee, President [Lyndon] Johnson sent a telegram, the day was officially proclaimed by the Mayor of New York, an orchestra assembled in the center field in front of the trinity of monuments to Ruth, [Lou] Gehrig, [Miller] Huggins; and high in the grandstands, billowing in the breeze of early autumn, were white banners that read: "Don't Quit, Mick," "We Love the Mick."

The banner had been held by hundreds of young boys whose dreams had   60
been fulfilled so often by Mantle, but also seated in the grandstands were older men, paunchy and balding, in whose middle-aged minds DiMaggio was still vivid and invincible, and some of them remembered how one month before, during a pregame exhibition at Old-Timers' Day in Yankee Stadium, DiMaggio had hit a pitch into the left-field seats, and suddenly thousands of people had jumped wildly to their feet, joyously screaming — the great DiMaggio had returned, they were young again, it was yesterday.

But on this sunny September day at the stadium, the feast day of Mickey Mantle, DiMaggio was not wearing No. 5 on his back or a black cap to cover his graying hair; he was wearing a black suit and white shirt and blue tie, and he stood in one corner of the Yankees' dugout waiting to be introduced by Red Barber, who was standing near home plate behind a silver microphone. In the outfield Guy Lombardo's Royal Canadians were playing soothing, soft music; and moving slowly back and forth over the sprawling green grass between the left-field bullpen and the infield were two carts driven by grounds keepers and containing dozens and dozens of large gifts for Mantle — a 6-foot, 100-pound Hebrew National salami, a Winchester rifle, a mink coat for Mrs. Mantle, a set of Wilson golf clubs, a year's supply of Chunky Candy. DiMaggio smoked a cigarette, but cupped it in his hands as if not wanting to be caught in the act by teenaged boys near enough to peek down into the dugout. Then, edging forward a step, DiMaggio poked his head out and looked up. He could see nothing above except the packed, towering green grandstands that seemed a mile high and moving, and he could see no clouds or blue sky, only a sky of faces. Then the announcer called out his name — "Joe DiMaggio!" — and suddenly there was a blast of cheering that grew louder and louder, echoing and reechoing within the big steel canyon, and DiMaggio stomped out his cigarette and climbed up the dugout steps and onto the soft green grass, the noise resounding in his ears, he could almost feel the breeze, the breath of 50,000 lungs upon him, 100,000 eyes watching his every move, and for the briefest instant as he walked he closed his eyes.

Then in his path he saw Mickey Mantle's mother, a smiling woman wearing an orchid, and he gently reached out for her elbow, holding it as he led her toward the microphone next to the other dignitaries lined up on the infield. Then he stood, very erect and without expression as the cheers softened and the stadium settled down.

Mantle was still in the dugout, in uniform, standing with one leg on the top step, and lined on both sides of him were the other Yankees who, when the ceremony was over, would play the Detroit Tigers. Then into the dugout, smiling, came Senator Robert Kennedy, accompanied by two tall curly-haired assistants with blue eyes, Fordham freckles. Jim Farley was the first on the field to notice the Senator, and Farley muttered, loud enough for others to hear, "Who the hell invited *him*?"

Toots Shor and some of the other committeemen standing near Farley looked into the dugout, and so did DiMaggio, his glance seeming cold, but he remained silent. Kennedy walked up and down within the dugout, shaking hands with the Yankees, but he did not walk onto the field.

"Senator," said Yankees' manager Johnny Keane, "why don't you sit down?"   65
Kennedy quickly shook his head, smiled. He remained standing, and then one Yankee came over and asked about getting relatives out of Cuba, and Kennedy called over one of his aides to take down the details in a notebook.

On the infield the ceremony went on, Mantle's gifts continued to pile up — a Mobilette motorbike, a Sooner Schooner wagon barbecue, a year's supply of Chock Full O' Nuts coffee, a year's supply of Topps Chewing Gum — and the Yankee players watched, and Maris seemed glum.

"Hey, Rog," yelled a man with a tape recorder, Murray Olderman, "I want to do a 30-second tape with you."

Maris swore angrily, shook his head.

"Why don't you ask Richardson? He's a better talker than me."

"Yes, but the fact that it comes from you . . ."   70

Maris swore again. But finally he went over and said in an interview that Mantle was the finest player of his era, a great competitor, a great hitter.

Fifteen minutes later, standing behind the microphone at home plate, Di-Maggio was telling the crowd, "I'm proud to introduce the man who succeeded me in center field in 1951," and from every corner of the stadium, the cheering, whistling, clapping came down. Mantle stepped forward. He stood with his wife and children, posed for the photographers kneeling in front. Then he thanked the crowd in a short speech, and, turning, shook hands with the dignitaries standing nearby. Among them now was Senator Kennedy, who had been spotted in the dugout five minutes before by Red Barber, and been called out and introduced. Kennedy posed with Mantle for a photographer, then shook hands with the Mantle children, and with Toots Shor and James Farley and others. DiMaggio saw him coming down the line and at the last second he backed away, casually, hardly anybody noticing it, and Kennedy seemed not to notice it either, just swept past, shaking more hands. . . .

Finishing his tea, putting aside the newspaper, DiMaggio went upstairs to dress, soon he was waving good-bye to Marie and driving toward his business appointment in downtown San Francisco with his partners in the retail television business. DiMaggio, while not a millionaire, has invested wisely and has always had, since his retirement from baseball, executive positions with big companies that have paid him well. He also was among the organizers of the Fisherman's National Bank of San Francisco last year, and, though it never came about, he demonstrated an acuteness that impressed those businessmen who had thought of him only in terms of baseball. He has had offers to manage big-league baseball teams but always has rejected them, saying, "I have enough trouble taking care of my own problems without taking on the responsibilities of 25 ball players."

So his only contact with baseball these days, excluding public appearances, is his unsalaried job as a batting coach each spring in Florida with the New York Yankees, a trip he would make once again on the following Sunday, three days away, if he could accomplish what for him is always the dreaded responsibility of packing, a task made no easier by the fact that he lately had fallen into the habit of keeping his clothes in two places — some hang in his closet at home, some hang in the back room of a saloon called Reno's.

Reno's is a dimly lit bar in the center of San Francisco. A portrait of DiMaggio   75
swinging a bat hangs on the wall, in addition to portraits of other star athletes, and the clientele consists mainly of the sporting crowd and newspapermen, people who know DiMaggio quite well and around whom he speaks freely on a number of subjects and relaxes as he can in few other places. The owner of the bar is Reno Barsocchini, a broad-shouldered and handsome man of 51 with graying wavy hair who began as a fiddler in Dago Mary's tavern 35 years ago. He later became a bartender there and elsewhere, including DiMaggio's Restaurant, and now he is probably DiMaggio's closest friend. He was the best man at the DiMaggio-Monroe wedding in 1954, and when they separated nine months later in Los Angeles, Reno rushed down to help DiMaggio with the packing and drove him back to San Francisco. Reno will never forget the day.

Hundreds of people were gathered around the Beverly Hills home that DiMaggio and Marilyn had rented, and photographers were perched in the trees watching the windows, and others stood on the lawn and behind the rose bushes waiting to snap pictures of anybody who walked out of the house. The newspapers that day played all the puns — "Joe Fanned on Jealousy"; "Marilyn and Joe — Out at Home" — and the Hollywood columnists, to whom DiMaggio was never an idol, never a gracious host, recounted instances of incompatibility, and Oscar Levant said it all proved that no man could be a success in two national pastimes. When Reno Barsocchini arrived, he had to push his way through the mob, then bang on the door for several minutes before being admitted. Marilyn Monroe was upstairs in bed. Joe DiMaggio was downstairs with his suitcases, tense and pale, his eyes bloodshot.

Reno took the suitcase and golf clubs out to DiMaggio's car, and then DiMaggio came out of the house, the reporters moving toward him, the lights flashing.

"Where are you going?" they yelled.

"I'm driving to San Francisco," he said, walking quickly.

"Is that going to be your home?"   80

"That is my home and always has been."

"Are you coming back?"

DiMaggio turned for a moment, looking up at the house.

"No," he said, "I'll never be back."

Reno Barsocchini, except for a brief falling-out over something he will not   85
discuss, has been DiMaggio's trusted companion ever since, joining him whenever
he can on the golf course or on the town, otherwise waiting for him in the bar with
other middle-aged men. They may wait for hours sometimes, waiting and knowing that when he arrives he may wish to be alone; but it does not seem to matter,
they are endlessly awed by him, moved by the mystique, he is a kind of male
Garbo. They know that he can be warm and loyal if they are sensitive to his wishes,
but they must never be late for an appointment to meet him. One man, unable to
find a parking place, arrived a half hour late once, and DiMaggio did not talk to
him again for three months. They know, too, when dining at night with DiMaggio,
that he generally prefers male companions and occasionally one or two young
women, but never wives; wives gossip, wives complain, wives are trouble, and men
wishing to remain close to DiMaggio must keep their wives at home.

When DiMaggio strolls into Reno's bar, the men wave and call out his name
and Reno Barsocchini smiles and announces, "Here's the Clipper!" — the "Yankee Clipper" being a nickname from his baseball days.

"Hey Clipper, Clipper," Reno had said two nights before, "where you been,
Clipper? . . . Clipper, how 'bout a belt?"

DiMaggio refused the offer of a drink, ordering instead a pot of tea, which he
prefers to all other beverages except before a date, when he will switch to vodka.

"Hey, Joe," a sports writer asked, a man researching a magazine piece on golf,
"why is it that a golfer, when he starts getting older, loses his putting touch first?
Like [Sam] Snead and [Ben] Hogan, they can still hit a ball well off the tee, but on
the greens they lose the strokes."

"It's the pressure of age," DiMaggio said, turning around on his barstool.   90
"With age you get jittery. It's true of golfers, it's true of any man when he gets into
his 50s. He doesn't take chances like he used to. The younger golfer, on the greens,
he'll stroke his putts better. The older man, he becomes hesitant. A little uncertain. Shaky. When it comes to taking chances, the younger man, even when
driving a car, will take chances that the older man won't."

"Speaking of chances," another man said, one of the group that had gathered
around DiMaggio, "did you see that guy on crutches in here last night?"

"Yeah, had his leg in a cast," a third said. "Skiing."

"I would never ski," DiMaggio said. "Men who ski must be doing it to impress
a broad. You see these men, some of them 40, 50, getting onto skis. And later you
see them all bandaged up, broken legs."

"But skiing's a very sexy sport, Joe. All the clothes, the tight pants, the fireplaces in the ski lodge, the bear rug — Christ nobody goes to ski. They just go out
there to get it cold so they can warm it up."

"Maybe you're right," DiMaggio said. "I might be persuaded."   95

"Want a belt, Clipper?" Reno asked.

DiMaggio thought for a second, then said, "All right — first belt tonight."

Now it was noon, a warm sunny day. DiMaggio's business meeting with the
television retailers had gone well; he had made a strong appeal to George Sha-

hood, president of Continental Television, Inc., which has eight retail outlets in Northern California, to put prices on color television sets and increase the sales volume, and Shahood had conceded it was worth a try. Then DiMaggio called Reno's bar to see if there were any messages, and now he was in Lefty O'Doul's car being driven along Fisherman's Wharf toward the Golden Gate Bridge en route to a golf course 30 miles upstate. Lefty O'Doul was one of the great hitters in the National League in the early thirties, and later he managed the San Francisco Seals when DiMaggio was the shining star. Though O'Doul is now 69, 18 years older than DiMaggio, he nevertheless possesses great energy and spirit, is a hard-drinking, boisterous man with a big belly and roving eye; and when DiMaggio, as they drove along the highway toward the golf club, noticed a lovely blonde at the wheel of a car nearby and exclaimed, "Look at *that* tomato!" O'Doul's head suddenly spun around, he took his eyes off the road, and yelled, "Where, *where?*" O'Doul's golf game is less than what it was — he used to have a two-handicap — but he still shoots in the 80s, as does DiMaggio.

DiMaggio's drives range between 250 and 280 yards when he doesn't sky them, and his putting is good, but he is distracted by a bad back that both pains him and hinders the fullness of his swing. On the first hole, waiting to tee off, DiMaggio sat back watching a foursome of college boys ahead swinging with such freedom. "Oh," he said with a sigh, "to have *their* backs."

DiMaggio and O'Doul were accompanied around the golf course by Ernie 100
Nevers, the former football star, and two brothers who are in the hotel and movie-distribution business. They moved quickly up and down the green hills in electric golf carts, and DiMaggio's game was exceptionally good for the first nine holes. But then he seemed distracted, perhaps tired, perhaps even reacting to a conversation of a few minutes before. One of the movie men was praising the film *Boeing, Boeing*, starring Tony Curtis and Jerry Lewis, and the man asked DiMaggio if he had seen it.

"No," DiMaggio said. Then he added, swiftly, "I haven't seen a film in eight years."

DiMaggio hooked a few shots, was in the woods. He took a No. 9 iron and tried to chip out. But O'Doul interrupted DiMaggio's concentration to remind him to keep the face of the club closed. DiMaggio hit the ball. It caromed off the side of his club, went skipping like a rabbit through the high grass down toward a pond. DiMaggio rarely displays any emotion on a golf course, but now, without saying a word, he took his No. 9 iron and flung it into the air. The club landed in a tree and stayed up there.

"Well," O'Doul said casually, "there goes *that* set of clubs."

DiMaggio walked to the tree. Fortunately the club had slipped to the lower branch, and DiMaggio could stretch up on the cart and get it back.

"Every time I get advice," DiMaggio muttered to himself, shaking his head 105
slowly and walking toward the pond, "I shank it."

Later, showered and dressed, DiMaggio and the others drove to a banquet about 10 miles from the golf course. Somebody had said it was going to be an elegant dinner, but when they arrived they could see it was more like a county fair; farmers were gathered outside a big barnlike building, a candidate for sheriff was distributing leaflets at the front door, and a chorus of homely ladies was inside singing "You Are My Sunshine."

"How did we get sucked into this?" DiMaggio asked, talking out of the side of his mouth, as they approached the building.

"O'Doul," one of the men said. "It's his fault. Damned O'Doul can't turn *any-thing* down."

"Go to hell," O'Doul said.

Soon DiMaggio and O'Doul and Ernie Nevers were surrounded by the   110
crowd, and the woman who had been leading the chorus came rushing over and said, "Oh, Mr. DiMaggio, it certainly is a pleasure having you."

"It's a pleasure being here, ma'am," he said, forcing a smile.

"It's too bad you didn't arrive a moment sooner. You'd have heard our singing."

"Oh, I heard it," he said, "and I enjoyed it very much."

"Good, good," she said. "And how are your brothers, Dom and Vic?"

"Fine. Dom lives near Boston. Vince is in Pittsburgh."   115

"Why, *hello* there, Joe," interrupted a man with wine on his breath, patting DiMaggio on the back, feeling his arm. "Who's gonna take it this year, Joe?"

"Well, I have no idea," DiMaggio said.

"What about the Giants?"

"Your guess is as good as mine."

"Well, you can't count the Dodgers out," the man said.   120

"You sure can't," DiMaggio said.

"Not with all that pitching."

"Pitching is certainly important," DiMaggio said.

Everywhere he goes the question seems the same, as if he has some special vision into the future of new heroes, and everywhere he goes, too, older men grab his hand and feel his arm and predict that he could still go out there and hit one, and the smile on DiMaggio's face is genuine. He tries hard to remain as he was — he diets, he takes steambaths, he is careful; and flabby men in the locker rooms of golf clubs sometimes steal peeks at him when he steps out of the shower, observing the tight muscles across his chest, the flat stomach, the long sinewy legs. He has a young man's body, very pale and little hair; his face is dark and lined, however, parched by the sun of several seasons. Still he is always an impressive figure at banquets such as this — an "immortal" sports writers called him, and that is how they have written about him and others like him, rarely suggesting that such heroes might ever be prone to the ills of mortal men, carousing, drinking, scheming; to suggest this would destroy the myth, would disillusion small boys, would infuriate rich men who own ball clubs and to whom baseball is a business dedicated to profit and in pursuit of which they trade mediocre players' flesh as casually as boys trade players' pictures on bubble-gum cards. And so the baseball hero must always act the part, must preserve the myth, and none does it better than DiMaggio, none is more patient when drunken old men grab an arm and ask, "Who's gonna take it this year, Joe?"

Two hours later, dinner and the speeches over, DiMaggio was slumped in O'Doul's car headed back to San Francisco. He edged himself up, however, when O'Doul pulled into a gas station in which a pretty red-haired girl sat on a stool, legs crossed, filing her fingernails. She was about 22, wore a tight black skirt and tighter white blouse. 125

"Look at *that*," DiMaggio said.

"Yeah," O'Doul said.

O'Doul turned away when a young man approached, opened the gas tank, began wiping the windshield. The young man wore a greasy white uniform on the front of which was printed the name "Burt." DiMaggio kept looking at the girl, but she was not distracted from her fingernails. Then he looked at Burt, who did not recognize him. When the tank was full, O'Doul paid and drove off. Burt returned to his girl; DiMaggio slumped down in the front seat and did not open his eyes again until they arrived in San Francisco.

"Let's go see Reno," DiMaggio said.

"No, I gotta go see my old lady," O'Doul said. So he dropped DiMaggio off in front of the bar, and a moment later Reno's voice was announcing in the smoky room, "Hey, here's the Clipper!" The men waved and offered to buy him a drink. DiMaggio ordered a vodka and sat for an hour at the bar talking to a half-dozen men around him. Then a blonde girl who had been with friends at the other end of the bar came over, and somebody introduced her to DiMaggio. He bought her a drink, offered her a cigarette. Then he struck a match and held it. His hand was unsteady. 130

"Is that me that's shaking?" he asked.

"It must be," said the blonde. "I'm calm."

Two nights later, having collected his clothes out of Reno's back room, DiMaggio boarded a jet; he slept crossways on three seats, then came down the steps as the sun began to rise in Miami. He claimed his luggage and golf clubs, put them into the trunk of a waiting automobile, and less than an hour later he was being driven into Fort Lauderdale, past palm-lined streets, toward the Yankee Clipper Hotel.

"All my life it seems I've been on the road traveling," he said, squinting through the windshield into the sun. "I never get a sense of being in any one place."

Arriving at the Yankee Clipper Hotel, DiMaggio checked into the largest suite. People rushed through the lobby to shake hands with him, to ask for his autograph, to say, "Joe, you look great." And early the next morning, and for the next 30 mornings, DiMaggio arrived punctually at the baseball park and wore his uniform with the famous No. 5, and the tourists seated in the sunny grandstands clapped when he first appeared on the field each time, and then they watched with nostalgia as he picked up a bat and played "pepper" with the younger Yankees, 135 some of whom were not even born when, 25 years ago this summer, he hit in 56 straight games and became the most celebrated man in America.

But the younger spectators in the Fort Lauderdale park, and the sports writers, too, were more interested in Mantle and Maris, and nearly every day there were news dispatches reporting how Mantle and Maris felt, what they did, what they said, even though they said and did very little except walk around the field frowning when photographers asked for another picture and when sports writers asked how they felt.

After seven days of this, the big day arrived — Mantle and Maris would swing a bat — and a dozen sports writers were gathered around the big batting cage that was situated beyond the left-field fence; it was completely enclosed in wire, meaning that no baseball could travel more than 30 or 40 feet before being trapped in rope; still Mantle and Maris would be swinging, and this, in spring, makes news.

Mantle stepped in first. He wore black gloves to help prevent blisters. He hit right-handed against the pitching of a coach named Vern Benson, and soon Mantle was swinging hard, smashing line drives against the nets, going *ahhh ahhh* as he followed through with his mouth open.

Then Mantle, not wanting to overdo it on his first day, dropped his bat in the dirt and walked out of the batting cage. Roger Maris stepped in. He picked up Mantle's bat.

"This damn thing must be 38 ounces," Maris said. He threw the bat down   140
into the dirt, left the cage, and walked toward the dugout on the other side of the field to get a lighter bat.

DiMaggio stood among the sports writers behind the cage, then turned when Vern Benson, inside the cage, yelled, "Joe, wanna hit some?"

"No chance," DiMaggio said.

"Com'on Joe," Benson said.

The reporters waited silently. Then DiMaggio walked slowly into the cage and picked up Mantle's bat. He took his position at the plate but obviously it was not the classic DiMaggio stance; he was holding the bat about two inches from the knob, his feet were not so far apart, and when DiMaggio took a cut at Benson's first pitch, fouling it, there was none of that ferocious follow-through, the blurred bat did not come whipping all the way around, the No. 5 was not stretched full across his broad back.

DiMaggio fouled Benson's second pitch, then he connected solidly with the   145
third, the fourth, the fifth. He was just meeting the ball easily, however, not smashing it, and Benson called out, "I didn't know you were a choke hitter, Joe."

"I am now." DiMaggio said, getting ready for another pitch.

He hit three more squarely enough, and then he swung again and there was a hollow sound.

"Ohhh," DiMaggio yelled, dropping his bat, his fingers stung. "I was waiting for that one." He left the batting cage, rubbing his hands together. The reporters watched him. Nobody said anything. Then DiMaggio said to one of them, not in anger or in sadness, but merely as a simply stated fact, "There was a time when you couldn't get me out of there."

Questions for Discussion

1. How does Gay Talese create a picture of DiMaggio at loose ends that nevertheless suggests his heroism?
2. What does Talese tell us about the position of sports in American popular culture?
3. Talese describes DiMaggio as "a kind of male Garbo," referring to the legendary, reclusive film star Greta Garbo (para. 85). The comparison suggests that DiMaggio's detachment was a masculine ideal. Does this ideal still resonate? How does it square with the image of today's superstar athletes? Does our media-crazy era demand more engagement from our heroes? Are we still capable of being "moved by the mystique" (para. 85)?
4. Talese has said that his work is a highly personal response to the world as an Italian American outsider. How does the authorial voice of an outsider add nuance to the profile of Joe DiMaggio?
5. Why is spring the silent season? Consider the title from the perspective of fishing and baseball.

Questions on Rhetoric and Style

1. What is the effect of juxtaposing details of Joe DiMaggio's legendary baseball prowess with details of his everyday life in San Francisco as a retired athlete?
2. Why does "The Silent Season of a Hero" open with a quotation from Hemingway's *The Old Man and the Sea*? Cite specific passages from Talese's essay to support your answer.
3. The "tall gray-haired man in a dark suit" in the first paragraph is obviously Joe DiMaggio, but Talese waits until the end of paragraph 2 to name him. What is the effect of delaying identification of the essay's subject?
4. Characterize the narrator. Does he step forward at any time? Who is the "man from New York" (para. 12)? Who is asked by the narrator to comment on DiMaggio?
5. Although DiMaggio was a baseball player, the essay sometimes sounds as if it's about a fisherman. Trace both the language of baseball and the language of fishing. Which is predominant?
6. Talese suggests — but doesn't come out and say — that Joe DiMaggio and Marilyn Monroe were competitive about their celebrity. How does Talese use Monroe's mythical status to develop his portrait of DiMaggio? Is he sympathetic to her? Does his profile of DiMaggio deepen our understanding of Monroe, or does she remain as tantalizingly out of reach as she seems to have been to DiMaggio?

7. Several parts of the essay — especially paragraphs 3 and 41 — evoke Hemingway. How do the images and language of those allusions create another level of meaning? How do they add to the portrait of DiMaggio?

8. What is the overall tone of the essay? How does Talese achieve his tone? How does the tone add a layer of meaning?

9. Talese notes that sportswriters have called DiMaggio an "immortal" (para. 124). How does the essay both support and debunk that myth?

10. Explain the assumptions Talese makes about his audience based on his portrait of DiMaggio as an aging hero.

Suggestions for Writing

1. Examine the parts of the selection that are about Marilyn Monroe, especially the anecdote about her performing for the troops in Korea (paras. 48–50). Write an essay about how, in the absence of details about why her marriage to DiMaggio failed, the language suggests that perhaps the marriage could not accommodate two egos as strong as DiMaggio's and Monroe's. Read other accounts of the marriage to see if they support or contradict Talese's, and refer to them in your essay.

2. Read "Sinatra Has a Cold," Gay Talese's profile of Frank Sinatra, which can be found at <bedfordstmartins.com/languageofcomp>. Compare and contrast it with "The Silent Season of the Hero." How is the author's voice similar or different? Compare the treatment of DiMaggio and Sinatra as embodiments of a masculine ideal.

3. Paragraphs 53–56 recount DiMaggio's 1941 hitting streak, which ended at a record-breaking fifty-six games. During this streak, the New York Yankees went from fourth place in the American League to victory in the World Series. The missing bat — returned by a rueful fan — seems to have been the magic charm. Compare this account with other tales of heroes who depend on the power of a sword, a shield, or other special piece of equipment.

The Proper Place for Sports

THEODORE ROOSEVELT

 Theodore Roosevelt (1858–1919) was only forty-two when he became the twenty-sixth president of the United States following William McKinley's assassination in 1901. During his first term he spearheaded the construction of the Panama Canal, and during his second he won the Nobel Peace Prize — the first American to do so — for his mediation in the Russo-Japanese War of 1904–1905. Prior to holding office, he commanded the famed Rough Riders, an all-volunteer cavalry that led the charge on San Juan Hill in the Spanish-American War, for which he was awarded the Congressional Medal of Honor. Roosevelt led what he called the "strenuous life," which included being a cowboy in the Wild West, going on safari in Africa, and exploring the Amazon basin. His letters to his children, originally published in 1919, capture Roosevelt's view that "for unflagging interest and enjoyment, a household of children, if things go reasonably well, certainly makes all other forms of success and achievement lose their importance by comparison." In the following 1903 letter to his son Ted, Roosevelt puts participation in sports in perspective.

White House, Oct. 4, 1903.

Dear Ted:

In spite of the "Hurry! Hurry!" on the outside of your envelope, I did not like to act until I had consulted Mother and thought the matter over; and to be frank with you, old fellow, I am by no means sure that I am doing right now. If it were not that I feel you will be so bitterly disappointed, I would strongly advocate your acquiescing in the decision to leave you off the second squad this year. I am proud of your pluck, and I greatly admire football — though it was not a game I was ever able to play myself, my qualities resembling Kermit's rather than yours. But the very things that make it a good game make it a rough game, and there is always the chance of your being laid up. Now, I should not in the least object to your being laid up for a season if you were striving for something worth while, to get on the Groton school team, for instance, or on your class team when you entered Harvard — for of course I don't think you will have the weight to entitle you to try for the 'varsity. But I am by no means sure that it *is* worth your while to run the risk of being laid up for the sake of playing in the second squad when you are a fourth former, instead of when you are a fifth former. I do not know that the risk is balanced by the reward. However, I have told the Rector that as you feel so strongly about it, I think that the chance of your damaging yourself in body is outweighed by the possibility of bitterness of spirit if you could not play. Understand me, I should think mighty little of you if you permitted chagrin to make

449

you bitter on some point where it was evidently right for you to suffer the cha-grin. But in this case I am uncertain, and I shall give you the benefit of the doubt. If, however, the coaches at any time come to the conclusion that you ought not to be in the second squad, why you must come off without grumbling.

I am delighted to have you play football. I believe in rough, manly sports. But I do not believe in them if they degenerate into the sole end of any one's existence. I don't want you to sacrifice standing well in your studies to any over-athleticism; and I need not tell you that character counts for a great deal more than either intel-lect or body in winning success in life. Athletic proficiency is a mighty good ser-vant, and like so many other good servants, a mighty bad master. Did you ever read Pliny's letter to Trajan, in which he speaks of [it] being advisable to keep the Greeks absorbed in athletics, because it distracted their minds from all serious pursuits, including soldiering, and prevented their ever being dangerous to the Romans? I have not a doubt that the British officers in the Boer War had their effi-ciency partly reduced because they had sacrificed their legitimate duties to an inordinate and ridiculous love of sports. A man must develop his physical prowess up to a certain point; but after he has reached that point there are other things that count more. In my regiment nine-tenths of the men were better horsemen than I was, and probably two-thirds of them better shots than I was, while on the average they were certainly hardier and more enduring. Yet after I had had them a very short while they all knew, and I knew too, that nobody else could command them as I could. I am glad you should play football; I am glad that you should box; I am glad that you should ride and shoot and walk and row as well as you do. I should be very sorry if you did not do these things. But don't ever get into the frame of mind which regards these things as constituting the end to which all your energies must be devoted, or even the major portion of your energies.

Yes, I am going to speak at Groton on prize day. I felt that while I was Presi-dent, and while you and Kermit were at Groton I wanted to come up there and see you, and the Rector wished me to speak, and so I am very glad to accept.

By the way, I am working hard to get Renown accustomed to automobiles. He is such a handful now when he meets them that I seriously mind encountering them when Mother is along. Of course I do not care if I am alone, or with another man, but I am uneasy all the time when I am out with Mother. Yesterday I tried Bleistein over the hurdles at Chevy Chase. The first one was new, high and stiff, and the old rascal never rose six inches, going slap through it. I took him at it again and he went over all right.

I am very busy now, facing the usual endless worry and discouragement, and trying to keep steadily in mind that I must not only be as resolute as Abraham Lincoln in seeking to achieve decent ends, but as patient, as uncomplaining, and as even-tempered in dealing, not only with knaves, but with the well-meaning foolish people, educated and uneducated, who by their unwisdom give the knaves their chance. 5

Questions for Discussion

1. How does Theodore Roosevelt balance his belief in the "strenuous life" with advising his son that his safety is also important?
2. In this letter, Roosevelt reluctantly supports his son's wish to play football. Why does he think it may not be wise for Ted to play as a fourth former (tenth grader)? How does Roosevelt support Ted's position and at the same time make clear his trepidation?
3. Consider this letter in light of the current generation of parents, considered by many to be overly involved in their children's lives. Could one accuse Roosevelt of being an early-twentieth-century soccer dad?
4. Compare Roosevelt's view of the importance of sports for children with Kris Vervaecke's view in "A Spectator's Notebook" (p. 461).
5. How is athletic proficiency "a mighty good servant, and like so many other good servants, a mighty bad master" (para. 2)?
6. How does the last paragraph of the letter send another message to both Roosevelt's son and to the modern reader?
7. Roosevelt is credited with having said, "In short, in life, as in a football game, the principle to follow is: Hit the line hard; don't foul and don't shirk, but hit the line hard!" In what ways does the letter to Ted offer similar advice? How is the advice tempered for his young son? Does the letter contradict the hit-the-line-hard quotation in any way?

Questions on Rhetoric and Style

1. Roosevelt argues against sports if they "degenerate into the sole end of any one's existence" (para. 2). What examples does he give to support his argument? Are they effective? Do they withstand the test of time? Can you apply his argument to participation in sports today?
2. What assumptions about his son underlie Roosevelt's argument?
3. Characterize the letter's tone. Do some parts seem more presidential than fatherly?
4. How does the first paragraph of the letter balance appeals to logos and pathos?
5. What is the effect of Roosevelt's allusions to Pliny's letter to Trajan and to the Boer War?
6. Analyze the following two sentences, considering the effects of Roosevelt's diction. In which ways does the language support or undermine his argument?

   Understand me, I should think mighty little of you if you permitted chagrin to make you bitter on some point where it was evidently right for you to suffer the chagrin. (para. 1)

   I don't want you to sacrifice standing well in your studies to any over-athleticism; and I need not tell you that character counts for a great deal more than either intellect or body in winning success in life. (para. 2)

7. Paragraphs 3 and 4 shift gears; one answers a question about a visit to Groton, and the other reports on Roosevelt's horses. How does each paragraph contribute to the establishment of ethos?

8. Paraphrase the last paragraph of the letter. Compare your language with the original. What is the effect of Roosevelt's indirection?

9. Roosevelt begins the letter by saying he did not hurry his response because he wanted to confer with Ted's mother. He doesn't mention her again until paragraph 4. What is the effect of this rhetorical decision?

10. How does Roosevelt achieve his measured response to what was obviously a sense of urgency in the letter to which he is responding? Look particularly at the ways he uses the word *if*.

Suggestions for Writing

1. Research the year 1903. Who do you think Roosevelt is calling *knaves* when he says he must be patient "not only with knaves, but with the well-meaning foolish people, educated and uneducated, who by their unwisdom give the knaves their chance" (para. 5)? Write about Roosevelt's resolution, patience, and even temper in dealing with them while in office.

2. Write your own version of the letter from Ted that Roosevelt is replying to, or write a response from Ted to his father's letter.

3. Write an essay in which you support, challenge, or qualify Roosevelt's assertion that "character counts for a great deal more than either intellect or body in winning success in life" (para. 2).

4. In paragraph 2, Roosevelt writes that "other things . . . count more" than physical prowess. Write an essay about the qualities that make someone like Roosevelt an effective leader, even if he is less physically powerful than the men he leads.

Kill 'Em! Crush 'Em! Eat 'Em Raw!

JOHN MCMURTRY

Born in Toronto in 1939, John McMurtry has worked as a professional football player, a print and television journalist, and an English teacher. He claims he became a philosopher "as a last resort." His writing on higher education and business criticizes the application of the global manufacturing model to social institutions. The following essay first appeared in 1971 In *Macleans*. In it, McMurtry draws on his experience as a football player to argue that society accepts the brutality of football because it mirrors the competitive economic practices that we blindly accept.

A few months ago my neck got a hard crick in it. I couldn't turn my head; to look left or right I'd have to turn my whole body. But I'd had cricks in my neck since I started playing grade-school football and hockey, so I just ignored it. Then I began to notice that when I reached for any sort of large book (which I do pretty often as a philosophy teacher at the University of Guelph) I had trouble lifting it with one hand. I was losing the strength in my left arm, and I had such a steady pain in my back I often had to stretch out on the floor of the room I was in to relieve the pressure.

A few weeks later I mentioned to my brother, an orthopedic surgeon, that I'd lost the power in my arm since my neck began to hurt. Twenty-four hours later I was in a Toronto hospital not sure whether I might end up with a wasted upper limb. Apparently the steady pounding I had received playing college and professional football in the late Fifties and early Sixties had driven my head into my backbone so that the discs had crumpled together at the neck — "acute herniation" — and had cut the nerves to my left arm like a pinched telephone wire (without nerve stimulation, of course, the muscles atrophy, leaving the arm crippled). So I spent my Christmas holidays in the hospital in heavy traction and much of the next three months with my neck in a brace. Today most of the pain has gone, and I've recovered most of the strength in my arm. But from time to time I still have to don the brace, and surgery remains a possibility.

Not much of this will surprise anyone who knows football. It is a sport in which body wreckage is one of the leading conventions. A few days after I went into hospital for that crick in my neck, another brother, an outstanding football player in college, was undergoing spinal surgery in the same hospital two floors above me. In his case it was a lower, more massive herniation, which every now and again buckled him so that he was unable to lift himself off his back for days at a time. By the time he entered the hospital for surgery he had already spent several months in bed. The operation was successful, but, as in all such cases, it will take him a year to recover fully.

These aren't isolated experiences. Just about anybody who has ever played football for any length of time, in high school, college or one of the professional leagues, has suffered for it later physically.

Indeed, it is arguable that body shattering is the very *point* of football, as killing and maiming are of war. (In the United States, for example, the game results in 15 to 20 deaths a year and about 50,000 major operations on knees alone.) To grasp some of the more conspicuous similarities between football and war, it is instructive to listen to the imperatives most frequently issued to the players by their coaches, teammates and fans. "Hurt 'em!" "Level 'em!" "Kill 'em!" "Take 'em apart!" Or watch for the plays that are most enthusiastically applauded by the fans. Where someone is "smeared," "knocked silly," "creamed," "nailed," "broken in two," or even "crucified." (One of my coaches when I played corner linebacker with the Calgary Stampeders in 1961 elaborated, often very inventively, on this language of destruction: admonishing us to "unjoin" the opponent, "make 'im remember you" and "stomp 'im like a bug.") Just as in hockey, where a fight will bring fans to their feet more often than a skillful play, so in football the mouth waters most of all for the really crippling block or tackle. For the kill. Thus the good teams are "hungry," the best players are "mean," and "casualties" are as much a part of the game as they are of a war.

The family resemblance between football and war is, indeed, striking. Their languages are similar: "field general," "long bomb," "blitz," "take a shot," "front line," "pursuit," "good hit," "the draft" and so on. Their principles and practices are alike: mass hysteria, the art of intimidation, absolute command and total obedience, territorial aggression, censorship, inflated insignia and propaganda, blackboard maneuvers and strategies, drills, uniforms, formations, marching bands and training camps. And the virtues they celebrate are almost identical: hyper-aggressiveness, coolness under fire and suicidal bravery. All this has been implicitly recognized by such jock-loving Americans as media stars General [George] Patton and President [Richard] Nixon, who have talked about war as a football game. Patton wanted to make his Second World War tank men look like football players. And Nixon, as we know, was fond of comparing attacks on Vietnam to football plays and drawing coachly diagrams on a blackboard for TV war fans.

One difference between war and football, though, is that there is little or no protest against football. Perhaps the most extraordinary thing about the game is that the systematic infliction of injuries excites in people not concern, as would be the case if they were sustained at, say, a rock festival, but a collective rejoicing and euphoria. Players and fans alike revel in the spectacle of a combatant felled into semiconsciousness, "blindsided," "clothes-lined" or "decapitated." I can remember, in fact, being chided by a coach in pro ball for not "getting my hat" injuriously into a player who was already lying helpless on the ground. (On another occasion, after the Stampeders had traded the celebrated Joe Kapp to BC, we were playing the Lions in Vancouver and Kapp was forced on one play to run with the ball. He was coming "down the chute," his bad knee wobbling uncertainly, so I simply dropped on him like a blanket. After I returned to the bench I was reproved for not exploiting the opportunity to unhinge his bad knee.)

After every game, of course, the papers are full of reports on the day's injuries, a sort of post-battle "body count," and the respective teams go to work with doctors and trainers, tape, whirlpool baths, cortisone and morphine to patch and deaden the wounds before the next game. Then the whole drama is reenacted — injured athletes held together by adhesive, braces and drugs — and the days following it are filled with even more feverish activity to put on the show yet again at the end of the next week. (I remember being so taped up in college that I earned the nickname "[M]ummy.") The team that survives this merry-go-round spectacle of skilled masochism with the fewest incapacitating injuries usually wins. It is a sort of victory by ordeal: "We hurt them more than they hurt us."

My own initiation into this brutal circus was typical. I loved the game from the moment I could run with a ball. Played shoeless on a green open field with no one keeping score and in a spirit of reckless abandon and laughter, it's a very different sport. Almost no one gets hurt and it's rugged, open and exciting (it still is for me). But then, like everything else, it starts to be regulated and institutionalized by adult authorities. And the fun is over.

So it was as I began the long march through organized football. Now there   10
was a coach and elders to make it clear by their behavior that beating other people was the only thing to celebrate and that trying to shake someone up every play was the only thing to be really proud of. Now there were severe rule enforcers, audiences, formally recorded victors and losers, and heavy equipment to permit crippling bodily moves and collisions (according to one American survey, more than 80% of all football injuries occur to fully equipped players). And now there was the official "given" that the only way to keep playing was to wear suffocating armor, to play to defeat, to follow orders silently and to renounce spontaneity for joyless drill. The game had been, in short, ruined. But because I loved to play and play skillfully, I stayed. And progressively and inexorably, as I moved through high school, college and pro leagues, my body was dismantled. Piece by piece.

I started off with torn ligaments in my knee at 13. Then, as the organization and the competition increased, the injuries came faster and harder. Broken nose (three times), broken jaw (fractured in the first half and dismissed as a "bad wisdom tooth," so I played with it for the rest of the game), ripped knee ligaments again. Torn ligaments in one ankle and a fracture in the other (which I remember feeling relieved about because it meant I could honorably stop drill-blocking a 270-pound defensive end). Repeated rib fractures and cartilage tears (usually carried, again, through the remainder of the game). More dislocations of the left shoulder than I can remember (the last one I played with because, as the Calgary Stampeder doctor said, it "couldn't be damaged any more"). Occasional broken or dislocated fingers and toes. Chronically hurt lower back (I still can't lift with it or change a tire without worrying about folding). Separated right shoulder (as with many other injuries, like badly bruised hips and legs, needled with morphine for the games). And so on. The last pro game I played — against Winnipeg Blue Bombers in the Western finals in 1961 — I had a recently dislocated left shoulder, a more recently wrenched right shoulder and a chronic pain center in one leg. I was so tied up with soreness I couldn't drive my car to the airport. But it never occurred to me or anyone else that I miss a play as a corner linebacker.

By the end of my football career, I had learned that physical injury — giving it and taking it — is the real currency of the sport. And that in the final analysis the "winner" is the man who can hit to kill even if only half his limbs are working. In brief, a warrior game with a warrior ethos into which (like almost everyone else I played with) my original boyish enthusiasm had been relentlessly taunted and conditioned.

In thinking back on how all this happened, though, I can pick out no villains. As with the social system as a whole, the game has a life of its own. Everyone grows up inside it, accepts it and fulfills its dictates as obediently as helots.[1] Far from ever questioning the principles of the activity, people simply concentrate on executing these principles more aggressively than anybody around them. The result is a group of people who, as the leagues become of a higher and higher class, are progressively insensitive to the possibility that things could be otherwise. Thus, in football, anyone who might question the wisdom or enjoyment of putting on heavy equipment on a hot day and running full speed at someone else with the intention of knocking him senseless would be regarded simply as not really a devoted athlete and probably "chicken." The choice is made straightforward. Either you, too, do your very utmost to efficiently smash and be smashed, or you admit incompetence or cowardice and quit. Since neither of these admissions is very pleasant, people generally keep any doubts they have to themselves and carry on.

Of course, it would be a mistake to suppose that there is more blind acceptance of brutal practices in organized football than elsewhere. On the contrary, a recent Harvard study has approvingly argued that football's characteristics of "impersonal acceptance of inflicted injury," an overriding "organization goal," the "ability to turn oneself on and off" and being, above all, "out to win" are of "inestimable value" to big corporations. Clearly, our sort of football is no sicker than the rest of our society. Even its organized destruction of physical well-being is not anomalous. A very large part of our wealth, work and time is, after all, spent in systematically destroying and harming human life. Manufacturing, selling and using weapons that tear opponents to pieces. Making ever bigger and faster predator-named cars with which to kill and injure one another by the million every year. And devoting our very lives to outgunning one another for power in an ever

---

[1]In ancient Sparta, slaves owned by the state rather than by private individuals. — Eds.

more destructive rat race. Yet all these practices are accepted without question by most people, even zealously defended and honored. Competitive, organized injuring is integral to our way of life, and football is simply one of the more intelligible mirrors of the whole process: a sort of colorful morality play showing us how exciting and rewarding it is to Smash Thy Neighbor.

Now it is fashionable to rationalize our collaboration in all this by arguing that, well, man *likes* to fight and injure his fellows and such games as football should be encouraged to discharge this original-sin urge into less harmful channels than, say, war. Public-show football, this line goes, plays the same sort of cathartic role as Aristotle said stage tragedy does: without real blood (or not much), it releases players and audience from unhealthy feelings stored up inside them.

As an ex-player in the seasonal coast-to-coast drama, I see little to recommend such a view. What organized football did to me was make me *suppress* my natural urges and re-express them in an alienating, vicious form. Spontaneous desires for free bodily exuberance and fraternization with competitors were shamed and forced under ("If it ain't hurtin' it ain't helpin'") and in their place were demanded armored mechanical moves and cool hatred of all opposition. Endless authoritarian drill and dressing-room harangues (ever wonder why competing teams can't prepare for a game in the same dressing room?) were the kinds of mechanisms employed to reconstruct joyful energies into mean and alien shapes. I am quite certain that everyone else around me was being similarly forced into this heavily equipped military precision and angry antagonism, because there was always a mutinous attitude about full-dress practices, and everybody (the pros included) had to concentrate incredibly hard for days to whip themselves into just one hour's hostility a week against another club. The players never speak of these things, of course, because everyone is so anxious to appear tough.

The claim that men like seriously to battle one another to some sort of finish is a myth. It only endures because it wears one of the oldest and most propagandized of masks — the romantic combatant. I sometimes wonder whether the violence all around us doesn't depend for its survival on the existence and preservation of this tough-guy disguise.

As for the effect of organized football on the spectator, the fan is not released from supposed feelings of violent aggression by watching his athletic heroes perform it so much as encouraged in the view that people-smashing is an admirable mode of self-expression. The most savage attackers, after all, are, by general agreement, the most efficient and worthy players of all (the biggest applause I ever received as a football player occurred when I ran over people or slammed them so hard they couldn't get up). Such circumstances can hardly be said to lessen the spectators' martial tendencies. Indeed it seems likely that the whole show just further develops and titillates the North American addiction for violent self-assertion. . . . Perhaps, as well, it helps explain why the greater the zeal of U.S. political leaders as football fans (Lyndon Johnson, Richard Nixon, Spiro Agnew), the more enthusiastic the commitment to hard-line politics. At any rate there seems to be a strong correlation between people who relish tough football and

15

people who relish intimidating and beating the hell out of commies, hippies, protest marchers and other opposition groups.

Watching well-advertised strong men knock other people round, make them hurt, is in the end like other tastes. It does not weaken with feeding and variation in form. It grows.

I got out of football in 1962. I had asked to be traded after Calgary had offered me a $25-a-week-plus-commissions off-season job as a clothing-store salesman. ("Dear Mr. Finks:" I wrote. [Jim Finks was then the Stampeders' general manager.] "Somehow I do not think the dialectical subtleties of Hegel, Marx and Plato would be suitably oriented amidst the environmental stimuli of jockey shorts and herringbone suits. I hope you make a profitable sale or trade of my contract to the East.") So the Stampeders traded me to Montreal. In a preseason intersquad game with the Alouettes I ripped the cartilages in my ribs on the hardest block I'd ever thrown. I had trouble breathing and I had to shuffle-walk with my torso on a tilt. The doctor in the local hospital said three weeks' rest, the coach said scrimmage in two days. Three days later I was back home reading philosophy.

20

Exploring the Text

1. John McMurtry's essay begins with a personal anecdote about the results of playing sports — especially football — since childhood. When he can no longer ignore his physical condition, he seeks treatment and is hospitalized. How does the anecdote lend credibility to his argument?

2. Paragraphs 5–7 compare and contrast football and war. Is this comparison convincing? How does the comparison appeal to logos?

3. In paragraph 9, the tone shifts. How is the shift achieved? Explain how the shift mirrors a transition in McMurtry's argument.

4. In paragraph 14, McMurtry cites a Harvard study showing that some of the more brutal characteristics of football players are valued in the business world. How do the study's findings support McMurtry's argument against the brutality of football?

5. McMurtry also addresses the argument that games such as football allow us to discharge our "original-sin urge into less harmful channels than, say, war" (para. 15). Cite passages where McMurtry counters this argument. Do you agree with him? Why or why not?

6. Consider the language of football, especially the words shared by the military. What sports other than football have a militaristic side?

7. Who is McMurtry's audience? Is it necessary for the reader to understand or care about football in order to understand what McMurtry is saying about society? Explain.

8. McMurtry characterizes General George Patton and President Richard Nixon as "jock-loving . . . media stars" (para. 6). Think of contemporary media stars who associate themselves with football or other sports. Does the association enhance or tarnish their image?

From *How I Learned to Ride the Bicycle*

FRANCES E. WILLARD

Frances Willard (1839–1898) is little known today, but in her own time she was famous. Born in western New York, she grew up on the prairie near Janesville, Wisconsin. She spent her childhood free of the usual constraints endured by girls of the time. From the age of sixteen on, however, she wore the long skirts, corsets, and high-heeled shoes required of women. She became a teacher and later served as president of Evanston College for Women. At thirty-five, Willard found the causes that would become her life's work: the women's movement and the temperance movement. The best-known and most dynamic president of the Women's Christian Temperance Union (WCTU), Willard was an outstanding educator, astute politician, pioneer suffragist, and strong advocate for the emancipation of women. When Willard was fifty-three, she was in poor health, and her doctor encouraged her to take outdoor exercise. Lady Henry Somerset, head of the British Women's Temperance Union, gave her a bicycle, which was nicknamed Gladys. In 1893, Willard wrote *How I Learned to Ride the Bicycle: Reflections of an Influential 19th Century Woman*, which tells how she met the challenge of learning how to ride a bicycle. The book's conclusion follows.

If I am asked to explain why I learned the bicycle, I should say I did it as an act of grace, if not of actual religion. The cardinal doctrine laid down by my physician was, "Live out of doors and take congenial exercise"; but from the day when, at sixteen years of age, I was enwrapped in the long skirts that impeded every footstep, I have detested walking and felt with a certain noble disdain that the conventions of life had cut me off from what in the freedom of my prairie home had been one of life's sweetest joys. Driving is not real exercise; it does not renovate the river of blood that flows so sluggishly in the veins of those who from any cause have lost the natural adjustment of brain to brawn. Horseback riding, which does promise vigorous exercise, is expensive. The bicycle, however, meets all the conditions and will ere long come within the reach of all. Therefore, in obedience to the laws of health, I learned to ride. I also wanted to help women to a wider world, for I hold that the more interests women and men can have in common, in thought, word, and deed, the happier will it be for the home. Besides, there was a special value to women in the conquest of the bicycle by a woman in her fifty-third year, and one who had so many comrades in the white-ribbon army of temperance workers that her action would be widely influential. Then there were three minor reasons:

I did it from pure natural love of adventure — a love long hampered and impeded, like a brook that runs underground, but in this enterprise bubbling up again with somewhat of its pristine freshness and taking its merry course as of old.

Second, from a love of acquiring this new implement of power and literally putting it underfoot.

Last, but not least, because a good many people thought I could not do it at my age.

It is needless to say that a bicycling costume was a prerequisite. This consisted 5
of a skirt and blouse of tweed, with belt, rolling collar, and loose cravat, the skirt three inches from the ground; a round straw hat, and walking shoes with gaiters. It was a simple, modest suit, to which no person of common sense could take exception.

As nearly as I can make out, reducing the problem to actual figures, it took me about three months, with an average of fifteen minutes' practice daily, to learn, first, to pedal; second, to turn; third, to dismount; and fourth, to mount independently this most mysterious animal. January 20th will always be a red-letter bicycle day, because although I had already mounted several times with no hand on the rudder, some good friend had always stood by to lend moral support; but summoning all my force, on this day, I mounted and started off alone. From that hour the spell was broken; Gladys was no more a mystery: I had learned all her kinks, had put a bridle in her teeth, and touched her smartly with the whip of victory. Consider, ye who are of a considerable chronology: in about thirteen hundred minutes, or, to put it more mildly, in twenty-two hours, or, to put it most mildly of all, in less than a single day as the almanac reckons time — but practically in two days of actual practice — amid the delightful surroundings of the great outdoors, and inspired by the bird-songs, the color and fragrance of an English posy-garden, in the company of devoted and pleasant comrades, I had made myself master of the most remarkable, ingenious, and inspiring motor ever yet devised upon this planet.

Moral: Go thou and do likewise!

Exploring the Text

1. How does learning to ride a bicycle become a parable on life, especially on the life of a woman, or a parable on the emancipation movement, in which Frances Willard was involved?

2. It is hard for us to imagine the nineteenth-century controversy over bicycle riding for women. British novelist John Galsworthy summed up the bicycle's role in the eventual demise of the Victorian woman:

   The bicycle . . . has been responsible for more movement in manners and morals than anything [else]. . . . Under its influence, wholly or in part, have wilted chaperones, long and narrow skirts, tight corsets, hair that would come down, black stockings, thick ankles, large hats, prudery and fear of the dark; under its influence, wholly or in part, have blossomed weekends, strong nerves, strong legs, strong language, knickers, knowledge of make and shape, knowledge of woods and pastures, equality of sex, good digestion and professional occupation — in four words, the emancipation of women.

What might the arguments against women's bicycle riding have been? How might Willard and other feminists have addressed these arguments?

3. During her two decades of leadership of the WCTU, Willard effectively organized women for direct political action — without violating the notion of women's "proper" roles — by referring to women as guardians and defenders of their homes and families and by focusing on women's traditional concerns. How does her account of learning to ride a bicycle support those principles? What evidence does her account provide of her skill at inspiring fundamentally conservative, apolitical churchwomen to take political action?

4. Willard's matter-of-fact account of why and how she learned to ride a bicycle is intended as an argument. Why is a strong argument necessary? What counterarguments does she present?

5. Acknowledging the weight of public opinion against her ideas is a strategy Willard probably developed as head of the WCTU. What other strategies does she employ that she might have learned as a political leader?

6. Willard's bicycle is nicknamed Gladys. In the final paragraph, Willard has "put a bridle in [Gladys's] teeth, and touched her smartly with the whip of victory." Why do you think Willard asked her readers to imagine Gladys as a horse?

7. Willard gives three major reasons and three minor reasons why learning to ride a bicycle was important. What is the effect of her hierarchy? Why do you think she organized her material this way?

8. Analyze the syntax of the final sentence. What is the effect of delaying the subject and the verb?

9. Why does Willard call the exhortation at the end of the piece the "Moral"?

A Spectator's Notebook

KRIS VERVAECKE

A native of Nebraska, Kris Vervaecke is a graduate of the Iowa Writers' Workshop. She has published essays and stories in literary magazines and in books such as *Of Mothers and Sons: Women Writers Talk about Having Sons and Raising Men, The Healing Circle: Authors Writing of Recovery,* and *Writers on Sports,* where this essay appeared.

When I was a girl, I played brutish softball on hot summer days in a cow pasture with the other girls in the neighborhood, a neighborhood which was actually a scattering of a few houses outside the city limits of Omaha. These were homes inhabited almost solely by females: There was the widow

Edgerton and her daughter, the Hellerman twin girls, the Kosinsky girl, two Martin girls, and three Vervaecke girls, of which I was the oldest. The Hellerman, Kosinsky, Martin, and Vervaecke fathers were gone all day and most evenings, some not returning even at night, except for Mr. Hellerman, who created a kind of father emergency for the rest of us by rolling into their driveway Monday through Friday evenings at 5:30 sharp. (Nancy Kosinsky's father did sometimes drink at home instead of out, which created another sort of father emergency, because he'd dress up in his Shriner's outfit and ride roughshod over everyone's lawns in his little Shriner's jeep, shearing through my mother's canna bed, sending up humiliations of red petals.) We envied the Hellerman girls, but the other mothers said that Mr. Hellerman was a very *nice* man, but not a *man's* man — a distinction I found confusing, along with the implication that a *real* woman would want a *man's man*.

No mother or father or brother ever came down to the pasture to coach or referee our games, so we girls were left to our own devices. Mary Hellerman and I were always the captains of opposing teams; no one challenged this arrangement because it was understood that the whole point of the game was to build tension between Mary and me until we had no choice but to lay down our bats and balls and injure each other.

The pretense for our fights was an alleged infraction of the rules, which were crudely drawn, like the diamond, in the rising dust. Mary would accuse me, or I'd accuse her, and our shouts ("You cheater! You fat, ugly liar!") would bring us close enough to smell each other. The Herefords would lift their heads in mild interest; the other girls would draw near. Then we'd sharpen our taunts until one of us landed the first slap. I still remember the satisfaction of smacking Mary's bony, sunburned arm. And the coarseness of her long brown hair, coated with sweat and dust, sticking to my fingers as I pulled it. She was several inches taller than I, which allowed me to punch her stomach. Her mother never seemed to make her cut her fingernails, so Mary left long furrows down my arms. Blood! What a thrill and relief it was to see it bubbling up through our sultry sleep of resignation and resentment.

Later some boys moved into the neighborhood, and most of the girls retreated inside to talk about them on the telephone. I played baseball and football with the boys: They were stuck halfway out of nowhere, too, and so they needed me and sometimes even weeny-armed Mary, to play. These games were also primitive, tackle-and-roll-in-the-cow-dirt affairs. Then, one January afternoon during my eighth-grade year, running laps around the gymnasium for seventh-period coed gym class, I broke out in a sweat. Perspiration spread under the sleeves of my prison blue uniform like twin maps of Texas, and, quite abruptly, it mattered to me that my corporeality was revealing itself so grossly in the presence of boys. In panic and humiliation, I plastered my arms to my sides, slowed down to a trot, and became a girl.

It would be years before it dawned on me that a game might be more than a prelude to a fight, more than a release from preadolescent boredom. Through the   5 eyes of my daughter and sons, who play in school and community league sports, I began to see a game as a sustaining drama dreamed up by the will and the scarcely imaginable possibilities of the body. And although I see that *the game* claims vital parts of their imaginations, I can never experience it in the same way.

Driving home from work, I catch part of a radio quiz show:

> GAME SHOW HOST: Question number one. Who won the 1991 Super Bowl?
> *BUZZ!*
> MALE CONTESTANT: The New York Giants!
> HOST: Sorry. I'm afraid that's not the right answer.
> MALE CONTESTANT: But it is! The Giants beat the Buffalo Bills, 20–19, in Tampa Stadium!
> HOST: Sorry! Who won the 1991 Super Bowl?
> *BUZZ!*
> FEMALE CONTESTANT: I don't know, and I don't care!
> HOST (also female): Yes!!! That's correct!!! [*BELLS RING AND WHISTLES SOUND.*] Yeah!!! Congratulations!!!

I'd be a whiz on that show. Although I grew up in the Nebraska vortex of Big Red football and *should* be capable of being swept up by my nation's preoccupation, even as a kid, I was too *embarrassed*. I hated it when everybody was supposed to dress in red, gather around the television set, and feel excited. Or maybe it is closer to the truth to say that I was embarrassed to find that it was over watching a football game that the passions of others were aroused, while *I*, who was usually the one to go around *feeling* things, could not manufacture even a fleeting rivalrous impulse toward the state of Oklahoma, a wind-worn, sun-dulled place much like the place I lived.

Years later, after living on the West Coast, I returned to Nebraska, showing up one autumn Saturday to do some research at the university library. In my characteristically oblivious way, I had failed to find out whether there was a home game, and so it took two hours to make my way through the traffic in Lincoln, and, finally parked, through the throngs of hoarse, red-polyester-suited people to the library door.

Where I found the door locked and library closed, because it was a Big Red Saturday.

Fortunately for me and my prejudices, my kids — Ben, Emily, and Andrew — were never interested in playing football. Basketball's their game, and sometimes soccer, or tennis. They run track and practice martial arts. When Ben went through a Dan Quayle phase when he was fifteen — deciding that when he was grown he would abandon the income bracket to which his mother belongs and possibly even vote Republican — he took up golf, practiced every day for an entire summer, and won the city championship for his age division. For a few moments, he was a kind of celebrity, at least to some sweet old men we ran into at the grocery store. I was proud of him, but he was already discarding the polo shirts he'd begun wearing and letting his golf clubs gather dust. He started paying more attention to politics and environmental policy and thinking about what he wanted to do with his life. I suspected it was closely listening to Republicans that soured him on golf, but I can't say for sure, because I wanted only to listen and observe, not pry. Sports has been one of the ways he's defined and differentiated himself, stretched far beyond and past his mother, surprising her with the slam dunk.

※ ※ ※

For me, the experience of raising children has no equivalent in terror and love.   10
For long stretches of years as a single parent, I've watched as *the game* dreamed up my sons and daughter, giving them things I could not, letting them shed, for the game's duration, grief, rage, loneliness, or boredom, and allowing them to take on skill and cunning, filling them with inspiration and determination, some-times awe.

December 1987. At ten years old, a stubby little blond boy, Ben sits in rapt attention during any game, understanding it intuitively, committing himself wholly. At a Kansas Jayhawks basketball game, I take him down to the court so he can watch his team jog into the locker room. We are so close to their immense, shining bodies that, as Milt Newton trots past (he'd scored eighteen points and accomplished several steals), Ben is able to scoop up, into his cupped palm, a few drops of Newton's sweat. For a moment, Ben holds his breath, staring down at his glistening palm. Then he straightens and begins carefully applying the sweat to his own skin, up and down his arms, patting it into his very pores.

August 1992. Over speed bumps so pronounced you need a forty-thousand-dollar vehicle to get to the other side with your teeth intact, I wind up the narrow road to the country club, to which we don't belong, to pick up Ben after his eigh-teen holes. He is nowhere to be seen. It's 105 degrees, and so I get out of the car, with my book, and settle myself under the stingy shade of an ornamental tree next to the parking lot.

"Mom!" I hear Ben say. "What are you doing?"

"Well, I'm just waiting for you," I say, bewildered.

"Get up! Get up!" he says.   15

After we're settled in the car, I ask what's wrong.

He struggles, not wanting to hurt my feelings. Wiping sweat from his fore-head, he then passes his hand over his eyes.

"Sitting in the grass?" he finally reproaches, a bit incredulous. I don't get it. "Mom, my God, you looked like a hippie!"

August 1995. Everything has been loaded into the car: clothes, photos of the family members and the dogs; Ben's iguana ("Jay") is resting securely among the rocks in his aquarium, wedged, in the backseat, between the lifting equipment and the reference books I insist he take. We've hugged and cried and said every-thing there is to say about his going off to college. He does not want me to drive to

the university with him, not this time; we've already done this for parent orientation and his enrollment in the honors program. He says he'll look like a baby if his
mom helps him move into the dorm.

"One more thing before I leave," he says. "Mom, will you watch this with me?"   20

He slides Michael Jordan's "Air Time" into the VCR, and, sitting together on
the couch, we endure the strains of the background music massacred by the
worn-out sound track on our VCR. As we watch Jordan's volitant performance,
his pure, vibrant grace and athleticism, the way, under pressure, his quotient of
joy increases — he fakes, spins, and drives through, dunking over the head of
somebody who's at least seven feet tall — Ben says, "I get chills, Mom, I really do."

Unsophisticated? My son, whose father died, as Jordan's did a few years ago, a
senseless, violent death: What spiritual toll does that exact on a child? What does
he understand the body to mean, knowing his father's body was robbed of life?

I remember his martial arts phase, which followed the Republican golf
phase, all the demonstrations I attended of Filipino, Korean, and Chinese stylized
fighting: Ben whirling nunchuks, throwing and catching knives, breaking the req-
uisite boards and bricks. At home, when his sister or brother or the dog came up
behind him, he'd leap up and chop the air, spinning off an instantaneous dram-
atization of his charged, secure masculinity. Then he'd get down on the floor
to reassure the startled dog. "It's okay, baby," he'd croon. "Benny would never
hurt you."

He doesn't need a role model, exactly, isn't interested in the personal or moral
failures of athletes, isn't drawn to their celebrity. Instead he needs the example of
pure jubilation in the body, the triumph of spirit, strength, determination, and
talent.

▓ ▓ ▓

I teach at a small liberal arts college thirty miles from where I live, a Division III   25
school with an active athletic program. While the college cannot offer athletic
scholarships, many of the students are there primarily to play sports, and it is
their athletic not scholastic achievement that inspires the college to find sufficient
financial aid for them to attend. These are mostly white kids from farms, or towns
such as Beebeetown, Mechanicsville, Altoona, Correctionville, or What Cheer,
Iowa. (I listen closely as my students tell me the names of their towns, hoping
for an ironic inflection, but I'm always disappointed.) Some of the students are
fairly bright, but, because they were stars of their high school classes — football,
wrestling, basketball, track, or golf — they haven't read any books.

I don't mean that they haven't read many books, or that they haven't read the
great books. I mean that, except for comic books, they haven't read even one
book, that is, you know, sitting down, opening a book, and reading it, beginning
sentence to the next, sentence by sentence, paragraph by paragraph, all the way to
the end. They've simply been passed from one class to the next without doing
the work.

"Do we really have to read the whole thing?" they ask me plaintively, as we begin the first book on the syllabus.

Because my children and I live in a university community that insists on higher educational standards than most (although, believe me, these standards are nothing to boast about), by the time my children were in fifth grade they could read and write better than most of my college freshmen. Because my children attend a public school where, although there are drugs and skirmishes and occasionally weapons, there is a reasonable expectation of safety and order and the opportunity to be educated, they will be able to compete with their academic achievements, not a reverse layup or three-point shot. They are fortunate because games are play for them. On the other hand, because my children are not particularly gifted athletes, they've not had the playing time or attention from coaches that their more talented or parent-coached peers have had. All three of them need those things, not because they will bring glory to their schools, but because we all need joy in our physicality. When I travel to a school in Altoona or someplace like it to attend one of my daughter's basketball games, at first I'm distracted by my awareness that this town is one of countless others where we're failing to sufficiently educate some, if not many, of the children. Then I pick a spot in the bleachers several rows behind where her team will sit and wait for my daughter to come jogging in.

As Emily bounces onto the floor in her green-and-gold uniform, her eyes scan the crowd to meet mine. She's always happy before a game, and now, a few minutes before the whistle, she's luminous with excitement. The girls warm up, shoot, huddle, then go to the bench. Emily's one of the shorter girls, but she moves fast. I take inordinate pride in the fact that it wouldn't occur to her to go out for cheerleading. Sometimes when I pick her up after practice, ready with food she can stuff into her mouth, she cannot contain her exuberance: "Mom, I swear to God! We worked so hard, it was the most fun I've had in my entire life!" Sometimes, watching them practice, I think back to our cow-pasture softball and wish, well, that Mary and I had learned to play the game.

The girls are on the sidelines, waiting for the game to begin. I look at Emily's golden brown head among all the other bright heads with their French and cornrow braids (the girls braid each others' hair as they ride the bus to the game). The whistle blows, the ball's in play; the air is filled with shouts and squeaking shoes and the bouncing of the ball. Each time there is a substitution of players I watch my daughter's slender back lift with hope then go slack with disappointment. Unlike most of the other parents, I do not give a damn whether West High's teams win State or anything else; I want all the kids to have their playing time. The game wears on; West High is once again kicking butt. Not until the last minute or two of the game, when her team has maintained a twenty-point lead over the second half, do Emily and several other girls get to play.

She maintains her composure until we get in the car, then crumples in humiliation. Once we're on the highway, forty miles to home, freezing rain coats

30

our windows, but I can't see well enough to find a safe place to pull off. I drive with trepidation over the slippery road, through the foggy darkness, while Emily cries so hard it sounds as though she will break apart. "Mommy, I'm such a failure!" she weeps. At first my attempts to comfort her only increase her misery, so I shut up. I'm left to listen and worry about the road and think my resentful thoughts. I remember all the years in elementary school when she was "benched" in the classroom — left to do bulletin boards for the teacher — because she'd already mastered what was being taught. I think about the studies that suggest that girls who compete in athletics are far less likely to drink or take drugs or become pregnant.

To make myself feel better, I remember her thirteenth birthday, when she was the high scorer on her team with nineteen points. I can still see her dribbling the ball down the court, passing, rebounding, shooting, so far from any self-consciousness about her body it was as though the game had dreamed her up, supplying her with a body that moved as though sure of itself and its momentary grace.

⠿ ⠿ ⠿

One of Ben's names for his younger brother, Andrew, is "Trancer." Years ago, when Andrew played outfield in Little League, he often faced *away* from the batter in deep contemplation, and it was only with difficulty that his coach or I would pull his attention away from his thoughts and redirect it toward the real danger he might be smacked in the back of the skull by the ball.

"Andrew, get your head in the game!" the coach would holler, but Andrew never actually did. It worked out better when he went out for track. Long-distance running gave him plenty of time to think. Until recently, I thought the last thing he'd ever want to be was a jock.

July 1996. A Saturday morning, the window open while I work at home, bringing in the breeze fragrant with freshly cut grass and the steady thump thump thump of the basketball on the driveway. Andrew, who has just turned fourteen, bounces a ball in order to think. Two hours might pass in bouncing and shooting hoops before he appears in the office, as if from a dream, to tell me what's on his mind.

He wanders in wearing a wrinkled T-shirt and shorts, barefoot, his dark hair mussed. I'm surprised again by how graceful and muscular he is, how tall — five-foot-ten last time I measured him — but it seems possible that he's grown another inch since I fed him breakfast.

He plops down on a chair next to mine. Up close there's a little acne and a few whiskers, new this year, and the chickenpox scar on his cheek from when he was three.

"Hi, Mom." Here's something familiar: It's obvious he hasn't gotten around to brushing his teeth. He's lost in thought. "I love you, Mom," he says absently.

"I love you," I say, patting his rather huge and hairy knee, adding, "You look like a derelict."

He registers this and looks pleased.   40

Then he wakes up, turns toward me, says in a voice heavy with portent, "To-morrow."

"Tomorrow," I say cheerfully, because this is my role: to refute the objections he'll make because he's scared to go to the two-week writing scholarship work-shop that begins the next day.

"It's going to suck! They'll treat us like babies, probably make us go to bed at ten o'clock!"

This will be the first time he's been away from home for two weeks, one of the few times he's ever been away, even to stay with family. Three summers ago, when he stayed at my mother's, he got so homesick he went on a hunger strike so that he could come home. Since that time, he's grown a foot, his voice has dropped an octave, and his shin bones are as thick as the beef bones we buy for the puppy to chew.

"Oh, I doubt it," I say. "They chose you based on your manuscripts and test   45
scores, so they know you're not babies."

"Yeah," he says. "But I bet everybody will already know each other except for me."

"They come from all over the state, so I don't know how they'd already know each other."

"Yeah, well, I don't care," he says, sounding satisfied. "They're probably all a bunch of nerds, anyway."

"Probably."

"What do you think?" he asks, pushing up the sleeve of his T-shirt, revealing   50
what I can genuinely describe to him as an amazingly well-developed biceps.

"Wow," I say, trying to take in the irony — or anti-irony — that all that grunting and weight lifting in the basement had been in preparation for a smart kids' workshop.

The next day I drive him to the university where the workshop will be held; after the three-hour orientation, I am to return to drive him to the dorm. At the appointed time, I pull into the parking lot. There is a cluster of girls at the shelter, surreptitiously watching the boys playing basketball. I scan the crowd of boys as they jump and shoot, and four times I think spot my son, but from this distance and with the sun in my eyes, I can't discern Andrew from the others. As I step out of the car to go look for him, he opens the passenger door.

"Mom!" he says. "Get in the car!"

His face is flushed, jaw set. Someone might see me, confirming the rumor he has a mother.

"How was it?" I ask, backing out.   55

"It sucks," he says. "We're on such a short leash. WE HAVE TO GO TO BED AT TEN O'CLOCK! And the boys are like all into role-playing games, though some of them are pretending to be intellectuals. It sucks so bad you wouldn't believe it. The books they go around recommending to each other are like science-fiction stuff they think is great literature."

"That's too bad," I say.

"It might be okay, though," he says. "Some of the kids are pretty cool."

"That's good," I say, noticing the lovely cumulus between us and the enormous sky.

"One kid asked me what kind of game system I have, and I said 'Game system?' And he said, 'You know like Sega or Super Nintendo,' and I said, 'Game system? I don't play game systems.'" 60

"You really shut him off," I say.

"Well, I didn't really shut him off," he says, hedging.

Trailing him down the hall of the dorm where he'll live for the next two weeks, I watch as he nods to the other boys. As he unlocks the door to his room, he whispers, "Nobody I couldn't take if I had to," and grins before giving me the briefest and most furtive of hugs good-bye.

Over the next two weeks, he phones only once, and, in a breezy tone, tells me he's having, definitely, the best time of his life. My friend who lives across the street from the dorm and has promised to spy on my child, reports that every evening Andrew's out shooting hoops with the R.A. and a couple of the other scholarship guys.

In the remarks at the closing ceremony, Andrew's muscles emerge as a kind of theme, and, in the final ritual of parting, each kid autographs my son's manly biceps. 65

❖ ❖ ❖

When I mention to Ben that I'm writing an essay about sports, he looks stricken. "I don't think that's a good idea, Mom," he says, honesty overriding tact. "I mean it's not something you can read about and understand in that way. You have to have a feel for it, an intuition. You have to *love* it."

"I'm not pretending to love it," I say a bit defensively.

Is there anything about sports I love?

Closing my eyes, I remember swinging my bat and solidly hitting the ball, the shudder of the connection a physical exultation traveling down my arm. I remember tossing the bat aside, and, as though suddenly released into the wild, racing through the shimmering heat, toeing each dried cow pie base and sliding into home.

I remember running hard, free of ambivalence, of pity. I remember the powdery dirt and the minty smell of the weeds and the unreasonable beauty of the sky. 70

"Mom," someone is calling. "*Mom!*"

I open my eyes.

"You're as bad as Andrew," Emily informs me. "Why are you just sitting here?"

"I was remembering when I was a kid, playing softball."

"Oh, my gosh," she says, mildly exasperated, "playing in the dirt with your friends doesn't count, Mom. I thought you were going to write about when I was the high scorer on my basketball team with nineteen points. On my thirteenth birthday, remember?" 75

"When did I say I was going to write about that?"

"You didn't, but I told you you should. It was so awesome. We were playing Southeast, the gym was packed, and everybody from Northwest was yelling my name. I kept throwing the ball up there, and it kept going in. My team was pounding the floor, yelling 'Em-i-ly!' Then I did a layup, and it won the game. Don't you remember?"

"Of course, I remember."

"Well, all right then," she says, satisfied. "*That's* the story to tell."

Exploring the Text

1. Kris Vervaecke describes as "brutish" the softball she played as a young girl in Nebraska (para. 1). What satisfactions did she derive from the game? How did the game define her and her nemesis, Mary Hellerman?
2. Vervaecke describes her neighborhood as "inhabited almost solely by females" (para. 1). How does that fact connect to the game she and her friends play? How might it connect to the end of Vervaecke's sports career, when she "became a girl" (para. 4)?
3. How does paragraph 5 provide a transition to Vervaecke's role as the mother of athletes?
4. How and why does Vervaecke characterize herself as an uninterested spectator (paras. 6–8)? What rhetorical strategies does she use? Are they effective?
5. At the beginning of the second section (para. 10), Vervaecke says that sports has given her children what she, as a single mother could not: "letting them shed, for the game's duration, grief, rage, loneliness, or boredom, and allowing them to take on skill and cunning, filling them with inspiration and determination, sometimes awe" (para. 10). How does each of the anecdotes that follow illustrate some part of that statement?
6. Why does Vervaecke begin the third section (para. 25), which is about a game in which her daughter Emily barely plays, by noting that the athletes who attend the college where she teaches have never read a book?
7. What is the connection between Andrew's enjoyment of the writing workshop and his highly developed biceps?
8. In what ways does the last section of the essay connect playing sports, watching sports, and motherhood — the main threads of the piece? Why does the essay end with Emily's exasperation at her mother's memory of playing softball?
9. Frances Willard, author of *How I Learned to Ride the Bicycle* (p. 459), grew up on the prairie in the Midwest more than a century before Vervaecke did. Willard writes of being forced to stop playing and to put on long skirts and a corset when she was sixteen. Compare and contrast Willard's experience with the experience Vervaecke describes when she "became a girl" (para. 4).

The Real New York Giants

Rick Reilly

Born in Boulder, Colorado, in 1958, Richard Paul "Rick" Reilly is a columnist for *Sports Illustrated*. His column on the last page of the magazine is so popular that fans have been known to read the magazine from back to front. He has also published a number of books, including the autobiographical *Who's Your Caddy?* (2003) and a golf novel, *Missing Links* (1996). Reilly is known for his humorous — and sometimes scathing — writing. This selection, published six months after the 2001 terrorist attacks on the World Trade Center, shows his serious side.

Talk about a rebuilding year. The New York City Fire Department football team starts its National Public Safety League season next week missing seven starters, 12 alums and two coaches. But the firemen are playing. Hell, yes, they're playing.

Says cornerback Mike Heffernan, whose brother John was among the Bravest who died in the collapse of the World Trade Center towers, "Somebody said to me, 'Probably not going to be a team this season, huh, Mike?' I told him, 'We'll have a team if we only have 10 guys. We're playing.'"

Most of the guys on the team have a nasty case of the WTC cough, which is what you get from digging week after week, up to 18 hours a day, and inhaling dust, smoke, glass particles, asbestos and, indeed, microscopic remains of their fallen comrades. But the guys are playing. "Damn right," says fullback Tom Narducci. "It's tradition."

But how? Forget about replacing the players. How do you replace the *men*? How does starting cornerback Danny Foley replace the starting cornerback on the other side — his brother, Tommy?

Last season, if it wasn't Danny pulling Tommy out of the pile, it was Tommy 5 pulling Danny out. "That was the most fun I ever had playing football," says Danny, 28, the younger of the two by four years. "We both played high school and college, so we never got to see each other play. On this team, we were always together."

After 10 straight days of digging through the rubble, it was Danny who found Tommy. One last time, Danny pulled Tommy out of the pile. "When we found him," says Danny, "it was kind of a relief. I promised my mom I wasn't coming home without Tommy — and I didn't. But a lot of families had nobody to bury."

Play football? How will they even get a play off? They lost their No. 1 and 1A quarterbacks, Paddy Lyons and Tom Cullen. It was Lyons who came into the game last May against the Orange County (Calif.) Lawmen and rescued his teammates. They trailed 14–0, but he led them to a 28–21 win. He was good at that kind of thing. He was with Squad 252, along with cornerback Tarel Coleman, and his friends believe those two rescued a lot of people that day before the steel-and-concrete sky collapsed on them.

How do you replace tight end Keith Glascoe, who was so good only a bum shoulder kept him off the New York Jets' roster in the early '90s? Or big lineman Bronko Pearsall, who insisted on singing *Wild Rover* after every game, win or lose?

Who's going to kick now that Billy Johnston is gone? Everybody called him Liam because he looked so bloody Irish. He was automatic on extra points, which was a luxury. Hell, there were years when the Bravest had to go for two after every touchdown just because they didn't have a kicker. Then they found Johnston.

They found Johnston again three weeks into the digging. Heffernan was there, and he helped carry his teammate out.   10

Even if you can replace the players who were lost, how do you replace all the other guys who made the team so damn much fun? Tommy Haskell was the tight ends coach and wrote the team newsletter. Mike Cawley set up the after-game beer parties. Danny Suhr, the first fireman to die that day, was the treasurer. Offensive coordinator Mike Stackpole lost his brother, Tim. Linebacker Zach Fletcher lost his twin brother, Andre.

How do you go on when so many guys are dead that you can't even retire their jerseys because you wouldn't have enough left to dress the team? How do you play a game draped in sorrow like that?

Came the first team meeting, and the club didn't get anywhere near its usual 60 guys. It got 120. All the lineup holes were patched. Guys who had retired signed up again. Guys who'd been asked 10 times said yes on the 11th. You cry together at enough funerals, you figure you can bleed together on a football field, too. One thing about firemen, they don't let each other fight battles alone.

Talk about a comeback year. "You've got to understand," says the team's president, Neil Walsh. "We all go to each other's weddings, christenings, graduations. I broke your brother in, and your dad broke me in, and I carried your son out of the pile. We're all brothers."

Not long ago a third-grade teacher found the team's water boy — Walsh's son   15
Ryan — sobbing uncontrollably in the boys' bathroom. "To him, all those guys were his uncles," says Walsh. "He couldn't handle losing them all in one day."

Some holes are easier to patch than others.

Exploring the Text

1. Rick Reilly's opening line suggests an ongoing conversation. What is the effect of that first line? What is the effect of the last sentence of that paragraph? Why do you think Reilly waited until the beginning of the next paragraph to quote one of the players?
2. Analyze the title "The Real New York Giants," considering the many ways it can be interpreted.
3. Reilly makes great use of rhetorical questions. How do the questions both comfort and provoke?
4. Reilly uses both concrete descriptions and figurative language. Find examples of each, and identify their purpose.

5. One of the essay's central images is pulling men out of "the pile." How does that image serve double duty?
6. What is the effect of ending the essay with the anecdote about third grader Ryan Walsh crying in the boys' bathroom? How does the anecdote tie Reilly's main ideas together?
7. Despite its conversational tone, this essay is also **elegiac**. How does Reilly achieve this?

For Fasting and Football, a Dedicated Game Plan

SAMUEL G. FREEDMAN

> Samuel G. Freedman (b. 1955) is a professor at Columbia University's Graduate School of Journalism. A staff reporter for the *New York Times* from 1981 to 1987, Freedman now writes the weekly "On Education" column for the *Times*, as well as articles about culture. He has also written for *Rolling Stone, New York,* and *Salon.* His nonfiction books cover topics ranging from black churches to Jewish identity in America to a New York City high school. The following essay is one of Freedman's "On Education" columns.

At 5 o'clock in the morning on game day, maybe the last game day of his football career, Ali Ahmad walked from the overnight darkness into the gleaming marble heart of the Golden Bakery. He wore his letter jacket from the Dearborn High Pioneers, with an orange chevron on each shoulder for his two years on the varsity and the stitching on the back spelling out his nickname, Flea. From a pocket of his sweats he pulled out a few dollars for a Pepsi and the meat-and-cheese pie called lahma ma jibini.

Since it was Ramadan, the Muslim holy month of daylight fasting, Ali would not eat or drink again until the sun set in nearly 14 hours. By then, Dearborn would be lining up against Crestwood High, knowing that a victory would put the Pioneers into the state playoffs and a loss would end the season with a mediocre record of 5–4. Weighing all of 135 pounds, Ali realized that he was not going to play any more football after high school. He would go back to watching it on television like the 6-year-old he had been when he discovered this crashing competition, much to the consternation of his parents, refugees from the more lethal forms of competition practiced in the Lebanese civil war.

If the kickoff on this October Friday was delayed a few minutes, Ali would be able to grab some crackers and a swig of Gatorade from the trainer. Otherwise, he would wait until halftime, having stashed a tuna sub in his locker for breaking the fast. As much as football meant to him, as much as it mattered to win, those things only counted for Ali if he was also staying true to Allah.

"To get through the fast," he put it, "I concentrate on the game."

The balance Ali struck was nothing unusual here in Dearborn, the center of   5
the largest Arab community in the Americas. About one-third of the students at Ali's high school are Muslim, and the proportion is similar on the football team. Khalil Dabaja at defensive back, Amir Rustom at linebacker, Mohammad Kassab at nose guard, Hassan Cheaib at fullback — they all have mastered the rhythms of the twin rituals of Islam and the gridiron.

Since Ramadan began in early October, the Muslim players have awakened at 4:30 for the predawn breakfast, shahoor; gone through an entire day of class without sustenance; resisted the temptation of a water break during practice; and started most of their Friday night games before full darkness allows for the evening meal of the iftar.

"When you start your day off fasting and you get to football at the end of the day, that's the challenge," said Hassan Cheaib, a 17-year-old senior. "You know you've worked hard. You know you've been faithful. And that makes you much tougher out on the field. You have to have a crazy mentality out on the field, and after fasting all day, you feel like a warrior."

Khalil Dabaja finds another kind of inspiration, one that puts even the intensity of football in perspective. "We fast so we can feel for the poor people, to know how they feel," said Khalil, 16, a junior. "I'm going through this hunger and thirst for 12, 13 hours. They're going through it for a lifetime."

The easy commingling of Ramadan and football season, Middle East and Middle America, has a value beyond the personal. It attests to a fundamental stability in American society, a capacity to absorb difference. Despite the global strains between the United States and much of the Islamic world because of both al Qaeda and Iraq, despite the domestic tensions brought on by the surveillance and detention of Muslims, this country has afforded a public tolerance for immigration and religion far greater than have the nations of Western Europe.

So Dearborn High is a place where the cafeteria serves halal chicken nuggets,   10
girls wear the hijab along with embroidered jeans, the Ramadan food drive gets equal time with the Key Club on morning announcements, and — to come back to football — Mohammad Kassab leads his Muslim teammates in al-Fateeha, the prayer that asks God's protection in both spiritual and physical ways, before every game. The divine one notwithstanding, Mohammad also has a favorite cheerleader hold his peanut-butter sandwich on the sideline for iftar.

While the first wave of Arab immigrants reached the Detroit area before World War II, they were predominantly Christians from Syria and Lebanon. The Muslim influx — Palestinian, Iraqi, Yemenite — has come largely in the last generation. At Dearborn High, most of the Muslim students are the children of Lebanese who fled the nation's civil war. By now, 20 years along, the parents have gone from being cooks and truck drivers to engineers, doctors and business owners. They have moved their families onto the city's affluent West Side, formerly the stronghold of white ethnics.

When David Mifsud, the Pioneers' coach, played for the team in the early 1980's, he knew one Muslim classmate. The players of that era were Haas, Kreger, Deorio, Szuba, Mason. Returning to Dearborn after college to start teaching at an elementary school, Mr. Mifsud was unprepared for the transformation. After a class aced a reading test, Mr. Mifsud threw a pizza party, only to learn that the Muslim pupils could not eat any because the pepperoni was pork.

These days, when the coach invites his team over for a barbecue, he has halal meat for the burgers.

This season asked for a greater sacrifice than the culinary. The last three games of the regular season fell during Ramadan, meaning many of Mr. Mifsud's 25 Muslim players were practicing and playing on empty stomachs.

After some exasperating mistakes — twice inside the 5-yard line without a touchdown against Allen Park, and falling for the fullback draw play all night against Monroe — the team risked missing the playoffs after having gone all the way to the semifinals last year.   15

Still, the coach made sure never to mention the fast, so as to not call attention to it. The responsibility belonged to the Muslim players themselves, like Ali Ahmad.

"Sometimes at practice one of the guys'll say, 'Let's just break, it's just one day,'" he said. "And I'll say: 'It's just a few more hours. You only got a couple more to go. It'll be worth it in the end.'"

Exploring the Text

1. How does Samuel Freedman make the connection between sports and religion?
2. Freedman opens his essay with a vivid image of a football player, not on the field, but in a bakery before dawn. How is the language like the language of sportswriting?
3. In paragraph 5, Freedman mentions balance, arguably the most important idea in this piece. How does Freedman's language throughout the column reflect this theme? Look especially at the parallels he sets up in paragraph 10.
4. Freedman uses words — *fundamental stability, sustenance, temptation, warrior,* and *sacrifice*, for example — that might be provocative. How do words like these help him achieve the essay's purpose?
5. Discuss ways that the sports field can absorb the tensions of the political world and neutralize political language.
6. What is the effect of the names Freedman lists in paragraphs 5 and 12? How do they help make Freedman's point about balance?
7. Freedman quotes two young football players in paragraphs 7 and 8. What does each one's view of fasting and football add to the essay?

8. Discuss paragraph 9. Do you agree that the United States has "a public tolerance for immigration and religion [that is] far greater than the nations of Western Europe" have? What evidence from recent events suggests that this is either true or false?

SAMUEL G. FREEDMAN ON WRITING

In the following interview with Samuel G. Freedman, he speaks about the challenges of writing on deadline and the strategies he uses under time constraints.

I think the great advantage in having come up as a daily newspaper reporter and having to write on deadline all the time is that you have to overcome whatever fear of it you might have because otherwise you just can't survive as a reporter. It is important to be able to function under deadline pressure because with a book you might spend 15 months. When you are writing a book or doing creative, fictional writing, no one is there to make you do the work, so you have to be even more self-disciplined. In fact, if you are working on a book, you have to tell yourself that even though completion might be months or even more than a year away, it is important to get a couple hundred words or even a thousand words written every day. My newspaper background was helpful for being able to focus even if it is just for a short amount of time. My writing is intermingled with teaching and parenting and all these other things, so it has been a long time since I have had the luxury of sitting down for 8 hours with nothing to do but work on my writing. It is much more common — especially in shorter pieces like my columns — that I have only an hour or two of writing time and the necessity is to concentrate very intensely during that time.

But one more thing that I want to say is that you have to resist the sense of panicking when you are on deadline and thinking, "I don't have time to review my notes, I don't have time to outline before I start to write." Something I tell my students and what I definitely abide by in my own writing is that I will always, no matter now tight the time is, make myself go back through all the notes, all the research material I have, and work out an outline for myself of what I want to write. I always tell my students the amount of time it takes you to do that you are going to more than recoup when you are writing because you are not going to get lost. You are going to know your direction. You are going to have the overall contour of the essay or article in your head before you start to write it.

Sometimes writers are concerned that [an outline] is going to restrain you or take your creativity away, but I disagree. To me, it is liberating. I always compare it to the way a good jazz musician has to know scales in order to improvise. If you don't know the scales, you can't improvise effectively. You don't just make it up. It is freedom within structure. So for me, the thought of writing, part fun, finding the right word, coming up with the right word, coming up with a terrific phrase, and using it in evocative detail — that freedom happens best for me within the overall structure of knowing what I want to say, how I want a piece to proceed from point A to point Z.

I tell students some practical advice [to help them balance the demands of the deadline with the need for depth — or truth]. If you are not sure about something, don't go to print with it. For instance, I had a student covering an election the other night. We are actually putting our stories on the Internet. The student filed a story that had a reference to an allegation of sexual harassment against a candidate in the City Council election. I said, "I'm not going to run this story, because I'd rather wait until tomorrow. You have to check to make sure that a suit has actually been filed. You have to find out if it has been dismissed or not. Is it waiting to be heard? What is the response of the person? If there is not a lawsuit and this is just a rumor, it shouldn't even be in the article." So, I guess one of the things I say is I'd rather be late and right, than first and wrong.

I try to give the students a sense of the importance of balancing. You know not everything is supposed to be balanced. I don't think if you are writing about a Holocaust survivor that you have to call up a Holocaust denier to get the other side of the story. But, for instance, a few of my students, just this week, are doing stories about gentrification in certain New York neighborhoods. The stories are very sympathetic to people who are being displaced by gentrification. I said to them, "That's fine and I do have sympathy, but you can't just have a story that doesn't even talk to the people who are moving into the neighborhood. Do they have no right to be heard from?" So, I was trying to teach them that you have got to hold two opposing ideas in your head at the same time and take them each seriously. That is part of our obligation as journalists.

Follow-up

Discuss which of Samuel Freedman's suggestions you find most helpful. Explain how you could apply them to your own writing.

Ex-Basketball Player (poetry)

JOHN UPDIKE

John Updike (b. 1932) grew up in Pennsylvania and attended Harvard University on a full scholarship, before graduating summa cum laude. At Harvard, he was president of the *Harvard Lampoon*. Updike is known for his careful craftsmanship and for writing about the world of the Protestant middle class. In his novels and short stories he often explores the interrelationship of sex, faith, and death. His series of novels about Harry "Rabbit" Angstrom, a former high-school basketball star, defined the suburban experience. Two of these novels won the Pulitzer Prize. Updike is also known for his criticism and poetry.

Pearl Avenue runs past the high-school lot,
Bends with the trolley tracks, and stops, cut off
Before it has a chance to go two blocks,
At Colonel McComsky Plaza. Berth's Garage
Is on the corner facing west, and there,   5
Most days, you'll find Flick Webb, who helps Berth out.

Flick stands tall among the idiot pumps —
Five on a side, the old bubble-head style,
Their rubber elbows hanging loose and low.
One's nostrils are two S's, and his eyes   10
An E and O. And one is squat, without
A head at all — more of a football type.

Once Flick played for the high-school team, the Wizards.
He was good: in fact, the best. In '46
He bucketed three hundred ninety points,   15
A county record still. The ball loved Flick.
I saw him rack up thirty-eight or forty
In one home game. His hands were like wild birds.

He never learned a trade, he just sells gas,
Checks oil, and changes flats. Once in a while,   20
As a gag, he dribbles an inner tube,
But most of us remember anyway.
His hands are fine and nervous on the lug wrench.
It makes no difference to the lug wrench, though.

Off work, he hangs around Mae's Luncheonette.   25
Grease-gray and kind of coiled, he plays pinball,
Smokes those thin cigars, nurses lemon phosphates.

Flick seldom says a word to Mae, just nods
Beyond her face toward bright applauding tiers
Of Necco Wafers, Nibs, and Juju Beads.   30

Exploring the Text

1. In addition to creating a portrait of Flick Webb, the former basketball star, John Updike also creates a setting. What details does he use to set the scene?
2. Updike uses figurative language sparingly. Consider the effects of personification and simile in this poem.
3. What statement does the poem make about high school sports?
4. Compare the effect of the following excerpt about a pickup basketball game from Updike's novel *Rabbit, Run* (1960) with the effect of "Ex-Basketball Player" (1957).

> Yet in his time Rabbit was famous through the county; in basketball in his junior year he set a B-league scoring record that in his senior year he broke with a record that was not broken until four years later, that is, four years ago.
>
> He sinks shots one-handed, two-handed, underhanded, flat-footed, and out of the pivot, jump, and set. Flat and soft the ball lifts. That his touch still lives in his hands elates him. He feels liberated from long gloom.

Prothalamion (poetry)

Maxine Kumin

Maxine Kumin, who was born in Philadelphia in 1925, now lives in New Hampshire. She has published eleven books of poetry, including *Up Country: Poems of New England* (1972) for which she received the Pulitzer Prize. She is also the author of a memoir, *Inside the Halo and Beyond: The Anatomy of a Recovery* (2000), four novels, a collection of short stories, more than twenty children's books, and four books of essays, most recently *Always Beginning: Essays on a Life in Poetry* (2000) and *Women, Animals, and Vegetables* (1994). She has served as consultant in poetry to the Library of Congress and as poet laureate of New Hampshire, and is a former chancellor of the Academy of American Poets.

The far court opens for us all July.
Your arm, flung up like an easy sail bellying,
comes down on the serve in a blue piece of sky
barely within reach, and you, following,
tip forward on the smash. The sun sits still   5
on the hard white canvas lip of the net. Five-love.

Salt runs behind my ears at thirty-all.
At game, I see the sweat that you're made of.
We improve each other, quickening so by noon
that the white game moves itself, the universe   *10*
contracted to the edge of the dividing line
you toe against — limbering for your service,
arm up, swiping the sun time after time —
and the square I live in, measured out with lime.

Exploring the Text

1. A *prothalamion* is a song celebrating a marriage. Why might Maxine Kumin have used it as the title of a poem about tennis? Find images in the poem that suggest celebration, weddings, love.
2. Edmund Spenser's "Prothalamion" was an occasional poem, written to celebrate the marriages of Ladies Katherine and Elizabeth Somerset in 1596. Read the Spencer poem online at <bedfordstmartins.com/languageofcomp>, and compare it with Kumin's. What is Kumin celebrating in her poem of the same name?
3. What statement does Kumin make about athletics in the poem?
4. How does the structure of Kumin's poem add a level of meaning? Look at the poem grammatically, and consider the effects of its line breaks.

Untitled (cartoon)

EDWARD KOREN

Edward Koren is best known for his work in the *New Yorker*, where he has published more than nine hundred cartoons. His cartoons have also appeared in the *New York Times, Newsweek, Time,* the *Boston Globe, Fortune, GQ,* and *Sports Illustrated.* In addition, they are included in the collections of museums at the Rhode Island School of Design and at Harvard, Princeton, and Cambridge universities, as well as at the Library of Congress. Koren attended Columbia College and received an MFA from Pratt Institute. He taught at Brown University for many years and received a Guggenheim Fellowship. He lives with his family in Vermont.

Exploring the Text

1. Consider the words and the images separately. What is the relationship between them? Do the images support the words or vice versa?

2. What point does the cartoon make about the relationship between sports and academics? Do you agree with Edward Koren's thesis?

3. What does the American flag add to the cartoon's impact?

4. This cartoon was originally published in the *New Yorker* in March 2002. What assumptions about its audience are evident in the cartoon?

5. A cartoon can be analyzed through the rhetorical triangle. Consider the cartoon, the artist, and the audience separately; then analyze the relationships among those three elements. Also consider the context: the time and place of the work's creation, and how and where it is viewed.

6. Essayist Roger Rosenblatt said, "There's no point in trying to say something serious about humor. It just gets depressing. Cartoons, especially, defy analysis. We only want to look and laugh." Do you agree or disagree? Why? What other purposes do cartoons serve besides inducing laughter?

Conversation

Focus on Body Image

Following are five selections that comment directly or indirectly on the issue of body image:

Sources
1. **Donna Britt,** *A Unique Take on Beauty*
2. *Sports Illustrated* (Cover), *Little Sister, Big Hit*
3. **Natalie Angier,** *Drugs, Sports, Body Image and G.I. Joe*
4. **American College of Sports Medicine,** *Disordered Eating and Body Image Disturbances May Be Underreported in Male Athletes*
5. **National Eating Disorders Association,** *Enhancing Male Body Image*

After using the questions to discuss individual selections, synthesize the pieces through one of the suggested assignments on page 492.

1. *A Unique Take on Beauty*

DONNA BRITT

In the following column from the *Washington Post*, Donna Britt discusses the September 20, 1999, *Sports Illustrated* cover featuring Serena Williams.

Before I get to U.S. Open champion Serena Williams's disconcerting cover photo on the new *Sports Illustrated*, I must point something out:

There are people on earth who sincerely find Sarah Jessica Parker beautiful.

Maybe that doesn't surprise you. After all, the vivacious actress, a recent best-actress Emmy nominee for HBO's "Sex in the City," is blond, slim and possesses ample upper-body upholstery. The fact that her face is unremarkable seems hardly to matter. Parker is, I've heard repeatedly, beautiful.

Ditto for the versatile actress who defeated Parker for the [1999] Emmy. Physically, Helen Hunt is much like Parker: blond, thin, busty for her small frame. So she, too, is beautiful. So is the wraithlike Gwyneth Pallid — I mean Paltrow, whom some have dared to compare to Grace Kelly. So are dozens of women on TV and onscreen whom I, and others, find merely pretty or profoundly average.

But to begrudge folks their opinion of these women is useless. Beauty is 5 entirely subjective, a matter truly in the eye of the beholder.

So let us behold Serena Williams. A guy I know who did recently said this:

"I don't watch tennis, but was channel-flipping and got the championship," said the man, who asked not to be identified. "I saw Serena and, said, 'Damn. . . . She was fine in a way that I almost never see on the airwaves.'"

I, too, watched Williams wrest the tournament from Martina Hingis in an excruciating battle. As impressed as I was with Williams's speed, thunderous speed, serve and body-hugging outfits, they weren't the reasons I couldn't stop staring.

Williams's physical presence is what struck me — and the fact that it's of a type I rarely see beamed from my TV set.

Serena is no light-and-lovely Halle Berry–Vanessa Williams type, nor a fine- 10 featured brown vision in the vein of Angela Bassett or Whitney Houston — recognized beauties who've all had some difficulty getting parts equal to their looks.

Serena's beauty is a motherland thing. She is, with her satin skin, cornrows and powerhouse voluptuousness, the female embodiment of Africa, unmistakable and undiluted. She is also, as my son used to say, "the bomb-diggity."

Now some may grouse at my bringing a subject as unworthy as appearance into the pristine arena of sports. They'd suggest that considering Williams's many gifts, attractiveness hardly matters. To which I respectfully respond:

Bull. Who really believes Michael Jordan's unprecedented popularity has nothing to do with his handsomeness? Or that soccer star Mia Hamm's wholesome prettiness doesn't help endear her to fans, or that hardbodied Gabrielle Reece, a men's mag fave, is the nation's best-known female volleyball player because of her serve?

For athletes, there's as much money to be made in looks as talent. But something more important than a paycheck is at stake with Serena.

In the video for TLC's hit single, "Unpretty," several young women struggle 15 with being judged by standards of beauty that reject full-figured and flatchested women and those with unfashionable features. I love the video's self-love message.

And that it shows how much looks still matter to most women and girls.

It's a credit to Williams's upbringing that she doesn't feel "unpretty" in a culture that long ignored and rejected beauty like hers. Some find Serena and sister Venus — who's also striking — confident to the point of intimidation. My son, 14, says Serena is "cute for a girl who looks like she could kick my butt."

Maybe Serena's muscularity explains why much of the media has yet to note her beauty. But buffness hasn't marred Lucy Lawless's sex-symbol status as TV's Xena. Her rippling bod still graces men's magazine covers. Could Williams's youth be the issue? Not if you consider how often the prettiness of Hingis, 18, is noted, as is 18-year-old Anna Kournikova's Kewpie-doll appeal.

The new *Sports Illustrated* clinched it. From hundreds of possible photos, *SI* chose one of Serena during play, her face contorted in a grimace. The shot highlights her athleticism, which I love, but diminishes her attractiveness. Oddly, the mag that invented swimsuit issues modestly obscures Serena's breasts with a strip of type.

Some, I suspect, don't know what to think of the Williams sisters' special   20
glamour.

Serena may be just the girl to help them. As smart, bubbly and open as she is attractive, she has everything that our most beloved sports heroes possess.

My hope is that America is smart and open enough to embrace Serena's "unique" beauty, which in fact can be found on vivid display all over the world. That would mean enfolding her as it does its Parkers and Hamms and more recently its Jennifer Lopezes, though that once-bountiful Latina seems blonder and thinner every day.

America should wrap its arms around Serena's beauty as well as her talent — not just for her sake, but for all the beautiful dark girls who never got their due.

Tennis star Serena Williams graces the Sept. 20 [1999] cover of *Sports Illustrated*.

Questions

1. Characterize Donna Britt's audience. What assumptions does she make about her readers?
2. What is Britt's basic argument? How does she use the cover of *Sports Illustrated* featuring Serena Williams to support it?
3. Britt says some might "grouse" at bringing the subject of appearance into what she calls the "pristine arena of sports" (para. 12). Why does she call the arena of sports pristine? Is she interested in what those who would "grouse" about this think? Why does she bring it up, and how does she counter the argument that looks don't matter in sports?
4. What other counterarguments does Britt offer? How does she address each one?
5. Britt lets *Sports Illustrated* off the hook by saying she suspects that some people "don't know what to think of the Williams sisters' special glamour" (para. 21). In the years since she wrote that, how has public opinion about the Williams sisters' looks changed?
6. Do you think attractiveness matters in an athlete? What effect has the physical attractiveness of athletes such as Maria Sharapova or Michael Jordan had on their careers?

2. *Little Sister, Big Hit*

SPORTS ILLUSTRATED

Following is the cover of *Sports Illustrated* that Donna Britt wrote about (p. 482).

Questions

1. Consider the layout of the *Sports Illustrated* cover. How much space does the photograph of Serena Williams take? What is the effect of obscuring part of the title of the magazine?

2. In "A Unique Take on Beauty" (p. 482), Donna Britt describes Williams's face on the cover as "contorted in a grimace" (para. 19). She says the shot "highlights her athleticism . . . but diminishes her attractiveness" (para. 19). Do you agree or disagree with Britt? Is a man less attractive if he is photographed in an intensely athletic moment?

3. Consider the text on the cover. Why do you think the articles on the National Football League (NFL) are advertised along with Williams's picture? Comment on calling Williams "Little Sister."

3. *Drugs, Sports, Body Image and G.I. Joe*

NATALIE ANGIER

In the following 1998 *New York Times* article, science writer Natalie Angier discusses the influence of the G.I. Joe doll since its introduction in 1964.

Which classic American doll has been a staple of childhood from the boomer babies onward, has won iconic, if politically freighted, status in our culture, and possesses a waist so small and hemispheric projections so pronounced that no real adult could approach them without the help of potentially dangerous body enhancement therapies?

Barbie? Well, yes. But Barbie has a male companion in the land of the outlandish physique, and his name is not Ken. Instead, we must look to a recent model of that old trooper, G.I. Joe, to see a match for Barbie's cartoon anatomy, and to find a doll that may be as insidious a role model for boys as Ms. Triple-D top, Size-2 bottom is for girls.

Some researchers worry that Joe and other action-hero figures may, in minor fashion, help fan the use of muscle-building drugs among young athletes, even as doctors and sports officials struggle to emphasize that such drugs are not only risky, illegal and unsporting, but, in many cases, worthless in enhancing performance.

Dr. Harrison G. Pope Jr., a psychiatrist at McLean Hospital in Belmont, Mass., has studied how the morphology of G.I. Joe has evolved since the doll was introduced in 1964. Just as Barbie has become gradually thinner and bustier, Dr. Pope said, so each new vintage of G.I. Joe has been more muscular and sharply defined, or "cut," than the model before.

The most extraordinary G.I. Joe on the market, "G.I. Joe Extreme," wears a red bandanna and an expression of rage. His biceps bulge so much that they are larger around than his waist, and, if ratcheted up to human size, they would be larger than even the arms of the grotesquely muscular Mr. Olympias of today, said Dr. Pope.

Hasbro Industries, maker of the G.I. Joe dolls, disagrees with Dr. Pope's contention that the body type of the standard Joe doll has changed much over the years. The company adds that it has stopped manufacturing the "Extreme" model, although a recent shopping expedition showed that the doll was still available in toy stores.

G.I. Joe is the only action figure that has been around long enough for Dr. Pope to be able to make comparisons between old and new models. But he said that a survey of other popular action figures, including the Power Rangers, Batman and Cyberforce Stryker showed the same excessive muscularity.

Dr. Pope said the dolls might be planting in boys' minds a template for a heman's body that cannot be attained without engaging in obsessive behaviors to build muscle and strip off fat, and then augmenting those efforts through the consumption of drugs like human growth hormone and anabolic steroids, which are synthetic versions of the male hormone, testosterone. . . .

"Prior to 1960, and the introduction of anabolic steroids, even the most dedicated bodybuilders couldn't get larger than a certain maximum size," Dr. Pope said. "Steroids made it possible for men to look as big as supermen, and now we see that standard reflected in our toys for the very young."

Given the ubiquitous images of muscularity, as well as the mounting demands on young athletes to sprint faster, vault higher, lift heavier and otherwise impress cadres of easily disgruntled sports fans, experts say it is not surprising that the use of muscle-enhancing drugs has reached pandemic proportions, even among barely pubescent boys. Some 18 percent of high school athletes in the United States are thought to use anabolic steroids, about twice the figure of [1988], according to some estimates.

Although performance-enhancing drugs are generally banned by athletic organizations, it is considered laughably easy to cheat and escape detection in drug screens. In addition, health food stores now offer a variety of "nutritional supplements" reputed to have anabolic properties. The supplements include creatine, DHEA, beta agonists and androstenedione, a precursor of testosterone . . . made famous by the baseball slugger Mark McGwire, who admitted with pride that he ate it. Such supplements are not strictly regulated, like drugs, their side effects are uncharted and their effectiveness is unproved.

Doctors have long emphasized the dangers of muscle-building drugs. The use of anabolic steroids lowers the levels of protective high-density lipoproteins, suppresses sperm production and raises the risk of heart attacks, strokes and liver disease.

The chronic use of human growth hormone in ultra-high doses has its own hazards, among them an increased risk of arthritic-type disorders, diabetes and some cancers.

Yet experts acknowledge that it is not enough to harangue athletes about the risks to their health. Surveys have shown that competitive athletes — who are, after all, quite young and still unconvinced of their mortality — say they would gladly trade years of their life for the chance at winning a gold medal or breaking a world record.

Arnold Schwarzenegger has pointed out that top-tier athletes are not in it for the sake of "fitness," and that they often go to grueling, distinctly unhealthy extremes in their training regimens; he has said that, when he was a competitive bodybuilder, he often worked out so intensively that he vomited afterward.

The great Alberto Salazar twice was given last rites at the end of a marathon after pushing himself so hard in the race that he nearly died at the finish line. What is the difference between overtraining and overcompeting yourself to death, and killing yourself slowly with steroids?

"We can be so hypocritical," said George Annas, chairman of the health law department in the Boston University School of Public Health. "We say, it's O.K. to spend 18 hours a day training, and we put our kids through all kinds of inhumane regimens that can border on child abuse, but take one drug and that's the end of it. We're really crazy about drugs."

According to many researchers, the paradoxical element in the seemingly unstoppable epidemic of doping, or using performance enhancing drugs, is that most of the drugs do not work nearly as well as billed.

Human growth hormone may increase muscle mass, but bigger does not necessarily mean stronger, said Shalender Bhasin, a professor of medicine and chief of the division of endocrinology metabolism and molecular medicine at Charles Drew University in Los Angeles. "Patients with acromegaly, who naturally overproduce growth hormone, often have muscle hypertrophy," he said. "But their muscles are weak."

As for the effectiveness of anabolic steroids and other types of testosterone supplements, scientists for years debated whether the drugs truly increased muscle mass and strength, or merely bloated muscle cells with water and encouraged athletes to train harder through a placebo effect.   20

[In 1996], Dr. Bhasin and his colleagues showed in a comprehensive report in the *New England Journal of Medicine* that super-high doses of testosterone given to healthy young men could increase muscle size and muscle strength, as measured by the ability to do exercises like bench-pressing and leg-squatting.

But the results were far from spectacular, and high-intensity, drug-free workouts proved nearly as good at building muscle strength as did exercise and testosterone combined. For reasons that remain unclear, said Dr. Bhasin, a pound of muscle gained through exercise is stronger than a pound of muscle gained through the grace of testosterone. He also emphasized that neither his study, nor any other that he knew of, had shown testosteronelike drugs capable of improving muscle performance — that is, the capacity of a muscle to do the sports maneuver an athlete wants it to do.

The extra muscle bulk that comes from steroid use may drag an athlete down without compensating for the added weight through better performance. For any event that requires moving against friction or gravity, Dr. Bhasin said, including sprinting, pole-vaulting or swimming, and for endurance activities like marathon running, taking testosterone may be counterproductive.

Some athletes know as much, and sneer at their doping friends. Whether performance drugs will ever be eliminated from sports, though, nobody can say. "I'm afraid I'm very cynical," Dr. Pope said. "From my research, I've seen that the use of steroids and other drugs has infiltrated deeper into sports than the vast majority of the public realizes. It's like asking, how can we turn back from nuclear weapons? The technology is there. The genie is out of the bottle."

It might help to begin by tinkering at Santa's workshop. Mattel has talked   25
about releasing a more realistic Barbie doll with a thicker waist and smaller bust. How about a G.I. "Love Handles" Joe?

Questions

1. Natalie Angier's lead plays off our expectation that Barbie will be the villain of the piece. Is the lead effective? What assumptions does Angier make about her audience?

2. Angier's article was first published in the *New York Times* on December 22. How is the date connected to her subject? How does the occasion affect the reader's relationship to the subject?
3. How does Angier establish credibility for her sources?
4. Consider paragraph 6, in which Angier reports on her conversation with a representative from the toy company that makes G.I. Joe. What is the effect of the order in which she shares the representative's comments?
5. What solutions does Angier offer for the problems associated with the unrealistic body image modeled by G.I. Joe?

4. *Disordered Eating and Body Image Disturbances May Be Underreported in Male Athletes*

AMERICAN COLLEGE OF SPORTS MEDICINE

The following selection, a press release from the American College of Sports Medicine, discusses body image disturbance and eating disorders among male athletes.

Fitness professionals urged to identify and assist those who show warning signs and symptoms of dangerous behavior

INDIANAPOLIS — Male athletes who constantly seek instant results from working out by frequently looking at themselves in mirrors or weighing themselves at the gym could be exhibiting a dangerous psychiatric condition that most consider only a threat to women's health.

An article published in the March/April 2003 issue of *ACSM's Health & Fitness Journal* reviews recent studies on disordered eating and body image in male athletes and concludes that instances of these conditions are underreported. As a result, health and fitness professionals should actively attempt to recognize clients at risk of developing a problem with disordered eating and body image and intervene when necessary.

In highlighting what many researchers consider to be a growing health concern among males, author Katherine A. Beals, R.D., Ph.D., points out the difficulty in accurately estimating the number of male athletes with disordered eating because few studies have included males. She indicates that women are still more commonly considered to exhibit such symptoms as anorexia nervosa and bulimia nervosa, but that reasons for any perceived gender gap could lie in how society responds to behavior and appearance among the genders. For example, a thin man may be considered "skinny," whereas a thin female may be labeled "anorexic." Furthermore, women who report body dissatisfaction generally want to lose weight, whereas men are evenly split between those desiring weight loss and those desiring weight gain.

The article notes that certain sports appear to place athletes at an increased risk, particularly sports that use weight classifications, such as wrestling and weightlifting. According to a study conducted by the NCAA, competitive wrestlers often shed 15 pounds or more utilizing dangerous methods like fasting, fluid restriction, and even vomiting. In another study, weightlifters reported a significantly greater rate of body dissatisfaction than other athletes.

Another form of body image disturbance found among some male athletes is muscle dysmorphia, described as "reverse anorexia," or the "Adonis Complex." This disorder is characterized by an inordinate preoccupation and dissatisfaction with body size and muscularity. Individuals with this condition see themselves as small and frail, even though they are actually large and muscular. These men tend to be at risk of abusing performance-enhancing drugs and supplements.

Beals cites a recent study that helps health and fitness professionals differentiate between muscle dysmorphia and a normal concern with body weight or a simple enthusiasm for weightlifting. She points out that the athletes with muscle dysmorphia will report a greater level of dissatisfaction with their appearance, constantly looking for compliments or approval from friends, yet expressing discomfort with the idea of having to expose their body, such as by taking off a shirt at the beach.

Health and fitness professionals should look for the signs of these problems, such as frequent mood swings, relentless exercise, and chronic fatigue, and carefully approach a male athlete demonstrating symptoms of disordered eating or body image problems. The author notes it is generally more difficult for males to seek treatment than females, due to the perception that these conditions are exclusive to women or the belief that they can handle it themselves. Once a male athlete has accepted such a problem, fitness professionals are strongly encouraged to refer him to the appropriate medical or health practitioner. The treatment team assembled to assist in the recovery from disordered eating and body image typically includes a physician, a psychologist, and a dietician.

Questions

1. How does the news release from the American College of Sports Medicine create a sense of urgency?
2. In the news release, Katherine A. Beals points out the difficulty in estimating the number of male athletes with disordered eating (para. 3). How does she explain the gender gap in reports of disordered eating?
3. What is the "Adonis Complex" (para. 5)? What particular risks does this condition cause male athletes to take?
4. Why are the warning signs in males with dysmorphia, or disordered eating, different from the warning signs in females?

5. *Enhancing Male Body Image*

NATIONAL EATING DISORDERS ASSOCIATION

The following information from the National Eating Disorders Association discusses male body image.

Recognize that bodies come in all different shapes and sizes. There is no one "right" body size. Your body is not, and should not, be exactly like anyone else's. Try to see your body as a facet of your uniqueness and individuality.

- **Focus** on the qualities in yourself that you like that are not related to appearance. Spend time developing these capacities rather than letting your appearance define your identity and your worth.

- **Look** critically at advertisements that push the "body building" message. Our culture emphasizes the V-shaped muscular body shape as the ideal for men. Magazines targeted at men tend to focus on articles and advertisements promoting weight lifting, body building or muscle toning. Do you know men who have muscular, athletic bodies but who are not happy? Are there dangers in spending too much time focusing on your body? Consider giving up your goal of achieving the "perfect" male body and work at accepting your body just the way it is.

- **Remember** that your body size, shape, or weight does not determine your worth as a person, or your identity as a man. In other words, you are not just your body. Expand your idea of "masculinity" to include qualities such as sensitivity, cooperation, caring, patience, having feelings, being artistic. Some men may be muscular and athletic, but these qualities in and of themselves do not make a person a "man."

- **Find** friends who are not overly concerned with weight or appearance. 5

- **Be assertive** with others who comment on your body. Let people know that comments on your physical appearance, either positive or negative, are not appreciated. Confront others who tease men about their bodies or who attack their masculinity by calling them names such as "sissy" or "wimp."

- **Demonstrate respect** for men who possess body types or who display personality traits that do not meet the cultural standard for masculinity; e.g., men who are slender, short, or overweight, gay men, men who dress colorfully or who enjoy traditional "non-masculine" activities such as dancing, sewing or cooking.

- **Be aware** of the negative messages you tell yourself about your appearance or body. Respond to negative self-talk with an affirmation. For example, if you start giving yourself a message like, "I look gross," substitute a positive affirmation, "I accept myself the way I am," or "I'm a worthwhile person, fat and all."

- **Focus** on the ways in which your body serves you and enables you to participate fully in life. In other words, appreciate how your body functions rather than obsessing about its appearance. For example, appreciate that your arms enable you to hold someone you love, your thighs enable you to run, etc.

- **Aim** for lifestyle mastery, rather than mastery over your body, weight, or appearance. Lifestyle mastery has to do with developing your unique gifts and potential, expressing yourself, developing meaningful relationships, learning how to solve problems, establishing goals, and contributing to life. View exercise and balanced eating as aspects of your overall approach to a life that emphasizes self-care. 10

Questions

1. Which of the bulleted suggestions in the selection are specific to men? Which could apply to both men and women?
2. Which suggestions are the most concrete? How do they differ from the more abstract suggestions? Which are easier to follow?
3. What is the effect of beginning each suggestion with a bold-faced verb? Is this tactic effective?

Entering the Conversation

As you respond to each of the following prompts, support your argument with references to at least three of the sources in Conversation: Focus on Body Image. For help using sources, see Chapter 3.

1. Write an essay explaining whether sports is a healthy or unhealthy influence on teenagers' thoughts about body image.

2. In 1991, Paul Solotaroff wrote a terrifying essay, "The Power and the Gory," about a bodybuilder's nightmare addiction to steroids. It ends with these words:

> Someone ought to post those words "There's only bad drugs and the sick . . . [people] who want to sell them to you" in every high school in the country. The latest estimate from a *USA Today* report is that there are half a million teenagers on juice these days, almost half of whom, according to a University of Kentucky study, [are] so naïve they think that steroids without exercise will build muscle. In this second stone age, the America of Schwarzkopf and

Schwarzenegger, someone needs to tell them that bigger isn't necessarily better. Sometimes, bigger is deader.

Create an education plan that might convince teenagers of the dangers of steroid use. In doing so, consider the role of the media and ways to use the media's power in order to encourage moderation and a healthy balance of exercise and competition.

3. According to the selections in Conversation: Focus on Body Image, how does the media create a single ideal body image that readers and viewers should aspire to? What is the effect of this image?

4. Discuss how the sports world's and the media's idealization of the human body undermines physical and mental health.

5. Compare and contrast the ways men and women are influenced by the idealization of the human form in sports or the media.

Student Writing

Rhetorical Analysis: Comparing Strategies

Following is a prompt that asks the writer to compare two passages describing the same event, the finish of the 1938 Pimlico Special.

The passages here — one an excerpt from *Seabiscuit* (2001) by Laura Hillenbrand and the other taken from sportswriter Grantland Rice's report at the time of the race — describe the finish of the 1938 Pimlico Special. Compare and contrast the voice of each writer.

Michele Mendelson, an eleventh-grade AP student, has written a response to this prompt. As you read her essay, consider the approach Michele takes in her comparison, and then answer the questions that follow about how she organized and developed it.

From Seabiscuit

Laura Hillenbrand

The horses strained onward, arcing around the far turn and rushing at the crowd. Woolf was still, his eyes trained on War Admiral's head. He could see that Seabiscuit was looking right at his opponent. War Admiral glared back at him, his eyes wide open. Woolf saw Seabiscuit's ears flatten to his head and knew that the moment Fitzsimmons had spoken of was near. One horse was going to crack.

As forty thousand voices shouted them on, War Admiral found something more. He thrust his head in front.

Woolf glanced at War Admiral's beautiful head, sweeping through the air like a sickle. He could see the depth of the colt's effort in his large amber eye, rimmed in crimson and white. "His eye was rolling in its socket as if the horse was in agony," Woolf later recalled.

An instant later, Woolf felt a subtle hesitation in his opponent, a wavering. He looked at War Admiral again. The colt's tongue shot out the side of his mouth. Seabiscuit had broken him.

Woolf dropped low over the saddle and called into Seabiscuit's ear, asking him for everything he had. Seabiscuit gave it to him. War Admiral tried to answer, clinging to Seabiscuit for a few strides, but it was no use. He slid from Seabiscuit's side as if gravity were pulling him backward. Seabiscuit's ears flipped up. Woolf made a small motion with his hand.

"So long, Charley." He had coined a phrase that jockeys would use for decades.

Galloping low with Woolf flat over his back, Seabiscuit flew into the lane, the clean peninsula of track narrowing ahead as the crowd pushed forward. A steeplechase fence in the infield had collapsed, and a line of men had crashed through the line of police and now stood upright on the inner rail near the wire, bending down toward Seabiscuit and rooting him on. Clem McCarthy's voice was breaking into his microphone. *"Seabiscuit by three! Seabiscuit by three!"* He had never heard such cheering. Arms waved and mouths gaped open in incredulity as Seabiscuit came on, his ears wagging. Thousands of hands reached out from the infield, stretching to brush his shoulders as he blew past.

When he could no longer hear War Admiral's hooves beating the track, Woolf looked back. He saw the black form some thirty-five feet behind, still struggling to catch him. He had been wrong about War Admiral: he was game. Woolf felt a stab of empathy. "I saw something in the Admiral's eyes that was pitiful," he would say later. "He looked all broken up. I don't think he will be good for another race. Horses, mister, can have crushed hearts just like humans."

Seabiscuit Tops Admiral by Three Lengths
before Pimlico Crowd of 40,000

Grantland Rice

Sets Track Record and Shows Superior Speed and Courage
Over Mile-and-Three-Sixteenths Route

Rises to Second Place in Turf Earnings, with Total of $340,000 —
Rice Says Victor Is Gamest That Ever Raced in U.S.

The drama and melodrama of this match race, held before a record crowd keyed to the highest tension I have ever seen in sport, set an all time mark.

You must get the picture from the start to absorb the thrill of this perfect autumn day over a perfect track. As the two thoroughbreds paraded to the post there was no emotional outburst. The big crowd was too full of tension, the type of tension that locks the human throat.

You looked at the odds flashed upon the mutual board — War Admiral, one to four, Seabiscuit two to one. Even those backing War Admiral, the great majority of the crowd, felt their pity for the son of Hard Tack and Swing On [Seabiscuit], who had come along the hard way and had churned up the dust of almost every track from the Great Lakes to the Gulf, from the Atlantic to the Pacific.

After two false starts, they were off. But it wasn't the fast-flying War Admiral who took the lead. It was Seabiscuit, taking the whip from Woolf, who got the jump. It was Seabiscuit who had a full-length lead as they passed the first furlong. The Admiral's supporters were dazed as the 'Biscuit not only held this lead but increased it to two lengths before they passed the first quarter.

The 'Biscuit was moving along as smoothly as a southern breeze. And then the first roar of the big crowd swept over Maryland. The Admiral was moving up. Stride by stride, Man o' War's favorite offspring was closing up the open gap. You could hear the roar from thousands of throats "Here he comes, here he comes!"

And the Admiral was under full steam. He cut away a length. He cut away another length as they came to the half-mile post — and now they were running head and head. The Admiral looked Seabiscuit in the eye at the three-quarters but Seabiscuit never got the look. He was too busy running with his shorter, faster stride.

For almost a half mile they ran as one horse, painted against the green, red and orange foliage of a Maryland countryside. They were neck and neck — head and head — nose and nose.

The great Admiral had thrown his challenge. You could see that he expected Seabiscuit to quit and curl up. But, Seabiscuit has never been that brand of horse. I had seen him before in two $100,000 races at Santa Anita, boxed out, knocked to his knees, taking the worst of all the racing luck — almost everything except facing a firing squad or a machine-gun nest — and yet, through all this barrage of trouble Seabiscuit was always there, challenging at the wire. I saw him run the fastest half-mile ever run at Santa Anita last March, when he had to do it in his pursuit of Stagehand.

So, when War Admiral moved up on even terms and 40,000 throats poured out their tribute to the Admiral, I still knew that the 'Biscuit would be alongside at the finish. The 'Biscuit had come up the hard way. That happens to be the only way worthwhile. The Admiral had known only the softer years — the softer type of competition. He had never before met a combination of a grizzly bear and a running fool.

Head and head they came to the mile. There wasn't a short conceded putt between them. It was a question now of the horse that had the heart. Seabiscuit had lost his two-length margin. His velvet had been shot away. He was on his own where all races are won — down the stretch. He had come to the great kingdom of all sport — the kingdom of the heart.

The Admiral had shown his reserve speed. From two lengths away he was now on even terms. But as they passed the mile post with three-sixteenths left — the vital test — the stretch that always tells the story — where 40,000 looked for the fleet War Admiral to move away — there was another story. Seabiscuit was still hanging on. Seabiscuit hadn't quit. With barely more than a final furlong left, the hard-way son of Hard Tack must have said to the Admiral — "Now, let's start running. Let's see who is the better horse."

Foot by foot and yard by yard, Woolf and Seabiscuit started moving away. Charlie Kurtzinger gave the Admiral the whip. But you could see from the stands that the Admiral suddenly knew he had nothing left in heart or feet to match this crazy five-year-old who all his life had known only the uphill, knockdown devil-take-the-loser route, any track — any distance — any weight — any time. And who the hell are you?

War Admiral had no answer. Down the final furlong the great-hearted 'Biscuit put on extra speed. He moved on by. Then he opened a small gap. Forty thousand expected the Admiral to move up, close the gap again. But the Admiral was through. He had run against too many plow horses and platers in his soft easy life. He had never tackled a Seabiscuit before.

He had never met a horse who could look him in the eye down the stretch and say to him, in horse language, "Now let's start traveling, kid. How do you feel? I feel great. This is down my alley."

Yard by yard Seabiscuit moved on ahead. Then it was length by length. Seabiscuit left the Admiral so far behind that it wasn't even a contest down the stretch. War Admiral might just as well have been chasing a will-o-the-wisp in a midnight swamp. He might just as well have been a poodle chasing a meat wagon. He had been outrun and outgamed — he had been run off the track by a battered five-year-old who had more speed and heart.

The race, they say, isn't to the swift. But it is always to the swift and the game. It so happened that Seabiscuit had these two important qualities in deep abundance. War Admiral could match neither flying feet nor fighting heart. Man o' War's brilliant son hung on with all he had until it came to the big showdown — to the point when the hard-way thoroughbred, the horse from the wrong side of the track, began really to run.

Draft

Michele Mendelson

In *Seabiscuit*, Laura Hillenbrand focuses on the bigger picture of the race, while Grantland Rice recreates the race in almost real time. Hillenbrand's "voice" slows time down so the reader has a chance to see every detail. Rice's "voice" recreates the race almost as a play-by-play, reminiscent of the radio reports that were most likely broadcast as the race was run.

Hillenbrand creates photographic images by using a zoom lens on the details of the race. Hillenbrand's camera eye sees only one of Seabiscuit's eyes, as he races around the track. Her description of Seabiscuit's "large amber eye, rimmed in crimson and white" brings the reader right up close to the beautiful horse. His strength — and vulnerability — are suggested by amber, with its meaning as an ancient and precious stone. The crimson and white rim around his eye reinforces the strain of the race. Hillenbrand takes a quick look at the "black form some thirty-five feet behind" Seabiscuit. It is Seabiscuit's main competitor, War Admiral. Focused as Hillenbrand is on Seabiscuit, however, War Admiral is just a blur. For a moment Hillenbrand takes us into the mind of Seabiscuit's jockey: "Woolf glanced at War Admiral's beautiful head, sweeping through the air like a sickle." He only has a second to notice both the horse's beauty and its potential for mayhem — the blade of a sickle cutting through the competition. Hillenbrand slows time down to help the reader notice and enjoy every detail of this near photo finish.

Rice's account is that of a live reporter on the scene, giving the play-by-play for a radio audience. He recreates the moment by describing the progress of the race "foot by foot and yard by yard" as the horses gallop away from the starting line. His account has no frills: "'Biscuit put on extra speed. He moved on by." His voice is objective as he repeats words to emphasize the movement of time: "Yard by yard Seabiscuit moved on ahead" shows the arduous process by which Seabiscuit took the lead. Rice does comment on War Admiral, saying he "might just as well have been a fat poodle chasing a meat wagon," but the metaphor ends up highlighting Seabiscuit's lean power and sense of purpose. Rice's report, though filled with excitement, is fact-filled when it comes to Seabiscuit. We know the horse's progress at every step. His more colorful observations are reserved for the competition.

Hillenbrand and Rice both recreate the excitement of the historic race. Each uses vivid details to recreate the movement of the horses and the closeness of the race. The sparing use of figurative language keeps the reader in the moment. The difference in the two writers' voices comes from their functions as reporters. Hillenbrand sends us snapshots; her details create a photo album of images that bring the race to life. Rice "films" the race in real time. He recreates the moment-by-moment excitement of the horses flying around the track.

Questions

1. What metaphor does Michele Mendelson use to describe the difference between the two accounts of the race? Do you agree with how she describes the difference?
2. Would Michele's essay have benefited from more examples? What other examples could she have used to highlight the differences between the two accounts? What examples would have highlighted the similarities?
3. Write a new conclusion to Michele's essay that comments on the two pieces as examples of sportswriting.

Grammar as Rhetoric and Style
Direct, Precise, and Active Verbs

Direct, precise, active verbs energize writing. Consider this sentence with verbs in bold from "Drugs, Sports, Body Image and G.I. Joe" by Natalie Angier (p. 486):

> The use of anabolic steroids **lowers** the levels of protective high-density lipoproteins, **suppresses** sperm production and **raises** the risk of heart attacks, strokes and liver disease.

The verbs in Angier's sentence tell you how the drug acts. The rhetorical effect of the three verbs is that they move the sentence forward with vigor and clarity so that you form a negative opinion about the drug's actions. In addition, the verbs contribute to Angier's confident, no-nonsense tone: she has no need for fancy descriptions when straightforward verbs will do.

Now consider another passage, this one from "The Silent Season of a Hero" by Gay Talese (p. 431), with its verbs, verb phrases, and verbals (adjectives made from verbs) in bold type:

> He **watched** until she **left**, **lost** in the crowd of the newly arrived tourists that **had** just **come** down the hill by cable car. Then he **sat** down again at the table in the restaurant, **finishing** his tea and **lighting** another cigarette, his fifth in the last half hour. It **was** 11:30 in the morning. None of the other tables **was occupied**, and the only sounds **came** from the bar, where a liquor salesman **was laughing** at something the headwaiter **had said**. But then the salesman, his briefcase under his arm, **headed** for the door, **stopping** briefly **to peek** into the dining room and **call** out, "**See** you later, Joe." Joe DiMaggio **turned** and **waved** at the salesman. Then the room **was** quiet again.

Talese uses the action verbs, verb phrases, and verbals to give you a sense of the scene's movement and drama. On the other hand, the two shortest sentences — both emphasizing silence and stasis rather than movement — rely on the linking verb *was*.

Once you've learned to recognize effective verbs in your reading, you'll become more aware of them in your own writing. You may find yourself working on the verbs in revisions rather than first drafts, but here are some suggestions for making even your first draft active and precise.

Direct Verbs

Use forms of *to be* and other linking verbs sparingly and with a specific reason. Often you can change a form of *to be* followed by a predicate adjective or a predicate noun into an action verb. Consider how the second sentence in each pair below sports a stronger verb than the first:

> An article published in the March/April 2003 issue of *ACSM's Health & Fitness Journal* is a review of recent studies.

> An article published in the March/April 2003 issue of *ACSM's Health & Fitness Journal* reviews recent studies.
>
> — AMERICAN COLLEGE OF SPORTS MEDICINE

> It is a testament to a fundamental stability in American society. . . .

> It attests to a fundamental stability in American society. . . .
>
> — SAMUEL G. FREEDMAN

> My left arm was weak.

> I was losing the strength in my left arm.
>
> — JOHN MCMURTRY

My arm is strong again.

I've recovered most of the strength in my arm.

— John McMurtry

Precise Verbs

While there is nothing wrong with the verbs *walks* and *looks* in the first sentence that follows, consider the precision of the verbs in the second sentence.

> As Emily walks onto the floor in her green-and-gold uniform, she looks for me.

> As Emily bounces onto the floor in her green-and-gold uniform, her eyes scan the crowd to meet mine.

— Kris Vervaecke

Similarly, in the first sentence that follows, *complain* is a perfectly serviceable verb — until you compare it with the more precise verb that the writer selects.

> Now some may complain about my bringing a subject as unworthy as appearance into the pristine arena of sports.

> Now some may grouse at my bringing a subject as unworthy as appearance into the pristine arena of sports.

— Donna Britt

Active Verbs

In addition to selecting a verb that is direct and creates a precise image, use verbs in the active voice — with an easy-to-picture subject doing something — unless you have a specific purpose for using the passive voice, where the subject is acted upon. Here, for example, in the final part of a sentence from "The Silent Season of a Hero," Gay Talese makes good use of the passive voice (p. 432, para. 10):

> Zio Pepe was among those who cheered when Joe DiMaggio returned to San Francisco after his first season with the New York Yankees and **was carried** along the wharf on the shoulders of the fishermen.

In this sentence, DiMaggio is acted upon by the fishermen. Why? Perhaps because Talese wanted *DiMaggio* to remain as the subject instead of switching away from *DiMaggio* and making *the fishermen* the subject.

By and large though, strong writers stick with the active voice, as Talese does in the following passage (p. 437, para. 54):

> In the forty-first game [of 1941] . . . DiMaggio **tied** an American League record that George Sisler **had set** in 1922.

Talese could have cast that sentence in the passive voice, as follows:

> In the forty-first game . . . an American League record **that had been set** by George Sisler in 1922 **was tied** by DiMaggio.

As is often the case, the use of passive voice in this example makes for a wordy sentence that is hard to follow.

• EXERCISE 1

Improve the following sentences by replacing one or more verbs in each with a more effective verb — that is, a more vivid, precise, and active verb.

1. My first college visit will always be remembered by me.
2. There are many technological advances available to make our lives easier.
3. In the middle of the night, sirens could be heard.
4. It was not very long before she regretted buying the expensive handbag.
5. The Graham technique is little esteemed by modern dancers today.
6. The college advisor said she could not make a suggestion about which school to apply to because she didn't know his SAT scores.
7. The team captain is responsible for scheduling practices and communicating with team members.
8. A decision was reached by the arbitration panel.
9. The local sheriff gave a warning to the college students about walking around with open containers.
10. The chief of surgery took the opportunity to thank the volunteers.
11. Do your children have fears about going away to camp?
12. Antigone was very protective of Oedipus in *Oedipus at Colonus*.

• EXERCISE 2

Identify the verbs and verbals in the following passages. Discuss how these verbs affect the tone of the passages.

Maybe Serena's muscularity explains why much of the media has yet to note her beauty. But buffness hasn't marred Lucy Lawless's sex-symbol status as TV's Xena. Her rippling bod still graces men's magazine covers. Could Williams's youth be the issue? Not if you consider how often the prettiness of Hingis, 18, is noted, as is 18-year-old Anna Kournikova's Kewpie-doll appeal.

The new *Sports Illustrated* clinched it. From hundreds of possible photos, *SI* chose one of Serena during play, her face contorted in a grimace. The shot highlights her athleticism, which I love, but diminishes her attractiveness. Oddly, the mag that invented swimsuit issues modestly obscures Serena's breasts with a strip of type.

— DONNA BRITT, "A Unique Take on Beauty"

She maintains her composure until we get in the car, then crumples in humiliation. Once we're on the highway, forty miles to home, freezing rain coats our windows, but I can't see well enough to find a safe place to pull off. I drive with trepidation over the slippery road, through the foggy darkness, while Emily cries so hard it sounds as though she will break apart. "Mommy, I'm such a failure!" she weeps. At first my attempts to comfort her only increase her misery, so I shut up. I'm left to listen and worry about the road and think my resentful thoughts. I remember all the years in elementary school when she was "benched" in the classroom — left to do bulletin boards for the teacher — because she'd already mastered what was being taught. I think about the studies that suggest that girls who compete in athletics are far less likely to drink or take drugs or become pregnant.

— KRIS VERVAECKE, "A Spectator's Notebook"

• EXERCISE 3

Analyze the verbs in the opening paragraph of "How I Learned to Ride the Bicycle" on pages 459–460. Which verbs are precise and vivid? Which are bland or in the passive voice? Do you think that Frances Willard uses the passive voice deliberately and effectively? Do the verbs she uses tip you off that this is an older piece? Are there strong verbs that mirror the exercise the author is advocating? Cite specific examples to support your view.

If I am asked to explain why I learned the bicycle, I should say I did it as an act of grace, if not of actual religion. The cardinal doctrine laid down by my physician was, "Live out of doors and take congenial exercise"; but from the day when at sixteen years of age, I was enwrapped in the long skirts that impeded every footstep, I have detested walking and felt with a certain noble disdain that the conventions of life had cut me off from what in the freedom of my prairie home had been one of life's sweetest joys. Driving is not real exercise; it does not renovate the river of blood that flows so sluggishly in the veins of those who from any cause have lost the natural adjustment of brain to brawn. Horseback riding, which does promise vigorous exercise, is expensive. The bicycle, however, meets all the conditions and will ere long come within the reach of all. Therefore, in obedience to the laws of health, I learned to ride.

• EXERCISE 4

Count the verbs in one of the passages in Exercise 2. Then categorize them into linking verbs and more vivid action verbs, and calculate the ratio. Do the same for several paragraphs of your own writing. Are you relying more on linking verbs, or are most of your verbs direct and precise action verbs?

Suggestions for Writing
Sports and Fitness

Now that you have examined a number of texts that focus on sports and fitness, explore this topic yourself by synthesizing your own ideas and the readings. You might want to do additional research or use readings from other classes as you write.

1. Read *The Old Man and the Sea* by Ernest Hemingway. Write an essay discussing whether you think Joe DiMaggio would have been a good fishing companion for the old man.

2. "The Proper Place for Sports" by Theodore Roosevelt appears on page 449. Kathleen Dalton, a historian and high school history teacher, subtitled her 2002 biography of Theodore Roosevelt, *The Strenuous Life*. In an interview, she explained that Roosevelt used that phrase to summarize his philosophy of life.

   > He urged Americans to turn their backs on the soft, easy indoor life they had been leading and embrace the challenges of the twentieth century with a spirit of adventure and courage. He praised physical activity — sports, mountain climbing, exploring, and fighting if necessary — and strenuous endeavor of all kinds, including building an empire and making America a major moral force in the world. He criticized spectators and urged them to participate in sports rather than merely watch them. He also argued that you could lead a strenuous life by working politically to make your country a better place or by writing a book or a poem or by being a caring mother who raised good kids.

   Dalton added that the subtitle has a direct connection to Roosevelt's own life. That is, Roosevelt

   > followed his own advice and lived his own kind of rugged strenuous life. He threw himself completely into each new endeavor — wrestling, bronco busting, mountain climbing, chopping trees, or exploring a dangerous uncharted river.

He also led a strenuous life of struggle by making a new man of himself again and again: he resisted illness and built a stronger body, he proved himself a true man by holding his own among western ranch hands and cowboys, he made himself a writer and reformer, and he made himself a leader and a political prophet without losing his sense of ethics.

Write about your own philosophy of life. In your essay, explain your thoughts on how to improve humankind, and examine the ways you have practiced what you preach.

3. "How I Learned to Ride the Bicycle" by Frances Willard appears on page 459. One could argue that the fashions of Frances Willard's day intentionally limited women and, certainly, that one of the strongest objections to women's bicycling had to do with clothing. Though bloomers (a shorter skirt worn over long trouserlike undergarments) had existed since 1848, it took nearly forty years before the first bloomer-clad women were seen riding bicycles in the United States. Read about clothing reform, and argue for or against its influence on the emancipation of women.

4. Working in groups, compare fashion magazines — men's and women's, if possible — from several decades. Create a visual showing how the ideal body image has changed. Indicate, perhaps with a timeline or graph, the pace and timing of the change. Show for which gender the change has been more radical.

5. Write an essay comparing the ways the media projects images of male and female athletes. Which images create more pressure to conform — images of male athletes or images of female athletes?

6. Write a personal narrative in which you describe the effect sports has had on your connection to family, community, or school. Has the experience been positive or negative?

7. Do some research on Title IX, the law that bans sex discrimination at schools receiving federal funds. What effect has this legislation had on participation in high school, college, and professional sports? Develop a thesis and then write about it, supporting it with your research sources. Be sure to consider the law's effect on male and female role models.

8. The following excerpt is from George Orwell's essay "The Sporting Spirit," published in 1945:

I am always amazed when I hear people saying that sport creates goodwill between nations, and that if only the common peoples of the world could meet one another at football or cricket, they would have no inclination to meet on the battlefield. Even if one didn't know from concrete examples (the 1936 Olympics, for instance) that international sporting contests lead to orgies of hatred, one could deduce it from general principles. . . . At the international level sport is frankly mimic warfare.

In an essay, agree or disagree with Orwell's view of sports.

9. Write a letter to Frances Willard (see p. 459) from champion bicyclist Lance Armstrong. Imagine how he might encourage or discourage Willard in her pursuit.

9

Language

How does the language we use reveal who we are?

In many people's opinion, to call the link between language and culture sacred would not be exaggeration. The language of our birth, the language of the first words we speak to our parents or those closest to us, creates a powerful bond and shapes our perception of the world. Yet few of us are fully aware of the way our language influences others or the extent to which language is used to manipulate our emotions, our politics, our decisions about whether and what to buy, and our thinking in general.

Although the United States is closely associated with English — some would be quick to point out, with American English rather than British English — we are accustomed to hearing a myriad of other languages. In many American cities, Spanish is as common as English, and some urban school districts have students who, jointly, speak more than a hundred languages. In addition, some Americans speak dialects of English as well as dialects of other languages. The writers we study these days, often the children of immigrants, tell of parents who speak not standard written English but rather "broken English," a term author Amy Tan analyzes in her essay "Mother Tongue." The way a person speaks can lead to stereotyped judgments about him or her and assumptions about a range of topics from IQ to economic class.

The politics of language adds another dimension to this discussion. An integral part of imperialism was the privileging of the colonizer's language over that of the colonized. We know that in mission schools Native Americans were punished for speaking their tribal languages instead of English. We know too that a certain British accent automatically signals to some an upper-class educated person. Unexamined assumptions about language allow us to be manipulated and misled by people in power, including advertisers as well as politicians.

The selections in this chapter examine all of these issues and many more. Is bilingual education a positive policy? Should English be the official language of the United States, sanctioned and enforced by legislation? What are the repercussions of immigrating to a country where one's native language is rarely heard, where one learns and writes in a "foreign" language? And how worrisome is it that many Americans speak only English? Should schools have foreign-language requirements, and how can we encourage students to branch out from the study of European languages to Asian and Arabic ones?

In his essay "If Black English Isn't a Language, Then Tell Me What Is," African American writer James Baldwin writes: "It goes without saying, then, that language is also a political instrument, means, and proof of power. It is the most vivid and crucial key to identity: it reveals the private identity, and connects one with, or divorces one from, the larger, public, or communal identity." In this chapter, you will explore language as both "political instrument, means, and proof of power" and "key to identity."

Aria: Memoir of a Bilingual Childhood

RICHARD RODRIGUEZ

 Richard Rodriguez is a literary scholar, memoirist, essayist, journalist, and television commentator known for his controversial positions — especially his stands against bilingual education and affirmative action. Born in 1944 in San Francisco to Mexican immigrants, he grew up in Sacramento, California. Rodriguez received a BA from Stanford University and an MA from Columbia University, and he studied for his doctorate at the University of California at Berkeley. He is best known for his autobiography, *Hunger of Memory: The Education of Richard Rodriguez* (1982). He is also the author of *Days of Obligation: An Argument with My Mexican Father* (1992), which was a finalist for the Pulitzer Prize, and *Brown: The Last Discovery of America* (2002). A former Fulbright Scholar, Rodriguez won a 1997 George Foster Peabody Award for broadcast journalism and received the Frankel Medal, the federal government's top honor for work in the humanities. Rodriguez is an editor at the Pacific News Service and a contributing editor for *Harper's* and *U.S. News and World Report*. The following selection, a chapter from *Hunger of Memory* (originally an essay for *The American Scholar*), contrasts the public world of Rodriguez's Catholic grammar school with the private and intimate world of his family.

1

I remember to start with that day in Sacramento — a California now nearly thirty years past — when I first entered a classroom, able to understand some fifty stray English words.

The third of four children, I had been preceded to a neighborhood Roman Catholic school by an older brother and sister. But neither of them had revealed very much about their classroom experiences. Each afternoon they returned, as they left in the morning, always together, speaking in Spanish as they climbed the five steps of the porch. And their mysterious books, wrapped in shopping-bag paper, remained on the table next to the door, closed firmly behind them.

An accident of geography sent me to a school where all my classmates were white, many the children of doctors and lawyers and business executives. All my classmates certainly must have been uneasy on that first day of school — as most children are uneasy — to find themselves apart from their families in the first institution of their lives. But I was astonished.

The nun said, in a friendly but oddly impersonal voice, "Boys and girls, this is Richard Rodriguez." (I heard her sound out: *Rich-heard Road-ree-guess.*) It was the first time I had heard anyone name me in English. "Richard," the nun repeated more slowly, writing my name down in her black leather book. Quickly I turned to see my mother's face dissolve in a watery blur behind the pebbled glass door.

Many years later there is something called bilingual education — a scheme pro- 5
posed in the late 1960s by Hispanic-American social activists, later endorsed by a congressional vote. It is a program that seeks to permit non-English-speaking children, many from lower-class homes, to use their family language as the language of school. (Such is the goal its supporters announce.) I hear them and am forced to say no: It is not possible for a child — any child — ever to use his family's language in school. Not to understand this is to misunderstand the public uses of schooling and to trivialize the nature of intimate life — a family's "language."

Memory teaches me what I know of these matters; the boy reminds the adult. I was a bilingual child, a certain kind — socially disadvantaged — the son of working-class parents, both Mexican immigrants.

In the early years of my boyhood, my parents coped very well in America. My father had steady work. My mother managed at home. They were nobody's victims. Optimism and ambition led them to a house (our home) many blocks from the Mexican south side of town. We lived among *gringos* and only a block from the biggest, whitest houses. It never occurred to my parents that they couldn't live wherever they chose. Nor was the Sacramento of the fifties bent on teaching them a contrary lesson. My mother and father were more annoyed than intimidated by those two or three neighbors who tried initially to make us unwelcome. ("Keep your brats away from my sidewalk!") But despite all they achieved, perhaps because they had so much to achieve, any deep feeling of ease, the confidence of "belonging" in public was withheld from them both. They regarded the people at work, the faces in crowds, as very distant from us. They were the others, *los gringos*. That term was interchangeable in their speech with another, even more telling, *los americanos*.

I grew up in a house where the only regular guests were my relations. For one day, enormous families of relatives would visit and there would be so many people that the noise and the bodies would spill out to the backyard and front porch. Then, for weeks no one came by. (It was usually a salesman who rang the door bell.) Our house stood apart. A gaudy yellow in a row of white bungalows. We were the people with the noisy dog. The people who raised pigeons and chickens. We were the foreigners on the block. A few neighbors smiled and waved. We waved back. But no one in the family knew the names of the old couple who lived next door; until I was seven years old, I did not know the names of the kids who lived across the street.

In public, my father and mother spoke a hesitant, accented, not always grammatical English. And they would have to strain — their bodies tense — to catch the sense of what was rapidly said by *los gringos*. At home they spoke Spanish. The language of their Mexican past sounded in counterpoint to the English of public society. The words would come quickly, with ease. Conveyed through those sounds was the pleasing, soothing, consoling reminder of being at home.

During those years when I was first conscious of hearing, my mother and father addressed me only in Spanish; in Spanish I learned to reply. By contrast, English (*inglés*), rarely heard in the house, was the language I came to associate with *gringos*. I learned my first words of English overhearing my parents speak to strangers. At five years of age, I knew just enough English for my mother to trust me on errands to stores one block away. No more.

I was a listening child, careful to hear the very different sounds of Spanish and English. Wide-eyed with hearing, I'd listen to sounds more than words. First, there were English (*gringo*) sounds. So many words were still unknown that when the butcher or the lady at the drugstore said something to me, exotic polysyllabic sounds would bloom in the midst of their sentences. Often, the speech of people in public seemed to me very loud, booming with confidence. The man behind the counter would literally ask, "What can I do for you?" But by being so firm and so clear, the sound of his voice said that he was a *gringo*; he belonged in public society.

I would also hear then the high nasal notes of middle-class American speech. The air stirred with sound. Sometimes, even now, when I have been traveling abroad for several weeks, I will hear what I heard as a boy. In hotel lobbies or airports, in Turkey or Brazil, some Americans will pass, and suddenly I will hear it again — the high sound of American voices. For a few seconds I will hear it with pleasure, for it is now the sound of *my* society — a reminder of home. But inevitably — already on the flight headed for home — the sound fades with repetition. I will be unable to hear it anymore.

When I was a boy, things were different. The accent of *los gringos* was never pleasing nor was it hard to hear. Crowds at Safeway or at bus stops would be noisy with sound. And I would be forced to edge away from the chirping chatter above me.

I was unable to hear my own sounds, but I knew very well that I spoke English poorly. My words could not stretch far enough to form complete thoughts. And the words I did speak I didn't know well enough to make into distinct sounds. (Listeners would usually lower their heads, better to hear what I was trying to say.) But it was one thing for *me* to speak English with difficulty. It was more troubling for me to hear my parents speak in public: their high-whining vowels and guttural consonants; their sentences that got stuck with "eh" and "ah" sounds; the confused syntax; the hesitant rhythm of sounds so different from the way *gringos* spoke. I'd notice, moreover, that my parents' voices were softer than those of *gringos* we'd meet.

I am tempted now to say that none of this mattered. In adulthood I am embarrassed by childhood fears. And, in a way, it didn't matter very much that my parents could not speak English with ease. Their linguistic difficulties had no serious consequences. My mother and father made themselves understood at the county hospital clinic and at government offices. And yet, in another way, it mattered very much — it was unsettling to hear my parents struggle with English. Hearing them, I'd grow nervous, my clutching trust in their protection and power weakened.

There were many times like the night at a brightly lit gasoline station (a blaring white memory) when I stood uneasily, hearing my father. He was talking to a teenaged attendant. I do not recall what they were saying, but I cannot forget the sounds my father made as he spoke. At one point his words slid together to form one word — sounds as confused as the threads of blue and green oil in the puddle next to my shoes. His voice rushed through what he had left to say. And, toward the end, reached falsetto notes, appealing to his listener's understanding. I looked away to the lights of passing automobiles. I tried not to hear anymore. But I heard only too well the calm, easy tones in the attendant's reply. Shortly afterward, walking toward home with my father, I shivered when he put his hand on my shoulder. The very first chance that I got, I evaded his grasp and ran on ahead into the dark, skipping with feigned boyish exuberance.

But then there was Spanish. *Español*: my family's language. *Español*: the language that seemed to me a private language. I'd hear strangers on the radio and in the Mexican Catholic church across town speaking in Spanish, but I couldn't really believe that Spanish was a public language, like English. Spanish speakers, rather, seemed related to me, for I sensed that we shared — through our language — the experience of feeling apart from *los gringos*. It was thus a ghetto Spanish that I heard and I spoke. Like those whose lives are bound by a barrio, I was reminded by Spanish of my separateness from *los otros, los gringos* in power. But more intensely than for most barrio children — because I did not live in a barrio — Spanish seemed to me the language of home. (Most days it was only at home that I'd hear it.) It became the language of joyful return.

A family member would say something to me and I would feel myself specially recognized. My parents would say something to me and I would feel embraced by the sounds of their words. Those sounds said: *I am speaking with ease in Spanish. I am addressing you in words I never use with* los gringos, *I recognize you as someone special, close, like no one outside. You belong with us. In the family.*

(Ricardo.)

At the age of five, six, well past the time when most other children no longer 20 easily notice the difference between sounds uttered at home and words spoken in public, I had a different experience. I lived in a world magically compounded of sounds. I remained a child longer than most; I lingered too long, poised at the edge of language — often frightened by the sounds of *los gringos*, delighted by the sounds of Spanish at home. I shared with my family a language that was startlingly different from that used in the great city around us.

For me there were none of the gradations between public and private society so normal to a maturing child. Outside the house was public society; inside the house was private. Just opening or closing the screen door behind me was an important experience. I'd rarely leave home all alone or without reluctance. Walking down the sidewalk, under the canopy of tall trees, I'd warily notice the — suddenly — silent neighborhood kids who stood warily watching me. Nervously, I'd arrive at the grocery store to hear there the sounds of the *gringo* — foreign to me — reminding me that in this world so big, I was a foreigner. But then I'd return. Walking back toward our house, climbing the steps from the sidewalk, when the front door was open in summer, I'd hear voices beyond the screen door talking in Spanish. For a second or two, I'd stay, linger there, listening. Smiling, I'd hear my mother call out, saying in Spanish (words): "Is that you, Richard?" All the while her sounds would assure me: *You are home now; come closer; inside. With us.*

"*Sí,*" I'd reply.

Once more inside the house I would resume (assume) my place in the family. The sounds would dim, grow harder to hear. Once more at home, I would grow less aware of that fact. It required, however, no more than the blurt of the doorbell to alert me to listen to sounds all over again. The house would turn instantly still while my mother went to the door. I'd hear her hard English sounds. I'd wait to hear her voice return to soft-sounding Spanish, which assured me, as surely as did the clicking tongue of the lock on the door, that the stranger was gone.

Plainly, it is not healthy to hear such sounds so often. It is not healthy to distinguish public words from private sounds so easily. I remained cloistered by sounds, timid and shy in public, too dependent on voices at home. And yet it needs to be emphasized: I was an extremely happy child at home. I remember many nights when my father would come back from work, and I'd hear him call out to my mother in Spanish, sounding relieved. In Spanish, he'd sound light and free notes he never could manage in English. Some nights I'd jump up just at hearing his voice. With *mis hermanos* I would come running into the room where he was with my mother. Our laughing (so deep was the pleasure!) became screaming. Like others who know the pain of public alienation, we transformed the knowledge of our public separateness and made it consoling — the reminder of intimacy. Excited, we joined our voices in a celebration of sounds. *We are speaking now the way we never speak out in public. We are alone — together,* voices sounded, surrounded to tell me. Some nights, no one seemed willing to loosen the hold sounds had on us. At dinner, we invented new words. (Ours sounded Spanish, but made sense only to us.) We pieced together new words by taking, say, an English verb and giving it Spanish endings. My mother's instructions at bedtime would be lacquered with mock-urgent tones. Or a word like *sí* would become, in several notes, able to convey added measures of feeling. Tongues explored the edges of words, especially the fat vowels. And we happily sounded that military drum roll, the twirling roar of the Spanish *r*. Family language: my family's sounds. The voices of my parents and sisters and brother. Their voices insisting: *You belong here. We are family members. Related. Special to one another. Listen!* Voices singing and sighing, rising, straining, then surging, teeming with pleasure that burst syllables into fragments of laughter. At times it seemed there was steady quiet only when, from another room, the rustling whispers of my parents faded and I moved closer to sleep.

2

Supporters of bilingual education today imply that students like me miss a great deal by not being taught in their family's language. What they seem not to recognize is that, as a socially disadvantaged child, I considered Spanish to be a private language. What I needed to learn in school was that I had the right — and the obligation — to speak the public language of *los gringos*. The odd truth is that my first-grade classmates could have become bilingual, in the conventional sense of that word, more easily than I. Had they been taught (as upper-middle-class children are often taught early) a second language like Spanish or French, they could have regarded it simply as that: another public language. In my case such bilingualism could not have been so quickly achieved. What I did not believe was that I could speak a single public language.

Without question, it would have pleased me to hear my teachers address me in Spanish when I entered the classroom. I would have felt much less afraid. I would have trusted them and responded with ease. But I would have delayed — for how long postponed? — having to learn the language of public society. I would have evaded — and for how long could I have afforded to delay? — learning the great lesson of school, that I had a public identity.

Fortunately, my teachers were unsentimental about their responsibility. What they understood was that I needed to speak a public language. So their voices would search me out, asking me questions. Each time I'd hear them, I'd look up in surprise to see a nun's face frowning at me. I'd mumble, not really meaning to answer. The nun would persist, "Richard, stand up. Don't look at the floor. Speak up. Speak to the entire class, not just to me!" But I couldn't believe that the English language was mine to use. (In part, I did not want to believe it.) I continued to mumble. I resisted the teacher's demands. (Did I somehow suspect that once I learned public language my pleasing family life would be changed?) Silent, waiting for the bell to sound, I remained dazed, diffident, afraid.

Because I wrongly imagined that English was intrinsically a public language and Spanish an intrinsically private one, I easily noted the difference between classroom language and the language of home. At school, words were directed to a general audience of listeners. ("Boys and girls.") Words were meaningfully ordered. And the point was not self-expression alone but to make oneself understood by many others. The teacher quizzed: "Boys and girls, why do we use that word in this sentence? Could we think of a better word to use there? Would the sentence change its meaning if the words were differently arranged? And wasn't there a better way of saying much the same thing?" (I couldn't say. I wouldn't try to say.)

Three months. Five. Half a year passed. Unsmiling, ever watchful, my teachers noted my silence. They began to connect my behavior with the difficult progress my older sister and brother were making. Until one Saturday morning three nuns arrived at the house to talk to our parents. Stiffly, they sat on the blue living room sofa. From the doorway of another room, spying the visitors, I noted the incongruity — the clash of two worlds, the faces and voices of school intruding upon the familiar setting of home. I overheard one voice gently wondering, "Do your children speak only Spanish at home, Mrs. Rodriguez?" While another voice added, "That Richard especially seems so timid and shy."

That Rich-heard!   30

With great tact the visitors continued, "Is it possible for you and your husband to encourage your children to practice their English when they are home?" Of course, my parents complied. What would they not do for their children's well-being? And how could they have questioned the Church's authority which those women represented? In an instant, they agreed to give up the language (the sounds) that had revealed and accentuated our family's closeness. The moment after the visitors left, the change was observed. *"Ahora,* speak to us *en inglés,"* my father and mother united to tell us.

At first, it seemed a kind of game. After dinner each night, the family gathered to practice "our" English. (It was still then *inglés,* a language foreign to us, so we felt drawn as strangers to it.) Laughing, we would try to define words we could not pronounce. We played with strange English sounds, often over-anglicizing our pronunciations. And we filled the smiling gaps of our sentences with familiar Spanish sounds. But that was cheating, somebody shouted. Everyone laughed. In school, meanwhile, like my brother and sister, I was required to attend a daily tutoring session. I needed a full year of special attention. I also needed my teachers to keep my attention from straying in class by calling out, *Rich-heard* — their English voices slowly prying loose my ties to my other name, its three notes, *Ri-car-do.* Most of all I needed to hear my mother and father speak to me in a moment of seriousness in broken — suddenly heartbreaking — English. The scene was inevitable: One Saturday morning I entered the kitchen where my parents were talking in Spanish. I did not realize that they were talking in Spanish however until, at the moment they saw me, I heard their voices change to speak English. Those *gringo* sounds they uttered startled me. Pushed me away. In that moment of trivial misunderstanding and profound insight, I felt my throat twisted by unsounded grief. I turned quickly and left the room. But I had no place to escape to with Spanish. (The spell was broken.) My brother and sisters were speaking English in another part of the house.

Again and again in the days following, increasingly angry, I was obliged to hear my mother and father: "Speak to us *en inglés.*" (*Speak.*) Only then did I determine to learn classroom English. Weeks after, it happened: One day in school I raised my hand to volunteer an answer. I spoke out in a loud voice. And I did not think it remarkable when the entire class understood. That day, I moved very far from the disadvantaged child I had been only days earlier. The belief, the calming assurance that I belonged in public, had at last taken hold.

Shortly after, I stopped hearing the high and loud sounds of *los gringos*. A more and more confident speaker of English, I didn't trouble to listen to *how* strangers sounded, speaking to me. And there simply were too many English-speaking people in my day for me to hear American accents anymore. Conversations quickened. Listening to persons who sounded eccentrically pitched voices, I usually noted their sounds for an initial few seconds before I concentrated on *what* they were saying. Conversations became content-full. Transparent. Hearing someone's *tone* of voice — angry or questioning or sarcastic or happy or sad — I didn't distinguish it from the words it expressed. Sound and word were thus tightly wedded. At the end of a day, I was often bemused, always relieved, to realize how "silent," though crowded with words, my day in public had been. (This public silence measured and quickened the change in my life.)

At last, seven years old, I came to believe what had been technically true since 35 my birth: I was an American citizen.

But the special feeling of closeness at home was diminished by then. Gone was the desperate, urgent, intense feeling of being at home; rare was the experience of feeling myself individualized by family intimates. We remained a loving family, but one greatly changed. No longer so close; no longer bound tight by the pleasing and troubling knowledge of our public separateness. Neither my older brother nor sister rushed home after school anymore. Nor did I. When I arrived home there would often be neighborhood kids in the house. Or the house would be empty of sounds.

Following the dramatic Americanization of their children, even my parents grew more publicly confident. Especially my mother. She learned the names of all the people on our block. And she decided we needed to have a telephone installed in the house. My father continued to use the word *gringo*. But it was no longer charged with the old bitterness or distrust. (Stripped of any emotional content, the word simply became a name for those Americans not of Hispanic descent.) Hearing him, sometimes, I wasn't sure if he was pronouncing the Spanish word *gringo* or saying gringo in English.

Matching the silence I started hearing in public was a new quiet at home. The family's quiet was partly due to the fact that, as we children learned more and more English, we shared fewer and fewer words with our parents. Sentences needed to be spoken slowly when a child addressed his mother or father. (Often the parent wouldn't understand.) The child would need to repeat himself. (Still the parent misunderstood.) The young voice, frustrated, would end up saying, "Never mind" — the subject was closed. Dinners would be noisy with the clinking of knives and forks against dishes. My mother would smile softly between her remarks; my father at the other end of the table would chew and chew at his food, while he stared over the heads of his children.

My *mother!* My *father!* After English became my primary language, I no longer knew what words to use in addressing my parents. The old Spanish words (those tender accents of sound) I had used earlier — *mamá* and *papá* — I couldn't use anymore. They would have been too painful reminders of how much had changed in my life. On the other hand, the words I heard neighborhood kids call *their* parents seemed equally unsatisfactory. *Mother* and *Father; Ma, Papa, Pa, Dad, Pop* (how I hated the all-American sound of that last word especially) — all these terms I felt were unsuitable, not really terms of address for *my* parents. As a result, I never used them at home. Whenever I'd speak to my parents, I would try to get their attention with eye contact alone. In public conversations, I'd refer to "my parents" or "my mother and father."

My mother and father, for their part, responded differently, as their children   40 spoke to them less. She grew restless, seemed troubled and anxious at the scarcity of words exchanged in the house. It was she who would question me about my day when I came home from school. She smiled at small talk. She pried at the edges of my sentences to get me to say something more. (What?) She'd join conversations she overheard, but her intrusions often stopped her children's talking. By contrast, my father seemed reconciled to the new quiet. Though his English improved somewhat, he retired into silence. At dinner he spoke very little. One night his children and even his wife helplessly giggled at his garbled English pronunciation of the Catholic Grace before Meals. Thereafter he made his wife recite the prayer at the start of each meal, even on formal occasions, when there were guests in the house. Hers became the public voice of the family. On official business, it was she, not my father, one would usually hear on the phone or in stores, talking to strangers. His children grew so accustomed to his silence that, years later, they would speak routinely of his shyness. (My mother would often try to explain: Both his parents died when he was eight. He was raised by an uncle who treated him like little more than a menial servant. He was never encouraged to speak. He grew up alone. A man of few words.) But my father was not shy, I realized, when I'd watch him speaking Spanish with relatives. Using Spanish, he was quickly effusive. Especially when talking with other men, his voice would spark, flicker, flare alive with sounds. In Spanish, he expressed ideas and feelings he rarely revealed in English. With firm Spanish sounds, he conveyed confidence and authority English would never allow him.

The silence at home, however, was finally more than a literal silence. Fewer words passed between parent and child, but more profound was the silence that resulted from my inattention to sounds. At about the time I no longer bothered to listen with care to the sounds of English in public, I grew careless about listening to the sounds family members made when they spoke. Most of the time I heard someone speaking at home and didn't distinguish his sounds from the words people uttered in public. I didn't even pay much attention to my parents' accented and ungrammatical speech. At least not at home. Only when I was with them in public would I grow alert to their accents. Though, even then, their sounds caused me less and less concern. For I was increasingly confident of my own public identity.

I would have been happier about my public success had I not sometimes recalled what it had been like earlier, when my family had conveyed its intimacy through a set of conveniently private sounds. Sometimes in public, hearing a stranger, I'd hark back to my past. A Mexican farmworker approached me downtown to ask directions to somewhere. "¿*Hijito*. . . ?" he said. And his voice summoned deep longing. Another time, standing beside my mother in the visiting room of a Carmelite convent, before the dense screen which rendered the nuns shadowy figures, I heard several Spanish-speaking nuns — their busy, singsong overlapping voices — assure us that yes, yes, we were remembered, all our family was remembered in their prayers. (Their voices echoed faraway family sounds.) Another day, a dark-faced old woman — her hand light on my shoulder — steadied herself against me as she boarded a bus. She murmured something I couldn't quite comprehend. Her Spanish voice came near, like the face of a never-before-seen relative in the instant before I was kissed. Her voice, like so many of the Spanish voices I'd hear in public, recalled the golden age of my youth. Hearing Spanish then, I continued to be a careful, if sad, listener to sounds. Hearing a Spanish-speaking family walking behind me, I turned to look. I smiled for an instant, before my glance found the Hispanic-looking faces of strangers in the crowd going by.

Today I hear bilingual educators say that children lose a degree of "individuality" by becoming assimilated into public society. (Bilingual schooling was popularized in the seventies, that decade when middle-class ethnics began to resist the process of assimilation — the American melting pot.) But the bilingualists simplistically scorn the value and necessity of assimilation. They do not seem to realize that there are *two* ways a person is individualized. So they do not realize that while one suffers a diminished sense of *private* individuality by becoming assimilated into public society, such assimilation makes possible the achievement of *public* individuality.

The bilingualists insist that a student should be reminded of his difference from others in mass society, his heritage. But they equate mere separateness with individuality. The fact is that only in private — with intimates — is separateness from the crowd a prerequisite for individuality. (An intimate draws me apart, tells me that I am unique, unlike all others.) In public, by contrast, full individuality is achieved, paradoxically, by those who are able to consider themselves members of the crowd. Thus it happened for me: Only when I was able to think of myself as an American, no longer an alien in *gringo* society, could I seek the rights and opportunities necessary for full public individuality. The social and political advantages I enjoy as a man result from the day that I came to believe that my name, indeed, is *Rich-heard Road-ree-guess*. It is true that my public society today is often impersonal. (My public society is usually mass society.) Yet despite the anonymity of the crowd and despite the fact that the individuality I achieve in public is often tenuous — because it depends on my being one in a crowd — I celebrate the day I acquired my new name. Those middle-class ethnics who scorn assimilation seem to me filled with decadent self-pity, obsessed by the burden of public life. Dangerously, they romanticize public separateness and they trivialize the dilemma of the socially disadvantaged.

My awkward childhood does not prove the necessity of bilingual education. My story discloses instead an essential myth of childhood — inevitable pain. If I rehearse here the changes in my private life after my Americanization, it is finally to emphasize the public gain. The loss implies the gain: The house I returned to each afternoon was quiet. Intimate sounds no longer rushed to the door to greet me. There were other noises inside. The telephone rang. Neighborhood kids ran past the door of the bedroom where I was reading my schoolbooks — covered with shopping-bag paper. Once I learned public language, it would never again be easy for me to hear intimate family voices. More and more of my day was spent hearing words. But that may only be a way of saying that the day I raised my hand in class and spoke loudly to an entire roomful of faces, my childhood started to end.

3

I grew up victim to a disabling confusion. As I grew fluent in English, I no longer could speak Spanish with confidence. I continued to understand spoken Spanish. And in high school, I learned how to read and write Spanish. But for many years I could not pronounce it. A powerful guilt blocked my spoken words; an essential glue was missing whenever I'd try to connect words to form sentences. I would be unable to break a barrier of sound, to speak freely. I would speak, or try to speak, Spanish, and I would manage to utter halting, hiccuping sounds that betrayed my unease.

When relatives and Spanish-speaking friends of my parents came to the house, my brother and sisters seemed reticent to use Spanish, but at least they managed to say a few necessary words before being excused. I never managed so gracefully. I was cursed with guilt. Each time I'd hear myself addressed in Spanish, I would be unable to respond with any success. I'd know the words I wanted to say, but I couldn't manage to say them. I would try to speak, but everything I said seemed to me horribly anglicized. My mouth would not form the words right. My jaw would tremble. After a phrase or two, I'd cough up a warm, silvery sound. And stop.

It surprised my listeners to hear me. They'd lower their heads, better to grasp what I was trying to say. They would repeat their questions in gentle, affectionate voices. But by then I would answer in English. No, no, they would say, we want you to speak to us in Spanish. (". . . *en español*.") But I couldn't do it. *Pocho* then they called me. Sometimes playfully, teasingly, using the tender diminutive — *mi pochito*. Sometimes not so playfully, mockingly, *Pocho*. (A Spanish dictionary defines that word as an adjective meaning "colorless" or "bland." But I heard it as a noun, naming the Mexican-American who, in becoming an American, forgets his native society.) "*¡Pocho!*" the lady in the Mexican food store muttered, shaking her head. I looked up to the counter where red and green peppers were strung like Christmas tree lights and saw the frowning face of the stranger. My mother laughed somewhere behind me. (She said that her children didn't want to practice "our Spanish" after they started going to school.) My mother's smiling voice made me suspect that the lady who faced me was not really angry at me. But, searching her face, I couldn't find the hint of a smile.

Embarrassed, my parents would regularly need to explain their children's inability to speak flowing Spanish during those years. My mother met the wrath of her brother, her only brother, when he came up from Mexico one summer with his family. He saw his nieces and nephews for the very first time. After listening to me, he looked away and said what a disgrace it was that I couldn't speak Spanish, "*su proprio idioma.*" He made that remark to my mother; I noticed, however, that he stared at my father.

I clearly remember one other visitor from those years. A long-time friend of my father from San Francisco would come to stay with us for several days in late August. He took great interest in me after he realized that I couldn't answer his questions in Spanish. He would grab me as I started to leave the kitchen. He would ask me something. Usually he wouldn't bother to wait for my mumbled response. Knowingly, he'd murmur: "*¿Ay Pocho, Pocho, adónde vas?*" And he would press his thumbs into the upper part of my arms, making me squirm with currents of pain. Dumbly, I'd stand there, waiting for his wife to notice us, for her to call him off with a benign smile. I'd giggle, hoping to deflate the tension between us, pretending that I hadn't seen the glittering scorn in his glance.

I remember that man now, but seek no revenge in this telling. I recount such incidents only because they suggest the fierce power Spanish had for many people I met at home; the way Spanish was associated with closeness. Most of those people who called me a *pocho* could have spoken English to me. But they would not. They seemed to think that Spanish was the only language we could use, that Spanish alone permitted our close association. (Such persons are vulnerable always to the ghetto merchant and the politician who have learned the value of speaking their clients' family language to gain immediate trust.) For my part, I felt that I had somehow committed a sin of betrayal by learning English. But betrayal against whom? Not against visitors to the house exactly. No, I felt that I had betrayed my immediate family. I *knew* that my parents had encouraged me to learn English. I *knew* that I had turned to English only with angry reluctance. But once I spoke English with ease, I came to *feel* guilty. (This guilt defied logic.) I felt that I had shattered the intimate bond that had once held the family close. This original sin against my family told whenever anyone addressed me in Spanish and I responded, confounded.

But even during those years of guilt, I was coming to sense certain consoling truths about language and intimacy. I remember playing with a friend in the backyard one day, when my grandmother appeared at the window. Her face was stern with suspicion when she saw the boy (the *gringo*) I was with. In Spanish she called out to me, sounding the whistle of her ancient breath. My companion looked up and watched her intently as she lowered the window and moved, still visible, behind the light curtain, watching us both. He wanted to know what she had said. I started to tell him, to say — to translate her Spanish words into English. The problem was, however, that though I knew how to translate exactly *what* she had told me, I realized that any translation would distort the deepest meaning of her message: It had been directed only to me. This message of intimacy could never be translated because it was not *in* the words she had used but passed *through* them. So any translation would have seemed wrong; her words would have been stripped of an essential meaning. Finally, I decided not to tell my friend anything. I told him that I didn't hear all she had said.

This insight unfolded in time. Making more and more friends outside my house, I began to distinguish intimate voices speaking through *English*. I'd listen at times to a close friend's confidential tone or secretive whisper. Even more remarkable were those instances when, for no special reason apparently, I'd become conscious of the fact that my companion was speaking only to me. I'd marvel just hearing his voice. It was a stunning event: to be able to break through his words, to be able to hear this voice of the other, to realize that it was directed only to me. After such moments of intimacy outside the house, I began to trust hearing intimacy conveyed through my family's English. Voices at home at last punctured sad confusion. I'd hear myself addressed as an intimate at home once again. Such moments were never as raucous with sound as past times had been when we had had "private" Spanish to use. (Our English-sounding house was never to be as noisy as our Spanish-speaking house had been.) Intimate moments were usually soft moments of sound. My mother was in the dining room while I did my homework nearby. And she looked over at me. Smiled. Said something — her words said nothing very important. But her voice sounded to tell me (*We are together*) I was her son.

(*Richard!*)

Intimacy thus continued at home; intimacy was not stilled by English. It is 55
true that I would never forget the great change of my life, the diminished occasions of intimacy. But there would also be times when I sensed the deepest truth about language and intimacy: *Intimacy is not created by a particular language; it is created by intimates.* The great change in my life as not linguistic but social. If, after becoming a successful student, I no longer heard intimate voices as often as I had earlier, it was not because I spoke English rather than Spanish. It was because I used public language for most of the day. I moved easily at last, a citizen in a crowded city of words.

4

This boy became a man. In private now, alone, I brood over language and intimacy — the great themes of my past. In public I expect most of the faces I meet to be the faces of strangers. (How do you do?) If meetings are quick and impersonal, they have been efficiently managed. I rush past the sounds of voices attending only to the words addressed to me. Voices seem planed to an even sur-face of sound, soundless. A business associate speaks in a deep baritone, but I pass through the timbre to attend to his words. The crazy man who sells me a news-paper every night mumbles something crazy, but I have time only to pretend that I have heard him say hello. Accented versions of English make little impression on me. In the rush-hour crowd a Japanese tourist asks me a question, and I inch past his accent to concentrate on what he is saying. The Eastern European immi-grant in a neighborhood delicatessen speaks to me through a marinade of sounds, but I respond to his words. I note for only a second the Texas accent of the telephone operator or the Mississippi accent of the man who lives in the apart-ment below me.

My city seems silent until some ghetto black teenagers board the bus I am on. Because I do not take their presence for granted, I listen to the sounds of their voices. Of all the accented versions of English I hear in a day, I hear theirs most intently. They are *the* sounds of the outsider. They annoy me for being loud — so self-sufficient and unconcerned by my presence. Yet for the same reason they seem to me glamorous. (A romantic gesture against public acceptance.) Listening to their shouted laughter, I realize my own quiet. Their voices enclose my isola-tion. I feel envious, envious of their brazen intimacy.

I warn myself away from such envy, however. I remember the black political activists who have argued in favor of using black English in schools. (Their argu-ment varies only slightly from that made by foreign-language bilingualists.) I have heard "radical" linguists make the point that black English is a complex and intricate version of English. And I do not doubt it. But neither do I think that black English should be a language of public instruction. What makes black English inappropriate in classrooms is not something *in* the language. It is rather what lower-class speakers make of it. Just as Spanish would have been a danger-ous language for me to have used at the start of my education, so black English would be a dangerous language to use in the schooling of teenagers for whom it reenforces feelings of public separateness.

This seems to me an obvious point. But one that needs to be made. In recent years there have been attempts to make the language of the alien public language. "Bilingual education, two ways to understand . . . ," television and radio commer-cials glibly announce. Proponents of bilingual education are careful to say that they want students to acquire good schooling. Their argument goes something like this: Children permitted to use their family language in school will not be so alienated and will be better able to match the progress of English-speaking chil-dren in the crucial first months of instruction. (Increasingly confident of their abilities, such children will be more inclined to apply themselves to their studies in the future.) But then the bilingualists claim another, very different goal. They say that children who use their family language in school will retain a sense of their individuality — their ethnic heritage and cultural ties. Supporters of bilin-gual education thus want it both ways. They propose bilingual schooling as a way of helping students acquire the skills of the classroom crucial for public success. But they likewise insist that bilingual instruction will give students a sense of their identity apart from the public.

Behind this screen there gleams an astonishing promise: One can become a public person while still remaining a private person. At the very same time one can be both! There need be no tension between the self in the crowd and the self apart from the crowd! Who would not want to believe such an idea? Who can be surprised that the scheme has won the support of many middle-class Americans? If the barrio or ghetto child can retain his separateness even while being publicly educated, then it is almost possible to believe that there is no private cost to be paid for public success. Such is the consolation offered by any of the current bilingual schemes. Consider, for example, the bilingual voters' ballot. In some American cities one can cast a ballot printed in several languages. Such a document implies that a person can exercise that most public of rights — the right to vote — while still keeping apart, unassimilated from public life.

It is not enough to say that these schemes are foolish and certainly doomed. Middle-class supporters of public bilingualism toy with the confusion of those Americans who cannot speak standard English as well as they can. Bilingual enthusiasts, moreover, sin against intimacy. An Hispanic-American writer tells me, "I will never give up my family language; I would as soon give up my soul." Thus he holds to his chest a skein of words, as though it were the source of his family ties. He credits to language what he should credit to family members. A convenient mistake. For as long as he holds on to words, he can ignore how much else has changed in his life.

It has happened before. In earlier decades, persons newly successful and ambitious for social mobility similarly seized upon certain "family words." Working-class men attempting political power took to calling one another "brother." By so doing they escaped oppressive public isolation and were able to unite with many others like themselves. But they paid a price for this union. It was a public union they forged. The word they coined to address one another could never be the sound (*brother*) exchanged by two in intimate greeting. In the union hall the word "brother" became a vague metaphor; with repetition a weak echo of the intimate sound. Context forced the change. Context could not be overruled. Context will always guard the realm of the intimate from public misuse.

Today nonwhite Americans call "brother" to strangers. And white feminists refer to their mass union of "sisters." And white middle-class teenagers continue to prove the importance of context as they try to ignore it. They seize upon the idioms of the black ghetto. But their attempt to appropriate such expressions invariably changes the words. As it becomes a public expression, the ghetto idiom loses its sound — its message of public separateness and strident intimacy. It becomes with public repetition a series of words, increasingly lifeless.

The mystery remains: intimate utterance. The communication of intimacy passes through the word to enliven its sound. But it cannot be held by the word.

Cannot be clutched or ever quoted. It is too fluid. It depends not on word but on person.

My grandmother! 65

She stood among my other relations mocking me when I no longer spoke Spanish. "*Pocho*," she said. But then it made no difference. (She'd laugh.) Our relationship continued. Language was never its source. She was a woman in her eighties during the first decade of my life. A mysterious woman to me, my only living grandparent. A woman of Mexico. The woman in long black dresses that reached down to her shoes. My one relative who spoke no word of English. She had no interest in *gringo* society. She remained completely aloof from the public. Protected by her daughters. Protected even by me when we went to Safeway together and I acted as her translator. Eccentric woman. Soft. Hard.

When my family visited my aunt's house in San Francisco, my grandmother searched for me among my many cousins. She'd chase them away. Pinching her granddaughters, she'd warn them all away from me. Then she'd take me to her room, where she had prepared for my coming. There would be a chair next to the bed. A dusty jellied candy nearby. And a copy of *Life en Español* for me to examine. "There," she'd say. I'd sit there content. A boy of eight. *Pocho*. Her favorite. I'd sift through the pictures of earthquake-destroyed Latin American cities and blond-wigged Mexican movie stars. And all the while I'd listen to the sound of my grandmother's voice. She'd pace round the room, searching through closets and drawers, telling me stories of her life. Her past. They were stories so familiar to me that I couldn't remember the first time I'd heard them. I'd look up sometimes to listen. Other times she'd look over at me. But she never seemed to expect a response. Sometimes I'd smile or nod. (I understood exactly what she was saying.) But it never seemed to matter to her one way or another. It was enough I was there. The words she spoke were almost irrelevant to that fact — the sounds she made. Content.

The mystery remained: intimate utterance.

I learn little about language and intimacy listening to those social activists who propose using one's family language in public life. Listening to songs on the radio, or hearing a great voice at the opera, or overhearing the woman downstairs singing to herself at an open window, I learn much more. Singers celebrate the human voice. Their lyrics are words. But animated by voice those words are subsumed into sounds. I listen with excitement as the words yield their enormous power to sound — though the words are never totally obliterated. In most songs the drama or tension results from the fact that the singer moves between word (sense) and note (song). At one moment the song simply "says" something. At another moment the voice stretches out the words — the heart cannot contain — and the voice moves toward pure sound. Words take flight.

Singing out words, the singer suggests an experience of sound most intensely 70 mine at intimate moments. Literally, most songs are about love. (Lost love; celebrations of loving; pleas.) By simply being occasions when sound escapes word, however, songs put me in mind of the most intimate moments of my life.

Finally, among all types of song, it is the song created by lyric poets that I find most compelling. There is no other public occasion of sound so important for me. Written poems exist on a page, at first glance, as a mere collection of words. And yet, despite this, without musical accompaniment, the poet leads me to hear the sounds of the words that I read. As song, the poem passes between sound and sense, never belonging for long to one realm or the other. As public artifact, the poem can never duplicate intimate sound. But by imitating such sound, the poem helps me recall the intimate times of my life. I read in my room — alone — and grow conscious of being alone, sounding my voice, in search of another. The poem serves then as a memory device. It forces remembrance. And refreshes. It reminds me of the possibility of escaping public words, the possibility that awaits me in meeting the intimate.

The poems I read are not nonsense poems. But I read them for reasons which, I imagine, are similar to those that make children play with meaningless rhyme. I have watched them before: I have noticed the way children create private languages to keep away the adult; I have heard their chanting riddles that go nowhere in logic but harken back to some kingdom of sound; I have watched them listen to intricate nonsense rhymes, and I have noted their wonder. I was never such a child. Until I was six years old, I remained in a magical realm of sound. I didn't need to remember that realm because it was present to me. But then the screen door shut behind me as I left home for school. At last I began my movement toward words. On the other side of initial sadness would come the realization that intimacy cannot be held. With time would come the knowledge that intimacy must finally pass.

I would dishonor those I have loved and those I love now to claim anything else. I would dishonor our closeness by holding on to a particular language and calling it my family language. Intimacy is not trapped within words. It passes through words. It passes. The truth is that intimates leave the room. Doors close. Faces move away from the window. Time passes. Voices recede into the dark. Death finally quiets the voice. And there is no way to deny it. No way to stand in the crowd, uttering one's family language.

The last time I saw my grandmother I was nine years old. I can tell you some of the things she said to me as I stood by her bed. I cannot, however, quote the message of intimacy she conveyed with her voice. She laughed, holding my hand. Her voice illumined disjointed memories as it passed them again. She remembered her husband, his green eyes, the magic name of Narciso. His early death. She remembered the farm in Mexico. The eucalyptus nearby. (Its scent, she remembered, like incense.) She remembered the family cow, the bell round its neck heard miles away. A dog. She remembered working as a seamstress. How she'd leave her daughters and son for long hours to go into Guadalajara to work. And how my mother would come running toward her in the sun — her bright yellow dress — to see her return. "*Mmmaaammmmmááááá,*" the old lady mimicked her daughter (my mother) to her son. She laughed. There was the snap of a cough. An aunt came into the room and told me it was time I should leave. "You can see her tomorrow," she promised. And so I kissed my grandmother's cracked face. And the last thing I saw was her thin, oddly youthful thigh, as my aunt rearranged the sheet on the bed.

At the funeral parlor a few days after, I knelt with my relatives during the rosary. Among their voices but silent, I traced, then lost, the sounds of individual aunts in the surge of the common prayer. And I heard at that moment what I have since heard often again — the sounds the women in my family make when they are praying in sadness. When I went up to look at my grandmother, I saw her through the haze of a veil draped over the open lid of the casket. Her face appeared calm — but distant and unyielding to love. It was not the face I remembered seeing most often. It was the face she made in public when the clerk at Safeway asked her some question and I would have to respond. It was her public face the mortician had designed with his dubious art.

Questions for Discussion

1. One way to read Richard Rodriguez's essay is as a discussion of two discrete educational philosophies. What are they?
2. What does Rodriguez mean when he says, "[I]n a way, it didn't matter very much that my parents could not speak English with ease. . . . And yet, in another way, it mattered very much" (para. 15)?
3. What does Rodriguez mean by calling Spanish a "private language" (para. 17)? Even if you do not speak more than one language, does your family have what you would characterize as a "private language"?
4. Rodriguez admits, "Matching the silence I started hearing in public was a new quiet at home" (para. 38). Later he says, "The silence at home, however, was finally more than a literal silence" (para. 41). Does he convince you that this change in family relationships is worthwhile in terms of his "dramatic Americanization" (para. 37)?
5. What does Rodriguez mean in the following statement: "[W]hile one suffers a diminished sense of *private* individuality by becoming assimilated into public society, such assimilation makes possible the achievement of *public* individuality" (para. 43)?
6. Rodriguez draws the following analogy in paragraph 58: "Just as Spanish would have been a dangerous language for me to have used at the start of my education, so black English would be a dangerous language to use in the schooling of teenagers for whom it reenforces feelings of public separateness." Do you find this analogy convincing? Why or why not?

Questions on Rhetoric and Style

1. What is an aria? Why do you think Rodriguez chose it for his title? Is it an appropriate title? Is it effective?
2. Explain how Rodriguez establishes his ethos in the opening four paragraphs and what it is.
3. Describe the tone of paragraph 5, where Rodriguez first raises the issue of bilingual education. Cite specific language to support your description.
4. Why does Rodriguez emphasize the sound of language? Is his doing so an appeal to logos, pathos, or both?
5. Although the entire essay is not strictly chronological, Rodriguez structures it with signals to chronology. What are they? Why are they effective?
6. How would you describe Rodriguez's attitude toward his parents? Does it change from one point in the essay to another? Identify specific passages.
7. In several sections, Rodriguez makes his point by narrative (such as the moment in school when he first hears his name). How does narrative contribute to the effectiveness of Rodriguez's argument?
8. Where in the essay does Rodriguez present his most straightforward argument? Is it effective? Would it have been more effective if it had been placed nearer the beginning?
9. What major counterarguments does Rodriguez address? (He does not address them all at once; identify specific passages.)
10. What weakness in reasoning are "middle-class ethnics" guilty of according to Rodriguez (para. 43)?
11. Rodriguez uses very little Spanish in this essay, in contrast to other writers whose heritage includes the Spanish language. What is the effect of this choice?
12. Who do you think is the intended audience for this essay? Cite passages to support your viewpoint.
13. What is the tone in the final paragraphs (beginning with para. 69)? Is it different from the tone in the rest of the essay? What would have been the effect of eliminating these last paragraphs?

Suggestions for Writing

1. Rodriguez makes the following statement in paragraph 5: "It is not possible for a child — any child — ever to use his family's language in school. Not to understand this is to misunderstand the public uses of schooling and to trivialize the nature of intimate life — a family's 'language.'" Write an essay defending, challenging, or modifying Rodriguez's assertion. Support your argument with evidence from your experience, observation, or reading.
2. Do you agree with Rodriguez or with supporters of bilingual education? After you have done some research, write an argument explaining your position.
3. Read part of a work by an author such as Cormac McCarthy or Gloria Anzaldúa, who includes entire passages of Spanish without translation. Write your responses

to this technique (regardless of whether you know Spanish) in a journal. How do the Spanish excerpts make you feel? Is understanding what is going on necessary? Does the inclusion of Spanish cause you to develop a specific attitude toward the author? If so, what is that attitude? You might discuss your responses in groups and then report back to the full class and try to discern patterns.

4. Turn Rodriguez's argument against itself. Using several passages from "Aria," write a letter to the author explaining how his own points undermine his position that bilingual education or any kind of policy that separates students on the basis of language is a disservice to the nonnative English speaker.

5. In a 1994 interview, Rodriguez makes the following comment about multiculturalism: "Multiculturalism, as it is expressed in the platitudes of the American campus, is not multiculturalism. It is an idea about culture that has a specific genesis, a specific history, and a specific politics. What people mean by multiculturalism is different hues of themselves. They don't mean Islamic fundamentalists or skinheads. They mean other brown and black students who share opinions like theirs. It isn't diversity. It's a pretense to diversity." Do you agree with Rodriguez that "multicultural centers" or "multicultural curriculum" or other similar projects are not truly diverse?

Politics and the English Language

GEORGE ORWELL

George Orwell (1903–1950) is the pseudonym of Eric Arthur Blair, a writer who was the son of an English civil servant during the Raj, the British rule of India. Orwell was educated in England, but when financial constraints prevented him from attending university, he joined the imperial police in Burma, an experience immortalized in his famous essay "Shooting an Elephant." He returned to England five years later, but in 1928 he moved to Paris. There he took on a series of menial jobs, which he described in his first book, *Down and Out in Paris and London* (1933). Orwell worked as a schoolteacher, fought on the side of the republicans in the Spanish civil war, and began writing for magazines, often speaking out against economic injustice. He finally gained recognition and considerable financial success with his novels *Animal Farm* (1945) and *Nineteen Eighty-four* (1949). The term *Orwellian* came to describe mechanisms used by totalitarian governments to manipulate the populace in order to enforce conformity. In the following essay, which first appeared in *Horizon* in 1946, Orwell explores the impact of totalitarian thinking on language.

Most people who bother with the matter at all would admit that the English language is in a bad way, but it is generally assumed that we cannot by conscious action do anything about it. Our civilization is decadent and our language — so the argument runs — must inevitably share in the general collapse. It follows that any struggle against the abuse of language is a sentimental archaism, like preferring candles to electric light or hansom cabs to aeroplanes. Underneath this lies the half-conscious belief that language is a natural growth and not an instrument which we shape for our own purposes.

Now, it is clear that the decline of a language must ultimately have political and economic causes: it is not due simply to the bad influence of this or that individual writer. But an effect can become a cause, reinforcing the original cause and producing the same effect in an intensified form, and so on indefinitely. A man may take to drink because he feels himself to be a failure, and then fail all the more completely because he drinks. It is rather the same thing that is happening to the English language. It becomes ugly and inaccurate because our thoughts are foolish, but the slovenliness of our language makes it easier for us to have foolish thoughts. The point is that the process is reversible. Modern English, especially written English, is full of bad habits which spread by imitation and which can be avoided if one is willing to take the necessary trouble. If one gets rid of these habits one can think more clearly, and to think clearly is a necessary first step towards political regeneration: so that the fight against bad English is not frivolous and is not the exclusive concern of professional writers. I will come back to this presently, and I hope that by that time the meaning of what I have said here will have become clearer. Meanwhile, here are five specimens of the English language as it is now habitually written.

These five passages have not been picked out because they are especially bad — I could have quoted far worse if I had chosen — but because they illustrate various of the mental vices from which we now suffer. They are a little below the average, but are fairly representative samples. I number them so that I can refer back to them when necessary:

(1) I am not, indeed, sure whether it is not true to say that the Milton who once seemed not unlike a seventeenth-century Shelley had not become, out of an experience ever more bitter in each year, more alien [*sic*] to the founder of that Jesuit sect which nothing could induce him to tolerate.

> — PROFESSOR HAROLD LASKI
> (Essay in *Freedom of Expression*)

(2) Above all, we cannot play ducks and drakes with a native battery of idioms which prescribes such egregious collocations of vocables as the Basic *put up with* for *tolerate* or *put at a loss* for *bewilder*.

> — PROFESSOR LANCELOT HOGBEN (*Interglossa*)

(3) On the one side we have the free personality: by definition it is not neurotic, for it has neither conflict nor dream. Its desires, such as they are, are transparent, for they are just what institutional approval keeps in the forefront of consciousness; another institutional pattern would alter their number and intensity; there is little in them that is natural, irreducible, or culturally dangerous. But *on the other side*, the social bond itself is nothing but the mutual reflection of these self-secure integrities. Recall the definition of love. Is not this the very picture of a small academic? Where is there a place in this hall of mirrors for either personality or fraternity?

> Essay on psychology in *Politics* (New York)

(4) All the "best people" from the gentlemen's clubs, and all the frantic fascist captains, united in common hatred of Socialism and bestial horror of the rising tide of the mass revolutionary movement, have turned to acts of provocation, to foul incendiarism, to medieval legends of poisoned wells, to legalize their own destruction of proletarian organizations, and rouse the agitated petty-bourgeoisie to chauvinistic fervor on behalf of the fight against the revolutionary way out of the crisis.

> — Communist pamphlet

(5) If a new spirit *is* to be infused into this old country, there is one thorny and contentious reform which must be tackled, and that is the humanization and galvanization of the B.B.C. Timidity here will bespeak canker and atrophy of the soul. The heart of Britain may be sound and of strong beat, for instance, but the

British lion's roar at present is like that of Bottom in Shakespeare's *Midsummer Night's Dream* — as gentle as any sucking dove. A virile new Britain cannot continue indefinitely to be traduced in the eyes, or rather ears, of the world by the effete languors of Langham Place, brazenly masquerading as "standard English." When the Voice of Britain is heard at nine o'clock, better far and infinitely less ludicrous to hear aitches honestly dropped than the present priggish, inflated, inhibited, school-ma'amish arch braying of blameless bashful mewing maidens!

—Letter in *Tribune*

Each of these passages has faults of its own, but, quite apart from avoidable ugliness, two qualities are common to all of them. The first is staleness of imagery; the other is lack of precision. The writer either had a meaning and cannot express it, or he inadvertently says something else, or he is almost indifferent as to whether his words mean anything or not. This mixture of vagueness and sheer incompetence is the most marked characteristic of modern English prose, and especially of any kind of political writing. As soon as certain topics are raised, the concrete melts into the abstract and no one seems able to think of terms of speech that are not hackneyed: prose consists less and less of *words* chosen for the sake of their meaning, and more and more of *phrases* tacked together like the sections of a prefabricated henhouse. I list below, with notes and examples, various of the tricks by means of which the work of prose-construction is habitually dodged:

Dying Metaphors

A newly invented metaphor assists thought by evoking a visual image, while on the other hand a metaphor which is technically "dead" (e.g., *iron resolution*) has in effect reverted to being an ordinary word and can generally be used without loss of vividness. But in between these two classes there is a huge dump of worn-out metaphors which have lost all evocative power and are merely used because they save people the trouble of inventing phrases for themselves. Examples are: *Ring the changes on, take up the cudgels for, toe the line, ride roughshod over, stand shoulder to shoulder with, play into the hands of, no axe to grind, grist to the mill, fishing in troubled waters, rift within the lute, on the order of the day, Achilles' heel, swan song, hotbed.* Many of these are used without knowledge of their meaning (what is a "rift," for instance?), and incompatible metaphors are frequently mixed, a sure sign that the writer is not interested in what he is saying. Some metaphors now current have been twisted out of their original meaning without those who use them even being aware of the fact. For example, *toe the line* is sometimes written *tow the line*. Another example is *the hammer and the anvil*, now always used with the implication that the anvil gets the worst of it. In real life it is always the anvil that breaks the hammer, never the other way about: a writer who stopped to think what he was saying would be aware of this, and would avoid perverting the original phrase.

Operators or Verbal False Limbs

These save the trouble of picking out appropriate verbs and nouns, and at the same time pad each sentence with extra syllables which give it an appearance of symmetry. Characteristic phrases are *render inoperative, militate against, make contact with, be subjected to, give rise to, give grounds for, have the effect of, play a leading part (role) in, make itself felt, take effect, exhibit a tendency to, serve the purpose of, etc., etc.* The keynote is, the elimination of simple verbs. Instead of being a single word, such as *break, stop, spoil, mend, kill,* a verb becomes a *phrase,* made up of a noun or adjective tacked on to some general-purposes verb such as *prove, serve, form, play, render.* In addition, the passive voice is wherever possible used in preference to the active, and noun constructions are used instead of gerunds (*by examination of* instead of *by examining*). The range of verbs is further cut down by means of the *-ize* and *de-* formations, and the banal statements are given an appearance of profundity by means of the *not un-* formation. Simple conjunctions and prepositions are replaced by such phrases as *with respect to, having regard to, the fact that, by dint of, in view of, in the interests of, on the hypothesis that;* and the ends of sentences are saved from anticlimax by such resounding commonplaces as *greatly to be desired, cannot be left out of account, a development to be expected in the near future, deserving of serious consideration, brought to a satisfactory conclusion,* and so on and so forth.

Pretentious Diction

Words like *phenomenon, element, individual* (as noun), *objective, categorical, effective, virtual, basic, primary, promote, constitute, exhibit, exploit, utilize, eliminate, liquidate* are used to dress up simple statement and give an air of scientific impartiality to biased judgments. Adjectives like *epoch-making, epic, historic, unforgettable, triumphant, age-old, inevitable, inexorable, veritable,* are used to dignify the sordid processes of international politics, while writing that aims at glorifying war usually takes on an archaic color, its characteristic words being: *realm, throne, chariot, mailed fist, trident, sword, shield, buckler, banner, jackboot, clarion.* Foreign words and expressions such as *cul de sac, ancien régime, deus ex machina, mutatis mutandis, status quo, Gleichschaltung, Weltanschauung,* are used to give an air of culture and elegance. Except for the useful abbreviations *i.e., e.g.,* and *etc.,* there is no real need for any of the hundreds of foreign phrases now current in English. Bad writers, and especially scientific, political and sociological writers, are nearly always haunted by the notion that Latin or Greek words are grander than Saxon ones, and unnecessary words like *expedite, ameliorate, predict, extraneous, deracinated, clandestine, subaqueous* and hundreds of others constantly gain ground from their Anglo-Saxon opposite numbers.[1] The jargon peculiar to Marxist writ-

---

[1]An interesting illustration of this is the way in which the English flower names which were in use till very recently are being ousted by Greek ones, *snapdragon* becoming *antirrhinum,*

ing (*hyena, hangman, cannibal, petty bourgeois, these gentry, lacquey, flunkey, mad dog, White Guard,* etc.) consists largely of words and phrases translated from Russian, German or French; but the normal way of coining a new word is to use a Latin or Greek root with the appropriate affix and, where necessary, the -*ize* formation. It is often easier to make up words of this kind (*deregionalize, impermissible, extramarital, non-fragmentary* and so forth) than to think up the English words that will cover one's meaning. The result, in general, is an increase in slovenliness and vagueness.

Meaningless Words

In certain kinds of writing, particularly in art criticism and literary criticism, it is normal to come across long passages which are almost completely lacking in meaning.[2] Words like *romantic, plastic, values, human, dead, sentimental, natural, vitality,* as used in art criticism, are strictly meaningless, in the sense that they not only do not point to any discoverable object, but are hardly ever expected to do so by the reader. When one critic writes, "The outstanding feature of Mr. X's work is its living quality," while another writes, "The immediately striking thing about Mr. X's work is its peculiar deadness," the reader accepts this as a simple difference of opinion. If words like *black* and *white* were involved, instead of the jargon words *dead* and *living,* he would see at once that language was being used in an improper way. Many political words are similarly abused. The word *Fascism* has now no meaning except in so far as it signifies "something not desirable." The words *democracy, socialism, freedom, patriotic, realistic, justice,* have each of them several different meanings which cannot be reconciled with one another. In the case of a word like *democracy,* not only is there no agreed definition, but the attempt to make one is resisted from all sides. It is almost universally felt that when we call a country democratic we are praising it: consequently the defenders of every kind of régime claim that it is a democracy, and fear that they might have to stop using the word if it were tied down to any one meaning. Words of this kind are often used in a consciously dishonest way. That is, the person who uses them has his own private definition, but allows his hearer to think he means something quite different. Statements like *Marshal Pétain*[3] *was a true patriot, The*

---

forget-me-not becoming *myosotis,* etc. It is hard to see any practical reason for this change of fashion: it is probably due to an instinctive turning-away from the more homely word and a vague feeling that the Greek word is scientific.

[2]Example: "Comfort's catholicity of perception and image, strangely Whitmanesque in range, almost the exact opposite in aesthetic compulsion, continues to evoke that trembling atmospheric accumulative hinting at a cruel, an inexorably serene timelessness. . . . Wrey Gardiner scores by aiming at simple bull's-eyes with precision. Only they are not so simple, and through this contented sadness runs more than the surface bitter-sweet of resignation."

[3]Henri Phillipe Pétain (1856–1951), head of the French government during the German occupation from 1940 to 1945, was convicted of treason in 1945. — Eds.

Soviet Press is the freest in the world, The Catholic Church is opposed to persecution, are almost always made with intent to deceive. Other words used in variable meanings, in most cases more or less dishonestly, are: *class, totalitarian, science, progressive, reactionary, bourgeois, equality.*

Now that I have made this catalogue of swindles and perversions, let me give another example of the kind of writing that they lead to. This time it must of its nature be an imaginary one. I am going to translate a passage of good English into modern English of the worst sort. Here is a well-known verse from *Ecclesiastes*:

> I returned and saw under the sun, that the race is not to the swift, nor the battle to the strong, neither yet bread to the wise, nor yet riches to men of understanding, nor yet favour to men of skill; but time and chance happeneth to them all.

Here it is in modern English: 10

> Objective consideration of contemporary phenomena compels the conclusion that success or failure in competitive activities exhibits no tendency to be commensurate with innate capacity, but that a considerable element of the unpredictable must invariably be taken into account.

This is a parody, but not a very gross one. Exhibit (3), above, for instance, contains several patches of the same kind of English. It will be seen that I have not made a full translation. The beginning and ending of the sentence follow the original meaning fairly closely, but in the middle the concrete illustrations — race, battle, bread — dissolve into the vague phrase "success or failure in competitive activities." This had to be so, because no modern writer of the kind I am discussing — no one capable of using phrases like "objective consideration of contemporary phenomena" — would ever tabulate his thoughts in that precise and detailed way. The whole tendency of modern prose is away from concreteness. Now analyse these two sentences a little more closely. The first contains forty-nine words but only sixty syllables, and all its words are those of everyday life. The second contains thirty-eight words of ninety syllables: eighteen of its words are from Latin roots, and one from Greek. The first sentence contains six vivid images, and only one phrase ("time and chance") that could be called vague. The second contains not a single fresh, arresting phrase, and in spite of its ninety syllables it gives only a shortened version of the meaning contained in the first. Yet without a doubt it is the second kind of sentence that is gaining ground in modern English. I do not want to exaggerate. This kind of writing is not yet universal, and outcrops of simplicity will occur here and there in the worst-written page. Still, if you or I were to write a few lines on the uncertainty of human fortunes, we should probably come much nearer to my imaginary sentence than to the one from *Ecclesiastes*.

As I have tried to show, modern writing at its worst does not consist in picking out words for the sake of their meaning and inventing images in order to make the meaning clearer. It consists in gumming together long strips of words which have already been set in order by someone else, and making the results presentable by sheer humbug. The attraction of this way of writing is that it is easy. It is easier — even quicker, once you have the habit — to say *In my opinion it is not an unjustifiable assumption that* than to say *I think*. If you use ready-made phrases, you not only don't have to hunt about for words; you also don't have to bother with the rhythms of your sentences, since these phrases are generally so arranged as to be more or less euphonious. When you are composing in a hurry — when you are dictating to a stenographer, for instance, or making a public speech — it is natural to fall into a pretentious, Latinized style. Tags like *a consideration which we should do well to bear in mind* or *a conclusion to which all of us would readily assent* will save many a sentence from coming down with a bump. By using stale metaphors, similes and idioms, you save much mental effort, at the cost of leaving your meaning vague, not only for your reader but for yourself. This is the significance of mixed metaphors. The sole aim of a metaphor is to call up a visual image. When these images clash — as in *The Fascist octopus has sung its swan song, the jackboot is thrown into the melting pot* — it can be taken as certain that the writer is not seeing a mental image of the objects he is naming; in other words he is not really thinking. Look again at the examples I gave at the beginning of this essay. Professor Laski (1) uses five negatives in fifty-three words. One of these is superfluous, making nonsense of the whole passage, and in addition there is the slip *alien* for akin, making further nonsense, and several avoidable pieces of clumsiness which increase the general vagueness. Professor Hogben (2) plays ducks and drakes with a battery which is able to write prescriptions, and, while disapproving of the everyday phrase *put up with*, is unwilling to look *egregious* up in the dictionary and see what it means; (3), if one takes an uncharitable attitude towards it, is simply meaningless: probably one could work out its intended meaning by reading the whole of the article in which it occurs. In (4), the writer knows more or less what he wants to say, but an accumulation of stale phrases chokes him like tea leaves blocking a sink. In (5), words and meaning have almost parted company. People who write in this manner usually have a general emotional meaning — they dislike one thing and want to express solidarity with another — but they are not interested in the detail of what they are saying. A scrupulous writer, in every sentence that he writes, will ask himself at least four questions, thus: What am I trying to say? What words will express it? What image or idiom will make it clearer? Is this image fresh enough to have an effect? And he will probably ask himself two more: Could I put it more shortly? Have I said anything that is avoidably ugly? But you are not obliged to go to all this trouble. You can shirk it by simply throwing your mind open and letting the ready-made phrases come crowding in. They will construct your sentences for you — even think your thoughts for you, to a certain extent — and at need they will perform the important service of partially concealing your meaning even from yourself. It is at this point that the special connection between politics and the debasement of language becomes clear.

In our time it is broadly true that political writing is bad writing. Where it is not true, it will generally be found that the writer is some kind of rebel, expressing his private opinions and not a "party line." Orthodoxy, of whatever color, seems to demand a lifeless, imitative style. The political dialects to be found in pamphlets, leading articles, manifestos, White Papers and the speeches of undersecretaries do, of course, vary from party to party, but they are all alike in that one almost never finds in them a fresh, vivid, homemade turn of speech. When one watches some tired hack on the platform mechanically repeating the familiar phrases — *bestial atrocities, iron heel, bloodstained tyranny, free peoples of the world, stand shoulder to shoulder* — one often has a curious feeling that one is not watching a live human being but some kind of dummy: a feeling which suddenly becomes stronger at moments when the light catches the speaker's spectacles and turns them into blank discs which seem to have no eyes behind them. And this is not altogether fanciful. A speaker who uses that kind of phraseology has gone some distance towards turning himself into a machine. The appropriate noises are coming out of his larynx, but his brain is not involved as it would be if he were choosing his words for himself. If the speech he is making is one that he is accustomed to make over and over again, he may be almost unconscious of what he is saying, as one is when one utters the responses in church. And this reduced state of consciousness, if not indispensable, is at any rate favorable to political conformity.

In our time, political speech and writing are largely the defence of the indefensible. Things like the continuance of British rule in India, the Russian purges and deportations, the dropping of the atom bombs on Japan, can indeed be defended, but only by arguments which are too brutal for most people to face, and which do not square with the professed aims of political parties. Thus political language has to consist largely of euphemism, question-begging and sheer cloudy vagueness. Defenceless villages are bombarded from the air, the inhabitants driven out into the countryside, the cattle machine-gunned, the huts set on fire with incendiary bullets: this is called *pacification*. Millions of peasants are robbed of their farms and sent trudging along the roads with no more than they can carry: this is called *transfer of population* or *rectification of frontiers*. People are imprisoned for years without trial, or shot in the back of the neck or sent to die of scurvy in Arctic lumber camps: this is called *elimination of unreliable elements*. Such phraseology is needed if one wants to name things without calling up mental pictures of them. Consider for instance some comfortable English professor defending Russian totalitarianism. He cannot say outright, "I believe in killing off your opponents when you can get good results by doing so." Probably, therefore, he will say something like this:

> While freely conceding that the Soviet régime exhibits certain features which the humanitarian may be inclined to deplore, we must, I think, agree that a certain curtailment of the right to political opposition is an unavoidable concomi-

tant of transitional periods, and that the rigors which the Russian people have been called upon to undergo have been amply justified in the sphere of concrete achievement.

The inflated style is itself a kind of euphemism. A mass of Latin words falls 15 upon the facts like soft snow, blurring the outlines and covering up all the details. The great enemy of clear language is insincerity. When there is a gap between one's real and one's declared aims, one turns as it were instinctively to long words and exhausted idioms, like a cuttlefish squirting out ink. In our age there is no such thing as "keeping out of politics." All issues are political issues, and politics itself is a mass of lies, evasions, folly, hatred and schizophrenia. When the general atmosphere is bad, language must suffer. I should expect to find — this is a guess which I have not sufficient knowledge to verify — that the German, Russian and Italian languages have all deteriorated in the last ten or fifteen years, as a result of dictatorship.

But if thought corrupts language, language can also corrupt thought. A bad usage can spread by tradition and imitation, even among people who should and do know better. The debased language that I have been discussing is in some ways very convenient. Phrases like *a not unjustifiable assumption, leaves much to be desired, would serve no good purpose, a consideration which we should do well to bear in mind*, are a continuous temptation, a packet of aspirins always at one's elbow. Look back through this essay, and for certain you will find that I have again and again committed the very faults I am protesting against. By this morning's post I have received a pamphlet dealing with conditions in Germany. The author tells me that he "felt impelled" to write it. I open it at random, and here is almost the first sentence that I see: "[The Allies] have an opportunity not only of achieving a radical transformation of Germany's social and political structure in such a way as to avoid a nationalistic reaction in Germany itself, but at the same time of laying the foundation of a cooperative and unified Europe." You see, he "feels impelled" to write — feels, presumably, that he has something new to say — and yet his words, like cavalry horses answering the bugle, group themselves automatically into the familiar dreary pattern. This invasion of one's mind by ready-made phrases (*lay the foundations, achieve a radical transformation*) can only be prevented if one is constantly on guard against them, and every such phrase anaesthetizes a portion of one's brain.

I said earlier that the decadence of our language is probably curable. Those who deny this would argue, if they produced an argument at all, that language merely reflects existing social conditions, and that we cannot influence its development by any direct tinkering with words and constructions. So far as the general tone or spirit of a language goes, this may be true, but it is not true in detail. Silly words and expressions have often disappeared, not through any evolutionary process but owing to the conscious action of a minority. Two recent examples were *explore every avenue* and *leave no stone unturned*, which were killed by the jeers of a few journalists. There is a long list of flyblown metaphors which could similarly be got rid of if enough people would interest themselves in the job; and it should also be possible to laugh the *not un-* formation out of existence,[4] to reduce the amount of Latin and Greek in the average sentence, to drive out foreign phrases and strayed scientific words, and, in general, to make pretentiousness unfashionable. But all these are minor points. The defence of the English language implies more than this, and perhaps it is best to start by saying what it does *not* imply.

To begin with it has nothing to do with archaism, with the salvaging of obsolete words and turns of speech, or with the setting up of a "standard English" which must never be departed from. On the contrary, it is especially concerned with the scrapping of every word or idiom which has outworn its usefulness. It has nothing to do with correct grammar and syntax, which are of no importance so long as one makes one's meaning clear, or with the avoidance of Americanisms, or with having what is called a "good prose style." On the other hand it is not concerned with fake simplicity and the attempt to make written English colloquial. Nor does it even imply in every case preferring the Saxon word to the Latin one, though it does imply using the fewest and shortest words that will cover one's meaning. What is above all needed is to let the meaning choose the word, and not the other way about. In prose, the worst thing one can do with words is to surrender to them. When you think of a concrete object, you think wordlessly, and then, if you want to describe the thing you have been visualizing you probably hunt about till you find the exact words that seem to fit it. When you think of something abstract you are more inclined to use words from the start, and unless you make a conscious effort to prevent it, the existing dialect will come rushing in and do the job for you, at the expense of blurring or even changing your meaning. Probably it is better to put off using words as long as possible and get one's meaning as clear as one can through pictures or sensations. Afterwards one can choose — not simply *accept* — the phrases that will best cover the meaning, and then switch round and decide what impression one's words are likely to make on another person. This last effort of the mind cuts out all stale or mixed images, all prefabricated phrases, needless repetitions, and humbug and vagueness generally. But one can often be in doubt about the effect of a word or a phrase, and one needs rules that one can rely on when instinct fails. I think the following rules will cover most cases:

(i) Never use a metaphor, simile or other figure of speech which you are used to seeing in print.

(ii) Never use a long word where a short one will do.

---

[4]One can cure oneself of the *not un-* formation by memorizing this sentence: *A not unblack dog was chasing a not unsmall rabbit across a not ungreen field.*

(iii)   If it is possible to cut a word out, always cut it out

(iv)   Never use the passive where you can use the active.

(v)   Never use a foreign phrase, a scientific word or a jargon word if you can think of an everyday English equivalent.

(vi)   Break any of these rules sooner than say anything outright barbarous.

These rules sound elementary, and so they are, but they demand a deep change of attitude in anyone who has grown used to writing in the style now fashionable. One could keep all of them and still write bad English, but one could not write the kind of stuff that I quoted in those five specimens at the beginning of this article.

I have not here been considering the literary use of language, but merely language as an instrument for expressing and not for concealing or preventing thought. Stuart Chase and others have come near to claiming that all abstract words are meaningless, and have used this as a pretext for advocating a kind of political quietism. Since you don't know what Fascism is, how can you struggle against Fascism? One need not swallow such absurdities as this, but one ought to recognize that the present political chaos is connected with the decay of language, and that one can probably bring about some improvement by starting at the verbal end. If you simplify your English, you are freed from the worst follies of orthodoxy. You cannot speak any of the necessary dialects, and when you make a stupid remark its stupidity will be obvious, even to yourself. Political language — and with variations this is true of all political parties, from Conservatives to Anarchists — is designed to make lies sound truthful and murder respectable, and to give an appearance of solidity to pure wind. One cannot change this all in a moment, but one can at least change one's own habits, and from time to time one can even, if one jeers loudly enough, send some worn-out and useless phrase — some *jackboot, Achilles' heel, hotbed, melting pot, acid test, veritable inferno* or other lump of verbal refuse — into the dustbin where it belongs.

Questions for Discussion

1. George Orwell argues against the "belief that language is a natural growth and not an instrument which we shape for our own purposes" (para. 1). Explain why you do or do not agree with Orwell's position.

2. In speeches by contemporary politicians, find examples of each type of writing problem that Orwell discusses: dying metaphors, operators or verbal false limbs, pretentious diction, and meaningless words. Explain why the examples you've cited are "swindles and perversions," as Orwell calls them (para. 9).

3. Why does Orwell object to "ready-made phrases" and "mixed metaphors" (para. 12)?

4. In paragraph 12, Orwell says that every writer "ask[s] himself at least four questions: What am I trying to say? What words will express it? What image or idiom

will make it clearer? Is this image fresh enough to have an effect?" What do you think of these questions? Do you agree or disagree that they are the most essential questions for writers to ask themselves? Explain why.

5. What does Orwell mean when he asserts, "But if thought corrupts language, language can also corrupt thought" (para. 16)?

6. Do you agree with Orwell that "correct grammar and syntax . . . are of no importance so long as one makes one's meaning clear" (para. 18)? Explain. If you do agree, cite examples from your own experience or reading that support your position.

Questions on Rhetoric and Style

1. What is Orwell's thesis? Does he actually state it, or is it implied?

2. How effective is Orwell's analogy of the cause and effect of alcohol abuse to the demise of language (para. 2)?

3. In each of the following paragraphs — paragraphs 4, 5, 12, 15, and 16 — Orwell uses at least one metaphor or simile. Identify each figure of speech. Then explain how it works and whether you find it rhetorically effective.

4. Orwell develops his ideas through extensive use of examples. Try rewriting paragraph 5, 6, 7, or 8 without examples. How does the effect of the paragraph change?

5. What is the purpose of the additional information provided in Orwell's footnotes for paragraphs 7 and 8? Why do you think Orwell chose to put the information in footnotes rather than in the main text?

6. Orwell wrote this essay before he was well known for his novels. He uses the first person, yet he does not directly state his qualifications to speak on language. How does he establish ethos? Should he have been more direct?

7. How would you describe the overall organization of this essay? Examine its movement, from the examples in the opening to the rules in the ending.

8. What is Orwell's purpose in writing this essay? How might the historical context of post–World War II affect that purpose? Cite specific passages to support your response.

9. How would you describe the tone of Orwell's essay? Can you sum it up in one word, or does the essay range from one tone to another? Cite specific passages to support your response.

10. Find examples in the essay where Orwell is guilty of the four faults that characterize the writing he is criticizing.

Suggestions for Writing

1. Using examples from your own writing, observation of popular culture, or reading of contemporary texts, explain why you do or do not agree with Orwell's opening statement that "the English language is in a bad way."

2. Working in groups, find examples of writing in current newspapers or magazines or a political speech that illustrate what Orwell calls "staleness of imagery" and

"lack of precision." Then, revise the writing by applying one or more of the six rules Orwell prescribes in the penultimate paragraph of his essay.

3. Write an essay agreeing or disagreeing with the following assertion by Orwell (para. 13): "In our time it is broadly true that political writing is bad writing. Where it is not true, it will generally be found that the writer is some kind of rebel, expressing his private opinions and not a 'party line.' Orthodoxy, of whatever color, seems to demand a lifeless, imitative style." Support your position with examples from political speeches, newspaper columns and articles, advertisements, and Web sites.

4. Orwell uses many terms that refer to language. Develop a glossary that has the following components: (1) the term as Orwell uses it, (2) a definition of the term, and (3) an example from your own reading (including advertisements). Include the following terms, along with any others you note: *mixed metaphor, pretentious diction, euphemism, parody, idiom, archaic language* ("*archaism*"), *dialect.*

5. Suppose "Politics and the English Language" were being reprinted in a specific contemporary magazine. Redesign the essay by adding visual images and graphic displays that will appeal to the magazine's audience. Do *not* change Orwell's language; simply download the essay from the Internet, and then redesign it by including graphs, charts, cartoon characters, icons, color, or different fonts. Explain the rhetorical effect that you intend these changes to have.

6. Compare and contrast paragraph 14 in Orwell's essay with the following paragraph from Toni Morrison's 1993 Nobel Prize speech. You can listen to this speech at <bedfordstmartins.com/languageofcomp>.

> The systematic looting of language can be recognized by the tendency of its users to forgo its nuanced, complex, mid-wifery properties for menace and subjugation. Oppressive language does more than represent violence; it is violence; does more than represent the limits of knowledge; it limits knowledge. Whether it is obscuring state language or the faux-language of mindless media; whether it is the proud but calcified language of the academy or the commodity driven language of science; whether it is the malign language of law-without-ethics, or language designed for the estrangement of minorities, hiding its racist plunder in its literary cheek — it must be rejected, altered and exposed. It is the language that drinks blood, laps vulnerabilities, tucks its fascist boots under crinolines of respectability and patriotism as it moves relentlessly toward the bottom line and the bottomed-out mind. Sexist language, racist language, theistic language — all are typical of the policing languages of mastery, and cannot, do not permit new knowledge or encourage the mutual exchange of ideas.

Mother Tongue

AMY TAN

Best-selling author Amy Tan (b. 1952) has written several novels, including *The Joy Luck Club* (1989), *The Kitchen God's Wife* (1991), *The Bonesetter's Daughter* (2001), and *Saving Fish from Drowning* (2005). Known for her portrayal of mother-daughter relationships, Tan draws on her Chinese heritage to depict the clash of traditional Chinese culture with modern-day American customs. Tan grew up in California, has an MA in linguistics, and worked as a business writer before turning to fiction. She is a member of the Rock Bottom Remainders, a band — including Dave Barry and Stephen King — that plays for charity events. Tan collected many of her nonfiction writings in *The Opposite of Fate: A Book of Musings* (2003). Among these is "Mother Tongue," an essay in which Tan explores "all the Englishes" that are part of her identity.

I am not a scholar of English or literature. I cannot give you much more than personal opinions on the English language and its variations in this country or others.

I am a writer. And by that definition, I am someone who has always loved language. I am fascinated by language in daily life. I spend a great deal of my time thinking about the power of language — the way it can evoke an emotion, a visual image, a complex idea, or a simple truth. Language is the tool of my trade. And I use them all — all the Englishes I grew up with.

Recently, I was made keenly aware of the different Englishes I do use. I was giving a talk to a large group of people, the same talk I had already given to half a dozen other groups. The nature of the talk was about my writing, my life, and my book, *The Joy Luck Club*. The talk was going along well enough, until I remembered one major difference that made the whole talk sound wrong. My mother was in the room. And it was perhaps the first time she had heard me give a lengthy speech, using the kind of English I have never used with her. I was saying things like "The intersection of memory upon imagination" and "There is an aspect of my fiction that relates to thus-and-thus" — a speech filled with carefully wrought grammatical phrases, burdened, it suddenly seemed to me, with nominalized forms, past perfect tenses, conditional phrases, all the forms of standard English that I had learned in school and through books, the forms of English I did not use at home with my mother.

Just last week, I was walking down the street with my mother, and I again found myself conscious of the English I was using, the English I do use with her. We were talking about the price of new and used furniture and I heard myself saying this: "Not waste money that way." My husband was with us as well, and he didn't notice any switch in my English. And then I realized why. It's because over the twenty years we've been together I've often used that same kind of English with him, and sometimes he even uses it with me. It has become our language of intimacy, a different sort of English that relates to family talk, the language I grew up with.

So you'll have some idea of what this family talk I heard sounds like, I'll quote   5 what my mother said during a recent conversation which I videotaped and then transcribed. During this conversation, my mother was talking about a political gangster in Shanghai who had the same last name as her family's, Du, and how the gangster in his early years wanted to be adopted by her family, which was rich by comparison. Later, the gangster became more powerful, far richer than my mother's family, and one day showed up at my mother's wedding to pay his respects. Here's what she said in part:

"Du Yusong having business like fruit stand. Like off the street kind. He is Du like Du Zong — but not Tsung-ming Island people. The local people call putong, the river east side, he belong to that side local people. That man want to ask Du Zong father take him in like become own family. Du Zong father wasn't look down on him, but didn't take seriously, until that man big like become a mafia. Now important person, very hard to inviting him. Chinese way, came only to show respect, don't stay for dinner. Respect for making big celebration, he shows up. Mean gives lots of respect. Chinese custom. Chinese social life that way. If too important won't have to stay too long. He come to my wedding. I didn't see, I heard it. I gone to boy's side, they have YMCA dinner. Chinese age I was nineteen."

You should know that my mother's expressive command of English belies how much she actually understands. She reads the *Forbes* report, listens to *Wall Street Week*, converses daily with her stockbroker, reads all of Shirley MacLaine's books with ease — all kinds of things I can't begin to understand. Yet some of my friends tell me they understand 50 percent of what my mother says. Some say they understand 80 to 90 percent. Some say they understand none of it, as if she were speaking pure Chinese. But to me, my mother's English is perfectly clear, perfectly natural. It's my mother tongue. Her language, as I hear it, is vivid, direct, full of observation and imagery. That was the language that helped shape the way I saw things, expressed things, made sense of the world.

Lately, I've been giving more thought to the kind of English my mother speaks. Like others, I have described it to people as "broken" or "fractured" English. But I wince when I say that. It has always bothered me that I can think of no other way to describe it other than "broken," as if it were damaged and needed to be fixed, as if it lacked a certain wholeness and soundness. I've heard other terms used, "limited English," for example. But they seem just a bad, as if everything is limited, including people's perceptions of the limited English speaker.

I know this for a fact, because when I was growing up, my mother's "limited" English limited *my* perception of her. I was ashamed of her English. I believed that her English reflected the quality of what she had to say. That is, because she expressed them imperfectly her thoughts were imperfect. And I had plenty of empirical evidence to support me: the fact that people in department stores, at banks, and at restaurants did not take her seriously, did not give her good service, pretended not to understand her, or even acted as if they did not hear her.

My mother has long realized the limitations of her English as well. When I was fifteen, she used to have me call people on the phone to pretend I was she. In this guise, I was forced to ask for information or even to complain and yell at people who had been rude to her. One time it was a call to her stockbroker in New York. She had cashed out her small portfolio and it just so happened we were going to go to New York the next week, our very first trip outside California. I had to get on the phone and say in an adolescent voice that was not very convincing, "This is Mrs. Tan." 10

And my mother was standing in the back whispering loudly, "Why he don't send me check, already two weeks late. So mad he lie to me, losing me money."

And then I said in perfect English, "Yes, I'm getting rather concerned. You had agreed to send the check two weeks ago, but it hasn't arrived."

Then she began to talk more loudly. "What he want, I come to New York tell him front of his boss, you cheating me." And I was trying to calm her down, make her be quiet, while telling the stockbroker, "I can't tolerate any more excuses. If I don't receive the check immediately, I am going to have to speak to your manager when I'm in New York next week." And sure enough, the following week there we were in front of this astonished stockbroker, and I was sitting there red-faced and quiet, and my mother, the real Mrs. Tan, was shouting at his boss in her impeccable broken English.

We used a similar routine just five days ago, for a situation that was far less humorous. My mother had gone to the hospital for an appointment, to find out about a benign brain tumor a CAT scan had revealed a month ago. She said she had spoken very good English, her best English, no mistakes. Still, she said, the hospital did not apologize when they said they had lost the CAT scan and she had come for nothing. She said they did not seem to have any sympathy when she told them she was anxious to know the exact diagnosis, since her husband and son had both died of brain tumors. She said they would not give her any more information until the next time and she would have to make another appointment for that. So she said she would not leave until the doctor called her daughter. She wouldn't budge. And when the doctor finally called her daughter, me, who spoke in perfect English — lo and behold — we had assurances the CAT scan would be found, promises that a conference call on Monday would be held, and apologies for any suffering my mother had gone through for a most regrettable mistake.

I think my mother's English almost had an effect on limiting my possibilities in life as well. Sociologists and linguists probably will tell you that a person's developing language skills are more influenced by peers. But I do think that the language spoken in the family, especially in immigrant families which are more 15 insular, plays a large role in shaping the language of the child. And I believe that it affected my results on achievement tests, IQ tests, and the SAT. While my English skills were never judged as poor, compared to math, English could not be considered my strong suit. In grade school I did moderately well, getting perhaps B's, sometimes B-pluses, in English and scoring perhaps in the sixtieth or seventieth percentile on achievement tests. But those scores were not good enough to override the opinion that my true abilities lay in math and science, because in those areas I achieved A's and scored in the ninetieth percentile or higher.

This was understandable. Math is precise; there is only one correct answer. Whereas, for me at least, the answers on English tests were always a judgment call, a matter of opinion and personal experience. Those tests were constructed around items like fill-in-the-blank sentence completion, such as "Even though Tom was _____, Mary thought he was _____." And the correct answer always seemed to be the most bland combinations of thoughts, for example, "Even though Tom was shy, Mary thought he was charming," with the grammatical structure "even though" limiting the correct answer to some sort of semantic opposites, so you wouldn't get answers like, "Even though Tom was foolish, Mary thought he was ridiculous." Well, according to my mother, there were very few limitations as to what Tom could have been and what Mary might have thought of him. So I never did well on tests like that.

The same was true with word analogies, pairs of words in which you were supposed to find some sort of logical, semantic relationship — for example, "*Sunset* is to *nightfall* as _____ is to _____." And here you would be presented with a list of four possible pairs, one of which showed the same kind of relationship: *red* is to *stoplight, bus* is to *arrival, chills* is to *fever, yawn* is to *boring*. Well, I could never think that way. I knew what the tests were asking, but I could not block out of my mind the images already created by the first pair, "*sunset* is to *nightfall*" — and I would see a burst of colors against a darkening sky, the moon rising, the lowering of a curtain of stars. And all the other pairs of words — red, bus, stoplight, boring — just threw up a mass of confusing images, making it impossible for me to sort out something as logical as saying: "A sunset precedes nightfall" is the same as "a chill precedes a fever." The only way I would have gotten that answer right would have been to imagine an associative situation, for example, my being disobedient and staying out past sunset, catching a chill at night, which turns into feverish pneumonia as punishment, indeed did happen to me.

I have thinking about all this lately, about my mother's English, about achievement tests. Because lately I've been asked, as a writer, why there are not more Asian Americans represented in American literature. Why are there few Asian Americans enrolled in creative writing programs? Why do so many Chinese students go into engineering? Well, these are broad sociological questions I can't begin to answer. But I have noticed in surveys — in fact, just last week — that Asian students, as a whole, always do significantly better on math achievement tests than in English. And this makes me think that there are other Asian-American students whose English spoken in the home might also be described as "broken" or "limited." And perhaps they also have teachers who are steering them away from writing and into math and science, which is what happened to me.

Fortunately, I happen to be rebellious in nature and enjoy the challenge of disproving assumptions made about me. I became an English-major my first year in college, after being enrolled as pre-med. I started writing nonfiction as a free-lancer the week after I was told by my former boss that writing was my worst skill and I should hone my talents toward account management.

But it wasn't until 1985 that I finally began to write fiction. And at first I   20 wrote using what I thought to be wittily crafted sentences, sentences that would finally prove I had mastery over the English language. Here's an example from the first draft of a story that later made its way into *The Joy Luck Club*, but without this line: "That was my mental quandary in its nascent state." A terrible line, which I can barely pronounce.

Fortunately, for reasons I won't get into today, I later decided I should envision a reader for the stories I would write. And the reader I decided upon was my mother, because these were stories about mothers. So with this reader in mind — and in fact she did read my early drafts — I began to write stories using all the Englishes I grew up with: the English I spoke to my mother, which for lack of a better term might be described as "simple"; the English she used with me, which for lack of a better term might be described as "broken"; my translation of her Chinese, which could certainly be described as "watered down"; and what I imagined to be her translation of her Chinese if she could speak in perfect English, her internal language, and for that I sought to preserve the essence, but neither an English nor a Chinese structure. I wanted to capture what language ability tests can never reveal: her intent, her passion, her imagery, the rhythms of her speech, and the nature of her thoughts.

Apart from what any critic had to say about my writing, I knew I had succeeded where it counted when my mother finished reading my book and gave me her verdict: "So easy to read."

Exploring the Text

1. Amy Tan opens her essay with "I am not a scholar of English or literature" and then states, in the next paragraph, "I am a writer." What is the difference? Is she appealing to ethos, logos, or pathos?
2. At several points in her essay, Tan relates anecdotes. How do they further her argument? Be sure to consider the anecdotes regarding Tan's giving a speech, the stockbroker, the CAT scan, and Tan's experience with the SATs. What would be the impact of omitting one of these anecdotes?
3. What is Tan's strategy in including a direct quotation from her mother (para. 6) rather than paraphrasing what she said?

4. Tan criticizes herself twice in this essay. In paragraph 3, she quotes a speech she gave "filled with carefully wrought grammatical phrases, burdened, it suddenly seemed to me, with nominalized forms, past perfect tenses, conditional phrases." What are nominalized forms, past perfect tenses, and conditional phrases? Why are they burdensome? At another point, Tan recalls a draft of *The Joy Luck Club* in which she wrote, "That was my mental quandary in its nascent state" (para. 20). Why does she call this a "terrible line"?

5. Tan divides the essay into three sections. Why? If there were no breaks, would the three sections be clear?

6. Why does Tan believe that envisioning a reader — specifically, her mother — encouraged her to write more authentically?

7. How would you describe Tan's attitude toward her mother in this essay?

8. Discuss how Tan broadens the essay to have relevance beyond her personal experience. How does she raise issues that are germane to a group as well as to herself?

From *Decolonising the Mind*

Ngugi wa Thiong'o

> Born in 1938 as James Thiong'o Ngugi, this celebrated novelist, playwright, and social critic changed his name to Ngugi wa Thiong'o to renounce the colonial ties of British-ruled Kenya, his birthplace. His family was active in the Mau-Mau war of independence, the subject of Ngugi's early works. He was educated at Makerere University in Kampala, Uganda, and the University of Leeds in England. A prolific fiction writer early in his career, he published *Weep Not, Child* (1964), *The River Between* (1965), and *A Grain of Wheat* (1967). Ngugi wrote these works in English, but in the 1970s he began writing and staging plays in his native Gikuyu language. This action, along with his harsh depiction of neocolonial Kenya in the novel *Petals of Blood* (1977), resulted in his arrest and imprisonment. Through efforts of human rights organizations, he was released, but he left Kenya in self-exile in 1982. He lived and traveled in Europe and the United States, and taught at New York University from 1993 until 2002, when he returned to Kenya. His nonfiction works include *Penpoints, Gunpoints, and Dreams: Towards a Critical Theory of African Americans and the State of Africa* (1998) and *Decolonising the Mind: The Politics of Language in African Literature* (1986), the source of the following selection on the interrelationship of language, power, and culture.

I

I was born into a large peasant family: father, four wives and about twenty-eight children. I also belonged, as we all did in those days, to a wider extended family and to the community as a whole.

We spoke Gĩkũyũ as we worked in the fields. We spoke Gĩkũyũ in and outside the home. I can vividly recall those evenings of storytelling around the fireside. It was mostly the grown-ups telling the children but everybody was interested and involved. We children would re-tell the stories the following day to other children who worked in the fields picking the pyrethrum flowers, tea-leaves or coffee beans of our European and African landlords.

The stories, with mostly animals as the main characters, were all told in Gĩkũyũ. Hare, being small, weak but full of innovative wit and cunning, was our hero. We identified with him as he struggled against the brutes of prey like lion, leopard, hyena. His victories were our victories and we learnt that the apparently weak can outwit the strong. We followed the animals in their struggle against hostile nature — drought, rain, sun, wind — a confrontation often forcing them to search for forms of co-operation. But we were also interested in their struggles amongst themselves, and particularly between the beasts and the victims of prey. These twin struggles, against nature and other animals, reflected real-life struggles in the human world.

Not that we neglected stories with human beings as the main characters. There were two types of characters in such human-centred narratives: the species of truly human beings with qualities of courage, kindness, mercy, hatred of evil, concern for others; and a man-eat-man two-mouthed species with qualities of greed, selfishness, individualism and hatred of what was good for the larger co-operative community. Co-operation as the ultimate good in a community was a constant theme. It could unite human beings with animals against ogres and beasts of prey, as in the story of how dove, after being fed with castor-oil seeds, was sent to fetch a smith working far away from home and whose pregnant wife was being threatened by these man-eating two-mouthed ogres.

There were good and bad story-tellers. A good one could tell the same story over and over again, and it would always be fresh to us, the listeners. He or she could tell a story told by someone else and make it more alive and dramatic. The differences really were in the use of words and images and the inflexion of voices to effect different tones.

We therefore learnt to value words for their meaning and nuances. Language was not a mere string of words. It had a suggestive power well beyond the imme-diate and lexical meaning. Our appreciation of the suggestive magical power of language was reinforced by the games we played with words through riddles, proverbs, transpositions of syllables, or through nonsensical but musically ar-ranged words.[1] So we learnt the music of our language on top of the content. The language, through images and symbols, gave us a view of the world, but it had a

5

---

[1]Example from a tongue twister: "Kaana ka Nikoora koona koora koora: na ko koora koona kaana ka Nikoora koora koora." I'm indebted to Wangui wa Goro for this example. "Nichola's child saw a baby frog and ran away: and when the baby frog saw Nichola's child it also ran

beauty of its own. The home and the field were then our pre-primary school but what is important, for this discussion, is that the language of our evening teach-ins, and the language of our immediate and wider community, and the language of our work in the fields were one.

And then I went to school, a colonial school, and this harmony was broken. The language of my education was no longer the language of my culture. I first went to Kamaandura, missionary run, and then to another called Maanguuū run by nationalists grouped around the Gĩkũyũ Independent and Karinga Schools Association. Our language of education was still Gĩkũyũ. The very first time I was ever given an ovation for my writing was over a composition in Gĩkũyũ. So for my first four years there was still harmony between the language of my formal educa-tion and that of the Limuru peasant community.

It was after the declaration of a state of emergency over Kenya in 1952 that all the schools run by patriotic nationalists were taken over by the colonial regime and were placed under District Education Boards chaired by Englishmen. English became the language of my formal education. In Kenya, English became more than a language: it was *the* language, and all the others had to bow before it in deference.

Thus one of the most humiliating experiences was to be caught speaking Gĩ-kũyũ in the vicinity of the school. The culprit was given corporal punishment — three to five strokes of the cane on bare buttocks — or was made to carry a metal plate around the neck with inscriptions such as I AM STUPID or I AM A DONKEY. Sometimes the culprits were fined money they could hardly afford. And how did the teachers catch the culprits? A button was initially given to one pupil who was supposed to hand it over to whoever was caught speaking his mother tongue. Whoever had the button at the end of the day would sing who had given it to him and the ensuing process would bring out all the culprits of the day. Thus children were turned into witch-hunters and in the process were being taught the lucrative value of being a traitor to one's immediate community.

The attitude to English was the exact opposite: any achievement in spoken or written English was highly rewarded; prizes, prestige, applause; the ticket to higher realms. English became the measure of intelligence and ability in the arts, the sciences, and all the other branches of learning. English became *the* main determinant of a child's progress up the ladder of formal education.

As you may know, the colonial system of education in addition to its apart-heid racial demarcation had the structure of a pyramid: a broad primary base, a narrowing secondary middle, and an even narrower university apex. Selections from primary into secondary were through an examination, in my time called Kenya African Preliminary Examination, in which one had to pass six subjects

10

---

away." A Gĩkũyũ speaking child has to get the correct tone and length of vowel and pauses to get it right. Otherwise it becomes a jumble of *k*'s and *r*'s and *na*'s.

ranging from Maths to Nature Study and Kiswahili. All the papers were written in English. Nobody could pass the exam who failed the English language paper no matter how brilliantly he had done in the other subjects. I remember one boy in my class of 1954 who had distinctions in all subjects except English, which he had failed. He was made to fail the entire exam. He went on to become a turn boy in a bus company. I who had only passes but a credit in English got a place at the Alliance High School, one of the most elitist institutions for Africans in colonial Kenya. The requirements for a place at the University, Makerere University College, were broadly the same: nobody could go on to wear the undergraduate red gown, no matter how brilliantly they had performed in all the other subjects unless they had a credit — not even a simple pass! — in English. Thus the most coveted place in the pyramid and in the system was only available to the holder of an English language credit card. English was the official vehicle and the magic formula to colonial elitedom.

Literary education was now determined by the dominant language while also reinforcing that dominance. Orature (oral literature) in Kenyan languages stopped. In primary school I now read simplified Dickens and Stevenson alongside Rider Haggard. Jim Hawkins, Oliver Twist, Tom Brown — not Hare, Leopard and Lion — were now my daily companions in the world of imagination. In secondary school, Scott and G. B. Shaw vied with more Rider Haggard, John Buchan, Alan Paton, Captain W. E. Johns. At Makerere I read English: from Chaucer to T. S. Eliot with a touch of Graham Greene.

Thus language and literature were taking us further and further from ourselves to other selves, from our world to other worlds.

What was the colonial system doing to us Kenyan children? What were the consequences of, on the one hand, this systematic suppression of our languages and the literature they carried, and on the other the elevation of English and the literature it carried? To answer those questions, let me first examine the relationship of language to human experience, human culture, and the human perception of reality.

II

Language, any language, has a dual character: it is both a means of communication and a carrier of culture. Take English. It is spoken in Britain and in Sweden and Denmark. But for Swedish and Danish people English is only a means of communication with non-Scandinavians. It is not a carrier of their culture. For the British, and particularly the English, it is additionally, and inseparably from its use as a tool of communication, a carrier of their culture and history. Or take Swahili in East and Central Africa. It is widely used as a means of communication across many nationalities. But it is not the carrier of a culture and history of many of those nationalities. However in parts of Kenya and Tanzania, and particularly in Zanzibar, Swahili is inseparably both a means of communication and a carrier of the culture of those people to whom it is a mother-tongue.

15

Language as communication has three aspects or elements. There is first what Karl Marx once called the language of real life,[2] the element basic to the whole notion of language, its origins and development: that is, the relations people enter into with one another in the labour process, the links they necessarily establish among themselves in the act of a people, a community of human beings, producing wealth or means of life like food, clothing, houses. A human community really starts its historical being as a community of co-operation in production through the division of labour; the simplest is between man, woman and child within a household; the more complex divisions are between branches of production such as those who are sole hunters, sole gatherers of fruits or sole workers in metal. Then there are the most complex divisions such as those in modern factories where a single product, say a shirt or a shoe, is the result of many hands and minds. Production is co-operation, is communication, is language, is expression of a relation between human beings and it is specifically human.

The second aspect of language as communication is speech and it imitates the language of real life, that is communication in production. The verbal signposts both reflect and aid communication or the relations established between human beings in the production of their means of life. Language as a system of verbal signposts makes that production possible. The spoken word is to relations between human beings what the hand is to the relations between human beings and nature. The hand through tools mediates between human beings and nature and forms the language of real life: spoken words mediate between human beings and form the language of speech.

The third aspect is the written signs. The written word imitates the spoken. Where the first two aspects of language as communication through the hand and the spoken word historically evolved more or less simultaneously, the written aspect is a much later historical development. Writing is representation of sounds with visual symbols, from the simplest knot among shepherds to tell the number in a herd or the hieroglyphics among the Agĩkũyũ gicaandi singers and poets of Kenya, to the most complicated and different letter and picture writing systems of the world today.

In most societies the written and the spoken languages are the same, in that they represent each other: what is on paper can be read to another person and be

---

[2]"The production of ideas, of conceptions, of consciousness, is at first directly interwoven with the material activity and the material intercourse of men, the language of real life. Conceiving, thinking, the mental intercourse of men, appear at this stage as the direct efflux of their material behaviour. The same applies to mental production as expressed in the language of politics, laws, morality, religion, metaphysics, etc., of a people. Men are the producers of their conceptions, ideas etc. — real, active men, as they are conditioned by a definite development of their productive forces and of the intercourse corresponding to these, up to its furthest form." Marx and Engels, German Ideology, the first part published under the title, *Feuerbach: Opposition of the Materialist and Idealist Outlooks*, London: 1973, p. 8.

received as that language which the recipient has grown up speaking. In such a society there is broad harmony for a child between the three aspects of language as communication. His interaction with nature and with other men is expressed in written and spoken symbols or signs which are both a result of that double interaction and a reflection of it. The association of the child's sensibility is with the language of his experience of life.

But there is more to it: communication between human beings is also the   20 basis and process of evolving culture. In doing similar kinds of things and actions over and over again under similar circumstances, similar even in their mutability, certain patterns, moves, rhythms, habits, attitudes, experiences and knowledge emerge. Those experiences are handed over to the next generation and become the inherited basis for their further actions on nature and on themselves. There is a gradual accumulation of values which in time become almost self-evident truths governing their conception of what is right and wrong, good and bad, beautiful and ugly, courageous and cowardly, generous and mean in their internal and external relations. Over a time this becomes a way of life distinguishable from other ways of life. They develop a distinctive culture and history. Culture embodies those moral, ethical and aesthetic values, the set of spiritual eyeglasses, through which they come to view themselves and their place in the universe. Values are the basis of a people's identity, their sense of particularity as members of the human race. All this is carried by language. Language as culture is the collective memory bank of a people's experience in history. Culture is almost indistinguishable from the language that makes possible its genesis, growth, banking, articulation and indeed its transmission from one generation to the next.

Language as culture also has three important aspects. Culture is a product of the history which it in turn reflects. Culture in other words is a product and a reflection of human beings communicating with one another in the very struggle to create wealth and to control it. But culture does not merely reflect that history, or rather it does so by actually forming images or pictures of the world of nature and nurture. Thus the second aspect of language as culture is as an image-forming agent in the mind of a child. Our whole conception of ourselves as a people, individually and collectively, is based on those pictures and images which may or may not correctly correspond to the actual reality of the struggles with nature and nurture which produced them in the first place. But our capacity to confront the world creatively is dependent on how those images correspond or not to that reality, how they distort or clarify the reality of our struggles. Language as culture is thus mediating between me and my own self; between my own self and other selves; between me and nature. Language is mediating in my very being. And this brings us to the third aspect of language as culture. Culture transmits or imparts those images of the world and reality through the spoken and the written language, that is through a specific language. In other words, the capacity to speak, the capacity to order sounds in a manner that makes for mutual comprehension between human beings is universal. This is the universality of language, a quality specific to human beings. It corresponds to the universality of the struggle against nature and that between human beings. But the particularity of sounds, the words, the word order into phrases and sentences, and the specific manner, or laws, of their ordering is what distinguishes one language from another. Thus a specific culture is not transmitted through language in its universality but in its particularity as the language of a specific community with a specific history. Written literature and orature are the main means by which a particular language transmits the images of the world contained in the culture it carries.

Language as communication and as culture are then products of each other. Communication creates culture: culture is a means of communication. Language carries culture, and culture carries, particularly through orature and literature, the entire body of values by which we come to perceive ourselves and our place in the world. How people perceive themselves affects how they look at their culture, at their politics and at the social production of wealth, at their entire relationship to nature and to other beings. Language is thus inseparable from ourselves as a community of human beings with a specific form and character, a specific history, a specific relationship to the world.

III

So what was the colonialist imposition of a foreign language doing to us children?

The real aim of colonialism was to control the people's wealth: what they produced, how they produced it, and how it was distributed; to control, in other words, the entire realm of the language of real life. Colonialism imposed its control of the social production of wealth through military conquest and subsequent political dictatorship. But its most important area of domination was the mental universe of the colonised, the control, through culture, of how people perceived themselves and their relationship to the world. Economic and political control can never be complete or effective without mental control. To control a people's culture is to control their tools of self-definition in relationship to others.

For colonialism this involved two aspects of the same process: the destruc-   25
tion or the deliberate undervaluing of a people's culture, their art, dances, religions, history, geography, education, orature and literature, and the conscious elevation of the language of the coloniser. The domination of a people's language by the languages of the colonising nations was crucial to the domination of the mental universe of the colonised.

Take language as communication. Imposing a foreign language, and suppressing the native languages as spoken and written, were already breaking the harmony previously existing between the African child and the three aspects of language. Since the new language as a means of communication was a product of and was reflecting the "real language of life" elsewhere, it could never as spoken or written properly reflect or imitate the real life of that community. This may in part explain why technology always appears to us as slightly external; *their* product and not *ours*. The word "missile" used to hold an alien far-away sound until I recently learnt its equivalent in Gīkūyū, *ngurukuhi*, and it made me apprehend it differently. Learning, for a colonial child, became a cerebral activity and not an emotionally felt experience.

But since the new, imposed languages could never completely break the native languages as spoken, their most effective area of domination was the third aspect of language as communication, the written. The language of an African child's formal education was foreign. The language of the books he read was foreign. The language of his conceptualisation was foreign. Thought, in him, took the visible form of a foreign language. So the written language of a child's upbringing in the school (even his spoken language within the school compound) became divorced from his spoken language at home. There was often not the slightest relationship between the child's written world, which was also the language of his schooling, and the world of his immediate environment in the family and the community. For a colonial child, the harmony existing between the three aspects of language as communication was irrevocably broken. This resulted in the disassociation of the sensibility of that child from his natural and social environment, what we might call colonial alienation. The alienation became reinforced in the teaching of history, geography, music, where bourgeois Europe was always the centre of the universe.

This disassociation, divorce, or alienation from the immediate environment becomes clearer when you look at colonial language as a carrier of culture.

Since culture is a product of the history of a people which it in turn reflects, the child was now being exposed exclusively to a culture that was a product of a world external to himself. He was being made to stand outside himself to look at himself. *Catching Them Young* is the title of a book on racism, class, sex, and politics in children's literature by Bob Dixon. "Catching them young" as an aim was even more true of a colonial child. The images of this world and his place in it implanted in a child take years to eradicate, if they ever can be.

Since culture does not just reflect the world in images but actually, through those very images, conditions a child to see that world in a certain way, the colonial child was made to see the world and where he stands in it as seen and defined by or reflected in the culture of the language of imposition. 30

And since those images are mostly passed on through orature and literature it meant the child would now only see the world as seen in the literature of his language of adoption. From the point of view of alienation, that is of seeing oneself from outside oneself as if one was another self, it does not matter that the imported literature carried the great humanist tradition of the best in Shakespeare, Goethe, Balzac, Tolstoy, Gorky, Brecht, Sholokhov, Dickens. The location of this great mirror of imagination was necessarily Europe and its history and culture and the rest of the universe was seen from that centre.

But obviously it was worse when the colonial child was exposed to images of his world as mirrored in the written languages of his coloniser. Where his own native languages were associated in his impressionable mind with low status, humiliation, corporal punishment, slow-footed intelligence and ability or downright stupidity, non-intelligibility and barbarism, this was reinforced by the world he met in the works of such geniuses of racism as a Rider Haggard or a Nicholas Monsarrat; not to mention the pronouncement of some of the giants of western intellectual and political establishment, such as Hume (". . . the negro is naturally inferior to the whites . . ."),[3] Thomas Jefferson (". . . the blacks . . . are inferior to the whites on the endowments of both body and mind . . ."),[4] or Hegel with his Africa comparable to a land of childhood still enveloped in the dark mantle of the night as far as the development of self-conscious history was concerned. Hegel's statement that there was nothing harmonious with humanity to be found in the African character is representative of the racist images of Africans and Africa such a colonial child was bound to encounter in the literature of the colonial languages.[5] The results could be disastrous.

Exploring the Text

1. Ngugi wa Thiong'o begins this excerpt with stories of his childhood. What is his purpose in starting out this way? How does this strategy contribute to the effectiveness of the argument he is building?
2. In paragraph 6, Ngugi begins, "We therefore learnt to value words for their meaning and nuances"; "therefore" signals a logical conclusion. Construct the logical chain of reasoning that leads to "therefore."
3. Footnote 1 offers an example of a Gĩkũyũ tongue twister. How does the information in the footnote contribute to achieving Ngugi's purpose? Why does the author not include it as a paragraph within the essay?
4. What does Ngugi mean in paragraph 7 when he says, "The language of my education was no longer the language of my culture"?

---

[3]Quoted in Eric Williams *A History of the People of Trinidad and Tobago*, London: 1964, p. 32.
[4]Eric Williams, ibid., p. 31.
[5]In references to Africa in the introduction to his lectures in *The Philosophy of History*, Hegel gives historical, philosophical, rational expression and legitimacy to every conceivable European racist myth about Africa. Africa is even denied her own geography where it does not correspond to the myth. Thus Egypt is not part of Africa; and North Africa is part of Europe. Africa proper is the especial home of ravenous beasts, snakes of all kinds. The African is not part of humanity. Only slavery to Europe can raise him, possibly, to the lower ranks of humanity. Slavery is good for the African. "Slavery is in and for itself *injustice*, for the essence of humanity is *freedom*; but for this man must be matured. The gradual abolition of slavery is therefore wiser and more equitable than its sudden removal." (Hegel *The Philosophy of History*, Dover edition, New York: 1956, pp. 91–99.) Hegel clearly reveals himself as the nineteenth-century Hitler of the intellect.

5. Do you think Ngugi is being unduly harsh when he asserts, "Thus children were turned into witch-hunters and in the process were being taught the lucrative value of being a traitor to one's immediate community" (para. 9)? Explain your response.

6. At the end of section I, Ngugi asks two questions (para. 14). In what ways does section II provide a framework for him to answer those questions? How does section II lay the foundation for section III?

7. What are the "three aspects or elements" of language as communication and language as culture that Ngugi discusses (para. 15)?

8. What does Ngugi mean by "the set of spiritual eyeglasses" in this statement: "Culture embodies those moral, ethical and aesthetic values, the set of spiritual eyeglasses, through which [human beings] come to view themselves and their place in the universe" (para. 20)?

9. What is the purpose of footnote 5, where Ngugi calls the German philosopher Hegel "the nineteenth-century Hitler of the intellect"? Would the tone of the essay change if this assertion was part of the body of the text?

10. Does Ngugi appeal principally to logos or pathos in this piece? Cite specific passages to support your response.

11. Ngugi argues that a specific culture can be transmitted only through the language native to that culture. Explain why you agree or disagree. Take into account American immigrant cultures where the generation born in the United States is no longer fluent in the original language.

12. Compare and contrast the viewpoints of Richard Rodriguez in "Aria" (p. 509) and of Ngugi wa Thiong'o in this essay. How are the experiences of the immigrant and the colonized similar and different?

Always Living in Spanish

Marjorie Agosín

Human rights activist, author, and professor at Wellesley College, Marjorie Agosín (b. 1955) is a descendant of Russian and Austrian Jews. She was born in Maryland and raised in Chile, but she left for the United States with her parents when the dictator Augusto Pinochet overthrew the government of Salvador Allende. Agosín's writings reflect her heritage, especially the experience of Jewish refugees, and she has received international acclaim for her work on behalf of poor women in developing countries. Agosín has written many books of fiction, memoirs, poetry, and essays. These include the collection of bilingual poems entitled *Dear Anne Frank* (1994); *A Cross and a Star: Memoirs of a Jewish Girl in Chile* (1995), about her mother; *Always from Somewhere Else: A Memoir of My Chilean Jewish Father* (1998); and *At the Threshold of Memory: New and Selected Poems* (2003). In the following essay, written in 1999, Agosín explores the passionate connection she feels with Spanish, her first language.

In the evenings in the northern hemisphere, I repeat the ancient ritual that I observed as a child in the southern hemisphere: going out while the night is still warm and trying to recognize the stars as it begins to grow dark silently. In the sky of my country, Chile, that long and wide stretch of land that the poets blessed and dictators abused, I could easily name the stars: the three Marias, the Southern Cross, and the three Lilies, names of beloved and courageous women.

But here in the United States, where I have lived since I was a young girl, the solitude of exile makes me feel that so little is mine, that not even the sky has the same constellations, the trees and the fauna the same names or sounds, or the rubbish the same smell. How does one recover the familiar? How does one name the unfamiliar? How can one be another or live in a foreign language? These are the dilemmas of one who writes in Spanish and lives in translation.

Since my earliest childhood in Chile I lived with the tempos and the melodies of a multiplicity of tongues: German, Yiddish, Russian, Turkish, and many Latin songs. Because everyone was from somewhere else, my relatives laughed, sang, and fought in a Babylon of languages. Spanish was reserved for matters of extreme seriousness, for commercial transactions, or for illnesses, but everyone's mother tongue was always associated with the memory of spaces inhabited in the past: the shtetl, the flowering and vast Vienna avenues, the minarets of Turkey, and the Ladino whispers of Toledo. When my paternal grandmother sang old songs in Turkish, her voice and body assumed the passion of one who was there in the city of Istanbul, gazing by turns toward the west and the east.

Destiny and the always ambiguous nature of history continued my family's enforced migration, and because of it I, too, became one who had to live and speak in translation. The disappearances, torture, and clandestine deaths in my country in the early seventies drove us to the United States, that other America that looked with suspicion at those who did not speak English and especially those who came from the supposedly uncivilized regions of Latin America. I had left a dangerous place that was my home, only to arrive in a dangerous place that was not: a high school in the small town of Athens, Georgia, where my poor English and my accent were the cause of ridicule and insult. The only way I could recover my usurped country and my Chilean childhood was by continuing to write in Spanish, the same way my grandparents had sung in their own tongues in diasporic sites.

The new and learned English language did not fit with the visceral emotions and themes that my poetry contained, but by writing in Spanish I could recover fragrances, spoken rhythms, and the passion of my own identity. Daily I felt the need to translate myself for the strangers living all around me, to tell them why we were in Georgia, why we ate differently, why we had fled, why my accent was so thick, and why I did not look Hispanic. Only at night, writing poems in Spanish, could I return to my senses, and soothe my own sorrow over what I had left behind.

This is how I became a Chilean poet who wrote in Spanish and lived in the southern United States. And then, one day, a poem of mine was translated and published in the English language. Finally, for the first time since I had left Chile,

I felt I didn't have to explain myself. My poem, expressed in another language, spoke for itself . . . and for me.

Sometimes the austere sounds of English help me bear the solitude of knowing that I am foreign and so far away from those about whom I write. I must admit I would like more opportunities to read in Spanish to people whose language and culture is also mine, to join in our common heritage and in the feast of our sounds. I would also like readers of English to understand the beauty of the spoken word in Spanish, that constant flow of oxytonic and paraoxytonic syllables (*Verde que te quiero verdo*), the joy of writing — of dancing — in another language. I believe that many exiles share the unresolvable torment of not being able to live in the language of their childhood.

I miss that undulating and sensuous language of mine, those baroque descriptions, the sense of being and feeling that Spanish gives me. It is perhaps for this reason that I have chosen and will always choose to write in Spanish. Nothing else from my childhood world remains. My country seems to be frozen in gestures of silence and oblivion. My relatives have died, and I have grown up not knowing a young generation of cousins and nieces and nephews. Many of my friends disappeared, others were tortured, and the most fortunate, like me, became guardians of memory. For us, to write in Spanish is to always be in active pursuit of memory. I seek to recapture a world lost to me on that sorrowful afternoon when the blue electric sky and the Andean cordillera bade me farewell. On that, my last Chilean day, I carried under my arm my innocence recorded in a little blue notebook I kept even then. Gradually that diary filled with memoranda, poems written in free verse, descriptions of dreams and of the thresholds of my house surrounded by cherry trees and gardenias. To write in Spanish is for me a gesture of survival. And because of translation, my memory has now become a part of the memory of many others.

Translators are not traitors, as the proverb says, but rather splendid friends in this great human community of language.

Exploring the Text

1. How would you describe Marjorie Agosín's opening strategy in the first two paragraphs? How effective are the two paragraphs in capturing the reader's attention and establishing the author's ethos?
2. What does Agosín mean by the allusion to "a Babylon of languages" (para. 3)?
3. What is the effect of the following statement, an example of antithesis, by Agosín: "I had left a dangerous place that was my home, only to arrive in a dangerous place that was not" (para. 4)?
4. Why is the first translation of a poem of Agosín's meaningful for her?
5. List the ways Agosín describes Spanish. How would you describe these descriptive terms? Contrast these descriptions with the way Agosín refers to English. How do the differences contribute to the effectiveness of her essay?

6. What is Agosín's thesis, or claim, in this essay? Find a sentence that seems closest to a directly stated thesis.

7. What does Agosín mean when she says, "To write in Spanish is for me a gesture of survival" (para. 8)?

8. How would you describe the tone of this essay? Cite specific passages to support your response.

9. This essay was published in *Poets & Writers*, a magazine for writers. Discuss why and how Agosín appeals to this audience.

10. Agosín alludes to the way her "grandparents had sung in their own tongues in diasporic sites" (para. 4). What does she mean by "diasporic sites"? Are they literal geographical places? Discuss the concept of diaspora as it applies to a group in the contemporary world (for example, the African diaspora, the Chinese diaspora).

Studying Islam, Strengthening the Nation

PETER BERKOWITZ AND MICHAEL McFAUL

Peter Berkowitz (b. 1959) teaches at George Mason University School of Law in Virginia. He has written widely on topics related to American constitutionalism and the Middle East. Michael McFaul (b. 1963) teaches in the department of political science at Stanford University. An associate at the Carnegie Endowment for International Peace and a well-known scholar and author, McFaul is an expert on United States–Russian relations and on American efforts to promote democracy abroad. Both Berkowitz and McFaul are research fellows at the Hoover Institution on War, Revolution, and Peace, a public policy research center at Stanford University. The following essay appeared in the *Washington Post* in 2005.

It remains painfully true, more than three years after Sept. 11, that even highly educated Americans know little about the Arab Middle East. And it is embarrassing how little our universities have changed to educate our nation and train experts on the wider Middle East.

For believers in a good liberal arts education, it has long been a source of consternation that faculties in political science, history, economics and sociology lack scholars who know Arabic or Persian and understand Islam. Since Sept. 11 it has become clear that this abdication of responsibility is more than an educational problem: It also poses a threat to our national security.

The case for bolstering faculty and curriculum resources devoted to the Muslim Middle East is, of course, obvious from an educational perspective. The region is vast. Islam represents one of the world's great religions and provides not only an intellectual feast for comparative study in the social sciences and humanities but also an indispensable comparison and contrast for more familiar religions and ways of life. Particularly in the era of globalization and the information revolution, there is little excuse for universities' continuing to betray the liberal ideal of educating students in the ways of all people.

Our national security interest in this area should also be obvious. As in the Cold War, the war against Islamic extremism will not be won in months or years but in decades. And as in the Cold War, the non-military components of the war will play a crucial role.

To fight the decades-long battle against communism, the United States invested billions in education and intelligence. The U.S. government sponsored centers of Soviet studies, provided foreign-language scholarships in Russian and Eastern European languages, and offered dual-competency grants to enable graduate students to acquire expertise both in security issues and in Russian culture.

In the early days of the Cold War, a mere handful of Soviet experts dominated scholarship and policy debates. Not coincidentally, this was the time when we made some of our greatest mistakes, such as treating the communist world as a monolithic bloc and considering all communist regimes to have the same degree of internal dissent. By the end of the Cold War, however, the effort to "know the enemy" had resulted in the training of tens of thousands of professors, government analysts and policymakers. Every interpretation of Soviet society or Kremlin behavior triggered an informed and exhaustive debate.

Today, there is not one tenured professor in the departments of political science at Harvard, Princeton, Stanford, Chicago or Yale universities who specializes in the politics of the wider Middle East. Some scholars do study Islam and the languages and countries of the people who profess it. Programs in and outside of universities aimed at comprehending and combating Islamic extremism also exist, but they are woefully underdeveloped and changing at a snail's pace. Everyone now recognizes that we lack "human intelligence" — covert agents, spies and informants — in the Middle East. But we also suffer from shortages of NSA linguists, academic scholars, and senior policymakers trained in the languages, cultures, politics and economics of the wider Middle East.

It is time to recognize our ignorance and address it. Universities, working in tandem with government and foundations, should take immediate steps. And in doing so, they should resist the temptation to simply amend existing faculties with programs in Middle Eastern studies centers that are not rooted firmly in the established faculties of the university. Programs set up this way promote a kind of intellectual ghettoization because of the misguided assumption from which they and the multitude of special-interest programs that have sprung up around the university derive: that in each area of human affairs there is a methodology distinctive to it.

Universities should encourage the study of Islam from within the various social sciences and humanities, the better to promote truly interdisciplinary conversation. And they should avoid concentrating resources on the Israeli-Palestinian conflict. The disproportionate weight it is often given in Middle East studies programs reflects the poisonous political proposition that Israel is the root source of all the ills that beset the Muslim world. Teaching and inquiry in the university must remain, to the extent possible, nonpolitical.

Universities need to make a priority of teaching Arabic, Persian and Turkish, 10 and it should be done not by part-time adjunct faculty but by tenured professors. The study of language opens doors to culture, history and politics. It disciplines the mind, and allows people to reach out to foreigners by showing them the respect that inheres in addressing them in their mother tongue.

It will not be easy to find the necessary faculty. During the Cold War, universities could draw on a pool of extraordinary European émigrés. But in educating scholars of the Muslim Middle East, we must start almost from scratch. We can provide incentives to bring PhD candidates from the region to study at U.S. universities, but we must understand that filling the large gaps in our universities is the work of a generation.

As for government, it should immediately foster a dramatic expansion of fellowships for graduate students to study Arabic, Persian and Turkish. And the government ought to provide grants to universities to fund undergraduate education in Islam. These investments would be a drop in the bucket of the federal budget and would bring huge rewards.

Major foundations can play their role, too, by, for example, creating mid-career fellowships for senior faculty in the social sciences and humanities to obtain new competencies in the study of the Islamic world. They could also use their financial leverage to endow new chairs in the study of the wider Middle East.

Dramatically increasing opportunities for the study of Arabic, Persian, Turkish and Islam in our universities is the right thing to do, to advance the cause of learning and America's interest in training people who can contribute to the spread of liberty abroad. We owe it to our universities to demand that they live up to their responsibility.

Exploring the Text

1. What rhetorical strategies do the authors use in the opening two paragraphs to establish a need for action and to stress the urgency of the problem they are about to discuss?

2. Why do Peter Berkowitz and Michael McFaul believe that studying Arabic, Persian, and Turkish is essential to understanding the Middle East?

3. Essential to the authors' argument are certain assumptions about the purpose and value of a liberal arts education. What are at least two of these assumptions?

4. Although the authors make what seems to be a straightforward argument, they make a number of appeals to pathos. Identify several of these appeals, and discuss their effectiveness.

5. Analyze the organizational structure of this essay. Consider the definition of the problem, counterarguments, supporting evidence, and proposed solution. Explain

why you do or do not find the organization effective. Could parts of the argument have been deleted? Or should parts have been expanded?

6. Would you characterize the authors' argument as one of values, policy, or fact? Explain, with reference to specific elements of the text.

7. What is the authors' tone in this essay? Discuss why it is appropriate to the purpose and audience.

8. Research whether some of the colleges and universities in your area — or those you are considering attending — have a foreign-language requirement for under-graduates. How many courses are usually required? What languages are offered? What do you think of the language requirements (or lack of them)?

Bilingualism in America: English Should Be the Official Language

S. I. HAYAKAWA

Samuel Ichiye Hayakawa (1906–1992) was born to Japanese immigrant parents in Vancouver, Canada. After receiving both a BA and an MA in Canada, he did his doctoral work at the University of Wisconsin. He had a distinguished academic career that culminated in his appointment as president of San Francisco State College in 1968. There he gained national attention for quelling student riots during the late 1960s. Then, from 1977 to 1983, he served as a U.S. senator from California. As senator, he introduced the English Language Amendment, an effort to make English the nation's official language. He is the author of several critically acclaimed books, including *Language in Thought and Action*. Hayakawa claimed, "Bilingualism for the individual is fine, but not for a country"; the following essay, first published in *USA Today* in 1989, explores that claim.

During the dark days of World War II, Chinese immigrants in California wore badges proclaiming their original nationality so they would not be mistaken for Japanese. In fact, these two immigrant groups long had been at odds with each other. However, as new English-speaking generations came along, the Chinese and Japanese began to communicate with one another. They found they had much in common and began to socialize. Today, they get together and form Asian-American societies.

Such are the amicable results of sharing the English language. English unites us as American-immigrants and native-born alike. Communicating with each other in a single, common tongue encourages trust, while reducing racial hostility and bigotry.

My appreciation of English has led me to devote my retirement years to championing it. Several years ago, I helped to establish U.S. English, a Washington D.C.–based public interest group that seeks an amendment to the U.S. Constitution declaring English our official language, regardless of what other languages we may use unofficially.

As an immigrant to this nation, I am keenly aware of the things that bind us as Americans and unite us as a single people. Foremost among these unifying forces is the common language we share. While it is certainly true that our love of freedom and devotion to democratic principles help to unite and give us a mutual purpose, it is English, our common language, that enables us to discuss our views and allows us to maintain a well-informed electorate, the cornerstone of democratic government.

Because we are a nation of immigrants, we do not share the characteristics of 5 race, religion, ethnicity, or native language which form the common bonds of society in other countries. However, by agreeing to learn and use a single, universally spoken language, we have been able to forge a unified people from an incredibly diverse population.

Although our 200-year history should be enough to convince any skeptic of the powerful unifying effects of a common language, some still advocate the official recognition of other languages. They argue that a knowledge of English is not part of the formula for responsible citizenship in this country.

Some contemporary political leaders, like the former mayor of Miami, Maurice Ferre, maintain that "Language is not necessary to the system. Nowhere does our Constitution say that English is our language." He also told the *Tampa Tribune* that, "Within ten years there will not be a single word of English spoken [in Miami] — English is not Miami's official language — [and] one day residents will have to learn Spanish or leave."

The U.S. Department of Education also reported that countless speakers at a conference on bilingual education "expounded at length on the need for and eventually of, a multilingual, multicultural United States of America with a national language policy citing English and Spanish as the two 'legal languages.'"

As a former resident of California, I am completely familiar with a system that uses two official languages, and I would not advise any nation to move in such a direction unless forced to do so. While it is true that India functions with ten official languages, I haven't heard anyone suggest that it functions particularly well because of its multilingualism. In fact, most Indians will concede that the situation is a chaotic mess which has led to countless problems in the government's efforts to manage the nation's business. Out of necessity, English still is used extensively in India as a common language.

Belgium is another clear example of the diverse effects of two officially recog- 10 nized languages in the same nation. Linguistic differences between Dutch- and French-speaking citizens have resulted in chronic political instability. Consequently, in the aftermath of the most recent government collapse, legislators are working on a plan to turn over most of its powers and responsibilities to the various regions, a clear recognition of the diverse effects of linguistic separateness.

There are other problems. Bilingualism is a costly and confusing bureaucratic nightmare. The Canadian government has estimated its bilingual costs to be nearly $400,000,000 per year. It is almost certain that these expenses will increase as a result of a massive expansion of bilingual services approved by the Canadian Parliament in 1988. In the United States, which has ten times the population of Canada, the cost of similar bilingual services easily would be in the billions.

We first should consider how politically infeasible it is that our nation ever could recognize Spanish as a second official language without opening the floodgates for official recognition of the more than 100 languages spoken in this country. How long would it take, under such an arrangement, before the United States started to make India look like a model of efficiency?

Even if we can agree that multilingualism would be a mistake, some would suggest that official recognition of English is not needed. After all, our nation has existed for over 200 years without this, and English as our common language has continued to flourish.

I could agree with this sentiment had government continued to adhere to its time-honored practice of operating in English and encouraging newcomers to learn the language. However, this is not the case. Over the last few decades, government has been edging slowly towards policies that place other languages on a par with English.

In reaction to the cultural consciousness movement of the 1960s and 1970s, 15
government has been increasingly reluctant to press immigrants to learn the English language, lest it be accused of "cultural imperialism." Rather than insisting that it is the immigrant's duty to learn the language of this country, the government has acted instead as if it has a duty to accommodate an immigrant in his native language.

A prime example of this can be found in the continuing debate over Federal and state policies relating to bilingual education. At times, these have come dangerously close to making the main goal of this program the maintenance of the immigrant child's native language, rather than the early acquisition of English.

As a former U.S. senator from California, where we spend more on bilingual education programs than any other state, I am very familiar with both the rhetoric and reality that lie behind the current debate on bilingual education. My experience has convinced me that many of these programs are shortchanging immigrant children in their quest to learn English.

To set the record straight from the start, I do not oppose bilingual education *if it is truly bilingual.* Employing a child's native language to teach him (or her) English is entirely appropriate. What is not appropriate is continuing to use the children of Hispanic and other immigrant groups as guinea pigs in an unproven program that fails to teach English efficiently and perpetuates their dependency on their native language.

Under the dominant method of bilingual education used throughout this country, non-English-speaking students are taught all academic subjects such as math, science, and history exclusively in their native language. English is taught as a separate subject. The problem with this method is that there is no objective way to measure whether a child has learned enough English to be placed in classes where academic instruction is entirely in English. As a result, some children have been kept in native language classes for six years.

Some bilingual education advocates, who are more concerned with main- 20 taining the child's use of their native language, may not see any problem with such a situation. However, those who feel that the most important goal of this program is to get children functioning quickly in English appropriately are alarmed.

In the Newhall School District in California, some Hispanic parents are raising their voices in criticism of its bilingual education program, which relies on native language instruction. Their children complain of systematically being segregated from their English-speaking peers. Now in high school, these students cite the failure of the program to teach them English first as the reason for being years behind their classmates.

Even more alarming is the Berkeley (Calif.) Unified School District, where educators have recognized that all-native-language instruction would be an inadequate response to the needs of their non-English-speaking pupils. Challenged by a student body that spoke more than four different languages and by budgetary constraints, teachers and administrators responded with innovative language programs that utilized many methods of teaching English. That school district is now in court answering charges that the education they provided was inadequate because it did not provide transitional bilingual education for every non-English speaker. What was introduced twenty years ago as an experimental project has become — despite inconclusive research evidence — the only acceptable method of teaching for bilingual education advocates.

When one considers the nearly 50 percent dropout rate among Hispanic students (the largest group receiving this type of instruction), one wonders about their ability to function in the English-speaking mainstream of this country. The school system may have succeeded wonderfully in maintaining their native language, but if it failed to help them to master the English language fully, what is the benefit?

Alternatives

If this method of bilingual education is not the answer, are we forced to return to the old, discredited, sink-or-swim approach? No, we are not, since, as shown in Berkeley and other school districts, there are a number of alternative methods that have been proven effective, while avoiding the problems of all-native-language instruction.

Sheltered English and English as a Second Language (ESL) are just two pro-   25
grams that have helped to get children quickly proficient in English. Yet, political
recognition of the viability of alternate methods has been slow in coming. In
1988, we witnessed the first crack in the monolithic hold that native language
instruction has had on bilingual education funds at the Federal level. In its reau-
thorization of Federal bilingual education, Congress voted to increase the percentage of funds available for alternate methods from 4 to 25 percent of the total.
This is a great breakthrough, but we should not be satisfied until 100 percent of
the funds are available for any program that effectively and quickly can get children functioning in English, regardless of the amount of native language instruction it uses.

My goal as a student of language and a former educator is to see all students
succeed academically, no matter what language is spoken in their homes. I want
to see immigrant students finish their high school education and be able to compete for college scholarships. To help achieve this goal, instruction in English
should start as early as possible. Students should be moved into English mainstream classes in one or, at the very most, two years. They should not continue to
be segregated year after year from their English-speaking peers.

Another highly visible shift in Federal policy that I feel demonstrates quite
clearly the eroding support of government for our common language is the
requirement for bilingual voting ballots. Little evidence ever has been presented
to show the need for ballots in other languages. Even prominent Hispanic organizations acknowledge that more than 90 percent of native-born Hispanics currently are fluent in English and more than half of that population is English
monolingual.

Furthermore, if the proponents of bilingual ballots are correct when they
claim that the absence of native language ballots prevents non-English-speaking
citizens from exercising their right to vote, then current requirements are clearly
unfair because they provide assistance to certain groups of voters while ignoring
others. Under current Federal law, native language ballots are required only for
certain groups: those speaking Spanish, Asian, or Native American languages.
European or African immigrants are not provided ballots in their native language, even in jurisdictions covered by the Voting Rights Act.

As sensitive as Americans have been to racism, especially since the days of the
civil rights movement, no one seems to have noticed the profound racism
expressed in the amendment that created the "bilingual ballot." Brown people,
like Mexicans and Puerto Ricans; red people, like American Indians; and yellow
people, like the Japanese and Chinese, are assumed not to be smart enough to
learn English. No provision is made, however, for non-English-speaking French-
Canadians in Maine or Vermont, or Yiddish-speaking Hasidic Jews in Brooklyn,
who are white and thus presumed to be able to learn English without difficulty.

Voters in San Francisco encountered ballots in Spanish and Chinese for the   30
first time in the elections of 1980, much to their surprise, since authorizing legislation had been passed by Congress with almost no debate, roll-call vote, or pub-

lic discussion. Naturalized Americans, who had taken the trouble to learn English to become citizens, were especially angry and remain so. While native language ballots may be a convenience to some voters, the use of English ballots does not deprive citizens of their right to vote. Under current voting law, non-English-speaking voters are permitted to bring a friend or family member to the polls to assist them in casting their ballots. Absentee ballots could provide another method that would allow a voter to receive this help at home.

Congress should be looking for other methods to create greater access to the ballot box for the currently small number of citizens who cannot understand an English ballot, without resorting to the expense of requiring ballots in foreign languages. We cannot continue to overlook the message we are sending to immigrants about the connection between English language ability and citizenship when we print ballots in other languages. The ballot is the primary symbol of civic duty. When we tell immigrants that they should learn English — yet offer them full voting participation in their native language — I fear our actions will speak louder than our words.

If we are to prevent the expansion of policies such as these, moving us further along the multilingual path, we need to make a strong statement that our political leaders will understand. We must let them know that we do not choose to reside in a "Tower of Babel." Making English our nation's official language *by law* will send the proper signal to newcomers about the importance of learning English and provide the necessary guidance to legislators to preserve our traditional policy of a common language.

Exploring the Text

1. How does S. I. Hayakawa appeal to ethos in this essay? Why is ethos particularly important when writing on this subject? Note instances of Hayakawa's appealing to ethos throughout his essay.

2. Outline Hayakawa's argument for making English the country's official language. What are his unstated assumptions?

3. Hayakawa states that he does not oppose bilingual education. What does he favor, and how does he present his views? On what does he base his claim that bilingual education programs "are shortchanging immigrant children in their quest to learn English" (para. 17)? Why does he assert that the "bilingual ballot" is racist (para. 29)?

4. As he develops his argument, does Hayakawa make stronger appeals to logos or pathos? Cite specific passages to support your response.

5. What counterarguments does Hayakawa address? Where in the essay does he address them?

6. What is Hayakawa's overall tone? Try describing it as two adjectives joined by *yet* or *but.*

From *Monkey Bridge* (fiction)

LAN CAO

Lan Cao (b. 1961) came alone to the United States from Vietnam in 1975 and lived with family friends in Farmington, Connecticut. After earning a BA from Mount Holyoke College and a JD from Yale University, she taught at Brooklyn Law School for six years. In 2001, she joined the faculty of the College of William and Mary Law School. Her specialty is international business transactions and trade law, and she has published widely in that area. The following selection is from her partially autobiographical novel, *Monkey Bridge* (1997), which was the first novel published by a Vietnamese American about the Vietnam conflict.

Every morning during that month of February 1975, while my mother paced the streets of Saigon and witnessed the country's preparation for imminent defeat, I followed Aunt Mary around the house, collecting words like a beggar gathering rain with an earthen pan. She opened her mouth, and out came a constellation of gorgeous sounds. Each word she uttered was a round stone, with the smoothness of something that had been rubbed and polished by the waves of a warm summer beach. She could swim straight through her syllables. On days when we studied together, I almost convinced myself that we would continue that way forever, playing with the movement of sound itself. I would listen as she tried to inspire me into replicating the "th" sound with the seductive powers of her voice. "Slip the tip of your tongue between your front teeth and pull it back real quick," she would coax and coax. Together, she and I sketched the English language, its curious cadence and rhythm, into the receptive Farmington landscape. Only with Aunt Mary and Uncle Michael could I give myself an inheritance my parents never gave me: the gift of language. The story of English was nothing less than the poetry of sound and motion. To this day, Aunt Mary's voice remains my standard for perfection.

My superior English meant that, unlike my mother and Mrs. Bay, I knew the difference between "cough" and "enough," "bough" and "through," "thorough," "dough" and "fought." Once I made it past the fourth or fifth week in Connecticut, the new language Uncle Michael and Aunt Mary were teaching me began gathering momentum, like tumbleweed in a storm. This was my realization: we have only to let one thing go — the language we think in, or the composition of our dream, the grass roots clinging underneath its rocks — and all at once everything goes. It had astonished me, the ease with which continents shift and planets change course, the casual way in which the earth goes about shedding the laborious folds of its memories. Suddenly, out of that difficult space between here and there, English revealed itself to me with the ease of thread unspooled. I began to understand the levity and weight of its sentences. First base, second base, home run. New terminologies were not difficult to master, and gradually the possibility of perfection began edging its way into my life. How did those numerous China-towns and Little Italys sustain the will to maintain a distance, the desire to inhabit the edge and margin of American life? A mere eight weeks into Farmington, and the American Dream was exerting a sly but seductive pull.

By the time I left Farmington to be with my mother, I had already created for myself a different, more sacred tongue. Khe Sanh, the Tet Offensive, the Ho Chi Minh Trail — a history as imperfect as my once obviously imperfect English — these were the things that had rushed me into the American melting pot. And when I saw my mother again, I was no longer the same person she used to know. Inside my new tongue, my real tongue, was an astonishing new power. For my mother and her Vietnamese neighbors, I became the keeper of the word, the only one with access to the light world. Like Adam, I had the God-given right to name all the fowls of the air and all the beasts of the field.

The right to name, I quickly discovered, also meant the right to stand guard over language and the right to claim unadulterated authority. Here was a language with an ocean's quiet mystery, and it would be up to me to render its vast-ness comprehensible to the newcomers around me. My language skill, my ability to decipher the nuances of American life, was what held it firmly in place, night after night, in our Falls Church living room.

Exploring the Text

1. In the passage from Lan Cao's *Monkey Bridge*, what is the attitude of the narrator toward acquiring English?
2. What does the narrator of *Monkey Bridge* mean by this statement: "This was my realization: we have only to let one thing go — the language we think in, or the composition of our dream, the grass roots clinging underneath its rocks — and all at once everything goes" (para. 2)?
3. What does the narrator of *Monkey Bridge* mean when she says that she "became the keeper of the word" (para. 3)?

From *Native Speaker* (fiction)

Chang-Rae Lee

Chang-Rae Lee (b. 1965) emigrated with his family to Westchester, New York, from Korea when he was three years old. After receiving a BA in English from Yale University and an MFA in writing from the University of Oregon, he worked as a financial analyst for a brief period before beginning his writing career. Today he teaches at Princeton University. His novel *Native Speaker* (1995) won the PEN/

Hemingway Award and the National Book Award. Lee is also the author of *A Gesture Life* (1999) and *Aloft* (2004).

"Henry Park," her voice would quiver. "Please recite our favorite verse." I'd choke, stumble, inside myself. And this was her therapy struck in sublime meter on my palms and the back of my calves.

> Till, like one slumber bound,
> Borne to the ocean, I float down, around,
> Into a sea of profound, of ever-spreading sound . . .

Peanut Butter Shelley, I'd murmur beneath my breath, unable to remember all the poet's womanly names. It was my first year of school, my first days away from the private realm of our house and tongue. I thought English would be simply a version of our Korean. Like another kind of coat you could wear. I didn't know what a difference in language meant then. Or how my tongue would tie in the initial attempts, stiffen so, struggle like an animal booby-trapped and dying inside my head. Native speakers may not fully know this, but English is a scabrous mouthful. In Korean, there are no separate sounds for *L* and *R*, the sound is singular and without a baroque Spanish trill or roll. There is no *B* and *V* for us, no *P* and *F*. I always thought someone must have invented certain words to torture us. *Frivolous. Barbarian.* I remember my father saying, Your eyes all *led*, staring at me after I'd smoked pot the first time, and I went to my room and laughed until I wept.

I will always make bad errors of speech. I remind myself of my mother and father, fumbling in front of strangers. Lelia says there are certain mental pathways of speaking that can never be unlearned. Sometimes I'll still say *riddle* for *little*, or *bent* for *vent*, though without any accent, and whoever is present just thinks I've momentarily lost my train of thought. But I always hear myself displacing the two languages, conflating them — maybe conflagrating them — for there's so much rubbing and friction, a fire always threatens to blow up between the tongues. Friction, affliction. In kindergarten, kids would call me "Marble Mouth" because I spoke in a garbled voice, my bound tongue wrenching itself to move in the right ways.

"Yo, China boy," the older black kids would yell at me across the blacktop, "what you doin' there, practicin'?"

Of course I was. I would rewhisper all the words and sounds I had messed up earlier that morning, trying to invoke how the one girl who always wore a baby-blue cardigan would speak.

"Thus flies foul our fearless night owl," she might say, the words forming so punctiliously on her lips, her head raised and neck straight and her eyes fixed on our teacher. Alice Eckles, I adored and despised her height and beauty and the oniony sheen of her skin. I knew she looked just like her parents — lanky, washed-out, lipless — and that when she spoke to them they answered her in the same even, lowing rhythm of ennui and supremacy she lorded over us.

Exploring the Text

1. What is the attitude of the narrator of Chang-Rae Lee's *Native Speaker* toward his younger self struggling to learn English?
2. In the final paragraph, why does the narrator of *Native Speaker* say he "adored and despised" Alice Eckles?
3. Compare and contrast the relationship between power and language that the narrators of *Monkey Bridge* (p. 568) and *Native Speaker* experience.
4. How do the distinctive styles of *Monkey Bridge* (p. 568) and *Native Speaker* reveal the writers' interaction with a new language?

For Mohammed Zeid of Gaza, Age 15 (poetry)
and
Why I Could Not Accept Your Invitation (poetry)

Naomi Shihab Nye

Poet, novelist, editor, and political activist Naomi Shihab Nye (b. 1952) is the daughter of a Palestinian father and American mother. She grew up in St. Louis, Missouri, visited Jerusalem for the first time when she was fourteen, and currently lives in San Antonio, Texas. Her works for children include the picture book *Sitti's Secret* (1994) and the novel *Habibi* (1996). Her poetry collections include *Different Ways to Pray* (1980), *Fuel* (1998), *19 Varieties of Gazelle: Poems of the Middle East* (2002), and *You and Yours* (2005). She has won many awards and fellowships, including four Pushcart Prizes (for best work from small presses), the Jane Addams Children's Book Award, and the Isabella Gardner Poetry Award. Nye, who has been a visiting writer all over the world, describes herself as "a wandering poet." An advocate for peaceful solutions to conflict, she often writes about miscommunications caused by disregarding or misusing language, as in the following two poems.

For Mohammed Zeid of Gaza, Age 15

There is no *stray* bullet, sirs.
No bullet like a worried cat
crouching under a bush,
no half-hairless puppy bullet
dodging midnight streets.   5
The bullet could not be a pecan
plunking the tin roof,
not hardly, no fluff of pollen
on October's breath,
no humble pebble at our feet.   10

So don't gentle it, please.

We live among stray thoughts,
tasks abandoned midstream.
Our fickle hearts are fat
with stray devotions, we feel at home   15
among bits and pieces,
all the wandering ways of words.

But this bullet had no innocence, did not
wish anyone well, you can't tell us otherwise
by naming it mildly, this bullet was never the friend   20
of life, should not be granted immunity
by soft saying — friendly fire, straying death-eye,
why have we given the wrong weight to what we do?

Mohammed, Mohammed, deserves the truth.
This bullet had no secret happy hopes,   25
it was not singing to itself with eyes closed
under the bridge.

Exploring the Text

1. Who is the speaker in "For Mohammed Zeid of Gaza, Age 15"?
2. What is the setting of the poem? Why is it important?
3. Usually, what part of speech is the word *gentle*? What is the effect of using it in this poem as a verb?
4. The speaker objects to a certain use of "stray" yet accepts another. What distinction is being made?
5. What metaphors for the bullet does the speaker reject? Why are they inappropriate?
6. Why does the speaker believe our hearts are "fickle" and "fat with stray devotions"?

7. What is the speaker's purpose in this poem? What does he or she want the audience to understand or feel?

Why I Could Not Accept Your Invitation

Besides the fact that your event
is coming up in three weeks
on the other side of the world
and you just invited me *now*,
your fax contained the following phrases: 5
action-research oriented initiative;
regionally based evaluation vehicles;
culture should impregnate all different sectors;
consumption of cultural products;
key flashpoints in thematic areas.   10
Don't get me wrong, I love what you are doing,
believing in art and culture,
there, in the country next to the country
my country has recently been devastating
in the name of democracy,   15
but that is not the language I live in
and so I cannot come.
I live in teaspoon, bucket, river, pain,
turtle sunning on a brick.
Forgive me. Culture is everything   20
right about now. But I cannot pretend
a scrap of investment in the language
that allows human beings to kill one another
systematically, abstractly, distantly.
The language wrapped around 37,000,   25
or whatever the number today,
dead and beautiful bodies thrown into holes
without any tiny, reasonable *goodbye*.

Exploring the Text

1. In "Why I Could Not Accept Your Invitation," what is wrong with the italicized phrases (lines 6–10), according to the speaker?
2. Is it significant that the invitation — possibly an invitation to attend a conference or to give a poetry reading — arrived via fax? Why or why not?
3. What examples of irony do you see in "Why I Could Not Accept Your Invitation"?

4. What does the speaker mean by "I live in teaspoon, bucket, river, pain, / turtle sunning on a brick"?
5. How would you describe the tone of this poem?
6. Discuss how these two poems by Naomi Shihab Nye might be interpreted as updated examples of George Orwell's points in "Politics and the English Language" (p. 529).

NAOMI SHIHAB NYE ON WRITING

In the following interview, Naomi Shihab Nye, author of the poems on pages 572 and 573, reflects on how language can become a means toward understanding and moderating conflict.

Renée Shea (RS): A number of poems in *You and Yours* are about the power of language to confuse, obscure, and mask meaning. How can we become more aware of this power — both to recognize it when we see it and to avoid doing it ourselves?

Naomi Shihab Nye (NSN): Writing regularly helps more than anything, I think. Placing ourselves into some kind of community where other people also value language, where we are called upon to speak honorably and honestly helps. So does attempting to shape some of the "difficult things" into language on a regular basis. I am astonished these days by people who "don't want to talk about it" when it comes to the complex, crisis-ridden issues of our times. I am haunted by false and manipulated language, and by all the people who don't write letters to the editor.
　　Language is a tool for creating empathy, not deepening division. What other kinds of questions might we ask one another; how can we find ways to communicate? I think there's a tendency, even in families these days, to "shut down" and stop speaking altogether if people don't agree. Tempers are flaring. We all have sharp edges.

RS: You've written of the power of words "to renew and uplift the spirit." How can we tap into that power, especially those of us who lack your natural fascination with language?

NSN: It might help to read more poetry, though that's probably unrealistic. Poetry has a way of moving us to a deeper place very quickly: we don't tend to read it in divisive situations though. At least we can read it to ourselves so we don't go entirely nuts! We all need voices we believe in, to uplift and enlarge us. It takes a little time to read, but we need to do that regularly, as regularly as we read headlines or watch TV. Sometimes students haven't discovered who those voices are for them yet. Exposure is everything, so we have to read widely until we find the voices. William Stafford's voice helps me live every day. W. S. Merwin's voice has guided me since I was eighteen. Even thinking of Robert Bly's voice or Mary Oliver's or Lucille Clifton's calms my heart. We need not only to *read* but to *absorb* the tenor and tone of wise, luminous voices that know more than we do. We need to soak in them and feel the way they enable consciousness to expand.

RS: **You're such a passionate and involved person who writes about issues near and dear to her. How do you harness that passion so that it gives your writing vitality without clouding your vision or making you so subjective that audiences doubt your credibility?**

NSN: I don't think anyone ever really "harnesses" passion. We try to find vessels to hold little bits of it. A "vessel" may be a story, essay, poem, song — something of a manageable, recognizable shape. I trust a lot in moments, small scenes with a finite framework — time, place, characters, conversation — and try to write those small scenes that we are living all the time, every day. They're human-sized, not gigantic, even if the passion or energy or conflict contained is much larger. I often tell my students that nothing is too small to write about, but many things may feel too large. Trust in the small containing the large. If we write too didactically or ideologically, one may argue with our "stance," but how can one argue with a scene from life?

Follow-up

After you have reflected on Naomi Shihab Nye's comments, freewrite on an issue to which you have a strong emotional attachment. Then rewrite the freewriting by including "small scenes" (as Nye says) that humanize the bigger issue.

Rumors, Lies, Innuendo (cartoon)

MIKE TWOHY

After receiving a master of fine arts degree in painting from the University of California, Berkeley in 1973, Mike Twohy applied his pop-art skills to cartooning. His comic strip *That's Life* is nationally syndicated, and his political cartoons are published in magazines from *Audubon* to the *Vegetarian Times*. The following political cartoon appeared in the *New Yorker*, where his cartoons have been published regularly since 1980.

Exploring the Text

1. What is the subject of Mike Twohy's cartoon?
2. How is the written text — the three individual words — related to the drawing?
3. What claim is Twohy making?
4. What evidence or data in the cartoon support the claim?
5. What are the unstated assumptions?
6. Do you find this cartoon persuasive? Funny? Thought-provoking? Explain your response.

Census Data on Language Use in the United States (table)

JAMES CRAWFORD

> James Crawford (b. 1949) is former executive director of the National Association for Bilingual Education. In the following table, Crawford uses U.S. Census data to show historical trends in language use in America.

CHART I. LANGUAGE SPOKEN AT HOME AND SELF-REPORTED ENGLISH-SPEAKING ABILITY, U.S. RESIDENTS, AGE 5 AND OLDER — 1980, 1990, AND 2000

	1980	%	1990	%	CHANGE IN 1980s	2000	%	CHANGE IN 1990s
All speakers age 5+	210,247,455	100.0	230,445,777	100.0	+9.6%	262,375,152	100.0	+13.9%
English only	187,187,415	89.0	198,600,798	86.2	+6.1%	215,423,557	82.1	+8.5%
Language other than English	23,060,040	11.0	31,844,979	13.8	+38.1%	46,951,595	17.9	+47.4%
Speaks English very well	12,879,004	6.1	17,862,477	7.8	+38.7%	25,631,188	9.8	+43.5%
. . . well	5,957,544	2.8	7,310,301	3.2	+22.7%	10,333,556	3.9	+41.4%
. . . not well	3,005,503	1.4	4,826,958	2.1	+60.6%	7,620,719	2.9	+57.9%
. . . not at all	1,217,989	0.6	1,845,243	0.8	+51.5%	3,366,132	1.3	+82.4%
. . . with some "difficulty"*	10,181,036	4.8	13,982,502	6.1	+37.3%	21,320,407	8.1	+52.5%
Total U.S. population	226,545,805	100.0	248,709,873	100.0	+9.8%	281,421,906	100.0	+13.2%
Foreign-born	14,079,906	6.2	19,767,316	7.9	+40.4%	31,107,889	11.1	+57.4%

*Includes all persons who report speaking English less than "very well," the threshold for full proficiency in English, as determined by the U.S. Department of Education.

Exploring the Text

1. What was the rate of increase from 1980 to 1990 and then from 1990 to 2000 in the number of U.S. residents who speak a language other than English? In 2000, what was the ratio of the percentage of the population who were fluent bilinguals to the percentage of the population who spoke languages other than English?

2. Based on James Crawford's table, what can you conclude about the population growth of speakers of languages other than English in comparison with the population growth of English-only speakers in the 1980s? in the 1990s?

3. What is the narrative of this table? That is, explain in writing what the table tells you visually.

4. How might the data in this table inform the debate on making English the nation's official language, referred to in S. I. Hayakawa's essay (p. 562)?

5. Develop a thesis that you could support using this table. (It need not be the *only* support you would need to develop the thesis.)

Conversation

Focus on Current Language Usage

The following five texts comment directly or indirectly on the language we speak, hear, and write.

Sources

1. **Geoffrey Nunberg,** *How Much Wallop Can a Simple Word Pack?*
2. **Daniel Okrent,** *The War of Words: A Dispatch from the Front Lines*
3. Letters to the Editor in Response to *The War of Words*
4. **Courtland Milloy,** *Pride to One Is Prejudice to Another*
5. **Ray Magliozzi,** *Help Us Overthrow the Tall/Short Mafia*

After you have read, studied, and synthesized these pieces, enter the conversation by responding to one of the prompts on page 589.

1. *How Much Wallop Can a Simple Word Pack?*

GEOFFREY NUNBERG

In the following article, Geoffrey Nunberg, a senior researcher and linguistics professor at Stanford University, examines the history and use of the word *terror* and its derivatives.

"The long-term defeat of terror will happen when freedom takes hold in the broader Middle East," President Bush said on June 28, [2004], as he announced the early transfer of sovereignty to the Iraqis.

The "defeat of terror" — the wording suggests that much has changed since Sept. 11, 2001. In his speech on that day, Mr. Bush said, "We stand together to win the war against terrorism," and over the following year the White House described the enemy as terrorism twice as often as terror. But in White House speeches over the past year, those proportions have been reversed. And the shift from "terrorism" to "terror" has been equally dramatic in major newspapers, according to a search of several databases.

Broad linguistic shifts like those usually owe less to conscious decisions by editors or speechwriters than to often unnoticed changes in the way people perceive their world. Terrorism may itself be a vague term, as critics have argued. But terror is still more amorphous and elastic, and alters the understanding not just of the enemy but of the war against it.

True, phrases like "terror plots" or "terror threat level" can make terror seem merely a headline writer's shortening of the word terrorism. But even there, "terror" draws on a more complex set of meanings. It evokes both the actions of terrorists and the fear they are trying to engender.

"Do we cower in the face of terror?" Mr. Bush asked on Irish television a few 5 days before the handover in Iraq, with terror doing double work.

And unlike "terrorism," "terror" can be applied to states as well as to insurgent groups, as in the President's frequent references to Saddam Hussein's "terror regime." Even if Mr. Hussein can't actually be linked to the attacks of Sept. 11, "terror" seems to connect them etymologically.

The modern senses of "terror" and "terrorism" reach back to a single historical moment: "la Terreur," Robespierre's Reign of Terror in 1793 and 1794.

"Terror," Robespierre said, "is nothing other than justice, prompt, severe, inflexible; it is therefore an emanation of virtue."

It was the ruthless severity of that emanation that moved Edmund Burke to decry "those hell-hounds called terrorists," in one of the first recorded uses of "terrorist" in English.

For Robespierre and his contemporaries, "terror" conveyed the exalted emo- 10 tion people may feel when face to face with the absolute. That was what led Albert Camus to describe terror as the urge that draws people to the violent certainties of totalitarianism, where rebellion hardens into ideology.

With time, though, the word's aura of sublimity faded. By 1880, "holy terror" was only a jocular name for an obstreperous child and "terrible" no longer suggested the sense of awe it had in "terrible swift sword." By the Jazz Age, "terrific" was just a wan superlative. Terror was still a name for intense fear, but it no longer connoted a social force.

"Terrorism," too, has drifted since its origin. By modern times, the word could refer only to the use of violence against a government, not on its behalf — though some still claimed the "terrorist" designation proudly, like the Russian revolutionaries who assassinated Czar Alexander II in 1881 and the Zionist Stern Gang (later the Lehi), which, in the 1940's used assassination and other violent means in hopes of driving the British occupiers out of Palestine.

It wasn't until the beginning of the post-colonial period that all groups rejected the terrorist label in favor of names like freedom fighters or mujahadeen. By then, "terrorism" was no longer a genuine -ism, but the name for a reprehensible strategy, often extended as a term of abuse for anyone whose methods seemed ruthless.

But the recent uses of "terror" seem to draw its disparate, superseded senses back together in a way that Burke might have found familiar. Today, it is again a name that encompasses both the dark forces that threaten "civilization" and the fears they arouse.

The new senses of the noun are signaled in another linguistic shift in the 15 press and in White House speeches. Just as "terrorism" has been replaced by "terror," so "war" is much more likely now to be followed by "on" rather than "against."

That "war on" pattern dates from the turn of the 20th century, when people adapted epidemiological metaphors like "the war on typhus" to describe campaigns against social evils like alcohol, crime and poverty — endemic conditions that could be mitigated but not eradicated. Society may declare a war on drugs or drunken driving, but no one expects total victory.

"The war on terror," too, suggests a campaign aimed not at human adversaries but at a pervasive social plague. At its most abstract, terror comes to seem as persistent and inexplicable as evil itself, without raising any inconvenient theological qualms. And in fact, the White House's use of "evil" has declined by 80 percent over the same period that its use of "terror" has been increasing.

Like wars on ignorance and crime, a "war on terror" suggests an enduring state of struggle — a "never ending fight against terror and its relentless onslaughts," as Camus put it in *The Plague*, his 1947 allegory on the rise and fall of Fascism. It is as if the language is girding itself for the long haul.

Questions

1. What is Geoffrey Nunberg's main point?
2. What is Nunberg's purpose in offering a historical perspective of the word *terror* and its derivatives?
3. What allusions does Nunberg make? What is the effect of these allusions?
4. Why does Nunberg include the analysis of "war *on*" versus "war *against*"? Do you see the analysis as peripheral or essential to his discussion of terror? Explain why.
5. Is Nunberg being critical of George W. Bush by using examples from his speeches? Cite specific passages to support your opinion.

2. *The War of Words: A Dispatch from the Front Lines*

Daniel Okrent

In the following article, Daniel Okrent, then public editor of the *New York Times*, discusses the use of *terrorist* and *terrorism* in the *Times* and the language used to report news from the Middle East.

Nothing provokes as much rage as what many perceive to be *The Times*'s policy on the use of "terrorist," "terrorism" and "terror." There is no policy, actually, but except in the context of Al Qaeda, or in direct quotations, these words, as explosive as what they describe, show up very rarely.

Among pro-Israeli readers (and nonreaders urged to write to me by media watchdog organizations), the controversy over variants of the T-word has become the stand-in for the Israel-Palestine conflict itself. When Israel's targeted assassinations of suspected sponsors of terrorism provoke retaliation, some pro-Palestinian readers argue that at any armed response against civilians by such groups as Hamas is morally equivalent. Critics on the other side say *The Times*'s general avoidance of the word "terrorism" is a political decision, and exactly what Hamas wants.

Here's what I want: A path out of this thicket, which is snarled with far more than "terror" and its derivative tendrils. I packed the preceding paragraph with enough verbal knots to secure the QE2, so I'll untangle them one by one.

"Pro-Israeli" and "pro-Palestinian": Adem Carroll of the Islamic Circle of North America has pointed out to me that both epithets represent value judgments. Are Ariel Sharon's policies pro-Israel? Not in the minds of his critics on the Israeli left. Is Mahmoud Abbas's negotiation policy pro-Palestinian? I doubt that supporters of Islamic jihad believe it is.

"Israel-Palestine conflict": I've heard from ardent Zionists who deplore this   5
usage because, they say, "There is no Palestine."

"Targeted assassinations": The Israel Defense Forces use this term; Palestinians believe it implicitly exonerates Israel for the deaths of nearby innocents. The Times tries to avoid it, but an editor's attempt at a substitute on Jan. 27 [2005] — "pinpoint killings" — was even more accepting of the Israeli line.

"Settlers": Are they merely settlers when they carry out armed actions against Palestinians?

"Groups such as Hamas": According to the European Union and the United States government, which are both cited regularly by an army of readers, Hamas is a terrorist organization. According to *Times* deputy foreign editor Ethan Bronner: "We use 'terrorist' sparingly because it is a loaded word. Describing the goals or acts of a group often serves readers better than repeating the term 'terrorist.' We make clear that Hamas seeks the destruction of Israel through violence but that it is also a significant political and social force among Palestinians, fielding candidates and clinics and day care centers." According to many *Times* critics, that just won't do.

There was one more bugbear in that overloaded paragraph up top: "Media watchdog organizations." That's what you call the noble guardians on your side; the other guy's dishonest advocates are "pressure groups." Both are accurate characterizations, but trying to squeeze them into the same sentence can get awfully clumsy. It's also clumsy to befog clear prose by worrying over words so obsessively that strong sentences get ground into grits. But closing one's ears to the complaints of partisans would also entail closing one's mind to the substance of their arguments.

The Armed Conflict in the Area Between Lebanon and Egypt may yield the   10
most linguistically volatile issues confronting *Times* editors, but I've encountered a ferocious tug-of-war between advocates of each of the following as well: Genital mutilation vs. genital cutting ("would you call ritual male circumcision 'genital mutilation'?"). Liberal vs. moderate ("you're simply trying to make liberalism look reasonable and inoffensive" as in calling Michael Bloomberg a "moderate Republican"). Abuse vs. torture ("if the Abu Ghraib victims had been American

soldiers," *The Times* "would have described it as torture"). Partial birth vs. intact dilation and extraction (the use of the former demonstrates that The Times "has embraced the terminology of anti-abortion forces"). "Iraqi forces" vs. "American-backed forces" ("aren't the Sunni insurgents Iraqis?"). Don't get me started on "insurgents," much less homeless vs. vagrant, affirmative action vs. racial preferences, or loophole vs. tax incentive.

Now a rugby scrum has gathered around the Bush Social Security plan. Republicans tout "personal accounts"; Democrats trash "private accounts." In this atmosphere, I don't think reporters have much choice other than to use "private" and "personal" interchangeably, and to interchange them often. Once one side of an ideological conflict has seized control of a word, it no longer has a meaning of its own; opting for one or the other would be a declaration that doesn't belong in the news reports.

Hijacking the language proves especially pernicious when government officials deodorize their programs with near-Orwellian euphemism. (If Orwell were writing "Politics and the English Language" today, he'd need a telephone book to contain his "catalog of swindles and perversions.") The Bush administration has been especially good at this; just count the number of times self-anointing phrases like "Patriot Act," "Clear Skies Act" or "No Child Left Behind Act" appear in *The Times*, at each appearance sounding as wholesome as a hymn. Even the most committed Republicans must recognize that such phrases could apply to measures guaranteeing the opposite of what they claim to accomplish.

When the next Democratic administration rolls around, Republicans will likely discover how it feels to be on the losing side of a propaganda war. (The Clinton White House wasn't very good at this: somehow, the Personal Responsibility and Work Opportunity Reconciliation Act of 1996, which remade federal welfare policy, never hit the top of the charts.)

The Times shouldn't play along. If the sports section calls the Orange Bowl the Orange Bowl, even if its formal name is the Federal Express Orange Bowl, why can't the news pages refer to the Public Education Act of 2002, or the Industrial Emissions Act of 2005? Similarly, editors could ban the use of "reform" as a description of legislative action. It's even worse than "moderate," something so benign in tone and banal in substance that it can be used to camouflage any depredations its sponsors propose. Who could oppose health care reform, Social Security reform or welfare reform, and who could tell me what any of them means? You could call the rule barring (or at least radically limiting) the use of these shameless beards the Save the Language Act.

Of course, reform of the use of "reform," or a consistent assault on any of the linguistic cosmetics used by politicians and interest groups to disfigure public debate, could bring on charges of bias (a word which itself has almost come to mean "something I disagree with").

But I think in some instances The Times's earnest effort to avoid bias can desiccate language and dilute meaning. In a January memo to the foreign desk,

15

former Jerusalem bureau chief James Bennet addressed the paper's gingerly use of the word "terrorism."

"The calculated bombing of students in a university cafeteria, or of families gathered in an ice cream parlor, cries out to be called what it is," he wrote. "I wanted to avoid the political meaning that comes with 'terrorism,' but I couldn't pretend that the word had no usage at all in plain English." Bennet came to believe that "not to use the term began to seem like a political act in itself."

I agree. While some Israelis and their supporters assert that any Palestinian holding a gun is a terrorist, there can be neither factual nor moral certainty that he is. But if the same man fires into a crowd of civilians, he has committed an act of terror, and he is a terrorist. My own definition is simple: an act of political violence committed against purely civilian targets is terrorism; attacks on military targets are not. The deadly October 2000 assault on the American destroyer Cole or the devastating suicide bomb that killed 18 American soldiers and 4 Iraqis in Mosul last December may have been heinous, but these were acts of war, not terrorism. Beheading construction workers in Iraq and bombing a market in Jerusalem are terrorism pure and simple.

Given the word's history as a virtual battle flag over the past several years, it would be tendentious for *The Times* to require constant use of it, as some of the paper's critics are insisting. But there's something uncomfortably fearful, and inevitably self-defeating, about struggling so hard to avoid it.

3. *Letters to the Editor in Response to* The War of Words

Following is a series of letters to Daniel Okrent in response to his article "The War of Words."

Re "The War of the Words: A Dispatch From the Front Lines" (March 6):

The right definition of terrorism is "acts of war by nongovernmental organizations." But the fact that this is the only definition that matches both intent and usage is irrelevant. "Terrorism" has no agreed-upon definition. We should therefore drop the use of the term. Palestinian bus bombers should be called "bus bombers." Hamas should be called a "quasi-military group." The attack on New York and Washington by Al Qaeda should be called an "attack."

— WARREN SELTZER, *Jerusalem, March 6, 2005*

You write: "The deadly October 2000 assault on the American destroyer Cole or the devastating suicide bomb that killed 18 American soldiers and 4 Iraqis in Mosul last December may have been heinous, but these were acts of war, not terrorism."

The bombing of the Cole was an "act of war"? Isn't war a conflict between legitimate governments, adhering to certain universally agreed-upon "rules"? As far as I know, no government declared war against the United States by attacking the Cole, just as no government declared war by attacking the World Trade Center and the Pentagon.

—Cathleen Medwick, *Somers, N.Y., March 6, 2005*

Supporters of Israel's policies have long dominated this war of words in the American news media. Otherwise, you and your colleagues might be debating whether to use "settlers" or "colonists" for the inhabitants of Israeli enclaves in the occupied territories: the former implies that they moved into uninhabited territory; the latter that someone else might already have been living there. Use of "colonists" brings charges of anti-Semitism, however, while "settlers," which is at least equally partisan, is widely treated as a neutral descriptive term.

Journalists at The New York Times will never satisfy everyone when writing about the Middle East. But trying not to ruffle feathers should take a back seat to accuracy and clarity.

—Robert Dimit, *New York, March 6, 2005*

Regarding the phrasing "Israel-Palestine conflict," you write, "I've heard from ardent Zionists who deplore this usage because they say, 'There is no Palestine.'" You failed to mention that most Palestinians, and other Arabs for that matter, say, "There is no Israel."

—Shlomo Singer, *New York, March 6, 2005*

You call terrorism "an act of political violence committed against purely civilian targets." By this definition the British and American bombing of Dresden was terrorism, as was the fire-bombing of Tokyo and the nuclear attacks on Hiroshima and Nagasaki. (Almost no one argues there was military value to these targets.) These were attacks meant to change people's minds by invoking fear. The same can be said for the German attacks on London, which were clearly aimed at the will of the British people. And, if you accept the argument that these attacks were military because they forced the diversion of military forces to stop them, then any civilian attack becomes a military one.

—John A. Kroll, *Tarpon Springs, Fla., March 6, 2005*

Terrorism is the intentional harming of innocent civilians for political purposes. The Times should have the courage to use this term correctly, consistently and as often (or seldom) as the facts require. Let the political chips fall where they may.

—John Tomasi, *Providence, March 6, 2005*
The writer is an associate professor of political science at Brown University.

The major point of disagreement I have with your article relates to Social Security privatization.

It is not as if Republicans have always called for "personal" accounts, and Democrats have always called it "privatization." The right has always (for some 60 years now) called for privatization, and to them the entire issue is a moral one, not an economic one. They only switched to "personal" when focus groups showed that "private" was failing the cause.

—Dana Beyer, *Chevy Chase, Md., March 6, 2005*

Questions

1. In his article, how does Daniel Okrent fulfill his duty as a commentator on journalistic issues? Does he offer information and interpretation objectively?
2. What is Okrent's main argument? Does it transcend the specific case of Israel and Palestine, or does it apply only to that conflict?
3. Okrent uses many metaphors and analogies. Identify three, and comment on their individual effectiveness. Then consider the overall effectiveness of Okrent's use of figurative language.
4. What does Okrent mean when he writes, "Hijacking the language proves especially pernicious when government officials deodorize their programs with near-Orwellian euphemism" (para. 12)? Try rewriting that sentence with entirely literal language — no metaphors and no allusions allowed.
5. What objections do the letters to the editor raise? Paraphrase at least three of them.

4. *Pride to One Is Prejudice to Another*

Courtland Milloy

In the following article, columnist Courtland Milloy comments on the names of sports teams derived from terms associated with Native Americans.

For some Native Americans, the birth of a white buffalo signifies prayers heard and consciousness raised. Several such births have been reported in recent years, and the prophesized enlightenment could take many forms. A new name for Washington's professional football team sure would be a welcome sign.

To illustrate the offensiveness of the name Redskins, I wrote a column Nov. 14 about an imaginary football game between the Whiteys and the Darkies. Of the responses I received, one stood out. Fellow [*Washington*] *Post* columnist Marc Fisher, writing in this space Thursday, noted that my effort was "a strong appeal to our sense of fairness." Then he added: "But it was based on a fallacy."

Notice how quickly that compliment gets undercut.

And Marc's claim that names such as Redskins are complimentary doesn't even last that long.

Citing the Southeastern Oklahoma State University Savages, he wrote, "Turns out that the chief of the Choctaw Nation defends the Savages. Instead of ripping the college for insensitivity, tribal officials are proud of the name and emphasize the school's support for the quarter of its students who are Indians."

That's not an example of pride. That's a sellout for school support.

Nevertheless, Marc's column was a succinct summation of the most common arguments for keeping the team name. As such, it offered insight into the mindset of the dominant culture — a people in denial about the nation's history of

racism. In justifying use of the name, they must rationalize oppression and minimize the harms done. It is truly a shame, for even some of the football players
don't like the name.

Pro Football Inc., in fighting a lawsuit that seeks to ban disparaging images of
native people in sports, has attempted to dismiss the plaintiffs as an inconsequen-
tial group of people that is representative of no one but themselves. In several
legal briefs, the plaintiffs are referred to as "a mere handful of activist American
Indians" and "fringe activist groups."

For his part, Marc cited two surveys — one by *Sports Illustrated*, another by
the University of Pennsylvania — which purport to show that a majority of
Native Americans are not offended by Indian mascots. Never mind that Native
American organizations have conducted their own surveys — using respondents
who are actually native peoples — and found that upward of 90 percent of those
polled are offended by these names and depictions.

And forget that on Nov. 4, the National Congress of American Indians —   10
11,000 members representing 187 nations meeting in Tulsa — voted to "oppose
the use of racist and demeaning 'Indian' sports mascots" and reiterated its support of the lawsuit against Pro Football Inc. The National Indian Education Association, the National Indian Youth Council and the Native American Rights Fund
are unified in their support of the plaintiffs.

"The real question," Marc wrote, "is whether the trumped-up sensitivities of
people who could be addressing, say, Indian poverty will be permitted to scrub
away history at thousands of schools."

And just who are these people with the fake sensitivities?

One plaintiff was Vine Deloria of the Standing Rock Sioux Tribe, who died
last week. He had served as a Marine in World War II and was a lawyer and professor of history at the University of Colorado. "This is not just a disenfranchised few calling for something only a handful would agree with," he said of the
lawsuit. "While American Indians, like other groups, are diverse in their views,
most share a deep feeling of offense at terms like Redskins. Enough is enough. We
don't want future generations of Indian children to bear this burden of discrimination."

Susan Harjo, the lead plaintiff, is a Muscogee (Creek) and daughter of Free-
land Douglas, a World War II hero. Douglas served as code breaker with the
Army's 45th Infantry Division, Company C, which helped liberate the Nazi concentration camps at Dachau. "These are mainstream people who fought for their
country and are now fighting for respect from their country," Harjo said.

Examples of such Native Americans as Deloria and Douglas are often   15
ignored by those who argue that the mascots or team names are inoffensive.

But times are changing. The U.S. Court of Appeals has refused to dismiss the
lawsuit, and each friend-of-the-court brief offered on behalf of the plaintiffs
sheds new light on just how abominable those names really are.

The prophecy of the white buffalo may yet come to pass.

Questions

1. What is the allusion in the title of Courtland Milloy's article? Is understanding this allusion essential to comprehending the article?
2. This article is a counterargument — that is, it is a response to a previous article. What is the previous article's argument? Does Courtland Milloy summarize it objectively?
3. Does Milloy make any concessions to the previous article's argument? If so, what are they?
4. What evidence does Milloy offer to refute the argument? How convincing is he?

5. *Help Us Overthrow the Tall/Short Mafia*

RAY MAGLIOZZI

In the following humorous essay, Ray Magliozzi, one of the hosts of the award-winning show *Car Talk* on National Public Radio, addresses the language of Starbucks, the coffee chain.

Our New Year's resolution for this coming year is going to involve Starbucks Coffee.

Now as good as their coffee is, they have unnecessarily complicated my life, and probably everyone else's life, too. I'm not even going to deal with the fact that they make you choose between a million different kinds of coffee, like decaf, macchiato, americano, skinny, ice, mocha, latte, schmatte, and all that stuff. We'll deal with that problem another time.

Today, I want to deal with their ridiculous size-related nomenclature. And I want to tell you what *we* can do to wipe it off the face of the earth. Keep reading, because this "resolution" includes an exciting call to action that we can *all* participate in.

Remember the old days, when you asked for a cup of coffee and someone would say "Large or small?" Well, apparently "large" and "small" weren't good enough for Starbucks. Noooooo. So they come out with "short" and "tall." That's pretentious, but it's not the end of the world. If it had stopped there, I wouldn't be asking the entire Car Talk Nation to rise up and join me in my Coffee Action today.

So what went wrong? Well, suddenly "tall" became "medium." So if you ask 5 for a "tall," you get a "medium." Well, I didn't want a "medium." I wanted *tall*! Tall is what!? *Big*! *Tall*! Right??

It turns out they've introduced a new size . . . above "tall." "Grande!" So now "grande" is large, "tall" is medium, and "short" is small. You follow me?

Then they add a whole other group of drinks, for which there is an even *larger* size than "grande." Now, in some drink categories, you can get a "venti"! That's apparently Italian for "humongous." And to make matters worse, you can't get a "short" in that category, so "tall" becomes "small!" I went in and asked for a "tall," and I got the smallest thing on the menu! And I'm sick of it!!! Sick, I say!

So for the last three months, every time I go into one of their stores, I end up having a fight with the poor guy with the nose ring behind the counter. I say "I want a small iced cappuccino," and the guy says, "You mean tall?" "*No, I don't mean tall*! I said small, and I mean small!" I duke it out with the guy while 10 people behind me are yelling and screaming to have me physically ejected from the store. Then I have to go down the street to Dunkin Donuts — where they still understand the words "large" and "small."

So here's my resolution, and I hope everyone reading this today will join me in this worthwhile project. I'm going to walk into Starbucks from now on and I'm going to refuse to play their game. I'm going to refuse to use their obtuse nomenclature.

From now on, I'm going to walk up to the counter and say, "Gimme 2 bucks worth." When they say, "Do you want tall, grande, short, venti . . ." I'm gonna say, "You figure it out. Here's my 2 bucks. Give me as much coffee as that'll buy." And if they have to fill the thing up three-quarters of the way, or give me a cup and a half, that's their problem.

So next time you walk into a Starbucks . . . just walk up to the counter and say "Give me a buck fifty's worth of decaf," and see what they do. It's kind of like Alice's Restaurant.[1] If we can get the whole country doing this, I think we may get them to stop this ridiculousness.

So wadda ya say? Are you with me on this? Good.

Wanna go out for a cup of coffee?

Questions

1. What solid information does Ray Magliozzi present that gives the article credibility?
2. What rhetorical strategies does the author employ: understatement? hyperbole? irony? parody?
3. Does the author have a serious point? If so, what is it?
4. What is the tone of this article? Does the title signal the tone of Magliozzi's article? Explain.

Entering the Conversation

As you respond to the following prompts, support your argument with references to at least three of the sources in Conversation: Focus on Current Language Usage. For help using sources, see Chapter 3.

1. Find an article related to terrorism or terrorist activities in two different newspapers, preferably two with different styles and even politics. Write an analysis of their use of language.

---

[1]"Alice's Restaurant" is a protest song written by Arlo Guthrie in the 1960s. — Eds.

2. Write a letter to the editor in response to either Geoffrey Nunberg (p. 579) or Courtland Milloy (p. 586). Keep in mind that your letter should be at least several paragraphs long, enough to flesh out your position. In your letter, refer to at least two *other* sources in Conversation: Focus on Current Language Usage.

3. Consider the issues raised in these readings, and develop a position about the "state of the language" that we speak, hear, and write every day. Do you think that we are living in a time with less and less regard for precision in language?

4. Emulating the lively, satiric style of Ray Magliozzi (p. 588), write a brief essay about the state of language in a context other than Starbucks. You might choose an example of prose from advertising, politics, or popular culture.

Student Writing

Reflection: Reflecting on "Different Englishes"

The following student's essay was written in response to this prompt:

Write a narrative explaining the different "Englishes," as Amy Tan calls them, that you speak and write. If your home language is not English, consider the reasons and ways you switch from it to English and vice versa. But even if English is the only language you know, you "code switch" with different audiences as you speak formally, write informal e-mails, use jargon with peers, and so forth. After your narrative, discuss how these different "Englishes" create different personae for you.

As you read this essay, consider how Nazanin Nikaein develops a distinctive voice and tone. How does she draw her reader in?

My Three Englishes

Nazanin Nikaein

My life consists of three Englishes; the regular English I use for my friends, the English mixed with Farsi for my parents and family, and a type of Spanglish I use with my Spanish-speaking friends or friends who know some Spanish. Language can be a big barrier between people, and sometimes it's easier to create a blend of two languages so that both the people can talk to one another.

"Salaam, chobee?" "Hi, I'm doing well." This is the result of the various "Englishes" in my life. My parents speak to me in Farsi, and I respond in English. Farsi was originally my first language, but now it's just an afterthought for me. If I want to say anything in that language, I have to stop and think about it as if it's a mathematical problem and I have to use an equation to find the answer. I try to say something in Farsi, and it comes out in Spanish or Hebrew. There are too many ways of saying one phrase, and it eventually comes out wrong when I try to say anything. It may be a blessing to know multiple languages, but it can be rough on your mind. There are certain phrases in one language that don't exist in another language. There are foods and technology that don't exist in other languages, and to talk about them you have to adopt the original language's version of it. *Internet* in Hebrew is simply *Internet*. But, on the other hand, *cheeseburger* in Hebrew doesn't even exist. When my family came here and heard the term *cheeseburger*, they were astonished and never even thought it possible to eat a burger with cheese. So in many ways, culture does affect our languages.

Attitude and society also play a big role in affecting our languages. When a Persian person tries to say something in English, it sounds strong and forceful, almost pushy. But that is just how the power of the Persian attitude comes out in English. Often people ask me to translate something from Farsi to English, but the translation is never accurate. The translation sounds almost rude, and it is hard to explain to people that that is not the way it was intended. Word-for-word translating is not a good idea; instead I have to rearrange the entire sentence to get the point through correctly. It is hard to switch languages because you also have to switch mindsets.

I have always wondered what it is like for people who speak multiple languages to switch languages around at a moment's notice. I asked my mother, who speaks three languages, what it's like, and she told me how at times she would have to think about it. She would have to stop and think because otherwise the wrong language would come out. I then asked her what language she thinks in, and she was stumped. I think in English, and if I try to think in Spanish or Farsi, it's hard, and often times nothing comes out. Most likely, our main language is the one we are able to think in, and I wonder if we can change languages. What would be wonderful would be if we had a way of mixing languages so that both sides could understand. That is exactly what people have done with Spanish and English. Spanglish is an amazing version of English mixed with Spanish terms and verbs that English and Spanish speakers can understand. It involves none of the switching between verbs and tenses that would otherwise be called for if switching languages.

We are lucky to live in a time where we can read novels written in other languages because there are people out there willing to sit down and translate them. The only downside is that the meanings are not always accurate. Switching languages is difficult for me, but getting everything correct in tense and tone is on a completely different level of difficulty.

Questions

1. What do you find most appealing or effective about Nazanin's essay?
2. Are the personal examples the author uses more appropriate than ones from other sources? If you were making suggestions for a revision, would you recommend adding external sources? Why or why not?
3. Are there places in the essay that would benefit from the addition of another personal example? Explain where and why.
4. How would you describe Nazanin's tone? Cite passages to support your response.

Grammar as Rhetoric and Style

Concise Diction

At the start of her essay "Mother Tongue," Amy Tan criticizes herself for writing that is "burdened . . . with nominalized forms, past perfect tenses, conditional phrases." Similarly, George Orwell (p. 529) lambasts "the *-ize* and *de-* formations," preferring direct verbs. He also cautions against complex or unusual words that "dress up simple statements," preferring economy of language. Both writers argue for clear, authentic writing using the most straightforward language possible.

Nominalization

Nominalization is the process that changes a verb into its noun form. The verb *discuss* becomes *discussion*, for instance; the verb *depend* becomes *dependence*; *recognize* becomes *recognition*. The noun forms often result in wordiness, stiffness, or awkward constructions, as the following examples (with added italics) show.

Rodriguez could have said:

I had the knowledge *that my* speech *in English was poor.*

Instead, he puts the emphasis on verbs and writes:

I knew very well *that I* spoke *English poorly.*

Showy Vocabulary

Having a large and diverse vocabulary gives a writer many choices and usually results in more precise writing. Inexperienced writers, however, often believe that fancier is better and try to show off words they know. In "Mother Tongue," Amy Tan looks back on a first draft of a story containing this line:

That was my mental *quandary* in its *nascent* state.

With a sense of humor about herself, she tells us that when she first wrote the questionable sentence she believed that a sentence with such elevated vocabulary "would finally prove I had mastery over the English language," but she realized it was "a terrible line" that needed revision. One such revision might read:

That was my *dilemma* in its *earliest* state.

The key to figuring out if a word is too showy is to ask yourself if the fancy word — for example, *pernicious* — is more precise than the more ordinary word — for example, *fatal* — or if you think the former is simply more impressive than the latter. *Pernicious* seems appropriate when Daniel Okrent says:

Hijacking the language proves especially *pernicious* when government officials deodorize their programs with near-Orwellian euphemism.

On the other hand, *pernicious* is inappropriate in a sentence such as:

We all heard the *pernicious* gunshots.

The only reason you might laugh when someone says to you, "Felicitations on your natal day!" is that that expression is so much more pompous than "Happy birthday!" — and much less authentic. Like Tan, you must make your own decisions because these choices are not a matter of hard-and-fast rules but rather of how you assess your audience's expectations and the effect your language will have.

Rhetorical and Stylistic Strategy

Writers who use nominalizations, *de-* and *-ize* verbs, and overly complex or unusual words may think these choices add elegance or complexity to their prose and the ideas they express. However, the opposite is true. A writer who relies on expressions that fall into these categories gives the impression of insecurity and perhaps even insincerity. Whenever possible, follow the aphorism "Less is more": less complexity, less length, and less obscurity will lead you toward clear and readable prose with an authentic voice.

• EXERCISE 1

Identify awkward or pretentious diction in the following sentences, and revise each sentence as necessary to improve clarity.

1. A person who has a dependence on constant approval from others is usually insecure.
2. Let's have a discussion of the essay you read for homework.

3. Khaya finally came to the realization that she preferred research to teaching.

4. A key step toward losing weight is to make a reduction in the amount of food you consume.

5. A supercilious manager rarely contributes to a felicitous workplace.

6. Recommendations are being made by the faculty for the honor society.

7. Colin filled out his application to work part-time during the holidays.

8. We should give serious consideration to the possibility of traveling to China this summer.

9. The president has every intention of hearing both viewpoints.

10. Before finalizing the meeting, the chair of the group offered a plethora of ideas.

11. Before Derrell made a serious purchase, such as a car, he made a study of the competition.

12. Many benefits accrue from residing in a heterogeneous community.

13. The press release gave an explanation for the senator's stance on homeland security.

14. A recalcitrant attitude has resulted from too many of our colleagues becoming mired in quotidian concerns.

15. Maya has a lot of sympathy for students who experience test anxiety.

• EXERCISE 2

In "Politics and the English Language," George Orwell cites the following paragraph as an example of "bad writing." Revise the paragraph by eliminating pretentious diction and improving clarity.

On the one side we have the free personality: by definition it is not neurotic, for it has neither conflict nor dream. Its desires, such as they are, are transparent, for they are just what institutional approval keeps in the forefront of consciousness; another institutional pattern would alter their number and intensity; there is little in them that is natural, irreducible, or culturally dangerous. But *on the other side*, the social bond itself is nothing but the mutual reflection of these self-secure integrities. Recall the definition of love. Is not this the very picture of a small academic? Where is there a place in this hall of mirrors for either personality or fraternity?

> ● **EXERCISE 3**
>
> Find an article in a newspaper, a memo from an organization, or a speech that contains examples of pretentious and awkward diction. Identify the examples, and explain their effect. Suggest ways to revise that would make the writing clearer. Do you think the writer is intentionally keeping the language obscure?

Suggestions for Writing

Language

Now that you have examined a number of readings and other texts that focus on language, explore one dimension of this issue by synthesizing your own ideas and the texts. You might want to do more research or use readings from other classes as you prepare for the following projects.

1. The following assertion by Greg Lewis, a pioneer of computer-based technology and author of several books of political analysis, appeared in the *Washington Dispatch* in 2003:

   > To succeed in America — with a number of relatively minor although often highly visible exceptions — it's important to speak, read, and understand English as most Americans speak it. There's nothing cruel or unfair in that; it's just the way it is. And when liberals try to downplay that fact in the name of diversity or multiculturalism . . . they're cynically appealing to a kind of cultural vanity that almost every one of us possesses. . . . In this case, however, the appeal to cultural vanity is destructive.

   Is bilingual education or class instruction and discussion in African American vernacular English (or Ebonics, as it is often called) a viable alternative to conducting classes in standard American English? Write an essay explaining your position.

2. Should language be legislated? Congress has debated whether English should be declared the national language of the United States. What would be the implication of such a law? Do you believe that it is in the interest of national unity to pass a law making English the national language? Write an essay explaining your view.

3. In "Decolonising the Mind" (p. 547), Ngugi wa Thiong'o describes being punished for speaking his tribal language at school. Research a similar prohibition and punishment system at U.S. boarding schools for Native Americans. Then

write an essay that describes the program (including time and place) and explains the logic behind it.

4. Trace the history and derivation of terms used to describe one ethnic group. What do members of the ethnic group themselves prefer to be called? For instance, discuss the differences among the terms *Hispanic, Latino/Latina,* and *Chicano/Chicana,* both to the general public and to the people who identify themselves by these terms. Another option is to discuss the meanings of the terms *colored, Negro, black, Afro-American, African American,* and *person of color* — again to the general public and to members of the group itself. Your essay should examine why certain terms win favor over others, as well as the politics and values associated with those terms.

5. Write an essay in which you agree or disagree with the following assertion:

> In classrooms and hallways and on the playground, young people are using inappropriate language more frequently than ever, teachers and principals say. Not only is it coarsening the school climate and social discourse, they say, it is evidence of a decline in language skills. Popular culture has made ugly language acceptable and hip, and many teachers say they only expect things to get uglier.
> —VALERIE STRAUSS, "More and More, Kids Say the Foulest Things"

6. Choose one of the following quotations, and explain why it speaks to you. Use examples from your own experience and reading to illustrate what the quotation means to you.

   • Who does not know another language, does not know his own. — GOETHE
   • Languages are the pedigree of nations. — SAMUEL JOHNSON
   • Language is a city to the building of which every human being brought a stone. — RALPH WALDO EMERSON

7. Some believe that the Internet is improving writing skills because everyone, especially younger people, spends so much time e-mailing, instant messaging, blogging, and chatting in forums. The very fact that young people are writing so frequently is bound to increase comfort level and may lead to the development of a creative style, they claim. Others argue that such activity only degrades writing skills because the language used is so informal, often a series of abbreviations, and the communication is usually a rapid-fire response rather than a sustained discussion. Write an essay explaining whether you think that writing online (in whatever form that might take) has a positive or negative impact on a person's writing. Feel free to use your own experience in your discussion.

8. Sports teams have been criticized for having names such as Redskins, the name of the Washington, D.C., football team. Many people believe such names devalue, even insult, the original meaning or subject of the name. Do you agree? Consider the names of several sports teams — local, college, or

professional — and take a position on whether the names should be changed to reflect more neutral terms.

9. Most professions — plumbers, lawyers, teachers, accountants, physicians — have their jargon, a language that practitioners use among themselves. In many ways, that language defines the user as a member of the community and sets them apart from others who do not "belong." Choose one profession or group (such as those who read graphic novels or listen to a particular type of music), describe key elements of that group's language, and analyze how the language defines the group as a community.

10. Advertisers are keenly aware of the importance of a product's name. Choose one specific type of product (for example, men's or women's cologne, cars, shampoos, lines of clothing, laundry detergents, medical remedies), and classify the names according to the connotations or images they suggest.

Science and Technology

How are advances in science and technology affecting the way we define our humanity?

At the 1833 meeting of the British Association, a group dedicated to the advancement of science, William Whewell first proposed the word *scientist.* Up to that time, cultivators of science were called "natural philosophers." The word *science*, derived from the Latin *scientia*, meaning "knowledge," had referred for centuries to almost any kind of knowledge, from how to plow to how to read or write poetry. Indeed we still think of science as a way of knowing about the world, and we trace the roots of modern Western science back to such early natural philosophers as Plato, Aristotle, and Eratosthenes.

In the nineteenth century, science came to refer specifically to the study of the physical world, connecting the discoveries of such early figures as Nicolaus Copernicus, Galileo Galilei, and Isaac Newton to those of Whewell's contemporaries Thomas Henry Huxley and Charles Darwin. Whewell, Huxley, and others called the workings of scientific investigation the "scientific method," and they sought to explain for a general audience what science is and what it does. It was during the nineteenth century, as the Industrial Revolution advanced, that science ceased being merely an academic pursuit and began having widespread application to everyday life. At the same time, the ethics of applied science first became a concern. Mary Shelley wrote her novel *Frankenstein*, a cautionary tale about the dangers of playing God through science, and Nedd Ludd destroyed a knitting frame, fearing that technology would replace workers with machines. From him we have the word *Luddite*, which we now apply to someone who fears or questions new technology.

In the early twentieth century, science continued to shift its purpose from the pursuit of abstract knowledge to the pursuit of practical technologies; first came the telegraph, then the phonograph, the telephone, the camera, and the lightbulb, to name just a few of those technologies we now cannot imagine living without. Through the work of Samuel Morse, Alexander Graham Bell, and Thomas Edison, science and technology became inextricably linked. The rapid pace of technological growth has only increased since that time, as some of the fantasies of science fiction have become the realities of life. Consider that Philo T. Farnsworth

599

invented the first electronic television in 1928. It took nearly forty years before television became ubiquitous. How much more quickly for the PC, which made its first appearance in 1981. And most people never even heard of the Internet before the early 1990s. Who can predict the rate of technological growth in the future?

While science has given us better nutrition, comfortable shelter, and modern medicine, it has also brought environmental pollution, nuclear weapons, and a frenetic pace to our lives. Is the pace of technological change now so fast as to be beyond our control? Have we created a monster, as Mary Shelley prophesized in *Frankenstein*? Do we live in a braver newer world than even Aldous Huxley (T. H. Huxley's grandson) could have imagined? Or will modern technology continue to improve our lives and even provide solutions for our environmental difficulties? With the rapid appearance of new technologies and with the looming possibility of genetic engineering changing our notion of life itself, the effects of science and technology on humanity are crucial concerns.

The selections in this chapter invite reflection on such matters. As you read, think about the discipline of science itself and also the purpose and effect of technology. Consider how science and technology may be changing the way we see ourselves and our world.

The Bird and the Machine

Loren Eiseley

Loren Eiseley (1907–1977) was born in Nebraska, studied science at the University of Nebraska in Lincoln, and completed graduate work in anthropology at the University of Pennsylvania. He taught at the University of Kansas, at Oberlin College, and finally at the University of Pennsylvania, where he chaired the department of anthropology and served as curator of early man at the university museum. He was also president of the American Institute of Human Paleontology. Eiseley is as well respected for his contributions to science as he is for his perceptive essays and lyrical writing style; for many readers his writing bridges the gap between science and the humanities. "The Bird and the Machine" comes from *The Immense Journey* (1957), his first collection of essays.

I suppose their little bones have years ago been lost among the stones and winds of those high glacial pastures. I suppose their feathers blew eventually into the piles of tumbleweed beneath the straggling cattle fences and rotted there in the mountain snows, along with dead steers and all the other things that drift to an end in the corners of the wire. I do not quite know why I should be thinking of birds over the *New York Times* at breakfast, particularly the birds of my youth half a continent away. It is a funny thing what the brain will do with memories and how it will treasure them and finally bring them into odd juxtapositions with other things, as though it wanted to make a design, or get some meaning out of them, whether you want it or not, or even see it.

It used to seem marvelous to me, but I read now that there are machines that can do these things in a small way, machines that can crawl about like animals, and that it may not be long now until they do more things — maybe even make themselves — I saw that piece in the *Times* just now. And then they will, maybe — well, who knows — but you read about it more and more with no one making any protest, and already they can add better than we and reach up and hear things through the dark and finger the guns over the night sky.

This is the new world that I read about at breakfast. This is the world that confronts me in my biological books and journals, until there are times when I sit quietly in my chair and try to hear the little purr of the cogs in my head and the tubes flaring and dying as the messages go through them and the circuits snap shut or open. This is the great age, make no mistake about it; the robot has been born somewhat appropriately along with the atom bomb, and the brain they say now is just another type of more complicated feedback system. The engineers have its basic principles worked out; it's mechanical, you know; nothing to get superstitious about; and man can always improve on nature once he gets the idea. Well, he's got it all right and that's why, I guess, that I sit here in my chair, with the article crunched in my hand, remembering those two birds and that blue mountain sunlight. There is another magazine article on my desk that reads "Machines Are Getting Smarter Every Day." I don't deny it, but I'll still stick with the birds. It's life I believe in, not machines.

Maybe you don't believe there is any difference. A skeleton is all joints and pulleys, I'll admit. And when man was in his simpler stages of machine building in the eighteenth century, he quickly saw the resemblances. "What," wrote Hobbes, "is the heart but a spring, and the nerves but so many strings, and the joints but so many wheels, giving motion to the whole body?"[1] Tinkering about in their shops it was inevitable in the end that men would see the world as a huge machine "subdivided into an infinite number of lesser machines."

The idea took on with a vengeance. Little automatons toured the country — dolls controlled by clockwork. Clocks described as little worlds were taken on tours by the designers. They were made up of moving figures, shifting scenes and other remarkable devices. The life of the cell was unknown. Man, whether he was conceived as possessing a soul or not, moved and jerked about like these tiny puppets. A human being thought of himself in terms of his own tools and implements. He had been fashioned like the puppets he produced and was only a more clever model made by a greater designer.

Then in the nineteenth century, the cell was discovered, and the single machine in its turn was found to be the product of millions of infinitesimal machines — the cells. Now, finally, the cell itself dissolves away into an abstract chemical machine — and that into some intangible, inexpressible flow of energy. The secret seems to lurk all about, the wheels get smaller and smaller, and they turn more rapidly, but when you try to seize it the life is gone — and so, by popular definition, some would say that life was never there in the first place. The wheels and the cogs are the secret and we can make them better in time — machines that will run faster and more accurately than real mice to real cheese.

I have no doubt it can be done, though a mouse harvesting seeds on an autumn thistle is to me a fine sight and more complicated, I think, in his multiform activity, than a machine "mouse" running a maze. Also, I like to think of the possible shape of the future brooding in mice, just as it brooded once in a rather ordinary mousy insectivore who became a man. It leaves a nice fine indeterminate sense of wonder that even an electronic brain hasn't got, because you know perfectly well that if the electronic brain changes, it will be because of something man has done to it. But what man will do to himself he doesn't really know. A certain scale of time and a ghostly intangible thing called change are ticking in him.

5

---

[1]Thomas Hobbes (1588–1679), an English social philosopher, thought that only a strong government — specifically, an absolute monarchy — could control conflicting individual interests.

Powers and potentialities like the oak in the seed, or a red and awful ruin. Either way, it's impressive; and the mouse has it, too. Or those birds, I'll never forget those birds — yet before I measured their significance, I learned the lesson of time first of all. I was young then and left alone in a great desert — part of an expedition that had scattered its men over several hundred miles in order to carry on research more effectively. I learned there that time is a series of planes existing superficially in the same universe. The tempo is a human illusion, a subjective clock ticking in our own kind of protoplasm.

As the long months passed, I began to live on the slower planes and to observe more readily what passed for life there. I sauntered, I passed more and more slowly up and down the canyons in the dry baking heat of midsummer. I slumbered for long hours in the shade of huge brown boulders that had gathered in tilted companies out on the flats. I had forgotten the world of men and the world had forgotten me. Now and then I found a skull in the canyons, and these justified my remaining there. I took a serene cold interest in these discoveries. I had come, like many a naturalist before me, to view life with a wary and subdued attention. I had grown to take pleasure in the divested bone.

I sat once on a high ridge that fell away before me into a waste of sand dunes. I sat through hours of a long afternoon. Finally, as I glanced beside my boot an indistinct configuration caught my eye. It was a coiled rattlesnake, a big one. How long he had sat with me I do not know. I had not frightened him. We were both locked in the sleep-walking tempo of the earlier world, baking in the same high air and sunshine. Perhaps he had been there when I came. He slept on as I left, his coils, so ill discerned by me, dissolving once more among the stones and gravel from which I had barely made him out.

Another time I got on a higher ridge among some tough little wind-warped   10
pines half covered over with sand in a basin-like depression that caught everything carried by the air up to those heights. There were a few thin bones of birds, some cracked shells of indeterminable age, and the knotty fingers of pine roots bulged out of shape from their long and agonizing grasp upon the crevices of the rock. I lay under the pines in the sparse shade and went to sleep once more.

It grew cold finally, for autumn was in the air by then, and the few things that lived thereabouts were sinking down into an even chillier scale of time. In the moments between sleeping and waking I saw the roots about me and slowly, slowly, a foot in what seemed many centuries, I moved my sleep-stiffened hands over the scaling bark and lifted my numbed face after the vanishing sun. I was a great awkward thing of knots and aching limbs, trapped up there in some long, patient endurance that involved the necessity of putting living fingers into rock and by slow, aching expansion bursting those rocks asunder. I suppose, so thin and slow was the time of my pulse by then, that I might have stayed on to drift still deeper into the lower cadences of the frost, or the crystalline life that glistens pebbles, or shines in a snowflake, or dreams in the meteoric iron between the worlds.

It was a dim descent, but time was present in it. Somewhere far down in that scale the notion struck me that one might come the other way. Not many months thereafter I joined some colleagues heading higher into a remote windy tableland where huge bones were reputed to protrude like boulders from the turf. I had drowsed with reptiles and moved with the century-long pulse of trees; now, lethargically, I was climbing back up some invisible ladder of quickening hours. There had been talk of birds in connection with my duties. Birds are intense, fast-living creatures — reptiles, I suppose one might say, that have escaped out of the heavy sleep of time, transformed fairy creatures dancing over sunlit meadows. It is a youthful fancy, no doubt, but because of something that happened up there among the escarpments of that range, it remains with me a lifelong impression. I can never bear to see a bird imprisoned.

We came into that valley through the trailing mists of a spring night. It was a place that looked as though it might never have known the foot of man, but our scouts had been ahead of us and we knew all about the abandoned cabin of stone that lay far up on one hillside. It had been built in the land rush of the last century and then lost to the cattlemen again as the marginal soils failed to take to the plow.

There were spots like this all over that country. Lost graves marked by unlettered stones and old corroding rim-fire cartridge cases lying where somebody had made a stand among the boulders that rimmed the valley. They are all that remain of the range wars; the men are under the stones now. I could see our cavalcade winding in and out through the mist below us: torches, the reflection of the truck lights on our collecting tins, and the far-off bumping of a loose dinosaur thigh bone in the bottom of a trailer. I stood on a rock a moment looking down and thinking what it cost in money and equipment to capture the past.

We had, in addition, instructions to lay hands on the present. The word had come through to get them alive — birds, reptiles, anything. A zoo somewhere abroad needed restocking. It was one of those reciprocal matters in which science involves itself. Maybe our museum needed a stray ostrich egg and this was the payoff. Anyhow, my job was to help capture some birds and that was why I was there before the trucks. 15

The cabin had not been occupied for years. We intended to clean it out and live in it, but there were holes in the roof and the birds had come in and were roosting in the rafters. You could depend on it in a place like this where everything blew away, and even a bird needed some place out of the weather and away from coyotes. A cabin going back to nature in a wild place draws them till they come in, listening at the eaves, I imagine, pecking softly among the shingles till they find a hole and then suddenly the place is theirs and man is forgotten.

Sometimes of late years I find myself thinking the most beautiful sight in the world might be the birds taking over New York after the last man has run away to the hills. I will never live to see it, of course, but I know just how it will sound because I've lived up high and I know the sort of watch birds keep on us. I've listened to sparrows tapping tentatively on the outside of air conditioners when they thought no one was listening, and I know how other birds test the vibrations that come up to them through the television aerials.

"Is he gone?" they ask, and the vibrations come up from below, "Not yet, not yet."

Well, to come back, I got the door open softly and I had the spotlight all ready to turn on and blind whatever birds there were so they couldn't see to get out through the roof. I had a short piece of ladder to put against the far wall where there was a shelf on which I expected to make the biggest haul. I had all the information I needed just like any skilled assassin. I pushed the door open, the hinges squeaking only a little. A bird or two stirred — I could hear them — but nothing flew and there was a faint starlight through the holes in the roof.

I padded across the floor, got the ladder up and the light ready, and slithered up the ladder till my head and arms were over the shelf. Everything was dark as pitch except for the starlight at the little place back of the shelf near the eaves. With the light to blind them, they'd never make it. I had them. I reached my arm carefully over in order to be ready to seize whatever was there and I put the flash on the edge of the shelf where it would stand by itself when I turned it on. That way I'd be able to use both hands. 20

Everything worked perfectly except for one detail — I didn't know what kind of birds were there. I never thought about it at all, and it wouldn't have mattered if I had. My orders were to get something interesting. I snapped on the flash and sure enough there was a great beating and feathers flying, but instead of my having them, they, or rather he, had me. He had my hand, that is, and for a small hawk not much bigger than my fist he was doing all right. I heard him give one short metallic cry when the light went on and my hand descended on the bird beside him; after that he was busy with his claws and his beak was sunk in my thumb. In the struggle I knocked the lamp over on the shelf, and his mate got her sight back and whisked neatly through the hole in the roof and off among the stars outside. It all happened in fifteen seconds and you might think I would have fallen down the ladder, but no, I had a professional assassin's reputation to keep up, and the bird, of course, made the mistake of thinking the hand was the enemy and not the eyes behind it. He chewed my thumb up pretty effectively and lacerated my hand with his claws, but in the end I got him, having two hands to work with.

He was a sparrow hawk and a fine young male in the prime of life. I was sorry not to catch the pair of them, but as I dripped blood and folded his wings carefully, holding him by the back so that he couldn't strike again, I had to admit the two of them might have been more than I could have handled under the circumstances. The little fellow had saved his mate by diverting me, and that was that. He was born to it, and made no outcry now, resting in my hand hopelessly, but peering toward me in the shadows behind the lamp with a fierce, almost indifferent glance. He neither gave nor expected mercy and something out of the high air passed from him to me, stirring a faint embarrassment.

I quit looking into that eye and managed to get my huge carcass with its fist full of prey back down the ladder. I put the bird in a box too small to allow him to injure himself by struggle and walked out to welcome the arriving trucks. It had been a long day, and camp still to make in the darkness. In the morning that bird would be just another episode. He would go back with the bones in the truck to a small cage in a city where he would spend the rest of his life. And a good thing, too. I sucked my aching thumb and spat out some blood. An assassin has to get used to these things. I had a professional reputation to keep up.

In the morning, with the change that comes on suddenly in that high country, the mist that had hovered below us in the valley was gone. The sky was a deep blue, and one could see for miles over the high outcroppings of stone. I was up early and brought the box in which the little hawk was imprisoned out onto the grass where I was building a cage. A wind as cool as a mountain spring ran over the grass and stirred my hair. It was a fine day to be alive. I looked up and all around and at the hole in the cabin roof out of which the other little hawk had fled. There was no sign of her anywhere that I could see.

"Probably in the next county by now," I thought cynically, but before begin- 25 ning work I decided I'd have a look at my last night's capture.

Secretively, I looked again all around the camp and up and down and opened the box. I got him right out in my hand with his wings folded properly and I was careful not to startle him. He lay limp in my grasp and I could feel his heart pound under the feathers but he only looked beyond me and up.

I saw him look that last look away beyond me into a sky so full of light that I could not follow his gaze. The little breeze flowed over me again, and nearby a mountain aspen shook all its tiny leaves. I suppose I must have had an idea then of what I was going to do, but I never let it come up into consciousness. I just reached over and laid the hawk on the grass.

He lay there a long minute without hope, unmoving, his eyes still fixed on that blue vault above him. It must have been that he was already so far away in heart that he never felt the release from my hand. He never even stood. He just lay with his breast against the grass.

In the next second after that long minute he was gone. Like a flicker of light, he had vanished with my eyes full on him, but without actually seeing even a premonitory wing beat. He was gone straight into that towering emptiness of light and crystal that my eyes could scarcely bear to penetrate. For another long moment there was silence. I could not see him. The light was too intense. Then from far up somewhere a cry came ringing down.

I was young then and had seen little of the world, but when I heard that cry 30 my heart turned over. It was not the cry of the hawk I had captured; for, by shifting my position against the sun, I was now seeing further up. Straight out of the sun's eye, where she must have been soaring restlessly above us for untold hours, hurtled his mate. And from far up, ringing from peak to peak of the summits over us, came a cry of such unutterable and ecstatic joy that it sounds down across the years and tingles among the cups on my quiet breakfast table.

I saw them both now. He was rising fast to meet her. They met in a great soaring gyre that turned to a whirling circle and a dance of wings. Once more, just once, their two voices, joined in a harsh wild medley of question and response, struck and echoed against the pinnacles of the valley. Then they were gone forever somewhere into those upper regions beyond the eyes of men.

I am older now, and sleep less, and have seen most of what there is to see and am not very much impressed any more, I suppose, by anything. "What Next in the Attributes of Machines?" my morning headline runs. "It Might Be the Power to Reproduce Themselves."

I lay the paper down and across my mind a phrase floats insinuatingly: "It does not seem that there is anything in the construction, constituents, or behavior of the human being which it is essentially impossible for science to duplicate and synthesize. On the other hand . . ."

All over the city the cogs in the hard, bright mechanisms have begun to turn. Figures move through computers, names are spelled out, a thoughtful machine selects the fingerprints of a wanted criminal from an array of thousands. In the laboratory an electronic mouse runs swiftly through a maze toward the cheese it can neither taste nor enjoy. On the second run it does better than a living mouse.

"On the other hand . . ." Ah, my mind takes up, on the other hand the machine does not bleed, ache, hang for hours in the empty sky in a torment of hope to learn the fate of another machine, nor does it cry out with joy nor dance in the air with the fierce passion of a bird. Far off, over a distance greater than space, that remote cry from the heart of heaven makes a faint buzzing among my breakfast dishes and passes on and away. 35

Questions for Discussion

1. In paragraph 3, Loren Eiseley states, "This is the new world that I read about at breakfast." What would you have to read in the morning paper in order to feel you were in a new world?
2. Eiseley speaks in paragraph 15 of "one of those reciprocal matters in which science involves itself." How is this matter reciprocal? What would be "one of those reciprocal matters" today?
3. In paragraph 17, Eiseley says, "the most beautiful sight in the world might be the birds taking over New York after the last man has run away to the hills." Would you find this sight beautiful, or do you see it differently? What might Eiseley say about the red-tailed hawks whose nest at the top of an apartment building on Fifth Avenue in Manhattan was dismantled in 2006 and then restored after a public outcry? (See www.palemale.com for more information.)
4. Identify a passage that indicates an epiphany. Describe it. What does it suggest about Eiseley's attitude toward science?

5. At the end of the essay, Eiseley leaves his thesis implicit. If he wanted to conclude with one, which sentence from the first three paragraphs might serve his purpose?
6. Reread the essential question posed at the beginning of this chapter. What does Eiseley's essay reveal about the relationship among science, technology, and humanity?

Questions on Rhetoric and Style

1. In paragraph 1, Eiseley presents imagery before exposition. What effect does this have?
2. In paragraph 1, Eiseley speaks of "odd juxtapositions." Give an example of an odd juxtaposition in the essay. What is its effect?
3. How do such statements as "make no mistake," "they say now," "you know," "nothing to get superstitious about," "I guess," "I don't deny it," and "I'll admit" in paragraphs 3 and 4 help create the tone of the essay?
4. What is the effect of directly addressing the audience in paragraph 4?
5. Eiseley uses cause and effect in paragraphs 4 through 7. Is this pattern of development effective? Could he have used a different pattern? Explain.
6. What is the effect of the verbs Eiseley uses in paragraph 20?
7. What is ironic about what Eiseley says in paragraph 24?
8. What is the effect of Eiseley's shift from present to past in paragraph 31?
9. The essay has appeals to logos, ethos, and pathos. How do all three work together to create a bridge between the humanities and science?

Suggestions for Writing

1. In the first paragraph, Eiseley says, "It is a funny thing what the brain will do with memories and how it will treasure them and finally bring them into odd juxtapositions with other things, as though it wanted to make a design, or get some meaning out of them, whether you want it or not, or even see it." In your experience, have you found Eiseley's comment to be true? Write about a memory that has behaved the way Eiseley describes here.
2. Beginning in paragraph 4, Eiseley argues with the position stated by Thomas Hobbes, that the world is essentially a complex machine. Since this essay was written over a half century ago, whose position has proved to be more valid? Write an essay supporting Eiseley or Hobbes.
3. Eiseley describes with great detail his adventure with the birds. Write a detailed account of an event in which an "advance," either scientific or technological, turned out to have an unexpected effect.
4. Paraphrase Eiseley's thesis about the relationship between humanity and technology. Write an essay that supports or refutes his position.
5. Write an essay analyzing Eiseley's rhetorical strategy. Consider his use of different patterns of development, his use of juxtapositions, and his appeals to logos, pathos, and ethos.

The Method of Scientific Investigation

T. H. HUXLEY

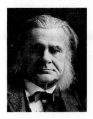 Thomas Henry Huxley (1825–1895), a distinguished British biologist and science writer, is widely considered the epitome of the scientific rationalist. Largely educated at home, he went on to study medicine at the University of London. After serving as a ship's doctor, he spent several years at sea on a scientific expedition to Australia. He was president of the Royal Society and authored many essays and books on science and education. Chief among Huxley's interests were the promotion of science as an important feature of education and the primacy of reason in all human affairs. To describe his own attitude toward belief in God and a spiritual reality, he coined the word *agnostic*. His books include *The Physical Basis of Life* (1868), *Science and Culture* (1881), and *Science and Education* (1899). The following essay, originally given as one of his "Six Lectures to Working Men," illustrates his rational approach to science and knowledge.

The method of scientific investigation is nothing but the expression of the necessary mode of working of the human mind. It is simply the mode at which all phenomena are reasoned about, rendered precise and exact. There is no more difference, but there is just the same kind of difference, between the mental operations of a man of science and those of an ordinary person, as there is between the operations and methods of a baker or of a butcher weighing out his goods in common scales, and the operations of a chemist in performing a difficult and complex analysis by means of his balance and finely graduated weights. It is not that the action of the scales in the one case, and the balance in the other, differ in the principles of their construction or manner of working; but the beam of one is set on an infinitely finer axis than the other, and of course turns by the addition of a much smaller weight.

You will understand this better, perhaps, if I give you some familiar example. You have all heard it repeated, I dare say, that men of science work by means of induction and deduction, and that by the help of these operations, they, in a sort of sense, wring from Nature certain other things, which are called natural laws, and causes, and that out of these, by some cunning skill of their own, they build up hypotheses and theories. And it is imagined by many, that the operations of the common mind can be by no means compared with these processes, and that they have to be acquired by a sort of special apprenticeship to the craft. To hear all these large words, you would think that the mind of a man of science must be constituted differently from that of his fellow men; but if you will not be frightened by terms, you will discover that you are quite wrong, and that all these terrible apparatus are being used by yourselves every day and every hour of your lives.

609

There is a well-known incident in one of Molière's plays, where the author makes the hero express unbounded delight on being told that he had been talking prose during the whole of his life. In the same way, I trust, that you will take comfort, and be delighted with yourselves, on the discovery that you have been acting on the principles of inductive and deductive philosophy during the same period. Probably there is not one here who has not in the course of the day had occasion to set in motion a complex train of reasoning, of the very same kind, though differing of course in degree, as that which a scientific man goes through in tracing the causes of natural phenomena.

A very trivial circumstance will serve to exemplify this. Suppose you go into a fruiterer's shop, wanting an apple — you take up one, and, on biting it, you find it is sour; you look at it, and see that it is hard and green. You take up another one, and that too is hard, green, and sour. The shopman offers you a third; but, before biting it, you examine it, and find that it is hard and green, and you immediately say that you will not have it, as it must be sour, like those that you have already tried.

Nothing can be more simple than that, you think; but if you will take the trouble to analyse and trace out into its logical elements what has been done by the mind, you will be greatly surprised. In the first place, you have performed the operation of induction. You found that, in two experiences, hardness and greenness in apples went together with sourness. It was so in the first case, and it was confirmed by the second. True, it is a very small basis, but still it is enough to make an induction from; you generalise the facts, and you expect to find sourness in apples where you get hardness and greenness. You found upon that a general law, that all hard and green apples are sour; and that, so far as it goes, is a perfect induction. Well, having got your natural law in this way, when you are offered another apple which you find is hard and green, you say, "All hard and green apples are sour; this apple is hard and green, therefore this apple is sour." That train of reasoning is what logicians call a syllogism, and has all its various parts and terms — its major premiss, its minor premiss, and its conclusion. And, by the help of further reasoning, which, if drawn out, would have to be exhibited in two or three other syllogisms, you arrive at your final determination, "I will not have that apple." So that, you see, you have, in the first place, established a law by induction, and upon that you have founded a deduction, and reasoned out the special particular case. Well now, suppose, having got your conclusion of the law, that at some time afterwards, you are discussing the qualities of apples with a friend: you will say to him, "It is a very curious thing, but I find that all hard and green apples are sour!" Your friend says to you, "But how do you know that?" You at once reply, "Oh, because I have tried them over and over again, and have always found them to be so." Well, if we were talking science instead of common sense, we should call that an experimental verification. And, if still opposed, you go further, and say, "I have heard from the people in Somersetshire and Devonshire, where a large number of apples are grown, that they have observed the same thing. It is also found to be the case in Normandy, and in North America. In short, I find it to be the universal experience of mankind wherever attention has been directed to the subject." Whereupon, your friend, unless he is a very unreasonable man, agrees with you, and is convinced that you are quite right in the conclusion you have drawn. He believes, although perhaps he does not know he believes it, that the more extensive verifications are — that the more frequently experiments have been made, and results of the same kind arrived at — that the more varied the conditions under which the same results are attained, the more certain is the ultimate conclusion, and he disputes the question no further. He sees that the experiment has been tried under all sorts of conditions, as to time, place, and people, with the same result; and he says with you, therefore, that the law you have laid down must be a good one, and he must believe it.

In science we do the same thing — the philosopher exercises precisely the same faculties, though in a much more delicate manner. In scientific inquiry it becomes a matter of duty to expose a supposed law to every possible kind of verification, and to take care, moreover, that this is done intentionally, and not left to a mere accident, as in the case of the apples. And in science, as in common life, our confidence in a law is in exact proportion to the absence of variation in the result of our experimental verifications. For instance, if you let go your grasp of an article you may have in your hand, it will immediately fall to the ground. That is a very common verification of one of the best established laws of nature — that of gravitation. The method by which men of science establish the existence of that law is exactly the same as that by which we have established the trivial proposition about the sourness of hard and green apples. But we believe it in such an extensive, thorough, and unhesitating manner because the universal experience of mankind verifies it, and we can verify it ourselves at any time; and that is the strongest possible foundation on which any natural law can rest.

So much, then, by way of proof that the method of establishing laws in science is exactly the same as that pursued in common life. Let us now turn to another matter (though really it is but another phase of the same question), and that is, the method by which, from the relations of certain phenomena, we prove that some stand in the position of causes towards the others.

I want to put the case clearly before you, and I will therefore show you what I mean by another familiar example. I will suppose that one of you, on coming down in the morning to the parlour of your house, finds that a tea-pot and some spoons which had been left in the room on the previous evening are gone — the window is open, and you observe the mark of a dirty hand on the window-frame, and perhaps, in addition to that, you notice the impress of a hob-nailed shoe on the gravel outside. All these phenomena have struck your attention instantly, and before two seconds have passed you say, "Oh, somebody has broken open the window, entered the room, and run off with the spoons and the tea-pot!" That speech is out of your mouth in a moment. And you will probably add, "I know there has; I am quite sure of it!" You mean to say exactly what you know; but in reality you are giving expression to what is, in all essential particulars, an hypothesis. You do not *know* it at all; it is nothing but an hypothesis rapidly framed in your own mind. And it is an hypothesis founded on a long train of inductions and deductions.

What are those inductions and deductions, and how have you got at this hypothesis? You have observed in the first place, that the window is open; but by a train of reasoning involving many inductions and deductions, you have probably arrived long before at the general law — and a very good one it is — that windows do not open of themselves; and you therefore conclude that something has opened the window. A second general law that you have arrived at in the same way is, that tea-pots and spoons do not go out of a window spontaneously, and you are satisfied that, as they are not now where you left them, they have been removed. In the third place, you look at the marks on the window-sill, and the shoe-marks outside, and you say that in all previous experience the former kind of mark has never been produced by anything else but the hand of a human being; and the same experience shows that no other animal but man at present wears shoes with hob-nails in them such as would produce the marks in the gravel. I do not know, even if we could discover any of those "missing links" that are talked about, that they would help us to any other conclusion! At any rate the law which states our present experience is strong enough for my present purpose. You next reach the conclusion that, as these kinds of marks have not been left by any other animal than man, or are liable to be formed in any other way than by a man's hand and shoe, the marks in question have been formed by a man in that way. You have, further, a general law, founded on observation and experience, and that, too, is I am sorry to say, a very universal and unimpeachable one — that some men are thieves; and you assume at once from all these premises — and that is what constitutes your hypothesis — that the man who made the marks outside and on the windowsill, opened the window, got into the room, and stole your tea-pot and spoons. You have now arrived at a *vera causa* — you have assumed a cause which, it is plain, is competent to produce all the phenomena you have observed. You can explain all these phenomena only by the hypothesis of a thief. But that is a hypothetical conclusion, of the justice of which you have no absolute proof at all; it is only rendered highly probable by a series of inductive and deductive reasonings.

I suppose your first action, assuming that you are a man of ordinary common sense, and that you have established this hypothesis to your own satisfaction, will very likely be to go off for the police, and set them on the track of the burglar, with the view to the recovery of your property. But just as you are starting with this object, some person comes in, and on learning what you are about, says, "My good friend, you are going on a great deal too fast. How do you know that the man who really made the marks took the spoons? It might have been a monkey that took them, and the man may have merely looked in afterwards." You would probably reply, "Well, that is all very well, but you see it is contrary to all experience of the way tea-pots and spoons are abstracted; so that, at any rate, your hypothesis is less probable than mine." While you are talking the thing over in this way, another friend arrives, one of the good kind of people that I was talking of a little while ago. And he might say, "Oh, my dear sir, you are certainly going on a great deal too fast. You are most presumptuous. You admit that all these occurrences took place when you were fast asleep, at a time when you could not possibly have known anything about what was taking place. How do you know that the laws of Nature are not suspended during the night? It may be that there has been some kind of supernatural interference in this case." In point of fact, he declares that your hypothesis is one of which you cannot at all demonstrate the truth, and that you are by no means sure that the laws of Nature are the same when you are asleep as when you are awake.

Well, now, you cannot at the moment answer that kind of reasoning. You feel that your worthy friend has you somewhat at a disadvantage. You will feel perfectly convinced in your own mind, however, that you are quite right, and you say to him, "My good friend, I can only be guided by the natural probabilities of the case, and if you will be kind enough to stand aside and permit me to pass, I will go and fetch the police." Well, we will suppose that your journey is successful, and that by good luck you meet with a policeman; that eventually the burglar is found with your property on his person, and the marks correspond to his hand and to his boots. Probably any jury would consider those facts a very good experimental verification of your hypothesis, touching the cause of the abnormal phenomena observed in your parlour, and would act accordingly.

Now, in this supposititious case, I have taken phenomena of a very common kind, in order that you might see what are the different steps in an ordinary process of reasoning, if you will only take the trouble to analyse it carefully. All the operations I have described, you will see, are involved in the mind of any man of sense in leading him to a conclusion as to the course he should take in order to make good a robbery and punish the offender. I say that you are led, in that case, to your conclusion by exactly the same train of reasoning as that which a man of science pursues when he is endeavouring to discover the origin and laws of the most occult phenomena. The process is, and always must be, the same; and precisely the same mode of reasoning was employed by Newton and Laplace in their endeavours to discover and define the causes of the movements of the heavenly bodies, as you, with your own common sense, would employ to detect a burglar. The only difference is, that the nature of the inquiry being more abstruse, every step has to be most carefully watched, so that there may not be a single crack or flaw in your hypothesis. A flaw or crack in many of the hypotheses of daily life may be of little or no moment as affecting the general correctness of the conclusions at which we may arrive; but, in a scientific inquiry, a fallacy, great or small, is always of importance, and is sure to be in the long run constantly productive of mischievous if not fatal results.

Do not allow yourselves to be misled by the common notion that an hypothesis is untrustworthy simply because it is an hypothesis. It is often urged, in respect to some scientific conclusion, that, after all, it is only an hypothesis. But what more have we to guide us in nine-tenths of the most important affairs of daily life than hypotheses, and often very ill-based ones? So that in science, where the evidence of an hypothesis is subjected to the most rigid examination, we may rightly pursue the same course. You may have hypotheses, and hypotheses. A man may say, if he likes, that the moon is made of green cheese: that is an hypothesis. But another man, who has devoted a great deal of time and attention to the subject, and availed himself of the most powerful telescopes and the results of the observations of others, declares that in his opinion it is probably composed of materials very similar to those of which our own earth is made up: and that is also only an hypothesis. But I need not tell you that there is an enormous difference in the value of the two hypotheses. That one which is based on sound scientific knowledge is sure to have a corresponding value; and that which is a mere hasty random guess is likely to have but little value. Every great step in our progress in discovering causes has been made in exactly the same way as that which I have detailed to you. A person observing the occurrence of certain facts and phenomena asks, naturally enough, what process, what kind of operation known to occur in Nature, applied to the particular case, will unravel and explain the mystery? Hence you have the scientific hypothesis; and its value will be proportionate to the care and completeness with which its basis had been tested and verified. It is in these matters as in the commonest affairs of practical life; the guess of the fool will be folly, while the guess of the wise man will contain wisdom. In all cases, you see that the value of the result depends on the patience and faithfulness with which the investigator applies to his hypothesis every possible kind of verification.

Questions for Discussion

1. What important implication about the faculty of reason does T. H. Huxley make in paragraphs 2 and 3? What conclusions can be drawn from this?
2. According to Huxley, what is induction (para. 5)? What is deduction (para. 5)? What is an example of an induction from paragraph 9? What is an example of a deduction?
3. How does a syllogism work (para. 5)? Develop a syllogism based on an induction, as Huxley does.
4. According to Huxley, what is the "strongest possible foundation on which any natural law can rest" (para. 6)? Do you see that consideration at work in daily life?
5. What does Huxley suggest about the relationship between knowledge and belief?
6. Reread the opening sentence. Do you agree with Huxley's statement? Why or why not?
7. How could you apply the ideas in Huxley's essay to your study of science in school?

Questions on Rhetoric and Style

1. Huxley's opening sentence states a claim. How adequately does Huxley support it in the first few paragraphs?

2. What is the effect of Huxley's direct address to "you," the audience, in paragraph 2?
3. How does Huxley use analogy to develop his argument in the first six paragraphs?
4. In paragraph 3, Huxley refers to Molière, the French playwright and satirist. What does this reference suggest about Huxley's consideration of his audience?
5. What is the effect of such word choices as *trivial* and *delicate* in paragraph 6?
6. In paragraph 8, Huxley uses humor to show the ways in which we use induction and deduction. How does this strategy help him establish ethos?
7. What is the effect of Huxley's including the hypothesis of the "worthy friend" in paragraphs 10 and 11?
8. What does Huxley mean by "supposititious case" in paragraph 12?
9. How effective is the analogy developed in paragraph 12?
10. How effectively does Huxley support his concluding argument?

Suggestions for Writing

1. Write an argument that supports, refutes, or qualifies Huxley's opening sentence.
2. In the final paragraph, Huxley writes, "It is in these matters as in the commonest affairs of practical life; the guess of the fool will be folly, while the guess of the wise man will contain wisdom." Write an essay that illustrates the truth of that statement.
3. Huxley uses analogies to develop his argument about scientific method. Develop an additional analogy that would support one of the positions he develops, and explain how your example illustrates the validity of that position.
4. Write an essay exploring the relationship between Huxley's views and what you do in your science class. Consider how accurately Huxley's position describes your experience.
5. What does Huxley's essay imply about the importance of scientific reasoning? Does the essay speak to readers today as it did to Huxley's audience in the late nineteenth century? Why or why not?

The Reach of Imagination

Jacob Bronowski

Jacob Bronowski (1908–1974) was born in Poland, lived in Germany during World War I, and moved to London in 1920. He studied at Cambridge University, earning his PhD in mathematics in 1933. After teaching at various universities in England, he went to the United States in 1964 to work at the Salk Institute for Biological Studies. Bronowski is highly regarded for his ability to write about complex subjects for general audiences. Among his books are *Science and Human Values* (1965) and the widely popular *The Ascent of Man* (1973), which grew out of his television series for the British Broadcasting Corporation. Bronowski described himself as a "mathematician trained in physics, who was taken into the life sciences in middle age by a series of lucky chances." About his work, Bronowski wrote, "All that I have written, though it has seemed to me so different from year to year, turns to the same centre: the uniqueness of man that grows out of his struggle (and his gift) to understand both nature and himself." The following selection is the text of a speech given to the American Academy of Arts and Letters, which appeared in *The American Scholar* in 1967.

For three thousand years, poets have been enchanted and moved and perplexed by the power of their own imagination. In a short and summary essay I can hope at most to lift one small corner of that mystery, and yet it is a critical corner. I shall ask, What goes on in the mind when we imagine? You will hear from me that one answer to this question is fairly specific: which is to say, that we can describe the working of the imagination. And when we describe it as I shall do, it becomes plain that imagination is a specifically *human* gift. To imagine is the characteristic act, not of the poet's mind, or the painter's, or the scientist's, but of the mind of man.

My stress here on the word *human* implies that there is a clear difference in this between the actions of men and those of other animals. Let me then start with a classical experiment with animals and children which Walter Hunter thought out in Chicago about 1910. That was the time when scientists were agog with the success of Ivan Pavlov in forming and changing the reflex actions of dogs, which Pavlov had first announced in 1903. Pavlov had been given a Nobel prize the next year, in 1904; although in fairness I should say that the award did not cite his work on the conditioned reflex, but on the digestive glands.

Hunter duly trained some dogs and other animals on Pavlov's lines. They were taught that when a light came on over one of three tunnels out of their cage, that tunnel would be open; they could escape down it, and were rewarded with food if they did. But once he had fixed that conditioned reflex, Hunter added to it a deeper idea: he gave the mechanical experiment a new dimension, literally —

the dimension of time. Now he no longer let the dog go to the lighted tunnel at once; instead, he put out the light, and then kept the dog waiting a little while before he let him go. In this way Hunter timed how long an animal can remember where he has last seen the signal light to his escape route.

The results were and are staggering. A dog or a rat forgets which one of three tunnels has been lit up within a matter of seconds — in Hunter's experiment, ten seconds at most. If you want such an animal to do much better than this, you must make the task much simpler: you must face him with only two tunnels to choose from. Even so, the best that Hunter could do was to have a dog remember for five minutes which one of two tunnels had been lit up.

I am not quoting these times as if they were exact and universal: they surely are not. Hunter's experiment, more than fifty years old now, had many faults of detail. For example, there were too few animals, they were oddly picked, and they did not all behave consistently. It may be unfair to test a dog for what he *saw*, when he commonly follows his nose rather than his eyes. It may be unfair to test any animal in the unnatural setting of a laboratory cage. And there are higher animals, such as chimpanzees and other primates, which certainly have longer memories than the animals that Hunter tried.

Yet when all these provisos have been made (and met, by more modern experiments) the facts are still startling and characteristic. An animal cannot recall a signal from the past for even a short fraction of the time that a man can — for even a short fraction of the time that a child can. Hunter made comparable tests with six-year-old children and found, of course, that they were incomparably better than the best of his animals. There is a striking and basic difference between a man's ability to imagine something that he saw or experienced and an animal's failure.

Animals make up for this by other and extraordinary gifts. The salmon and the carrier pigeon can find their way home as we cannot; they have, as it were, a practical memory that man cannot match. But their actions always depend on some form of habit: on instinct or on learning, which reproduce by rote a train of known responses. They do not depend, as human memory does, on calling to mind the recollection of absent things.

Where is it that the animal falls short? We get a clue to the answer, I think when Hunter tells us how the animals in his experiment tried to fix their recollection. They most often pointed themselves at the light before it went out, as some gun dogs point rigidly at the game they scent — and get the name *pointer* from the posture. The animal makes ready to act by building the signal into its action. There is a primitive imagery in its stance, it seems to me; it is as if the animal were trying to fix the light in its mind by fixing it in its body. And indeed, how else can a dog mark and (as it were) name one of three tunnels, when he has no such words as *left* and *right*, and no such numbers as *one, two, three*? The directed gesture of attention and readiness is perhaps the only symbolic device that the dog commands to hold on to the past, and thereby to guide himself into the future.

I used the verb *to imagine* a moment ago, and now I have some ground for giving it a meaning. To *imagine* means to make images and to move them about inside one's head in new arrangements. When you and I recall the past, we imagine it in this direct and homely sense. The tool that puts the human mind ahead of the animal is imagery. For us, memory does not demand the preoccupation that it demands in animals, and it lasts immensely longer, because we fix it in images or other substitute symbols. With the same symbolic vocabulary we spell out the future — not one but many futures, which we weigh one against another.

I am using the word *image* in a wide meaning, which does not restrict it to the mind's eye as a visual organ. An image in my usage is what Charles Peirce called a *sign*, without regard for its sensory quality. Peirce distinguished between different forms of signs, but there is no reason to make his distinction here, for the imagination works equally with them all, and that is why we call them all images.

Indeed, the most important images for human beings are simply words, which are abstract symbols. Animals do not have words, in our sense; there is no specific center for language, in the brain of any animal, as there is in the human brain. In this respect at least we know that the human imagination depends on a configuration in the brain that has only evolved in the last one or two million years. In the same period, evolution has greatly enlarged the front lobes in the human brain, which govern the sense of the past and the future; and it is a fair guess that they are probably the seat of our other images. (Part of the evidence for this guess is that damage to the front lobes in primates reduces them to the state of Hunter's animals.) If the guess turns out to be right, we shall know why man has come to look like a highbrow or an egghead: because otherwise there would not be room in his head for his imagination.

The images play out for us events which are not present to our senses, and thereby guard the past and create the future — a future that does not yet exist, and may never come to exist in that form. By contrast, the lack of symbolic ideas, or their rudimentary poverty, cuts off an animal from the past and the future alike, and imprisons him in the present. Of all the distinctions between man and animal, the characteristic gift which makes us human is the power to work with symbolic images: the gift of imagination.

This is really a remarkable finding. When Philip Sidney in 1580 defended poets (and all unconventional thinkers) from the Puritan charge that they were liars, he said that a maker must imagine things that are not. Halfway between Sidney and us, William Blake said, "What is now proved was once only imagin'd." About the same time, in 1796, Samuel Taylor Coleridge for the first time distinguished between the passive fancy and the active imagination, "the living Power and prime Agent of all human Perception." Now we see that they were right, and precisely right: the human gift is the gift of imagination — and that is not just a literary phrase.

Nor is it just a literary gift; it is, I repeat, characteristically human. Almost everything that we do that is worth doing is done in the first place in the mind's eye. The richness of human life is that we have many lives; we live the events that do not happen (and some that cannot) as vividly as those that do; and if thereby we die a thousand deaths, that is the price we pay for living a thousand lives. (A cat, of course, has only nine.) Literature is alive to us because we live its images, but so is any play of the mind — so is chess: the lines of play that we foresee and try in our heads and dismiss are as much a part of the game as the moves that we make. John Keats said that the unheard melodies are sweeter, and all chess players sadly recall that the combinations that they planned and which never came to be played were the best.

I make this point to remind you, insistently, that imagination is the manipu-   15
lation of images in one's head; and that the rational manipulation belongs to that, as well as the literary and artistic manipulation. When a child begins to play games with things that stand for other things, with chairs or chessmen, he enters the gateway to reason and imagination together. For the human reason discovers new relations between things not by deduction, but by that unpredictable blend of speculation and insight that scientists call induction, which — like other forms of imagination — cannot be formalized. We see it at work when Walter Hunter inquires into a child's memory, as much as when Blake and Coleridge do. Only a restless and original mind would have asked Hunter's questions and could have conceived his experiments, in a science that was dominated by Pavlov's reflex arcs and was heading toward the behaviorism[1] of John Watson.

Let me find a spectacular example for you from history. What is the most famous experiment that you had described to you as a child? I will hazard that it is the experiment that Galileo is said to have made in Sidney's age, in Pisa about 1590, by dropping two unequal balls from the Leaning Tower. There, we say, is a man in the modern mold, a man after our own hearts: he insisted on questioning the authority of Aristotle and St. Thomas Aquinas, and seeing with his own eyes whether (as they said) the heavy ball would reach the ground before the light one. Seeing is believing.

Yet seeing is also imagining. Galileo did challenge the authority of Aristotle, and he did look hard at his mechanics. But the eye that Galileo used was the mind's eye. He did not drop balls from the Leaning Tower of Pisa — and if he had, he would have got a very doubtful answer. Instead, Galileo made an imaginary experiment in his head, which I will describe as he did years later in the book he wrote after the Holy Office silenced him: the *Discorsi . . . intorno à due nuove scienze* (Discourses Concerning Two New Sciences), which was smuggled out to be printed in the Netherlands in 1638.

Suppose, said Galileo, that you drop two unequal balls from the tower at the same time. And suppose that Aristotle is right — suppose that the heavy ball falls faster, so that it steadily gains on the light ball, and hits the ground first. Very well. Now imagine the same experiment done again, with only one difference: this time the two unequal balls are joined by a string between them. The heavy ball will again move ahead, but now the light ball holds it back and acts as a drag or

---

[1]Branch of psychology that argues that analysis of behavior is the best way to understand the patient's mental state. — Eds.

brake. So the light ball will be speeded up and the heavy ball will be slowed down; they must reach the ground together because they are tied together, but they cannot reach the ground as quickly as the heavy ball alone. Yet the string between them has turned the two balls into a single mass which is heavier than either ball — and surely (according to Aristotle) this mass should therefore move faster than either ball? Galileo's imaginary experiment has uncovered a contradiction; he says trenchantly, "You see how, from your assumption that a heavier body falls more rapidly than a lighter one, I infer that a (still) heavier body falls more slowly." There is only one way out of the contradiction: the heavy ball and the light ball must fall at the same rate, so that they go on falling at the same rate when they are tied together.

This argument is not conclusive, for nature might be more subtle (when the two balls are joined) than Galileo has allowed. And yet it is something more important: it is suggestive, it is stimulating, it opens a new view — in a word, it is imaginative. It cannot be settled without an actual experiment, because nothing that we imagine can become knowledge until we have translated it into, and backed it by, real experience. The test of imagination is experience. But then, that is as true of literature and the arts as it is of science. In science, the imaginary experiment is tested by confronting it with physical experience; and in literature, the imaginative conception is tested by confronting it with human experience. The superficial speculation in science is dismissed because it is found to falsify nature; and the shallow work of art is discarded because it is found to be untrue to our own nature. So when Ella Wheeler Wilcox died in 1919, more people were reading her verses than Shakespeare's; yet in a few years her work was dead. It had been buried by its poverty of emotion and its trivialness of thought: which is to say that it had been proved to be as false to the nature of man as, say, Jean Baptiste Lamarck[2] and Trofim Lysenko[3] were false to the nature of inheritance. The strength of the imagination, its enriching power and excitement, lies in its interplay with reality — physical and emotional.

I doubt if there is much to choose here between science and the arts: the imagination is not much more free, and not much less free, in one than in the other. All great scientists have used their imagination freely, and let it ride them to outrageous conclusions without crying "Halt!" Albert Einstein fiddled with imaginary experiments from boyhood, and was wonderfully ignorant of the facts that they were supposed to bear on. When he wrote the first of his beautiful papers on the random movement of atoms, he did not know that the Brownian motion which it predicted could be seen in any laboratory. He was sixteen when he invented the paradox that he resolved ten years later, in 1905, in the theory of rel-

20

---

[2]Jean Baptiste Lamarck (1744–1829), French naturalist who argued that acquired traits can be passed down to future generations. — Eds.
[3]Trofim Lysenko (1898–1976), Soviet agriculturalist who applied Lamarck's ideas to agriculture and used the Soviet propaganda machine to discredit agricultural genetics, resulting in the imprisonment and death of hundreds of scientists. — Eds.

ativity, and it bulked much larger in his mind than the experiment of Albert Michelson and Edward Morley which had upset every other physicist since 1881.[4] All his life Einstein loved to make up teasing puzzles like Galileo's, about falling lifts and the detection of gravity; and they carry the nub of the problems of general relativity on which he was working.

Indeed, it could not be otherwise. The power that man has over nature and himself, and that a dog lacks, lies in his command of imaginary experience. He alone has the symbols which fix the past and play with the future, possible and impossible. In the Renaissance, the symbolism of memory was thought to be mystical, and devices that were invented as mnemonics (by Giordano Bruno, for example, and by Robert Fludd) were interpreted as magic signs. The symbol is the tool which gives man his power, and it is the same tool whether the symbols are images or words, mathematical signs or mesons. And the symbols have a reach and a roundness that goes beyond their literal and practical meaning. They are the rich concepts under which the mind gathers many particulars into one name, and many instances into one general induction. When a man says *left* and *right*, he is outdistancing the dog not only in looking for a light; he is setting in train all the shifts of meaning, the overtones and the ambiguities, between *gauche* and *adroit* and *dexterous*, between *sinister* and the sense of right. When a man counts *one, two, three*, he is not only doing mathematics; he is on the path to the mysticism of numbers in Pythagoras and Vitruvius and Kepler[5], to the Trinity and the signs of the Zodiac.

I have described imagination as the ability to make images and to move them about inside one's head in new arrangements. This is the faculty that is specifically human, and it is the common root from which science and literature both spring and grow and flourish together. For they do flourish (and languish) together; the great ages of science are the great ages of all the arts, because in them powerful minds have taken fire from one another, breathless and higgledy-piggledy, without asking too nicely whether they ought to tie their imagination to falling balls or a haunted island. Galileo and Shakespeare, who were born in the same year, grew into greatness in the same age; when Galileo was looking through his telescope at the moon, Shakespeare was writing *The Tempest*; and all Europe was in ferment, from Johannes Kepler to Peter Paul Rubens, and from the first table of logarithms by John Napier to the authorized version of the Bible.

Let me end with a last and spirited example of the common inspiration of literature and science, because it is as much alive today as it was three hundred years

---

[4]From 1881 to 1887 Michelson (1852–1931) and Morley (1838–1923) repeatedly failed to prove the existence of a luminiferous aether, which was thought to be the medium through which light travels. — Eds.

[5]Each of these figures, Pythagoras (582 B.C.E.–507 B.C.E.), Vitruvius (c. 80 B.C.E.–c. 25 B.C.E.), and Johannes Kepler (1571–1630) believed, in his own way, that mathematics could reveal the divine. — Eds.

ago. What I have in mind is man's ageless fantasy, to fly to the moon. I do not display this to you as a high scientific enterprise; on the contrary, I think we have more important discoveries to make here on earth than wait for us, beckoning, at the horned surface of the moon. Yet I cannot belittle the fascination which that ice-blue journey has had for the imagination of men, long before it drew us to our television screens to watch the tumbling of astronauts. Plutarch and Lucian, Ariosto and Ben Jonson wrote about it, before the days of Jules Verne and H. G. Wells and science fiction. The seventeenth century was heady with new dreams and fables about voyages to the moon. Kepler wrote one full of deep scientific ideas, which (alas) simply got his mother accused of witchcraft. In England, Francis Godwin wrote a wild and splendid work, *The Man in the Moone*, and the astronomer John Wilkins wrote a wild and learned one, *The Discovery of a New World*. They did not draw a line between science and fancy; for example, they all tried to guess just where in the journey the earth's gravity would stop. Only Kepler understood that gravity has no boundary, and put a law to it — which happened to be the wrong law.

All this was a few years before Isaac Newton was born, and it was all in his head that day in 1666 when he sat in his mother's garden, a young man of twenty-three, and thought about the reach of gravity. This was how he came to conceive his brilliant image, that the moon is like a ball which has been thrown so hard that it falls exactly as fast as the horizon, all the way round the earth. The image will do for any satellite, and Newton modestly calculated how long therefore an astronaut would take to fall round the earth once. He made it ninety minutes, and we have all seen now that he was right; but Newton had no way to check that. Instead he went on to calculate how long in that case the distant moon would take to round the earth, if indeed it behaves like a thrown ball that falls in the earth's gravity, and if gravity obeyed a law of inverse squares. He found that the answer would be twenty-eight days.

In that telling figure, the imagination that day chimed with nature, and made   25
a harmony. We shall hear an echo of that harmony on the day when we land on the moon, because it will be not a technical but an imaginative triumph, that reaches back to the beginning of modern science and literature both. All great acts of imagination are like this, in the arts and in science, and convince us because they fill out reality with a deeper sense of rightness. We start with the simplest vocabulary of images, with *left* and *right* and *one, two, three*, and before we know how it happened the words and the numbers have conspired to make a match with nature: we catch in them the pattern of mind and matter as one.

Exploring the Text

1. What is Jacob Bronowski's definition of *imagination*? Do you agree with it? Have you thought of imagination this way before? If you disagree with Bronowski's definition, suggest another and explain why it is better.

2. Bronowski says images "guard the past and create the future" (para. 12). What does he mean?

3. Bronowski refers to a wide range of authorities, from Ivan Pavlov (a biologist) to Charles Peirce (a philosopher and mathematician), to Galileo (an astronomer), and to Albert Einstein (a physicist), as well as to Philip Sidney, William Blake, Samuel Taylor Coleridge, and William Shakespeare (all poets). What is the effect of such a diversity of references?

4. How effective is Bronowski's analogy to chess in paragraph 14? What makes it effective or ineffective?

5. What is the relationship between paragraphs 16 and 17?

6. Based on what you learned about deduction and induction from T. H. Huxley's essay (p. 609), what do you think of Bronowski's statement that induction "cannot be formalized" (para. 15)?

7. In paragraph 19, what does Bronowski present as common to science and literature?

8. How effectively does the example of Isaac Newton in paragraph 24 support Bronowski's thesis?

9. In his conclusion, Bronowski states that landing on the moon would be "not a technical but an imaginative triumph." Now that astronauts have gone to the moon, do you think of it as a technical or imaginative triumph?

The Future of Happiness

Mihaly Csikszentmihalyi

> Born in Hungary in 1934, Mihaly Csikszentmihalyi (pronounced Chick-SENT-mee-high) now lives in the United States. He received his doctorate from the University of Chicago in 1965, where he went on to become chair of the psychology department. Currently, he is Davidson Professor of Psychology and Management at the Claremont Graduate University in Claremont, California. Csikszentmihalyi is the author of several popular books about his theories, including *Flow: The Psychology of Optimal Experience* (1990) and *Finding Flow: The Psychology of Engagement with Everyday Life* (1997). "The Future of Happiness" appeared in the collection *The Next Fifty Years: Science in the First Half of the Twenty-first Century* (2002).

One issue that will become central in the next fifty years is how we shall use the ability to control the genetic makeup of the human species. In the past, our ancestors used crude methods of genetic selection to determine which kinds of children survived to reproductive age. Now we are being handed the dubious gift of reaching the same goal through the auspices of science.

Long before anyone suspected the existence of genes, farmers recognized that the traits of parents were passed down to the offspring, and thus they could improve the yield of pumpkins or the size of pigs by selectively breeding the best specimens with each other. It was then easy to apply this principle to human beings. Plato devotes a large part of the fifth book of his *Republic* to the question of how to apply the practices used to breed hunting dogs to producing rulers for the perfect State he envisions. In chapter 459, for instance, he writes:

> [T]he best of either sex should be united with the best as often, and the inferior with the inferior as seldom as possible; and . . . they should rear the offspring of the one sort of union, but not of the other, if the flock is to be maintained in first-rate condition. Now these goings on must be a secret which the rulers only know, or there will be a further danger of . . . rebellion.

Earlier, in chapter 415 of Book III, he writes, "And God proclaims as a first principle to the rulers . . . that there is nothing which they should so anxiously guard, or of which they should be such good guardians, as of the purity of the race." In fact, all known societies have practiced what in retrospect we could label "eugenics" or "genetic engineering." These practices were often justified in terms that have nothing to do with biology — such as religion or custom — but presumably they were carried out because they were seen as contributing to the survival of the group. It is useful to remember that the idea of all persons having the right to reproduce is a recent one; previous societies survived by granting that privilege primarily to individuals who were likely to produce above-average children.

Positive practices encouraged the mating of individuals with desirable phenotypic traits — including health, strength, and beauty — and material success, such as wealth or power. Differential reproduction was achieved by various means: The almost universal practice of obtaining a dowry or brideswealth before marriage ensured that the future parents would have enough resources and kin support to bring up children who would not become a burden to the community.

Negative practices discouraged reproduction among individuals with traits that a given society deemed undesirable. Some of these were little more than natural tendencies: For instance, poor, unhealthy individuals were less likely to marry and have children. But other means were much more active, ranging from castration to infanticide. Often a cultural practice that seemed to have an entirely different purpose might nevertheless have a substantial eugenic impact. For instance, the Russian Orthodox Church adopted the ritual of immersing naked newborn infants in cold water in order to infuse them with the grace of the Holy Ghost and protect their souls from eternal damnation. An incidental consequence of this practice was that less than healthy infants would not survive baptism, thus removing their genes from the gene pool. One can only speculate whether such rituals survived primarily because of the peace of mind they conferred on the devout or the genetic advantages they provided. Presumably they were overdetermined, in that both sets of advantages supported their existence relative to alternatives open to the culture at the time.

Most of these practices were hit-or-miss, without any foundation in an understanding of how different traits are transmitted from one generation to the next. But this situation is about to change drastically in the coming decades. Currently two of the liveliest branches of the human sciences are behavioral genetics, which tries to ascertain the degree of inheritability of such behavioral traits as schizophrenia, propensity to divorce, political beliefs, and even happiness, and evolutionary psychology, which searches out the mechanisms by which these traits are selected and transmitted from one generation to the next. Both approaches assume that nature and nurture are implicated in shaping our behavior, thoughts, and emotions — although, contrary to the learning bias of the last century, they favor nature more.

This trend is bound to be magnified tremendously in the next half century as a result of advances in genetics. Although few important traits are likely to depend on the action of a single or even a few genes, some genetic engineers are confident that the era of "designer babies" is at hand. Even if their optimism is misplaced, it would be foolish to ignore the impending decisions we may soon confront. It is interesting that leading human geneticists, of whom my colleagues and I interviewed close to one hundred in a recent study, have rarely taken the more controversial aspects of their work seriously. Most argue that it has no relation to anything resembling eugenics. They scoff at the possibility of human cloning and see little likelihood that their discoveries can be misused. Almost unanimously, they claim no special knowledge about or responsibility for potential applications of genetic engineering; they insist that this is a political decision, to be taken by society at large — even though "society" lacks the specialized understanding to make informed decisions. The situation is not unlike what was happening in atomic physics a little over a half century ago, when even such a universal thinker as Niels Bohr maintained into the 1940s that experiments with nuclear fission could have no possible practical applications.

But ready or not, the choices will soon have to be made, and they will determine our future. For instance, let us suppose that it will be possible soon to substantially increase g, the general-intelligence factor that underlies the linguistic and mathematical skills prized by the educational system and useful in other spheres of life as well. Is this a good idea? Several commentators have pointed out that society is already stratified by intelligence to a troublesome extent. Whereas in the recent past people could be considered successful if they were hardworking, honest, friendly, or virtuous, without necessarily being "book smart," nowadays abstract reasoning skills are becoming a prerequisite for any kind of material or social success. If we find ways to enhance this trait genetically, the trend may become exponential. As the division between "supersmart" and average individuals increases, so will the gap between their economic and political power. Endogamy based on intelligence — already in effect — will become more pronounced, as no one with an IQ over 200 would dream of marrying someone with an IQ of less than 150. If the engineering affects the germline, these divisions will be transmitted automatically to the next generation.

But what if, in an unlikely burst of egalitarianism, we found ways to enhance everyone's intelligence — to raise the baseline for the entire human race? Would that be a good idea? The answer is that we don't know. Most biological and psychological functions that are useful in small doses are dangerous when they become excessive. As Aristotle noted, virtues become vices when taken to the extreme: Courage turns into foolhardiness, prudence into indecisiveness. The ambiguous relation of genius to insanity suggests that too much intelligence may have its own handicaps — excessive sensitivity, for example, leading to proneness to anxiety and depression. Or, to the extent that rational intelligence is linked to self-centered attitudes à la Ayn Rand[1], it may result in a species even more unfeeling and cruel than we are now.

A more basic issue is whether, having the means, we should aim for uniformity or diversity in fiddling with the human genome. The pressure for uniformity is going to be great: Everybody will want to have children who are intelligent, good-looking (by standard conceptions of beauty), ambitious, and successful. Diversity is risky. Who would want to wager on the unknown, the untested? Yet the biologist E. O. Wilson's arguments in favor of biodiversity also apply to psychological traits; the prospect of an increasingly homogeneous race is not only frightening to our humanistic sensibilities but potentially dangerous from the strict perspective of survival. Because the future is largely unforeseeable, the best strategy is to have a diverse pool of potentialities from which adaptive responses to new situations may emerge, instead of locking ourselves into a pattern that is best in terms of present conditions.

If human genetic engineering will be market-driven (instead of being dictated by a central computer that will determine how many warriors, workers, and drones society will need in the next generation), it is likely that the most intense selective pressure will be for producing happy children. When parents are asked what they hope for their children, the typical answer is that they hope the kids will be well educated and have good jobs, but above all else that they will be happy in whatever path they choose for themselves. Contemporary parents seem to agree with Aristotle, in that they understand that while every other good is a means to an end, happiness is *the* good in itself: It is what we hope to achieve through education, money, beauty, and intelligence. If it becomes possible to produce happiness through genetic manipulation, that may well become parents' first priority.

According to behavioral geneticists studying identical and fraternal twins reared together and apart, at least 50 percent of happiness is genetically inherited. One might have some justifiable reservations about how "happiness" is measured in such studies, but the fact that there is a set point of happiness different from one individual to the next and relatively impervious to external ups and downs seems well established. Of course, the general level of happiness in a population is also affected by economic conditions (having more money is related to happiness, up to a point, but past the threshold of income that would be average in Por-

10

---

[2]Ayn Rand (1905–1982), author and philosopher. Rand founded the Objectivist movement, which argued that the purpose of life is the pursuit of one's own happiness. — Eds.

tugal or South Korea additional income does not correspond to more happiness), the political situation, and many other external variables. Nevertheless, one's genetic inheritance plays an important role.

So let us suppose that in the decades ahead it will be possible to enhance the likelihood of our children's happiness through genetic engineering. Are we going to do them a favor by availing ourselves of this opportunity? Will society, and the species as a whole, benefit from such a choice? In speculating on what the answers to these questions may be, we might start by reviewing the little we know about happiness at this point.

In the first place, it seems clear that people's self-report of how happy they are is a fairly valid measure of their happiness. It correlates highly with the perception of family and friends, with the incidence of pathologies and relevant behaviors — in short, people who think they are happy also look and act like happy people are supposed to. They tend to be extroverted, they have stable relationships, they live healthy and productive lives. So far, so good.

But there might be some interesting downsides as well. For instance, one of the most widely accepted definitions of happiness is that it is a state in which one does not desire anything else. Happy people tend not to value material possessions highly, are less affected by advertising and propaganda, are not as driven by desire for power and achievement. Why would they? They are happy already, right? The prospect of a society of happy people should be enough to send shivers down the spine of our productive system, built on ever-escalating consumption, on never-satisfied desire.

Will academic psychology be of any help in providing answers to these impending choices? Until about two decades ago, the discipline had very little to say about happiness. It was considered too "soft" an issue for serious scientific study. To make a difference in this quandary, psychology will have to focus once again on its original object, the psyche — not as an ephemeral, mystical, soul-like substance but as a set of the very concrete phenomena that transpire in our consciousness as our attention is turned to apprehending, integrating, and responding both to external stimuli and to internal states (that is, thoughts and emotions). The stream of consciousness is considered by most scientists, including psychologists, to be too subjective for rigorous study, while in fact it is the most objective datum we have access to. Scientific facts and the knowledge based on them is hearsay that I am glad to accept on faith, but the events in consciousness, such as fear, joy, anger, hope — to them I have immediate access and their reality is beyond question.

For my part, I determined to develop a systematic phenomenology that would find answers to the following kinds of questions: How do people's thoughts, feelings, goals, and actions fluctuate during an average day? During a lifetime? How are these components of the stream of consciousness related to each other? When do people feel happy in everyday life? Any one of these questions could in turn generate dozens of further ones, including investigations of how age, gender, ethnicity, and other such differences affect consciousness and how patterns measured at one time relate to patterns measured years later. Among the things we learned is that people who are engaged in challenging activities with clear goals tend to be happier than those who lead relaxing, pleasurable lives. The less one works just for oneself, the larger the scope of one's relationships and commitments, the happier a person is likely to be.

It is also important to realize that consciousness has its own specific reality, which is immediately destroyed when one begins to analyze it in terms appropriate to less complex systems. For one thing, it is an open system, whose states constantly change through time. What's on my mind now, for instance, cannot have been accurately predicted by what was on my mind a minute ago, even if you had all the information about my brain chemistry, genetic background, past learning, and so forth, sixty seconds earlier. What happens between time 1 and time 2 is that any sound, sight, feeling, or idea that enters consciousness during that minute may set my thoughts and feelings on an entirely new and unpredictable course.

This indeterminacy can be seen most clearly in creative activity. It is generally thought that the elements of a poem (or a sonata, a painting, a scientific theory) could be retrieved from the poet's mind if we had enough information about the contents of that mind. That is, in a distant analogy to the homuncular theory of embryonic development, we believe that the creative work is contained — even if only in some microscopic or codified form — within the creator. But that is not the case. A poet may start with a single word or phrase — a word or phrase that is meaningless or ordinary but which at that particular moment seems compelling to him. Why the word or phrase is suddenly meaningful might be explained if you knew what the poet was thinking or feeling just before. But what happens next is not: The word may suggest ideas and associations that were not predictable, and these in turn open up new directions of thought and feeling, which lead to more words, and so on in an expanding circle of meaning that is the result of an emerging, autonomous, self-organizing system — still based on the poet's past consciousness but no longer reducible to it.

One need not turn to creativity to illustrate this process. Let's take a more universal event, the reaction of parents to their newborn child. Genetic and evolutionary psychology can tell us a great deal about how and why parents bond with their offspring. Parenting is one of the oldest human experiences; it has been the experience of every generation since the beginnings of our species. Nevertheless, even if one knows everything about babies and birth, seeing one's own child for the first time is an event so *sui generis* that nothing can adequately prepare one for it. Its nuances depend on how one feels about one's spouse, one's financial situation, one's life in general — to say nothing of the baby's physical appearance and behavior — and all of these elements are striving to achieve meaningful combination with the main event, the birth of the baby. You can guess what that combination will look like by knowing as much as possible about the parent, but the prediction will be imprecise, because too many of the variable factors that affect the parent's consciousness are external.

If psychology were to take the stream of consciousness for its territory, it 20 might begin to provide the kind of knowledge that we will need to make enlightened choices about the sort of future we want. With every increase in knowledge, our responsibilities increase. In the past, we were like passengers on the slow coach of evolution. Now evolution is more like a rocket hurtling through space, and we are no longer passengers but its pilots. What kind of human beings are we going to create? Flesh-and-blood copies of our machines and computers? Or beings with a consciousness open to the cosmos, organisms that are joyfully evolving in unprecedented directions?

Psychology is beginning to show signs of moving in the latter direction. At various centers in the United States and abroad, topics like wisdom, life goals, intrinsic motivation, spirituality — all of which would have been outside the pale a few decades ago — are being investigated by serious scholars. During his recent presidency of the American Psychological Association, Martin E. P. Seligman established within the profession a "Positive Psychology" movement, which reaches beyond the traditional goals of healing mental afflictions. Among its accomplishments so far has been the development of a list of "strengths" that are ubiquitous across times and cultures — such as wisdom, valor, perseverance, and integrity. As a next step, the knowledge of how such strengths are cultivated is being assembled. Eventually this knowledge should permeate the profession, giving it equal weight with the practice of therapy and prevention. We will need such a science to confront successfully the challenges of the next fifty years.

Exploring the Text

1. What is Mihaly Csikszentmihalyi referring to as a "dubious gift"? How is it dubious? How is it a gift?

2. In paragraph 2, Csikszentmihalyi says, "it is useful to remember that the idea of all persons having the right to reproduce is a recent one; previous societies survived by granting that privilege primarily to individuals who were likely to produce above-average children." How does he prove this radical statement? Are his examples convincing? Explain.

3. In paragraph 5, the author writes of "the learning bias of the last century." How does his language in that phrase influence your understanding of his position?

4. What does Csikszentmihalyi suggest about the relationship of science, technology, and politics (para. 6)? What might be the positive and negative effects of this relationship? What would be the ideal relationship?

5. What is the effect of Csikszentmihalyi's reference to E. O. Wilson, the eminent evolutionary biologist, in paragraph 9? Do you accept his argument? If yes, what rhetorical move did you find most convincing? If no, what rhetorical move would you have made to make the argument more convincing?

6. Do you agree with Csikszentmihalyi's posited characteristics of happiness (para. 14)? What would be the effect of a population like the one described?

7. What is ironic about the relationship between happiness and pleasure (para. 16)?

8. According to Csikszentmihalyi in paragraph 18, what accounts for the indeterminacy of human consciousness? Which of the two examples of indeterminacy — creativity (para. 18), or parental response to a birth (para. 19) — do you find more compelling? Why?

9. Paragraph 20 echoes the ideas of Loren Eiseley's "The Bird and the Machine" (p. 601). However, Csikszentimihalyi believes we will be able to choose to have humans evolve into something more than a model of a machine, while Eiseley believes that feelings like the joy of the two birds who reunite under the blue sky are impossible to replicate. Compare the way the two writers use figurative language and rhetorical questions to examine the possibilities and limitations of human and animal existence in the present and the future.

10. What quality could you add to Csikszentmihalyi's "list of 'strengths'" in the final paragraph? Why is that quality important?

The Blank Slate

STEVEN PINKER

Steven Pinker was born in Montreal, Canada, in 1954. He received a BA from McGill University and a PhD from Harvard. He taught for twenty-one years in the Department of Brain and Cognitive Sciences at the Massachusetts Institute of Technology and for two years at Stanford. Later, he moved to Harvard, where he is now a professor in the psychology department. Pinker writes about the nature of language and cognitive science; among his books are *The Language Instinct* (1994), *How the Mind Works* (1997), and *The Blank Slate* (2002). His essays have appeared in a variety of publications, including the *New York Times*, *Time*, the *New Yorker*, *Technology Review*, and *Slate*. Selected for inclusion in *The Best American Science and Nature Writing* (2003), the essay included here, "The Blank Slate," first appeared in *Discover*.

If you read the pundits in newspapers and magazines, you may have come across some remarkable claims about the malleability of the human psyche. Here are a few from my collection of clippings:

- Little boys quarrel and fight because they are encouraged to do so.
- Children enjoy sweets because their parents use them as rewards for eating vegetables.
- Teenagers get the idea to compete in looks and fashion from spelling bees and academic prizes.
- Men think the goal of sex is an orgasm because of the way they were socialized.

If you find these assertions dubious, your skepticism is certainly justified. In all cultures little boys quarrel, children like sweets, teens compete for status, and men pursue orgasms without the slightest need of encouragement or socialization. In each case, the writers made their preposterous claims without a shred of evidence — without even a nod to the possibility that they were saying something common sense might call into question.

Intellectual life today is beset with a great divide. On one side is a militant denial of human nature, a conviction that the mind of a child is a blank slate that is subsequently inscribed by parents and society. For much of the past century, psychology has tried to explain all thought, feeling, and behavior with a few simple mechanisms of learning by association. Social scientists have tried to explain all customs and social arrangements as a product of the surrounding culture. A long list of concepts that would seem natural to the human way of thinking — emotions, kinship, the sexes — are said to have been "invented" or "socially constructed."

At the same time, there is a growing realization that human nature won't go away. Anyone who has had more than one child, or been in a heterosexual relationship, or noticed that children learn language but house pets don't has recognized that people are born with certain talents and temperaments. An acknowledgment that we humans are a species with a timeless and universal psychology pervades the writings of great political thinkers, and without it we cannot explain the recurring themes of literature, religion, and myth. Moreover, the modern sciences of mind, brain, genes, and evolution are showing that there is something to the commonsense idea of human nature. Although no scientist denies that learning and culture are crucial to every aspect of human life, these processes don't happen by magic. There must be complex innate mental faculties that enable human beings to create and learn culture.

Sometimes the contradictory attitudes toward human nature divide people   5
into competing camps. The blank slate camp tends to have greater appeal among those in the social sciences and humanities than it does among biological scientists. And until recently, it was more popular on the political left than it was on the right.

But sometimes both attitudes coexist uneasily inside the mind of a single person. Many academics, for example, publicly deny the existence of intelligence. But privately, academics are *obsessed* with intelligence, discussing it endlessly in admissions, in hiring, and especially in their gossip about one another. And despite their protestations that it is a reactionary concept, they quickly invoke it to oppose executing a murderer with an I.Q. of 64 or to support laws requiring the removal of lead paint because it may lower a child's I.Q. by five points. Similarly, those who argue that gender differences are a reversible social construction do not treat them that way in their advice to their daughters, in their dealings with the opposite sex, or in their unguarded gossip, humor, and reflections on their lives.

No good can come from this hypocrisy. The dogma that human nature does not exist, in the face of growing evidence from science and common sense that it does, has led to contempt among many scholars in the humanities for the concepts of evidence and truth. Worse, the doctrine of the blank slate often distorts science itself by making an extreme position — that culture alone determines behavior — seem moderate, and by making the moderate position — that behavior comes from an interaction of biology and culture — seem extreme.

For example, many policies on parenting come from research that finds a correlation between the behavior of parents and of their children. Loving parents have confident children, authoritative parents (neither too permissive nor too punitive) have well-behaved children, parents who talk to their children have children with better language skills, and so on. Thus everyone concludes that parents should be loving, authoritative, and talkative, and if children don't turn out well, it must be the parents' fault.

Those conclusions depend on the belief that children are blank slates. It ignores the fact that parents provide their children with genes, not just an environment. The correlations may be telling us only that the same genes that make adults loving, authoritative, and talkative make their children self-confident, well behaved, and articulate. Until the studies are redone with adopted children (who get only their environment from their parents), the data are compatible with the possibility that genes make all the difference, that parenting makes all the difference, or anything in between. Yet the extreme position — that parents are everything — is the only one researchers entertain.

The denial of human nature has not just corrupted the world of intellectuals   10 but has harmed ordinary people. The theory that parents can mold their children like clay has inflicted child-rearing regimes on parents that are unnatural and sometimes cruel. It has distorted the choices faced by mothers as they try to balance their lives, and it has multiplied the anguish of parents whose children haven't turned out as hoped. The belief that human tastes are reversible cultural preferences has led social planners to write off people's enjoyment of ornament, natural light, and human scale and forced millions of people to live in drab cement boxes. And the conviction that humanity could be reshaped by massive social engineering projects has led to some of the greatest atrocities in history.

The phrase "blank slate" is a loose translation of the medieval Latin term *tabula rasa* — scraped tablet. It is often attributed to the seventeenth-century English philosopher John Locke, who wrote that the mind is "white paper void of all characters." But it became the official doctrine among thinking people only in the first half of the twentieth century, as part of a reaction to the widespread belief in the intellectual or moral inferiority of women, Jews, nonwhite races, and non-Western cultures.

Part of the reaction was a moral repulsion from discrimination, lynchings, forced sterilizations, segregation, and the Holocaust. And part of it came from empirical observations. Waves of immigrants from southern and eastern Europe filled the cities of America and climbed the social ladder. African Americans took advantage of "Negro colleges" and migrated northward, beginning the Harlem Renaissance. The graduates of women's colleges launched the first wave of feminism. To say that women and minority groups were inferior contradicted what people could see with their own eyes.

Academics were swept along by the changing attitudes, but they also helped direct the tide. The prevailing theories of mind were refashioned to make racism and sexism as untenable as possible. The blank slate became sacred scripture. According to the doctrine, any differences we see among races, ethnic groups, sexes, and individuals come not from differences in their innate constitution but from differences in their experiences. Change the experiences — by reforming parenting, education, the media, and social rewards — and you can change the person. Also, if there is no such thing as human nature, society will not be saddled with such nasty traits as aggression, selfishness, and prejudice. In a reformed environment, people can be prevented from learning these habits.

In psychology, behaviorists like John B. Watson and B. F. Skinner simply banned notions of talent and temperament, together with all the other contents of the mind, such as beliefs, desires, and feelings. This set the stage for Watson's famous boast: "Give me a dozen healthy infants, well-formed, and my own specified world to bring them up in, and I'll guarantee to take any one at random and train him to become any type of specialist I might select — doctor, lawyer, artist, merchant-chief, and yes, even beggar-man and thief, regardless of his talents, penchants, tendencies, abilities, vocations, and race of his ancestors."

Watson also wrote an influential child-rearing manual recommending that parents give their children minimum attention and love. If you comfort a crying baby, he wrote, you will reward the baby for crying and thereby increase the frequency of crying behavior. 15

In anthropology, Franz Boas wrote that differences among human races and ethnic groups come not from their physical constitution but from their *culture*. Though Boas himself did not claim that people were blank slates — he only argued that all ethnic groups are endowed with the same mental abilities — his students, who came to dominate American social science, went further. They insisted not just that *differences* among ethnic groups must be explained in terms of culture (which is reasonable) but that *every aspect* of human existence must be explained in terms of culture (which is not). "Heredity cannot be allowed to have acted any part in history," wrote Alfred Kroeber. "With the exception of the instinctoid reactions in infants to sudden withdrawals of support and to sudden loud noises, the human being is entirely instinctless," wrote Ashley Montagu.

In the second half of the twentieth century, the ideals of the social scientists of the first half enjoyed a well-deserved victory. Eugenics, social Darwinism, overt expressions of racism and sexism, and official discrimination against women and minorities were on the wane, or had been eliminated, from the political and intellectual mainstream in Western democracies.

At the same time, the doctrine of the blank slate, which had been blurred with ideals of equality and progress, began to show cracks. As new disciplines such as cognitive science, neuroscience, evolutionary psychology, and behavioral genetics flourished, it became clearer that thinking is a biological process, that the brain is not exempt from the laws of evolution, that the sexes differ above the neck as well as below it, and that people are not psychological clones. Here are some examples of the discoveries.

Natural selection tends to homogenize a species into a standard design by concentrating the effective genes and winnowing out the ineffective ones. This suggests that the human mind evolved with a universal complex design. Beginning in the 1950s, the linguist Noam Chomsky of the Massachusetts Institute of Technology argued that a language should be analyzed not in terms of the list of sentences people utter but in terms of the mental computations that enable them to handle an unlimited number of new sentences in the language. These computations have been found to conform to a universal grammar. And if this universal grammar is embodied in the circuitry that guides babies when they listen to speech, it could explain how children learn language so easily.

Similarly, some anthropologists have returned to an ethnographic record that used to trumpet differences among cultures and have found an astonishingly detailed set of aptitudes and tastes that all cultures have in common. This shared way of thinking, feeling, and living makes all of humanity look like a single tribe, which the anthropologist Donald Brown of the University of California at Santa Barbara has called the universal people. Hundreds of traits, from romantic love to humorous insults, from poetry to food taboos, from exchange of goods to mourning the dead, can be found in every society ever documented.

One example of a stubborn universal is the tangle of emotions surrounding the act of love. In all societies, sex is at least somewhat "dirty." It is conducted in private, pondered obsessively, regulated by custom and taboo, the subject of gossip and teasing, and a trigger for jealous rage. Yet sex is the most concentrated source of physical pleasure granted by the nervous system. Why is it so fraught with conflict? For a brief period in the 1960s and 1970s, people dreamed of an erotopia in which men and women could engage in sex without hang-ups and inhibitions. "If you can't be with the one you love, love the one you're with," sang Stephen Stills. "If you love somebody, set them free," sang Sting.

But Sting also sang, "Every move you make, I'll be watching you." Even in a time when, seemingly, anything goes, most people do not partake in sex as casually as they partake in food or conversation. The reasons are as deep as anything in biology. One of the hazards of sex is a baby, and a baby is not just any seven-pound object but, from an evolutionary point of view, our reason for being. Every time a woman has sex with a man, she is taking a chance at sentencing herself to years of motherhood, and she is forgoing the opportunity to use her finite repro-

ductive output with some other man. The man, for his part, may be either implicitly committing his sweat and toil to the incipient child or deceiving his partner
about such intentions.

On rational grounds, the volatility of sex is a puzzle, because in an era with
reliable contraception, these archaic entanglements should have no claim on our
feelings. We should be loving the one we're with, and sex should inspire no more
gossip, music, fiction, raunchy humor, or strong emotions than eating or talking
does. The fact that people are tormented by the Darwinian economics of babies
they are no longer having is testimony to the long reach of human nature.

Although the minds of normal human beings work in pretty much the same way,
they are not, of course, identical. Natural selection reduces genetic variability but
never eliminates it. As a result, nearly every one of us is genetically unique. And
these differences in genes make a difference in mind and behavior, at least quanti-
tatively. The most dramatic demonstrations come from studies of the rare people
who *are* genetically identical, identical twins.

Identical twins think and feel in such similar ways that they sometimes suspect they are linked by telepathy. They are similar in verbal and mathematical
intelligence, in their degree of life satisfaction, and in personality traits such as
introversion, agreeableness, neuroticism, conscientiousness, and openness to
experience. They have similar attitudes toward controversial issues such as the
death penalty, religion, and modern music. They resemble each other not just in
paper-and-pencil tests but in consequential behavior such as gambling, divorc-
ing, committing crimes, getting into accidents, and watching television. And they
boast dozens of shared idiosyncrasies such as giggling incessantly, giving interminable answers to simple questions, dipping buttered toast in coffee, and, in the
case of Abigail van Buren and the late Ann Landers, writing indistinguishable
syndicated advice columns. The crags and valleys of their electroencephalograms
(brain waves) are as alike as those of a single person recorded on two occasions,
and the wrinkles of their brains and the distribution of gray matter across cortical
areas are similar as well.

Identical twins (who share all their genes) are far more similar than fraternal
twins (who share just half their genes). This is as true when the twins are separated at birth and raised apart as when they are raised in the same home by the
same parents. Moreover, biological siblings, who also share half their genes, are
far more similar than adoptive siblings, who share no more genes than strangers.
Indeed, adoptive siblings are barely similar at all. These conclusions come from
massive studies employing the best instruments known to psychology. Alternative explanations that try to push the effects of the genes to zero have by now been
tested and rejected.

People sometimes fear that if the genes affect the mind at all they must determine it in every detail. That is wrong, for two reasons. The first is that most effects
of genes are probabilistic. If one identical twin has a trait, there is often no more

25

than an even chance that the other twin will have it, despite having a complete genome in common (and in the case of twins raised together, most of their environment in common as well).

The second reason is that the genes' effects can vary with the environment. Although Woody Allen's fame may depend on genes that enhance a sense of humor, he once pointed out that "we live in a society that puts a big value on jokes. If I had been an Apache Indian, those guys didn't need comedians, so I'd be out of work."

Studies of the brain also show that the mind is not a blank slate. The brain, of course, has a pervasive ability to change the strengths of its connections as the result of learning and experience — if it didn't, we would all be permanent amnesiacs. But that does not mean that the structure of the brain is mostly a product of experience. The study of the brains of twins has shown that much of the variation in the amount of gray matter in the prefrontal lobes is genetically caused. And these variations are not just random differences in anatomy like fingerprints; they correlate significantly with differences in intelligence.

People born with variations in the typical brain plan can vary in the way their minds work. A study of Einstein's brain showed that he had large, unusually shaped inferior parietal lobules, which participate in spatial reasoning and intuitions about numbers. Gay men are likely to have a relatively small nucleus in the anterior hypothalamus, a nucleus known to have a role in sex differences. Convicted murderers and other violent, antisocial people are likely to have a relatively small and inactive prefrontal cortex, the part of the brain that governs decision making and inhibits impulses. These gross features of the brain are almost certainly not sculpted by information coming in from the senses. That, in turn, implies that differences in intelligence, scientific genius, sexual orientation, and impulsive violence are not entirely learned.

The doctrine of the blank slate had been thought to undergird the ideals of equal rights and social improvement, so it is no surprise that the discoveries undermining it have often been met with fear and loathing. Scientists challenging the doctrine have been libeled, picketed, shouted down, and subjected to searing invective.

This is not the first time in history that people have tried to ground moral principles in dubious factual assumptions. People used to ground moral values in the doctrine that Earth lay at the center of the universe and that God created mankind in his own image in a day. In both cases, informed people eventually reconciled their moral values with the facts, not just because they had to give a nod to reality, but also because the supposed connections between the facts and morals — such as the belief that the arrangement of rock and gas in space has something to do with right and wrong — were spurious to begin with.

We are now living, I think, through a similar transition. The blank slate has been widely embraced as a rationale for morality, but it is under assault from science. Yet just as the supposed foundations of morality shifted in the centuries following Galileo and Darwin, our own moral sensibilities will come to terms with the scientific findings, not just because facts are facts but because the moral credentials of the blank slate are just as spurious. Once you think through the issues, the two greatest fears of an innate human endowment can be defused.

One is the fear of inequality. Blank is blank, so if we are all blank slates, the reasoning goes, we must all be equal. But if the slate of a newborn is not blank, different babies could have different things inscribed on their slates. Individuals, sexes, classes, and races might differ innately in their talents and inclinations. The fear is that if people do turn out to be different, it would open the door to discrimination, oppression, or eugenics.

But none of this follows. For one thing, in many cases the empirical basis of 35 the fear may be misplaced. A universal human nature does not imply that *differences* among groups are innate. Confucius could have been right when he wrote, "Men's natures are alike; it is their habits that carry them far apart."

More important, the case against bigotry is not a factual claim that people are biologically indistinguishable. It is a moral stance that condemns judging an *individual* according to the average traits of certain *groups* to which the individual belongs. Enlightened societies strive to ignore race, sex, and ethnicity in hiring, admissions, and criminal justice because the alternative is morally repugnant. Discriminating against people on the basis of race, sex, or ethnicity would be unfair, penalizing them for traits over which they have no control. It would perpetuate the injustices of the past and could rend society into hostile factions. None of these reasons depends on whether groups of people are or are not genetically indistinguishable.

Far from being conducive to discrimination, a conception of human nature is the reason we oppose it. Regardless of I.Q. or physical strength or any other trait that might vary among people, all human beings can be assumed to have certain traits in common. No one likes being enslaved. No one likes being humiliated. No one likes being treated unfairly. The revulsion we feel toward discrimination and slavery comes from a conviction that however much people vary on some traits, they do not vary on these.

A second fear of human nature comes from a reluctance to give up the age-old dream of the perfectibility of man. If we are forever saddled with fatal flaws and deadly sins, according to this fear, social reform would be a waste of time. Why try to make the world a better place if people are rotten to the core and will just foul it up no matter what you do?

But this, too, does not follow. If the mind is a complex system with many faculties, an antisocial desire is just one component among others. Some faculties may endow us with greed or lust or malice, but others may endow us with sympathy, foresight, self-respect, a desire for respect from others, and an ability to learn from experience and history. Social progress can come from pitting some of these faculties against others.

For example, suppose we are endowed with a conscience that treats certain other beings as targets of sympathy and inhibits us from harming or exploiting them. The philosopher Peter Singer of Princeton University has shown that moral improvement has proceeded for millennia because people have expanded the mental dotted line that embraces the entities considered worthy of sympathy. The circle has been poked outward from the family and village to the clan, the tribe, the nation, the race, and most recently to all of humanity. This sweeping change in sensibilities did not require a blank slate. It could have arisen from a moral gadget with a single knob or slider that adjusts the size of the circle embracing the entities whose interests we treat as comparable to our own.

Some people worry that these arguments are too fancy for the dangerous world we live in. Since data in the social sciences are never perfect, shouldn't we err on the side of caution and stick with the null hypothesis that people are blank slates? Some people think that even if we were certain that people differed genetically or harbored ignoble tendencies, we might still want to promulgate the fiction that they didn't.

This argument is based on the fallacy that the blank slate has nothing but good moral implications and a theory that admits a human nature has nothing but bad ones. In fact, the dangers go both ways. Take the most horrifying example of all, the abuse of biology by the Nazis, with its pseudoscientific nonsense about superior and inferior races. Historians agree that bitter memories of the Holocaust were the main reason that human nature became taboo in intellectual life after the Second World War.

But historians have also documented that Nazism was not the only ideologically inspired holocaust of the twentieth century. Many atrocities were committed by Marxist regimes in the name of egalitarianism, targeting people whose success was taken as evidence of their avarice. The kulaks ("bourgeois peasants") were exterminated by Lenin and Stalin in the Soviet Union. Teachers, former landlords, and "rich peasants" were humiliated, tortured, and murdered during China's Cultural Revolution. City dwellers and literate professionals were worked to death or executed during the reign of the Khmer Rouge in Cambodia.

And here is a remarkable fact: Although both Nazi and Marxist ideologies led to industrial-scale killing, *their biological and psychological theories were opposites.* Marxists had no use for the concept of race, were averse to the notion of genetic inheritance, and were hostile to the very idea of a human nature rooted in biology. Marx did not explicitly embrace the blank slate, but he was adamant that human nature has no enduring properties. "All history is nothing but a continuous transformation of human nature," he wrote. Many of his followers did embrace it. "It is on a blank page that the most beautiful poems are written," said Mao. "Only the newborn baby is spotless," ran a Khmer Rouge slogan. This philosophy led to the persecution of the successful and of those who produced more crops on their private family plots than on communal farms. And it made these regimes not just dictatorships but totalitarian dictatorships, which tried to control every aspect of life from art and education to child rearing and sex. After all, if the mind is structureless at birth and shaped by its experience, a society that wants the right kind of minds must control the experience.

None of this is meant to impugn the blank slate as an evil doctrine, any more than a belief in human nature is an evil doctrine. Both are separated by many steps from the evil acts committed under their banners, and they must be evaluated on factual grounds. But the fact that tyranny and genocide can come from an anti-innatist belief system as readily as from an innatist one does upend the common misconception that biological approaches to behavior are uniquely sinister. And the reminder that human nature is the source of our interests and needs as well as our flaws encourages us to examine claims about the mind objectively, without putting a moral thumb on either side of the scale.

45

Exploring the Text

1. What is the effect of beginning the essay with four bulleted statements?
2. What hypocrisy does Steven Pinker refer to at the beginning of paragraph 7?
3. What does Pinker imply through his references to Franz Boas, Alfred Kroeber, and Ashley Montagu (para. 16)? In what ways do the references appeal to ethos, logos, or pathos?
4. Among the discoveries Pinker discusses in the text following paragraph 18, which one do you find most compelling as evidence supporting his claim? Why?
5. How do the examples from music in paragraphs 21 and 22 support Pinker's purpose?
6. What reasons does Pinker give to support his suggestion that the human mind is neither a blank slate nor purely determined?
7. What effect does the qualifier "not entirely" have in paragraph 30?
8. To what does Pinker refer when he mentions "the belief that the arrangement of rock and gas in space has something to do with right and wrong" (para. 31)? What is Pinker's attitude toward this belief? What would T. H. Huxley think about this hypothesis if he were to apply the scientific method to it?
9. How effectively does Pinker refute the legitimacy of the two fears he introduces in paragraph 33?
10. Describe the argument and the logical flaw Pinker identifies in paragraph 42.
11. What is Pinker's main idea in the conclusion of the essay?

STEVEN PINKER ON WRITING

In this interview, Steven Pinker, author of the preceding essay "The Blank Slate," speaks about how he considers his audience when he writes.

Robin Dissin Aufses (RA): Since you're trained as a scientist, how much and how consciously do you shift to write for a general audience?

Steven Pinker (SP): I try to put myself in the shoes of someone who has not been part of the academic world and does not know the jargon, or the reasons that particular scientific issues are interesting and important.

RA: What do you consider the two or three most important qualities of good writing?

SP: Respect for the intelligence of the readers. Attention to prose style, omitting needless words, putting the new information later in the sentence, and the use of deep rather than superficial analogies. I try to monitor my use of terms that are second nature to people in my field but that are meaningless to outsiders. I also avoid technical terms that add no conceptual precision. Why use *murine* when it just means "mouse"?

RA: What do you see as the difference between writing for the specialized community of your peers and writing for general readers?

SP: More background knowledge can be taken for granted in writing for peers.

RA: Do you usually ask someone to read and comment on early drafts of your work? If so, does this exchange help to target your audience?

SP: Yes, always. I generally get some intelligent nonacademics to give me comments, but I also find that academia has become so specialized that an academic in some other field is as much of a beginner as a layperson.

RA: It may be a stereotype, but we usually don't imagine that scientific thinkers are enthusiastic about writing. Do you enjoy writing? Do you do any other kind of writing?

SP: Judging from both quality and quantity, I'd say that scientists are more enthusiastic about writing than academics in the humanities, many of whom crank out reams of turgid jargon. Like many writers, I often find that I enjoy having written more than I enjoy writing, though it can be exhilarating when it flows. I write op-ed pieces and essays for newspapers and magazines, but no fiction.

RA: Who are the science writers you admire or who have influenced you? Who are the other writers you admire or [who] have influenced you?

SP: Richard Dawkins, the early Stephen Jay Gould, Thomas Schelling, Dan Dennett. Among psychologists, George Miller, and my graduate advisor Roger Brown.

RA: What role does writing play in the courses you teach? Do you make a special point of including assignments or work that requires students to write?

SP: I not only assign writing, but also require that students rewrite a paper in light of the feedback they receive from their teaching assistant. The rewrite counts for as much of the grade as the original paper. That is because for most people good writing comes from revising. My books go through five to seven drafts.

Follow-up

Write your own answers to questions 2 through 5. Compare your answers with Pinker's. Reflect on the differences between your responses and his, and write about how his answers can help you as a writer. Read Pinker's answers to questions 1, 6, and 7. How might his responses help you consider audience?

Silence and the Notion of the Commons

Ursula Franklin

Ursula Franklin was born in Germany in 1921 and educated there, earning her PhD in physics at the Technical University of Berlin. She emigrated to Canada and became a scientist at the Ontario Research Foundation. In 1967, she became the first woman professor of metallurgy and materials science at the University of Toronto, where she is currently professor emeritus. One of the founders of the Canadian Research Center for the Advancement of Women, Franklin is an activist for social issues and for peace. Her highly regarded *The Real World of Technology* (1989) is a study of the social impact of technology. The following essay is based on a lecture Franklin gave in 1993 at a conference on acoustic technology. Referring to technology, Franklin asks, "How does one talk about something that is both fish and water, means as well as end?"

In a technological world, where the acoustic environment is largely artificial, silence takes on new dimensions, be it in terms of the human need for silence (perhaps a person's right to be free from acoustic assault), of communication, or of intentional modification of the environment.

Before we had a technologically mediated society, before we had electronics and electro-magnetic devices, sound was rightly seen as being ephemeral, sound was coupled to its source, and lasted only a very short time. This is very different from what we see in a landscape: however much we feel that the landscape might be modified, however much we feel that there is a horrible building somewhere in front of a beautiful mountain, on the scale of the soundscape, the landscape is permanent. What is put up is there. That's very different from the traditional soundscape. What modern technology has brought to sound is the possibility of doing two things: to separate the sound from the source and to make the sound permanent. In addition, modern devices make it possible to decompose, recompose, analyze and mix sounds, to change the initial magnitude and sustainability of sound, as well as to change all the characteristics that link the sound with its source. R Murray Schafer called this "schizophonia," separating the sound from the source. We now have easy access to the multitude of opportunities that result from overcoming that coupling.

The social impact of this technology is significant. Prior to these developments there was a limitation to sound and sound penetration. If you heard a bagpipe band there was a limit to the amount of time it would play; if you found it displeasing you could patiently wait until the players got exhausted. But with a recording of a bagpipe band, you are out of luck. It's never going to be exhausted. Electronics, then, have altered the modern soundscape. While modern technology is a source of joy in modern composition, through the opening of many doors for expression, it is also the source of a good number of problems related to the soundscape, problems which society as a whole must adjust to, cope with, and possibly ameliorate.

But then there is not only sound, there is silence. Silence is affected by these same technological developments, the same means of separating sound from source and overcoming the ephemeral nature of a soundscape. I have attempted to define silence and to analyze the attributes that make it valuable. Defining silence as the absence of external or artificially generated sound is fine, but it's a little bit shallow, because silence in many ways is very much more than the absence of sound. Absence of sound is a condition necessary to silence but it is not sufficient in itself to define what we mean by silence. When one thinks about the concept of silence, one notices that there has to be somebody who listens before you can say there is silence. Silence, in addition to being an absence of sound, is defined by a listener, by hearing.

A further attribute, or parameter of silence, from my point of view, comes out of the question: *why is it that we worry about silence?* I feel that one comes to the root of the meaning and practice of silence only when one asks, *why is it that we value and try to establish silence?* Because silence is an enabling environment. This is the domain that we have traditionally associated with silence, the enabling condition in which unprogrammed and unprogrammable events can take place. That is the silence of contemplation; it is the silence when people get in touch with themselves; it is the silence of meditation and worship. The distinctive character of this domain of silence is that it is an enabling condition that opens up the possibility of unprogrammed, unplanned, and unprogrammable happenings.

In this light we understand why, as Christians, traditional Quakers found it necessary in the seventeenth century, when they were surrounded by all the pomp and circumstance of the church of England, to reject it. We understand why they felt any ritual, in the sense of its programmed nature and predictability, to be a straitjacket rather than a comfort, and why they said to the amazement of their contemporaries: *we worship God in silence.* Their justification for the practice of silence was that they required it to hear God's voice. Beyond the individual's centering, beyond the individual effort of meditation, there was the need for *collective* silence. Collective silence is an enormously powerful event. There are contemporaneous accounts of Quaker meetings under heavy persecution in England, when thousands of people met silently on a hillside. Then out of the silence, one person — unappointed, unordained, unexpected, and unprogrammed — might speak, to say: *Out of the silence there can come a ministry.* The message is not essentially within that person, constructed in their intellect, but comes out of the silence to them. This isn't just history and theory. I think that if any one of you attended Quaker meetings, particularly on a regular basis, you would find that, suddenly, out of the silence, somebody speaks about something that had just entered *your* mind. It's an uncanny thing. The strength of collective silence is probably one of the most powerful spiritual forces.

Now, in order for something like this to happen, a lot of things are required. There is what Quakers call: *to be with heart and mind prepared.* But there is also the collective decision to be silent. And to be silent in order to let unforeseen, unforeseeable, and unprogrammed things happen. Such silence, I repeat, is the environment that enables the unprogrammed. I feel it is very much at risk.

I will elaborate on this, but first I want to say: there is another silence. There is the silence that enables a programmed, a planned, event to take place. There is the silence in which you courteously engage so that I might be heard: in order for one to be heard all the others have to be silent. But in many cases silence is not taken on voluntarily and it is this false silence of which I am afraid. It is not the silence only of the padded cell, or of solitary confinement; it is the silence that is enforced by the megaphone, the boom box, the PA system, and any other device that stifles other sounds and voices in order that a planned event can take place.

There is a critical juncture between the planned and the unplanned, the programmed and the unplannable that must be kept in mind. I feel very strongly that our present technological trends drive us toward a decrease in the space — be it in the soundscape, the landscape, or the mindscape — in which the unplanned and unplannable can happen. Yet silence has to remain available in the soundscape, the landscape, and the mindscape. Allowing openness to the unplannable, to the unprogrammed, is the core of the strength of silence. It is also the core of our individual and collective sanity. I extend that to the collectivity because, as a community, as a people, we are threatened just as much, if not more, by the impingement of the programmed over the silent, over that which enables the unprogrammed. Much of the impingement goes unnoticed, uncommented upon, since it is much less obvious than the intrusion of a structure into the landscape. While we may not win all the battles at City Hall to preserve our trees, at least there is now a semi-consciousness that this type of struggle is important.

Where can one go to get away from the dangers of even the gentle presence of   10
programmed music, or Muzak, in our public buildings? Where do I protest that upon entering any place, from the shoe store to the restaurant, I am deprived of the opportunity to be quiet? Who has asked my permission to put that slop into the elevator I may have to use umpteen times every day? Many such "background" activities are intentionally manipulative. This is not merely "noise" that can be dealt with in terms of noise abatement. There are two aspects to be stressed in this context. One is that the elimination of silence is being done without anybody's consent. The other is that one really has to stop and think and analyze in order to see just how manipulative these interventions can be.

For instance, in the Toronto Skydome, friends tell me that the sound environment is coupled and geared to the game: if the home team misses, there are mournful and distressing sounds over the PA; when the home team scores there is a sort of athletic equivalent of the Hallelujah Chorus. Again, the visitor has no choice; the programmed soundscape is part of the event. You cannot be present at the game without being subjected to that mood manipulation. I wonder if music will soon be piped into the voter's booth, maybe an upbeat, slightly military tune: *"Get on with it. Get the votes in."* Joking aside, soundscape manipulation is a serious issue. Who on earth has given anybody the right to manipulate the sound environment?

Now, I want to come back to the definition of silence and introduce the notion of the commons, because the soundscape essentially doesn't belong to anyone in particular. What we are hearing, I feel, is very much the privatization of the soundscape, in the same manner in which the enclosure laws in Britain destroyed the commons of old. There was a time when in fact every community had what was called "the commons," an area that belonged to everybody and where sheep could graze — a place important to all, belonging to all. The notion of the commons is deeply embedded in our social mind as something that all share. There are many "commons" that we take for granted and for millenia, clean air and clean water were the norm. Because of the ephemeral nature of sound in the past, silence was not considered part of the commons. Today, the technology to preserve and multiply sound and separate it from its source has resulted in our sudden awareness that silence, too, is a common good. Silence, which we need in order that unprogrammed and unprogrammable things can take place, is being removed from common access without much fuss and civic bother. It is being privatized.

This is another illustration of an often-observed occurrence related to the impact of technology: that things considered in the past to be normal or ordinary become rare or extraordinary, while those things once considered rare and unusual become normal and routine. Flying is no longer a big deal, but a hand-made dress or a home-cooked meal may well be special. We essentially consider polluted water as normal now, and people who can afford it drink bottled water. It is hard to have bottled silence. But money still can buy distance from sound. Today, when there is civic anger, it is with respect to "noise" — like airport noise, etc. There is not yet such anger with respect to the manipulative elimination of silence from the soundscape.

There are those of us who have acknowledged and seen the deterioration of the commons as far as silence is concerned, who have seen that the soundscape is not only polluted by noise — so that one has to look for laws related to noise abatement — but also that the soundscape has become increasingly polluted through the private use of sound in the manipulative dimension of setting and programming moods and conditions. There is a desperate need for awareness of this, and for awareness of it in terms of the collectivity, rather than just individual needs. I feel very much that this is a time for civic anger. This is a time when one has to say: *town planning is constrained by by-laws on height, density, and other features; what are town planning's constraints in relation to silence?*

You may ask, what would I suggest? First of all, we must insist that, as human beings in a society, we have a right to silence. Just as we feel we have the right to walk down the street without being physically assaulted by people and preferably without being visually assaulted by ugly outdoor advertising, we also have the right not to be assaulted by sound, and in particular, not to be assaulted by sound that is there solely for the purpose of profit. Now is the time for civic rage, as well as civic education, but also for some action. 15

Think of the amount of care that goes into the regulation of parking, so that our good, precious, and necessary cars have a place to be well and safe. That's very important to society. I have yet to see, beyond hospitals, a public building that has a quiet room. Is not our sanity at least as important as the safety of our cars? One should begin to think: are there places, even in conferences like this, that are hassle-free, quiet spaces, where people can go? There were times when one could say to a kid: *"Where did you go?"* — *"Out."* — *"What did you do?"* — *"Nothing."*

That sort of blessed time is past. The kid is programmed. We are programmed. And we don't even ask for a quiet space anymore.

One possible measure, relatively close at hand, is to set aside, as a normal matter of human rights, in those buildings over which we have some influence, a quiet room. Further, I highly recommend starting committee meetings with two minutes of silence, and ending them with a few minutes of silence, too. I sit on committees that have this practice, and find that it not only can expedite the business before the committee, but also contributes to a certain amount of peacefulness and sanity. One can start a lecture with a few minutes of silence, and can close it the same way. There can be a few minutes of silence before a shared meal. Such things help, even if they help only in small ways. I do think even small initiatives make silence "visible" as an ever-present part of life. I now invite you to have two minutes of silence before we go on into the question period. Let us be quiet together.

Exploring the Text

1. Do you agree with the claim Ursula Franklin makes in the first sentence? What examples would you use to illustrate how "silence takes on new dimensions"?
2. How does Franklin's selection of detail in paragraph 3 contribute to her tone?
3. In paragraphs 6 and 7, Franklin italicizes three phrases or sentences. How do those italicized statements support her argument? What effect do the italics have?
4. What is the irony that Franklin describes in paragraph 8?
5. What is the effect of the parallelism in "the soundscape, the landscape, or the mindscape" (para. 9)?
6. What is a more contemporary example of the "elimination of silence" that Franklin discusses in paragraphs 10 and 11? How might this "elimination" be manipulative? Do we have a right to silence, as Franklin claims?
7. In paragraph 13, Franklin says that "things considered in the past to be normal or ordinary become rare or extraordinary, while those things once considered rare and unusual become normal and routine." Give two examples from your observation that support her claim.
8. How would following Franklin's recommendations be beneficial (para. 15)? What might make following her recommendations difficult?
9. What is the effect of Franklin's two concluding sentences?
10. As mentioned, this essay was originally a lecture Franklin gave at a conference on acoustic technology. What rhetorical strategies does she use to connect to her audience?

Into the Electronic Millennium

SVEN BIRKERTS

Sven Birkerts (b. 1951) graduated from the University of Michigan and has taught writing at Bennington College, Emerson College, Mount Holyoke, Amherst, and Harvard. One of our most outspoken critics of technology, he has won many awards for his critiques of literature, society, and technology. His essays have appeared in a wide variety of publications including the *New York Times Book Review*, the *New York Review of Books*, the *Atlantic Monthly, Harper's*, and the *New Republic*. The following essay is taken from *The Gutenberg Elegies: The Fate of Reading in an Electronic Age* (1994).

The order of print is linear, and is bound to logic by the imperatives of syntax. Syntax is the substructure of discourse, a mapping of the ways that the mind makes sense through language. Print communication requires the active engagement of the reader's attention, for reading is fundamentally an act of translation. Symbols are turned into their verbal referents and these are in turn interpreted. The print engagement is essentially private. While it does represent an act of communication, the contents pass from the privacy of the sender to the privacy of the receiver. Print also posits a time axis; the turning of pages, not to mention the vertical descent down the page, is a forward-moving succession, with earlier contents at every point serving as a ground for what follows. Moreover, the printed material is static — it is the reader, not the book, that moves forward. The physical arrangements of print are in accord with our traditional sense of history. Materials are layered; they lend themselves to rereading and to sustained attention. The pace of reading is variable, with progress determined by the reader's focus and comprehension.

The electronic order is in most ways opposite. Information and contents do not simply move from one private space to another, but they travel along a network. Engagement is intrinsically public, taking place within a circuit of larger connectedness. The vast resources of the network are always there, potential, even if they do not impinge on the immediate communication. Electronic communication can be passive, as with television watching, or interactive, as with computers. Contents, unless they are printed out (at which point they become part of the static order of print) are felt to be evanescent. They can be changed or deleted with the stroke of a key. With visual media (television, projected graphs, highlighted "bullets") impression and image take precedence over logic and concept, and detail and linear sequentiality are sacrificed. The pace is rapid, driven by jump-cut increments, and the basic movement is laterally associative rather than vertically cumulative. The presentation structures the reception and, in time, the expectation about how information is organized.

Further, the visual and nonvisual technology in every way encourages in the user a heightened and ever-changing awareness of the present. It works against historical perception, which must depend on the inimical notions of logic and sequential succession. If the print medium exalts the word, fixing it into permanence, the electronic counterpart reduces it to a signal, a means to an end.

Transitions like the one from print to electronic media do not take place without rippling or, more likely, *reweaving* the entire social and cultural web. The tendencies outlined above are already at work. We don't need to look far to find their effects. We can begin with the newspaper headlines and the millennial lamentations sounded in the op-ed pages: that our educational systems are in decline; that our students are less and less able to read and comprehend their required texts, and that their aptitude scores have leveled off well below those of previous generations. Tag-line communication, called "bite-speak" by some, is destroying the last remnants of political discourse; spin doctors and media consultants are our new shamans. As communications empires fight for control of all information outlets, including publishers, the latter have succumbed to the tyranny of the bottom line; they are less and less willing to publish work, however worthy, that will not make a tidy profit. And, on every front, funding for the arts is being cut while the arts themselves appear to be suffering a deep crisis of relevance. And so on.

Every one of these developments is, of course, overdetermined, but there can   5
be no doubt that they are connected, perhaps profoundly, to the transition that is underway.

Certain other trends bear watching. One could argue, for instance, that the entire movement of postmodernism in the arts is a consequence of this same macroscopic shift. For what is postmodernism at root but an aesthetic that rebukes the idea of an historical time line, as well as previously uncontested assumptions of cultural hierarchy. The postmodern artifact manipulates its stylistic signatures like Lego blocks and makes free with combinations from the formerly sequestered spheres of high and popular art. Its combinatory momentum and relentless referencing of the surrounding culture mirror perfectly the associative dynamics of electronic media.

One might argue likewise, that the virulent debate within academia over the canon and multiculturalism may not be a simple struggle between the entrenched ideologies of white male elites and the forces of formerly disenfranchised gender, racial, and cultural groups. Many of those who would revise the canon (or end it altogether) are trying to outflank the assumption of historical tradition itself. The underlying question, avoided by many, may be not only whether the tradition is relevant, but whether it might not be too taxing a system for students to comprehend. Both the traditionalists and the progressives have valid arguments, and we must certainly have sympathy for those who would try to expose and eradicate the hidden assumptions of bias in the Western tradition. But it also seems clear that this debate could only have taken the form it has in a society that has begun to come loose from its textual moorings. To challenge repression is salutary. To challenge history itself, proclaiming it to be simply an archive of repressions and justifications, is idiotic.*

Then there are the more specific sorts of developments. Consider the multibillion-dollar initiative by Whittle Communications to bring commercially sponsored education packages into the classroom. The underlying premise is staggeringly simple: If electronic media are the one thing that the young are at ease with, why not exploit the fact? Why not stop bucking television and use it instead, with corporate America picking up the tab in exchange for a few minutes of valuable airtime for commercials? As the *Boston Globe* reports:

> Here's how it would work:
>
> Participating schools would receive, free of charge, $50,000 worth of electronic paraphernalia, including a satellite dish and classroom video monitors. In return, the schools would agree to air the show.
>
> The show would resemble a network news program, but with 18- to 24-year-old anchors.
>
> A prototype includes a report on a United Nations Security Council meeting on terrorism, a space shuttle update, a U2 music video tribute to Martin Luther King, a feature on the environment, a "fast fact" ('Arachibutyrophobia is the fear of peanut butter sticking to the roof of your mouth') and two minutes of commercial advertising.
>
> "You have to remember that the children of today have grown up with the visual media," said Robert Calabrese [Billerica School Superintendent]. "They know no other way and we're simply capitalizing on that to enhance learning."

Calabrese's observation on the preconditioning of a whole generation of students raises troubling questions: Should we suppose that American education will begin to tailor itself to the aptitudes of its students, presenting more and more of its materials in newly packaged forms? And what will happen when educators find that not very many of the old materials will "play" — that is, capture

---

*The outcry against the modification of the canon can be seen as a plea for old reflexes and routines. And the cry for multicultural representation may be a last-ditch bid for connection to the fading legacy of print. The logic is simple. When a resource is threatened — made scarce — people fight over it. In this case the struggle is over textual power in an increasingly nontextual age. The future of books and reading is what is at stake, and a dim intuition of this drives the contending factions.

As Katha Pollitt argued so shrewdly in her much-cited article in *The Nation*: If we were a nation of readers, there would be no issue. No one would be arguing about whether to put Toni Morrison on the syllabus because her work would be a staple of the reader's regular diet anyway. These lists are suddenly so important because they represent, very often, the only serious works that the student is ever likely to be exposed to. Whoever controls the lists comes out ahead in the struggle for the hearts and minds of the young.

student enthusiasm? Is the *what* of learning to be determined by the *how*? And at what point do vicious cycles begin to reveal their viciousness?

A collective change of sensibility may already be upon us. We need to take seriously the possibility that the young truly "know no other way," that they are not made of the same stuff that their elders are. In her *Harper's* magazine debate with Neil Postman, Camille Paglia observed:

> Some people have more developed sensoriums than others. I've found that most people born before World War II are turned off by the modern media. They can't understand how we who were born after the war can read and watch TV at the same time. But we *can*. When I wrote my book, I had earphones on, blasting rock music or Puccini and Brahms. The soap operas — with the sound turned down — flickered on my TV. I'd be talking on the phone at the same time. Baby boomers have a multilayered, multitrack ability to deal with the world.

I don't know whether to be impressed or depressed by Paglia's ability to disperse her focus in so many directions. Nor can I say, not having read her book, in what ways her multitrack sensibility has informed her prose. But I'm baffled by what she means when she talks about an ability to "deal with the world." From the context, "dealing" sounds more like a matter of incessantly repositioning the self within a barrage of onrushing stimuli.

Paglia's is hardly the only testimony in this matter. A *New York Times* article on the cult success of Mark Leyner (author of *I Smell Esther Williams* and *My Cousin, My Gastroenterologist*) reports suggestively:

> His fans say, variously, that his writing is like MTV, or rap music, or rock music, or simply like everything in the world put together: fast and furious and intense, full of illusion and allusion and fantasy and science and excrement.
>
> Larry McCaffery, a professor of literature at San Diego State University and co-editor of *Fiction International*, a literary journal, said his students get excited about Mr. Leyner's writing, which he considers important and unique: "It speaks to them, somehow, about this weird milieu they're swimming through. It's this dissolving, discontinuous world." While older people might find Mr. Leyner's world bizarre or unreal, Professor McCaffery said, it doesn't seem so to people who grew up with Walkmen and computers and VCR's, with so many choices, so much bombardment, that they have never experienced a sensation singly.

The article continues:

> There is no traditional narrative, although the book is called a novel. And there is much use of facts, though it is called fiction. Seldom does the end of a sentence have any obvious relation to the beginning. "You don't know where you're going, but you don't mind taking the leap," said R. J. Cutler, the producer of "Heat," who invited Mr. Leyner to be on the show after he picked up the galleys of his book and found it mesmerizing. "He taps into a specific cultural perspective where thoughtful literary world view meets pop culture and the TV generation."

My final exhibit — I don't know if it qualifies as a morbid symptom as such — is drawn from a *Washington Post Magazine* essay on the future of the Library of Congress, our national shrine to the printed word. One of the individuals interviewed in the piece is Robert Zich, so-called "special projects czar" of the institution. Zich, too, has seen the future, and he is surprisingly candid with his interlocutor. Before long, Zich maintains, people will be able to get what information they want directly off their terminals. The function of the Library of Congress (and perhaps libraries in general) will change. He envisions his library becoming more like a museum: "Just as you go to the National Gallery to see its Leonardo or go to the Smithsonian to see the Spirit of St. Louis and so on, you will want to go to libraries to see the Gutenberg or the original printing of Shakespeare's plays or to see Lincoln's hand-written version of the Gettysburg Address."

Zich is outspoken, voicing what other administrators must be thinking privately. The big research libraries, he says, "and the great national libraries and their buildings will go the way of the railroad stations and the movie palaces of an earlier era which were really vital institutions in their time . . . Somehow folks moved away from that when the technology changed."

And books? Zich expresses excitement about Sony's hand-held electronic book, and a miniature encyclopedia coming from Franklin Electronic Publishers. "Slip it in your pocket," he says. "Little keyboard, punch in your words and it will do the full text searching and all the rest of it. Its limitation, of course, is that it's devoted just to that one book." Zich is likewise interested in the possibility of memory cards. What he likes about the Sony product is the portability: one machine, a screen that will display the contents of whatever electronic card you feed it.

I cite Zich's views at some length here because he is not some Silicon Valley research and development visionary, but a highly placed executive at what might be called, in a very literal sense, our most conservative public institution. When men like Zich embrace the electronic future, we can be sure it's well on its way.

Others might argue that the technologies cited by Zich merely represent a modification in the "form" of reading, and that reading itself will be unaffected, as there is little difference between following words on a pocket screen or a printed page. Here I have to hold my line. The context cannot but condition the process. Screen and book may exhibit the same string of words, but the assumptions that underlie their significance are entirely different depending on whether we are staring at a book or a circuit-generated text. As the nature of looking — at the natural world, at paintings — changed with the arrival of photography and mechanical reproduction, so will the collective relation to language alter as new modes of dissemination prevail.

Whether all of this sounds dire or merely "different" will depend upon the reader's own values and priorities. I find these portents of change depressing, but also exhilarating — at least to speculate about. On the one hand, I have a great feeling of loss and a fear about what habitations will exist for self and soul in the future. But there is also a quickening, a sense that important things are on the line. As Heraclitus once observed, "The mixture that is not shaken soon stagnates." Well, the mixture is being shaken, no doubt about it. And here are some of the kinds of developments we might watch for as our "proto-electronic" era yields to an all-electronic future:

1. *Language erosion.* There is no question but that the transition from the culture of the book to the culture of electronic communication will radically alter the ways in which we use language on every societal level. The complexity and distinctiveness of spoken and written expression, which are deeply bound to traditions of print literacy, will gradually be replaced by a more telegraphic sort of "plainspeak." Syntactic masonry is already a dying art. Neil Postman and others have already suggested what losses have been incurred by the advent of telegraphy and television — how the complex discourse patterns of the nineteenth century were flattened by the requirements of communication over distances. That tendency runs riot as the layers of mediation thicken. Simple linguistic prefab is now the norm, while ambiguity, paradox, irony, subtlety, and wit are fast disappearing. In their place, the simple "vision thing" and myriad other "things." Verbal intelligence, which has long been viewed as suspect as the act of reading, will come to seem positively conspiratorial. The greater part of any articulate person's energy will be deployed in dumbing-down her discourse.

Language will grow increasingly impoverished through a series of vicious 20 cycles. For, of course, the usages of literature and scholarship are connected in fundamental ways to the general speech of the tribe. We can expect that curricula will be further streamlined, and difficult texts in the humanities will be pruned and glossed. One need only compare a college textbook from twenty years ago to its contemporary version. A poem by Milton, a play by Shakespeare — one can hardly find the text among the explanatory notes nowadays. Fewer and fewer people will be able to contend with the so-called masterworks of literature or ideas. Joyce, Woolf, Soyinka, not to mention the masters who preceded them, will go unread, and the civilizing energies of their prose will circulate aimlessly between closed covers.

2. *Flattening of historical perspectives.* As the circuit supplants the printed page, and as more and more of our communications involve us in network processes — which of their nature plant us in a perpetual present — our perception of history will inevitably alter. Changes in information storage and access are bound to impinge on our historical memory. The depth of field that is our sense of the past is not only a linguistic construct, but is in some essential way represented by the book and the physical accumulation of books in library spaces. In the contemplation of the single volume, or mass of volumes, we form a picture of time past as a growing deposit of sediment; we capture a sense of its depth and dimensionality. Moreover, we meet the past as much in the presentation of words in books of specific vintage as we do in any isolated fact or statistic. The database, useful as it is, expunges this context, this sense of chronology, and admits us to a weightless order in which all information is equally accessible.

If we take the etymological tack, history (cognate with "story") is affiliated in complex ways with its texts. Once the materials of the past are unhoused from their pages, they will surely *mean* differently. The printed page is itself a link, at least along the imaginative continuum, and when that link is broken, the past can only start to recede. At the same time it will become a body of disjunct data available for retrieval and, in the hands of our canny dream merchants, a mythology. The more we grow rooted in the consciousness of the now, the more it will seem utterly extraordinary that things were ever any different. The idea of a farmer plowing a field — an historical constant for millennia — will be something for a theme park. For, naturally, the entertainment industry, which reads the collective unconscious unerringly, will seize the advantage. The past that has slipped away will be rendered ever more glorious, ever more a fantasy play with heroes, villains, and quaint settings and props. Small-town American life returns as "Andy of Mayberry" — at first enjoyed with recognition, later accepted as a faithful portrait of how things used to be.

3. *The waning of the private self.* We may even now be in the first stages of a process of social collectivization that will over time all but vanquish the ideal of the isolated individual. For some decades now we have been edging away from the perception of private life as something opaque, closed off to the world; we increasingly accept the transparency of a life lived within a set of systems, electronic or otherwise. Our technologies are not bound by season or light — it's always the same time in the circuit. And so long as time is money and money matters, those circuits will keep humming. The doors and walls of our habitations matter less and less — the world sweeps through the wires as it needs to, or as we need it to. The monitor light is always blinking; we are always potentially on-line.

I am not suggesting that we are all about to become mindless, soulless robots, or that personality will disappear altogether into an oceanic homogeneity. But certainly the idea of what it means to be a person living a life will be much changed. The figure-ground model, which has always featured a solitary self before a background that is the society of other selves, is romantic in the extreme. It is ever less tenable in the world as it is becoming. There are no more wildernesses, no more lonely homesteads, and, outside of cinema, no more emblems of the exalted individual.

The self must change as the nature of subjective space changes. And one of the many incremental transformations of our age has been the slow but steady destruction of subjective space. The physical and psychological distance between individuals has been shrinking for at least a century. In the process, the figure-ground image has begun to blur its boundary distinctions. One day we will conduct our public and private lives within networks so dense, among so many channels of instantaneous information, that it will make almost no sense to speak of the differentiations of subjective individualism.

We are already captive in our webs. Our slight solitudes are transected by codes, wires, and pulsations. We punch a number to check in with the answering

25

machine, another to tape a show that we are too busy to watch. The strands of the web grow finer and finer — this is obvious. What is no less obvious is the fact that they will continue to proliferate, gaining in sophistication, merging functions so that one can bank by phone, shop via television, and so on. The natural tendency is toward streamlining: The smart dollar keeps finding ways to shorten the path, double-up the function. We might think in terms of a circuit-board model, picturing ourselves as the contact points. The expansion of electronic options is always at the cost of contractions in the private sphere. We will soon be navigating with ease among cataracts of organized pulsations, putting out and taking in signals. We will bring our terminals, our modems, and menus further and further into our former privacies; we will implicate ourselves by degrees in the unitary life, and there may come a day when we no longer remember that there was any other life.

Exploring the Text

1. Analyze Sven Birkerts's diction in paragraph 4. What does the diction reveal about the tone Birkerts is trying to set?
2. What is the effect of including the comment by Katha Pollitt within the footnote to paragraph 7?
3. In paragraph 11, Birkerts wonders whether to be impressed or depressed by "Paglia's ability to disperse her focus." As you read Paglia's statement, did you find yourself impressed or depressed? Why?
4. Do you agree with what "others might argue" in paragraph 17? How adequately does Birkerts support the analogy he makes between looking and reading at the end of the paragraph?
5. Analyze the diction in paragraph 21. In an essay about technology, discuss why Birkerts use so many words that have to do with nature. Are these choices in diction deliberate, or is our language "naturally" prone to these expressions? Is the language literal? figurative? ironic?
6. How effectively does paragraph 24 answer the essay's essential question: how are advances in science and technology affecting the way we define our humanity? Explain.
7. Considering that so many of us have our own bedrooms, drive our own cars, plug ourselves into headphones, and so on, do you agree with the claims Birkerts makes in paragraph 25? Why or why not?
8. How do Birkerts's references to such sources as the *Boston Globe, Harper's*, the *New York Times*, and the *Washington Post Magazine* support his argument?
9. Which of the predictions Birkerts makes in paragraphs 19–25 do you believe have occurred/been realized?

Transsexual Frogs

Elizabeth Royte

Elizabeth Royte (b. 1960) has written about science and the environment for a variety of publications including *National Geographic*, the *New York Times Magazine*, *Harper's*, the *New Yorker*, *Outside*, *Smithsonian*, and *Discover*. She has a BA in English from Bard College. She currently lives in Brooklyn, New York. Her book *The Tapir's Morning Bath: Mysteries of the Tropical Rain Forest and the Scientists Who Are Trying to Solve Them* (2001) was named a *New York Times* Notable Book. "Transsexual Frogs," in which she describes the work of scientist Tyrone Hayes of the University of California at Berkeley, is included in *The Best American Science Writing* (2004). She is the author of *Garbage Land: On the Secret Trail of Trash*, named *New York Times* Notable Book of 2005.

Tyrone Hayes stands out in the overwhelmingly white field of biology, and his skin color isn't the half of it. To use his own idiom, Hayes is several standard deviations from the norm. At the University of California at Berkeley, he glides around his lab wearing nylon shorts and rubber flip-flops, with a gold hoop in one ear and his beard braided into two impish points. Not counting his four inches of thick, upstanding hair, Hayes is just over five feet tall, with smooth features and warm eyes. He drives a truck littered with detritus human, amphibian, and reptilian. He keeps his pocket money in a baby's sock. "Hey, wassup?" he'll say to anyone, from the president of the United States on down. He can't help the informality, he says. "Tyrone can only be Tyrone."

Hayes, 35, is a professor at Berkeley, where he has taught human endocrinology since 1994. His research centers on frogs, of which he keeps enormous colonies. Frogs make convenient study subjects for anyone interested in how hormones affect physical development. Their transformation from egg to tadpole to adult is rapid, and it's visible to the naked eye. With their permeable skin, frogs are especially vulnerable to environmental factors such as solar radiation or herbicides. That vulnerability has lately garnered Hayes more attention than his appearance ever has.

The controversy began in 1998, when a company called Syngenta asked Hayes to run safety tests on its product atrazine. Syngenta is the world's largest agribusiness company, with $6.3 billion in sales of crop-related chemicals and other products in 2001 alone. Atrazine is the most widely used weed killer in the United States. To test its safety, Hayes put trace amounts of the compound in the water tanks in which he raised African clawed frogs. When the frogs were fully grown, they appeared normal. But when Hayes looked closer, he found problems. Some male frogs had developed multiple sex organs, and some had both ovaries and testes. There were also males with shrunken larynxes, a crippling handicap for a frog intent on mating. The atrazine apparently created hermaphrodites at a concentration one-thirtieth the safe level set by the Environmental Protection Agency for drinking water.

The next summer Hayes loaded a refrigerated 18-wheel truck with 500 half-gallon buckets and headed east, followed by his students. He parked near an Indiana farm, a Wyoming river, and a Utah pond, filled his buckets with 18,000 pounds of water, and headed back to Berkeley. He thawed the frozen water, poured it into hundreds of individual tanks, and dropped in thousands of leopard-frog eggs collected en route. To find out if frogs in the wild showed hermaphroditism, Hayes dissected juveniles from numerous sites. To see if frogs were vulnerable as adults, and if the effects were reversible, he exposed them to atrazine at different stages of their development.

Hayes published his first set of findings last April, in the *Proceedings of the* 5 *National Academy of Sciences.* He published the second set in October, in *Nature.* Both times the media went a little crazy. The two studies showed equally dramatic results: 40 percent of male frogs were feminized; 80 percent had diminished larynxes. Wild frogs collected from areas with atrazine showed the same number of abnormalities. Could the chemical also affect humans? The beginning of an answer may be emerging. Workers at a Louisiana plant where atrazine is manufactured are now suing their employer, saying they were nine times as likely to get prostate cancer as the average Louisianan.

Inside Berkeley's Valley Life Sciences building, Hayes approaches a set of double doors and lifts his thigh, doggy style, toward the wall. The doors respond to a security card in his pocket and swing wide onto an empty corridor. It's 7 A.M., but Hayes has been here since 4:30 this morning, when he came to "make water" — mix the chemical cocktails in which he's raising 3,000 leopard frogs in a crowded basement lab. He deftly shakes crickets — frog breakfast — from a plastic bag into dozens of tanks. On another shelf, tadpoles swim in one set of deli cups while metamorphs, which have both tails and legs, swim in another. Escaped crickets dart around the room. Strips of colored tape adorn each tank, each color denoting a particular mix of compounds. In this quadruple-blind experiment, neither Hayes nor his assistants know exactly what they're testing. Except for the notorious Red Yellow Red.

We peek into the suspect tank. "They're not doing too well, are they?" Hayes says, brushing a cricket off his neck with a practiced flick. The frogs are listless. Their heads tilt at a creepy angle. "Everything we put in this mixture died within a week, except for frogs that have adapted to that environment. So I had to look it up." Red Yellow Red, the codebook said, is the brew that runs off a Nebraska cornfield in springtime. "These frogs took a month longer than average to metamorphose, and then they were smaller than average," Hayes says. "That's wrong: Usually a longer metamorphosis means a bigger frog." He dumps in another meal of crickets and delivers the kicker: "This mixture from the cornfield has a lower dose than what's in the drinking water there."

The problem, Hayes knows, goes well beyond frogs that loiter near cornfields. According to James Hanken, a biologist at Harvard University who heads a task force on declining amphibian populations, "at least one-third to one-half of all living species of amphibian that have been examined in this regard are on their way down, and out." Researchers have offered a number of explanations for the die-off: attacks of parasites, exposure to radiation or ultraviolet light, fungal infections, climate change, habitat loss, competition with exotic species, and pesticides. Atrazine is used in more than 80 countries, primarily on corn and sorghum fields. By interfering with frog reproduction, Hayes wonders, could it be part of the problem?

Atrazine is a synthetic chemical that belongs to the triazine class of herbicides. Its technical name is 2-chloro-4-ethylamino-6-isopropylamine-1,3,5-triazine. In the United States, farmers apply around 60 million pounds of atrazine a year. Nearly all of it eventually degrades in the environment, but usually not before it's reapplied. The EPA permits up to three parts per billion of atrazine in drinking water. Every year, as waters drain down the Mississippi River basin, they accumulate 1.2 million pounds of atrazine before reaching the Gulf of Mexico.

Like the smoke from factory chimneys, pesticides cross borders. Atrazine   10 molecules easily attach to dust particles: Researchers have found it in clouds, fog, and snow. In Iowa the herbicide has been documented at 40 parts per billion in rainwater. According to the U.S. Geological Survey, atrazine contaminates well water and groundwater in states where the compound isn't even used. "It's hard to find an atrazine-free environment," Hayes says. In Switzerland, where it is banned, atrazine occurs at one part per billion, even in the Alps. Hayes says that's still enough to turn some male frogs into females.

Hayes talks rapidly as he walks from the basement lab. He'll also talk rapidly as he drives to his children's school in an hour, as he eats at a nearby restaurant, and as he types e-mail. "I'll calm down after lunch," he promises. "Here's how we think it works. Testosterone is a precursor to estrogen. In male frogs, it makes their voice boxes grow and their vocal sacs develop. But atrazine, in frogs, switches on a gene that makes the enzyme aromatase, which turns testosterone to estrogen. Normally, males don't make aromatase; it's silent. In these males, the estrogen induces the growth of ovaries, eggs, and yolk." We're at the double doors, and Hayes lifts his thigh again. "So you've got two things happening: The frog is demasculinized, and it's also feminized."

And the females that get extra estrogen? "It wouldn't happen," Hayes says. "There's a feedback mechanism. The excess hormone would decrease stimulation of the ovary, which would then cut off its production of estrogen."

Because hormones, not genes, regulate the structure of reproductive organs, vertebrates are particularly vulnerable to their environment during early development. Frogs are most susceptible just before they metamorphose. Unfortunately, that change occurs in the spring, when atrazine levels peak in waterways. "All it takes is a single application to affect the frog's development," Hayes says.

Theo Colborn, a senior scientist with the World Wildlife Fund who has spent nearly 15 years studying endocrine-disrupting chemicals in the environment, calls Hayes's work a breakthrough. "At a time when other developmental biologists were taking a broad, traditional approach, he was taking long-term effects into consideration," she says. "No one had looked at the histology the way he has. Everyone was so hung up on limb deformities in frogs that they forgot about other effects. His work may explain why frogs are disappearing."

Hayes has always been fond of frogs. He grew up in a modest neighborhood of brick houses outside Columbia, South Carolina. The development had been drained of its marsh, but snakes, turtles, and amphibians abounded. Hayes followed them and learned their ways. As a teenager, he dug a pond in his backyard, hoping to breed turtles. He kept lizards. His father brought him boxes of *National Geographic* from houses in which he had installed carpet. The boy read them all. "Those magazines were the beginning of it," Romeo Hayes says. "Even then he knew he wanted to be a scientist." The television was always on in the Hayes household, even during meals, and Tyrone paid particular attention to the nature specials. When he began dating, he took girlfriends to the Congaree Swamp, nine miles away. The young women assumed he had other things in mind, but his motives were always the same: He wanted help catching frogs.

The summer after sixth grade, Hayes taught himself to play basketball. "That was the only way I knew for blacks to get into college," he says. Through high school he wrestled, struggling with a hypothyroid condition to make weight. Entranced by the pop star Prince, he wore frilly shirts and velvet jackets, winning Best-Dressed Student five years in a row. "I wanted a hoop earring, but my mother forbade it," he says. Within days of arriving at college, he pierced his ear himself. (These days, Hayes wears a coat and tie to meetings. "But it's a real *Men in Black* kind of suit," one former student says. "And he wears a skullcap.")

Geography and family circumstances narrowed expectations. Hayes's father had been the first on his side of the family to attend high school. Hayes had never heard of an academic scholarship; he had never known anyone who left South Carolina to go to school. But his high PSAT scores brought a sheaf of recruitment letters to his house. He wrote a personal statement about his interest in armadillo biology and mailed it to Harvard. It was the only school to which he applied. "I'd heard of it on *Green Acres* and figured it must be good," he says, without a trace of irony.

Once on scholarship in Cambridge, Hayes thought he'd become a doctor. Then he began working with the biologist Bruce Waldman on kin recognition in toads. Waldman recognized Hayes's talent for asking challenging research questions and his skill in the field and the lab. He treated the freshman like a grad student. Soon Hayes was studying environmental effects on tadpole metamorphosis. "I realized what a person who enjoyed what I did might do for a living," Hayes says. "I saw the whole picture coming together."

15

Still, nothing in his background had prepared him for Harvard's social and academic pressures. "Most blacks at Harvard were from private schools," Hayes says. "They knew what was going on. Their parents had gone to school there. They flew to Bermuda at spring break." Hayes felt out of place. He didn't join any campus groups and spent all his time in the laboratory. "It was the only place I felt at home," he says. "I had four finals to study for and didn't know how to organize my time. I couldn't get advice from my dad." His grades fell, and he was placed on academic probation. Hayes nearly dropped out at that point, but Waldman and Kathy Kim, the girlfriend he later married, persuaded him to stick it out. In 1989 he graduated with departmental honors and moved to Berkeley, where he earned his Ph.D. at the age of 24.

"You think Tyrone is manic now, you should have seen him in those years," says Nigel Noriega, a research scientist in reproductive toxicology at the EPA. At Berkeley, Hayes's weight ballooned from 135 pounds to 260 pounds in six months. To get back into fighting shape, he ran 18 miles a day, often with an infant in a stroller. He went for days without sleep, then set the alarm to ring after just a few minutes. He was running a shape-shifting experiment on himself.

He drove his students to the edge as well. Lab assistants, drawn in by his dynamism, became exhausted and depressed. "It was hard; we barely saw the light of day," says Roger Liu, who spent the better part of 10 years in Hayes's lab. The results of their experiments would be so far in the future that they lost sight of their goals. Still, they loved Hayes. "Tyrone treated undergrads like grad students and grad students like postdocs," Noriega says, echoing Hayes's assessment of Waldman. "You could ask him for anything." When Hayes found attendance flagging at his 6:30 A.M. lab meetings, he started baking, at 2 A.M., to lure students in. When he worried about his charges walking to the lab in the dark, he picked them up at 4 in the morning, shining a spotlight into their windows to wake them.

From the outset, Hayes's lab attracted minority students and soon became far and away the most diverse in the department. The department of integrative biology is only 3 percent black and has produced just four black Ph.D.'s in its history. (Noriega is one.) Now nearly 20 percent of his lecture class is black. Hayes says he concentrates on selecting talented students who need nurturing. This semester's crop of researchers comes from Vietnam, India, Pakistan, Thailand, Tunisia, Mexico, Guatemala, Canada, and the United States.

"Maybe minority students think they'll make some kind of connection with me," Hayes says, shrugging. Or maybe they appreciate his holistic approach to science. He often brings his two children — Tyler, 10, and Kassina, 7 — into the lab with him, and he watches over his students with the same paternal eye. "The lab was like a family," Liu says. "Dad got pissed, the siblings fought, but we were happy."

Last year, at the departmental graduation, the students gave Hayes a standing ovation. This past spring he won the College of Letters and Science's award for Distinguished Research Mentoring; a week later he won its Distinguished

20

Teaching Award. "Tyrone reveals that science is inbred and flawed and political, just like art and music," Noriega says. "But he's still striving for its bright and shining truth. He lays all this out, and you see it's still worth it."

Even after all the weirdness with Syngenta.   25

Like all chemical companies, Syngenta has to have its products tested for safety before the EPA will approve them. The company came to Hayes in 1997 because he had experience with hormones and amphibians: He had developed an assay in which frogs exposed to estrogen mimics turned from green to red. "This was a chance to use my research," Hayes says. "Also, not that many labs are set up to travel and collect eggs, establish a colony, and breed. I had a big lab, with lots of people willing to move 3,000 frogs from tanks to deli cups."

Hayes says that when he informed Syngenta about atrazine's negative low-dose effects in August 2001, the company treated his data like a hot potato. "They told me, 'That's not what you were contracted to do. We don't acknowledge your work,'" Hayes says. "I sent them all my raw data, and they FedExed it back to me." Ronald Kendall, an environmental toxicologist at Texas Tech University and a leader of Syngenta's atrazine-testing panel, insists that Hayes told the team only about the frogs' shrunken larynxes, not their hermaphroditism: "We didn't learn about gonadal effects until a hormone meeting late in November." Rather than keep quiet about his findings, Hayes quit his contract and repeated his experiments. The week before he was scheduled to share his data with the EPA, he received 500 computer viruses.

After Hayes quit his contract, Syngenta funded some of Kendall's colleagues at Texas Tech to replicate the work. They produced almost no hermaphrodites at the atrazine levels Hayes had tested. The lab conditions in Texas differed from conditions in the Berkeley basement. For example, the Texas experimenters raised their frogs in glass instead of plastic tanks, at higher population densities, and at cooler temperatures, and they fed them differently. "But if the effect is robust, as Hayes claims it is, you should still be able to see it under slightly different conditions," says James Carr, a comparative endocrinologist on the Texas Tech team.

Hayes accused the Texas team of raising unhealthy frogs in tanks with uncontrolled atrazine levels. "Their animals were underfed and overcrowded," he says. "How can you tell if their gonads are deformed if the animals don't develop properly?" In response, the Texas team crafted an 18-page defense, to which Hayes responded with 22 pages of his own. The Texas team says it was difficult to compare the health of their animals with the health of Hayes's because he didn't report hatching success, mortality, survivorship, and other data. Hayes responds: "They've had all my information on protocols and SOPs since 1999. They signed off on this work. They even visited my lab."

While the scientists sparred, workers at Syngenta's atrazine plant in St.   30
Gabriel, Louisiana, stole the spotlight when their cancer rates became public. At

least 14 of 600 employees who'd been at the plant for more than 10 years had developed prostate cancer — a rate nine times as high as that of the general statewide population.

Had Syngenta inadvertently tested atrazine on humans? Studies of farm laborers who worked with the compound showed rates of certain cancers double to eight times the national average, but those exposures were intermittent and not exclusive, because workers handle many types of chemicals. In St. Gabriel, atrazine represented 80 percent of the plant's production, and it was made year-round. Atrazine dust covered the walls and floors, countertops and lunch tables.

Hayes's frog data were alarming, but they probably wouldn't have persuaded the EPA to ban atrazine. The cancer findings may. This past summer, the Natural Resources Defense Council persuaded the agency to launch a criminal investigation of Syngenta for suppressing data on the herbicide's potential risks to the environment and to human health. The EPA has since extended the deadline for its atrazine review. In addition to the cases in Louisiana, laboratory studies have linked atrazine to hormonally responsive cancers in humans and lab animals. Studies have also suggested that it disrupts the production of hormones such as testosterone, prolactin (which stimulates the production of breast milk), progesterone, estrogen, and the thyroid hormones that regulate metabolism.

Nonetheless, Hayes doesn't jump to condemn atrazine. He says he hasn't studied humans, but it is unlikely they'd be affected because atrazine doesn't accumulate in tissues the way DDT does. Others aren't so sure. "Why would anyone think these pesticides *wouldn't* affect us?" the World Wildlife Fund's Theo Colborn says. "No matter the species, we all have similar signaling systems in our bodies, similar chemical reactions. That's why we've always tested drugs on animals." Human kidneys filter atrazine, and humans don't spend a lot of time swimming in pesticide-laced water, the way frogs do. But human fetuses do live in water.

"Our big concern is pregnant females," Colborn says. "There have been enough studies on farm families to show that babies conceived in the spring, when runoff is highest, have far higher rates of birth defects than babies conceived at other times." But what component of the runoff is toxic and at what levels? That may be impossible to say, because scientists don't run lethal-dose experiments on humans. Faced with this uncertainty, how cautious should we be? When pressed, Hayes says that if his wife was pregnant, he'd advise her against drinking water from much of the Midwest — his children too. "If there's a .01 percent freak chance that something could happen, why take that chance?"

The mystery of amphibian decline continues to intrigue Hayes. He believes a 35 combination of many different effects may stress frogs' immune systems and that atrazine may be a part of it.

He dreams of testing his ideas with the perfect field experiment, one without unquantifiable variables, and he knows just where he'd enact it. "We'd go to

Biosphere 2, in Arizona," he says. "We'd bring in all our own air, our own water. We'd set up farm plots with corn. We'd bring in our own frogs, study every compound and its impact on the corn, the corn pests, the nontarget organisms." There's a gleam in Hayes's eyes. The thought of all those animals, the long hours, the phalanx of tired graduate students — it all makes his blood rise. "Nobody knows what these compounds actually do," he says. "I want to figure it out from beginning to end."

Exploring the Text

1. Considering that the essay is titled according to the topic of study, transsexual frogs, why does Elizabeth Royte begin with the scientist rather than with the science?

2. In paragraphs 8 and 14, Royte quotes scientists James Hanken and Theo Colborn. What is the rhetorical effect of these references?

3. In paragraph 10, Royte writes, "In Switzerland, where it is banned, atrazine occurs at one part per billion, even in the Alps." What does this point suggest about the gravity of the scientific problem Hayes is studying?

4. Paragraphs 15–24 profile Tyrone Hayes. How does Royte bring him to life? Consider especially her use of concrete details and strong verbs.

5. Why is paragraph 25 just one sentence? Reread it and the paragraph preceding it. Do you believe Hayes can discover a "bright and shining truth" despite the "weirdness with Syngenta"?

6. What do you find most interesting about Hayes's work?

7. Why does Royte begin paragraph 31 with a question rather than a statement?

8. What is the effect of switching back and forth between the profile of the scientist and a description of his work?

9. How do Hayes's ideas in paragraph 33 exemplify the scientific process described by T. H. Huxley (p. 609)?

10. In paragraph 34, Royte asks, "Faced with this uncertainty, how cautious should we be?" How would you answer this?

11. In the final paragraph, Royte describes what Hayes regards as the "perfect field experiment." What does the improbability of conducting such an experiment suggest about the nature of science in our time?

Sonnet — To Science (poetry)

EDGAR ALLAN POE

Edgar Allan Poe (1809–1849) was born in Boston but lived most of his life in Baltimore, Maryland. He briefly attended West Point Academy, and later worked as a journalist and critic. Poe is chiefly known as a romantic poet and writer of psychologically gripping horror stories. Among his most famous works are the poems "The Raven" and "Annabel Lee" and the short stories "The Tell-Tale Heart," "The Fall of the House of Usher," and "The Cask of Amontillado." "Sonnet — To Science" may come as a surprise to those readers who know Poe merely as a writer of gruesome horror stories.

Science! true daughter of Old Time thou art!
   Who alterest all things with thy peering eyes.
Why preyest thou thus upon the poet's heart,
   Vulture, whose wings are dull realities?
How should he love thee? or how deem thee wise?   *5*
   Who wouldst not leave him in his wandering
To seek for treasure in the jeweled skies,
   Albeit he soared with an undaunted wing?
Hast thou not dragged Diana[1] from her car?
   And driven the Hamadryad[2] from the wood   *10*
To seek a shelter in some happier star?
   Hast thou not torn the Naiad[3] from her flood,
The Elfin from the green grass, and from me
The summer dream beneath the tamarind tree?

Exploring the Text

1. What effect does Edgar Allan Poe's figurative language have on the presentation of Science?
2. According to Poe's speaker, what has Science done for him?
3. According to Poe's speaker, how has Science changed the world?
4. Is this ode to Science more laudatory or critical? Cite specific language to support your response.

---

[1]Diana was the ancient Roman goddess of the moon and of hunting.
[2]According to ancient Greek myth, Hamadryad was a tree nymph who died when the tree she lived in died.
[3]Both the ancient Greeks and the ancient Romans identified the Naiad as a river nymph.

When I Heard the Learn'd Astronomer
(poetry)

WALT WHITMAN

> Walt Whitman (1819–1892) was born on Long Island in New York. He worked as a teacher, a printer, and a journalist before making his name as a poet. Known widely for his free verse as well as his democratic spirit, Whitman is one of the most influential poets in the English language. His major work is *Leaves of Grass.* Among the famous poems from that collection are "Facing West from California's Shores," "Crossing Brooklyn Ferry," and "When Lilacs Last in the Dooryard Bloom'd," about Abraham Lincoln. While Whitman is well known for his lengthy and sprawling verse, his short poem, "When I Heard the Learn'd Astronomer" is justly famous as well.

When I heard the learn'd astronomer,
When the proofs, the figures, were ranged in columns before me,
When I was shown the charts and diagrams, to add, divide, and measure
    them,
When I sitting heard the astronomer where he lectured with much applause
    in the lecture-room,
How soon unaccountable I became tired and sick,   5
Till rising and gliding out I wander'd off by myself,
In the mystical moist night-air, and from time to time,
Look'd up in perfect silence at the stars.

Exploring the Text

1. Walt Whitman's poem is delivered as a periodic sentence, which puts its main clause after a series of phrases or clauses. What is the effect of this syntax?
2. How does the presentation of scientific data affect the speaker?
3. What is the effect of the series of participles: "sitting," "rising and gliding"?
4. What does the speaker imply about the relationship between science and nature?
5. Is Whitman's attitude similar to Edgar Allan Poe's (p. 663)? Explain.
6. How might Whitman regard T. H. Huxley's essay (p. 609)? Loren Eiseley's (p. 601)? Based on this poem, do you think Whitman would be a kindred spirit to either Huxley or Eiseley? Explain.

Super-Toys Last All Summer Long (fiction)

BRIAN ALDISS

Born in 1925 in Norfolk, England, Brian Aldiss is a prolific author of short stories, criticism, novels, drama, and poetry. He is most widely known as a writer of science fiction. He was awarded the title of Officer of the Order of the British Empire in 2005 in recognition of his contribution to literature. *A.I.: Artificial Intelligence,* the 2001 science fiction film directed by Steven Spielberg, is based on Aldiss's 1969 short story "Super-Toys Last All Summer Long," which follows.

In Mrs. Swinton's garden, it was always summer. The lovely almond trees stood about it in perpetual leaf. Monica Swinton plucked a saffron-colored rose and showed it to David.

"Isn't it lovely?" she said.

David looked up at her and grinned without replying. Seizing the flower, he ran with it across the lawn and disappeared behind the kennel where the mower-vator crouched, ready to cut or sweep or roll when the moment dictated. She stood alone on her impeccable plastic gravel path.

She had tried to love him.

When she made up her mind to follow the boy, she found him in the court-yard floating the rose in his paddling pool. He stood in the pool engrossed, still wearing his sandals. 5

"David, darling, do you have to be so awful? Come in at once and change your shoes and socks."

He went with her without protest into the house, his dark head bobbing at the level of her waist. At the age of three, he showed no fear of the ultrasonic dryer in the kitchen. But before his mother could reach for a pair of slippers, he wriggled away and was gone into the silence of the house.

He would probably be looking for Teddy.

Monica Swinton, twenty-nine, of graceful shape and lambent eye, went and sat in her living room, arranging her limbs with taste. She began by sitting and thinking; soon she was just sitting. Time waited on her shoulder with the maniac slowth it reserves for children, the insane, and wives whose husbands are away improving the world. Almost by reflex, she reached out and changed the wave-length of her windows. The garden faded; in its place, the city center rose by her left hand, full of crowding people, blowboats, and buildings (but she kept the sound down). She remained alone. An overcrowded world is the ideal place in which to be lonely.

The directors of Synthank were eating an enormous luncheon to celebrate the 10 launching of their new product. Some of them wore the plastic face-masks popular at the time. All were elegantly slender, despite the rich food and drink they were putting away. Their wives were elegantly slender, despite the food and drink they too were putting away. An earlier and less sophisticated generation would have regarded them as beautiful people, apart from their eyes.

Henry Swinton, Managing Director of Synthank, was about to make a speech.

"I'm sorry your wife couldn't be with us to hear you," his neighbor said.

"Monica prefers to stay at home thinking beautiful thoughts," said Swinton, maintaining a smile.

"One would expect such a beautiful woman to have beautiful thoughts," said the neighbor.

Take your mind off my wife, you bastard, thought Swinton, still smiling.   15

He rose to make his speech amid applause.

After a couple of jokes, he said, "Today marks a real breakthrough for the company. It is now almost ten years since we put our first synthetic life-forms on the world market. You all know what a success they have been, particularly the miniature dinosaurs. But none of them had intelligence.

"It seems like a paradox that in this day and age we can create life but not intelligence. Our first selling line, the Crosswell Tape, sells best of all, and is the most stupid of all." Everyone laughed.

"Though three-quarters of the overcrowded world are starving, we are lucky here to have more than enough, thanks to population control. Obesity's our problem, not malnutrition. I guess there's nobody round this table who doesn't have a Crosswell working for him in the small intestine, a perfectly safe parasite tape-worm that enables its host to eat up to fifty percent more food and still keep his or her figure. Right?" General nods of agreement.

"Our miniature dinosaurs are almost equally stupid. Today, we launch an   20
intelligent synthetic life-form — a full-size serving-man.

"Not only does he have intelligence, he has a controlled amount of intelligence. We believe people would be afraid of a being with a human brain. Our serving-man has a small computer in his cranium.

"There have been mechanicals on the market with mini-computers for brains — plastic things without life, super-toys — but we have at last found a way to link computer circuitry with synthetic flesh."

David sat by the long window of his nursery, wrestling with paper and pencil. Finally, he stopped writing and began to roll the pencil up and down the slope of the desk-lid.

"Teddy!" he said.

Teddy lay on the bed against the wall, under a book with moving pictures and   25
a giant plastic soldier. The speech-pattern of his master's voice activated him and he sat up.

"Teddy! I can't think what to say!"

Climbing off the bed, the bear walked stiffly over to cling to the boy's leg. David lifted him and set him on the desk.

"What have you said so far?"

"I've said —" He picked up his letter and stared hard at it. "I've said, 'Dear Mummy, I hope you're well just now. I love you . . .'"

There was a long silence, until the bear said, "That sounds fine. Go downstairs and give it to her." 30

Another long silence.

"It isn't quite right. She won't understand."

Inside the bear, a small computer worked through its program of possibilities. "Why not do it again in crayon?"

When David did not answer, the bear repeated his suggestion. "Why not do it again in crayon?"

David was staring out of the window. "Teddy, you know what I was thinking? 35 How do you tell what are real things from what aren't real things?"

The bear shuffled its alternatives. "Real things are good."

"I wonder if time is good. I don't think Mummy likes time very much. The other day, lots of days ago, she said that time went by her. Is time real, Teddy?"

"Clocks tell the time. Clocks are real. Mummy has clocks so she must like them. She has a clock on her wrist next to her dial."

David started to draw a jumbo jet on the back of his letter. "You and I are real, Teddy, aren't we?"

The bear's eyes regarded the boy unflinchingly. "You and I are real, David." It 40 specialized in comfort.

Monica walked slowly about the house. It was almost time for the afternoon post to come over the wire. She punched the Post Office number on the dial on her wrist, but nothing came through. A few minutes more.

She could take up her painting. Or she could dial her friends. Or she could wait till Henry came home. Or she could go up and play with David. . . .

She walked out into the hall and to the bottom of the stairs.

"David!"

No answer. She called again and a third time. 45

"Teddy!" she called, in sharper tones.

"Yes, Mummy!" After a moment's pause, Teddy's head of golden fur appeared at the top of the stairs.

"Is David in his room, Teddy?"

"David went into the garden, Mummy."

"Come down here, Teddy!" 50

She stood impassively, watching the little furry figure as it climbed down from step to step on its stubby limbs. When it reached the bottom, she picked it up and carried it into the living room. It lay unmoving in her arms, staring up at her. She could feel just the slightest vibration from its motor.

"Stand there, Teddy. I want to talk to you." She set him down on a tabletop, and he stood as she requested, arms set forward and open in the eternal gesture of embrace.

"Teddy, did David tell you to tell me he had gone into the garden?"

The circuits of the bear's brain were too simple for artifice. "Yes, Mummy."

"So you lied to me." 55

"Yes. Mummy."

"Stop calling me Mummy! Why is David avoiding me? He's not afraid of me, is he?"

"No. He loves you."

"Why can't we communicate?"

"David's upstairs." 60

The answer stopped her dead. Why waste time talking to this machine? Why not simply go upstairs and scoop David into her arms and talk to him, as a loving mother should to a loving son? She heard the sheer weight of silence in the house, with a different quality of silence pouring out of every room. On the upper landing, something was moving very silently — David, trying to hide away from her. . . .

He was nearing the end of his speech now. The guests were attentive; so was the Press, lining two walls of the banqueting chamber, recording Henry's words and occasionally photographing him.

"Our serving-man will be, in many senses, a product of the computer. Without computers, we could never have worked through the sophisticated biochemics that go into synthetic flesh. The serving-man will also be an extension of the computer — for he will contain a computer in his own head, a microminiaturized computer capable of dealing with almost any situation he may encounter in the home. With reservations, of course." Laughter at this; many of those present knew the heated debate that had engulfed the Synthank boardroom before the decision had finally been taken to leave the serving-man neuter under his flawless uniform.

"Amid all the triumphs of our civilization — yes, and amid the crushing problems of overpopulation too — it is sad to reflect how many millions of people suffer from increasing loneliness and isolation. Our serving-man will be a boon to them: he will always answer, and the most vapid conversation cannot bore him.

"For the future, we plan more models, male and female — some of them 65 without the limitations of this first one, I promise you! — of more advanced design, true bio-electronic beings.

"Not only will they possess their own computer, capable of individual programming; they will be linked to the World Data Network. Thus everyone will be able to enjoy the equivalent of an Einstein in their own homes. Personal isolation will then be banished forever!"

He sat down to enthusiastic applause. Even the synthetic serving-man, sitting at the table dressed in an unostentatious suit, applauded with gusto.

Dragging his satchel, David crept round the side of the house. He climbed on to the ornamental seat under the living-room window and peeped cautiously in.

His mother stood in the middle of the room. Her face was blank, its lack of expression scared him. He watched fascinated. He did not move; she did not move. Time might have stopped, as it had stopped in the garden.

At last she turned and left the room. After waiting a moment, David tapped on the window. Teddy looked round, saw him, tumbled off the table, and came over to the window. Fumbling with his paws, he eventually got it open.

They looked at each other.

"I'm no good, Teddy. Let's run away!"

"You're a very good boy. Your Mummy loves you."

Slowly, he shook his head. "If she loved me, then why can't I talk to her?"

"You're being silly, David. Mummy's lonely. That's why she had you."

"She's got Daddy. I've got nobody 'cept you, and I'm lonely."

Teddy gave him a friendly cuff over the head. "If you feel so bad, you'd better go to the psychiatrist again."

"I hate that old psychiatrist — he makes me feel I'm not real." He started to run across the lawn. The bear toppled out of the window and followed as fast as its stubby legs would allow.

Monica Swinton was up in the nursery. She called to her son once and then stood there, undecided. All was silent.

Crayons lay on his desk. Obeying a sudden impulse, she went over to the desk and opened it. Dozens of pieces of paper lay inside. Many of them were written in crayon in David's clumsy writing, with each letter picked out in a color different from the letter preceding it. None of the messages was finished.

"My dear Mummy, How are you really, do you love me as much —"

"Dear Mummy, I love you and Daddy and the sun is shining —"

"Dear dear Mummy, Teddy's helping me write to you. I love you and Teddy —"

"Darling Mummy, I'm your one and only son and I love you so much that some times —"

"Dear Mummy, you're really my Mummy and I hate Teddy —"

"Darling Mummy, guess how much I love —"

"Dear Mummy, I'm your little boy not Teddy and I love you but Teddy —"

"Dear Mummy, this is a letter to you just to say how much how ever so much —"

Monica dropped the pieces of paper and burst out crying. In their gay inaccurate colors, the letters fanned out and settled on the floor.

Henry Swinton caught the express home in high spirits, and occasionally said a word to the synthetic serving-man he was taking home with him. The serving-man answered politely and punctually, although his answers were not always entirely relevant by human standards.

The Swintons lived in one of the ritziest city-blocks, half a kilometer above the ground. Embedded in other apartments, their apartment had no windows to the outside; nobody wanted to see the overcrowded external world. Henry unlocked the door with his retina pattern-scanner and walked in, followed by the serving-man.

At once, Henry was surrounded by the friendly illusion of gardens set in eternal summer. It was amazing what Whologram could do to create huge mirages in small spaces. Behind its roses and wisteria stood their house; the deception was complete: a Georgian mansion appeared to welcome him.

"How do you like it?" he asked the serving-man.

"Roses occasionally suffer from black spot."

"These roses are guaranteed free from any imperfections." 95

"It is always advisable to purchase goods with guarantees, even if they cost slightly more."

"Thanks for the information," Henry said dryly. Synthetic lifeforms were less than ten years old, the old android mechanicals less than sixteen; the faults of their systems were still being ironed out, year by year.

He opened the door and called to Monica.

She came out of the sitting-room immediately and flung her arms round him, kissing him ardently on cheek and lips. Henry was amazed.

Pulling back to look at her face, he saw how she seemed to generate light and 100 beauty. It was months since he had seen her so excited. Instinctively, he clasped her tighter.

"Darling, what's happened?"

"Henry, Henry — oh, my darling, I was in despair . . . but I've just dialed the afternoon post and — you'll never believe it! Oh, it's wonderful!"

"For heavens sake, woman, what's wonderful?"

He caught a glimpse of the heading on the photostat in her hand, still moist from the wall-receiver: Ministry of Population. He felt the color drain from his face in sudden shock and hope.

"Monica . . . oh . . . Don't tell me our number's come up!" 105

"Yes, my darling, yes, we've won this week's parenthood lottery! We can go ahead and conceive a child at once!"

He let out a yell of joy. They danced round the room. Pressure of population was such that reproduction had to be strict, controlled. Childbirth required government permission. For this moment, they had waited four years. Incoherently they cried their delight.

They paused at last, gasping and stood in the middle of the room to laugh at each other's happiness. When she had come down from the nursery, Monica had de-opaqued the windows so that they now revealed the vista of garden beyond. Artificial sunlight was growing long and golden across the lawn — and David and Teddy were staring through the window at them.

Seeing their faces, Henry and his wife grew serious.

"What do we do about them?" Henry asked. 110

"Teddy's no trouble. He works well."

"Is David malfunctioning?"

"His verbal communication center is still giving trouble. I think he'll have to go back to the factory again."

"Okay. We'll see how he does before the baby's born. Which reminds me — I have a surprise for you: help just when help is needed! Come into the hall and see what I've got."

As the two adults disappeared from the room, boy and bear sat down beneath the standard roses. 115

"Teddy — I suppose Mummy and Daddy are real, aren't they?"

Teddy said, "You ask such silly questions, David. Nobody knows what *real* really means. Let's go indoors."

"First I'm going to have another rose!" Plucking a bright pink flower, he carried it with him into the house. It could lie on the pillow as he went to sleep. Its beauty and softness reminded him of Mummy.

Exploring the Text

1. What are some early indications that Brian Aldiss's story is set in the future?
2. What clues are there about the nature of David and Teddy? What in the text leads the reader to suspect that the mother is the robotic creature?
3. Paragraph 40 concludes with the statement, "It specialized in comfort." What is the tone of this statement?
4. To which characters does the title refer?
5. With which character does the reader sympathize? Is this ironic?
6. Considering that this story was published in 1969, which details are especially prescient?
7. What do paragraphs 90–118 suggest about Aldiss's attitude toward values? What do they suggest about the relationship between technology and humanity?
8. If you have seen the movie *A.I.*, how does it compare with the short story?

The Cosmic Calendar

Carl Sagan

Carl Sagan (1934–1996) received both undergraduate degrees and a doctorate in astronomy and astrophysics from the University of Chicago, and he taught on the faculty of Stanford Medical School, Harvard University, and Cornell University. At Cornell he was a professor of astronomy and space sciences. Sagan received numerous awards for his scientific work and for his writing, including the NASA Exceptional Scientific Achievement Medal. Among his books are the nonfiction *Cosmos* (1980), based on his television series for PBS; *Broca's Brain* (1993); and a novel, *Contact*

(1985). "The Cosmic Calendar" appears in *The Dragons of Eden* (1977), Sagan's Pulitzer Prize–winning book about the evolution of human intelligence.

What seest thou else
In the dark backward and abysm of time?

— Wm. Shakespeare
The Tempest

The world is very old, and human beings are very young. Significant events in our personal lives are measured in years or less; our lifetimes in decades; our family genealogies in centuries; and all of recorded history in millennia. But we have been preceded by an awesome vista of time, extending for prodigious periods into the past, about which we know little — both because there are no written records and because we have real difficulty in grasping the immensity of the intervals involved.

Yet we are able to date events in the remote past. Geological stratification and radioactive dating provide information on archaeological, paleontological and geological events; and astrophysical theory provides data on the ages of planetary surfaces, stars, and the Milky Way Galaxy, as well as an estimate of the time that has elapsed since that extraordinary event called the Big Bang — an explosion that involved all of the matter and energy in the present universe. The Big Bang may be the beginning of the universe, or it may be a discontinuity in which information about the earlier history of the universe was destroyed. But it is certainly the earliest event about which we have any record.

The most instructive way I know to express this cosmic chronology is to imagine the fifteen-billion-year lifetime of the universe (or at least its present incarnation since the Big Bang) compressed into the span of a single year. Then every billion years of Earth history would correspond to about twenty-four days of our cosmic year, and one second of that year to 475 real revolutions of the Earth about the sun. [In Figures 1, 2, and 3] I present the cosmic chronology in three forms: a list of some representative pre-December dates; a calendar for the month of December; and a closer look at the late evening of New Year's Eve. On this scale, the events of our history books — even books that make significant efforts to deprovincialize the present — are so compressed that it is necessary to give a second-by-second recounting of the last seconds of the cosmic year. Even then, we find events listed as contemporary that we have been taught to consider as widely separated in time. In the history of life, an equally rich tapestry must have been woven in other periods — for example, between 10:02 and 10:03 on the morning of April 6th or September 16th. But we have detailed records only for the very end of the cosmic year.

The chronology corresponds to the best evidence now available. But some of it is rather shaky. No one would be astounded if, for example, it turns out that plants colonized the land in the Ordovician rather than the Silurian Period; or

Pre-December Dates

Big Bang	January 1
Origin of the Milky Way Galaxy	May 1
Origin of the solar system	September 9
Formation of the Earth	September 14
Origin of life on Earth	~ September 25
Formation of the oldest rocks known on Earth	October 2
Date of oldest fossils (bacteria and blue-green algae)	October 9
Invention of sex (by microorganisms)	~ November 1
Oldest fossil photosynthetic plants	November 12
Eukaryotes (first cells with nuclei) flourish	November 15

~ = approximately.

FIGURE 1

Cosmic Calendar
DECEMBER

Sunday	Monday	Tuesday	Wednesday	Thursday	Friday	Saturday
	1 Significant oxygen atmosphere begins to develop on Earth.	**2**	**3**	**4**	**5** Extensive vulcanism and channel formation on Mars.	**6**
7	**8**	**9**	**10**	**11**	**12**	**13**
14	**15**	**16** First worms.	**17** Precambrian ends. Paleozoic Era and Cambrian Period begin. Invertebrates flourish.	**18** First oceanic plankton. Trilobites flourish.	**19** Ordovician Period. First fish. First vertebrates.	**20** Silurian Period. First vascular plants. Plants begin colonization of land.
21 Devonian Period begins. First insects. Animals begin colonization of land.	**22** First amphibians. First winged insects.	**23** Carboniferous Period. First trees. First reptiles.	**24** Permian Period begins. First dinosaurs.	**25** Paleozoic Era ends. Mesozoic Era begins.	**26** Triassic Period. First mammals.	**27** Jurassic Period. First birds.
28 Cretaceous Period. First flowers. Dinosaurs become extinct.	**29** Mesozoic Era ends. Cenozoic Era and Tertiary Period begin. First cetaceans. First primates.	**30** Early evolution of frontal lobes in the brains of primates. First hominids. Giant mammals flourish.	**31** End of the Pliocene Period. Quatenary (Pleistocene and Holocene) Period. First humans.			

FIGURE 2

that segmented worms appeared earlier in the Precambrian Period than indicated. Also, in the chronology of the last ten seconds of the cosmic year, it was obviously impossible for me to include all significant events; I hope I may be

December 31

Origin of *Proconsul* and *Ramapithecus*, probable ancestors of apes and men	~ 1:30 P.M.
First humans	~10:30 P.M.
Widespread use of stone tools	11:00 P.M.
Domestication of fire by Peking man	11:46 P.M.
Beginning of most recent glacial period	11:56 P.M.
Seafarers settle Australia	11:58 P.M.
Extensive cave painting in Europe	11:59 P.M.
Invention of agriculture	11:59:20 P.M.
Neolithic civilization; first cities	11:59:35 P.M.
First dynasties in Sumer, Ebla and Egypt; development of astronomy	11:59:50 P.M.
Invention of the alphabet; Akkadian Empire	11:59:51 P.M.
Hammurabic legal codes in Babylon; Middle Kingdom in Egypt	11:59:52 P.M.
Bronze metallurgy; Mycenaean culture; Trojan War; Olmec culture: invention of the compass	11:59:53 P.M.
Iron metallurgy; First Assyrian Empire; Kingdom of Israel; founding of Carthage by Phoenicia	11:59:54 P.M.
Asokan India; Ch'in Dynasty China; Periclean Athens; birth of Buddha	11:59:55 P.M.
Euclidean geometry; Archimedean physics; Ptolemaic astronomy; Roman Empire; birth of Christ	11:59:56 P.M.
Zero and decimals invented in Indian arithmetic; Rome falls; Moslem conquests	11:59:57 P.M.
Mayan civilization; Sung Dynasty China; Byzantine empire; Mongol invasion; Crusades	11:59:58 P.M.
Renaissance in Europe; voyages of discovery from Europe and from Ming Dynasty China; emergence of the experimental method in science	11:59:59 P.M.
Widespread development of science and technology; emergence of a global culture; acquisition of the means for self-destruction of the human species; first steps in spacecraft planetary exploration and the search for extraterrestrial intelligence	Now: The first second of New Year's Day

FIGURE 3

excused for not having explicitly mentioned advances in art, music and literature or the historically significant American, French, Russian and Chinese revolutions.

The construction of such tables and calendars is inevitably humbling. It is disconcerting to find that in such a cosmic year the Earth does not condense out of interstellar matter until early September; dinosaurs emerge on Christmas Eve; flowers arise on December 28th; and men and women originate at 10:30 P.M. on New Year's Eve. All of recorded history occupies the last ten seconds of December

31; and the time from the waning of the Middle Ages to the present occupies little more than one second. But because I have arranged it that way, the first cosmic year has just ended. And despite the insignificance of the instant we have so far occupied in cosmic time, it is clear that what happens on and near Earth at the beginning of the second cosmic year will depend very much on the scientific wisdom and the distinctly human sensitivity of mankind.

Exploring the Text

1. Does Carl Sagan use simile, metaphor, or analogy as his basic rhetorical device? Explain.
2. In paragraph 4, why does Sagan acknowledge the possibility of error in Figures 1 to 3?
3. How does Sagan's calendar affect your view of human history?
4. What is the effect of Sagan's mentioning omissions of art, music, literature, and political revolutions (para. 4)?
5. What does Sagan's last sentence imply?
6. How effectively do Figures 1 to 3 confirm or expand Sagan's points?
7. In his book *Faster* (1999), author and journalist James Gleick says that in a nanosecond, light travels the distance of one foot. How does such a measurement inform a reading of Sagan's calendar?
8. How does Sagan's idea for the cosmic calendar exemplify Jacob Bronowski's ideas about science (see p. 616)?

Food Fight (cagtoon)

GAHAN WILSON

Author, cartoonist, and illustrator Gahan Wilson was born in 1930 and is known for his dark humor, often featuring atomic mutants and subway monsters. His short stories have appeared in *Fantasy and Science Fiction*, and he has written book and movie reviews for that publication as well as *The Twilight Zone Magazine* and *Realms of Fantasy*. He has also created a computer game titled *Gahan Wilson's The Ultimate Haunted House*. His cartoons have appeared in the *New Yorker*, the *National Lampoon, Colliers, Look*, and *Fantasy and Science Fiction*. In 2005 he received the National Cartoonist Society Milton Caniff Lifetime Achievement Award.

Exploring the Text

1. What comes to mind when you read the title "Food Fight"? Does the cartoon fulfill your expectations?

FOOD FIGHT BY GAHAN WILSON

There have been outcries against our nation's efforts to genetically manipulate the food we eat and export.

The big corporations claim they're only helping edibles fight off bugs and other natural enemies.

They say that consumers who worry about the use of human-genome technology suffer from overactive imaginations.

It hasn't occurred to them that unless we slow down this acceleration of evolution or enact a similar program for ourselves . . .

our food's increasing ability to adapt to a hostile environment may result in a reversal of the food chain.

And that would serve us right.

2. How are the humans depicted in the drawings throughout this cartoon?
3. Why are the foods anthropomorphized?
4. What commentary does the parallelism of frames 1 and 4 make?
5. How do you interpret the final commentary, "And that would serve us right"? Is the cartoonist being ironic or serious?
6. Read the print commentaries all the way through as a continuous stream. What is the tone? How does the interaction of print text with the cartoons change that tone?
7. What is Wilson's argument? How does he set up an us-versus-them situation?
8. The graphic novel is increasingly considered a serious genre of fiction. What case can you make for this sequence to be called a "graphic short story" rather than a cartoon? What difference would such a title make?

Conversation

Focus on the Ethics of Genetic Technology

The following five selections comment directly or indirectly on the ethical issues surrounding genetic technology.

Sources

1. **Lewis Thomas,** *On Cloning a Human Being*
2. **Philip M. Boffey,** *Fearing the Worst Should Anyone Produce a Cloned Baby*
3. **David Ewing Duncan,** *DNA as Destiny*
4. **Rick Weiss,** *Pet Clones Spur Call for Limits*
5. **Marilynn Marchione and Lindsey Tanner,** *More Couples Screening Embryos for Gender*

After you have read, studied, and synthesized these pieces, enter the conversation by responding to one of the prompts on page 695.

1. *On Cloning a Human Being*

LEWIS THOMAS

In the following essay from *The Medusa and the Snail* (1979), biologist and physician Lewis Thomas discusses the possibility of cloning.

It is now theoretically possible to recreate an identical creature from any animal or plant, from the DNA contained in the nucleus of any somatic cell. A single plant root-tip cell can be teased and seduced into conceiving a perfect copy of the whole plant; a frog's intestinal epithelial cell possesses the complete instructions needed for a new, same frog. If the technology were further advanced, you could do this with a human being, and there are now startled predictions all over the place that this will in fact be done, someday, in order to provide a version of immortality for carefully selected, especially valuable people.

The cloning of humans is on most of the lists of things to worry about from Science, along with behavior control, genetic engineering, transplanted heads, computer poetry, and the unrestrained growth of plastic flowers.

Cloning is the most dismaying of prospects, mandating as it does the elimination of sex with only a metaphoric elimination of death as compensation. It is almost no comfort to know that one's cloned, identical surrogate lives on, especially when the living will very likely involve edging one's real, now aging self off to side, sooner or later. It is hard to imagine anything like filial affection or respect for a single, unmated nucleus; harder still to think of one's new, self-generated self

678

as anything but an absolute, desolate orphan. Not to mention the complex interpersonal relationship involved in raising one's self from infancy, teaching the language, enforcing discipline, instilling good manners, and the like. How would you feel if you became an incorrigible juvenile delinquent by proxy, at the age of fifty-five?

The public questions are obvious. Who is to be selected, and on what qualifications? How to handle the risks of misused technology, such as self-determined cloning by the rich and powerful but socially objectionable, or the cloning by governments of dumb, docile masses for the world's work? What will be the effect on all the uncloned rest of us of human sameness? After all, we've accustomed ourselves through hundreds of millennia to the continual exhilaration of uniqueness; each of us is totally different, in a fundamental sense, from all the other four billion. Selfness is an essential fact of life. The thought of human nonselfness, precise sameness, is terrifying, when you think about it.

Well, don't think about it, because it isn't a probable possibility, not even as a   5
long shot for the distant future, in my opinion. I agree that you might clone some people who would look amazingly like their parental cell donors, but the odds are that they'd be almost as different as you or me, and certainly more different than any of today's identical twins.

The time required for the experiment is only one of the problems, but a formidable one. Suppose you wanted to clone a prominent, spectacularly successful diplomat, to look after the Middle East problems of the distant future. You'd have to catch him and persuade him, probably not very hard to do, and extirpate a cell. But then you'd have to wait for him to grow up through embryonic life and then for at least forty years more, and you'd have to be sure all observers remained patient and unmeddlesome through his unpromising, ambiguous childhood and adolescence.

Moreover, you'd have to be sure of recreating his environment, perhaps down to the last detail. "Environment" is a word which really means people, so you'd have to do a lot more cloning than just the diplomat himself.

This is a very important part of the cloning problem, largely overlooked in our excitement about the cloned individual himself. You don't have to agree all the way with B. F. Skinner to acknowledge that the environment does make a difference, and when you examine what we really mean by the word "environment" it comes down to other human beings. We use euphemisms and jargon for this, like "social forces," "cultural influences," even Skinner's "verbal community," but what is meant is the dense crowd of nearby people who talk to, listen to, smile or frown at, give to, withhold from, nudge, push, caress, or flail out at the individual. No matter what the genome says, these people have a lot to do with shaping a character. Indeed, if all you had was the genome, and no people around, you'd grow a sort of vertebrate plant, nothing more.

So, to start with, you will undoubtedly need to clone the parents. No question about this. This means the diplomat is out, even in theory, since you couldn't have

gotten cells from both his parents at the time when he was himself just recognizable as an early social treasure. You'd have to limit the list of clones to people
already certified as sufficiently valuable for the effort, with both parents still alive.
The parents would need cloning and, for consistency, their parents as well. I suppose you'd also need the usual informed-consent forms, filled out and signed, not
easy to get if I know parents, even harder for grandparents.

But this is only the beginning. It is the whole family that really influences the   10
way a person turns out, not just the parents, according to current psychiatric
thinking. Clone the family.

Then what? The way each member of the family develops has already been
determined by the environment set around him, and this environment is more
people, people outside the family, schoolmates, acquaintances, lovers, enemies,
car-pool partners, even, in special circumstances, peculiar strangers across the
aisle on the subway. Find them, and clone them.

But there is no end to the protocol. Each of the outer contacts has his own
surrounding family, and his and their outer contacts. Clone them all.

To do the thing properly, with any hope of ending up with a genuine duplicate
of a single person, you really have no choice. You must clone the world, no less.

We are not ready for an experiment of this size, nor, I should think, are we
willing. For one thing, it would mean replacing today's world by an entirely identical world to follow immediately, and this means no new, natural, spontaneous,
random, chancy children. No children at all, except for the manufactured doubles
of those now on the scene. Plus all those identical adults, including all of today's
politicians, all seen double. It is too much to contemplate.

Moreover, when the whole experiment is finally finished, fifty years or so   15
from now, how could you get a responsible scientific reading on the outcome?
Somewhere in there would be the original clonee, probably lost and overlooked,
now well into middle age, but everyone around him would be precise duplicates
of today's everyone. It would be today's same world, filled to overflowing with
duplicates of today's people and their same, duplicated problems, probably all
resentful at having had to go through our whole thing all over, sore enough at the
clonee to make endless trouble for him, if they found him.

And obviously, if the whole thing were done precisely right, they would still
be casting about for ways to solve the problem of universal dissatisfaction, and
sooner or later they'd surely begin to look around at each other, wondering who
should be cloned for his special value to society, to get us out of all this. And so it
would go, in regular cycles, perhaps forever.

I once lived through a period when I wondered what Hell could be like, and I
stretched my imagination to try to think of a perpetual sort of damnation. I have
to confess, I never thought of anything like this.

I have an alternative suggestion, if you're looking for a way out. Set cloning
aside, and don't try it. Instead, go in the other direction. Look for ways to get
mutations more quickly, new variety, different songs. Fiddle around, if you must

fiddle, but never with ways to keep things the same, no matter who, not even yourself. Heaven, somewhere ahead, has got to be a change.

Questions

1. How has the scientific knowledge of cloning changed since the 1970s, when Lewis Thomas wrote that cloning is "theoretically possible"? How does this change affect your view of Thomas's piece?
2. What does Thomas mean when he refers to cloning as "the most dismaying of prospects" (para. 3)?
3. Is society even today ready to address the questions Thomas raises in paragraph 4? Why or why not?
4. Why does Thomas say, "You must clone the world, no less," in paragraph 13? Is he exaggerating?
5. Do you agree with Thomas's conclusion? Why or why not?

2. *Fearing the Worst Should Anyone Produce a Cloned Baby*

Philip M. Boffey

In the following article from *The Best American Science and Nature Writing* (2004), Philip Boffey looks at the fears associated with cloning. Boffey's article first appeared in the *New York Times* in 2004.

Experts increasingly suspect that a fringe cult's claim to have cloned a human baby is a publicity-seeking hoax, especially now that the group seems to be evading genetic tests that might prove its claim. The cult's deep-seated belief that space aliens created the human race by cloning is so wacko that all of its other claims become suspect. But with several renegade groups supposedly racing to produce the first cloned baby, it is almost inevitable that sooner or later someone will succeed. It's time to start preparing ourselves mentally for that eventuality.

Until now, there has been widespread support in Congress for a ban on cloning to produce babies — the only real debate has been over the use of cloned embryos to find cures for disease. Even scientists who want to pursue therapeutic cloning have been happy to endorse a ban on reproductive cloning for safety reasons. Judging from animal tests, there is just too much risk that a cloned baby would be born with birth defects or face medical problems as it ages. But if the renegade cloners ever present a healthy baby who is shown by genetic tests to be a cloned copy of an adult, the safety argument will become less persuasive. It will then be imperative to look much harder at the ethical and moral implications of reproductive cloning.

The public's fear and fascination with cloning, as expressed in popular culture, focuses on some highly improbable scenarios. *The Boys from Brazil*, a 1978 movie based on a novel, featured a plot by Nazi doctors to produce a cadre of young Hitler clones to start a Fourth Reich. Although the villains tried to give the young Hitlers the same home life as the original, the writers slid past the overwhelming probability that even Hitler himself, introduced into a different historical context, would not have the same career trajectory.

The most recent *Star Wars* movie, last year's *Attack of the Clones*, featured an army of clones derived from the genes of an aggressive bounty hunter, modified to ensure willingness to follow military orders. The image of a horde of unthinking, cloned attackers is a classic science-fiction nightmare. But producing such an army with today's techniques would require a huge number of women to supply the eggs and bear the fetal clones to term, a problem that is often glossed over in horror stories. On a more individual scale, the new *Star Trek* movie, *Nemesis*, pits a good spaceship captain against his evil younger clone. The younger version went bad because of his harsh treatment when exiled to hellish mines on a remote world, a nice reminder that genes alone do not dictate destiny.

Over the years, people have fretted that cloning practiced widely might eliminate the need for men (women could bear children asexually), might exacerbate the male-female ratio (cultures that revere males could clone only them), and might reduce the genetic diversity that comes from mingling genes in sexual reproduction. But those scenarios suppose that cloning might indeed become the preferred means of reproduction, an event that would seem to require an unlikely mass change in human preferences or a totalitarian regime to impose its will. In a democratic, free-market society, commercial entities might well promote cloning, but such marketing has not turned in vitro fertilization or the freezing of bodies for later resurrection into mass commodities.

Some critics fear that cloning could usher in a new eugenics, in which nations or individuals might try to improve the average capabilities of the next generation by cloning the likes of an Einstein, Mozart, Michael Jordan, or Marilyn Monroe. Such genetic enhancement has in fact been endorsed by some eminent scientists in the past, and no doubt there are individuals who might want offspring with particular talents. Yet sperm banks with seed from famous and accomplished men have existed for some time with no sign of a mass rush to use them.

In its report on human cloning last year, the President's Council on Bioethics worried that cloning to produce children could disrupt the normal relationships between generations and within families, could turn children into manufactured products rather than independent beings, and could put undue pressure on a cloned child living in the shadow of a genetically identical adult. Most of the panel's concerns were necessarily speculative, and some of its worries seem overdrawn. Twins seem to do just fine with the same genome, for example, so it is not clear that having a twin a generation older would be all that burdensome. Nor is it clear that families with a cloned child would face more confusing relationships than already exist in today's divorced, blended, and extended families. On the other hand, cloning could prove medically useful for couples worried about passing on genetic diseases, infertile individuals who could not have a biologically related child any other way, or parents needing a compatible tissue donor to cure a sick child.

For the immediate future, Congress would be wise to ban reproductive cloning as far too risky while allowing therapeutic cloning to proceed. But sooner or later technical advances may diminish the risks. The nation needs to focus on what to do then.

Questions

1. Do you agree with Philip Boffey that cloning is an "eventuality" that we should prepare for? How would we prepare?
2. Boffey does not state his ethical position on cloning, but what clues in the reading suggest his position?
3. Of the two concerns Boffey discusses in paragraph 2, which is more important? Why?
4. Why does Boffey believe mass cloning is unlikely? Is his argument compelling? Why or why not?
5. How persuasive is Boffey's dismissal of the three concerns he identifies in paragraph 7?

3. *DNA as Destiny*

DAVID EWING DUNCAN

In the following essay, David Ewing Duncan examines DNA testing. First published in *Wired*, this piece is included in *The Best American Science and Nature Writing* (2003).

I feel naked. Exposed. As if my skin, bone, muscle tissue, cells, have all been peeled back, down to a tidy swirl of DNA. It's the basic stuff of life, the billions of nucleotides that keep me breathing, walking, craving, and just being. Eight hours ago, I gave a few cells, swabbed from inside my cheek, to a team of geneticists. They've spent the day extracting DNA and checking it for dozens of hidden diseases. Eventually, I will be tested for hundreds more. They include, as I will discover, a nucleic time bomb ticking inside my chromosomes that might one day kill me.

For now I remain blissfully ignorant, awaiting the results of an office at Sequenom, one of scores of biotech startups incubating in the canyons north of San Diego. I'm waiting to find out if I have a genetic proclivity for cancer, cardiac disease, deafness, Alzheimer's, or schizophrenia.

This, I'm told, is the first time a healthy human has ever been screened for the full gamut of genetic disease markers. Everyone has errors in his or her DNA, glitches that may trigger a heart spasm or cause a brain tumor. I'm here to learn mine.

Waiting, I wonder if I carry some sort of Pandora gene, a hereditary predisposition to peek into places I shouldn't. Morbid curiosity is an occupational hazard for a writer, I suppose, but I've never been bothered by it before. Yet now I find myself growing nervous and slightly flushed. I can feel my pulse rising, a cardiovascular response that I will soon discover has, for me, dire implications.

In the coming days, I'll seek a second opinion, of sorts. Curious about where   5
my genes come from, I'll travel to Oxford and visit an "ancestral geneticist" who has agreed to examine my DNA for links back to progenitors whose mutations have been passed on to me. He will reveal the seeds of my individuality and the roots of the diseases that may kill me — and my children.

For now, I wait in an office at Sequenom, a sneak preview of a trip to the DNA doctor, circa 2008. The personalized medicine being pioneered here and elsewhere prefigures a day when everyone's genome will be deposited on a chip or stored on a gene card tucked into a wallet. Physicians will forecast illnesses and prescribe preventive drugs custom-fitted to a patient's DNA, rather than the one-size-fits-all pharmaceuticals that people take today. Gene cards might also be used to find that best-suited career, or a DNA-compatible mate, or, more darkly, to deny someone jobs, dates, and meds because their nucleotides don't measure up. It's a scenario Andrew Niccol imagined in his 1997 film, *Gattaca*, where embryos in a not-too-distant future are bioengineered for perfection and where genism — discrimination based on one's DNA — condemns the lesser-gened to scrubbing toilets.

The *Gattaca*-like engineering of defect-free embryos is at least twenty or thirty years away, but Sequenom and others plan to take DNA testing to the masses in just a year or two. The prize: a projected $5 billion market for personalized medicine by 2006 and billions, possibly hundreds of billions, more for those companies that can translate the errors in my genome and yours into custom pharmaceuticals.

Sitting across from me is the man responsible for my gene scan: Andi Braun, chief medical officer at Sequenom. Tall and sinewy, with a long neck, glasses, and short gray hair, Braun, forty-six, is both jovial and German. Genetic tests are already publicly available for Huntington's disease and cystic fibrosis, but Braun points out that these illnesses are relatively rare. "We are targeting diseases that impact millions," he says in a deep Bavarian accent, envisioning a day when genetic kits that can assay the whole range of human misery will be available at Wal-Mart, as easy to use as a home pregnancy test.

But a kit won't tell me if I'll definitely get a disease, just if I have a bum gene. What Sequenom and others are working toward is pinning down the probability that, for example, a colon cancer gene will actually trigger a tumor. To know this, Braun must analyze the DNA of thousands of people and tally how many have the colon cancer gene, how many actually get the disease, and how many don't. Once these data are gathered and crunched, Braun will be able to tell you, for instance, that if you have the defective gene, you have a 40 percent chance, or maybe a 75 percent chance, of getting the disease by age fifty, or ninety. Environmental factors such as eating right — or wrong — and smoking also weigh in. "It's a little like predicting the weather," says Charles Cantor, the company's cofounder and chief scientific officer.

Braun tells me that, for now, his tests offer only a rough sketch of my genetic 10 future. "We can't yet test for everything, and some of the information is only partially understood," he says. It's a peek more through a rudimentary eyeglass than a Hubble Space Telescope. Yet I will be able to glimpse some of the internal programming bequeathed to me by evolution and that I, in turn, have bequeathed to my children — Sander, Danielle, and Alex, ages fifteen, thirteen, and seven. They are a part of this story, too. Here's where I squirm, because as a father I pass on not only the ingredients of life to my children but the secret codes of their demise — just as I have passed on my blue eyes and a flip in my left brow that my grandmother called "a little lick from God." DNA is not only the book of life, it is also the book of death, says Braun: "We're all going to die, *ja?*"

Strictly speaking, Braun is not looking for entire genes, the long strings of nucleotides that instruct the body to grow a tooth or create white blood cells to attack an incoming virus. He's after single nucleotide polymorphisms, or SNPs (pronounced "snips"), the tiny genetic variations that account for nearly all differences in humans.

Imagine DNA as a ladder made of rungs — 3 billion in all — spiraling upward in a double helix. Each step is base pair, designated by two letters from the nucleotide alphabet of G, T, A, and C. More than 99 percent of these base pairs are identical in all humans, with only about one in a thousand SNPs diverging to make us distinct. For instance, you might have a CG that makes you susceptible to diabetes, and I might have a CC, which makes it far less likely I will get this disease.

This is all fairly well known: Genetics 101. What's new is how startups like Sequenom have industrialized the SNP identification process. Andi Braun and Charles Cantor are finding thousands of new SNPs a day, at a cost of about a penny each.

Braun tells me that there are possibly a million SNPs in each person, though only a small fraction are tightly linked with common ailments. These disease-causing SNPs are fueling a biotech bonanza; the hope is that after finding them, the discoverers can design wonder drugs. In the crowded SNP field, Sequenom vies with Iceland-based deCode Genetics and American companies such as Millennium Pharmaceuticals, Orchid BioSciences, and Celera Genomics, as well as multinationals like Eli Lilly and Roche Diagnostics. "It's the Oklahoma Land Grab right now," says Toni Schuh, Sequenom's CEO.

The sun sets outside Braun's office as my results arrive, splayed across his com- 15 puter screen like tarot cards. I'm trying to maintain a steely, reportorial facade, but my heart continues to race.

Names of SNPs pop up on the screen: connexin 26, implicated in hearing loss; factor V leiden, which causes blood clots; and alpha-1 antitrypsin deficiency, linked to lung and liver disease. Beside each SNP are codes that mean nothing to me: 13q11-q12, 1q23, 14q32.1. Braun explains that these are addresses on the human genome; the P.O. box numbers of life. For instance, 1q23 is the address for a mutant gene that causes vessels to shrink and impede the flow of blood — it's on chromosome 1. Thankfully, my result is negative. "So, David, you will not get the varicose veins. That's good, *ja?*" says Braun. One gene down, dozens to go.

Next up is the hemochromatosis gene. This causes one's blood to retain too much iron, which can damage the liver. As Braun explains it, somewhere in the past, an isolated human community lived in an area where the food was poor in iron. Those who developed a mutation that stores high levels of iron survived, and those who didn't became anemic and died, failing to reproduce. However, in these iron-rich times, hemochromatosis is a liability. Today's treatment? Regular bleeding. "You tested negative for this mutation," says Braun. "You do not have to be bled."

I'm also clean for cystic fibrosis and for a SNP connected to lung cancer.

Then comes the bad news. A line of results on Braun's monitor shows up red and is marked "MT," for mutant type. My body's programming code is faulty. There's a glitch in my system. Named ACE (for angiotensin-I converting enzyme), this SNP means my body makes an enzyme that keeps my blood pressure spiked. In plain English, I'm a heart attack risk.

My face drains of color as the news sinks in. I'm not only defective, but down   20
the road, every time I get anxious about my condition, I'll know that I have a much higher chance of dropping dead. I shouldn't be surprised, since I'm told everyone has some sort of disease-causing mutation. Yet I realize that my decision to take a comprehensive DNA test has been based on the rather ridiculous assumption that I would come out of this with a clean genetic bill of health. I almost never get sick, and, at age forty-four, I seldom think about my physical limitations or death. This attitude is buttressed by a family largely untouched by disease. The women routinely thrive into their late eighties and nineties. One great-aunt lived to age one hundred and one; she used to bake me cupcakes in her retirement home when I was a boy. And some of the Duncan menfolk are pushing ninety-plus. My parents, now entering their seventies, are healthy. In a flash of red MTs, I'm glimpsing my own future, my own mortality. I'm slated to keel over, both hands clutching at my heart.

"Do you have any history in your family of high blood pressure or heart disease?" asks Matthew McGinniss, a Sequenom geneticist standing at Braun's side.

"No," I answer, trying to will the color back into my face. Then a second MT pops up on the screen — another high blood pressure mutation. My other cardiac indicators are OK, which is relatively good news, though I'm hardly listening now. I'm already planning a full-scale assault to learn everything I can about fighting heart disease — until McGinniss delivers an unexpected pronouncement. "These mutations are probably irrelevant," he says. Braun agrees: "It's likely that you carry a gene that keeps these faulty ones from causing you trouble — DNA that we have not yet discovered."

The SNPs keep rolling past, revealing more mutations, including a type 2 diabetes susceptibility, which tells me I may want to steer clear of junk food. More bad news: I don't have a SNP called CCR5 that prevents me from acquiring HIV, nor one that seems to shield smokers from lung cancer. "*Ja*, that's my favorite," says Braun, himself a smoker. "I wonder what Philip Morris would pay for that."

By the time I get home, I realize that all I've really learned is, I might get heart disease, and I could get diabetes. And I should avoid smoking and unsafe sex — as if I didn't already know this. Obviously, I'll now watch my blood pressure, exercise more, and lay off the Cap'n Crunch. But beyond this, I have no idea what to make of the message Andi Braun has divined from a trace of my spit.

Looking for guidance, I visit Ann Walker, director of the Graduate Program for Genetic Counseling at the University of California at Irvine. Walker explains the whats and hows, and the pros and cons, of DNA testing to patients facing hereditary disease, pregnant couples concerned with prenatal disorders, and anyone else contemplating genetic evaluation. It's a tricky job because, as I've learned, genetic data are seldom clear-cut.

Take breast cancer, Walker says. A woman testing positive for BRCA1, the main breast cancer gene, has an 85 percent chance of actually getting the cancer by age seventy, a wrenching situation, since the most effective method of prevention is a double mastectomy. What if a woman has the operation and it turns out she's among those 15 percent who carry the mutation but will never get the cancer? Not surprisingly, one study, conducted in Holland, found that half of the healthy women whose mothers developed breast cancer opt not to be tested for the gene, preferring ignorance and closer monitoring. Another example is the test for APoE, the Alzheimer's gene. Since the affliction has no cure, most people don't want to know their status. But some do. A positive result, says Walker, allows them to put their affairs in order and prepare for their own dotage. Still, the news can be devastating. One biotech executive told me that a cousin of his committed suicide when he tested positive for Huntington's, having seen the disease slowly destroy his father.

Walker pulls out a chart and asks about my family's medical details, starting with my grandparents and their brothers and sisters: what they suffered and died from, and when. My Texas grandmother died at ninety-two after a series of strokes. My ninety-one-year-old Missouri grandmom was headed to a vacation in Mexico with her eighty-eight-year-old second husband when she got her death sentence — ovarian cancer. The men died younger: my grandfathers in their late sixties, though they both have brothers still alive and healthy in their nineties. To the mix, Walker adds my parents and their siblings, all of whom are alive and healthy in their sixties and seventies; then my generation; and finally our children. She looks up and smiles: "This is a pretty healthy group."

Normally, Walker says, she would send me home. Yet I'm sitting across from her, not because my parents carry some perilous SNP, but as a healthy man who is after a forecast of future maladies. "We have no real training yet for this," she says,

25

and tells me the two general rules of genetic counseling: No one should be screened unless there is an effective treatment or readily available counseling; and the information should not bewilder people or present them with unnecessary trauma.

Many worry that these prime directives may be ignored by Sequenom and other startups that need to launch products to survive. FDA testing for new drugs can take up to ten years, and many biotech firms feel pressure to sell something in the interim. "Most of these companies need revenue," says the University of Pennsylvania's Arthur Caplan, a top bioethicist. "And the products they've got now are diagnostic. Whether they are good ones, useful ones, necessary ones, accurate ones, seems less of a concern than that they be sold." Caplan also notes that the FDA does not regulate these tests. "If it was a birth control test, the FDA would be all over it."

I ask Caplan about the *Gattaca* scenario of genetic discrimination. Will a   30 woman dump me if she finds out about my ACE? Will my insurance company hike my rate? "People are denied insurance and jobs right now," he says, citing sickle cell anemia, whose sufferers and carriers, mostly black, have faced job loss and discrimination. No federal laws exist to protect us from genism, or from insurers and employers finding out our genetic secrets. "Right now, you're likely going to be more disadvantaged than empowered by genetic testing," says Caplan.

After probing my genetic future, I jet to England to investigate my DNA past. Who are these people who have bequeathed me this tainted bloodline? From my grandfather Duncan, an avid genealogist, I already know that my paternal ancestors came from Perth, in south-central Scotland. We can trace the name back to an Anglican priest murdered in Glasgow in 1680 by a mob of Puritans. His six sons escaped and settled in Shippensburg, Pennsylvania, where their descendants lived until my great-great-grandfather moved west to Kansas City in the 1860s.

In an Oxford restaurant, over a lean steak and a heart-healthy merlot, I talk with geneticist Bryan Sykes, a linebacker-sized fifty-five-year-old with a baby face and an impish smile. He's a molecular biologist at the university's Institute of Molecular Medicine and the author of the best-selling *Seven Daughters of Eve*. Sykes first made headlines in 1994 when he used DNA to directly link a 5,000-year-old body discovered frozen and intact in an Austrian glacier to a twentieth-century Dorset woman named Marie Mosley. This stunning genetic connection between housewife and hunter-gatherer launched Sykes's career as a globe-trotting genetic gumshoe. In 1995, he confirmed that bones dug up near Ekaterinburg, Russia, were the remains of Czar Nicholas II and his family by comparing the body's DNA with that of the czar's living relatives, including Britain's Prince Philip. Sykes debunked explorer Thor Heyerdahl's *Kon-Tiki* theory by tracing Polynesian genes to Asia, not the Americas, and similarly put the lie to the *Clan of the Cave Bear* hypothesis, which held that the Neanderthal interbred with our ancestors, the Cro-Magnon, when the two subspecies coexisted in Europe 15,000 years ago.

Sykes explains to me that a bit of DNA called mtDNA is key to his investigations. A circular band of genes residing separately from the twenty-three chromosomes of the double helix, mtDNA is passed down solely through the maternal line. Sykes used mtDNA to discover something astounding: Nearly every European can be traced back to just seven women living 10,000 to 45,000 years ago. In his book, Sykes gives these seven ancestors hokey names and tells us where they most likely lived: Ursula, in Greece (circa 43,000 B.C.), and Velda, in northern Spain (circa 15,000 B.C.), to name two of the "seven daughters of Eve." (Eve was the ur-mother who lived 150,000 years ago in Africa.)

Sykes has taken swab samples from the cheeks of more than 10,000 people, charging $220 to individually determine a person's mtDNA type. "It's not serious genetics," Sykes admits, "but people like to know their roots. It makes genetics less scary and shows us that, through our genes, we are all very closely related." He recently expanded his tests to include non-Europeans. The Asian daughters of Eve are named Emiko, Nene, and Yumio, and their African sisters are Lamia, Latifa, and Ulla, among others.

Before heading to England, I had mailed Sykes a swab of my cheek cells. Over our desserts in Oxford he finally offers up the results. "You are descended from Helena," he pronounces. "She's the most common daughter of Eve, accounting for some 40 percent of Europeans." He hands me a colorful certificate, signed by him, that heralds my many-times-great-grandma and tells me that she lived 20,000 years ago in the Dordogne Valley of France. More interesting is the string of genetic letters from my mtDNA readout that indicate I'm mostly Celtic, which makes sense. But other bits of code reveal traces of Southeast Asian DNA, and even a smidgen of Native American and African. 35

This doesn't quite have the impact of discovering that I'm likely to die of a heart attack. Nor am I surprised about the African and Indian DNA, since my mother's family has lived in the American South since the seventeenth century. But Southeast Asian? Sykes laughs. "We are all mutts," he says. "There is no ethnic purity. Somewhere over the years, one of the thousands of ancestors who contributed to your DNA had a child with someone from Southeast Asia." He tells me a story about a blond, blue-eyed surfer from Southern California who went to Hawaii to apply for monies awarded only to those who could prove native Hawaiian descent. The grant-givers laughed — until his DNA turned up traces of Hawaiian.

The next day, in Sykes's lab, we have one more test: running another ancestry marker in my Y chromosome through a database of 10,000 other Ys to see which profile is closest to mine. If my father was in the database, his Y chromosome would be identical, or possibly one small mutation off. A cousin might deviate by one tick. Someone descended from my native county of Perth might be two or three mutations removed, indicating that we share a common ancestor hundreds of years ago. Sykes tells me these comparisons are used routinely in paternity cases. He has another application. He is building up Y-chromosome profiles of surnames: men with the same last name whose DNA confirms that they are related to common ancestors.

After entering my mtDNA code into his laptop, Sykes looks intrigued, then surprised, and suddenly moves to the edge of his seat. Excited, he reports that the closest match is, incredibly, him — Bryan Sykes! "This has never happened," he says, telling me that I am a mere one mutation removed from him, and two from the average profile of a Sykes. He has not collected DNA from many other Duncans, he says, though it appears as if sometime in the past 400 years a Sykes must have ventured into Perth and then had a child with a Duncan. "That makes us not-so-distant cousins," he says. We check a map of Britain on his wall, and sure enough, the Sykes family's homeland of Yorkshire is less than 200 miles south of Perth.

The fact that Sykes and I are members of the same extended family is just a bizarre coincidence, but it points to applications beyond simple genealogy. "I've been approached by the police to use my surnames data to match up with DNA from an unknown suspect found at a crime scene," says Sykes. Distinctive genetic markers can be found at the roots of many family trees. "This is possible, to narrow down a pool of suspects to a few likely surnames. But it's not nearly ready yet."

Back home in California, I'm sweating on a StairMaster at the gym, wondering about my heart. I wrap my hands around the grips and check my pulse: 129. Normal. I pump harder and top out at 158. Also normal. I think about my visit a few days earlier — prompted by my gene scan — to Robert Superko, a cardiologist. After performing another battery of tests, he gave me the all clear — except for one thing. Apparently, I have yet another lame heart gene, the atherosclerosis susceptibility gene ATHS, a SNP that causes plaque in my cardiac bloodstream to build up if I don't exercise far more than average — which I do, these days, as a slightly obsessed biker and runner. "As long as you exercise, you'll be fine," Superko advised, a bizarre kind of life sentence that means that I must pedal and jog like a madman or face — what? A triple bypass?

Pumping on the StairMaster, I nudge the setting up a notch, wishing, in a way, that I either knew for sure I was going to die on, say, February 17, 2021, or that I hadn't been tested at all. As it is, the knowledge that I have an ACE and ATHS deep inside me will be nagging me every time I get short of breath.

The last results from my DNA workup have also come in. Andi Braun has tested me for seventy-seven SNPs linked to lifespan in order to assess when and how I might get sick and die. He has given me a score of .49 on his scale. It indicates a lifespan at least 20 percent longer than that of the average American male, who, statistically speaking, dies in his seventy-fourth year. I will likely live, then, to the age of eighty-eight. That's forty-four years of StairMaster to go.

Braun warns that this figure does not take into account the many thousands of other SNPs that affect my life, not to mention the possibility that a piano could fall on my head.

That night, I put my seven-year-old, Alex, to bed. His eyes droop under his bright white head of hair as I finish reading *Captain Underpants* aloud. Feeling his little heart beating as he lies next to me on his bed, I wonder what shockers await him inside his nucleotides, half of which I gave him. As I close the book and then sing him to sleep, I wonder if he has my culprit genes. I don't know, because he hasn't been scanned. For now, he and the rest of humanity are living in nearly the same blissful ignorance as Helena did in long-ago Dordogne. But I do know one thing: Alex has my eyebrow, the "lick of God." I touch his flip in the dark, and touch mine. He stirs, but it's not enough to wake him.

Questions

1. As mentioned in the headnote, this essay originally appeared in *Wired*, a cutting-edge magazine about technology and culture. What assumptions does David Ewing Duncan make about his audience's knowledge and interests?
2. In paragraphs 7, 14, and 29, what does Duncan imply about the motives behind DNA testing?
3. What is the effect of the reference to tarot cards in paragraph 15?
4. Considering how attitudes can influence health, is the information the author receives in paragraph 19 and reflects on in paragraph 20 desirable? Would you want to receive such information? Explain.
5. What purpose does the account of Duncan's visit to Sykes's lab serve (paras. 37–39)?
6. What is the effect of Duncan's appeal to pathos at the end of the essay?

4. *Pet Clones Spur Call for Limits*

RICK WEISS

In the following article, which appeared in the *Washington Post* in 2005, Rick Weiss looks at pet cloning.

Clone a cat, go to jail — or at least pay a fine.

That is the goal of animal welfare activists who announced yesterday [2005] that they are seeking state and federal restrictions on the small but growing pet-cloning industry.

Spearheaded by the American Anti-Vivisection Society in suburban Philadelphia, the effort takes aim at companies such as Genetic Savings and Clone Inc., the California enterprise that last year began to fill orders for cloned cats. The clones — which have sold for $50,000 each — are genetic duplicates of customers' deceased pets and represent the leading edge of an emerging commercial sector that advocates predict could eventually reap billions of dollars for corporate cloners.

Several companies are racing to compete with Genetic Savings and Clone, the industry leader, which has produced about a half-dozen cloned cats and aims to achieve the more difficult goal of cloning a dog this year. Some companies are already selling fish genetically engineered to glow in the dark, while one has said it will soon produce cats engineered to not cause reactions in people allergic to felines.

Yesterday the AAVS announced it had petitioned the Agriculture Depart-   5
ment to regulate pet-cloning companies as it does other animal research labs under the Animal Welfare Act. The act demands minimum standards of animal care and detailed reporting of the fates of laboratory animals.

The group has also been working with a California lawmaker to intro-duce state legislation that would ban the sale of cloned or genetically engi-neered pets.

"Pet cloning companies offer false hope of never having to let go of a pet and are causing harm to animals in the process," the AAVS concluded in a report released yesterday, "Pet Cloning: Separating Facts From Fluff."

Managers of Genetics Savings and Clone reacted quickly to the charges, con-vening a news conference immediately after one sponsored by the AAVS. They denied emphatically that their enterprise takes advantage of grieving pet owners or harms animals.

"We bend over backwards to make sure people are doing this for the right reasons," said the company's president, Lou Hawthorne. Nonetheless, he said, "we're open to additional oversight, provided it makes sense."

Scientists who have cloned cattle, sheep and other farm animals have   10
reported high rates of biological abnormalities, and unexpected deaths during gestation and in the first days of life. Hawthorne said that has not been the case with cats, though he declined yesterday to release specific numbers, which he said he hopes to publish in a scientific journal.

But critics said the process raises other concerns, including the welfare of egg donor and surrogate-mother animals that must undergo multiple surgeries as part of the process of making clones.

The potential for consumer fraud is also an issue. Clones tend to be ordered by people who are grieving the loss of a much-loved pet and who may have unre-alistically high expectations of their clones. Although they share identical genetic profiles, clones do not always resemble originals because coat patterns are not strictly genetically determined. Personalities and behavior patterns are even less predictable on the basis of genetics alone.

"Consumers are likely under the impression that a clone is a carbon copy. We believe they are being misled," AAVS policy analyst Crystal Miller-Spiegel said.

David Magnus, director of Stanford University's Center for Biomedical Ethics, spoke more bluntly.

"People are not getting what they think they're getting," Magnus said. "This is   15
a $50,000 rip-off."

In fact, Genetic Savings and Clone announced this week that it is reducing the price of its clones to $32,000 per kitten, part of a business plan that Haw-thorne said aims to make the company profitable in the next few years.

"I think it's going to be a multibillion-dollar market," he said. "There will be thousands of dogs and cats [cloned] every year."

Not if the AAVS has anything to say about it. At a minimum, the group's petition to the USDA says, pet-cloning companies should have to register as a "research facility" subject to the same degree of federal oversight that university and other research labs withstand. Currently they are effectively unregulated because they are not classified as animal research labs, breeders or kennels.

The California legislation, under development by assembly member Lloyd E. Levine, a Democrat from Van Nuys, would outlaw the sale or transport of cloned or engineered pets, which could include larger mammals such as horses and calves meant as "companion animals."

Levine's bill, like the AAVS report, reflects perhaps the most glaring concern   20
of pet-cloning opponents: the enormous glut of homeless pets already. Last year, about 1.5 million dogs and cats passed through California's shelters, and two-thirds of them were euthanized, the bill's preamble notes.

"Pet cloning serves no good purpose, does harm to animals and should be banned," said Richard Hayes, executive director of the Center for Genetics and Society, a public affairs organization based in Oakland. "Assembly member Levine's proposal is long overdue, and other states should follow his lead."

Questions

1. Are you surprised by the fifty-thousand-dollar fee for pet clones? Why or why not?
2. Consider the name Genetic Savings and Clone. Are you surprised to be reading about such a company in the *Washington Post* rather than in, say, the parody newspaper the *Onion*? Explain.
3. How does paragraph 12 inform the discussion of the relationship between genetics and environment, between nature and nurture?
4. Which quoted source is most persuasive? Why?
5. Which of the classic appeals does the "glut of homeless pets" speak to (para. 20)?
6. What is the main point Rick Weiss makes in the article? Is he objective? If not, which side does he support?

5. *More Couples Screening Embryos for Gender*

Marilynn Marchione and Lindsey Tanner

In the following news story from the Associated Press, Marilynn Marchione and Lindsey Tanner report on the results of a survey of couples using fertility clinics that offer embryo screening.

Boy or girl? Almost half of U.S. fertility clinics that offer embryo screening say they allow couples to choose the sex of their child, the most extensive survey of the practice suggests.

Sex selection without any medical reason to warrant it was performed in about 9 percent of all embryo screenings last year, the survey found.

Another controversial procedure — helping parents conceive a child who could supply compatible cord blood to treat an older sibling with a grave illness — was offered by 23 percent of clinics, although only 1 percent of screenings were for that purpose in 2005.

For the most part, couples are screening embryos for the right reasons — to avoid passing on dreadful diseases, said Dr. William Gibbons, who runs a fertility clinic in Baton Rouge, La., and is president of the Society for Assisted Reproductive Technology, which assisted with the survey.

"There are thousands of babies born now that we know are going to be free of   5 lethal and/or devastating genetic diseases. That's a good thing," he said.

However, the survey findings also confirm many ethicists' fears that Americans increasingly are seeking "designer babies" not just free of medical defects but also possessing certain desirable traits.

"That's a big problem if that's true," Boston University ethicist George Annas said of the sex selection finding. "This is not a risk-free technique," he said referring to in vitro fertilization, which can over-stimulate a woman's ovaries and bring the risk of multiple births.

"I don't think a physician can justify doing that to a patient" for sex selection alone, Annas said.

Survey results were published on the Internet Wednesday by the medical journal Fertility and Sterility and will appear in print later.

The survey was led by Susanna Baruch, a lawyer at Johns Hopkins Univer-   10 sity's Genetics and Public Policy Center in Washington, D.C., with the cooperation of the reproductive medicine society. It involved an online survey of 415 fertility clinics, of which 190 responded.

They were asked about pre-implantation genetic diagnosis, or PGD, which can be done as part of in vitro fertilization, when eggs and sperm are mixed in a lab dish and the resulting embryos implanted directly into the womb. In PGD, a single cell from an embryo that is three to five days old is removed to allow its genes and chromosomes to be analyzed.

About 1 of every 20 in vitro pregnancy attempts in the United States last year used PGD, the survey found.

Two-thirds of the time it was to detect abnormalities that would keep the embryo from developing normally and doom the pregnancy attempt.

In 12 percent of cases, PGD was used to detect single-gene disorders like those that cause cystic fibrosis. Three percent of cases were to detect problems that mostly affect males, because they have only one copy of certain genes.

However, these cases are different from those done purely for gender prefer-   15 ence. A whopping 42 percent of clinics that offer PGD said they had done so for non-medically related sex selection. Nearly half of those clinics said they would only offer sex selection for a second or subsequent child.

"That's really startling," University of Pennsylvania ethicist Arthur Caplan said of the high number of PGD for sex selection alone. "Family balancing seems like a morally persuasive reason to some people," but doing gender selection just because a couple doesn't want any girls, or any boys, is troubling, he said.

One doctor who offers it takes a different view.

"It performs a much desired service. We're making people happy," said Dr. Jeffrey Steinberg, medical director of Fertility Institutes, which has clinics in Los Angeles, Las Vegas and Guadalajara, Mexico.

Many countries ban PGD or restrict it to prevention of serious inherited diseases. Many people from foreign countries travel to the United States to obtain it, especially from countries like China and Canada.

Baruch said the survey was intended to get a realistic view of what was 20 going on.

"This is the first time anyone has tried to quantify how often PGD is done and what it's being offered for," she said.

Questions

1. According to paragraph 4, Dr. William Gibbons, head of a fertility clinic in Louisiana, believes that most "couples are screening embryos for the right reasons." What does he consider the right reasons? What would you consider the right reasons?
2. According to Marilynn Marchione and Lindsey Tanner, what health issues are associated with gender screening?
3. What ethical issues do the authors examine?
4. Ethicist Arthur Caplan notes that the high number of PGDs (pre-implantation genetic diagnoses) for sex selection alone is "really startling" (para. 16). What does he find morally disturbing about it?
5. Do you think Dr. Jeffrey Steinberg's defense of PGD is convincing (para. 18)? Explain.

Entering the Conversation

As you respond to the following prompts, support your argument with references to at least three of the sources in Conversation: Focus on the Ethics of Genetic Technology. For help using sources, see Chapter 3.

1. Write a letter to the editor of your local newspaper in response to an issue raised by the readings.

2. Consider the nature of human cloning, DNA testing, or PGD (pre-implantation gender diagnosis). Then write an essay in which you discuss the pros and cons and argue for or against the practice.

3. Write a feature article for your school newspaper about genetic engineering. In addition to using at least three of the preceding sources, include a source from independent research that you conduct.

4. Knowing that the word *science* comes from the Latin word meaning "knowledge," consider science itself as an intellectual activity, as a means of learning about the world. Many people today recognize the necessity of balancing the human need to know with moral and ethical responsibilities. Science and technology bring wonders and terrors; considering the baleful as well as hopeful promises that increased knowledge creates, should we place limits on scientific knowledge? How do you classify cloning, stem-cell research, DNA testing, PGD, genetic engineering, and the possibility of what David Ewing Duncan calls "genism"? Are the issues associated with them scientific, legal, ethical, or social, or a combination of these? Develop a thesis that addresses these concerns, and write an essay on the nature of scientific knowledge and its limits.

5. Several of the texts in this Conversation section argue that those who resist, as well as those who blindly embrace, the advances of science sometimes forget that humans are more than the sum of their genetic makeup. Write an essay in which you argue for either nature or nurture as the most important factor in human development. Be sure to acknowledge the counterargument.

Student Writing

Counterargument: Responding to a Newspaper Column

The following prompt asks the writer to respond to the question of privacy in cyberspace.

In her article, "What's a Mother to Do" (read the article at <bedfordstmartins .com/languageofcomp>), journalist Ruth Marcus expresses her frustration over trying to balance respecting her children's privacy with protecting them when they use the Internet. She writes: "Do gentle parents read their children's e-mail? Install software to intercept their instant messages? Keep track of who's in their chat rooms? Read their blogs? Even for those who insist they wouldn't read an old-fashioned diary or eavesdrop on a telephone call, privacy in cyberspace poses difficult issues."

Write an essay explaining why parents should or should not monitor the Internet communications of their children.

Read high school student Jenna Odett's essay, and consider the rhetorical strategies she uses to make her argument. Then answer the questions about her technique and its effectiveness.

Internet Privacy

Jenna Odett

Privacy is a touchy subject, but in the context of parenting, Ruth Marcus poses
the question of what allowance children should have for confidentiality on the Internet.
Or more aptly, what limitations should parents impose on their children because of their
fear of the Internet? Obviously software companies are marketing a product to make
money and are trying to generate a fear that may or may not exist. Additionally, if
parents decide to monitor e-mail, instant messages, chat rooms, and blogs (with or
without their children knowing) and find out that their son or daughter is mean or catty
or looking at gross porn, what next? The article points out some simple and basic truths:
first, in relation to Internet pornography, "teenage boys will be teenage boys," and
second, "mean girls tend to get even meaner in cyberspace." If the major concerns of
parents are porn and meanness (and not sketchy strangers or learning to make homemade
bombs), then it is important to realize these issues have been dealt with since the dawn
of the porn industry and the beginning of time, and monitoring may not be useless but is
certainly not necessary.

I am not a parent, and I have not faced a single dilemma as a parent, but why
is snooping so important? If parents are genuinely concerned about what is going on
in the lives and minds of their children, why not just ask them? Many parents have
conversations with their teenage kids about sex and drugs — if Ruth Marcus ultimately
felt "sick and guilty" about using a trial surveillance test once, she should know she was
just the pawn of a software company. If parents are going to discuss and deliberate and
waver about whether or not they are invading their child's privacy, or if they should, I
really think they don't know their children. One thing parents should know, and shouldn't
have to snoop around to find it, is what their child is like. If a child has a private issue or
conversation and doesn't share it with his or her parent, I say good job! Everyone has to
learn independent decision-making at some point.

I know how much time I spend on the Internet every day; it is probably too much
time, considering the endless opportunities present outside my computer room. However,
I'm fairly certain my mother has no idea what I'm doing most of the time, and explaining
it wouldn't really help . . . because it makes no sense. We spend countless hours chatting
and cyber flirting and illegally downloading music, but it's relatively harmless time
wasting. If my mom is worried that I'm talking to creepy strangers or searching online for
Web sites that give instructions for making homemade bombs, then using software to
intercept my activity would be helpful, if I hadn't already been abducted or set off my
bomb by the time I actually got off the computer and my mom figured out how to use the

software. Truth is, I have no interest in talking to people I didn't invite to my buddy list, or making bombs, or worrying that my mom is pretending to be a private detective.

Online privacy is a controversial issue globally, but it shouldn't really have to be at home. Parents need to calm down and try to accept that while young people spend a ton of time on the computer, they are not necessarily being mischievous. It's even possible we're doing our homework. If parents used to dread conversations about safe sex and the dangers of underage drinking and drug abuse, I suppose Ruth Marcus is onto something — have a talk about "the rules of the Internet road." Let children know certain expectations, be confident parents, and know your kid won't prove you wrong. Spend the money you save on the IM monitoring program on a family dinner out, where you can enjoy your children face to face.

Questions

1. Describe the tone of Jenna's essay. Cite passages to support your response.
2. How does Jenna establish ethos in the essay? How does she appeal to pathos and logos?
3. Is Jenna's argument convincing? How would you craft a counterargument?
4. Comment on Jenna's use of the first person. Does it strengthen or weaken her argument?

Grammar as Rhetoric and Style

Coordination in the Compound Sentence

Coordination confers equal value and significance on two or more elements in a sentence. You can use coordination to join words, phrases, and even independent clauses that could be sentences in their own right. When you use coordination to combine two sentences, the result is a *compound sentence*. Compound sentences can be created using coordinating conjunctions (*and, but, or, not, for, so, yet*) and correlative conjunctions (*not only . . . but also; either . . . or; just as . . . so also*); however, you can also use a semicolon alone or coupled with a conjunctive adverb (*however, indeed, thus, moreover, in fact, therefore, nevertheless*), as we've done in this sentence.

In the following compound sentences, you can see how removing the coordinating conjunction or the semicolon from each of the original sentences and separating the previously joined ideas into two or three sentences make each author's meaning less clear. Without the coordinating conjunction or the semicolon, a reader cannot immediately figure out the relationship between the ideas in the sentences.

Coordinating Conjunctions Joining Main Clauses

Morbid curiosity is an occupational hazard for a writer, I suppose. I've never been bothered by it before.

Morbid curiosity is an occupational hazard for a writer, I suppose, but I've never been bothered by it before.

— DAVID EWING DUNCAN

We essentially consider polluted water as normal now. People who can afford it drink bottled water.

We essentially consider polluted water as normal now, **and** people who can afford it drink bottled water.

— URSULA FRANKLIN

Semicolons Joining Main Clauses

That is the silence of contemplation. It is the silence when people get in touch with themselves. It is the silence of meditation and worship.

That is the silence of contemplation; it is the silence when people get in touch with themselves; it is the silence of meditation and worship.

— URSULA FRANKLIN

Nature was then. This is now.
Nature was then; this is now.

— SVEN BIRKERTS

Semicolons and Conjunctive Adverbs Joining Main Clauses

Now he no longer let the dog go to the lighted tunnel at once. He put out the light, and then kept the dog waiting a little while before he let him go.

Now he no longer let the dog go to the lighted tunnel at once; instead, he put out the light, and then kept the dog waiting a little while before he let him go.

— JACOB BRONOWSKI

Punctuation of Sentences That Contain Coordination

A comma indicates a pause in a sentence; a semicolon indicates a full stop in a sentence that joins two complete thoughts, as you can see in this very sentence. Using a semicolon is an effective way to establish coordination between two sentences. Think of the semicolon as a fulcrum between two equal weights, such as you find in the middle of a seesaw or teeter-totter; you know what happens when the two sides try to support different weights.

Comma Splices

If you omit the conjunction or semicolon and instead place only a comma between main clauses, you are splicing the clauses. Grammatically, *splicing* means "joining loosely or ineffectively." As demonstrated in the following example, you can eliminate a comma splice by using a coordinating conjunction, a semicolon, or even a period.

Incorrect

She began by sitting and thinking, soon she was just sitting.

Correct

COMMA AND A COORDINATING CONJUNCTION	She began by sitting and thinking, but soon she was just sitting.
SEMICOLON	She began by sitting and thinking; soon she was just sitting.
	— BRIAN ALDISS
SEMICOLON AND A CONJUNCTIVE ADVERB	She began by sitting and thinking; however, soon she was just sitting.
TWO SEPARATE SENTENCES	She began by sitting and thinking. Soon she was just sitting.

As you can see, the correct way to fix a comma splice is to divide it into two separate sentences or turn it into a compound sentence using coordination.

Rhetorical and Stylistic Strategy

Writers make deliberate decisions regarding coordination.

On the most basic level, writers use coordinating conjunctions to smooth two shorter sentences into a single longer one that is more cohesive. In the following example, *it* refers to the theory that parents can "mold their children like clay."

It has distorted the choices faced by others as they try to balance their lives, and it has multiplied the anguish of parents whose children haven't turned out as hoped.

— SVEN BIRKERTS

If Birkerts had put a period after *lives* and begun the next sentence with *it*, the result would have been two abrupt sentences. The simple addition of *and* that turns two simple sentences into a compound sentence also adds to the fluency of the prose. In this case, joining the two also emphasizes that the two results (distorting and multiplying) are equally detrimental.

In fact, the job of conjunctions is to specify the relationship between two ideas. If the ideas contrast, then *but*, *yet*, or *however* signals that connection.

Flying is no longer a big deal, but a handmade dress or a home-cooked meal may well be special.

— URSULA FRANKLIN

If they are related through cause and effect, *thus, for,* or *therefore* signals that connection.

> Long before anyone suspected the existence of genes, farmers recognized that the traits of parents were passed down to the offspring, and thus they could improve the yield of pumpkins or the size of pigs by selectively breeding the best specimens with each other.
>
> — MIHALY CSIKSZENTMIHALYI

In both of these examples, the first clause contrasts with the second. The conjunction makes that connection clear to the reader.

A writer might choose a semicolon instead of a period or a conjunction to signal that two ideas are closely related, as shown in the following example.

> Parenting is one of the oldest human experiences; it has been the experience of every generation since the beginnings of our species.
>
> — MIHALY CSIKSZENTMIHALYI

In this example, the second point grows out of the first, and the semicolon stresses the closeness. As in the following sentence, a semicolon may also emphasize balance or alternation: it is not this; it is that.

> The garden faded; in its place, the city center rose by her left hand, full of crowding people, blowboats, and buildings."
>
> — BRIAN ALDISS

In this example, the second clause emphasizes what has replaced the garden. The pattern is: the garden is gone; a city center replaced it. It's the same space but a different scene. In a similar example, Aldiss writes:

> He did not move; she did not move.
>
> — BRIAN ALDISS

The semicolon links the two independent clauses that are parallel except for the pronoun. The result is stillness — in perfect balance.

Caution: Starting a Sentence with a Coordinating Conjunction

Because people often overuse conjunctions such as *and* and *but*, some books and teachers discourage student writers from beginning sentences with those words. You might have been taught that such a practice is incorrect; however, professional writers do sometimes begin sentences with coordinating conjunctions. This practice is perfectly acceptable and often quite effective as long as you don't overuse it. But don't just take our word for it; read the last two sentences of Steven Pinker's essay:

> But the fact that tyranny and genocide can come from an anti-innatist belief system as readily as from an innatist one does upend the common misconception

that biological approaches to behavior are uniquely sinister. And the reminder that human nature is the source of our interests and needs as well as our flaws encourages us to examine claims about the mind objectively, without putting a moral thumb on either side of the scale.

In the first instance, Pinker uses *but* as a transition from his previous sentence. In the second instance, he uses *and* to emphasize the point he makes in that sentence. Now look at how Ursula Franklin uses *yet* in this sentence:

> I feel very strongly that our present technological trends drive us toward a decrease in the space — be it in the soundscape, the landscape, or the mindscape — in which the unplanned and unplannable can happen. Yet silence has to remain available in the soundscape, the landscape, and the mindscape.

If Franklin had made this a single sentence, it would have been exceptionally long and fairly difficult to follow. By breaking it into two sentences and joining them with a coordinating conjunction at the start of the second, she stresses the difference and varies the rhythm of the passage.

Polysyndeton and Asyndeton

The inclusion or exclusion of conjunctions may have a strong rhetorical effect, influencing pace and emphasis, and adding complexity. The use of many conjunctions has the effect of speeding up the pace of a sentence, and stressing the connections among things linked, as you will see in the examples of *polysyndeton* below.

Polysyndeton   The deliberate use of a series of conjunctions.

> *When you get to college you may study history and psychology and literature and mathematics and botany.*

In the following example, Aldiss uses polysyndeton in a series of individual sentences. The result is an emphasis on the choices — the "or" — and a marchlike pace:

> She could take up her painting. Or she could dial her friends. Or she could wait till Henry came home. Or she could go up and play with David.
>
> — BRIAN ALDISS

Here's the beginning of a passage by E. B. White from his celebrated essay "Once More to the Lake." White could have omitted the crossed-out conjunctions and still have produced grammatically correct sentences — in some cases, by using a semicolon instead of the conjunction. He chose, however, to use the conjunctions, thus speeding up the pace of his narration.

> Peace ~~and~~ goodness and jollity. The only thing that was wrong, now, really, was the sound of the place, an unfamiliar nervous sound of the outboard motors.

This was the note that jarred, the one thing that would sometimes break the illusion and set the years moving. In those other summertimes all motors were inboard; ~~and~~ when they were at a little distance, the noise they made was a sedative, an ingredient of summer sleep. They were one-cylinder and two-cylinder engines, ~~and~~ some were make-and-break and some were jump-spark, ~~but~~ they all made a sleepy sound across the lake. The one-luggers throbbed and fluttered, ~~and~~ the twin-cylinder ones purred and purred, ~~and~~ that was a quiet sound, too.

Asyndeton   The deliberate omission of conjunctions.

> *From his wealthy parents he received his wardrobe, his car, his tuition, his vacation, his attitude.*

Omission of conjunctions, on the other hand, has the ironic effect of separating ideas more distinctly, giving them greater emphasis, as you see in Abraham Lincoln's famous example of asyndeton.

> [A]nd that government of the people, by the people, for the people, shall not perish from the earth.
>
> — ABRAHAM LINCOLN, GETTYSBURG ADDRESS

• EXERCISE 1

Eliminate the comma splices in the following sentences.

1. Chocolate ice cream is delicious, vanilla is tasty too.
2. Preparing for your English final is important, so is preparing for your math exam.
3. I would love to go out with you this evening, I have to wash my hair.
4. I am lying about why I do not want to go out with him, it is wrong to do that.
5. Cousins Matthew, Nicholas, and Aidan were all born during the same year, they will grow up to be great friends.
6. Maura loves to play soccer, field hockey, and volleyball, however she is so busy at school now that she has no time to play any sports.
7. Kaitlin loves to check out a book from the library, sit down with a snack and read for hours, she reads books in both English and French, so selecting a title sometimes takes her a long time.
8. Alison wants to buy a hybrid car this year, as a result, she will spend less money on gas and also help the environment.
9. Either my parents will drive us to the movies, we will take the bus.
10. Pythons are not venomous snakes, they squeeze the life out of their prey rather than poison it, they are large enough to suffocate a person, pythons are not generally dangerous to humans.

• EXERCISE 2

Combine each of the following pairs of sentences into a smoother sentence by using a coordinating conjunction or a conjunctive adverb. Remember to punctuate correctly.

1. Aidan James is an excellent pitcher. His father is an excellent pitcher too.
2. Cell phones have become practically ubiquitous. Some people like them. Some people hate them.
3. Digital cameras have made taking pictures easier. Digital cameras have made developing pictures cheaper.
4. When Charles Dickens wrote *Great Expectations* he was paid by the word. When Victor Hugo wrote *Les Miserables* he was paid by the word also. Some speculate that this contributed to the descriptive style of both authors.
5. I learned how to type in high school. This was one of the most important classes that I took. I type all the time.

• EXERCISE 3

The following paragraph from Steven Pinker relies primarily on coordination, but the punctuation (and capitalization) has been removed. Add appropriate punctuation, and explain the reasons for your choices. Then compare your version with the original on page 632.

The denial of human nature has not just corrupted the world of intellectuals but has harmed ordinary people the theory that parents can mold their children like clay has inflicted child-rearing regimes on parents that are unnatural and sometimes cruel it has distorted the choices faced by mothers as they try to balance their lives and it has multiplied the anguish of parents whose children haven't turned out as hoped the belief that human tastes are reversible cultural preferences has led social planners to write off people's enjoyment of ornament natural light and human scale and forced millions of people to live in drab cement boxes and the conviction that humanity could be reshaped by massive social engineering projects has led to some of the greatest atrocities in history.

• EXERCISE 4

Identify the examples of coordination in the following paragraphs, and explain their rhetorical effects. Pay attention to the way the writers use coordination to signal relationships, to emphasize a point, or to vary the rhythm of a paragraph.

I was young then and had seen little of the world, but when I heard that cry my heart turned over. It was not the cry of the hawk I had captured; for, by shifting my position against the sun, I was now seeing further up. Straight out of the sun's eye, where she must have been soaring restlessly above us for untold hours, hurtled his mate. And from far up, ringing from peak to peak of the summits over us, came a cry of such unutterable and ecstatic joy that it sounds down across the years and tingles among the cups on my quiet breakfast table.

—Loren Eiseley

Language will grow increasingly impoverished through a series of vicious cycles. For, of course, the usages of literature and scholarship are connected in fundamental ways to the general speech of the tribe. We can expect that curricula will be further streamlined, and difficult texts in the humanities will be pruned and glossed. One need only compare a college textbook from twenty years ago to its contemporary version. A poem by Milton, a play by Shakespeare — one can hardly find the text among the explanatory notes nowadays. Fewer and fewer people will be able to contend with the so-called masterworks of literature or ideas. Joyce, Woolf, Soyinka, not to mention the masters who preceded them will go unread, and the civilizing energies of their prose will circulate aimlessly between closed covers.

— Sven Birkerts

• EXERCISE 5

Find several examples of compound sentences in a respected national magazine and analyze their effect.

Suggestions for Writing
Science and Technology

Now that you have examined a number of texts that focus on science and technology, explore this topic yourself by synthesizing your own ideas and the texts. You might want to do more research or use readings from other classes as you write.

1. Write a letter to your science teacher in which you discuss one of the issues raised by the selections in this chapter. Then ask for his or her perspective on the issue, and explain why you need or want that perspective.

2. Considering how technology has altered American lifestyles — either within your own lifetime or between the time your parents were your age and now — write an essay that directly addresses the essential question found at the beginning of this chapter. Refer to at least three of the texts to support your position.

3. For centuries, people have argued about whether human behavior is more the result of nature or nurture — that is, whether it is determined more by heredity or environment. Write an essay in which you discuss both sides of the question and argue for the primacy of one force over the other. Refer to at least three of the texts in this chapter as you discuss the issue.

4. Based on what you have read in this chapter, write an essay predicting how technology will affect human beings in 2050. Alternatively, write a short story set in that year, illustrating the future effects of technology on daily life as Brian Aldiss did nearly forty years ago, when he wrote "Super-Toys Last All Summer Long" (p. 665).

5. Writers such as Sven Birkerts (p. 647) or even Ursula Franklin (p. 641) might be viewed by some as misoneists or Luddites for their critical attitude toward the value of new technologies. Write an essay assessing the nature of their claims regarding electronic technology, and decide whether the term *misoneists* or *Luddites* is appropriate for them.

6. As Carl Sagan has done with his "Cosmic Calendar" (p. 671), graphically illustrate a scientific concept discussed in one of the texts in this chapter. Write an essay that explains how the graph supports that text.

7. Write a poem that refutes the position developed by either of the poems in this chapter: Edgar Allan Poe's "Sonnet — To Science" (p. 663) or Walt Whitman's "When I Heard the Learn'd Astronomer" (p. 664). As you do so, imitate the form and style of either Poe or Whitman.

8. About electronic communication, Sven Birkerts writes, "With visual media (television, projected graphs, highlighted 'bullets') impression and image take precedence over logic and concept, and detail and linear sequentiality are sacrificed" (p. 647, para. 2). Write an essay about your positive or negative views of technology. Then deliver the same content through a recording, video, PowerPoint presentation, Web site, or another electronic medium. What changes as you move from an essay to a more visual medium? What remains the same? Is Birkerts's claim a sound one?

11

Popular Culture

To what extent does pop culture reflect our society's values?

Popular culture is a term that once characterized mass-produced or low-brow culture: pop music, potboilers and page-turners, movies, comics, advertising, and radio and television. Its audience was the masses. Opposite popular culture were highbrow forms of entertainment: opera, fine art, classical music, traditional theater, and literature. These were the realm of the wealthy and educated classes.

Today, the line between high and pop culture has blurred, partially because of the ways in which pop culture revises and reinvents earlier high forms. For example, *Great Expectations*, the Oscar-winning film of the 1940s, was based on the popular Victorian novel by Charles Dickens. Recast as a twenty-first-century star vehicle, with Gwyneth Paltrow, Ethan Hawke, and Robert DiNiro, the latest version is set in modern-day New York. Pop culture is often at the leading edge of what will become established culture: the avant-garde — sometimes the very young or those at the margins of society — discovers; the laggards later adopt. For example, the work of 1980s graffitist Jean-Michel Basquiat commands high prices in today's art market, and he is considered a leading figure in contemporary art.

Popular culture moves through our world at warp speed. The political news in the morning is the talk-show host's monologue at night. Homemade videos are posted on the Internet, become cultural phenomena overnight, and are just as quickly forgotten. Albums and movies are exchanged on peer-to-peer networks months before they are officially released. Rap music uses samples from a decade ago — now considered old school — and mash-ups raise the stakes even higher by sampling and remixing current albums. How does the public cope with this onslaught?

In the past, popular culture was generally assumed to be superficial; training, experience, and reflection were not essential to appreciate it or produce it. Now, however, appreciating the importance of both high culture and pop culture has become the hallmark of an educated person. When reading popular culture, we can ask many of the same questions that we ask when reading high culture: Does

707

the art form say something new? What does the piece tell us about ourselves? Popular culture also spawns new questions: What is pop? What is the right balance between pop culture and high culture? Does each generation bring something new to a remake, or is something lost with time? Does pop culture respect its roots? What is the relationship between pop culture and commerce? Do commercial interests control what is offered to the public, or does the public ultimately have its own say? In the end, does old-fashioned word of mouth still tell us what's hot and what's not?

The selections in this chapter are about media that you can access. Listen to the music discussed here; watch the films and TV shows; find the art online, or see it in a museum. The connections made in this chapter prompt a conversation between the past and the present; enter the conversation, consider both, and imagine the future.

High-School Confidential:
Notes on Teen Movies

DAVID DENBY

David Denby (b. 1943), who lives in New York City, is a staff writer and film critic for the *New Yorker* and the former film critic for *New York*. His writing has also appeared in the *Atlantic Monthly*, the *New York Review of Books*, and the *New Republic*. In 1990, Denby received a National Magazine Award for his pieces on high-end audio. His first book, *Great Books: My Adventures with Homer, Rousseau, Woolf, and Other Indestructible Writers of the Western World* (1996), was a finalist for the National Book Critics Circle Award. Denby is also the editor of *Awake in the Dark: An Anthology of Film Criticism from 1915 to the Present* (1977). *American Sucker* (2004) chronicles Denby's misadventures in amateur investing during the dot-com boom and bust. The essay that follows was originally published in the *New Yorker* in May 1999.

The most hated young woman in America is a blonde — well, sometimes a redhead or a brunette, but usually a blonde. She has big hair flipped into a swirl of gold at one side of her face or arrayed in a sultry mane, like the magnificent pile of a forties movie star. She's tall and slender, with a waist as supple as a willow, but she's dressed in awful, spangled taste: her outfits could have been put together by warring catalogues. And she has a mouth on her, a low, slatternly tongue that devastates other kids with such insults as "You're vapor, you're Spam!" and "Do I look like Mother Teresa? If I did, I probably wouldn't mind talking to the geek squad." She has two or three friends exactly like her, and together they dominate their realm — the American high school as it appears in recent teen movies. They are like wicked princesses, who enjoy the misery of their subjects. Her coronation, of course, is the senior prom, when she expects to be voted "most popular" by her class. But, though she may be popular, she is certainly not liked, so her power is something of a mystery. She is beautiful and rich, yet in the end she is preeminent because . . . she is preeminent, a position she works to maintain with Joan Crawford-like tenacity. Everyone is afraid of her; that's why she's popular.

She has a male counterpart. He's usually a football player, muscular but dumb, with a face like a beer mug and only two ways of speaking — in a conspiratorial whisper, to a friend; or in a drill sergeant's sudden bellow. If her weapon is the snub, his is the lame but infuriating prank — the can of Sprite emptied into a knapsack, or something sticky, creamy, or adhesive deposited in a locker. Sprawling and dull in class, he comes alive in the halls and in the cafeteria. He hurls people against lockers; he spits, pours, and sprays; he has a projectile relationship with food. As the crown prince, he claims the best-looking girl for himself, though in a perverse display of power he may invite an outsider or an awkward girl — a "dog" — to the prom, setting her up for some special humiliation. When we first see him, he is riding high, and virtually the entire school colludes in his tyranny. No authority figure — no teacher or administrator — dares correct him.

Thus the villains of the recent high-school movies. Not every American teen movie has these two characters, and not every social queen or jock shares all the attributes I've mentioned. (Occasionally, a handsome, dark-haired athlete can be converted to sweetness and light.) But as genre figures these two types are hugely familiar; that is, they are a common memory, a collective trauma, or at least a social and erotic fantasy. Such movies . . . as *Disturbing Behavior, She's All That, Ten Things I Hate about You,* and *Never Been Kissed* depend on them as stock figures. And they may have been figures in the minds of the Littleton shooters, Eric Harris and Dylan Klebold, who imagined they were living in a school like the one in so many of these movies — a poisonous system of status, snobbery, and exclusion.

Do genre films reflect reality? Or are they merely a set of conventions that refer to other films? Obviously, they wouldn't survive if they didn't provide emotional satisfaction to the people who make them and to the audiences who watch them. A half century ago, we didn't need to see ten Westerns a year in order to learn that the West got settled. We needed to see it settled ten times a year in order to provide ourselves with the emotional gratifications of righteous violence. By drawing his gun only when he was provoked, and in the service of the good, the classic Western hero transformed the gross tangibles of the expansionist drive (land, cattle, gold) into a principle of moral order. The gangster, by contrast, is a figure of chaos, a modern, urban person, and in the critic Robert Warshow's formulation he functions as a discordant element in an American society devoted to a compulsively "positive" outlook. When the gangster dies, he cleanses viewers of their own negative feelings.

High-school movies are also full of unease and odd, mixed-up emotions. 5 They may be flimsy in conception; they may be shot in lollipop colors, garlanded with mediocre pop scores, and cast with goofy young actors trying to make an impression. Yet this most commercial and frivolous of genres harbors a grievance against the world. It's a very specific grievance, quite different from the restless anger of such fifties adolescent-rebellion movies as *The Wild One,* in which someone asks Marlon Brando's biker "What are you rebelling against?" and the biker replies "What have you got?" The fifties teen outlaw was against anything that adults considered sacred. But no movie teenager now revolts against adult authority, for the simple reason that adults have no authority. Teachers are rarely more than a minimal, exasperated presence, administrators get turned into a joke, and parents are either absent or distantly benevolent. It's a teen world bounded by school, mall, and car, with occasional moments set in the fast-food outlets where the kids work, or in the kids' upstairs bedrooms, with their pinups and rack stereo systems. The enemy is not authority; the enemy is other teens and the social system that they impose on one another.

The bad feeling in these movies may strike grownups as peculiar. After all, from a distance American kids appear to be having it easy these days. The teen audience is facing a healthy job market; at home, their parents are stuffing the den with computers and the garage with a bulky S.U.V. But most teens aren't thinking about the future job market. Lost in the eternal swoon of late adolescence, they're thinking about their identity, their friends, and their clothes. Adolescence is the present-tense moment in American life. Identity and status are fluid: abrupt, devastating reversals are always possible. (In a teen movie, a guy who swallows a bucket of cafeteria coleslaw can make himself a hero in an instant.) In these movies, accordingly, the senior prom is the equivalent of the shoot-out at the O.K. Corral; it's the moment when one's worth as a human being is settled at last. In the rather pedestrian new comedy *Never Been Kissed*, Drew Barrymore, as a twenty-five-year-old newspaper reporter, goes back to high school pretending to be a student, and immediately falls into her old, humiliating pattern of trying to impress the good-looking rich kids. Helplessly, she pushes for approval, and even gets herself chosen prom queen before finally coming to her senses. She finds it nearly impossible to let go.

Genre films dramatize not what happens but how things feel — the emotional coloring of memory. They fix subjectivity into fable. At actual schools, there is no unitary system of status; there are many groups to be a part of, many places to excel (or fail to excel), many avenues of escape and self-definition. And often the movies, too, revel in the arcana of high-school cliques. In . . . *Disturbing Behavior*, a veteran student lays out the cafeteria ethnography for a newcomer: Motorheads, Blue Ribbons, Skaters, Micro-geeks ("drug of choice: Stephen Hawking's *A Brief History of Time* and a cup of jasmine tea on Saturday night"). Subjectively, though, the social system in *Disturbing Behavior* (a high-school version of *The Stepford Wives*) and in the other movies still feels coercive and claustrophobic: humiliation is the most vivid emotion of youth, so in memory it becomes the norm.

The movies try to turn the tables. The kids who cannot be the beautiful ones, or make out with them, or avoid being insulted by them — these are the heroes of the teen movies, the third in the trio of character types. The female outsider is usually an intellectual or an artist. (She scribbles in a diary, she draws or paints.) Physically awkward, she walks like a seal crossing a beach, and is prone to drop her books and dither in terror when she stands before a handsome boy. Her clothes, which ignore mall fashion, scandalize the social queens. Like them, she has a tongue, but she's tart and grammatical, tending toward feminist pungency and precise diction. She may mask her sense of vulnerability with sarcasm or with

Plathian rue (she's stuck in the bell jar), but even when she lashes out she can't hide her craving for acceptance.

The male outsider, her friend, is usually a mass of stuttering or giggling sexual gloom: he wears shapeless clothes; he has an undeveloped body, either stringy or shrimpy; he's sometimes a Jew (in these movies, still the generic outsider). He's also brilliant, but in a morose, preoccupied way that suggests masturbatory absorption in some arcane system of knowledge. In a few special cases, the outsider is not a loser but a disengaged hipster, either saintly or satanic. (Christian Slater has played this role a couple of times.) This outsider wears black and keeps his hair long, and he knows how to please women. He sees through everything, so he's ironic by temperament and genuinely indifferent to the opinion of others — a natural aristocrat, who transcends the school's contemptible status system. There are whimsical variations on the outsider figure, too. In the recent *Rushmore*, an obnoxious teen hero, Max Fischer (Jason Schwartzman), runs the entire school: he can't pass his courses but he's a dynamo at extracurricular activities, with a knack for staging extraordinary events. He's a con man, a fund-raiser, an entrepreneur — in other words, a contemporary artist.

In fact, the entire genre, which combines self-pity and ultimate vindication, might be called "Portrait of the Filmmaker as a Young Nerd." Who can doubt where Hollywood's twitchy, nearsighted writers and directors ranked — or feared they ranked — on the high-school totem pole? They are still angry, though occasionally the target of their resentment goes beyond the jocks and cheerleaders of their youth. Consider this anomaly: the young actors and models on the covers of half the magazines published in this country, the shirtless men with chests like burnished shields, the girls smiling, glowing, tweezed, full-lipped, full-breasted (but not too full), and with skin so honeyed that it seems lacquered — these are the physical ideals embodied by the villains of the teen movies. The social queens and jocks, using their looks to dominate others, represent an American barbarism of beauty. Isn't it possible that the detestation of them in teen movies is a veiled strike at the entire abs-hair advertising culture, with its unobtainable glories of perfection? A critic of consumerism might even see a spark of revolt in these movies. But only a spark.

My guess is that these films arise from remembered hurts which then get recast in symbolic form. For instance, a surprising number of the outsider heroes have no mother. Mom has died or run off with another man; her child, only half loved, is ill equipped for the emotional pressures of school. The motherless child, of course, is a shrewd commercial ploy that makes a direct appeal to the members of the audience, many of whom may feel like outsiders, too, and unloved, or not loved enough, or victims of some prejudice or exclusion. But the motherless child also has powers, and will someday be a success, an artist, a screenwriter. It's the wound and the bow all over again, in cargo pants.

As the female nerd attracts the attention of the handsomest boy in the senior class, the teen movie turns into a myth of social reversal — a Cinderella fantasy.

Initially, his interest in her may be part of a stunt or a trick: he is leading her on, perhaps at the urging of his queenly girlfriend. But his gaze lights her up, and we see how attractive she really is. Will she fulfill the eternal specs? She wants her prince, and by degrees she wins him over, not just with her looks but with her superior nature, her essential goodness. In the male version of the Cinderella trip, a few years go by, and a pale little nerd (we see him at a reunion) has become rich. All that poking around with chemicals paid off. Max Fischer, of *Rushmore*, can't miss being richer than Warhol.

So the teen movie is wildly ambivalent. It may attack the consumerist ethos that produces winners and losers, but in the end it confirms what it is attacking. The girls need the seal of approval conferred by the converted jocks; the nerds need money and a girl. Perhaps it's no surprise that the outsiders can be validated only by the people who ostracized them. But let's not be too schematic: the outsider who joins the system also modifies it, opens it up to the creative power of social mobility, makes it bend and laugh, and perhaps this turn of events is not so different from the way things work in the real world, where merit and achievement stand a good chance of trumping appearance. The irony of the Littleton shootings is that Klebold and Harris, who were both proficient computer heads, seemed to have forgotten how the plot turns out. If they had held on for a few years they might have been working at a hip software company, or have started their own business, while the jocks who oppressed them would probably have wound up selling insurance or used cars. That's the one unquestionable social truth the teen movies reflect: geeks rule.

There is, of course, a menacing subgenre, in which the desire for revenge turns bloody. Thirty-one years ago, Lindsay Anderson's semi-surrealistic *If . . .* was set in an oppressive, class-ridden English boarding school, where a group of rebellious students drive the school population out into a courtyard and open fire on them with machine guns. In Brian De Palma's 1976 masterpiece *Carrie*, the pale, repressed heroine, played by Sissy Spacek, is courted at last by a handsome boy but gets violated — doused with pig's blood — just as she is named prom queen. Stunned but far from powerless, Carrie uses her telekinetic powers to set the room afire and burn down the school. *Carrie* is the primal school movie, so wildly lurid and funny that it exploded the clichés of the genre before the genre was quite set: the heroine may be a wrathful avenger, but the movie, based on a Stephen King book, was clearly a grinning-gargoyle fantasy. So, at first, was *Heathers*, in which Christian Slater's satanic outsider turns out to be a true devil. He and his girlfriend (played by a very young Winona Ryder) begin gleefully knocking off the rich, nasty girls and the jocks, in ways so patently absurd that their revenge seems a mere wicked dream. I think it's unlikely that these movies had a direct effect on the actions of the Littleton shooters, but the two boys would surely have recognized the emotional world of *Heathers* and *Disturbing Behavior* as their own. It's a place where feelings of victimization join fantasy, and you experience the social élites as so powerful that you must either become them or kill them.

But enough. It's possible to make teen movies that go beyond these fixed 15 polarities — insider and outsider, blonde-bitch queen and hunch-shouldered nerd. In Amy Heckerling's 1995 comedy *Clueless*, the big blonde played by Alicia Silverstone is a Rodeo Drive clotheshorse who is nonetheless possessed of extraordinary virtue. Freely dispensing advice and help, she's almost ironically good — a designing goddess with a cell phone. The movie offers a sun-shiny satire of Beverly Hills affluence, which it sees as both absurdly swollen and generous in spirit. The most original of the teen comedies, *Clueless* casts away self-pity. So does *Romy and Michele's High School Reunion* (1997), in which two gabby, lovable friends, played by Mira Sorvino and Lisa Kudrow, review the banalities of their high-school experience so knowingly that they might be criticizing the teen-movie genre itself. And easily the best American film of the year so far is Alexander Payne's *Election*, a high-school movie that inhabits a different aesthetic and moral world altogether from the rest of these pictures. *Election* shreds everyone's fantasies and illusions in a vision of high school that is bleak but supremely just. The movie's villain, an over-achieving girl (Reese Witherspoon) who runs for class president, turns out to be its covert heroine, or, at least, its most poignant character. A cross between Pat and Dick Nixon, she's a lower-middle-class striver who works like crazy and never wins anyone's love. Even when she's on top, she feels excluded. Her loneliness is produced not by malicious cliques but by her own implacable will, a condition of the spirit that may be as comical and tragic as it is mysterious. *Election* escapes all the clichés; it graduates into art.

Questions for Discussion

1. David Denby suggests that Columbine High School in Colorado — at least in the minds of the two student shooters — was "a poisonous system of status, snobbery, and exclusion" (para. 3), peopled with stock villains like the ones in teen movies. Do you believe the teen movies Denby mentions are accurate portrayals of high school life? In the teen movies you've seen, what parts are accurate? exaggerated? just plain wrong?

2. What is Denby's opinion of teen movies? Does he find anything redeeming in them? Do you agree that it is the "most commercial and frivolous of genres" (para. 5)?

3. Consider Denby's statement that "[a]dolescence is the present-tense moment in American life" (para. 6). Is it valid? Is adolescence a particularly American phenomenon? How might adolescence be different in other parts of the world?

4. Do Denby's stock characters — jock, cheerleader, male and female nerds — appear in current teen movies or television shows? Are there characters who transcend these classifications? Explain.

5. Denby mentions three movies that "go beyond [the] fixed polarities" (para. 15): *Clueless*, *Romy and Michele's High School Reunion*, and *Election*. Do you agree? Do any recent teen movies transcend the genre? Explain.

6. Denby suggests that teen movies "harbor a grievance against the world" (para. 5). The enemy is certainly not parents, teachers, or other authority figures but "other teens and the social system that they impose on one another" (para. 5). Why have teen movies changed from the days of movies such as *Wild in the Streets* or *Rebel Without a Cause*, when teenagers rebelled against authority?

Questions on Rhetoric and Style

1. What rhetorical strategies does Denby use in the first paragraph to create a picture of the female villain of teen movies? Consider irony, hyperbole, metaphor, colloquialisms, and opposition.

2. How does Denby's description of the male villain in paragraph 2 differ from that of the female villain in the first paragraph? What does the difference suggest about how males and females are portrayed in film and other media?

3. Where do you detect changes in Denby's tone? How does Denby achieve these changes?

4. Why does the essay have a break between paragraphs 3 and 4? What turn does the essay make here?

5. How does the essay answer the rhetorical questions that begin paragraph 4?

6. The essay makes several appeals to ethos. Denby is a well-known film critic. How does he use the expertise of others — implicitly and explicitly — to support his argument?

7. What is Denby's central argument? What are his secondary arguments? How does he bring them together?

8. In paragraph 10, Denby says the genre of teen movies might be called "Portrait of the Filmmaker as a Young Nerd," an allusion to James Joyce's novel *Portrait of the Artist as a Young Man*. What is the effect of the allusion? Does the allusion strengthen the point Denby makes at the end of the paragraph — that "[a] critic of consumerism might even see a spark of revolt in these movies. But only a spark"? Or is the allusion irrelevant?

9. The "wound and the bow" (para. 11) refers to the theory that pain or unhappiness in an artist's childhood is inextricably tied to strength and creativity later in the artist's life. How does Denby tie that theory to teen movies?

10. In paragraph 13, Denby argues that the two teenage boys who killed classmates, teachers, and then themselves at Columbine High School did not learn the lesson of teen movies: "geeks rule." How does he support this argument?

11. In the last two paragraphs, Denby discusses teen movies that go beyond the genre. How do these examples bolster his argument?

12. Who is the likely audience for this essay? How does Denby consider audience in his essay?

Suggestions for Writing

1. Denby argues that "geeks rule" (para. 13). Write an essay in which you support, challenge, or qualify his assertion.

2. In an essay, answer Denby's rhetorical questions: "Do genre films reflect reality? Or are they merely a set of conventions that refer to other films?" (para. 4). Use your own experiences and teen movies you have seen as evidence.

3. Using Denby's descriptions of stock teen-movie characters, analyze characters in popular television shows. Consider whether they are faithful to the types he identifies.

4. Write an outline for a screenplay that overturns the conventions of teen movies. Who would you cast as the characters?

5. Write an analysis of a teen-movie character who seems to transcend the genre as Denby defines it. Does that character's uniqueness challenge or support Denby's theories about why "geeks rule" in teen movies?

Corn-Pone Opinions

MARK TWAIN

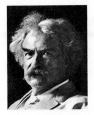 Mark Twain (1835–1910) is the pseudonym of Samuel Langhorne Clemens. Best known as a novelist — *The Adventures of Huckleberry Finn* (1884), *Tom Sawyer* (1876), and *A Connecticut Yankee in King Arthur's Court* (1889) are among his most famous — Twain also worked as a typesetter, a riverboat pilot, a miner, a reporter, and an editor. His early writings reflect his pre–Civil War upbringing in their idyllic images as well as in their reminders of some of America's least acceptable social realities. Twain spent his life observing and reporting on his surroundings, and his work provides a glimpse into the mind-set of the late nineteenth century. "Corn-Pone Opinions," which was found in his papers after his death, was first published in 1923 in *Europe and Elsewhere*. In it, Twain comments — not always approvingly — on word of mouth as the spreader of popular opinion and culture.

Fifty years ago, when I was a boy of fifteen and helping to inhabit a Missourian village on the banks of the Mississippi, I had a friend whose society was very dear to me because I was forbidden by my mother to partake of it. He was a gay and impudent and satirical and delightful young black man — a slave — who daily preached sermons from the top of his master's woodpile, with me for sole audience. He imitated the pulpit style of the several clergymen of the village, and did it well, and with fine passion and energy. To me he was a wonder. I believed he was the greatest orator in the United States and would some day be heard from. But it did not happen; in the distribution of rewards he was overlooked. It is the way, in this world.

He interrupted his preaching, now and then, to saw a stick of wood; but the sawing was a pretense — he did it with his mouth; exactly imitating the sound the bucksaw makes in shrieking its way through the wood. But it served its purpose; it kept his master from coming out to see how the work was getting along. I listened to the sermons from the open window of a lumber room at the back of the house. One of his texts was this:

"You tell me whar a man gits his corn pone, en I'll tell you what his 'pinions is."

I can never forget it. It was deeply impressed upon me. By my mother. Not upon my memory, but elsewhere. She had slipped in upon me while I was absorbed and not watching. The black philosopher's idea was that a man is not independent, and cannot afford views which might interfere with his bread and butter. If he would prosper, he must train with the majority; in matters of large

717

moment, like politics and religion, he must think and feel with the bulk of his neighbors, or suffer damage in his social standing and in his business prosperities. He must restrict himself to corn-pone opinions — at least on the surface. He must get his opinions from other people; he must reason out none for himself; he must have no first-hand views.

I think Jerry was right, in the main, but I think he did not go far enough. 5

1. It was his idea that a man conforms to the majority view of his locality by calculation and intention. This happens, but I think it is not the rule.

2. It was his idea that there is such a thing as a first-hand opinion; an original opinion; an opinion which is coldly reasoned out in a man's head, by a searching analysis of the facts involved, with the heart unconsulted, and the jury room closed against outside influences. It may be that such an opinion has been born somewhere, at some time or other, but I suppose it got away before they could catch it and stuff it and put it in the museum.

I am persuaded that a coldly-thought-out and independent verdict upon a fashion in clothes, or manners, or literature, or politics, or religion, or any other matter that is projected into the field of our notice and interest, is a most rare thing — if it has indeed ever existed.

A new thing in costume appears — the flaring hoopskirt, for example — and the passers-by are shocked, and the irreverent laugh. Six months later everybody is reconciled; the fashion has established itself; it is admired, now, and no one laughs. Public opinion resented it before, public opinion accepts it now, and is happy in it. Why? Was the resentment reasoned out? Was the acceptance reasoned out? No. The instinct that moves to conformity did the work. It is our nature to conform; it is a force which not many can successfully resist. What is its seat? The inborn requirement of self-approval. We all have to bow to that; there are no exceptions. Even the woman who refuses from first to last to wear the hoop skirt comes under that law and is its slave; she could not wear the skirt and have her own approval; and that she must have, she cannot help herself. But as a rule our self-approval has its source in but one place and not elsewhere — the approval of other people. A person of vast consequences can introduce any kind of novelty in dress and the general world will presently adopt it — moved to do it, in the first place, by the natural instinct to passively yield to that vague something recognized as authority, and in the second place by the human instinct to train with the multitude and have its approval. An empress introduced the hoopskirt, and we know the result. A nobody introduced the bloomer, and we know the result. If Eve should come again, in her ripe renown, and reintroduce her quaint styles — well, we know what would happen. And we should be cruelly embarrassed, along at first.

The hoopskirt runs its course and disappears. Nobody reasons about it. One 10 woman abandons the fashion; her neighbor notices this and follows her lead; this influences the next woman; and so on and so on, and presently the skirt has vanished out of the world, no one knows how nor why, nor cares, for that matter. It will come again, by and by and in due course will go again.

Twenty-five years ago, in England, six or eight wine glasses stood grouped by each person's plate at a dinner party, and they were used, not left idle and empty; to-day there are but three or four in the group, and the average guest sparingly uses about two of them. We have not adopted this new fashion yet, but we shall do it presently. We shall not think it out; we shall merely conform, and let it go at that. We get our notions and habits and opinions from outside influences; we do not have to study them out.

Our table manners, and company manners and street manners change from time to time, but the changes are not reasoned out; we merely notice and conform. We are creatures of outside influences; as a rule we do not think, we only imitate. We cannot invent standards that will stick; what we mistake for standards are only fashions, and perishable. We may continue to admire them, but we drop the use of them. We notice this in literature. Shakespeare is a standard, and fifty years ago we used to write tragedies which we couldn't tell from — from somebody else's; but we don't do it any more, now. Our prose standard, three quarters of a century ago, was ornate and diffuse; some authority or other changed it in the direction of compactness and simplicity, and conformity followed, without argument. The historical novel starts up suddenly, and sweeps the land. Everybody writes one, and the nation is glad. We had historical novels before; but nobody read them, and the rest of us conformed — without reasoning it out. We are conforming in the other way, now, because it is another case of everybody.

The outside influences are always pouring in upon us, and we are always obeying their orders and accepting their verdicts. The Smiths like the new play; the Joneses go to see it, and they copy the Smith verdict. Morals, religions, politics, get their following from surrounding influences and atmospheres, almost entirely; not from study, not from thinking. A man must and will have his own approval first of all, in each and every moment and circumstance of his life — even if he must repent of a self-approved act the moment after its commission, in order to get his self-approval again: but, speaking in general terms, a man's self-approval in the large concerns of life has its source in the approval of the peoples about him, and not in a searching personal examination of the matter. Mohammedans are Mohammedans because they are born and reared among that sect, not because they have thought it out and can furnish sound reasons for being Mohammedans; we know why Catholics are Catholics; why Presbyterians are Presbyterians; why Baptists are Baptists; why Mormons are Mormons; why thieves are thieves; why monarchists are monarchists; why Republicans are Republicans and Democrats, Democrats. We know it is a matter of association and sympathy, not reasoning and examination; that hardly a man in the world has an opinion upon morals, politics, or religion which he got otherwise than through his associations and sympathies. Broadly speaking, there are none but corn-pone opinions. And broadly speaking, corn-pone stands for self-approval. Self-approval is acquired mainly from the approval of other people. The result is conformity. Sometimes conformity has a sordid business interest — the bread-and-butter interest — but not in most cases, I think. I think that in the majority of cases it is unconscious and not calculated; that it's born of the human being's natural yearning to stand well with his fellows and have their inspiring approval and praise — a yearning which is commonly so strong and so insistent that it cannot be effectually resisted, and must have its way. A political emergency brings out the corn-pone opinion in fine force in its two chief varieties — the pocket-book variety, which has its origin in self-interest, and the bigger variety, the senti-mental variety — the one which can't bear to be outside the pale; can't bear to be in disfavor; can't endure the averted face and the cold shoulder; wants to stand well with his friends, wants to be smiled upon, wants to be welcome, wants to hear the precious words, "He's on the right track!" Uttered, perhaps by an ass, but still an ass of high degree, an ass whose approval is gold and diamonds to a smaller ass, and confers glory and honor and happiness, and membership in the herd. For these gauds many a man will dump his life-long principles into the street, and his conscience along with them. We have seen it happen. In some millions of instances.

Men think they think upon great political questions, and they do; but they think with their party, not independently; they read its literature, but not that of the other side; they arrive at convictions, but they are drawn from a partial view of the matter in hand and are of no particular value. They swarm with their party, they feel with their party, they are happy in their party's approval; and where the party leads they will follow, whether for right and honor, or through blood and dirt and a mush of mutilated morals.

In our late canvass half of the nation passionately believed that in silver lay   15
salvation, the other half as passionately believed that that way lay destruction. Do you believe that a tenth part of the people, on either side, had any rational excuse for having an opinion about the matter at all? I studied that mighty question to the bottom — came out empty. Half of our people passionately believe in high tariff, the other half believe otherwise. Does this mean study and examination, or only feeling? The latter, I think. I have deeply studied that question, too — and didn't arrive. We all do no end of feeling, and we mistake it for thinking. And out of it we get an aggregation which we consider a boon. Its name is Public Opinion. It is held in reverence. It settles everything. Some think it the Voice of God.

Questions for Discussion

1. According to Mark Twain, "It is our nature to conform" (para. 9); he also says that we do so for self-approval. The two statements seem contradictory; how does Twain connect conformity and self-approval?

2. Twain makes a distinction between standards and fashions. What is the difference? What examples does he provide for each? How does the distinction apply to the twenty-first century?

3. Twain's essay is ultimately a denunciation of cultural chauvinism. What consequences does he suggest are the result of "corn-pone opinions"? Which are explicit? Which are implicit?

4. The last paragraph begins with a reference to a "late canvass" in which "half the nation passionately believed" in one path and "the other half passionately believed" in another. To what was Twain probably referring? Does he take sides? How does he distinguish between thinking and feeling?

5. In what two ways does a political emergency bring out corn-pone opinions? What does Twain mean by "an ass of high degree" (para. 13)?

Questions on Rhetoric and Style

1. What is Twain's purpose in "Corn-Pone Opinions"?

2. Trace Twain's use of the personal pronoun. What is the effect of changing from *I* to *we*?

3. Twain claims he got the idea of corn-pone opinions from a young slave with a talent for preaching. What does the anecdote add to his argument? Does it detract in any way?

4. How does Twain expand Jerry's definition of corn-pone opinions? What is the effect of numbering the two items in which he begins to expand Jerry's definition?

5. Identify Twain's appeals to logos. Do the subjects of the appeals (hoopskirts, bloomers, wineglasses) strengthen the appeals or weaken them?

6. Explain the irony of Twain's qualification of Jerry's statement about calculation and intention in paragraph 6.

7. Why is paragraph 13 so long? Where, if anywhere, could Twain have broken it up? What is the effect of the series of subordinate clauses in the middle of the paragraph?

8. What is the effect of the parallelism in the two long sentences that make up paragraph 14?

9. What is the effect of capitalizing "Public Opinion" and "Voice of God" at the end of the essay?

10. How does a phrase such as "helping to inhabit" in the first paragraph contribute to the tone of the essay?

11. Find examples of understatement and hyperbole. Discuss their effects.

Suggestions for Writing

1. Write your own version of "Corn-Pone Opinions," giving examples from contemporary culture and politics. Do you end up making the same argument as Twain, or do you think Americans are more independent thinkers now? Explain why.

2. Twain says he believed that the slave Jerry was "the greatest orator in the United States" (para. 1) but that "in the distribution of rewards he was overlooked." Write about how Jerry might have viewed his situation.

3. Do you agree or disagree with Twain's assertion that "[I]t is our nature to conform" (para. 9)? Explain why.

4. Refute Twain's view of Public Opinion by defending word of mouth as the most reliable communicator of cultural innovation.

5. Find examples of prose that are (a) ornate and diffuse and (b) compact and simple. In paragraph 12, Twain contrasts prose styles that are "ornate and diffuse" with those that are characterized by "compactness and simplicity." Find examples of each, and write an essay comparing and contrasting the effects of the two prose styles.

Godzilla vs. the Giant Scissors:
Cutting the Antiwar Heart out of a Classic

Brent Staples

Born in 1951 and raised in Chester, Pennsylvania, Brent Staples is an editorial writer for the *New York Times* and an influential commentator on American politics and culture. He earned a BA with honors from Widener University and studied at the University of Chicago on a Danforth Fellowship. There he earned a PhD in psychology. In 1994, he published a memoir, *Parallel Time: Growing Up in Black and White*, which won the Anisfield-Wolf Book Award. His essays, such as "Just Walk on By: Black Men and Public Spaces," are frequently anthologized. The essay that follows appeared on the op-ed page of the *New York Times* in May 2005.

Film directors who once stood helpless while studios recut their movies can now console themselves with "directors' cuts" put out on DVD. This option was not available to the influential Japanese director Ishiro Honda, whose 1954 classic *Godzilla* — known in Japan as "Gojira" — made a household name of the towering reptile who stomped a miniature Tokyo into the ground while raking the landscape with his fiery thermonuclear breath.

A fire-breathing reptile is pretty much the same in any language. But the butchered version of the film that swept the world after release in the United States was stripped of the political subtext — and the anti-American, antinuclear messages — that had saturated the original. The uncut version of the film is due out on home video early next year, and should push serious Godzilla fans to rethink the 50-year evolution of the series. It should also show them that they were hoodwinked by the denatured Americanized version that dominated many of their childhoods in the late 20th century. At the same time, Godzilla fans are on the edge of their seats about a new film that should be released in the United States soon.

The original "Gojira" was never intended as a conventional monster-on-the-loose movie. Nor did it resemble the farcical rubber-suit wrestling matches or the domesticated movies (with Godzilla cast as a mammoth household pet) that the series degenerated into during the 1960s and 70s.

As the historian William Tsutsui reminded us in last year's cult classic, "Godzilla on My Mind," the 1954 movie was a dark, poetic production that dealt openly with Japanese misgivings about the nuclear menace, environmental degradation and the traumatic experience associated with World War II.

The nuclear annihilations of Hiroshima and Nagasaki were still fresh in 5 mind when the famous Toho Company embarked on the "Gojira" project in 1954. But Japanese fear of nuclear catastrophe was given fresh impetus in the spring of that year, when the United States detonated a huge hydrogen bomb at Bikini Atoll in the central Pacific. Japanese fishermen aboard a trawler were exposed to nuclear fallout. Japanese consumers panicked and declined to eat fish after irradiated tuna was found to have slipped into the nation's food supply.

In the film, the H-bomb blast awakens and irradiates a dinosaur that has somehow escaped extinction. The reptile strides ashore and begins his trademark devastation of the Tokyo landscape. The nuclear antecedents were not at all lost on Honda, a World War II veteran who passed through the bombed-out city of Hiroshima and witnessed the damage firsthand. Honda later said that he envisioned the fiery breath of Godzilla as a way of "making radiation visible," and of showing the world that nuclear power could never be tamed.

He also told an interviewer: "Believe it or not, we naively hoped that the end of Godzilla was going to coincide with the end of nuclear testing."

That was clearly a tall order for a monster movie. But Honda's message never had a chance because most of the world never received it. The American company that bought the rights to distribute the film in this country cut a large chunk from Honda's original film and rearranged the plot. The biggest change involved splicing in Raymond Burr, who played an American reporter chronicling the devastation for the press. Dialogue that dealt heavily with human suffering, the morality of all-out war — and the temptation to play God with weapons of mass destruction — was left on the American cutting room floor.

The exclusion of the antinuclear theme in the American version is hardly surprising. Hollywood had little stomach for anti-American rhetoric during the McCarthyite 1950s. But the American production of "Godzilla" that starred Matthew Broderick a half-century later showed that Hollywood did not understand the monster, either.

The sleek, animated "American" Godzilla somehow managed to be less scary   10
than the Japanese actor in the latex suit. Part of the problem is that the American Godzilla relied on stealth and cunning instead of the brute force displayed by the original. Some fans felt like walking out when the American Godzilla, confronted by a military threat, turned and ran. The essence of Godzilla is that he keeps stomping relentlessly forward, no matter what you throw his way.

It is fitting, then, that the American Godzilla is K.O.'ed by the real thing in the 28th and perhaps final installment, "Godzilla Final Wars," which should make it into general release in America sometime soon. It's also fitting that the original Godzilla movie, which was dismembered a half-century ago in America, is finally being shown in its full and uncut form.

Exploring the Text

1. An essential assumption of Brent Staples's essay is the belief that popular culture can communicate an important message. How does he share that assumption with the reader? What is the message of the original Japanese version of *Godzilla*?

2. Who is Staples's audience in addition to "serious *Godzilla* fans" (para. 2)? Does Staples give the impression that he himself is a fan? How does he characterize the serious fan?

3. In paragraph 10, Staples says, "The essence of Godzilla is that he keeps stomping relentlessly forward, no matter what you throw his way." What might the American Godzilla stand for?

4. Despite its serious subject, there is an undercurrent of humor in Staples's essay. How does Staples create the mock serious tone? Cite specific passages. What effect does it have on his message?

5. In paragraph 10, Staples compares the American Godzilla to the original. What is the effect of the images he creates for each one?

6. Staples's essay heralds both the rerelease of the original version of *Godzilla* and a new American film version. Watch several versions of *Godzilla*, and then discuss the ways they reflect the hopes and anxieties of the times in which they were made.

BRENT STAPLES ON WRITING

In this excerpt from an interview with Brent Staples, whose work appears on page 723, he speaks about his career as a writer, including early influences.

Robin Dissin Aufses (RA): Were there specific events or people that influenced you to become a writer?

Brent Staples (BS): Writers stand apart from events, making mental notes about them. I realized after writing my memoir, *Parallel Time*, published in 1994, that I had always done this, even as a child. My family moved often while I was growing up; we'd had seven different addresses by the time I reached eighth grade. I arrived in a new neighborhood long after the kids there had established their friendships; my family moved on before I'd had a chance to break into things. This placed me naturally into the posture of the outsider, the posture of the observer. It stood me in good stead when I began to write professionally. The men in my family are monologuists by birth. They tell stories all the time. I grew up listening to my father and his brothers weaving long stories — mainly remembrances of family life — for hours on end. My most important influence, of course, was my mother. This was the 1950s and just about all mothers were stay-at-home mothers. My mother and father married when she was eighteen — and she had her first child a little over a year later. By the time I was nine, she'd had four children —

and we were naturally a handful. Story time at our house was pretty unique. My mother sat us in a circle on the floor and asked those of us who could talk to make up stories — on the spot. I suppose this gave me a natural sense of narrative.

RA: Were there other writers or teachers who influenced you?

BS: The novelist Saul Bellow was the first writer I'd ever seen in the flesh. He taught at the University of Chicago when I was there. I can still remember the huge headlines and all the celebration when he received the Nobel Prize — just after the novel *Humboldt's Gift*, which was modeled on the life of the poet Delmore Schwartz. The novel hit the street in 1975, when I was going on twenty-four. I was surprised to find that the novel contained a detailed representation of the university and the surrounding neighborhood, the Hyde Park section of Chicago. Reading it changed the way I thought about fiction. Prior to that time, I'd believed that novels were made up entirely out of the writer's imagination. I saw from watching Saul Bellow, however, that part of the writer's job was to fold reality into books. You can tell from *Parallel Time* how much the discovery startled me.

I have never taken a writing course. . . . All of the training in my case was practice, beginning in my twenties. I tried to write essays and pieces of reportage that were broad appraisals of the subject at hand. Whenever I speak to young people about writing — and I often do — I say: don't let anyone tell you that writing is a mystical activity. I tell them: writing is like bricklaying. You learn from watching or being taught by other people. Walk down the street in a neighborhood constructed of brick and you see buildings of all shapes and sizes. Some are square. Some have turrets. Some are squat. Some are tall. Each building was built by laying bricks end to end. Words are like bricks, sentences are like courses of bricks. Simple declarative sentences are stretched end to end in an illuminating way to make stories, chapters, and books. I also tell young people that writing is work — and that ninety percent of writing is actually rewriting what you have written. The only way to write is to "apply your butt to the seat" — as one of my newspaper editors used to say.

Follow-up

Write a narrative or an essay discussing the people — in your family, at school, from your reading — who influenced the way you feel about writing. Consider both the positive and negative attitudes you have toward writing, as well as the people who influenced those attitudes.

From *We Talk, You Listen*

VINE DELORIA JR.

A Standing Rock Sioux, Vine Deloria Jr. (1933–2005) was born in Martin, South Dakota. He received a master of theology degree from the Lutheran School of Theology in 1964 and a law degree from the University of Chicago in 1970. Deloria was a leading Native American scholar whose research, writings, and teaching covered history, law, religion, and political science. He has been hailed as one of the great religious thinkers of the twentieth century. Deloria wrote many books including *Custer Died for Your Sins* (1969), an influential study of Indian affairs that helped launch the field of Native American studies. The following essay, from *We Talk, You Listen: New Tribes, New Turf* (1970), looks at media stereotypes of Native Americans and other minorities, as well as at ethnic studies programs in universities, as they existed almost four decades ago.

One reason that Indian people have not been heard from until recently is that we have been completely covered up by movie Indians. Western movies have been such favorites that they have dominated the public's conception of what Indians are. It is not all bad when one thinks about the handsome Jay Silverheels bailing the Lone Ranger out of a jam, or Ed Ames rescuing Daniel Boone with some clever Indian trick. But the other mythologies that have wafted skyward because of the movies have blocked out any idea that there might be real Indians with real problems.

Other minority groups have fought tenaciously against stereotyping, and generally they have been successful. Italians quickly quashed the image of them as mobsters that television projected in *The Untouchables*. Blacks have been successful in getting a more realistic picture of the black man in a contemporary setting because they have had standout performers like Bill Cosby and Sidney Poitier to represent them.

Since stereotyping was highlighted by motion pictures, it would probably be well to review the images of minority groups projected in the movies in order to understand how the situation looks at present. Perhaps the first aspect of stereotyping was the tendency to exclude people on the basis of their inability to handle the English language. Not only were racial minorities excluded, but immigrants arriving on these shores were soon whipped into shape by ridicule of their English.

Traditional stereotypes pictured the black as a happy watermelon-eating darky whose sole contribution to American society was his indiscriminate substitution of the "d" sound for "th." Thus a black always said "dis" and "dat," as in "lift dat bale." The "d" sound carried over and was used by white gangsters to indicate disfavor with their situation, as in "dis is de end, ya rat." The important thing was to indicate that blacks were like lisping children not yet competent to undertake the rigors of economic opportunities and voting.

Mexicans were generally portrayed as shiftless and padded out for siesta, without any redeeming qualities whatsoever. Where the black had been handicapped by his use of the "d," the Mexican suffered from the use of the double "e." This marked them off as a group worth watching. Mexicans, according to the stereotype, always said "theenk," "peenk," and later "feenk." Many advertisements today still continue this stereotype, thinking that it is cute and cuddly.

These groups were much better off than Indians were. Indians were always devoid of any English whatsoever. They were only allowed to speak when an important message had to be transmitted on the screen. For example, "many pony soldiers die" was meant to indicate that Indians were going to attack the peaceful settlers who happened to have broken their three hundredth treaty moments before. Other than that Indian linguistic ability was limited to "ugh" and "kemo sabe" (which means honky in some obscure Indian language).

The next step was to acknowledge that there was a great American dream to which any child could aspire. (It was almost like the train in the night that Richard Nixon heard as a child anticipating the dream fairy.) The great American dream was projected in the early World War II movies. The last reel was devoted to a stirring proclamation that we were going to win the war and it showed factories producing airplanes, people building ships, and men marching in uniform to the transports. There was a quick pan of a black face before the scene shifted to scenes of orchards, rivers, Mount Rushmore, and the Liberty Bell as we found out what we were fighting for.

The new images expressed a profound inability to understand why minority groups couldn't "make it" when everybody knew that America was all about freedom and equality. By projecting an image of everyone working hard to win the war, the doctrine was spread that America was just one big happy family and that there really weren't any differences so long as we had to win the war.

It was a rare war movie in the 1940s that actually showed a black or a Mexican as a bona fide fighting man. When they did appear it was in the role of cooks or orderlies serving whites. In most cases this was a fairly accurate statement of their situation, particularly with respect to the Navy.

World War II movies were entirely different for Indians. Each platoon of red-blooded white American boys was equipped with its own set of Indians. When the platoon got into trouble and was surrounded, its communications cut off except for one slender line to regimental headquarters, and that line tapped by myriads of Germans, Japanese, or Italians, the stage was set for the dramatic episode of the Indians.

John Wayne, Randolph Scott, Sonny Tufts, or Tyrone Power would smile broadly as he played his ace, which until this time had been hidden from view. From nowhere, a Navaho, Comanche, Cherokee, or Sioux would appear, take the telephone, and in some short and inscrutable phraseology communicate such a plenitude of knowledge to his fellow tribesman (fortunately situated at the general's right hand) that fighting units thousands of miles away would instantly perceive the situation and rescue the platoon. The Indian would disappear as mysteriously as he had come, only to reappear the next week in a different battle to perform his esoteric rites. Anyone watching war movies during the '40s would have been convinced that without Indian telephone operators the war would have been lost irretrievably, in spite of John Wayne.

Indians were America's secret weapon against the forces of evil. The typing spoke of a primitive gimmick, and it was the strangeness of Indians that made them visible, not their humanity. With the Korean War era and movies made during the middle '50s, other minority groups began to appear and Indians were pushed into the background. This era was the heyday of the "All-American Platoon." It was the ultimate conception of intergroup relations. The "All-American Platoon" was a "one each": one black, one Mexican, one Indian, one farm boy from Iowa, one Southerner who hated blacks, one boy from Brooklyn, one Polish boy from the urban slums of the Midwest, one Jewish intellectual, and one college boy. Every possible stereotype was included and it resulted in a portrayal of Indians as another species of human being for the first time in moving pictures.

The platoon was always commanded by a veteran of grizzled countenance who had been at every battle in which the United States had ever engaged. The whole story consisted in killing off the members of the platoon until only the veteran and the college boy were left. The Southerner and the black would die in each other's arms singing "Dixie." The Jewish intellectual and the Indian formed some kind of attachment and were curiously the last ones killed. When the smoke cleared, the college boy, with a prestige wound in the shoulder, returned to his girl, and the veteran reconciled with his wife and checked out another platoon in anticipation of taking the same hill in the next movie.

While other groups have managed to make great strides since those days, Indians have remained the primitive unknown quantity. Dialogue has reverted back to the monosyllabic grunt and even pictures that attempt to present the Indian side of the story depend upon unintelligible noises to present their message. The only exception to this rule is a line famed for its durability over the years. If you fall asleep during the Late Show and suddenly awaken to the words "go in peace, my son," it is either an Indian chief bidding his son good bye as the boy heads for college or a Roman Catholic priest forgiving Paul Newman or Steve McQueen for killing a hundred men in the preceding reel.

Anyone raising questions about the image of minority groups as portrayed in 15 television and the movies is automatically suspect as an un-American and subversive influence on the minds of the young. The historical, linguistic, and cultural differences are neatly blocked out by the fad of portraying members of minority groups in roles which formerly were reserved for whites. Thus Burt Reynolds played a Mohawk detective busy solving the crime problem in New York City. Diahann Carroll played a well-to-do black widow with small child in a television series that was obviously patterned after the unique single-headed white family.

In recent years the documentary has arisen to present the story of Indian people and a number of series on Black America have been produced. Indian documentaries are singularly the same. A reporter and television crew hasten to either the Navaho or Pine Ridge reservation, quickly shoot reels on poverty conditions, and return East blithely thinking that they have captured the essence of Indian life. In spite of the best intentions, the eternal yearning to present an exciting story of a strange people overcomes, and the endless cycle of poverty-oriented films continues.

This type of approach continually categorizes the Indian as an incompetent boob who can't seem to get along and who is hopelessly mired in a poverty of his own making. Hidden beneath these documentaries is the message that Indians really *want* to live this way. No one has yet filmed the incredible progress that is being made by the Makah tribe, the Quinaults, Red Lake Chippewas, Gila River Pima-Waricopas, and others. Documentaries project the feeling that reservations should be eliminated because the conditions are so bad. There is no effort to present the bright side of Indian life.

With the rise of ethnic studies programs and courses in minority-group history, the situation has become worse. People who support these programs assume that by communicating the best aspects of a group they have somehow solved the major problems of that group in its relations with the rest of society. By emphasizing that black is beautiful or that Indians have contributed the names of rivers to the road map, many people feel that they have done justice to the group concerned.

One theory of interpretation of Indian history that has arisen in the past several years is that all of the Indian war chiefs were patriots defending their lands. This is the "patriot chief" interpretation of history. Fundamentally it is a good theory in that it places a more equal balance to interpreting certain Indian wars as wars of resistance. It gets away from the tendency, seen earlier in this century, to classify all Indian warriors as renegades. But there is a tendency to overlook the obvious renegades: Indians who were treacherous and would have been renegades had there been no whites to fight. The patriot chiefs interpretation also conveniently overlooks the fact that every significant leader of the previous century was eventually done in by his own people in one way or another. Sitting Bull was killed by Indian police working for the government. Geronimo was captured by an army led by Apache scouts who sided with the United States.

If the weak points of each minority group's history are to be covered over by a sweetness-and-light interpretation based on what we would like to think happened rather than what did happen, we doom ourselves to decades of further racial strife. Most of the study programs today emphasize the goodness that is inherent in the different minority communities, instead of trying to present a balanced story. There are basically two schools of interpretation running through all of these efforts as the demand for black, red, and brown pride dominates the programs.

One theory derives from the "All-American Platoon" concept of a decade ago. Under this theory members of the respective racial minority groups had an important role in the great events of American history. Crispus Attucks, a black, almost single-handedly started the Revolutionary War, while Eli Parker, the Seneca Indian general, won the Civil War and would have concluded it sooner had not there been so many stupid whites abroad in those days. This is the "cameo" theory of history. It takes a basic "manifest destiny" white interpretation of history and lovingly plugs a few feathers, woolly heads, and sombreros into the famous events of American history. No one tries to explain what an Indian is who was helping the whites destroy his own people, since we are now all Americans and have these great events in common.

The absurdity of the cameo school of ethnic pride is self-apparent. Little Mexican children are taught that there were some good Mexicans at the Alamo. They can therefore be happy that Mexicans have been involved in the significant events of Texas history. Little is said about the Mexicans on the other side at the Alamo. The result is a denial of a substantial Mexican heritage by creating the feeling that "we all did it together." If this trend continues I would not be surprised to discover that Columbus had a Cherokee on board when he set sail from Spain in search of the Indies.

The cameo school smothers any differences that existed historically by presenting a history in which all groups have participated through representatives. Regardless of Crispus Attucks's valiant behavior during the Revolution, it is doubtful that he envisioned another century of slavery for blacks as a cause worth defending.

The other basic school of interpretation is a projection backward of the material blessings of the white middle class. It seeks to identify where all the material wealth originated and finds that each minority group *contributed* something. It can therefore be called the contribution school. Under this conception we should all love Indians because they contributed corn, squash, potatoes, tobacco, coffee, rubber, and other agricultural products. In like manner, blacks and Mexicans are credited with Carver's work on the peanut, blood transfusion, and tacos and tamales.

The ludicrous implication of the contribution school visualizes the minority groups clamoring to enter American society, lined up with an abundance of foods and fancies, presenting them to whites in a never ending stream of generosity. If the different minority groups were given an overriding two-percent royalty on their contributions, the same way whites have managed to give themselves royalties for their inventions, this school would have a more realistic impact on minority groups.

The danger with both of these types of ethnic studies theories is that they present an unrealistic account of the role of minority groups in American history.

Certainly there is more to the story of the American Indian than providing cocoa and popcorn for Columbus's landing party. When the clashes of history are smoothed over in favor of a mushy togetherness feeling, then people begin to wonder what has happened in the recent past that has created the conditions of today. It has been the feeling of younger people that contemporary problems have arisen because community leadership has been consistently betraying them. Older statesmen are called Uncle Toms, and the entire fabric of accumulated wisdom and experience of the older generation of minority groups is destroyed. . . .

Under present conceptions of ethnic studies there can be no lasting benefit either to minority groups or to society at large. The pride that can be built into children and youth by acknowledgment of the validity of their group certainly cannot be built by simply transferring symbols and interpretations arising in white culture history into an Indian, black, or Mexican setting. The result will be to make the minority groups bear the white man's burden by using his symbols and stereotypes as if they were their own.

There must be a drive within each minority group to understand its own uniqueness. This can only be done by examining what experiences were relevant to the group, not what experiences of white America the group wishes itself to be represented in. As an example, the discovery of gold in California was a significant event in the experience of white America. The discovery itself was irrelevant to the western Indian tribes, but the migrations caused by the discovery of gold were vitally important. The two histories can dovetail around this topic but ultimately each interpretation must depend upon its orientation to the group involved.

What has been important and continues to be important is the Constitution of the United States and its continual adaptation to contemporary situations. With the Constitution as a framework and reference point, it would appear that a number of conflicting interpretations of the experience of America could be validly given. While they might conflict at every point as each group defines to its own satisfaction what its experience has meant, recognition that within the Constitutional framework we are engaged in a living process of intergroup relationships would mean that no one group could define the meaning of American society to the exclusion of any other.

Self-awareness of each group must define a series of histories about the American experience. Manifest destiny has dominated thinking in the past because it has had an abstract quality that appeared to interpret experiences accurately. Nearly every racial and ethnic group has had to bow down before this conception of history and conform to an understanding of the world that it did not ultimately believe. Martin Luther King, Jr., spoke to his people on the basis of self-awareness the night before he died. He told them that they as a people would reach the promised land. Without the same sense of destiny, minority groups will simply be adopting the outmoded forms of stereotyping by which whites have deluded themselves for centuries.

We can survive as a society if we reject the conquest-oriented interpretation of the Constitution. While some Indian nationalists want the whole country back, a guarantee of adequate protection of existing treaty rights would provide a meaningful compromise. The Constitution should provide a sense of balance between groups as it has between conflicting desires of individuals.

As each group defines the ideas and doctrines necessary to maintain its own sense of dignity and identity, similarities in goals can be drawn that will have relevance beyond immediate group aspirations. Stereotyping will change radically because the ideological basis for portraying the members of any group will depend on that group's values. Plots in books and movies will have to show life as it is seen from within the group. Society will become broader and more cosmopolitan as innovative themes are presented to it. The universal sense of inhumanity will take on an aspect of concreteness. From the variety of cultural behavior patterns we can devise a new understanding of humanity.

The problem of stereotyping is not so much a racial problem as it is a problem of limited knowledge and perspective. Even though minority groups have suffered in the past by ridiculous characterizations of themselves by white society, they must not fall into the same trap by simply reversing the process that has stereotyped them. Minority groups must thrust through the rhetorical blockade by creating within themselves a sense of "peoplehood." This ultimately means the creation of a new history and not mere amendments to the historical interpretations of white America.

Exploring the Text

1. Vine Deloria Jr. introduces his subject by reviewing the stereotyping of minorities in the films of the 1940s and 1950s. How does this lay the groundwork for his argument? Why is this rhetorical strategy effective?

2. What audience is Deloria addressing? How does he establish ethos?

3. Deloria's essay was published in 1970. Has the media's treatment of African Americans and Latinos changed since then? Has the media's treatment of Native Americans changed?

4. In the second half of the essay, the focus shifts from ethnic stereotyping to ethnic studies programs. How does Deloria connect the two? How does he make the transition?

5. In paragraph 7, Deloria says, "The great American dream was projected in the early World War II movies." Consider the ways that dream was perceived — and did or did not come true — for the different ethnic groups Deloria mentions. How was the dream different for Native Americans? How did the portrayal of ethnic groups change in the 1950s? Why does Deloria believe the portrayal of Native Americans caused them to remain "the primitive unknown quantity"?

6. Though Deloria's argument is serious, he uses hyperbole and understatement as rhetorical strategies. Find examples of each. Are they effective, or do they undermine his seriousness?

7. Compare the way Deloria invokes the U.S. Constitution in paragraph 29 ("within the constitutional framework we are engaged in a living process of intergroup relationships") with what writer Ralph Ellison said when asked whether institutions existed to preserve the gains of the Harlem Renaissance ("We have the Constitution and the Bill of Rights, and we have jazz").

8. How might Deloria respond to the current trend of political correctness that questions the use of Indian names and images for sports teams?

9. According to Deloria, "The problem of stereotyping is not so much a racial problem as it is a problem of limited knowledge and perspective" (para. 33). Defend or challenge his assertion.

Dreaming America

Danyel Smith

> Danyel Smith (b. 1965) is a former editor-at-large for Time Inc. and the former editor-in-chief of *Vibe*. She has written for the *Village Voice*, *Rolling Stone*, *Spin*, the *San Francisco Bay Guardian*, and the *New York Times*, among other publications. Smith also wrote the introduction to *Vibe's* book on Tupac Shakur. Smith is the author of the novels *More Like Wrestling* (2003) and *Bliss* (2005). In addition, she comments regularly on culture on VH1, WNYC, and CNN. Born and raised in California, Smith now lives in Brooklyn, New York. The following essay first appeared in *Spin*.

The music is my life.

Is New York, New York, really the birthplace of hip hop? Is this ultimate city — the preferred setting for most modern-day film fables — the place where the seed took hold? Where the rhymes first flowed and a culture took form? This compressed, dirty place, this mainstream cultural stronghold, is the steamy-hot/snowy region where a generation found an identity, where all the . . . went down?

It's where DJ Scott LaRock died and Slick Rick went to prison. Where Run found Christ and Griff got dismissed. Where sneakers became the rule and not the exception: where Latifah grew Treach, and where the Guru *squoze* hip hop out of Bird's horn.

And here she is, Ms. Hip Hop, generic girl-fan. In that place. The city. Looking around for the elusive ticket, the line, the string that tied it all together and turned the music into a thing, a movement — music.

She is a native Californian in New York for the third time. She never stays long. She always flies back West, over the mountains and the lakes, relieved when she sees Lake Tahoe, ecstatic when she spots the Golden Gate Bridge, its yawning red span as welcoming as a familiar mouth upturned in a smile. Then she knows she is in California, a subdivision of the U.S.A. as long and thin as she would like to be — a huge state broken up into sprawling counties, the seductively warm state she calls her home. California has its glories, and it holds on tight to its trophies — the Eagles, Sly and the Family Stone, Jefferson Airplane, Tower of Power. But as grand and forthright as Cali hip hop is circa 1993 — the Coup, Snoop Dogg, Souls of Mischief — in the East lay the lungs and heart of hip hop and so the West holds court in its long shadow.

Tommy Boy president Monica Lynch asked, "Has New York fallen the . . . off?" a long time ago, like maybe it would jar East Coast B-boys and -girls into action. But to no avail. The cast pumps hip hop blood, but out West are the sinewy appendages, out West is where folks are waking and talking it.

New York beckons, though, like an old buddy with gossip, like a preacher who just might know the Truth. The buildings are older, the street fumes stronger, every other car is a taxi. The periodicals seem vital, seem to have more than a tenuous connection to the city. The trains hiss and moan and chug. The place is cutthroat, envious, and mean. Pleasantries are hoarded like money and doled out without enthusiasm. California is one big country town compared with Manhattan and the surrounding boroughs. California piles on big-city makeup in L.A. and Oakland, San Diego and San Francisco — but really, the place is spread out like a big cabbage farm, like the far-flung desert it is.

But cabbage farm or no, in urban southern California, even a mostly middle-class Catholic schoolgirl like Ms. Hip Hop knows which neighborhood is blue and which is red. She knows when to hit the asphalt in the parking lot of Shakey's or Astro Burger because boys are shooting bullets in the air or at certain cars because their varsity hoop squad lost. Or because they won.

She remembers when "urban" didn't have a negative connotation, when urban meant of or having to do with a city or a metropolis. She remembers when "city" didn't mean dank and dark and poor. She vaguely recalls when black people weren't automatically associated with cities and urbanity. She's read about it, about when African-Americans lived mostly on farms and in the "country" and in the South. Arrested Development's Speech reminisces about that era in "Tennessee." Making myth of the post-sharecropping era and country life, he talks convincingly, painfully about climbing the trees his forefathers hung from. It sounds so cleansing and sad and fine. Just as American black people are automatically associated with cities and all of their ills, Speech wants the old life, the old values, the old ways — back to the earth. To being "natural." As if that state — "naturalness" — is an option at this point in Western civilization.

The Catholic schoolgirl, the smart hip hop girl — she is ever anxious for peace for her people and her own state of mind. She wildly reaches for this "oldness," this better way of being. But even as a mind-set, while she stands on the streets of New York or West Los Angeles or Fresno or Kettleman or Napa, California — it doesn't work. Images of wooden porches and backyard cornstalks, or roosters pecking and kente cloth flowing, the brightly painted pictures in her desperate imagination fade like a mirage in an old cartoon: quickly and completely in its place are frowns and guns, televisions and straightened hair, housing projects and stucco single-family homes. Fast cars and loud music. Hip hop MC Breed and Too Short. Onyx and Ice Cube.

Still she looks for hip hop's heart in New York City, believing she can find it, thinking naively that if she sees it, she could define it and the definition would make a difference in all that she sees, in all that her mind conjures and remembers. So she presses on.

Exploring the Text

1. Although "Dreaming America" is unconventional in style, Danyel Smith uses some traditional rhetorical strategies. How does she appeal to logos, pathos, and ethos?

2. How does Smith use "Ms. Hip Hop, generic girl fan" (para. 4), to comment on music, the meaning of *urban*, and the differences between New York and California?

3. How would you characterize the audience for whom Smith is writing? What assumptions does she make about their interests and knowledge?

4. Find examples of figurative language. What is their effect on the tone of the essay? How does the figurative language help develop the character of both the narrator and Ms. Hip Hop?

5. How does Smith extend the analogies between city and country life, Eastern and Western cities, and past and present to include hip-hop music?

6. Characterize the way Smith refers to both hip-hop and other musicians. What is the purpose of the references? How do they provide credibility?

7. What is Smith's argument? How does she use examples to support her unstated thesis?

8. What does "New York beckons . . . like an old buddy with gossip" mean (para. 7)? Create a simile that describes the place you live.

9. Smith says, "[T]he Guru *squoze* hip hop out of Bird's horn" (para. 3). She is referring to the rap group Gang Starr's sampling of the music of Charlie "Bird" Parker, jazz saxophonist and inventor of bebop. Listen to Parker's music. How are bebop and hip-hop similar?

From *Show and Tell* (graphic essay)

SCOTT MCCLOUD

Scott McCloud (b. 1960) decided to become a comics artist when he was in tenth grade. After graduating from Syracuse University with a degree in illustration, McCloud worked in the production department of DC Comics until he began publishing his own comic series, "Zot!" and "Destroy!!" McCloud is the author of *Understanding Comics: The Invisible Art* (1993) and *Reinventing Comics* (2000). In *Understanding Comics*, from which the following excerpts are taken, a caricature of McCloud guides the reader through a study of what he calls sequential art by tracing the relationship between words and images.

Exploring the Text

1. Scott McCloud begins with a series of sixteen panels of a boy demonstrating how his toy robot turns into an airplane. Six of the panels have no words, yet the vignette manages to establish both pathos and ethos. How does McCloud accomplish this? Consider the drawings and the words separately, and then consider them together.

2. Why does McCloud use the show-and-tell vignette to open the piece? How does it support the piece's main idea?

3. On page 741, McCloud defines comics (although he says it isn't *his* definition) as "words and pictures in combination." He suggests that this is essentially show-and-tell. Trace how he uses classification to expand and refine his definition. How does he provide examples for each of his categories?

4. On page 745, McCloud uses dance as a metaphor to explain the possibilities in the relationship between words and images. Do you consider the words or the illustrations more powerful in illustrating that relationship? Can either stand alone?

5. What audience is McCloud addressing? In what ways does he acknowledge that audience? How does he establish ethos?

6. McCloud uses comic-book conventions such as exaggerated facial expressions to show emotion and a character walking left to right to create a sense of slowness and difficulty. Find other examples of these conventions, and compare them to the conventions of language he employs.

7. Charles McGrath, an editor of the *New York Times Book Review*, wrote in a 2004 essay "Not Funnies," that comic books are "what novels used to be — an accessible, vernacular form with mass appeal." He says that if the "highbrows" are right, they are a "form perfectly suited to our dumbed-down culture and collective attention deficit." How might Scott McCloud respond to McGrath and the "highbrows"? How does McCloud address the gap between high and low culture?

8. How would you describe the tone of "Show and Tell" (p. 738)? How does McCloud create it? Are the words or images more instrumental in creating the tone? Are there places where the words and images create different tones?

139

140

153

154

155

WHEN A SCENE SHOWS YOU ALL YOU *"NEED"* TO KNOW, LIKE *THIS* ONE, THE LATITUDE FOR **SCRIPTING** GROWS *ENORMOUSLY.*

I MAY BE ALONE LIKE THIS FOR A VERY LONG TIME.

IT COULD BECOME AN *INTERNAL MONOLOGUE.*

(INTERDEPENDENT)

PERHAPS SOMETHING WILDLY *INCONGRUOUS*

"MISSION CONTROL, MISSION CONTROL, DO YOU READ ME?"

(PARALLEL)

MAYBE IT'S ALL JUST A BIG *ADVERTISEMENT!*

YOU'LL *Love* THE TASTE!

(INTERDEPENDENT)

OR A CHANCE TO RUMINATE ON *BROADER TOPICS.*

THIS IS THE WAY THE WORLD ENDS...

THIS IS THE WAY THE WORLD ENDS...

(INTERDEPENDENT)

161

Popular Culture in the Aftermath of Sept. 11 Is a Chorus without a Hook, a Movie without an Ending

Teresa Wiltz

Teresa Wiltz is a staff writer for the *Washington Post*. This essay appeared in the *Washington Post* on November 19, 2001.

In the first few weeks following that day, once we'd stopped reeling from the initial shock, there was a collective throat-clearing, and then came tumbling forth the pronouncements: Vanity has taken a hit. Irony, so beloved by smarty-pants, was on life support. Comedy would be careful.

Such declarations are the punditocracy equivalent of calling the Super Bowl — three seasons in advance.

Popular culture, that which shapes how we see ourselves and how others see us, is in a state of flux. A change is gonna come. Or will it?

It is true, of course, that a certain earnestness has crept into the national zeitgeist,[1] blotting out — for now, at least — our normal, unique brand of optimistic cynicism. In her latest video, blue-eyed soul singer Pink urges us all to "Get This Party Started" as she dances against the backdrop of a giant flag. Celebs attending the Emmy Awards earlier this month were asked to tone down the sartorial glitz. And just a week ago Sunday, in a much-publicized gathering, movie execs met with White House officials — again — to suss out just what Hollywood could do for the war-on-terrorism effort.

But amid the earnestness, there is contradiction. A couple of weeks ago, the 5 No. 1 CD in the nation was a "God Bless America" compilation. New Agey popster Enya's feel-good CD, "A Day without Rain," ranked No. 2. The following week, both CDs were nudged out by gansta rapper DMX's downtrodden CD "The Great Depression." And last week Michael Jackson's latest CD, "Invincible," reigned, followed by Enrique Iglesias's "Escape" — that is until midweek, when Britney Spears wiggled her way to the top of the charts.

---

[1]German, "spirit of the time."

So what does it say that we go from blessing America to wallowing in the great depression to feeling invincible but desperately in need of escape?

That we're fickle, sure. But more importantly: Even a national tragedy of cataclysmic proportions can alter our cultural DNA by only so much. Popular culture is, as one observer put it, a daily Rorschach test, a peek into the American id as it flips and flops about. It's also a business, a huge one, arguably our biggest international export. And as with any business, it is the consumer who has the ultimate say.

Says Robert Thompson, professor of media and culture at Syracuse University and past president of the International Popular Culture Association: "We may be surprised at how capable American popular culture is of dissolving even the most horrible of historical events."

And now, in the wake of an unprecedented home front attack, peddlers of pop are grappling for ways to appear relevant. To strike just the right notes: empathetic yet resolved; patriotic but not profiteering.

If they've found the answers, they're not telling. Entertainers and execs con- 10 tacted by *The Washington Post* were, for the most part, zipping lips. When asked about how their work would be affected by Sept. 11, most of them, from Steven Spielberg to Dr. Dre, decided to pass on the question. Some pleaded busy schedules; others, like Conan O'Brien, frankly admitted that they weren't stepping anywhere near that date.

Then there's Jack Valenti, chairman of the Motion Picture Association of America, who's more than happy to offer up his take on the future of popular culture. Which is to say, he doesn't see it changing much: As long as there's a great story to tell, he doesn't see a problem if somewhere along the way a building or two is blown up. Forget about forecasting trends in entertainment. The public's desire to be entertained is a constant.

Valenti does see, however, among the American public a strong yearning for escape, a desire reflected by the impressive box office figures ($156.7 million) of Disney's *Monsters, Inc.*, an animated flick about facing one's worst fears.

"It's spiritually beautiful," says Valenti, fresh from his meeting with studio and White House officials. "That box office take is spiritually beautiful."

As Valenti sees it, box office takes will continue to be beautiful — and the opening weekend totals for *Harry Potter and the Sorcerer's Stone* (a record-setting $93.5 million) indicate likewise.

"In times of peril, in times of uncertainty, people don't want to be in a con- 15 stant state of perpetual anxiety," he says. "People want to enjoy storytelling, which for a couple of hours at least will transport them away."

Even so, storytellers, like the rest of us, are faced with how to interpret the recent life-changing turn of events.

"It's affected me personally," says mystery writer Walter Mosley, who recently published *Futureland*, a "pre-apocalyptic" collection of sci-fi stories with echoes of Sept. 11.

"It happened right outside my window; I watched it happen. I don't even yet know what that means. On the other hand, my work has kind of gone on the way it has before.

"I don't know what will happen next," he says. "But what's happened so far, as terrible as it is, is not enough to change the nature of the course of the nation. . . . Our concept of how the world works hasn't really been altered as of yet. We're still thinking people should be going out spending money and making capitalism function. There's a great desire, among the people and among our leaders, that life go back to normal. Whatever that is."

Indeed, "normal" is a murky concept for a nation with the attention span of a   20
gnat, where race, class and religion often form a combustible mix, where box office numbers are "spiritual" and Madison Avenue pledges to "keep America rolling." With zero-percent financing, of course.

Comfort in Continuity

Great, sweeping cultural changes happen in waves, one incremental change lapping over another microscopic blip, gradually building in intensity. It's only afterward that we look back and realize that we've been hit by a tsunami. After all, the '60s — or what we like to think of as happening in the '60s — didn't occur all at once: First there was the civil rights movement, then the assassinations, Vietnam and eventually Watergate. Somewhere in all that came the pill, women's lib and a revolution in pop music. By the time the '60s were in full force, it was, well, 1975.

"September 11 is what I'd call a 'second order change,'" says futurist and psychological anthropologist Doug Raybeck, who describes the gradual changes of the '60s as "first order changes." "It took us to a place we'd never been before. We've lost our innocence, lost our invulnerability, and we're in the process of losing our naivete."

So, what happens to a culture when irrevocable change happens in an instant?

Most of what we've seen post–Sept. 11 is quick and reactive.

Television was first to weigh in and, for the most part, came off looking   25
heavy-handed: NBC's *Third Watch* cobbled together a two-part episode about the World Trade Center attacks; *West Wing* creator Aaron Sorkin whipped out a quick treatise on terrorism.

Pop singers and rappers, from U2's Bono to Alicia Keys to Ja Rule, crammed into the studio to produce a remake of Marvin Gaye's "What's Going On." (Proceeds originally were planned to benefit AIDS patients, but the WTC and Pentagon survivors and relatives were quickly added to the list of beneficiaries.) Movie studios pushed back the release dates or postponed the production of a few films deemed too violent or involving acts of terrorism.

But many folks found comfort in continuity, the succor found in cultural chicken soup. The sitcom *Friends* has been extended for another season in the wake of its overwhelming popularity since the attacks. And those predictions that violent films would be offensive were wiped out by the success of movies like *13 Ghosts, From Hell, Training Day* and *The Heist,* all of which feature no small amount of bloodshed.

Perhaps it's the American way, to channel anger and grief through a weird mix of violence and humor.

Soon came the e-mails passed from office cubicle to office cubicle, jokes about Miss Cleo predicting that Osama bin Laden would die on a national holiday ("Any day you die gwan be an American holiday") and the animated mini-flick depicting a cartoon bin Laden being sexually assaulted by the Gimp from "Pulp Fiction."

There are also dozens of interactive games on the Internet, like the graphic 30 "Nuke Bin Laden," where you can use a revolver, baseball bat, nuclear bomb or box cutter to pulverize "the evil one." Or the pictures of bin Laden posing with his "family" — a trio of pigs.

But in the corporate arena of the nation's networks, Sept. 11–related humor seemed almost verboten at first. Late-night hosts David Letterman and Jay Leno stayed off the air the first week after the attacks. Now Taliban jokes are a steady part of their patter — including dancing bin Ladens, much like the dancing Judge Itos from O. J. Simpson days. *Saturday Night Live* took a pointed jab at the government's handling of D.C.'s anthrax cases: In a mock news conference, Chris Kattan, playing the National Institutes of Health's Anthony Fauci, proclaimed, "We cleaned the State Department, the White House, the Supreme Court and the Capitol building with state-of-the-art decontamination equipment . . ." As for decontaminating post offices, "Fauci" says, "We've given each post office some baby wipes and a DustBuster."

So far, smart-aleck humor prevails, as on the "America's Mad as Hell Humor Page," which offers to provide "humor in a time of grief."

But there are few voices like the darkly sardonic Internet comic strip "Get Your War On," where cynics ponder which is worse, bin Laden as president or anthrax, and depressives wonder, "Maybe I should write a poem about my feelings since September 11; that might help! What rhymes with alcohol-saturated dread?"

Lockdown and Lock Step?

"How can we have popular culture if everyone is afraid to say anything but 'God Bless America'?" observes Kevin Jones, a former studio executive who produced the Gwyneth Paltrow film *Duets.*

Still, not everyone is singing that tune. 35

One recent Saturday night at the Birchmere, the mood was mellow, even somber. Buppies and bohos sat clustered at tables, ordering fried chicken nuggets and sipping on Coronas. Onstage, D.C. native Meshell Ndegeocello, an alternasoul singer-musician, served up humor, pathos, politics and a thumping bass line with scathing anti-war commentary.

"Express yourself," Ndegeocello said. "Soon we won't be able to. We'll all be on lockdown."

She pulled out a picture, her newly acquired "Bling-Bling Jesus," a glittery picture of Christ that she bought in sardonic obedience to what she sees as President Bush's entreaties: "God Bless America. Keep shopping; we are open for business."

For Ndegeocello, patriotism is a complicated affair. There is the pressure she believes artists feel to make another "We Are the World" record, to spend their own cash in expensive studio time and then forward the proceeds to charity.

"It's hard to love where you come from when the truth is buried so deep," she said "You can be gung-ho patriotic. . . . But understand, people are struggling every day.   40

"I pray for Brother Bush, I really do. When he says Osama bin Laden wasn't elected. Well [expletive], neither were you."

Her words were met with laughter — and a standing ovation.

Ndegeocello's work is outside the mainstream; dissent is a part of her oeuvre. But others who make a living fighting the powers that be have been strangely silent. Rage Against the Machine declined to be interviewed for this article, as did rapper Mos Def and alternative folkie Ani DiFranco.

"In the public eye at this point, you better show some sort of sympathy or love for America or it will be construed wrong," says hip-hop journalist and Bay Area radio personality Dave "Davey D" Cook. "For artists, every gesture is scrutinized. The messages, whether intentional or not, have been delivered hard and fast to people. Line up, get in lock step and God help you if you aren't.

"I see a few songs that are on the whole 'Wave the flag, I love America' tip," Cook says. "The big question is: Is this the record company trying to capitalize on people's emotions? Or are the artists really feeling that way? Time will tell."   45

There is an intolerance of those who do speak up, and an attempt to control the images we see: *Politically Incorrect*'s Bill Maher was criticized for following up on neoconservative Dinesh D'Souza's assertion that the terrorists behind the Sept. 11 attacks were not cowards. Maher had added: "We have been the cowards, lobbing cruise missiles from 2,000 miles away." (Maher declined to be interviewed for this article.)

Then there's "Boondocks" comic strip creator Aaron McGruder, who found his work pulled from the *New York Daily News* and *Long Island Newsday* after his strip questioned the CIA's role in funding the Taliban.

And radio giant Clear Channel suggested, in the days after Sept. 11, that its 1,170 stations refrain from playing a list of potentially offensive songs, among them John Lennon's "Imagine" and the entire catalogue of Rage Against the Machine. Then there's Davey D, who for years hosted a public affairs show on KMEL-FM, own by Clear Channel in San Francisco, until being fired soon after the attacks. The station manager said that Cook was let go because of "extreme financial pressure" and that nine others were also fired. Cook's supporters, in an e-mail campaign, see no coincidence in the fact that his show was canceled after he interviewed Rep. Barbara Lee (D.-Calif.), the only member of Congress to vote against authorizing the use of force against anyone associated with the terrorist attacks.

"When you have a national project, which any war is, that tends not to be the healthiest environment for a huge, diverse conversation of varying ideas," says Syracuse's Thompson. "The diversity of voices is going to recede a bit."

Hollywood, Reporting for Duty

One impulse has definitely been at work since Sept. 11: The urge to compare this war to previous ones, to put things into some sort of context by claiming, for example, that the attacks were this generation's Pearl Harbor.   50

Comparisons are at once instructive and useless. There is an ocean of difference between where we were then and where we are now. In World War II, the enemy was clearly defined, not some amorphous concept.

The day after the Japanese attacked Pearl Harbor, Franklin Delano Roosevelt told Congress, in passionate tones, "We will not only defend ourselves to the utmost, but will make very certain that this form of treachery shall never endanger us again."

Then, radio was the primary means of communication; in many ways, programming quickly returned to normal after the attacks. (The development of television, which had begun in the '30s, was postponed by the war. The technology was seen as too expensive in times of sacrifice.)

"One can listen to the radio programs of mid-December 1941 and often be unaware that the nation had just entered a world war," says Thompson.

Hollywood, on the other hand, jumped on the war effort, working with the   55 government to produce propaganda films as a part of a campaign to thwart Nazi influence in South America, according to Toby Miller, professor of cultural studies at New York University. Orson Welles, working with Carmen Miranda, directed *It's All True*, an anti-racism film distributed in Brazil. Walt Disney, a reported anti-Semite who was struggling to resuscitate his failing company, created *Saludos Amigos* and *The Three Caballeros*, cartoons featuring Donald Duck. (The government reportedly paid for part of Disney's production costs and distributed the films for free.)

Disney's collaboration with the government didn't end there: The company produced military training films, and Army troops actually moved into the studios for eight months, camping on the floors and setting up their own mess kitchen on the premises. (Immediately after Sept. 11, Disney postponed the release of *Big Trouble* and *Bad Company* because of the films' violent content.)

During World War II, in many instances, there was no attempt to be racially sensitive: In "Tokio Jokio," the wily Bugs Bunny triumphed over dimwitted, buck-toothed, nearsighted Japanese soldiers; in "Scrap the Japs," Popeye declared, "I've never met a Jap that wasn't yellow."

"To convince a population to go out and shoot people, you had to make [the enemy] other than human," Thompson says.

After the war, B movies in which the Soviet Union was cast as the evil one started to proliferate. The '60s brought glamorous spies to both the big and little screens, from James Bond to the Avengers and the man from U.N.C.L.E. Never mind that the nation was exploding with its own internal war over Vietnam.

Music, of course, was a different matter. The cultural revolution was fought   60
through songs like Bob Dylan's "The Times They Are a-Changin'," and Edwin Starr's admonitions of "War! What is it good for? Absolutely nothing!" Redemption, the counterculture proposed, could be found through sex, drugs, avoiding the draft — and of course, rock-and-roll.

But with the president called "Tricky Dick" by detractors, the Pentagon Papers and Watergate burglars, a new cynicism started creeping into the country's consciousness.

"The idea of a strong U.S. . . . was really rocked by the revealing of the Pentagon Papers and the Watergate revelations," says New York University's Miller. TV shows like *M*A*S*H*, sly and subversive — not to mention funny as hell — rejected the gung-ho values of a previous generation. *M*A*S*H* obliquely criticized government; with its wink-wink approach, just who was being criticized was in the eyes and ears of the beholder.

It wasn't until the late '70s and early '80s that we were ready to deal with films about Vietnam — *The Deer Hunter, Apocalypse Now, Coming Home.*

It's not likely that we will return to the days following 1941, when Frank Capra made a series of films dubbed "Why We Fight." Sixty years later, Hollywood execs emerge from the meeting with the White House's Karl Rove and announce that they want to help in any way possible. But it's not producing propaganda.

Wait and See

Most likely, it will be years before our culture is ready to deconstruct the events of   65
September.

It is anyone's guess what will be. The war changes daily, events seemingly tumbling over one another. For now, with no new outbreaks of anthrax infections and last week's advances in Afghanistan, we are sleeping a little easier. For now.

"Trying to predict the endgame right now is the biggest mistake you can make," says Scott Donaton, editor of *Advertising Age.* "In New York, for a couple of days you could cross the street across the traffic and no one beeped. But life gets back to normal more quickly than you think. We can't boil it down to earnest patriotism. That's not what we are."

TV talk show host Ananda Lewis says she already sees signs that some people are tiring of it all. She was surprised, she says, when television stations outside

New York and Washington told her they weren't interested in more shows about Sept. 11.

"I really think everybody would be about the healing process right now," says Lewis. "That seems to be true of only the areas that were affected. Which is sad, because it trivializes something to just a news event."

It won't be just a news event if things get worse. Or another plane falls from the sky — and this time it's not an accident. Or smallpox hits Tulsa. Then perhaps you'll see a society in which no one wants to leave home and people find release instead through virtual ski trips: A specially rigged treadmill and some goggles and you're there, on the Alps. It could happen.

Or maybe last week's advances in Afghanistan will take a turn and tens of thousands of young men and women will die in a protracted ground war. Maybe we'll see civil liberties erode in the name of fighting the evildoers, until our rights are nothing more than a wistful thought. And then, perhaps, we'll see a new brand of protest music on MTV and BET.

"Remember 'Hell no, we won't go'?" asks hip-hop impresario Russell Simmons, whose latest endeavor, *Def Poetry Jam*, was picked up by HBO in the days after Sept. 11. "I'm hopeful that young people will have something to contribute. Three rappers are more important than three heads of states talking."

Maybe right now there's an aspiring rapper with a turntable in his bedroom trying to work through his fears. Or maybe next month, three geeks in a storefront will get the corporate backing for their video game "Crush al Qaeda." Or maybe in 10 years some eager director will be maxing out her credit cards to make an indie flick.

We're shape-shifting.

It's anyone's guess what that final shape will look like.

Just like staking it all on the Redskins three years down the road in Super Bowl XXXIX, there are no sure bets.

Exploring the Text

1. In the second paragraph of Teresa Wiltz's essay, she compares predicting the effects of September 11 on pop culture with calling the Super Bowl three years in advance, yet she and the people she interviews make predictions anyway. How does she maintain her credibility and the credibility of her sources?

2. In what different ways does Wiltz define popular culture?

3. The tone of the essay shifts several times. Find the transition points, and consider why Wiltz might have shifted the tone at each spot.

4. Wiltz cites several experts on the subject of popular culture. What does each offer? She also mentions people who declined to be interviewed for the essay. What is the effect of including their names, even without their statements?

5. In the section "Comfort in Continuity," Wiltz quotes futurist and psychological anthropologist Doug Raybeck, who classifies change in two categories: first-order

change, such as the gradual changes of the sixties, and second-order change, such as the change that happens nearly overnight. How does Wiltz connect Raybeck's ideas to the changes predicted for popular culture? In retrospect, is her analysis correct?

6. Wiltz begins the section "Lockdown and Lock Step?" with a rhetorical question from a former studio executive (para. 34). How does Wiltz answer the question?

7. Wiltz compares the effects of September 11 on popular culture with the effects of the attack on Pearl Harbor on popular culture. What are the similarities? the differences?

8. The last section of the essay is called "Wait and See." In what ways is Wiltz prescient about the change — or lack of change — in popular culture since September 11, 2001?

Emily Dickinson and Elvis Presley in Heaven (poetry)

HANS OSTROM

Hans Ostrom (b. 1954) grew up in Sierra City, California. His grandfather, a Swedish immigrant, worked in gold mines in the Sierra Nevada mountain range. Ostrom, Distinguished Professor of English at the University of Puget Sound, teaches composition, creative writing, rhetoric, and literature and is codirector of African American studies. He is the author of *A Langston Hughes Encyclopedia* (2001) and *Langston Hughes: A Study of the Short Fiction* (1993). His articles, poems, and short stories have appeared in a variety of magazines and journals. He is also the author of the novel *Three to Get Ready* (1991) and two poetry collections, *Subjects Apprehended* (2000) and *The Coast Starlight: Collected Poems, 1976–2006* (2006).

They call each other E. Elvis picks
wildflowers near the river and brings
them to Emily. She explains half-rhymes to him.

In heaven Emily wears her hair long, sports
Levis and western blouses with rhinestones.　　　　　5
Elvis is lean again, wears baggy trousers

and T-shirts, a letterman's jacket from Tupelo High.
They take long walks and often hold hands.
She prefers they remain just friends. Forever.

Emily's poems now contain naugahyde, Cadillacs,　　　10
Electricity, jets, TV, Little Richard and Richard
Nixon. The rock-a-billy rhythm makes her smile.

Elvis likes himself with style. This afternoon
he will play guitar and sing "I Taste a Liquor
Never Brewed" to the tune of "Love Me Tender."   *15*

Emily will clap and harmonize. Alone
in their cabins later, they'll listen to the river
and nap. They will not think of Amherst

or Las Vegas. They know why God made them
roommates. It's because America   *20*
was their hometown. It's because

God is a thing
without feathers. It's because
God wears blue suede shoes.

··

Exploring the Text

1. What does Hans Ostrom's pairing of Elvis Presley and Emily Dickinson suggest about the poem's idea of heaven?
2. The poem depends somewhat on the reader's familiarity with the works of Dickinson and Presley. Look up the references you don't recognize — such as Dickinson's poems "I taste a liquor never brewed" and "Hope is that thing with feathers," Presley's song "Love Me Tender," Little Richard, Amherst, and naugahyde. Then reconsider Ostrom's poem with all the blanks filled in.
3. What is the intention and effect of the period after "friends" in line 9?
4. In nearly every stanza, Ostrom uses enjambment — when one line ends without a pause and continues into the next line for its meaning. What is the effect?
5. In the last two stanzas, Ostrom says God made Presley and Dickinson roommates for three reasons. What do these reasons suggest about the importance of pop culture in America?

Sanctuary: For Harry Potter the Movie

NIKKI GIOVANNI

Nikki Giovanni (b. 1943) grew up in Cincinnati, Ohio, but in summers returned to her birthplace in Knoxville, Tennessee, to visit her grandparents. She graduated from Fisk University with honors in history and went on to graduate school at the University of Pennsylvania. Since 1987, she has been a professor of writing and literature at Virginia Polytechnic Institute and State University. Giovanni has written volumes of poetry, illustrated children's books, and three collections of essays, including *Sacred Cows . . . and Other Edibles* (1988). Among Giovanni's many awards and honors are three NAACP Image Awards. The following "not quite poem" comes from *Quilting the Black-Eyed Pea: Poems and Not Quite Poems* (2002).

The movie should have started with drums. Small drums maybe bongos then trap drums then the full complement of jazz drums. Silhouetted figures straddling drums. Male figures riding really big deep drums. Hands flying. Sweat flicking through the air. A spiral of light with a certain . . . well . . . heaviness implied.   5
Followed by a Quiet. Then the Savannah. A community of elephants. The camera moving in on the baby trailing just slightly behind its mother. The bull elephant turns his head upward testing the air. Something is awry. The bull elephant drops behind the community. He wants to bring up the rear. He   10
seems to know something. The bull elephant suddenly charges into the bush and we hear the 40 OD six go off. The bull elephant continues toward the bush and we hear over and above the drumming the report of gunfire. The elephants turn to gather round the fallen bull. The elephants try to keep him on his feet   15
but the bull elephant is mortally wounded. The alpha female takes up the charge while the other females surround the baby. The alpha female is repeatedly shot. the shots are in rhythm with the drumming. The juvenile elephants take up the fight while the females try to get the baby elephant away. A barrage of   20
gunfire . . . rhythmic . . . sweaty . . . heavy . . . insistent . . . intrudes. Dust is swirling. Then silence. A wearisome silence. The settling dust can almost be heard. Then the buzzing of flies. A dark cloud of hundreds no thousands of flies heads toward us. The camera however does not move. As the dust settles and just before the   25
flies land we see, surrounded by the carnage, still standing . . . standing still . . . the baby elephant. The object of this search. He is looking at all the death and destruction. He is trying to decide: Should I live? Do I want to live with these memories? He sees the men coming toward him with nets and chains. He has to decide: 30
Will I live? Do I want to live . . . like this . . . with these people who have destroyed everything I cherish? Then we see a flicker of light. A promise perhaps. Surely a sign of hope. Live and tell the story. Live and sing the song of your people.

"Live! and have your blooming in the noise of the whirlwind."   35
— GWENDOLYN BROOKS, *In the Mecca*

Harry Potter was just a boy who lived. Like all of us. On the forced marches to uninhabitable reservations. Through the smallpox-infested blankets. From the stench and starvation of middle passage. From the auction blocks where the unimagin- 40
able took place. From the ghettos of Europe and in the inner cities of America. From the enforced hopelessness that only a song . . . that only an imagined grandmother's hum . . . only a dream of a better day could assuage . . . A bright star . . . like a real fat shooting star comes from the back of the screen. 45
We see a bungalow that is near destruction. We hear the questioning voices of people running to the scene. A giant swoops down from the sky on a motorcycle. He hits the kickstand down runs into the house and emerges with something bundled in a blanket. He jumps back on the cycle and heads into the 50
sky. As the light from the cycle shoots out we follow it to the farthermost point where it turns into a streetlight dimming out. Two distinguished figures are peering into the sky . . . waiting . . . hoping . . . sending comforting looks to each other. Then *voilà*! The cycle comes down. A giant steps off with the bun- 55
dle. The waiting man and woman discuss the wisdom of the baby being left with these people. "They are all the family Harry's got. Harry needs time, even in this sterile environment, to understand what has happened and how famous he is. He needs time to prepare himself," says the waiting man. "And you think," challenges 60
the woman, "*these people* can provide the help?" The man looks at her gently: "They are all he has. We must try to do the right thing." In the background we hear a song coming up "boop boop a boom you went to school to learn girl what you never never knew before . . . *i* before *e* except after *c* and how 65
2 plus 2 are four . . ."

We now cut to a man and a woman sitting in a café. There are two glasses of wine, the man drinking a red and the woman having a not too expensive champagne. It is late afternoon. The sun is setting wide and very red. The man, a young man in about his 70
midthirties, is saying to the woman, "You know this sky reminds me of something I can't remember." "That's silly," she says. "How can you remember nothing?" "No. Well, yes. Oh well. There was a giant once named Hagrid. Hagrid was a friend of my mother and father's. He loved me. And I, he. He saved me from 75
evil by telling me who I am. And where I came from." The background music is from the *New World* Symphony. The man looks deep into the eyes of the woman. It is obvious he cares for her

very much. "You never asked me about my scar," he says. She looks into her champagne glass then at the ring on her finger 80 then up at him. "I know an evil thing struck you and left a mark I know that. But, no, I haven't asked, Harry, because I know when you know I love you no matter what, you will share your thoughts about it with me." "Well, it was my mother, you know. It was my mother's love that protected me from harm. It was the love my 85 mother threw over me when the evil came that kept evil from being able to touch me. After the bloodshed and the bloodletting I know that some of my blood is in evil and some evil is in my blood. But I am neither the white man you think I am nor the Black man I hope to be. I'm just the boy who lived and in living 90 I have to find my way." He called for the check and paid. They stood. "Want to go to Aruba? We can walk the beach and talk . . ." "Oh, Harry, it takes all day to get to Aruba . . ." "Not when you're with a magical guy . . ." And off they go talking about Hagrid and Hogwarts and Dumbledore and McGonagall and Ron and 95 Hermione and Mountain Trolls and the Mirror of Erised and Quidditch and baby elephants and manatees and the vanishing Savannah and . . .

Exploring the Text

1. How does the text use a different film genre to comment on the Harry Potter story and movie?

2. What is Nikki Giovanni's purpose in opening with the scene of drums and elephants?

3. What is the effect of the line from the Gwendolyn Brooks poem that Giovanni uses to make the transition to Harry Potter (l. 35)?

4. What does Giovanni mean when she writes, "Harry Potter was just a boy who lived"? Is she criticizing the Harry Potter novels? Praising them?

5. How would you characterize the genre of Giovanni's text? Is it a prose poem? An essay? A stream-of-consciousness commentary? Why do you think she chose this form?

6. How does Giovanni's interpretation of the Harry Potter movie jibe with yours? What other ways can readers and viewers interpret the Harry Potter movies and novels?

7. What is suggested by the title of the "not quite poem"? Consider the different meanings of the word *sanctuary*.

The Innocent Eye Test (painting)

MARK TANSEY

A well-known New York City artist, Mark Tansey was born in California in 1949, the son of two art historians. His work has been described as surrealistic and post-modern; his subject matter is often ironic. He uses photographic images from popular culture, academia, and art history, relocating and recombining them in order to comment on humanity. *The Innocent Eye Test* (1981), a painting that hangs in New York's Metropolitan Museum of Art, comments on the relationship between the artist and the viewer, an important concern of Tansey's. The image shows a cow examining *Young Bull*, a 1647 oil painting by Paulus Potter that hangs in the Mauritshuis in The Hague. In the background is one of Monet's *Haystack* paintings from the early 1890s.

Exploring the Text

1. Who or what is being tested in *Innocent Eye Test*? What does the painting say about art criticism? How do the details complicate the answer to who is testing whom?
2. Identify and analyze the visual and historical information in this painting.
3. Visual art can be analyzed through the rhetorical triangle (see Chapter 1). Consider the painting, the artist, and the audience separately, and then analyze the relationships among these three elements.

4. A hallmark of postmodern art is the appropriation — quoting or borrowing — of other art. What has Mark Tansey borrowed in this painting? What is the relationship between the old and the new? How does the appropriation create a conversation between the artist and the viewer? the past and the present?
5. American novelist William S. Burroughs (1914–1997) is credited with noting that there is no such thing as an innocent bystander. Does Tansey's painting make the same point, or does it refute it?

Focus on Television

The following five documents comment directly or indirectly on the effects of television.

Sources
1. **Steven Johnson,** *Watching TV Makes You Smarter*
2. **Corbett Trubey,** *The Argument against TV*
3. **Julia Scott,** *He Doesn't Like to Watch*
4. **Anthony DiVivo,** *TV Turnoff Week* (detail from a poster)
5. **George Gerbner and Todd Gitlin,** *Is Media Violence Free Speech?*

After you have read, studied, and synthesized these pieces, enter the conversation by responding to one of the prompts on page 787.

1. *Watching TV Makes You Smarter*

STEVEN JOHNSON

The following excerpt from *Everything Bad Is Good for You* appeared in the *New York Times Magazine* in 2005.

The Sleeper Curve

SCIENTIST A: Has he asked for anything special?
SCIENTIST B: Yes, this morning for breakfast . . . he requested something called "wheat germ, organic honey and tiger's milk."
SCIENTIST A: Oh, yes. Those were the charmed substances that some years ago were felt to contain life-preserving properties.
SCIENTIST B: You mean there was no deep fat? No steak or cream pies or . . . hot fudge?
SCIENTIST A: Those were thought to be unhealthy.
— from Woody Allen's *Sleeper*

On Jan. 24, the Fox network showed an episode of its hit drama *24*, the real-time thriller known for its cliffhanger tension and often-gruesome violence. Over the preceding weeks, a number of public controversies had erupted around *24*, mostly focused on its portrait of Muslim terrorists and its penchant for torture scenes. The episode that was shown on the 24th only fanned the flames higher: in one scene, a terrorist enlists a hit man to kill his child for not fully supporting the jihadist cause; in another scene, the secretary of defense authorizes the torture of his son to uncover evidence of a terrorist plot.

But the explicit violence and the post-911 terrorist anxiety are not the only elements of *24* that would have been unthinkable on prime-time network television 20 years ago. Alongside the notable change in content lies an equally notable change in form. During its 44 minutes — a real-time hour, minus 16 minutes for commercials — the episode connects the lives of 21 distinct characters, each with a clearly defined "story arc," as the Hollywood jargon has it: a defined personality with motivations and obstacles and specific relationships with other characters. Nine primary narrative threads wind their way through those 44 minutes, each drawing extensively upon events and information revealed in earlier episodes. Draw a map of all those intersecting plots and personalities, and you get structure that — where formal complexity is concerned — more closely resembles *Middlemarch* than a hit TV drama of years past like *Bonanza*.

For decades, we've worked under the assumption that mass culture follows a path declining steadily toward lowest-common-denominator standards, presumably because the "masses" want dumb, simple pleasures and big media companies try to give the masses what they want. But as that *24* episode suggests, the exact opposite is happening: the culture is getting more cognitively demanding, not less. To make sense of an episode of *24*, you have to integrate far more information than you would have a few decades ago watching a comparable show. Beneath the violence and the ethnic stereotypes, another trend appears: to keep up with entertainment like *24*, you have to pay attention, make inferences, track shifting social relationships. This is what I call the Sleeper Curve: the most debased forms of mass diversion — video games and violent television dramas and juvenile sitcoms — turn out to be nutritional after all.

I believe that the Sleeper Curve is the single most important new force alter- 5 ing the mental development of young people today, and I believe it is largely a force for good: enhancing our cognitive faculties, not dumbing them down. And yet you almost never hear this story in popular accounts of today's media. Instead, you hear dire tales of addiction, violence, mindless escapism. It's assumed that shows that promote smoking or gratuitous violence are bad for us, while those that thunder against teen pregnancy or intolerance have a positive role in society. Judged by that morality-play standard, the story of popular culture over the past 50 years — if not 500 — is a story of decline: the morals of the stories have grown darker and more ambiguous, and the antiheroes have multiplied.

The usual counterargument here is that what media have lost in moral clarity, they have gained in realism. The real world doesn't come in nicely packaged public-service announcements, and we're better off with entertainment like "The Sopranos" that reflects our fallen state with all its ethical ambiguity. I happen to be sympathetic to that argument, but it's not the one I want to make here. I think there is another way to assess the social virtue of pop culture, one that looks at media as a kind of cognitive workout, not as a series of life lessons. There may indeed be more "negative messages" in the mediasphere today. But that's not the only way to evaluate whether our television shows or video games are having a positive impact. Just as important — if not more important — is the kind of thinking you have to do to make sense of a cultural experience. That is where the Sleeper Curve becomes visible.

Televised Intelligence

Consider the cognitive demands that televised narratives place on their viewers. With many shows that we associate with "quality" entertainment — *The Mary Tyler Moore Show, Murphy Brown, Frasier* — the intelligence arrives fully formed in the words and actions of the characters on-screen. They say witty things to one another and avoid lapsing into tired sitcom clichés, and we smile along in our living rooms, enjoying the company of these smart people. But assuming we're bright enough to understand the sentences they're saying, there's no intellectual labor involved in enjoying the show as a viewer. You no more challenge your mind by watching these intelligent shows than you challenge your body watching *Monday Night Football.* The intellectual work is happening on-screen, not off.

But another kind of televised intelligence is on the rise. Think of the cognitive benefits conventionally ascribed to reading: attention, patience, retention, the parsing of narrative threads. Over the last half-century, programming on TV has increased the demands it places on precisely these mental faculties. This growing complexity involves three primary elements: multiple threading, flashing arrows and social networks.

According to television lore, the age of multiple threads began with the arrival in 1981 of *Hill Street Blues*, the Steven Bochco police drama invariably praised for its "gritty realism." Watch an episode of *Hill Street Blues* side by side with any major drama from the preceding decades — *Starsky and Hutch*, for instance, or *Dragnet* — and the structural transformation will jump out at you. The earlier shows follow one or two lead characters, adhere to a single dominant plot and reach a decisive conclusion at the end of the episode. Draw an outline of the narrative threads in almost every *Dragnet* episode, and it will be a single line: from the initial crime scene, through the investigation, to the eventual cracking of the case. A typical *Starsky and Hutch* episode offers only the slightest variation on this linear formula: the introduction of a comic subplot that usually appears only at the tail ends of the episode, creating a structure that looks like the graph below. The vertical axis represents the number of individual threads, and the horizontal axis is time.

DRAGNET (ANY EPISODE)

STARSKY AND HUTCH (ANY EPISODE)

A *Hill Street Blues* episode complicates the picture in a number of profound   10
ways. The narrative weaves together a collection of distinct strands — sometimes as many as 10, though at least half of the threads involve only a few quick
scenes scattered through the episode. The number of primary characters — and
not just bit parts — swells significantly. And the episode has fuzzy borders: picking up one or two threads from previous episodes at the outset and leaving one
or two threads open at the end. Charted graphically, an average episode looks
like this:

HILL STREET BLUES (EPISODE 85)

Critics generally cite *Hill Street Blues* as the beginning of "serious drama"
native in the television medium — differentiating the series from the single-
episode dramatic programs from the 50's, which were Broadway plays performed
in front of a camera. But the *Hill Street* innovations weren't all that original;
they'd long played a defining role in popular television, just not during the
evening hours. The structure of a *Hill Street* episode — and indeed of all the
critically acclaimed dramas that followed, from *thirtysomething* to *Six Feet
Under* — is the structure of a soap opera. *Hill Street Blues* might have sparked a
new golden age of television drama during its seven-year run, but it did so by
using a few crucial tricks that *Guiding Light* and *General Hospital* mastered long
before.

Bochco's genius with *Hill Street* was to marry complex narrative structure
with complex subject matter. *Dallas* had already shown that the extended, interwoven threads of the soap-opera genre could survive the weeklong interruptions
of a prime-time show, but the actual content of *Dallas* was fluff. (The most probing issue it addressed was the question, now folkloric, of who shot J.R.) *All in the
Family* and *Rhoda* showed that you could tackle complex social issues, but they
did their tackling in the comfort of the sitcom living room. *Hill Street* had richly
drawn characters confronting difficult social issues and a narrative structure to
match.

Since *Hill Street* appeared, the multi-threaded drama has become the most
widespread fictional genre on prime time: *St. Elsewhere, L.A. Law, thirtysomething, Twin Peaks, N.Y.P.D. Blue, E.R., The West Wing, Alias, Lost.* (The only
prominent holdouts in drama are shows like *Law and Order* that have essentially
updated the venerable *Dragnet* format and thus remained anchored to a single
narrative line.) Since the early 80's, however, there has been a noticeable increase

in narrative complexity in these dramas. The most ambitious show on TV to date, *The Sopranos*, routinely follows up to a dozen distinct threads over the course of an episode, with more than 20 recurring characters. An episode from late in the first season looks like this:

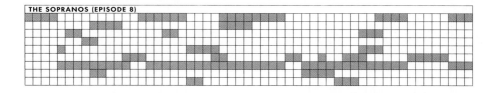

The total number of active threads equals the multiple plots of *Hill Street*, but here each thread is more substantial. The show doesn't offer a clear distinction between dominant and minor plots; each story line carries its weight in the mix. The episode also displays a chordal mode of storytelling entirely absent from *Hill Street*: a single scene in *The Sopranos* will often connect to three different threads at the same time, layering one plot atop another. And every single thread in this *Sopranos* episode builds on events from previous episodes and continues on through the rest of the season and beyond.

Put those charts together, and you have a portrait of the Sleeper Curve rising 15 over the past 30 years of popular television. In a sense, this is as much a map of cognitive changes in the popular mind as it is a map of on-screen developments, as if the media titans decided to condition our brains to follow ever-larger numbers of simultaneous threads. Before *Hill Street*, the conventional wisdom among television execs was that audiences wouldn't be comfortable following more than three plots in a single episode, and indeed, the *Hill Street* pilot, which was shown in January 1981, brought complaints from viewers that the show was too complicated. Fast-forward two decades, and shows like *The Sopranos* engage their audiences with narratives that make *Hill Street* look like *Three's Company*. Audiences happily embrace that complexity because they've been trained by two decades of multi-threaded dramas.

Multi-threading is the most celebrated structural feature of the modern television drama, and it certainly deserves some of the honor that has been doled out to it. And yet multi-threading is only part of the story.

The Case for Confusion

Shortly after the arrival of the first-generation slasher movies — *Halloween, Friday the 13th* — Paramount released a mock-slasher flick called *Student Bodies*, parodying the genre just as the *Scream* series would do 15 years later. In one scene, the obligatory nubile teenage baby sitter hears a noise outside a suburban house; she opens the door to investigate, finds nothing and then goes back inside. As the door shuts behind her, the camera swoops in on the doorknob, and we see that she has left the door unlocked. The camera pulls back and then swoops down again for emphasis. And then a flashing arrow appears on the screen, with text that helpfully explains: "Unlocked!"

That flashing arrow is parody, of course, but it's merely an exaggerated version of a device popular stories use all the time. When a sci-fi script inserts into some advanced lab a nonscientist who keeps asking the science geeks to explain what they're doing with that particle accelerator, that's a flashing arrow that gives the audience precisely the information it needs in order to make sense of the ensuing plot. ("Whatever you do, don't spill water on it, or you'll set off a massive explosion!") These hints serve as a kind of narrative hand-holding. Implicitly, they say to the audience, "We realize you have no idea what a particle accelerator is, but here's the deal: all you need to know is that it's a big fancy thing that explodes when wet." They focus the mind on relevant details: "Don't worry about whether the baby sitter is going to break up with her boyfriend. Worry about that guy lurking in the bushes." They reduce the amount of analytic work you need to do to make sense of a story. All you have to do is follow the arrows.

By this standard, popular television has never been harder to follow. If narrative threads have experienced a population explosion over the past 20 years, flashing arrows have grown correspondingly scarce. Watching our pinnacle of early 80's TV drama, *Hill Street Blues*, we find there's an informational wholeness to each scene that differs markedly from what you see on shows like *The West Wing* or *The Sopranos* or *Alias* or *E.R.*

Hill Street has ambiguities about future events: will a convicted killer be exe- 20 cuted? Will Furillo marry Joyce Davenport? Will Renko find it in himself to bust a favorite singer for cocaine possession? But the present-tense of each scene explains itself to the viewer with little ambiguity. There's an open question or a mystery driving each of these stories — how will it all turn out? — but there's no mystery about the immediate activity on the screen. A contemporary drama like *The West Wing*, on the other hand, constantly embeds mysteries into the present-tense events: you see characters performing actions or discussing events about which crucial information has been deliberately withheld. Anyone who has watched more than a handful of *The West Wing* episodes closely will know the feeling: scene after scene refers to some clearly crucial but unexplained piece of information, and after the sixth reference, you'll find yourself wishing you could rewind the tape to figure out what they're talking about, assuming you've missed something. And then you realize that you're supposed to be confused. The open question posed by these sequences is not "How will this turn out in the end?" The question is "What's happening right now?"

The deliberate lack of hand-holding extends down to the microlevel of dialogue as well. Popular entertainment that addresses technical issues — whether they are the intricacies of passing legislation, or of performing a heart bypass, or of operating a particle accelerator — conventionally switches between two modes of information in dialogue: texture and substance. Texture is all the arcane verbiage provided to convince the viewer that they're watching Actual Doctors at Work; substance is the material planted amid the background texture that the viewer needs to make sense of the plot.

Conventionally, narratives demarcate the line between texture and substance by inserting cues that flag or translate the important data. There's an unintentionally comical moment in the 2004 blockbuster *The Day After Tomorrow* in which the beleaguered climatologist (played by Dennis Quaid) announces his theory about the imminent arrival of a new ice age to a gathering of government officials. In his speech, he warns that "we have hit a critical desalinization point!" At this moment, the writer-director Roland Emmerich — a master of brazen arrow-flashing — has an official follow with the obliging remark: "It would explain what's driving this extreme weather." They might as well have had a flashing "Unlocked!" arrow on the screen.

The dialogue on shows like *The West Wing* and *E.R.*, on the other hand, doesn't talk down to its audiences. It rushes by, the words accelerating in sync with the high-speed tracking shots that glide through the corridors and operating rooms. The characters talk faster in these shows, but the truly remarkable thing about the dialogue is not purely a matter of speed; it's the willingness to immerse the audience in information that most viewers won't understand. Here's a typical scene from *E.R.*:

[WEAVER and WRIGHT push a gurney containing a 16-year-old girl. Her parents, Janna and Frank MIKAMI, follow close behind. CARTER and LUCY fall in.]

WEAVER: 16-year-old, unconscious, history of biliary atresia.

CARTER: Hepatic coma?

WEAVER: Looks like it.

MR. MIKAMI: She was doing fine until six months ago.

CARTER: What medication is she on?

MRS. MIKAMI: Ampicillin, tobramycin, vitamins A, D and K.

LUCY: Skin's jaundiced.

WEAVER: Same with the sclera. Breath smells sweet.

CARTER: Fetor hepaticus?

WEAVER: Yep.

LUCY: What's that?

WEAVER: Her liver's shut down. Let's dip a urine. [To CARTER] Guys, it's getting a little crowded in here, why don't you deal with the parents? Start lactulose, 30 cc's per NG.

CARTER: We're giving medicine to clean her blood.

WEAVER: Blood in the urine, two-plus.

CARTER: The liver failure is causing her blood not to clot.

MRS. MIKAMI: Oh, God. . . .

CARTER: Is she on the transplant list?

MR. MIKAMI: She's been Status 2a for six months, but they haven't been able to find her a match.

CARTER: Why? What's her blood type?

MR. MIKAMI: AB.

[This hits CARTER like a lightning bolt. LUCY gets it, too. They share a look.]

There are flashing arrows here, of course — "The liver failure is causing her blood not to clot" — but the ratio of medical jargon to layperson translation is remarkably high. From a purely narrative point of view, the decisive line arrives at the very end: "AB." The 16-year-old's blood type connects her to an earlier plot line, involving a cerebral-hemorrhage victim who — after being dramatically revived in one of the opening scenes — ends up brain-dead. Far earlier, before the liver-failure scene above, Carter briefly discusses harvesting the hemorrhage victim's organs for transplants, and another doctor makes a passing reference to his blood type being the rare AB (thus making him an unlikely donor). The twist here revolves around a statistically unlikely event happening at the E.R. — an otherwise perfect liver donor showing up just in time to donate his liver to a recipient with the same rare blood type. But the show reveals this twist with remarkable subtlety. To make sense of that last "AB" line — and the look of disbelief on Carter's and Lucy's faces — you have to recall a passing remark uttered earlier regarding a character who belongs to a completely different thread. Shows like *E.R.* may have more blood and guts than popular TV had a generation ago, but when it comes to storytelling, they possess a quality that can only be described as subtlety and discretion.

Even Bad TV Is Better

Skeptics might argue that I have stacked the deck here by focusing on relatively highbrow titles like *The Sopranos* or *The West Wing*, when in fact the most significant change in the last five years of narrative entertainment involves reality TV. Does the contemporary pop cultural landscape look quite as promising if the representative show is *Joe Millionaire* instead of *The West Wing*?

I think it does, but to answer that question properly, you have to avoid the tendency to sentimentalize the past. When people talk about the golden age of television in the early 70's — invoking shows like *The Mary Tyler Moore Show* and *All in the Family* — they forget to mention how awful most television programming was during much of that decade. If you're going to look at pop-culture trends, you have to compare apples to apples, or in this case, lemons to lemons. The relevant comparison is not between *Joe Millionaire* and *MASH*; it's between *Joe Millionaire* and *The Newlywed Game*, or between *Survivor* and *The Love Boat*.

What you see when you make these head-to-head comparisons is that a rising tide of complexity has been lifting programming at the bottom of the quality
spectrum and at the top. *The Sopranos* is several times more demanding of its
audiences than *Hill Street* was, and *Joe Millionaire* has made comparable advances
over *Battle of the Network Stars*. This is the ultimate test of the Sleeper Curve theory: even the junk has improved.

If early television took its cues from the stage, today's reality programming is
reliably structured like a video game: a series of competitive tests, growing more
challenging over time. Many reality shows borrow a subtler device from gaming
culture as well: the rules aren't fully established at the outset. You learn as you
play.

On a show like *Survivor* or *The Apprentice*, the participants — and the audi-   30
ence — know the general objective of the series, but each episode involves new
challenges that haven't been ordained in advance. The final round of the first season of *The Apprentice*, for instance, threw a monkey wrench into the strategy that
governed the play up to that point, when Trump announced that the two remaining apprentices would have to assemble and manage a team of subordinates who
had already been fired in earlier episodes of the show. All of a sudden the overarching objective of the game — do anything to avoid being fired — presented a
potential conflict to the remaining two contenders: the structure of the final
round favored the survivor who had maintained the best relationships with his
comrades. Suddenly, it wasn't enough just to have clawed your way to the top;
you had to have made friends while clawing. The original *Joe Millionaire* went so
far as to undermine the most fundamental convention of all — that the show's
creators don't openly lie to the contestants about the prizes — by inducing a construction worker to pose as man of means while 20 women competed for his
attention.

Reality programming borrowed another key ingredient from games: the
intellectual labor of probing the system's rules for weak spots and opportunities.
As each show discloses its conventions, and each participant reveals his or her
personality traits and background, the intrigue in watching comes from figuring
out how the participants should best navigate the environment that has been created for them. The pleasure in these shows comes not from watching other people
being humiliated on national television; it comes from depositing other people in
a complex, high-pressure environment where no established strategies exist and
watching them find their bearings. That's why the water-cooler conversation
about these shows invariably tracks in on the strategy displayed on the previous
night's episode: why did Kwame pick Omarosa in that final round? What devious
strategy is Richard Hatch concocting now?

When we watch these shows, the part of our brain that monitors the emotional lives of the people around us — the part that tracks subtle shifts in intona-
tion and gesture and facial expression — scrutinizes the action on the screen,
looking for clues. We trust certain characters implicitly and vote others off the

island in a heartbeat. Traditional narrative shows also trigger emotional connections to the characters, but those connections don't have the same participatory effect, because traditional narratives aren't explicitly about strategy. The phrase "Monday-morning quarterbacking" describes the engaged feeling that spectators have in relation to games as opposed to stories. We absorb stories, but we second-guess games. Reality programming has brought that second-guessing to prime time, only the game in question revolves around social dexterity rather than the physical kind.

The Rewards of Smart Culture

The quickest way to appreciate the Sleeper Curve's cognitive training is to sit down and watch a few hours of hit programming from the late 70's on Nick at Nite or the SOAPnet channel or on DVD. The modern viewer who watches a show like *Dallas* today will be bored by the content — not just because the show is less salacious than today's soap operas (which it is by a small margin) but also because the show contains far less information in each scene, despite the fact that its soap-opera structure made it one of the most complicated narratives on television in its prime. With *Dallas*, the modern viewer doesn't have to think to make sense of what's going on, and not having to think is boring. Many recent hit shows — *24, Survivor, The Sopranos, Alias, Lost, The Simpsons, E.R.* — take the opposite approach, layering each scene with a thick network of affiliations. You have to focus to follow the plot, and in focusing you're exercising the parts of your brain that map social networks, that fill in missing information, that connect multiple narrative threads.

Of course, the entertainment industry isn't increasing the cognitive complexity of its products for charitable reasons. The Sleeper Curve exists because there's money to be made by making culture smarter. The economics of television syndication and DVD sales mean that there's a tremendous financial pressure to make programs that can be watched multiple times, revealing new nuances and shadings on the third viewing. Meanwhile, the Web has created a forum for annotation and commentary that allows more complicated shows to prosper, thanks to the fan sites where each episode of shows like *Lost* or *Alias* is dissected with an intensity usually reserved for Talmud scholars. Finally, interactive games have trained a new generation of media consumers to probe complex environments and to think on their feet, and that gamer audience has now come to expect the same challenges from their television shows. In the end, the Sleeper Curve tells us something about the human mind. It may be drawn toward the sensational where content is concerned — sex does sell, after all. But the mind also likes to be challenged; there's real pleasure to be found in solving puzzles, detecting patterns or unpacking a complex narrative system.

In pointing out some of the ways that popular culture has improved our 35 minds, I am not arguing that parents should stop paying attention to the way their children amuse themselves. What I am arguing for is a change in the criteria we use to determine what really is cognitive junk food and what is genuinely nourishing. Instead of a show's violent or tawdry content, instead of wardrobe malfunctions or the F-word, the true test should be whether a given show engages or sedates the mind. Is it a single thread strung together with predictable punch lines every 30 seconds? Or does it map a complex social network? Is your on-screen character running around shooting everything in sight, or is she trying to solve problems and manage resources? If your kids want to watch reality TV, encourage them to watch *Survivor* over *Fear Factor*. If they want to watch a mystery show, encourage *24* over *Law and Order*. If they want to play a violent game, encourage Grand Theft Auto over Quake. Indeed, it might be just as helpful to have a rating system that used mental labor and not obscenity and violence as its classification scheme for the world of mass culture.

Kids and grown-ups each can learn from their increasingly shared obsessions. Too often we imagine the blurring of kid and grown-up cultures as a series of violations: the 9-year-olds who have to have nipple broaches explained to them thanks to Janet Jackson; the middle-aged guy who can't wait to get home to his Xbox. But this demographic blur has a commendable side that we don't acknowledge enough. The kids are forced to think like grown-ups: analyzing complex social networks, managing resources, tracking subtle narrative intertwinings, recognizing long-term patterns. The grown-ups, in turn, get to learn from the kids: decoding each new technological wave, parsing the interfaces and discovering the intellectual rewards of play. Parents should see this as an opportunity, not a crisis. Smart culture is no longer something you force your kids to ingest, like green vegetables. It's something you share.

Questions

1. Steven Johnson calls his theory — that the "most debased forms of mass diversion" (para. 4) turn out to be good for us, after all — the "Sleeper Curve," after a scene in a Woody Allen movie. How does using one form of popular culture to examine another form affect Johnson's argument?

2. How do the charts accompanying the essay illustrate Johnson's points? How important is it to know the television programs to which the charts refer? Can the charts stand on their own?

3. In the section "Televised Intelligence," Johnson equates the intellectual demands of television to those ascribed to reading. Do multiple threading, flashing arrows, and social networks match up with attention, patience, retention, and the need to follow several narrative threads? What qualities do they have in common? What are their differences?

4. Examine the ways that Johnson provides counterarguments and responds to them.

5. What economic explanation does Johnson offer for why television has become more intellectually demanding?

2. *The Argument against TV*

CORBETT TRUBEY

Corbett Trubey wrote the following essay in 1999 for the online magazine *Lotus* on the occasion of TV Turnoff Week.

From April 22–28, various anti-media groups will be sponsoring "TV Turnoff Week," a challenge to the 98 percent of Americans who own at least one television to switch it off and find something better to do. For those of us who prefer our entertainment live, interactive and complete with DJs, vinyl and 30-foot speaker stacks, this might seem like a breeze. In all reality though, the omnipresent box sitting somewhere in our homes, workplaces, and just about everywhere else has a much greater hold on our lives than we think. Do we really know what we're up against?

Television has grown over the past 60 years from an experimental form of image transmission available only to the middle and upper classes, to the ultimate in low-end entertainment. People like to think that television is one of the best inventions of the 20th century, and it just might have been. Unfortunately, our old friends greed and sloth entered the picture and transformed it into a 24-hour ad-plastered, brainwashing, individuality bleaching, stereotyping, couch-potato-making tool of society. Never in the history of civilization has one manufactured product (along with an industry consisting of millions of people and billions of dollars) been able to induce such widespread passivity for hours on end.

The hours add up. The average American spends nine years of their life glued to the box. Imagine for a moment that you're one of these average Americans (it might be a stretch, but just do it anyway). In the span of your nine-year affair with television, what do you think you've accomplished? Imagine spending nine years pursuing other activities . . . you could have earned a PhD, achieved master DJ status, or cultivated a garden that amazes you every spring.

The television audience is divided into two categories: passive and interpretive. If you're the passive type, you're simply picking up the remote and foregoing the role of participant in the real world. Passive viewers are prone to resembling zombies after a good while and will exit their experience getting nothing more than wasted time. If you're an active viewer, you have an advantage. Unlike passive viewers, you're actually taking in what you see and forming an opinion on it. It might not be anything more than a little emotional stimulation, but at least there is meaning given to what an active viewer has watched.

Regardless of these two categories, everyone watching is a television viewer, a role defined by its passivity. You sit, you face forward, you are entertained. Many of us have grown up around television and can't imagine life without it. It's one of our favorite escapes from reality. From soap operas to crime dramas, stepping into a fantasy world takes our mind off whatever we choose not to deal with. 5

One question still remains: *What are we getting done?* The stream of images that flow into our brain when we watch television is doing nothing more than keeping us indoors and preoccupied with an alternate reality, lulled into physical and mental inactivity. It's no wonder then that a study done on teenagers ages 13 to 17 showed that only 25 percent could name the city where the U.S. Constitution was written, while 75 percent knew where you would find the zip code 90210. Is this how we're supposed to be enlightening ourselves?

What's even scarier about this waste of time is that it influences what we say, think, feel, wear and do. By the time we reach the age of 65, we will have seen over two million commercials. It would be completely irrational to think that not one of those ads affects us. Liberal consumerism is a dominant theme in modern society. The freedom to spend, spend, spend, and accumulate as much crap as possible is brought to you by . . . you get the picture.

So is this what we've turned into? A bunch of MTV-addicted, Jerry Springer–loving mall rats? Hell no! We are all unique individuals capable of free and creative thought, and while television can make us laugh and think, we all know that there are much better forms of entertainment to indulge in. We can all go out and shake our asses all night. We can all engage in deep illuminating conversations with our closest buds. And one thing's for damn sure, we can all read a book.

In a society that increasingly values work over pleasure, our leisure time has become a precious commodity. Making the most of the hours that we have to ourselves is essential. There's a big, beautiful world out there, and not even the widest TV screen or the sweetest *Animal Planet* documentary can compare to the real view. Television is just an infinitesimal speck compared to all the things you can do in your free time, and the longer you take to get off your butt and do it, the more time you waste watching other people have all the fun. This might explain why everybody wants to be on TV.

The next step is to face the challenge and turn off the television. Considering   10
what you might be able to do with a little less programming in your diet, does taking part in TV Turnoff Week sound all that bad? Get together with some friends and unplug it together if it makes it easier. Then, when you're all in the same room together, you can discuss what you'd like to see with the nine years of your life you've just gained. What's most important is that we all need to elevate above the blatant commercialism and mindlessness of television, and to sit pretty on a plane where we can enjoy a richer and more fulfilling existence.

Facts about Television Viewing

- Number of videos rented daily in the US: 6 million
- Number of public library items checked out daily: 3 million
- Hours per year the average American youth watches television: 1,500
- Hours per year the average American youth spends in school: 900
- Number of violent acts the average American child sees on TV by age 18: 200,000
- Percent increase in network news coverage of homicide between 1990 and 1995: 336

- Percentage of local TV news broadcast time devoted to advertising: 30
- Percentage devoted to public service announcements: 0.7
- Number of medical studies since 1985 linking excessive television watching to increasing rates of obesity: 12
- Chance that an American falls asleep with the TV on at least three nights a week: 1 in 4

Resources on Television Viewing:

- The Center for Screen-Time Awareness: tvturnoff.org
- Center for a New American Dream: www.newdream.org
  Another informative site dedicated to reducing consumption with lots of fun interactive stuff
- Adbusters: www.adbusters.org
  Slick, hilarious ad spoofs and information on other anti-media campaigns (they also publish an excellent magazine)
- Whitedot: www.whitedot.org
  The UK version of TV Free America; also big supporters of TV Turnoff Week
- The Kill Your TV Website: turnoffyourtv.com
  Links, cartoons, and plenty of thoughtful comments

Questions

1. What assumptions about his audience does Corbett Trubey make in paragraph 1?
2. How does the occasion for which Trubey is writing affect the reader's relationship with the subject?
3. What is the effect of the question that ends paragraph 1? Do you agree with Trubey's answer?
4. How does Trubey's use of classification strengthen his argument?
5. In paragraph 6, Trubey uses figures from a study but does not document the source. Does this kind of citation affect his credibility?
6. Do the lists at the end of the essay strengthen Trubey's argument?

3. *He Doesn't Like to Watch*

It's TV Turnoff Week, and its mastermind explains why thousands of culture jammers might be disrupting a sports bar near you.

Julia Scott

In the following 2005 interview from the online magazine *Salon*, Julia Scott talks with Kalle Lasn, editor-in-chief of Adbusters.org and patriarch of TV Turnoff Week.

That intrusive moment — in a bar, on a subway, at the airport — when a loud television dominates a public place was the original inspiration for TV-B-Gone, a lightweight remote control created by San Francisco engineer Mitch Altman. TV-B-Gone can hang on a keychain and can turn off almost any television, anywhere. The device was so popular that it sold out within hours of its launch in October 2004. And now Altman's remotes are in particular demand, as Adbusters magazine promotes their use in conjunction with TV Turnoff Week. . . .

After Adbusters started it in 1994 with the goal of improving our quality of life, TV Turnoff Week has become a bit of a mainstay. The TV Turnoff Network, a Washington group that promotes TV Turnoff Week mostly in schools, estimates that 7.6 million people participated in the campaign last year. Still, publicity for the event has waned in recent years, so Adbusters took a more radical approach. The magazine's staff believes that some 2,500 TV-B-Gone devices have been bought so far through Adbusters' Web site; there's no way to tell how they'll be distributed in its "JammerGroup" network of more than 10,000 people. But, for $15 a pop, the small army can (temporarily) silence that fuzzy white noise in restaurants, coin laundries and waiting rooms.

But does every public TV need to be turned off? Do nature shows get privileged treatment? And does culture jamming run the risk of becoming more annoying than watching Bill O'Reilly in the grocery checkout lane? Salon spoke with Kalle Lasn, Adbusters' editor in chief and the patriarch of TV Turnoff Week, from his home in Vancouver.

Why did you decide to combine TV-B-Gone with TV Turnoff week? We brainstormed here at Adbusters and figured that TV Turnoff Week was losing a bit of its oomph over the last few years . . . TV-B-Gone has given our TV Turnoff Week campaign, which was sort of dormant, a bit of magic. TV-B-Gone doesn't exactly give us our voices back, but it helps us get some control. It shuts up that corporate, commercial ad agency voice. In public spaces, they have the right to put up a TV, but I think that we the people who have to live in those public spaces have the right to switch those things off.

How do you see this working? I go to a bank every Saturday here in Vancouver. When I'm standing in line I have this group of three TV sets that I'm looking at, whether I like it or not. Last Saturday, I had my TV-B-Gone with me while I was standing in line, and I pressed the button and I switched those TVs off. It was a beautiful moment. It was a moment where I felt that we were in control, rather than the bank with its TV sets.

People's reactions were interesting. Before, everybody was kind of standing there with their heads slightly lifted toward the TV sets. Nobody was talking to each other. But a few seconds after those TVs went off, people were suddenly talking to each other and looking around. It felt like real life again. It was an epiphany — and the bank didn't even notice.

But when is it appropriate to turn off someone else's TVs? I think everybody has to decide for themselves what's off-limits. I know there are some edgy people who will, for the sheer fun of it, switch everything off. But I was at the airport the other day, and there was a big TV set that a number of people were watching, and for some reason I didn't want to switch it off because it was some nature show. I think it's a decision that people can make in the moment it's happening.

Do you anticipate a number of television vigilantes who will go into stores and bars, switching TVs off? I think the real question here isn't whether there's going to be a few vigilantes who switch off TV sets. The question is, what right do airports and bank managers have to force us to watch TV in public places?

If you treat this device as a little lark, you're missing the point. It's the tip of the iceberg in addressing an incredibly polluted mental environment that is now causing mental diseases to the point where the World Health Organization is predicting that by the year 2020, mental diseases will be more widespread than heart disease. We live in an age of mood disorders and anxiety attacks, where depression has gone up by 300 percent in two generations. It's gotten to the point where there are ads in fortune cookies, and here in Vancouver, you walk into the bathroom and a TV set suddenly goes on in front of you.

What do you think of someone going into a sports bar — where people 10 **have gone to watch a game — and turning the TV off there? Do you think that's a justified use?** Well, we've done that, and occasionally we had to hightail it out of there really fast because there was going to be a fight. But at the beginning of movements like this one, I think a certain amount of civil disobedience, even if it gets physical after a while, is good.

But are you sacrificing any educational aspect of TV Turnoff Week this way? I don't think the educational component has been sacrificed; I think what has been sacrificed is the debate over the larger issues: What is happening in our mental commons? What does a commercial do to you? What does media concentration really mean for a democracy? How can so many Americans still think there was a connection between Saddam Hussein and al-Qaida? There's an incredible amount of disinformation floating around.

Questions

1. The interview's come-on states that "culture jammers might be disrupting a sports bar near you." Does the interview address that threat? In what other directions does the interview take the reader?
2. Julia Scott focuses the interview on the TV-B-Gone device created by a San Francisco engineer. It can hang on a keychain and, when activated, can turn off almost any TV anywhere. What is the interviewer's bias toward the device? How is her bias apparent in her questions?
3. Describe the tone of the interview. Does the tone affect the credibility of the interviewee? of the interviewer? Explain.
4. How does the interview address the political nature of TV Turnoff Week?

4. *TV Turnoff Week* (detail from a poster)

ANTHONY DIVIVO

The following poster by Anthony DiVivo advertises TV Turnoff Week.

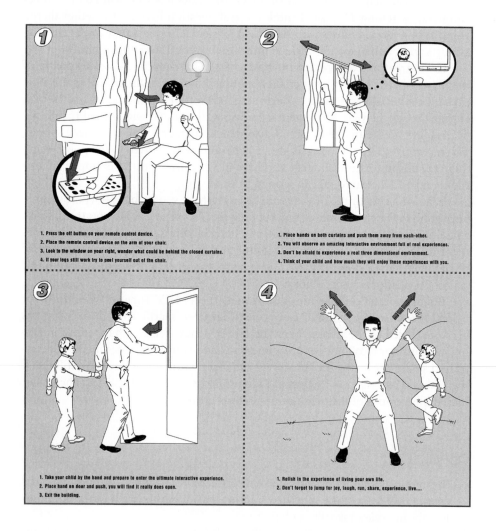

Questions

1. What is the purpose of Anthony DiVivo's poster? How do the illustrations address this purpose?
2. How does the poster create a tone? Are the words, which are difficult to read, necessary?
3. The inspiration for DiVivo's poster was an airline safety card. Does this connection add to the poster's effectiveness? Explain.

5. *Is Media Violence Free Speech?*

GEORGE GERBNER AND TODD GITLIN

The following debate on media violence was originally posted in 1997 on the Web site *Hot Wired*.

No

George Gerbner is the former dean of the Annenberg School of Communication at the University of Pennsylvania. In 1996, he founded the Cultural Environment Movement to examine the role of media violence in American society. He says media violence is tantamount to censorship by media conglomerates who effectively shut out diverse points of view.

Yes

A high-profile veteran of the 1960s peace movement, Todd Gitlin has become a leading U.S. commentator and author on media and culture issues. In his essays and books, he has called the crusade against media violence "hollow" and "cheap." He says media violence isn't dangerous, it's just stupid.

Gerbner Starts:

Formula-driven media violence is not an expression of crime statistics, popularity, or freedom. It is de facto censorship driven by global marketing, imposed on creative people, foisted on the children of the world. Far from inciting to mayhem, media violence is an instrument of fear and social control.

Violence dominates television news and entertainment, particularly what we call "happy violence" — cool, swift, painless, and always leading to a happy ending in order to deliver the audience to the next commercial message in a receptive mood.

The Cultural Indicators Project has found that heavy viewers are more likely   5
to overestimate their chances of involvement in violence; to believe that their neighborhoods are unsafe; to state that fear of crime is a very serious personal problem; and to assume that crime is rising, regardless of the facts.

Heavy viewers express a greater sense of insecurity and mistrust than comparable groups of light viewers. They are more likely to be dependent on authority and to support repression if it is presented as enhancing their security.

Gitlin Responds:

Television violence is mainly redundant, stupid, and ugly. The deepest problem with TV violence is not that it causes violence — the evidence for this is very thin. The problem is that the profiteers of television in the United States — the networks, the program suppliers, and the advertisers — are essentially subsidized (e.g., via tax write-offs) to program this formulaic stuff.

Professor Gerbner may well be right about TV watchers — the more violence they watch, the more dangerous they think the world is. They may therefore support heavy-handed, authoritarian responses to crime.

But consider the case of Japan. There is far more vile media violence — including more widely available violent pornography — in Japan than in the United States. But there is less real-world violence — particularly sexual violence — in Japan than in the United States. This is not to say that television is healthy for American society. To the contrary.

It would help to provide alternatives. We could use some government-subsidized programs devoted to something other than mindless, transitory entertainment. We could tax television sets, as in Great Britain, or subsidize public broadcasting through taxes, as in Canada, or — in a more American mode — charge fees to networks, which now avail themselves of the public airwaves, buy and sell licenses, and amass immense profits, all without charge. 10

Gerbner Rebuts:

"The case of Japan" argument surprises me from Professor Gitlin. It is the knee-jerk retort of apologists, of whom Mr. Gitlin is certainly not one. The argument assumes that media violence is the only, or major and always decisive, influence on human social behavior — extensio ad absurdum. Media violence (or any other single factor) is one of many factors interacting with other influences in any culture that contribute to real-world violence.

I completely agree that the main problem behind violence is virtual commercial monopoly over the public's airways. No other democracy delivers its cultural environment to a marketing operation.

But apologists might also argue that the free-market environment delivers programming tailored to its audience. However, our studies show that violence actually depresses ratings. Instead of popularity, the mechanisms of global marketing drive televised violence. Producers for global markets look for a dramatic formula that needs no translation, speaks "action" in any language, fits every culture. That formula is violence.

The V-chip is not the solution. That technology merely protects the industry from the parents, rather than the other way around. It only facilitates business as usual. Programming needs to be diversified, not just "rated." A better government regulation is antitrust, which could create a level playing field, admitting new entries and a greater diversity of ownership, employment, and representation. That would reduce violence to its legitimate role and frequency.

Gitlin Explains:

By citing the case of Japan, I mean simply to restore some balance to a discussion that, like so many other American debates, gets pinned to single-cause theories and sound-bite nostrums. TV versions of violence are egregious, coarsening, and 15 produce a social fear and anesthesia which damage our capacity to face reality, but I think many liberals have gone overboard in thinking that if they clean up television, they have accomplished a great deal to rub out violence in the real world. To make television more discriminating, intelligent, and various would be an achievement worthy in its own right, but let's not kid ourselves: The deepest sources of murderous American violence are stupefying inequality, terrible poverty, a nihilistic drug-saturated culture, and an easy recourse to guns. TV's contribution is a target of convenience for a political culture that makes it difficult to grow up with a sense of belonging to a decent society.

I'm not against the V-chip as such, since any device that enables parents to redress the imbalance of power they suffer under the invasion of television is all to the good. Given the power of nihilistic corporations over TV programs, any reasonable off-switch is defensible. But again, let's not kid ourselves about just how easy it will be to address the problem of TV violence all by itself. The Hollywood mania for dumb-bunny action is driven — as Professor Gerbner rightly says — by the export imperative. Entertainment is America's second-largest export in dollar value. The industry is not going to go quietly.

Gerbner Speaks:

The V-chip is a sideshow and a diversion. I have observed this game since the 1970s. It is called "the carrot and the stick." Legislators posture in public, shaking the stick; and then vote the carrot of multibillion dollar windfalls for the same companies they pretend to threaten. They may even extract some meaningless concessions to calm the waters, take the heat off their media clients — who are among their major bankrollers — and call it a victory.

But the industry knows better. The cover story of the 14 August 1996 issue of the trade journal *Broadcasting & Cable* is titled "The Man Who Made the V-chip." Pictured on the cover is "the man," liberal House Democrat Edward J. Markey, who should know better. The cover story is titled "Why the Markey Chip Won't Hurt You." In fact, it can only help the industry. It's like the major polluters saying, "We shall continue business as usual, but don't worry, we'll also sell you gas masks to 'protect your children' and have a 'free choice!'"

There is no free market in television. Viewers are sold to the highest bidders at the lowest cost. That drives both violence and drivel on television. The giveaway of the public airways to private exploitation damages our children and swamps any effort toward democracy. Only a broad citizen movement can turn this around.

Gitlin Responds:

V-chips or the like are sure to come — they are perfectly tailored to the American can-do attitude that there is a technological fix for every social problem. Though I don't regard them as pernicious — parents deserve all the technohelp they can get — I agree with Dr. Gerbner that the irresponsibility of the broadcasters is the

20

fundamental issue. They are nihilists who spend many millions of dollars to buy a supine government. Pat Robertson's willingness to sell his "Christian" channel to Rupert Murdoch, master exploiter of brainless smirkiness and sexual innuendo, shows what kind of values are in play among the movers and shakers.

The problem of TV goes far beyond violence. The speed-up of imagery undermines the capacity to pay attention. Flashy sensation clogs up the synapses. The cheapening of violence — not so much the number of incidents as their emptiness and lightweight gruesomeness — leads to both paranoia and anesthesia. The coarsening of TV inhibits seriousness. The glut of entertainment cheers consumers on primitive levels. Whiz-bang new technologies like high-definition TV will offer sharper images of banality.

To the idea of a citizen's movement, hooray! At the least, let all who want a more vital America — and more vital arts — support antitrust action against the media oligopoly.

Gerbner's Last Word:

We agree: The problem goes beyond violence, ratings, or any single factor, to the heart of the system. Television is driven not by the creative people who have something to tell, but by global conglomerates that have something to sell.

Citizens own the airways. We should demand that it be free and fair, and not just "rated." Besides, the current so-called rating system is fundamentally flawed.

Ratings flash on during opening credits, but never again. Producers rate their own programs, resulting in inconsistencies across networks. Ratings designed by the industry is like letting the fox (no pun intended) guard the chicken coop.   25

So — don't just agonize; organize! The Cultural Environment Movement (CEM) is a nonprofit organization with members and supporters worldwide, united in working for freedom and fairness in media. . . .

Gitlin's Last Word:

The moneymaking machines that control as much of the culture as they can get their hands on will make just as many moral-sounding reforms as they think they need to keep Congress and the FCC off their backs. They will trim an ax-murder here, insert a V-chip there, and later — when public-interest groups and the FCC have taken their attention elsewhere — throw in another ax-murder, or six. The reforms, most likely transitory, will have a pleasant ring and will gain much well-meaning support. In the meantime, for the foreseeable future, the culture — the unofficial curriculum of American children — will remain infantile, degraded, and, among other things, tolerant of and conducive to a violent nihilism. Those who have access to the Web will feel that they have broken free of the tripe, but this is at least half-fanciful. Much of what goes on the Web, however decentralized and freely chosen, is as glib, shallow, and weightless as commercial TV. The great Fun Leviathan churns on.

I have been trying to argue in these few words that we are imprisoned in a mania for easy sensation. We have more and more delivery systems for hollow toys. The virtual eclipses virtue. This year's shoddy goods displace last year's. The freedom to choose is debased into the pursuit of the next kick. The frantic search for electronic sensation does violence to the reflection and deliberation that a democracy needs. No quick fixes, no "just say no" is adequate. It would make sense to curb our own hunger for distraction, as we need to curb the reach of the moguls who now lord it over the catering business.

Is market-driven culture a reflection of the population, or a toxic side-effect of global capitalism?

Questions

1. Although this selection is labeled a debate, on what aspects of the subject do George Gerbner and Todd Gitlin agree?
2. Why does Gitlin use Japan as an example of the effects of media violence? How does Gerbner respond?
3. What are Gerbner's and Gitlin's views of the V-chip?
4. According to Gitlin and Gerbner, what are the results of excessive TV violence?

Entering the Conversation

As you respond to the following prompts, support your argument with references to at least three sources in Conversation: Focus on Television. For help using sources, see Chapter 3.

1. Write an essay explaining whether you view television as beneficial or detrimental to society.

2. Analyze a contemporary television series according to the criteria Steven Johnson supplies in "Watching TV Makes You Smarter" (p. 766): multiple threading, flashing arrows, and social networks. Use your analysis to counter an anti-television argument.

3. In the foreword to *Amusing Ourselves to Death*, media critic Neil Postman (1931–2003) suggests that the vision of Aldous Huxley's *Brave New World* (1932) turned out to be more terrifyingly true than the vision George Orwell created in *Nineteen Eighty-four* (1949):

   What Orwell feared were those who would ban books. What Huxley feared was that there would be no reason to ban a book, for there would be no one who wanted to read one. Orwell feared those who would deprive us of information. Huxley feared those who would give us so much that we would be reduced to passivity and egoism. Orwell feared that the truth would be concealed from us. Huxley feared the truth would be drowned in a sea of irrelevance. Orwell feared we would become a captive culture. Huxley feared we would become a trivial culture, preoccupied with some equivalent of the feelies, the orgy porgy, and the centrifugal bumblepuppy. As Huxley remarked in *Brave New World Revisited*, the civil libertarians and rationalists who are ever on the alert to oppose tyranny "failed to take into account man's almost infinite appetite for distractions." In *1984*, Huxley added, people are controlled by inflicting pain. In *Brave New World*, they are controlled by inflicting pleasure. In short, Orwell feared that what we hate will ruin us. Huxley feared that what we love will ruin us.

Write an essay explaining the extent to which you believe television has proven Postman right or wrong. Refer to at least three sources.

4. Using the arguments and evidence in "Conversation: Focus on Television," answer the following questions: Should we have a TV Turnoff Week? Is it just hype? How would you modify it?

Student Writing

Visual Rhetoric: Interpreting a Painting

The following prompt asks students to comment on Mark Tansey's painting *The Innocent Eye Test*, which appears on page 764.

Write an essay about what or who is being tested in the painting. What does the painting say about art criticism? How do the details complicate the answer to who is testing whom?

Emily Fine, an eleventh-grade AP English student, analyzed the visual text and wrote the essay that appears here. Read the essay carefully, keeping in mind your own expertise on writing about visual texts. Then answer the questions at the end of the essay to help you focus on the essay's strengths and weaknesses.

The Innocent Eye Test: Who Is Tested?

Emily Fine

The Innocent Eye Test is a painting by Mark Tansey that uses humor to explore art criticism. Tansey's references to Paulus Potter's *Young Bull* and Monet's *Haystack* help him test the viewer and express his ideas about art critics. Tansey tests the viewer's ability to understand or identify a work of art and shows the unreliability of art critics, which then complicates our understanding of who is testing whom.

Mark Tansey's test of the viewers of his artwork is made clear through its title, *The Innocent Eye Test*. In his painting, the "innocent eye" is the cow's, and his response to *The Young Bull* will let the businessmen and scientists in the painting know just how successful Potter's painting actually is. Will the reaction of the viewers of Potter's painting be similarly as "innocent" as the cow's, unbiased and open-minded enough to make a conclusion of his painting on their own? The moment anyone views artwork, their facial expressions show their true thought on the piece. Tansey wants the viewers to be able to hold true to their initial reaction rather than conform to the ideas of others. Thus, he objects to art criticism as well, wanting viewers to decide for themselves the value of an artwork, whether or not the critic is reliable. With the use of Monet's *Haystack* in the background, Tansey may also be testing the viewers' ability to identify art, or whether they are cultured. If they are, it might also mean that they are biased in observing his artwork, something Tansey does not hope for. His painting tests the viewers and gives ideas of art criticism, which can mean that there is yet another test for the viewers — their ability to establish the meaning of a painting. His artwork obviously has many meanings, and how a person interprets it says something about his or her character. Some may see it as no more than a humorous painting of a cow observing a life-size painting of a cow, while others will go deeper in analyzing its hidden messages. Therefore, Tansey's painting is a test of the viewer, and in some cases, a person may receive more than one test depending on his or her perception of the artwork.

As noted previously, Tansey comments on art criticism through his painting. He believes people should trust their initial responses when viewing an artwork. Using educated businessmen and scientists in his painting, who are attentively awaiting the cow's response, can mean that one's initial "innocent" response is more valuable than any educated art critic's. The professional-looking men can also serve a second meaning. They are all wearing glasses with the exception of one man holding a mop, which may be because the cow's possible dissatisfaction is likely to create an unwanted bowel movement. The fact that the men are wearing glasses indicates that they are unable to decipher the meaning of Potter's painting without the help of their glasses and a real cow to tell them if the painted cow was a success. If Tansey's painting is interpreted this way, he is also saying that art critics are not reliable, and no matter how scholarly they may be, they might not be able to interpret a painting. If they can, there are always other meanings, and all viewers have their own preferences, which allow them to determine their appreciation for a particular work of art on their own.

Who is testing whom becomes complicated after noting the possible meanings of Tansey's artwork. Tansey is testing the viewer in more than one way, though it is possible that the details of his painting can imply that it is the art viewers who are testing the art critics. The art viewers are aware of how they perceive the piece to be, and this makes them capable of testing the art critics, if they are open-minded and do not reflect on the artwork from solely their own point of view. More literally, Tansey's painting is a test for the cow. The men in the painting are eager to know the cow's response, which will then tell them the true value of Potter's artwork since the cow is "innocent." Though taken figuratively, who is testing whom becomes even more complicated. Tansey can be testing the viewer or, more specifically, the art critic and what he is actually testing is open to interpretation. Any individual is capable of finding another meaning in the painting, or another test presented by Tansey, but in order for this to happen, the viewer must observe the artwork without the predisposed ideas from an art critic. Tansey's *Innocent Eye Test* is a humorous work of art that holds many meanings, as well as tests for different people.

The *Innocent Eye Test* by Mark Tansey reveals his beliefs about art criticism, while he tests the viewer in various ways. He does this by referring to Paulus Potter's *Young Bull* and Monet's *Haystack*. He tests the viewer's ability to interpret artwork without regard to the analyses of others, and implies that art critics are partial and not always reliable. It is up to the viewer to observe the artwork independently and provide an explanation of their own. That is the beauty of art, something that art critics, pushing their personal opinions into the minds of others, take away.

Questions

1. What is this essay's strength?
2. Look carefully at the painting, which is reproduced on page 764. Is Emily's description accurate? What other elements of the painting would you have discussed?
3. This essay is written in the third person. How would the use of *I* have strengthened or weakened the essay?
4. Would the use of outside sources have helped Emily develop her thesis? What sources would you have consulted? How would you use them in an essay that analyzes a visual text?

Grammar as Rhetoric and Style

Modifiers

A modifier may be a one-word adverb or adjective; a phrase, such as a prepositional phrase or a participial phrase; or a clause, such as an adjective clause. At its best, a modifier describes, focuses, or qualifies the nouns, pronouns, and verbs it modifies. But when a writer overuses or incorrectly uses modifiers, the result may be verbose or even flowery writing.

Here is how David Denby describes the "most hated young woman in America" in "High School Confidential: Notes on Teen Movies":

> a blonde — well, sometimes a redhead or a brunette, but usually a blonde. She has big hair, flipped into a swirl of gold at one side of her face or arrayed in a sultry mane. . . . She's tall and slender, with a waist as supple as a willow, but she's dressed in awful, spangled taste.

These sentences include single-word adjectives (*sultry, tall, slender, supple, awful, spangled*), a participle followed by two prepositional phrases (*flipped into a swirl of gold*), and several other prepositional phrases (*at one side of her face*; *in a sultry mane*; *with a waist . . .* ; *in awful, spangled taste*). When we call attention to all of them like this, the modification may seem heavy, but in the passage itself, all the modifiers do *not* amount to overkill because Denby paces them.

Let's look more closely at another Denby sentence with a participial phrase as a modifier:

> Sprawling and dull in class, he comes alive in the halls and in the cafeteria.

Here Denby has essentially combined two sentences: "He is sprawling and dull in class. He comes alive in the halls and in the cafeteria." The result is a smoother, single sentence that focuses on the difference between the subject's behavior in and out of class.

In Vine Deloria's "We Talk, You Listen," the author uses a couple of key single-word adverbs to qualify and focus his meaning:

> The discovery itself was irrelevant to the western Indian tribes, but the migrations caused by the discovery of gold were vitally important. The two histories can dovetail around this topic but ultimately each interpretation must depend upon its orientation to the group involved.

Deloria qualifies — and stresses — the importance of the migrations with the adverb *vitally*. He then focuses his view of that significance by specifying *ultimately*, meaning "in the final analysis."

Rhetorical and Stylistic Strategy

Modifiers can enliven, focus, and qualify ideas. The *placement* of modifiers can add to or detract from these effects. Note the following example by Denby.

> Physically awkward, she walks like a seal crossing a beach, and is prone to drop her books and dither in terror when she stands before a handsome boy.

The modifiers that describe the girl gather steam, and finally, in a prepositional phrase at the end of the sentence, they contrast her with the handsome boy. Note the different effect if the handsome boy comes into the sentence before the awkward girl drops her books and dithers:

> When she stands before the handsome boy, physically awkward, she walks like a seal crossing a beach, and is prone to drop her books and dither in terror.

Announcing the handsome boy early in the sentence undercuts the contrast between the girl and the boy that Denby wants to stress.

In the accompanying panel from page 140 in Scott McCloud's comic-book guide to reading comic books, note how the modifiers reinforce the changes in our reading habits that occur as we age. Note also the progression in the drawings: the very young boy in the first frame grows into the older man by the third; the narrator shows up in the fourth to finish his commentary. In addition to the drawings, McCloud has the advantage of the text's graphic flexibility: little punctuation besides dashes, and boldface and italics to stress certain words.

The first frame begins the progression with the modifier *as children* and describes picture books as having *pictures galore*. The second begins with *then*, showing time moving on, stressing text with *more* and minimizing pictures with *occasional*. The third places us *finally* as grown-ups, and our books have no pictures *at all*. Quite a switch from *galore*! In the last frame, McCloud's qualifier *perhaps* suggests further ruin in the future: *sadly . . . no books at all*.

Consider the effect of the modifier *now* in this sentence from Mark Twain:

> We are conforming in the other way, now, because it is another case of everybody.

The placement of *now* in the middle of the sentence reinforces *the other way* and reminds us that Twain is making a point about the mercurial nature of public opinion.

Cautions

Studying how accomplished writers use modifiers helps us understand how to use them effectively. Following are some cautions to keep in mind when using modifiers in your own writing.

1. *Do not use too many modifiers.* David Denby gives a clear visual image of the evil high-school cheerleader by using a variety of modifiers. However, less experienced writers may overwrite by including too many adjectives, as shown in the following example:

The bright yellow compact car with the pun-laden, out-of-state vanity plates was like beautiful, warm sunshine on the gray, dreary Tuesday afternoon.

2. *Do not rely on adjectives when strong verbs are more effective.* Instead of writing, "Elani walked with a confident and quick stride," perhaps say, "Elani strutted" or "Elani strode."

3. *Beware of adding too many qualifiers.* Be especially careful about *really* and *very*.

   • "Troy felt really sad" might be expressed as "Troy felt discouraged" or "despondent." Or it might simply be stated as "Troy felt sad."
   • Similarly, "The mockingbird's song is very beautiful" is probably just as well stated as "The mockingbird's song is beautiful" or, introducing a strong verb, as "The mockingbird serenades."

You need not avoid qualifiers altogether, but if you find yourself using them over and over, it's time to check whether they're *really very* effective.

• EXERCISE 1

Rewrite each of the following sentences to make the modifiers more effective.

1. Dolores offered a rather unique view of the situation.
2. I had difficulty understanding my teacher because he talked so quickly and softly.
3. Michael was so very excited about the beginning of lacrosse season that he could barely sleep.
4. Susan talked with self-assurance about movies she hadn't even seen.
5. The skyline was amazing on the beautiful evening.

• EXERCISE 2

Discuss the following paragraph from Teresa Wiltz's "Popular Culture in the Aftermath of Sept. 11. . . ." Focus on the writer's modifiers. Look carefully at the adjectives Wiltz uses to describe the most immediate changes. Look also at the qualifiers she uses — *for now, at least, again* — and consider how they suit the purpose of the essay.

It is true, of course, that a certain earnestness has crept into the national zeitgeist, blotting out — for now, at least — our normal, unique brand of optimistic cynicism. In her latest video, blue-eyed soul singer Pink urges us all to "Get This Party Started" as she dances against the backdrop of a giant flag. Celebs attending the Emmy Awards earlier this month were asked to tone down the sartorial glitz. And just a week ago Sunday, in a much-publicized gathering, movie execs met with White House officials — again — to suss out just what Hollywood could do for the war-on-terrorism effort.

● **EXERCISE 3**

Identify the modifiers, both words and phrases, in the following paragraph from "The Argument against TV" by Corbett Trubey. Are the modifiers effective, or are they excessive? Cite specific examples to support your view.

Television has grown over the past 60 years from an experimental form of image transmission available only to the middle and upper classes, to the ultimate in low-end entertainment. People like to think that television is one of the best inventions of the 20th century, and it just might have been. Unfortunately, our old friends greed and sloth entered the picture and transformed it into a 24-hour ad-plastered, brainwashing, individuality bleaching, stereotyping, couch-potato-making tool of society. Never in the history of civilization has one manufactured product (along with an industry consisting of millions of people and billions of dollars) been able to induce such widespread passivity for hours on end.

● **EXERCISE 4**

Most of the modifiers have been removed from the following paragraph from "We Talk, You Listen" by Vine Deloria Jr.

In recent years the documentary has arisen to present the story of Indian people and a number of series on Black America have been produced. Indian documentaries are the same. A reporter and television crew hasten to either the Navaho or Pine Ridge reservation, shoot reels on conditions, and return East thinking that they have captured the essence of Indian life. In spite of the intentions, the yearning to present a story of a people overcomes, and the cycle of films continues.

· Read the paragraph aloud, and listen to its cadence.
· Add the following modifiers: *quickly, best, poverty-oriented, strange, blithely, eternal, endless, exciting.* Use them to improve the paragraph's effectiveness.
· Compare your version to the original (see para. 16, p. 730).
· Discuss the rhetorical effect of the modifiers in this paragraph.

- **EXERCISE 5**

Following are examples of authors' skillful use of modifiers, both single words and phrases. In each, identify the modifier or modifiers, and discuss the effect they create. Then write a sentence or passage of your own, emulating the writer's technique.

1. Other minority groups have fought tenaciously against stereotyping, and generally they have been successful.   — VINE DELORIA JR.

2. He's usually a football player, muscular but dumb, with a face like a beer mug and only two ways of speaking — in a conspiratorial whisper to a friend; or in a drill sergeant's sudden bellow. — DAVID DENBY

3. Broadly speaking, there are none but corn-pone opinions. And broadly speaking, corn-pone stands for self-approval.   — MARK TWAIN

4. Flashy sensation clogs up the synapses. The cheapening of violence — not so much the number of incidents as their emptiness and lightweight gruesomeness — leads to both paranoia and anesthesia.
   —TODD GITLIN

5. Violence dominates television news and entertainment, particularly what we call "happy violence" — cool, swift, painless, and always leading to a happy ending in order to deliver the audience to the next commercial message in a receptive mood.   — GEORGE GERBNER

6. On Jan. 24, the Fox network showed an episode of its hit drama *24*, the real-time thriller known for its cliffhanger tension and often-gruesome violence.   — STEVEN JOHNSON

7. A fire-breathing reptile is pretty much the same in any language. But the butchered version of the film that swept the world after release in the United States was stripped of the political subtext — and the anti-American, antinuclear messages — that had saturated the original.
   — BRENT STAPLES

Suggestions for Writing
Popular Culture

Now that you have examined a number of readings and other texts that focus on popular culture, explore one dimension of the topic by synthesizing your own ideas and the texts. You might want to do more research or use readings from other classes as you prepare for the following projects.

1. In his essay "High-School Confidential: Notes on Teen Movies" (p. 709), David Denby suggests that the teen movies from the turn of this century reflect the secret wishes — and geekiness — of their screenwriters and directors. Watch a movie about teens from an earlier time — *Rebel without a Cause* (1955) or *Splendor in the Grass* (1961), for example — and discuss what the film said about the filmmakers of the era.

2. "Dreaming America" by Danyel Smith (p. 734) refers to several different genres of popular music. Listen to an assortment of songs by the artists mentioned in her piece. Make a CD of the music, and write the liner notes in which you explain why you chose the songs and how you decided the order in which they appear.

3. Write an essay in which you apply Steven Johnson's or Corbett Trubey's arguments about television (pp. 766 and 777) to another form of popular culture, such as advertisements, movies, or music.

4. Write a sermon using "Emily Dickinson and Elvis Presley in Heaven" as a starting point.

5. Each of the following statements addresses the subject of media. Select one that interests you, and write an essay that defends or challenges its assertion. To support your argument, refer to your own experience with media and to the selections in this chapter.

   > The one function TV news performs very well is that when there is no news, we give it to you with the same emphasis as if there were.
   >
   > — DAVID BRINKLEY, American TV network news anchor

   > Whoever controls the media — the images — controls the culture.
   >
   > — ALLEN GINSBERG, poet

   > If you want to use television to teach somebody something, you have first to teach somebody how to use television.   — UMBERTO ECO, philosopher

   > Visual chaos is not good for anyone. Billboard companies should not be allowed to sell what they don't own — our field of vision and our civic pride.
   >
   > — MEG MAGUIRE, president, Scenic America

6. Watch a pair of films in which one is a remake of another. *Seven Samurai* and *Magnificent Seven*, *The Shop around the Corner* and *You've Got Mail*, *Fingers* and *The Beat That My Heart Skipped* are some examples. Then write about how the remake was changed for a new audience and how the new version honors the old.

7. Write a review of a concert, CD, movie, or graphic novel. Keep in mind that reviews are arguments either applauding artists, criticizing them, or both.

8. In "Corn-Pone Opinions," Mark Twain distinguishes between fashion and standards. Is it the same as the difference, discussed on pages 707–708, between what was once considered popular culture and high culture? Write about what you see as the difference between fashion and standards.

12

Nature

What is our responsibility to nature?

The ancient Greeks were on to something when they divided the natural world into earth, air, fire, and water. We need these resources for our basic needs: trees give fruit for sustenance and lumber for shelter, fields provide grain, and pastures feed animals that become meat. Rivers and oceans deliver fish; fire and air and water provide warmth, breath, and life itself. We harvest the bounty that nature brings. But we do not simply use nature as a resource; we also look to nature for recreation, inspiration, and solace. It is not surprising, therefore, that we refer to the source of sunrises and earthquakes, hurricanes and flowers, deluge and drought, mosquito buzz and birdsong as Mother Nature.

Throughout history we have tried to conquer the wilderness, tame the jungles, and master the elements, and we are still trying to conquer space. But are nature and humankind necessarily in conflict? We created civilization to protect us from the undesirable features of the outdoors and, to some degree, from harm. But now our experience of the natural world is so mediated that many of us know it only as it is presented on television. Has our relationship with nature changed so drastically that nature now exists *within* civilization, as contemporary naturalist Bill McKibben suggests? Do we now contain nature rather than being contained by it?

In recent years, humankind's attitude toward the natural world has changed. Before Rachel Carson and others began to alert us to the dangers of pollution, most people simply didn't think about the environment. And looking back over the last half century, it is hard to imagine what may be in store for us over the next fifty years. Are we yet to see the consequences of what we have already done to alter the environment?

Once we begin to protect the environment, our fundamental relationship with our world changes. We're still dwarfed by the awesome power of nature, but if we are creating conditions that may change nature itself, whether through pollution, development of open land, or global warming, then we need to consider our responsibility. Can we do enough right now to protect our world? Will we eventually become an endangered species?

The selections in this chapter consider nature from many angles. As you read, consider your responsibility to nature. What might we expect from it, and what might it expect from us?

From *Silent Spring*

RACHEL CARSON

Rachel Carson (1907–1964) was educated at Johns Hopkins University and conducted research at the Marine Biological Laboratory in Woods Hole, Massachusetts. She worked as a biologist for the U.S. Fish and Wildlife Service and served as chief editor of publications from 1947 to 1952. She wrote many books and articles about the sea, including *Under the Sea-Wind* (1941); *The Sea around Us* (1951), which won a National Book Award; and *The Edge of the Sea* (1955). Carson was among the first scientists to raise environmental issues for the general public, and her views and insights have greatly influenced the environmental movement. The readings that follow — "A Fable for Tomorrow" and "The Obligation to Endure" — are the first two chapters of *Silent Spring* (1962), a book that "changed the course of history," according to former vice president Al Gore. It led to John F. Kennedy's presidential commission on the environment, as well as the banning of the use of the poison DDT in agriculture.

I. A Fable for Tomorrow

There was once a town in the heart of America where all life seemed to live in harmony with its surroundings. The town lay in the midst of a checkerboard of prosperous farms, with fields of grain and hillsides of orchards where, in spring, white clouds of bloom drifted above the green fields. In autumn, oak and maple and birch set up a blaze of color that flamed and flickered across a backdrop of pines. Then foxes barked in the hills and deer silently crossed the fields, half hidden in the mists of the fall mornings.

Along the roads, laurel, viburnum and alder, great ferns and wildflowers delighted the traveler's eye through much of the year. Even in winter the roadsides were places of beauty, where countless birds came to feed on the berries and on the seed heads of the dried weeds rising above the snow. The countryside was, in fact, famous for the abundance and variety of its bird life, and when the flood of migrants was pouring through in spring and fall people traveled from great distances to observe them. Others came to fish the streams, which flowed clear and cold out of the hills and contained shady pools where trout lay. So it had been from the days many years ago when the first settlers raised their houses, sank their wells, and built their barns.

Then a strange blight crept over the area and everything began to change. Some evil spell had settled on the community: mysterious maladies swept the flocks of chickens; the cattle and sheep sickened and died. Everywhere was a shadow of death. The farmers spoke of much illness among their families. In the town the doctors had become more and more puzzled by new kinds of sickness appearing among their patients. There had been several sudden and unexplained deaths, not only among adults but even among children, who would be stricken suddenly while at play and die within a few hours.

There was a strange stillness. The birds, for example — where had they gone? Many people spoke of them, puzzled and disturbed. The feeding stations in the backyards were deserted. The few birds seen anywhere were moribund; they trembled violently and could not fly. It was a spring without voices. On the mornings that had once throbbed with the dawn chorus of robins, catbirds, doves, jays, wrens, and scores of other bird voices there was now no sound; only silence lay over the fields and woods and marsh.

On the farms the hens brooded, but no chicks hatched. The farmers complained that they were unable to raise any pigs — the litters were small and the young survived only a few days. The apple trees were coming into bloom but no bees droned among the blossoms, so there was no pollination and there would be no fruit.

The roadsides, once so attractive, were now lined with browned and withered vegetation as though swept by fire. These, too, were silent, deserted by all living things. Even the streams were now lifeless. Anglers no longer visited them, for all the fish had died.

In the gutters under the eaves and between the shingles of the roofs, white granular powder still showed a few patches; some weeks before it had fallen like snow upon the roofs and the lawns, the fields and streams.

No witchcraft, no enemy action had silenced the rebirth of new life in this stricken world. The people had done it themselves.

This town does not actually exist, but it might easily have a thousand counterparts in America or elsewhere in the world. I know of no community that has experienced all the misfortunes I describe. Yet every one of these disasters has actually happened somewhere, and many real communities have already suffered a substantial number of them. A grim specter has crept upon us almost unnoticed, and this imagined tragedy may easily become a stark reality we all shall know.

What has already silenced the voices of spring in countless towns in America? This book is an attempt to explain.

II. The Obligation to Endure

The history of life on earth has been a history of interaction between living things and their surroundings. To a large extent, the physical form and the habits of the earth's vegetation and its animal life have been molded by the environment. Considering the whole span of earthly time, the opposite effect, in which life actually modifies its surroundings, has been relatively slight. Only within the moment of time represented by the present century has one species — man — acquired significant power to alter the nature of his world.

During the past quarter century this power has not only increased to one of disturbing magnitude but it has changed in character. The most alarming of all man's assaults upon the environment is the contamination of air, earth, rivers, and sea with dangerous and even lethal materials. This pollution is for the most part irrecoverable; the chain of evil it initiates not only in the world that must support life but in living tissues is for the most part irreversible. In this now universal contamination of the environment, chemicals are the sinister and little-recognized partners of radiation in changing the very nature of the world — the very nature of its life. Strontium 90, released through nuclear explosions into the air, comes to earth in rain or drifts down as fallout, lodges in soil, enters into the grass or corn or wheat grown there, and in time takes up its abode in the bones of a human being, there to remain until his death. Similarly, chemicals sprayed on croplands or forests or gardens lie long in soil, entering into living organisms, passing from one to another in a chain of poisoning and death. Or they pass mysteriously by underground streams until they emerge and, through the alchemy of air and sunlight, combine into new forms that kill vegetation, sicken cattle, and work unknown harm on those who drink from once pure wells. As Albert Schweitzer[1] has said, "Man can hardly even recognize the devils of his own creation."

It took hundreds of millions of years to produce the life that now inhabits the earth — eons of time in which that developing and evolving and diversifying life reached a state of adjustment and balance with its surroundings. The environment, rigorously shaping and directing the life it supported, contained elements that were hostile as well as supporting. Certain rocks gave out dangerous radiation; even within the light of the sun, from which all life draws its energy, there were short-wave radiations with power to injure. Given time — time not in years but in millennia — life adjusts, and a balance has been reached. For time is the essential ingredient; but in the modern world there is no time.

The rapidity of change and the speed with which new situations are created follow the impetuous and heedless pace of man rather than the deliberate pace of nature. Radiation is no longer merely the background radiation of rocks, the bombardment of cosmic rays, the ultraviolet of the sun that have existed before there was any life on earth; radiation is now the unnatural creation of man's tampering with the atom. The chemicals to which life is asked to make its adjustment are no longer merely the calcium and silica and copper and all the rest of the minerals washed out of the rocks and carried in rivers to the sea; they are the synthetic creations of man's inventive mind, brewed in his laboratories, and having no counterparts in nature.

To adjust to these chemicals would require time on the scale that is nature's; it would require not merely the years of a man's life but the life of generations. 15

---

[1]Albert Schweitzer (1875–1965), a French philosopher, musician, and medical missionary, spent much of his life in Africa. He won the 1952 Nobel Peace Prize. — Eds.

And even this, were it by some miracle possible, would be futile, for the new chemicals come from our laboratories in an endless stream; almost five hundred annually find their way into actual use in the United States alone. The figure is staggering and its implications are not easily grasped — 500 new chemicals to which the bodies of men and animals are required somehow to adapt each year, chemicals totally outside the limits of biologic experience.

Among them are many that are used in man's war against nature. Since the mid-1940s over 200 basic chemicals have been created for use in killing insects, weeds, rodents, and other organisms described in the modern vernacular as "pests"; and they are sold under several thousand different brand names.

These sprays, dusts, and aerosols are now applied almost universally to farms, gardens, forests, and homes — nonselective chemicals that have the power to kill every insect, the "good" and the "bad," to still the song of birds and the leaping of fish in the streams, to coat the leaves with a deadly film, and to linger on in soil — all this though the intended target may be only a few weeds or insects. Can anyone believe it is possible to lay down such a barrage of poisons on the surface of the earth without making it unfit for all life? They should not be called "insecticides," but "biocides."

The whole process of spraying seems caught up in an endless spiral. Since DDT was released for civilian use, a process of escalation has been going on in which ever more toxic materials must be found. This has happened because insects, in a triumphant vindication of Darwin's principle of the survival of the fittest, have evolved super races immune to the particular insecticide used, hence a deadlier one has always to be developed — and then a deadlier one than that. It has happened also because, for reasons to be described later, destructive insects often undergo a "flareback," or resurgence, after spraying, in numbers greater than before. Thus the chemical war is never won, and all life is caught in its violent crossfire.

Along with the possibility of the extinction of mankind by nuclear war, the central problem of our age has therefore become the contamination of man's total environment with such substances of incredible potential for harm — substances that accumulate in the tissues of plants and animals and even penetrate the germ cells to shatter or alter the very material of heredity upon which the shape of the future depends.

Some would-be architects of our future look toward a time when it will be 20 possible to alter the human germ plasm by design. But we may easily be doing so now by inadvertence, for many chemicals, like radiation, bring about gene mutations. It is ironic to think that man might determine his own future by something so seemingly trivial as the choice of an insect spray.

All this has been risked — for what? Future historians may well be amazed by our distorted sense of proportion. How could intelligent beings seek to control a few unwanted species by a method that contaminated the entire environment and brought the threat of disease and death even to their own kind? Yet this is precisely what we have done. We have done it, moreover, for reasons that collapse the moment we examine them. We are told that the enormous and expanding use of pesticides is necessary to maintain farm production. Yet is our real problem not one of *overproduction?* Our farms, despite measures to remove acreages from production and to pay farmers *not* to produce, have yielded such a staggering excess of crops that the American taxpayer in 1962 is paying out more than one billion dollars a year as the total carrying cost of the surplus-food storage program. And is the situation helped when one branch of the Agriculture Department tries to reduce production while another states, as it did in 1958, "It is believed generally that reduction of crop acreages under provisions of the Soil Bank will stimulate interest in use of chemicals to obtain maximum production on the land retained in crops."

All this is not to say there is no insect problem and no need of control. I am saying, rather, that control must be geared to realities, not to mythical situations, and that the methods employed must be such that they do not destroy us along with the insects.

The problem whose attempted solution has brought such a train of disaster in its wake is an accompaniment of our modern way of life. Long before the age of man, insects inhabited the earth — a group of extraordinarily varied and adaptable beings. Over the course of time since man's advent, a small percentage of the more than half a million species of insects have come into conflict with human welfare in two principal ways: as competitors for the food supply and as carriers of human disease.

Disease-carrying insects become important where human beings are crowded together, especially under conditions where sanitation is poor, as in time of natural disaster or war or in situations of extreme poverty and deprivation. Then control of some sort becomes necessary. It is a sobering fact, however, as we shall presently see, that the method of massive chemical control has had only limited success, and also threatens to worsen the very conditions it is intended to curb.

Under primitive agricultural conditions the farmer had few insect problems. 25
These arose with the intensification of agriculture — the devotion of immense acreages to a single crop. Such a system set the stage for explosive increases in specific insect populations. Single-crop farming does not take advantage of the principles by which nature works; it is agriculture as an engineer might conceive it to be. Nature has introduced great variety into the landscape, but man has displayed a passion for simplifying it. Thus he undoes the built-in checks and balances by which nature holds the species within bounds. One important natural check is a limit on the amount of suitable habitat for each species. Obviously then, an insect that lives on wheat can build up its population to much higher levels on a farm devoted to wheat than on one in which wheat is intermingled with other crops to which the insect is not adapted.

The same thing happens in other situations. A generation or more ago, the towns of large areas of the United States lined their streets with the noble elm tree. Now the beauty they hopefully created is threatened with complete destruction as disease sweeps through the elms, carried by a beetle that would have only limited chance to build up large populations and to spread from tree to tree if the elms were only occasional trees in a richly diversified planting.

Another factor in the modern insect problem is one that must be viewed against a background of geologic and human history: the spreading of thousands of different kinds of organisms from their native homes to invade new territories. This worldwide migration has been studied and graphically described by the British ecologist Charles Elton in his recent book *The Ecology of Invasions.* During the Cretaceous Period, some hundred million years ago, flooding seas cut many land bridges between continents and living things found themselves confined in what Elton calls "colossal separate nature reserves." There, isolated from others of their kind, they developed many new species. When some of the land masses were joined again, about 15 million years ago, these species began to move out into new territories — a movement that is not only still in progress but is now receiving considerable assistance from man.

The importation of plants is the primary agent in the modern spread of species, for animals have almost invariably gone along with the plants, quarantine being a comparatively recent and not completely effective innovation. The United States Office of Plant Introduction alone has introduced almost 200,000 species and varieties of plants from all over the world. Nearly half of the 180 or so major insect enemies of plants in the United States are accidental imports from abroad, and most of them have come as hitchhikers on plants.

In new territory, out of reach of the restraining hand of the natural enemies that kept down its numbers in its native land, an invading plant or animal is able to become enormously abundant. Thus it is no accident that our most troublesome insects are introduced species.

These invasions, both the naturally occurring and those dependent on human assistance, are likely to continue indefinitely. Quarantine and massive chemical campaigns are only extremely expensive ways of buying time. We are faced, according to Dr. Elton, "with a life-and-death need not just to find new technological means of suppressing this plant or that animal"; instead we need the basic knowledge of animal populations and their relations to their surroundings that will "promote an even balance and damp down the explosive power of outbreaks and new invasions." 30

Much of the necessary knowledge is now available but we do not use it. We train ecologists in our universities and even employ them in our governmental agencies but we seldom take their advice. We allow the chemical death rain to fall as though there were no alternative, whereas in fact there are many, and our ingenuity could soon discover many more if given opportunity.

Have we fallen into a mesmerized state that makes us accept as inevitable that which is inferior or detrimental, as though having lost the will or the vision to demand that which is good? Such thinking, in the words of the ecologist Paul

Shepard, "idealizes life with only its head out of water, inches above the limits of toleration of the corruption of its own environment . . . Why should we tolerate a diet of weak poisons, a home in insipid surroundings, a circle of acquaintances who are not quite our enemies, the noise of motors with just enough relief to prevent insanity? Who would want to live in a world which is just not quite fatal?"

Yet such a world is pressed upon us. The crusade to create a chemically sterile, insect-free world seems to have engendered a fanatic zeal on the part of many specialists and most of the so-called control agencies. On every hand there is evidence that those engaged in spraying operations exercise a ruthless power. "The regulatory entomologists . . . function as prosecutor, judge and jury, tax assessor and collector and sheriff to enforce their own orders," said Connecticut entomologist Neely Turner. The most flagrant abuses go unchecked in both state and federal agencies.

It is not my contention that chemical insecticides must never be used. I do contend that we have put poisonous and biologically potent chemicals indiscriminately into the hands of persons largely or wholly ignorant of their potentials for harm. We have subjected enormous numbers of people to contact with these poisons, without their consent and often without their knowledge. If the Bill of Rights contains no guarantee that a citizen shall be secure against lethal poisons distributed either by private individuals or by public officials, it is surely only because our forefathers, despite their considerable wisdom and foresight, could conceive of no such problem.

I contend, furthermore, that we have allowed these chemicals to be used with little or no advance investigation of their effect on soil, water, wildlife, and man himself. Future generations are unlikely to condone our lack of prudent concern for the integrity of the natural world that supports all life.   35

There is still very limited awareness of the nature of the threat. This is an era of specialists, each of whom sees his own problem and is unaware of or intolerant of the larger frame into which it fits. It is also an era dominated by industry, in which the right to make a dollar at whatever cost is seldom challenged. When the public protests, confronted with some obvious evidence of damaging results of pesticide applications, it is fed little tranquilizing pills of half truth. We urgently need an end to these false assurances, to the sugar coating of unpalatable facts. It is the public that is being asked to assume the risks that the insect controllers calculate. The public must decide whether it wishes to continue on the present road, and it can do so only when in full possession of the facts. In the words of Jean Rostand,[2] "The obligation to endure gives us the right to know."

---

[2]Jean Rostand (1894–1977), a French biologist, science writer, and philosopher, spoke against nuclear proliferation. — Eds.

Questions for Discussion

1. Why does Rachel Carson begin with "There was once a town . . . ," as though she were writing a fairy tale? Is this a fairy tale of sorts? How does Carson present the town in paragraphs 1 and 2?
2. Carson claims in paragraph 12 that "[t]he most alarming of . . . assaults upon the environment is the contamination of air, earth, rivers, and sea with dangerous and even lethal materials." Is contamination still the most alarming assault on the environment, or has another problem taken its place?
3. In paragraph 16, Carson claims that humankind is engaged in a "war against nature" and describes the targets of that war. Do you agree that targeting certain things for destruction (or at least control) means we are at war with nature? Can we be at war with something that is not our intended target? Explain.
4. Carson says the products used to kill bugs should be called "biocides" instead of "insecticides." Why? What is the difference?
5. What has changed since Carson wrote *Silent Spring*? Has the natural environmental improved? Has it declined? Since Carson's time, have we become more concerned with the effect we have on nature — or less concerned?
6. What does Rostand mean by our "obligation to endure"? How is our "right to know" related to this obligation?

Questions on Rhetoric and Style

1. Why does Carson begin "A Fable for Tomorrow" with imagery rather than exposition? What is the effect?
2. How do Carson's tone, style, and purpose change in paragraphs 9 and 10? Why do they change? How does Carson's voice change from "A Fable for Tomorrow" to "The Obligation to Endure"? How does the difference serve the writer's rhetorical purpose?
3. Why does Carson call the problem a "train of disaster" (para. 23)? What is the effect of this metaphor?
4. How does Carson appeal to authority in paragraph 27? Where else in the selection does she appeal to authority? What is the effect of her use of statistics in paragraph 28?
5. What are the "agencies" to which Carson refers (para. 33)? Why are they reduced to "so-called control agencies"?
6. Why doesn't Carson mention her "contention" until she is nearly finished with the piece? Is her argument inductive or deductive? How do you know? Also, why does she tell the reader what her "contentions" *aren't* before stating what they *are*? What response from her readers might she anticipate at this point in their reading?
7. Carson says that the public "is fed little tranquilizing pills of half truth" when it contests the use of pesticides (para. 36). Why is this metaphor effective?
8. What do you think Carson's purpose was in ending the final paragraph (and the chapter) with someone else's words?

Suggestions for Writing

1. In imitation of Rachel Carson, write an update of "A Fable for Tomorrow."

2. In paragraph 19, Carson says, "Along with the possibility of the extinction of mankind by nuclear war, the central problem of our age has therefore become the contamination of man's total environment." Write an essay in which you defend, challenge, or qualify the validity of this statement.

3. Carson writes in paragraph 35, "Future generations are unlikely to condone our lack of prudent concern for the integrity of the natural world that supports all life." As a member of one of the generations after Carson's, write a letter to her, to someone of her generation, or to a polluter of today. In the letter, identify and explain your response to Carson's statement.

4. Carson concludes with the words of French biologist and philosopher Jean Rostand: "The obligation to endure gives us the right to know." Write an essay that defends or challenges Rostand's claim as it relates to our relationship to the natural world today.

5. Carson writes, "If the Bill of Rights contains no guarantee that a citizen shall be secure against lethal poisons distributed either by private individuals or by public officials, it is surely only because our forefathers, despite their considerable wisdom and foresight, could conceive of no such problem." Imagine that the framers of the Constitution were here today, and write an essay explaining how they might use the Constitution to protect the environment.

6. Considering that *Silent Spring* was written more than forty years ago, should we be optimistic or pessimistic in our attitude toward the preservation of the natural world? As you answer this question, consider what has changed since Carson's time in our approach toward the environment.

From *Nature*

RALPH WALDO EMERSON

Ralph Waldo Emerson (1803–1882), perhaps best known for his essay "Self-Reliance," was one of America's most influential thinkers and writers. After graduating from Harvard Divinity School, he followed nine generations of his family into the ministry but practiced for only a few years. Known as a great orator, Emerson made his living as a popular lecturer on a wide range of topics. From 1821 to 1826, he taught in city and country schools and later served on a number of school boards, including the Concord School Committee and the Board of Overseers of Harvard College. Central to Emerson's thought is recognizing the spiritual relationship between humans and the natural world. In 1836, he and other like-minded intellectuals, including Henry David Thoreau, founded the Transcendental Club, and that same year he published his influential essay "Nature," the first three chapters of which are included here.

I. Nature

To go into solitude, a man needs to retire as much from his chamber as from society. I am not solitary whilst I read and write, though nobody is with me. But if a man would be alone, let him look at the stars. The rays that come from those heavenly worlds, will separate between him and what he touches. One might think the atmosphere was made transparent with this design, to give man, in the heavenly bodies, the perpetual presence of the sublime. Seen in the streets of cities, how great they are! If the stars should appear one night in a thousand years, how would men believe and adore; and preserve for many generations the remembrance of the city of God which had been shown! But every night come out these envoys of beauty, and light the universe with their admonishing smile.

The stars awaken a certain reverence, because though always present, they are inaccessible; but all natural objects make a kindred impression, when the mind is open to their influence. Nature never wears a mean appearance. Neither does the wisest man extort her secret, and lose his curiosity by finding out all her perfection. Nature never became a toy to a wise spirit. The flowers, the animals, the mountains, reflected the wisdom of his best hour, as much as they had delighted the simplicity of his childhood.

When we speak of nature in this manner, we have a distinct but most poetical sense in the mind. We mean the integrity of impression made by manifold natural objects. It is this which distinguishes the stick of timber of the wood-cutter, from the tree of the poet. The charming landscape which I saw this morning, is indubitably made up of some twenty or thirty farms. Miller owns this field, Locke that, and Manning the woodland beyond. But none of them owns the landscape. There is a property in the horizon which no man has but he whose eye can integrate all the parts, that is, the poet. This is the best part of these men's farms, yet to this their warranty-deeds give no title.

To speak truly, few adult persons can see nature. Most persons do not see the sun. At least they have a very superficial seeing. The sun illuminates only the eye of the man, but shines into the eye and the heart of the child. The lover of nature is he whose inward and outward senses are still truly adjusted to each other; who has retained the spirit of infancy even into the era of manhood. His intercourse with heaven and earth, becomes part of his daily food. In the presence of nature, a wild delight runs through the man, in spite of real sorrows. Nature says, — he is my creature, and maugre[1] all his impertinent griefs, he shall be glad with me. Not the sun or the summer alone, but every hour and season yields its tribute of delight; for every hour and change corresponds to and authorizes a different state of the mind, from breathless noon to grimmest midnight. Nature is a setting that fits equally well a comic or a mourning piece. In good health, the air is a cordial of incredible virtue. Crossing a bare common, in snow puddles, at twilight, under a clouded sky, without having in my thoughts any occurrence of special good fortune, I have enjoyed a perfect exhilaration. I am glad to the brink of fear. In the woods too, a man casts off his years, as the snake his slough, and at what period soever of life, is always a child. In the woods, is perpetual youth. Within these plantations of God, a decorum and sanctity reign, a perennial festival is dressed, and the guest sees not how he should tire of them in a thousand years. In the woods, we return to reason and faith. There I feel that nothing can befall me in life, — no disgrace, no calamity, (leaving me my eyes,) which nature cannot repair. Standing on the bare ground, — my head bathed by the blithe air, and uplifted into infinite space, — all mean egotism vanishes. I become a transparent eye-ball; I am nothing; I see all; the currents of the Universal Being circulate through me; I am part or particle of God. The name of the nearest friend sounds then foreign and accidental: to be brothers, to be acquaintances, — master or servant, is then a trifle and a disturbance. I am the lover of uncontained and immortal beauty. In the wilderness, I find something more dear and connate[2] than in streets or villages. In the tranquil landscape, and especially in the distant line of the horizon, man beholds somewhat as beautiful as his own nature.

The greatest delight which the fields and woods minister, is the suggestion of an occult relation between man and the vegetable. I am not alone and unacknowledged. They nod to me, and I to them. The waving of the boughs in the storm, is new to me and old. It takes me by surprise, and yet is not unknown. Its effect is like that of a higher thought or a better emotion coming over me, when I deemed I was thinking justly or doing right.

5

---

[1]Despite. — Eds.
[2]Sympathetic. — Eds.

Yet it is certain that the power to produce this delight, does not reside in nature, but in man, or in a harmony of both. It is necessary to use these pleasures with great temperance. For, nature is not always tricked in holiday attire, but the same scene which yesterday breathed perfume and glittered as for the frolic of the nymphs, is overspread with melancholy today. Nature always wears the colors of the spirit. To a man laboring under calamity, the heat of his own fire hath sadness in it. Then, there is a kind of contempt of the landscape felt by him who has just lost by death a dear friend. The sky is less grand as it shuts down over less worth in the population.

II. Commodity

Whoever considers the final cause of the world, will discern a multitude of uses that enter as parts into that result. They all admit of being thrown into one of the following classes; Commodity; Beauty; Language; and Discipline.

Under the general name of Commodity, I rank all those advantages which our senses owe to nature. This, of course, is a benefit which is temporary and mediate, not ultimate, like its service to the soul. Yet although low, it is perfect in its kind, and is the only use of nature which all men apprehend. The misery of man appears like childish petulance, when we explore the steady and prodigal provision that has been made for his support and delight on this green ball which floats him through the heavens. What angels invented these splendid ornaments, these rich conveniences, this ocean of air above, this ocean of water beneath, this firmament of earth between? this zodiac of lights, this tent of dropping clouds, this striped coat of climates, this fourfold year? Beasts, fire, water, stones, and corn serve him. The field is at once his floor, his work-yard, his play-ground, his garden, and his bed.

> "More servants wait on man
> Than he 'll take notice of." — [3]

Nature, in its ministry to man, is not only the material, but is also the process and the result. All the parts incessantly work into each other's hands for the profit of man. The wind sows the seed; the sun evaporates the sea; the wind blows the vapor to the field; the ice, on the other side of the planet, condenses rain on this; the rain feeds the plant; the plant feeds the animal; and thus the endless circulations of the divine charity nourish man.

The useful arts are reproductions or new combinations by the wit of man, of the same natural benefactors. He no longer waits for favoring gales, but by means of steam, he realizes the fable of Æolus's bag, and carries the two and thirty winds in the boiler of his boat. To diminish friction, he paves the road with iron bars, and, mounting a coach with a ship-load of men, animals, and merchandise

10

---

[3] The quotation is from *Man* by English poet George Herbert (1593–1633). — Eds.

behind him, he darts through the country, from town to town, like an eagle or a swallow through the air. By the aggregate of these aids, how is the face of the world changed, from the era of Noah to that of Napoleon! The private poor man hath cities, ships, canals, bridges, built for him. He goes to the post-office, and the human race run on his errands; to the book-shop, and the human race read and write of all that happens, for him; to the court-house, and nations repair his wrongs. He sets his house upon the road, and the human race go forth every morning, and shovel out the snow, and cut a path for him.

But there is no need of specifying particulars in this class of uses. The catalogue is endless, and the examples so obvious, that I shall leave them to the reader's reflection, with the general remark, that this mercenary benefit is one which has respect to a farther good. A man is fed, not that he may be fed, but that he may work.

III. Beauty

A nobler want of man is served by nature, namely, the love of Beauty.

The ancient Greeks called the world κόσμος,[4] beauty. Such is the constitution of all things, or such the plastic power of the human eye, that the primary forms, as the sky, the mountain, the tree, the animal, give us a delight *in and for themselves*; a pleasure arising from outline, color, motion, and grouping. This seems partly owing to the eye itself. The eye is the best of artists. By the mutual action of its structure and of the laws of light, perspective is produced, which integrates every mass of objects, of what character soever, into a well colored and shaded globe, so that where the particular objects are mean and unaffecting, the landscape which they compose, is round and symmetrical. And as the eye is the best composer, so light is the first of painters. There is no object so foul that intense light will not make beautiful. And the stimulus it affords to the sense, and a sort of infinitude which it hath, like space and time, make all matter gay. Even the corpse has its own beauty. But besides this general grace diffused over nature, almost all the individual forms are agreeable to the eye, as is proved by our endless imitations of some of them, as the acorn, the grape, the pine-cone, the wheat-ear, the egg, the wings and forms of most birds, the lion's claw, the serpent, the butterfly, sea-shells, flames, clouds, buds, leaves, and the forms of many trees, as the palm.

For better consideration, we may distribute the aspects of Beauty in a threefold manner.

1. First, the simple perception of natural forms is a delight. The influence of the forms and actions in nature, is so needful to man, that, in its lowest functions, it seems to lie on the confines of commodity and beauty. To the body and mind which have been cramped by noxious work or company, nature is medicinal and

15

---

[4]*Cosmos*, Greek for "universe" or "order." Emerson is equating *order* with *beauty*. — Eds.

restores their tone. The tradesman, the attorney comes out of the din and craft of the street, and sees the sky and the woods, and is a man again. In their eternal calm, he finds himself. The health of the eye seems to demand a horizon. We are never tired, so long as we can see far enough.

But in other hours, Nature satisfies by its loveliness, and without any mixture of corporeal benefit. I see the spectacle of morning from the hill-top over against my house, from day-break to sun-rise, with emotions which an angel might share. The long slender bars of cloud float like fishes in the sea of crimson light. From the earth, as a shore, I look out into that silent sea. I seem to partake its rapid transformations: the active enchantment reaches my dust, and I dilate and conspire with the morning wind. How does Nature deify us with a few and cheap elements! Give me health and a day, and I will make the pomp of emperors ridiculous. The dawn is my Assyria; the sun-set and moon-rise my Paphos,[5] and unimaginable realms of faerie; broad noon shall be my England of the senses and the understanding; the night shall be my Germany of mystic philosophy and dreams.

Not less excellent, except for our less susceptibility in the afternoon, was the charm, last evening, of a January sunset. The western clouds divided and subdivided themselves into pink flakes modulated with tints of unspeakable softness; and the air had so much life and sweetness, that it was a pain to come within doors. What was it that nature would say? Was there no meaning in the live repose of the valley behind the mill, and which Homer or Shakspeare could not re-form for me in words? The leafless trees become spires of flame in the sunset, with the blue east for their back-ground, and the stars of the dead calices of flowers, and every withered stem and stubble rimed with frost, contribute something to the mute music.

The inhabitants of cities suppose that the country landscape is pleasant only half the year. I please myself with the graces of the winter scenery, and believe that we are as much touched by it as by the genial influences of summer. To the attentive eye, each moment of the year has its own beauty, and in the same field, it beholds, every hour, a picture which was never seen before, and which shall never be seen again. The heavens change every moment, and reflect their glory or gloom on the plains beneath. The state of the crop in the surrounding farms alters the expression of the earth from week to week. The succession of native plants in the pastures and roadsides, which makes the silent clock by which time tells the summer hours, will make even the divisions of the day sensible to a keen observer. The tribes of birds and insects, like the plants punctual to their time, follow each other, and the year has room for all. By water-courses, the variety is greater. In July, the blue pontederia or pickerel-weed blooms in large beds in the shallow parts of our pleasant river, and swarms with yellow butterflies in contin-

---

[5]City in Cyprus. At its height, in the ninth century B.C.E., the Assyrian empire controlled much of the Middle East, including Cyprus. — Eds.

ual motion. Art cannot rival this pomp of purple and gold. Indeed the river is a perpetual gala, and boasts each month a new ornament.

But this beauty of Nature which is seen and felt as beauty, is the least part. The shows of day, the dewy morning, the rainbow, mountains, orchards in blossom, stars, moonlight, shadows in still water, and the like, if too eagerly hunted, become shows merely, and mock us with their unreality. Go out of the house to see the moon, and 't is mere tinsel; it will not please as when its light shines upon your necessary journey. The beauty that shimmers in the yellow afternoons of October, who ever could clutch it? Go forth to find it, and it is gone: 't is only a mirage as you look from the windows of diligence.

2. The presence of a higher, namely, of the spiritual element is essential to its perfection. The high and divine beauty which can be loved without effeminacy, is that which is found in combination with the human will. Beauty is the mark God sets upon virtue. Every natural action is graceful. Every heroic act is also decent, and causes the place and the bystanders to shine. We are taught by great actions that the universe is the property of every individual in it. Every rational creature has all nature for his dowry and estate. It is his, if he will. He may divest himself of it; he may creep into a corner, and abdicate his kingdom, as most men do, but he is entitled to the world by his constitution. In proportion to the energy of his thought and will, he takes up the world into himself. "All those things for which men plough, build, or sail, obey virtue;" said Sallust.[6] "The winds and waves," said Gibbon,[7] "are always on the side of the ablest navigators." So are the sun and moon and all the stars of heaven. When a noble act is done — perchance in a scene of great natural beauty; when Leonidas and his three hundred martyrs consume one day in dying, and the sun and moon come each and look at them once in the steep defile of Thermopylæ; when Arnold Winkelried, in the high Alps, under the shadow of the avalanche, gathers in his side a sheaf of Austrian spears to break the line for his comrades, are not these heroes entitled to add the beauty of the scene to the beauty of the deed? When the bark of Columbus nears the shore of America; — before it, the beach lined with savages, fleeing out of all their huts of cane; the sea behind; and the purple mountains of the Indian Archipelago around, can we separate the man from the living picture? Does not the New World clothe his form with her palm-groves and savannahs as fit drapery? Ever does natural beauty steal in like air, and envelope great actions. When Sir Harry Vane was dragged up the Tower-hill, sitting on a sled, to suffer death, as the champion of the English laws, one of the multitude cried out to him, "You never sate on so glorious a seat." Charles II, to intimidate the citizens of London, caused the patriot Lord Russel to be drawn in an open coach, through the principal streets of

20

---

[6]Sallust (86–34 B.C.E.), Roman historian. — Eds.

[7]Edward Gibbon (1737–1794), English historian and author of *The History of the Decline and Fall of the Roman Empire.* — Eds.

the city, on his way to the scaffold. "But," his biographer says, "the multitude imagined they saw liberty and virtue sitting by his side." In private places, among sordid objects, an act of truth or heroism seems at once to draw to itself the sky as its temple, the sun as its candle. Nature stretcheth out her arms to embrace man, only let his thoughts be of equal greatness. Willingly does she follow his steps with the rose and the violet, and bend her lines of grandeur and grace to the decoration of her darling child. Only let his thoughts be of equal scope, and the frame will suit the picture. A virtuous man is in unison with her works, and makes the central figure of the visible sphere. Homer, Pindar, Socrates, Phocion, associate themselves fitly in our memory with the geography and climate of Greece. The visible heavens and earth sympathize with Jesus. And in common life, whosoever has seen a person of powerful character and happy genius, will have remarked how easily he took all things along with him, — the persons, the opinions, and the day, and nature became ancillary to a man.

3. There is still another aspect under which the beauty of the world may be viewed, namely, as it becomes an object of the intellect. Beside the relation of things to virtue, they have a relation to thought. The intellect searches out the absolute order of things as they stand in the mind of God, and without the colors of affection. The intellectual and the active powers seem to succeed each other, and the exclusive activity of the one, generates the exclusive activity of the other. There is something unfriendly in each to the other, but they are like the alternate periods of feeding and working in animals; each prepares and will be followed by the other. Therefore does beauty, which, in relation to actions, as we have seen, comes unsought, and comes because it is unsought, remain for the apprehension and pursuit of the intellect; and then again, in its turn, of the active power. Nothing divine dies. All good is eternally reproductive. The beauty of nature reforms itself in the mind, and not for barren contemplation, but for new creation.

All men are in some degree impressed by the face of the world; some men even to delight. This love of beauty is Taste. Others have the same love in such excess, that, not content with admiring, they seek to embody it in new forms. The creation of beauty is Art.

The production of a work of art throws a light upon the mystery of humanity. A work of art is an abstract or epitome of the world. It is the result or expression of nature, in miniature. For, although the works of nature are innumerable and all different, the result or the expression of them all is similar and single. Nature is a sea of forms radically alike and even unique. A leaf, a sun-beam, a landscape, the ocean, make an analogous impression on the mind. What is common to them all, — that perfectness and harmony, is beauty. The standard of beauty is the entire circuit of natural forms, — the totality of nature; which the Italians expressed by defining beauty "il piu nell' uno."[8] Nothing is quite beautiful

---

[8]Italian, "the many in one." — Eds.

alone: nothing but is beautiful in the whole. A single object is only so far beautiful as it suggests this universal grace. The poet, the painter, the sculptor, the musician, the architect, seek each to concentrate this radiance of the world on one point, and each in his several work to satisfy the love of beauty which stimulates him to produce. Thus is Art, a nature passed through the alembic[9] of man. Thus in art, does nature work through the will of a man filled with the beauty of her first works.

The world thus exists to the soul to satisfy the desire of beauty. This element I call an ultimate end. No reason can be asked or given why the soul seeks beauty. Beauty, in its largest and profoundest sense, is one expression for the universe. God is the all-fair. Truth, and goodness, and beauty, are but different faces of the same All. But beauty in nature is not ultimate. It is the herald of inward and eternal beauty, and is not alone a solid and satisfactory good. It must stand as a part, and not as yet the last or highest expression of the final cause of Nature.

Questions for Discussion

1. Explain Ralph Waldo Emerson's attitude toward nature in paragraphs 1 and 2.
2. In paragraph 4, Emerson writes, "I become a transparent eye-ball; I am nothing; I see all; the currents of the Universal Being circulate through me; I am part or particle of God." From those words, how would you describe Emerson's mental state here, and what has brought it about?
3. In paragraph 6, Emerson says, "Nature always wears the colors of the spirit." What does he mean? Do you agree? In paragraph 4, Emerson says, "Crossing a bare common, in snow puddles, at twilight, under a clouded sky . . . I have enjoyed a perfect exhilaration." Does this contradict his statement in paragraph 6? Explain how the relationship that Emerson describes between humans and nature works.
4. In paragraphs 7–9, what does Emerson suggest about the human condition?
5. In paragraph 10, what is Emerson's attitude toward the "useful arts" — what people now call technology? Would Emerson have the same attitude today? Why or why not?
6. In Part III of the selection, Emerson says that in regard to nature, loving its beauty is a nobler response than using it as a commodity. Do you agree or disagree? Explain why.
7. In paragraph 20, Emerson writes, "Nature stretcheth out her arms to embrace man, only let his thoughts be of equal greatness." What does he mean? What does this statement imply about the relationship between nature and humankind?

---

[9]A device that purifies or refines. — Eds.

Questions on Rhetoric and Style

1. What is the effect of the comparisons (including figurative language) and distinctions that Ralph Waldo Emerson makes in paragraphs 1 and 2? In the conclusion to the first paragraph, Emerson says the stars give an "admonishing smile." What does he mean by this phrase? How does Emerson characterize nature? What is the purpose of this characterization?

2. Identify the juxtapositions in paragraph 4. What is their effect? Is there a relationship among the juxtapositions that suggests a larger point? Explain.

3. In paragraph 8, Emerson speaks of "this green ball which floats him through the heavens." What is the effect of this metaphor? How does the repetition in the rest of the paragraph ("this ocean of air above, this ocean of water beneath, this . . . this . . .") contribute to this effect?

4. What three aspects of the beauty of nature does Emerson delineate in Part III? How does he use simile and metaphor to develop the first aspect? How do the rhetorical questions in paragraph 20 serve to develop the second aspect?

5. What is the relationship between paragraphs 19 and 20? What is the effect of the paradox that concludes paragraph 20?

6. In Part III, what distinction does Emerson make between "barren contemplation" and "new creation"?

7. How does Emerson unite truth, goodness, and beauty in the final paragraph? Why is this a fitting conclusion for this section?

Suggestions for Writing

1. Write an essay in which you support, challenge, or qualify Emerson's main idea in Part I.

2. In Part II, Emerson presents an optimistic view of the "useful arts." In the voice of a modern-day environmentalist such as Rachel Carson (p. 798), discuss whether his view holds true today.

3. Write a letter to Emerson describing an experience you have had with nature. Explain how it was similar or different from the experience he describes in Part II.

4. Select a powerful, challenging, or thought-provoking statement from Emerson — such as "The production of a work of art throws a light upon the mystery of humanity. A work of art is an abstract or epitome of the world." Write an essay that supports, qualifies, or refutes its assertion. Use evidence from your reading, as well as your own knowledge and experience, to defend your position.

5. Read the poem "Thanatopsis" by William Cullen Bryant, a contemporary of Emerson's, at <bedfordstmartins.com/languageofcomp>, and write an essay comparing it with Emerson's essay "Nature."

The Clan of One-Breasted Women

TERRY TEMPEST WILLIAMS

Terry Tempest Williams was born in Nevada in 1955. She studied at the University of Utah, where she became a professor of English. She has also been naturalist-in-residence at the Utah Museum of Natural History. Williams's work has appeared in the *New Yorker*, *Orion*, the *New York Times*, the *Nation*, and *The Best American Essays* (2000). Williams has won a Guggenheim Fellowship and a Lannan Literary Fellowship. Among her books are the essay collections *An Unspoken Hunger: Stories from the Field* (1995) and *Refuge: An Unnatural History of Family and Place* (1989), from which the following selection is taken. The essay is based on her family's experience in Utah, where she lives and writes on social and environmental issues.

I belong to a Clan of One-breasted Women. My mother, my grandmothers, and six aunts have all had mastectomies. Seven are dead. The two who survive have just completed rounds of chemotherapy and radiation.

I've had my own problems: two biopsies for breast cancer and a small tumor between my ribs diagnosed as "a border-line malignancy."

This is my family history.

Most statistics tell us breast cancer is genetic, hereditary, with rising percentages attached to fatty diets, childlessness, or becoming pregnant after thirty. What they don't say is living in Utah may be the greatest hazard of all.

We are a Mormon family with roots in Utah since 1847. The word-of-wisdom, a religious doctrine of health, kept the women in my family aligned with good foods: no coffee, no tea, tobacco, or alcohol. For the most part, these women were finished having their babies by the time they were thirty. And only one faced breast cancer prior to 1960. Traditionally, as a group of people, Mormons have a low rate of cancer.

Is our family a cultural anomaly? The truth is we didn't think about it. Those who did, usually the men, simply said, "bad genes." The women's attitude was stoic. Cancer was part of life. On February 16, 1971, the eve before my mother's surgery, I accidently picked up the telephone and overheard her ask my grandmother what she could expect.

"Diane, it is one of the most spiritual experiences you will ever encounter."

I quietly put down the receiver.

Two days later, my father took my three brothers and me to the hospital to visit her. She met us in the lobby in a wheelchair. No bandages were visible. I'll never forget her radiance, the way she held herself in a purple velour robe and how she gathered us around her.

"Children, I am fine. I want you to know I felt the arms of God around me."   10

We believed her. My father cried. Our mother, his wife, was thirty-eight years old.

Two years ago, after my mother's death from cancer, my father and I were having dinner together. He had just returned from St. George where his construction company was putting in natural gas lines for towns in southern Utah. He spoke of his love for the country: the sandstoned landscape, bare-boned and beautiful. He had just finished hiking the Kolob trail in Zion National Park. We got caught up in reminiscing, recalling with fondness our walk up Angel's Landing on his fiftieth birthday and the years our family had vacationed there. This was a remembered landscape where we had been raised.

Over dessert, I shared a recurring dream of mine. I told my father that for years, as long as I could remember, I saw this flash of light in the night in the desert. That this image had so permeated my being, I could not venture south without seeing it again, on the horizon, illuminating buttes and mesas.

"You did see it," he said.

"Saw what?" I asked, a bit tentative.   15

"The bomb. The cloud. We were driving home from Riverside, California. You were sitting on your mother's lap. She was pregnant. In fact, I remember the date, September 7, 1957. We had just gotten out of the Service. We were driving north, past Las Vegas. It was an hour or so before dawn, when this explosion went off. We not only heard it, but felt it. I thought the oil tanker in front of us had blown up. We pulled over and suddenly, rising from the desert floor, we saw it, clearly, this golden-stemmed cloud, the mushroom. The sky seemed to vibrate with an eerie pink glow. Within a few minutes, a light ash was raining on the car."

I stared at my father. This was new information to me.

"I thought you knew that," my father said. "It was a common occurrence in the fifties."

It was at this moment I realized the deceit I had been living under. Children growing up in the American Southwest, drinking contaminated milk from contaminated cows, even from the contaminated breasts of their mother, my mother — members, years later, of the Clan of One-breasted Women.

It is a well-known story in the Desert West, "The Day We Bombed Utah," or per-   20
haps, "The Years We Bombed Utah."[1] Above ground atomic testing in Nevada took place from January 27, 1951, through July 11, 1962. Not only were the winds blowing north, covering "low use segments of the population" with fallout and leaving sheep dead in their tracks, but the climate was right. The United States of the 1950s was red, white, and blue. The Korean War was raging. McCarthyism was rampant. Ike was it and the Cold War was hot. If you were against nuclear testing, you were for a Communist regime.

---

[1]Fuller, John G., *The Day We Bombed Utah* (New York: New American Library, 1984).

Much has been written about this "American nuclear tragedy." Public health was secondary to national security. The Atomic Energy Commissioner, Thomas Murray said, "Gentlemen, we must not let anything interfere with this series of tests, nothing."[2]

Again and again, the American public was told by its government, in spite of burns, blisters, and nausea, "It has been found that the tests may be conducted with adequate assurance of safety under conditions prevailing at the bombing reservations."[3] Assuaging public fears was simply a matter of public relations. "Your best action," an Atomic Energy Commission booklet read, "is not to be worried about fallout." A news release typical of the times stated, "We find no basis for concluding that harm to any individual has resulted from radioactive fallout."[4]

On August 30, 1979, during Jimmy Carter's presidency, a suit was filed entitled "Irene Allen vs. the United States of America." Mrs. Allen was the first to be alphabetically listed with twenty-four test cases, representative of nearly 1200 plaintiffs seeking compensation from the United States government for cancers caused from nuclear testing in Nevada.

Irene Allen lived in Hurricane, Utah. She was the mother of five children and had been widowed twice. Her first husband with their two oldest boys had watched the tests from the roof of the local high school. He died of leukemia in 1956. Her second husband died of pancreatic cancer in 1978.

In a town meeting conducted by Utah Senator Orrin Hatch, shortly before the suit was filed, Mrs. Allen said, "I am not blaming the government, I want you to know that, Senator Hatch. But I thought if my testimony could help in any way so this wouldn't happen again to any of the generations coming up after us . . . I am really happy to be here this day to bear testimony of this."[5]

God-fearing people. This is just one story in an anthology of thousands.

On May 10, 1984, Judge Bruce S. Jenkins handed down his opinion. Ten of the plaintiffs were awarded damages. It was the first time a federal court had determined that nuclear tests had been the cause of cancers. For the remaining fourteen test cases, the proof of causation was not sufficient. In spite of the split decision, it was considered a landmark ruling.[6] It was not to remain so for long.

In April, 1987, the 10th Circuit Court of Appeals overturned Judge Jenkins' ruling on the basis that the United States was protected from suit by the legal doc-

25

---

[2]Szasz, Ferenc M., "Downwind from the Bomb," *Nevada Historical Society Quarterly*, Fall 1987 Vol. XXX, No. 3, p. 185.
[3]Fradkin, Philip L., *Fallout* (Tucson: University of Arizona Press, 1989), 98.
[4]Ibid., 109.
[5]Town meeting held by Senator Orrin Hatch in St. George, Utah, April 17, 1979, transcript, 26–28.
[6]Fradkin, Op. cit., 228.

trine of sovereign immunity, the centuries-old idea from England in the days of absolute monarchs.[7]

In January, 1988, the Supreme Court refused to review the Appeals Court decision. To our court system, it does not matter whether the United States Government was irresponsible, whether it lied to its citizens or even that citizens died from the fallout of nuclear testing. What matters is that our government is immune. "The King can do no wrong."

In Mormon culture, authority is respected, obedience is revered, and independent thinking is not. I was taught as a young girl not to "make waves" or "rock the boat."

"Just let it go —" my mother would say. "You know how you feel, that's what counts."

For many years, I did just that — listened, observed, and quietly formed my own opinions within a culture that rarely asked questions because they had all the answers. But one by one, I watched the women in my family die common, heroic deaths. We sat in waiting rooms hoping for good news, always receiving the bad. I cared for them, bathed their scarred bodies and kept their secrets. I watched beautiful women become bald as cytoxan, cisplatin and adriamycin were injected into their veins. I held their foreheads as they vomited green-black bile and I shot them with morphine when the pain became inhuman. In the end, I witnessed their last peaceful breaths, becoming a midwife to the rebirth of their souls. But the price of obedience became too high.

The fear and inability to question authority that ultimately killed rural communities in Utah during atmospheric testing of atomic weapons was the same fear I saw being held in my mother's body. Sheep. Dead sheep. The evidence is buried.

I cannot prove that my mother, Diane Dixon Tempest, or my grandmothers, Lettie Romney Dixon and Kathryn Blackett Tempest, along with my aunts contracted cancer from nuclear fallout in Utah. But I can't prove they didn't.

My father's memory was correct, the September blast we drove through in 1957 was part of Operation Plumbbob, one of the most intensive series of bomb tests to be initiated. The flash of light in the night in the desert I had always thought was a dream developed into a family nightmare. It took fourteen years, from 1957 to 1971, for cancer to show up in my mother — the same time, Howard L. Andrews, an authority on radioactive fallout at the National Institutes of Health, says radiation cancer requires to become evident.[8] The more I learn about what it means to be a "downwinder," the more questions I drown in.

30

35

---

[7]U.S. vs. Allen, 816 Federal Reporter, 2d/1417 (10th Circuit Court 1987), cert. denied, 108 S. Ct. 694 (1988).
[8]Fradkin, Op. cit., 116.

What I do know, however, is that as a Mormon woman of the fifth generation of "Latter-Day-Saints," I must question everything, even if it means losing my faith, even if it means becoming a member of a border tribe among my own people. Tolerating blind obedience in the name of patriotism or religion ultimately takes our lives.

When the Atomic Energy Commission described the country north of the Nevada Test Site as "virtually uninhabited desert terrain," my family members were some of the "virtual uninhabitants."

One night, I dreamed women from all over the world circling a blazing fire in the desert. They spoke of change, of how they hold the moon in their bellies and wax and wane with its phases. They mocked at the presumption of even-tempered beings and made promises that they would never fear the witch inside themselves. The women danced wildly as sparks broke away from the flames and entered the night sky as stars.

And they sang a song given to them by Shoshoni grandmothers:

> *Ah ne nah, nah*
> *nin nah nah —*
> *Ah ne nah, nah*
> *nin nah nah —*
> *Nyaga mutzi*
> *oh ne nay —*
> *Nyaga mutzi*
> *oh ne nay —* [9]

The women danced and drummed and sang for weeks, preparing themselves   40
for what was to come. They would reclaim the desert for the sake of their children, for the sake of the land.

A few miles downwind from the fire circle, bombs were being tested. Rabbits felt the tremors. Their soft leather pads on paws and feet recognized the shaking sands while the roots of mesquite and sage were smoldering. Rocks were hot from the inside out and dust devils hummed unnaturally. And each time there was another nuclear test, ravens watched the desert heave. Stretch marks appeared. The land was losing its muscle.

The women couldn't bear it any longer. They were mothers. They had suffered labor pains but always under the promise of birth. The red hot pains

---

[9]This song was sung by the Western Shoshone women as they crossed the line at the Nevada Test Site on March 18, 1988, as part of their "Reclaim the Land" action. The translation they gave was: "Consider the rabbits how gently they walk on the earth. Consider the rabbits how gently they walk on the earth. We remember them. We can walk gently also. We remember them. We can walk gently also."

beneath the desert promised death only as each bomb became a stillborn. A contract had been broken between human beings and the land. A new contract was being drawn by the women who understood the fate of the earth as their own.

Under the cover of darkness, ten women slipped under the barbed wire fence and entered the contaminated country. They were trespassing. The walked toward the town of Mercury in moonlight, taking their cues from coyote, kit fox, antelope squirrel, and quail. They moved quietly and deliberately through the maze of Joshua trees. When a hint of daylight appeared they rested, drinking tea and sharing their rations of food. The women closed their eyes. The time had come to protest with the heart, that to deny one's genealogy with the earth was to commit treason against one's soul.

At dawn, the women draped themselves in mylar, wrapping long streamers of silver plastic around their arms to blow in the breeze. They wore clear masks that became the faces of humanity. And when they arrived on the edge of Mercury, they carried all the butterflies of a summer day in their wombs. They paused to allow their courage to settle.

The town which forbids pregnant women and children to enter because of 45 radiation risks to their health was asleep. The women moved through the streets as winged messengers, twirling around each other in slow motion, peeking inside homes and watching the easy sleep of men and women. They were astonished by such stillness and periodically would utter a shrill note or low cry just to verify life.

The residents finally awoke to what appeared as strange apparitions. Some simply stared. Others called authorities, and in time, the women were apprehended by wary soldiers dressed in desert fatigues. They were taken to a white, square building on the other edge of Mercury. When asked who they were and why they were there, the women replied, "We are mothers and we have come to reclaim the desert for our children."

The soldiers arrested them. As the ten women were blindfolded and handcuffed, they began singing:

> *You can't forbid us everything*
> *You can't forbid us to think —*
> *You can't forbid our tears to flow*
> *And you can't stop the songs that we sing.*

The women continued to sing louder and louder, until they heard the voices of their sisters moving across the mesa.

> *Ah ne nah, nah*
> *nin nah nah —*
> *Ah ne nah, nah*
> *nin nah nah —*
> *Nyaga mutzi*

oh ne nay —
Nyaga mutzi
oh ne nay —

"Call for re-enforcement," one soldier said.

"We have," interrupted one woman. "We have — and you have no idea of our   50
numbers."

On March 18, 1988, I crossed the line at the Nevada Test Site and was arrested with nine other Utahns for trespassing on military lands. They are still conducting nuclear tests in the desert. Ours was an act of civil disobedience. But as I walked toward the town of Mercury, it was more than a gesture of peace. It was a gesture on behalf of the Clan of One-breasted Women.

As one officer cinched the handcuffs around my wrists, another frisked my body. She found a pen and a pad of paper tucked inside my left boot.

"And these?" she asked sternly.

"Weapons," I replied.

Our eyes met. I smiled. She pulled the leg of my trousers back over my boot.   55

"Step forward, please," she said as she took my arm.

We were booked under an afternoon sun and bussed to Tonapah, Nevada. It was a two-hour ride. This was familiar country to me. The Joshua trees standing their ground had been named by my ancestors who believed they looked like prophets pointing west to the promised land. These were the same trees that bloomed each spring, flowers appearing like white flames in the Mojave. And I recalled a full moon in May when my mother and I had walked among them, flushing out mourning doves and owls.

The bus stopped short of town. We were released. The officials thought it was a cruel joke to leave us stranded in the desert with no way to get home. What they didn't realize is that we were home, soul-centered and strong, women who recognized the sweet smell of sage as fuel for our spirits.

Exploring the Text

1. The first section of the essay (paras. 1–19) begins and ends with a reference to the title. Why do you think Terry Tempest Williams frames this section this way? How does it affect the tone?

2. Williams claims that "[t]raditionally, as a group of people, Mormons have a low rate of cancer" (para. 5). What are some of the possible reasons for this?

3. Research the story that a group of women warriors called the Amazons each slashed off one breast to get better leverage when using bow and arrow. How effectively does Williams use the reference to this legend?

4. What is the effect of repeating the word *contaminated* three times in paragraph 19?

5. At paragraph 20, why does Williams interrupt the story of her own family's illness to tell the story of Irene Allen's family?

6. Williams says in paragraph 22, "Assuaging public fears was simply a matter of public relations" by the government. What does she mean? Is she being ironic, or is she giving a matter-of-fact description of public policy at the time?

7. Why does Williams put a section break between paragraphs 29 and 30? Why is there no smooth transition from the Supreme Court case to Mormon culture?

8. What is the effect of the footnotes Williams includes and of the reference to the National Institutes of Health in paragraph 35?

9. In paragraph 43, Williams writes, "The time had come to protest with the heart, that to deny one's genealogy with the earth was to commit treason against one's soul." What underlying assumption connects her support to this claim?

10. In paragraphs 43 and 58, how does Williams give the impression of a spiritual presence in nature?

11. What is the rhetorical effect of shifting between narration, exposition, and argument in this essay?

Message to President Franklin Pierce

CHIEF SEATTLE

Chief Seattle (c.1786–1866), or Satala, was born in the Pacific Northwest. He became chief of the Suquamish and Duwamish tribes in what is now Washington state. He converted to Catholicism in the late 1840s. An advocate of peace who promoted trade with the "white man," he became so prominent that the city of Seattle was named for him. The selection that follows is Chief Seattle's reply to a treaty offered by Governor Isaac Stevens, Commissioner of Indian Affairs. Since the text was delivered orally, there are several versions of it in existence. The one here is believed to be close to the original.

We know that the white man does not understand our ways. One portion of the land is the same to him as the next, for he is a stranger who comes in the night and takes from the land whatever he needs. The earth is not his brother, but his enemy, and when he has conquered it, he moves on. He leaves his fathers' graves, and his children's birthright is forgotten. The sight of your cities pains the eyes of the red man. But perhaps it is because the red man is a savage and does not understand.

There is no quiet place in the white man's cities. No place to hear the leaves of spring or the rustle of insect's wings. But perhaps because I am a savage and do not understand, the clatter only seems to insult the ears. The Indian prefers the soft sound of the wind darting over the face of the pond, the smell of the wind itself cleansed by a mid-day rain, or scented with the piñon pine. The air is precious to the red man. For all things share the same breath — the beasts, the trees, the man. Like a man dying for many days, he is numb to the stench.

What is man without the beasts? If all the beasts were gone, men would die from great loneliness of spirit, for whatever happens to the beasts also happens to man. All things are connected. Whatever befalls the earth befalls the sons of the earth.

It matters little where we pass the rest of our days; they are not many. A few more hours, a few more winters, and none of the children of the great tribes that once lived on this earth, or that roamed in small bands in the woods, will be left to mourn the graves of a people once as powerful and hopeful as yours.

The whites, too, shall pass — perhaps sooner than other tribes. Continue to contaminate your bed, and you will one night suffocate in your own waste. When the buffalo are all slaughtered, the wild horses all tamed, the secret corners of the forest heavy with the scent of many men, and the view of the ripe hills blotted by talking wires, where is the thicket? Gone. Where is the eagle? Gone. And what is it to say goodby to the swift and the hunt, the end of living and the beginning of survival? We might understand if we knew what it was that the white man dreams, what he describes to his children on the long winter nights, what visions he burns into their minds, so they will wish for tomorrow. But we are savages. The white man's dreams are hidden from us.

Exploring the Text

1. What is the effect of the contrasts and juxtapositions in the first paragraph?
2. How does Chief Seattle's use of the word *savage* three times serve his rhetorical purpose?
3. According to Chief Seattle, what are several differences between the "white man" and the "red man"? How does Seattle's admonition of the "white man" speak to our situation in the twenty-first century?
4. Chief Seattle's message begins, "We know that the white man does not understand our ways." He later says, "We might understand if we knew what it was that the white man dreams" (para. 5). What is the effect of this reversal?
5. If the message included here is a reply to a treaty offered by Governor Isaac Stevens, Commissioner of Indian Affairs, why do you think Chief Seattle writes not to Stevens but to President Franklin Pierce?
6. How might President Pierce have responded?
7. The speech included here is one of many versions. Many are apocryphal, and this one might be inauthentic in part. Read a few versions on the Internet. Compare and contrast two different versions and discuss the impact of the differences.

An Entrance to the Woods

WENDELL BERRY

A farmer, environmentalist, teacher, and writer, Wendell Berry was born in Kentucky in 1934. He is also a critic of technology and government. After living in both New York and California and teaching at New York University in the 1960s he returned to Kentucky, where he now lives, farms, and teaches at the University of Kentucky. Berry writes novels, essays, and poetry, winning acclaim in all three genres. Among his essay collections are *The Gift of Good Land* (1982), *Standing by Words* (1983), *Home Economics* (1987), and *Recollected Essays: 1965–1980* (1987), which includes "An Entrance to the Woods," the 1971 essay that follows.

On a fine sunny afternoon at the end of September I leave my work in Lexington and drive east on I-64 and the Mountain Parkway. When I leave the Parkway at the little town of Pine Ridge I am in the watershed of the Red River in the Daniel Boone National Forest. From Pine Ridge I take Highway 715 out along the narrow ridgetops, a winding tunnel through the trees. And then I turn off on a Forest Service Road and follow it to the head of a foot trail that goes down the steep valley wall of one of the tributary creeks. I pull my car off the road and lock it, and lift on my pack.

It is nearly five o'clock when I start walking. The afternoon is brilliant and warm, absolutely still, not enough air stirring to move a leaf. There is only the steady somnolent trilling of insects, and now and again in the woods below me the cry of a pileated woodpecker. Those, and my footsteps on the path, are the only sounds.

From the dry oak woods of the ridge I pass down into the rock. The foot trails of the Red River Gorge all seek these stony notches that little streams have cut back through the cliffs. I pass a ledge overhanging a sheer drop of the rock, where in a wetter time there would be a waterfall. The ledge is dry and mute now, but on the face of the rock below are the characteristic mosses, ferns, liverwort, meadow rue. And here where the ravine suddenly steepens and narrows, where the shadows are long-lived and the dampness stays, the trees are different. Here are beech and hemlock and poplar, straight and tall, reaching way up into the light. Under them are evergreen thickets of rhododendron. And wherever the dampness is there are mosses and ferns. The faces of the rock are intricately scalloped with veins of ironstone, scooped and carved by the wind.

Finally from the crease of the ravine I am following there begins to come the trickling and splashing of water. There is a great restfulness in the sounds these small streams make; they are going down as fast as they can, but their sounds seem leisurely and idle, as if produced like gemstones with the greatest patience and care.

A little later, stopping, I hear not far away the more voluble flowing of the   5
creek. I go on down to where the trail crosses and begin to look for a camping
place. The little bottoms along the creek here are thickety and weedy, probably
having been kept clear and cropped or pastured not so long ago. In the more open
places are little lavender asters, and the even smaller-flowered white ones that
some people call beeweed or farewell-summer. And in low wet places are the richly
flowered spikes of great lobelia, the blooms an intense startling blue, exquisitely
shaped. I choose a place in an open thicket near the stream, and make camp.

It is a simple matter to make camp. I string up a shelter and put my air mat-
tress and sleeping bag in it, and I am ready for the night. And supper is even
simpler, for I have brought sandwiches for this first meal. In less than an hour all
my chores are done. It will still be light for a good while, and I go over and sit
down on a rock at the edge of the stream.

And then a heavy feeling of melancholy and lonesomeness comes over me.
This does not surprise me, for I have felt it before when I have been alone at
evening in wilderness places that I am not familiar with. But here it has a quality
that I recognize as peculiar to the narrow hollows of the Red River Gorge. These
are deeply shaded by the trees and by the valley walls, the sun rising on them late
and setting early; they are more dark than light. And there will often be little
rapids in the stream that will sound, at a certain distance, exactly like people talking. As I sit on my rock by the stream now, I could swear that there is a party of
campers coming up the trail toward me, and for several minutes I stay alert, listening for them, their voices seeming to rise and fall, fade out and lift again, in
happy conversation. When I finally realize that it is only the sound the creek is
making, though I have not come here for company and do not want any, I am
inexplicably sad.

These are haunted places, or at least it is easy to feel haunted in them, alone at
nightfall. As the air darkens and the cool of the night rises, one feels the imma-
nence of the wraiths of the ancient tribesmen who used to inhabit the rock
houses of the cliffs; of the white hunters from east of the mountains; of the farmers who accepted the isolation of these nearly inaccessible valleys to crop the narrow bottoms and ridges and pasture their cattle and hogs in the woods; of the
seekers of quick wealth in timber and ore. For though this is a wilderness place, it
bears its part of the burden of human history. If one spends much time here and
feels much liking for the place, it is hard to escape the sense of one's predecessors.
If one has read of the prehistoric Indians whose flint arrowpoints and pottery and
hominy holes and petroglyphs have been found here, then every rock shelter and
clifty spring will suggest the presence of those dim people who have disappeared
into the earth. Walking along the ridges and the stream bottoms, one will come
upon the heaped stones of a chimney, or the slowly filling depression of an old
cellar, or will find in the spring a japonica bush or periwinkles or a few jonquils
blooming in a thicket that used to be a dooryard. Wherever the land is level
enough there are abandoned fields and pastures. And nearly always there is the
evidence that one follows in the steps of the loggers.

That sense of the past is probably one reason for the melancholy that I feel. But I know that there are other reasons.

One is that, though I am here in body, my mind and my nerves too are not yet altogether here. We seem to grant to our high-speed roads and our airlines the rather thoughtless assumption that people can change places as rapidly as their bodies can be transported. That, as my own experience keeps proving to me, is not true. In the middle of the afternoon I left off being busy at work, and drove through traffic to the freeway, and then for a solid hour or more I drove sixty or seventy miles an hour, hardly aware of the country I was passing through, because on the freeway one does not have to be. The landscape has been subdued so that one may drive over it at seventy miles per hour without any concession whatsoever to one's whereabouts. One might as well be flying. Though one is in Kentucky one is not experiencing Kentucky; one is experiencing the highway, which might be in nearly any hill country east of the Mississippi.

Once off the freeway, my pace gradually slowed, as the roads became progressively more primitive, from seventy miles an hour to a walk. And now, here at my camping place, I have stopped altogether. But my mind is still keyed to seventy miles an hour. And having come here so fast, it is still busy with the work I am usually doing. Having come here by the freeway, my mind is not so fully here as it would have been if I had come by the crookeder, slower state roads; it is incalculably farther away than it would have been if I had come all the way on foot, as my earliest predecessors came. When the Indians and the first white hunters entered this country they were altogether here as soon as they arrived, for they had seen and experienced fully everything between here and their starting place, and so the transition was gradual and articulate in their consciousness. Our senses, after all, were developed to function at foot speeds; and the transition from foot travel to motor travel, in terms of evolutionary time, has been abrupt. The faster one goes, the more strain there is on the senses, the more they fail to take in, the more confusion they must tolerate or gloss over — and the longer it takes to bring the mind to a stop in the presence of anything. Though the freeway passes through the very heart of this forest, the motorist remains several hours' journey by foot from what is living at the edge of the right-of-way.

But I have not only come to this strangely haunted place in a short time and too fast. I have in that move made an enormous change: I have departed from my life as I am used to living it, and have come into the wilderness. It is not fear that I feel; I have learned to fear the everyday events of human history much more than I fear the everyday occurrences of the woods; in general, I would rather trust myself to the woods than to any government that I know of. I feel, instead, an uneasy awareness of severed connections, of being cut off from all familiar places and of being a stranger where I am. What is happening at home? I wonder, and I know I can't find out very easily or very soon.

Even more discomforting is a pervasive sense of unfamiliarity. In the places I am most familiar with — my house, or my garden, or even the woods near home that I have walked in for years — I am surrounded by associations; everywhere I look I am reminded of my history and my hopes; even unconsciously I am comforted by any number of proofs that my life on the earth is an established and a going thing. But I am in this hollow for the first time in my life. I see nothing that I recognize. Everything looks as it did before I came, as it will when I am gone. When I look over at my little camp I see how tentative and insignificant it is. Lying there in my bed in the dark tonight, I will be absorbed in the being of this place, invisible as a squirrel in his nest.

Uneasy as this feeling is, I know it will pass. Its passing will produce a deep pleasure in being here. And I have felt it often enough before that I have begun to understand something of what it means:

Nobody knows where I am. I don't know what is happening to anybody else in the world. While I am here I will not speak, and will have no reason or need for speech. It is only beyond this lonesomeness for the places I have come from that I can reach the vital reality of a place such as this. Turning toward this place, I confront a presence that none of my schooling and none of my usual assumptions have prepared me for: the wilderness, mostly unknowable and mostly alien, that is the universe. Perhaps the most difficult labor for my species is to accept its limits, its weakness and ignorance. But here I am. This wild place where I have camped lies within an enormous cone widening from the center of the earth out across the universe, nearly all of it a mysterious wilderness in which the power and the knowledge of men count for nothing. As long as its instruments are correct and its engines run, the airplane now flying through this great cone is safely within the human freehold; its behavior is as familiar and predictable to those concerned as the inside of a man's living room. But let its instruments or its engines fail, and at once it enters the wilderness where nothing is foreseeable. And these steep narrow hollows, these cliffs and forested ridges that lie below, are the antithesis of flight.

Wilderness is the element in which we live encased in civilization, as a mollusk lives in his shell in the sea. It is a wilderness that is beautiful, dangerous, abundant, oblivious of us, mysterious, never to be conquered or controlled or second-guessed, or known more than a little. It is a wilderness that for most of us most of the time is kept out of sight, camouflaged, by the edifices and the busyness and the bothers of human society.

And so, coming here, what I have done is strip away the human facade that usually stands between me and the universe, and I see more clearly where I am. What I am able to ignore much of the time, but find undeniable here, is that all wildernesses are one: there is profound joining between this wild stream deep in one of the folds of my native country and the tropical jungles, the tundras of the north, the oceans and the deserts. Alone here, among the rocks and the trees, I see that I am alone also among the stars. A stranger here, unfamiliar with my surroundings, I am aware also that I know only in the most relative terms my whereabouts within the black reaches of the universe. And because the natural processes are here so little qualified by anything human, this fragment of the wilderness is also joined to other times; there flows over it a nonhuman time to be told by the growth and death of the forest and the wearing of the stream. I feel drawing out beyond my comprehension perspectives from which the growth and the death of a large poplar would seem as continuous and sudden as the raising and the lowering of a man's hand, from which men's history in the world, their brief clearing of the ground, will seem no more than the opening and shutting of an eye.

And so I have came here to enact — not because I want to but because, once here, I cannot help it — the loneliness and the humbleness of my kind. I must see in my flimsy shelter, pitched here for two nights, the transience of capitols and cathedrals. In growing used to being in this place, I will have to accept a humbler and a truer view of myself than I usually have.

A man enters and leaves the world naked. And it is only naked — or nearly so — that he can enter and leave the wilderness. If he walks, that is; and if he doesn't walk it can hardly be said that he has entered. He can bring only what he can carry — the little that it takes to replace for a few hours or a few days an animal's fur and teeth and claws and functioning instincts. In comparison to the usual traveler with his dependence on machines and highways and restaurants and motels — on the economy and the government, in short — the man who walks into the wilderness is naked indeed. He leaves behind his work, his household, his duties, his comforts — even, if he comes alone, his words. He immerses himself in what he is not. It is a kind of death.

The dawn comes slow and cold. Only occasionally, somewhere along the creek or 20 on the slopes above, a bird sings. I have not slept well, and I waken without much interest in the day. I set the camp to rights, and fix breakfast, and eat. The day is clear, and high up on the points and ridges to the west of my camp I can see the sun shining on the woods. And suddenly I am full of an ambition: I want to get up where the sun is; I want to sit still in the sun up there among the high rocks until I can feel its warmth in my bones.

I put some lunch into a little canvas bag, and start out, leaving my jacket so as not to have to carry it after the day gets warm. Without my jacket, even climbing, it is cold in the shadow of the hollow, and I have a long way to go to get to the sun. I climb the steep path up the valley wall, walking rapidly, thinking only of the sunlight above me. It is as though I have entered into a deep sympathy with those tulip poplars that grow so straight and tall out of the shady ravines, not growing a branch worth the name until their heads are in the sun. I am so concentrated on the sun that when some grouse flush from the undergrowth ahead of me, I am thunderstruck; they are already planing down into the underbrush again before I can get my wits together and realize what they are.

The path zigzags up the last steepness of the bluff and then slowly levels out. For some distance it follows the backbone of a ridge, and then where the ridge is narrowest there is a great slab of bare rock lying full in the sun. This is what I have been looking for. I walk out into the center of the rock and sit, the clear warm light falling unobstructed all around. As the sun warms me I begin to grow comfortable not only in my clothes, but in the place and the day. And like those light-seeking poplars of the ravines, my mind begins to branch out.

Southward, I can hear the traffic on the Mountain Parkway, a steady continuous roar — the corporate voice of twentieth-century humanity, sustained above the transient voices of its members. Last night, except for an occasional airplane passing over, I camped out of reach of the sounds of engines. For long stretches of time I heard no sounds but the sounds of the woods.

Near where I am sitting there is an inscription cut into the rock:

A · J · SARGENT

fEB · 2ꝭ · 1903

Those letters were carved there more than sixty-six years ago. As I look around me I realize that I can see no evidence of the lapse of so much time. In every direction I can see only narrow ridges and narrow deep hollows, all covered with trees. For all that can be told from this height by looking, it might still be 1903 — or, for that matter, 1803 or 1703, or 1003. Indians no doubt sat here and looked over the country as I am doing now; the visual impression is so pure and strong that I can almost imagine myself one of them. But the insistent, the overwhelming, evidence of the time of my own arrival is in what I can hear — that roar of the highway off there in the distance. In 1903 the continent was still covered by a great ocean of silence, in which the sounds of machinery were scattered at wide intervals of time and space. Here, in 1903, there were only the natural sounds of the place. On a day like this, at the end of September, there would have been only the sounds of a few faint crickets, a woodpecker now and then, now and then the wind. But today, two-thirds of a century later, the continent is covered by an ocean of engine noise, in which silences occur only sporadically and at wide intervals.

From where I am sitting in the midst of this island of wilderness, it is as though I am listening to the machine of human history — a huge flywheel building speed until finally the force of its whirling will break it in pieces, and the world with it. That is not an attractive thought, and yet I find it impossible to escape, for it has seemed to me for years now that the doings of men no longer occur within nature, but that the natural places which the human economy has so far spared now survive almost accidentally within the doings of men. This wilderness of the Red River now carries on its ancient processes *within* the human climate of war and waste and confusion. And I know that the distant roar of engines, though it may *seem* only to be passing through this wilderness, is really bearing down upon it. The machine is running now with a speed that produces blindness — as to the driver of a speeding automobile the only thing stable, the only thing not a mere blur on the edge of the retina, is the automobile itself —

25

and the blindness of a thing with power promises the destruction of what cannot be seen. That roar of the highway is the voice of the American economy; it is sounding also wherever strip mines are being cut in the steep slopes of Appalachia, and wherever cropland is being destroyed to make roads and suburbs, and wherever rivers and marshes and bays and forests are being destroyed for the sake of industry or commerce.

No. Even here where the economy of life is really an economy — where the creation is yet fully alive and continuous and self-enriching, where whatever dies enters directly into the life of the living — even here one cannot fully escape the sense of an impending human catastrophe. One cannot come here without the awareness that this is an island surrounded by the machinery and the workings of an insane greed, hungering for the world's end — that ours is a "civilization" of which the work of no builder or artist is symbol, nor the life of any good man, but rather the bulldozer, the poison spray, the hugging fire of napalm, the cloud of Hiroshima.

Though from the high vantage point of this stony ridge I see little hope that I will ever live a day as an optimist, still I am not desperate. In fact, with the sun warming me now, and with the whole day before me to wander in this beautiful country, I am happy. A man cannot despair if he can imagine a better life, and if he can enact something of its possibility. It is only when I am ensnarled in the meaningless ordeals and the ordeals of meaninglessness, of which our public and political life is now so productive, that I lose the awareness of something better, and feel the despair of having come to the dead end of possibility.

Today, as always when I am afoot in the woods, I feel the possibility, the reasonableness, the practicability of living in the world in a way that would enlarge rather than diminish the hope of life. I feel the possibility of a frugal and protective love for the creation that would be unimaginably more meaningful and joyful than our present destructive and wasteful economy. The absence of human society, that made me so uneasy last night, now begins to be a comfort to me. I am afoot in the woods. I am alive in the world, this moment, without the help or the interference of any machine. I can move without reference to anything except the lay of the land and the capabilities of my own body. The necessities of foot travel in this steep country have stripped away all superfluities. I simply could not enter into this place and assume its quiet with all the belongings of a family man, property holder, etc. For the time, I am reduced to my irreducible self. I feel the lightness of body that a man must feel who has just lost fifty pounds of fat. As I leave the bare expanse of the rock and go in under the trees again, I am aware that I move in the landscape as one of its details.

Walking through the woods, you can never see far, either ahead or behind, so you move without much of a sense of getting anywhere or of moving at any certain speed. You burrow through the foliage in the air much as a mole burrows through 30 the roots in the ground. The views that open out occasionally from the ridges afford a relief, a recovery of orientation, that they could never give as mere "scenery," looked at from a turnout at the edge of a highway.

The trail leaves the ridge and goes down a ravine into the valley of a creek where the night chill has stayed. I pause only long enough to drink the cold clean water. The trail climbs up onto the next ridge.

It is the ebb of the year. Though the slopes have not yet taken on the bright colors of the autumn maples and oaks, some of the duller trees are already shedding. The foliage has begun to flow down the cliff faces and the slopes like a tide pulling back. The woods is mostly quiet, subdued, as if the pressure of survival has grown heavy upon it, as if above the growing warmth of the day the cold of winter can be felt waiting to descend.

At my approach a big hawk flies off the low branch of an oak and out over the treetops. Now and again a nuthatch hoots, off somewhere in the woods. Twice I stop and watch an ovenbird. A few feet ahead of me there is a sudden movement in the leaves, and then quiet. When I slip up and examine the spot there is nothing to be found. Whatever passed there has disappeared, quicker than the hand that is quicker than the eye, a shadow fallen into a shadow.

In the afternoon I leave the trail. My walk so far has come perhaps three-quarters of the way around a long zigzagging loop that will eventually bring me back to my starting place. I turn down a small unnamed branch of the creek where I am camped, and I begin the loveliest part of the day. There is nothing here resembling a trail. The best way is nearly always to follow the edge of the stream, stepping from one stone to another. Crossing back and forth over the water, stepping on or over rocks and logs, the way ahead is never clear for more than a few feet. The stream accompanies me down, threading its way under boulders and logs and over little falls and rapids. The rhododendron overhangs it so closely in places that I can go only by stooping. Over the rhododendron are the great dark heads of the hemlocks. The streambanks are ferny and mossy. And through this green tunnel the voice of the stream changes from rock to rock; subdued like all the other autumn voices of the woods, it seems sunk in a deep contented meditation on the sounds of *l*.

The water in the pools is absolutely clear. If it weren't for the shadows and ripples you would hardly notice that it is water; the fish would seem to swim in the air. As it is, where there is no leaf floating, it is impossible to tell exactly where the plane of the surface lies. As I walk up on a pool the little fish dart every which way out of sight. And then after I sit still a while, watching, they come out again. Their shadows flow over the rocks and leaves on the bottom. Now I have come into the heart of the woods. I am far from the highway and can hear no sound of it. All around there is a grand deep autumn quiet, in which a few insects dream their summer songs. Suddenly a wren sings way off in the underbrush. A redbreasted nuthatch walks, hooting, headfirst down the trunk of a walnut. An ovenbird walks out along the limb of a hemlock and looks at me, curious. The

35

little fish soar in the pool, turning their clean quick angles, their shadows seeming barely to keep up. As I lean and dip my cup in the water, they scatter. I drink, and go on.

When I get back to camp it is only the middle of the afternoon or a little after. Since I left in the morning I have walked something like eight miles. I haven't hurried — have mostly poked along, stopping often and looking around. But I am tired, and coming down the creek I have got both feet wet. I find a sunny place, and take off my shoes and socks and set them to dry. For a long time then, lying propped against the trunk of a tree, I read and rest and watch the evening come.

All day I have moved through the woods, making as little noise as possible. Slowly my mind and my nerves have slowed to a walk. The quiet of the woods has ceased to be something that I observe; now it is something that I am a part of. I have joined it with my own quiet. As the twilight draws on I no longer feel the strangeness and uneasiness of the evening before. The sounds of the creek move through my mind as they move through the valley, unimpeded and clear.

When the time comes I prepare supper and eat, and then wash kettle and cup and spoon and put them away. As far as possible I get things ready for an early start in the morning. Soon after dark I go to bed, and I sleep well.

I wake long before dawn. The air is warm and I feel rested and wide awake. By the light of a small candle lantern I break camp and pack. And then I begin the steep climb back to the car.

The moon is bright and high. The woods stands in deep shadow, the light   40
falling soft through the openings of the foliage. The trees appear immensely tall, and black, gravely looming over the path. It is windless and still; the moonlight pouring over the country seems more potent than the air. All around me there is still that constant low singing of the insects. For days now it has continued without letup or inflection, like ripples on water under a steady breeze. While I slept it went on through the night, a shimmer on my mind. My shoulder brushes a low tree overhanging the path and a bird that was asleep on one of the branches startles awake and flies off into the shadows, and I go on with the sense that I am passing near to the sleep of things.

In a way this is the best part of the trip. Stopping now and again to rest, I linger over it, sorry to be going. It seems to me that if I were to stay on, today would be better than yesterday, and I realize it was to renew the life of that possibility that I came here. What I am leaving is something to look forward to.

Exploring the Text

1. What is the immediate effect of the descriptive detail in Berry's first five paragraphs? Given Wendell Berry's involvement in the setting in those five paragraphs,

are you surprised by the mood that comes over him in paragraph 7? What is responsible for that mood?

2. In the second sentence of paragraph 8, there is an example of anaphora in the four clauses beginning with *of*. How does this anaphora serve Berry's rhetorical purpose?

3. How would you paraphrase the main idea Berry develops in paragraphs 10 and 11?

4. What is the effect of the simile at the beginning of paragraph 16: "Wilderness is the element in which we live encased in civilization, as a mollusk lives in his shell in the sea"?

5. Berry is clearly a lover of nature. Why doesn't he present a more romantic picture in paragraph 20? Looking at the essay as a whole, how are the descriptions of nature emblematic of Berry himself?

6. According to Berry in paragraphs 26–27, what is changing in the nature of the relationship between humanity and nature? Is the shift as profound as he suggests? Note the difference in tone between paragraphs 26–27 and paragraphs 34–35. How does this shift reflect what Berry sees as the changing relationship between humanity and nature?

7. How does Berry's paragraph 29 compare with paragraph 4 of "Nature" by Ralph Waldo Emerson (p. 807)?

8. William Cullen Bryant's poem "Inscription for the Entrance to a Wood" begins:

> Stranger, if thou hast learned a truth which needs
> No school of long experience, that the world
> Is full of guilt and misery, and hast seen
> Enough of all its sorrows, crimes, and cares,
> To tire thee of it, enter this wild wood
> And view the haunts of nature.

What evidence in Berry's essay suggests that he was influenced by Bryant's poem? Explain, making reference to specific passages in Berry's essay.

2004 Nobel Peace Prize Speech

WANGARI MUTA MAATHAI

Wangari Muta Maathai (b. 1940) was the first woman from central or eastern Africa to earn a PhD. Born in Kenya, she was educated there and at Mount St. Scholastica College in Atchison, Kansas, and at the University of Pittsburgh. An activist and environmentalist, she founded the Green Belt Movement in 1977, which has planted tens of millions of trees on farms and at schools and churches in Kenya. Other African countries have adopted the movement's methods. In 1991, when Maathai was arrested and imprisoned, the first of many times, for her revolutionary environmental activities, an Amnesty International letter-writing campaign helped free her. She went on to become one of the most effective environmental activists in the world, accepting a position as visiting fellow at Yale University in 2002 and receiving the Nobel Peace Prize in 2004. She has since been elected to parliament, and she now serves as deputy minister of the environment, natural resources, and wildlife in Kenya. In 2006 she published a memoir titled *Unbowed*.

Your Majesties
Your Royal Highnesses
Honourable Members of the Norwegian Nobel Committee
Excellencies
Ladies and Gentlemen

I stand before you and the world humbled by this recognition and uplifted by the honour of being the 2004 Nobel Peace Laureate.

As the first African woman to receive this prize, I accept it on behalf of the people of Kenya and Africa, and indeed the world. I am especially mindful of women and the girl child. I hope it will encourage them to raise their voices and take more space for leadership. I know the honour also gives a deep sense of pride to our men, both old and young. As a mother, I appreciate the inspiration this brings to the youth and urge them to use it to pursue their dreams.

Although this prize comes to me, it acknowledges the work of countless individuals and groups across the globe. They work quietly and often without recognition to protect the environment, promote democracy, defend human rights and ensure equality between women and men. By so doing, they plant seeds of peace. I know they, too, are proud today. To all who feel represented by this prize I say use it to advance your mission and meet the high expectations the world will place on us.

This honour is also for my family, friends, partners and supporters throughout the world. All of them helped shape the vision and sustain our work, which was often accomplished under hostile conditions. I am also grateful to the people of Kenya — who remained stubbornly hopeful that democracy could be realized and their environment managed sustainably. Because of this support, I am here today to accept this great honour. 5

I am immensely privileged to join my fellow African Peace laureates, Presidents Nelson Mandela and F. W. de Klerk, Archbishop Desmond Tutu, the late Chief Albert Luthuli, the late Anwar el-Sadat and the UN Secretary General, Kofi Annan.

I know that African people everywhere are encouraged by this news. My fellow Africans, as we embrace this recognition, let us use it to intensify our commitment to our people, to reduce conflicts and poverty and thereby improve their quality of life. Let us embrace democratic governance, protect human rights and protect our environment. I am confident that we shall rise to the occasion. I have always believed that solutions to most of our problems must come from us.

In this year's prize, the Norwegian Nobel Committee has placed the critical issue of environment and its linkage to democracy and peace before the world. For their visionary action, I am profoundly grateful. Recognizing that sustainable development, democracy and peace are indivisible is an idea whose time has come. Our work over the past 30 years has always appreciated and engaged these linkages.

My inspiration partly comes from my childhood experiences and observations of Nature in rural Kenya. It has been influenced and nurtured by the formal education I was privileged to receive in Kenya, the United States and Germany. As I was growing up, I witnessed forests being cleared and replaced by commercial plantations, which destroyed local biodiversity and the capacity of the forests to conserve water.

Excellencies, ladies and gentlemen,   10

In 1977, when we started the Green Belt Movement, I was partly responding to needs identified by rural women, namely lack of firewood, clean drinking water, balanced diets, shelter and income.

Throughout Africa, women are the primary caretakers, holding significant responsibility for tilling the land and feeding their families. As a result, they are often the first to become aware of environmental damage as resources become scarce and incapable of sustaining their families.

The women we worked with recounted that unlike in the past, they were unable to meet their basic needs. This was due to the degradation of their immediate environment as well as the introduction of commercial farming, which replaced the growing of household food crops. But international trade controlled the price of the exports from these small-scale farmers and a reasonable and just income could not be guaranteed. I came to understand that when the environment is destroyed, plundered or mismanaged, we undermine our quality of life and that of future generations.

Tree planting became a natural choice to address some of the initial basic needs identified by women. Also, tree planting is simple, attainable and guarantees quick, successful results within a reasonable amount of time. This sustains interest and commitment.

So, together, we have planted over 30 million trees that provide fuel, food,   15
shelter, and income to support their children's education and household needs. The activity also creates employment and improves soils and watersheds. Through their involvement, women gain some degree of power over their lives, especially their social and economic position and relevance in the family. This work continues.

Initially, the work was difficult because historically our people have been persuaded to believe that because they are poor, they lack not only capital, but also knowledge and skills to address their challenges. Instead they are conditioned to believe that solutions to their problems must come from "outside." Further, women did not realize that meeting their needs depended on their environment being healthy and well managed. They were also unaware that a degraded environment leads to a scramble for scarce resources and may culminate in poverty and even conflict. They were also unaware of the injustices of international economic arrangements.

In order to assist communities to understand these linkages, we developed a citizen education program, during which people identify their problems, the causes and possible solutions. They then make connections between their own personal actions and the problems they witness in the environment and in society. They learn that our world is confronted with a litany of woes: corruption, violence against women and children, disruption and breakdown of families, and disintegration of cultures and communities. They also identify the abuse of drugs and chemical substances, especially among young people. There are also devastating diseases that are defying cures or occurring in epidemic proportions. Of particular concern are HIV/AIDS, malaria and diseases associated with malnutrition.

On the environment front, they are exposed to many human activities that are devastating to the environment and societies. These include widespread destruction of ecosystems, especially through deforestation, climatic instability, and contamination in the soils and waters that all contribute to excruciating poverty.

In the process, the participants discover that they must be part of the solutions. They realize their hidden potential and are empowered to overcome inertia and take action. They come to recognize that they are the primary custodians and beneficiaries of the environment that sustains them.

Entire communities also come to understand that while it is necessary to hold their governments accountable, it is equally important that in their own relationships with each other, they exemplify the leadership values they wish to see in their own leaders, namely justice, integrity and trust.   20

Although initially the Green Belt Movement's tree planting activities did not address issues of democracy and peace, it soon became clear that responsible governance of the environment was impossible without democratic space. Therefore, the tree became a symbol for the democratic struggle in Kenya. Citizens were mobilised to challenge widespread abuses of power, corruption and environmental mismanagement. In Nairobi's Uhuru Park, at Freedom Corner, and in many parts of the country, trees of peace were planted to demand the release of prisoners of conscience and a peaceful transition to democracy.

Through the Green Belt Movement, thousands of ordinary citizens were mobilized and empowered to take action and effect change. They learned to overcome fear and a sense of helplessness and moved to defend democratic rights.

In time, the tree also became a symbol for peace and conflict resolution, especially during ethnic conflicts in Kenya when the Green Belt Movement used peace trees to reconcile disputing communities. During the ongoing rewriting of the Kenyan constitution, similar trees of peace were planted in many parts of the country to promote a culture of peace. Using trees as a symbol of peace is in keeping with a widespread African tradition. For example, the elders of the Kikuyu carried a staff from the thigi tree that, when placed between two disputing sides, caused them to stop fighting and seek reconciliation. Many communities in Africa have these traditions.

Such practises are part of an extensive cultural heritage, which contributes both to the conservation of habitats and to cultures of peace. With the destruction of these cultures and the introduction of new values, local biodiversity is no longer valued or protected, and as a result, it is quickly degraded and disappears. For this reason, the Green Belt Movement explores the concept of cultural biodiversity, especially with respect to indigenous seeds and medicinal plants.

As we progressively understood the causes of environmental degradation, we saw the need for good governance. Indeed, the state of any county's environment is a reflection of the kind of governance in place, and without good governance there can be no peace. Many countries, which have poor governance systems, are also likely to have conflicts and poor laws protecting the environment.

In 2002, the courage, resilience, patience and commitment of members of the Green Belt Movement, other civil society organizations, and the Kenyan public culminated in the peaceful transition to a democratic government and laid the foundation for a more stable society.

Excellencies, friends, ladies and gentlemen,

It is 30 years since we started this work. Activities that devastate the environment and societies continue unabated. Today we are faced with a challenge that calls for a shift in our thinking, so that humanity stops threatening its life-support system. We are called to assist the Earth to heal her wounds and in the process heal our own — indeed, to embrace the whole creation in all its diversity, beauty and wonder. This will happen if we see the need to revive our sense of belonging to a larger family of life, with which we have shared our evolutionary process.

In the course of history, there comes a time when humanity is called to shift to a new level of consciousness, to reach a higher moral ground. A time when we have to shed our fear and give hope to each other.

That time is now.

The Norwegian Nobel Committee has challenged the world to broaden the understanding of peace: there can be no peace without equitable development; and there can be no development without sustainable management of the environment in a democratic and peaceful space. This shift is an idea whose time has come.

I call on leaders, especially from Africa, to expand democratic space and build fair and just societies that allow the creativity and energy of their citizens to flourish. Those of us who have been privileged to receive education, skills, and experiences and even power must be role models for the next generation of leadership. In this regard, I would also like to appeal for the freedom of my fellow laureate Aung San Suu Kyi so that she can continue her work for peace and democracy for the people of Burma and the world at large.

Culture plays a central role in the political, economic and social life of communities. Indeed, culture may be the missing link in the development of Africa. Culture is dynamic and evolves over time, consciously discarding retrogressive traditions, like female genital mutilation (FGM), and embracing aspects that are good and useful.

Africans, especially, should rediscover positive aspects of their culture. In accepting them, they would give themselves a sense of belonging, identity and self-confidence.

Ladies and Gentlemen,   35

There is also need to galvanize civil society and grassroots movements to catalyse change. I call upon governments to recognize the role of these social movements in building a critical mass of responsible citizens, who help maintain checks and balances in society. On their part, civil society should embrace not only their rights but also their responsibilities.

Further, industry and global institutions must appreciate that ensuring economic justice, equity and ecological integrity are of greater value than profits at any cost. The extreme global inequities and prevailing consumption patterns continue at the expense of the environment and peaceful co-existence. The choice is ours.

I would like to call on young people to commit themselves to activities that contribute toward achieving their long-term dreams. They have the energy and creativity to shape a sustainable future. To the young people I say, you are a gift to your communities and indeed the world. You are our hope and our future.

The holistic approach to development, as exemplified by the Green Belt Movement, could be embraced and replicated in more parts of Africa and beyond. It is for this reason that I have established the Wangari Maathai Foundation to ensure the continuation and expansion of these activities. Although a lot has been achieved, much remains to be done.

Excellencies, ladies and gentlemen,   40

As I conclude I reflect on my childhood experience when I would visit a stream next to our home to fetch water for my mother. I would drink water straight from the stream. Playing among the arrowroot leaves I tried in vain to pick up the strands of frogs' eggs, believing they were beads. But every time I put my little fingers under them they would break. Later, I saw thousands of tadpoles: black, energetic and wriggling through the clear water against the background of the brown earth. This is the world I inherited from my parents.

Today, over 50 years later, the stream has dried up, women walk long distances for water, which is not always clean, and children will never know what they have lost. The challenge is to restore the home of the tadpoles and give back to our children a world of beauty and wonder.

Thank you very much.

Exploring the Text

1. Wangari Muta Maathai addresses her audience several times, at the beginning of her speech and again in paragraphs 10, 27, 35, and 40. What is the purpose of this repetition? Does each address serve a unique purpose, or are they all the same? Do you think the occasion affected Maathai's decision to use multiple addresses? Explain.

2. In accepting the Nobel Peace Prize, Maathai discusses democracy and the natural environment more than she discusses peace. Explain why you do or do not agree that they are inextricably linked to peace, as she says.

3. In paragraph 13, Maathai says, "I came to understand that when the environment is destroyed, plundered or mismanaged, we undermine our quality of life and that of future generations." What is the underlying assumption that connects her claim and support in this statement?

4. Based on paragraph 15, what were the main impediments to the work of the Green Belt Movement? What is the relationship between paragraphs 15 and 16?

5. In paragraph 16, Maathai discusses the importance of education. Do you agree with her views?

6. What is the rhetorical effect of recognizing, as Maathai does throughout, the power of the Nobel Peace Prize?

7. Maathai says, "That time is now" (para. 30), when discussing the need for a shift in our consciousness regarding our relationship with the natural world. Do you agree with her sense of urgency? Why or why not?

8. How does Maathai use examples from her youth, including the one about tadpoles (para. 41), to appeal to ethos?

9. How does the context of this speech — the occasion of the Nobel Peace Prize and Maathai's status as a "first" — influence its content and tone?

Against Nature

Joyce Carol Oates

Joyce Carol Oates was born in Lockport, New York, in 1938. With a typewriter that she received at age fourteen, Oates wrote "novel after novel" in high school and college in order to train herself to be a writer. Oates, who received a bachelor's degree from Syracuse University and a master's in English from the University of Wisconsin, is currently the Roger S. Berlind Distinguished Professor of the Humanities at Princeton. She is the youngest author ever to receive the National Book Award — for her novel *Them* (1969). A highly regarded novelist, playwright, poet, and journalist, Oates is highly prolific, having published over thirty novels and numerous other works including the novels *Black Water* (1992), *We Were the Mulvaneys* (1996), and *The Falls* (2004). Her work often addresses the violence and suspense lurking beneath ordinary life. "Against Nature," in which she offers a "dissenting opinion," as the *New York Times* put it, is from her 1988 collection, *(Woman) Writer: Occasions and Opportunities*.

We soon get through with Nature. She excites an expectation which she cannot satisfy.
— Thoreau, *Journal*, 1854

Sir, if a man has experienced the inexpressible, he is under no obligation to attempt to express it.
— Samuel Johnson

T*he writer's resistance to Nature.*
    It has no sense of humor: in its beauty, as in its ugliness, or its neutrality, there is no laughter.
    It lacks a moral purpose.
    It lacks a satiric dimension, registers no irony.
    Its pleasures lack resonance, being accidental; its horrors, even when premeditated, are equally perfunctory, "red in tooth and claw," et cetera.   5
    It lacks a symbolic subtext — excepting that provided by man.
    It has no (verbal) language.
    It has no interest in ours.
    It inspires a painfully limited set of responses in "nature writers" — REVERENCE, AWE, PIETY, MYSTICAL ONENESS.
    It eludes us even as it prepares to swallow us up, books and all.   10

I was lying on my back in the dirt gravel of the towpath beside the Delaware and Raritan Canal, Titusville, New Jersey, staring up at the sky and trying, with no success, to overcome a sudden attack of tachycardia that had come upon me out of nowhere — such attacks are always "out of nowhere," that's their charm — and all around me Nature thrummed with life, the air smelling of moisture and sunlight, the canal reflecting the sky, red-winged blackbirds testing their spring calls; the usual. I'd become the jar in Tennessee, a fictitious center,[1] or parenthesis, aware beyond my erratic heartbeat of the numberless heartbeats of the earth, its pulsing, pumping life, sheer life, incalculable. Struck down in the midst of motion — I'd been jogging a minute before — I was "out of time" like a fallen, stunned boxer, privileged (in an abstract manner of speaking) to be an involuntary witness to the random, wayward, nameless motion on all sides of me.
    Paroxysmal tachycardia can be fatal, but rarely; if the heartbeat accelerates to 250–270 beats a minute you're in trouble, but the average attack is about 100–150 beats and mine seemed about average; the trick now was to prevent it from getting worse. Brainy people try brainy strategies, such as thinking calming thoughts, pseudo-mystic thoughts, *If I die now it's a good death*, that sort of thing,

---

[1]Reference to "Anecdote of the Jar," a poem by Wallace Stevens. — Eds.

if I die this is a good place and good time; the idea is to deceive the frenzied heart-beat that, really, you don't care: you hadn't any other plans for the afternoon. The important thing with tachycardia is to prevent panic! you must prevent panic! otherwise you'll have to be taken by ambulance to the closest emergency room, which is not so very nice a way to spend the afternoon, really. So I contemplated the blue sky overhead. The earth beneath my head. Nature surrounding me on all sides; I couldn't quite see it but I could hear it, smell it, sense it, there is something *there*, no mistake about it. Completely oblivious to the predicament of the indi-vidual but that's only "natural," after all, one hardly expects otherwise.

When you discover yourself lying on the ground, limp and unresisting, head in the dirt, and, let's face it, helpless, the earth seems to shift forward as a pres-ence; hard, emphatic, not mere surface but a genuine force — there is no other word for it but *presence*. To keep in motion is to keep in time, and to be stopped, stilled, is to be abruptly out of time, in another time dimension perhaps, an alien one, where human language has no resonance. Nothing to be said about it expresses it, nothing touches it, it's an absolute against which nothing human can be measured. . . . Moving through space and time by way of your own volition you inhabit an interior consciousness, a hallucinatory consciousness, it might be said, so long as breath, heartbeat, the body's autonomy hold; when motion is stopped you are jarred out of it. The interior is invaded by the exterior. The out-side wants to come in, and only the self's fragile membrane prevents it.

The fly buzzing at Emily's death.[2]

Still, the earth *is* your place. A tidy grave site measured to your size. Or, from another angle of vision, one vast democratic grave. 15

Let's contemplate the sky. Forget the crazy hammering heartbeat, don't listen to it, don't start counting, remember that there is a clever way of breathing that conserves oxygen as if you're lying below the surface of a body of water breathing through a very thin straw but you *can* breathe through it if you're careful, if you don't panic; one breath and then another and then another, isn't that the story of all lives? careers? Just a matter of breathing. Of course it is. But contemplate the sky, it's there to be contemplated. A mild shock to see it so blank, blue, a thin airy ghostly blue, no clouds to disguise its emptiness. You are beginning to feel not only weightless but near-bodiless, lying on the earth like a scrap of paper about to be blown off. Two dimensions and you'd imagined you were three! And there's the sky rolling away forever, into infinity — if "infinity" can be "rolled into" — and the forlorn truth is, that's where you're going too. And the lovely blue isn't even blue, is it? isn't even there, is it? a mere optical illusion, isn't it? no matter what art has urged you to believe.

Early Nature memories. Which it's best not to suppress.

. . . Wading, as a small child, in Tonawanda Creek near our house, and after-ward trying to tear off, in a frenzy of terror and revulsion, the sticky fat black

---

[2]Reference to "I heard a fly buzz, when I died," a poem by Emily Dickinson. —Eds.

bloodsuckers that had attached themselves to my feet, particularly between my toes.

. . . Coming upon a friend's dog in a drainage ditch, dead for several days, evidently the poor creature had been shot by a hunter and left to die, bleeding to death, and we're stupefied with grief and horror but can't resist sliding down to where he's lying on his belly, and we can't resist squatting over him, turning the body over.

. . . The raccoon, mad with rabies, frothing at the mouth and tearing at his   20
own belly with his teeth, so that his intestines spill out onto the ground . . . a sight I seem to remember though in fact I did not see. I've been told I did not see.

Consequently, my chronic uneasiness with Nature mysticism; Nature adoration; Nature-as-(moral)-instruction-for-mankind. My doubt that one can, with philosophical validity, address "Nature" as a single coherent noun, anything other than a Platonic, hence discredited, is-ness. My resistance to "Nature writing" as a genre, except when it is brilliantly fictionalized in the service of a writer's individual vision — Thoreau's books and *Journal*, of course, but also, less known in this country, the miniaturist prose poems of Colette (*Flowers and Fruit*) and Ponge (*Taking the Side of Things*)[3] — in which case it becomes yet another, and ingenious, form of storytelling. The subject is *there* only by the grace of the author's language.

Nature has no instructions for mankind except that our poor beleaguered humanist-democratic way of life, our fantasies of the individual's high worth, our sense that the weak, no less than the strong, have a right to survive, are absurd. When Edmund of *King Lear*[4] said excitedly, "Nature, be thou my goddess!" he knew whereof he spoke.

In any case, where *is* Nature, one might (skeptically) inquire. Who has looked upon her/its face and survived?

But isn't this all exaggeration, in the spirit of rhetorical contentiousness? Surely Nature is, for you, as for most reasonably intelligent people, a "perennial" source of beauty, comfort, peace, escape from the delirium of civilized life; a respite from the ego's ever-frantic strategies of self-promotion, as a way of ensuring (at least in fantasy) some small measure of immortality? Surely Nature, as it is understood in the usual slapdash way, as human, if not dilettante, *experience* (hiking in a national park, jogging on the beach at dawn, even tending, with the usual comical frustrations, a suburban garden), is wonderfully consoling; a place where, when you go there, it has to take you in?[5] — a palimpsest of sorts you choose to read,

---

[3]Colette was a twentieth-century French novelist known for sophisticated love stories; Francois Ponge was a twentieth-century French poet noted for his prose poems. — Eds.
[4]Edmund is the evil brother in Shakespeare's *King Lear*. — Eds.
[5]Allusion to the definition of home in Robert Frost's poem "Death of the Hired Man." — Eds.

layer by layer, always with care, always cautiously, in proportion to your psychological strength?

Nature: as in Thoreau's upbeat Transcendentalist mode ("The indescribable innocence and beneficence of Nature, — such health, such cheer, they afford forever! and such sympathy have they ever with our race, that all Nature would be affected . . . if any man should ever for a just cause grieve"), and not in Thoreau's grim mode ("Nature is hard to be overcome but she must be overcome"). 25

Another way of saying, not *Nature-in-itself* but *Nature-as-experience*.

The former, Nature-in-itself, is, to allude slantwise to Melville, a blankness ten times blank;[6] the latter is what we commonly, or perhaps always, mean when we speak of Nature as a noun, a single entity — something of *ours*. Most of the time it's just an activity, a sort of hobby, a weekend, a few days, perhaps a few hours, staring out the window at the mind-dazzling autumn foliage of, say, northern Michigan, being rendered speechless — temporarily — at the sight of Mt. Shasta, the Grand Canyon, Ansel Adams's[7] West. Or Nature writ small, contained in the back yard. Nature filtered through our optical nerves, our "senses," our fiercely romantic expectations. Nature that pleases us because it mirrors our souls, or gives the comforting illusion of doing so.

Nature as the self's (flattering) mirror, but not ever, no, never, Nature-in-itself.

Nature is mouths, or maybe a single mouth. Why glamorize it, romanticize it? — well, yes, but we must, we're writers, poets, mystics (of a sort) aren't we, precisely what else are we to do but glamorize and romanticize and generally exaggerate the significance of anything we focus the white heat of our "creativity" upon? And why not Nature, since it's there, common property, mute, can't talk back, allows us the possibility of transcending the human condition for a while, writing prettily of mountain ranges, white-tailed deer, the purple crocuses outside this very window, the thrumming dazzling "life force" we imagine we all support. Why not?

Nature *is* more than a mouth — it's a dazzling variety of mouths. And it pleases the senses, in any case, as the physicists' chill universe of numbers certainly does not. 30

Oscar Wilde on our subject:

Nature is no great mother who has borne us. She is our creation. It is in our brain that she quickens to life. Things are because we see them, and what we see, and how we see it, depends on the Arts that have influenced us. To look at a thing is very different from seeing a thing . . . At present, people see fogs, not because there are fogs, but because poets and painters have taught them the mysterious loveliness of such effects. There may have been fogs for centuries in London. I dare say there were. But no one saw them. They did not exist until Art had

---

[6] Allusion to the description of the white whale in Herman Melville's *Moby Dick.* — Eds.
[7] Reference to Ansel Adams, a photographer of the American West. — Eds.

invented them . . . Yesterday evening Mrs. Arundel insisted on my going to the window and looking at the glorious sky, as she called it. And so I had to look at it . . . And what was it? It was simply a very second-rate Turner,[8] a Turner of a bad period, with all the painter's worst faults exaggerated and over-emphasized.

—"The Decay of Lying," 1889

(If we were to put it to Oscar Wilde that he exaggerates, his reply might well be, "Exaggeration? I don't know the meaning of the word.")

Walden, that most artfully composed of prose fictions, concludes, in the rhapsodic chapter "Spring," with Henry David Thoreau's contemplation of death, decay, and regeneration as it is suggested to him, or to his protagonist, by the spectacle of vultures feeding off carrion. There is a dead horse close by his cabin, and the stench of its decomposition, in certain winds, is daunting. Yet "the assurance it gave me of the strong appetite and inviolable health of Nature was my compensation for this. I love to see that Nature is so rife with life that myriads can be afforded to be sacrificed and suffered to prey upon one another; that tender organizations can be so serenely squashed out of existence like pulp, — tadpoles which herons gobble up, and tortoises and toads run over in the road; and that sometimes it has rained flesh and blood! . . . The impression made on a wise man is that of universal innocence."

Come off it, Henry David. You've grieved these many years for your elder brother, John, who died a ghastly death of lockjaw: you've never wholly recovered from the experience of watching him die. And you know or must know, that you're fated too to die young of consumption. . . . But this doctrinaire Transcendentalist passage ends *Walden* on just the right note. It's as impersonal, as coolly detached, as the Oversoul itself: a "wise man" filters his emotions through his brain.

Or through his prose.

Nietzsche: "We all pretend to ourselves that we are more simple-minded than we 35 are: that is how we get a rest from our fellow men."

> Once out of nature I shall never take
> My bodily form from any natural thing.
> But such a form as Grecian goldsmiths make
> Of hammered gold and gold enamelling
> To keep a drowsy Emperor awake;
> Or set upon a golden bough to sing
> To lords and ladies of Byzantium
> Of what is past, or passing, or to come.
>
> —William Butler Yeats, "Sailing to Byzantium"

---

[8]English painter J. M. W. Turner (c. 1775–1851), who was known for his paintings of the sea and sunsets. — Eds.

Yet even the golden bird is a "bodily form [taken from a] natural thing." No, it's impossible to escape!

The writer's resistance to Nature.

Wallace Stevens: "In the presence of extraordinary actuality, consciousness takes the place of imagination."

Once, years ago, in 1972 to be precise, when I seemed to have been another person, related to the person I am now as one is related, tangentially, sometimes embarrassingly, to cousins not seen for decades — once, when we were living in London, and I was very sick, I had a mystical vision. That is, I "had" a "mystical vision" — the heart sinks: such pretension — or something resembling one. A fever dream, let's call it. It impressed me enormously and impresses me still, though I've long since lost the capacity to see it with my mind's eye, or even, I suppose, to believe in it. There is a statute of limitations on "mystical visions," as on romantic love.

I was very sick, and I imagined my life as a thread, a thread of breath, or heartbeat, or pulse, or light — yes, it was light, radiant light; I was burning with fever and I ascended to that plane of serenity that might be mistaken for (or *is*, in fact) Nirvana, where I had a waking dream of uncanny lucidity:

My body is a tall column of light and heat.
My body is not "I" but "it."
My body is not one but many.

My body, which "I" inhabit, is inhabited as well by other creatures, unknown   40
to me, imperceptible — the smallest of them mere sparks of light.

My body, which I perceive as substance, is in fact an organization of infinitely complex, overlapping, imbricated structures, radiant light their manifestation, the "body" a tall column of light and blood heat, a temporary agreement among atoms, like a high-rise building with numberless rooms, corridors, corners, elevator shafts, windows. . . . In this fantastical structure the "I" is deluded as to its sovereignty, let alone its autonomy in the (outside) world; the most astonishing secret is that the "I" doesn't exist! — but it behaves as if it does, as if it were one and not many.

In any case, without the "I" the tall column of light and heat would die, and the microscopic life particles would die with it . . . will die with it. The "I," which doesn't exist, is everything.

But Dr. Johnson is right, the inexpressible need not be expressed.
And what resistance, finally? There is none.

This morning, an invasion of tiny black ants. One by one they appear, out of nowhere — that's their charm too! — moving single file across the white Parsons table where I am sitting, trying without much success to write a poem. A poem of only three or four lines is what I want, something short, tight, mean; I want it to hurt like a white-hot wire up the nostrils, small and compact and turned in upon itself with the density of a hunk of rock from the planet Jupiter. . . .

But here come the black ants: harbingers, you might say, of spring. One by one by one they appear on the dazzling white table and one by one I kill them with a forefinger, my deft right forefinger, mashing each against the surface of the table and then dropping it into a wastebasket at my side. Idle labor, mesmerizing, effortless, and I'm curious as to how long I can do it — sit here in the brilliant March sunshine killing ants with my right forefinger — how long I, and the ants, can keep it up.   45

After a while I realize that I can do it a long time. And that I've written my poem.

Exploring the Text

1. What is the purpose of the list that begins the essay?
2. What is ironic in the lengthy first sentence of paragraph 11? What is the effect of "the usual" at the end of that sentence?
3. What is the purpose and likely effect of the three nature memories Joyce Carol Oates includes in paragraphs 18–20? How do her memories compare with your own?
4. In paragraph 22, Oates writes, "Nature has no instructions for mankind except that our poor beleaguered humanist-democratic way of life, our fantasies of the individual's high worth, our sense that the weak, no less than the strong, have a right to survive, are absurd." What is her tone here? Do you agree with what she says?
5. What is the effect of the rhetorical questions in paragraph 24?
6. What does Oates imply about Nature in her references to Nietzsche, William Butler Yeats, and Wallace Stevens?
7. Read carefully paragraphs 38 and 39. How does the experience recounted there compare with that presented in the first part of Ralph Waldo Emerson's essay (p. 807)?
8. Oates concludes with a discussion of "harbingers . . . of spring" (para. 45). What is the likely effect of her conclusion on the reader?
9. How does Oates use both humor and understatement to develop her essay?
10. How might Ralph Waldo Emerson (p. 807) or Wendell Berry (p. 825) reply to Oates? How would *you* reply?
11. The sources Oates quotes are primarily other creative writers. What is her purpose in relying on this type of source? Would her argument have been more effective if she had included a wider variety of sources?

A White Heron (fiction)

SARAH ORNE JEWETT

Sarah Orne Jewett (1849–1909) was born in Maine. As a young girl she accompanied her father, a country doctor, on his visits with patients, an experience which, at least in part, inspired her to write stories about rural New England. She began writing as a child, and at nineteen she had a story published in the *Atlantic Monthly*. One major theme in Jewett's work is the powerful influence of nature. *A White Heron and Other Stories* was published in 1886, and her most famous work, *The Country of the Pointed Firs*, was published a decade later.

I

The woods were already filled with shadows one June evening, just before eight o'clock, though a bright sunset still glimmered faintly among the trunks of the trees. A little girl was driving home her cow, a plodding, dilatory, provoking creature in her behavior, but a valued companion for all that. They were going away from whatever light there was, and striking deep into the woods, but their feet were familiar with the path, and it was no matter whether their eyes could see it or not.

There was hardly a night the summer through when the old cow could be found waiting at the pasture bars; on the contrary, it was her greatest pleasure to hide herself away among the high huckleberry bushes, and though she wore a loud bell she had made the discovery that if one stood perfectly still it would not ring. So Sylvia had to hunt for her until she found her, and call Co'! Co'! with never an answering Moo, until her childish patience was quite spent. If the creature had not given good milk and plenty of it, the case would have seemed very different to her owners. Besides, Sylvia had all the time there was, and very little use to make of it. Sometimes in pleasant weather it was a consolation to look upon the cow's pranks as an intelligent attempt to play hide and seek, and as the child had no playmates she lent herself to this amusement with a good deal of zest. Though this chase had been so long that the wary animal herself had given an unusual signal of her whereabouts, Sylvia had only laughed when she came upon Mistress Moolly at the swamp-side, and urged her affectionately homeward with a twig of birch leaves. The old cow was not inclined to wander farther, she even turned in the right direction for once as they left the pasture, and stepped along the road at a good pace. She was quite ready to be milked now, and seldom stopped to browse. Sylvia wondered what her grandmother would say because they were so late. It was a great while since she had left home at half-past five o'clock, but everybody knew the difficulty of making this errand a short one. Mrs. Tilley had chased the hornéd torment too many summer evenings herself to blame any one else for lingering, and was only thankful as she waited that she had Sylvia, nowadays, to give such valuable assistance. The good woman suspected that Sylvia loitered occasionally on her own account; there never was such a child for straying about out-of-doors since the world was made! Everybody said that it was a good change for a little maid who had tried to grow for eight years in a crowded manufacturing town, but, as for Sylvia herself, it seemed as if she never had been alive at all before she came to live at the farm. She thought often with wistful compassion of a wretched geranium that belonged to a town neighbor.

"'Afraid of folks,'" old Mrs. Tilley said to herself, with a smile, after she had made the unlikely choice of Sylvia from her daughter's houseful of children, and was returning to the farm. "'Afraid of folks,' they said! I guess she won't be troubled no great with 'em up to the old place!" When they reached the door of the lonely house and stopped to unlock it, and the cat came to purr loudly, and rub against them, a deserted pussy, indeed, but fat with young robins, Sylvia whispered that this was a beautiful place to live in, and she never should wish to go home.

The companions followed the shady wood-road, the cow taking slow steps and the child very fast ones. The cow stopped long at the brook to drink, as if the pasture were not half a swamp, and Sylvia stood still and waited, letting her bare feet cool themselves in the shoal water, while the great twilight moths struck softly against her. She waded on through the brook as the cow moved away, and listened to the thrushes with a heart that beat fast with pleasure. There was a stirring in the great boughs overhead. They were full of little birds and beasts that seemed to be wide awake, and going about their world, or else saying good-night to each other in sleepy twitters. Sylvia herself felt sleepy as she walked along. However, it was not much farther to the house, and the air was soft and sweet. She was not often in the woods so late as this, and it made her feel as if she were a part of the gray shadows and the moving leaves. She was just thinking how long it seemed since she first came to the farm a year ago, and wondering if everything went on in the noisy town just the same as when she was there, the thought of the great red-faced boy who used to chase and frighten her made her hurry along the path to escape from the shadow of the trees.

Suddenly this little woods-girl is horror-stricken to hear a clear whistle not very far away. Not a bird's-whistle, which would have a sort of friendliness, but a boy's whistle, determined, and somewhat aggressive. Sylvia left the cow to whatever sad fate might await her, and stepped discreetly aside into the bushes, but she was just too late. The enemy had discovered her, and called out in a very cheerful and persuasive tone, "Halloa, little girl, how far is it to the road?" and trembling Sylvia answered almost inaudibly, "A good ways."

She did not dare to look boldly at the tall young man, who carried a gun over his shoulder, but she came out of her bush and again followed the cow, while he walked alongside.

"I have been hunting for some birds," the stranger said kindly, "and I have lost my way, and need a friend very much. Don't be afraid," he added gallantly. "Speak up and tell me what your name is, and whether you think I can spend the night at your house, and go out gunning early in the morning."

Sylvia was more alarmed than before. Would not her grandmother consider her much to blame? But who could have foreseen such an accident as this? It did not seem to be her fault, and she hung her head as if the stem of it were broken, but managed to answer "Sylvy," with much effort when her companion again asked her name.

Mrs. Tilley was standing in the doorway when the trio came into view. The cow gave a loud moo by way of explanation.

"Yes, you'd better speak up for yourself, you old trial! Where'd she tuck her- 10
self away this time, Sylvy?" But Sylvia kept an awed silence; she knew by instinct that her grandmother did not comprehend the gravity of the situation. She must be mistaking the stranger for one of the farmer-lads of the region.

The young man stood his gun beside the door, and dropped a lumpy game-bag beside it; then he bade Mrs. Tilley good-evening, and repeated his wayfarer's story, and asked if he could have a night's lodging.

"Put me anywhere you like," he said. "I must be off early in the morning, before day; but I am very hungry, indeed. You can give me some milk at any rate, that's plain."

"Dear sakes, yes," responded the hostess, whose long slumbering hospitality seemed to be easily awakened. "You might fare better if you went out to the main road a mile or so, but you're welcome to what we've got. I'll milk right off, and you make yourself at home. You can sleep on husks or feathers," she proffered graciously. "I raised them all myself. There's good pasturing for geese just below here towards the ma'sh. Now step round and set a plate for the gentleman, Sylvy!" And Sylvia promptly stepped. She was glad to have something to do, and she was hungry herself.

It was a surprise to find so clean and comfortable a little dwelling in this New England wilderness. The young man had known the horrors of its most primitive housekeeping, and the dreary squalor of that level of society which does not rebel at the companionship of hens. This was the best thrift of an old-fashioned farm-stead, though on such a small scale that it seemed like a hermitage. He listened eagerly to the old woman's quaint talk, he watched Sylvia's pale face and shining gray eyes with ever growing enthusiasm, and insisted that this was the best supper he had eaten for a month, and afterward the new-made friends sat down in the door-way together while the moon came up.

Soon it would be berry-time, and Sylvia was a great help at picking. The cow 15
was a good milker, though a plaguy thing to keep track of, the hostess gossiped frankly, adding presently that she had buried four children, so Sylvia's mother, and a son (who might be dead) in California were all the children she had left. "Dan, my boy, was a great hand to go gunning," she explained sadly. "I never

wanted for pa'tridges or gray squer'ls while he was to home. He's been a great wand'rer, I expect, and he's no hand to write letters. There, I don't blame him, I'd ha' seen the world myself if it had been so I could."

"Sylvy takes after him," the grandmother continued affectionately, after a minute's pause. "There ain't a foot o' ground she don't know her way over, and the wild creatures counts her one o' themselves. Squer'ls she'll tame to come an' feed right out o' her hands, and all sorts o' birds. Last winter she got the jay-birds to bangeing here, and I believe she'd 'a' scanted herself of her own meals to have plenty to throw out amongst 'em, if I hadn't kep' watch. Anything but crows, I tell her, I'm willin' to help support, — though Dan he had a tamed one o' them that did seem to have reason same as folks. It was round here a good spell after he went away. Dan an' his father they didn't hitch, — but he never held up his head ag'in after Dan had dared him an' gone off."

The guest did not notice this hint of family sorrows in his eager interest in something else.

"So Sylvy knows all about birds, does she?" he exclaimed, as he looked round at the little girl who sat, very demure but increasingly sleepy, in the moonlight. "I am making a collection of birds myself. I have been at it ever since I was a boy." (Mrs. Tilley smiled.) "There are two or three very rare ones I have been hunting for these five years. I mean to get them on my own ground if they can be found."

"Do you cage 'em up?" asked Mrs. Tilley doubtfully, in response to this enthusiastic announcement.

"Oh no, they're stuffed and preserved, dozens and dozens of them," said the ornithologist, "and I have shot or snared every one myself. I caught a glimpse of a white heron a few miles from here on Saturday, and I have followed it in this direction. They have never been found in this district at all. The little white heron, it is," and he turned again to look at Sylvia with the hope of discovering that the rare bird was one of her acquaintances. 20

But Sylvia was watching a hop-toad in the narrow footpath.

"You would know the heron if you saw it," the stranger continued eagerly. "A queer tall white bird with soft feathers and long thin legs. And it would have a nest perhaps in the top of a high tree, made of sticks, something like a hawk's nest."

Sylvia's heart gave a wild beat; she knew that strange white bird, and had once stolen softly near where it stood in some bright green swamp grass, away over at the other side of the woods. There was an open place where the sunshine always seemed strangely yellow and hot, where tall, nodding rushes grew, and her grandmother had warned her that she might sink in the soft black mud underneath and never be heard of more. Not far beyond were the salt marshes just this side the sea itself, which Sylvia wondered and dreamed much about, but never had seen, whose great voice could sometimes be heard above the noise of the woods on stormy nights.

"I can't think of anything I should like so much as to find that heron's nest," the handsome stranger was saying. "I would give ten dollars to anybody who could show it to me," he added desperately, "and I mean to spend my whole vacation hunting for it if need be. Perhaps it was only migrating, or had been chased out of its own region by some bird of prey."

Mrs. Tilley gave amazed attention to all this, but Sylvia still watched the toad, not divining, as she might have done at some calmer time, that the creature wished to get to its hole under the door-step, and was much hindered by the unusual spectators at that hour of the evening. No amount of thought, that night, could decide how many wished-for treasures the ten dollars, so lightly spoken of, would buy.

The next day the young sportsman hovered about the woods, and Sylvia kept him company, having lost her first fear of the friendly lad, who proved to be most kind and sympathetic. He told her many things about the birds and what they knew and where they lived and what they did with themselves. And he gave her a jack-knife, which she thought as great a treasure as if she were a desert-islander. All day long he did not once make her troubled or afraid except when he brought down some unsuspecting singing creature from its bough. Sylvia would have liked him vastly better without his gun; she could not understand why he killed the very birds he seemed to like so much. But as the day waned, Sylvia still watched the young man with loving admiration. She had never seen anybody so charming and delightful; the woman's heart, asleep in the child, was vaguely thrilled by a dream of love. Some premonition of that great power stirred and swayed these young creatures who traversed the solemn woodlands with soft-footed silent care. They stopped to listen to a bird's song; they pressed forward again eagerly, parting the branches, — speaking to each other rarely and in whispers; the young man going first and Sylvia following, fascinated, a few steps behind, with her gray eyes dark with excitement.

She grieved because the longed-for white heron was elusive, but she did not lead the guest, she only followed, and there was no such thing as speaking first. The sound of her own unquestioned voice would have terrified her, — it was hard enough to answer yes or no when there was need of that. At last evening began to fall, and they drove the cow home together, and Sylvia smiled with pleasure when they came to the place where she heard the whistle and was afraid only the night before.

II

Half a mile from home, at the farther edge of the woods, where the land was highest, a great pine-tree stood, the last of its generation. Whether it was left for a boundary mark, or for what reason, no one could say; the woodchoppers who had felled its mates were dead and gone long ago, and a whole forest of sturdy trees, pines and oaks and maples, had grown again. But the stately head of this old pine towered above them all and made a landmark for sea and shore miles and miles away. Sylvia knew it well. She had always believed that whoever climbed to the top of it could see the ocean; and the little girl had often laid her hand on the great rough trunk and looked up wistfully at those dark boughs that the wind always stirred, no matter how hot and still the air might be below. Now she thought of the tree with a new excitement, for why, if one climbed it at break of day, could not one see all the world, and easily discover from whence the white heron flew, and mark the place, and find the hidden nest?

What a spirit of adventure, what wild ambition! What fancied triumph and delight and glory for the later morning when she could make known the secret! It was almost too real and too great for the childish heart to bear.

All night the door of the little house stood open and the whippoorwills came   30 and sang upon the very step. The young sportsman and his old hostess were sound asleep, but Sylvia's great design kept her broad awake and watching. She forgot to think of sleep. The short summer night seemed as long as the winter darkness, and at last when the whippoorwills ceased, and she was afraid the morning would after all come too soon, she stole out of the house and followed the pasture path through the woods, hastening toward the open ground beyond, listening with a sense of comfort and companionship to the drowsy twitter of a half-awakened bird, whose perch she had jarred in passing. Alas, if the great wave of human interest which flooded for the first time this dull little life should sweep away the satisfactions of an existence heart to heart with nature and the dumb life of the forest!

There was the huge tree asleep yet in the paling moonlight, and small and silly Sylvia began with utmost bravery to mount to the top of it, with tingling, eager blood coursing the channels of her whole frame, with her bare feet and fingers, that pinched and held like bird's claws to the monstrous ladder reaching up, up, almost to the sky itself. First she must mount the white oak tree that grew alongside, where she was almost lost among the dark branches and the green leaves heavy and wet with dew; a bird fluttered off its nest, and a red squirrel ran to and fro and scolded pettishly at the harmless housebreaker. Sylvia felt her way easily. She had often climbed there, and knew that higher still one of the oak's upper branches chafed against the pine trunk, just where its lower boughs were set close together. There, when she made the dangerous pass from one tree to the other, the great enterprise would really begin.

She crept out along the swaying oak limb at last, and took the daring step across into the old pine-tree. The way was harder than she thought; she must reach far and hold fast, the sharp dry twigs caught and held her and scratched her like angry talons, the pitch made her thin little fingers clumsy and stiff as she went round and round the tree's great stem, higher and higher upward. The sparrows and robins in the woods below were beginning to wake and twitter to the dawn, yet it seemed much lighter there aloft in the pine-tree, and the child knew she must hurry if her project were to be of any use.

The tree seemed to lengthen itself out as she went up, and to reach farther and farther upward. It was like a great main-mast to the voyaging earth; it must truly have been amazed that morning through all its ponderous frame as it felt this determined spark of human spirit wending its way from higher branch to branch. Who knows how steadily the least twigs held themselves to advantage this light, weak creature on her way! The old pine must have loved his new dependent. More than all the hawks, and bats, and moths, and even the sweet voiced thrushes, was the brave, beating heart of the solitary gray-eyed child. And the tree stood still and frowned away the winds that June morning while the dawn grew bright in the east.

Sylvia's face was like a pale star, if one had seen it from the ground, when the last thorny bough was past, and she stood trembling and tired but wholly triumphant, high in the tree-top. Yes, there was the sea with the dawning sun making a golden dazzle over it, and toward that glorious east flew two hawks with slow-moving pinions. How low they looked in the air from that height when one had only seen them before far up, and dark against the blue sky. Their gray feathers were as soft as moths; they seemed only a little way from the tree, and Sylvia felt as if she too could go flying away among the clouds. Westward, the woodlands and farms reached miles and miles into the distance; here and there were church steeples, and white villages, truly it was a vast and awesome world.

The birds sang louder and louder. At last the sun came up bewilderingly 35 bright. Sylvia could see the white sails of ships out at sea, and the clouds that were purple and rose-colored and yellow at first began to fade away. Where was the white heron's nest in the sea of green branches, and was this wonderful sight and pageant of the world the only reward for having climbed to such a giddy height? Now look down again, Sylvia, where the green marsh is set among the shining birches and dark hemlocks; there where you saw the white heron once you will see him again; look, look! a white spot of him like a single floating feather comes up from the dead hemlock and grows larger, and rises, and comes close at last, and goes by the landmark pine with steady sweep of wing and outstretched slender neck and crested head. And wait! wait! do not move a foot or a finger, little girl, do not send an arrow of light and consciousness from your two eager eyes, for the heron has perched on a pine bough not far beyond yours, and cries back to his mate on the nest and plumes his feathers for the new day!

The child gives a long sigh a minute later when a company of shouting catbirds comes also to the tree, and vexed by their fluttering and lawlessness the solemn heron goes away. She knows his secret now, the wild, light, slender bird that floats and wavers, and goes back like an arrow presently to his home in the green world beneath. Then Sylvia, well satisfied, makes her perilous way down again, not daring to look far below the branch she stands on, ready to cry sometimes because her fingers ache and her lamed feet slip. Wondering over and over again what the stranger would say to her, and what he would think when she told him how to find his way straight to the heron's nest.

"Sylvy, Sylvy!" called the busy old grandmother again and again, but nobody answered, and the small husk bed was empty and Sylvia had disappeared.

The guest waked from a dream, and remembering his day's pleasure hurried to dress himself that might it sooner begin. He was sure from the way the shy little girl looked once or twice yesterday that she had at least seen the white heron, and now she must really be made to tell. Here she comes now, paler than ever, and her worn old frock is torn and tattered, and smeared with pine pitch. The grandmother and the sportsman stand in the door together and question her, and the splendid moment has come to speak of the dead hemlock-tree by the green marsh.

But Sylvia does not speak after all, though the old grandmother fretfully rebukes her, and the young man's kind, appealing eyes are looking straight in her own. He can make them rich with money; he has promised it, and they are poor now. He is so well worth making happy, and he waits to hear the story she can tell.

No, she must keep silence! What is it that suddenly forbids her and makes her 40 dumb? Has she been nine years growing and now, when the great world for the first time puts out a hand to her, must she thrust it aside for a bird's sake? The murmur of the pine's green branches is in her ears, she remembers how the white heron came flying through the golden air and how they watched the sea and the morning together, and Sylvia cannot speak; she cannot tell the heron's secret and give its life away.

Dear loyalty, that suffered a sharp pang as the guest went away disappointed later in the day, that could have served and followed him and loved him as a dog loves! Many a night Sylvia heard the echo of his whistle haunting the pasture path as she came home with the loitering cow. She forgot even her sorrow at the sharp report of his gun and the sight of thrushes and sparrows dropping silent to the ground, their songs hushed and their pretty feathers stained and wet with blood. Were the birds better friends than their hunter might have been, — who can tell? Whatever treasures were lost to her, woodlands and summer-time, remember! Bring your gifts and graces and tell your secrets to this lonely country child!

Exploring the Text

1. What is the effect of the imagery in the first paragraph?
2. Look up *sylvan* in the dictionary. What does Sarah Orne Jewett suggest by using *Sylvia* as the name of her protagonist?
3. In paragraph 2, Jewett writes, "The good woman suspected that Sylvia loitered occasionally on her own account; there never was such a child for straying about out-of-doors since the world was made!" In terms of the voice, what is the relationship between the two clauses that make up this sentence?
4. How does Sylvia regard the stranger and his request (para. 8)?
5. What is the significance of the hunter being an ornithologist?
6. What is Jewett's attitude toward the stranger? Use specific evidence to support your argument.
7. Jewett concludes paragraph 30: "Alas, if the great wave of human interest which flooded for the first time this dull little life should sweep away the satisfactions of an existence heart to heart with nature and the dumb life of the forest!" Considering especially such diction as "dull," little," and "dumb," what is Jewett's attitude toward Sylvia?

8. What is the effect of Jewett's use of personification throughout the story?
9. How does this story fit with — or reflect on — the works of nonfiction that comprise most of this chapter?

The Tables Turned (poetry)

WILLIAM WORDSWORTH

William Wordsworth (1770–1850) is one of the most famous and influential poets of the Western world and one of the premier Romantics. Widely known for his reverence of nature and the power of his lyrical verse, he lived in the Lake District in northern England, where he was inspired by the natural beauty of the landscape. With Samuel Taylor Coleridge, he published *Lyrical Ballads* in 1798; the collection, which changed the direction of English poetry, begins with Coleridge's "Rime of the Ancient Mariner" and includes Wordsworth's "Lines Composed a Few Miles above Tintern Abbey." Among Wordsworth's other most famous works are "The World Is Too Much with Us," a sonnet; "Ode: Intimations of Immortality"; and "The Prelude or Growth of a Poet's Mind," an autobiographical poem. "The Tables Turned," also from *Lyrical Ballads*, is an early Romantic poem in which the speaker enjoins his reader to greet nature.

Up! up! my Friend, and quit your books,
Or surely you'll grow double.
Up! up! my Friend, and clear your looks,
Why all this toil and trouble?

The sun, above the mountain's head,   5
A freshening lustre mellow
Through all the long green fields has spread,
His first sweet evening yellow.

Books! 'tis a dull and endless strife:
Come, hear the woodland linnet,   10
How sweet his music! on my life,
There's more of wisdom in it.

And hark! how blithe the throstle sings!
He, too, is no mean preacher:
Come forth into the light of things,   15
Let Nature be your Teacher.

She has a world of ready wealth,
Our minds and hearts to bless —

Spontaneous wisdom breathed by health,
Truth breathed by cheerfulness.   *20*

One impulse from a vernal wood
May teach you more of man,
Of moral evil and of good,
Than all the sages can.

Sweet is the lore which Nature brings;   *25*
Our meddling intellect
Misshapes the beauteous forms of things:—
We murder to dissect.

Enough of Science and of Art;
Close up these barren leaves;   *30*
Come forth, and bring with you a heart
That watches and receives.

Exploring the Text

1. How would you characterize the speaker of this poem?
2. What does the poem suggest about the source of knowledge about humanity and the world? How does it characterize the human intellect?
3. What is the effect of such diction as "mean," "vernal," "meddling," and "beauteous"? Do you think the effect is the same now as it was in William Wordsworth's time?
4. What does Wordsworth mean by the statement, "We murder to dissect" (l. 28)?
5. The young man in Sarah Orne Jewett's "A White Heron" (p. 848) is identified as an ornithologist. Which quatrain from Wordsworth might best be used to comment on Jewett's portrayal of that character? Why?
6. How might Joyce Carol Oates (p. 840) respond to this poem?

Cloud the Issue or Clear the Air?
(advertisement)

Royal Dutch/Shell

> The following advertisement for the major oil company Royal Dutch/Shell has appeared in several national magazines.

OR CLEAR THE AIR?

T   A CHOICE?

Shell believes that action needs to be taken now. We are delivering on our commitment to reduce greenhouse gas emissions from our operations. We're working to increase the provision of cleaner burning natural gas and encouraging the use of lower-carbon fuels for homes and transport. It's all part of our commitment to sustainable development, balancing economic progress with environmental care and social responsibility. Solutions to the future won't come easily, particularly in today's business climate, but you can't find them if you don't keep looking.

WE WELCOME YOUR INPUT. CONTACT US ON THE INTERNET AT WWW.SHELL.COM OR
EMAIL US AT 'TELL-SHELL@SI.SHELL.COM' OR WRITE TO US AT: 'THE PROFITS & PRINCIPLES DEBATE',
SHELL INTERNATIONAL LTD, SHELL CENTRE, LONDON SE1 7NA, UK.

Exploring the Text

1. Based on your reading of this ad, how would you define Royal Dutch/Shell's position on global warming, or climate change?
2. What is the effect of the word choices *heated debate*, *hot air*, and *today's business climate*?
3. Note how the ad juxtaposes *profits* with *principles*, *cloud the issue* with *clear the air*, *serious threat* with *hot air*, and *economic progress* with *environmental care and social responsibility*. What is the rhetorical effect of these juxtapositions?
4. What claim, support, and assumption does this ad present?
5. Does the ad appeal most to ethos, logos, or pathos? Explain.
6. After reading and thinking about the ad, how do you feel about the Shell company? How do you feel about the issues raised by the ad?

Kindred Spirits (painting)

ASHER B. DURAND

Asher B. Durand (1796–1886), a successful engraver, was inspired by Thomas Cole to become a painter. Durand later became a major representative of the Hudson River School of painting. His *Kindred Spirits*, a masterpiece of American landscape painting, depicts premier American landscape artist Thomas Cole (1801–1848) and romantic poet William Cullen Bryant (1794–1878) in the Catskill Mountains of New York State in 1849. Bryant's eulogy at Cole's funeral inspired Durand to paint their friendship in the natural world they both loved so well.

Exploring the Text

1. What do you notice first in this painting? Is the painting pleasing? Why?
2. William Cullen Bryant's famous poem "Thanatopsis," found at <bedfordstmartins.com/languageofcomp>, begins:

To him who in the love of Nature holds
Communion with her visible forms, she speaks
A various language; for his gayer hours
She has a voice of gladness, and a smile
And eloquence of beauty, and she glides
Into his darker musings, with a mild
And healing sympathy, that steals away
Their sharpness, ere he is aware.

How does *Kindred Spirits* illustrate Bryant's words?

3. What might the painter be suggesting with the overarching tree limb?
4. The phrase "kindred spirits" is taken from "Sonnet to Solitude" at <bedfordstmartins .com/languageofcomp>, which is a poem about the healing power of nature by John Keats. It expresses a theme dear to both Thomas Cole and William Cullen Bryant, and may be meant to refer to the two figures in the painting. Might nature be a third kindred spirit? Why or why not?
5. How might Ralph Waldo Emerson (p. 807) respond to the painting? How might Joyce Carol Oates (p. 840)?

Focus on Climate Change

The following texts each present a view on the issue of climate change.

Sources
1. **Bill McKibben,** *It's Easy Being Green*
2. **Richard Conniff,** from *Counting Carbons*
3. **Edward O. Wilson,** From *The Future of Life*
4. **Melissa Farlow and Randy Olson,** *Ice Blankets*
5. **Indur M. Goklany,** *Is Climate Change the 21st Century's Most Urgent Environmental Problem?*
6. **Daniel Glick,** *GeoSigns: The Big Thaw*

After you have read, studied, and synthesized these pieces, enter the conversation by responding to one of the prompts on page 888.

1. *It's Easy Being Green*

BILL MCKIBBEN

In the following essay from *Mother Jones,* Bill McKibben discusses the use of fossil fuels versus renewable energy.

The more I surveyed my new car, the happier I got. "New car" is one of those phrases that make Americans unreasonably happy to begin with. And this one — well, it was a particularly shiny metallic blue. Better yet, it was the first Honda Civic hybrid electric sold in the state of Vermont: I'd traded in my old Civic (40 miles to the gallon), and now the little screen behind the steering wheel was telling me that I was getting 50, 51, 52 miles to the gallon. Even better yet, I was doing nothing strange or difficult or conspicuously ecological. If you didn't know there was an electric motor assisting the small gas engine — well, you'd never know. The owner's manual devoted far more space to the air bags and the heating system. It didn't look goofily Jetsonish like Honda's first hybrid, the two-seater Insight introduced in 2000. Instead, it looked like a Civic, the most vanilla car ever produced. "Our goal was to make it look, for lack of a better word, normal," explained Kevin Bynoe, spokesman for American Honda.

And the happier I got, the angrier I got. Because, as the Honda and a raft of other recent developments powerfully proved, energy efficiency, energy conservation, and renewable energy are ready for prime time. No longer the niche province of incredibly noble backyard tinkerers distilling biodiesel from used vegetable oil or building homes from Earth rammed into tires, the equipment and attitudes necessary to radically transform our energy system are now mainstream enough for those of us too lazy or too busy to try anything that seems hard. And yet the switch toward sensible energy still isn't happening. A few weeks before I picked up my car, an overwhelming bipartisan vote in the Senate had rejected calls to increase the mileage of the nation's new car fleet by 2015 — to increase it to 36 mpg, not as good as the Civic I'd traded in to buy this hybrid. The administration was pressing ahead with its plan for more drilling and refining. The world was suffering the warmest winter in history as more carbon dioxide pushed global temperatures ever higher. And people were dying in conflicts across wide swaths of the world, the casualties — at least in some measure — of America's insatiable demand for energy.

In other words, the gap between what we could be doing and what we are doing has never been wider. Consider:

- The Honda I was driving was the third hybrid model easily available in this country, following in the tire tracks of the Insight and the Toyota Prius. They take regular gas, they require nothing in the way of special service, and they boast waiting lists. And yet Detroit, despite a decade of massive funding from the Clinton administration, can't sell you one. Instead, after September 11, the automakers launched a massive campaign (zero financing, red, white, and blue ads) to sell existing stock, particularly the gas-sucking SUVs that should by all rights come with their own little Saudi flags on the hood.

- Even greater boosts in efficiency can come when you build or renovate a home. Alex Wilson, editor of *Environmental Building News*, says the average American house may be 20 percent more energy efficient than it was two decades ago, but simple tweaks like better windows and bulkier insulation could save 30 to 50 percent more energy with "very little cost implication." And yet building codes do almost nothing to boost such technologies, and the Bush administration is fighting to roll back efficiency gains for some appliances that Clinton managed to push through. For instance, air-conditioner manufacturers recently won a battle in the Senate to let them get away with making their machines only 20 percent more efficient, not the 30 percent current law demands. The difference in real terms? Sixty new power plants across the country by 2030.

- Or consider electric generation. For a decade or two, environmentalists had their fingers crossed when they talked about renewables. It was hard to imagine most Americans really trading in their grid connection for backyard solar panels with their finicky batteries. But such trade-offs are less necessary by the day. Around the world, wind power is growing more quickly than any other form of energy — Denmark, Germany, Spain, and

India all generate big amounts of their power from ultra-modern wind turbines. But in this country, where the never-ending breeze across the High Plains could generate twice as much electricity as the country uses, progress has been extraordinarily slow. (North Dakota, the windiest state in the union, has exactly four turbines.) Wind power is finally beginning to get some serious attention from the energy industry, but the technology won't live up to its potential until politicians stop subsidizing fossil fuels and give serious boosts to the alternatives.

And not all those politicians are conservative, either. In Massachusetts, even some true progressives, like the gubernatorial candidate Robert Reich, can't bring themselves to endorse a big wind installation proposed for six miles off Cape Cod. They have lots of arguments, most of which boil down to NIVOMD (Not in View of My Deck), a position particularly incongruous since Cape Cod will sink quickly beneath the Atlantic unless every weapon in the fight against global warming is employed as rapidly a possible.

What really haunts energy experts is the sense that, for the first time since the oil shocks of the early 1970s, the nation could have rallied around the cause of energy conservation and renewable alternatives last fall. In the wake of September 11, they agree, the president could have announced a pair of national goals — capture Osama and free ourselves from the oil addiction that leaves us endlessly vulnerable. "President Bush's failure will haunt me for decades," says Alan Durning, president of Northwest Environment Watch. "Bush had a chance to advance, in a single blow, three pressing national priorities: national security, economic recovery, and environmental protection. All the stars were aligned." If only, says Brent Blackwelder, president of Friends of the Earth, Bush had set a goal, like JFK and the space program. "We could totally get off oil in three decades." Instead, the president used the crisis to push for drilling in the Arctic National Wildlife Refuge, a present to campaign contributors that would yield a statistically insignificant new supply ten years down the road.

It's not just new technologies that Bush could have pushed, of course. Americans were, at least for a little while, in the mood to do something, to make some sacrifice, to rally around some cause. In the words of Charles Komanoff, a New York energy analyst, "The choice is between love of oil and love of country," and at least "in the initial weeks after September 11, it seemed that Americans were awakening at last to the true cost of their addiction to oil." In an effort to take advantage of that political window, Komanoff published a booklet showing just how simple it would be to cut America's oil use by 5 or 10 percent — not over the years it will take for the new technologies to really kick in, but over the course of a few weeks and with only minor modifications to our way of life.

For instance, he calculated, we could save 7 percent of the gasoline we use simply by eliminating one car trip in fourteen. The little bit of planning required to make sure you visit the grocery store three times a week instead of four would

5

leave us with endlessly more oil than sucking dry the Arctic. Indeed, Americans are so energy-profligate that even minor switches save significant sums — if half the drivers in two-car households switched just a tenth of their travel to their more efficient vehicle, we'd instantly save 1 percent of our oil. Keep the damn Explorer; just leave it in the driveway once a week and drive the Camry.

A similar menu of small changes — cutting back on one airplane trip in seven, turning down the thermostat two degrees, screwing in a few compact fluorescent bulbs — and all of a sudden our endlessly climbing energy usage begins to decline. Impossible? Americans won't do it? Look at California. With the threat of power shortages looming and with some clever incentives provided by government and utilities, Californians last year found an awful lot of small ways to save energy that really added up: 79 percent reported taking some steps, and a third of households managed to cut their electric use by more than 20 percent. Not by becoming a Third World nation (the state's economy continued to grow), not by living in caves, not by suffering — but by turning off the lights when they left the room. In just the first six months of 2001, the Colorado energy guru Amory Lovins pointed out recently, "customers wiped out California's previous five to ten years of demand growth." Now the same companies that were scrambling to build new plants for the Golden State a year ago are backing away from their proposals, spooked by the possibility of an energy glut.

It's only in Washington, in fact, that nobody gets it. If you go to Europe or Asia, you'll find nations increasingly involved in planning for a different energy future: Every industrial country but the United States signed on to the Kyoto agreement at the last international conference on global warming, and some of those nations may actually meet their targets for carbon dioxide reductions. The Dutch consumer demand for green power outstrips even the capacity of their growing wind farms, while the Germans have taken the logical step of raising taxes on carbon-based fuels and eliminating them on renewable sources. Reducing fossil fuel use is an accepted, inevitable part of the political process on the Continent, the same way that "fighting crime" is in this country, and Europeans look with growing disgust at the depth of our addiction — only the events of September 11 saved America from a wave of universal scorn when Bush backed away from the Kyoto pact.

And in state capitols and city halls around this country, local leaders are   10 beginning to act as well. Voters in San Francisco last year overwhelmingly approved an initiative to require municipal purchases of solar and wind power; in Seattle, the mayor's office announced an ambitious plan to meet or beat the Kyoto targets within the confines of the city and four suburbs.

Perhaps such actions might be expected in San Francisco and Seattle. But in June of 2001, the Chicago city government signed a contract with Commonwealth Edison to buy 10 percent of its power from renewables, a figure due to increase to 20 percent in five years. And in Salt Lake City, of all places, Mayor Rocky Anderson announced on the opening day of the Winter Olympics that his city, too, was going to meet the Kyoto standards — already, in fact, crews were at work changing lightbulbs in street lamps and planning new mass transit.

Even many big American corporations have gone much further than the Bush administration. As Alex Wilson, the green building expert, points out, "Corporations are pretty good at looking at the bottom line, which is directly affected by operating costs. They're good with numbers." If you can make your product with half the energy, well, that's just as good as increasing sales — and if you can put a windmill on the cover of your annual report, that's gravy.

In short, what pretty much everyone outside the White House has realized is this: The great economic shift of this century will be away from fossil fuels and toward renewable energy. That shift will happen with or without George W. Bush — there are too many reasons, from environmental to economic to geopolitical necessity, for it not to. But American policy can slow down the transition, perhaps by decades, and that is precisely what the administration would like to see. They have two reasons: One is the enormous debt they owe to the backers of their political careers, those coal and oil and gas guys who dictated large sections of the new energy policy. Those industries want to wring every last penny from their mines, their drill rigs, and their refineries — and if those extra decades mean that the planet's temperature rises a few degrees, well, that's business.

The other reason is just as powerful, though — it's the fear that Americans will blame their leaders if prices for gas go up too quickly. It's not an idle fear — certainly it was shared by Bill Clinton, who did nothing to stem the nation's love affair with SUVs, and by Al Gore, who, during his presidential campaign, demanded that the Strategic Petroleum Reserve be opened to drive down prices at the pump. But that's what makes Bush's post-September silence on this issue so sad. For once a U.S. president had the chance to turn it all around — to say that this was a sacrifice we needed to make and one that any patriot would support. It's tragically likely he will have the same opportunity again in the years ahead, and tragically unlikely that he will take it.

In the meantime, there's work to be done in statehouses and city halls. And at   15
the car lot — at least the ones with the Honda and Toyota signs out front. "This Civic has a slightly different front end and a roof-mounted antenna," says Honda's Bynoe. "But other than that, it looks like a regular Civic, and it drives like one too. It's not necessarily for hard-core enviros. You don't have to scream about it at the top of your lungs. It's just a car." But a very shiny blue. And I just came back from a trip to Boston: 59 miles to the gallon.

Questions

1. What is Bill McKibben's tone in the first two paragraphs? How does it change as the essay continues? Would the essay suffer if McKibben ended it after paragraph 14? Explain.
2. What is the effect of the three bulleted points in paragraph 3? To what values does McKibben appeal with these points?

3. What is McKibben's most compelling argument? How persuasive is it?
4. While the use of the acronym NIVOMD (para. 4) may be humorous (it's an awkward play on NIMBY, which stands for Not in My Backyard), what serious issue does it suggest?
5. Do you agree that McKibben's suggestion is something "any patriot would support," as he says in paragraph 14?
6. According to information from the text, how would you characterize McKibben politically? How might such a characterization influence a reader?

2. *Counting Carbons*

How much greenhouse gas does your family produce?

RICHARD CONNIFF

In the following selection from a 2005 article in *Discover*, Richard Conniff writes about the amount of carbon dioxide the typical American produces while going about his or her everyday life.

Not long ago, the Rolling Stones announced plans to ensure that an upcoming tour would not contribute to global warming: They had signed on to two forestry projects in Scotland, which would plant 2,800 trees, one for every 60 fans in the audience, and thus render the entire tour "carbon neutral." Better still, the Stones got a mobile phone company to pick up the extra cost of the saplings, about 20 cents a ticket.

My first impulse was to laugh. Mick Jagger is a great performer, but he also personifies the jet-set lifestyle, blithely tripping from villa to penthouse on a gaudy 40-year-long plume of fossil-fuel exhaust. How could one tree possibly remove the carbon dioxide produced in getting thousands of rock-and-roll fans, let alone lights, amps, and the Stones themselves, to various stadiums on the tour? Does a pine seedling really work that hard?

My second, less gratifying impulse was to wonder, What if they're right, or at least moving in the right direction? If you believe, along with almost every scientist who has studied the issue, that global warming poses a genuine threat to humanity, doesn't this suggest that we should be doing something about it?

What would it mean to apply in our daily lives, just for argument, the kind of reductions called for in the Kyoto Protocol on greenhouse-gas emissions? At the most elementary level, could we do the math? Could we figure out how much carbon dioxide and other greenhouse gases our cars, our homes, and our work produce? Given how invested we have become in the automotive way of life, would it even be possible to reduce emissions significantly? And if we started down this line of thinking, would emissions counting join low-carb diets and real estate one-upmanship as favorite topics of cocktail party bores? Or forget the cocktail parties: Once we confronted the mathematics of a Sunday drive, would there be anything left to do, in a guilt-free way, other than crawl under a rock?

Under pressure from the Kyoto Protocol, which went into effect in February 5 [2005] for just about every country except the United States and Australia, people elsewhere have actually begun to think about such questions, often in ways that are startling for their scale and severity. Researchers at Oxford University recently proposed demolishing 80,000 inefficient homes a year — many of them century-old structures in town and city centers — to achieve the British goal of a 60 percent reduction in greenhouse-gas emissions by 2050. (The proposal also included building 220,000 low-carbon-emission homes a year.) In Switzerland, which is watching its Alpine ice disappear, technicians set out to wrap part of a glacier in insulating foam.

Even die-hard Alaskan antienvironmentalists have begun to warm up to the idea of imposing limits on greenhouse-gas emissions, according to *The Wall Street Journal*, because homes on the coast there are already beginning to slip into rising seas. The Government Accountability Office recently reported that 180 Alaskan coastal villages are threatened because of melting sea ice and permafrost. Moving just one of them, Shishmaref, with 600 residents, would cost taxpayers $180 million.

Detroit's Big Three automakers have also tacitly accepted global warming as a political reality, agreeing in April to a 6 percent reduction in greenhouse-gas emissions from new vehicles sold in Canada by 2010. (They continue, however, to fight a California law requiring a 30 percent reduction in 10 years.)

Despite criticisms that the Kyoto Protocol limitations are too expensive, too difficult, or too heavily targeted against developed nations, one American company has gone well beyond Kyoto, apparently without giving up its competitive edge. By tinkering with manufacturing processes, DuPont says it has already cut its greenhouse-gas emissions by 72 percent from 1990 levels, despite a 33 percent increase in production. It has also reduced total energy use by 7 percent from 1990 levels, saving $2 billion.

Saying that DuPont can do it, on the other hand, doesn't necessarily make it any easier for the rest of us. Calculating greenhouse-gas emissions turns out to be dismayingly complex, and figuring out how to reduce or mitigate these emissions is even more difficult.

The first time I bothered to consider my own family's contribution to global 10 warming was late one night last winter when my teenage son had taken the car on a long and unnecessary errand. As I sat up waiting for him, I scribbled the mileage and the upfront costs of his journey on the back of an envelope. Then, because of the idea of wasting money wasn't going to get his attention, I started to work out the greenhouse-gas emissions. I fussed over the calculations for a while, then I threw the envelope in the trash and went to bed, partly because I knew my son would just say I was being a jerk but mostly because the numbers were too large to believe.

Experts on greenhouse-gas emissions tell me that every time my car burns a gallon of gasoline, I am putting more than 25 pounds of carbon dioxide into the atmosphere as well as a smaller amount of methane, nitrous oxide, and various other toxic gases. It is easy to stumble over this fact. A single gallon of gasoline weighs only about 6 pounds. Otherwise, I couldn't carry a gas can down the highway to refill my tank. Moreover, when I put that gallon of gas in the engine, it *burns*, all too quickly. So by what dark magic could there be 25 pounds of junk released in the process?

Look at it another way: A 747 passenger jet traveling from New York to London emits about 880,000 pounds of carbon dioxide. But that is more than the plane's maximum takeoff weight. The fuel on board weighs only about 300,000 pounds.

So I did some more calculations the next day (when my son was lying low with a $113 speeding ticket): Gasoline and jet fuel (kerosene) are about 90 percent carbon. Combustion causes almost every atom of carbon in the fuel to combine with two atoms of oxygen, producing carbon dioxide. Despite our tendency to think of it as weightless, oxygen is in fact 1.33 times heavier than carbon. So the original 6 pounds of carbon combine with 15 or 16 pounds of oxygen, minus some soot, water, and other by-products, and, bingo, by driving 21 miles down the road, my car has just disturbed the balance of the planet's carbon cycle by producing 19 pounds of CO_2. Emissions released in manufacturing and transporting the gas to market add another 6 pounds to the total, meaning that effectively my car has launched 25 pounds of CO_2 into the atmosphere, where scientists say it will linger for hundreds or even thousands of years, helping to trap solar heat and turn the atmosphere into a greenhouse. . . .

For a lot of people and organizations feeling stuck on the wrong side of the global-warming balance sheet, one solution is to offset the emissions they cannot eliminate. In essence, they pay somebody else not to pollute, or they pay for activities like planting trees that are assumed to remove carbon dioxide from the atmosphere. As a practical alternative for individual consumers, the retail market in emissions offsets is promising — but not yet ready for prime time.

Most trading in carbon dioxide offsets now occurs only on a large scale. It works like this: One company installs new equipment to cut its emissions by 5,000 tons. Then it sells the right to emit 5,000 tons to a buyer for whom new equipment would be too costly. To avoid simply swapping pollution from one place to another, these so-called cap-and-trade systems usually involve a gradual, government-ordered reduction in overall emissions. As the cheaper reductions get put into place, participants move on to the more difficult reductions, and the trades become steadily more pricey. Selling emissions rights helps defray the cost of making reductions.

To some people, reforestation projects, like the ones the Rolling Stones arranged, seem like the most appealing way to offset emissions. In one case, a power company paid $13.7 million to reforest 100,000 acres of U.S. Fish and Wildlife Service land in Mississippi in the expectation that every acre of trees would absorb enough carbon dioxide to offset 150 tons of greenhouse-gas emissions over the life span of the trees. But critics say such these schemes are much less effective than advertised.

"Basically, they're selling a warm, fuzzy feeling," says Dennis King, a University of Maryland researcher and the author of an EPA-funded study of carbon sequestration. Young trees don't actually start to sequester significant amounts of carbon dioxide for 20 years, he says, and it takes a tree 100 years to remove a measly 3,000 pounds of carbon dioxide from the atmosphere — assuming the tree survives drought, fire, flood, disease, and other afflictions. But, King says, the buyer "gets to dump a ton of carbon into the atmosphere with 100 percent certainty" today. Moreover, most of the carbon that gets sequestered in these forestry projects will eventually be released again when the trees die and decompose — or get harvested. "The numbers don't look good when you work them out," King says.

The danger of such projects is that they risk discrediting the market in greenhouse-gas emissions just as it is starting to get off the ground. One Swiss multinational, the Holcim Group, recently pulled out of a mitigation scheme, with an executive predicting that loose accounting standards will produce "other Enrons" among the companies developing such projects and "other Arthur Andersens" among the auditors.

Proponents of offsets are acutely aware of the need to protect the credibility of their burgeoning market. The Chicago Climate Exchange, the leading marketplace, started trading carbon dioxide emissions in 2003, with members like IBM and International Paper committing themselves to a voluntary schedule of reductions. Exchange chairman Richard Sandor says it uses the National Association of Securities Dealers to audit its transactions. A company that fails to deliver on emissions-reduction claims, he says, can expect to be treated the same as a company that overstates its earnings. This is a polite way of saying that CEOs could end up in court and their company stock in the doghouse.

But determining what is a legitimate way to reduce greenhouse-gas emissions — and how to account for it — is going to be a long, messy process. Moreover, the scale of the problem is unlike anything previously attempted. For instance, Statoil, the Norwegian energy company, has engineered a drilling platform in the North Sea to pump a million tons of carbon dioxide back underground every year. Construction alone cost $100 million. Geologists believe that it is a permanent way to keep carbon dioxide out of the atmosphere. [20]

The problem, says climate scientist Ken Caldeira of Lawrence Livermore National Laboratory, is that even assuming a modest attack on global warming, "we would need to build one of these a day for the next 50 years to maybe get halfway there."

So where does this leave my family and yours as we roll down the highway trailing our vast burden of greenhouse-gas emissions? Individuals can also buy offsets to compensate for the things we haven't yet figured out how to reduce. But how many? A shortcut is to take the share of greenhouse-gas emissions under the average American's individual control — call it 10 tons, for simplicity — and multiply that by the number of people in the household. For my family of five, I would need 50 tons of offsets a year.

JUST PLANT A FEW TREES, RIGHT?

Trees draw carbon dioxide out of the atmosphere through photosynthesis, so one potential way to offset some greenhouse-gas emissions is to plant more forests. But most trees don't sequester significant amounts of carbon during the first few years after planting. Moreover, when trees succumb to forest fires or begin to decay, they release carbon back into the atmosphere.

An acre of fast-growing softwood trees, such as pines, can take in as much as 5 tons of carbon dioxide a year as they enter their peak years of growth at around age 15. Hardwood trees grow more slowly but tend to keep their carbon locked away longer. An acre of walnut trees, for example, can take in as much as 2.2 tons of carbon dioxide a year as the trees enter their peak years of growth at around age 25.

The graphic below gives a rough indication of how many walnut trees would have to be planted—and allowed to mature for at least 25 years—to offset the carbon emissions of a typical family of four and the nation at large from just one year.

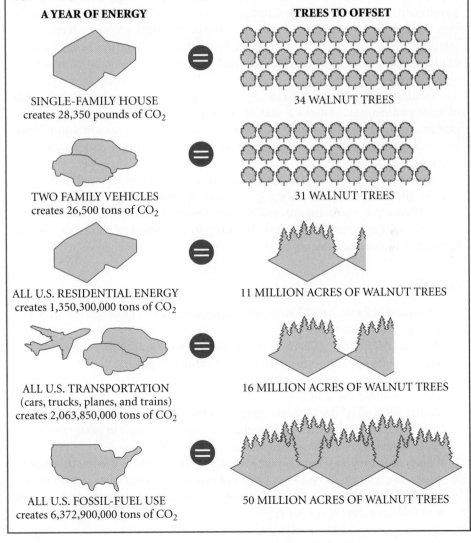

A YEAR OF ENERGY

SINGLE-FAMILY HOUSE
creates 28,350 pounds of CO_2

TWO FAMILY VEHICLES
creates 26,500 tons of CO_2

ALL U.S. RESIDENTIAL ENERGY
creates 1,350,300,000 tons of CO_2

ALL U.S. TRANSPORTATION
(cars, trucks, planes, and trains)
creates 2,063,850,000 tons of CO_2

ALL U.S. FOSSIL-FUEL USE
creates 6,372,900,000 tons of CO_2

TREES TO OFFSET

34 WALNUT TREES

31 WALNUT TREES

11 MILLION ACRES OF WALNUT TREES

16 MILLION ACRES OF WALNUT TREES

50 MILLION ACRES OF WALNUT TREES

You can get your offsets wholesale at about $1.30 a ton. An individual can register with the Chicago Climate Exchange as an exchange participant for a one-time fee of $250, then contact a broker to place an order. The typical minimum order is 2,500 tons. But Amerex, a Houston brokerage, says it will take smaller orders, with a base commission of $150. The hitch for me is that trades on the Chicago Climate Exchange are anonymous, and buyers do not know what kind of offset projects they have purchased until after a transaction is complete. So you can get stuck with offsets involving reforestation projects.

The gold standard in offsets are the ones that pay other people to use less fossil fuels — the only way to get at the root of the global-warming problem. Several services come close to fitting the bill. The Better World Club, an environmentally oriented alternative to AAA, sells offsets to help people "travel guilt free." But it has donated money for only one project so far, a $13,000 replacement of inefficient oil-burning furnaces in public schools in Portland, Oregon. TerraPass, a start-up by students at the University of Pennsylvania's Wharton School, offsets emissions by investing in wind power and reduction of methane emissions in agriculture. But it's also small.

I ended up at the Solar Electric Light Fund, a nonprofit that installs hundreds   25
of solar photovoltaic systems a year in developing countries. According to www
.self.org, a $100 donation prevents 10 tons of greenhouse-gas emissions from kerosene lanterns and diesel generators in places like Bhutan and Tanzania — and it's tax deductible.

I went to bed thinking that, for $500, I had at last made my household carbon neutral. But in the middle of the night I woke up from a dream in which Inuits balanced on a vast mathematical and moral equation made of ice, which was rapidly melting. I lay there in the dark, listening to the sound of warm air rushing through the heating ducts.

Questions

1. What effect does Richard Conniff achieve by opening the piece with an anecdote about the Rolling Stones?
2. How effective are the statistics in paragraph 5? Looking at the article as a whole, does Conniff appeal most to ethos, logos, or pathos? Explain.
3. In paragraph 10, Conniff reports that his response to "counting carbons" was frustrating "because the numbers were too large to believe." What is your own response? What effect does the information included in the table on page 871 have? Does it make the problem seem hopeless, as Conniff suggests in paragraph 10, or understandable and perhaps manageable?
4. What is the strongest point Conniff makes? Why do you think it is the strongest?
5. What is the relationship between Conniff's text and the visual data in the table on page 871? How do the data support Conniff's argument? How do the data enhance your understanding of the issue?

3. From *The Future of Life*

EDWARD O. WILSON

In the following excerpt from *The Future of Life* (2002), acclaimed scientist Edward O. Wilson creates an imaginary debate between "the economist" and "the environmentalist."

The economist is focused on production and consumption. These are what the world wants and needs, he says. He is right, of course. Every species lives on production and consumption. The tree finds and consumes nutrients and sunlight; the leopard finds and consumes the deer. And the farmer clears both away to find space and raise corn — for consumption. The economist's thinking is based on precise models of rational choice and near-horizon time lines. His parameters are the gross domestic product, trade balance, and competitive index. He sits on corporate boards, travels to Washington, occasionally appears on television talk shows. The planet, he insists, is perpetually fruitful and still underutilized.

The ecologist has a different worldview. He is focused on unsustainable crop yields, overdrawn aquifers, and threatened ecosystems. His voice is also heard, albeit faintly, in high government and corporate circles. He sits on nonprofit foundation boards, writes for *Scientific American*, and is sometimes called to Washington. The planet, he insists, is exhausted and in trouble.

The Economist

"Ease up. In spite of two centuries of doomsaying, humanity is enjoying unprecedented prosperity. There are environmental problems, certainly, but they can be solved. Think of them as the detritus of progress, to be cleared away. The global economic picture is favorable. The gross national products of the industrial countries continue to rise. Despite their recessions, the Asian tigers are catching up with North America and Europe. Around the world, manufacture and the service economy are growing geometrically. Since 1950 per-capita income and meat production have risen continuously. Even though the world population has increased at an explosive 1.8 percent each year during the same period, cereal production, the source of more than half the food calories of the poorer nations and the traditional proxy of worldwide crop yield, has more than kept pace, rising from 275 kilograms per head in the early 1950s to 370 kilograms by the 1980s. The forests of the developed countries are now regenerating as fast as they are being cleared, or nearly so. And while fibers are also declining steeply in most of the rest of the world — a serious problem, I grant — no global scarcities are expected in the foreseeable future. Agriforestry has been summoned to the rescue: more than 20 percent of industrial wood fiber now comes from tree plantations.

"Social progress is running parallel to economic growth. Literacy rates are climbing, and with them the liberation and empowerment of women. Democracy, the gold standard of governance, is spreading country by country. The communication revolution powered by the computer and the Internet has accelerated the globalization of trade and the evolution of a more irenic international culture.

"For two centuries the specter of Malthus[1] troubled the dreams of futurists.   5
By rising exponentially, the doomsayers claimed, population must outstrip the limited resources of the world and bring about famine, chaos, and war. On occasion this scenario did unfold locally. But that has been more the result of political mismanagement than Malthusian mathematics. Human ingenuity has always found a way to accommodate rising populations and allow most to prosper. The green revolution, which dramatically raised crop yields in the developing countries, is the outstanding example. It can be repeated with new technology. Why should we doubt that human entrepreneurship can keep us on an upward turning curve?

"Genius and effort have transformed the environment to the benefit of human life. We have turned a wild and inhospitable world into a garden. Human dominance is Earth's destiny. The harmful perturbations we have caused can be moderated and reversed as we go along."

The Environmentalist

"Yes, it's true that the human condition has improved dramatically in many ways. But you've painted only half the picture, and with all due respect the logic it uses is just plain dangerous. As your worldview implies, humanity has learned how to create an economy-driven paradise. Yes again — but only on an infinitely large and malleable planet. It should be obvious to you that Earth is finite and its environment increasingly brittle. No one should look to GNPs and corporate annual reports for a competent projection of the world's long-term economic future. To the information there, if we are to understand the real world, must be added the research reports of natural-resource specialists and ecological economists. They are the experts who seek an accurate balance sheet, one that includes a full accounting of the costs to the planet incurred by economic growth.

"This new breed of analysts argues that we can no longer afford to ignore the dependency of the economy and social progress on the environmental resource base. It is the *content* of economic growth, with natural resources factored in, that counts in the long term, not just the yield in products and currency. A country that levels its forests, drains its aquifers, and washes its topsoil downriver without measuring the cost is a country traveling blind. It faces a shaky economic future. It suffers the same delusion as the one that destroyed the whaling industry. As harvesting and processing techniques were improved, the annual catch of whales rose, and the industry flourished. But the whale populations declined in equal measure until they were depleted. Several species, including the blue whale, the

---

[1]Thomas Malthus (1766–1834), demographer and economist, predicted that the human population would exceed its food supply by the middle of the nineteenth century. — Eds.

largest animal species in the history of Earth, came close to extinction. Where-upon most whaling was called to a halt. Extend that argument to falling ground water, drying rivers, and shrinking per-capita arable land, and you get the picture.

"Suppose that the conventionally measured global economic output, now at about $31 trillion, were to expand at a healthy 3 percent annually. By 2050 it would in theory reach $138 trillion. With only a small leveling adjustment of this income, the entire world population would be prosperous by current standards. Utopia at last, it would seem! What is the flaw in the argument? It is the environ-ment crumbling beneath us. If natural resources, particularly fresh water and arable land, continue to diminish at their present per-capita rate, the economic boom will lose steam, in the course of which — and this worries me even if it doesn't worry you — the effort to enlarge productive land will wipe out a large part of the world's fauna and flora.

"The appropriation of productive land — the ecological footprint — is 10 already too large for the planet to sustain, and it's growing larger. A recent study building on this concept estimated that the human population exceeded Earth's sustainable capacity around the year 1978. By 2000 it had overshot by 1.4 times that capacity. If 12 percent of land were now to be set aside in order to protect the natural environment, as recommended in the 1987 Brundtland Report, Earth's sustainable capacity will have been exceeded still earlier, around 1972. In short, Earth has lost its ability to regenerate — unless global consumption is reduced, or global production is increased, or both."

By dramatizing these two polar views of the economic future, I don't wish to imply the existence of two cultures with distinct ethos. All who care about both the economy and environment, and that includes the vast majority, are members of the same culture. The gaze of our two debaters is fixed on different points in the space-time scale in which we all dwell. They differ in the factors they take into account in forecasting the state of the world, how far they look into the future, and how much they care about nonhuman life. Most economists today, and all but the most politically conservative of their public interpreters, recognize very well that the world has limits and the human population cannot afford to grow much larger. They know that humanity is destroying biodiversity. They just don't like to spend a lot of time thinking about it.

Notes

The data and arguments in the dialogue between economist and ecologist were drawn from many sources. Among the most up-to-date were the series *Living Planet Report* (1998 and 1999) of the World Wide Fund for Nature (Gland, Switzerland), the New Economics Foundation (London), and the World Conser-vation Monitoring Center (Cambridge, England); and *World Resources 2000–2001: People and Ecosystems — The Fraying Web of Life*, produced by the World Resources Institute in collaboration with the United Nations Development and

Environment Programmes and the World Bank (Oxford: Elsevier Science, 2000; Washington, D.C.: World Resources Institute, 2000; summary available at www .elsevier.com/locate/worldresources).

Questions

1. Edward O. Wilson, a Harvard professor and a curator at the Museum of Comparative Zoology at Harvard, has won two Pulitzer Prizes. What impact might these facts have on you or another reader?
2. In this selection, Wilson posits two different points of view about the future of life. Paraphrase each one. Which one makes more sense to you? How would you describe a third point of view?
3. Which of the views presented most expresses Wilson's own? How do you know?
4. Has your attitude toward the economy or the environment been influenced by Wilson's views? Explain.

4. *Ice Blankets*

MELISSA FARLOW AND RANDY OLSON

The following photograph appeared in *National Geographic* in 2006.

Draping a ski slope on Austria's Pitztal Glacier, synthetic blankets reflect solar radiation to slow summer melting. Such drastic measures to save the slopes may prove futile. If current temperature trends hold, 50 to 80 percent of remaining Alpine glacier ice could vanish by 2100. The loss would alter the region's ecosystems — not to mention its economy.

Questions

1. What was your first reaction upon seeing this photograph?
2. What does the photograph suggest about the natural environment in terms of climate change?
3. How would the voices in Edward O. Wilson's essay (p. 873) respond to the photograph?
4. Consider the relationship between the photograph and the accompanying text. Is the text necessary?

5. *Is Climate Change the 21st Century's Most Urgent Environmental Problem?*

INDUR M. GOKLANY

In the following essay, scholar Indur M. Goklany examines the impact of climate change.

Introduction

Some have argued that the Kyoto Protocol and other schemes for immediately mitigating greenhouse gas (GHG) emissions are justified because human-induced global warming is, in the words of the 42nd U.S. President, William J. Clinton, "the overriding environmental challenge" facing the globe today. Another argument, advanced by those who are more cautious and perhaps less prone to hyperbole, is that the impacts of global warming — on top of myriad other global public health and environmental threats — may prove to be the proverbial "straw that broke the camel's back." They suggest that climate change will overwhelm human and natural systems by increasing the prevalence of climate-sensitive diseases, reducing agricultural productivity in developing countries, raising sea levels, and altering ecosystems, forests, and biodiversity worldwide.

In this paper, we first examine global warming impacts to date — the good, bad and indifferent effects. We next analyze the impacts of global warming into the foreseeable [future]. Thirdly, we ask whether it is more effective to rely on mitigation (emission reduction) strategies, or on adaptation approaches to climate change impacts. (In this analysis, "adaptation" implies measures, approaches, or strategies that would help cope with, take advantage of, or reduce vulnerability to the impacts of global warming.)

Global Warming Impacts to Date

According to the Intergovernmental Panel on Climate Change (IPCC), over the last century or more, the earth has warmed 0.4 to 0.8°C, perhaps due in part to man's influence. Over this period, there have been changes in many climate-sensitive environmental indicators or sectors of the economy — some for the better, others for the worse, and for others, neither better nor worse (good, bad and indifferent changes).

The Good   For many critical climate-sensitive sectors and indicators, matters have actually improved, especially during the last half century. Global agricultural productivity has never been greater, for instance.

An acre of cropland sustains about twice as many people today as it did in   5
1900, and it sustains them better. Based on nutrition and affordability of food, people have never been fed better or more cheaply. Between 1961 and 2001, global food supplies per person increased 24 percent, although global population almost doubled. Between 1969–71 and 1998–2000, the number of people in developing countries suffering from chronic hunger declined from 35 percent to 17 percent or, in absolute terms, from 917 million to 799 million despite a 79 percent growth in population in developing countries.

In wealthier countries, deaths due to climate-sensitive infectious and parasitic diseases are now the exception rather than the rule. Such deaths are declining in most developing countries thanks to better nutrition and public-health measures. Accordingly, from 1960 to 2000, the global infant mortality rate dropped by 57 percent, and global life expectancy at birth increased from 50.2 to 66.5 years. However, in the last 10 to 15 years, these improving trends have been reversed in many sub-Saharan African and former communist countries, not because of climate change, but because of increasing poverty, AIDS, and malaria.

Another climate change concern is that severe weather events could become more extreme and, therefore, more destructive. Indeed, increased population and wealth have put more people and property at risk. For example, this factor has contributed to an increase in U.S. property losses from floods and hurricanes over the last century. Significantly, there are no clear trends in losses in terms of the fraction of wealth that these losses represent.

More significant, based upon nine-year averages, U.S. death rates due to hurricanes, tornados, floods, and lightning decreased between 60 and 99 percent, compared with their earlier peaks during this century (overall deaths declined between 46 and 97 percent). Similarly, globally, the average deaths per year from climate and weather related events declined by over 95 percent between the 1930s and 2000–2003, while death rates declined overall by 98.5 percent (see Figure 1).

The Bad   For other climate-sensitive indicators matters have, indeed, worsened. So far, however, human-caused warming has had little to do with these declines.

Consider sea level rise. Mean sea level is rising at a rate of about 0.1 to 0.2 mm   10
per year. While it is not known what fraction, if any, might be due to any human-caused warming, the IPCC's Science Assessment notes that there was no detectable acceleration of sea level rise during the 20th century. Suffice it to say, so

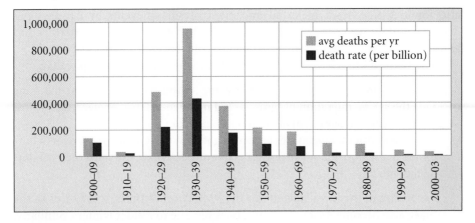

FIGURE 1 Global deaths and death rates from climate-related disasters (includes deaths from drought, extreme temperature, famine, flood, slides, wave/surge, wild fires, windstorm), 1900–2003. SOURCES: Emergency Disasters Data Base (2004), McEvedy & Jones (1978), and FAO (2004).

far, any accelerated sea level rise due to man-made warming is unlikely to have caused anything other than a minor impact on human or natural systems compared to other environmental stresses (such as development of coastlines, conversion of lands for aquaculture, drainage for other human land uses, sediment diversion due to dam construction, construction of seawalls, and subsidence owing to water, oil and gas extraction).

Agricultural demand for water — probably the largest threat to freshwater species — continues to increase. Meanwhile, threats to terrestrial biodiversity — primarily the conversion of habitat to agricultural uses — have not diminished. Forested area declined by 124 million hectares (306 million acres) in tropical and subtropical nations between 1990 and 2000. This decline, which occurred largely because increases in food demand outstripped increases in agricultural yields in those nations, is unrelated to global warming. During the same period, forest cover in the rest of the world (mainly wealthy nations) expanded by 28 million hectares (69 million acres) primarily because technology-based, high yield agriculture has reduced the demand for cropland in those countries.

The Indifferent As the higher latitudes have become warmer, spring has arrived earlier since the 1960s. As a result, we observe "earlier breeding or first singing of birds, earlier arrival of migrant birds, earlier appearance of butterflies, earlier choruses and spawning in amphibians, earlier shooting and flowering of plants. This has been accompanied by later arrival of autumn and autumn colours in some places.

A meta-analysis of trends for 99 species of birds, butterflies and alpine herbs, found significant range shifts averaging 6.1 km per decade towards the poles. It also found a significant mean advancement of spring events by 2.3 days per decade based on data for 172 species of shrubs, herbs, trees, birds, butterflies and amphibians. Clearly, there have been changes, but are these changes adverse?

The Finnish branch of the World Wildlife Fund notes, for example, that:

> Thanks to the warming trend, the growing season has grown . . . At the same time the spring migration of birds, including finches, larks, wagtails, and swifts, has begun an average of ten days earlier than before.
>
> The warmer temperatures have brought new, more southerly species of butterflies to Finland. Many existing types of butterflies have extended their habitats further north.

According to the Royal Society for the Protection of Birds, some birds in the U.K. have also become more abundant, possibly due to milder winters. Similarly, the ranges of 15 butterfly species in the U.K. have expanded substantially since the 1970s, "almost certainly" because of warming (whether or not human-induced). Butterflies also appear earlier in the year and some have been able to spawn an extra generation during the summer. In addition, some moths, crickets and dragonflies have migrated into the U.K.

With respect to vegetation, a study of the earliest flowering dates of 385 wild-flower species in the United Kingdom shows that on average they bloomed more than 4.5 days earlier in the 1990s compared to their 1954 to 1990 average, with 16 percent blooming significantly earlier, while 3 percent bloomed significantly later. One plant bloomed fully 55 days earlier. Similarly, the ranges of flowering plants and mosses seem to have expanded in the parts of Antarctica that have warmed. Soil invertebrates have also advanced with changes in vegetation.

Obviously, warming (whether due to man's activities or nature's machinations) seems to have a measurable impact on the distribution and abundance of species but it is far from clear whether these changes are beneficial or detrimental. More importantly, the major current threats to species come from habitat modification and loss, water diversions, and invasive species, perhaps in that order, rather from climate change.

Summary   Despite any warming, by virtually any climate-sensitive measure of human well-being, human welfare has improved over the last century. While some credit for increasing agricultural and forest productivity is probably due to higher carbon dioxide concentrations and higher wintertime temperatures, most of these improvements are due to technological progress driven by market — and science — based economic growth, technology, and trade. Such progress has also reduced human vulnerability to the effects of climate change. As a result, technological progress has so far had a greater impact on the climate-sensitive measures than has climate change itself.

On the other hand, matters may actually have deteriorated for some climate-sensitive environmental indicators, such as the loss of habitat and forests, and threats to biodiversity. However, so far, climate change (human-induced or not), while contributing to change, seems to be responsible for little, if any, of this deterioration.

On the basis of current evidence, it is difficult to sustain the notion that cli- 20 mate change is the greatest threat to public health or the environment today. But what about the future?

Questions

1. In the first paragraph, what does Indur M. Goklany's phrase "less prone to hyperbole" suggest about his argument?
2. How would you paraphrase what Goklany characterizes as "the good," "the bad," and "the indifferent"?
3. What is the main point indicated by Figure 1?
4. What is Goklany's main idea? How does it compare with other views of climate change? Which view makes more sense to you?

6. *GeoSigns: The Big Thaw*

DANIEL GLICK

In the following 2004 essay from *National Geographic*, journalist Daniel Glick looks at the nature and effects of climate change.

"If we don't have it, we don't need it," pronounces Daniel Fagre as we throw on our backpacks. We're armed with crampons, ice axes, rope, GPS receivers, and bear spray to ward off grizzlies, and we're trudging toward Sperry Glacier in Glacier National Park, Montana. I fall in step with Fagre and two other research scientists from the U.S. Geological Survey Global Change Research Program. They're doing what they've been doing for more than a decade: measuring how the park's storied glaciers are melting.

So far, the results have been positively chilling. When President Taft created Glacier National Park in 1910, it was home to an estimated 150 glaciers. Since then the number has decreased to fewer than 30, and most of those remaining have shrunk in area by two-thirds. Fagre predicts that within 30 years most if not all of the park's namesake glaciers will disappear.

"Things that normally happen in geologic time are happening during the span of a human lifetime," says Fagre. "It's like watching the Statue of Liberty melt."

Scientists who assess the planet's health see indisputable evidence that Earth has been getting warmer, in some cases rapidly. Most believe that human activity, in particular the burning of fossil fuels and the resulting buildup of greenhouse gases in the atmosphere, have influenced this warming trend. In the past decade scientists have documented record-high average annual surface temperatures and have been observing other signs of change all over the planet: in the distribution of ice, and in the salinity, levels, and temperatures of the oceans.

"This glacier used to be closer," Fagre declares as we crest a steep section, his glasses fogged from exertion. He's only half joking. A trailside sign notes that since 1901, Sperry Glacier has shrunk from more than 800 acres to 300 acres. "That's out of date," Fagre says, stopping to catch his breath. "It's now less than 250 acres." 5

Everywhere on Earth ice is changing. The famed snows of Kilimanjaro have melted more than 80 percent since 1912. Glaciers in the Garhwal Himalaya in India are retreating so fast that researchers believe that most central and eastern Himalayan glaciers could virtually disappear by 2035. Arctic sea ice has thinned significantly over the past half century, and its extent has declined by about 10 percent in the past 30 years. NASA's repeated laser altimeter readings show the edges of Greenland's ice sheet shrinking. Spring freshwater ice breakup in the Northern Hemisphere now occurs nine days earlier than it did 150 years ago, and autumn freeze-up ten days later. Thawing permafrost has caused the ground to subside more than 15 feet in parts of Alaska. From the Arctic to Peru, from Switzerland to the equatorial glaciers of Irian Jaya in Indonesia, massive ice fields, monstrous glaciers, and sea ice are disappearing, fast.

When temperatures rise and ice melts, more water flows to the seas from glaciers and ice caps, and ocean water warms and expands in volume. This combination of effects has played the major role in raising average global sea level between four and eight inches in the past hundred years, according to the intergovernmental Panel on Climate Change (IPCC).

Scientists point out that sea levels have risen and fallen substantially over Earth's 4.6-billion-year history. But the recent rate of global sea level rise has departed from the average rate of the past two to three thousand years and is rising more rapidly — about one-tenth of an inch a year. A continuation or acceleration of that trend has the potential to cause striking changes in the world's coastlines.

Driving around Louisiana's Gulf Coast, Windell Curole can see the future, and it looks pretty wet. In southern Louisiana coasts are literally sinking by about three feet a century, a process called subsidence. A sinking coastline and a rising ocean combine to yield powerful effects. It's like taking the global sea-level-rise problem and moving it along at fast-forward.

The seventh-generation Cajun and manager of the South Lafourche Levee District navigates his truck down an unpaved mound of dirt that separates civilization from inundation, dry land from a swampy horizon. With his French-tinged lilt, Curole points to places where these bayous, swamps, and fishing villages portend a warmer world: his high school girlfriend's house partly submerged, a cemetery with water lapping against the white tombs, his grandfather's former hunting camp now afloat in a stand of skeleton oak snags. "We live in a place of almost land, almost water," says the 52-year-old Curole. 10

Rising sea level, sinking land, eroding coasts, and temperamental storms are a fact of life for Curole. Even relatively small storm surges in the past two decades have overwhelmed the system of dikes, levees, and pump stations that he manages, upgraded in the 1990s to forestall the Gulf of Mexico's relentless creep. "I've probably ordered more evacuations than any other person in the country," Curole says.

The current trend is consequential not only in coastal Louisiana but around the world. Never before have so many humans lived so close to the coasts: More than a hundred million people worldwide live within three feet of mean sea level. Vulnerable to sea-level rise, Tuvalu, a small country in the South Pacific, has already begun formulating evacuation plans. Megacities where human populations have concentrated near coastal plains or river deltas — Shanghai, Bangkok, Jakarta, Tokyo, and New York — are at risk. The projected economic and humanitarian impacts on low-lying, densely populated, and desperately poor countries like Bangladesh are potentially catastrophic. The scenarios are disturbing even in wealthy countries like the Netherlands, with nearly half its landmass already at or below sea level.

Rising sea level produces a cascade of effects. Bruce Douglas, a coastal researcher at Florida International University, calculates that every inch of sea-level rise could result in eight feet of horizontal retreat of sandy beach shorelines due to erosion. Furthermore, when salt water intrudes into freshwater aquifers, it threatens sources of drinking water and makes raising crops problematic. In the Nile Delta, where many of Egypt's crops are cultivated, widespread erosion and saltwater intrusion would be disastrous — since the country contains little other arable land.

In some places marvels of human engineering worsen effects from rising seas in a warming world. The system of channels and levees along the Mississippi effectively stopped the millennia-old natural process of rebuilding the river delta with rich sediment deposits. In the 1930s, oil and gas companies began to dredge shipping and exploratory canals, tearing up the marshland buffers that helped dissipate tidal surges. Energy drilling removed vast quantities of subsurface liquid, which studies suggest increased the rate at which the land is sinking. Now Louisiana is losing approximately 25 square miles of wetlands every year, and the state is lobbying for federal money to help replace the upstream sediments that are the delta's lifeblood.

Local projects like that might not do much good in the very long run, though, depending on the course of change elsewhere on the planet. Part of Antarctica's Larsen Ice Shelf broke apart in early 2002. Although floating ice does not change sea level when it melts (any more than a glass of water will overflow when the ice cubes in it melt), scientists became concerned that the collapse could foreshadow the breakup of other ice shelves in Antarctica and allow increased glacial discharge into the sea from ice sheets on the continent. If the West Antarctic ice sheet were to break up, which scientists consider very unlikely this century, it alone contains enough ice to raise sea level by nearly 20 feet. 15

Even without such a major event, the IPCC projected in its 2001 report that sea level will rise anywhere between 4 and 35 inches by the end of the century. The high end of that projection — nearly three feet — would be "an unmitigated disaster," according to Douglas.

Down on the bayou, all of those predictions make Windell Curole shudder. "We're the guinea pigs," he says, surveying his aqueous world from the relatively lofty vantage point of a 12-foot high earthen berm. "I don't think anybody down here looks at the sea-level-rise problem and puts their heads in the sand." That's because soon there may not be much sand left.

Rising sea level is not the only change Earth's oceans are undergoing. The ten-year-long World Ocean Circulation Experiment, launched in 1990, has helped researchers to better understand what is now called the ocean conveyor belt.

Oceans, in effect, mimic some functions of the human circulatory system. Just as arteries carry oxygenated blood from the heart to the extremities, and veins return blood to be replenished with oxygen, oceans provide life-sustaining circulation to the planet. Propelled mainly by prevailing winds and differences in water density, which changes with the temperature and salinity of the seawater, ocean currents are critical in cooling, warming, and watering the planet's terrestrial surfaces — and in transferring heat from the Equator to the Poles.

The engine running the conveyor belt is the density-driven thermohaline circulation ("thermo" for heat and "haline" for salt). Warm, salty water flows from the tropical Atlantic north toward the Pole in surface currents like the Gulf Stream. This saline water loses heat to the air as it is carried to the far reaches of the North Atlantic. The coldness and high salinity together make the water more dense, and it sinks deep into the ocean. Surface water moves in to replace it. The deep, cold water flows into the South Atlantic, Indian, and Pacific Oceans, eventually mixing again with warm water and rising back to the surface.   20

Changes in water temperature and salinity, depending on how drastic they are, might have considerable effects on the ocean conveyor belt. Ocean temperatures are rising in all ocean basins and at much deeper depths than previously thought, say scientists at the National Oceanic and Atmospheric Administration (NOAA). Arguably, the largest oceanic change ever measured in the era of modern instruments is in the declining salinity of the subpolar seas bordering the North Atlantic.

Robert Gagosian, president and director of the Woods Hole Oceanographic Institution, believes that oceans hold the key to potential dramatic shifts in the Earth's climate. He warns that too much change in ocean temperature and salinity could disrupt the North Atlantic thermohaline circulation enough to slow down or possibly halt the conveyor belt — causing drastic climate changes in time spans as short as a decade.

The future breakdown of the thermohaline circulation remains a disturbing, if remote, possibility. But the link between changing atmospheric chemistry and the changing oceans is indisputable, says Nicholas Bates, a principal investigator for the Bermuda Atlantic Time-series Study station, which monitors the temperature, chemical composition, and salinity of deep-ocean water in the Sargasso Sea southeast of the Bermuda Triangle.

Oceans are important sinks, or absorption centers, for carbon dioxide, and take up about a third of human-generated CO_2. Data from the Bermuda monitoring programs show that CO_2 levels at the ocean surface are rising at about the same rate as atmospheric CO_2. But it is in the deeper levels where Bates has observed even greater change. In the waters between 250 and 450 meters (820 and 1,476 feet) deep, CO_2 levels are rising at nearly twice the rate as in the surface waters. "It's not a belief system; it's an observable scientific fact," Bates says. "And it shouldn't be doing that unless something fundamental has changed in this part of the ocean."

While scientists like Bates monitor changes in the oceans, others evaluate CO_2 levels in the atmosphere. In Vestmannaeyjar, Iceland, a lighthouse attendant opens a large silver suitcase that looks like something out of a James Bond movie, telescopes out an attached 15-foot rod, and flips a switch, activating a computer that controls several motors, valves, and stopcocks. Two two-and-a-half-liter flasks in the suitcase fill with ambient air. In North Africa, an Algerian monk at Assekrem does the same. Around the world, collectors like these are monitoring the cocoon of gases that compose our atmosphere and permit life as we know it to persist. 25

When the weekly collection is done, all the flasks are sent to Boulder, Colorado. There, Pieter Tans, a Dutch-born atmospheric scientist with NOAA's Climate Monitoring and Diagnostics Laboratory, oversees a slew of sensitive instruments that test the air in the flasks for its chemical composition. In this way Tans helps assess the state of the world's atmosphere.

By all accounts it has changed significantly in the past 150 years.

Walking through the various labs filled with cylinders of standardized gas mixtures, absolute manometers, and gas chromatographs, Tans offers up a short history of atmospheric monitoring. In the late 1950s a researcher named Charles Keeling began measuring CO_2 in the atmosphere above Hawaii's 13,679-foot Mauna Loa. The first thing that caught Keeling's eye was how [the] CO_2 level rose and fell seasonally. That made sense since, during spring and summer, plants take in CO_2 during photosynthesis and produce oxygen in the atmosphere. In the fall and winter, when plants decay, they release greater quantities of CO_2 through respiration and decay. Keeling's vacillating seasonal curve became famous as a visual representation of the Earth "breathing."

Something else about the way the Earth was breathing attracted Keeling's attention. He watched as [the] CO_2 level not only fluctuated seasonally, but also rose year after year. Carbon dioxide level has climbed from about 315 parts per million (ppm) from Keeling's first readings in 1958 to more than 375 ppm today. A primary source for this rise is indisputable: humans' prodigious burning of carbon-laden fossil fuels for their factories, homes, and cars.

Tans shows me a graph depicting levels of three key greenhouse gases — CO₂, methane, and nitrous oxide — from the year 1000 to the present. The three gases together help keep Earth, which would otherwise be an inhospitably cold orbiting rock, temperate by orchestrating an intricate dance between the radiation of heat from Earth back to space (cooling the planet) and the absorption of radiation in the atmosphere (trapping it near the surface and thus warming the planet).   30

Tans and most other scientists believe that greenhouse gases are at the root of our changing climate. "These gases are a climate-change driver," says Tans, poking his graph definitively with his index finger. The three lines on the graph follow almost identical patterns: basically flat until the mid-1800s, then all three move upward in a trend that turns even more sharply upward after 1950. "This is what we did," says Tans, pointing to the parallel spikes. "We have very significantly changed the atmospheric concentration of these gases. We know their radiative properties," he says. "It is inconceivable to me that the increase would not have a significant effect on climate."

Exactly how large that effect might be on the planet's health and respiratory system will continue to be a subject of great scientific and political debate — especially if the lines on the graph continue their upward trajectory.

Eugene Brower, an Inupiat Eskimo and president of the Barrow Whaling Captains' Association, doesn't need fancy parts-per-million measurements of CO₂ concentrations or long-term sea-level gauges to tell him that his world is changing.

"It's happening as we speak," the 56-year-old Brower says as we drive around his home in Barrow, Alaska — the United States' northernmost city — on a late August day. In his fire chief's truck, Brower takes me to his family's traditional ice cellars, painstakingly dug into the permafrost, and points out how his stores of muktuk — whale skin and blubber — recently began spoiling in the fall because melting water drips down to his food stores. Our next stop is the old Bureau of Indian Affairs school building. The once impenetrable permafrost that kept the foundation solid has bucked and heaved so much that walking through the school is almost like walking down the halls of an amusement park fun house. We head to the eroding beach and gaze out over open water. "Normally by now the ice would be coming in," Brower says, scrunching up his eyes and scanning the blue horizon.

We continue our tour. Barrow looks like a coastal community under siege.   35
The ramshackle conglomeration of weather-beaten houses along the seaside gravel road stands protected from fall storm surges by miles-long berms of gravel and mud that block views of migrating gray whales. Yellow bulldozers and graders patrol the coast like sentries.

The Inupiat language has words that describe many kinds of ice. *Piqaluyak* is salt-free multiyear sea ice. *Ivuniq* is a pressure ridge. *Sarri* is the word for pack ice, *tuvaqtaq* is bottom-fast ice, and shore-fast ice is *tuvaq*. For Brower, these words are the currency of hunters who must know and follow ice patterns to track bearded seals, walruses, and bowhead whales.

There are no words, though, to describe how much, and how fast, the ice is changing. Researchers long ago predicted that the most visible impacts from a globally warmer world would occur first at high latitudes: rising air and sea temperatures, earlier snowmelt, later ice freeze-up, reductions in sea ice, thawing permafrost, more erosion, increases in storm intensity. Now all those impacts have been documented in Alaska. "The changes observed here provide an early warning system for the rest of the planet," says Amanda Lynch, an Australian researcher who is the principal investigator on a project that works with Barrow's residents to help them incorporate scientific data into management decisions for the city's threatened infrastructure.

Before leaving the Arctic, I drive to Point Barrow alone. There, at the tip of Alaska, roughshod hunting shacks dot the spit of land that marks the dividing line between the Chukchi and Beaufort Seas. Next to one shack someone has planted three eight-foot sticks of white driftwood in the sand, then criss-crossed their tops with whale baleen, a horny substance that whales of the same name use to filter life-sustaining plankton out of seawater. The baleen, curiously, looks like palm fronds.

So there, on the North Slope of Alaska, stand three makeshift palm trees. Perhaps they are no more than an elaborate Inupiat joke, but these Arctic palms seem an enigmatic metaphor for the Earth's future.

Questions

1. Which of Daniel Glick's observations and claims do you find most compelling? Why?
2. Cite examples of Glick's use of statistics and appeals to authority. What are their effects? Why does Glick shift from authority to personal experience as he moves toward his conclusion? What other kinds of evidence does Glick use? Which is most persuasive?
3. Does Glick's use of such disparate locations as Louisiana, Shanghai, Bangkok, the Netherlands, Jakarta, Tokyo, Florida, Bangladesh, and Egypt influence your view of the subject of climate change? Explain.
4. Does the ironic and surprising information Glick discusses in paragraphs 14–16 affect your view of the problems associated with climate change? Explain.
5. Does the discussion of language in paragraph 36 influence your view of the problem Glick discusses? Explain.
6. Considering that outside the scientific community some people deny the reality of global warming, what is the effect of the word *how* in paragraph 32? Should we refer to the issue as one of "global warming" or one of "climate change"?
7. Is the problem as severe as Glick suggests? Explain.

Entering the Conversation

As you respond to the following prompts, support your argument with references to at least three of the sources in Conversation: Focus on Climate Change. For help using sources, see Chapter 3.

1. Take an especially provocative statement from Edward O. Wilson (p. 873), and write an essay that supports, challenges, or refutes its argument.

2. Discuss some of the important concerns about the nature of climate change, and suggest possible steps we might take to address them.

3. Write an article for your school newspaper discussing what the average citizen can do to become more environmentally conscious. You may include your own ideas and/or ideas of others, as long as you properly cite them.

4. Write a letter to the editor of your local newspaper about the problem of climate change.

5. Write an argument from the perspective of either the economist or the environmentalist as characterized by Edward O. Wilson.

6. Write an essay explaining whether global warming is more a scientific or a political issue.

DANIEL GLICK ON WRITING

In this exchange, writer Daniel Glick, whose essay appears on page 881, talks about revision.

Lawrence Scanlon (LS): It's been said that "all writing is rewriting." Do you agree?

Daniel Glick (DG): The statement seems a little facile. I've written first drafts that I consider to be good writing. I don't think writing is easy, and I do a lot of revisions — but sometimes the first draft of inspiration can be quite exhilarating. Sometimes the first blush — the torrent of words that emerges before you're too obsessed with structure, precision, and flow — is a real rush. I often feel that my first draft is the real creative outpouring, almost magical, where something appears on the page (or a computer screen) that simply didn't exist before you wrote it. That said, burnishing a piece through revisions and rewriting can also be an exciting process.

LS: **After you have finished traveling and researching, how do you decide which materials will go into your work, since there is so much?**

DG: It's part of the magic I was referring to. Often, after filling several notebooks with dozens of interviews, reading several books, diving into all manner of research materials, and making research trips, when I sit down to write, I do so without looking at my notes at all. That exercise allows me to put down on paper the material that jumps out at me as the most important pieces of the article. Then I go back and check my notes to see what I've forgotten, and of course to make sure I've been accurate in my recollections.

LS: **How do you keep track of the information you gather in your research, and how do you decide what to include and what to leave out as you revise?**

DG: There's an important concept in writing good nonfiction: learning how to take an interesting topic and turning it into a compelling narrative. Often, while I'm reporting, I'm thinking about what's important, even dreaming at night about how I'm going to tell the story. I jot down notes, go for long walks, and muse a lot. At the end of the day, it's a very difficult and painful process to figure out what gets left on the cutting-room floor. It's a matter of thinking about what's essential and building from there. Honestly, I keep track of a lot of the information in my head. The important stuff usually sticks.

LS: **When writing and revising an article on a topic you have researched, do you tend to use all of the information you have discovered, or just the information that supports your argument?**

DG: As tortured as the words "fair and balanced" are because of their misrepresentation, I always try to give voice to the complexities of a story. There are very few stories that I've done where I don't learn something about "the other side of a story." I think it's vital to keep an open mind and do a lot of homework before writing a story. I pride myself on never writing a story until I've done eighty-five percent of my reporting. Then I let my reporting tell the story.

LS: **As a reporter, your revisions are not always self-motivated — because you have an editor (which in some ways is like having a teacher) offering comments, suggestions, indicating areas that aren't clear, those** needing development, and the like. What happens when you don't agree (or like) an editor's comments — or take — on your work?

DG: I learned in journalism school that all editing is a negotiation, and that's true with every edit I've done since then. For space. For style. For emphasis. The truth is, often the writer comes out on the short end of those negotiations. What I try to do is to work with my editor along the way — during story development, consulting about choices for reporting trips and sources, and even discussing possible narrative approaches. I try to get some buy-in early on so neither my editor nor I will be surprised. When things get tough, I make my last stand over matters of fact: I will never let something appear under my byline that I know is not true.

LS: Do you have friends or colleagues . . . read your work before you send it to an editor? Do you just send your work cold and ask, "What do you think?" Or do you pose specific questions about tone or an opening or a closing, and so forth?

DG: For my longer pieces, I almost always have a friend — often another writer I like and trust — read my first draft. I work so hard on my manuscripts, sometimes rewriting the first paragraph fifty times or more, that I have blind spots about whether things work or not. Sometimes I know the material so well that I forget that I didn't understand it when I started the project, and I need to be reminded to take my readers by the hand and lead them gently through the process of understanding new concepts. Bottom line: Everybody needs an editor. And the cleaner the copy is when I turn it in to my "real" editor, the more likely the "real" edit will go smoothly.

LS: What strategies do you use when writing a piece on a controversial topic such as global warming in order not to alienate your more conservative readers?

DG: I've never shied away from writing about a subject. Frankly, the more controversial, the more I like to write about it. But the more controversial the subject, the more I feel the responsibility to do a lot of homework, to understand all sides of a story. I don't care about alienating my more conservative readers per se. I strive to be accurate, disciplined, well-researched, cogent, and thoughtful. It is all I can do.

LS: Were you always a good writer? Does writing come naturally to you, or do you have to work at it, as most students do?

DG: I never published anything longer than a want ad until I was almost thirty years old. I always loved words, but more as a reader than as a writer. . . . (I was a good speller once, before spell-check.) I guess I have a little more alacrity with putting words on paper than some people. But of course I have to work at it. Writing is really hard work. I've always liked reading more than I liked writing. [In high school] I was a little weird — I took extra literature classes as my electives. I had one high-school English teacher in particular who really conveyed his love of the written word, of the art of a good story, of the strange and wonderful lives of so many writers.

Follow-up

Discuss your major concerns about revising your essays. What types of issues do you focus on — grammar and word choice, introduction, overall structure? Which practices that Daniel Glick describes can you apply to your own writing?

Student Writing

Visual Rhetoric: Analyzing a Political Cartoon

The following prompt asks the writer to respond to a visual text: Herb Block's (whose pen name is Herblock) classic cartoon, "This is the Forest Primeval —," published in 1929.

> Discuss the rhetorical strategies and style elements that political cartoonist Herblock uses in this cartoon. What is his purpose? How does he develop his argument?

As you read Katy Whitman's response, consider the techniques she used to "close read" the visual text. Then answer the questions about how she develops her argument and how you might change or expand it.

A Plea for Moderation:
Analysis of "This is the Forest Primeval—"

Katy Whitman

In his 1929 drawing, "This is the forest primeval—" Herb Block addresses the issue of clear-cutting American forests. Block borrows a phrase from Henry Wadsworth Longfellow's poem "Evangeline" to suggest the devastation that will occur if we continue to deplete America's natural resources. In his first daily cartoon for the *Chicago Daily News*, the juxtaposition of Block's words and images predict the barren wasteland we will encounter in the future.

"This is the forest primeval" is the opening of Longfellow's poem about Evangeline and her fiancé Gabriel, who were Acadians. The first few lines describe the unspoiled landscape of what is now Nova Scotia, but the poem is a tragedy about the Great Expulsion of 1755, when, on the eve of the Seven Years War between France and

Great Britain, all Acadians (French-speaking settlers) were expelled from present-day Nova Scotia and scattered by the British to English-speaking colonies in America. Block's words suggest an idyllic time, but the context of the poem suggests violence and heartbreak to come, which is more in keeping with the cartoon's images.

The term *primeval forest* is used interchangeably with *old-growth forest* to refer to wooded areas that have been untouched by humans. The cartoon's depiction of an endless stand of tree stumps suggests anything but an old-growth forest. Each tree stump shows the marks of the axe used to cut down the tree, and the hill and clouds in the background seem the backdrop of a desert rather than a forest. Block's image of clear-cut forestry, a practice very much in use in 1929, warns America about its dangerous habits.

Block, with a simple drawing and one poetic line, told us what we now know well: nature is not interminable, and its resources will run out. His subject, the clearcutting of forests, is presented to his audience, readers of the *Chicago Daily News* through the "voice" of a straightforward drawing and a literary allusion. Block's cartoon is emotionally stirring. The terrifying desert of used-up trees warns Americans of an infertile, inhospitable future. He establishes ethos with his reference to Longfellow's phrase "this is the forest primeval," its very familiarity reminding us of the fleeting nature of the idyllic forest. These words, paired with Block's straightforward drawing, rationally outline his argument: through overuse, the land will return to a primordial state — not the idyllic state of old-growth forests, but one of lifeless devastation. By showing what lies in America's future, Block suggests that we not only have the ability to stop the devastation, but we also have an obligation to save our landscape.

Questions

1. Is Katy's argument effective? Can you see another way to read the cartoon?
2. Would the essay have benefited from outside information about clear-cut forestry?
3. Katy's essay argues that Herblock's cartoon is a warning about the consequences of how we treat the environment. What would you add to her argument?
4. Herblock's cartoon appeared at the dawn of the Great Depression. How would you use this information to expand Katy's argument?

Grammar as Rhetoric and Style

Cumulative, Periodic, and Inverted Sentences

Most of the time, writers of English use the following standard sentence patterns:

Subject/Verb (SV)

My father cried.   — TERRY TEMPEST WILLIAMS

Subject/Verb/Subject complement (SVC)

Even the streams were now lifeless.   — RACHEL CARSON

Subject/Verb/Direct object (SVO)

We believed her.   — TERRY TEMPEST WILLIAMS

Subject/Verb/Indirect object/Direct object (SVIO)

Tans shows me a graph.   — DANIEL GLICK

To make longer sentences, writers often coordinate two or more of the standard sentence patterns or subordinate one sentence pattern to another. (See the grammar lesson about coordination on page 698 and the grammar lesson about subordination on page 999.) Here are examples of both techniques.

Coordinating patterns

        S   V   O

Yet every one of these disasters has actually happened somewhere, and many

        S   V   O

real communities have already suffered a substantial number of them.

                                                 — RACHEL CARSON

Subordinating one pattern to another

              S   V   S   V   O

And when they arrived on the edge of Mercury, they carried all the butter-

                                         I

flies of a summer day in their wombs.

                                           — TERRY TEMPEST WILLIAMS

The downside to sticking with standard sentence patterns, coordinating them, or subordinating them is that too many standard sentences in a row become monotonous. So writers break out of the standard patterns now and then by using a more unusual pattern, such as the **cumulative sentence**, the **periodic sentence**, or the **inverted sentence**.

Cumulative Sentence

The cumulative, or so-called loose, sentence begins with a standard sentence pattern (shown here underlined) and adds multiple details *after* it. The details can take the form of subordinate clauses or different kinds of phrases. These details accumulate, or pile up — hence, the name *cumulative*.

The women moved through the streets as winged messengers, twirling around each other in slow motion, peeking inside homes and watching the easy sleep of men and women.   — TERRY TEMPEST WILLIAMS

Here's another cumulative sentence, this one from Wendell Berry's *An Entrance to the Woods*:

> It is a <u>wilderness</u> that is beautiful, dangerous, abundant, oblivious of us, mysterious, never to be conquered or controlled or second-guessed, or known more than a little.

Periodic Sentence

The periodic sentence *begins* with multiple details and holds off a standard sentence pattern — or at least its predicate (shown here underlined) — until the end.

> Crossing a bare common, in snow puddles, at twilight, under a clouded sky, without having in my thoughts any occurrence of special good fortune, <u>I have enjoyed a perfect exhilaration.</u>   — Ralph Waldo Emerson

The following periodic sentence by Daniel Glick starts out by filling the reader in on all the details before stating the main clause.

> Often, after filling several notebooks with dozens of interviews, reading several books, diving into all manner of research materials, and making research trips, when I sit down to write, <u>I do so without looking at my notes at all.</u>

Inverted Sentence

In every standard English sentence pattern, the subject comes before the verb (SV). But if a writer chooses, he or she can invert the standard sentence pattern and put the verb before the subject (VS). This is called an **inverted sentence.** Here are a couple of examples:

> Everywhere was a shadow of death.   — Rachel Carson

> Under them are evergreen thickets of rhododendron.   — Wendell Berry

Rhetorical and Stylistic Strategy

When you use an unusual sentence pattern — cumulative, periodic, or inverted — you call attention to that sentence because its pattern contrasts significantly with the pattern of the sentences surrounding it. You can use unusual sentence patterns to emphasize a point, as well as to control sentence rhythm, increase tension, or create a dramatic impact. In other words, using the unusual pattern helps you avoid monotony in your writing.

Cumulative

Look at this cumulative sentence by Wendell Berry:

> It is a wilderness that is beautiful, dangerous, abundant, oblivious of us, mysteri-
> ous, never to be conquered or controlled or second-guessed, or known more
> than a little.

The independent clause in the sentence focuses on one word: *wilderness*. Then the
sentence accumulates a string of modifiers that describe nature's ambiguity. It is
"beautiful" and "abundant" but also "dangerous" and "mysterious." Berry ends
with phrases that emphasize nature's independence: "never to be conquered or
controlled or second-guessed, or known more than a little." Using a cumulative
sentence allows Berry to include all of these modifiers in one smooth sentence,
rather than using a series of shorter sentences that repeat "wilderness." Furthermore, this accumulation of modifiers takes the reader into the scene just as the
writer experiences it, one detail at a time.

Periodic

In the following periodic sentence, Ralph Waldo Emerson packs the front of the
sentence with phrases providing elaborate detail:

> Crossing a bare common, in snow puddles, at twilight, under a clouded sky,
> without having in my thoughts any occurrence of special good fortune, I have
> enjoyed a perfect exhilaration.

The vivid descriptions engage us, so that by the end of the sentence we can feel (or
at least imagine) the exhilaration Emerson feels. By placing the descriptions at the
beginning of the sentence, Emerson demonstrates how nature can ascend from
the physical ("snow puddles," "clouded sky") to the psychological ("without . . .
thoughts of . . . good fortune"), and finally to the spiritual ("perfect exhilaration").

Could Emerson have written this as a cumulative sentence? He probably
could have by moving things around — "I have enjoyed a perfect exhilaration as I
was crossing . . ." — and then providing the details. In some ways, the impact of
the descriptive detail would be similar.

Whether you choose to place detail at the beginning or end of a sentence
often depends on the surrounding sentences. Unless you have a good reason,
though, you probably should not put one cumulative sentence after another or
one periodic sentence after another. Instead, by shifting sentence patterns, you
can vary sentence length and change the rhythm of your sentences.

Inverted

The inverted sentence pattern slows the reader down, because it is simply more
difficult to comprehend inverted word order. Take this example from Emerson's
"Nature":

V   S

In the woods, is perpetual youth.

In this example, Emerson calls attention to "woods" and "youth," minimizing the verb "is" and juxtaposing a place ("woods") with a state of being ("youth"). Consider the difference if he had written:

S   V

Perpetual youth is in the woods.

This "revised" version is easier to read quickly, and even though the meaning is essentially the same, the emphasis is different. In fact, to understand the full impact, we need to consider the sentence in its context. If you look back at Emerson's essay "Nature," you'll see that his sentence is a short one among longer, more complex sentences. That combination of inversion and contrasting length makes the sentence — and the idea it conveys — stand out.

A Word about Punctuation

It is important to follow the normal rules of comma use when punctuating unusual sentence patterns. In a cumulative sentence, the descriptors that follow the main clause need to be set off from it and one another with commas, as in the example from Terry Tempest Williams. Likewise, in a periodic sentence, the series of clauses or phrases that precede the subject should be set off from the subject and one another by commas, as in the Emerson example. When writing an inverted sentence, you may be tempted to insert a comma between the verb and the subject because of the unusual order — but don't.

• EXERCISE 1

Identify each of the following sentences as periodic, cumulative, or inverted, and punctuate each correctly.

1. Now when I had mastered the language of this water and had come to know every trifling feature that bordered the great river as familiarly as I knew the letters of the alphabet I had made a valuable acquisition.
   — MARK TWAIN

2. In all things of nature there is something of the marvelous. — ARISTOTLE

3. Instead of being at the mercy of wild beasts earthquakes landslides and inundations modern man is battered by the elemental forces of his own psyche.   — CARL JUNG

4. Nature like a loving mother is ever trying to keep land and sea mountain and valley each in its place to hush the angry winds and waves

> balance the extremes of heat and cold of rain and drought that peace harmony and beauty may reign supreme.
>
> — ELIZABETH CADY STANTON

• EXERCISE 2

Craft a periodic, cumulative, or inverted sentence by filling in the blanks.

1. Among the tangle of weeds and brush were _____.

2. Hoping _____, knowing _____, but realizing _____, the candidate _____.

3. All his life he would remember that perfect moment when she entered the room _____, _____, _____.

4. If you _____ and if you _____, then _____.

5. Into the clouds soared _____.

• EXERCISE 3

Identify each of the following sentences as periodic, cumulative, or inverted, and discuss the impact of using that pattern. (Each sentence is a direct quotation from essays in this chapter, so you might want to check the context of the sentence to appreciate its impact more fully. Note that some sentences use more than one unusual pattern.)

1. Similarly, chemicals sprayed on croplands or forests or gardens lie long in soil, entering into living organisms, passing from one to another in a chain of poisoning and death.
   — RACHEL CARSON, para. 12

2. Among them are many that are used in man's war against nature.
   — RACHEL CARSON, para. 16

3. . . . mounting a coach with a ship-load of men, animals, and merchandise behind him, he darts through the country, from town to town, like an eagle or a swallow through the air.
   — RALPH WALDO EMERSON, para. 10

4. I see the spectacle of morning from the hill-top over against my house, from day-break to sunrise, with emotions which an angel might share.   — RALPH WALDO EMERSON, para. 16

5. Not less excellent, except for our less susceptibility in the afternoon was the charm, last event, of a January sunset.
   — RALPH WALDO EMERSON, para. 17

6. When a noble act is done, — perchance in a scene of great natural beauty, when Leonidas and his three hundred martyrs consume one day in dying, and the sun and moon come each and look at them once in the steep defile of Thermopylae, when Arnold Winkelreid, in the high Alps, under the shadow of the avalanche, gathers in his side a sheaf of Austrian spears to break the line for his comrades; are not these heroes entitled to add the beauty of the scene to the beauty of the dead? — RALPH WALDO EMERSON, para. 20

7. When the buffalo are all slaughtered, the wild horses all tamed, the secret corners of the forest heavy with the scent of many men, and the view of the ripe hills blotted by talking wires, where is the thicket? — CHIEF SEATTLE, para. 5

8. And here where the ravine suddenly steepens and narrows, where the shadows are long-lived and the dampness stays, the trees are different. — WENDELL BERRY, para. 3

9. Even more discomforting is a pervasive sense of unfamiliarity. — WENDELL BERRY, para. 13

10. And why not Nature, since it's there, common property, mute, can't talk back, allows us the possibility of transcending the human condition for a while, writing prettily of mountain ranges, white-tailed deer, the purple crocuses outside this very window, the thrumming dazzling "life force" we imagine we all support. — JOYCE CAROL OATES, para. 29

11. Even here where the economy of life is really an economy — where the creation is yet fully alive and continuous and self-enriching, where whatever dies enters directly into the life of the living — even here one cannot fully escape the sense of an impending human catastrophe. — WENDELL BERRY, para. 27

• EXERCISE 4

Fiction writers often use unusual sentence patterns. Find examples of cumulative, periodic, and inverted sentences in "The White Heron" by Sarah Orne Jewett, and discuss her purpose in using them.

• EXERCISE 5

Following are five examples of unusual sentence patterns. Choose two or three, then write your own sentences, using each example as a model.

1. Neither in its clearness, its colour, its fantasy of motion, its calmness of space, depth, and reflection or its wrath, can water be conceived by a low-lander, out of sight of sea. — JOHN RUSKIN, *Modern Painters*

2. There are hills, rounded, blunt, burned, squeezed up out of chaos, chrome and vermilion painted, aspiring to the snow-line.
— MARY AUSTIN, "The Land of Little Rain"

3. The yucca bristles with bayonet-pointed leaves, dull green, growing shaggy with age, tipped with panicles of fetid, greenish bloom.
— MARY AUSTIN, "The Land of Little Rain"

4. Scores of millions of years before man had risen from the shores of the ocean to perceive its grandeur and to venture forth upon its turbulent waves, this eternal sea existed, larger than any other of the earth's features, vaster than the sister oceans combined, wild, terrifying in its immensity and imperative in its universal role.
— JAMES MICHENER, *Hawaii*

5. Something will have gone out of us as a people if we ever let the remaining wilderness be destroyed; if we permit the last virgin forests to be turned into comic books and plastic cigarette cases; if we drive the few remaining members of the wild species into zoos or to extinction; if we pollute the last clear air and dirty the last clean streams and push our paved roads through the last of the silence, so that never again will Americans be free in their own country from the noise, the exhausts, the stinks of human and automotive waste. And so that never again can we have the change to see ourselves single, separate, vertical and individual in the world, part of the environment of trees and rocks and soil, brother to the other animals, part of the natural world and competent to belong in it.
— WALLACE STEGNER, "Wilderness Letter"

Suggestions for Writing

Nature

Now that you have examined a number of readings and other texts focusing on nature, explore one dimension of this topic by synthesizing your own ideas and the selections. You might want to do more research or use readings from other classes as you prepare for the following projects.

1. Take a walk in a favorite natural place close to where you live — in the woods, or out on the prairie, or along the beach, or in the desert. Then write to one of the authors in this chapter, comparing your impressions of nature with those he or she presents.

2. Research a local environmental issue — the development of open land, hunting or fishing regulations, wildlife protection, auto emissions, or any

other important concern. Then write a letter to the editor of your local newspaper in which you take a position on the issue. Refer to at least three sources from the chapter to support your position.

3. Write an essay in which you compare the ways in which two authors in this chapter use research to support their arguments.

4. Write a personal essay that answers this chapter's essential question: What is our responsibility to nature?

5. Write an essay evaluating and comparing the classic appeals to ethos, pathos, and logos used by two or more of the authors in this chapter.

6. Write an essay explaining how one of the visual texts illustrates a major idea espoused by one of the authors in the chapter.

7. Imagine what a person living fifty years in the future might say to us now about the effect we have had on the environment. Employing both exposition and argument, write a "report from the future" warning our society about the consequences of our treatment of the natural world.

8. Select one of the following statements about nature, and write an essay that explores its validity. To support your essay, refer to your personal experience and to the selections in this chapter.

   - The West of which I speak is but another name for the Wild; and what I have been preparing to say is, that in Wildness is the preservation of the World. — HENRY DAVID THOREAU
   - Sometimes we forget that nature also means us. Termites build mounds; we build cities. All of our being — juices, flesh and spirit — is nature. — DIANE ACKERMAN
   - A true conservationist is a man who knows that the world is not given by his fathers but borrowed from his children.
     — JOHN JAMES AUDUBON
   - In every walk with Nature one receives far more than he seeks.
     — JOHN MUIR
   - To waste, to destroy our natural resources, to skin and exhaust the land instead of using it so as to increase its usefulness, will result in undermining in the days of our children the very prosperity which we ought by right to hand down to them amplified and developed.
     — THEODORE ROOSEVELT
   - The goal of life is living in agreement with nature. — ZENO

9. View former vice president Al Gore's documentary film *An Inconvenient Truth*. Write a review of the film in the voice of one of the writers you've read in this chapter.

Politics

What is the relationship between the citizen and the state?

Politics, the process by which groups make decisions, is part of all human interactions. When we study history, the social sciences, religion, or business, we learn about politics; whenever we read the newspaper or watch the news on television, we see politics in action; and when we discuss issues with our classmates and friends or involve ourselves in our community, we engage in politics. Politics is as much the context for our daily lives as it is for government legislation and international affairs. Thus one could argue that politics is the cause of all social change.

Democratic governments, such as the one in which we live, exercise power through the will of the people. With that power comes responsibility, even the responsibility to dissent if necessary. So what is the nature of patriotism in a democracy? Is it loyalty to the government or loyalty to the ideals of the nation? How is American patriotism colored by the fact that our country was born out of a revolution? In this chapter, writers on American politics from Henry David Thoreau to Tim O'Brien examine the rights of citizens to resist, and remind us of the connection between political action and social change.

For Americans, former subjects of a colonial power, colonialism is an especially interesting subject. Is our view of colonialism affected by our nation's origin? Does colonialism ever have positive benefits? And how does patriotism work when the government is a foreign power? The selections in this chapter raise those questions and also remind us of the effects of both colonialism and postcolonialism on language, culture, social change, and global politics.

Educated citizens — the root of the word *politics* is the Greek word for *citizen* — must know about the politics of the world as well as the politics of their own country. This chapter presents a variety of voices and perspectives on national and world politics. The selections examine the interrelationships among citizens, their states, and the world. Here you will read classic voices delivering sardonic criticism and lofty idealism; you will encounter the immediacy of personal reflections on the nature and experience of war; and you will read contemporary reflections on the lingering effects of colonialism in the modern world.

On Seeing England for the First Time

JAMAICA KINCAID

 Jamaica Kincaid was born in 1949 on the Caribbean island of Antigua, then a British colony. She came to the United States as a teenager to work as an au pair in New York City, where she then attended the New School for Social Research. Kincaid became a staff writer for the *New Yorker* in 1975 and published much of her short work there. Perhaps her most widely known work is "Girl" from *At the Bottom of the River* (1985), a collection of essays, and *Annie John* (1985), a novel. *A Small Place* (1988), her book-length essay on the tensions between tourists and the native people of the Caribbean, followed. Among her later books are *My Garden* (1999), the novel *Mr. Potter* (2002), and the nonfiction *Among Flowers: A Walk in the Himalaya* (2005). The autobiographical essay included here originally appeared in *Transition* in 1991 and later that year was excerpted in *Harper's*.

When I saw England for the first time, I was a child in school sitting at a desk. The England I was looking at was laid out on a map gently, beautifully, delicately, a very special jewel: it lay on a bed of sky blue — the background of the map — its yellow form mysterious, because though it looked like a leg of mutton, it could not really look like anything so familiar as a leg of mutton because it was England — with shadings of pink and green, unlike any shadings of pink and green I had seen before, squiggly veins of red running in every direction. England was a special jewel all right, and only special people got to wear it. The people who got to wear England were English people. They wore it well and they wore it everywhere: in jungles, in deserts, on plains, on top of the highest mountains, on all the oceans, on all the seas, in places where they were not welcome, in places they should not have been. When my teacher had pinned this map up on the blackboard, she said, "This is England" — and she said it with authority, seriousness, and adoration, and we all sat up. It was as if she had said, "This is Jerusalem, the place you will go to when you die but only if you have been good." We understood then — we were meant to understand then — that England was to be our source of myth and the source from which we got our sense of reality, our sense of what was meaningful, our sense of what was meaningless — and much about our own lives and much about the very idea of us headed that last list.

At the time I was a child sitting at my desk seeing England for the first time, I was already very familiar with the greatness of it. Each morning before I left for school, I ate a breakfast of half a grapefruit, an egg, bread and butter and a slice of cheese, and a cup of cocoa; or half a grapefruit, a bowl of oat porridge, bread and butter and a slice of cheese, and a cup of cocoa. The can of cocoa was often left on the table in front of me. It had written on it the name of the company, the year the company was established, and the words "Made in England." Those words "Made in England," were written on the box the oats came in too. They would also have been written on the box the shoes I was wearing came in; a bolt of gray linen cloth lying on the shelf of a store from which my mother had bought three yards to make the uniform that I was wearing had written along its edge those three words. The shoes I wore were made in England; so were my socks and cotton undergarments and the satin ribbons I wore tied at the end of two plaits of my hair. My father, who might have sat next to me at breakfast, was a carpenter and cabinet maker. The shoes he wore to work would have been made in England, as were his khaki shirt and trousers, his underpants and undershirt, his socks and brown felt hat. Felt was not the proper material from which a hat that was expected to provide shade from the hot sun should be made, but my father must have seen and admired a picture of an Englishman wearing such a hat in England, and this picture that he saw must have been so compelling that it caused him to wear the wrong hat for a hot climate most of his long life. And this hat — a brown felt hat — became so central to his character that it was the first thing he put on in the morning as he stepped out of bed and the last thing he took off before he stepped back into bed at night. As we sat at breakfast a car might go by. The car, a Hillman or a Zephyr, was made in England. The very idea of the meal itself, breakfast, and its substantial quality and quantity was an idea from England; we somehow knew that in England they began the day with this meal called breakfast and a proper breakfast was a big breakfast. No one I knew liked eating so much food so early in the day; it made us feel sleepy, tired. But this breakfast business was Made in England like almost everything else that surrounded us, the exceptions being the sea, the sky, and the air we breathed.

At the time I saw this map — seeing England for the first time — I did not say to myself, "Ah, so that's what it looks like," because there was no longing in me to put a shape to those three words that ran through every part of my life, no matter how small; for me to have had such a longing would have meant that I lived in a certain atmosphere, an atmosphere in which those three words were felt as a burden. But I did not live in such an atmosphere. My father's brown felt hat would develop a hole in its crown, the lining would separate from the hat itself, and six weeks before he thought that he could not be seen wearing it — he was a very vain man — he would order another hat from England. And my mother taught me to eat my food in the English way: the knife in the right hand, the fork in the left, my elbows held still close to my side, the food carefully balanced on my fork and then brought up to my mouth. When I had finally mastered it, I overheard her saying to a friend, "Did you see how nicely she can eat?" But I knew then that I enjoyed my food more when I ate it with my bare hands, and I continued to do so when she wasn't looking. And when my teacher showed us the map, she asked us to study it carefully, because no test we would ever take would be complete without this statement: "Draw a map of England."

I did not know then that the statement "Draw a map of England" was something far worse than a declaration of war, for in fact a flat-out declaration of war would have put me on alert, and again in fact, there was no need for war — I had long ago been conquered. I did not know then that this statement was part of a process that would result in my erasure, not my physical erasure, but my erasure all the same. I did not know then that this statement was meant to make me feel in awe and small whenever I heard the word "England": awe at its existence, small because I was not from it. I did not know very much of anything then — certainly not what a blessing it was that I was unable to draw a map of England correctly.

After that there were many times of seeing England for the first time. I saw 5 England in history. I knew the names of all the kings of England. I knew the names of their children, their wives, their disappointments, their triumphs, the names of people who betrayed them; I knew the dates on which they were born and the dates they died. I knew their conquests and was made to feel glad if I figured in them; I knew their defeats. I knew the details of the year 1066 (the Battle of Hastings, the end of the reign of the Anglo-Saxon kings) before I knew the details of the year 1832 (the year slavery was abolished). It wasn't as bad as I make it sound now; it was worse. I did like so much hearing again and again how Alfred the Great, traveling in disguise, had been left to watch cakes, and because he wasn't used to this the cakes got burned, and Alfred burned his hands pulling them out of the fire, and the woman who had left him to watch the cakes screamed at him. I loved King Alfred. My grandfather was named after him; his son, my uncle, was named after King Alfred; my brother is named after King Alfred. And so there are three people in my family named after a man they have never met, a man who died over ten centuries ago. The first view I got of England then was not unlike the first view received by the person who named my grandfather.

This view, though — the naming of the kings, their deeds, their disappointments — was the vivid view, the forceful view. There were other views, subtler ones, softer, almost not there — but these were the ones that made the most lasting impression on me, these were the ones that made me really feel like nothing. "When morning touched the sky" was one phrase, for no morning touched the sky where I lived. The mornings where I lived came on abruptly, with a shock of heat and loud noises. "Evening approaches" was another, but the evenings where I lived did not approach; in fact, I had no evening — I had night and I had day and they came and went in a mechanical way: on, off; on, off. And then there were gentle mountains and low blue skies and moors over which people took walks for nothing but pleasure, when where I lived a walk was an act of labor, a burden, something only death or the automobile could relieve. And there were things that a small turn of a head could convey — entire worlds, whole lives would depend on this thing, a certain turn of a head. Everyday life could be quite tiring, more tiring than anything I was told not to do. I was told not to gossip, but they did that all the time. And they ate so much food, violating another of those rules they taught me: do not indulge in gluttony. And the foods they ate actually: if only sometime I could eat cold cuts after theater, cold cuts of lamb and mint sauce, and Yorkshire pudding and scones, and clotted cream, and sausages that came from up-country (imagine, "up-country"). And having troubling thoughts at twilight, a good time to have troubling thoughts, apparently; and servants who stole and left in the middle of a crisis, who were born with a limp or some other kind of deformity, not nourished properly in their mother's womb (that last part I figured out for myself; the point was, oh to have an untrustworthy servant); and wonderful cobbled streets onto which solid front doors opened; and people whose eyes were blue and who had fair skins and who smelled only of lavender, or sometimes sweet pea or primrose. And those flowers with those names: delphiniums, foxgloves, tulips, daffodils, floribunda, peonies; in bloom, a striking display, being cut and placed in large glass bowls, crystal, decorating rooms so large twenty families the size of mine could fit in comfortably but used only for passing through. And the weather was so remarkable because the rain fell gently always, only occasionally in deep gusts, and it colored the air various shades of gray, each an appealing shade for a dress to be worn when a portrait was being painted; and when it rained at twilight, wonderful things happened: people bumped into each other unexpectedly and that would lead to all sorts of turns of events — a plot, the mere weather caused plots. I saw that people rushed: they rushed to catch trains, they rushed toward each other and away from each other; they rushed and rushed and rushed. That word: rushed! I did not know what it was to do that. It was too hot to do that, and so I came to envy people who would rush, even though it had no meaning to me to do such a thing. But there they are again. They loved their children; their children were sent to their own rooms as a punishment, rooms larger than my entire house. They were special, everything about them said so, even their clothes; their clothes rustled, swished, soothed. The world was theirs, not mine; everything told me so.

If now as I speak of all this I give the impression of someone on the outside looking in, nose pressed up against a glass window, that is wrong. My nose was pressed up against a glass window all right, but there was an iron vise at the back of my neck forcing my head to stay in place. To avert my gaze was to fall back into something from which I had been rescued, a hole filled with nothing, and that was the word for everything about me, nothing. The reality of my life was conquests, subjugation, humiliation, enforced amnesia. I was forced to forget. Just for instance, this: I lived in a part of St. John's, Antigua, called Ovals. Ovals was made up of five streets, each of them named after a famous English seaman — to be quite frank, an officially sanctioned criminal: Rodney Street (after George Rodney), Nelson Street (after Horatio Nelson), Drake Street (after Francis Drake), Hood Street, and Hawkins Street (after John Hawkins). But John Hawkins was knighted after a trip he made to Africa, opening up a new trade, the slave trade. He was then entitled to wear as his crest a Negro bound with a cord. Every single person living on Hawkins Street was descended from a slave. John Hawkins's ship, the one in which he transported the people he had bought and kidnapped, was called *The Jesus*. He later became the treasurer of the Royal Navy and rear admiral.

Again, the reality of my life, the life I led at the time I was being shown these views of England for the first time, for the second time, for the one-hundred-millionth time, was this: the sun shone with what sometimes seemed to be a deliberate cruelty; we must have done something to deserve that. My dresses did not rustle in the evening air as I strolled to the theater (I had no evening, I had no theater; my dresses were made of a cheap cotton, the weave of which would give way after not too many washings). I got up in the morning, I did my chores (fetched water from the public pipe for my mother, swept the yard), I washed myself, I went to a woman to have my hair combed freshly every day (because before we were allowed into our classroom our teachers would inspect us, and children who had not bathed that day, or had dirt under their fingernails, or whose hair had not been combed anew that day, might not be allowed to attend class). I ate that breakfast. I walked to school. At school we gathered in an auditorium and sang a hymn, "All Things Bright and Beautiful," and looking down on us as we sang were portraits of the Queen of England and her husband; they wore jewels and medals and they smiled. I was a Brownie. At each meeting we would form a little group around a flagpole, and after raising the Union Jack, we would say, "I promise to do my best, to do my duty to God and the Queen; to help other people every day and obey the scouts' law."

Who were these people and why had I never seen them, I mean really seen them, in the place where they lived? I had never been to England. No one I knew had ever been to England, or I should say, no one I knew had ever been and returned to tell me about it. All the people I knew who had gone to England had stayed there. Sometimes they left behind them their small children, never to see them again. England! I had seen England's representatives. I had seen the governor general at the public grounds at a ceremony celebrating the Queen's birthday. I had seen an old princess and I had seen a young princess. They had both been extremely not beautiful, but who of us would have told them that? I had never seen England, really seen it, I had only met a representative, seen a picture, read books, memorized its history. I had never set foot, my own foot, in it.

The space between the idea of something and its reality is always wide and deep 10
and dark. The longer they are kept apart — idea of thing, reality of thing — the wider the width, the deeper the depth, the thicker and darker the darkness. This space starts out empty, there is nothing in it, but it rapidly becomes filled up with obsession or desire or hatred or love — sometimes all of these things, sometimes some of these things, sometimes only one of these things. The existence of the world as I came to know it was a result of this: idea of thing over here, reality of thing way, way over there. There was Christopher Columbus, an unlikable man, an unpleasant man, a liar (and so, of course, a thief) surrounded by maps and

schemes and plans, and there was the reality on the other side of that width, that depth, that darkness. He became obsessed, he became filled with desire, the hatred came later, love was never a part of it. Eventually, his idea met the longed-for reality. That the idea of something and its reality are often two completely different things is something no one ever remembers; and so when they meet and find that they are not compatible, the weaker of the two, idea or reality, dies. That idea Christopher Columbus had was more powerful than the reality he met, and so the reality he met died.

And so finally, when I was a grown-up woman, the mother of two children, the wife of someone, a person who resides in a powerful country that takes up more than its fair share of a continent, the owner of a house with many rooms in it and of two automobiles, with the desire and will (which I very much act upon) to take from the world more than I give back to it, more than I deserve, more than I need, finally then, I saw England, the real England, not a picture, not a painting, not through a story in a book, but England, for the first time. In me, the space between the idea of it and its reality had become filled with hatred, and so when at last I saw it I wanted to take it into my hands and tear it into little pieces and then crumble it up as if it were clay, child's clay. That was impossible, and so I could only indulge in not-favorable opinions.

There were monuments everywhere; they commemorated victories, battles fought between them and the people who lived across the sea from them, all vile people, fought over which of them would have dominion over the people who looked like me. The monuments were useless to them now, people sat on them and ate their lunch. They were like markers on an old useless trail, like a piece of old string tied to a finger to jog the memory, like old decoration in an old house, dirty, useless, in the way. Their skins were so pale, it made them look so fragile, so weak, so ugly. What if I had the power to simply banish them from their land, send boat after boatload of them on a voyage that in fact had no destination, force them to live in a place where the sun's presence was a constant? This would rid them of their pale complexion and make them look more like me, make them look more like the people I love and treasure and hold dear, and more like the people who occupy the near and far reaches of my imagination, my history, my geography, and reduce them and everything they have ever known to figurines as evidence that I was in divine favor, what if all this was in my power? Could I resist it? No one ever has.

And they were rude, they were rude to each other. They didn't like each other very much. They didn't like each other in the way they didn't like me, and it occurred to me that their dislike for me was one of the few things they agreed on.

I was on a train in England with a friend, an English woman. Before we were in England she liked me very much. In England she didn't like me at all. She didn't like the claim I said I had on England, she didn't like the views I had of England. I didn't like England, she didn't like England, but she didn't like me not liking it too. She said, "I want to show you my England, I want to show you the England that I know and love." I had told her many times before that I knew England and I didn't want to love it anyway. She no longer lived in England; it was her own country, but it had not been kind to her, so she left. On the train, the conductor was rude to her; she asked something, and he responded in a rude way. She became ashamed. She was ashamed at the way he treated her; she was ashamed at the way he behaved. "This is the new England," she said. But I liked the conductor being rude; his behavior seemed quite appropriate. Earlier this had happened: we had gone to a store to buy a shirt for my husband; it was meant to be a special present, a special shirt to wear on special occasions. This was a store where the Prince of Wales has his shirts made, but the shirts sold in this store are beautiful all the same. I found a shirt I thought my husband would like and I wanted to buy him a tie to go with it. When I couldn't decide which one to choose, the salesman showed me a new set. He was very pleased with these, he said, because they bore the crest of the Prince of Wales, and the Prince of Wales had never allowed his crest to decorate an article of clothing before. There was something in the way he said it; his tone was slavish, reverential, awed. It made me feel angry; I wanted to hit him. I didn't do that. I said, my husband and I hate princes, my husband would never wear anything that had a prince's anything on it. My friend stiffened. The salesman stiffened. They both drew themselves in, away from me. My friend told me that the prince was a symbol of her Englishness, and I could see that I had caused offense. I looked at her. She was an English person, the sort of English person I used to know at home, the sort who was nobody in England but somebody when they came to live among the people like me. There were many people I could have seen England with; that I was seeing it with this particular person, a person who reminded me of the people who showed me England long ago as I sat in church or at my desk, made me feel silent and afraid, for I wondered if, all these years of our friendship, I had had a friend or had been in the thrall of a racial memory.

I went to Bath — we, my friend and I, did this, but though we were together, 15 I was no longer with her. The landscape was almost as familiar as my own hand, but I had never been in this place before, so how could that be again? And the streets of Bath were familiar, too, but I had never walked on them before. It was all those years of reading, starting with Roman Britain. Why did I have to know about Roman Britain? It was of no real use to me, a person living on a hot, drought-ridden island, and it is of no use to me now, and yet my head is filled with this nonsense, Roman Britain. In Bath, I drank tea in a room I had read about in a novel written in the eighteenth century. In this very same room, young women wearing those dresses that rustled and so on danced and flirted and sometimes disgraced themselves with young men, soldiers, sailors, who were on their way to Bristol or someplace like that, so many places like that where so many adventures, the outcome of which was not good for me, began. Bristol, England. A sentence that began "That night the ship sailed from Bristol, England" would end not so good for me. And then I was driving through the countryside in an

English motorcar, on narrow winding roads, and they were so familiar, though I had never been on them before; and through little villages the names of which I somehow knew so well though I had never been there before. And the country-side did have all those hedges and hedges, fields hedged in. I was marveling at all the toil of it, the planting of the hedges to begin with and then the care of it, all that clipping, year after year of clipping, and I wondered at the lives of the people who would have to do this, because wherever I see and feel the hands that hold up the world, I see and feel myself and all the people who look like me. And I said, "Those hedges" and my friend said that someone, a woman named Mrs. Rothchild, worried that the hedges weren't being taken care of properly; the farmers couldn't afford or find the help to keep up the hedges, and often they replaced them with wire fencing. I might have said to that, well if Mrs. Rothchild doesn't like the wire fencing, why doesn't she take care of the hedges herself, but I didn't. And then in those fields that were now hemmed in by wire fencing that a privileged woman didn't like was planted a vile yellow flowering bush that pro-duced an oil, and my friend said that Mrs. Rothchild didn't like this either; it ruined the English countryside, it ruined the traditional look of the English countryside.

It was not at that moment that I wished every sentence, everything I knew, that began with England would end with "and then it all died; we don't know how, it just all died." At that moment, I was thinking, who are these people who forced me to think of them all the time, who forced me to think that the world I knew was incomplete, or without substance, or did not measure up because it was not England; that I was incomplete, or without substance, and did not measure up because I was not English. Who were these people? The person sitting next to me couldn't give me a clue; no one person could. In any case, if I had said to her, I find England ugly, I hate England; the weather is like a jail sentence, the English are a very ugly people, the food in England is like a jail sentence, the hair of English people is so straight, so dead looking, the English have an unbearable smell so different from the smell of people I know, real people of course, she would have said that I was a person full of prejudice. Apart from the fact that it is I — that is, the people who look like me — who made her aware of the unpleas-antness of such a thing, the idea of such a thing, prejudice, she would have been only partly right, sort of right: I may be capable of prejudice, but my prejudices have no weight to them, my prejudices have no force behind them, my prejudices remain opinions, my prejudices remain my personal opinion. And a great feeling of rage and disappointment came over me as I looked at England, my head full of personal opinions that could not have public, my public, approval. The people I come from are powerless to do evil on grand scale.

The moment I wished every sentence, everything I knew, that began with England would end with "and then it all died, we don't know how, it just all died" was when I saw the white cliffs of Dover. I had sung hymns and recited poems that were about a longing to see the white cliffs of Dover again. At the time I sang the hymns and recited the poems, I could really long to see them again because I had never seen them at all, nor had anyone around me at the time. But there we were, groups of people longing for something we had never seen. And so there they were, the white cliffs, but they were not that pearly majestic thing I used to sing about, that thing that created such a feeling in these people that when they died in the place where I lived they had themselves buried facing a direction that would allow them to see the white cliffs of Dover when they were resurrected, as surely they would be. The white cliffs of Dover, when finally I saw them, were cliffs, but they were not white; you would only call them that if the word "white" meant something special to you; they were dirty and they were steep; they were so steep, the correct height from which all my views of England, starting with the map before me in my classroom and ending with the trip I had just taken, should jump and die and disappear forever.

Questions for Discussion

1. What is ironic about the title, "On Seeing England for the First Time"?
2. In paragraph 4, Jamaica Kincaid says, "I had long ago been conquered." What does she mean?
3. How does Kincaid regard the British influence under which she was raised? Refer to specific passages.
4. How do Kincaid's childhood memories of school compare with your own?
5. In paragraph 10, Kincaid writes, "The space between the idea of something and its reality is always wide and deep and dark." What does she mean?
6. At the end of paragraph 12, Kincaid says, in reference to power, "No one ever has [resisted it]." Do you think this is true? Explain.
7. What is the effect of the shirt-shopping example Kincaid provides (para. 14)? What does it contribute to your understanding of Kincaid's attitude toward England?
8. Where in the essay does Kincaid's epiphany occur? Support your claim with evidence from the text.
9. Having read the essay, how do you regard Kincaid?

Questions on Rhetoric and Style

1. In the opening paragraph, how does Kincaid build up detail to develop a clearly ironic tone?
2. How does the use of parallelism serve Kincaid's rhetorical purpose in the first paragraph?
3. What is the effect of the mutton simile that Kincaid uses in paragraph 1? What is the effect of retracting that simile within the same clause?
4. In paragraphs 1 and 2, Kincaid uses listing as a technique. What is the effect? How does this effect serve her purpose?

5. Kincaid writes in paragraph 5 that "there were many times of seeing England for the first time." What is her purpose for developing this paradox?

6. In paragraph 11, Kincaid says she has "the desire and will . . . to take from the world more than I give back to it, more than I deserve, more than I need." What effect does such a statement have on the reader?

7. Kincaid uses the phrases "extremely not beautiful" (para. 9) and "not-favorable" (para. 11). Why not simply say "ugly" or "homely" or "unfavorable"? How does Kincaid's diction contribute to her purpose?

8. Kincaid uses repetition in paragraph 16. She mentions "my prejudices" four times. What is the effect of the repetition as she confesses to the reader?

9. What is the rhetorical effect of the phrase "as surely they would be" in paragraph 17?

10. What is the effect of Kincaid's attitude toward her friend? How does her description of this relationship affect her ethos?

11. Throughout the essay Kincaid conveys her anger and her sense of injustice with various appeals to pathos. How does she also appeal to logos? Identify specific examples.

Suggestions for Writing

1. Reread paragraph 10, which begins, "The space between the idea of something and its reality is always wide and deep and dark." Has there ever been a time in your life when an idea and reality have come into conflict? Write an essay explaining how your experience supports Kincaid's observation.

2. Many readers note the bitter voice in this essay. Does Kincaid present a narrator who becomes bitter as the piece develops, or is the speaker's voice consistently bitter from the beginning? Use specific references to support your answer.

3. We consider education as a liberating process, a "leading out," according to its etymology. This essay presents a different view. Explain how Kincaid uses her youthful experience to present education as an oppressive rather than a generative force.

4. Has there ever been a time in your life when you saw something "for the first time" many times? Write an essay explaining that experience.

5. Read carefully paragraphs 12 and 16, noting particularly where Kincaid comments on the universality of power and prejudice as she concludes each paragraph. Write an essay supporting or challenging her analysis.

6. Some readers may consider Kincaid's criticism of England and its people as extreme and may characterize her essay as polemical. Write an essay that discusses Kincaid's views of England, and evaluate the success of her argument.

A Modest Proposal

JONATHAN SWIFT

 Perhaps best known for *Gulliver's Travels* (1726), which has mistakenly come to be thought of as a children's novel, Jonathan Swift (1667–1745) was born in Ireland to English parents. He was educated at Trinity College, was ordained a minister, and was appointed dean of Saint Patrick's Cathedral in Dublin in 1713. For years he addressed the political problems of his day by publishing pamphlets on contemporary social issues, some of them anonymously. For one, it is widely believed that a reward of 300 pounds was offered to anyone who would "discover" the authorship. Among these pamphlets is the well-known essay "A Modest Proposal for Preventing the Children of Poor People in Ireland from Being a Burden to Their Parents or Country, and for Making Them Beneficial to the Publick," widely known as "A Modest Proposal." As a model of elegant prose and cogent argument, it has gained deserved fame. After reading it, you will understand what *Swiftian* means and why Swift is regarded as one of the world's premier satirists.

It is a melancholy object to those who walk through this great town or travel in the country, when they see the streets, the roads, and cabin doors, crowded with beggars of the female sex, followed by three, four, or six children, all in rags and importuning every passenger for an alms. These mothers instead of being able to work for their honest livelihood, are forced to employ all their time in strolling to beg sustenance for their helpless infants: who as they grow up either turn thieves for want of work, or leave their dear native country to fight for the pretender in Spain, or sell themselves to the Barbadoes.

I think it is agreed by all parties that this prodigious number of children in the arms, or on the backs, or at the heels of their mothers, and frequently of their fathers, is in the present deplorable state of the kingdom a very great additional grievance; and, therefore, whoever could find out a fair, cheap, and easy method of making these children sound, useful members of the commonwealth, would deserve so well of the public as to have his statute set up for a preserver of the nation.

But my intention is very far from being confined to provide only for the children of professed beggars; it is of a much greater extent, and shall take in the whole number of infants at a certain age who are born of parents in effect as little able to support them as those who demand our charity in the streets.

As to my own part, having turned my thoughts for many years upon this important subject, and maturely weighed the several schemes of our projectors, I have always found them grossly mistaken in their computation. It is true, a child just dropped from its dam may be supported by her milk for a solar year, with little other nourishment; at most not above the value of 2s., which the mother may certainly get, or the value in scraps, by her lawful occupation of begging; and it is exactly at one year old that I propose to provide for them in such a manner as instead of being a charge upon their parents or the parish, or wanting food and raiment for the rest of their lives, they shall on the contrary contribute to the feeding, and partly to the clothing, of many thousands.

There is likewise another great advantage in my scheme, that it will prevent   5
those voluntary abortions, and that horrid practice of women murdering their bastard children, alas! too frequent among us! sacrificing the poor innocent babes I doubt more to avoid the expense than the shame, which would move tears and pity in the most savage and inhuman breast.

The number of souls in this kingdom being usually reckoned one million and a half, of these I calculate there may be about 200,000 couple whose wives are breeders; from which number I subtract 30,000 couple who are able to maintain their own children (although I apprehend there cannot be so many, under the present distress of the kingdom); but this being granted, there will remain 170,000 breeders. I again subtract 50,000 for those women who miscarry, or whose children die by accident or disease within the year. There only remain 120,000 children of poor parents annually born. The question therefore is, how this number shall be reared and provided for? which, as I have already said, under the present situation of affairs, is utterly impossible by all the methods hitherto proposed. For we can neither employ them in handicraft of agriculture; we neither build houses (I mean in the country) nor cultivate land; they can very seldom pick up a livelihood by stealing, till they arrive at six years old, except where they are of towardly parts, although I confess they learn the rudiments much earlier; during which time they can, however, be properly looked upon only as probationers; as I have been informed by a principal gentleman in the county of Cavan, who protested to me that he never knew above one or two instances under the age of six, even in a part of the kingdom so renowned for the quickest proficiency in that art.

I am assured by our merchants, that a boy or a girl before twelve years old is no salable commodity; and even when they come to this age they will not yield above 3£ or 3£ 2s. 6d.[1] at most on the exchange; which cannot turn to account either to the parents or kingdom, the charge of nutriment and rags having been at least four times that value.

I shall now therefore humbly propose my own thoughts, which I hope will not be liable to the least objection.

I have been assured by a very knowing American of my acquaintance in London, that a young healthy child well nursed is at a year old a most delicious,

---

[1] 3 pounds, 2 shillings, 6 pence (denominations of English money).

nourishing, and wholesome food, whether stewed, roasted, baked, or broiled; and I make no doubt that it will equally serve in a fricassee or a ragout.

I do therefore humbly offer it to public consideration that of the 120,000 children already computed, 20,000 may be reserved for breed, whereof only one-fourth part to be males; which is more than we allow to sheep, black cattle, or swine; and my reason is, that these children are seldom the fruits of marriage, a circumstance not much regarded by our savages; therefore one male will be sufficient to serve four females. That the remaining 100,000 may, at a year old, be offered in sale to the persons of quality and fortune through the kingdom; always advising the mother to let them suck plentifully in the last month, so as to render them plump and fat for a good table. A child will make two dishes at an entertainment for friends; and when the family dines alone, the fore and hind quarter will make a reasonable dish, and seasoned with a little pepper or salt will be very good boiled on the fourth day, especially in winter.

I have reckoned upon a medium that a child just born will weigh 12 pounds, and in a solar year, if tolerably nursed, will increase to 28 pounds.

I grant this food will be somewhat dear, and therefore very proper for landlords, who, as they have already devoured most of the parents, seem to have the best title to the children.

Infants' flesh will be in season throughout the year, but more plentiful in March, and a little before and after: for we are told by a grave author, an eminent French physician, that fish being a prolific diet, there are more children born in Roman Catholic countries about nine months after Lent than at any other season; therefore, reckoning a year after Lent, the markets will be more glutted than usual, because the number of popish infants is at least three to one in this kingdom: and therefore it will have one other collateral advantage, by lessening the number of papists among us.

I have already computed the charge of nursing a beggar's child (in which list I reckon all cottagers, laborers, and four-fifths of the farmers) to be about 2s. per annum, rags included; and I believe no gentleman would repine to give 10s. for the carcass of a good fat child, which, as I have said, will make four dishes of excellent nutritive meat, when he has only some particular friend or his own family to dine with him. Thus the squire will learn to be a good landlord, and grow popular among the tenants; the mother will have 8s. net profit, and be fit for work till she produces another child.

Those who are more thrifty (as I must confess the times require) may flay the carcass; the skin of which artificially dressed will make admirable gloves for ladies, and summer boots for fine gentlemen.

As to our city of Dublin, shambles may be appointed for this purpose in the most convenient parts of it, and butchers we may be assured will not be wanting: although I rather recommend buying the children alive, and dressing them hot from the knife as we do roasting pigs.

A very worthy person, a true lover of his country, and whose virtues I highly esteem, was lately pleased in discoursing on this matter to offer a refinement upon my scheme. He said that many gentlemen of this kingdom, having of late destroyed their deer, he conceived that the want of venison might be well supplied by the bodies of young lads and maidens, not exceeding fourteen years of age nor under twelve; so great a number of both sexes in every country being now ready to starve for want of work and service; and these to be disposed of by their parents, if alive, or otherwise by their nearest relations. But with due deference to so excellent a friend and so deserving a patriot, I cannot be altogether in his sentiments; for as to the males, my American acquaintance assured me from frequent experience that their flesh was generally tough and lean, like that of our school-boys by continual exercise, and their taste disagreeable; and to fatten them would not answer the charge. Then as to the females, it would, I think, with humble submission be a loss to the public, because they soon would become breeders themselves: and besides, it is not improbable that some scrupulous people might be apt to censure such a practice (although indeed very unjustly), as a little bordering upon cruelty; which, I confess, has always been with me the strongest objection against any project, how well soever intended.

But in order to justify my friend, he confessed that this expedient was put into his head by the famous Psalmanazar, a native of the island Formosa, who came from thence to London about twenty years ago: and in conversation told my friend, that in his country when any young person happened to be put to death, the executioner sold the carcass to persons of quality as a prime dainty; and that in his time the body of a plump girl of fifteen, who was crucified for an attempt to poison the emperor, was sold to his imperial majesty's prime minister of state, and other great mandarins of the court, in joints from the gibbet, at 400 crowns. Neither indeed can I deny, that if the same use were made of several plump young girls in this town, who without one single groat to their fortunes cannot stir abroad without a chair, and appear at the playhouse and assemblies in foreign fineries which they never will pay for, the kingdom would not be the worse.

Some persons of a desponding spirit are in great concern about the vast number of poor people, who are aged, diseased, or maimed, and I have been desired to employ my thoughts what course may be taken to ease the nation of so grievous an encumbrance. But I am not in the least pain upon that matter, because it is very well known that they are every day dying and rotting by cold and famine, and filth and vermin, as fast as can be reasonably expected. And as to the young laborers, they are now in as hopeful condition: They cannot get work, and consequently pine away for want of nourishment, to a degree that if at any time they are accidentally hired to common labor, they have not strength to perform it; and thus the country and themselves are happily delivered from the evils to come.

I have too long digressed, and therefore shall return to my subject. I think the advantages by the proposal which I have made are obvious and many, as well as of the highest importance. 20

For first, as I have already observed, it would greatly lessen the number of papists, with whom we are yearly overrun, being the principal breeders of the nation as well as our most dangerous enemies; and who stay at home on purpose to deliver the kingdom to the Pretender, hoping to take their advantage by the absence of so many good Protestants, who have chosen rather to leave their country than stay at home and pay tithes against their conscience to an Episcopal curate.

Secondly, The poor tenants will have something valuable of their own, which by law may be made liable to distress and help to pay their landlord's rent, their corn and cattle being already seized, and money a thing unknown.

Thirdly, Whereas the maintenance of 100,000 children from two years old and upward, cannot be computed at less that 10s a-piece per annum, the nation's stock will be thereby increased £50,000 per annum, beside the profit of a new dish introduced to the tables of all gentlemen of fortune in the kingdom who have any refinement in taste. And the money will circulate among ourselves, the goods being entirely of our own growth and manufacture.

Fourthly, The constant breeders beside the gain of 8s. sterling per annum by the sale of their children, will be rid of the charge of maintaining them after the first year.

Fifthly, This food would likewise bring great custom to taverns where the vintners will certainly be so prudent as to procure the best receipts for dressing it to perfection, and consequently have their houses frequented by all the fine gentlemen, who justly value themselves upon their knowledge in good eating; and a skilful cook who understands how to oblige his guests, will contrive to make it as expensive as they please.

Sixthly, This would be a great inducement to marriage, which all wise nations have either encouraged by rewards or enforced by laws and penalties. It would increase the care and tenderness of mothers toward their children, when they were sure of a settlement for life to the poor babes, provided in some sort by the public, to their annual profit instead of expense. We should see an honest emulation among the married women, which of them would bring the fattest child to the market. Men would become as fond of their wives during the time of their pregnancy as they are now of their mares in foal, their cows in calf, their sows when they are ready to farrow; nor offer to beat or kick them (as is too frequent a practice) for fear of a miscarriage.

Many other advantages might be enumerated. For instance, the addition of some thousand carcasses in our exportation of barreled beef, the propagation of swine's flesh, and improvement in the art of making good bacon, so much wanted among us by the great destruction of pigs, too frequent at our table; which are no way comparable in taste or magnificence to a well-grown, fat, yearling child, which roasted whole will make a considerable figure at a lord mayor's feast or any other public entertainment. But this and many others I omit, being studious of brevity.

Supposing that 1,000 families in this city would be constant customers for infants' flesh, besides others who might have it at merry-meetings, particularly at weddings and christenings, I compute that Dublin would take off annually about

20,000 carcasses; and the rest of the kingdom (where probably they will be sold somewhat cheaper) the remaining 80,000.

I can think of no one objection that will possibly be raised against this proposal unless it should be urged that the number of people will be thereby much lessened in the kingdom. This I freely own, and it was indeed one principal design in offering it to the world. I desire the reader will observe, that I calculate my remedy for this one individual kingdom of Ireland and for no other that ever was, is, or I think ever can be upon earth. Therefore let no man talk to me of other expedients: of taxing our absentees at 5s. a pound: of using neither clothes nor household furniture except what is of our own growth and manufacture: of utterly rejecting the materials and instruments that promote foreign luxury: of curing the expensiveness of pride, vanity, idleness, and gaming in our women: of introducing a vein of parsimony, prudence, and temperance: of learning to love our country, in the want of which we differ even from Laplanders and the inhabitants of Topinamboo: of quitting our animosities and factions; nor acting any longer like the Jews, who were murdering one another at the very moment their city was taken: of being a little cautious not to sell our country and conscience for nothing: of teaching landlords to have at least one degree of mercy toward their tenants: lastly, of putting a spirit of honesty, industry, and skill into our shopkeepers; who, if a resolution could now be taken to buy only our native goods, would immediately unite to cheat and exact upon us in the price the measure, and the goodness, nor could ever yet be brought to make one fair proposal of just dealing, though often and earnestly invited to it.

Therefore I repeat, let no man talk to me of these and the like expedients, till   30
he has at least some glimpse of hope that there will be ever some hearty and sincere attempt to put them in practice.

But as to myself, having been wearied out for many years with offering vain, idle, visionary thoughts, and at length utterly despairing of success, I fortunately fell upon this proposal; which, as it is wholly new, so it has something solid and real, of no expense and little trouble, full in our own power, and whereby we can incur no danger in disobliging England. For this kind of commodity will not bear exportation, the flesh being of too tender a consistence to admit a long continuance in salt, although perhaps I could name a country which would be glad to eat up our whole nation without it.

After all, I am not so violently bent upon my own opinion as to reject any offer proposed by wise men, which shall be found equally innocent, cheap, easy, and effectual. But before something of that kind shall be advanced in contradiction to my scheme, and offering a better, I desire the author or authors will be pleased maturely to consider two points. First, as things now stand, how they will be able to find food and raiment for 100,000 useless mouths and backs. And secondly, there being a round million of creatures in human figure throughout this kingdom, whose subsistence put into a common stock would leave them in debt 2,000,000£, sterling, adding those who are beggars by profession to the bulk of farmers, cottagers, and laborers, with the wives and children who are beggars in effect; I desire those politicians who dislike my overture, and may perhaps be so bold as to attempt an answer, that they will first ask the parents of these mortals, whether they would not at this day think it a great happiness to have been sold for food at a year old in the manner I prescribe, and thereby have avoided such a perpetual scene of misfortunes as they have since gone through by the oppression of landlords, the impossibility of paying rent without money or trade, the want of common sustenance, with neither house nor clothes to cover them from the inclemencies of the weather, and the most inevitable prospect of entailing the like or greater miseries upon their breed for ever.

I profess, in the sincerity of my heart, that I have not the least personal interest in endeavoring to promote this necessary work, having no other motive than the public good of my country, by advancing our trade, providing for infants, relieving the poor, and giving some pleasure to the rich. I have no children by which I can propose to get a single penny; the youngest being nine years old, and my wife past childbearing.

Questions for Discussion

1. What were the social conditions in Ireland that occasioned the writing of Jonathan Swift's essay? Does the essay indicate what Swift considers to be the causes of these conditions? Does Swift target anybody in particular with his satire? How can you tell?
2. At what point in the essay did you recognize that Swift's proposal is meant to be satiric? Do you think a modern audience would get the joke faster than Swift's contemporaries did?
3. Would a modern audience be more or less offended by Swift's proposal? Explain your reasoning.
4. Of the six advantages Swift enumerates (paras. 21–26), which one might be considered the most sardonic? Explain.
5. Explain how Swift uses the essay to satirize both his subject and the vehicle he employs — that is, a political proposal itself.
6. What is Swift's overall purpose?
7. The modern reader may notice the misogyny in Swift's essay. Does it affect your opinion of the essay? Does it make Swift's criticism of society less powerful?
8. Several eighteenth-century writers made allusions to "A Modest Proposal" in the titles of their satiric essays. For example, Philip Skelton made his irony obvious by calling an essay "Some Proposals for the Revival of Christianity." Why do you think Swift's title was considered such a useful satiric tool?

Questions on Rhetoric and Style

1. How does Swift want the reader to view his speaker? That is, how would Swift want his reader to describe the persona he adopts?

2. Note Swift's diction in the first seven paragraphs. How does it show quantification and dehumanization? Explain the purpose of Swift's specific word choices.

3. At the beginning of the essay, Swift explains the anticipated results before revealing the actual proposal. Explain the rhetorical purpose of such a strategy.

4. In paragraph 9, why doesn't Swift end the sentence after the word *food*? Explain the purpose and effect of the modifiers included there.

5. Identify examples of appeals other than the classical appeals, such as appeals to thrift, economy, and patriotism. Explain the rhetorical strategy behind each example.

6. Consider the additional proposal that Swift mentions in paragraph 17. Explain the rhetorical strategy at work in that paragraph.

7. Which targets does Swift ironically identify in paragraphs 21 and 22? Note the rhetorical progression of paragraphs 21–26. By using such a method, what is Swift satirizing?

8. What are the assumptions behind each of Swift's claims in paragraphs 21–26? Explain them.

9. Read carefully paragraphs 29–31. What are the "expedients" that Swift discusses there? How does irony serve his rhetorical purpose in this section?

10. To what do the "vain, idle, visionary thoughts" (para. 31) refer? What is Swift's tone here?

11. How does the final paragraph of the essay contribute to Swift's rhetorical purpose?

12. By publishing such an outrageous text, what might Swift have hoped to bring about among the people of Ireland?

Suggestions for Writing

1. "A Modest Proposal" is remarkably consistent in its ironic voice throughout. There are, however, some places where Swift's own voice intrudes. Write an essay showing how these breaks in tone reveal Swift's own attitude toward his subject.

2. Read carefully paragraphs 20–26. Then write an essay explaining how Swift uses resources of language to develop his positions. Consider diction, voice, pacing, and other rhetorical features to support your position.

3. Write an essay explaining the influence of Swift on a contemporary example of satire. One example, by political commentator Christopher Buckley about mad cow disease, was published in the *New Yorker* (April 15, 1996) and titled "A Modest Proposal." Another example might be the satiric news program *The Colbert Report.*

4. In response to a current concern or issue, write your own modest proposal in the style of Swift for publication in your school literary magazine or newspaper.

5. Write a response to Swift in the voice of a government official sympathetic to Swift's views, or in the voice of someone who takes the proposal seriously, challenging Swift's argument.

From *The Destruction of Culture*

CHRIS HEDGES

Educated at Colgate University and at the Harvard Divinity School, Chris Hedges (b. 1956) has worked as a foreign correspondent for over two decades. He has witnessed war close up all over the world, particularly in the Balkans, Central America, and the Middle East. In 2002, he shared the Pulitzer Prize for coverage of global terrorism. His most recent book, *Losing Moses on the Freeway* (2005), is about the importance of the Ten Commandments to our time. The essay included here, "The Destruction of Culture," is taken from a chapter in his book *War Is a Force That Gives Us Meaning* (2002). Referring to the book, General Wesley K. Clark — former NATO Supreme Allied Commander in Europe — says, "War is a culture of its own, [Hedges] warns, and it can undercut and ultimately destroy the civil societies that engage in it."

In wartime the state seeks to destroy its own culture. It is only when this destruction has been completed that the state can begin to exterminate the culture of its opponents. In times of conflict authentic culture is subversive. As the cause championed by the state comes to define national identity, as the myth of war entices a nation to glory and sacrifice, those who question the value of the cause and the veracity of the myths are branded internal enemies.

Art takes on a whole new significance in wartime. War and the nationalist myth that fuels it are the purveyors of low culture — folklore, quasi-historical dramas, kitsch, sentimental doggerel, and theater and film that portray the glory of soldiers in past wars or current wars dying nobly for the homeland. This is why so little of what moves us during wartime has any currency once war is over. The songs, books, poems, and films that arouse us in war are awkward and embarrassing when the conflict ends, useful only to summon up the nostalgia of war's comradeship.

States at war silence their own authentic and humane culture. When this destruction is well advanced they find the lack of critical and moral restraint useful in the campaign to exterminate the culture of their opponents. By destroying authentic culture — that which allows us to question and examine ourselves and our society — the state erodes the moral fabric. It is replaced with a warped version of reality. The enemy is dehumanized; the universe starkly divided between the forces of light and the forces of darkness. The cause is celebrated, often in overt religious forms, as a manifestation of divine or historical will. All is dedicated to promoting and glorifying the myth, the nation, the cause.

The works of the writers in Serbia, such as Danilo Kis and Milovan Djilas, were mostly unavailable during the war. It remains hard even now to find their books. In Croatia the biting satires of Miroslav Krleža, who wrote one of the most searing portraits of Balkan despots, were forgotten. Writers and artists were inconvenient. They wrote about social undercurrents that were ignored by a new crop of self-appointed nationalist historians, political scientists, and economists.

National symbols — flags, patriotic songs, sentimental dedications — invade and take over cultural space. Art becomes infected with the platitudes of patriotism. More important, the use of a nation's cultural resources to back up the war effort is essential to mask the contradictions and lies that mount over time in the drive to sustain war. Cultural or national symbols that do not support the crusade are often ruthlessly removed.

In Bosnia the ethnic warlords worked hard to wipe out all the records of cohabitation between ethnic groups. The symbols of the old communist regime — one whose slogan was "Brotherhood and Unity" — were defaced or torn down. The monuments to partisan fighters who died fighting the Germans in World War II, the lists of names clearly showing a mix of ethnic groups, were blown up in Croatia. The works of Ivo Andrić, who wrote some of the most lyrical passages about a multiethnic Bosnia, were edited by the Bosnian Serbs and selectively quoted to support ethnic cleansing.

All groups looked at themselves as victims — the Croats, the Muslims, and the Serbs. They ignored the excesses of their own and highlighted the excesses of the other in gross distortions that fueled the war. The cultivation of victimhood is essential fodder for any conflict. It is studiously crafted by the state. All cultural life is directed to broadcast the injustices carried out against us. Cultural life soon becomes little more than the drivel of agitprop. The message that the nation is good, the cause just, and the war noble is pounded into the heads of citizens in everything from late-night talk shows to morning news programs to films and popular novels. The nation is soon thrown into a trance from which it does not awake until the conflict ends. In parts of the world where the conflict remains unresolved, this trance can last for generations.

I walked one morning a few years ago down the deserted asphalt tract that slices through the center of the world's last divided capital, Nicosia, on the island of Cyprus. At one spot on the asphalt dividing line was a small painted triangle. For fifteen minutes each hour, Turkish troops, who control the northern part of the island, were allowed to move from their border posts and stand inside the white triangular lines. The arrangement was part of a deal laboriously negotiated by the United Nations to give Greek Cypriots and Turkish Cypriots access to several disputed areas along the 110-mile border that separates the north from the south. The triangle was a potent reminder that once the folly of war is over, folly itself is often all that remains. . . .

War, just as it tears down old monuments, demands new ones. These new monuments glorify the state's uniform and unwavering call for self-sacrifice and ultimately self-annihilation. Those who find meaning in the particular, who embrace affirmation not through the collective of the nation but through the love of another individual regardless of ethnic or national identity, are dangerous to the emotional and physical domination demanded by the state. Only one message is acceptable.

A soldier who is able to see the humanity of the enemy makes a troubled and ineffective killer. To achieve corporate action, self-awareness and especially self-criticism must be obliterated. We must be transformed into agents of a divinely inspired will, as defined by the state, just as those we fight must be transformed into the personification of unmitigated evil. There is little room for individuality in war.

The effectiveness of the myths peddled in war is powerful. We often come to doubt our own perceptions. We hide these doubts, like troubled believers, sure that no one else feels them. We feel guilty. The myths have determined not only how we should speak but how we should think. The doubts we carry, the scenes we see that do not conform to the myth are hazy, difficult to express, unsettling. And as the atrocities mount, as civil liberties are stripped away (something, with the "War on Terror," already happening to hundreds of thousands of immigrants in the United States), we struggle uncomfortably with the jargon and clichés. But we have trouble expressing our discomfort because the collective shout has made it hard for us to give words to our thoughts.

This self-doubt is aided by the monstrosity of war. We gape and wonder at the collapsing towers of the World Trade Center. They crumble before us, and yet we cannot quite comprehend it. What, really, did we see? In wartime an attack on a village where women and children are killed, an attack that does not conform to the myth peddled by our side, is hard to fathom and articulate. We live in wartime with a permanent discomfort, for in wartime we see things so grotesque and fantastic that they seem beyond human comprehension. War turns human reality into a bizarre carnival that does not seem part of our experience. It knocks us off balance.

On a chilly, rainy day in March 1998 I was in a small Albanian village in Kosovo, twenty-five miles west of the provincial capital of Pristina. I was waiting with a few thousand Kosovar Albanian mourners for a red Mercedes truck to rumble down the dirt road and unload a cargo of fourteen bodies. A group of distraught women, seated on wooden planks set up on concrete blocks, was in the dirt yard.

When the truck pulled into the yard I climbed into the back. Before each corpse, wrapped in bloodstained blankets and rugs, was lifted out for washing and burial I checked to see if the body was mutilated. I pulled back the cloth to uncover the faces. The gouged-out eyes, the shattered skulls, the gaping rows of broken teeth, and the sinewy strands of flayed flesh greeted me. When I could not see clearly in the fading light I flicked on my Maglite. I jotted each disfigurement in my notebook.

The bodies were passed silently out of the truck. They were laid on crude wooden coffin lids placed on the floor of the shed. The corpses were wound in

10

15

white shrouds by a Muslim cleric in a red turban. The shed was lit by a lone kerosene lamp. It threw out a ghastly, uneven, yellowish light. In the hasty effort to confer some dignity on the dead, family members, often weeping, tried to wash away the bloodstains from the faces. Most could not do it and had to be helped away.

It was not an uncommon event for me. I have seen many such dead. Several weeks later it would be worse. I would be in a warehouse with fifty-one bodies, including children, even infants, women, and the elderly from the town of Prekaz. I had spent time with many of them. I stared into their lifeless faces. I was again in the twilight zone of war. I could not wholly believe what I saw in front of me.

This sense that we cannot trust what we see in wartime spreads throughout the society. The lies about the past, the eradication of cultural, historical, and religious monuments that have been part of a landscape for centuries, all serve to shift the ground under which we stand. We lose our grip. Whole worlds vanish or change in ways we cannot fully comprehend. A catastrophic terrorist strike will have the same effect.

In Bosnia the Serbs, desperately trying to deny the Muslim character of Bosnia, dynamited or plowed over libraries, museums, universities, historic monuments, and cemeteries, but most of all mosques. The Serbs, like the Croats, also got rid of monuments built to honor their own Serb or Croat heroes during the Communist era. These monuments championed another narrative, a narrative of unity among ethnic groups that ran contrary to the notion of ancient ethnic hatreds. The partisan monuments that honored Serb and Croat fighters against the Nazis honored, in the new narrative, the wrong Serbs and Croats. For this they had to be erased.

This physical eradication, coupled with intolerance toward any artistic endeavor that does not champion the myth, formed a new identity. The Serbs, standing in flattened mud fields, were able to deny that there were ever churches or mosques on the spot because they had been removed. The town of Zvornik in Serb-held Bosnia once had a dozen mosques. The 1991 census listed 60 percent of its residents as Muslim Slavs. By the end of the war the town was 100 percent Serb. Branko Grujic, the Serb-appointed mayor, informed us: "There never were any mosques in Zvornik."

No doubt he did not believe it. He knew that there had been mosques in Zvornik. But his children and grandchildren would come to be taught the lie. Serbs leaders would turn it into accepted historical fact. There are no shortage of villages in Russia or Germany or Poland where all memory of the Jewish community is gone because the physical culture has been destroyed. And, when mixed with the strange nightmarish quality of war, it is hard to be completely sure of your own memories. 20

The destruction of culture sees the state or the group prosecuting the war take control of the two most important mediums that transmit information to the nation — the media and the schools. The alleged "war crimes" of the enemy, real and imagined, are played and replayed night after night, rousing a nation to fury. In the Middle East and the Balkans, along with many other parts of the world, children are taught to hate. In Egypt pupils are told Jews are interlopers on Arab land. Israel does not appear on schoolroom maps. In Jordan, children learn that Christians are "infidels" who "must be forced into submission," that the Jewish Torah is "perverted," and that Jews have only "their own evil practices" to blame for the Holocaust. Syrian schoolbooks exhort students to "holy war" and paint pictures of Israelis "perpetrating beastly crimes and horrendous massacres," burying people alive in battle and dancing drunk in Islamic holy places in Jerusalem. And Israel, despite efforts in secular state schools to present a more balanced view of Arab history, allows state-funded religious schools to preach that Jewish rule should extend from the Nile in Egypt to the Euphrates in Iraq and that the kingdom of Jordan is occupied Jewish land.

The reinterpretation of history and culture is dizzying and dangerous. But it is the bedrock of the hatred and intolerance that leads to war.

On June 28, 1914, Gavrilo Princip shot and killed Archduke Franz Ferdinand of Austria in a Sarajevo street, an act that set off World War I. But what that makes him in Bosnia depends on which lesson plan you pick up.

"A hero and a poet," says a textbook handed to high school students in the Serb-controlled region of this divided country. An "assassin trained and instructed by the Serbs to commit this act of terrorism," says a text written for Croatian students. "A nationalist whose deed sparked anti-Serbian rioting that was only stopped by the police from all three ethnic groups," reads the Muslim version of the event.

In communist Yugoslavia, Princip was a hero. But with the partition of 25 Bosnia along ethnic lines, huge swathes of history are reinterpreted. The Muslim books, for example, portray the Ottoman Empire's rule over Bosnia, which lasted 500 years, as a golden age of enlightenment; the Serbs and Croats condemn it as an age of "brutal occupation."

These texts have at least one thing in common: a distaste for [Marshal] Tito, the Communist leader who ruled the country from 1945 to 1980 and was a staunch opponent of the nationalist movements that now hold power. And Tito's state pioneered the replacement of history with myth, forcing schoolchildren to memorize mythical stories about Tito's life and aphorisms.

By the time today's books in the Balkans reach recent history, the divergence takes on ludicrous proportions; each side blames the others for the Bosnian war and makes no reference to crimes or mistakes committed by its own leaders or fighters.

The Muslims are taught that the Serbs "attacked our country" and started the war. The Serbs a told that "Muslims, with the help of mujahadeen fighters from Pakistan, Iraq and Iran, launched a campaign of genocide against the Serbs that almost succeeded."

The Croatian students learn that Croatian forces in "the homeland war" fought off "Serbian and Muslim aggressors."

Even the classics get twisted into a political diatribe. I saw a pro-Milošević 30 production of *Hamlet* in Belgrade that was scripted to convey the message that usurping authority, even illegitimate authority, only brings chaos and ruin. Hamlet was portrayed as a bold and decisive man, constantly training for battle. He was not consumed by questions about the meaning of existence or a desire to withdraw from society, but the steely drive to seize power, even if it plunged the kingdom into chaos. Horatio, usually portrayed as a thoughtful and humane scholar, was the incarnation of evil.

Hamlet's treachery was illustrated at the conclusion of the play when Prince Fortinbras of Norway entered Elsinore to view the carnage. Fortinbras, dressed to look like the chief European representative at the time in Bosnia, Carl Bildt, walked onstage with a Nazi marching song as his entrance music. He unfolded maps showing how, with the collapse of authority, he had now carved up Serbian territory among foreign powers.

"Here is a *Hamlet* for our time," the director, Dejan Krstović, told me. "We want to show audiences what happens when individuals tamper with power and refuse to sublimate their own ambitions for the benefit of the community.

"Because of Hamlet, the bodies pile up on the altar of authority and the system collapses. Because of Hamlet, the foreign prince, Fortinbras, who for us represents the new world order, comes in from the outside and seizes control, as has happened to the Serbs throughout their history."

Every reporter struggles with how malleable and inaccurate memory can be when faced with trauma or stress. Witnesses to war, even moments after a killing or an atrocity, often cannot remember what took place in front of them. They struggle to connect disparate images. And those who see events with some coherency find there is an irreversible pull to twist the facts to conform to the myth. Truth, in such moments, is too nuanced and contradictory for most to swallow. It is best left untouched.

I went one rainy afternoon to the Imperial War Museum in Vienna, mostly to 35 see the rooms dedicated to the 1878 Bosnian rebellion and the assassination of Archduke Franz Ferdinand. His car, peppered with bullet holes, and the blood-stained couch on which he died are on display. But I also wandered through the other rooms designed to honor the bloodlust and forgotten skirmishes of the Austro-Hungarian Empire. When I finished with the World War I exhibit I looked for the room dedicated to World War II. There wasn't one. And when I inquired at the desk, I was told there was no such exhibit in the city. World War II, at least in terms of the collective memory of the Austrian nation, unlike in Germany, might as well have not existed. Indeed, in one of the great European perversions of memory, many Austrians had come to think of themselves as victims of that war.

The destruction of culture plays a crucial role in the solidification of a wartime narrative. When the visible and tangible symbols of one's past are destroyed or denied, the past can be recreated to fit the myth. It is left only to those on the margins to keep the flame of introspection alive, although the destruction of culture is often so great that full recovery is impossible. Yugoslavia, a country that had a vibrant theater and cinema, has seen its cultural life wither, with many of its best talents living in exile or drinking themselves to death in bars in Belgrade or Vienna.

Most societies never recover from the self-inflicted wounds made to their own culture during wartime. War leaves behind not memory but amnesia. Once wars end, people reach back to the time before the catastrophe. The books, plays, cinema take up the established cultural topics; authors and themes are often based on issues and ideas that predated the war. In post-war Germany it was as if Weimar had never ended, as if the war was just some bad, horrible dream from which everyone had just awoken and no one wanted to discuss.

This is why the wall of names that is the Vietnam Veterans Memorial is so important. It was not a project funded or organized by the state but by those who survived and insisted we not forget. It was part of America's battle back to truth, part of our desire for forgiveness. It ultimately held out to us as a nation the opportunity for redemption, although the state has prodded us back towards the triumphalism that led us into Vietnam.

But just as the oppressors engage in selective memory and myth, so do the victims, building unassailable monuments to their own suffering. It becomes impossible to examine, to dispute, or to criticize the myths that have grown up around past suffering of nearly all in war. The oppressors are painted by the survivors as monsters, the victims paint themselves as holy innocents. The oppressors work hard to bury inconvenient facts and brand all in wartime with the pitch of atrocity. They strive to reduce victims to their moral level. Each side creates its own narrative. Neither is fully true.

Until there is a common vocabulary and a shared historical memory there is no   40
peace in any society, only an absence of war. The fighting may have stopped in Bosnia or Cyprus but this does not mean the war is over. The search for a common narrative must, at times, be forced upon a society. Few societies seem able to do this willingly. The temptation, as with the Turks and the Armenian genocide, is to forget or ignore, to wallow in the lie. But reconciliation, self-awareness, and finally the humility that makes peace possible come only when culture no longer serves a cause or a myth but the most precious and elusive of all human narratives — truth.

Exploring the Text

1. Why does Chris Hedges open his essay with both exposition and argument? Where in the text does he shift between exposition, narration, and argument? What is the effect of shifting modes of discourse in this way?
2. Note how Hedges effects transitions. For example, what is the relationship between paragraphs 12 and 13? between 15 and 16?
3. What is the effect of the highly descriptive details in paragraphs 14 and 15? Does it detract from his argument or strengthen it?

4. Do you agree with Hedges's claim that "the two most important mediums that transmit information to the nation [are] the media and the schools" (para. 21)? Explain.

5. How do paragraphs 23–29 support the assertion Hedges makes in paragraph 22?

6. What does Hedges mean by *culture*? Provide examples to support what you think he means. What does Hedges think the purpose of culture is? Do you agree? Explain.

7. In paragraph 38, Hedges claims that the Vietnam Veterans Memorial is important because it was funded and organized "by those who survived," rather than by the government. Visit <www.nps.gov/archive/vivi/home.htm> for more information about the memorial. Do you agree that it offers our nation "an opportunity for redemption"? Explain. Do you agree with Hedges's claim that the "state has prodded us back towards the triumphalism that led us into Vietnam"?

8. Reread the final paragraph, and then reread the quotation from Senator Hiram Johnson with which Hedges begins the chapter. How effectively has Hedges illustrated the meaning of Johnson's assertion?

9. What do you think is Hedges's most interesting or provocative statement? Why?

10. Has reading this essay affected your thinking regarding culture? regarding war? Explain.

CHRIS HEDGES ON WRITING

In the following interview, Chris Hedges, author of "The Destruction of Culture" (p. 922), discusses the role of research in his work and the conversation he sees himself in with other writers, including those from the past. As you read, think about your own experience working with sources.

Renée Shea (RS): Once you have an idea for a topic, do you do a great deal of research before you start writing, or do you jump in and then do research as you find it necessary?

Chris Hedges (CH): Research is key. Especially in my case, where I'm writing about other cultures and countries, you cannot understand the issues you're writing about if you don't understand the history of the people you're writing about, their religion, their social and political orientation. The writers who deal most effectively with these issues are not always the historians or journalists but the poets, playwrights, and novelists. One of the techniques I always used when I covered a foreign country was to go to avant-garde theater productions written by contemporary playwrights because I found that they were often dealing with the most important social and cultural struggles, those that were not seen on the surface.

You have to read a lot because journalism by its very nature is superficial. It will describe the events of the day, and if it's done well, it will be enlightening, but you have to put it in context. And you're not going to get that context from newspapers but from books. When I covered the war in Yugoslavia, I read a tremendous amount about the World War II period, the partisans under Tito, who fought the Germans, the conflicts with the royalists; I visited the battle sites; I often interviewed old fighters. I rarely wrote about this [background] stuff, but it was important for me to understand what was happening. Any writer who wants to write with any kind of depth and insight into any situation has to look at what it is he is writing about from every possible angle and not be restricted to journalism and history. It's important to understand: many of the greatest insights into a culture come from artists.

RS: Do you deliberately seek out views counter to your own to incorporate and address in your work?

CH: One of the marks of good journalists or historians or researchers is that willingness to have their own assumptions shattered. As a journalist, you walk into a situation you are covering and you think you understand it. You think you put all the pieces together, and then as you report the story, you find out that you're wrong — it's not the way you thought. One of my problems with academics who would come over to the Middle East or the Balkans is that they become invested in a thesis they had hammered out in the cloistered environment of the academy. Now some of them did a more credible job, but some academics worked hard only to justify their own thesis. And that's dishonest.

One of the most exciting things about being a writer and investigating other cultures and other ways of being is that you realize that the view from your own perspective, once you are able to study the issues, is often extremely different if not wrong.

All good writing is a form of self-awareness and, perhaps, even a form of self-criticism. That recognition comes from listening and absorbing very closely the position and the experience of "the other," not seeing the world through your own narrow prism, but understanding there are many ways to look at reality and many ways to experience the same reality. As long as we certify "the other" as incomprehensible because they're incomprehensible to us, the conflicts are by nature intractable.

RS: Literature is clearly part of your thinking: it's in your head. In "The Destruction of Culture," you refer to *Hamlet,* for instance. How do you call up such references: are they just in your mind, or do you keep a notebook of quotations?

CH: The most precious objects that I own are my books, and I have about five thousand of them. I am incapable most of the time of remembering my own telephone number, but I remember something I read twenty years ago. I don't lend my books because I underline them, I mark them up in the margins, and I have an emotional relationship to great literature because having lived in moments of extremity, it was often great writers such as Shakespeare, Proust, Dostoyevsky, Faulkner who alone spoke to me. When you are a foreign correspondent, in my case a war correspondent, you have a lonely existence. It was the plays of Shakespeare that kept me sane.

Great writers understand human nature; they understand the darkness that all of us carry within us, the capacity that all of us have to commit acts of evil, even acts of atrocity. Joseph Conrad, of course, did this very well. When you're living in a disintegrating society, when you're living around horrible violence, you grasp for those [writers] who understand the complexity of human beings but who also affirm those values of humanity — the values of tenderness, of loving, of protection, of nurturing life — that often seem so rare in the world you're witnessing.

I memorize a lot. I think memorization is extremely important if you want to be a good writer. In the same way that an aspiring painter will go to a museum and copy masters like Goya or Rubens, writers have to ingest great writing so that they can understand cadences, alliteration, and break the habit of clichés. I acted in a lot of Shakespeare's plays in college, so by the time I was in my early twenties I had memorized hundreds of lines of Shakespeare. I remember reading *In Search of Lost Time* by Marcel Proust in Bosnia. What Proust can do, like all great writers, is explain a reality we know is real but have never been able to describe before, and those things are like depth charges to a writer because suddenly something so visceral, so true, that you've carried within you but have never been able to put into words has been put into words for you.

RS: How do you keep track of what you're reading when you do research? Do you keep extensive notes?

CH: I take some notes but not many. You want to be a little careful. If someone has been writing about an issue that you want to write about, you don't want to have detailed notes in front of you because then it becomes hard to express it in your own words. It could be a kind of inadvertent plagiarism that you want to guard against. So when I do take notes from a book, they're sparse. There may be a particular idea that a great writer such as Reinhold Niebuhr explains. I may jot down a couple of ideas or go back and reread some of my underlining, but then I want to make sure it's in my words. Obviously, if you're quoting directly or explaining an idea, you have to footnote and you have to be very clear that it comes from a particular writer.

We build on those who come before us, and the contributions we make are often not giant leaps but small steps — and we always have to be clear and open about the traditions we came out of, and the writers, philosophers, and thinkers who have informed us.

Follow-up

Keep a log of your reading and writing processes as you develop an essay for one of the Conversation sections of this book. In what ways are your processes similar to those of Chris Hedges? In what ways are they different? What advice from Hedges might help you use sources more effectively?

National Prejudices

OLIVER GOLDSMITH

Born in Ireland, Oliver Goldsmith (1731–1774) was a member of the intellectual circle surrounding Dr. Samuel Johnson. Goldsmith is most widely known for the novel *The Vicar of Wakefield* (1766) and the play *She Stoops to Conquer* (1771). Both deal with a series of misfortunes that end happily. He was also the author of the nursery tale "Goody Two-Shoes," from which we derive the source of the common expression. "National Prejudices," the essay that follows, might seem surprisingly critical for a writer whose works are known to have a sunny disposition. It was published anonymously in the *British Magazine* in August 1760, and while some scholars doubt his authorship, most regard it as Goldsmith's work.

As I am one of that sauntering tribe of mortals, who spend the greatest part of their time in taverns, coffee-houses, and other places of public resort, I have thereby an opportunity of observing an infinite variety of characters, which, to a person of a contemplative turn, is a much higher entertainment than a view of all the curiosities of art or nature. In one of these my late rambles, I accidentally fell into the company of half-a-dozen gentlemen, who were engaged in a warm dispute about some political affair; the decision of which, as they were equally divided in their sentiments, they thought proper to refer to me, which naturally drew me in for a share of the conversation.

Amongst a multiplicity of other topics, we took occasion to talk of the different characters of the several nations of Europe; when one of the gentlemen, cocking his hat, and assuming such an air of importance as if he had possessed all the merit of the English nation in his own person, declared that the Dutch were a parcel of avaricious wretches; the French a set of flattering sycophants; that the Germans were drunken sots, and beastly gluttons; and the Spaniards proud, haughty, and surly tyrants: but that in bravery, generosity, clemency, and in every other virtue, the English excelled all the world.

This very learned and judicious remark was received with a general smile of approbation by all the company — all, I mean, but your humble servant; who, endeavouring to keep my gravity as well as I could, and reclining my head upon my arm, continued for some time in a posture of affected thoughtfulness, as if I had been musing on something else, and did not seem to attend to the subject of conversation; hoping, by this means, to avoid the disagreeable necessity of explaining myself, and thereby depriving the gentleman of his imaginary happiness.

But my pseudo-patriot had no mind to let me escape so easily: not satisfied that his opinion should pass without contradiction, he was determined to have it ratified by the suffrage of everyone in the company; for which purpose, addressing himself to me with an air of inexpressible confidence, he asked me if I was not of the same way of thinking. As I am never forward in giving my opinion, especially when I have reason to believe that it will not be agreeable; so, when I am obliged to give it, I always hold it for a maxim to speak my real sentiments. I therefore told him, that, for my own part, I should not have ventured to talk in such peremptory strain, unless I had made the tour of Europe, and examined the manners of the several nations with great care and accuracy; that, perhaps a more impartial judge would not scruple to affirm, that the Dutch were more frugal and industrious, the French more temperate and polite, the Germans more hardy and patient of labour and fatigue, and the Spaniards more staid and sedate, than the English; who, though undoubtedly brave and generous, were at the same time rash, headstrong, and impetuous, too apt to be elated with prosperity, and to despond in adversity.

I could easily perceive, that all the company began to regard me with a jealous   5
eye before I had finished my answer; which I had no sooner done than the patriotic gentleman observed, with a contemptuous sneer, that he was greatly surprised how some people could have the conscience to live in a country which they did not love, and to enjoy the protection of a government, to which in their hearts they were inveterate enemies. Finding that by this modest declaration of my sentiments, I had forfeited the good opinion of my companions, and given them

occasion to call my political principles in question, and well knowing that it was in vain to argue with men who were so very full of themselves, I threw down my reckoning, and retired to my own lodgings, reflecting on the absurd and ridiculous nature of national prejudice and prepossession.

Among all the famous sayings of antiquity, there is none that does greater honour to the author, or affords greater pleasure to the reader (at least if he be a person of a generous and benevolent heart), than that of the philosopher, who being asked what countryman he was, replied that he was a citizen of the world. How few are there to be found in modern times who can say the same, or whose conduct is consistent with such a profession! We are now become so much Englishmen, Frenchmen, Dutchmen, Spaniards, or Germans, that we are no longer citizens of the world; so much the natives of one particular spot, or members of one petty society, that we no longer consider ourselves as the general inhabitants of the globe, or members of that grand society which comprehends the whole human kind.

Did these prejudices prevail only among the meanest and lowest of the people, perhaps they might be excused, as they have few, if any opportunities of correcting them by reading, travelling, or conversing with foreigners; but the misfortune is, that they infect the minds, and influence the conduct even of our gentlemen; of those, I mean, who have every title to this appellation but an exemption from prejudice, which, however, in my opinion, ought to be regarded as the characteristical mark of a gentleman: for let a man's birth be ever so high, his station ever so exalted, or his fortune ever so large, yet, if he is not free from the national and all other prejudices, I should make bold to tell him, that he had a low and vulgar mind, and had no just claim to the character of a gentleman. And, in fact, you will always find, that those are most apt to boast of national merit, who have little or no merit of their own to depend on; than which, to be sure, nothing is more natural: the slender vine twists around the sturdy oak for no other reason in the world, but because it has not strength sufficient to support itself.

Should it be alleged in defense of national prejudice, that it is the natural and necessary growth of love to our country, and that therefore the former cannot be destroyed without hurting the latter; I answer that this is a gross fallacy and delusion. That it is the growth of love to our country, I will allow; but that it is the natural and necessary growth of it, I absolutely deny. Superstition and enthusiasm too are the growth of religion; but whoever took it in his head to affirm, that they are the necessary growth of this noble principle? They are, if you will, the bastard sprouts of this heavenly plant; but not its natural and genuine branches, and may safely enough be lopt off, without doing any harm to the parent stock: nay, perhaps, 'till once they are lopt off, this goodly tree can never flourish in perfect health and vigour.

Is it not very possible that I may love my own country, without hating the natives of other countries? That I may exert the most heroic bravery, the most undaunted resolution, in defending its laws and liberty, without despising all the rest of the world as cowards and poltroons? Most certainly it is: and if it were not — but what need I suppose what is absolutely impossible? — but if it were not I must own I should prefer the title of the ancient philosopher, namely, a citizen of the world, to that of an Englishman, a Frenchman, an European, or to any other appellation whatever.

Exploring the Text

1. How does Oliver Goldsmith's use of the word *prejudice* differ from the way we use it?
2. In the first paragraph, Goldsmith identifies himself as one of the "sauntering tribe." What does he mean? How does this phrase establish his tone?
3. What do you suppose Goldsmith's attitude is toward his country?
4. In paragraph 5, what does Goldsmith mean by "jealous eye"? Analyze the response of the "patriotic gentleman" in paragraph 5.
5. In paragraph 6, the speaker says, "[We] no longer consider ourselves as the general inhabitants of the globe, or members of that grand society which comprehends the whole human kind." This essay was written in 1760. Have you today ever considered yourself a citizen of the world? Explain how Goldsmith speaks to that issue in our time.
6. Comment on the effects of each of the following rhetorical strategies: irony and analogy (para. 7), metaphor (para. 8), and rhetorical questions (para. 9).
7. If you encountered people who regard themselves in the way that Goldsmith describes in paragraph 5, how would you respond to them?
8. What does Goldsmith imply about the nature of pride and prejudices? Where do people today draw the line? Do we also hold national prejudices? How do our prejudices resemble and differ from those Goldsmith describes?

Thoughts on Peace in an Air Raid

Virginia Woolf

A prolific novelist, critic, and essayist, Virginia Woolf (1882–1941) was born in London. Her novels, particularly *Mrs. Dalloway* (1925) and *To the Lighthouse* (1927), are renowned for their penetrating psychological insight. Woolf's works are noted for the interior monologue, or stream of consciousness. She is also known for her nonfiction, especially for such major works as *The Common Reader* (1925), *A Room of One's Own* (1929), and *Three Guineas* (1938). Severely depressed over the war in Europe and anxious about her own sanity, she drowned herself in 1941. Woolf wrote the following essay in 1940, and published it in her *Collected Essays*, Volume Four. It also appears in *The Death of a Moth and Other Essays* (1942).

The Germans were over this house last night and the night before that. Here they are again. It is a queer experience, lying in the dark and listening to the zoom of a hornet, which may at any moment sting you to death. It is a sound that interrupts cool and consecutive thinking about peace. Yet it is a sound — far more than prayers and anthems — that should compel one to think about peace. Unless we can think peace into existence we — not this one body in this one bed but millions of bodies yet to be born — will lie in the same darkness and hear the same death rattle overhead. Let us think what we can do to create the only efficient air-raid shelter while the guns on the hill go pop pop pop and the searchlights finger the clouds and now and then, sometimes close at hand, sometimes far away, a bomb drops.

Up there in the sky young Englishmen and young German men are fighting each other. The defenders are men, the attackers men. Arms are not given to Englishwomen either to fight the enemy or to defend herself. She must lie weaponless tonight. Yet if she believes that the fight going on up in the sky is a fight by the English to protect freedom, by the Germans to destroy freedom, she must fight, so far as she can, on the side of the English. How far can she fight for freedom without firearms? By making arms, or clothes or food. But there is another way of fighting for freedom without arms: we can fight with the mind. We can make ideas that will help the young Englishman who is fighting up in the sky to defeat the enemy.

But to make ideas effective, we must be able to fire them off. We must put them into action. And the hornet in the sky rouses another hornet in the mind. There was one zooming in *The Times* this morning — a woman's voice saying, "Women have not a word to say in politics." There is no woman in the Cabinet; nor in any responsible post. All the idea-makers who are in a position to make ideas effective are men. That is a thought that damps thinking, and encourages irresponsibility. Why not bury the head in the pillow, plug the ears, and cease this futile activity of idea-making? Because there are other tables besides officer tables and conference tables. Are we not leaving the young Englishman without a weapon that might be of value to him if we give up private thinking, tea-table thinking, because it seems useless? Are we not stressing our disability because our ability exposes us perhaps to abuse, perhaps to contempt? "I will not cease from mental fight," Blake wrote. Mental fight means thinking against the current, not with it.

That current flows fast and furious. It issues in a spate of words from the loudspeakers and the politicians. Every day they tell us that we are a free people, fighting to defend freedom. That is the current that has whirled the young airman up into the sky and keeps him circling there among the clouds. Down here, with a roof to cover us and a gas-mask handy, it is our business to puncture gas-bags and discover seeds of truth. It is not true that we are free. We are both prisoners tonight — he boxed up in his machine with a gun handy; we lying in the dark with a gas-mask handy. If we were free we should be out in the open, dancing, at the play, or sitting at the window talking together. What is it that prevents us? "Hitler!" the loudspeakers cry with one voice. Who is Hitler? What is he? Aggressiveness, tyranny, the insane love of power made manifest, they reply. Destroy that, and you will be free.

The drone of the planes is now like the sawing of a branch overhead. Round and round it goes, sawing and sawing at a branch directly above the house. Another sound begins sawing its way in the brain. "Women of ability" — it was Lady Astor[1] speaking in *The Times* this morning — "are held down because of a subconscious Hitlerism in the hearts of men." Certainly we are held down. We are equally prisoners tonight — the Englishmen in their planes, the Englishwomen in their beds. But if he stops to think he may be killed; and we too. So let us think for him. Let us try to drag up into consciousness the subconscious Hitlerism that holds us down. It is the desire for aggression; the desire to dominate and enslave. Even in the darkness we can see that made visible. We can see shop windows blazing; and women gazing; painted women; dressed-up women; women with crimson lips and crimson fingernails. They are slaves who are trying to enslave. If we could free ourselves from slavery we should free men from tyranny. Hitlers are bred by slaves.

A bomb drops. All the windows rattle. The anti-aircraft guns are getting active. Up there on the hill under a net tagged with strips of green and brown stuff to imitate the hues of autumn leaves guns are concealed. Now they all fire at once. On the nine o'clock radio we shall be told "Forty-four enemy planes were shot down during the night, ten of them by anti-aircraft fire." And one of the terms of peace, the loudspeakers say, is to be disarmament. There are to be no more guns, no army, no navy, no air force in the future. No more young men will be trained to fight with arms. That rouses another mind-hornet in the chambers of the brain — another quotation. "To fight against a real enemy, to earn undying honour and glory by shooting total strangers, and to come home with my breast covered with medals and decorations, that was the summit of my hope. . . . It was for this that my whole life so far had been dedicated, my education, training, everything. . . ."

Those were the words of a young Englishman who fought in the last war. In the face of them, do the current thinkers honestly believe that by writing "Disarmament" on a sheet of paper at a conference table they will have done all that is needful? Othello's occupation will be gone; but he will remain Othello.[2] The young airman up in the sky is driven not only by the voices of loudspeakers; he is driven by voices in himself — ancient instincts, instincts fostered and cherished by education and tradition. Is he to be blamed for those instincts? Could we switch off the maternal instinct at the command of a table full of politicians? Suppose that imperative among the peace terms was: "Child-bearing is to be restricted to a very small class of specially selected women," would we submit? Should we not say, "The maternal instinct is a woman's glory. It was for this that

---

[1]Nancy Witcher Astor (1879–1964), Viscountess Astor, first woman to serve in the British House of Commons. — Eds.

[2]Venetian general, title character in *Othello* by William Shakespeare. — Eds.

my whole life has been dedicated, my education, training, everything. . . ." But if it were necessary, for the sake of humanity, for the peace of the world, that child-bearing should be restricted, the maternal instinct subdued; women would attempt it. Men would help them. They would honour them for their refusal to bear children. They would give them other openings for their creative power. That too must make part of our fight for freedom. We must help the young Englishmen to root out from themselves the love of medals and decorations. We must create more honourable activities for those who try to conquer in themselves their fighting instinct, their subconscious Hitlerism. We must compensate the man for the loss of his gun.

The sound of sawing overhead has increased. All the searchlights are erect. They point at a spot exactly above this roof. At any moment a bomb may fall on this very room. One, two, three, four, five, six . . . the seconds pass. The bomb did not fall. But during those seconds of suspense all thinking stopped. All feeling, save one dull dread, ceased. A nail fixed the whole being to one hard board. The emotion of fear and of hate is therefore sterile, unfertile. Directly that fear passes, the mind reaches out and instinctively revives itself by trying to create. Since the room is dark it can create only from memory. It reaches out to the memory of other Augusts — in Bayreuth, listening to Wagner; in Rome, walking over the Campagna; in London. Friends' voices come back. Scraps of poetry return. Each of those thoughts, even in memory, was far more positive, reviving, healing, and creative than the dull dread made of fear and hate. Therefore if we are to compensate the young man for the loss of his glory and of his gun, we must give him access to the creative feelings. We must make happiness. We must free him from the machine. We must bring him out of his prison into the open air. But what is the use of freeing the young Englishman if the young German and the young Italian remain slaves?

The searchlights, wavering across the flat, have picked up the plane now. From this window one can see a little silver insect turning and twisting in the light. The guns go pop pop pop. Then they cease. Probably the raider was brought down behind the hill. One of the pilots landed safe in a field near here the other day. He said to his captors, speaking fairly good English, "How glad I am that the fight is over!" Then an Englishman gave him a cigarette, and an Englishwoman made him a cup of tea. That would seem to show that if you can free the man from the machine, the seed does not fall upon altogether stony ground. The seed may be fertile.

At last all the guns have stopped firing. All the searchlights have been extin- 10
guished. The natural darkness of a summer's night returns. The innocent sounds of the country are heard again. An apple thuds to the ground. An owl hoots, winging its way from tree to tree. And some half-forgotten words of an old English writer come to mind: "The huntsmen are up in America. . . ."[3] Let us send

---

[3]"The huntsmen are up in America, and they are already past their first sleep in Persia." — Sir Thomas Browne (1605–1682), from "The Garden of Cyrus." — Eds.

these fragmentary notes to the huntsmen who are up in America, to the men and women whose sleep has not yet been broken by machine-gun fire, and in the belief that they will rethink them generously and charitably, perhaps shape them into something serviceable. And now, in the shadowed half of the world, to sleep.

Exploring the Text

1. What is the effect of beginning the essay in the first-person plural, present tense?
2. In paragraph 2, what kind of fighting does Virginia Woolf call on women to do?
3. How do the hornet metaphor (para. 3) and the sawing simile (para. 5) serve Woolf's purpose as she argues for women to fight the war?
4. Woolf includes a quotation from the *Times* in paragraph 3 and offers examples to support its validity. How would the change in women's social and political status in England since 1940 affect Woolf's thesis?
5. In paragraph 5, Woolf writes, "Hitlers are bred by slaves." How can such a paradoxical statement be accurate? What is the effect of following that short sentence with the abrupt three-word sentence in paragraph 6?
6. What are the purpose and effect of the rhetorical questions in paragraph 7? Woolf concludes paragraph 7 with the aphoristic statement "We must compensate the man for the loss of his gun." What does she mean?
7. In paragraph 8, Woolf refers to "this roof" and "this very room," and counts the seconds. What is the effect of such details?
8. What is Woolf's attitude toward war and peace as revealed in the last two paragraphs? How does Woolf try to appeal to Americans?
9. Woolf writes of the English fighters. Does her essay speak to American fighters as well?
10. Explain whether you believe that Woolf's suggestions about the relationship between gender and warfare, between gender and aggression are still relevant.

On the Duty of Civil Disobedience

Henry David Thoreau

Henry David Thoreau (1817–1862) was a philosopher, poet, essayist, and naturalist as well as an outspoken social critic. Born in Concord, Massachusetts, he was educated at Harvard and worked at a variety of professions, from land surveyor to teacher to pencil maker. Strongly influenced by his neighbor and friend Ralph Waldo Emerson, Thoreau considered himself a fierce patriot who honored his country and its ideals, if not always its government. He spoke out against the war with Mexico and criticized the Fugitive Slave Act, and he defended the abolitionist John Brown. Thoreau is best known for *Walden, or Life in the Woods*

(p. 276), published in 1854, which presents his account of living in a cabin on Walden Pond for two years. Originally delivered as a lecture, "On the Duty of Civil Disobedience" is Thoreau's response to his arrest and incarceration for not paying a poll tax. Its influence has been enormous, deeply affecting such twentieth-century figures as Gandhi and Martin Luther King Jr.

I heartily accept the motto, — "That government is best which governs least"; and I should like to see it acted up to more rapidly and systematically. Carried out, it finally amounts to this, which I also believe, — "That government is best which governs not at all"; and when men are prepared for it, that will be the kind of government which they will have. Government is at best but an expedient; but most governments are usually, and all governments are sometimes, inexpedient. The objections which have been brought against a standing army, and they are many and weighty, and deserve to prevail, may also at last be brought against a standing government. The standing army is only an arm of the standing government. The government itself, which is only the mode which the people have chosen to execute their will, is equally liable to be abused and perverted before the people can act through it. Witness the present Mexican war, the work of comparatively a few individuals using the standing government as their tool; for, in the outset, the people would not have consented to this measure.

This American government, — what is it but a tradition, though a recent one, endeavoring to transmit itself unimpaired to posterity, but each instant losing some of its integrity? It has not the vitality and force of a single living man; for a single man can bend it to his will. It is a sort of wooden gun to the people themselves. But it is not the less necessary for this; for the people must have some complicated machinery or other, and hear its din, to satisfy that idea of government which they have. Governments show thus how successfully men can be imposed on, even impose on themselves, for their own advantage. It is excellent, we must all allow. Yet this government never of itself furthered any enterprise, but by the alacrity with which it got out of its way. *It* does not keep the country free. *It* does not settle the West. *It* does not educate. The character inherent in the American people has done all that has been accomplished; and it would have done somewhat more, if the government had not sometimes got in its way. For government is an expedient by which men would fain succeed in letting one another alone; and, as has been said, when it is most expedient, the governed are most let alone by it. Trade and commerce, if they were not made of India-rubber, would never manage to bounce over the obstacles which legislators are continually putting in their way; and, if one were to judge these men wholly by the effects of their actions and not partly by their intentions, they would deserve to be classed and punished with those mischievous persons who put obstructions on railroads.

But, to speak practically and as a citizen, unlike those who call themselves no-government men, I ask for, not at once no government, but *at once* a better government. Let every man make known what kind of government would command his respect, and that will be one step toward obtaining it.

After all, the practical reason why, when the power is once in the hands of the people, a majority are permitted, and for a long period continue, to rule, is not because they are most likely to be in the right, nor because this seems fairest to the minority, but because they are physically the strongest. But a government in which the majority rule in all cases cannot be based on justice, even as far as men understand it. Can there not be a government in which majorities do not virtually decide right and wrong, but conscience? — in which majorities decide only those questions to which the rule of expediency is applicable? Must the citizen ever for a moment, or in the least degree, resign his conscience to the legislator? Why has every man a conscience, then? I think that we should be men first, and subjects afterward. It is not desirable to cultivate a respect for the law, so much as for the right. The only obligation which I have the right to assume, is to do at any time what I think right. It is truly enough said, that a corporation has no conscience; but a corporation of conscientious men is a corporation *with* a conscience. Law never made men a whit more just; and, by means of their respect for it, even the well-disposed are daily made the agents of injustice. A common and natural result of an undue respect for law is, that you may see a file of soldiers, colonel, captain, corporal, privates, powder-monkeys, and all, marching in admirable order over hill and dale to the wars, against their wills, ay, against their common sense and consciences, which makes it very steep marching indeed, and produces a palpitation of the heart. They have no doubt that it is a damnable business in which they are concerned; they are all peaceably inclined. Now, what are they? Men at all? or small movable forts and magazines, at the service of some unscrupulous man in power? Visit the Navy-Yard, and behold a marine, such a man as an American government can make, or such as it can make a man with its black arts, — a mere shadow and reminiscence of humanity, a man laid out alive and standing, and already, as one may say, buried under arms with funeral accompaniments, though it may be, —

> Not a drum was heard, not a funeral note.
> As his corse to the rampart we hurried;
> Not a soldier discharged his farewell shot
> O'er the grave where our hero we buried.[1]

The mass of men serve the state thus, not as men mainly, but as machines, with their bodies. They are the standing army, and the militia, jailers, constables, posse comitatus, &c. In most cases there is no free exercise whatever of the judgment or of the moral sense; but they put themselves on a level with wood and earth and stones; and wooden men can perhaps be manufactured that will serve

5

---

[1]From an early nineteenth-century song. — Eds.

the purpose as well. Such command no more respect than men of straw or a lump of dirt. They have the same sort of worth only as horses and dogs. Yet such as these even are commonly esteemed good citizens. Others, — as most legislators, politicians, lawyers, ministers, and office-holders, — serve the state chiefly with their heads; and, as they rarely make any moral distinctions, they are as likely to serve the Devil, without *intending* it, as God. A very few, as heroes, patriots, martyrs, reformers in the great sense, and *men*, serve the state with their consciences also, and so necessarily resist it for the most part; and they are commonly treated as enemies by it. A wise man will only be useful as a man, and will not submit to be "clay," and "stop a hole to keep the wind away,"[2] but leave that office to his dust at least: —

> I am too high-born to be propertied,
> To be a secondary at control,
> Or useful serving-man and instrument
> To any sovereign state throughout the world.[3]

He who gives himself entirely to his fellow-men appears to them useless and selfish; but he who gives himself partially to them is pronounced a benefactor and philanthropist.

How does it become a man to behave toward this American government today? I answer, that he cannot without disgrace be associated with it. I cannot for an instant recognize that political organization as *my* government which is the *slave's* government also.

All men recognize the right of revolution; that is, the right to refuse allegiance to, and to resist, the government, when its tyranny or its inefficiency are great and unendurable. But almost all say that such is not the case now. But such was the case, they think, in the Revolution of '75. If one were to tell me that this was a bad government because it taxed certain foreign commodities brought to its ports, it is most probable that I should not make an ado about it, for I can do without them. All machines have their friction; and possibly this does enough good to counterbalance the evil. At any rate, it is a great evil to make a stir about it. But when the friction comes to have its machine, and oppression and robbery are organized, I say, let us not have such a machine any longer. In other words, when a sixth of the population of a nation which has undertaken to be the refuge of liberty are slaves, and a whole country is unjustly overrun and conquered by a foreign army, and subjected to military law, I think that it is not too soon for honest men to rebel and revolutionize. What makes this duty the more urgent is the fact, that the country so overrun is not our own, but ours is the invading army.

---

[2]*Hamlet* 5.1.236–237. — Eds.
[3]*King John* 5.1.79–82. — Eds.

Paley, a common authority with many on moral questions, in his chapter on the "Duty of Submission to Civil Government," resolves all civil obligation into expediency; and he proceeds to say, "that so long as the interest of the whole society requires it, that is, so long as the established government cannot be resisted or changed without public inconveniency, it is the will of God that the established government be obeyed, and no longer. —— This principle being admitted, the justice of every particular case of resistance is reduced to a computation of the quantity of the danger and grievance on the one side, and of the probability and expense of redressing it on the other. Of this, he says, every man shall judge for himself. But Paley appears never to have contemplated those cases to which the rule of expediency does not apply, in which a people, as well as an individual, must do justice, cost what it may. If I have unjustly wrested a plank from a drowning man, I must restore it to him though I drown myself. This, according to Paley, would be inconvenient. But he that would save his life, in such a case, shall lose it. This people must cease to hold slaves, and to make war on Mexico, though it cost them their existence as a people.

In their practice, nations agree with Paley; but does any one think that Massachusetts does exactly what is right at the present crisis? 10

> A drab of state, a cloth-'o-silver slut,
> To have her train borne up, and her soul trail in the dirt.[4]

Practically speaking, the opponents to a reform in Massachusetts are not a hundred thousand politicians at the South, but a hundred thousand merchants and farmers here, who are more interested in commerce and agriculture than they are in humanity, and are not prepared to do justice to the slave and to Mexico, *cost what it may*. I quarrel not with far-off foes, but with those who, near at home, cooperate with, and do the bidding of, those far away, and without whom the latter would be harmless. We are accustomed to say, that the mass of men are unprepared; but improvement is slow, because the few are not materially wiser or better than the many. It is not so important that many should be as good as you, as that there be some absolute goodness somewhere; for that will leaven the whole lump. There are thousands who are *in opinion* opposed to slavery and to the war, who yet in effect do nothing to put an end to them; who, esteeming themselves children of Washington and Franklin, sit down with their hands in their pockets, and say that they know not what to do, and do nothing; who even postpone the question of freedom to the question of free-trade, and quietly read the prices-current along with the latest advices from Mexico, after dinner, and, it may be, fall asleep over them both. What is the price-current of an honest man and a patriot today? They hesitate, and they regret, and sometimes they petition; but they do nothing in earnest and with effect. They will wait, well disposed, for others to remedy the

---

[4]From a work by Cyril Tourneur (c. 1575–1626). —Eds.

evil, that they may no longer have it to regret. At most, they give only a cheap vote, and a feeble countenance and God-speed, to the right, as it goes by them. There are nine hundred and ninety-nine patrons of virtue to one virtuous man. But it is easier to deal with the real possessor of a thing than with the temporary guardian of it.

All voting is a sort of gaming, like checkers or backgammon, with a slight moral tinge to it, a playing with right and wrong, with moral questions; and betting naturally accompanies it. The character of the voters is not staked. I cast my vote, perchance, as I think right; but I am not vitally concerned that that right should prevail. I am willing to leave it to the majority. Its obligation, therefore, never exceeds that of expediency. Even voting *for the right* is *doing* nothing for it. It is only expressing to men feebly your desire that it should prevail. A wise man will not leave the right to the mercy of chance, nor wish it to prevail through the power of the majority. There is but little virtue in the action of masses of men. When the majority shall at length vote for the abolition of slavery, it will be because they are indifferent to slavery, or because there is but little slavery left to be abolished by their vote. *They* will then be the only slaves. Only *his* vote can hasten the abolition of slavery who asserts his own freedom by his vote.

I hear of a convention to be held at Baltimore, or elsewhere, for the selection of a candidate for the Presidency, made up chiefly of editors, and men who are politicans by profession; but I think, what is it to any independent, intelligent, and respectable man what decision they may come to? shall we not have the advantage of his wisdom and honesty, nevertheless? Can we not count upon some independent votes? Are there not many individuals in the country who do not attend conventions? But no: I find that the respectable man, so called, has immediately drifted from his position, and despairs of his country, when his country has more reason to despair of him. He forthwith adopts one of the candidates thus selected as the only *available* one, thus proving that he is himself *available* for any purposes of the demagogue. His vote is of no more worth than that of any unprincipled foreigner or hireling native, who may have been bought. O for a man who is *a man*, and, as my neighbor says, has a bone in his back which you cannot pass your hand through! Our statistics are at fault: The population has been returned too large. How many *men* are there to a square thousand miles in this country? Hardly one. Does not America offer any inducement for men to settle here? The American has dwindled into an Odd Fellow, — one who may be known by the development of his organ of gregariousness, and a manifest lack of intellect and cheerful self-reliance; whose first and chief concern, on coming into the world, is to see that the Almshouses are in good repair; and, before yet he has lawfully donned the virile garb, to collect a fund for the support of the widows and orphans that may be; who, in short, ventures to live only by the aid of the Mutual Insurance company, which has promised to bury him decently.

It is not a man's duty, as a matter of course, to devote himself to the eradication of any, even the most enormous wrong; he may still properly have other concerns to engage him; but it is his duty, at least, to wash his hands of it, and, if he gives it no thought longer, not to give it practically his support. If I devote myself to other pursuits and contemplations, I must first see, at least, that I do not pursue them sitting upon another man's shoulders. I must get off him first, that he may pursue his contemplations too. See what gross inconsistency is tolerated. I have heard some of my townsmen say, "I should like to have them order me out to help put down an insurrection of the slaves, or to march to Mexico; — see if I would go"; and yet these very men have each, directly by their allegiance, and so indirectly, at least, by their money, furnished a substitute. The soldier is applauded who refuses to serve in an unjust war by those who do not refuse to sustain the unjust government which makes the war; is applauded by those whose own act and authority he disregards and sets at naught; as if the State were penitent to that degree that it hired one to scourge it while it sinned, but not to that degree that it left off sinning for a moment. Thus, under the name of Order and Civil Government, we are all made at last to pay homage to and support our own meanness. After the first blush of sin comes its indifference; and from immoral it becomes, as it were, *un*moral, and not quite unnecessary to that life which we have made.

The broadest and most prevalent error requires the most disinterested virtue to sustain it. The slight reproach to which the virtue of patriotism is commonly liable, the noble are most likely to incur. Those who, while they disapprove of the character and measures of a government, yield to it their allegiance and support, are undoubtedly its most conscientious supporters, and so frequently the most serious obstacles to reform. Some are petitioning the State to dissolve the Union, to disregard the requisitions of the President. Why do they not dissolve it themselves, — the union between themselves and the States, — and refuse to pay their quota into its treasury? Do not they stand in the same relation to the State, that the State does to the Union? And have not the same reasons prevented the State from resisting the Union, which have prevented them from resisting the State?

How can a man be satisfied to entertain an opinion merely, and enjoy *it*? Is there any enjoyment in it, if his opinion is that he is aggrieved? If you are cheated out of a single dollar by your neighbor, you do not rest satisfied with knowing that you are cheated, or with saying that you are cheated, or even with petitioning him to pay you your due; but you take effectual steps at once to obtain the full amount, and see that you are never cheated again. Action from principle, the perception and the performance of right, changes things and relations; it is essentially revolutionary, and does not consist wholly with anything which was. It not only divides states and churches, it divides families; ay, it divides the *individual*, separating the diabolical in him from the divine.

Unjust laws exist: Shall we be content to obey them, or shall we endeavor to amend them, and obey them until we have succeeded, or shall we transgress them at once? Men generally, under such a government as this, think that they ought to wait until they have persuaded the majority to alter them. They think that, if they

15

should resist, the remedy would be worse than the evil. But it is the fault of the government itself that the remedy *is* worse than the evil. *It* makes it worse. Why is it not more apt to anticipate and provide for reform? Why does it not cherish its wise minority? Why does it cry and resist before it is hurt? Why does it not encourage its citizens to be on the alert to point out its faults, and *do* better than it would have them? Why does it always crucify Christ, and excommunicate Copernicus and Luther, and pronounce Washington and Franklin rebels?

One would think, that a deliberate and practical denial of its authority was the only offence never contemplated by government; else, why has it not assigned its definite, its suitable and proportionate penalty? If a man who has no property refuses but once to earn nine shillings for the State, he is put in prison for a period unlimited by any law that I know, and determined only by the discretion of those who placed him there; but if he should steal ninety times nine shillings from the State, he is soon permitted to go at large again.

If the injustice is part of the necessary friction of the machine of government, let it go, let it go: Perchance it will wear smooth, — certainly the machine will wear out. If the injustice has a spring, or a pulley, or a rope, or a crank, exclusively for itself, then perhaps you may consider whether the remedy will not be worse than the evil; but if it is of such a nature that it requires you to be the agent of injustice to another, then, I say, break the law. Let your life be a counter friction to stop the machine. What I have to do is to see, at any rate, that I do not lend myself to the wrong which I condemn.

As for adopting the ways which the State has provided for remedying the evil, I know not of such ways. They take too much time, and a man's life will be gone. I have other affairs to attend to. I came into this world, not chiefly to make this a good place to live in, but to live in it, be it good or bad. A man has not everything to do, but something; and because he cannot do *everything*, it is not necessary that he should do *something* wrong. It is not my business to be petitioning the Governor or the Legislature any more than it is theirs to petition me; and, if they should not hear my petition, what should I do then? But in this case the State has provided no way: Its very Constitution is the evil. This may seem to be harsh and stubborn and unconciliatory; but it is to treat with the utmost kindness and consideration the only spirit that can appreciate or deserves it. So is all change for the better, like birth and death, which convulse the body.

I do not hesitate to say, that those who call themselves Abolitionists should at once effectually withdraw their support, both in person and property, from the government of Massachusetts, and not wait till they constitute a majority of one, before they suffer the right to prevail through them. I think that it is enough if they have God on their side, without waiting for that other one. Moreover, any man more right than his neighbors constitutes a majority of one already.[5]

20

---

[5]An allusion to a statement by John Knox (1505?–1572), a religious reformer, who said, "A man with God is always in the majority." — Eds.

I meet this American government, or its representative, the State government, directly, and face to face, once a year — no more — in the person of its tax-gatherer; this is the only mode in which a man situated as I am necessarily meets it; and it then says distinctly, Recognize me; and the simplest, the most effectual, and, in the present posture of affairs, the indispensablest mode of treating with it on this head, of expressing your little satisfaction with and love for it, is to deny it then. My civil neighbor, the tax-gatherer, is the very man I have to deal with, — for it is, after all, with men and not with parchment that I quarrel, — and he has voluntarily chosen to be an agent of the government. How shall he ever know well what he is and does as an officer of the government, or as a man, until he is obliged to consider whether he shall treat me, his neighbor, for whom he has respect, as a neighbor and well-disposed man, or as a maniac and disturber of the peace, and see if he can get over this obstruction to his neighborliness without a ruder and more impetuous thought or speech corresponding with his action. I know this well, that if one thousand, if one hundred, if ten men whom I could name, — if ten *honest* men only, — ay, if *one* HONEST man, in this State of Massachusetts, *ceasing to hold slaves*, were actually to withdraw from this copartnership, and be locked upon the county jail therefor, it would be the abolition of slavery in America. For it matters not how small the beginning may seem to be: What is once well done is done forever. But we love better to talk about it. That we say is our mission. Reform keeps many scores of newspapers in its service, but not one man. If my esteemed neighbor, the State's ambassador, who will devote his days to the settlement of the question of human rights in the Council Chamber, instead of being threatened with the prisons of Carolina, were to sit down the prisoner of Massachusetts, that State which is so anxious to foist the sin of slavery upon her sister, — though at present she can discover only an act of inhospitality to be the ground of a quarrel with her, — the Legislature would not wholly waive the subject the following winter.

Under a government which imprisons any unjustly, the true place for a just man is also a prison. The proper place today, the only place which Massachusetts has provided for her freer and less desponding spirits, is in her prisons, to be put out and locked out of the State by her own act, as they have already put themselves out by their principles. It is there that the fugitive slave, and the Mexican prisoner on parole, and the Indian come to plead the wrongs of his race, should find them; on that separate, but more free and honorable ground, where the State places those who are not *with* her, but *against* her, — the only house in a slave State in which a free man can abide with honor. If any think that their influence would be lost there, and their voices no longer afflict the ear of the State, that they would not be as an enemy within its walls, they do not know by how much truth is stronger than error, nor how much more eloquently and effectively he can combat injustice who has experienced a little in his own person. Cast your whole vote, not a strip of paper merely, but your whole influence. A minority is powerless while it conforms to the majority; it is not even a minority then; but it is irresistible when it clogs by its whole weight. If the alternative is to keep all just men in prison, or give up war and slavery, the State will not hesitate which to choose. If a thousand men were not to pay their tax-bills this year, that would not be a violent and bloody measure, as it would be to pay them, and enable the State to commit violence and shed innocent blood. This is, in fact, the definition of a peaceable revolution, if any such is possible. If the tax-gatherer, or any other public officer, asks me, as one has done, "But what shall I do?" my answer is, "If you really wish to do anything, resign your office." When the subject has refused allegiance, and the officer has resigned his office, then the revolution is accomplished. But even suppose blood should flow. Is there not a sort of blood shed when the conscience is wounded? Through this wound a man's real manhood and immortality flow out, and he bleeds to an everlasting death. I see this blood flowing now.

I have contemplated the imprisonment of the offender, rather than the seizure of his goods, — though both will serve the same purpose, — because they who assert the purest right, and consequently are most dangerous to a corrupt State, commonly have not spent much time in accumulating property. To such the State renders comparatively small service, and a slight tax is wont to appear exorbitant, particularly if they are obliged to earn it by special labor with their hands. If there were one who lived wholly without the use of money, the State itself would hesitate to demand it of him. But the rich man, — not to make any invidious comparison, — is always sold to the institution which makes him rich. Absolutely speaking, the more money, the less virtue; for money comes between a man and his objects, and obtains them for him; and it was certainly no great virtue to obtain it. It puts to rest many questions which he would otherwise be taxed to answer; while the only new question which it puts is the hard but superfluous one, how to spend it. Thus his moral ground is taken from under his feet. The opportunities of living are diminished in proportion as what are called the "means" are increased. The best thing a man can do for his culture when he is rich is to endeavor to carry out those schemes which he entertained when he was poor. Christ answered the Herodians according to their condition. "Show me the tribute-money," said he; — and one took a penny out of his pocket; — if you use money which has the image of Caesar on it, and which he has made current and valuable, that is, *if you are men of the State,* and gladly enjoy the advantages of Caesar's government, then pay him back some of his own when he demands it; "Render therefore to Caesar that which is Caesar's, and to God those things which are God's,"[6] — leaving them no wiser than before as to which was which; for they did not wish to know.

When I converse with the freest of my neighbors, I perceive that, whatever they may say about the magnitude and seriousness of the question, and their regard for the public tranquility, the long and the short of the matter is, that they

---

[6]Matt. 22:16–21. — Eds.

cannot spare the protection of the existing government, and they dread the consequences to their property and families of disobedience to it. For my own part, I should not like to think that I ever rely on the protection of the State. But, if I deny the authority of the State when it presents its tax-bill, it will soon take and waste all my property, and so harass me and my children without end. This is hard. This makes it impossible for a man to live honestly, and at the same time comfortably, in outward respects. It will not be worth the while to accumulate property; that would be sure to go again. You must hire or squat somewhere, and raise but a small crop, and eat that soon. You must live within yourself, and depend upon yourself always tucked up and ready for a start, and not have many affairs. A man may grow rich in Turkey even, if he will be in all respects a good subject of the Turkish government. Confucius said: "If a state is governed by the principles of reason, poverty and misery are subjects of shame; if a state is not governed by the principles of reason, riches and honors are the subjects of shame." No: Until I want the protection of Massachusetts to be extended to me in some distant Southern port, where my liberty is endangered, or until I am bent solely on building up an estate at home by peaceful enterprise, I can afford to refuse allegiance to Massachusetts, and her right to my property and life. It costs me less in every sense to incur the penalty of disobedience to the State, than it would to obey. I should feel as if I were worth less in that case.

Some years ago, the State met me in behalf of the Church and commanded   25
me to pay a certain sum toward the support of a clergyman whose preaching my father attended, but never I myself. "Pay," it said, "or be locked up in the jail." I declined to pay. But, unfortunately, another man saw fit to pay it. I did not see why the schoolmaster should be taxed to support the priest, and not the priest the schoolmaster; for I was not the State's schoolmaster, but I supported myself by voluntary subscription. I did not see why the lyceum should not present its tax-bill, and have the State to back its demand, as well as the Church. However, at the request of the selectmen, I condescended to make some such statement as this in writing: — "Know all men by these presents, that I, Henry Thoreau, do not wish to be regarded as a member of any incorporated society which I have not joined." This I gave to the town clerk; and he has it. The State, having thus learned that I did not wish to be regarded as a member of that church, has never made a like demand on me since; though it said that it must adhere to its original presumption that time. If I had known how to name them, I should then have signed off in detail from all the societies which I never signed on to; but I did not know where to find a complete list.

I have paid no poll-tax for six years. I was put into a jail once on this account, for one night; and, as I stood considering the walls of solid stone, two or three feet thick, the door of wood and iron, a foot thick, and the iron grating which strained the light, I could not help being struck with the foolishness of that institution which treated me as if I were mere flesh and blood and bones, to be locked up. I wondered that it should have concluded at length that this was the best use it could put me to, and had never thought to avail itself of my services in some way. I saw that, if there was a wall of stone between me and my townsmen, there was a still more difficult one to climb or break through, before they could get to be as free as I was. I did not for a moment feel confined, and the walls seemed a great waste of stone and mortar. I felt as if I alone of all my townsmen had paid my tax. They plainly did not know how to treat me, but behaved like persons who are underbred. In every threat and in every compliment there was a blunder; for they thought that my chief desire was to stand the other side of that stone wall, I could not but smile to see how industriously they locked the door on my meditations, which followed them out again without let or hindrance, and *they* were really all that was dangerous. As they could not reach me, they had resolved to punish my body; just as boys, if they cannot come at some person against whom they have a spite, will abuse his dog. I saw that the State was half-witted, that it was timid as a lone woman with her silver spoons, and that it did not know its friends from its foes, and I lost all my remaining respect for it, and pitied it.

Thus the State never intentionally confronts a man's sense, intellectual or moral, but only his body, his senses. It is not armed with superior wit or honesty, but with superior physical strength. I was not born to be forced. I will breathe after my own fashion. Let us see who is the strongest. What force has a multitude? They only can force me who obey a higher law than I. They force me to become like themselves. I do not hear of *men* being *forced* to live this way or that by masses of men. What sort of life were that to live? When I meet a government which says to me, "Your money or your life," why should I be in haste to give it my money? It may be in a great strait, and not know what to do: I cannot help that. It must help itself; do as I do. It is not worth the while to snivel about it. I am not responsible for the successful working of the machinery of society. I am not the son of the engineer. I perceive that, when an acorn and a chestnut fall side by side, the one does not remain inert to make way for the other, but both obey their own laws, and spring and grow and flourish as best they can, till one, perchance, overshadows and destroys the other. If a plant cannot live according to its nature, it dies; and so a man.

The night in prison was novel and interesting enough. The prisoners in their shirt-sleeves were enjoying a chat and the evening air in the doorway, when I entered. But the jailer said, "Come, boys, it is time to lock up"; and so they dispersed, and I heard the sound of their steps returning into the hollow apartments. My roommate was introduced to me by the jailer, as "a first-rate fellow and a clever man." When the door was locked, he showed me where to hang my hat, and how he managed matters there. The rooms were white-washed once a month; and this one, at least, was the whitest, most simply furnished, and probably the neatest apartment in the town. He naturally wanted to know where I came from, and what brought me there; and, when I had told him, I asked him in my turn how he came there, presuming him to be an honest man, of course; and, as the world goes, I believe he was. "Why," said he, "they accuse me of burning a barn; but I never did it." As near as I could discover, he had probably gone to bed in a barn when drunk, and smoked his pipe there; and so a barn was burnt. He had the reputation of being a clever man, had been there some three months waiting for his trial to come on, and would have to wait as much longer; but he was quite domesticated and contented, since he got his board for nothing, and thought that he was well-treated.

He occupied one window, and I the other; and I saw, that, if one stayed there long, his principal business would be to look out the window. I had soon read all the tracts that were left there, and examined where former prisoners had broken out, and where a grate had been sawed off, and heard the history of the various occupants of that room; for I found that even here there was a history and a gossip which never circulated beyond the walls of the jail. Probably this is the only house in the town where verses are composed, which are afterward printed in a circular form, but not published. I was shown quite a long list of verses which were composed by some young men who had been detected in an attempt to escape, who avenged themselves by singing them.

I pumped my fellow-prisoner as dry as I could, for fear I should never see him again; but at length he showed me which was my bed, and left me to blow out the lamp. 30

It was like travelling into a far country, such as I had never expected to behold, to lie there for one night. It seemed to me that I never had heard the town-clock strike before, nor the evening sounds of the village; for we slept with the windows open, which were inside the grating. It was to see my native village in the light of the Middle Ages, and our Concord was turned into a Rhine stream, and visions of knights and castles passed before me. They were the voices of old burghers that I heard in the streets. I was an involuntary spectator and auditor of whatever was done and said in the kitchen of the adjacent village-inn, — a wholly new and rare experience to me. It was a closer view of my native town. I was fairly inside of it. I never had seen its institutions before. This is one of its peculiar institutions; for it is a shire town. I began to comprehend what its inhabitants were about.

In the morning, our breakfasts were put through the hole in the door, in small oblong-square tin pans, made to fit, and holding a pint of chocolate, with brown bread, and an iron spoon. When they called for the vessels again, I was green enough to return what bread I had left; but my comrade seized it, and said that I should lay that up for lunch or dinner. Soon after he was let out to work at haying in a neighboring field, whither he went every day, and would not be back till noon; so he bade me good-day, saying that he doubted if he should see me again.

When I came out of prison, — for some one interfered, and paid that tax, — I did not perceive that great changes had taken place on the common, such as he observed who went in a youth, and emerged a tottering and gray-headed man;

and yet a change had to my eyes come over the scene, — the town, a State, and country, — greater than any mere time could effect. I saw yet more distinctly the State in which I lived. I saw to what extent the people among whom I lived could be trusted as good neighbors and friends; that their friendship was for summer weather only; that they did not greatly propose to do right; that they were a distinct race from me by their prejudices and superstitions, as the Chinamen and Malays are; that, in their sacrifices to humanity, they ran no risks, not even to their property; that, after all, they were not so noble but they treated the thief as he had treated them, and hoped, by a certain outward observance and a few prayers, and by walking in a particular straight though useless path from time to time, to save their souls. This may be to judge my neighbors harshly; for I believe that many of them are not aware that they have such an institution as the jail in their village.

It was formerly the custom in our village, when a poor debtor came out of jail, for his acquaintances to salute him, looking through their fingers, which were crossed to represent the grating of a jail window. "How do ye do?" My neighbors did not thus salute me, but first looked at me, and then at one another, as if I had returned from a long journey. I was put into jail as I was going to the shoemaker's to get a shoe which was mended. When I was let out the next morning, I proceeded to finish my errand, and having put on my mended shoe, joined a huckleberry party, who were impatient to put themselves under my conduct; and in half an hour, — for the horse was soon tackled, — was in the midst of a huckleberry field, on one of our highest hills, two miles off, and then the State was nowhere to be seen.

This is the whole history of "My Prisons." 35

I have never declined paying the highway tax, because I am as desirous of being a good neighbor as I am of being a bad subject; and, as for supporting schools, I am doing my part to educate my fellow-countrymen now. It is for no particular item in the tax-bill that I refuse to pay it. I simply wish to refuse allegiance to the State, to withdraw and stand aloof from it effectually. I do not care to trace the course of my dollar, if I could, till it buys a man or a musket to shoot one with, — the dollar is innocent, — but I am concerned to trace the effects of my allegiance. In fact, I quietly declare war with the State, after my fashion, though I will still make what use and get what advantage of her I can, as is usual in such cases.

If others pay the tax which is demanded of me, from a sympathy with the State, they do but what they have already done in their own case, or rather they abet injustice to a greater extent than the State requires. If they pay the tax from a mistaken interest in the individual taxed, to save his property, or prevent his going to jail, it is because they have not considered wisely how far they let their private feelings interfere with the public good.

This, then, is my position at present. But one cannot be too much on his guard in such a case, lest his action be biased by obstinacy, or an undue regard for the opinions of men. Let him see that he does only what belongs to himself and to the hour.

I think sometimes, Why, this people mean well; they are only ignorant; they would do better if they knew how; why give your neighbors this pain to treat you as they are not inclined to? But I think again, this is no reason why I should do as they do, or permit others to suffer much greater pain of a different kind. Again, I sometimes say to myself, When many millions of men, without heat, without ill will, without personal feeling of any kind, demand of you a few shillings only, without the possibility, such is their constitution, of retracing or altering their present demand, and without the possibility, on your side, of appeal to any other millions, why expose yourself to this overwhelming brute force? You do not resist cold and hunger, the winds and the waves, thus obstinately; you quietly submit to a thousand similar necessities. You do not put your head into the fire. But just in proportion as I regard this as not wholly a brute force, partly a human force, and consider that I have relations to those millions as to so many millions of men, and not of mere brute or inanimate things, I see that appeal is possible, first and instantaneously, from them to the Maker of them, and, secondly, from them to themselves. But, if I put my head deliberately into the fire, there is no appeal to fire or to the Maker of fire, and I have only myself to blame. If I could convince myself that I have any right to be satisfied with men as they are, and to treat them according, and not according, in some respects, to my requisitions and expectations of what they and I ought to be, then, like a good Mussulman and fatalist, I should endeavor to be satisfied with things as they are, and say it is the will of God. And, above all, there is this difference between resisting this and a purely brute or natural force, that I can resist this with some effect; but I cannot expect, like Orpheus, to change the nature of the rocks and trees and beasts.

I do not wish to quarrel with any man or nation. I do not wish to split hairs, to make fine distinctions, or set myself up as better than my neighbors. I seek rather, I may say, even an excuse for conforming to the laws of the land. I am but too ready to conform to them. Indeed, I have reason to suspect myself on this head; and each year, as the tax-gatherer comes round, I find myself disposed to review the acts and position of the general and State governments, and the spirit of the people, to discover a pretext for conformity.   40

> We must affect our country as our parents;
> And if at any time we alienate
> Our love or industry from doing it honor.
> We must respect effects and teach the soul
> Matter of conscience and religion.
> And not desire of rule or benefit.

I believe that the State will soon be able to take all my work of this sort out of my hands, and then I shall be no better a patriot than my fellow-countrymen. Seen from a lower point of view, the Constitution, with all its faults, is very good; the law and the courts are very respectable; even this State and this American government are, in many respects, very admirable and rare things, to be thankful for, such as a great many have described them; but seen from a point of view a little higher, they are what I have described them; seen from a higher still, and the highest, who shall say what they are, or that they are worth looking at or thinking of at all?

However, the government does not concern me much, and I shall bestow the fewest possible thoughts on it. It is not many moments that I live under a government, even in this world. If a man is thought-free, fancy-free, imagination-free, that which *is not* never for a long time appearing *to be* to him, unwise rulers or reformers cannot fatally interrupt him.

I know that most men think differently from myself; but those whose lives are by profession devoted to the study of these or kindred subjects, content me as little as any. Statesmen and legislators, standing so completely within the institution, never distinctly and nakedly behold it. They speak of moving society, but have no resting-place without it. They may be men of a certain experience and discrimination, and have no doubt invented ingenious and even useful systems, for which we sincerely thank them; but all their wit and usefulness lie within certain not very wide limits. They are wont to forget that the world is not governed by policy and expediency. Webster never goes behind government, and so cannot speak with authority about it. His words are wisdoms to those legislators who contemplate no essential reform in the existing government; but for thinkers, and those who legislate for all time, he never once glances at the subject. I know of those whose serene and wise speculations on this theme would soon reveal the limits of his mind's range and hospitality. Yet, compared with the cheap professions of most reformers, and the still cheaper wisdom and eloquence of politicians in general, his are almost the only sensible and valuable words, and we thank Heaven for him. Comparatively, he is always strong, original, and, above all, practical. Still his quality is not wisdom, but prudence. The lawyer's truth is not Truth, but consistency, or a consistent expediency. Truth is always in harmony with herself, and is not concerned chiefly to reveal the justice that may consist with wrong-doing. He well deserves to be called, as he has been called, the Defender of the Constitution. There are really no blows to be given by him but defensive ones. He is not a leader, but a follower. His leaders are the men of '87. "I have never made an effort," he says, "and never propose to make an effort; I have never countenanced an effort, and never mean to countenance an effort, to disturb the arrangement as originally made, by which the various States came into the Union."[7] Still thinking of the sanction which the Constitution gives to slavery, he says, "Because it was a part of the original compact, — let it stand." Notwithstanding his special acuteness and ability, he is unable to take a fact out of its

---

[7]From an 1845 speech by Daniel Webster about the admission of Texas to the United States. —Eds.

merely political relations, and behold it as it lies absolutely to be disposed of by the intellect, — what, for instance, it behooves a man to do here in America today with regard to slavery, but ventures, or is driven, to make some such desperate answer as the following, while professing to speak absolutely, and as a private man, — from which what new and singular code of social duties might be inferred? "The manner," says he, "in which the governments of those States where slavery exists are to regulate it, is for their own consideration, under their responsibility to their constituents, to the general laws of propriety, humanity, and justice, and to God. Associations formed elsewhere, springing from a feeling of humanity, or any other cause, have nothing whatever to do with it. They have never received any encouragement from me, and they never will."

They who know of no purer sources of truth, who have traced up its stream no higher, stand, and wisely stand, by the Bible and the Constitution, and drink at it there with reverence and humility; but they who behold where it comes trickling into this lake or that pool, gird up their loins once more, and continue their pilgrimage toward its fountain-head.

No man with a genius for legislation has appeared in America. They are rare in the history of the world. There are orators, politicians, and eloquent men, by the thousand; but the speaker has not yet opened his mouth to speak, who is capable of settling the much-vexed questions of the day. We love eloquence for its own sake, and not for any truth which it may utter, or any heroism it may inspire. Our legislators have not yet learned the comparative value of free-trade and of freedom, of union, and of rectitude, to a nation. They have no genius or talent for comparatively humble questions of taxation and finance, commerce and manufactures and agriculture. If we were left solely to the wordy wit of legislators in Congress for our guidance, uncorrected by the seasonable experience and the effectual complaints of the people, America would not long retain her rank among the nations. For eighteen hundred years, though perchance I have no right to say it, the New Testament has been written; yet where is the legislator who has wisdom and practical talent enough to avail himself of the light which it sheds on the science of legislation?

The authority of government, even such as I am willing to submit to, — for I will cheerfully obey those who know and can do better than I, and in many things even those who neither know nor can do so well, — is still an impure one: To be strictly just, it must have the sanction and consent of the governed. It can have no pure right over my person and property but what I concede to it. The progress from an absolute to a limited monarchy, from a limited monarchy to a democracy, is a progress toward a true respect for the individual. Even the Chinese philosopher was wise enough to regard the individual as the basis of the empire. Is a democracy, such as we know it, the last improvement possible in government? Is it not possible to take a step further towards recognizing and organizing the rights of man? There will never be a really free and enlightened State, until the State comes to recognize the individual as a higher and independent power, from which all its own power and authority are derived, and treats him accordingly. I please myself with imagining a State at last which can afford to be just to all men, and to treat the individual with respect as a neighbor; which even would not think it inconsistent with its own repose, if a few were to live aloof from it, not meddling with it, nor embraced by it, who fulfilled all the duties of neighbors and fellowmen. A State which bore this kind of fruit, and suffered it to drop off as fast as it ripened, would prepare the way for a still more perfect and glorious State, which also I have imagined, but not yet anywhere seen.

Exploring the Text

1. In paragraph 1, what distinction does Henry David Thoreau make between the government and the people? Why does he begin the essay this way? Why does Thoreau not begin the essay with his stay in jail?

2. Why does Thoreau refer to civil disobedience not merely as a right but as a duty?

3. Describe the tone Thoreau establishes in paragraph 2.

4. What are the two government policies Thoreau most objects to? Explain his objection.

5. In paragraph 20, Thoreau states that "any man more right than his neighbors constitutes a majority of one already." What does he mean by this? How does this support his thesis?

6. In paragraph 36, Thoreau distinguishes among different types of taxes. Why?

7. What is the effect of the metaphor about friction in paragraph 8?

8. One characteristic of Thoreau's style is the aphorism. For example, in paragraph 4, he writes, "It is not desirable to cultivate a respect for the law, so much as for the right." Find other examples of Thoreau's aphorisms. You might find some in paragraphs 9–10 and 20–22. What is the rhetorical effect of such statements?

9. Which of the three classic appeals dominates in paragraph 21, where Thoreau gives the government a human face? Defend your answer.

10. Note how Thoreau qualifies his argument in paragraph 40. How does using this strategy serve his rhetorical purpose?

11. Compare and contrast Thoreau's "Civil Disobedience" to Martin Luther King Jr.'s "Letter from Birmingham Jail" by focusing on one of the following: purpose, definition of a just law, or figurative language.

12. Under the circumstances Thoreau describes, is civil disobedience a duty, as he says? Explain how Thoreau's essay speaks to our own time. Is the essay dated? Is it still relevant?

Every Dictator's Nightmare

WOLE SOYINKA

Wole Soyinka was born Akinwande Oluwole Soyinka in 1934 in Nigeria, when it was still a British protectorate. He was educated there and in England. A fierce advocate for freedom and liberty of the individual, he was jailed without being officially charged or tried between 1965 and 1969 for civil disobedience during the Nigerian civil war. While imprisoned, he wrote a diary, later published as *The Man Died: Prison Notes of Wole Soyinka* (1972). Best known as a playwright of both satirical comedies and philosophical plays, Soyinka is one of Africa's most prolific and important writers. He was awarded the Nobel Prize in Literature in 1986, the first African to receive that honor. He has been a visiting professor at Harvard, Columbia, Yale, Cambridge, and other universities. Soyinka continues to be a strong political and cultural voice for freedom and against oppression. "Every Dictator's Nightmare," the essay that follows, was originally published in the *New York Times Magazine* in April 1999.

With the blood-soaked banner of religious fanaticism billowing across the skies as one prominent legacy of this millennium, Martin Luther's famous theses against religious absolutism struck me early as a strong candidate for the best idea of the last thousand years. By progressive association, so did the microprocessor and its implications — the liberalization of access to knowledge, and a quantum boost for the transmission of ideas. There is, however, a nobler idea that has spread by its own power in this millennium and that has now begun to flourish: the idea that certain fundamental rights are inherent to all humanity.

Humankind has always struggled to assert certain values in their own right, values that the individual intuitively felt belonged to each person as part of natural existence. It is difficult to imagine a period when such values were not pursued in spasmodic acts of dissent from norms that appeared to govern society even in its most rudimentary form. Even after years of conformity to hallowed precedents, a few dissidents always arise, and they obtain their primary impulse in crucial instances from the individual's seizure of his or her subjective worth.

In the devolution of authority to one individual as the head of a collective, a system of checks on arbitrary authority is prevalent. Take, for instance, monarchical rule among the Yoruba, the people now concentrated in western Nigeria. At the apex is a quasi-deified personage, endowed with supreme authority over his subjects. To preserve the mystic aura of such a ruler, he is never seen to eat or drink. In earlier times, he was not permitted to speak directly to his people but had to employ an intermediary voice, a spokesman. For the highest-ranked kings in the Yoruban world, the *ekeji orisa* (companions to the deities), it was forbidden even to see their faces. Despite the social and psychological distance between the leader and his subjects, the monarch was pledged to rule within a strict contract of authority. Transgression of a taboo, say, or failure to fulfill ceremonial duties on time, resulted in fines, rituals of appeasement or a period of ostracism. The major crime, however, was abuse of power, excessive authoritarianism and a trampling on the rights of the citizenry. For this category of crimes, there was only one response: the king, on being found guilty, was given a covered calabash and invited to retreat to his inner chambers. He understood the sentence: he must never again be seen among the living.

Sometimes, of course, an individual manages to convert collective authority into a personal monopoly. In these instances, society is characterized by tensions, palpable or hidden, between the suppressed rights of the people and the power rapacity of one individual. But where does society ground its claims, its resistant will, in such circumstances? We know that rebellion may be triggered by recollections of more equitable relationships, by material expropriation or by a cultural transgression that affects the spiritual well-being of the community or individual. Such rebellion finds its authority in the belief, in one citizen after another, that the ruler has violated a fundamental condition of human existence.

The *droit du seigneur*, the "right" that confers on the lord the pleasure of deflowering, on her marriage night, the bride of any of his vassals — on what does the ritually cuckolded groom finally ground his rebellion other than a subjective sense of self-worth? What of the Yoruban monarch who, even today in certain parts of my world, tries to exercise his "right" to *gbese le* — that is, to place his royal slipper, symbolically, on any woman who catches his fancy, and thus assign her to his harem? The manor lord's entitlement to compulsory labor from his peasants, the ownership of another being as a slave, the new age of enslavement of womanhood in countries like Afghanistan — the challenges to these and other so-called rights surely commence with the interrogation of self-worth, expanding progressively toward all examination of the common worth of the human entity as a unit of irreducible properties and rights.

It took centuries for societies to influence one another to the critical extent needed to incite the philosophic mind to address the concept of the human race in general, and not simply as members of a specific race or occupants of a geographical space. In its rudimentary beginnings, each society remained limited by a process that codified its own now-recognizable collective interests against all others, like the Magna Carta and the Bill of Rights. Such oaths of fealty by petty chieftains imposed duties on the suzerain but also entrenched their own equally arbitrary mechanisms of authority and coercion over the next level of society. This sometimes resulted in the bizarre alliance of the monarch with his lowest vassals against his overreaching barons and chieftains.

Like race and citizenship, religion was not far behind in the exclusionist philosophy of rights, formulating codes to protect the rights of the faithful but denying the same to others — the Cross against the Crescent, Buddhist versus Hindu, the believer against the infidel. Or simply religion versus secularism. Ground into powder beneath the hooves of the contending behemoths of religion, ideology and race, each social unit ponders, at least periodically, how he or she differs from cattle or sheep, from the horses that pull the carriages of majesty, even when such choices are the mere expressions of the collective will. If order alone, ornamentation, social organization, technology, bonding and even productive structures were all that defined the human species, then what significant properties marked out Homo sapiens as distinct from the rest of the living species?

Polarizations within various micro-worlds — us versus the inferior them — have long been armed with industrious rationalizations. Christian and Islamic theologians throughout history have quarried their scriptures for passages that stress the incontestable primacy of an unseen and unknowable Supreme Deity who has conferred authority on them. And to what end? Largely to divide the world into us and the rest. The great philosophical minds of Europe, like Hume, Hegel and Kant, bent their prodigious talents to separating the species into those with rights and those with none, founded on the convenient theory that some people were human and others less so. The Encyclopedists of France, products of the so-called Age of Reason, remain the most prolific codifiers of the human (and other) species on an ambitiously comprehensive scale, and their scholarly industry conferred a scientific benediction on a purely commercial project that saw millions of souls dragged across the ocean to serve as beasts of burden. Religion and commerce — far older professions than the one that is sometimes granted that distinction, but of an often-identical temperament — were reinforced by the authority of new scientific theories to divide humanity into higher and lower manifestations of the species. The dichotomy of the world was complete.

It took the near triumph of fascism to bring the world to its senses. The horror of the Holocaust finally took the rulers of the world back to the original question: what is the true value of humanity? It is to be doubted if the victorious three meeting in Yalta actually went into any profound philosophical niceties in the discussions that resulted in the United Nations, that partial attempt to reverse the dichotomizing course of humanity. That course, taken to its ultimate conclusion, had just resulted in an attempted purification of the species, the systematic elimination of millions in gas chambers and a war that mired the potential of Europe in the blood of its youth. After all, the concept of the master race was not new, but it was never before so obsessively articulated and systematically pursued. It was time to rethink the entire fate of humanity. The conversations at Yalta, conversations that led to the birth of the United Nations, were a partial answer to that question.

The first stage was to render the new thinking in concrete terms, to enshrine 10 in a charter of rights the product of the bruising lessons of the immediate past: the United Nations and the Universal Declaration of Human Rights. The informing recognition is that long-suppressed extract of the intuition that humanity had guarded through evolution, one that had been proposed, compromised, amended, vitiated, subverted but never abandoned: that, for all human beings, there do exist certain fundamental rights.

The idea already exists in the Bible, in the Koran, in the Bhagavad-Gita, in the Upanishads, but always in curtailed form, relativist, patriarchal, always subject to the invisible divine realms whose interpreters are mortals with distinct secular agendas, usually allied to the very arbitrary controls that are a contradiction to such ideas. Quiet, restrained, ignored by but also blissfully indifferent to the so-called world religions, Ifa, the corpus of Yoruban spiritual precepts and secular philosophy, its origins lost in antiquity but preserved and applied til today, annunciates identical ideas through Orunmila, the god of divination:

> *Dandan enia l'ayan ko mu ire lo s'aye . . . Ipo rere naa ni aye-amotan ohung-bogbo, ayo nnigbagbogbo, igbesi laisi ominu tabi iberu ota.*

> Certainly, it is the human being that was elected to bring values to the world . . . and his place of good is the knowledge of all things, joy at all times, freedom from anxiety and freedom from fear of the enemy. [Irosu Wori]

Humanity has been straining to seize the fullness of this doctrine, the right to knowledge, the freedom from anxiety, the right to security of existence as inherent to the species. It is only the process of promulgating its pertinence to all mankind that has been long and costly. The kernel of the idea, therefore, is both timeless and new. Its resurrection — the concrete seizure of the idea within this millennium, answering the exigencies of politics, religion and power and securing it within the bedrock of universality — was a destiny that would first be embraced by France.

There, alas, the events that gave new life to this idea did not encourage its adoption on a universal scale, indeed not even durably within France itself. The restoration of slavery by Napoleon was surely the most blatant contradiction of the idea, but this did not much trouble the Emperor.

Still, the idea had taken hold, the idea of the rights of man as a universal principle. It certainly motored the passion of the genuine idealists in the abolition of the slave trade, who must always be distinguished from those to whom abolition was simply a shrewd commercial calculation. The idea of the American Declaration of Independence — an idea that still lacks full realization — that "all men are created equal, that they are endowed by their Creator with certain unalienable Rights" is an adumbration of that original idea from which the French Revolution obtained its inspiration, one that has continued to convulse the unjust order of the world wherever it has been grasped: the fundamental rights of man.

It is an idea whose suppression is the main occupation of dictatorships — be these military or civilian, of the right or the left, secular or theocratic. It is, however, their nightmare, their single province of terror, one that they cannot exorcise, not even through the most unconscionable pogroms, scorched-earth campaigns and crimes against humanity. It is an idea that has transformed the lives of billions and remains poised to liberate billions more, since it is an idea that will not settle for tokenism or for relativism — it implicitly links the liberation of one

15

to the liberation of all. Its gospel of universalism is anchored in the most affective impulse that cynics attribute to the choices made by humanity, self-love, but one that now translates humanity as one's own self.

Exploring the Text

1. In paragraph 1, Wole Soyinka mentions three very important ideas of the last millennium. What are they? Discuss Soyinka's choices. What do you think are three important ideas of the last millennium? Do you agree with Soyinka's choice for the best idea?
2. What are the effects of the juxtapositions and rhetorical questions in paragraph 7?
3. Paragraph 11 refers to religious texts as sources for the great idea Soyinka espouses. How can you reconcile his view there with his criticism of religion in paragraphs 7 and 8?
4. In paragraph 12, Soyinka says, "The kernel of the idea . . . is both timeless and new." What does he mean by this paradoxical statement?
5. Of the three institutions Soyinka identifies as hindrances to individual rights, which does he feel is the worst? Provide evidence to support your inference.
6. What is ironic in the sentence about the Encyclopedists of France (para. 8)?
7. What is Soyinka's tone in paragraph 13? Point to specific evidence within the paragraph to support your argument.
8. Given the title of the essay, "Every Dictator's Nightmare," why does Soyinka address that idea in only the last two paragraphs?
9. What are some current events that illustrate the relevance of Soyinka's ideas today?
10. How does what Soyinka says in paragraph 6 compare with Oliver Goldsmith's ideas in "National Prejudices" (p. 932)?

On the Rainy River (fiction)

Tim O'Brien

> Tim O'Brien (b. 1946) grew up in a small town in Minnesota. In 1968, he received a BA from Macalester College and, soon thereafter, a draft notice. He served as a soldier in the Vietnam War and wrote about his experiences in his memoir, *If I Die in a Combat Zone* (1973). O'Brien won the National Book Award in 1979 for a novel about the war, *Going after Cacciato*. "On the Rainy River," the story that follows, is from *The Things They Carried* (1990), a work of fiction that O'Brien based on his war experiences and in which he placed himself as the protagonist.

This is one story I've never told before. Not to anyone. Not to my parents, not to my brother or sister, not even to my wife. To go into it, I've always thought, would only cause embarrassment for all of us, a sudden need to be elsewhere, which is the natural response to a confession. Even now, I'll admit, the story makes me squirm. For more than twenty years I've had to live with it, feeling the shame, trying to push it away, and so by this act of remembrance, by putting the facts down on paper, I'm hoping to relieve at least some of the pressure on my dreams. Still, it's a hard story to tell. All of us, I suppose, like to believe that in a moral emergency we will behave like the heroes of our youth, bravely and forthrightly, without thought of personal loss or discredit. Certainly that was my conviction back in the summer of 1968. Tim O'Brien: a secret hero. The Lone Ranger. If the stakes ever became high enough — if the evil were evil enough, if the good were good enough — I would simply tap a secret reservoir of courage that had been accumulating inside me over the years. Courage, I seemed to think, comes to us in finite quantities, like an inheritance, and by being frugal and stashing it away and letting it earn interest, we steadily increase our moral capital in preparation for that day when the account must be drawn down. It was a comforting theory. It dispensed with all those bothersome little acts of daily courage; it offered hope and grace to the repetitive coward; it justified the past while amortizing the future.

In June of 1968, a month after graduating from Macalester College, I was drafted to fight a war I hated. I was twenty-one years old. Young, yes, and politically naive, but even so the American war in Vietnam seemed to me wrong. Certain blood was being shed for uncertain reasons. I saw no unity of purpose, no consensus on matters of philosophy or history or law. The very facts were shrouded in uncertainty: Was it a civil war? A war of national liberation or simple aggression? Who started it, and when, and why? What really happened to the USS *Maddox* on that dark night in the Gulf of Tonkin? Was Ho Chi Minh a Communist stooge, or a nationalist savior, or both, or neither? What about the Geneva Accords? What about SEATO and the Cold War? What about dominoes? America was divided on these and a thousand other issues, and the debate had spilled out across the floor of the United States Senate and into the streets, and smart men in pinstripes could not agree on even the most fundamental matters of public policy. The only certainty that summer was moral confusion. It was my view then, and still is, that you don't make war without knowing why. Knowledge, of course, is always imperfect, but it seemed to me that when a nation goes to war it must have reasonable confidence in the justice and imperative of its cause. You can't fix your mistakes. Once people are dead, you can't make them undead.

In any case those were my convictions, and back in college I had taken a modest stand against the war. Nothing radical, no hothead stuff, just ringing a few doorbells for Gene McCarthy, composing a few tedious, uninspired editorials for the campus newspaper. Oddly, though, it was almost entirely an intellectual activity. I brought some energy to it, of course, but it was the energy that accompanies almost any abstract endeavor; I felt no personal danger; I felt no sense of an impending crisis in my life. Stupidly, with a kind of smug removal that I can't begin to fathom, I assumed that the problems of killing and dying did not fall within my special province.

The draft notice arrived on June 17, 1968. It was a humid afternoon, I remember, cloudy and very quiet, and I'd just come in from a round of golf. My mother and father were having lunch out in the kitchen. I remember opening up the letter, scanning the first few lines, feeling the blood go thick behind my eyes. I remember a sound in my head. It wasn't thinking, just a silent howl. A million things all at once — I was too *good* for this war. Too smart, too compassionate, too everything. It couldn't happen. I was above it. I had the world . . . [licked] — Phi Beta Kappa and summa cum laude and president of the student body and a full-ride scholarship for grad studies at Harvard. A mistake maybe — a foul-up in the paperwork. I was no soldier. I hated Boy Scouts. I hated camping out. I hated dirt and tents and mosquitoes. The sight of blood made me queasy, and I couldn't tolerate authority, and I didn't know a rifle from a slingshot. I was a *liberal*, for Christ sake: If they needed fresh bodies, why not draft some back-to-the-stone-age hawk? Or some dumb jingo in his hard hat and Bomb Hanoi button, or one of LBJ's pretty daughters, or [General William] Westmoreland's whole handsome family — nephews and nieces and baby grandson. There should be a law, I thought. If you support a war, if you think it's worth the price, that's fine, but you have to put your own precious fluids on the line. You have to head for the front and hook up with an infantry unit and help spill the blood. And you have to bring along your wife, or your kids, or your lover. A *law*, I thought.

I remember the rage in my stomach. Later it burned down to a smoldering   5
self-pity, then to numbness. At dinner that night my father asked what my plans were. "Nothing," I said. "Wait."

I spent the summer of 1968 working in an Armour meatpacking plant in my hometown of Worthington, Minnesota. The plant specialized in pork products, and for eight hours a day I stood on a quarter-mile assembly line — more properly, a disassembly line — removing blood clots from the necks of dead pigs. My job title, I believe, was Declotter. After slaughter, the hogs were decapitated, split down the length of the belly, pried open, eviscerated, and strung up by the hind hocks on a high conveyer belt. Then gravity took over. By the time a carcass reached my spot on the line, the fluids had mostly drained out, everything except for thick clots of blood in the neck and upper chest cavity. To remove the stuff, I used a kind of water gun. The machine was heavy, maybe eighty pounds, and was suspended from the ceiling by a heavy rubber cord. There was some bounce to it, an elastic up-and-down give, and the trick was to maneuver the gun with your whole body, not lifting with the arms, just letting the rubber cord do the work for you. At one end was a trigger; at the muzzle end was a small nozzle and a steel roller brush. As a carcass passed by, you'd lean forward and swing the gun up against the clots and squeeze the trigger, all in one motion, and the brush would whirl and water would come shooting out and you'd hear a quick splattering sound as the clots dissolved into a fine red mist. It was not pleasant work. Goggles were a necessity, and a rubber apron, but even so it was like standing for eight hours a day under a lukewarm blood-shower. At night I'd go home smelling of pig. It wouldn't go away. Even after hot bath, scrubbing hard, the stink was always there — like old bacon, or sausage, a dense greasy pig-stink that soaked deep into my skin and hair. Among other things, I remember, it was tough getting dates that summer. I felt isolated; I spent a lot of time alone. And there was also that draft notice tucked away in my wallet.

In the evenings I'd sometimes borrow my father's car and drive aimlessly around town, feeling sorry for myself, thinking about the war and the pig factory and how my life seemed to be collapsing toward slaughter. I felt paralyzed. All around me the options seemed to be narrowing, as if I were hurtling down a huge black funnel, the whole world squeezing in tight. There was no happy way out. The government had ended most graduate school deferments; the waiting lists for the National Guard and Reserves were impossibly long; my health was solid; I didn't qualify for CO [conscientious objector] status — no religious grounds, no history as a pacifist. Moreover, I could not claim to be opposed to war as a matter of general principle. There were occasions, I believed, when a nation was justified in using military force to achieve its ends, to stop a Hitler or some comparable evil, and I told myself that in such circumstances I would've willingly marched off to the battle. The problem, though, was that a draft board did not let you choose your war.

Beyond all this, or at the very center, was the raw fact of terror. I did not want to die. Not ever. But certainly not then, not there, not in a wrong war. Driving up Main Street, past the courthouse and the Ben Franklin store, I sometimes felt the fear spreading inside me like weeds. I imagined myself dead. I imagined myself doing things I could not do — charging an enemy position, taking aim at another human being.

At some point in mid-July I began thinking seriously about Canada. The border lay a few hundred miles north, an eight-hour drive. Both my conscience and my instincts were telling me to make a break for it, just take off and run like hell and never stop. In the beginning the idea seemed purely abstract, the word Canada printing itself out in my head; but after a time I could see particular shapes and images, the sorry details of my own future — a hotel room in Winnipeg, a battered old suitcase, my father's eyes as I tried to explain myself over the telephone. I could almost hear his voice, and my mother's. Run, I'd think. Then I'd think, Impossible. Then a second later I'd think, *Run*.

It was a kind of schizophrenia. A moral split. I couldn't make up my mind. I feared the war, yes, but I also feared exile. I was afraid of walking away from my own life, my friends and my family, my whole history, everything that mattered to me. I feared losing the respect of my parents. I feared the law. I feared ridicule and censure. My hometown was a conservative little spot on the prairie, a place where

10

tradition counted, and it was easy to imagine people sitting around a table down at the old Gobbler Café on Main Street, coffee cups poised, the conversation slowly zeroing in on the young O'Brien kid, how the damned sissy had taken off for Canada. At night, when I couldn't sleep, I'd sometimes carry on fierce arguments with those people. I'd be screaming at them, telling them how much I detested their blind, thoughtless, automatic acquiescence to it all, their simple-minded patriotism, their prideful ignorance, their love-it-or-leave-it platitudes, how they were sending me off to fight a war they didn't understand and didn't want to understand. I held them responsible. By God, yes, I *did*. All of them — I held them personally and individually responsible — the polyestered Kiwanis boys, the merchants and farmers, the pious churchgoers, the chatty housewives, the PTA and the Lions club and the Veterans of Foreign Wars and the fine upstanding gentry out at the country club. They didn't know Bao Dai from the man in the moon. They didn't know history. They didn't know the first thing about Diem's tyranny, or the nature of Vietnamese nationalism, or the long colonialism of the French — this was all too damned complicated, it required some reading — but no matter, it was a war to stop the Communists, plain and simple, which was how they liked things, and you were a . . . [traitor] if you had second thoughts about killing or dying for plain and simple reasons.

I was bitter, sure. But it was so much more than that. The emotions went from outrage to terror to bewilderment to guilt to sorrow and then back again to outrage. I felt a sickness inside me. Real disease.

Most of this I've told before, or at least hinted at, but what I have never told is the full truth. How I cracked. How at work one morning, standing on the pig line, I felt something break open in my chest. I don't know what it was. I'll never know. But it was real, I know that much, it was a physical rupture — a cracking-leaking-popping feeling. I remember dropping my water gun. Quickly, almost without thought, I took off my apron and walked out of the plant and drove home. It was midmorning, I remember, and the house was empty. Down in my chest there was still that leaking sensation, something very warm and precious spilling out, and I was covered with blood and hog-stink, and for a long while I just concentrated on holding myself together. I remember taking a hot shower. I remember packing a suitcase and carrying it out to the kitchen, standing very still for a few minutes, looking carefully at the familiar objects all around me. The old chrome toaster, the telephone, the pink and white Formica on the kitchen counters. The room was full of bright sunshine. Everything sparkled. My house, I thought. My life. I'm not sure how long I stood there, but later I scribbled out a short note to my parents.

What it said, exactly, I don't recall now. Something vague. Taking off, will call, love Tim.

I drove north.

It's a blur now, as it was then, and all I remember is a sense of high velocity 15 and the feel of the steering wheel in my hands. I was riding on adrenaline. A giddy feeling, in a way, except there was the dreamy edge of impossibility to it — like running a dead-end maze — no way out — it couldn't come to a happy conclusion and yet I was doing it anyway because it was all I could think of to do. It was pure light, fast and mindless. I had no plan. Just hit the border at high speed and crash through and keep on running. Near dusk I passed through Bemidji, then turned northeast toward International Falls. I spent the night in the car behind a closed-down gas station a half mile from the border. In the morning, after gassing up, I headed straight west along the Rainy River, which separates Minnesota from Canada, and which for me separated one life from another. The land was mostly wilderness. Here and there I passed a motel or bait shop, but otherwise the country unfolded in great sweeps of pine and birch and sumac. Though it was still August, the air already had the smell of October, football season, piles of yellow-red leaves, everything crisp and clean. I remember a huge blue sky. Off to my right was the Rainy River, wide as a lake in places, and beyond the Rainy River was Canada.

For a while I just drove, not aiming at anything, then in the late morning I began looking for a place to lie low for a day or two. I was exhausted, and scared sick, and around noon I pulled into an old fishing resort called the Tip Top Lodge. Actually it was not a lodge at all, just eight or nine tiny yellow cabins clustered on a peninsula that jutted northward into the Rainy River. The place was in sorry shape. There was a dangerous wooden dock, an old minnow tank, a flimsy tar paper boathouse along the shore. The main building, which stood in a cluster of pines on high ground, seemed to lean heavily to one side, like a cripple, the roof sagging toward Canada. Briefly, I thought about turning around, just giving up, but then I got out of the car and walked up to the front porch.

The man who opened the door that day is the hero of my life. How do I say this without sounding sappy? Blurt it out — the man saved me. He offered exactly what I needed, without questions, without any words at all. He took me in. He was there at the critical time — a silent, watchful presence. Six days later, when it ended, I was unable to find a proper way to thank him, and I never have, and so, if nothing else, this story represents a small gesture of gratitude twenty years overdue.

Even after two decades I can close my eyes and return to that porch at the Tip Top Lodge. I can see the old guy staring at me. Elroy Berdahl: eighty-one years old, skinny and shrunken and mostly bald. He wore a flannel shirt and brown work pants. In one hand, I remember, he carried a green apple, a small paring knife in the other. His eyes had the bluish gray color of a razor blade, the same polished shine, and as he peered up at me I felt a strange sharpness, almost painful, a cutting sensation, as if his gaze were somehow slicing me open. In part, no doubt, it was my own sense of guilt, but even so I'm absolutely certain that the old man took one look and went right to the heart of things — a kid in trouble. When I asked for a room, Elroy made a little clicking sound with his tongue. He nodded, led me out to one of the cabins, and dropped a key in my hand. I remember smiling at him. I also remember wishing I hadn't. The old man shook his head as if to tell me it wasn't worth the bother.

"Dinner at five-thirty," he said. "You eat fish?"

"Anything," I said.   20

Elroy grunted and said, "I'll bet."

We spent six days together at the Tip Top Lodge. Just the two of us. Tourist season was over, and there were no boats on the river, and the wilderness seemed to withdraw into a great permanent stillness. Over those six days Elroy Berdahl and I took most of our meals together. In the mornings we sometimes went out on long hikes into the woods, and at night we played Scrabble or listened to records or sat reading in front of his big stone fireplace. At times I felt the awkwardness of an intruder, but Elroy accepted me into his quiet routine without fuss or ceremony. He took my presence for granted, the same way he might've sheltered a stray cat — no wasted sighs or pity — and there was never any talk about it. Just the opposite. What I remember more than anything is the man's willful, almost ferocious silence. In all that time together, all those hours, he never asked the obvious questions: Why was I there? Why alone? Why so preoccupied? If Elroy was curious about any of this, he was careful never to put it into words.

My hunch, though, is that he already knew. At least the basics. After all, it was 1968, and guys were burning draft cards, and Canada was just a boat ride away. Elroy Berdahl was no hick. His bedroom, I remember, was cluttered with books and newspapers. He killed me at the Scrabble board, barely concentrating, and on those occasions when speech was necessary he had a way of compressing large thoughts into small, cryptic packets of language. One evening, just at sunset, he pointed up at an owl circling over the violet-lighted forest to the west.

"Hey, O'Brien," he said. "There's Jesus."

The man was sharp — he didn't miss much. Those razor eyes. Now and then   25
he'd catch me staring out at the river, at the far shore, and I could almost hear the tumblers clicking in his head. Maybe I'm wrong, but I doubt it.

One thing for certain, he knew I was in desperate trouble. And he knew I couldn't talk about it. The wrong word — or even the right word — and I would've disappeared. I was wired and jittery. My skin felt too tight. After supper one evening I vomited and went back to my cabin and lay down for a few moments and then vomited again; another time, in the middle of the afternoon, I began sweating and couldn't shut it off. I went through whole days feeling dizzy with sorrow. I couldn't sleep; I couldn't lie still. At night I'd toss around in bed, half awake, half dreaming, imagining how I'd sneak down to the beach and quietly push one of the old man's boats out into the river and start paddling my way toward Canada. There were times when I thought I'd gone off the psychic edge. I couldn't tell up from down, I was just falling, and late in the night I'd lie there watching weird pictures spin through my head. Getting chased by the Border Patrol — helicopters and searchlights and barking dogs — I'd be crashing through the woods, I'd be

down on my hands and knees — people shouting out my name — the law closing in on all sides — my hometown draft board and the FBI and the Royal Canadian Mounted Police. It all seemed crazy and impossible. Twenty-one years old,
an ordinary kid with all the ordinary dreams and ambitions, and all I wanted was
to live the life I was born to — a mainstream life — I loved baseball and ham-
burgers and cherry Cokes — and now I was off on the margins of exile, leaving
my country forever, and it seemed so impossible and terrible and sad.

I'm not sure how I made it through those six days. Most of it I can't remember. On two or three afternoons, to pass some time, I helped Elroy get the place
ready for winter, sweeping down the cabins and hauling in the boats, little chores
that kept my body moving. The days were cool and bright. The nights were very
dark. One morning the old man showed me how to split and stack firewood, and
for several hours we just worked in silence out behind his house. At one point, I
remember, Elroy put down his maul and looked at me for a long time, his lips
drawn as if framing a difficult question, but then he shook his head and went
back to work. The man's self-control was amazing. He never pried. He never put
me in a position that required lies or denials. To an extent, I suppose, his reticence
was typical of that part of Minnesota, where privacy still held value, and even if
I'd been walking around with some horrible deformity — four arms and three
heads — I'm sure the old man would've talked about everything except those
extra arms and heads. Simple politeness was part of it. But even more than that, I
think, the man understood that words were insufficient. The problem had gone
beyond discussion. During that long summer I'd been over and over the various
arguments, all the pros and cons, and it was no longer a question that could be
decided by an act of pure reason. Intellect had come up against emotion. My conscience told me to run, but some irrational and powerful force was resisting, like a
weight pushing me toward the war. What it came down to, stupidly, was a sense of
shame. Hot, stupid shame. I did not want people to think badly of me. Not my
parents, not my brother and sister, not even the folks down at the Gobbler Café. I
was ashamed to be there at the Tip Top Lodge. I was ashamed of my conscience,
ashamed to be doing the right thing.

Some of this Elroy must've understood. Not the details, of course, but the
plain fact of crisis.

Although the old man never confronted me about it, there was one occasion
when he came close to forcing the whole thing out into the open. It was early
evening, and we'd just finished supper, and over coffee and dessert I asked him
about my bill, how much I owed so far. For a long while the old man squinted
down at the tablecloth.

"Well, the basic rate," he said, "is fifty bucks a night. Not counting meals. This
makes four nights, right?" 30

I nodded. I had three hundred and twelve dollars in my wallet.

Elroy kept his eyes on the tablecloth. "Now that's an on-season price. To be
fair, I suppose we should knock it down a peg or two." He leaned back in his chair.
"What's a reasonable number, you figure?"

"I don't know," I said. "Forty?"

"Forty's good. Forty a night. Then we tack on food — say another hundred? Two hundred sixty total?"

"I guess."

He raised his eyebrows. "Too much?"

"No, that's fair. It's fine. Tomorrow, though . . . I think I'd better take off tomorrow."

Elroy shrugged and began clearing the table. For a time he fussed with the dishes, whistling to himself as if the subject had been settled. After a second he slapped his hands together.

"You know what we forgot?" he said. "We forgot wages. Those odd jobs you done. What we have to do, we have to figure out what your time's worth. Your last job — how much did you pull in an hour?"

"Not enough," I said.

"A bad one?"

"Yes. Pretty bad."

Slowly then, without intending any long sermon, I told him about my days at the pig plant. It began as a straight recitation of the facts, but before I could stop myself I was talking about the blood clots and the water gun and how the smell had soaked into my skin and how I couldn't wash it away. I went on for a long time. I told him about wild hogs squealing in my dreams, the sounds of butchery, slaughterhouse sounds, and how I'd sometimes wake up with that greasy pig-stink in my throat.

When I was finished, Elroy nodded at me.

"Well, to be honest," he said, "when you first showed up here, I wondered about all that. The aroma, I mean. Smelled like you was awful damned fond of pork chops." The old man almost smiled. He made a snuffling sound, then sat down with a pencil and a piece of paper. "So what'd this crud job pay? Ten bucks an hour? Fifteen?"

"Less."

Elroy shook his head. "Let's make it fifteen. You put in twenty-five hours here, easy. That's three hundred seventy-five bucks total wages. We subtract the two hundred sixty for food and lodging, I still owe you a hundred and fifteen."

He took four fifties out of his shirt pocket and laid them on the table.

"Call it even," he said.

"No."

"Pick it up. Get yourself a haircut."

The money lay on the table for the rest of the evening. It was still there when I went back to my cabin. In the morning, though, I found an envelope tacked to my door. Inside were the four fifties and a two-word note that said EMERGENCY FUND.

The man knew.

Looking back after twenty years, I sometimes wonder if the events of that summer didn't happen in some other dimension, a place where your life exists before you've lived it, and where it goes afterward. None of it ever seemed real. During my time at the Tip Top Lodge I had the feeling that I'd slipped out of my own skin, hovering a few feet away while some poor yo-yo with my name and face tried to make his way toward a future he didn't understand and didn't want. Even now I can see myself as I was then. It's like watching an old home movie: I'm young and tan and fit. I've got hair — lots of it. I don't smoke or drink. I'm wearing faded blue jeans and a white polo shirt. I can see myself sitting on Elroy Berdahl's dock near dusk one evening, the sky a bright shimmering pink, and I'm finishing up a letter to my parents that tells what I'm about to do and why I'm doing it and how sorry I am that I'd never found the courage to talk to them about it. I ask them not to be angry. I try to explain some of my feelings, but there aren't enough words, and so I just say that it's a thing that has to be done. At the end of the letter I talk about the vacations we used to take up in this north country, at a place called Whitefish Lake, and how the scenery here reminds me of those good times. I tell them I'm fine. I tell them I'll write again from Winnipeg or Montreal or wherever I end up.

On my last full day, the sixth day, the old man took me out fishing on the Rainy 55 River. The afternoon was sunny and cold. A stiff breeze came in from the north, and I remember how the little fourteen-foot boat made sharp rocking motions as we pushed off from the dock. The current was fast. All around us, I remember, there was a vastness to the world, an unpeopled rawness, just the trees and the sky and the water reaching out toward nowhere. The air had the brittle scent of October.

For ten or fifteen minutes Elroy held a course upstream, the river choppy and silver-gray, then he turned straight north and put the engine on full throttle. I felt the bow lift beneath me. I remember the wind in my ears, the sound of the old outboard Evinrude. For a time I didn't pay attention to anything, just feeling the cold spray against my face, but then it occurred to me that at some point we must've passed into Canadian waters, across that dotted line between two different worlds, and I remember a sudden tightness in my chest as I looked up and watched the far shore come at me. This wasn't a daydream. It was tangible and real. As we came in toward land, Elroy cut the engine, letting the boat fishtail lightly about twenty yards off shore. The old man didn't look at me or speak. Bending down, he opened up his tackle box and busied himself with a bobber and a piece of wire leader, humming to himself, his eyes down.

It struck me then that he must've planned it. I'll never be certain, of course, but I think he meant to bring me up against the realities, to guide me across the river and to take me to the edge and to stand a kind of vigil as I chose a life for myself.

I remember staring at the old man, then at my hands, then at Canada. The shoreline was dense with brush and timber. I could see tiny red berries on the bushes. I could see a squirrel up in one of the birch trees, a big crow looking at me from a boulder along the river. That close — twenty yards — and I could see the delicate latticework of the leaves, the texture of the soil, the browned needles beneath the pines, the configurations of geology and human history. Twenty yards. I could've done it. I could've jumped and started swimming for my life. Inside me, in my chest, I felt a terrible squeezing pressure. Even now, as I write this, I can still feel that tightness. And I want you to feel it — the wind coming off the river, the waves, the silence, the wooded frontier. You're at the bow of a boat on the Rainy River. You're twenty-one years old, you're scared, and there's a hard squeezing pressure in your chest.

What would you do?

Would you jump? Would you feel pity for yourself? Would you think about 60
your family and your childhood and your dreams and all you're leaving behind? Would it hurt? Would it feel like dying? Would you cry, as I did?

I tried to swallow it back. I tried to smile, except I was crying.

Now, perhaps, you can understand why I've never told this story before. It's not just the embarrassment of tears. That's part of it, no doubt, but what embarrasses me much more, and always will, is the paralysis that took my heart. A moral freeze: I couldn't decide, I couldn't act, I couldn't comport myself with even a pretense of modest human dignity.

All I could do was cry. Quietly, not bawling, just the chest-chokes.

At the rear of the boat Elroy Berdahl pretended not to notice. He held a fishing rod in his hands, his head bowed to hide his eyes. He kept humming a soft, monotonous little tune. Everywhere, it seemed, in the trees and water and sky, a great worldwide sadness came pressing down on me, a crushing sorrow, sorrow like I had never known it before. And what was so sad, I realized, was that Canada had become a pitiful fantasy. Silly and hopeless. It was no longer a possibility. Right then, with the shore so close, I understood that I would not do what I should do. I would not swim away from my hometown and my country and my life. I would not be brave. That old image of myself as a hero, as a man of conscience and courage, all that was just a threadbare pipe dream. Bobbing there on the Rainy River, looking back at the Minnesota shore, I felt a sudden swell of helplessness come over me, a drowning sensation, as if I had toppled overboard and was being swept away by the silver waves. Chunks of my own history flashed by. I saw a seven-year-old boy in a white cowboy hat and a Lone Ranger mask and a pair of holstered six-shooters; I saw a twelve-year-old Little League shortstop pivoting to turn a double play; I saw a sixteen-year-old kid decked out for his first prom, looking spiffy in a white tux and a black bow tie, his hair cut short and flat, his shoes freshly polished. My whole life seemed to spill out into the river, swirling away from me, everything I had ever been or ever wanted to be. I couldn't get my breath; I couldn't stay afloat; I couldn't tell which way to swim. A hallucination, I suppose, but it was as real as anything I would ever feel. I saw my parents calling to me from the far shoreline. I saw my brother and sister, all the townsfolk, the mayor and the entire Chamber of Commerce and all my old teachers and girlfriends and high school buddies. Like some weird sporting event: everybody screaming from the sidelines, rooting me on — a loud stadium roar. Hotdogs and popcorn — stadium smells, stadium heat. A squad of cheerleaders did cartwheels along the banks of the Rainy River; they had megaphones and pompoms and smooth brown thighs. The crowd swayed left and right. A marching band played fight songs. All my aunts and uncles were there, and Abraham Lincoln, and Saint George, and a nine-year-old girl named Linda who had died of a brain tumor back in fifth grade, and several members of the United States Senate, and a blind poet scribbling notes, and LBJ, and Huck Finn, and Abbie Hoffman, and all the dead soldiers back from the grave, and the many thousands who were later to die — villagers with terrible burns, little kids without arms or legs — yes, and the Joint Chiefs of Staff were there, and a couple of popes, and a first lieutenant named Jimmy Cross, and the last surviving veteran of the American Civil War, and Jane Fonda dressed up as Barbarella, and an old man sprawled beside a pigpen, and my grandfather, and Gary Cooper, and a kind-faced woman carrying an umbrella and a copy of Plato's *Republic*, and a million ferocious citizens waving flags of all shapes and colors — people in hard hats, people in headbands — they were all whooping and chanting and urging me toward one shore or the other. I saw faces from my distant past and distant future. My wife was there. My unborn daughter waved at me, and my two sons hopped up and down, and a drill sergeant named Blyton sneered and shot up a finger and shook his head. There was a choir in bright purple robes. There was a cabbie from the Bronx. There was a slim young man I would one day kill with a hand grenade along a red clay trail outside the village of My Khe.

The little aluminum boat rocked softly beneath me. There was the wind and 65
the sky.

I tried to will myself overboard.

I gripped the edge of the boat and leaned forward and thought, *Now.*

I did try. It just wasn't possible.

All those eyes on me — the town, the whole universe — and I couldn't risk the embarrassment. It was as if there were an audience to my life, that swirl of faces along the river, and in my head I could hear people screaming at me. Traitor! they yelled. Turncoat! . . . . I felt myself blush. I couldn't tolerate it. I couldn't endure the mockery, or the disgrace, or the patriotic ridicule. Even in my imagination, the shore just twenty yards away, I couldn't make myself be brave. It had nothing to do with morality. Embarrassment, that's all it was.

And right then I submitted. 70

I would go to the war — I would kill and maybe die — because I was embarrassed not to.

That was the sad thing. And so I sat in the bow of the boat and cried.

It was loud now. Loud, hard crying.

Elroy Berdahl remained quiet. He kept fishing. He worked his line with the tips of his fingers, patiently, squinting out at his red and white bobber on the Rainy River. His eyes were flat and impassive. He didn't speak. He was simply there, like the river and the late-summer sun. And yet by his presence, his mute watchfulness, he made it real. He was the true audience. He was a witness, like God, or like the gods, who look on in absolute silence as we live our lives, as we make our choices or fail to make them.

"Ain't biting," he said. 75

Then after a time the old man pulled in his line and turned the boat back toward Minnesota.

I don't remember saying goodbye. That last night we had dinner together, and I went to bed early, and in the morning Elroy fixed breakfast for me. When I told him I'd be leaving, the old man nodded as if he already knew. He looked down at the table and smiled.

At some point later in the morning it's possible that we shook hands — I just don't remember — but I do know that by the time I'd finished packing the old man had disappeared. Around noon, when I took my suitcase out to the car, I noticed that his old black pickup truck was no longer parked in front of the house. I went inside and waited for a while, but I felt a bone certainty that he wouldn't be back. In a way, I thought, it was appropriate. I washed up the breakfast dishes, left his two hundred dollars on the kitchen counter, got into the car, and drove south toward home.

The day was cloudy. I passed through towns with familiar names, through the pine forests and down to the prairie, and then to Vietnam, where I was a soldier, and then home again. I survived, but it's not a happy ending. I was a coward. I went to the war.

Exploring the Text

1. What is the rhetorical effect of the first seven sentences? Based on the opening, what were your expectations of the story to follow?
2. This is a fictional story in which Tim O'Brien has used himself — or a character by the same name — as the protagonist. Describe how you determine which details are factual and which are imaginative. What is the effect of mixing fact and fiction?
3. Reread the questions in paragraph 2. Are they rhetorical? What purpose do they serve? Could we ask similar questions about events today?
4. What is the narrator's conflict (para. 9)? How does this conflict relate to the theme of this chapter?
5. Why does O'Brien address the reader directly in paragraphs 58–60? How would you answer his questions?
6. Identify the rhetorical strategies O'Brien uses in paragraph 64. What are the effects of these strategies in this long paragraph?
7. What is the effect of collapsing time in the final paragraph? What is the rhetorical effect of the irony in this paragraph?
8. If you have read *The Adventures of Huckleberry Finn* by Mark Twain, compare Huck's conflict about doing what he has been taught is "the right thing" — turning

Jim in — with O'Brien's statement at the end of paragraph 27. How are the situations of the two protagonists similar?

Conversation with an American Writer
(poetry)

YEVGENY YEVTUSHENKO

Yevgeny Yevtushenko was born in 1933 in Russia, then part of the Soviet Union, and became one of its most outspoken writers. His poem "Babi Yar" (1962) deals with a mass murder at a ravine where in 1941 Nazis killed tens of thousands of Jews during the German occupation of Russia. Much of Yevtushenko's work criticizes governmental limitations on personal freedom and discusses the effects of censorship. He traveled and lectured in the United States in the early 1960s, and his work was popular on college campuses in the 1960s and 1970s. Later, Yevtushenko embraced environmental concerns. He has taught in the United States at the University of Oklahoma and at Queens College in New York City. He wrote the following poem in response to praise that Western writers bestowed on him for his heroic political voice.

"You have courage,"
                    they tell me.
It's not true.
                    I was never courageous.
I simply felt it unbecoming   5
to stoop to the cowardice of my colleagues.

I've shaken no foundations.
I simply mocked at pretense
                              and inflation.
Wrote articles.   10
              Scribbled no denunciations.
And tried to speak all
                      on my mind.
Yes,
    I defended men of talent,   15
branding the hacks,
                    the would-be writers.
But this, in general, we should always do;
and yet they keep stressing my courage.
Oh, our descendants will burn with bitter shame   20
to remember, when punishing vile acts,

that most peculiar
            time,
                    when
plain honesty   25
            was labeled "courage" . . .

Exploring the Text

1. Why does Yevgeny Yevtushenko deny the words of praise he quotes in the first line?
2. What are some of the actions Yevtushenko offers as examples of honesty?
3. What distinction does the poem make between courage and honesty?
4. Does the speaker of the poem understate the importance of his actions? Explain.
5. Is the poem optimistic or pessimistic about the future? Explain.
6. What does the poem suggest about honesty and courage as political values?
7. How does Yevtushenko's view of courage compare with Tim O'Brien's (p. 961)?

Guernica (painting)

PABLO PICASSO

Widely regarded as the twentieth century's most respected and influential painter, Pablo Picasso (1881–1973) painted *Guernica*, an eleven-foot-tall, twenty-six-foot-wide mural in 1937. It was his response to the bombing of the Basque capital in the Spanish civil war. The bombing had been carried out by Nazis at the behest of Francisco Franco, who went on to rule Spain as dictator from 1939 to 1975. Thousands of people in Guernica were killed or wounded, and the town was destroyed. The painting is housed in the Museo Nacional Centro de Arte Reina Sofía in Madrid.

Exploring the Text

1. Look carefully at the elements of *Guernica*, specifically the burning woman, the horse, the warrior with the broken sword, the crying woman with the child, and the bull. How does each element contribute to the painting's theme — the apocalyptic horrors of war?
2. Discuss the style of *Guernica*. If you have studied art history, you may know that Picasso was a prime practitioner of Cubist fragmentation. How does such a method serve the meaning of this painting?
3. In the painting, Pablo Picasso uses only black, white, and gray. What is the effect of the absence of color?
4. Picasso once said, "Painting is not made to decorate apartments. It is an instrument for offensive and defensive war against the enemy." How does *Guernica*

exemplify this statement? What, if anything, has replaced fine art as a political statement in the post-Picasso world?

5. How does the painting appeal to ethos, logos, and pathos?

6. A tapestry of *Guernica* hangs at the United Nations building in New York City. What is its rhetorical effect as a mural in this setting?

Depictions of Guernica

In February 2003, Colin Powell, then U.S. secretary of state, delivered a speech at the United Nations. During Powell's talk, a tapestry depicting Pablo Picasso's *Guernica* was covered so that the audience would not see it. U.N. officials claim they covered the image to provide a neutral backdrop for television camera crews. Two national magazines that address political and cultural issues, the *New Yorker* and *Harper's*, responded to that event with their covers.

Exploring the Text

1. Why would authorities at the United Nations decide to cover *Guernica* during a political speech? What rhetorical purpose would covering it serve?

2. Which of the classic appeals do both *Harper's* and the *New Yorker* use in their covers?

3. What assumptions about their audiences — their readers' familiarity with history and art, their awareness of current events — do both publications evidently hold?

4. From these two covers, what inferences can you make about the political attitudes of each magazine? Explain.

5. Considering these covers as examples of visual rhetoric, what claim do they make?

6. Compare and contrast the two covers. How does each cover depict the draping? What images from the original does each cover show? Is one more powerful than the other? Explain.

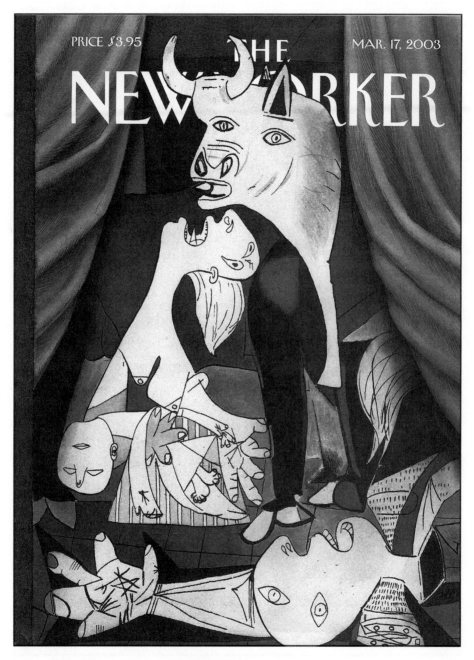

Cover of the *New Yorker*, March 17, 2003

HARPER'S

HARPER'S MAGAZINE / APRIL 2003 $5.95

CAUSE FOR DISSENT
Ten Questions for the Bush Regime
By *Lewis H. Lapham*

◆

NO MORE UNTO THE BREACH
Part II: The Unconquerable World
By *Jonathan Schell*

A HOUSE UNDIVIDED
Andrea Palladio and the Science of Happiness
By *Dave Hickey*

AJAX IS ALL ABOUT ATTACK
A story by Jim Shepard

Also: Francine Prose, Daniel Lazare

◆

Cover of *Harper's*, April 2003

Conversation

Focus on Colonialism

The following five texts comment directly or indirectly on colonialism:

Sources
1. **George Orwell**, *Shooting an Elephant*
2. **Chinua Achebe**, *The Empire Fights Back*
3. **Eavan Boland**, *In Which the Ancient History I Learn Is Not My Own* (poetry)
4. **National Park Service**, *Christiansted: Official Map and Guide* (travel brochure)
5. **Bombay Company**, *What Part of You Lives in Bombay?* (advertisement)

After you have read, studied, and synthesized these pieces, enter the conversation by responding to one of the suggested prompts on page 995.

1. *Shooting an Elephant*

GEORGE ORWELL

In the following narrative, autobiographical essay written in 1936, George Orwell talks about his experience in British-occupied Burma in the 1920s.

In Moulmein, in Lower Burma, I was hated by large numbers of people — the only time in my life that I have been important enough for this to happen to me. I was sub-divisional police officer of the town, and in an aimless, petty kind of way anti-European feeling was very bitter. No one had the guts to raise a riot, but if a European woman went through the bazaars alone somebody would probably spit betel juice over her dress. As a police officer I was an obvious target and was baited whenever it seemed safe to do so. When a nimble Burman tripped me up on the football field and the referee (another Burman) looked the other way, the crowd yelled with hideous laughter. This happened more than once. In the end the sneering yellow faces of young men that met me everywhere, the insults hooted after me when I was at a safe distance, got badly on my nerves. The young Buddhist priests were the worst of all. There were several thousands of them in the town and none of them seemed to have anything to do except stand on street corners and jeer at Europeans.

All this was perplexing and upsetting. For at that time I had already made up my mind that imperialism was an evil thing and the sooner I chucked up my job and got out of it the better. Theoretically — and secretly, of course — I was all for the Burmese and all against their oppressors, the British. As for the job I was doing, I hated it more bitterly than I can perhaps make clear. In a job like that you see the dirty work of Empire at close quarters. The wretched prisoners huddling in the stinking cages of the lock-ups, the grey, cowed faces of the long-term convicts, the scarred buttocks of the men who had been flogged with bamboos — all these oppressed me with an intolerable sense of guilt. But I could get nothing into perspective. I was young and ill-educated and I had had to think out my problems in the utter silence that is imposed on every Englishman in the East. I did not even know that the British Empire is dying, still less did I know that it is a great deal better than the younger empires that are going to supplant it. All I knew was that I was stuck between my hatred of the empire I served and my rage against the evil-spirited little beasts who tried to make my job impossible. With one part of my mind I thought of the British Raj as an unbreakable tyranny, as something clamped down, *in saecula saeculorum*[1] upon the will of prostrate peoples; with another part I thought that the greatest joy in the world would be to drive a bayonet into a Buddhist priest's guts. Feelings like these are the normal by-products of imperialism; ask any Anglo-Indian official, if you can catch him off duty.

One day something happened which in a roundabout way was enlightening. It was a tiny incident in itself, but it gave me a better glimpse than I had had before of the real nature of imperialism — the real motives for which despotic governments act. Early one morning the sub-inspector at a police station the other end of the town rang me up on the phone and said that an elephant was ravaging the bazaar. Would I please come and do something about it? I did not know what I could do, but I wanted to see what was happening and I got on to a pony and started out. I took my rifle, an old .44 Winchester and much too small to kill an elephant, but I thought the noise might be useful *in terrorem*.[2] Various Burmans stopped me on the way and told me about the elephant's doings. It was not, of course, a wild elephant, but a tame one which had gone "must." It had been chained up, as tame elephants always are when their attack of "must" is due, but on the previous night it had broken its chain and escaped. Its mahout, the only person who could manage it when it was in that state, had set out in pursuit, but had taken the wrong direction and was now twelve hours' journey away, and in the morning the elephant had suddenly reappeared in the town. The Burmese population had no weapons and were quite helpless against it. It had already destroyed somebody's bamboo hut, killed a cow and raided some fruit-stalls and devoured the stock; also it had met the municipal rubbish van and, when the driver jumped out and took to his heels, had turned the van over and inflicted violences upon it.

The Burmese sub-inspector and some Indian constables were waiting for me in the quarter where the elephant had been seen. It was a very poor quarter, a

---

[1] Latin, "for ever and ever." — Eds.
[2] A legal term meaning "to scare a person into complying with terms." — Eds.

labyrinth of squalid bamboo huts, thatched with palm-leaf, winding all over a steep hillside. I remember that it was a cloudy, stuffy morning at the beginning of the rains. We began questioning the people as to where the elephant had gone and, as usual, failed to get any definite information. That is invariably the case in the East; a story always sounds clear enough at a distance, but the nearer you get to the scene of events the vaguer it becomes. Some of the people said that the elephant had gone in one direction, some said that he had gone in another, some professed not even to have heard of any elephant. I had almost made up my mind that the whole story was a pack of lies, when we heard yells a little distance away. There was a loud, scandalized cry of "Go away, child! Go away this instant!" and an old woman with a switch in her hand came round the corner of a hut, violently shooing away a crowd of naked children. Some more women followed, clicking their tongues and exclaiming; evidently there was something that the children ought not to have seen. I rounded the hut and saw a man's dead body sprawling in the mud. He was an Indian, a black Dravidian coolie, almost naked, and he could not have been dead many minutes. The people said that the elephant had come suddenly upon him round the corner of the hut, caught him with its trunk, put its foot on his back and ground him into the earth. This was the rainy season and the ground was soft, and his face had scored a trench a foot deep and a couple of yards long. He was lying on his belly with arms crucified and head sharply twisted to one side. His face was coated with mud, the eyes wide open, the teeth bared and grinning with an expression of unendurable agony. (Never tell me, by the way, that the dead look peaceful. Most of the corpses I have seen looked devilish.) The friction of the great beast's foot had stripped the skin from his back as neatly as one skins a rabbit. As soon as I saw the dead man I sent an orderly to a friend's house nearby to borrow an elephant rifle. I had already sent back the pony, not wanting it to go mad with fright and throw me if it smelt the elephant.

The orderly came back in a few minutes with a rifle and five cartridges, and meanwhile some Burmans had arrived and told us that the elephant was in the paddy fields below, only a few hundred yards away. As I started forward practically the whole population of the quarter flocked out of the houses and followed me. They had seen the rifle and were all shouting excitedly that I was going to shoot the elephant. They had not shown much interest in the elephant when he was merely ravaging their homes, but it was different now that he was going to be shot. It was a bit of fun to them, as it would be to an English crowd; besides they wanted the meat. It made me vaguely uneasy. I had no intention of shooting the elephant — I had merely sent for the rifle to defend myself if necessary — and it is always unnerving to have a crowd following you. I marched down the hill, looking and feeling a fool, with the rifle over my shoulder and an ever-growing army of people jostling at my heels. At the bottom, when you got away from the huts, there was a metalled road and beyond that a miry waste of paddy fields a thousand yards across, not yet ploughed but soggy from the first rains and dotted with coarse grass. The elephant was standing eight yards from the road, his left side towards us. He took not the slightest notice of the crowd's approach. He was

5

tearing up bunches of grass, beating them against his knees to clean them and stuffing them into his mouth.

I had halted on the road. As soon as I saw the elephant I knew with perfect certainty that I ought not to shoot him. It is a serious matter to shoot a working elephant — it is comparable to destroying a huge and costly piece of machinery — and obviously one ought not to do it if it can possibly be avoided. And at that distance, peacefully eating, the elephant looked no more dangerous than a cow. I thought then and I think now that his attack of "must" was already passing off; in which case he would merely wander harmlessly about until the mahout came back and caught him. Moreover, I did not in the least want to shoot him. I decided that I would watch him for a little while to make sure that he did not turn savage again, and then go home.

But at that moment I glanced round at the crowd that had followed me. It was an immense crowd, two thousand at the least and growing every minute. It blocked the road for a long distance on either side. I looked at the sea of yellow faces above the garish clothes — faces all happy and excited over this bit of fun, all certain that the elephant was going to be shot. They were watching me as they would watch a conjurer about to perform a trick. They did not like me, but with the magical rifle in my hands I was momentarily worth watching. And suddenly I realized that I should have to shoot the elephant after all. The people expected it of me and I had got to do it; I could feel their two thousand wills pressing me forward, irresistibly. And it was at this moment, as I stood there with the rifle in my hands, that I first grasped the hollowness, the futility of the white man's dominion in the East. Here was I, the white man with his gun, standing in front of the unarmed native crowd — seemingly the leading actor of the piece; but in reality I was only an absurd puppet pushed to and fro by the will of those yellow faces behind. I perceived in this moment that when the white man turns tyrant it is his own freedom that he destroys. He becomes a sort of hollow, posing dummy, the conventionalized figure of a sahib.[3] For it is the condition of his rule that he shall spend his life in trying to impress the "natives," and so in every crisis he has got to do what the "natives" expect of him. He wears a mask, and his face grows to fit it. I had got to shoot the elephant. I had committed myself to doing it when I sent for the rifle. A sahib has got to act like a sahib; he has got to appear resolute, to know his own mind and do definite things. To come all that way, rifle in hand, with two thousand people marching at my heels, and then to trail feebly away, having done nothing — no, that was impossible. The crowd would laugh at me. And my whole life, every white man's life in the East, was one long struggle not to be laughed at.

But I did not want to shoot the elephant. I watched him beating his bunch of grass against his knees, with that preoccupied grandmotherly air that elephants have. It seemed to me that it would be murder to shoot him. At that age I was not

---

[3]In colonial India, the title used to address a European. — Eds.

squeamish about killing animals, but I had never shot an elephant and never wanted to. (Somehow it always seems worse to kill a *large* animal.) Besides, there was the beast's owner to be considered. Alive, the elephant was worth at least a hundred pounds; dead, he would only be worth the value of his tusks, five pounds, possibly. But I had got to act quickly. I turned to some experienced-looking Burmans who had been there when we arrived, and asked them how the elephant had been behaving. They all said the same thing: he took no notice of you if you left him alone, but he might charge if you went too close to him.

It was perfectly clear to me what I ought to do. I ought to walk up to within, say, twenty-five yards of the elephant and test his behavior. If he charged, I could shoot; if he took no notice of me, it would be safe to leave him until the mahout came back. But also I knew that I was going to do no such thing. I was a poor shot with a rifle and the ground was soft mud into which one would sink at every step. If the elephant charged and I missed him, I should have about as much chance as a toad under a steam-roller. But even then I was not thinking particularly of my own skin, only of the watchful yellow faces behind. For at that moment, with the crowd watching me, I was not afraid in the ordinary sense, as I would have been if I had been alone. A white man mustn't be frightened in front of "natives"; and so, in general, he isn't frightened. The sole thought in my mind was that if anything went wrong those two thousand Burmans would see me pursued, caught, trampled on and reduced to a grinning corpse like that Indian up the hill. And if that happened it was quite probable that some of them would laugh. That would never do. There was only one alternative. I shoved the cartridges into the magazine and lay down on the road to get a better aim.

The crowd grew very still, and a deep, low, happy sigh, as of people who see   10
the theatre curtain go up at last, breathed from innumerable throats. They were going to have their bit of fun after all. The rifle was a beautiful German thing with cross-hair sights. I did not then know that in shooting an elephant one would shoot to cut an imaginary bar running from ear-hole to ear-hole. I ought, therefore, as the elephant was sideways on, to have aimed straight at his ear-hole; actually I aimed several inches in front of this, thinking the brain would be further forward.

When I pulled the trigger I did not hear the bang or feel the kick — one never does when a shot goes home — but I heard the devilish roar of glee that went up from the crowd. In that instant, in too short a time, one would have thought, even for the bullet to get there, a mysterious, terrible change had come over the elephant. He neither stirred nor fell, but every line of his body had altered. He looked suddenly stricken, shrunken, immensely old, as though the frightful impact of the bullet had paralysed him without knocking him down. At last, after what seemed a long time — it might have been five seconds, I dare say — he sagged flabbily to his knees. His mouth slobbered. An enormous senility seemed to have settled upon him. One could have imagined him thousands of years old. I fired again into the same spot. At the second shot he did not collapse but climbed with desperate slowness to his feet and stood weakly upright, with legs sagging and head drooping. I fired a third time. That was the shot that did for him. You could see the agony of it jolt his whole body and knock the last remnant of strength from his legs. But in falling he seemed for a moment to rise, for as his hind legs collapsed beneath him he seemed to tower upward like a huge rock toppling, his trunk reaching skywards like a tree. He trumpeted, for the first and only time. And then down he came, his belly towards me, with a crash that seemed to shake the ground even where I lay.

I got up. The Burmans were already racing past me across the mud. It was obvious that the elephant would never rise again, but he was not dead. He was breathing very rhythmically with long rattling gasps, his great mound of a side painfully rising and falling. His mouth was wide open — I could see far down into caverns of pale pink throat. I waited a long time for him to die, but his breathing did not weaken. Finally I fired my two remaining shots into the spot where I thought his heart must be. The thick blood welled out of him like red velvet, but still he did not die. His body did not even jerk when the shots hit him, the tortured breathing continued without a pause. He was dying, very slowly and in great agony, but in some world remote from me where not even a bullet could damage him further. I felt that I had got to put an end to that dreadful noise. It seemed dreadful to see the great beast lying there, powerless to move and yet powerless to die, and not even to be able to finish him. I sent back for my small rifle and poured shot after shot into his heart and down his throat. They seemed to make no impression. The tortured gasps continued as steadily as the ticking of a clock.

In the end I could not stand it any longer and went away. I heard later that it took him half an hour to die. Burmans were bringing dahs and baskets even before I left, and I was told they had stripped his body almost to the bones by the afternoon.

Afterwards, of course, there were endless discussions about the shooting of the elephant. The owner was furious, but he was only an Indian and could do nothing. Besides, legally I had done the right thing, for a mad elephant has to be killed, like a mad dog, if its owner fails to control it. Among the Europeans opinion was divided. The older men said I was right, the younger men said it was a damn shame to shoot an elephant for killing a coolie,[4] because an elephant was worth more than any damn Coringhee coolie. And afterwards I was very glad that the coolie had been killed; it put me legally in the right and it gave me a sufficient pretext for shooting the elephant. I often wondered whether any of the others grasped that I had done it solely to avoid looking a fool.

---

[4]An unskilled Indian laborer. — Eds.

Questions

1. What is George Orwell's attitude toward imperialism, toward the native peoples, and toward his own position in Burma? Give evidence supporting your claim.
2. In paragraph 3, Orwell's narrator says that the incident of shooting the elephant "in a roundabout way was enlightening. It was a tiny incident in itself, but it gave me a better glimpse than I had had before of the real nature of imperialism — the real motives for which despotic governments act." What does he see as "the real nature of imperialism," and how does this incident reveal that nature?
3. In paragraph 6, the narrator says, "As soon as I saw the elephant I knew with perfect certainty that I ought not to shoot him." Why then does he decide to shoot it? Cite specific factors that influence his decision.
4. Explain the opinions of the Europeans about the killing of the elephant, as presented in the final paragraph. At the conclusion of the essay, how do you feel toward Orwell?
5. Describe Orwell's position concerning human motives. Support or challenge his position using evidence drawn from your readings, observations, and experiences.

2. *The Empire Fights Back*

Chinua Achebe

In the following excerpt from his book *Home and Exile*, Nigerian writer Chinua Achebe looks at British impressions of Africa as delivered in literature.

I will begin . . . with a question: what did I do with my experience of classroom rebellion over *Mister Johnson*?[1] Anyone familiar with the gossip in African literature may have heard that it was that book that made me decide to write. I am not even sure that I have not said it somewhere myself, in one of those occasional seizures of expansive ambition we have to sum up the whole world in a single, neat metaphor. Of course we need such moments now and again to stir things up in our lives. But other times we must be content to stay modest and level-headed, more factual. What *Mister Johnson* did do for me was not to change my course in life and turn me from something else into a writer; I was born that way. But it did open my eyes to the fact that my home was under attack and that my home was not merely a house or a town but, more importantly, an awakening story in whose ambience my own existence had first begun to assemble its fragments into a coherence and meaning; the story I had begun to learn consciously the moment I descended from the lorry that brought me to my father's house in Ogidi, the story

---

[1]A 1939 novel by the writer Joyce Cary, who had served as an administrator and soldier in Nigeria, Achebe's country. — Eds.

that, seventeen years later at the university, I still had only a sketchy, tantalizing knowledge of, and over which even today, decades later, I still do not have sufficient mastery, but about which I can say one thing: that it is not the same story Joyce Cary intended me to have.

For me there are three reasons for becoming a writer. The first is that you have an overpowering urge to tell a story. The second, that you have intimations of a unique story waiting to come out. And the third, which you learn in the process of becoming, is that you consider the whole project worth the considerable trouble — I have sometimes called it terms of imprisonment — you will have to endure to bring it to fruition. For me, those three factors were present, and would have been present had Joyce Cary never been born, or set foot in Nigeria. History, however, had contrived a crossing of our paths, and such crossings may sometimes leave their footmarks, faint or loud, on memory. And if they do, they should be acknowledged.

Another question. Was there any way Joyce Cary could have written a Nigerian novel that we Nigerian students could have accepted as our story? My answer, in retrospect, must be: not likely. And my reason would not be the obvious fact that Cary was a European, but rather because he was the product of a tradition of presenting Africa that he had absorbed at school and Sunday school, in magazines and in British society in general, at the end of the nineteenth century. In theory, a good writer might outgrow these influences, but Cary did not.

In their Introduction to *The Africa That Never Was*, Hammond and Jablow tell us that the large number of writers they studied "were not, and could not be, selected for literary merit" and that there were many more "bad" writers than "good" ones in their sample. (Which, I dare say, is hardly surprising.) They then identify [Joseph] Conrad, Cary, [Graham] Greene and Huxley (not Aldous but Elspeth) among the better writers (which is still OK by me — it only tells us how bad the bad ones must be). But when they proceed to praise these four for their handling of Africa in their books, I don't quite know what to make of it:

> The better writers, such as Conrad, Cary, Greene and Huxley . . . use the conventions of the tradition with skill and subtlety. Each of them has an unmistakably individual style in which he or she selectively exploits the conventions, without allowing the writing to become overwhelmed by them. They all have more to say about Africa than the merely conventional clichés, along with the talent to say it well.[2]

I suppose we can all differ as to the exact point where good writing becomes overwhelmed by racial cliché. But overwhelmed or merely undermined, literature is always badly served when an author's artistic insight yields place to stereotype

5

---

[2]Dorothy Hammond and Alta Jablow, *The Africa That Never Was* (Prospect Heights, Ill.: Waveland Press, 1992), p. 9.

and malice. And it becomes doubly offensive when such a work is arrogantly proffered to you as your story. Some people may wonder if, perhaps, we were not too touchy, if we were not oversensitive. We really were not. And I have a somewhat unusual reason for saying so.

Although my classmates and I would not have known it at the time, the London publishing house of Methuen had brought out the year before, in 1951, a little book titled simply *West Africa*. Its author, F. J. Pedler, was a highly respected public servant in Britain, with considerable experience of West Africa. Although the book was not entirely free of the stereotypes of contemporary British colonial writing, it was in some ways remarkably advanced for its time, and even for today. One small example will suffice. "It is misleading," Mr. Pedler wrote, "when Europeans talk of Africans buying a wife."[3] Although he did not mention Joyce Cary by name it is inconceivable that he would not have been aware of him or of his much celebrated novel *Mister Johnson*, in which that very stereotype was exploited for all it was worth in the episode in which Johnson, after much haggling, buys himself a local girl, Bamu, as wife.

But what I find truly remarkable about Pedler's book is the prominence he gave to, and the faith he had in, African literature that was not even in existence yet: "A country's novels reveal its social condition. West Africa has no full-length novels, but a few short stories may serve the purpose. We quote from two recent publications which show how educated West Africans themselves describe some of the features of social life in their own country." Pedler then proceeded to summarize for his reader two short stories published in a magazine in 1945 in the British colony of the Gold Coast. He devoted almost three pages of his short book to this matter and then concluded as follows: "Here is a dramatic treatment of a contemporary social phenomenon which leaves one with the hope that more West Africans may enter the field of authorship and give us authentic stories of the lives of their own people."[4]

These brief quotations speak volumes to us on the issue of peoples and their stories. We should note Pedler's phrases: West Africans themselves; their own country; authentic stories; of their own people. Without calling any names this extraordinary Englishman seemed to be engaged in a running argument against an age-old practice: the colonization of one people's story by another. In sidestepping Joyce Cary and all the other high-profile practitioners of this brand of writing and going, in search of authenticity, to two unpretentious short stories written by two completely unknown West African authors whose names did not ring any bell at all, Pedler was putting himself decisively and prophetically on the side of the right of a people to take back their own narrative. And because he was British, and because we, the students at Ibadan, did not even know of him, nor he

---

[3]F. J. Pedler, *West Africa* (London: Methuen & Co., 1951), p. 32.
[4]Both quotes from Pedler, *West Africa*, p. 49; 50.

presumably of us, our little rebellion in class one year after his book can, in retrospect, assume the status of a genuine, disinterested service to literature, and transcend the troubling impression it might otherwise easily create, of a white/black, British/Nigerian divide.

Incidentally Pedler's prayer for West African novels was instantly answered. There was already in the works, as we now know, a startling literary concoction from the pen of a Nigerian coppersmith, Amos Tutuola, which Faber would publish in 1952. It may not have been the social realism which F. J. Pedler had presumably hoped for but an odyssey in peculiar English, which roamed about from realism to magic and back again, as in old Africa. But no matter, *The Palm-Wine Drinkard* opened the floodgates to modern West African writing. Hot on its heels came another Nigerian, Cyprian Ekwensi, with *People of the City*; Camara Laye of Guinea with *L'Enfant Noir*, my *Things Fall Apart*; Mongo Beti of Cameroon and his countryman, Ferdinand Oyono, with *Poor Christ of Bomba* and *Houseboy*, respectively; Cheikh Hamidou Kane of Senegal with *Ambiguous Adventure*.

Looking back now on that incredible 1950s decade and all the intersecting events I have been describing, each of which seemed at first sight to be about its own separate little errand but then chanced upon these others on a large, open space such as is used to hold a big market once in eight days and abandoned again to a profound and watchful emptiness till another market-day — looking back on all this, it does become easy to indulge a temptation to see History as mindful, purposeful; and to see the design behind this particular summons and rendezvous as the signal at long last to end Europe's imposition of a derogatory narrative upon Africa, a narrative designed to call African humanity into question.

As we have seen, Captain John Lok's voyage to West Africa in 1561 provided an early model of what would become a powerful and enduring tradition. One of his men had described the Negroes as "a people of beastly living, without a God, laws, religion."[5] Three hundred and fifty years later we find that this model, like the Energizer Bunny, is still running strong, beating away on its tin drum. "Unhuman" was how Joyce Cary, in the early part of our own century, saw his African dancers. One generation before him, Joseph Conrad had created a memorable actor/narrator who could be greatly troubled by the mere thought of his Africans being human, like himself: "Well, you know, that was the worst of it — this suspicion of their not being inhuman."[6]

Questions

1. What did Chinua Achebe learn from *Mister Johnson*?
2. According to Achebe, what are the three reasons for becoming a writer? Which one do you think is most important? Why?

---

[5]Hammond and Jablow, p. 20.
[6]Joseph Conrad, *Heart of Darkness* (New York: W. W. Norton, 1988), p. 37.

3. In paragraph 3, Achebe analyzes the sources of Joyce Cary's impressions of Africa. What are they? Achebe says in paragraph 3 that "a good writer might outgrow [the] influences" of prejudice. Do you agree?
4. How does Achebe's attitude toward *The Africa That Never Was* differ from his attitude toward the contemporaneous *West Africa*?
5. Among the books he lists in paragraph 9, Achebe includes one of his own, *Things Fall Apart*. Achebe took the title from a line in a poem by the Irish poet W. B. Yeats. Explain the significance of this.
6. Read paragraph 10 carefully, noting that it is one sentence. What statement does Achebe make there about the "derogatory narrative"? Paraphrase his thesis.

3. *In Which the Ancient History I Learn Is Not My Own* (poetry)

EAVAN BOLAND

In the following poem, Irish poet Eavan Boland examines national history and identity.

The linen map
hung from the wall.
The linen was shiny
and cracked in places.
The cracks were darkened by grime.   5
It was fastened to the classroom wall with
a wooden batten on
a triangle of knotted cotton.

The colours
were faded out   10
so the red of Empire —
the stain of absolute possession —
the mark once made from Kashmir
to the oast-barns[1] of the Kent
coast south of us was   15
underwater coral.

Ireland was far away
and farther away
every year.
I was nearly an English child.   20

———————
[1]A kiln for drying hops or malt.

I could list the English kings.
I could name the famous battles.
I was learning to recognize
God's grace in history.

And the waters   *25*
of the Irish sea,
their shallow weave
and cross-grained blue green
had drained away
to the pale gaze   *30*
of a doll's china eyes —
a stare without recognition or memory.

We have no oracles,
no rocks or olive trees,
no sacred path to the temple   *35*
and no priestesses.
The teacher's voice had a London accent.
This was London. 1952.
It was Ancient History Class.
She put the tip   *40*

of the wooden
pointer on the map.
She tapped over ridges and dried-
out rivers and cities buried in
the sea and seascapes which   *45*
had once been land.
And stopped.
Remember this, children.

The Roman Empire was
the greatest Empire   *50*
ever known —
until our time of course —
while the Delphic Oracle
was reckoned to be
the exact centre   *55*
of the earth.

Suddenly
I wanted
to stand in front of it.

I wanted to trace over   *60*
and over the weave of my own country.
To read out names
I was close to forgetting.
Wicklow. Kilruddery. Dublin.

To ask   *65*
where exactly
was my old house?
Its brass One and Seven.
Its flight of granite steps.
Its lilac tree whose scent   *70*
stayed under your fingernails
for days.

For days —
she was saying — even months,
the ancients traveled   *75*
to the Oracle.
They brought sheep and killed them.
They brought questions about tillage and war.
They rarely left with more
than an ambiguous answer.   *80*

Questions

1. The Romans conquered Britain but did not conquer Ireland. How does knowing this affect your reading of "In Which the Ancient History I Learn Is Not My Own"?
2. In lines 17–19, the speaker says, "Ireland was far away / and farther away / every year." What does the speaker mean?
3. What does the speaker mean by "God's grace in history" (l. 24)?
4. What is ironic in line 39, "It was Ancient History Class"?
5. What is significant about the qualifier "until our time of course" in line 52?
6. What are the implications of the final stanza?
7. What point does Eavan Boland's poem make about imperialism?

4. *Christiansted: Official Map and Guide*

NATIONAL PARK SERVICE

The following U.S. National Park Service travel brochure for tourists in St. Croix, Virgin Islands, discusses the history of the island's capital, Christiansted.

Christiansted

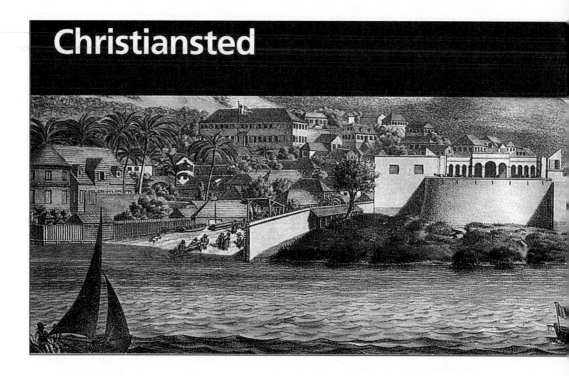

Denmark was a latecomer in the race for colonies in the New World. Columbus' voyages to the Caribbean gave Spain a monopoly in the region for well over a century. But after the English planted a colony in the Lesser Antilles in 1624, the French, the Dutch, and eventually Danes joined the scramble for empire. Seeking islands on which to cultivate sugar as well as an outlet for trade, the Danish West India & Guinea Company (a group of nobles and merchants chartered by the Crown) took possession of St. Thomas in 1672 and its neighbor St. John in 1717. Because neither island was well suited to agriculture, the company in 1733 purchased St. Croix — a larger, flatter, and more fertile island, 40 miles south — from France. Colonization of St. Croix began the next year, after troops put down a slave revolt on St. John.

For their first settlement, the Danes chose a good harbor on the northeast coast, the site of an earlier French village named Bassin. Their leader Frederick Moth was a man of some vision. Among his accomplishments were a plan for a new town, which he named Christiansted in honor of the reigning monarch, King Christian VI, and a survey of the island into plantations of 150 acres, which were offered at bargain prices to new settlers. The best land came under cultivation and dozens of sugar factories began operating. Population approached 10,000, of which nearly 9,000 were slaves imported from West Africa to work in the fields.

Christiansted National Historic Site
St. Croix, Virgin Islands

National Park Service
U.S. Department of the Interior

Even with this growth St. Croix's economy did not flourish. The planters chaffed under the restrictive trading practices of the DWI&G Company. This monopoly so burdened planters with regulations that they persuaded the king to take over the islands in 1755. Crown administration coincided with the beginning of a long period of growth for the cane sugar industry. St. Croix became the capital of the "Danish Islands of America," as they were then called, and royal governors took up residence in Christiansted. For the next century and a half, the town's fortunes were tied to St. Croix's sugar industry. Between 1760 and 1820 the economy boomed. Population rose dramatically, in part because free-trade policies and neutrality attracted settlers from other islands — hence the prevalence of English culture on this Danish island with a French name — and exports of sugar and rum soared. Capital was available, sugar prices were high, labor cheap. Planters, merchants, and traders — most of them — reaped great profits, which were reflected in the fine architecture of town and country. This golden age was, within a few decades, eclipsed by the rise of the beet sugar industry in Europe and North America. A drop in the price of cane sugar, an increase in planters' debts, drought, hurricanes, and the rising cost of labor after slavery was abolished in 1848 all contributed to economic decline. As the 19th century wore on, St. Croix became little more than a marginal sugar producer, her era of fabulous wealth now a thing of the past. When the United States purchased the Danish West

Indies in 1917, it was for the islands' strategic harbors, not their agriculture. The lovely town of Christiansted is a link to the old way of life here, with all its elegance, complexity, and contradiction.

Questions

1. The second paragraph concludes, "Population approached 10,000, of which nearly 9,000 were slaves imported from West Africa to work in the fields." Consider the diction in that sentence. What is the effect of the word *imported*? What is the effect of calling those 9,000 people "slaves" rather than "people who were enslaved"?
2. Paragraph 3 describes St. Croix as a "Danish island with a French name." Find out more about St. Croix, noting its distance from France and Denmark. What was it about this island that attracted the interest of the French and the Danish?
3. Look carefully at the portrait of Christiansted by the Danish artist Theodore C. Sabroe. What is the effect of the painting's pastoral and idyllic images?
4. Are there any unintended ironies in the brochure? What does the text reveal about the attitude and purpose of the government department that generated the brochure?

5. *What Part of You Lives in Bombay?*

BOMBAY COMPANY

The following is an advertisement for the furniture store Bombay.

Questions

1. There is little text in this ad, and one word — the name of the company and the place name — is repeated. How does the palm tree, a logo of the company, relate to the scene in the ad? How does relying more on the visual image and less on the text itself contribute to the ad's effectiveness?
2. In what ways does the visual image appeal to pathos? Consider the juxtaposition of the closed space of a chair with the open spaces, both literal and figurative, of books, a window, and light.
3. What is the impact of the written text? What images does the allusion to Bombay bring to mind? What is the impact of putting the one sentence into the form of a question? What if the text at the bottom right had read, "A part of each of us lives in Bombay"? What difference would this have made in the effectiveness of the ad?
4. Advertisements are said to have a narrative or story. What story does this ad tell or seek to tell?
5. How would you respond to the question posed by the ad?

Entering the Conversation

As you respond to the following prompts, support your argument with references to the sources in Conversation: Focus on Colonialism. For help using sources, see Chapter 3.

1. Assume you want to teach an audience of middle-school students about colonialism. In words and sentences middle-school students can understand,

explain what colonialism is, and discuss its effects in the modern world. Consider the effects on the governing nations and on the colonies. Use your knowledge of history and current events, and refer to at least two of the texts in Conversation: Focus on Colonialism.

2. What factual information could someone glean about colonialism from the texts in this chapter? Refer to all of the sources as you enumerate the facts.

3. Write an essay in which you discuss the individual's struggle against the power of the colonizer.

4. Reread carefully the St. Croix tourist brochure (p. 991) and the Bombay advertisement (p. 994). Imagine you are George Orwell (p. 979), Chinua Achebe (p. 985), or Eavan Boland (p. 989). In that writer's voice, compose an argument in response to the brochure or the ad.

5. George Orwell says of the imperialist, "He wears a mask, and his face grows to fit it." Write an essay exploring the implications of this statement.

Student Writing

Argument: Responding to a Quotation

The following prompt invites the student to enter this chapter's conversation.

> In "Shooting an Elephant" (p. 979), George Orwell observes that "when the white man turns tyrant it is his own freedom that he destroys," and that this man "wears a mask, and his face grows to fit it." Consider the implications of Orwell's observations about human nature in political situations. Then write an essay in which you support, refute, or qualify the paradoxes that Orwell presents. To support your argument, refer to the selections in this chapter as well as to your knowledge of history and current events

Consider this essay by Elisabeth Baseman, an eleventh-grade student, as a text you are studying. Analyze the rhetorical strategies Elisabeth employs.

Political Paradoxes

Elisabeth Baseman

We went to war over weapons of mass destruction in Iraq, only to discover that they didn't exist. The 2004 election was considered by many to require a selection of the lesser of two evils. The 2006 State of the Union address focused on alternative fuels, but we remain foreign oil–dependent, fuel-guzzling consumers. Why does it seem that the modern American political system is forever in a downward spiral? America is currently controlled by the rich upper class, and if power becomes too concentrated in any one spot, everyone suffers. Those in control, like the oil companies, suffer along with the middle class, who pay increasingly steep rates for fuel, and who suffer with the lower class, who can't even afford cars. Everyone knows that power corrupts, but power also punishes those who have it if they don't share. Orwell discusses the paradoxical aspects of power in his essay "Shooting an Elephant." He writes, "[W]hen the white man turns tyrant it is his own freedom that he destroys," and "he [the white man] wears a mask, and his face grows to fit it."

When power is concentrated in one spot, just as a sunbeam focused with a magnifying glass ignites a pile of dry leaves, it becomes a danger to both those who wield it and those who are subjected to it. Those who abuse power are eventually burnt by it. Britain, once the largest empire in the world, should be very familiar with this phenomenon. One would think that those in power would be able to contain those apparently powerless dissenters, but this is not the case. England colonized North America, but then made the mistake of tightening its grip. Colonists were outraged at new taxes and trade restrictions, and rose up in arms. In response to the call for revolution, Thomas Jefferson wrote in the Declaration of Independence, "When a long train of abuses and usurpations, pursuing invariably the same Object evinces a design to reduce them under absolute Despotism, it is their right, it is their duty, to throw off such Government, and to provide new Guards for their future security." Henry David Thoreau also firmly believed that it is the right and duty of the people to resist injustice, claiming that the only place for an honorable citizen in an unjust society is a prison cell. Thus, England lost a very valuable asset in America, due to the ironic power paradox.

In politics, nothing is what it seems. Every society wears Orwell's "mask." Jamaica Kincaid provides us with a clear example of this strange truth. Growing up, she was constantly taught to worship England and everything English, even though she never had any real contact with the nation itself. She came to believe everything that she was told, that the English all had blue eyes and fair skin and smelled like lavender and had "untrustworthy" servants (she imagined that this was desirable). However, when Kincaid finally traveled to England, she found nothing the way it had been portrayed. The English discriminated against her because of her skin color, and were extremely rude. She found that it was perfectly acceptable for the English to criticize their country, but if she ever spoke a harsh word about England, she was alienated. Just as Kincaid points out the linings of the mask worn by England, Jonathan Swift exposes the true face of England and Ireland through his satire in "A Modest Proposal." Swift, or rather the persona he invents to use in the passage, ultimately recommends solving poverty, hunger, and the like by slaughtering one-year-old babies for use as food and leather clothing, suggesting that this would be a plausible notion for the upper and middle classes. He attacks the upper and middle classes, and especially landlords, stating that eating children is not so very far off from what they are already doing. Swift's character appeals only to logos, which he uses to suggest that those in control of England had no sympathy. His essay, on the other hand, appeals to the reader's sense of ethics and compassion. Contrary to what Swift's words suggest, during this time England was portraying itself as the very height of culture and everything good. Even in American society we sometimes wear a mask. We claim to go to war for freedom, humanity, or our own defense, when many times the real reason is to gain territory, political influence, or wealth.

One fascinating — and disturbing — aspect of politics and power is behavior during conflict. Chris Hedges describes how in war, both sides each try to convince themselves that they are the sole victims. During war, truth disappears altogether. No doubt each side's argument contains elements of truth, but neither in the end is reliable from the point of view of one who is not involved in the conflict. In his book, *War Is a Force That Gives Us Meaning*, Hedges explains that the same picture of civilian casualties was used by both sides to rally support. The side that was victimized obviously claimed it had been unjustly attacked and called for retaliation — its people were happy to believe and responded. The side that had done the killing actually claimed that it had done nothing, but that the victims had killed themselves. The Palestinian hierarchy was able to convince its people that they had not really attacked Israel, and that the Israelis had fired missiles at themselves in order to have an excuse for military action. Surprisingly, the people gladly believed the bogus story and supported the war. How can this be? It seems that in wartime we don't care what the truth is as long as we are given something to believe that corroborates the side we are being encouraged to support. This works in the government's favor, making it easy to unite its people behind a cause and increase the war effort, but it eventually detracts from society. Mindless belief in government propaganda can turn the public into unconscious, unintelligent drones, and when the next election comes around, guess who will (or won't) be voting?

Power and politics are two sticky, volatile subjects that are not as friendly as we would like them to be. Even the closest-to-ideal governments functioning today are not free from power abuse and sinister political manipulation. In other words, there is always something going on behind the scenes. But due to the paradoxes explored by Orwell, as nature takes its course, those who abuse their power or use politics for selfish interests are punished for it. This kind of Darwinian cycle helps to support the claims of political writers throughout history, from the great Enlightenment thinkers such as John Locke, who claimed that all human beings are born with certain natural rights, governed by natural laws, to such contemporary voices as Wole Soyinka, who says in "Every Dictator's Nightmare" that "certain fundamental rights are inherent to all humanity." It would appear that Nature is constantly acting to protect our rights. And the problems with power and politics can only be resolved when all political power is spread evenly for *all*. This fact has been accepted over the centuries by Thomas Jefferson, Henry David Thoreau, Martin Luther King Jr., and every American child. Now, all that has to be done is to live by it.

Questions

1. What is Elisabeth's central assertion in this essay?
2. How does she establish ethos?
3. Discuss at least one quotation as an appeal to pathos and another as an appeal to logos.
4. Identify at least five rhetorical strategies in this student essay, including allusion, rhetorical questions, and figurative language.
5. How do the features discussed in questions 1 through 4 contribute to the effectiveness of the essay?
6. Elisabeth wrote most of this essay in third person, although she occasionally used the first-person plural, *we*. How would the use of *I* throughout the essay change its effectiveness? Would *I* have strengthened or weakened the essay?
7. Discuss Elisabeth's use of sources. Would using fewer have weakened or strengthened her argument? Explain.

Grammar as Rhetoric and Style
Subordination in the Complex Sentence

Subordination is the use of a subordinating conjunction to make the meaning of one clause dependent on another clause. One way that writers build longer sentences that are logical and clear is through subordination. Although there are different types of subordination, involving both clauses and phrases, we are focusing here on the **complex sentence** — that is, a sentence formed by an **independent clause** and a **dependent clause** that begins with a subordinating conjunction.

Just because a clause is subordinate does not mean that what it says is unimportant. The ideas in both clauses contribute to the meaning of the sentence. It is the job of subordination to tell us how those ideas are related. This ability to connect ideas is the reason subordination is so effective; by using *because*, you tell your reader that one thing causes another; by using *when*, you indicate that two things are related chronologically. Thus, you can show the logical relationships in a rather lengthy sentence so that the length in no way impedes clarity.

Note the relationship between the dependent and independent clauses in the following sentence:

> When a nimble Burman tripped me up on the football field and the referee (another Burman) looked the other way, the crowd yelled with hideous laughter.
>
> — GEORGE ORWELL

In this example, Orwell uses the subordinate clause to establish the chronology of events that lead to the main action of the sentence — that is, his being laughed at by the crowd.

Subordinating conjunctions (underlined below) can be classified by the relationships they indicate:

Contrast or Concession: *although, even though, though, while, whereas*

> <u>Although the book was not entirely free of the stereotypes of contemporary British colonial writing</u>, it was in some ways remarkably advanced for its time.
>
> — CHINUA ACHEBE

Cause and Effect or Reason: *because, since, so that*

> <u>Because neither island was well suited to agriculture</u>, the company in 1733 purchased St. Croix — a larger, flatter, and more fertile island, 40 miles south — from France.
>
> — NATIONAL PARK SERVICE, CHRISTIANSTED: OFFICIAL MAP AND GUIDE

Condition: *if, once, unless*

> I can think of no one objection that will possibly be raised against this proposal <u>unless it should be urged that the number of people will be thereby much lessened in the kingdom</u>.
>
> — JONATHAN SWIFT

Time: *when, whenever, after, before, as, once, since, while*

> I had committed myself to doing it [killing the elephant] <u>when I sent for the rifle</u>.
>
> — GEORGE ORWELL

Punctuation

Correct punctuation adds clarity to longer sentences. The rule of thumb is: use a comma to set off a subordinate clause that opens a sentence. Each of the opening clauses in the preceding examples from Achebe and the National Park Service — one starting with *although*, another with *because* — is set off with a comma. Note that the comma comes not after the subordinating conjunction but after the entire clause. If you read the examples aloud, you'll probably find yourself naturally pausing at the end of the subordinate clause.

When the subordinate clause follows the independent clause, it gets a little trickier. Most of the time there is no comma at all because the dependent clause is necessary to the meaning of the sentence; this is called a *restrictive clause*. The sentence you just read is an example: the clause "because the dependent clause is necessary . . ." is essential to the meaning of the sentence. In some cases, however, the dependent clause adds information but is not necessary to the meaning of the sentence. For example:

> It is left only to those on the margins to keep the flame of introspection alive, although the destruction of culture is often so great that full recovery is impossible.
>
> — CHRIS HEDGES

Here the subordinate clause is not essential to the meaning of the sentence, so it is set off with a comma; this is called a *nonrestrictive clause.*

Keep in mind that a dependent clause cannot stand alone. When you're using a dependent clause, be careful not to end up with a *sentence fragment* — that is, a dependent clause followed by a period. To correct a sentence fragment, simply attach it to the independent clause.

Rhetorical and Stylistic Strategy

One strategy is to use subordination to blend short sentences into more graceful, longer sentences. Consider the following two sentences:

> It was still August. The air already had the smell of October, football season, piles of yellow-red leaves, everything crisp and clean.

Both are complete sentences. As readers, we understand them easily. The relationship between the two is temporal. But consider the difference with the addition of a subordinating conjunction:

> Though it was still August, the air already had the smell of October, football season, piles of yellow-red leaves, everything crisp and clean.
>
> — TIM O'BRIEN

Here the conjunction *though* indicates a contrast between the summer months and the smell of the air. Combining the two short sentences does not make the resulting sentence more difficult to understand; on the contrary, the longer sentence is easier to understand because it leaves nothing to chance.

A writer has to determine which clause should be dependent and which should be independent in a complex sentence. Although one clause is just as important as the other, the independent clause usually carries the most force, so you should put the idea you want to emphasize in an independent clause. Sometimes the choice is obvious because the relationship is chronological or cause and effect, but other times either clause could be independent. Consider the following example:

> Although my classmates and I would not have known it at the time, the London publishing house of Methuen had brought out the year before, in 1951, a little book titled simply *West Africa.*
>
> — CHINUA ACHEBE

What would the difference in effect have been if Achebe had written the following?

Although the London publishing house of Methuen had brought out the year before, in 1951, a little book titled simply *West Africa*, my classmates and I would not have known it at the time.

Both examples indicate that the relationship between the two clauses is one of contrast. But the second example puts the emphasis on Achebe and his classmates when, in fact, the publication of *West Africa* is the main event in the sentence and deserves more emphasis; the publication of the book affected Achebe and friends, not vice versa.

Where to place the subordinate clause is another choice a writer must make. For instance, examine the dependent clause in the following example:

Though it was still August, the air already had the smell of October, football season, piles of yellow-red leaves, everything crisp and clean.

—TIM O'BRIEN

The dependent clause ("Though it was still August") could have been put at the end of the sentence or even in the middle. Why do you think O'Brien placed it at the beginning? Perhaps placing the dependent clause in the middle of all those descriptive phrases would have muddled the sentence, making it difficult to decipher. As for putting it at the end, consider this example:

The air already had the smell of October, football season, piles of yellow-red leaves, everything crisp and clean, though it was still August.

The effect is different. In the original sentence, O'Brien signals at the outset that something is unusual: "Though it was still August." However, if this clause appears at the end of the sentence, it gets buried. By the time we've read about the smell of things associated with autumn, the fact that "it was still August" seems beside the point.

• **EXERCISE 1**

Combine each of the following pairs of sentences into one sentence, using subordination. You might shift the order of the sentences, and in some cases you may have to change the wording slightly. Be sure to punctuate correctly.

1. The investigators have gathered and analyzed all the evidence. We may expect a full report.

2. Tom had listened to the music of Bruce Springsteen for years. He had no idea a live performance could be so exciting.

3. The team has suffered its share of injuries this year. It could have improved its performance by giving Flynn more time on the field.

4. We will not be able to resolve this situation amicably. We must be willing to leave our prejudices at the door.

5. The crime rate has escalated near the mall. Many people have stopped shopping at the mall.

6. Rose Henderson has the qualifications to become a first-rate senator. Most of us knew she did not have a good chance to be elected. We worked hard on her campaign.

7. Lan Cao is a law professor at the College of William and Mary. She is also the author of the novel *Monkey Bridge.*

8. I'm not feeling well today. I plan to leave the office early.

9. Apple offered a free iPod with every MacBook. Sales of the MacBook improved dramatically.

10. The affluent population of Dallas, Texas, is increasing steadily. Housing prices are rising beyond what someone with a middle-class salary can afford.

11. We all realize the necessity for increased security. We need to protect our civil liberties.

12. Thousands of vacationers travel to our national parks in search of solitude and fresh air. Other people prefer the excitement of casinos and amusement parks.

• EXERCISE 2

Identify each subordinate clause in the following sentences, and explain its effect. All are direct quotations from the readings in this chapter.

1. When I saw England for the first time, I was a child in school sitting at a desk. — JAMAICA KINCAID

2. If now as I speak of all this I give the impression of someone on the outside looking in, nose pressed up against a glass window, that is wrong. — JAMAICA KINCAID

3. Although the old man never confronted me about it, there was one occasion when he came close to forcing the whole thing out into the open. — TIM O'BRIEN

4. Once people are dead, you can't make them undead. — TIM O'BRIEN

5. If he charged, I could shoot; if he took no notice of me, it would be safe to leave him until the mahout came back. — GEORGE ORWELL

6. Therefore if we are to compensate the young man for the loss of his glory and of his gun, we must give him access to the creative feelings. — VIRGINIA WOOLF

7. As the 19th century wore on, St. Croix became little more than a marginal sugar producer.   — NATIONAL PARK SERVICE

8. If I have unjustly wrestled a plank from a drowning man, I must restore it to him though I drown myself.   — HENRY DAVID THOREAU

9. A minority is powerless while it conforms to the majority.
                                                      — HENRY DAVID THOREAU

10. There will never be a really free and enlightened State, until the State comes to recognize the individual as a higher and independent power, from which all its own power and authority are derived, and treats him accordingly.   — HENRY DAVID THOREAU

• EXERCISE 3

Analyze the use of subordinate clauses in the following passages. Pay particular attention to how the writer varies sentence patterns.

1. I suppose we can all differ as to the exact point where good writing becomes overwhelmed by racial cliché. But overwhelmed or undermined, literature is always badly served when an author's artistic insight yields place to stereotype and malice. And it becomes doubly offensive when such a work is arrogantly proffered to you as your story. Some people may wonder if, perhaps, we were not too touchy, if we were not oversensitive. We really were not. And I have a somewhat unusual reason for saying so.   — CHINUA ACHEBE

2. All this was perplexing and upsetting. For at that time I had already made up my mind that imperialism was an evil thing and the sooner I chucked up my job and got out of it the better. Theoretically — and secretly, of course — I was all for the Burmese and all against their oppressors, the British.... Feelings like these are the normal by-products of imperialism; ask any Anglo-Indian official, if you can catch him off duty....

   Afterwards, of course, there were endless discussions about the shooting of the elephant. The owner was furious, but he was only an Indian and could do nothing. Besides, legally I had done the right thing, for a mad elephant has to be killed, like a mad dog, if its owner fails to control it. Among the Europeans opinion was divided. The older men said I was right, the younger men said it was a damn shame to shoot an elephant for killing a coolie, because an elephant was worth more than any damn Coringhee coolie. And afterwards I was very glad that the coolie had been killed; it put me legally in the right and it gave me sufficient pretext for shooting the elephant. I often wondered whether any of the others grasped that I had done it solely to avoid looking a fool. — GEORGE ORWELL

3. In wartime the state seeks to destroy its own culture. It is only when this destruction has been completed that the state can begin to exterminate the culture of its opponents. In times of conflict authentic culture is subversive. As the cause championed by the state comes to define national identity, as the myth of war entices a nation to glory and sacrifice, those who question the value of the cause and the veracity of the myths are branded internal enemies. — CHRIS HEDGES

4. A minority is powerless while it conforms to the majority; it is not even a minority then; but it is irresistible when it clogs by its whole weight. If the alternative is to keep all just men in prison, or give up war and slavery, the State will not hesitate which to choose. If a thousand men were not to pay their tax-bills this year, that would not be a violent and bloody measure, as it would be to pay them, and enable the State to commit violence and shed innocent blood. This is, in fact, the definition of a peaceable revolution, if any such is possible. If the tax-gatherer, or any other public officer, asks me, as one has done, "But what shall I do?" my answer is, "If you really wish to do anything, resign your office." When the subject has refused allegiance and the officer has resigned his office, then the revolution is accomplished. — HENRY DAVID THOREAU

- **EXERCISE 4**

In a national magazine that features writing on cultural and political subjects, find a passage that is effective in its use of subordination. Discuss how each subordinate clause works to support the speaker's rhetorical purpose.

Suggestions for Writing

Politics

Now that you have examined a number of texts that focus on politics, explore one dimension of this topic by synthesizing your own ideas and the readings. You might want to do more research or use readings from other classes as you discuss and prepare for the following projects.

1. Read the following section from a translation of an ancient text, the *Tao Te Ching* by Lao-tzu, a Chinese philosopher who lived in the sixth century B.C. Then write an essay in which you support or refute Lao-tzu's claims about political leadership. Use your knowledge of history and current events, and refer to the texts in this chapter to support your argument.

   When the Master governs, the people
   are hardly aware that he exists.
   Next best is a leader who is loved.
   Next, one who is feared.
   The worst is one who is despised.

   If you don't trust the people,
   you make them untrustworthy.

   The Master doesn't talk, he acts.
   When his work is done,
   the people say, "Amazing:
   we did it, all by ourselves!"

2. Henry David Thoreau's objections to slavery and to what he saw as unjustified war prompted the writing of the essay "Civil Disobedience" (p. 939), which strongly influenced both Gandhi and Martin Luther King Jr. as they opposed injustice. In "On the Rainy River" (p. 961), Tim O'Brien considers civil disobedience as a response to what he also considers an unjust war. Reflect on the state of our society today, and write an essay in which you apply Thoreau's ideas to our time. Is civil disobedience an appropriate response to perceived injustice today? Why or why not?

3. Assuming the voice of one of the contemporary writers in this chapter, or in your own informed voice, write a letter to one of the earlier writers (for example, Jonathan Swift, Henry David Thoreau, Oliver Goldsmith, Virginia Woolf) about political issues. In your letter, refer to current political problems that would interest the earlier writer. Your letter may take the form of a request for information or guidance, a complaint or polemic defending or challenging the writer's views, or a complimentary letter telling the writer how prescient he or she was.

4. In paragraph 3 of "Shooting an Elephant" (p. 979), George Orwell says that the incident of shooting the elephant "in a roundabout way was enlightening. It was a tiny incident in itself, but it gave me a better glimpse than I had had before of the real nature of imperialism — the real motives for which despotic governments act." He implies that governments act from the same petty impulses that drive human beings in response to pressures. Write an essay in which you support, refute, or qualify Orwell's position concerning despotic governments. Use evidence from your

knowledge of history and from other readings in this chapter to support your position.

5. Consider the importance of appealing to ethos in political writing. To take three examples, Virginia Woolf, Chris Hedges, and Tim O'Brien all write from personal experience. How important is that experience to the relationships established between the speaker, the text, and the reader, as illustrated by Aristotle's rhetorical triangle? Would ethos be equally served if these three writers had not personally experienced what they report but instead had based their writings on research or on the accounts of others? Referring to at least two of the texts, write an argument about the importance of personal experience as support for an argument.

6. Peruse the Harper's Index, a compilation of unusual political facts, at <harpers.org/HarpersIndex.html>. Select a compelling statement as a thesis statement or as a statement to defend or challenge, and use the readings in this chapter as evidence.

7. Write a thoughtful essay on the relationship between the citizen and the state in our time. Refer to at least three of the texts in this chapter to support your position.

8. About the legacy of George Orwell, political commentator Christopher Hitchens writes:

> His importance to the century just past, and therefore his status as a figure in history as well as literature, derives from the extraordinary salience of the subjects he "took on," and stayed with, and never abandoned. As a consequence, we commonly use the term "Orwellian" in one of two ways. To describe a state of affairs as "Orwellian" is to imply crushing tyranny and fear and conformism. To describe a piece of writing as "Orwellian" is to recognize that human resistance to these terrors is unquenchable.

   Write an essay in which you apply Hitchens's second definition of *Orwellian* to "Shooting an Elephant" and to at least two other texts in this chapter.

9. Each of the following statements addresses the nature of politics. Select one that interests you, and write an essay defending or challenging its assertion. To support your argument, refer to your knowledge of history and to the selections in this chapter.

> No cause is left but the most ancient of all, the one, in fact, that from the beginning of our history has determined the very existence of politics, the cause of freedom versus tyranny. — HANNAH ARENDT

> We are not afraid to entrust the American people with unpleasant facts, foreign ideas, alien philosophies, and competitive values. For a nation that is afraid to let its people judge the truth and falsehood in an open market is a nation that is afraid of its people. — JOHN F. KENNEDY

In our age there is no such thing as "keeping out of politics." All issues are political issues, and politics itself is a mass of lies, evasions, folly, hatred and schizophrenia.   — GEORGE ORWELL

Injustice anywhere is a threat to justice everywhere. — MARTIN LUTHER KING JR.

Nobody made a greater mistake than he who did nothing because he could do
only a little.   — EDMUND BURKE

Do not put such unlimited power into the hands of husbands. Remember all
men would be tyrants if they could.   — ABIGAIL ADAMS

What we think, or what we know, or what we believe is, in the end, of little consequence. The only consequence is what we do.   — JOHN RUSKIN

If we are to survive, we are to have ideas, vision, and courage. These things are
rarely produced by communities. Everything that matters in our intellectual
and moral life begins with an individual confronting his own mind and conscience in a room by himself.   — ARTHUR SCHLESINGER JR.

Glossary

alliteration   The repetition of the same sound or letter at the beginning of consecutive words or syllables.

allusion   An indirect reference, often to another text or an historic event.

analogy   An extended comparison between two seemingly dissimilar things.

anaphora   The repetition of words at the beginning of successive clauses.

anecdote   A short account of an interesting event.

annotation   Explanatory or critical notes added to a text.

antecedent   The noun to which a later pronoun refers.

antimetabole   The repetition of words in an inverted order to sharpen a contrast.

antithesis   Parallel structure that juxtaposes contrasting ideas.

aphorism   A short, astute statement of a general truth.

appositive   A word or phrase that renames a nearby noun or pronoun.

archaic diction   The use of words common to an earlier time period; antiquated language.

argument   A statement put forth and supported by evidence.

Aristotelian triangle   A diagram that represents a rhetorical situation as the relationship among the speaker, the subject, and the audience (see rhetorical triangle).

assertion   An emphatic statement; declaration. An assertion supported by evidence becomes an argument.

assumption   A belief or statement taken for granted without proof.

asyndeton   Leaving out conjunctions between words, phrases, clauses.

attitude   The speaker's position on a subject as revealed through his or her tone.

audience   One's listener or readership; those to whom a speech or piece of writing is addressed.

authority   A reliable, respected source — someone with knowledge.

bias   Prejudice or predisposition toward one side of a subject or issue.

cite   Identifying a part of a piece of writing as being derived from a source.

claim   An assertion, usually supported by evidence.

close reading   A careful reading that is attentive to organization, figurative language, sentence structure, vocabulary, and other literary and structural elements of a text.

colloquial/ism   An informal or conversational use of language.

common ground   Shared beliefs, values, or positions.

complex sentence   A sentence that includes one independent clause and at least one dependent clause.

concession   A reluctant acknowledgment or yielding.

connotation   That which is implied by a word, as opposed to the word's literal meaning (see denotation).

context   Words, events, or circumstances that help determine meaning.

coordination   Grammatical equivalence between parts of a sentence, often through a coordinating conjunction such as *and*, or *but*.

counterargument   A challenge to a position; an opposing argument.

credible   Worthy of belief; trustworthy.

cumulative sentence   An independent clause followed by subordinate clauses or phrases that supply additional detail.

declarative sentence   A sentence that makes a statement.

deduction   Reasoning from general to specific.

denotation   The literal meaning of a word; its dictionary definition.

dialectal journal   A double-column journal in which one writes a quotation in one column and reflections on that quotation in the other column.

diction   Word choice.

documentation   Bibliographic information about the sources used in a piece of writing.

elegiac   Mournful over what has passed or been lost; often used to describe tone.

epigram   A brief witty statement.

ethos   A Greek term referring to the character of a person; one of Aristotle's three rhetorical appeals (see logos and pathos).

explication of text   Explanation of a text's meaning through an analysis of all of its constituent parts, including the literary devices used; also called close reading.

facts   Information that is true or demonstrable.

figurative language   The use of tropes or figures of speech; going beyond literal meaning to achieve literary effect.

figure of speech   An expression that strives for literary effect rather than conveying a literal meaning.

fragment   A word, phrase, or clause that does not form a full sentence.

hortatory   Urging, or strongly encouraging.

hyperbole   Exaggeration for the purpose of emphasis.

imagery   Vivid use of language that evokes a reader's senses (sight, smell, taste, touch, hearing).

imperative sentence   A sentence that requests or commands.

induction   Reasoning from specific to general.

inversion   A sentence in which the verb precedes the subject.

irony   A contradiction between what is said and what is meant; incongruity between action and result.

juxtaposition   Placement of two things side by side for emphasis.

logos   A Greek term that means "word"; an appeal to logic; one of Aristotle's three rhetorical appeals (see ethos and pathos) .

metaphor   A figure of speech or trope through which one thing is spoken of as though it were something else, thus making an implicit comparison.

metonymy   Use of an aspect of something to represent the whole.

modifier   A word, phrase, or clause that qualifies or describes another word, phrase, or clause.

narration   Retelling an event or series of events.

nominalization   Turning a verb or adjective into a noun.

occasion   An aspect of context; the cause or reason for writing.

omniscient narrator   An all-knowing, usually third-person narrator.

oxymoron   A figure of speech that combines two contradictory terms.

pacing   The relative speed or slowness with which a story is told or an idea is presented.

paradox   A statement that seems contradictory but is actually true.

parallelism   The repetition of similar grammatical or syntactical patterns.

parody   A piece that imitates and exaggerates the prominent features of another; used for comic effect or ridicule.

pathos   A Greek term that refers to suffering but has come to be associated with broader appeals to emotion; one of Aristotle's three rhetorical appeals (see ethos and logos).

periodic sentence   A sentence that builds toward and ends with the main clause.

persona   The speaker, voice, or character assumed by the author of a piece of writing.

personification   Assigning lifelike characteristics to inanimate objects.

polemic   An argument against an idea, usually regarding philosophy, politics, or religion.

polysyndeton The deliberate use of a series of conjunctions.

premise; major, minor Two parts of a syllogism. The concluding sentence of a syllogism takes its predicate from the major premise and its subject from the minor premise.

Major premise: All mammals are **warm-blooded.**

Minor premise: All **horses** are mammals.

Conclusion: All **horses** are **warm-blooded** (see syllogism).

pronoun A word used to replace a noun or noun phrase.

propaganda A negative term for writing designed to sway opinion rather than present information.

purpose One's intention or objective in a speech or piece of writing.

refute To discredit an argument, particularly a counterargument.

rhetoric The study of effective, persuasive language use; according to Aristotle, use of the "available means of persuasion."

rhetorical modes Patterns of organization developed to achieve a specific purpose; modes include but are not limited to narration, description, comparison and contrast, cause and effect, definition, exemplification, classification and division, process analysis, and argumentation.

rhetorical question A question asked more to produce an effect than to summon an answer.

rhetorical triangle A diagram that represents a rhetorical situation as the relationship among the speaker, the subject, and the audience (see Aristotelian triangle).

satire An ironic, sarcastic, or witty composition that claims to argue for something, but actually argues against it.

scheme A pattern of words or sentence construction used for rhetorical effect.

sentence patterns The arrangement of independent and dependent clauses into known sentence constructions — such as simple, compound, complex, or compound-complex.

sentence variety Using a variety of sentence patterns to create a desired effect.

simile A figure of speech that uses "like" or "as" to compare two things.

simple sentence A statement containing a subject and predicate; an independent clause.

source A book, article, person, or other resource consulted for information.

speaker A term used for the author, speaker, or the person whose perspective (real or imagined) is being advanced in a speech or piece of writing.

straw man A logical fallacy that involves the creation of an easily refutable position; misrepresenting, then attacking an opponent's position.

style The distinctive qualitiy of speech or writing created by the selection and arrangement of words and figures of speech.

subject   In rhetoric, the topic addressed in a piece of writing.

subordinate clause   Created by a subordinating conjunction, a clause that modifies an independent clause.

subordination   The dependence of one syntactical element on another in a sentence.

syllogism   A form of deductive reasoning in which the conclusion is supported by a major and minor premise (see premise; major, and minor).

syntax   Sentence structure.

synthesize   Combining or bringing together two or more elements to produce something more complex.

thesis   The central idea in a work to which all parts of the work refer.

thesis statement   A statement of the central idea in a work, may be explicit or implicit.

tone   The speaker's attitude toward the subject or audience.

topic sentence   A sentence, most often appearing at the beginning of a paragraph, that announces the paragraph's idea and often unites it with the work's thesis.

trope   Artful diction; the use of language in a nonliteral way; also called a figure of speech.

understatement   Lack of emphasis in a statement or point; restraint in language often used for ironic effect.

voice   In grammar, a term for the relationship between a verb and a noun (active or passive voice). In rhetoric, a distinctive quality in the style and tone of writing.

zeugma   A construction in which one word (usually a verb) modifies or governs — often in different, sometimes incongruent ways—two or more words in a sentence.

Text Credits

Chinua Achebe. "The Empire Fights Back." From *Home and Exile* by Chinua Achebe. Copyright © 2001 by Chinua Achebe. Used by permission of Oxford University Press, Inc.

Marjorie Agosin. "Always Living in Spanish." First published in *Poets & Writers* (March/April 1999). Copyright © 1999 by Marjorie Agosin. Translated by Celeste Kostopulos-Cooperman. Reprinted with permission.

Brian Aldiss. "Super-toys Last All Summer Long." First published in *Harper's Bazaar*, December 1969. Copyright © 1969 by Brian Aldiss. Reprinted with permission.

Sherman Alexie. "Superman and Me." Originally published in the *Los Angeles Times*, April 19, 1998. Copyright © 1997 by Sherman Alexie. Reprinted with permission of the author. All rights reserved.

Lori Arviso Alvord, M.D. and **Elizabeth Cohen Van Pelt.** "Walking the Path Between Worlds." From *The Scalpel and the Silver Bear* by Lori Arviso Alvord, M.D. and Elizabeth Cohen Van Pelt. Copyright © 1999 by Lori Arviso Alvord and Elizabeth Cohen Van Pelt. Used by permission of Bantam Books, a division of Random House, Inc.

American College of Sports Medicine. "Disordered Eating and Body Image Disturbances May Be Underreported in Male Athletes" by Christa Dickey and Jim Gavin. Copyright 1993. Courtesy of the American College of Sports Medicine. www.acsm.org.

Natalie Angier. "Drugs, Sports, Body Image, and G.I. Joe." From *The New York Times*, December 22, 1998. Copyright © 1998 by The New York Times Company. Reprinted with permission. All rights reserved.

Robin D. Aufses. "The Simple Declarative Sentence: A Conversation with Brent Staples." Copyright © 2005, the College Board, www.collegeboard.com. Reproduced with permission.

James Baldwin. "A Talk to Teachers." Originally published in *Saturday Review*. Collected in *The Price of the Ticket*, published by St. Martin's Press. Copyright © 1963 by James Baldwin. Reprinted by arrangement with the James Baldwin Estate.

Mark Bauerlein and **Sandra Stotsky.** "Why Johnny Won't Read." Originally published in *The Washington Post*, January 25, 2005. Copyright © 2005 by Mark Bauerlein and Sandra Stotsky. Reprinted with permission of the authors.

Peter Berkowitz and **Michael McFaul.** "Studying Islam, Strengthening the Nation." From the *Washington Post*, April 12, 2005.

Suzanne Berne. "Where Nothing Says Everything." From *The New York Times*, April 21, 2002. Copyright © 2002 by The New York Times Company. Reprinted with permission. All rights reserved.

Wendell Berry. "An Entrance to the Woods." From *The Unforeseen Wilderness*. Copyright © 1981, 1990, and 2006 by Wendell Berry. Reprinted with permission of Shoemaker & Hoard Publishers.

John Betjeman. "In Westminster Abbey." From BEST LOVED POEMS by John Betjeman. Copyright John Betjeman. Reprinted by permission of John Murray Publishers Ltd.

Sven Birkerts. "Into the Electronic Millennium." First published in *The Guttenberg Elegies* by Sven Birkerts. Copyright © 1994 by Sven Birkerts. Reprinted by permission of Faber & Faber, Inc., an affiliate of Farrar, Straus & Giroux, LLC.

Philip M. Boffey. "Fearing the Worst Should Anyone." From *The New York Times*, January 1, 2003. Copyright © 2003 by The New York Times Company. Reprinted by permission. All rights reserved.

Eavan Boland. "In Which the Ancient History I Learn Is Not My Own." From *In A Time of Violence* by Eavan Boland. Copyright © 1994 by Eavan Boland. Used by permission of W.W. Norton & Company, Inc.

Leon Botstein. "Let Teenagers Try Adulthood." From *The New York Times*, May 17, 1999. Copyright © 1999 by The New York Times Company. Reprinted with permission. All rights reserved.

British Broadcasting Company. "Earl Spencer's Eulogy to Diana, September 5, 1997." Copyright © 1997. Reprinted by permission.

Donna Britt. "A Unique Take on Beauty." From the *Washington Post*. Copyright © 1999 by The Washington Post. Reprinted with permission.

Bill Broadway. "New and Newer Versions of Scriptures." From *The Washington Post*, February 19, 2005, B9. Copyright © 2005 The Washington Post. Reprinted with permission.

Amitai Etzioni. "The New Community." From *The Spirit of Community: Rights, Responsibilities, and the Communitarian Agenda* by Amitai Etzioni. Copyright © 1993 by Amitai Etzioni. Used by permission of Crown Publishers, a division of Random House, Inc.

Ursula Franklin. "Silence and the Notion of the Commons." Originally published in *Musicworks 59*. Reprinted with permission. *Musicworks Magazine* specializes in sound exploration and contemporary sound arts. Visit www.musicworks.ca

Samuel G. Freedman. "For Fasting and Football, a Dedicated Game Plan." From *The New York Times*, October 26, 2005. Copyright © 2005 by The New York Times Company. Reprinted with permission. All rights reserved.

Marilyn Gardner. "More working parents play 'beat the clock.'" From *The Christian Science Monitor*. © 2004 The Christian Science Monitor. Reproduced with permission from the June 2, 2004 issue of *The Christian Science Monitor*. www.csmonitor.com.

Lou Gehrig. "Farewell Speech." ™ 2006 Lou Gehrig, licensed by CMG Worldwide, Inc. www.lougehrig.com. Reprinted with permission.

Nikki Giovanni. "Sanctuary: For Harry Potter, the Movie." From *Quilting the Black-Eyed Pea* by Nikki Giovanni. Copyright © 2002 by Nikki Giovanni. Reprinted with permission of HarperCollins Publishers.

Todd Gitlin. "The Liberal Arts in an Age of Info-Glut." Originally published by *The Chronicle of Higher Education, Inc.* Copyright © 1998. Reprinted with permission of the author. "Is Media Violence Free Speech? A debate between George Gerbner and Todd Gitlin." From *Hot Wired*, a Web site created by *Wired* magazine, June 1997. Copyright © 1994/97 by George Gerbner and Todd Gitlin. Reprinted with permission of the authors and publisher.

Daniel Glick. "Geosigns: The Big Thaw." From *National Geographic*, September 2004. Copyright © 2004 National Geographic. Used by permission.

Indur M. Goklany. "Is Climate Change the 21st Century's Most Urgent Environmental Problem?" A Linwood University, Economic Policy Lecture 7 (2005). Reprinted with permission.

Ellen Goodman. "In Praise of a Snail's Pace." From the *Washington Post*, August 13, 2005. © 2005 Washington Post. Reprinted with permission.

Stephen Jay Gould. "Women's Brains." Copyright © 1980 by Stephen Jay Gould. Reprinted by permission of The Estate of Stephen Jay Gould.

Garrett Hardin. "Lifeboat Ethics: The Case Against Helping the Poor." From *Psychology Today*, September 1974. Copyright © 1974 Sussex Publishers, Inc. Reprinted with permission of the publisher.

S. I. Hayakawa. "Bilingualism in America: English Should Be the Official Language." Originally published in *USA Today*, 1989. Reprinted with permission of Alan Hayakawa.

Chris Hedges. "The Destruction of Culture." From *War Is a Force That Gives Us Meaning* by Chris Hedges. Copyright © 2002 by Chris Hedges. Used with permission of Public Affairs, a member of Perseus Books, LLC.

Jody Heyman. "We Can Afford to Give Parents a Break." First published in THE WASHINGTON POST, May 14, 2006. Copyright © 2006 Jody Heyman. Reprinted with permission of the author.

Laura Hillenbrand. "Gravity." From *SeaBiscuit: An American Legend* by Laura Hillenbrand. Copyright © 2001 by Laura Hillenbrand. Used by permission of Random House, Inc.

Jane Howard. "In Search of the Good Family." From *Families* by Jane Howard. Originally published in *Atlantic Magazine* (1978). Copyright © 1978 by Jane Howard. Reprinted with permission.

Ann Hulbert. "Boy Problems." Originally printed in *The New York Times*, April 3, 2005. Copyright 2005 by Ann Hulbert. Reprinted with permission of the Wylie Agency, Inc.

Steven Johnson. "Watching TV Makes You Smarter." Excerpt from *Everything Bad Is Good for You* by Steven Johnson. Copyright © 2005 by Steven Johnson. Used by permission of Riverhead Books, an imprint of Penguin Group (USA) Inc.

Jamaica Kincaid. "On Seeing England for the First Time." © 1991 by Jamaica Kincaid. Reprinted with permission of The Wylie Agency, Inc.

Martin Luther King Jr. "Letter from Birmingham Jail." Copyright © 1963 Martin Luther King Jr. Copyright © renewed 1991 by Coretta Scott King. Reprinted with arrangement with the Estate of Martin Luther King Jr., c/o Writers House as agent for the proprietor New York, NY.

Maxine Kumin. "Prothalamion." From *Selected Poems 1960–1990* by Maxine Kumin. Copyright © 1965 by Maxine Kumin. Used with permission of W.W. Norton & Company, Inc.

Cheryl Langevine. "The Case for Staying Home." From *Time*, March 22, 2004. © 2004 Time, Inc. Reprinted by permission.

Stephen Lewis. "AIDS Has a Woman's Face." Keynote by Stephen Lewis, UN Special Envoy on HIV/AIDS in Africa, to the "Microbicides 2004" conference in London, Tuesday, March 30, 2004. Reprinted by permission of the Stephen Lewis Foundation.

Wangari Muta Maathai. Nobel Lecture given by The Nobel Peace Prize Laureate 2004 (Oslo, December 10, 2004). Copyright © The Nobel Foundation, Stockholm, 2004. Reprinted with permission.

Tom Magliozzi and **Ray Magliozzi.** "Help Us Overthrow the Tall/Short Mafia." From *In Our Humble Opinion* by Tom Magliozzi and Ray Magliozzi. Copyright © 2000 by Tom Magliozzi and Ray Magliozzi. Used by permission of Perigee Books, an imprint of Penguin Group (USA) Inc.

Marilynn Marchione and **Lindsey Tanner.** "More Couples Screening Embryos for Gender." From *Associated Press*, September 21, 2006. Copyright © 2006. Reprinted with permission.

Buzz McClain. "Don't Call Me Mr. Mom! What Not to Say to an At-Home Dad." From www.slowlane.com. October 2000. Copyright © 2000, Buzz McClain. Reprinted with permission of the author.

Scott McCloud. Chapter Six, pages 136–161 from *Understanding Comics* by Scott McCloud. Copyright © 1993, 1994 by Scott McCloud. Reprinted by permission of HarperCollins Publishers.

Bill McKibben. "It's Easy Being Green." Originally published in *Mother Jones*, July/August 2002. Copyright © 2002 by Bill McKibben. Reprinted with permission of the author.

John McMurtry. "Kill 'Em! Crush 'Em! Eat 'Em Raw!" Originally published in *Maclean's*, October 1971. Reprinted with permission of the author.

Christopher Mele. "Sick Parents Go to Work, Stay Home When Kids Are Ill." From *USA Today*, May 22, 2002. Copyright © 2002. Reprinted by permission.

Courtland Milloy. "Pride to One Is Prejudice to Another." From the *Washington Post*, November 21, 2005. Copyright © 2005. Reprinted by permission of The Washington Post Writers Group.

Steven Mitchell. "#17 When the Master governs...all by ourselves." From TAO TE CHING by Lao Tzu, a new English version, with Foreword and Notes by Stephen Mitchell. Translation copyright © 1988 Stephen Mitchell. Reprinted by permission of HarperCollins Publishers.

Aurora Levins Morales. "Child of the Americas." From *Getting Home Alive* by Aurora Levins Morales. Copyright © 1986 by Aurora Levins Morales. Reprinted with permission of the publisher.

Kyoko Mori. "School." From *Polite Lies: On Being a Woman Caught Between Cultures* by Kyoko Mori. Copyright © 1997 by Kyoko Mori. Reprinted by permission of Henry Holt and Company, LLC.

Ngugi wa Thiong'o. Excerpt from *Decolonising the Mind* by Ngugi wa Thiong'o. Copyright © 1986 by Ngugi wa Thiong'o. Published by Heinemann, a division of Reed Elsevier, Inc., Portsmouth, NH. Reprinted with permission. All rights reserved.

Floyd Norris. "US Students Fare Badly in International Survey of Math Skills." From *The New York Times*, December 7, 2004. Copyright © 2004 by The New York Times Company, Inc. Reprinted with permission. All rights reserved.

Geoffrey Nunberg. "The -Ism Schism: How Much Wallop Can a Simple Word Pack?" From *The New York Times*, July 11, 2004. Copyright © 2004 by The New York Times Company. Reprinted with permission. All rights reserved.

Naomi Shihab Nye. "For Mohammed Zeid of Gaza, Age 15" and "Why I Could Not Accept Your Invitation." From *You and Yours* by Naomi Shihab Nye. Copyright © 2005 by Naomi Shihab Nye. Reprinted with permission from the author.

Joyce Carol Oates. "Against Nature." From *Woman Writer: Occasions and Opportunities* by Joyce Carol Oates. Copyright © 1988 by The Ontario Review. Used by permission of Dutton, a division of Penguin Group (USA), Inc.

Tim O'Brien. "On the Rainy River." From *The Things They Carried* by Tim O'Brien. Copyright © 1990 by Tim O'Brien. Reprinted by permission of Houghton Mifflin Company. All rights reserved.

Sandra Day O'Connor and **Roy Remer.** "Not By Math Alone." Originally published in THE WASHINGTON POST, March 25, 2006, p. A19. Copyright © 2006 by Sandra Day O'Connor. Reprinted with permission of the author.

Claudia O'Keefe. "The Traveling Bra Salesman's Lesson." From *The Economist*, 2005. Copyright © 2005 The Economist Newspaper Ltd. Reprinted with permission. Future reproduction prohibited. All rights reserved. www.economist.com.

jorie T. Parson, Executrix. Reprinted with permission of the publisher. Reprinted with permission of The Society of Authors as the Literary Representative of the Estate of Virginia Woolf.

Yevgeny Yevtushenko. "Conversation with an American Writer." Reprinted with permission of the author.

Picture Credits

11, TOLES © 2005 *The Washington Post*. Reprinted with permission of UNIVERSAL PRESS SYNDICATE. All rights reserved; **27,** © *The New Yorker* Collection 2005 Roz Chast from cartoonbank.com. All Rights Reserved; **50,** Courtesy of DaimlerChrysler. Used with permission; **79,** © 2004 *The Breeze*; **89,** © Robert Eric/Corbis Sygma; **102,** © Mary Evans Picture Library/The Image Works; **141,** Katherine McKabe; **147–48,** Reproduced with permission of the National Endowment for the Arts; **163,** Collection of the Norman Rockwell Museum at Stockbridge, Norman Rockwell Museum Art Collection Trust. Printed by permission of the Norman Rockwell Family Agency. Copyright © 1984 the Norman Rockwell Family Entities; **179,** Andrew Shurtleff/AP/Wide World Photos; **191,** Virginia Historical Society, Richmond, Virginia; **233,** © Corbis; **234,** Jeff Parker/© *Florida Today*; **260,** © Arty Pomerantz/The Image Works; **276,** © Bettmann/Corbis; **312,** © 2004 AFP. Photo: Francois Guillot/AFP/Getty Images; **315,** Picture courtesy of VVA Chapter 172; www.vietnamreflections.com; **316,** © Henryk Kaiser/Stock Connection; **349,** © Richard Howard Photography; **356,** © Ann Ronan Picture Library/HIP/The Image Works; **376,** Photo: Peter Frey/Courtesy of The University of Georgia; **405,** CATHY © 1997 Cathy Guisewite. Reprinted with permission of UNIVERSAL PRESS SYNDICATE. All rights reserved; **431,** © Katy Winn/Corbis; **449,** © NMPFT/RPS/SSPL/The Image Works; **476,** Courtesy of Sara Barrett; **481,** © *The New Yorker* Collection 2002 Edward Koren from cartoonbank.com. All Rights Reserved; **485,** Mary Schilpp/*Sports Illustrated*; **509,** © Roger Ressmeyer/CORBIS; **529,** © Bettmann/CORBIS; **574,** Photo by Michael Nye. Reprinted courtesy of BOA Editions, Ltd.; **576,** © *The New Yorker* Collection 1998 Mike Twohy from cartoonbank.com. All Rights Reserved; **577,** © 2002 by James Crawford. All rights reserved; **601,** Collections of the University of Pennsylvania Archives; **609,** © SSPL/The Image Works; **640,** © Rick Friedman/CORBIS; **676,** © *The New Yorker* Collection 1999 Gahan Wilson from cartoonbank.com. All Rights Reserved; **709,** Courtesy of *The New Yorker*; **717,** © Roger Viollet/TOPHAM/The Image Works; **725,** Courtesy of *The New York Times*; **764,** "The Innocent Eye Test": Mark Tansey, *The Innocent Eye Test*, 1981. Oil on canvas, 78 × 120" (198.1 × 304.8 cm). © Copyright Mark Tansey. Photo: Courtesy of Gagosian Gallery, New York, NY; **782,** TV Turnoff Week poster: © Anthony DiVivio Design; **798,** Rachel Carson: © Bettmann/CORBIS; **807,** © Mary Evans Picture Library/The Image Works; **858–59,** Image provided courtesy of Royal Dutch Shell plc; **861,** Asher Brown Durand, *Kindred Spirits*, 1849. Oil on canvas, 44 × 36 inches. Courtesy Walton Family Foundation; **871,** Counting Carbons graphic: Used with permission of *Discover* Magazine, PARS International Corp.; icons courtesy of Bryon Thompson Illustration; **876,** Ice blankets/National Geographic: Credit: Melissa Farlow/National Geographic Image Collection; **888,** Daniel Glick: © Jillian Lloyd. Courtesy of Public Affairs; **892,** © The Herb Block Foundation; **904,** © Jeremy Bembaron/CORBIS Sygma; **914,** © Ann Ronan Picture Library/HIP/The Image Works; **929,** © Kim Hedges. Courtesy of Public Affairs; **976,** © 2008 Estate of Pablo Picasso/Artists Rights Society (ARS), New York. Photo: John Bigelow Taylor/Art Resource, NY; **977,** Cover Art by Harry Bliss/ © 2003 Condé Nast Publications Inc.; **978,** *Guernica* (detail) by Pablo Picasso © 2008 Estate of Pablo Picasso/Artists Rights Society (ARS) New York City and John Bigelow Taylor/Art Resource, New York City. Photomontage by Penny Gentieu. Cover image courtesy *Harper's* Magazine; **992–93,** Christiansted brochure: Detail of a lithograph by Theodore C. Sabroe. Courtesy of The Danish Royal Library. Courtesy, National Park Service; **995,** Photo: Nathan Schroder/Greg Booth + Associates. Courtesy of the Bombay Furniture Company.

Index